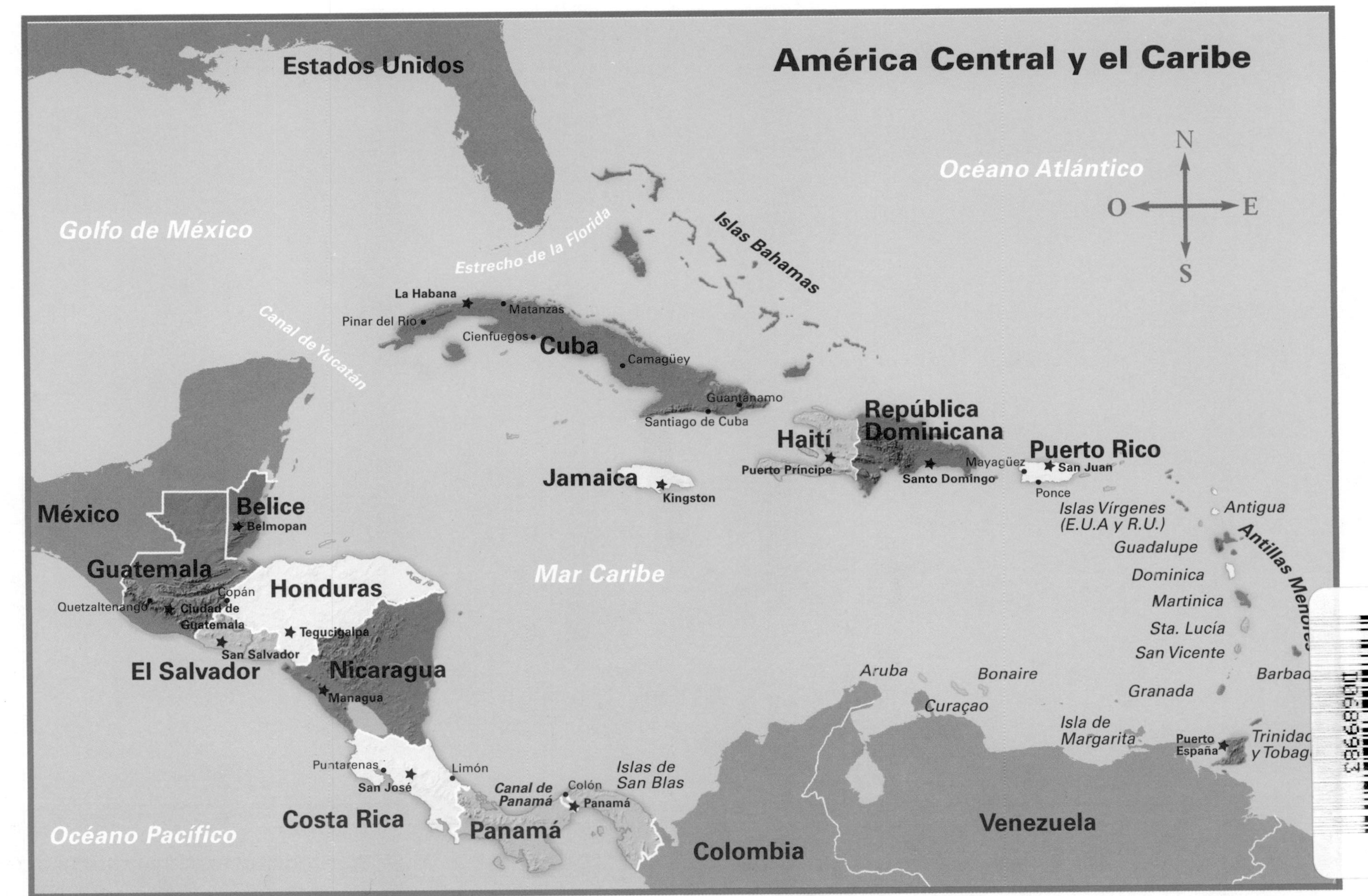
América Central y el Caribe
Estados Unidos
Golfo de México
Océano Atlántico
N
O
E
S
Estrecho de la Florida
Islas Bahamas
Canal de Yucatán
La Habana
Pinar del Río
Matanzas
Cienfuegos
Cuba
Camagüey
Guantánamo
Santiago de Cuba
República Dominicana
Haití
Puerto Príncipe
Santo Domingo
Puerto Rico
Mayagüez
San Juan
Ponce
Jamaica
Kingston
México
Belice
Belmopan
Guatemala
Copán
Quetzaltenango
Ciudad de Guatemala
Honduras
Tegucigalpa
San Salvador
El Salvador
Nicaragua
Managua
Mar Caribe
Islas Vírgenes (E.U.A y R.U.)
Antigua
Antillas Menores
Guadalupe
Dominica
Martinica
Sta. Lucía
San Vicente
Barbad
Granada
Aruba
Bonaire
Curaçao
Isla de Margarita
Puerto España
Trinidad y Tobag
Puntarenas
San José
Limón
Canal de Panamá
Colón
Panamá
Islas de San Blas
Océano Pacífico
Costa Rica
Colombia
Venezuela

Instructor's Annotated Edition

VISTAS

Introducción a la lengua española

SECOND EDITION

José A. Blanco

Philip Redwine Donley, Late

Austin Community College

Boston, Massachusetts

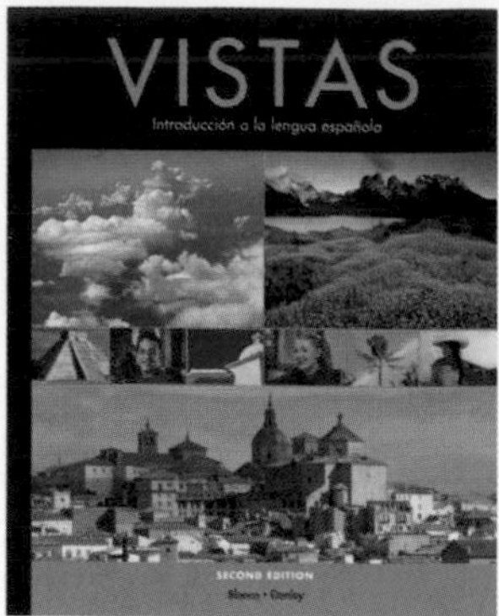

The **VISTAS, Second Edition,** cover celebrates the diversity of the Spanish-speaking world you will find throughout the text and all its ancillaries. Cover photos include images of Chile, Mexico, Peru, and Spain.

Publisher: José A. Blanco
President: Stephen Pekich
Editorial Director: Denise St. Jean
Art Director: Linda Jurras
Design Manager: Polo Barrera
Project Managers: Armando Brito, Kristen Odlum Chapron
Staff Editors: María Cinta Aparisi, María Isabel García, Sarah Kenney, Paola Ríos Schaaf, Alicia Spinner
Contributing Writers and Editors: Mary Ann Dellinger, Gabriela Ferland, Adriana Lavergne
Design, Production, and Manufacturing Team: Linde Gee; Oscar Díez, Mauricio Henao, Jonathan Gorey, Compset, Inc.; Gustavo Cinci

Student Text ISBN 1-59334-340-X
Instructor's Annotated Edition ISBN 1-59334-341-8

Library of Congress Card Number: 2004102458

1 2 3 4 5 6 7 8 9 VH 09 08 07 06 05 04

Instructor's Annotated Edition

Table of Contents

The VISTAS Story

Vista Higher Learning, the publisher of **VISTAS**, was founded with one mission: to raise the teaching of Spanish to a higher level. Years of experience working with textbook publishers convinced us that more could be done to offer you superior tools and to give your students a more profound learning experience. Along the way, we questioned everything about the way textbooks support the teaching of Spanish.

In fall 2000, the result was **VISTAS**, a textbook and coordinated package of print and technology ancillaries that looked different and *were* different. We took a fresh look at introductory college Spanish and found that hundreds of Spanish instructors nationwide liked what they saw. In just three years, **VISTAS** became the most successful new introductory Spanish textbook to be published in the last decade. More than 300 schools across the country have adopted **VISTAS**, and well over 100,000 students have used it to learn Spanish.

Over the last three years, we have been listening to the instructors and students using the First Edition, gathering their invaluable feedback in order to incorporate it into the Second Edition. The result is **VISTAS 2/e**, an even better and more comprehensive program that will work more effectively and seamlessly in your classes.

To those instructors who used **VISTAS 1/e** and are continuing with the Second Edition, we thank you for partnering with us these past few years and for your ongoing belief both in the program and in us as a new enterprise dedicated to innovative, focused, and captivating products. To those who are new to the Second Edition we welcome you and thank you for choosing **VISTAS**.

We hope that you and your students enjoy using **VISTAS**. Please contact us with your questions, comments, and reactions.

Vista Higher Learning
31 St. James Avenue
Boston, MA 02116-4104
TOLLFREE: 800-618-7375
TELEPHONE: 617-426-4910
FAX: 617-426-5215
www.vistahigherlearning.com

Getting to Know VISTAS

VISTAS 2/e retains the highly successful underpinnings of the First Edition. It takes a fresh, student-friendly approach to introductory Spanish aimed at making students' learning and instructors' teaching easier, more enjoyable, and more successful. At the same time, **VISTAS** takes a communicative approach to language learning. It develops students' speaking, listening, reading, and writing skills so that they will be able to express their own ideas and interact with others meaningfully and for real-life purposes. It emphasizes frequently used vocabulary, and it presents grammar as a tool for effective communication. Finally, because cultural knowledge is an integral part of both language learning and successful communication, **VISTAS** introduces students to the everyday lives of Spanish speakers, as well as the countries of the Spanish-speaking world.

Whereas other introductory college Spanish programs are based on many of these same pedagogical principles, **VISTAS** continues to offer features that make it truly different.

- **VISTAS** was the first introductory college Spanish textbook to incorporate graphic design—page layout, use of colors, typefaces, and other graphic elements—as an integral part of the learning process. To enhance learning and make navigation easy, lesson sections are color-coded and appear either completely on one page or on spreads of two facing pages. The textbook pages themselves are also visually dramatic, with an array of photos, drawings, realia, charts, graphs, diagrams, and word lists, all designed for both instructional impact and visual appeal.
- **VISTAS** offers student sidebars with on-the-spot linguistic, cultural, and language-learning information, as well as **recursos** boxes with on-page correlations of student supplements, to increase students' comfort level and to save them time.
- **VISTAS** integrates video with the student textbook in a distinct, more cohesive way up-front in each lesson's **Fotonovela** section and throughout every lesson's **Estructura** section.
- **VISTAS** provides a unique four-part practice sequence for virtually every grammar point. It moves from form-focused **¡Inténtalo!** exercises to directed, yet meaningful, **Práctica** exercises to communicative, interactive **Comunicación** activities, and lastly to cumulative, open-ended **Síntesis** activities.
- **VISTAS** incorporates groundbreaking, text-specific technology, specially designed to expand students' learning and instructors' teaching options. It was the first program to include a Video CD-ROM, and it is now the first to offer an online version of the textbook, **VISTAS** eText.

Before you delve into the remainder of the front matter in your Instructor's Annotated Edition (pages IAE-6 – IAE-16), it is strongly recommended that you familiarize yourself with the following pages of the StudentText front matter: page iii (To the Student), pages xiv–xxv (**VISTAS**-At-A-Glance), pages xxvi–xxvii (Video Program), and pages xxviii–xxix (Icons and Ancillaries).

Getting to Know Your Instructor's Annotated Edition

VISTAS, Second Edition, offers you the most thoroughly developed Instructor's Annotated Edition ever written for introductory college Spanish. In response to instructor input, the **Second Edition** IAE features a new trim size larger than that of the student text, as well as enhanced surrounding side and bottom panels for increased readability. It features slightly reduced student text pages overprinted with answers to all activities with discrete responses and places a wealth of teaching resources at your fingertips. The annotations were written to complement and support varied teaching styles, to extend the already rich contents of the student textbook, and to save you time in class preparation and course management.

Because the **VISTAS 2/e** IAE is a relatively new kind of teaching resource, this section is designed as a quick orientation to the principal types of instructor annotations you will find in it. As you familiarize yourself with them, it is important to know that the annotations are suggestions only. Any Spanish questions, sentences, models, or simulated instructor-student exchanges are not meant to be prescriptive or limiting. You are encouraged to view these suggested "scripts" as flexible points of departure that will help you achieve your instructional goals.

On the Lesson Opening Page

- **Lesson Goals** A list of the lexical, grammatical, and socio-cultural goals of the lesson, including language-learning strategies and skill-building techniques
- **A primera vista** Personalized questions based on the full-page photograph for jump-starting the lesson
- **Instructional Resources** A correlation, including page references, to all student and instructor supplements available to reinforce the lesson

In the Side Panels

- **Section Goals** A list of the lexical, grammatical, and/or socio-cultural goals of the corresponding section
- **Instructional Resources** A correlation, including page references, to all ancillaries
- **Suggestion** Teaching suggestions for leading into the corresponding section, working with on-page materials, and carrying out specific activities, as well as quick ways to start classes or activities by recycling language or ideas
- **Expansion** Expansions and variations on activities
- **Script** Printed transcripts of the audio recordings on the Textbook CDs for the first **Práctica** activity in each **Contextos** section and the **Estrategia** and **Ahora escucha** features in each **Escuchar** section
- **Possible Response** Answers based on known vocabulary, grammar, and language functions that students might produce
- **Video Recap** Questions to help students recall the events of the previous lesson's **Fotonovela** episode
- **Video Synopsis** Summaries in the **Fotonovela** sections that recap that lesson's video module
- **Expresiones útiles** Suggestions for introducing upcoming **Estructura** grammar points incorporated into the **Fotonovela** episode

- **Estrategia** Suggestions for working with the reading, writing, and listening strategies presented in the **Lectura, Escritura,** and **Escuchar** sections, respectively
- **Tema** Ideas for presenting and expanding the writing assignment topic in **Escritura**
- **Writing Sample** Samples of writing that students might produce in Spanish in response to the writing task in each **Escritura,** based on language students have studied up to that point
- **El país en cifras** Additional information expanding on the data presented for each Spanish-speaking country featured in the **Panorama** sections
- **¡Increíble pero cierto!** Curious facts about a lesser-known aspect of the country featured in the **Panorama** sections
- **Section-specific Annotations** Suggestions for presenting, expanding, varying, and reinforcing individual instructional elements
- **Student Text Sidebar Annotations** Suggestions for incorporating the information provided in sidebars (**¡Atención!, Ayuda, Nota cultural,** etc.)
- **Successful Language Learning** Tips and strategies to enhance students' language-learning experience
- **The Affective Dimension** Suggestions for managing and/or reducing students' language-learning anxieties

In the *Teaching Options* Boxes

- **Extra Practice, Pairs, Small Groups, and Large Groups** Additional activities over and above those already in the student textbook
- **Game** Games that practice the language of the section and/or recycle previously learned language
- **TPR** Total Physical Response activities that engage students physically in learning Spanish
- **Enfoque cultural** Additional cultural information related to the **Enfoque cultural** in **Fotonovela**
- **Variación léxica** Extra information related to the **Variación léxica** in **Contextos** and/or the Spanish-speaking countries in **Panorama**
- **Worth Noting** More detailed information about an interesting aspect of the history, geography, culture, or people of the Spanish-speaking countries in **Panorama**
- **Heritage Speakers** Suggestions and activities tailored to heritage speakers, who in many colleges and universities are enrolled in the same introductory courses as non-heritage speakers
- **Video** Techniques and activities for using the **VISTAS** video program with **Fotonovela** and other lesson sections
- **Proofreading Activity** Activities exclusive to the **Escritura** sections that guide students in the development of good proofreading skills. Each item contains errors related to a structure taught in the lesson's **Estructura** section or, in **Lecciones 10–18**, a spelling rule taught in **Ortografía**
- **Evaluation** Suggested rubrics in **Escritura** and **Proyecto** for grading students' writing efforts and oral presentations

Please check our website (**www.vistahigherlearning.com**) for additional teaching support and program updates.

General Teaching Considerations

Orienting Students to the Student Textbook

Because **VISTAS 2/e** treats interior and graphic design as an integral part of students' language-learning experience, you may want to take a few minutes to orient students to the student textbook. Have them flip through one lesson, and point out that all lessons are organized exactly the same way. Also point out how the major sections of each lesson are color-coded for easy navigation: red for **Contextos**, purple for **Fotonovela**, blue for **Estructura**, green for **Adelante**, orange for **Panorama**, and gold for **Vocabulario**. Let them know that, because of these design elements, they can be confident that they will always know "where they are" in their textbook.

Emphasize that sections are self-contained, occupying either a full page or a spread of two facing pages, thereby eliminating "bad breaks" and the need to flip back and forth to do activities or to work with explanatory material. Finally, call students' attention to the use of color to highlight key information in elements such as charts, diagrams, word lists, and activity **modelos**, titles, and sidebars.

Flexible Lesson Organization

VISTAS 2/e uses a flexible lesson organization designed to meet the needs of diverse teaching styles, institutions, and instructional goals. For example, you can begin with the lesson opening page and progress sequentially through a lesson. If you do not want to devote class time to grammar, you can assign the **Estructura** explanations for outside study, freeing up class time for other purposes like developing oral communication skills; building listening, reading, or writing skills; learning more about the Spanish-speaking world; or working with the video program. You might decide to work extensively with the **Adelante** and **Panorama** sections in order to focus on students' reading, writing, listening, and oral presentation skills and their knowledge of the Spanish-speaking world. On the other hand, you might prefer to skip these sections entirely, exploiting them periodically in response to your students' interests as the opportunity arises. If you plan on using the **VISTAS** Testing Program, however, be aware that its tests and exams check language presented in **Contextos**, **Estructura**, and the **Expresiones útiles** boxes of **Fotonovela**.

Identifying Active Vocabulary

All words and expressions taught in the illustrations and **Más vocabulario** lists in **Contextos** are considered active, testable vocabulary. Any items in the **Variación léxica** boxes, however, are intended for receptive learning and are presented for enrichment only. The words and expressions in the **Expresiones útiles** boxes in **Fotonovela**, as well as words in charts, word lists, **¡Atención!** sidebars, and sample sentences in **Estructura** are also part of the active vocabulary load. At the end of each lesson, **Vocabulario** provides a convenient one-page summary of the items students should know and that may appear on tests and exams. You will want to point this out to students. You might also tell them that an easy way to study from **Vocabulario** is to cover up the Spanish half of each section, leaving only the English equivalents exposed. They can then quiz themselves on the Spanish items. To focus on the English equivalents of the Spanish entries, they simply reverse this process.

Taking into Account the Affective Dimension

While many factors contribute to the quality and success rate of learning experiences, two factors are particularly germane to language learning. One is students' beliefs about how language is learned; the other is language-learning anxiety.

As studies show and experienced instructors know, students often come to modern languages courses either with a lack of knowledge about how to approach language learning or with mistaken notions about how to do so. For example, many students believe that making mistakes when speaking the target language must be avoided because doing so will lead to permanent errors. Others are convinced that learning another language is like learning any other academic subject. In other words, they believe that success is guaranteed, provided they attend class regularly, learn the assigned vocabulary words and grammar rules, and study for exams. In fact, in a study of college-level beginning language learners in the United States, over one-third of the participants thought that they could become fluent if they studied the language for only one hour a day for two years or less. Mistaken and unrealistic beliefs such as these can cause frustration and ultimately demotivation, thereby significantly undermining students' ability to achieve a successful language-learning experience.

Another factor that can negatively impact students' language-learning experiences is language-learning anxiety. As Professor Elaine K. Horwitz of The University of Texas at Austin and Senior Consulting Editor of **VISTAS 1/e** wrote, "Surveys indicate that up to one-third of American foreign language students feel moderately to highly anxious about studying another language. Physical symptoms of foreign language anxiety can include heart-pounding or palpitations, sweating, trembling, fast breathing, and general feelings of unease." The late Dr. Philip Redwine Donley, **VISTAS** co-author and author of articles on language-learning anxiety, spoke with many students who reported feeling nervous or apprehensive in their classes. They mentioned freezing when called on by their instructors or going inexplicably blank when taking tests. Some so dreaded their classes that they skipped them or dropped the course.

VISTAS contains several features aimed at reducing students' language anxiety and supporting their successful language-learning. First of all, its highly structured, visually dramatic interior design was conceived as a learning tool to make students feel comfortable with the content and confident about navigating the lessons. The Instructor's Annotated Edition includes recurring *Affective Dimension* annotations with suggestions for managing and/or reducing language-learning anxieties, as well as *Successful Language Learning* annotations with learning strategies for enhancing students' learning experiences. In addition, the student text provides a wealth of helpful sidebars that assist students by making immediately relevant connections with new information or reminding them of previously learned concepts.

Student Sidebars

¡Atención!	Provides active, testable information about the vocabulary or grammar point
Ayuda	Offers specific grammar and vocabulary reminders related to a particular activity
Consejos	Suggests pertinent language-learning strategies
Consúltalo	References related material introduced in previous or upcoming lessons
¡Lengua viva!	Presents immediately relevant information on everyday language use
Nota cultural	Provides a wide range of cultural information relevant to the topic of an activity or section

General Suggestions for Using the VISTAS *Panorama cultural* Video

The **Panorama cultural** video contains documentary and travelogue footage of each country featured in the lessons' **Panorama** section. The images were chosen for visual appeal, diversity of topics, and information of interest that goes beyond the materials about each country that are presented in the textbook. Like the conversations in the **Fotonovela** video, the voice-overs for the video segments represent comprehensible input. Each was written to make the most of the vocabulary and grammar students learned in the corresponding and previous lessons while still providing a small amount of unknown language. The effect on students as they watch will be that of viewing a documentary in their first language, because all footage is authentic and all narration is exclusively in Spanish. A special effort was also made to concentrate on one unique social or historical aspect of each country in such a way as to avoid promoting stereotypes of Spanish-speaking culture.

Panorama cultural Video Table of Contents

Lesson	Country	Topic	Lesson	Country	Topic
1	Los Estados Unidos	Los hispanos en Nueva York	11	Argentina	El tango
1	Canadá	Los hispanos en Montreal	12	Panamá	Los deportes en el mar
2	España	El Festival de San Fermín	13	Colombia	Las fiestas y los parques
3	Ecuador	Las Islas Galápagos	14	Venezuela	Las costas y las montañas
4	México	Teotihuacán	15	Bolivia	El Salar de Uyuni
5	Puerto Rico	El Viejo San Juan	16	Nicaragua	Masaya
6	Cuba	La santería	16	La República Dominicana	La bachata y el merengue
7	Perú	Los deportes de aventura	17	El Salvador	El maíz
8	Guatemala	Antigua y Chichicastenango	17	Honduras	Copán
9	Chile	La Isla de Pascua	18	Paraguay	El mate
10	Costa Rica	Monteverde y Tortuguero	18	Uruguay	Las estancias

Activities for the **Panorama cultural** video are located in the Video Manual section of the **VISTAS 2/e** Workbook/Video Manual. They follow a process approach of pre-viewing, while-viewing, and post-viewing and use a variety of formats to prepare students for watching the video segments, to focus them while watching, and to check comprehension after they have watched the footage.

When showing the **Panorama cultural** video in your classes, you might also want to implement a process approach. You could start with an activity that prepares students for the video segment by taking advantage of what they learned in previous lessons. This could be followed by an activity that students do while you play parts or all of the video segment. The final activity, done in the same class period or in the next one as warm-up, could recap what students saw and heard and move beyond the video segment's topic. The following suggestions for working with the **Panorama cultural** video in class can be carried out as described or expanded upon in any number of ways.

Before viewing

- After students have practiced the lesson's vocabulary and grammar and worked through the **Panorama** section of the student textbook, mention the video segment's title and ask them to guess what the segment might be about.
- Have pairs make a list of the lesson vocabulary they expect to hear in the video segment.
- Read the class a list of true-false or multiple-choice questions about the video. Students must use what they learned in the **Panorama** section to guess the answers. Confirm their guesses after watching the segment.

While viewing

- Show the video segment with the audio turned off and ask students to use lesson vocabulary and structures to describe what is happening. Have them confirm their guesses by showing the segment again with the audio on.
- Have students refer to the list of words they brainstormed before viewing the video and put a check in front of any words they actually see in the segment.
- First, have students simply watch the video. Then, show it again and ask students to take notes on what they see and hear. Finally, have them compare their notes in pairs or groups for confirmation.
- Photocopy the segment's videoscript from the Instructor's Resource Manual and white out words and expressions related to the lesson theme. Distribute the scripts for pairs or groups to complete as cloze paragraphs.
- After having introduced the lesson's theme using the lesson-opening page, show the video segment *before* moving on to **Contextos** to jump-start the lesson's new vocabulary, grammar, and cultural focus. Have students tell you what vocabulary and grammar they recognize from previous lessons. Briefly present the new lesson's theme and grammar structures for recognition.

After viewing

- Have students say what aspects of the information presented in the **Panorama** section of their textbook are observable in the video segment.
- Ask groups to write a brief summary of the content of the video segment. Have them exchange papers with another group for peer editing.
- Ask students to discuss any aspects of the featured country of which they were unaware before watching. Encourage them to say why they didn't expect those aspects to be true of the country in question.
- Have students pick one characteristic about the country that they learned from watching the video segment. Have them research more about that topic and write a brief composition to expand on it.

General Suggestions for Using the VISTAS *Fotonovela* Video

The **Fotonovela** section in each of the student textbook's lessons and the **VISTAS** **Fotonovela** video were created as interlocking pieces. All photos in **Fotonovela** are actual video stills from the corresponding video module, while the printed conversations are abbreviated versions of the video module's dramatic segment. Both the **Fotonovela** conversations and their expanded video versions represent comprehensible input at the discourse level; they were purposely written to use language from the corresponding lesson's **Contextos** and **Estructura** sections. Thus, as of **Lección 2**, they recycle known language, preview grammar points students will study later in the lesson, and, in keeping with the concept of "i + 1," contain a small amount of unknown language.

Because the **Fotonovela** sections and the **VISTAS** **Fotonovela** video are so closely connected, you may use them in many different ways. For instance, you can use **Fotonovela** as an advance organizer, presenting it before showing the video module. You can also show the video module first and follow up with **Fotonovela.** You can even use **Fotonovela** as a stand-alone, video-independent section.

Depending on your teaching preferences and campus facilities, you might decide to show all video modules in class or to assign them solely for viewing outside of the classroom. You could begin by showing the first one or two modules in class to familiarize yourself and students with the characters, storyline, style, "flashbacks," and **Resumen** sections. After that, you could work in class only with **Fotonovela** and have students view the remaining video modules outside of class. No matter which approach you choose, students have ample materials to support viewing the video independently and processing it in a meaningful way. For each video module, there are **Reacciona a la fotonovela** activities in the **Fotonovela** section of the corresponding textbook lesson and video activities in the Student Activities Manual.

You might also want to use the **VISTAS** **Fotonovela** video in class when working with the **Estructura** sections. You could play the parts of the dramatic episode that correspond to the video stills in the grammar explanations or show selected scenes and ask students to identify certain grammar points.

You could also focus on the video's **Resumen** sections. In these, one of the main video characters recaps the dramatic episode by reminiscing about its key events. These reminiscences, which emphasize the lesson's active vocabulary and grammar points, take the form of footage pulled out of the dramatic episode and repeated in black and white images. The main character who "hosts" each **Resumen** begins and ends the section with a few lines that do not appear in the live segment. These sentences provide a new, often humorous setting for the host character's reminiscences, as well as additional opportunities for students to process language they have been studying within the context of the video storyline.

In class, you could play the parts of the **Resumen** section that exemplify individual grammar points as you progress through each **Estructura** section. You could also wait until you complete an **Estructura** section and review it by showing the corresponding **Resumen** section in its entirety.

VISTAS and *the Standards for Foreign Language Learning*

Since 1982, when the *ACTFL Proficiency Guidelines* were first published, that seminal document and its subsequent revisions have influenced the teaching of modern languages in the United States. **VISTAS** was written with the concerns and philosophy of the *ACTFL Proficiency Guidelines* in mind, incorporating a proficiency-oriented approach from its planning stages.

VISTAS' pedagogy was also informed from its inception by the *Standards for Foreign Language Learning in the 21st Century*. First published in 1996 under the auspices of the National Standards in Foreign Language Education Project, the Standards are organized into five goal areas, often called the Five Cs: Communication, Cultures, Connections, Comparisons, and Communities.

Since **VISTAS** takes a communicative approach to the teaching and learning of Spanish, the Communication goal is central to the student text. For example, the diverse formats used in **Comunicación** and **Síntesis** activities—pair work, small group work, class circulation, information gap, task-based, and so forth—engage students in communicative exchanges, providing and obtaining information, and expressing feelings and emotions. The **Proyecto** sections guide students in presenting information, concepts, and ideas to their classmates on a variety of topics *and* in varied ways—oral, written, recorded, and videotaped.

The Cultures goal is most evident in the lessons' **Enfoque cultural** boxes **Nota cultural** student sidebars, and **Panorama** sections, but **VISTAS** also weaves culture into virtually every page, exposing students to the multiple facets of practices, products, and perspectives of the Spanish-speaking world. In keeping with the Connections goal, students can connect with other disciplines such as geography, history, fine arts, and science in the **Proyecto** and **Panorama** sections; they can acquire information and recognize distinctive cultural viewpoints in the non-literary and literary texts of the **Lectura** sections. The **Estructura** sections, with their clear explanations and special *Compare & Contrast* sections, reflect the Comparisons goal, while the Communities goal is particularly visible in the **Recursos para la investigación** boxes of the **Proyecto** sections. Students can work toward the Connections and Communities goal when they do the **Panorama** sections' **Conexión Internet** activities, as well as the activities and information on the VISTAS website. In addition, special Standards icons appear on the student text pages of your IAE to call out sections that have a particularly strong relationship with the Standards. These are a few examples of how **VISTAS** was written with the Standards firmly in mind, but you will find many more as you work with the student textbook and its ancillaries.

COURSE PLANNING

The entire **VISTAS** program was developed with an eye to flexibility and ease of use in a wide variety of course configurations. **VISTAS** can be used in courses taught on a semester or quarter system, and in courses that complete the book in two, three, or four semesters. Here are some sample course plans that illustrate how **VISTAS** can be used in a variety of academic situations. Visit the **VISTAS** website (**www.vistahigherlearning.com**) for more course planning tips and detailed suggestions, as well as an essay on course planning by the late Dr. Philip Redwine Donley, **VISTAS** co-author. You should, of course, feel free to organize your courses in the way that best suits your students' needs and your instructional objectives.

Two-Semester System

The following chart illustrates how **VISTAS** can be completed in a two-semester course. This division of material allows the present, the present progressive, and the preterite tenses to be presented in the first semester; the second semester focuses on the imperfect tense, the subjunctive, and the perfect tenses.

Semester 1	Semester 2
Lecciones 1–9	Lecciones 10–18

Three-Semester System

This chart shows how **VISTAS** can be used in a three-semester course. The lessons are equally divided among the three semesters, allowing students to absorb the material at a steady pace.

Semester 1	Semester 2	Semester 3
Lecciones 1–6	Lecciones 7–12	Lecciones 13–18

Four-Semester System

The following chart shows one way to configure the **VISTAS** materials for a four-semester course of study. This arrangement allots only four lessons to the first and fourth semesters; this gives students time to get their bearings in the first semester and permits extra time for review in the fourth semester.

Semester 1	Semester 2	Semester 3	Semester 4
Lecciones 1–4	Lecciones 5–9	Lecciones 10–14	Lecciones 15–18

Quarter System

In the following chart, the **VISTAS** materials are organized in three balanced segments for use in the quarter system, allowing ample time for learning and review in each quarter.

First Quarter	Second Quarter	Third Quarter
Lecciones 1–6	Lecciones 7–12	Lecciones 13–18

LESSON PLANNING

VISTAS has been carefully planned to meet your instructional needs, whether you teach on a semester or quarter system and whether you plan to use the textbook for two, three, or four semesters or over three quarters. Vocabulary presentations and grammar topics have been methodically designed for maximum instructional flexibility.

The following lesson plan for **Lección 1** illustrates how **VISTAS 2/e** can be used in a two-semester program with five contact hours per week. It deals with order of presentation rather than specific instructional techniques and suggestions because those are provided in the annotations of the **VISTAS 2/e** IAE and because complete, detailed lesson plans are posted on the **VISTAS 2/e** website (**www.vistahigherlearning.com**). There you will find lesson plans for two-semester courses, quarter courses, and essays by the late Dr. Philip Redwine Donley, **VISTAS** co-author, about how to use **VISTAS** with the following types of course configurations: two-semester courses with three contact hours per week; two-semester courses with five contact hours per week; and courses that meet over three and four semesters.

Sample Lesson Plan for *Lección 1*

Day 1

1. Introduce yourself and present the course syllabus.
2. Present the **Lección 1** objectives.
3. Preview the **Contextos** section; present the **Contextos** vocabulary.
4. Work through the **Práctica** activities with the class; have students read over the **Comunicación** activities for the next class.
5. Preview the **Fotonovela** and the **Expresiones útiles**.
6. Have students read through the **Fotonovela** and prepare the first **Reacciona a la fotonovela** activity for the next class.

Day 2

1. Review **Contextos** vocabulary; have the class do the **Comunicación** activities.
2. Present the **Fotonovela** and **Expresiones útiles**.
3. Do the first **Reacciona a la fotonovela** activity with the class.
4. Have your students do the next three **Reacciona a la fotonovela** activities.
5. Preview the **Pronunciación** section and **Estructura 1.1**.
6. Have students read **Estructura 1.1** and prepare the **Inténtalo** and **Práctica** activities for the next class.

Day 3

1. Review the **Expresiones útiles**.
2. Go over the **Pronunciación** section with the class and work through the corresponding activities.
3. Present **Estructura 1.1**.
4. Work through the **Inténtalo** and **Práctica** activities with the class.
5. Have your students do the **Comunicación** activity in class.
6. Preview **Estructura 1.2**.
7. Have students read **Estructura 1.2** and prepare the **Inténtalo** and **Práctica** activities for the next class.

Day 4

1. Review **Estructura 1.1.**
2. Present **Estructura 1.2** and work through the **Inténtalo** and **Práctica** activities with the class.
3. Have your students do the **Comunicación** activities during class.
4. Preview **Estructura 1.3.**
5. Have your students read **Estructura 1.3** and prepare the **Inténtalo** and **Práctica** activities for the next class.

Day 5

1. Review **Estructura 1.2.**
2. Present **Estructura 1.3** and work through the **Inténtalo** and **Práctica** activities with the class.
3. Have your students do the **Comunicación** activities during class.
4. Preview **Estructura 1.4.**
5. Have your students read **Estructura 1.4** and prepare the **Inténtalo** and **Práctica** activities for the next class.

Day 6

1. Quickly review **Estructura 1.3.**
2. Present **Estructura 1.4** and work through the **Inténtalo** and **Práctica** activities with the class.
3. Have your students do the **Comunicación** activities and the **Síntesis** activity.
4. Assign material from the **Adelante** section as desired for integrated practice and review.

Day 7

1. Go over assigned material from the **Adelante** section.
2. Review **Lección 1** with the class.
3. Have your students prepare to take one of the four **Pruebas** for **Lección 1** during the next class session.

Day 8

1. Administer one of the four **Pruebas** for **Lección 1.**
2. Preview the **Lección 2** objectives.
3. Have your students read the **Contextos** section and prepare the **Práctica** activities for the next class.

The lesson plan presented here is not prescriptive. You should feel free to present lesson materials as you see fit, tailoring them to your own teaching preferences and to your students' learning styles. You may, for example, want to allow extra time for concepts students find challenging. You may want to allot less time to topics they comprehend without difficulty or to group topics together when making assignments. Based on your students' needs, you may want to omit certain topics or activities altogether. If you have fewer than five contact hours per semester or are on a quarter system, you will find the **VISTAS** program very flexible: simply pick and choose from its array of instructional resources and sequence them in the way that makes the most sense for your program.

VISTAS

Introducción a la lengua española

SECOND EDITION

José A. Blanco

Philip Redwine Donley, Late
Austin Community College

Boston, Massachusetts

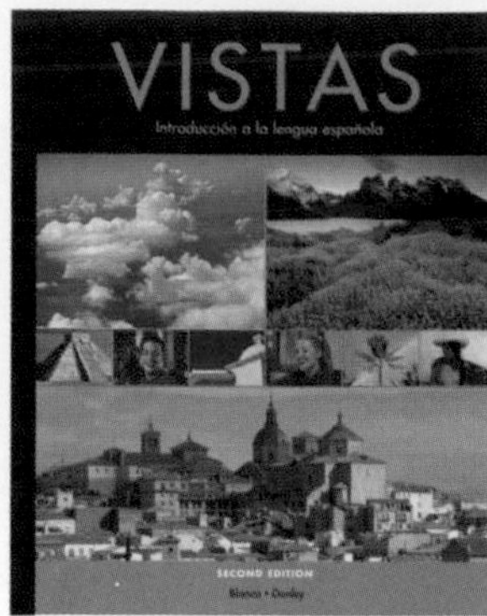

The **VISTAS, Second Edition,** cover celebrates the diversity of the Spanish-speaking world you will find throughout the text and all its ancillaries. Cover photos include images of Chile, Mexico, Peru, and Spain.

Publisher: José A. Blanco
President: Stephen Pekich
Editorial Director: Denise St. Jean
Art Director: Linda Jurras
Design Manager: Polo Barrera
Project Managers: Armando Brito, Kristen Odlum Chapron
Staff Editors: María Cinta Aparisi, María Isabel García, Sarah Kenney, Paola Ríos Schaaf, Alicia Spinner
Contributing Writers and Editors: Mary Ann Dellinger, Carmela Fazzino-Farah, Gabriela Ferland, Adriana Lavergne, Magdalena Malinowska, Lourdes Murray-Eljach
Design, Production, and Manufacturing Team: Linde Gee; Oscar Díez, Mauricio Henao, Jonathan Gorey; Gustavo Cinci

Student Text ISBN 1-59334-340-X
Instructor's Annotated Edition ISBN 1-59334-341-8

Library of Congress Card Number: 2004102457

1 2 3 4 5 6 7 8 9 VH 09 08 07 06 05 04

TO THE STUDENT

To Vista Higher Learning's great pride and gratification, **VISTAS** became the best-selling new introductory college Spanish program in more than a decade in its first edition. It is now our distinct pleasure to welcome you to **VISTAS**, **Second Edition**, your gateway to the Spanish language and to the vibrant, diverse cultures of the Spanish-speaking world.

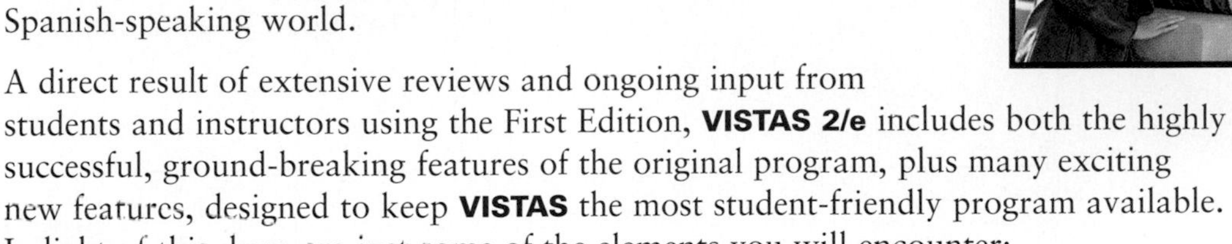

A direct result of extensive reviews and ongoing input from students and instructors using the First Edition, **VISTAS 2/e** includes both the highly successful, ground-breaking features of the original program, plus many exciting new features, designed to keep **VISTAS** the most student-friendly program available. In light of this, here are just some of the elements you will encounter:

Original, hallmark features

- A unique, easy-to-navigate design built around color-coded sections that appear either completely on one page or on spreads of two facing pages
- Integration of an appealing video, up-front in each lesson of the student text
- Practical, high-frequency vocabulary in meaningful contexts
- Clear, comprehensive grammar explanations with high-impact graphics and other special features that make structures easier to learn and use
- Ample guided, focused practice to make you comfortable with the vocabulary and grammar you are learning and to give you a solid foundation for communication
- An emphasis on communicative interactions with a classmate, small groups, the full class, and your instructor
- Careful development of reading, writing, and listening skills incorporating learning strategies and a process approach
- Integration of the culture of the everyday lives of Spanish speakers and coverage of the entire Spanish-speaking world
- Unprecedented learning support through on-the-spot student sidebars and on-page correlations of the print and technology ancillaries for each lesson section
- A complete set of print and technology ancillaries to help you learn Spanish more easily

New to the Second Edition

- Revised grammar scope and sequence for improved coverage within and across lessons
- Jump-start **A primera vista** activities on each lesson's opening page
- Engaging information gap activities in diverse formats
- Increased coverage of culture and opportunities for reading
- New ancillaries like Vocabulary CDs, **Panorama cultural** Video, DVDs, and the online **VISTAS** eText, all closely integrated with your student text

VISTAS 2/e has eighteen lessons, each of which is organized exactly the same way. To familiarize yourself with the organization of the text, as well as its *original* and *new* features, turn to page xiv and take the **at-a-glance** tour.

table of contents

	contextos	fotonovela

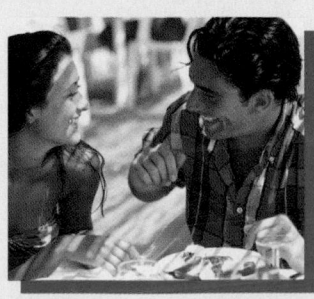

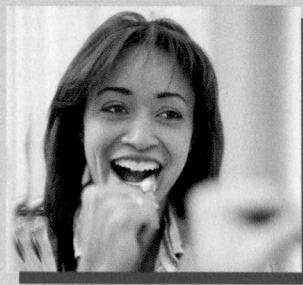

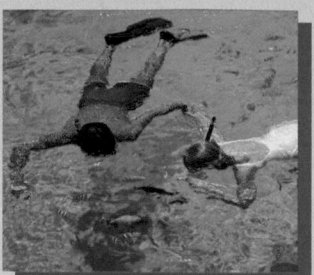

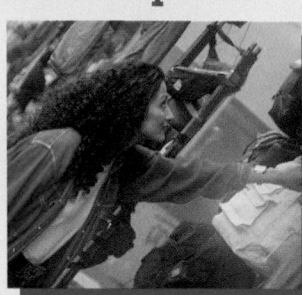

table of contents

	contextos	fotonovela

estructura	adelante	panorama

table of contents

	contextos	fotonovela
Lección 9		

Lección 9
Las fiestas

Lección 10
En el consultorio

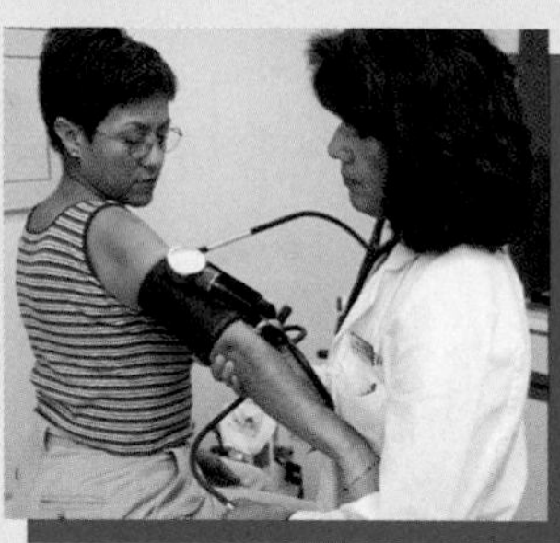

Lección 11
La tecnología

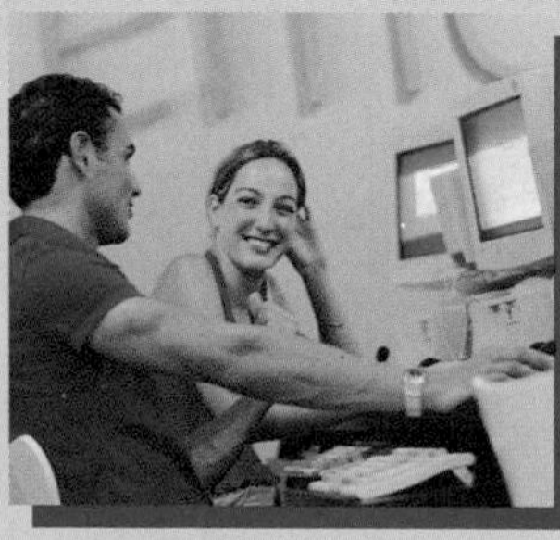

Lección 12
La vivienda

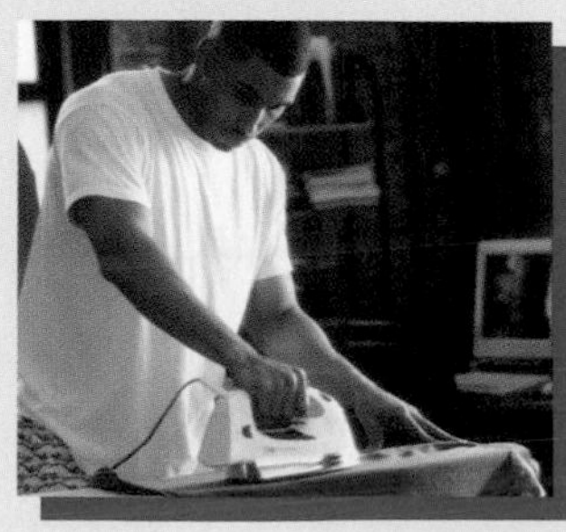

table of contents

	contextos	fotonovela

Lección 13
La naturaleza

Lección 14
En la ciudad

Lección 15
El bienestar

Lección 16
El mundo del trabajo

	contextos	fotonovela

Lección 17
Un festival de arte

Lección 18
Las actualidades

Consulta (*Reference*)

estructura	adelante	panorama

Lesson Openers
outline the content and features of each lesson

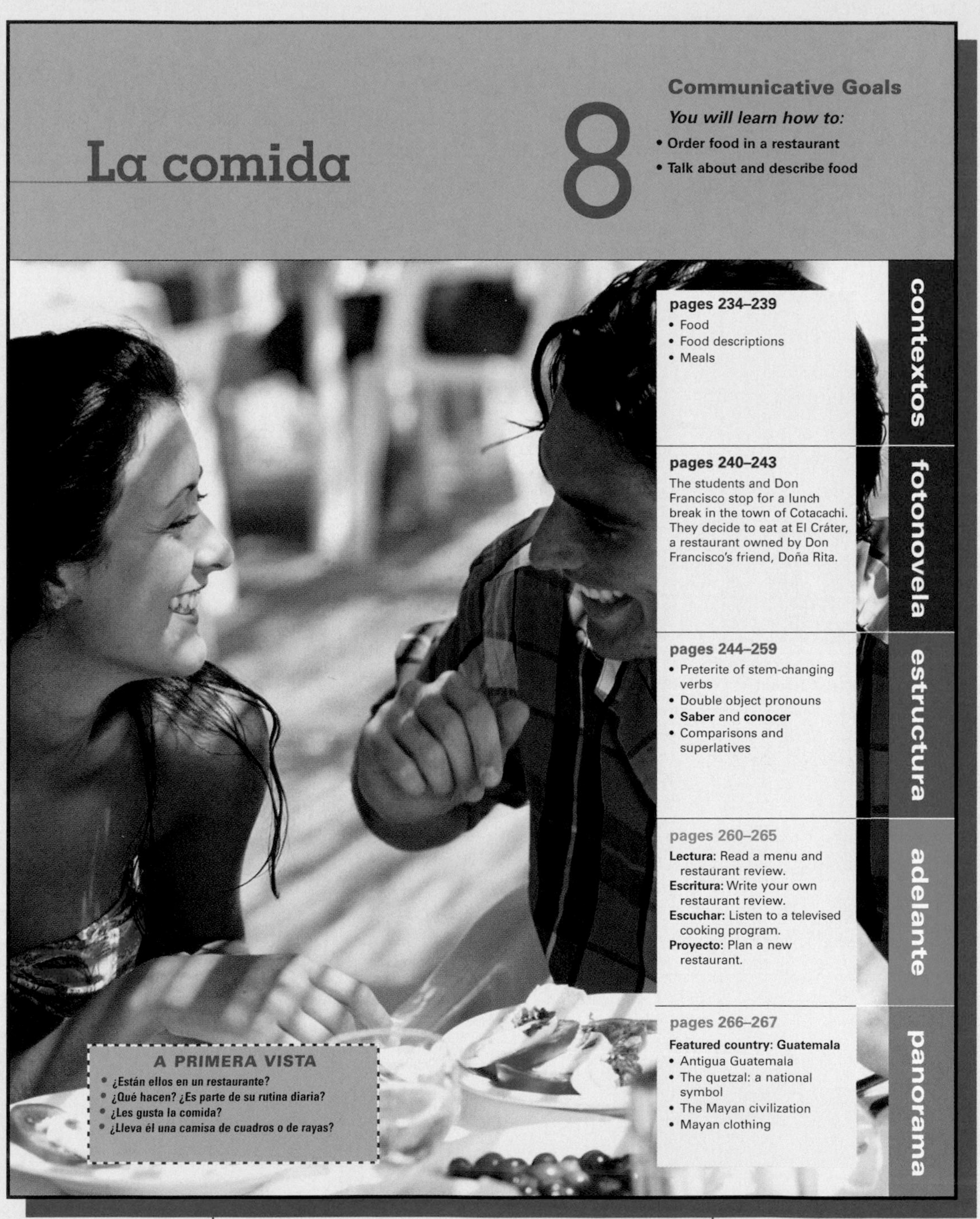

La comida
8
Communicative Goals
You will learn how to:
• Order food in a restaurant
• Talk about and describe food
contextos
pages 234–239
• Food
• Food descriptions
• Meals
fotonovela
pages 240–243
The students and Don Francisco stop for a lunch break in the town of Cotacachi. They decide to eat at El Cráter, a restaurant owned by Don Francisco's friend, Doña Rita.
estructura
pages 244–259
• Preterite of stem-changing verbs
• Double object pronouns
• Saber and conocer
• Comparisons and superlatives
adelante
pages 260–265
Lectura: Read a menu and restaurant review.
Escritura: Write your own restaurant review.
Escuchar: Listen to a televised cooking program.
Proyecto: Plan a new restaurant.
panorama
pages 266–267
Featured country: Guatemala
• Antigua Guatemala
• The quetzal: a national symbol
• The Mayan civilization
• Mayan clothing
A PRIMERA VISTA
• ¿Están ellos en un restaurante?
• ¿Qué hacen? ¿Es parte de su rutina diaria?
• ¿Les gusta la comida?
• ¿Lleva él una camisa de cuadros o de rayas?

New! A primera vista activities jump-start the lessons, allowing you to use the Spanish you know to talk about the photos.

Communicative goals highlights the real-life tasks you will be able to carry out in Spanish by the end of each lesson.

Contextos
presents vocabulary in meaningful contexts

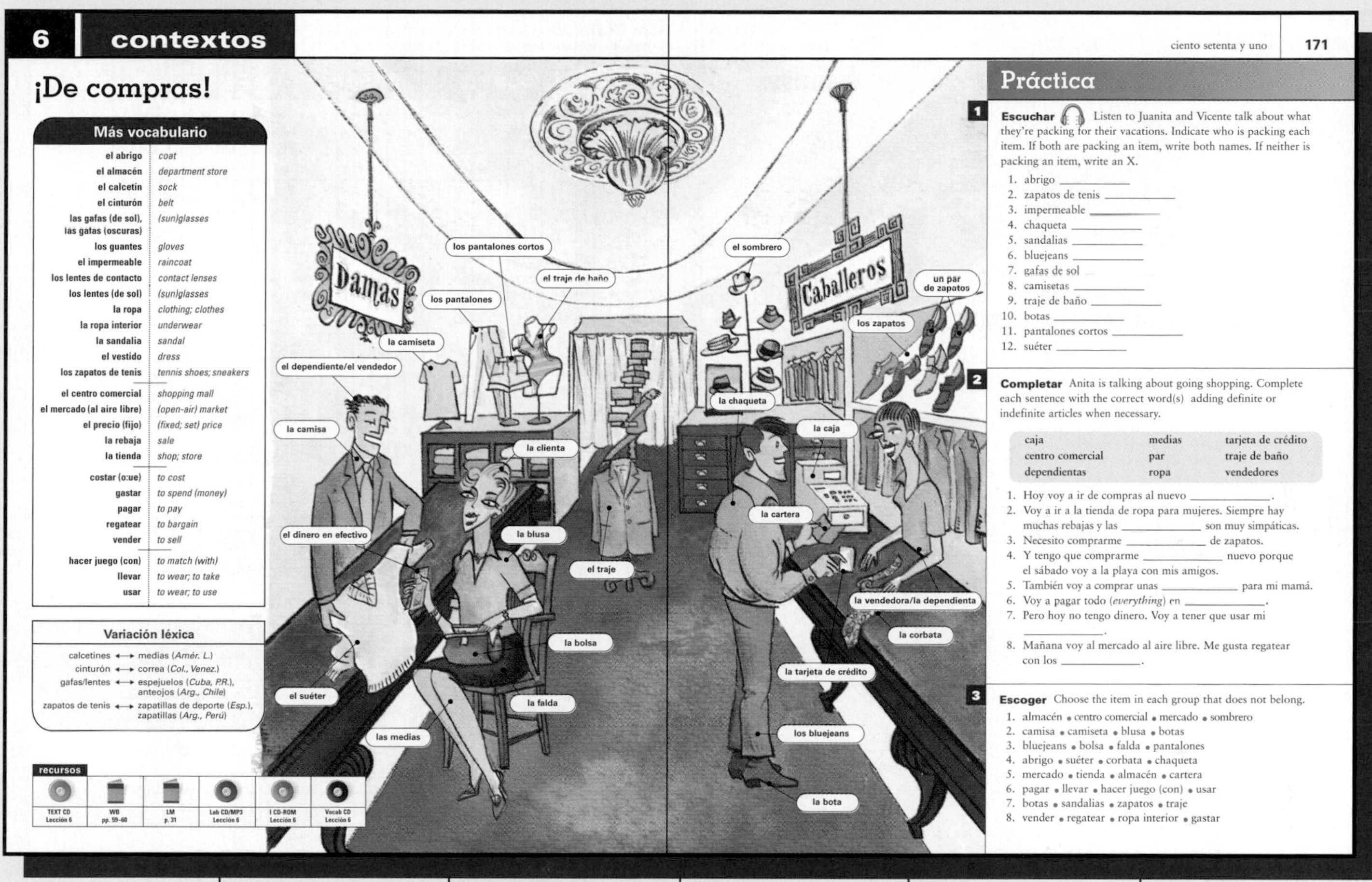

6 contextos

¡De compras!

Más vocabulario

el abrigo	*coat*
el almacén	*department store*
el calcetín	*sock*
el cinturón	*belt*
las gafas (de sol), las gafas (oscuras)	*(sun)glasses*
los guantes	*gloves*
el impermeable	*raincoat*
los lentes de contacto	*contact lenses*
los lentes (de sol)	*(sun)glasses*
la ropa	*clothing; clothes*
la ropa interior	*underwear*
la sandalia	*sandal*
el vestido	*dress*
los zapatos de tenis	*tennis shoes; sneakers*
el centro comercial	*shopping mall*
el mercado (al aire libre)	*(open-air) market*
el precio (fijo)	*(fixed; set) price*
la rebaja	*sale*
la tienda	*shop; store*
costar (o:ue)	*to cost*
gastar	*to spend (money)*
pagar	*to pay*
regatear	*to bargain*
vender	*to sell*
hacer juego (con)	*to match (with)*
llevar	*to wear; to take*
usar	*to wear; to use*

Variación léxica

calcetines ←→ medias (*Amér. L.*)
cinturón ←→ correa (*Col., Venez.*)
gafas/lentes ←→ espejuelos (*Cuba, P.R.*), anteojos (*Arg., Chile*)
zapatos de tenis ←→ zapatillas de deporte (*Esp.*), zapatillas (*Arg., Perú*)

recursos

TEXT CD Lección 6	WB pp. 59–60	LM p. 31	Lab CD/MP3 Lección 6	I CD-ROM Lección 6	Vocab CD Lección 6

ciento setenta y uno 171

Práctica

1 Escuchar Listen to Juanita and Vicente talk about what they're packing for their vacations. Indicate who is packing each item. If both are packing an item, write both names. If neither is packing an item, write an X.

1. abrigo ___________
2. zapatos de tenis ___________
3. impermeable ___________
4. chaqueta ___________
5. sandalias ___________
6. bluejeans ___________
7. gafas de sol ___________
8. camisetas ___________
9. traje de baño ___________
10. botas ___________
11. pantalones cortos ___________
12. suéter ___________

2 Completar Anita is talking about going shopping. Complete each sentence with the correct word(s) adding definite or indefinite articles when necessary.

caja	medias	tarjeta de crédito
centro comercial	par	traje de baño
dependientas	ropa	vendedores

1. Hoy voy a ir de compras al nuevo ___________.
2. Voy a ir a la tienda de ropa para mujeres. Siempre hay muchas rebajas y las ___________ son muy simpáticas.
3. Necesito comprarme ___________ de zapatos.
4. Y tengo que comprarme ___________ nuevo porque el sábado voy a la playa con mis amigos.
5. También voy a comprar unas ___________ para mi mamá.
6. Voy a pagar todo (*everything*) en ___________.
7. Pero hoy no tengo dinero. Voy a tener que usar mi ___________.
8. Mañana voy al mercado al aire libre. Me gusta regatear con los ___________.

3 Escoger Choose the item in each group that does not belong.

1. almacén • centro comercial • mercado • sombrero
2. camisa • camiseta • blusa • botas
3. bluejeans • bolsa • falda • pantalones
4. abrigo • suéter • corbata • chaqueta
5. mercado • tienda • almacén • cartera
6. pagar • llevar • hacer juego (con) • usar
7. botas • sandalias • zapatos • traje
8. vender • regatear • ropa interior • gastar

Más vocabulario boxes call out other important theme-related vocabulary in easy-to-reference Spanish-English lists.

Illustrations High-frequency vocabulary is introduced through expansive, full-color illustrations.

Práctica This section always begins with a listening exercise and continues with activities that practice the new vocabulary in meaningful contexts.

Variación léxica presents alternate words and expressions used throughout the Spanish-speaking world.

New! Recursos The icons in the **recursos** boxes are color-coded to match those of the actual components, making it even easier for you to know exactly what print and technology ancillaries you can use to reinforce and expand on every section of every lesson.

Contextos
practices vocabulary in a variety of formats

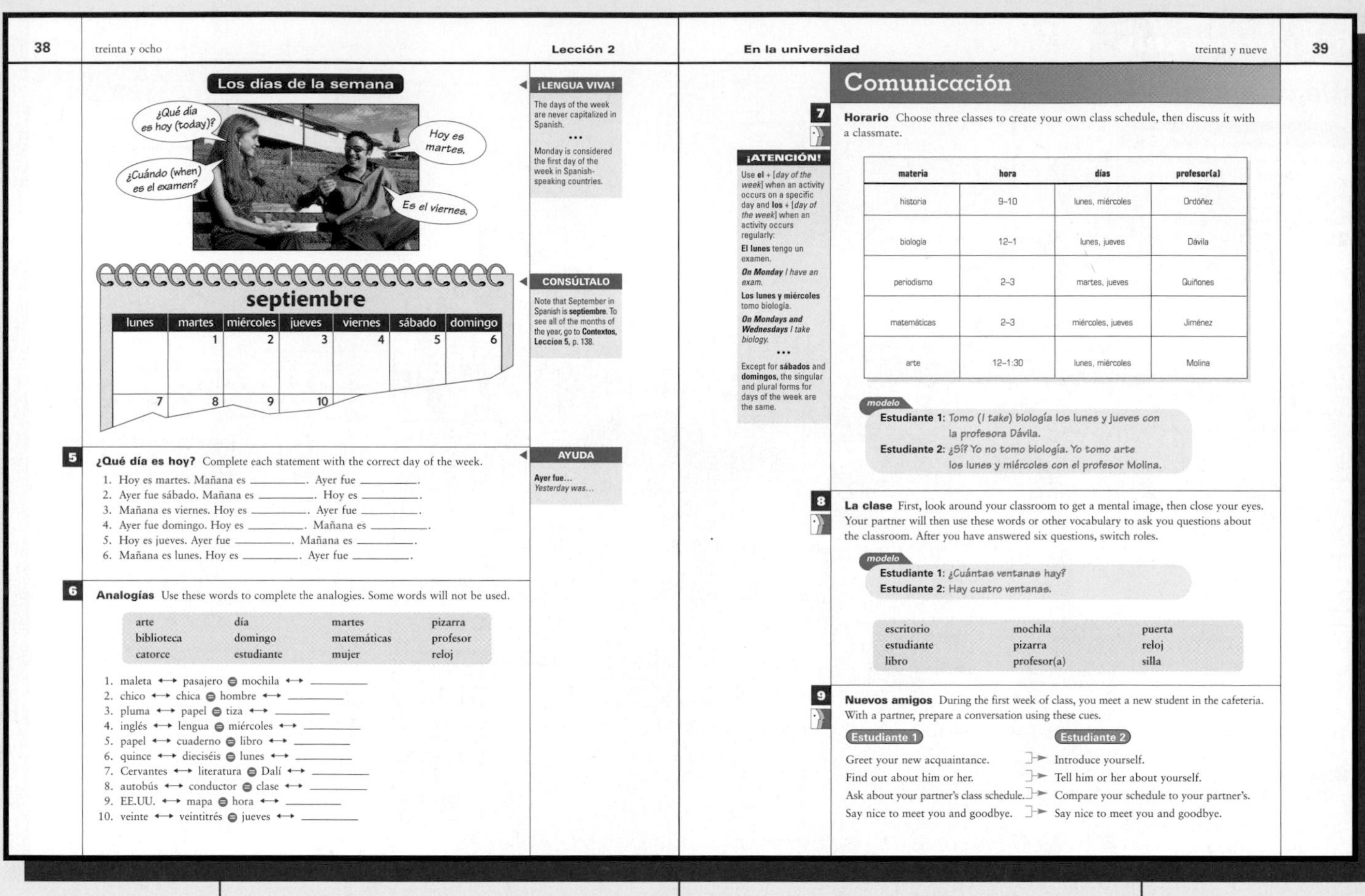

38 treinta y ocho **Lección 2**

Los días de la semana

¿Qué día es hoy (today)?
Hoy es martes.
¿Cuándo (when) es el examen?
Es el viernes.

septiembre

lunes	martes	miércoles	jueves	viernes	sábado	domingo
	1	2	3	4	5	6
7	8	9	10			

¡LENGUA VIVA!

The days of the week are never capitalized in Spanish.

• • •

Monday is considered the first day of the week in Spanish-speaking countries.

CONSÚLTALO

Note that September in Spanish is **septiembre**. To see all of the months of the year, go to **Contextos, Leccion 5**, p. 138.

5 **¿Qué día es hoy?** Complete each statement with the correct day of the week.

1. Hoy es martes. Mañana es ________. Ayer fue ________.
2. Ayer fue sábado. Mañana es ________. Hoy es ________.
3. Mañana es viernes. Hoy es ________. Ayer fue ________.
4. Ayer fue domingo. Hoy es ________. Mañana es ________.
5. Hoy es jueves. Ayer fue ________. Mañana es ________.
6. Mañana es lunes. Hoy es ________. Ayer fue ________.

AYUDA

Ayer fue...
Yesterday was...

6 **Analogías** Use these words to complete the analogies. Some words will not be used.

arte	día	martes	pizarra
biblioteca	domingo	matemáticas	profesor
catorce	estudiante	mujer	reloj

1. maleta ⟷ pasajero ⊜ mochila ⟷ ________
2. chico ⟷ chica ⊜ hombre ⟷ ________
3. pluma ⟷ papel ⊜ tiza ⟷ ________
4. inglés ⟷ lengua ⊜ miércoles ⟷ ________
5. papel ⟷ cuaderno ⊜ libro ⟷ ________
6. quince ⟷ dieciséis ⊜ lunes ⟷ ________
7. Cervantes ⟷ literatura ⊜ Dalí ⟷ ________
8. autobús ⟷ conductor ⊜ clase ⟷ ________
9. EE.UU. ⟷ mapa ⊜ hora ⟷ ________
10. veinte ⟷ veintitrés ⊜ jueves ⟷ ________

En la universidad treinta y nueve 39

Comunicación

7 **Horario** Choose three classes to create your own class schedule, then discuss it with a classmate.

materia	hora	días	profesor(a)
historia	9–10	lunes, miércoles	Ordóñez
biología	12–1	lunes, jueves	Dávila
periodismo	2–3	martes, jueves	Quiñones
matemáticas	2–3	miércoles, jueves	Jiménez
arte	12–1:30	lunes, miércoles	Molina

modelo

Estudiante 1: *Tomo (I take) biología los lunes y jueves con la profesora Dávila.*

Estudiante 2: *¿Sí? Yo no tomo biología. Yo tomo arte los lunes y miércoles con el profesor Molina.*

¡ATENCIÓN!

Use **el** + [*day of the week*] when an activity occurs on a specific day and **los** + [*day of the week*] when an activity occurs regularly:

El lunes tengo un examen.

***On Monday** I have an exam.*

Los lunes y miércoles tomo biología.

***On Mondays and Wednesdays** I take biology.*

• • •

Except for **sábados** and **domingos,** the singular and plural forms for days of the week are the same.

8 **La clase** First, look around your classroom to get a mental image, then close your eyes. Your partner will then use these words or other vocabulary to ask you questions about the classroom. After you have answered six questions, switch roles.

modelo

Estudiante 1: *¿Cuántas ventanas hay?*

Estudiante 2: *Hay cuatro ventanas.*

escritorio	mochila	puerta
estudiante	pizarra	reloj
libro	profesor(a)	silla

9 **Nuevos amigos** During the first week of class, you meet a new student in the cafeteria. With a partner, prepare a conversation using these cues.

Estudiante 1		Estudiante 2
Greet your new acquaintance.	→	Introduce yourself.
Find out about him or her.	→	Tell him or her about yourself.
Ask about your partner's class schedule.	→	Compare your schedule to your partner's.
Say nice to meet you and goodbye.	→	Say nice to meet you and goodbye.

Práctica exercises reinforce the vocabulary through varied and engaging formats.

Student sidebars provide handy, on-the-spot information that helps you complete the activities.

Comunicación activities allow you to use the vocabulary creatively in interactions with a partner, a small group, or the entire class.

Icons provide on-the-spot visual cues for various types of activities: pair, small group, listening-based, video-related, handout-based, and information gap. For a legend explaining all icons used in the student text, see page xxviii.

Fotonovela
tells the story of four students traveling in Ecuador

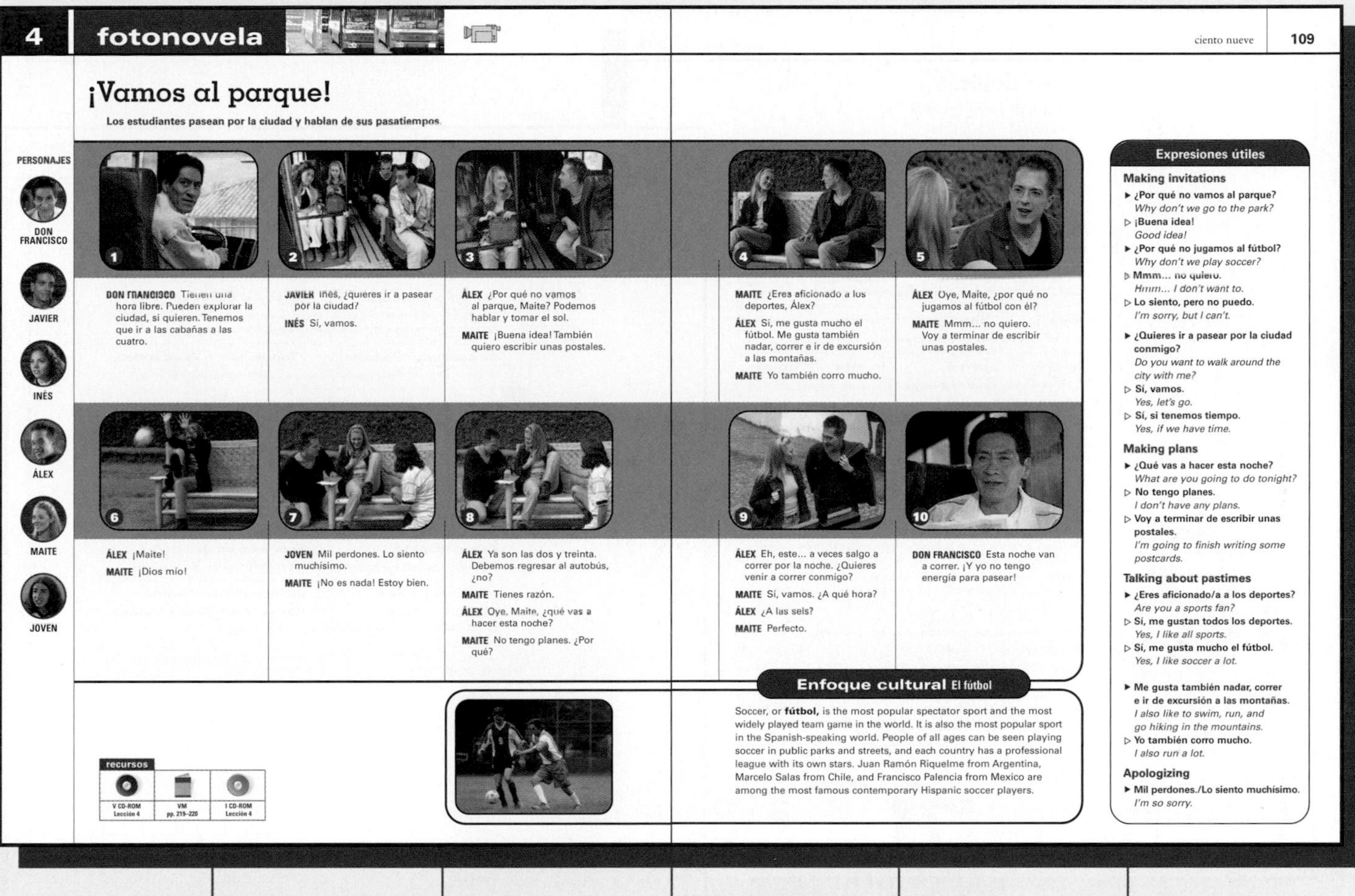
4 fotonovela

ciento nueve 109

¡Vamos al parque!

Los estudiantes pasean por la ciudad y hablan de sus pasatiempos.

PERSONAJES: DON FRANCISCO, JAVIER, INÉS, ÁLEX, MAITE, JOVEN

1 **DON FRANCISCO** Tienen una hora libre. Pueden explorar la ciudad, si quieren. Tenemos que ir a las cabañas a las cuatro.

2 **JAVIER** Inés, ¿quieres ir a pasear por la ciudad?
INÉS Sí, vamos.

3 **ÁLEX** ¿Por qué no vamos al parque, Maite? Podemos hablar y tomar el sol.
MAITE ¡Buena idea! También quiero escribir unas postales.

4 **MAITE** ¿Eres aficionado a los deportes, Álex?
ÁLEX Sí, me gusta mucho el fútbol. Me gusta también nadar, correr e ir de excursión a las montañas.
MAITE Yo también corro mucho.

5 **ÁLEX** Oye, Maite, ¿por qué no jugamos al fútbol con él?
MAITE Mmm... no quiero. Voy a terminar de escribir unas postales.

6 **ÁLEX** ¡Maite!
MAITE ¡Dios mío!

7 **JOVEN** Mil perdones. Lo siento muchísimo.
MAITE ¡No es nada! Estoy bien.

8 **ÁLEX** Ya son las dos y treinta. Debemos regresar al autobús, ¿no?
MAITE Tienes razón.
ÁLEX Oye, Maite, ¿qué vas a hacer esta noche?
MAITE No tengo planes. ¿Por qué?

9 **ÁLEX** Eh, este... a veces salgo a correr por la noche. ¿Quieres venir a correr conmigo?
MAITE Sí, vamos. ¿A qué hora?
ÁLEX ¿A las seis?
MAITE Perfecto.

10 **DON FRANCISCO** Esta noche van a correr. ¡Y yo no tengo energía para pasear!

Expresiones útiles

Making invitations
- ¿Por qué no vamos al parque? *Why don't we go to the park?*
- ¡Buena idea! *Good idea!*
- ¿Por qué no jugamos al fútbol? *Why don't we play soccer?*
- Mmm... no quiero. *Hmm... I don't want to.*
- Lo siento, pero no puedo. *I'm sorry, but I can't.*
- ¿Quieres ir a pasear por la ciudad conmigo? *Do you want to walk around the city with me?*
- Sí, vamos. *Yes, let's go.*
- Sí, si tenemos tiempo. *Yes, if we have time.*

Making plans
- ¿Qué vas a hacer esta noche? *What are you going to do tonight?*
- No tengo planes. *I don't have any plans.*
- Voy a terminar de escribir unas postales. *I'm going to finish writing some postcards.*

Talking about pastimes
- ¿Eres aficionado/a a los deportes? *Are you a sports fan?*
- Sí, me gustan todos los deportes. *Yes, I like all sports.*
- Sí, me gusta mucho el fútbol. *Yes, I like soccer a lot.*
- Me gusta también nadar, correr e ir de excursión a las montañas. *I also like to swim, run, and go hiking in the mountains.*
- Yo también corro mucho. *I also run a lot.*

Apologizing
- Mil perdones./Lo siento muchísimo. *I'm so sorry.*

Enfoque cultural El fútbol

Soccer, or **fútbol**, is the most popular spectator sport and the most widely played team game in the world. It is also the most popular sport in the Spanish-speaking world. People of all ages can be seen playing soccer in public parks and streets, and each country has a professional league with its own stars. Juan Ramón Riquelme from Argentina, Marcelo Salas from Chile, and Francisco Palencia from Mexico are among the most famous contemporary Hispanic soccer players.

recursos: V CD-ROM Lección 4 | VM pp. 219–220 | I CD-ROM Lección 4

Personajes The photo-based conversations take place among a cast of recurring characters—four college students on vacation in Ecuador and the bus driver who accompanies them.

***Fotonovela* Video** The **Fotonovela** episode appears in the **Fotonovela** Video Program. To learn more about the video, turn to page xxvi.

Conversations Taken from the **Fotonovela** video, the conversations reinforce vocabulary from **Contextos**. They also preview structures from the upcoming **Estructura** section in context *and* in a comprehensible way.

Enfoque cultural provides detailed cultural information on a topic related to the **Fotonovela** conversation.

Expresiones útiles organizes new, active words and expressions by language function so you can focus on using them for real-life, practical purposes.

Pronunciación & Ortografía present the rules of Spanish pronunciation and spelling

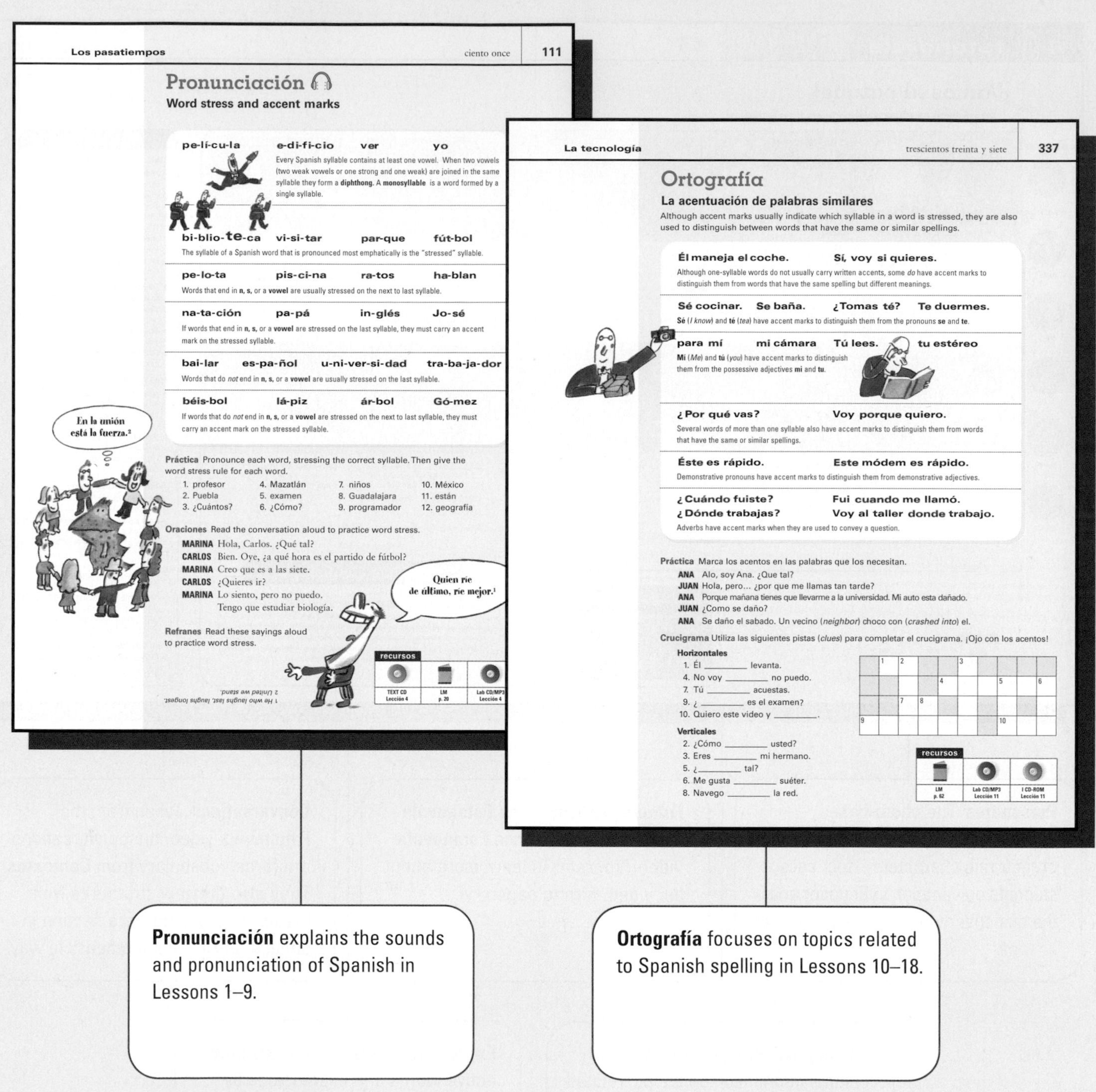

Pronunciación explains the sounds and pronunciation of Spanish in Lessons 1–9.

Ortografía focuses on topics related to Spanish spelling in Lessons 10–18.

Estructura
presents Spanish grammar in a graphic-intensive format

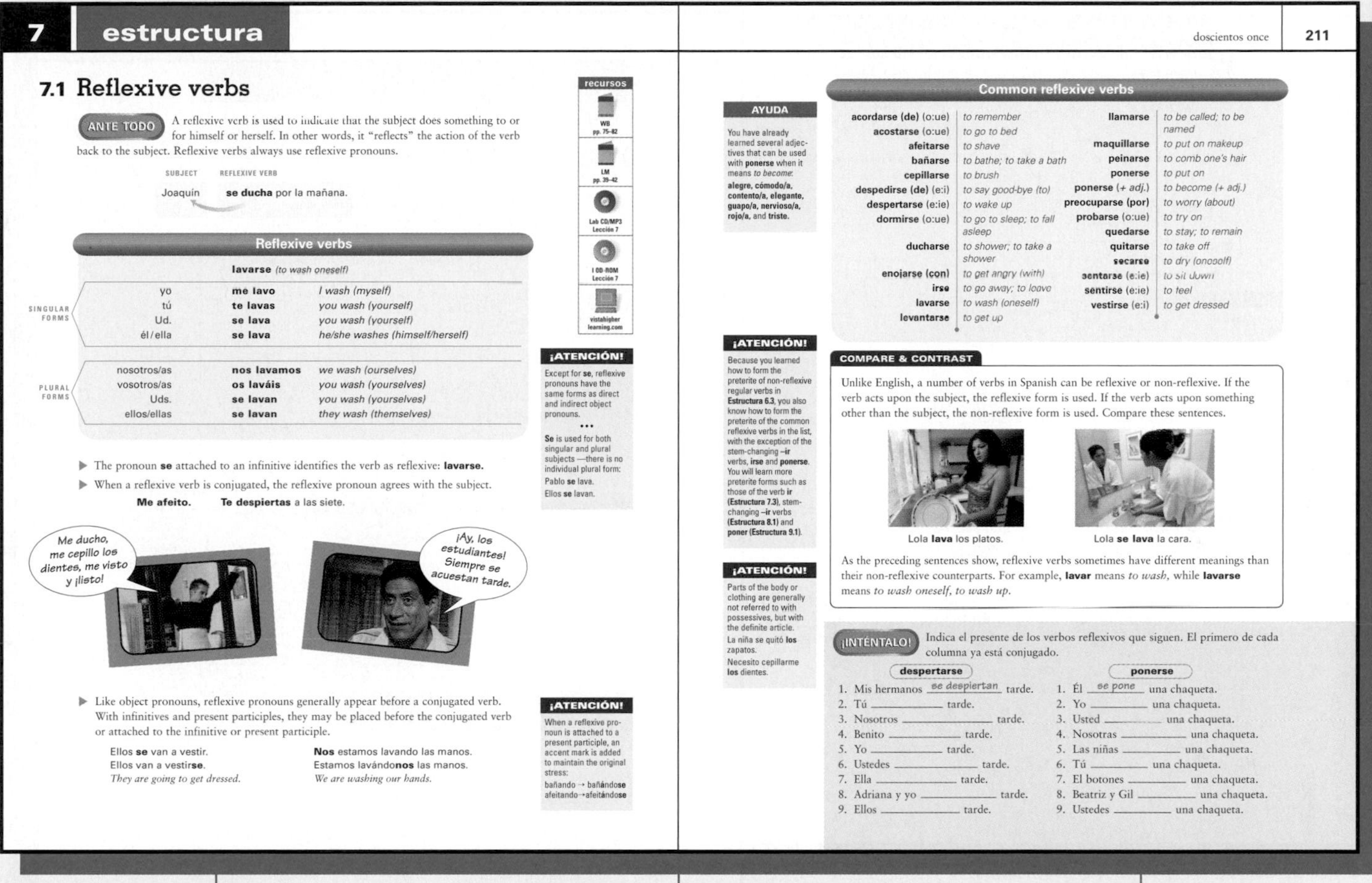

7 **estructura**

7.1 Reflexive verbs

ANTE TODO A reflexive verb is used to indicate that the subject does something to or for himself or herself. In other words, it "reflects" the action of the verb back to the subject. Reflexive verbs always use reflexive pronouns.

SUBJECT REFLEXIVE VERB
Joaquín **se ducha** por la mañana.

Reflexive verbs

		lavarse *(to wash oneself)*	
SINGULAR FORMS	yo	**me lavo**	*I wash (myself)*
	tú	**te lavas**	*you wash (yourself)*
	Ud.	**se lava**	*you wash (yourself)*
	él/ella	**se lava**	*he/she washes (himself/herself)*
PLURAL FORMS	nosotros/as	**nos lavamos**	*we wash (ourselves)*
	vosotros/as	**os laváis**	*you wash (yourselves)*
	Uds.	**se lavan**	*you wash (yourselves)*
	ellos/ellas	**se lavan**	*they wash (themselves)*

▶ The pronoun **se** attached to an infinitive identifies the verb as reflexive: **lavarse.**

▶ When a reflexive verb is conjugated, the reflexive pronoun agrees with the subject.

Me afeito. **Te despiertas** a las siete.

Me ducho, me cepillo los dientes, me visto y ¡listo!

¡Ay, los estudiantes! Siempre se acuestan tarde.

▶ Like object pronouns, reflexive pronouns generally appear before a conjugated verb. With infinitives and present participles, they may be placed before the conjugated verb or attached to the infinitive or present participle.

Ellos **se** van a vestir.
Ellos van a vestir**se**.
They are going to get dressed.

Nos estamos lavando las manos.
Estamos lavándo**nos** las manos.
We are washing our hands.

recursos: WB pp. 75–82; LM pp. 39–42; Lab CD/MP3 Lección 7; I CD-ROM Lección 7; vistahigherlearning.com

¡ATENCIÓN!
Except for **se**, reflexive pronouns have the same forms as direct and indirect object pronouns.
• • •
Se is used for both singular and plural subjects —there is no individual plural form:
Pablo **se** lava.
Ellos **se** lavan.

¡ATENCIÓN!
When a reflexive pronoun is attached to a present participle, an accent mark is added to maintain the original stress:
bañando → bañ**á**ndo**se**
afeitando → afeit**á**ndo**se**

doscientos once 211

AYUDA
You have already learned several adjectives that can be used with **ponerse** when it means *to become*:
alegre, cómodo/a, contento/a, elegante, guapo/a, nervioso/a, rojo/a, and **triste.**

Common reflexive verbs

acordarse (de) (o:ue)	*to remember*	**llamarse**	*to be called; to be named*
acostarse (o:ue)	*to go to bed*	**maquillarse**	*to put on makeup*
afeitarse	*to shave*	**peinarse**	*to comb one's hair*
bañarse	*to bathe; to take a bath*	**ponerse**	*to put on*
cepillarse	*to brush*	**ponerse** (+ *adj.*)	*to become (+ adj.)*
despedirse (de) (e:i)	*to say good-bye (to)*	**preocuparse (por)**	*to worry (about)*
despertarse (e:ie)	*to wake up*	**probarse** (o:ue)	*to try on*
dormirse (o:ue)	*to go to sleep; to fall asleep*	**quedarse**	*to stay; to remain*
ducharse	*to shower; to take a shower*	**quitarse**	*to take off*
		secarse	*to dry (oneself)*
enojarse (con)	*to get angry (with)*	**sentarse** (e:ie)	*to sit down*
irse	*to go away; to leave*	**sentirse** (e:ie)	*to feel*
lavarse	*to wash (oneself)*	**vestirse** (e:i)	*to get dressed*
levantarse	*to get up*		

¡ATENCIÓN!
Because you learned how to form the preterite of non-reflexive regular verbs in **Estructura 6.3**, you also know how to form the preterite of the common reflexive verbs in the list, with the exception of the stem-changing **–ir** verbs, **irse** and **ponerse**. You will learn more preterite forms such as those of the verb **ir** (**Estructura 7.3**), stem-changing **–ir** verbs (**Estructura 8.1**) and **poner** (**Estructura 9.1**).

COMPARE & CONTRAST

Unlike English, a number of verbs in Spanish can be reflexive or non-reflexive. If the verb acts upon the subject, the reflexive form is used. If the verb acts upon something other than the subject, the non-reflexive form is used. Compare these sentences.

Lola **lava** los platos.

Lola **se lava** la cara.

As the preceding sentences show, reflexive verbs sometimes have different meanings than their non-reflexive counterparts. For example, **lavar** means *to wash*, while **lavarse** means *to wash oneself, to wash up*.

¡ATENCIÓN!
Parts of the body or clothing are generally not referred to with possessives, but with the definite article.
La niña se quitó **los** zapatos.
Necesito cepillarme **los** dientes.

¡INTÉNTALO! Indica el presente de los verbos reflexivos que siguen. El primero de cada columna ya está conjugado.

despertarse	ponerse
1. Mis hermanos *se despiertan* tarde.	1. Él *se pone* una chaqueta.
2. Tú ________ tarde.	2. Yo ________ una chaqueta.
3. Nosotros ________ tarde.	3. Usted ________ una chaqueta.
4. Benito ________ tarde.	4. Nosotras ________ una chaqueta.
5. Yo ________ tarde.	5. Las niñas ________ una chaqueta.
6. Ustedes ________ tarde.	6. Tú ________ una chaqueta.
7. Ella ________ tarde.	7. El botones ________ una chaqueta.
8. Adriana y yo ________ tarde.	8. Beatriz y Gil ________ una chaqueta.
9. Ellos ________ tarde.	9. Ustedes ________ una chaqueta.

Ante todo eases you into the grammar with definitions of grammatical terms, reminders about what you already know of English grammar, and Spanish grammar you have learned in earlier lessons.

Compare & contrast focuses on aspects of grammar that native speakers of English may find difficult, clarifying similarities and differences between Spanish and English.

Diagrams To clarify concepts, clear and easy-to-grasp grammar explanations are reinforced by diagrams that colorfully present sample words, phrases, and sentences.

Charts To help you learn, colorful, easy-to-use charts call out key grammatical structures and forms, as well as important related vocabulary.

Student sidebars provide you with on-the-spot linguistic, cultural, or language-learning information directly related to the materials in front of you.

¡Inténtalo! exercises offer an easy first step in your practice of each new grammar point. They get you working with the grammar right away in simple, easy-to-understand formats.

Estructura
provides directed and communicative practice

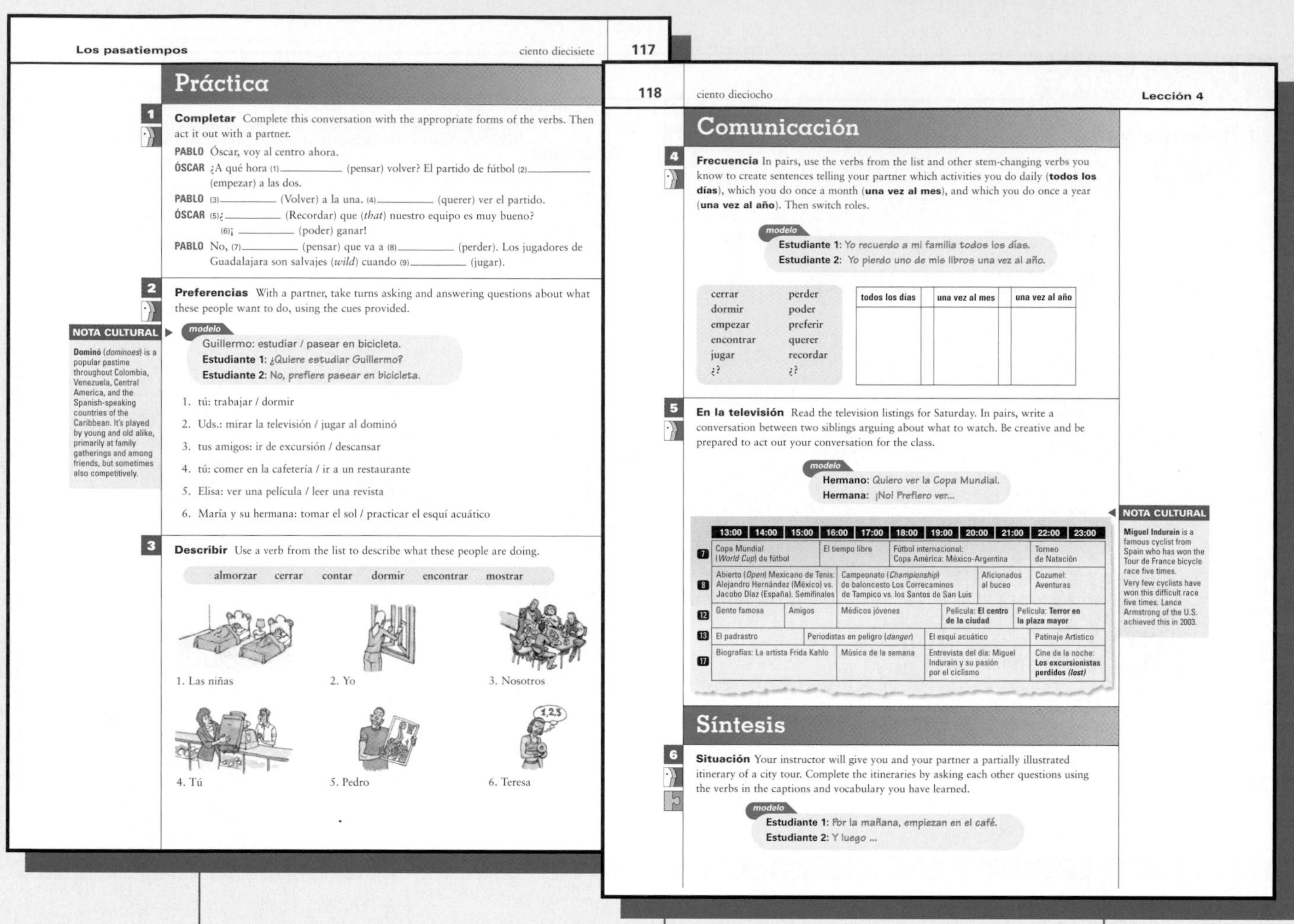
Los pasatiempos ciento diecisiete 117

Práctica

1 Completar Complete this conversation with the appropriate forms of the verbs. Then act it out with a partner.

PABLO Óscar, voy al centro ahora.
ÓSCAR ¿A qué hora (1)________ (pensar) volver? El partido de fútbol (2)________ (empezar) a las dos.
PABLO (3)________ (Volver) a la una. (4)________ (querer) ver el partido.
ÓSCAR (5)¿________ (Recordar) que (*that*) nuestro equipo es muy bueno? (6)¿________ (poder) ganar!
PABLO No, (7)________ (pensar) que va a (8)________ (perder). Los jugadores de Guadalajara son salvajes (*wild*) cuando (9)________ (jugar).

2 Preferencias With a partner, take turns asking and answering questions about what these people want to do, using the cues provided.

NOTA CULTURAL
Dominó (*dominoes*) is a popular pastime throughout Colombia, Venezuela, Central America, and the Spanish-speaking countries of the Caribbean. It's played by young and old alike, primarily at family gatherings and among friends, but sometimes also competitively.

modelo
Guillermo: estudiar / pasear en bicicleta.
Estudiante 1: *¿Quiere estudiar Guillermo?*
Estudiante 2: *No, prefiere pasear en bicicleta.*

1. tú: trabajar / dormir
2. Uds.: mirar la televisión / jugar al dominó
3. tus amigos: ir de excursión / descansar
4. tú: comer en la cafetería / ir a un restaurante
5. Elisa: ver una película / leer una revista
6. María y su hermana: tomar el sol / practicar el esquí acuático

3 Describir Use a verb from the list to describe what these people are doing.

almorzar cerrar contar dormir encontrar mostrar

1. Las niñas 2. Yo 3. Nosotros
4. Tú 5. Pedro 6. Teresa

118 ciento dieciocho Lección 4

Comunicación

4 Frecuencia In pairs, use the verbs from the list and other stem-changing verbs you know to create sentences telling your partner which activities you do daily (**todos los días**), which you do once a month (**una vez al mes**), and which you do once a year (**una vez al año**). Then switch roles.

modelo
Estudiante 1: *Yo recuerdo a mi familia todos los días.*
Estudiante 2: *Yo pierdo uno de mis libros una vez al año.*

cerrar, dormir, empezar, encontrar, jugar, ¿?
perder, poder, preferir, querer, recordar, ¿?

todos los días	una vez al mes	una vez al año

5 En la televisión Read the television listings for Saturday. In pairs, write a conversation between two siblings arguing about what to watch. Be creative and be prepared to act out your conversation for the class.

modelo
Hermano: *Quiero ver la Copa Mundial.*
Hermana: *¡No! Prefiero ver...*

	13:00	14:00	15:00	16:00	17:00	18:00	19:00	20:00	21:00	22:00	23:00
7	Copa Mundial (*World Cup*) de fútbol			El tiempo libre		Fútbol internacional: Copa América: México-Argentina				Torneo de Natación	
8	Abierto (*Open*) Mexicano de Tenis: Alejandro Hernández (México) vs. Jacobo Díaz (España). Semifinales			Campeonato (*Championship*) de baloncesto Los Correcaminos de Tampico vs. los Santos de San Luis				Aficionados al buceo		Cozumel: Aventuras	
12	Gente famosa		Amigos	Médicos jóvenes				Película: **El centro de la ciudad**		Película: **Terror en la plaza mayor**	
13	El padrastro			Periodistas en peligro (*danger*)			El esquí acuático			Patinaje Artístico	
17	Biografías: La artista Frida Kahlo			Música de la semana			Entrevista del día: Miguel Induráin y su pasión por el ciclismo			Cine de la noche: **Los excursionistas perdidos** (*lost*)	

NOTA CULTURAL
Miguel Induráin is a famous cyclist from Spain who has won the Tour de France bicycle race five times. Very few cyclists have won this difficult race five times. Lance Armstrong of the U.S. achieved this in 2003.

Síntesis

6 Situación Your instructor will give you and your partner a partially illustrated itinerary of a city tour. Complete the itineraries by asking each other questions using the verbs in the captions and vocabulary you have learned.

modelo
Estudiante 1: *Por la mañana, empiezan en el café.*
Estudiante 2: *Y luego ...*

Práctica activities provide a wide range of guided, yet meaningful exercises that weave current and previously learned vocabulary together with the current grammar point.

Comunicación offers opportunities for creative expression using the lesson's grammar and vocabulary. These take place with a partner, in small groups, or with the whole class.

Síntesis integrates the current grammar point with previously learned points, providing built-in, consistent review and recycling as you progress through the text.

New! Information Gap activities engage you and a partner in problem-solving and other situations based on handouts your instructor gives you. However, you and your partner each have only half of the information you need, so you must work together to accomplish the task at hand.

Expanded! New reading-based activities involving authentic documents, dialogues, and other brief texts provide increased reading opportunities throughout the textbook.

Expanded! Increased *Nota cultural* sidebars expand coverage of the cultures of the Spanish-speaking peoples and countries with a special emphasis on everyday-life practices. In Spanish as of Lesson 7, the cultural notes also provide additional reading practice.

Adelante

Lectura develops reading skills in the context of the lesson theme

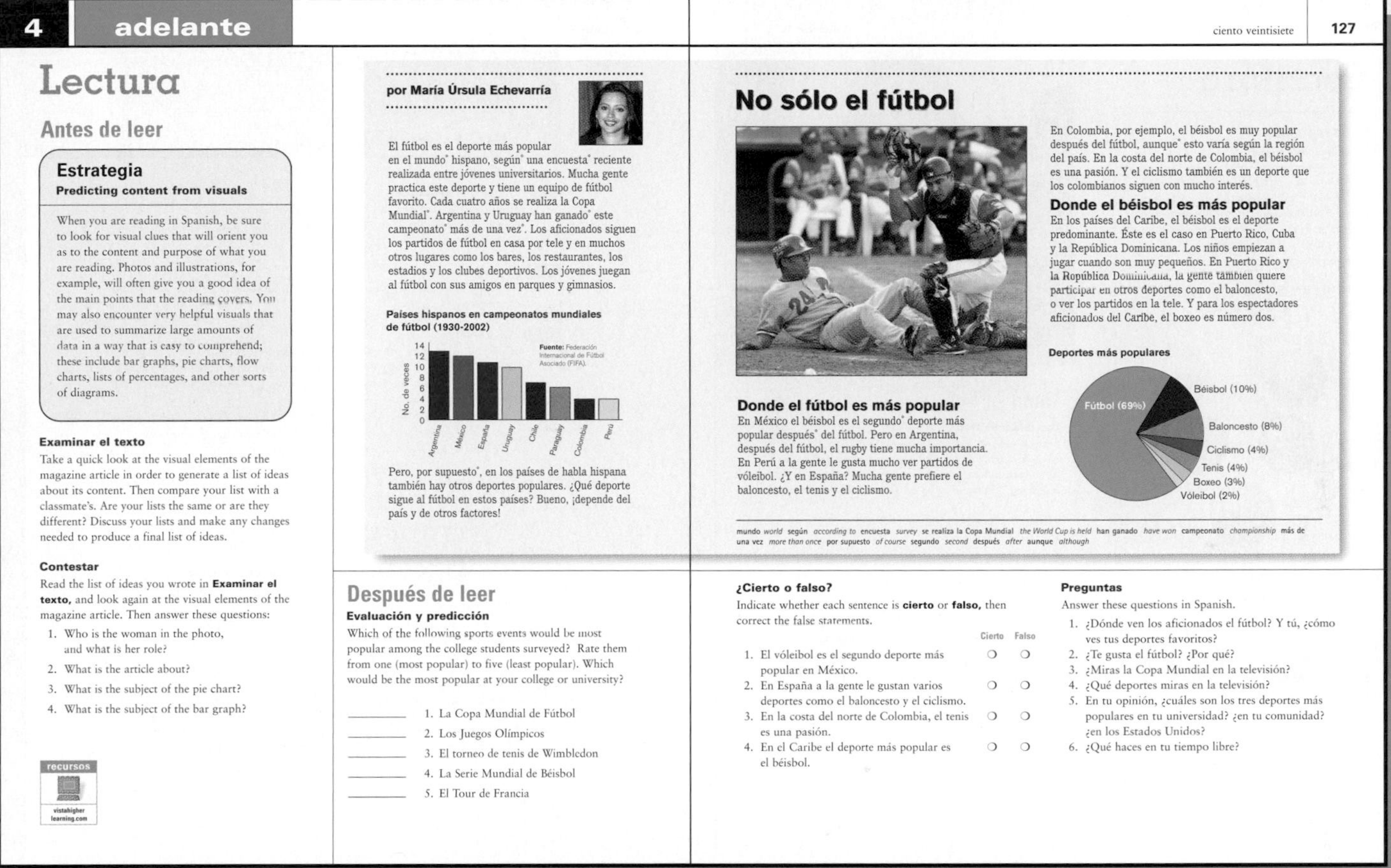

4 adelante | ciento veintisiete 127

Lectura

Antes de leer

Estrategia
Predicting content from visuals

When you are reading in Spanish, be sure to look for visual clues that will orient you as to the content and purpose of what you are reading. Photos and illustrations, for example, will often give you a good idea of the main points that the reading covers. You may also encounter very helpful visuals that are used to summarize large amounts of data in a way that is easy to comprehend; these include bar graphs, pie charts, flow charts, lists of percentages, and other sorts of diagrams.

Examinar el texto

Take a quick look at the visual elements of the magazine article in order to generate a list of ideas about its content. Then compare your list with a classmate's. Are your lists the same or are they different? Discuss your lists and make any changes needed to produce a final list of ideas.

Contestar

Read the list of ideas you wrote in **Examinar el texto,** and look again at the visual elements of the magazine article. Then answer these questions:

1. Who is the woman in the photo, and what is her role?
2. What is the article about?
3. What is the subject of the pie chart?
4. What is the subject of the bar graph?

recursos vistahigher learning.com

No sólo el fútbol

por María Úrsula Echevarría

El fútbol es el deporte más popular en el mundo hispano, según una encuesta reciente realizada entre jóvenes universitarios. Mucha gente practica este deporte y tiene un equipo de fútbol favorito. Cada cuatro años se realiza la Copa Mundial. Argentina y Uruguay han ganado este campeonato más de una vez. Los aficionados siguen los partidos de fútbol en casa por tele y en muchos otros lugares como los bares, los restaurantes, los estadios y los clubes deportivos. Los jóvenes juegan al fútbol con sus amigos en parques y gimnasios.

Países hispanos en campeonatos mundiales de fútbol (1930-2002)

Pero, por supuesto, en los países de habla hispana también hay otros deportes populares. ¿Qué deporte sigue al fútbol en estos países? Bueno, ¡depende del país y de otros factores!

Donde el fútbol es más popular

En México el béisbol es el segundo deporte más popular después del fútbol. Pero en Argentina, después del fútbol, el rugby tiene mucha importancia. En Perú a la gente le gusta mucho ver partidos de vóleibol. ¿Y en España? Mucha gente prefiere el baloncesto, el tenis y el ciclismo.

En Colombia, por ejemplo, el béisbol es muy popular después del fútbol, aunque esto varía según la región del país. En la costa del norte de Colombia, el béisbol es una pasión. Y el ciclismo también es un deporte que los colombianos siguen con mucho interés.

Donde el béisbol es más popular

En los países del Caribe, el béisbol es el deporte predominante. Éste es el caso en Puerto Rico, Cuba y la República Dominicana. Los niños empiezan a jugar cuando son muy pequeños. En Puerto Rico y la República Dominicana, la gente también quiere participar en otros deportes como el baloncesto, o ver los partidos en la tele. Y para los espectadores aficionados del Caribe, el boxeo es número dos.

Deportes más populares

mundo *world* **según** *according to* **encuesta** *survey* **se realiza la Copa Mundial** *the World Cup is held* **han ganado** *have won* **campeonato** *championship* **más de una vez** *more than once* **por supuesto** *of course* **segundo** *second* **después** *after* **aunque** *although*

Después de leer

Evaluación y predicción

Which of the following sports events would be most popular among the college students surveyed? Rate them from one (most popular) to five (least popular). Which would be the most popular at your college or university?

_______ 1. La Copa Mundial de Fútbol
_______ 2. Los Juegos Olímpicos
_______ 3. El torneo de tenis de Wimbledon
_______ 4. La Serie Mundial de Béisbol
_______ 5. El Tour de Francia

¿Cierto o falso?

Indicate whether each sentence is **cierto** or **falso,** then correct the false statements.

	Cierto	Falso
1. El vóleibol es el segundo deporte más popular en México.	❍	❍
2. En España a la gente le gustan varios deportes como el baloncesto y el ciclismo.	❍	❍
3. En la costa del norte de Colombia, el tenis es una pasión.	❍	❍
4. En el Caribe el deporte más popular es el béisbol.	❍	❍

Preguntas

Answer these questions in Spanish.

1. ¿Dónde ven los aficionados el fútbol? Y tú, ¿cómo ves tus deportes favoritos?
2. ¿Te gusta el fútbol? ¿Por qué?
3. ¿Miras la Copa Mundial en la televisión?
4. ¿Qué deportes miras en la televisión?
5. En tu opinión, ¿cuáles son los tres deportes más populares en tu universidad? ¿en tu comunidad? ¿en los Estados Unidos?
6. ¿Qué haces en tu tiempo libre?

Antes de leer presents valuable reading strategies and pre-reading activities that strengthen your reading abilities in Spanish.

Readings are specifically related to the lesson theme and recycle vocabulary and grammar you have learned. The selections in Lessons 1–12 are cultural texts, while those in Lessons 13–18 are literary pieces.

Después de leer includes post-reading exercises that review and check your comprehension of the reading.

New! Three cultural and three literary readings are new to **VISTAS, Second Edition**. Lessons 4, 7, and 11 feature high-interest, culturally-oriented texts; Lessons 13, 15, and 17 offer new highly accessible, theme-related poems.

Adelante

Escritura develops writing skills in the context of the lesson theme

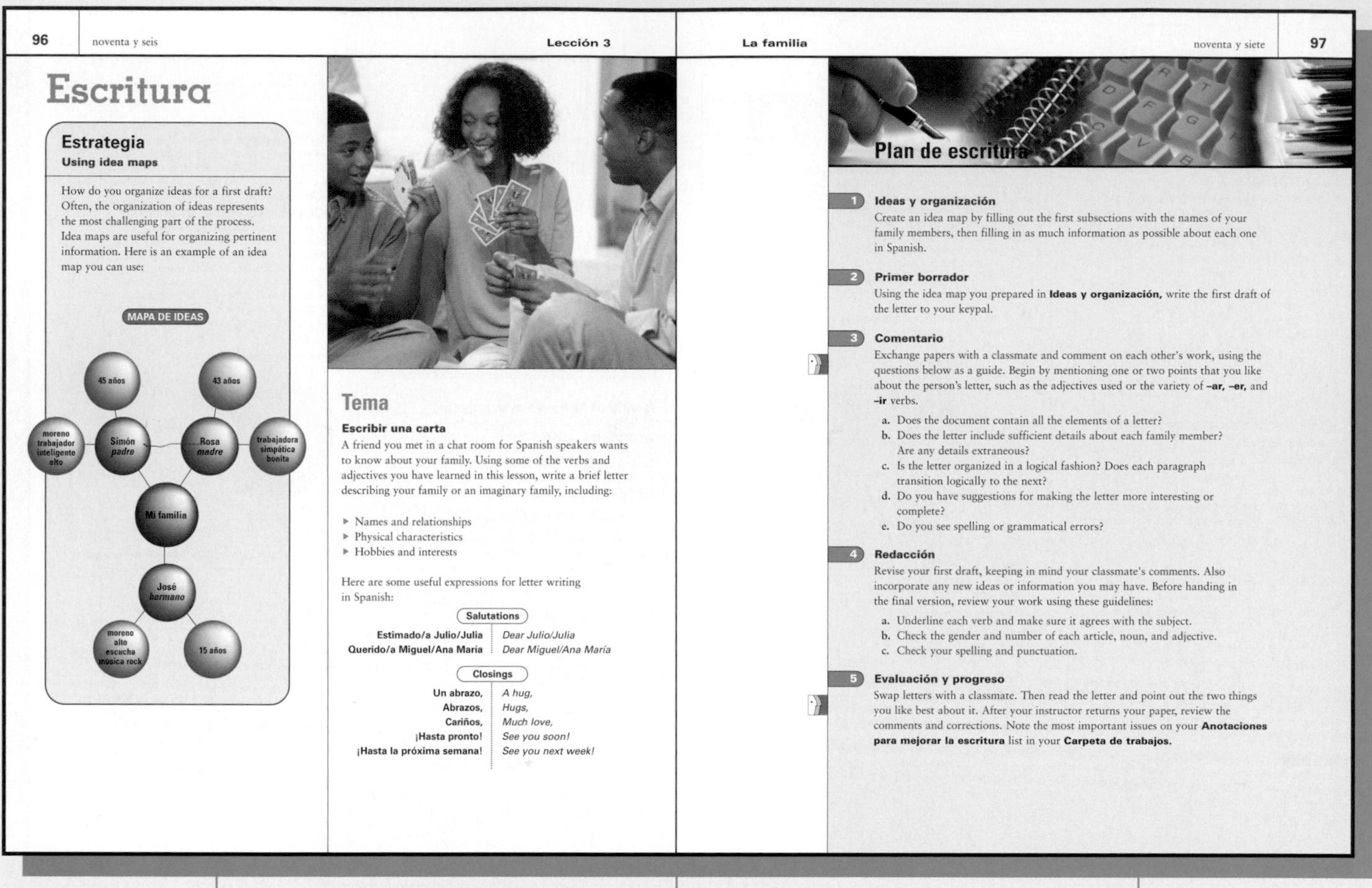

96 noventa y seis Lección 3

Escritura

Estrategia
Using idea maps

How do you organize ideas for a first draft? Often, the organization of ideas represents the most challenging part of the process. Idea maps are useful for organizing pertinent information. Here is an example of an idea map you can use:

Tema

Escribir una carta

A friend you met in a chat room for Spanish speakers wants to know about your family. Using some of the verbs and adjectives you have learned in this lesson, write a brief letter describing your family or an imaginary family, including:

- Names and relationships
- Physical characteristics
- Hobbies and interests

Here are some useful expressions for letter writing in Spanish:

Salutations

Estimado/a Julio/Julia	*Dear Julio/Julia*
Querido/a Miguel/Ana María	*Dear Miguel/Ana María*

Closings

Un abrazo,	*A hug,*
Abrazos,	*Hugs,*
Cariños,	*Much love,*
¡Hasta pronto!	*See you soon!*
¡Hasta la próxima semana!	*See you next week!*

La familia noventa y siete 97

Plan de escritura

1 **Ideas y organización**
Create an idea map by filling out the first subsections with the names of your family members, then filling in as much information as possible about each one in Spanish.

2 **Primer borrador**
Using the idea map you prepared in **Ideas y organización**, write the first draft of the letter to your keypal.

3 **Comentario**
Exchange papers with a classmate and comment on each other's work, using the questions below as a guide. Begin by mentioning one or two points that you like about the person's letter, such as the adjectives used or the variety of **-ar, -er,** and **-ir** verbs.

a. Does the document contain all the elements of a letter?
b. Does the letter include sufficient details about each family member? Are any details extraneous?
c. Is the letter organized in a logical fashion? Does each paragraph transition logically to the next?
d. Do you have suggestions for making the letter more interesting or complete?
e. Do you see spelling or grammatical errors?

4 **Redacción**
Revise your first draft, keeping in mind your classmate's comments. Also incorporate any new ideas or information you may have. Before handing in the final version, review your work using these guidelines:

a. Underline each verb and make sure it agrees with the subject.
b. Check the gender and number of each article, noun, and adjective.
c. Check your spelling and punctuation.

5 **Evaluación y progreso**
Swap letters with a classmate. Then read the letter and point out the two things you like best about it. After your instructor returns your paper, review the comments and corrections. Note the most important issues on your **Anotaciones para mejorar la escritura** list in your **Carpeta de trabajos.**

Estrategia provides strategies that help you prepare for the writing task presented in the next section.

Tema describes the writing topic and includes suggestions for approaching it.

Plan de escritura takes you step-by-step through the writing process, including planning, creating a first draft, peer review, and checking your work.

Adelante

Escuchar & Proyecto provide more listening practice and a task-based project

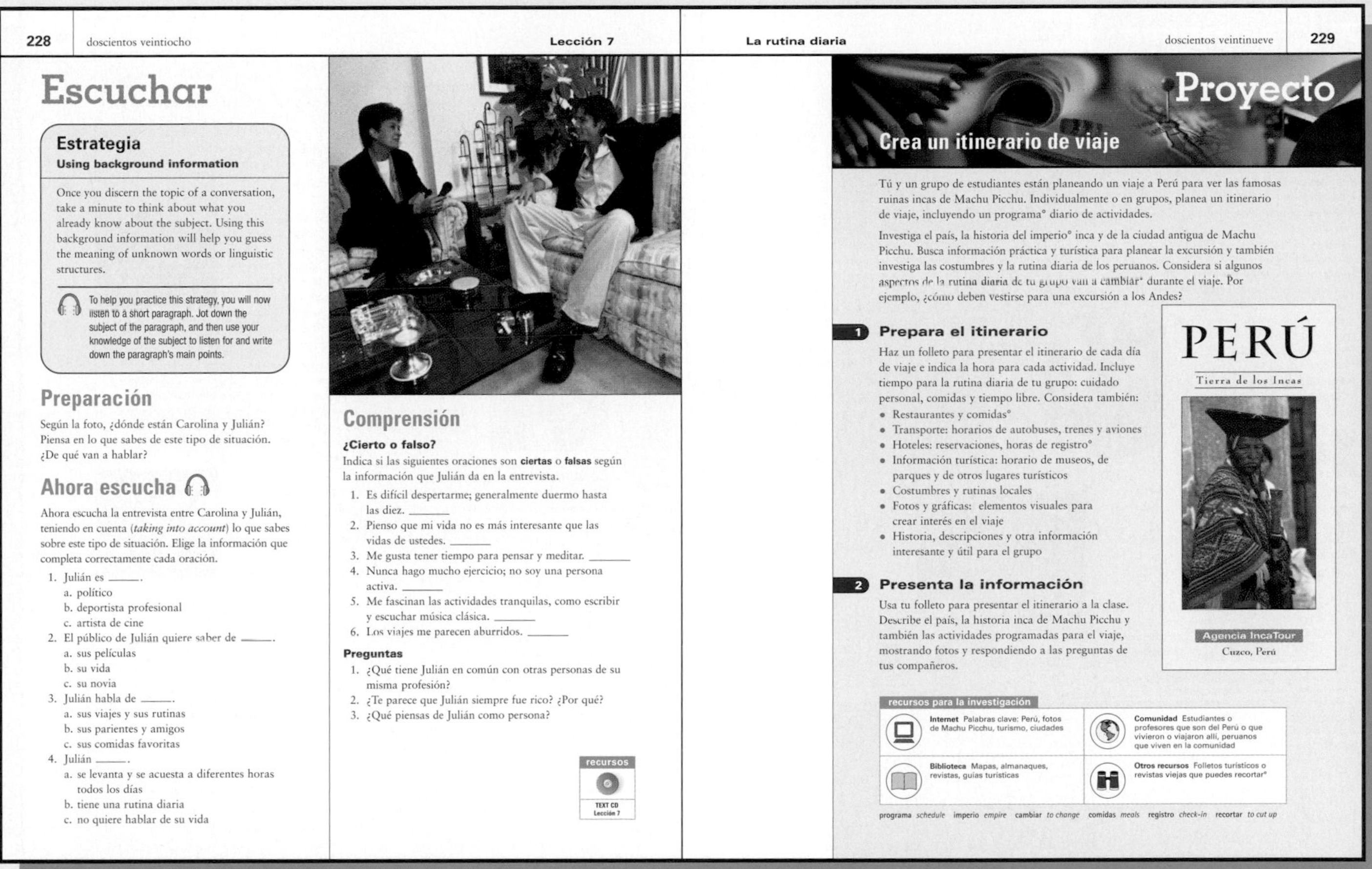

Escuchar presents a recorded conversation or narration to develop your listening skills in Spanish. **Estrategia** and **Preparación** prepare you for listening to the recorded passage.

Ahora escucha tracks you through the passage, and **Comprensión** checks your understanding of what you heard.

Proyecto gets you involved in a project by researching and creating a tangible product such as a brochure, a radio broadcast, or a Web page.

Recursos para la investigación points you toward research resources on the Web, in the library, and in your community.

Panorama
presents the nations of the Spanish-speaking world

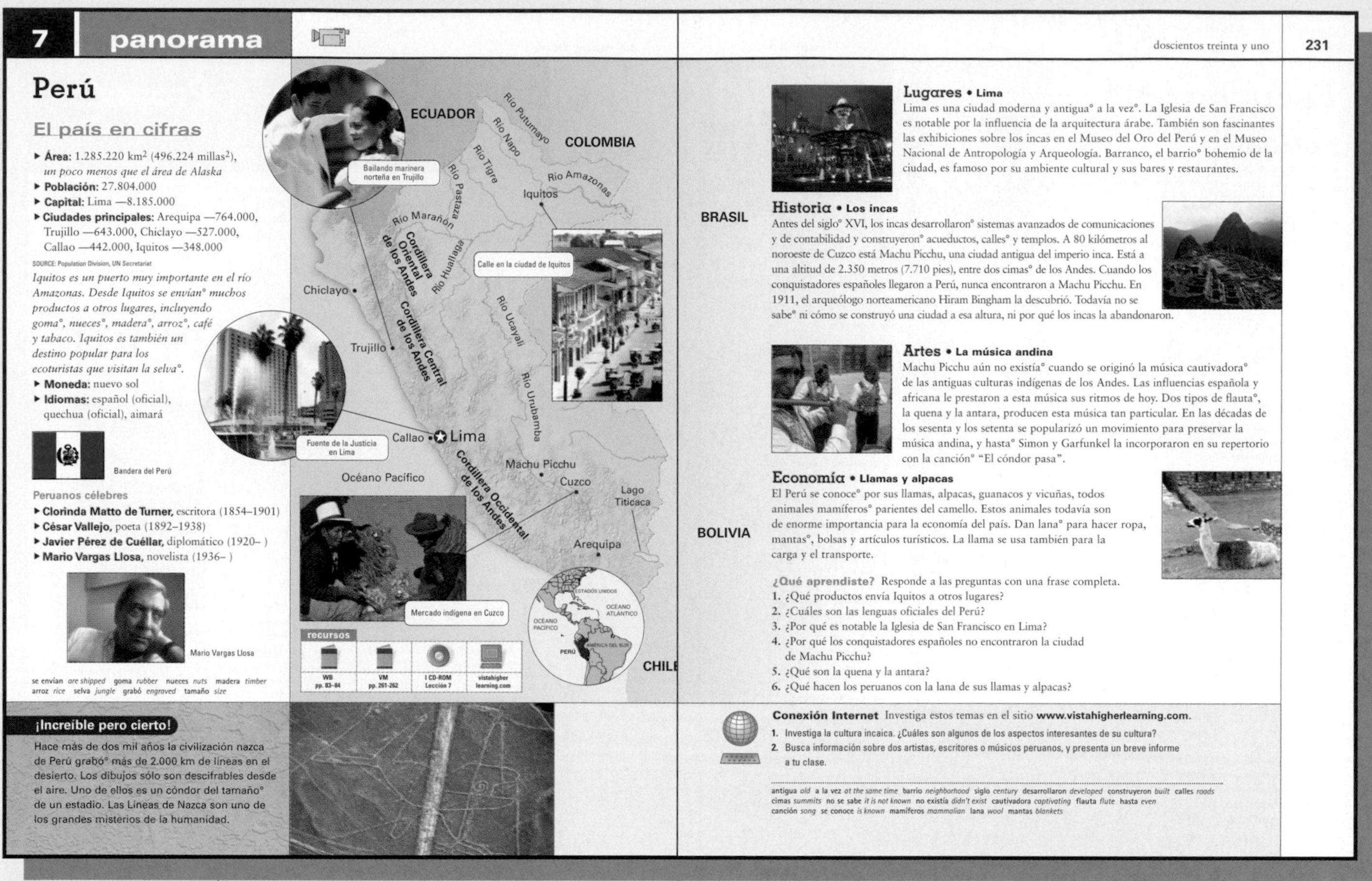

7 panorama

Perú

El país en cifras

- **Área:** 1.285.220 km² (496.224 millas²), *un poco menos que el área de Alaska*
- **Población:** 27.804.000
- **Capital:** Lima —8.185.000
- **Ciudades principales:** Arequipa —764.000, Trujillo —643.000, Chiclayo —527.000, Callao —442.000, Iquitos —348.000

SOURCE: Population Division, UN Secretariat

Iquitos es un puerto muy importante en el río Amazonas. Desde Iquitos se envían° muchos productos a otros lugares, incluyendo goma°, nueces°, madera°, arroz°, café y tabaco. Iquitos es también un destino popular para los ecoturistas que visitan la selva°.

- **Moneda:** nuevo sol
- **Idiomas:** español (oficial), quechua (oficial), aimará

Bandera del Perú

Peruanos célebres

- **Clorinda Matto de Turner,** escritora (1854–1901)
- **César Vallejo,** poeta (1892–1938)
- **Javier Pérez de Cuéllar,** diplomático (1920–)
- **Mario Vargas Llosa,** novelista (1936–)

Mario Vargas Llosa

se envían *are shipped* goma *rubber* nueces *nuts* madera *timber* arroz *rice* selva *jungle* grabó *engraved* tamaño *size*

Bailando marinera norteña en Trujillo

Calle en la ciudad de Iquitos

Fuente de la Justicia en Lima

Mercado indígena en Cuzco

recursos

WB pp. 83–84	VM pp. 261–262	I CD-ROM Lección 7	vistahigherlearning.com

¡Increíble pero cierto!

Hace más de dos mil años la civilización nazca de Perú grabó° más de 2.000 km de líneas en el desierto. Los dibujos sólo son descifrables desde el aire. Uno de ellos es un cóndor del tamaño° de un estadio. Las Líneas de Nazca son uno de los grandes misterios de la humanidad.

doscientos treinta y uno 231

Lugares • Lima

Lima es una ciudad moderna y antigua° a la vez°. La Iglesia de San Francisco es notable por la influencia de la arquitectura árabe. También son fascinantes las exhibiciones sobre los incas en el Museo del Oro del Perú y en el Museo Nacional de Antropología y Arqueología. Barranco, el barrio° bohemio de la ciudad, es famoso por su ambiente cultural y sus bares y restaurantes.

Historia • Los incas

Antes del siglo° XVI, los incas desarrollaron° sistemas avanzados de comunicaciones y de contabilidad y construyeron° acueductos, calles° y templos. A 80 kilómetros al noroeste de Cuzco está Machu Picchu, una ciudad antigua del imperio inca. Está a una altitud de 2.350 metros (7.710 pies), entre dos cimas° de los Andes. Cuando los conquistadores españoles llegaron a Perú, nunca encontraron a Machu Picchu. En 1911, el arqueólogo norteamericano Hiram Bingham la descubrió. Todavía no se sabe° ni cómo se construyó una ciudad a esa altura, ni por qué los incas la abandonaron.

Artes • La música andina

Machu Picchu aún no existía° cuando se originó la música cautivadora° de las antiguas culturas indígenas de los Andes. Las influencias española y africana le prestaron a esta música sus ritmos de hoy. Dos tipos de flauta°, la quena y la antara, producen esta música tan particular. En las décadas de los sesenta y los setenta se popularizó un movimiento para preservar la música andina, y hasta° Simon y Garfunkel la incorporaron en su repertorio con la canción° "El cóndor pasa".

Economía • Llamas y alpacas

El Perú se conoce° por sus llamas, alpacas, guanacos y vicuñas, todos animales mamíferos° parientes del camello. Estos animales todavía son de enorme importancia para la economía del país. Dan lana° para hacer ropa, mantas°, bolsas y artículos turísticos. La llama se usa también para la carga y el transporte.

¿Qué aprendiste? Responde a las preguntas con una frase completa.

1. ¿Qué productos envía Iquitos a otros lugares?
2. ¿Cuáles son las lenguas oficiales del Perú?
3. ¿Por qué es notable la Iglesia de San Francisco en Lima?
4. ¿Por qué los conquistadores españoles no encontraron la ciudad de Machu Picchu?
5. ¿Qué son la quena y la antara?
6. ¿Qué hacen los peruanos con la lana de sus llamas y alpacas?

Conexión Internet Investiga estos temas en el sitio **www.vistahigherlearning.com**.

1. Investiga la cultura incaica. ¿Cuáles son algunos de los aspectos interesantes de su cultura?
2. Busca información sobre dos artistas, escritores o músicos peruanos, y presenta un breve informe a tu clase.

antigua *old* a la vez *at the same time* barrio *neighborhood* siglo *century* desarrollaron *developed* construyeron *built* calles *roads* cimas *summits* no se sabe *it is not known* no existía *didn't exist* cautivadora *captivating* flauta *flute* hasta *even* canción *song* se conoce *is known* mamíferos *mammalian* lana *wool* mantas *blankets*

El país en cifras presents interesting, key facts about the featured country.

Maps point out major cities, rivers, and geographical features and situate the country in the context of its immediate surroundings and the world.

Readings A series of brief paragraphs explores facets of the country's culture such as history, places, fine arts, literature, and aspects of everyday life.

¡Increíble pero cierto! highlights an intriguing fact about the country or its people.

Conexión Internet offers Internet activities on the **VISTAS** Web Site for additional avenues of discovery.

New! *Panorama cultural* Video The authentic footage of this video takes you to the featured Spanish-speaking country, letting you experience the sights and sounds of an aspect of its culture. To learn more about the video, turn to page xxvii.

Vocabulario
summarizes all the active vocabulary of the lesson

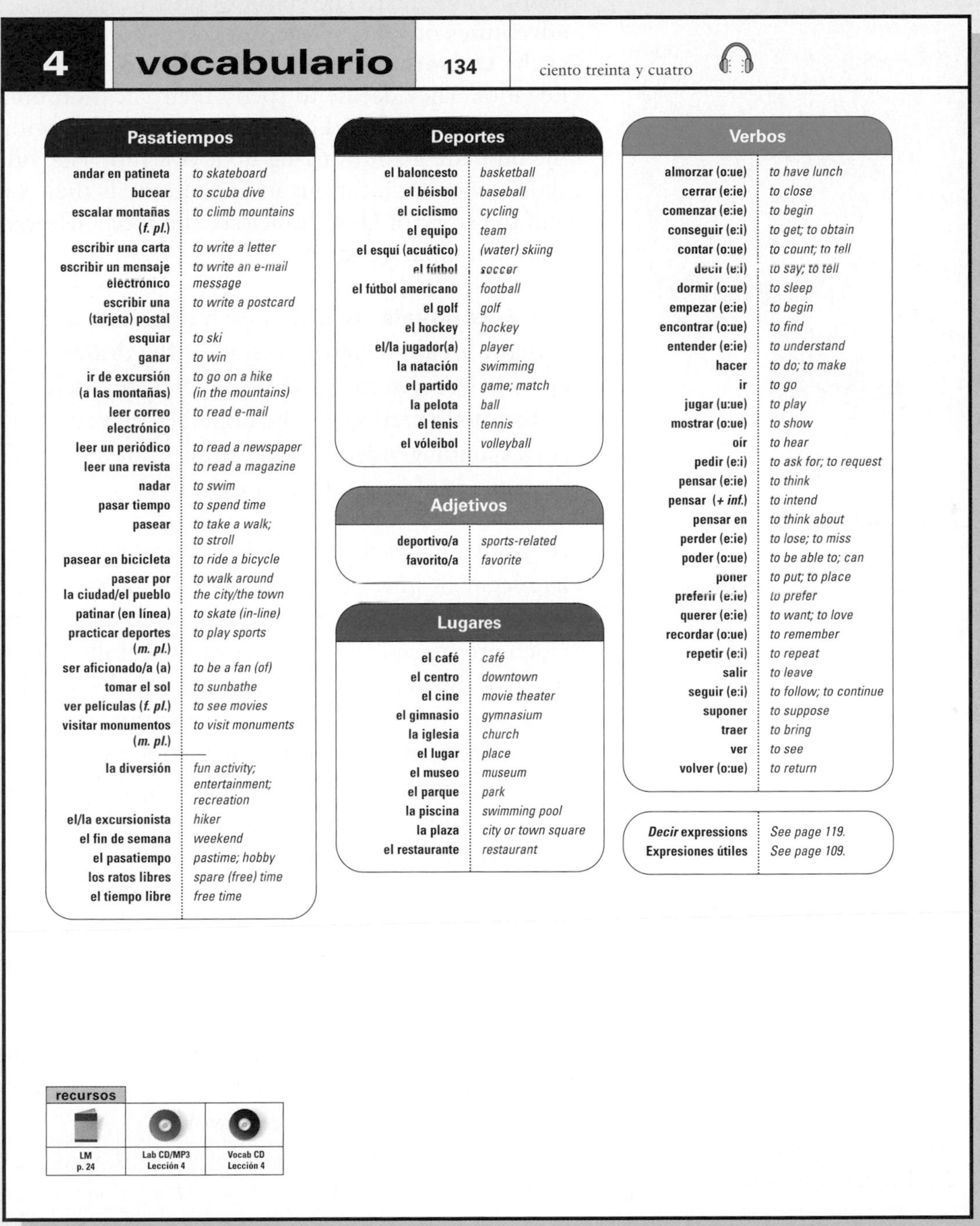

4 **vocabulario** 134 ciento treinta y cuatro

Pasatiempos

andar en patineta	*to skateboard*
bucear	*to scuba dive*
escalar montañas (*f. pl.*)	*to climb mountains*
escribir una carta	*to write a letter*
escribir un mensaje electrónico	*to write an e-mail message*
escribir una (tarjeta) postal	*to write a postcard*
esquiar	*to ski*
ganar	*to win*
ir de excursión (a las montañas)	*to go on a hike (in the mountains)*
leer correo electrónico	*to read e-mail*
leer un periódico	*to read a newspaper*
leer una revista	*to read a magazine*
nadar	*to swim*
pasar tiempo	*to spend time*
pasear	*to take a walk; to stroll*
pasear en bicicleta	*to ride a bicycle*
pasear por la ciudad/el pueblo	*to walk around the city/the town*
patinar (en línea)	*to skate (in-line)*
practicar deportes (*m. pl.*)	*to play sports*
ser aficionado/a (a)	*to be a fan (of)*
tomar el sol	*to sunbathe*
ver películas (*f. pl.*)	*to see movies*
visitar monumentos (*m. pl.*)	*to visit monuments*
la diversión	*fun activity; entertainment; recreation*
el/la excursionista	*hiker*
el fin de semana	*weekend*
el pasatiempo	*pastime; hobby*
los ratos libres	*spare (free) time*
el tiempo libre	*free time*

Deportes

el baloncesto	*basketball*
el béisbol	*baseball*
el ciclismo	*cycling*
el equipo	*team*
el esquí (acuático)	*(water) skiing*
el fútbol	*soccer*
el fútbol americano	*football*
el golf	*golf*
el hockey	*hockey*
el/la jugador(a)	*player*
la natación	*swimming*
el partido	*game; match*
la pelota	*ball*
el tenis	*tennis*
el vóleibol	*volleyball*

Adjetivos

deportivo/a	*sports-related*
favorito/a	*favorite*

Lugares

el café	*café*
el centro	*downtown*
el cine	*movie theater*
el gimnasio	*gymnasium*
la iglesia	*church*
el lugar	*place*
el museo	*museum*
el parque	*park*
la piscina	*swimming pool*
la plaza	*city or town square*
el restaurante	*restaurant*

Verbos

almorzar (o:ue)	*to have lunch*
cerrar (e:ie)	*to close*
comenzar (e:ie)	*to begin*
conseguir (e:i)	*to get; to obtain*
contar (o:ue)	*to count; to tell*
decir (e:i)	*to say; to tell*
dormir (o:ue)	*to sleep*
empezar (e:ie)	*to begin*
encontrar (o:ue)	*to find*
entender (e:ie)	*to understand*
hacer	*to do; to make*
ir	*to go*
jugar (u:ue)	*to play*
mostrar (o:ue)	*to show*
oír	*to hear*
pedir (e:i)	*to ask for; to request*
pensar (e:ie)	*to think*
pensar (+ *inf.*)	*to intend*
pensar en	*to think about*
perder (e:ie)	*to lose; to miss*
poder (o:ue)	*to be able to; can*
poner	*to put; to place*
preferir (e:ie)	*to prefer*
querer (e:ie)	*to want; to love*
recordar (o:ue)	*to remember*
repetir (e:i)	*to repeat*
salir	*to leave*
seguir (e:i)	*to follow; to continue*
suponer	*to suppose*
traer	*to bring*
ver	*to see*
volver (o:ue)	*to return*

***Decir* expressions**	*See page 119.*
Expresiones útiles	*See page 109.*

recursos

LM p. 24	Lab CD/MP3 Lección 4	Vocab CD Lección 4

New! Recorded vocabulary The headset icon at the top of the page and the **recursos** box at the bottom of the page highlight that the active lesson vocabulary is recorded for convenient study on both the Lab Audio Program and the new Vocabulary CDs.

FOTONOVELA VIDEO PROGRAM

Fully integrated with your textbook, the **VISTAS** video contains eighteen episodes, one for each lesson of the text. The episodes present the adventures of four college students who are studying at the **Universidad de San Francisco** in Quito, Ecuador. They decide to spend their vacation break on a bus tour of the Ecuadorian countryside with the ultimate goal of hiking up a volcano. The video, shot in various locations in Ecuador, tells their story and the story of Don Francisco, the tour bus driver who accompanies them.

The **Fotonovela** section in each textbook lesson is actually an abbreviated version of the dramatic episode featured in the video. Therefore, each **Fotonovela** section can be done before you see the corresponding video episode, after it, or as a section that stands alone in its own right.

As you watch each video episode, you will first see a live segment in which the characters interact using vocabulary and grammar you are studying. As the video progresses, the live segments carefully combine new vocabulary and grammar with previously taught language. You will then see a **Resumen** section in which one of the main video characters recaps the live segment, emphasizing the grammar and vocabulary you are studying within the context of the episode's key events.

In addition, in most of the video episodes, there are brief pauses to allow the characters to reminisce about their home country. These flashbacks—montages of real-life images shot in Spain, Mexico, Puerto Rico, and various parts of Ecuador—connect the theme of the video to everyday life in various parts of the Spanish-speaking world.

THE CAST

Here are the main characters you will meet when you watch the **VISTAS** video:

From Ecuador,
Inés Ayala Loor

From Spain,
María Teresa (Maite) Fuentes de Alba

From México,
Alejandro (Álex) Morales Paredes

From Puerto Rico,
Javier Gómez Lozano

And, also from Ecuador,
don Francisco Castillo Moreno

PANORAMA CULTURAL VIDEO PROGRAM

The new **Panorama cultural** video is integrated with the **Panorama** section in each lesson of **VISTAS, Second Edition**. Each segment is 2–3 minutes long and consists of documentary footage from each of the countries featured. The images were specially chosen for interest level and visual appeal, while the all-Spanish narrations were carefully written to reflect the vocabulary and grammar covered in the textbook.

As you watch the video segments, you will experience a diversity of images and topics: cities, monuments, traditions, festivals, archaeological sites, geographical wonders, and more. You will be transported to each Spanish-speaking country including the United States and Canada, thereby having the opportunity to expand your cultural perspectives with information directly related to the content of **VISTAS, Second Edition**.

ICONS AND RECURSOS BOXES

Icons

Familiarize yourself with these icons that appear throughout **VISTAS, Second Edition**.

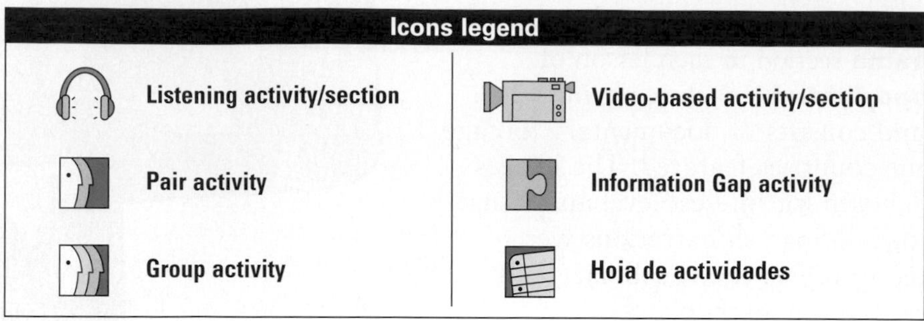

- The Information Gap activities and those involving **Hojas de actividades** (*activity sheets*) require handouts that your instructor will give you.
- You will see the listening icon in each lesson's **Contextos**, **Pronunciación**, **Escuchar** and **Vocabulario** sections.
- The video icon appears in the **Fotonovela** and the **Panorama** sections of each lesson.

Recursos

Recursos boxes let you know exactly what print and technology ancillaries you can use to reinforce and expand on every section of the lessons in your textbook. They even include page numbers when applicable. In **VISTAS 2/e**, the colors of the icons match those of the actual ancillaries, making it even easier for you to use the complete program. See the next page for a description of the ancillaries.

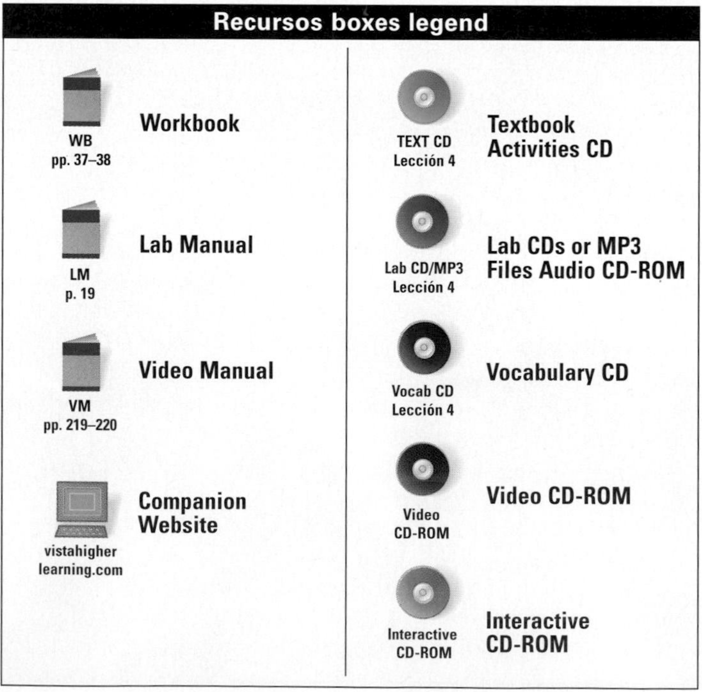

STUDENT ANCILLARIES

- **Workbook/Video Manual**
  The Workbook/Video Manual contains the workbook activities for each textbook lesson, activities for the **Fotonovela** Video, and new pre-, while-, and post-viewing activities for the **Panorama cultural** Video.
- **Lab Manual**
  The Lab Manual contains lab activities for each textbook lesson for use with the Lab Audio Program.
- **Lab Audio Program**
  18 CDs or 1 MP3 Files Audio CD-ROM
- **Textbook Activities CDs***
  The Textbook Activities CDs contain the audio recordings for the listening-based activities in the student text.
- **New! Vocabulary CDs***
  The Vocabulary CDs contain recordings of the active vocabulary in each lesson of the student text.
- ***Fotonovela* Video CD-ROM***
  The **Fotonovela** Video CD-ROM provides the complete **Fotonovela** Video Program with videoscripts, note-taking capabilities and navigation tools.
- **Significant Revision! Interactive CD-ROMs***
  These interactive CD-ROMs, overwhelmingly popular among students, contain multimedia practice of the language taught in each lesson. Improved **Panorama** sections feature interactive geographical maps, comprehension checks, and footage from the new **Panorama Cultural** Video Program.
- **VHL Intro Spanish Pocket Dictionary and Language Guide***
  The VHL Intro Spanish Pocket Dictionary and Language Guide is a portable reference for Spanish words, expressions, idioms, and more, created expressly to complement and extend the student text.
- **Web-SAM** (online Workbook/Video Manual/Lab Manual)
- **New! VISTAS eText**
  The **VISTAS eText** is a ground-breaking online version of **VISTAS 2/e**. It allows students to interact with the textbook, do practice activities, complete tests, and communicate with their instructors and e-partners online. For instructors, it also has complete classroom management tools.
- **Expanded! Companion Website***
  (www.vistahigherlearning.com)

**Free with purchase of a new Student Text*

INSTRUCTOR ANCILLARIES

- **New! Instructor's Annotated Edition (IAE)**
  The IAE contains a wealth of teaching information. The expanded trim size and enhanced design of **VISTAS 2/e** make the annotations and facsimile student pages easier to read and reference in the classroom.
- **Expanded! Instructor's Resource Manual (IRM)**
  The IRM contains Tapescripts, Videoscripts, English translations of both the **Fotonovela** conversations and the **Panorama cultural** Video, **Hojas de actividades** for selected textbook activities, **Vocabulario adicional** handouts for each lesson, and answers to the **¡Inténtalo!** and **Práctica** activities in the student text.
- **New! Information Gap Activities Booklet**
  This booklet contains the handouts for the information gap activities in the student text, plus additional activities.
- **New! Workbook/Video Manual/Lab Manual Answer Key**
- **Major Revision! Testing Program**
  The tests and exams are more contextualized and communicative and include reading sections. Two new communicative tests are offered for each lesson. Optional sections now include alternate listening sections and test items for the **Fotonovela** Video, the **Panorama** sections, and the **Panorama cultural** Video.
- **Testing Program Audio CD**
- **Major Revision! Test Files CD-ROM**
- **New! *Panorama cultural* Video Program (VHS)**
  The **Panorama cultural** Video Program consists of authentic footage from each of the Spanish-speaking countries featured in each lesson's Panorama section. The images were specifically chosen for interest level and visual appeal, while the all-Spanish narrations were specially written to reflect the vocabulary and grammar taught in the text.
- ***Fotonovela* Video Program (VHS)**
  This specially-shot video, a favorite among students using **VISTAS, 1/e**, is closely and distinctively integrated with each lesson of the textbook.
- **New! *Contextos* and *Estructura* Presentations CD-ROM**
  This CD-ROM contains images of the Overhead Transparencies and Microsoft PowerPoint® presentations of the grammar explanations in the **Estructura** sections of the student text.
- **New! DVD**
  Both the complete **Fotonovela** Video and the new **Panorama cultural** Video are available on DVD.
- **Overhead Transparencies**
  The Transparencies consist of the maps of the countries of the Spanish-speaking world, the **Contextos** vocabulary drawings, and other selected illustrations from the student text.

acknowledgments

On behalf of its authors and editors, Vista Higher Learning expresses its sincere appreciation to the many college professors nationwide who contributed their ideas and suggestions to **VISTAS, First Edition**. We are grateful to the more than fifty members of the Spanish-teaching community who participated in focus groups and class tested materials at the initial stages of the program, as well as the more than sixty instructors who reviewed it. Their insights and detailed comments were invaluable to us as we created the First Edition.

- **VISTAS, Second Edition** is the direct result of extensive reviews and ongoing input from both students and instructors using the First Edition. Accordingly, we gratefully acknowledge those who shared their suggestions, recommendations, and ideas as we prepared this Second Edition.
- A special nod of gratitude goes to Mary Ellen Brines of Alma College and her students for their generous feedback.
- We extend our appreciation to Julio Rivera and his students at Foothill College for their valuable input.
- We thank Dr. Antonio Velásquez of McMaster University in Ontario, Canada for his contributions regarding the presence and influence of the Spanish language and Hispanic cultures in Canada.
- We acknowledge Mary Ann Dellinger of Virginia Military Institute for her work with us on the First Edition, and we thank her for her contributions to the Instructor's Annotated Edition of **VISTAS 2/e**.
- We thank Mercedes Valle of the University of Massachusetts, Amherst and Smith College for her contributions to the **VISTAS 2/e** Testing Program.
- We express our gratitude to José Cruz of Fayetteville Technical Community College for his thorough comments and suggestions for improving the **VISTAS 1/e** Web-SAM that have resulted in an enhanced Web-SAM for **VISTAS 2/e**.
- We express our sincere appreciation to the almost one hundred instructors using **VISTAS 1/e** who completed our online review. Their comments and suggestions were instrumental in shaping the entire **VISTAS 2/e** program.
- Finally, we extend a special thank-you to the six instructors who provided in-depth reviews of **VISTAS 1/e** based on the everyday use of the materials in their classrooms. Their ideas played a critical role in helping us to fine-tune virtually every page of every lesson.

In-depth reviewers

María I. Fleck
Cerritos College, CA

Jerome Miner
Knox College, IL

Michael Panbehchi
Virginia Commonwealth University, VA

Joyce Pinkard
Fresno City College, CA

Claire Reetz
Florida Community College, Jacksonville, FL

Julio C. Rivera
Foothill College, CA

Reviewers

Amanda Amend
St. Michael's College, VT

Renée Andrade
Mount San Antonio College, CA

David Arbesú Fernández
University of Massachusetts, Amherst, MA

Rafael Arias
Los Angeles Valley College, LA

Emily Ballou
University of Calgary, Canada

Amy R. Barber
Grove City College, PA

Allen Bertsche
Augustana College, IL

Jane Harrington Bethune
Salve Regina University, RI

Patrick Brady
Tidewater Community College, VA

Mary Ellen Brines
Alma College, MI

Veronica Burke
Lyon College, AR

Karen Burrell
Mary Washington College, VA

Billy Bussell-Thompson
Hofstra University, NY

Danielle Cahill
Christopher Newport University, VA

Fernando Canto-Lugo
Yuba Community College, CA

Patricia H. Carlin
University of Central Arkansas, AR

Irene Chico-Wyatt
University of Kentucky, KY

Kimberly Contag
Minnesota State University, Mankato MN

Lisa Contreras
Transylvania University, KY

Marzia Corni-Benson
Indian Hills Community College, IA

Linda Crawford
Salve Regina University, RI

José Cruz
Fayetteville Technical Community College, NC

Maria D. Delgado-Hellin
Willamette University, OR

Rocío Domínguez
Carnegie Mellon University, PA

Deborah M. Edson
Tidewater Community College, VA

John L. Finan
William Rainey Harper College, IL

María I. Fleck
Cerritos College, CA

Roberto Fuertes-Manjón
Midwestern State University, TX

Adalberto García
Midwestern State University, TX

Lourdes Girardi
Glendale Community College, CA

James Grabowska
Minnesota State University, Mankato MN

Linda Hollabaugh
Midwestern State University, TX

Patricia G. Horner
Stanly Community College, NC

Nan Hussey
Houghton College, NY

Chuck Hutchings
Central Oregon Community College, OR

Alfonso Illingworth-Rico
Eastern Michigan University, MI

Franklin Inojosa
Richard J. Daley College, IL

Joseph C. Jeter
Alabama A & M University, AL

Eric Jewell
Truman State University, MO

Steven D. Kirby
Eastern Michigan University, MI

M. Phillip Kristiansen
University of the Ozarks, AR

Lora Looney
University of Portland, OR

Reviewers

Esteban E. Loustaunau
Augustana College, IL

Bernard Manker
Grand Rapids Community College, MI

Carol Marshall
Truman State University, MO

Gianna M. Martella
Western Oregon University, OR

Vidal Martín
Everett Community College, WA

Laurie Mattas
College of DuPage, IL

Haven McBee
Middle Tennessee State University, TN

Suzanne McLaughlin
Chemeketa Community College, OR

Jerome Miner
Knox College, IL

Carrie Mittleman
University of Massachusetts, Amherst, MA

Charles H. Molano
Dodge City Community College, KS

Karen-Jean Muñoz
Florida Community College, Jacksonville, FL

Nancy C. Mustafa
Virginia Commonwealth University, VA

M. Margarita Nodarse
Barry University, FL

Kathleen D. O'Connor
Tidewater Community College, VA

Milagros Ojermark
Diablo Valley College, CA

Daniel Onorato
Modesto Junior College, CA

Michael Panbehchi
Virginia Commonwealth University, VA

John Parrack
University of Central Arkansas, AR

Peregrina Pereiro
Washburn University, KS

Gladys A. Perez
University of Portland, OR

Martha Perez
Kirkwood Community College, Iowa City, IA

Inmaculada Pertusa
University of Kentucky, KY

Joyce Pinkard
Fresno City College, CA

Ruth Ellen Porter
Brewton-Parker College, GA

Karry Putzy
Kirkwood Community College, Iowa City, IA

Richard Reid
Grand Rapids Community College, MI

Claire Reetz
Florida Community College, Jacksonville, FL

Rita Ricaurte
Nebraska Wesleyan University, NE

Julio C. Rivera
Foothill College, CA

Anthony J. Robb
Rowan University, NJ

Cathy A. Robison
Clemson University, SC

Theresa E. Ruiz-Velasco
College of Lake County, IL

José Carlos Saa-Ramos
Washburn University, KS

Jan Satterlee
Richland Community College, IL

Kathy Schmidt
Minneapolis Community Technical College, MN

Mary Shea
Napa Valley College, CA

Juanita Shettlesworth
Tennessee Technological University, TN

Roger Simpson
Clemson University, SC

Laurel Sparks
North Dakota State University, ND

Daniela Stewart
Everett Community College, WA

Cristobal Trillo
Joliet Junior College, IL

Alejandro Varderi
Borough of Manhattan Community College of CUNY, NY

David J. Viera
Tennessee Technological University, TN

Keith Watts
Grand Valley State University, MI

James Reese Weckler
Minnesota State University, Moorhead, MN

Georgina Whittingham
Oswego, State University of New York, NY

Terri Wilbanks
University of South Alabama, AL

Diane Wright
Grand Valley State University, MI

Laura Yocom
Centralia College, WA

Mary F. Yudin
Mary Washington College, VA

Hola, ¿qué tal?

1

Communicative Goals

You will learn how to:

- Greet people in Spanish
- Say goodbye
- Identify yourself and others
- Talk about the time of day

contextos

pages 2–5
- Greetings and leave-takings
- Identifying yourself and others
- Expressions of courtesy

fotonovela

pages 6–9
Mrs. Ramos, from the travel agency Ecuatur, greets the students and hands out their travel papers. Don Francisco, the driver, introduces himself and asks the students to board the bus.

estructura

pages 10–25
- Nouns and articles
- Numbers 0-30
- Present tense of **ser**
- Telling time

adelante

pages 26–31
Lectura: Read a telephone list.
Escritura: Create an address list in Spanish.
Escuchar: Listen to a conversation in a bus station.
Proyecto: Research the influence of Hispanic culture in a U.S. or Canadian city.

panorama

pages 32–33
Featured Countries: Estados Unidos y Canadá
- Cities and states with the largest Hispanic populations
- Influence of Hispanic culture in the U.S. and Canada

A PRIMERA VISTA
- Guess what the people in the photo are saying:
  a. Adiós b. Hola c. Salsa
- Most likely they would also say:
  a. Gracias b. Fiesta c. Buenos días
- The women are:
  a. amigas b. chicos c. señores

Lesson Goals

In **Lección 1** students will be introduced to the following:
- terms for greetings and leave-takings
- identifying where one is from
- expressions of courtesy
- nouns and articles (definite and indefinite)
- numbers 0–30
- present tense of **ser**
- telling time
- recognizing cognates
- reading a telephone list rich in cognates
- writing a telephone/address list in Spanish
- listening for known vocabulary
- the influence of Hispanic cultures on cities in the United States and Canada
- cultural and demographic information about Hispanics in the United States and Canada

A primera vista Have students look at the photo. Ask: *What do you think the young women are doing?* Say: *It is common in Hispanic cultures for friends to greet each other with a kiss (or two) on the cheek.* Ask: *How do you greet your friends?*

INSTRUCTIONAL RESOURCES

Workbook/Video Manual: WB Activities, pp. 1–10
Laboratory Manual: Lab Activities, pp. 1–6
Workbook/Video Manual: Video Activities, pp. 213–214; pp. 249–250
Instructor's Resource Manual: **Vocabulario adicional**, pp. 177–178; **¡Inténtalo!** & **Práctica** Answers, pp. 197–198; **Fotonovela** Translations, p. 139; Textbook CD Tapescript, p. 85; Lab CDs Tapescript, pp. 1–5; **Fotonovela** Videoscript, p. 103; **Panorama cultural** Videoscript, p. 127
Info Gap Activities Booklet, pp. 1–4
Overhead Transparencies: #9, #10, #11, #12
Lab Audio CD/MP3 **Lección 1**
Panorama cultural DVD/Video
Fotonovela DVD/Video
Testing Program, pp. 1–12
Testing Program Audio CD
Test Files CD-ROM
Companion website
Presentations CD-ROM
Textbook CD
Vocabulary CD
Interactive CD-ROM
Video CD-ROM
Web-SAM

Section Goals

In **Contextos**, students will learn and practice:

- basic greetings
- introductions
- courtesy expressions

Instructional Resources
Transparencies, #9, #10
Textbook CD
Vocabulary CD
WB/VM: Workbook, pp. 1–2
Lab Manual, p. 1
Lab CD/MP3 ***Lección 1***
IRM: ***Vocab. adicional****, p. 177;*
Práctica *Answers, pp. 197–198;*
Tapescript, pp. 1–5; p. 85
Interactive CD-ROM
Companion website: www.vistahigherlearning.com
Presentations CD-ROM

Suggestions

- To familiarize students right away with the meanings of headings used in the lessons and important vocabulary for classroom interactions, you can pass out **Vocabulario adicional: Más vocabulario para la clase de español**, from the IRM.
- For complete lesson plans, go to **www.vistahigherlearning.com** to access the instructor's part of the **VISTAS** companion website.
- With books closed, write a few greetings, farewells, and courtesy expressions on the board, explain their meaning, and model their pronunciation. Go around the class greeting students, making introductions, and encouraging responses. Then have students open to pages 2–3 or project **Transparency #9** and ask them to identify which conversations seem to be exchanges between friends and which seem more formal. Overlay **Transparency #10** or use the printed text to draw attention to the use of **Ud.** vs. **tú** in these conversations. Explain situations in which each form is appropriate.

Successful Language Learning Encourage your students to make flash cards to help them memorize new vocabulary words.

Hola, ¿qué tal?

Más vocabulario

Buenos días.	*Good morning.*
Buenas tardes.	*Good afternoon.*
Buenas noches.	*Good evening./night.*
Hasta la vista.	*See you later.*
Hasta pronto.	*See you soon.*
¿Cómo se llama usted?	*What's your name? (form.)*
Le presento a...	*I would like to introduce (name) to you. (form.)*
Te presento a...	*I would like to introduce (name) to you. (fam.)*
nombre	*name*
¿Cómo estás?	*How are you? (fam.)*
No muy bien.	*Not very well.*
¿Qué pasa?	*What's happening?; What's going on?*
por favor	*please*
De nada.	*You're welcome.*
No hay de qué.	*You're welcome.*
Lo siento.	*I'm sorry.*
(Muchas) gracias.	*Thank you (very much); Thanks (a lot).*

Variación léxica

Items are presented for recognition purposes only.

Buenos días. ⟷ Buenas.
De nada. ⟷ A la orden.
Lo siento. ⟷ Perdón.
¿Qué tal? ⟷ ¿Qué hubo? (*Col.*)
chau ⟷ ciao

recursos

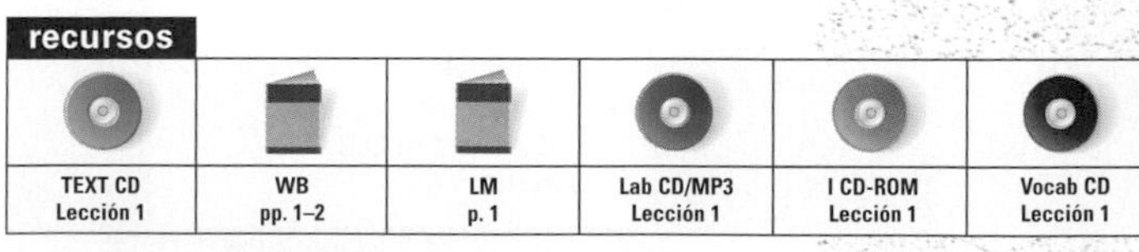

1

ELENA Patricia, éste es el señor Perales.
PATRICIA Encantada.
SEÑOR PERALES Igualmente. ¿De dónde es usted, señorita?
PATRICIA Soy de México. ¿Y usted?
SEÑOR PERALES De Puerto Rico.

2

TOMÁS ¿Qué tal, Alberto?
ALBERTO Regular. ¿Y tú?
TOMÁS Bien. ¿Qué hay de nuevo?
ALBERTO Nada.

3

SEÑOR VARGAS Buenas tardes, señora Wong. ¿Cómo está usted?
SEÑORA WONG Muy bien, gracias. ¿Y usted, señor Vargas?
SEÑOR VARGAS Bien, gracias.
SEÑORA WONG Hasta mañana, señor Vargas. Saludos a la señora Vargas.
SEÑOR VARGAS Adiós.

TEACHING OPTIONS

Variación léxica Point out that **Buenas, Chévere,** and **¿Qué hubo?** (often pronounced **¿Quihubo?**) are all colloquial. You may add that another common equivalent of **¿Qué tal?** is **¿Cómo te va?**
Extra Practice Bring family photos or magazine photos in which people are shown greeting each other. Ask groups to write dialogue captions for each photo. Remind the class to use formal and informal expressions as appropriate.

Small Groups Have small groups role-play an original conversation in which older adults, children, and college-age people interact. Verify that the groups are using formal and informal expressions as appropriate. Have a few groups present their conversations to the class.
Extra Practice After calling a name, greet that student and ask a question related to the day's lesson.

4
BERTA Hasta luego, Tere.
TERESA Chau, Berta. Nos vemos mañana.
5
CARMEN Buenas tardes. Me llamo Carmen. ¿Cómo te llamas tú?
ANTONIO Buenas tardes. Me llamo Antonio. Mucho gusto.
CARMEN El gusto es mío. ¿De dónde eres?
ANTONIO Soy de los Estados Unidos, de California.

AYUDA

In Spanish, people can be addressed either formally or informally. Dialogues 1 and 3 are formal exchanges and use **usted** (*you*) forms. Dialogues 2, 4, and 5 are informal and use the familiar **tú** (*you*) form or other informal expressions. You will learn more about this in **Estructura 1.3**.

Práctica

1 Escuchar Listen to each question or statement, then choose the correct response.

1. a. Muy bien, gracias. b. Me llamo Graciela. b
2. a. Lo siento. b. Mucho gusto. b
3. a. Soy de Puerto Rico. b. No muy bien. a
4. a. No hay de qué. b. Regular. a
5. a. Mucho gusto. b. Hasta pronto. b
6. a. Nada. b. Igualmente. a
7. a. Me llamo Guillermo Montero. b. Muy bien, gracias. b
8. a. Buenas tardes. ¿Cómo estás? b. El gusto es mío. a
9. a. Saludos a la Sra. Ramírez. b. Encantada. b
10. a. Adiós. b. Regular. b

2 Escoger For each expression, write another word or phrase that expresses a similar idea.

modelo
¿Cómo estás?
¿Qué tal?

1. De nada. No hay de qué.
2. Encantado. Mucho gusto.
3. Adiós. Chau o Hasta luego/mañana/pronto.
4. Te presento a Antonio. Éste es Antonio
5. Hasta la vista. Hasta luego.
6. Mucho gusto. El gusto es mío.

3 Ordenar Work with a classmate to put this scrambled conversation in order. Then act it out.

—Muy bien, gracias. Soy Rosabel.
—Soy del Ecuador. ¿Y tú?
—Mucho gusto, Rosabel.
—Hola. Me llamo Carlos. ¿Cómo estás?
—Soy de Argentina.
—Igualmente. ¿De dónde eres, Carlos?

CARLOS Hola. Me llamo Carlos. ¿Cómo estás?
ROSABEL Muy bien, gracias. Soy Rosabel.
CARLOS Mucho gusto, Rosabel.
ROSABEL Igualmente. ¿De dónde eres, Carlos?
CARLOS Soy del Ecuador. ¿Y tú?
ROSABEL Soy de Argentina.

1 Suggestion Before students listen, ask them to read the possible answers provided and jot down the questions or statements they think would elicit those responses. After they have listened and completed the activity, go over the answers to check whether students' predictions were accurate.

1 Tapescript 1. ¿Cómo te llamas? 2. Te presento a Juan Pablo. 3. ¿De dónde es usted? 4. Muchas gracias. 5. Nos vemos. 6. ¿Qué pasa? 7. ¿Cómo está usted? 8. Buenas tardes, señor Fernández. 9. Susana, éste es el señor Ramírez. 10. ¿Qué tal? *Textbook CD*

2 Expansion Have students provide the question or statement that would elicit each item in this activity. Ex: 1. —**Gracias.** —**De nada.**

3 Suggestion Have volunteer pairs read their conversations to the whole class.

3 Expansion In small groups, have students write a new conversation. Then ask each group to rewrite its conversation, scrambling the order of the exchanges. The groups then trade the scambled conversations and put them in logical order.

TEACHING OPTIONS

Game Divide the class into two groups. Create original statements and questions based on the **Más vocabulario** and the illustrated conversations. Indicate one group member at a time, alternating between groups. The indicated group member should respond to your statement or question. Each correct response wins the group a point. The group with the most points at the end of the game wins.

Heritage Speakers Have heritage speakers mention other greetings and expressions of courtesy that are used in their countries of origin or that they know about. Ask them to tell where in the Spanish-speaking world the expressions are used. Write them on the board. Ask volunteers to use these expressions in a conversation.

4 Suggestion Review the pairs' responses with the whole class.

4 Expansion Have pairs or small groups create conversations that include the expressions used in **Actividad 4**. Ask volunteers to present their conversations to the class.

5 Suggestions
- Be sure to discuss the **modelo** with the whole class before assigning the activity to pairs. After students have completed the activity, have eight pairs of students role-play one of the corrected mini-conversations. Ask them to substitute their own names and personal information where possible.
- Have volunteers write each conversation on the board. Work together as a class to identify and explain any errors.

¡Lengua viva! Have students locate examples of the titles in **Actividad 5**. Then have them create short sentences in which they use the titles with people they know.

4 Completar Work with a partner to complete these exchanges.

modelo
Estudiante 1: ¿Cómo estás?
Estudiante 2: Muy bien, gracias.

1. **Estudiante 1:** Buenos días.
   Estudiante 2: Buenos días. ¿Qué tal?
2. **Estudiante 1:** ¿Cómo te llamas?
   Estudiante 2: Me llamo Carmen Sánchez.
3. **Estudiante 1:** ¿De dónde eres?
   Estudiante 2: De México.
4. **Estudiante 1:** Te presento a Marisol.
   Estudiante 2: Encantado/a.
5. **Estudiante 1:** Gracias.
   Estudiante 2: De nada.
6. **Estudiante 1:** ¿Qué tal?
   Estudiante 2: Regular.
7. **Estudiante 1:** ¿Qué pasa?
   Estudiante 2: Nada.
8. **Estudiante 1:** ¡Hasta la vista!
   Estudiante 2: Answers will vary.

5 Cambiar Work with a partner and correct the second part of each conversation to make it logical. Answers will vary.

modelo
Estudiante 1: ¿Qué tal?
Estudiante 2: ~~No hay de qué.~~ Bien. ¿Y tú?

1. **Estudiante 1:** Hasta mañana, señora Ramírez. Saludos al señor Ramírez.
   Estudiante 2: *Muy bien, gracias.*
2. **Estudiante 1:** ¿Qué hay de nuevo, Alberto?
   Estudiante 2: *Sí, me llamo Alberto. ¿Cómo te llamas tú?*
3. **Estudiante 1:** Gracias, Tomás.
   Estudiante 2: *Regular. ¿Y tú?*
4. **Estudiante 1:** Miguel, ésta es la señorita Perales.
   Estudiante 2: *No hay de qué, señorita.*
5. **Estudiante 1:** ¿De dónde eres, Antonio?
   Estudiante 2: *Muy bien, gracias. ¿Y tú?*
6. **Estudiante 1:** ¿Cómo se llama usted?
   Estudiante 2: *El gusto es mío.*
7. **Estudiante 1:** ¿Qué pasa?
   Estudiante 2: *Hasta luego, Alicia.*
8. **Estudiante 1:** Buenas tardes, señor. ¿Cómo está usted?
   Estudiante 2: *Soy de Puerto Rico.*

¡LENGUA VIVA!

The titles **señor, señora,** and **señorita** are abbreviated **Sr., Sra.** and **Srta.** Note that these abbreviations are capitalized.

•••

There is no Spanish equivalent for the English title *Ms.;* women are addressed as **señora** or **señorita.**

TEACHING OPTIONS

Extra Practice Read some phrases to the class and ask if the class would use them with another student of the same age or with an older person. Ex: **1. Te presento a Luis.** (student) **2. Muchas gracias, señor.** (older person) **3. ¿Cómo estás?** (student) **4. Buenos días, doctor Soto.** (older person) **5. ¿De dónde es usted, señora?** (older person) **6. Chau, Teresa.** (student) **7. ¿Cómo se llama usted?** (older person) **8. No hay de qué, señor Perales.** (older person)

Game Prepare a series of response statements using language in **Contextos**. Divide the class into two groups and invite students to guess the question or statement that would have elicited each of your response statements. Read a statement at a time. The team to correctly guess the question or statement first wins the point. Ex: **Me llamo Lupe Torres Garza. (¿Cómo se llama usted? / ¿Cómo te llamas?)** The team with the most correct guesses wins.

Comunicación

6 **Diálogos** With a partner, complete and act out these conversations. Answers will vary.

Conversación 1
—Hola. Me llamo Teresa. ¿Cómo te llamas tú?
—________________________________
—Soy de Puerto Rico. ¿Y tú?
—________________________________

Conversación 2
—________________________________
—Muy bien, gracias. ¿Y usted, señora López?
—________________________________
—Hasta luego, señora. Saludos al señor López.
—________________________________

Conversación 3
—________________________________
—Regular. ¿Y tú?
—________________________________
—Nada.

7 **Conversaciones** This is the first day of class. Write four short conversations based on what the people in this scene would say. Answers will vary.

8 **Situaciones** In groups of three, write and act out these situations. Answers will vary.

1. On your way out of class on the first day of school, you strike up a conversation with the two students who were sitting next to you. You find out each student's name and where he or she is from before you say goodbye and go to your next class.
2. At the next class you meet up with a friend and find out how he or she is doing. As you are talking, your friend Elena enters. Introduce her to your friend.
3. As you're leaving the bookstore, you meet your parents' friends Mrs. Sánchez and Mr. Rodríguez. You greet them and ask how each person is. As you say goodbye, you send greetings to Mrs. Rodríguez.
4. Make up and act out a real-life situation that you and your classmates can imagine yourselves in.

6 Expansions
- Have the class work in small groups to write a few mini-conversations modeled on this activity. Then ask them to copy the dialogues, omitting a few exchanges. Each group should exchange its mini-conversations with another group, which will fill in the blanks.
- Have students rephrase **Conversaciones 1** and **3** in the formal register and **Conversación 2** in the informal register.

7 Suggestion Have students brainstorm who the people in the illustration are and what they are talking about. Ask students which groups would be speaking to each other in the **Ud.** form, and which would be using the **tú** form.

8 Suggestion Have each group pick a situation to prepare and perform. Tell groups not to memorize the conversations, but to recreate them.

The Affective Dimension Point out that if students rehearse the situations a few times, they will feel more comfortable with the material and less anxious when they are asked to present it before the class.

TEACHING OPTIONS

Extra Practice Have students circulate around the classroom and conduct unrehearsed mini-conversations in Spanish with other students, using the words and expressions that they have learned on pages 2–3. As students are carrying out the activity, circulate around the room, monitoring your students' work and offering assistance if requested.

Heritage Speakers Ask heritage speakers to role-play some of the conversations and situations in these **Comunicación** activities, modeling correct pronunciation and intonation for the class. Remind students that there are regional differences in the way English is pronounced, and that the same is true of Spanish. Help clarify unfamiliar vocabulary as necessary.

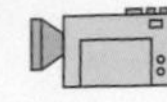

Section Goals

In **Fotonovela** students will:

- receive comprehensible input from free-flowing discourse
- learn functional phrases that preview lesson grammatical structures

Instructional Resources
WB/VM: Video Activities, pp. 213–214
***Fotonovela** DVD/Video (Start 00:02:18)*
Video CD-ROM
*IRM: **Fotonovela** Translations, p. 139, Videoscript, p. 103*
Interactive CD-ROM

Video Synopsis Don Francisco, the bus driver, and Sra. Ramos, a representative of Ecuatur, meet the four travelers at the university. Sra. Ramos passes out travel documents. Inés and Maite introduce themselves, as do Javier and Álex. The travelers board the bus.

Suggestions

- Have students cover the Spanish captions and guess the plot based only on the video stills. Record their predictions, and, after students have watched the video, compare their predictions to what actually happened in the episode.
- Tell students that all items in **Expresiones útiles** on page 7 are active vocabulary for which they are responsible. Pronounce each item and have the class repeat. Also, practice the **Expresiones útiles** by using them in short conversations with individual students.

¡Todos a bordo!

NATIONAL STANDARDS communication cultures

Los cuatro estudiantes, don Francisco y la Sra. Ramos se reúnen (*meet*) en la universidad.

PERSONAJES

DON FRANCISCO

SRA. RAMOS

ÁLEX

JAVIER

INÉS

MAITE

1

SRA. RAMOS Buenos días, chicos. Yo soy Isabel Ramos de la agencia Ecuatur.

DON FRANCISCO Y yo soy don Francisco, el conductor.

2

SRA. RAMOS Bueno, ¿quién es María Teresa Fuentes de Alba?

MAITE ¡Soy yo!

SRA. RAMOS Ah, bien. Aquí tienes los documentos de viaje.

MAITE Gracias.

3

SRA. RAMOS ¿Javier Gómez Lozano?

JAVIER Aquí... soy yo.

6

JAVIER ¿Qué tal? Me llamo Javier.

ÁLEX Mucho gusto, Javier. Yo soy Álex. ¿De dónde eres?

JAVIER De Puerto Rico. ¿Y tú?

ÁLEX Yo soy de México.

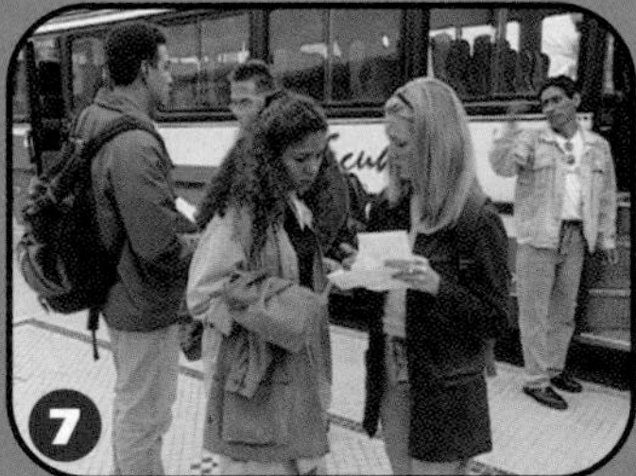
7

DON FRANCISCO Bueno, chicos, ¡todos a bordo!

8

INÉS Con permiso.

recursos

V CD-ROM Lección 1	VM pp. 213–214	I CD-ROM Lección 1

TEACHING OPTIONS

Video Tips General suggestions for using video clips in the classroom can be found on page IAE-12 of this Instructor's Annotated Edition.

¡Todos a bordo! Play the **¡Todos a bordo!** segment of this video module once and ask the class to write down the basic greetings they hear. Play this segment a second time and ask the class to make a list of all the expressions the characters use to identify themselves. Then play the **¡Todos a bordo!** segment for a third time, asking the class to write down all the courtesy expressions they hear, including ways to say "pleased to meet you" and "excuse me."

SRA. RAMOS Y tú eres Inés Ayala Loor, ¿verdad?

INÉS Sí, yo soy Inés.

SRA. RAMOS Y tú eres Alejandro Morales Paredes, ¿no?

ÁLEX Sí, señora.

INÉS Hola. Soy Inés.

MAITE Encantada. Yo me llamo Maite. ¿De dónde eres?

INÉS Soy del Ecuador, de Portoviejo. ¿Y tú?

MAITE De España. Soy de Madrid, la capital. Oye, ¿qué hora es?

INÉS Son las diez y tres minutos.

ÁLEX Perdón.

DON FRANCISCO ¿Y los otros?

SRA. RAMOS Son todos.

DON FRANCISCO Está bien.

Expresiones útiles

Identifying yourself and others

- ▸ **¿Cómo se llama usted?** *What's your name?*
- ▹ **Yo soy don Francisco, el conductor.** *I'm Don Francisco, the driver.*
- ▸ **¿Cómo te llamas?** *What's your name?*
- ▹ **Me llamo Javier.** *My name is Javier.*
- ▸ **¿Quién es... ?** *Who is... ?*
- ▹ **Aquí... soy yo.** *Here... that's me.*
- ▸ **Tú eres... , ¿verdad?/¿no?** *You are ..., right?/no?*
- ▹ **Sí, señora.** *Yes, ma'am.*

Saying what time it is

- ▸ **¿Qué hora es?** *What time is it?*
- ▹ **Es la una.** *It's one o'clock.*
- ▹ **Son las dos.** *It's two o'clock.*
- ▹ **Son las diez y tres minutos.** *It's 10:03.*

Saying "excuse me"

- ▸ **Con permiso.** *Pardon me; Excuse me. (to request permission)*
- ▸ **Perdón.** *Pardon me; Excuse me. (to get someone's attention or to ask forgiveness)*

When starting a trip

- ▸ **¡Todos a bordo!** *All aboard!*
- ▸ **¡Buen viaje!** *Have a good trip!*

Getting a friend's attention

- ▸ **Oye...** *Listen...*

Enfoque cultural Saludos y presentaciones

In the Hispanic world, it is customary for men and women to shake hands when meeting someone for the first time and when saying hello and goodbye to people they already know. Men greet female friends and family members with a brief kiss on the cheek, and they greet males they know well with an **abrazo**—a quick hug and pat on the back. Women of all ages frequently greet good friends, family members, and other loved ones with a brief kiss on one or both cheeks.

Suggestion Have students volunteer to read individual parts of the **Fotonovela** episode aloud. Then have students get together in groups of six to act out the episode. Have one or two groups present the episode to the class.

Expresiones útiles Identify forms of the verb **ser** and point out some subject pronouns. Identify time-telling expressions. Tell your students that they will learn more about these concepts in **Estructura.**

Successful Language Learning Tell your students that their conversational skills will grow more quickly as they learn each lesson's **Expresiones útiles**. This feature is designed to teach phrases that will be useful in conversation, and it will also help students understand key phrases in each **Fotonovela**.

TEACHING OPTIONS

Enfoque cultural Point out that greeting friends, family members, and loved ones with a kiss on one or both cheeks is not unique to the Spanish-speaking world; this custom is common in many European countries and in other parts of the world. Mention also that the concept of an appropriate personal space as it is understood in the United States differs from that of the Hispanic world. Linguists have determined that in the United States friends and acquaintances generally stand or sit at least 18 inches apart while chatting. In Hispanic cultures, however, 18 inches would probably seem like an excessive distance between friends who are having a conversation. It is not considered unusual for casual acquaintances to stand or sit closer to each other.

1 Expansion Give these true-false statements to the class as items 8–10: **8. Maite es de la capital de España. (Cierto) 9. Son las tres y diez minutos. (Falso. Son las diez y tres minutos.) 10. Inés es de Quito, la capital del Ecuador. (Falso. Inés es de Portoviejo.)**

2 Expansion Ask students to suggest any other statements each of the **Fotonovela** characters makes.

¡Lengua viva! Ask students how they might address **Sra. Ramos (doña Isabel)**.

3 Suggestion Go over the activity by asking volunteers to take the roles of Maite and Inés.

4 Possible Response
E1: Buenas tardes. ¿Cómo te llamas?
E2: Hola. Me llamo Felipe. Y tú, ¿cómo te llamas?
E1: Me llamo Denisa. Mucho gusto.
E2: El gusto es mío.
E1: ¿Cómo estás?
E2: Bien, gracias.
E1: ¿De dónde eres?
E2: Soy de Venezuela.
E1: ¡Buen viaje!
E2: Gracias. ¡Adiós!

The Affective Dimension Point out that many people feel a bit nervous about speaking in front of a group. Encourage your students to think of anxious feelings as extra energy that will help them accomplish their goals.

Reacciona a la fotonovela

1 **¿Cierto o falso?** Indicate if each statement is **cierto** or **falso**. Then correct the false statements.

	Cierto	Falso	
1. Javier y Álex son pasajeros (*passengers*).	✓	○	
2. Javier Gómez Lozano es el conductor.	○	✓	Don Francisco es el conductor.
3. Inés Ayala Loor es de la agencia Ecuatur.	○	✓	Isabel Ramos es de la agencia Ecuatur.
4. Inés es del Ecuador.	✓	○	
5. Maite es de España.	✓	○	
6. Javier es de Puerto Rico.	✓	○	
7. Álex es del Ecuador.	○	✓	Álex es de México.

NOTA CULTURAL

Maite is a shortened version of the name **María Teresa**.

Other popular "combination names" in Spanish are **Juanjo: Juan José** and **Maruja: María Eugenia**.

2 **Identificar** Indicate which person would make each statement. One name will be used twice.

1. Yo soy de México. ¿De dónde eres tú? Álex
2. ¡Atención! ¡Todos a bordo! Don Francisco
3. ¿Yo? Soy de la capital de España. Maite
4. Y yo soy del Ecuador. Inés
5. ¿Qué hora es, Inés? Maite
6. Yo soy de Puerto Rico. ¿Y tú? Javier

ÁLEX INÉS MAITE

DON FRANCISCO JAVIER

¡LENGUA VIVA!

In Spanish-speaking countries, **don** and **doña** are used with men's and women's first names to show respect: **don Francisco, doña Rita.** Note that these words are not capitalized.

3 **Completar** Complete this slightly altered version of the conversation that Inés and Maite had.

INÉS Hola. ¿Cómo te (1) llamas?
MAITE Me llamo Maite. ¿Y (2) tú?
INÉS Inés. Mucho (3) gusto.
MAITE (4) El gusto es mío.
INÉS ¿De (5) dónde eres?
MAITE (6) De España. ¿Y (7) tú?
INÉS Del (8) Ecuador.

4 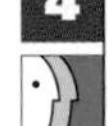 **Conversar** Imagine that you are chatting with a traveler you just met at the airport. With a partner, prepare a conversation using these cues. Some answers will vary.

Estudiante 1	Estudiante 2
Say "good afternoon" to your partner and ask for his or her name. →	Say hello and what your name is. Then ask what your partner's name is.
Say what your name is and that you are glad to meet your partner. →	Say that the pleasure is yours.
Ask how your partner is. →	Say that you're doing well, thank you.
Ask where your partner is from. →	Say where you're from.
Wish your partner a good trip. →	Say thank you and goodbye.

TEACHING OPTIONS

Pairs Ask students to work in pairs to ad-lib the exchanges between don Francisco and Sra. Ramos, Inés and Maite, and Álex and Javier. Tell them to convey the general meaning using vocabulary and expressions they know, and assure them that they don't have to stick to the original exchanges word for word. Then, ask volunteers to present their exchanges to the class.

Extra Practice Choose four or five lines of the **Fotonovela** to use as a dictation. Read the lines twice slowly to give students an opportunity to write. Then read them again at normal speed to allow students to correct any errors or fill in any gaps. You may have students correct their own work by checking it against the **Fotonovela** text.

NOTA CULTURAL

The **Real Academia Española** (Royal Spanish Academy) is based in Madrid, Spain. Founded in 1713, the goal of the RAE is to preserve and update the Spanish language throughout the Spanish-speaking world.

Pronunciación

The Spanish alphabet

The Spanish alphabet consisted of 30 letters until 1994, when the **Real Academia Española** removed **ch (che)** and **ll (elle)**. You may still see **ch** and **ll** listed as separate letters in reference works printed before 1994. Two Spanish letters, **ñ (eñe)** and **rr (erre)**, don't appear in the English alphabet. The letters **k (ka)** and **w (doble ve)** are used only in words of foreign origin.

Letra	Nombre(s)	Ejemplos	Letra	Nombre(s)	Ejemplos
a	a	**a**diós	ñ	eñe	ma**ñ**ana
b	be	**b**ien, pro**b**lema	o	o	**o**nce
c	ce	**c**osa, **c**ero	p	pe	**p**rofesor
d	de	**d**iario, na**d**a	q	cu	**q**ué
e	e	**e**studiante	r	ere	**r**egular, seño**r**a
f	efe	**f**oto	rr	erre	ca**rr**o
g	ge	**g**racias, **G**erardo, re**g**ular	s	ese	**s**eñor
h	hache	**h**ola	t	te	**t**ú
i	i	**I**gualmente	u	u	**u**sted
j	jota	**J**avier	v	ve	**v**ista, nue**v**o
k	ka, ca	**k**ilómetro	w	doble ve	*walkman*
l	ele	**l**ápiz	x	equis	e**x**istir, Mé**x**ico
m	eme	**m**apa	y	i griega, ye	**y**o
n	ene	**n**acionalidad	z	zeta, ceta	**z**ona

El alfabeto Repeat the Spanish alphabet and example words after your instructor.

Práctica Spell these words aloud in Spanish.

1. nada
2. maleta
3. quince
4. muy
5. hombre
6. por favor
7. San Fernando
8. Estados Unidos
9. Puerto Rico
10. España
11. Javier
12. Ecuador
13. Maite
14. gracias
15. Nueva York

Refranes Read these sayings aloud.

Ver es creer.[1]
En boca cerrada no entran moscas.[2]

1 Seeing is believing.
2 Silence is golden.

recursos

TEXT CD Lección 1	LM p. 2	Lab CD/MP3 Lección 1	I CD-ROM Lección 1

Section Goals

In **Pronunciación** students will be introduced to:

- the Spanish alphabet and how it contrasts with the English alphabet
- the names of the letters

Instructional Resources
Textbook CD
Lab Manual, p. 2
*Lab CD/MP3 **Lección 1***
IRM: Tapescript, pp. 1–5; p. 85
Interactive CD-ROM

Suggestions

- Model pronunciation of the Spanish alphabet and the example words. Have your students repeat them.
- You may want to point out that the expressions **b alta** and **v baja** are sometimes used to distinguish these two letters. A detailed explanation of the pronunciation of Spanish **b** and **v** can be found in **Lección 5, Pronunciación**, page 145.
- Draw attention to any posters, signs, or maps in the classroom. Point out individual letters and ask the class to identify them in Spanish.
- Write on the board the Spanish abbreviations of several famous organizations (Ex: **ONU, OPEP**), and have students spell them out. Explain what each represents. Ex: **ONU** = **Organización de Naciones Unidas** (*United Nations, UN*), **OPEP** = **Organización de Países Exportadores de Petróleo** (*Organization of Petroleum-Exporting Countries, OPEC*)

El alfabeto/Práctica/Refranes
These exercises are recorded on the Textbook CD. You may want to play the CD so students practice the pronunciation point by listening to Spanish spoken by speakers other than yourself.

TEACHING OPTIONS

Extra Practice Do a dictation activity in which you spell out a list of words in Spanish to the class. Spell each word twice to allow students sufficient time to write. After you have finished, write your list on the board or project it on a transparency and have your students check their work. You can also have students spell their names in Spanish.

Extra Practice Here are four more **refranes** to use for practicing the alphabet: **De tal palo, tal astilla** (*A chip off the old block*); **Los ojos son el espejo del alma** (*Eyes are the window to the soul*); **El rayo nunca cae dos veces en el mismo lugar** (*Lightning never strikes twice in the same place*); **No dejes para mañana lo que puedas hacer hoy** (*Don't put off until tomorrow what you can do today*).

Section Goals

In **Estructura 1.1**, students will be introduced to:
- gender of nouns
- definite and indefinite articles

Instructional Resources
WB/VM: Workbook, p. 3
Lab Manual, p. 3
Lab CD/MP3 ***Lección 1***
IRM: ***¡Inténtalo!*** *&* ***Práctica***
Answers, pp. 197–198;
Tapescript, pp. 1–5
Interactive CD-ROM
Companion website:
www.vistahigherlearning.com
Presentations CD-ROM

Suggestions

- Write these nouns from **Fotonovela** on the board: **conductor, agencia, documentos, universidades**. Ask volunteers what each means. Point out the different endings and introduce gender in Spanish. Explain what a noun is and give examples of people (**chicos**), places (**universidad**), things (**documentos**), and ideas (**nacionalidad**). Ask volunteers to point out which of these nouns are singular or plural and why.
- Point out that while nouns for male beings are generally masculine and those for female beings are generally feminine, grammatical gender doesn't necessarily reflect the actual gender of the noun.
- Point out patterns of noun endings **–o, –a; –or, –ora**. Stress that **–ista** can refer to males or females and give additional examples: **el/la artista, el/la dentista**.

1.1 Nouns and articles

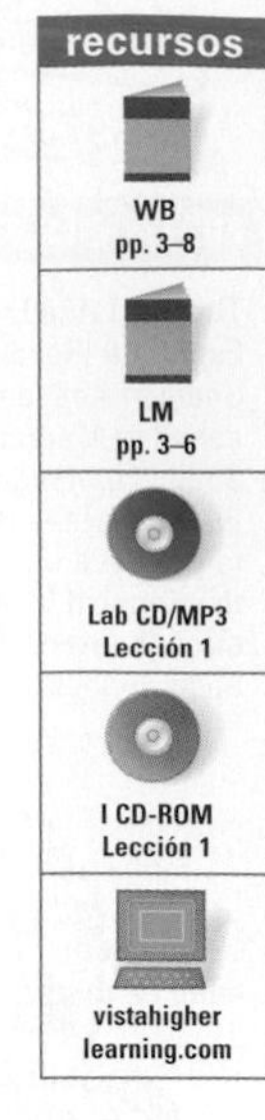

recursos
WB pp. 3–8
LM pp. 3–6
Lab CD/MP3 Lección 1
I CD-ROM Lección 1
vistahigherlearning.com

Spanish nouns

ANTE TODO A noun is a word used to identify people, animals, places, things, or ideas. Unlike English, all Spanish nouns, even those that refer to non-living things, have gender; that is, they are considered either masculine or feminine. As in English, nouns in Spanish also have number, meaning that they are either singular or plural.

Nouns that refer to living things

Masculine nouns		Feminine nouns	
el hombre	*the man*	**la mujer**	*the woman*
ending in –o		**ending in –a**	
el chico	*the boy*	**la chica**	*the girl*
el pasajero	*the (male) passenger*	**la pasajera**	*the (female) passenger*
ending in –or		**ending in –ora**	
el conductor	*the (male) driver*	**la conductora**	*the (female) driver*
el profesor	*the (male) teacher*	**la profesora**	*the (female) teacher*
ending in –ista		**ending in –ista**	
el turista	*the (male) tourist*	**la turista**	*the (female) tourist*

▶ As shown above, nouns that refer to males, like **el hombre**, are generally masculine, while nouns that refer to females, like **la mujer**, are generally feminine.

▶ Many nouns that refer to male beings end in **–o** or **–or**. Their corresponding feminine forms end in **–a** and **–ora**, respectively.

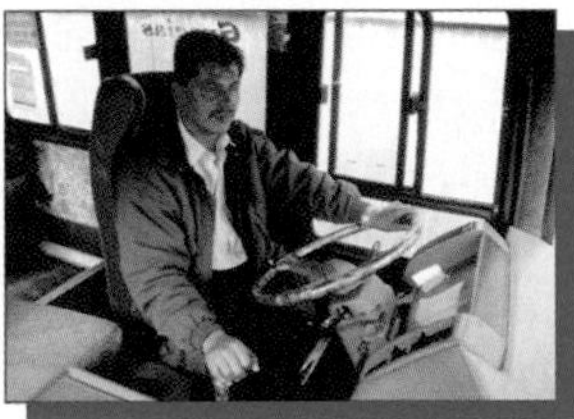
el conductor

la profesora

▶ The masculine and feminine forms of nouns that end in **–ista,** like **turista**, are the same, so gender is indicated by the article **el** (masculine) or **la** (feminine). Some other nouns have identical masculine and feminine forms.

el joven *the youth; the young man*	**la** joven *the youth; the young woman*
el estudiante *the (male) student*	**la** estudiante *the (female) student*

¡LENGUA VIVA!

Profesor(a) and **turista** are *cognates*— words that share similar spellings and meanings in Spanish and English. Recognizing cognates will help you determine the meaning of many Spanish words. Here are some other cognates: **la administración, el animal, el apartamento, el cálculo, el color, la decisión, la historia, la música, el restaurante, el/la secretario/a**

CONSEJOS

Cognates can certainly be very helpful in your study of Spanish. Beware, however, of "false" cognates, those that have similar spellings in Spanish and English, but different meanings:
la carpeta *file folder*
el conductor *driver*
el éxito *success*
la fábrica *factory*

TEACHING OPTIONS

Extra Practice Write ten singular nouns on the board. Make sure the nouns represent a mix of the different types of noun endings taught. In a rapid-response drill, call on students to give the appropriate gender. For **–ista** words, accept either masculine or feminine, but clarify that both are used. You may also do this as a completely oral drill by not writing the words on the board.

Game Divide the class into groups of three to four students. Bring in photos or magazine pictures, point to various objects or people, and say the Spanish noun without saying the article. Call on groups to indicate the object or person's gender. Give a point for each correct answer. Deduct a point for each incorrect answer. The group with the most points at the end wins.

Nouns that refer to non-living things

Masculine nouns		Feminine nouns	
ending in *-o*		**ending in *-a***	
el cuaderno	*the notebook*	**la cosa**	*the thing*
el diario	*the diary*	**la escuela**	*the school*
el diccionario	*the dictionary*	**la grabadora**	*the tape recorder*
el número	*the number*	**la maleta**	*the suitcase*
el video	*the video*	**la palabra**	*the word*
ending in *-ma*		**ending in *-ción***	
el problema	*the problem*	**la lección**	*the lesson*
el programa	*the program*	**la conversación**	*the conversation*
ending in *-s*		**ending in *-dad***	
el autobús	*the bus*	**la nacionalidad**	*the nationality*
el país	*the country*	**la comunidad**	*the community*

¡LENGUA VIVA!

The Spanish word for *video* can be pronounced with the stress on the **i** or the **e**. For that reason, you might see the word written with or without an accent: **video** or **vídeo**.

- As shown above, certain noun endings are strongly associated with a specific gender, so you can use them to determine if a noun is masculine or feminine.
- Because the gender of nouns that refer to non-living things cannot be determined by foolproof rules, you should memorize the gender of each noun you learn. It is helpful to memorize each noun with its corresponding article, **el** for masculine and **la** for feminine.
- Another reason to memorize the gender of every noun is that there are common exceptions to the rules of gender. For example, **el mapa** (*map*) and **el día** (*day*) end in **-a,** but are masculine. **La mano** (*hand*) ends in **-o,** but is feminine.

Plural of nouns

- In Spanish, nouns that end in a vowel form the plural by adding **-s.** Nouns that end in a consonant add **-es**. Nouns that end in **-z** change the **-z** to **-c**, then add **-es**.

el chic**o** → los chic**os** | la nacionalida**d** → las nacionalida**des**

el diari**o** → los diari**os** | el paí**s** → los paí**ses**

la palabr**a** → las palabr**as** | el profeso**r** → los profeso**res**

el problem**a** → los problem**as** | el lápi**z** (*pencil*) → los lápi**ces**

¡ATENCIÓN!

In general, when a singular noun has an accent mark on the last syllable, the accent is dropped from the plural form:
la lección → **las lecciones**
el autobús → **los autobuses**
You will learn more about accent marks in **Lección 4, Pronunciación,** p. 111.

- You use the masculine plural form of the noun to refer to a group that includes both males and females.

1 pasajer**o** + 2 pasajer**as** = 3 pasajer**os**

2 chic**os** + 2 chic**as** = 4 chic**os**

Suggestions

- Work through the list of nouns, modeling their pronunciation. Point out patterns of gender, including word endings **–ma**, **–ción**, and **–dad**. Give cognate nouns with these endings and ask students to indicate the gender. Ex: **diagrama**, **acción**, **personalidad**. Point out common exceptions to gender agreement rules for **el mapa**, **el día**, and **la mano**.
- Stress the addition of **–s** to nouns that end in vowels and **–es** to nouns that end in consonants. Write ten nouns on the board and ask volunteers to give the plural forms, along with the appropriate articles.
- Stress that even if a group contains 100 women and one man, the masculine plural form and article are used. Point to three male students and ask if the group is **los** or **las estudiantes** (**los**). Next, point to three female students and ask the same question (**las**). Then indicate a group of males and females and ask for the correct term to refer to them (**los estudiantes**).

¡Atención! Point out that these words lose the written accent in the plural form in order to keep the stress on the same syllable as in the singular noun.

The Affective Dimension
Tell your students that many people feel anxious when learning grammar. Tell them that grammar will seem less intimidating if they think of it as a description of how the language works instead of a list of strict rules.

TEACHING OPTIONS

TPR Assign a different definite article to each of four students. Then line up ten students, each of whom is assigned a noun. Include a mix of masculine, feminine, singular, and plural nouns. Say one of the nouns (without the article), and that student must step forward. The student assigned the corresponding article has five seconds to join the noun student.

Game Divide the class into two teams, A and B. Indicate one team member at a time, alternating between teams. Give a singular noun to the member of team A. He or she must repeat it, preceded by the correct definite article. The corresponding member of team B must correctly supply the plural and definite article. Give a point per correct answer. Deduct a point for each wrong answer. The team with the most points at the end of play wins.

Suggestions

- Write **¿El, la, los o las?** on the board and ask students to identify the correct definite article for the following words. **1. hombre (el) 2. computadora (la) 3. profesor (el) 4. universidades (las) 5. turistas (los/las) 6. diccionario (el) 7. problema (el) 8. mujeres (las)**
- Write **¿Un, una, unos o unas?** on the board and ask students to identify the correct indefinite article for the following words. **1. pasajeros (unos) 2. chico (un) 3. escuela (una) 4. lecciones (unas) 5. autobuses (unos) 6. maleta (una) 7. programas (unos) 8. cosa (una)**
- Do a pair of conversion activities. Students respond with the article and the noun: **Definido → Indefinido 1. los turistas (unos turistas) 2. la computadora (una computadora) 3. el hombre (un hombre) 4. las mujeres (unas mujeres) 5. el programa (un programa) 6. el hacha (un hacha) Indefinido → Definido 1. unas lecciones (las lecciones) 2. una maleta (la maleta) 3. unos lápices (los lápices) 4. unas pasajeras (las pasajeras) 5. un diario (el diario) 6. una foto (la foto)**

Spanish articles

ANTE TODO As you know, English often uses definite articles (**the**) and indefinite articles (**a, an**) before nouns. Spanish also has definite and indefinite articles. Unlike English, Spanish articles vary in form because they agree in gender and number with the nouns they modify.

Definite articles

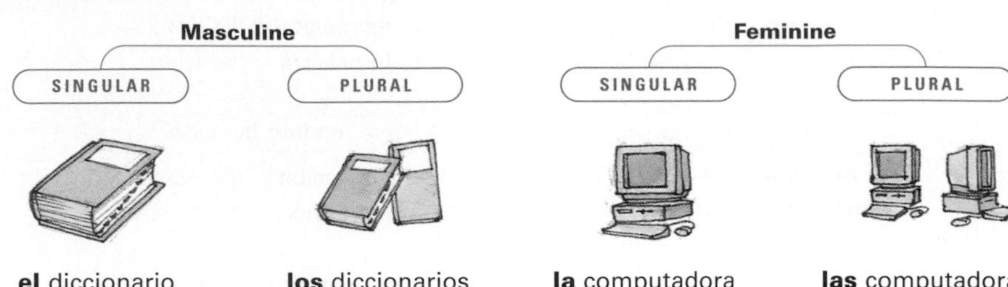

el diccionario *the dictionary* — **los** diccionarios *the dictionaries* — **la** computadora *the computer* — **las** computadoras *the computers*

▶ Spanish has four forms that are equivalent to the English definite article *the*. You use definite articles to refer to specific nouns.

¡LENGUA VIVA!
Feminine singular nouns that begin with **a-** or **ha-** require the masculine articles **el** and **un**. This is done in order to avoid repetition of the **a** sound:
el agua *water*
las aguas *waters*
un hacha *ax*
unas hachas *axes*

Indefinite articles

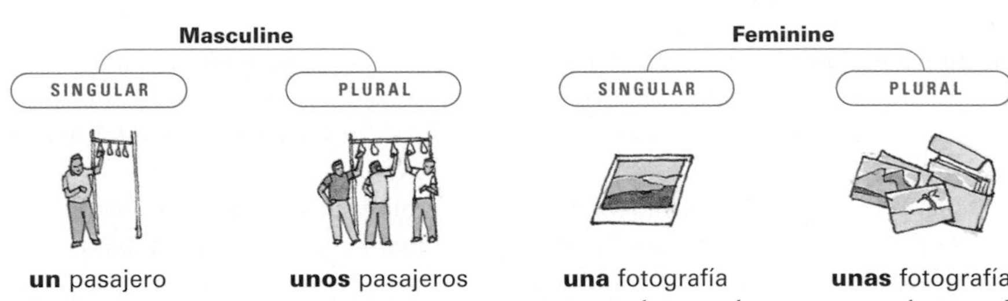

un pasajero *a (one) passenger* — **unos** pasajeros *some passengers* — **una** fotografía *a (one) photograph* — **unas** fotografías *some photographs*

▶ Spanish has four forms that are equivalent to the English indefinite article, which according to context may mean *a*, *an*, or *some*. You use indefinite articles to refer to unspecified persons or things.

¡LENGUA VIVA!
Since **la fotografía** is feminine, so is its shortened form, **la foto**, even though it ends in **–o**.

¡INTÉNTALO! Provide a definite article for each noun in the first column and an indefinite article for each noun in the second column. The first item has been done for you.

¿el, la, los o las?

1. __la__ chica
2. __el__ chico
3. __la__ maleta
4. __los__ cuadernos
5. __el__ lápiz
6. __las__ mujeres

¿un, una, unos o unas?

1. __un__ autobús
2. __unas__ escuelas
3. __una__ computadora
4. __unos__ hombres
5. __una__ señora
6. __unos__ lápices

TEACHING OPTIONS

Extra Practice Hold up or point to objects whose names students are familiar with (**diccionario, lápiz, computadora, foto[grafía]**, and so forth). Ask students to indicate the appropriate definite article and the noun. Include a mix of singular and plural nouns. Do the same exercise but substitute indefinite articles for definite articles.

Pairs Have pairs write down a mix of ten singular and plural nouns, *without their articles*. Have them exchange their list with another pair. Each pair then has to write down the appropriate definite or indefinite article for each item. You will assign which group concentrates on definite articles and which one concentrates on indefinite articles. After pairs have finished, have them exchange lists and correct them.

Práctica

1 **¿Singular o plural?** If the word is singular, make it plural. If it is plural, make it singular.

1. el número los números
2. un diario unos diarios
3. la estudiante las estudiantes
4. el conductor los conductores
5. el país los países
6. las cosas la cosa
7. unos turistas un turista
8. las nacionalidades la nacionalidad
9. unas computadoras una computadora
10. los problemas el problema
11. una fotografía unas fotografías
12. los profesores el profesor
13. unas señoritas una señorita
14. el hombre los hombres
15. la grabadora las grabadoras
16. la señora las señoras

2 **Identificar** For each drawing, provide the noun with its corresponding definite and indefinite articles.

las maletas, unas maletas

1. la computadora, una computadora

2. los cuadernos, unos cuadernos

3. las mujeres, unas mujeres

4. el chico, un chico

5. la escuela, una escuela

6. las fotos, unas fotos

7. los autobuses, unos autobuses

8. el diario, un diario

Comunicación

3 **Charadas** In groups, play a game of charades. Individually, think of two nouns for each charade, for example, a boy using a computer (**un chico; una computadora**). The first person to guess correctly acts out the next charade.

1 Expansion Reverse the activity by reading the on-page answers and having students convert the singular to plural and vice versa. Make sure they close their books. Give the nouns in random order.

2 Expansion Bring in photos or magazine pictures that illustrate items whose names students know. Ask students to indicate the definite article and the noun. Include a mix of singular and plural nouns. Repeat the exercise with indefinite articles.

3 Suggestion Explain the basic rules of charades relevant to what students know at this point: (1) the student acting out the charade may not speak and (2) he or she may show the number of syllables by using fingers.

3 Expansion Split the class into two teams with volunteers from each team acting out the charades. Give a point to each team for correctly guessing the charade. Deduct a point for incorrect guesses. The team with the most points wins.

TEACHING OPTIONS

Video Show the video again to offer more input on singular and plural nouns and their articles. With their books closed, have students write down every noun and article that they hear. After viewing the video, ask volunteers to list the nouns and articles they heard. Explain that the **las** used when telling time refers to **las horas** (Ex: **Son las cinco** = **Son las cinco horas**).

Extra Practice Slowly read a short passage from a novel, story, or poem written in Spanish, preferably one with a great number of nouns and articles. As a listening exercise, have students write down every noun and article they hear, even unfamiliar ones (the articles may cue when nouns appear).

Section Goals

In **Estructura 1.2** students will be introduced to:
- numbers 0–30
- the verb form **hay**

Instructional Resources
WB/VM: Workbook, p. 4
Lab Manual, p. 4
*Lab CD/MP3 **Lección 1***
*IRM: **¡Inténtalo! & Práctica** Answers, pp. 197–198; Tapescript, pp. 1–5*
Info Gap Activities Booklet, pp. 1–2
Interactive CD-ROM
Companion website: www.vistahigherlearning.com
Presentations CD-ROM

Suggestions

- Introduce numbers by asking students how many of them can count to ten in Spanish. Hold up varying numbers of fingers and ask students to shout out the corresponding number in Spanish.
- Assign each student a number which they must remember. When finished, have the student assigned **uno** recite his or her number aloud, then **dos, tres,** etc. Help anyone who struggles with his or her number.
- Go through the numbers, modeling the pronunciation of each. Write individual numbers on the board and call on students at random to say the number.
- Emphasize the variable forms of **uno** and **veintiuno**, giving examples of each. Ex: **veintiún profesores, veintiuna profesoras.**
- Ask questions like the following: **¿Cuántos estudiantes hay en la clase? (Hay quince estudiantes en la clase.)**

1.2 Numbers 0–30

Los números 0 a 30

0	cero				
1	uno	**11**	once	**21**	veintiuno
2	dos	**12**	doce	**22**	veintidós
3	tres	**13**	trece	**23**	veintitrés
4	cuatro	**14**	catorce	**24**	veinticuatro
5	cinco	**15**	quince	**25**	veinticinco
6	seis	**16**	dieciséis	**26**	veintiséis
7	siete	**17**	diecisiete	**27**	veintisiete
8	ocho	**18**	dieciocho	**28**	veintiocho
9	nueve	**19**	diecinueve	**29**	veintinueve
10	diez	**20**	veinte	**30**	treinta

- The number **uno** (*one*) and numbers ending in **–uno**, such as **veintiuno**, have more than one form. Before masculine nouns, **uno** shortens to **un**. Before feminine nouns, **uno** changes to **una**.

  un hombre → veinti**ún** hombres   **una** mujer → veinti**una** mujeres

- To ask *how many* people or things there are, use **cuántos** before masculine nouns and **cuántas** before feminine nouns.

- The Spanish equivalent of both *there is* and *there are* is **hay**. Use **¿Hay...?** to ask *Is there...?* or *Are there...?* Use **no hay** to express *there is not* or *there are not*.

¡ATENCIÓN!

The numbers sixteen through nineteen can also be written as three words: **diez y seis, diez y siete...**

The forms **uno** and **veintiuno** are used when counting (**uno, dos, tres...veinte, veintiuno, veintidós...**). They are also used when the number *follows* a noun, even if the noun is feminine: **la lección uno.**

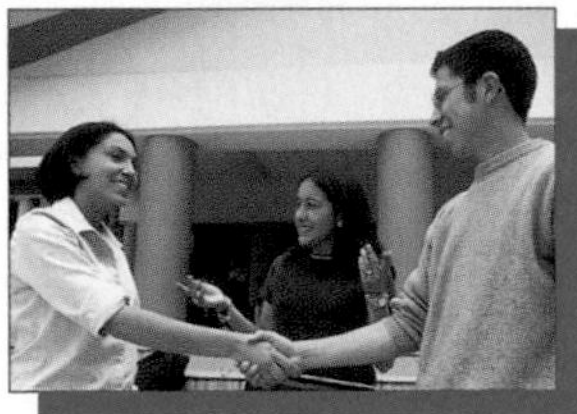

—¿**Cuántos** estudiantes **hay**?
How many students are there?

—**Hay** tres estudiantes en la foto.
There are three students in the photo.

—¿**Hay** chicas en la fotografía?
Are there girls in the picture?

—**Hay** cuatro chicos, y **no hay** chicas.
There are four guys, and there are no girls.

¡INTÉNTALO! Provide the Spanish words for these numbers.

1. **7** siete
2. **16** dieciséis
3. **29** veintinueve
4. **1** uno
5. **0** cero
6. **15** quince
7. **21** veintiuno
8. **9** nueve
9. **23** veintitrés
10. **11** once
11. **30** treinta
12. **4** cuatro
13. **12** doce
14. **28** veintiocho
15. **14** catorce
16. **10** diez
17. **2** dos
18. **5** cinco
19. **22** veintidós
20. **13** trece

TEACHING OPTIONS

TPR Assign ten students a number from 0–30 and line them up in front of the class. Call out one of the numbers at random, and have the student assigned that number take a step forward. When two students have stepped forward, ask them to repeat their numbers. Then ask individuals to add (Say: **Suma**) or subtract (Say: **Resta**) the two numbers.

Game Hand out Bingo cards with B-I-N-G-O across the top of five columns. The 25 squares underneath will contain random numbers. From a hat, draw letters and numbers and call them out in Spanish. The first student that can fill in a number in each one of the lettered columns yells **¡Bingo!** and wins.

Práctica

1 **Contar** Following the pattern, provide the missing numbers in Spanish.

1. 1, 3, 5, .., 29 — 7, 9, 11, 13, 15, 17, 19, 21, 23, 25, 27
2. 2, 4, 6, .., 30 — 8, 10, 12, 14, 16, 18, 20, 22, 24, 26, 28
3. 3, 6, 9, .., 30 — 12, 15, 18, 21, 24, 27
4. 30, 28, 26, .., 0 — 24, 22, 20, 18, 16, 14, 12, 10, 8, 6, 4, 2
5. 30, 25, 20, .., 0 — 15, 10, 5
6. 28, 24, 20, .., 0 — 16, 12, 8, 4

2 **Resolver** Solve these math problems with a partner.

AYUDA

+ → **más**
– → **menos**
= → **es/son**

modelo

5 + 3 =
Estudiante 1: *cinco más tres son...*
Estudiante 2: *ocho*

1. **2 + 15 =** Dos más quince son diecisiete.
2. **20 – 1 =** Veinte menos uno son diecinueve.
3. **5 + 7 =** Cinco más siete son doce.
4. **18 + 12 =** Dieciocho más doce son treinta.
5. **3 + 22 =** Tres más veintidós son veinticinco.
6. **6 – 3 =** Seis menos tres son tres.
7. **11 + 12 =** Once más doce son veintitrés.
8. **7 – 7 =** Siete menos siete es cero.
9. **8 + 5 =** Ocho más cinco son trece.
10. **23 – 14 =** Veintitrés menos catorce son nueve.

3 **¿Cuántos hay?** How many persons or things are there in these drawings?

modelo

Hay cuatro maletas.

1. Hay veinte lápices.

2. Hay un hombre.

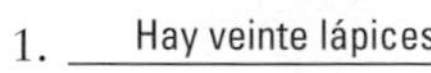

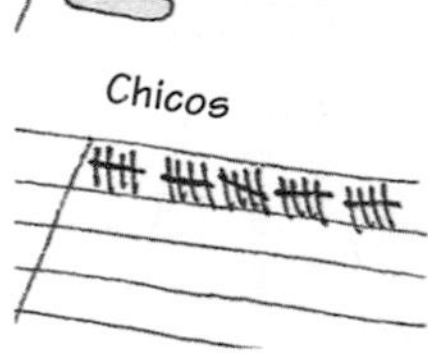

3. Hay veinticinco chicos.

4. Hay una conductora.

5. Hay cuatro fotos.

6. Hay treinta cuadernos.

7. Hay seis turistas.

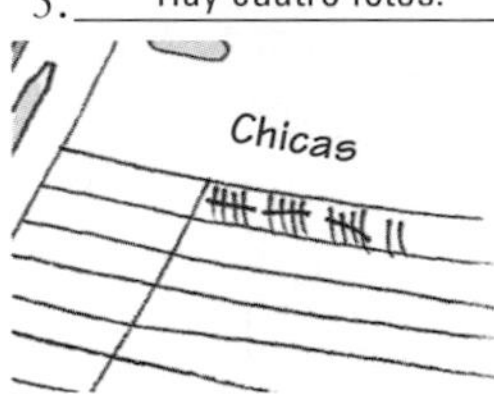

8. Hay diecisiete chicas.

1 Suggestion Before beginning the activity, make sure students know each pattern: odds (**los números impares**), evens (**los números pares**), count by threes (**contar de tres en tres**).

1 Expansion Ask the class to list the prime numbers (**los números primos**) up to 30. Explain that a prime number is any number that can only be divided by itself and 1. Prime numbers to 30 are: 1, 2, 3, 5, 7, 11, 13, 17, 19, 23, 29.

2 Expansion Do simple multiplication problems. Introduce the phrase (**multiplicado**) **por**. Ex: **Cinco multiplicado por cinco son...** (**veinticinco**) or **Cinco por cinco son...** (**veinticinco**).

3 Suggestion Have students read the directions and model sentence. Cue student responses by asking questions related to the drawings. Ex: **¿Cuántos lápices hay?** (**Hay veinte lápices.**)

3 Expansion Hold up or point to classroom objects and ask how many there are. Since students won't know the names of many of the items, a simple number or **hay** + the number will suffice to signal comprehension. Ex: **—¿Cuántos bolígrafos hay aquí? —(Hay) Dos.**

TEACHING OPTIONS

TPR Give ten students a card that contains a number from 0–30 (you may want to assign numbers in fives to simplify the activity). The card must be visible to the other students. Then call out simple math problems (addition, subtraction) involving the assigned numbers. When the first two numbers are called, each student steps forward. The student whose assigned number completes the math problem then has five seconds to join them.

Extra Practice Ask questions about the university and the town or city in which it's located. Ex: **¿Cuántos profesores hay en el departamento de español? ¿Cuántas universidades hay en ____? ¿Cuántas pizzerías hay en ___?** Encourage students to guess the number. If a number exceeds 30, write that number on the board and model its pronunciation.

4 Suggestion For items 3, 4, 7, and 9, ask students **¿Cuántos/as hay?** If there are no examples of the item listed, students should say **No hay** ____.

4 Expansion After completing the activity, call on individual students to give rapid responses to the same items. Mix up the order of items to make the activity more challenging. See if the students can remember the number of items from the first time through the activity.

5 Suggestion Remind students that they will be forming sentences with **hay** and a number. Give them four minutes to do the activity. You might also have them write out their answers.

5 Expansion After pairs have finished analyzing the drawing, call on individual students to respond. Convert the statements into questions in Spanish. Ask: **¿Cuántos chicos hay? ¿Cuántas mujeres hay?**

Suggestion See the Info Gap Activities Booklet for an additional activity to practice the material presented in this section.

Comunicación

NATIONAL communication STANDARDS

4 **En la clase** With a classmate, take turns asking and answering these questions about your classroom. Answers will vary.

1. ¿Cuántos estudiantes hay?
2. ¿Cuántos profesores hay?
3. ¿Hay una computadora?
4. ¿Hay una maleta?
5. ¿Cuántos mapas hay?
6. ¿Cuántos lápices hay?
7. ¿Hay cuadernos?
8. ¿Cuántas grabadoras hay?
9. ¿Hay hombres?
10. ¿Cuántas mujeres hay?

5 **Preguntas** With a classmate, take turns asking and answering questions about the drawing. Talk about: Answers will vary.

1. How many children there are
2. How many women there are
3. If there are some photographs
4. If there is a boy
5. How many notebooks there are
6. If there is a bus
7. If there are tourists
8. How many pencils there are
9. If there is a man
10. How many computers there are

TEACHING OPTIONS

Pairs Have each student draw a scene similar to the one on this page. Of course, stick figures are perfectly acceptable! Give them three minutes to draw the scene. Then pairs take turns describing what is in their partner's picture. Encourage students to include multiple numbers of particular items (**cuadernos**, **maletas**, **lápices**, and so forth).

Pairs Divide students into pairs. Give half of the pairs magazine pictures that contain images of words that are familiar to them or that are close cognates. Give the other half descriptions of those pictures, including **hay** in the description. Ex: **En esta foto hay dos mujeres, un chico y una chica.** Pairs walk around the room to match the descriptions with the corresponding pictures.

1.3 Present tense of ser

Subject pronouns

ANTE TODO In order to use verbs, you will need to learn about subject pronouns. A subject pronoun replaces the name or title of a person or thing and acts as the subject of a verb. In both Spanish and English, subject pronouns are divided into three groups: first person, second person, and third person.

Subject pronouns

	SINGULAR		PLURAL	
FIRST PERSON	**yo**	*I*	**nosotros**	*we* (masculine)
			nosotras	*we* (feminine)
SECOND PERSON	**tú**	*you* (familiar)	**vosotros**	*you* (masc., fam.)
	usted (Ud.)	*you* (formal)	**vosotras**	*you* (fem., fam.)
			ustedes (Uds.)	*you* (form.)
THIRD PERSON	**él**	*he*	**ellos**	*they* (masc.)
	ella	*she*	**ellas**	*they* (fem.)

¡LENGUA VIVA!

In Latin America, **ustedes** is used as the plural for both **tú** and **usted**. In Spain, however, **vosotros** and **vosotras** are used as the plural of **tú**, and **ustedes** is used only as the plural of **usted.**

•••

Usted and **ustedes** are abbreviated as **Ud.** and **Uds.**, or occasionally as **Vd.** and **Vds.**

▶ Spanish has two subject pronouns that mean *you* (singular). Use **tú** when addressing a friend, a family member, or a child you know well. Use **usted** to address a person with whom you have a formal or more distant relationship, such as a superior at work, a professor, or an older person.

▶ The masculine plural forms **nosotros**, **vosotros**, and **ellos** refer to a group of males or to a group of males and females. The feminine plural forms **nosotras**, **vosotras**, and **ellas** can refer only to groups made up exclusively of females.

nosotros, vosotros, ellos

nosotros, vosotros, ellos

nosotras, vosotras, ellas

▶ There is no Spanish equivalent of the English subject pronoun *it*. Generally it is not expressed in Spanish.

Es un problema.
It's a problem.

Es una computadora.
It's a computer.

Section Goals

In **Estructura 1.3** students will be introduced to:

- subject pronouns
- present tense of the verb **ser**
- using **ser** to identify, to indicate possession, to describe origin, and to talk about professions or occupations

Instructional Resources
WB/VM: Workbook, pp. 5–6
Lab Manual, p. 5
*Lab CD/MP3 **Lección 1***
*IRM: **Vocab. adicional**, p. 178; **¡Inténtalo!** & **Práctica** Answers, pp. 197–198; Tapescript, pp. 1–5*
Interactive CD-ROM
Companion website: www.vistahigherlearning.com
Presentations CD-ROM

Suggestions

- Point to yourself and say: **Yo soy profesor(a)**. Then walk up to a student and say: **Tú eres...** Correct student response should be **estudiante**. Once the pattern has been established, include other subject pronouns and forms of **ser** while indicating other students. Ex: **Él es...**, **Ella es...**, **Ellos son...**
- Remind students of familiar and formal forms of address they learned in **Contextos**.
- You may want to point out that while **Ud.** and **Uds.** are part of the second person *you*, they use third person forms.
- Point out that **nosotros/as** and **vosotros/as** are the only subject pronouns that indicate gender.
- While the **vosotros/as** forms are listed in verb paradigms in **VISTAS,** they will not be actively practiced.

TEACHING OPTIONS

Extra Practice Explain that students are to give subject pronouns based on your (the instructor's) point of view. Ex: Point to yourself (**yo**), a female student (**ella**), everyone in the class (**nosotros**).
Extra Practice Ask students to indicate whether the following people would be addressed as **tú** or **Ud.** Ex: a roommate, a friend's grandfather, a doctor, a neighbor's child

Heritage Speakers Ask heritage speakers how they address elder members of their family such as parents, grandparents, aunts and uncles—whether they use **tú** or **Ud.** Also ask them if they use **vosotros/as** or not (they typically won't unless they or their family are from Spain).

Suggestions

- Work through the explanation and the forms of **ser** in the chart. Emphasize that **es** is used for **Ud.**, **él**, and **ella**, and that **son** is used for **Uds.**, **ellos**, and **ellas**. Context or the use of subject pronouns or names will determine who is being addressed or talked about.
- Explain that **ser** is used to identify people and things. At this point there is no need to explain that **estar** also means *to be*; it will be introduced in **Lección 2**.
- Explain the meaning of **¿quién?** and ask questions about who students in the class are. Ex: ____, **¿quién es ella? Sí, es ____. ¿Quién soy yo? Sí, soy el profesor/la profesora ____**. Introduce **¿qué?** and ask questions about items in the class. Ex: **¿Qué es esto? Sí, es un mapa.**
- Point out the construction of **ser** + **de** to indicate possession. Stress that there is no *'s* in Spanish. (Direct students to the **¡Atención!** sidebar.) Pick up objects belonging to students and ask questions. Ex: **¿De quién es este cuaderno? (Es de ____.) ¿De quién son estos libros? (Son de ____.)**

¡Atención! Introduce the contraction **de + el = del**. Emphasize that **de** and other definite articles do not make contractions and support with examples. Ex: **Soy del estado de ____. El diccionario no es de la profesora de ____.** Also use examples of possession to illustrate the contraction. Ex: **¿Es este mapa del presidente de la universidad?**

The present tense of *ser*

ANTE TODO In **Contextos** and **Fotonovela**, you have already used several forms of the present tense of **ser** (*to be*) to identify yourself and others and to talk about where you and others are from. **Ser** is an irregular verb, which means its forms don't follow the regular patterns that most verbs follow. You need to memorize the forms, which appear in the following chart.

ser

		ser (*to be*)	
SINGULAR FORMS	yo	**soy**	*I am*
	tú	**eres**	*you are* (fam.)
	Ud./él/ella	**es**	*you are* (form.); *he/she is*
PLURAL FORMS	nosotros/as	**somos**	*we are*
	vosotros/as	**sois**	*you are* (fam.)
	Uds./ellos/ellas	**son**	*you are* (form.); *they are*

Uses of *ser*

▶ To identify people and things

—¿Quién **es** él?
Who is he?

—**Es** Javier Gómez Lozano.
He's Javier Gómez Lozano.

—¿Qué **es**?
What is it?

—**Es** un mapa de España.
It's a map of Spain.

▶ To express possession, with the preposition **de**

—¿**De** quién **es**?
Whose is it?

—**Es** el diario **de** Maite.
It's Maite's diary.

—**Es** la computadora **de** Álex.
It's Alex's computer.

—¿**De** quiénes **son**?
Whose are they?

—**Son** los lápices **de** la chica.
They are the girl's pencils.

—**Son** las maletas **del** chico.
They are the boy's suitcases.

¡ATENCIÓN!

When **de** is followed by the article **el**, the two combine to form the contraction **del**. **De** does *not* contract with **la, las,** or **los.**

•••

There is no Spanish equivalent of the English construction [*noun*] +'s (*Maite's*). In its place, Spanish uses [*noun*] + **de** + [*owner*]: **el diario de Maite**.

TEACHING OPTIONS

Extra Practice As a rapid response drill, call out subject pronouns and have students respond with the correct form of **ser**. Ex: **tú** (**eres**), **Uds.** (**son**), and so forth. Reverse the drill by starting with forms of **ser**. Students must give the subject pronouns. Accept multiple answers for **es** and **son**.

TPR Take a small beanbag or rubber ball and toss it to individual students for them to catch. When a student catches the ball, call on another student to indicate whose ball it is. Ex: **Es de ____.** Take two beanbags or balls and toss them to different students to elicit the response **Son de ____ y ____.**

¡LENGUA VIVA!

Some geographic locations can be referred to either with or without a definite article:

Soy de Ecuador./Soy del Ecuador.

• • •

Sometimes a definite article is a part of a proper name, as in **El Salvador, El Paso, and Los Ángeles.** In these cases, **de** and **el** do not contract:

Soy de El Salvador.

▶ To express origin, using the preposition **de**

—¿**De** dónde **es** Javier?
Where is Javier from?

—Es **de** Puerto Rico.
He's from Puerto Rico.

—¿**De** dónde **es** Inés?
Where is Inés from?

—**Es del** Ecuador.
She's from Ecuador.

¡ATENCIÓN!

Unlike English, Spanish does not use the indefinite article (**un, una**) after **ser** when referring to professions, unless accompanied by an adjective or other description:

Marta es profesora.

Marta es una profesora excelente.

You will learn more about adjectives in **Estructura 3.1**, pp. 78–80.

▶ To express profession or occupation

Don Francisco **es conductor**.
Don Francisco is a driver.

Yo **soy estudiante**.
I am a student.

¡INTÉNTALO! Provide the correct present forms of **ser** in the column. The first item has been done for you.

1. Gabriel ___es___
2. Juan y yo (*m.*) ___somos___
3. Óscar y Flora ___son___
4. Adriana ___es___
5. las turistas ___son___
6. el chico ___es___
7. los conductores ___son___
8. el señor y la señora Ruiz ___son___

Suggestions

- Explain **ser** + **de** to express origin. Start practicing this construction by indicating where you are from. Ex: **Soy de** ____. You may also want to further practice and contrast **de** + **el**. Ex: **Soy del estado de** ____**/de la región (de)** ____. Introduce **¿de dónde?** and ask students where they are from. Ex: ____, **¿de dónde eres?** After student answers, ask another student: **¿De dónde es** ____**? (Es de** ____**.)**
- Explain the use of **ser** to describe professions or occupations. Say: **Yo soy profesor(a) de español. ¿Qué eres tú?** Response: **Soy estudiante.** Say: **Sí, eres estudiante.** If students want to name occupations or professions, give them the necessary vocabulary. (See **Vocabulario adicional** for **Lección 16** in the IRM.) Ex: ____ **es recepcionista.**
- Point out that the indefinite articles **un** and **una** are not used in these constructions with **ser** and professions: **Él es arquitecto. Somos artistas.**

Note: At this point you may want to present **Vocabulario adicional: Más vocabulario para los países**, from the IRM.

TEACHING OPTIONS

Extra Practice Write cognates on the board and ask students to identify the professions of famous people. Ex: **actor/actriz, presidente, artista, pianista**. Ask: **¿Qué es Brad Pitt? (Es actor.) ¿Quién es presidente?** (____ **es presidente.**)

Pairs Have pairs of students interview each other. Write on the board the questions they should ask. Include: **¿Quién eres?, ¿De dónde eres?** After students interview each other, call on students to report the information they gathered from their partner. Students begin by saying: **Él/Ella es...**

1 Suggestion Review **tú** and **Ud.**, asking students which pronoun they would use in a formal situation and which they would use in an informal situation.

1 Expansion Once students have identified the correct subject pronouns, ask them to give the form of **ser** they would use when *addressing* each person and when *talking about* each person.

2 Expansion Give names of additional well-known Spanish speakers and ask students to tell where they are from. Have students give the country names in English if they don't know the Spanish equivalent. Ex: **¿De dónde es Andy García? (Es de Cuba.)**

3 Suggestion Inform students that they can answer the second part of the question (**¿De quién es?**) with any answer they wish. Have students take turns asking and answering questions.

Práctica

1 **Pronombres** What subject pronouns would you use to a) talk to these people directly and b) talk about them?

1. una chica tú, ella
2. el presidente de México Ud./ él
3. tres chicas y un chico Uds., ellos
4. un estudiante tú, él
5. la señora Ochoa Ud., ella
6. dos profesoras Uds., ellas

2 **Identidad y origen** With a partner, take turns asking and answering questions about these people: **¿Quién es?/¿Quiénes son?** and **¿De dónde es?/¿De dónde son?**

modelo

Ricky Martin (Puerto Rico)
Estudiante 1: *¿Quién es?* **Estudiante 1:** *¿De dónde es?*
Estudiante 2: *Es Ricky Martin.* **Estudiante 2:** *Es de Puerto Rico.*

1. Enrique Iglesias (España)
   E1: ¿Quién es? E2: Es Enrique Iglesias. E1: ¿De dónde es? E2: Es de España.
2. Sammy Sosa (República Dominicana)
   E2: ¿Quién es? E1: Es Sammy Sosa. E2: ¿De dónde es? E1: Es de la República Dominicana.
3. Rebecca Lobo y Martin Sheen (Estados Unidos) E1: ¿Quiénes son? E2: Son Rebecca Lobo y Martin Sheen. E1: ¿De dónde son? E2: Son de los Estados Unidos.
4. Carlos Santana y Salma Hayek (México) E2: ¿Quiénes son? E1: Son Carlos Santana y Salma Hayek. E2: ¿De dónde son? E1: Son de México.
5. Shakira (Colombia)
   E1: ¿Quién es? E2: Es Shakira. E1: ¿De dónde es? E2: Es de Colombia.
6. Antonio Banderas y Penélope Cruz (España) E2: ¿Quiénes son? E1: Son Antonio Banderas y Penélope Cruz. E2: ¿De dónde son? E1: Son de España.
7. Edward James Olmos y Jimmy Smits (Estados Unidos) E1: ¿Quiénes son? E2: Son Edward James Olmos y Jimmy Smits. E1: ¿De dónde son? E2: Son de los Estados Unidos.
8. Gloria Estefan (Cuba) E2: ¿Quién es? E1: Es Gloria Estefan. E1: ¿De dónde es? E1: Es de Cuba.

3 **¿Qué es?** Ask your partner what each object is and to whom it belongs.

modelo

Estudiante 1: *¿Qué es?* **Estudiante 1:** *¿De quién es?*
Estudiante 2: *Es una grabadora.* **Estudiante 2:** *Es del profesor.*

1. E1: ¿Qué es? E2: Es una maleta. E1: ¿De quién es? E2: Es de la Sra. Valdés.

2. E1: ¿Qué es? E2: Es un cuaderno. E1: ¿De quién es? E2: Es de Gregorio.

3. E1: ¿Qué es? E2: Es una computadora. E1: ¿De quién es? E2: Es de Rafael.

4. E1: ¿Qué es? E2: Es un diario. E1: ¿De quién es? E2: Es de Marisa.

TEACHING OPTIONS

Video Replay the video segment, having students focus on subject pronouns and the verb **ser**. Ask them to copy down as many examples of sentences that use forms of **ser** as they can. Stop the video where appropriate to ask comprehension questions on what the characters said.

Heritage Speakers Encourage heritage speakers to describe themselves and their family briefly. Make sure they use the cognates **familia**, **mamá**, and **papá**. Call on students to report the information given. Ex: **Francisco es de la Florida. La mamá de Francisco es de España. Ella es profesora. El papá de Francisco es de Cuba. Él es dentista.**

Comunicación

4 **Preguntas** Using the items in the word bank, ask your partner questions about the ad. Be imaginative in your responses. Answers will vary.

¿Quién?	¿De dónde?	¿Cuántos?
¿Qué?	¿De quién?	¿Cuántas?

SOMOS ECUATURISTA, S.A.

El autobús nacional del Ecuador

- 25 autobuses en total
- 30 conductores del Ecuador
- pasajeros internacionales
- mapas de las regiones del país

¡Todos a bordo!

5 **¿Quién es?** In small groups, take turns pretending to be a person from Spain, Mexico, Puerto Rico, Cuba, or the United States who is famous in these professions. Your partners will try to guess who you are. Answers will vary.

actor *actor*	deportista *athlete*	escritor(a) *writer*
actriz *actress*	cantante *singer*	músico/a *musician*

modelo

Estudiante 3: ¿Eres de Puerto Rico?
Estudiante 1: Sí. Soy de Puerto Rico.
Estudiante 2: ¿Eres hombre?
Estudiante 1: No. Soy mujer.
Estudiante 3: ¿Eres escritora?
Estudiante 1: No. Soy actriz.
Estudiante 2: ¿Eres Rita Moreno?
Estudiante 1: ¡Sí! ¡Sí!

NOTA CULTURAL

Rita Moreno, a Puerto Rican actress, is the only female performer to have won all four prestigious entertainment awards: the Oscar, the Emmy, the Grammy, and the Tony. She played Anita in *West Side Story*, a role for which she won an Oscar.

4 Suggestion If students ask, explain that the abbreviation **S.A.** in the ad stands for **sociedad anónima** and is equivalent to English *Inc.* (*Incorporated*).

4 Expansion Ask volunteers to make true-false statements about the ad. Classmates have to indicate whether the statements are true or false and correct false statements.

5 Suggestion You may want to have students brainstorm a list of names in the categories suggested and have three students read the **modelo** aloud.

TEACHING OPTIONS

Small Groups Bring in personal photos or magazine pictures that show people. In small groups, have students invent stories about the people: who they are, where they're from, what they do. Circulate around the room and assist with unfamiliar vocabulary as necessary, but encourage students to use terms they already know.

Game Hand out individual strips of paper with names of famous people on them. There should be several duplicates of each name. Then give descriptions of one of the famous people (**Es de ____,** **Es** [profession]), including cognate adjectives if you wish (**inteligente, pesimista**). The first person to stand and indicate that the name they have is the one you're describing (**¡Yo lo tengo!**) wins that round.

Section Goals

In **Estructura 1.4** students will be introduced to:
- asking and telling time
- times of day

Instructional Resources
Transparency #11
WB/VM: Workbook, pp. 7–8
Lab Manual, p. 6
Lab CD/MP3 ***Lección 1***
IRM: ***¡Inténtalo! & Práctica*** *Answers, pp. 197–198; Tapescript, pp. 1–5*
Info Gap Activities Booklet, pp. 3–4
Interactive CD-ROM
Companion website: www.vistahigherlearning.com
Presentations CD-ROM

Suggestions

- To prepare students for telling time, review **es** and **son** and their meanings and the numbers to 30.
- Introduce **es la una** and **son las dos (tres, cuatro...)**. Remind students that **las** in time constructions refers to **las horas**. Introduce **y cinco (diez, veinte...)**, **y quince/cuarto**, and **y treinta/media**.
- Project **Transparency #11**, use a paper plate clock, or any other clock where you can quickly move the hands to different positions and display a number of different times for students to identify. Ask: **¿Qué hora es?** Concentrate on this until students are relatively comfortable with expressing the time in Spanish.
- Introduce **menos diez (cuarto, veinte...)** and explain this method of telling time in Spanish. It typically takes students longer to master this aspect of telling time. Spend about five minutes with your moveable-hands clock and ask students to indicate the times given.

1.4 Telling time

ANTE TODO In both English and Spanish, the verb *to be* (**ser**) and numbers are used to tell time.

▶ To ask what time it is, use **¿Qué hora es?** When telling time, use **es + la** with **una** and **son + las** with all other hours.

Es la una.

Son las dos.

Son las seis.

▶ As in English, you express time from the hour to the half-hour in Spanish by adding minutes.

Son las cuatro **y cinco.**

Son las once **y veinte.**

▶ You may use either **y cuarto** or **y quince** to express fifteen minutes or quarter past the hour. For thirty minutes or half past the hour, you may use either **y media** or **y treinta**.

Es la una **y cuarto.**

Son las doce **y media.**

Son las nueve **y quince.**

Son las siete **y treinta.**

▶ You express time from the half-hour to the hour in Spanish by subtracting minutes or a portion of an hour from the next hour.

Es la una **menos cuarto.**

Son las tres **menos quince.**

Son las ocho **menos veinte.**

Son las tres **menos diez.**

TEACHING OPTIONS

Extra Practice Draw a large clock face on the board with its numbers but without its hands. Say a time and ask a volunteer to come up to the board and draw the hands to indicate that time. The rest of the class verifies whether their classmate has written the correct time or not. Continue until several volunteers have participated.

Pairs Have pairs take turns telling each other what time their classes are this semester/quarter. (Ex: **Tengo una clase a las...**) For each time given, the other student draws a clock face with the corresponding time. The first student verifies whether this is the correct time or not.

¡LENGUA VIVA!

Other useful expressions for telling time:

Son las doce (del día).
It is twelve o'clock (p.m.).

Son las doce (de la noche).
It is twelve o'clock (a.m.).

▶ To ask at what time a particular event takes place, use the phrase **¿A qué hora (...)?** To state at what time something takes place, use the construction **a la(s)** + *time*.

¿A qué hora es la clase de biología? *(At) what time is biology class?*	La clase es **a las dos**. *The class is at two o'clock.*
¿A qué hora es la fiesta? *(At) what time is the party?*	**A las ocho** *At eight*

▶ Here are some useful words and phrases associated with telling time:

Son las ocho **en punto**. *It's 8 o'clock on the dot/sharp.*	Son las nueve **de la mañana**. *It's 9 a.m. (in the morning).*
Es **el mediodía**. *It's noon.*	Son las cuatro y cuarto **de la tarde**. *It's 4:15 p.m. (in the afternoon).*
Es **la medianoche**. *It's midnight.*	Son las diez y media **de la noche**. *It's 10:30 p.m. (at night).*

Oye, ¿qué hora es?
Son las diez y tres minutos.

Oiga, ¿qué hora es?
Son las diez.

¡INTÉNTALO! Practice telling time by completing these sentences. The first item has been done for you.

1. (1:00 a.m.) Es la ___una___ de la mañana.
2. (2:50 a.m.) Son las tres ___menos___ diez de la mañana.
3. (4:15 p.m.) Son las cuatro y ___cuarto/quince___ de la tarde.
4. (8:30 p.m.) Son las ocho y ___media/treinta___ de la noche.
5. (9:15 a.m.) Son las nueve y quince de la ___mañana___.
6. (12:00 p.m.) Es el ___mediodía/Son las doce___.
7. (6:00 a.m.) Son las seis de la ___mañana___.
8. (4:05 p.m.) Son las cuatro y cinco de la ___tarde___.
9. (12:00 a.m.) Es la ___medianoche/Son las doce___.
10. (3:45 a.m.) Son las cuatro menos ___cuarto/quince___ de la mañana.

Suggestions

- Review **¿Qué hora es?** and introduce **¿A qué hora?** and make sure students know the difference between them. Ask a few questions to clarify. Ex: **¿Qué hora es? ¿A qué hora es la clase de español?**
- Go over **en punto, mediodía, medianoche**. Explain that **medio/a** means half in Spanish.
- Go over **de la mañana/tarde/noche**. Ask students what time it is now.
- You may wish to explain that Hispanics tend to view times of day differently than English speakers do. In many countries, only after someone has eaten lunch does one say **Buenas tardes**. Similarly with the evening, Hispanics tend to view 6:00 and even 7:00 as **de la tarde**, not **de la noche**.

¡Lengua viva! Introduce the Spanish equivalents for noon (**las doce del día**) and midnight (**las doce de la noche**).

TEACHING OPTIONS

Extra Practice Hand out slips of paper with clock faces depicting certain times on them to half of the class. Hand out the corresponding times written out in Spanish to the other half of the class. Students must find their partner. To increase difficulty, include duplicates of each time with **de la mañana** or **de la tarde/noche** on the written-out times and a sun or a moon on the clock faces so that students find only one partner.

Heritage Speakers Ask heritage speakers if they generally tell time as presented in the text or if they use different constructions. Some ways Hispanics use time constructions include (1) forgoing **menos** and using a number from 31–59 and (2) asking the question **¿Qué horas son?** Stress, however, that the constructions presented in the text are the ones students should focus on.

1 Expansion Have students draw clock faces showing the times presented in the activity. Then they exchange their drawings with a partner to verify accuracy.

2 Suggestion Model the pronunciation of the two ways of saying 4:15 in the model sentence. Point out that some of the clocks and watches also indicate the part of day (morning, afternoon, or evening) as well as the hour. Have students include this information in their responses.

2 Expansion At random, give times shown in activity. Students must give the number of the clock or watch described. Ex: **Es la una de la mañana. (Es el número 2.)**

3 Expansions
- Have partners switch roles and ask and answer the questions again. Alternatively, have each student who asked questions the first time pair up with a student from another pair who answered questions. The new pair then switches roles.
- Have students come up with three original items to ask their partner, based on the items in the activity. The partner should respond with actual times. Ex: **—¿A qué hora es el programa *ER*? —Es a las diez.**

Práctica

1 Ordenar Put these times in order, from the earliest to the latest.

a. Son las dos de la tarde. 4
b. Son las once de la mañana. 2
c. Son las siete y media de la noche. 6
d. Son las seis menos cuarto de la tarde. 5
e. Son las dos menos diez de la tarde. 3
f. Son las ocho y veintidós de la mañana. 1

2 ¿Qué hora es? Give the times shown on each clock or watch.

modelo

Son las cuatro y cuarto/quince de la tarde.

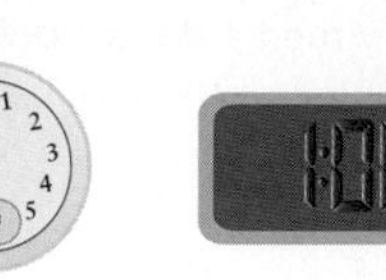

1. Son las doce y media.

2. Es la una de la mañana.

3. Son las cinco y cuarto.

4. Son las ocho y diez.

5. Son las cinco y media/treinta.

6. Son las once menos cuarto/quince.

7. Son las dos y doce de la tarde.

8. Son las siete y cinco.

9. Son las cuatro menos cinco.

10. Son las doce menos veinticinco de la noche.

NOTA CULTURAL

Many Spanish-speaking countries use both the 12-hour clock and the 24-hour clock (that is, military time). The 24-hour clock is commonly used in written form on signs and schedules. For example, 1p.m. is 13h, 2 p.m. is 14h and so on. See the photo on p. 30 for a sample schedule.

3 ¿A qué hora? Ask your partner at what time these events take place. Your partner will answer according to the cues provided.

modelo

la clase de matemáticas (2:30 p.m.)
Estudiante 1: *¿A qué hora es la clase de matemáticas?*
Estudiante 2: *Es a las dos y media de la tarde.*

1. el programa *Las cuatro amigas* (*11:30 a.m.*)
2. el drama *La casa de Bernarda Alba* (*7:00 p.m.*)
3. el programa *Las computadoras* (*8:30 a.m.*)
4. la clase de español (*10:30 a.m.*)
5. la clase de biología (*9:40 a.m. sharp*)
6. la clase de historia (*10:50 a.m.*)
7. el partido (*game*) de béisbol (*5:15 p.m.*)
8. el partido de tenis (*12:45 p.m. sharp*)
9. el partido de baloncesto (*basketball*) (*7:45 p.m.*)
10. la fiesta (*8:30 p.m.*)

1. E1: ¿A qué hora es el programa *Las cuatro amigas*? E2: Es a las once y media/treinta de la mañana.
2. E1: ¿A qué hora es el drama *La casa de Bernada Alba*? E2: Es a las siete de la noche.
3. E1: ¿A qué hora es el programa *Las computadoras*? E2: Es a las ocho y media/treinta de la mañana.
4. E1: ¿A qué hora es la clase de español? E2: Es a las diez y media/treinta de la mañana.
5. E1: ¿A qué hora es la clase de biología? E2: Es a las diez menos veinte de la mañana en punto.
6. E1: ¿A qué hora es la clase de historia? E2: Es a las once menos diez de la mañana.
7. E1: ¿A qué hora es el partido de béisbol? E2: Es a las cinco y cuarto de la tarde.
8. E1: ¿A qué hora es el partido de tenis? E2: Es a la una menos cuarto de la tarde en punto.
9. E1: ¿A qué hora es el partido de baloncesto? E2: Es a las ocho menos cuarto de la noche.
10. E1: ¿A qué hora es la fiesta? E2: Es a las ocho y media/treinta de la noche.

NOTA CULTURAL

La casa de Bernarda Alba is a famous play by Spanish poet and playwright **Federico García Lorca** (1898-1936). Lorca was one of the most famous writers of the 20th century and a close friend of Spain's most talented artists, including the painter Salvador Dalí and the filmmaker Luis Buñuel.

TEACHING OPTIONS

Pairs Have students work with a partner to create an original conversation similar to the one in **Actividad 3**. They should do at least the following in their conversation: (1) greet each other appropriately, (2) ask for the time, (3) ask what time a particular class is, (4) say good-bye. Have pairs present their conversations in front of the rest of the class.

Extra Practice Give certain times of the day and ask students whether those times are typical times to be awake for **un médico**, **un estudiante**, or **los dos** (*both*). Ex: **Son las cinco menos cuarto de la mañana. (un médico) Es la medianoche. (un estudiante)**

Comunicación

4 **En la televisión** With a partner, take turns asking and answering questions about these television listings. Answers will vary.

modelo

Estudiante 1: *¿A qué hora es el documental Las computadoras?*
Estudiante 2: *Es a las nueve en punto de la noche.*

NOTA CULTURAL

Telenovelas are the Latin American version of soap operas, but they differ from North American soaps in many ways. Many **telenovelas** are prime-time shows enjoyed by a large segment of the population. They seldom run for more than one season and they are sometimes based on famous novels.

TV Hoy – Programación

11:00 am	Telenovela: *Cuatro viajeros y un autobús*
12:00 pm	Película: *El cóndor* (drama)
2:00 pm	Telenovela: *Dos mujeres y dos hombres*
3:00 pm	Programa juvenil: *Fiesta*
3:30 pm	Telenovela: *¡Sí, sí, sí!*
4:00 pm	Telenovela: *El diario de la Sra. González*
5:00 pm	Telenovela: *Tres mujeres*
6:00 pm	Noticias
7:00 pm	Especial musical: *Música folklórica de México*
7:30 pm	La naturaleza: *Jardín secreto*
8:00 pm	Noticiero: *Veinticuatro horas*
9:00 pm	Documental: *Las computadoras*

5 **Preguntas** With a partner, answer these questions based on your own knowledge. Some answers will vary.

1. Son las tres de la tarde en Nueva York. ¿Qué hora es en Los Ángeles? Es el mediodía./ Son las doce.
2. Son las ocho y media en Chicago. ¿Qué hora es en Miami? Son las nueve y media.
3. Son las dos menos cinco en San Francisco. ¿Qué hora es en San Antonio? Son las cuatro menos cinco.
4. ¿A qué hora es el programa *60 Minutes*?; ¿A qué hora es el programa *Today Show*? 7:00 p.m. hora del este; 7:00 a.m. hora del este

6 **Más preguntas** Using the questions in the previous activity as a model, make up four questions of your own. Then, get together with a classmate and take turns asking and answering each other's questions. Answers will vary.

Síntesis

7 **Situación** With a partner, play the roles of a journalism student interviewing a visiting literature professor (**profesor(a) de literatura**) from Venezuela. Be prepared to act out the conversation for your classmates. Answers will vary.

Estudiante	Profesor(a) de literatura
Ask professor his/her name	→ Ask student his/her name
Ask professor what time his/her literature class is	→ Ask student where he/she is from
Ask how many students are in his/her class	→ Ask to whom his/her tape recorder belongs
Say thank you and goodbye.	→ Say thank you and you are pleased to meet him/her.

4 Suggestion Before beginning the activity, have students look over the schedule and point out cognates and predict their meanings. Help them with the meanings of other programming categories: **película, programa juvenil, noticias/noticiero**.

4 Expansion Ask students questions about what time some popular TV programs are shown. Ex: **—¿A qué hora es el programa "Will y Grace"? —Es a las ocho.**

5 Suggestion Remind students that there are four time zones in the continental United States, and that when it is noon in the Eastern Time zone, it is three hours earlier in the Pacific Time zone.

6 Expansion Have pairs choose the two most challenging questions to share with the class.

7 Suggestion Point out that this activity synthesizes everything students have learned in this chapter: greetings and leave-takings, nouns and articles, numbers 0–30 and **hay**, the verb **ser**, and telling time. Spend a few moments reviewing these topics.

Suggestion See the Info Gap Activities Booklet for an additional activity to practice the material presented in this section.

TEACHING OPTIONS

Small Groups Have small groups of students prepare skits. Groups can choose any situation they wish, provided that they use material presented in the **Contextos** and **Estructura** sections. Possible situations include: meeting to go on an excursion (as in **Fotonovela**), meeting in between classes, introducing friends to professors, and so forth.

Heritage Speakers Have heritage speakers interview classmates. They should use vocabulary and structures presented in **Lección 1**. Then they report their findings to the class.

Heritage Speakers Ask heritage speakers what **novelas** are currently featured on Spanish-language television and the channel (**canal**) and time when they are shown.

Lectura

Section Goals

In **Lectura** students will:

- learn to recognize cognates
- use suffixes to recognize cognates
- read a telephone list rich in cognates

Instructional Resource
Companion website:
www.vistahigherlearning.com

Estrategia Tell students that cognates are words in one language that have identical or similar counterparts in another language. True cognates are close in meaning, so recognizing Spanish words that are cognates of English words can help them read Spanish. Have students look at the cognates in this **Estrategia** box. Write some of the common suffix correspondences between Spanish and English on the board: **–ción/–sión** = *–tion/–sion* (**nación, decisión**); **–ante/–ente** = *–ant/–ent* (**importante, inteligente, elegante**); **–ia/–ía** = *–y* (**farmacia, sociología, historia**); **–dad** = *–ty* (**oportunidad, universidad**).

The Affective Dimension Tell students that reading in Spanish will be less anxiety-provoking if they follow the advice in the **Estrategia** sections, which are designed to reinforce and improve reading comprehension skills.

Examinar el texto Ask students to tell you what type of text **Teléfonos importantes** is and how they can tell. (It's a list and it contains names and telephone numbers.)

Cognados Ask students to mention any cognates they see in the phone list. Discuss the cognates and explain any discrepancies with the list of corresponding suffixes given above. Ex: **policía** = police, *not* policy

Antes de leer

Estrategia

Recognizing cognates

As you learned earlier in this lesson, cognates are words that share similar meanings and spellings in two or more languages. When reading in Spanish, it's helpful to look for cognates and use them to guess the meaning of what you're reading. But watch out for false cognates. For example, **librería** means *bookstore*, not *library*, and **embarazada** means *pregnant*, not *embarrassed*. Look at this list of Spanish words, paying special attention to prefixes and suffixes. Can you guess the meaning of each word?

importante	oportunidad
farmacia	cultura
inteligente	activo
dentista	sociología
decisión	espectacular
televisión	restaurante
médico	policía

Examinar el texto

Glance quickly at the reading selection and guess what type of document it is. Explain your answer.

Cognados

Read the document and make a list of the cognates you find. Guess their English equivalents, then compare your answers with those of a classmate.

recursos

Teléfonos importantes

Policía

Médico

Dentista

Pediatra

Farmacia

Banco Central

Aerolíneas Nacionales

Cine Metro

Hora/Temperatura

Profesora Salgado (universidad)

Felipe (oficina)

Gimnasio Gente Activa

Restaurante Roma

Supermercado Famoso

Librería El Inteligente

TEACHING OPTIONS

Heritage Speakers Ask heritage speakers to model reading and writing the numbers in **Teléfonos importantes**, and to discuss how digits are grouped and punctuated (periods instead of hyphens). For example, 732.5722 may be pronounced by a combination of tens, **siete, treinta y dos, cincuenta y siete, veintidós**, or hundreds and tens, **setecientos treinta y dos, cincuenta y siete, veintidós**.

Extra Practice Write some of these Spanish words on the board and have students name the English cognate: **democracia, actor, eficiente, nacionalidad, diferencia, guitarrista, artista, doctora, dificultad, exploración**. Then write on the board some of these words with less obvious cognates: **ciudad, ciencia, población, número, signo, remedio**.

54.11.11
54.36.92
54.87.11
53.14.57
54.03.06
54.90.83
54.87.40
53.45.96
53.24.81
54.15.33
54.84.99
54.36.04
53.75.44
54.77.23
54.66.04

Después de leer

¿Cierto o falso?

Indicate whether each statement is **cierto** or **falso.** Then correct the false statements.

1. There is a child in this household.
   Cierto
2. To renew a prescription you would dial 54.90.83.
   Falso. To renew a prescription you would dial 54.03.06.
3. If you wanted the exact time and information about the weather you'd dial 53.24.81.
   Cierto
4. Felipe probably works outdoors.
   Falso. Felipe works in an office.
5. This household probably orders a lot of Chinese food.
   Falso. They probably order a lot of Italian food.
6. If you had a toothache, you would dial 54.87.11.
   Cierto
7. You would dial 54.87.40 to make a flight reservation.
   Cierto
8. To find out if a best-selling book was in stock, you would dial 54.66.04.
   Cierto
9. If you needed information about aerobics classes, you would dial 54.15.33.
   Falso. If you needed information about aerobics class you would call Gimnasio Gente Activa at 54.36.04.
10. You would call **Cine Metro** to find out what time a movie starts.
    Cierto

Hacer una lista

Make your own list of phone numbers like the one shown in this reading. Include emergency phone numbers as well as frequently called numbers. Use as many cognates from the reading as you can.

¿Cierto o falso?

- Go over Items 1–10 orally with the whole class. If students have trouble inferring the answer to any question, help them identify the cognate or provide additional corresponding context clues.
- Ask students to work with a partner to use cognates and context clues to determine whether each statement is **cierto** or **falso**. Go over the answers with the whole class.

Hacer una lista

- With the whole class, brainstorm possible categories of phone numbers students may wish to include in their lists. Begin an idea map on the board or overhead projector, jotting down the students' responses in Spanish, explaining unfamiliar vocabulary as necessary.
- You may wish to have students include e-mail addesses (**direcciones electrónicas**) in their lists.

TEACHING OPTIONS

Variación léxica How a Spanish speaker answers the telephone may reveal where that person is from. A telephone call in Mexico is likely answered **¿Bueno?**. In other parts of the Spanish-speaking world you may hear the greetings **Diga, Dígame, Óigame**, and even **Aló**.

Small Groups In groups of three, have students read aloud entries from their lists. The listeners should copy down the items they hear. Have group members switch roles so each has a chance to read. Have groups compare and contrast their lists.

Heritage Speakers Ask heritage speakers to share phone etiquette they may know, such as answering the phone or the equivalents of "Is ____ there?" (**¿Está ____?**), "Speaking" (**Soy yo.** or **Al habla.**), and identifying oneself, "This is ____." (**Habla ____.** or **Soy ____.**)

Section Goals

In **Escritura** students will:

- learn to write a telephone/ address list in Spanish
- integrate lesson vocabulary, including cognates, and structures

Tema

- Introduce students to standard headings (**Nombre, Teléfono, Dirección electrónica**) used in a telephone/address list. Students may wish to add notes pertaining to home (**número de casa**) or office (**número de oficina**) telephone numbers, fax numbers (**número de fax**), or office hours (**horas de oficina**).
- Tell students that to find electronic resources for students of Spanish, they may enter the key words *Spanish Language* into an Internet search engine.
- Some students may find it helpful to brainstorm what headings or additional notes they wish to include for each type of entry, creating a type of template that they can reuse.

The Affective Dimension

Tell the class that they will feel less anxious about writing in a foreign language if they follow the step-by-step advice in the **Estrategia, Tema,** and **Plan de escritura** sections.

Escritura

Estrategia

Writing in Spanish

Why do we write? All writing has a purpose. For example, we may write a poem to reveal our innermost feelings, a letter to impart information, or an essay to persuade others to accept a point of view. Proficient writers are not born, however. Writing requires time, thought, effort, and a lot of practice. Here are some tips to help you write more effectively in Spanish.

DO

- Try to write your ideas in Spanish
- Use the grammar and vocabulary that you know
- Use your textbook for examples of style, format, and expression in Spanish
- Use your imagination and creativity
- Put yourself in your reader's place to determine if your writing is interesting

AVOID

- Translating your ideas from English to Spanish
- Simply repeating what is in the textbook or on a web page
- Using a dictionary until you have learned how to use foreign language dictionaries

Tema

Hacer una lista

Create a telephone/address list that includes important names, numbers, and websites that will be helpful to you in your study of Spanish. Make whatever entries you can in Spanish without using a dictionary. You might want to include this information:

- The names, phone numbers, and e-mail addresses of at least four classmates
- Your professor's name, e-mail address, and office hours
- Three phone numbers and e-mail addresses of campus offices or locations related to your study of Spanish
- Five electronic resources for students of Spanish, such as chat rooms, international keypal sites, and sites dedicated to the study of Spanish as a second language

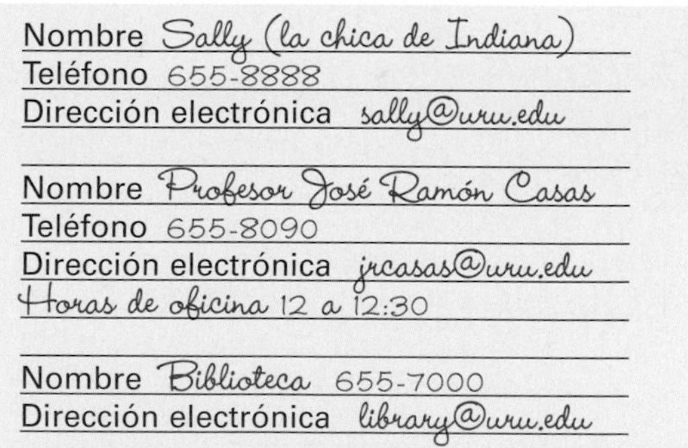

Nombre Sally (la chica de Indiana)
Teléfono 655-8888
Dirección electrónica sally@uru.edu

Nombre Profesor José Ramón Casas
Teléfono 655-8090
Dirección electrónica jrcasas@uru.edu
Horas de oficina 12 a 12:30

Nombre Biblioteca 655-7000
Dirección electrónica library@uru.edu

TEACHING OPTIONS

Proofreading Activity Copy onto the board or a transparency the following items containing mistakes as a proofreading activity.

1. **Telefonos importants**
2. **Direccion electrónico**
3. **Hora de oficina: 12 a 2**
4. **Nombre: David (amiga de Jaime)**
5. **Teléfon (del oficina) 407-2925**

Spanish Characters on the Word Processor

	Macintosh	PC (Windows)
á Á, etc.	*alt* + *e* then *a* or *A*, etc.	*ctrl* + ' then *a* or *A*, etc.
ñ Ñ	*alt* + *n* then *n* or *N*	*ctrl* + *shift* + ~ then *n* or *N*
ü Ü	*alt* + *u* then *u* or *U*	*ctrl* + *shift* + : then *u* or *U*
¿	*alt* + *shift* + ?	*ctrl* + *alt* + *shift* + ?
¡	*alt* + !	*ctrl* + *alt* + *shift* + !

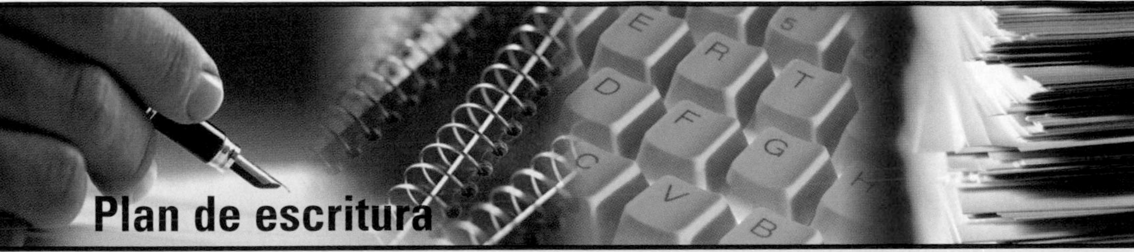

Plan de escritura

1 **Ideas y organización**
Begin by making a list of all your campus resources, including your professor, campus facilities, and your classmates. Then spend some time exploring web resources and jotting down the addresses of several sites. Choose various types of web pages; they shouldn't all be keypal sites or chat rooms.

2 **Primer borrador**
Using the lists you prepared in **Ideas y organización**, write a first draft of the new section for your telephone/address book.

3 **Comentario**
Exchange first drafts with a classmate and comment on each other's work using the questions below as a guide. Begin by mentioning what you like best about his or her telephone/address book, such as the organization of the entries, or a resource you didn't know about.

a. Is all the required information included and logically organized?
b. Are the websites included pertinent to Spanish students?
c. Do the entries appear in Spanish whenever possible?
d. Do you have any suggestions for additional or different entries in Spanish?
e. Are there any spelling or grammatical errors?

4 **Redacción**
Revise your first draft, keeping in mind your classmate's comments. Also incorporate any new ideas or information you may have. Before handing in the final version, use these suggestions to help you review your work:

a. Be sure you have included as much Spanish as possible.
b. Check for errors in spelling and punctuation.

5 **Evaluación y progreso**
Share your final draft with three classmates. Note the addresses of campus resources or websites mentioned on your classmates' lists; you might want to add them to your list. After your instructor has returned your paper, keep your list on hand with your other study aids.

Comentario
- Go over questions a–e with the whole class so peer readers understand their task. Then have pairs of students exchange lists. Allow five minutes for reading and comments. Allow five minutes for discussing comments.
- Have students read **Redacción** as homework. Ask them to rewrite their drafts incorporating the peer comments and following the directions in **Redacción**. Tell them to prepare a clean copy of their final draft to hand in.

Evaluación y progreso
Give the class five minutes to exchange and read the final drafts of their lists. Then have students hand them in.

Writing Sample Here is an example of a well-organized and annotated telephone/address list.

Números de urgencia
Policía 677-1000
Bomberos 677-1100
Hospital 677-2000

La universidad
Teléfono 677-3000
Página de Internet:
www.uru.edu

Profesores
Nombre Profesora Julia Gil (literatura)
Teléfono 677-3434
Dirección electrónica
jgil@uru.edu
Horas de oficina
10:30 a 12:00

Nombre Profesor Juan José Alarcón (español comercial)
Teléfono 677-3437
Dirección electrónica
jjalarcon@uru.edu
Horas de oficina
12:00 a 2:00

Biblioteca
Teléfono 677-3400

Café Alegre
Teléfono 677-3450

EVALUATION: Lista

Criteria	Scale
Content	1 2 3 4 5
Organization	1 2 3 4 5
Accuracy	1 2 3 4 5
Creativity	1 2 3 4 5

Scoring	
Excellent	18–20 points
Good	14–17 points
Satisfactory	10–13 points
Unsatisfactory	< 10 points

Section Goals

In **Escuchar** students will:

- listen to sentences containing familiar and unfamiliar vocabulary
- learn the strategy of listening for known vocabulary
- answer questions based on the content of a recorded conversation

Instructional Resources
Textbook CD
IRM: Tapescript, p. 85

Estrategia
Script Creo que hay… este… treinta pasajeros en el autobús que va a Guayaquil.

The Affective Dimension
Tell your students that many people feel nervous about their ability to comprehend what they hear in a foreign language. Tell them that they will probably feel less anxious if they follow the advice for increasing listening comprehension in the **Estrategia** sections.

Suggestion Have students look at the photo and describe what they see. Guide them to guess where they think Dr. Cavazos and Srta. Martínez are and what they are talking about.

Ahora escucha
Script DR. CAVAZOS: Buenos días, señorita.
SRTA. MARTÍNEZ: Buenos días, señor. ¿En qué le puedo servir?
C: Yo soy el doctor Alejandro Cavazos. Voy a Quito. Aquí tiene mi boleto. Deseo facturar mis maletas.
M: ¿Alejandro Cavazos? ¿C-A-V-A-Z-O-S?
C: Sí, señorita.
M: ¿Un viaje de ida y vuelta a Quito?
C: Sí.
M: ¿Cuántas maletas tiene usted? ¿Tres?
C: Dos.
M: Bueno, aquí tiene usted su boleto.
C: Muchas gracias, señorita.
M: No hay de qué, doctor Cavazos. ¡Buen viaje!
C: Gracias. ¡Adiós!

Escuchar

Estrategia

Listening for words you know

You can get the gist of a conversation by listening for words and phrases you already know.

 To help you practice this strategy, listen to the following sentence and make a list of the words you have already learned.

Preparación

Based on the photograph, what do you think Dr. Cavazos and Srta. Martínez are talking about? How would you get the gist of their conversation, based on what you know about Spanish?

Ahora escucha 

Now you are going to hear Dr. Cavazos's conversation with Srta. Martínez. List the familiar words and phrases each person says.

Dr. Cavazos	Srta. Martínez
1. ______	9. ______
2. ______	10. ______
3. ______	11. ______
4. ______	12. ______
5. ______	13. ______
6. ______	14. ______
7. ______	15. ______
8. ______	16. ______

With a classmate, use your lists of familiar words as a guide to come up with a summary of what happened in the conversation.

recursos

TEXT CD
Lección 1

Comprensión

Identificar

Who would say the following things, Dr. Cavazos or Srta. Martínez?

1. Me llamo… Dr. Cavazos
2. De nada. Srta. Martínez
3. Gracias. Muchas gracias. Dr. Cavazos
4. Aquí tiene usted los documentos de viaje, señor. Srta. Martínez
5. Usted tiene tres maletas, ¿no? Srta. Martínez
6. Tengo dos maletas. Dr. Cavazos
7. Hola, señor. Srta. Martínez
8. ¿Viaja usted a Buenos Aires? Srta. Martínez

Contestar

1. Does this scene take place in the morning, afternoon, or evening? How do you know? The scene takes place in the morning, as indicated by **Buenos días.**
2. How many suitcases does Dr. Cavazos have? two
3. Using the words you already know to determine the context, what might the following words and expressions mean?
   - boleto
   - un viaje de ida y vuelta
   - pasaporte
   - ¡Buen viaje!

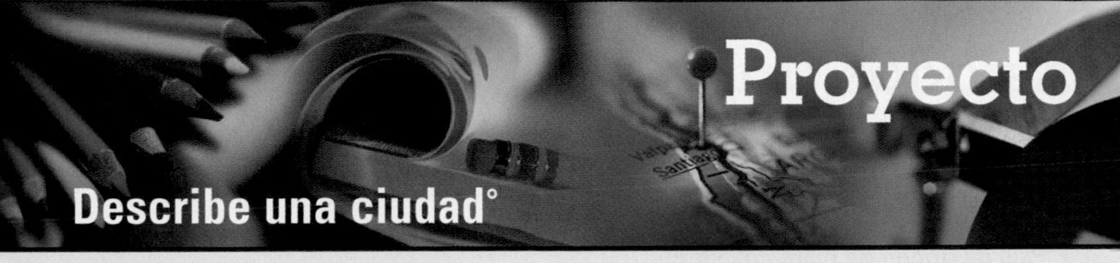

Proyecto

Describe una ciudad°

Imagine that you are a journalist reporting on the influence of Hispanic cultures on cities in the United States and Canada. You have been asked to present a report to a Spanish class, focusing on one American or Canadian city.

1 Prepara una presentación

Prepare a brief presentation about how Hispanic cultures have influenced a city in the United States or Canada. Using the research tools in **Recursos para la investigación,** choose a city and take notes about how it has been affected by Hispanic cultures. Your presentation might include these elements:

- A description of the city, its location, its history, and its population
- Explanations of how the city has been influenced by Hispanic cultures: for example, its cuisine, arts, politics, and architecture
- Descriptions and photos of famous people, places, and things in the city that are related to Hispanic cultures

2 Presenta la información

Using an outline and your photos, tell the class about the city you chose and how it reflects the influence of Hispanic cultures. Make your presentation vivid so that your classmates will want to learn more about Hispanic cultures in the United States and Canada. Use as much Spanish as possible in your presentation, especially to greet the class, to introduce youself, to say where you are from, and to state that you are a journalist (**Soy periodista**).

recursos para la investigación

Internet Palabras clave°: United States, Canada, city, cities, Hispanic influence(s)

Comunidad Faculty members and residents of your community who have lived in the city you chose

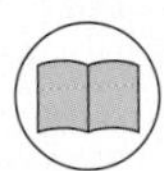

Biblioteca° Almanacs, encyclopedias, history books, maps, newspapers

Otros recursos° Brochures from travel agencies

ciudad *city* Palabras clave *keywords* Biblioteca *library* Otros recursos *other resources*

Section Goals

In **Proyecto** students will:
- learn about how Hispanic cultures have influenced a city in the United States or Canada
- use Spanish as they research and interact with the wider world
- incorporate Spanish in an oral presentation

Suggestion Students might need a week to complete the project, so at the beginning of that time period, have them open their books to this page and glance over **Proyecto**. Explain that they are going to use their research skills to prepare a brief presentation in which they describe how Hispanic cultures have influenced a city in the United States or Canada (**ciudad estadounidense/canadiense**).

Prepara una presentación
- If they choose a city they live in or visit, students may seek information from Hispanic members of the community, the Hispanic Chapter of the Chamber of Commerce, or other Hispanic organizations.
- Students' presentations will be more interesting if they incorporate visual aids such as posters and brochures, or integrate music or audio recordings.

Presenta la información
- To prepare, students may practice before a small group of friends who can critique the presentation or before a mirror.
- You may wish to do a few presentations at a time until all students have had a chance to present.

EVALUATION: Descripción

Criteria	Scale
Content	1 2 3 4
Comprehensibility	1 2 3 4
Organization	1 2 3 4
Accuracy	1 2 3 4
Creativity	1 2 3 4

Scoring	
Excellent	18–20 points
Good	14–17 points
Satisfactory	10–13 points
Unsatisfactory	< 10 points

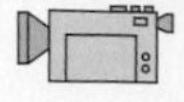

Section Goal

In **Panorama** students will read statistics and cultural information about Hispanics in the United States and Canada.

Instructional Resources
Transparency #12
WB/VM: Workbook, pp. 9–10; Video Activities, pp. 249–250
***Panorama cultural** DVD/Video*
Interactive CD-ROM
IRM: Videoscript, p. 127
Companion website: www.vistahigherlearning.com
Presentations CD-ROM

Suggestion Have students look at the map of the United States and Canada or project **Transparency #12**. Have volunteers read aloud the labeled cities and geographic features. Model Spanish pronunciation of names as necessary. Have students jot down as many names of places and geographic features with Hispanic origins as they can. Ask volunteers to share their lists with the class. Write the names they mention on the board and model their pronunciation. Ex: **Alamosa está en Colorado.**

El país en cifras Have volunteers read the bulleted headings in **El país en cifras**. Point out cognates and clarify unfamiliar words. Explain that numerals in Spanish have a comma where English would use a decimal point (**3,5%**) and have a period where English would use a comma (**12.268.000**). Explain that **EE.UU.** is the abbreviation of **Estados Unidos**, the doubling of the initial letters indicating plural. Model the pronunciation of **Florida** (accent on the second syllable) and point out that it is often used with an article (**la Florida**) by Spanish speakers.

¡Increíble pero cierto! Don't expect students to produce numbers greater than 30 at this point. Explain phrases such as **se estima** and **grupo minoritario**.

Note: Population figures represent metropolitan areas.

Estados Unidos

National Standards: connections, cultures

El país en cifras°

- **Población° de EE.UU.:** 288 millones
- **Población de origen hispano:** 39 millones
- **País de origen de hispanos en EE.UU.:**

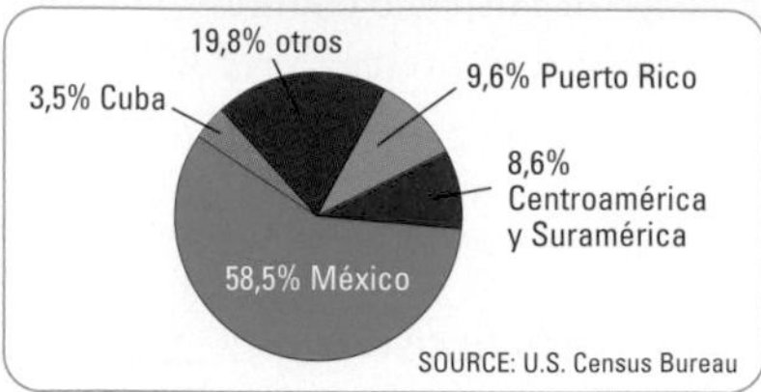

- **Estados con la mayor población hispana:**

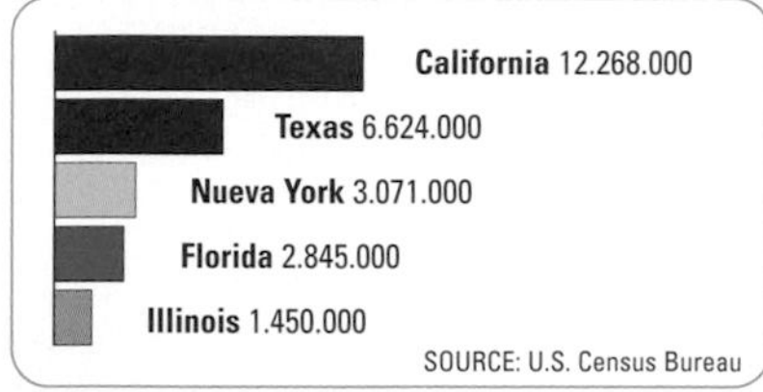

Canadá

El país en cifras

- **Población del Canadá:** 32 millones
- **Población de origen hispano:** 300.000
- **País de origen de hispanos en Canadá:**

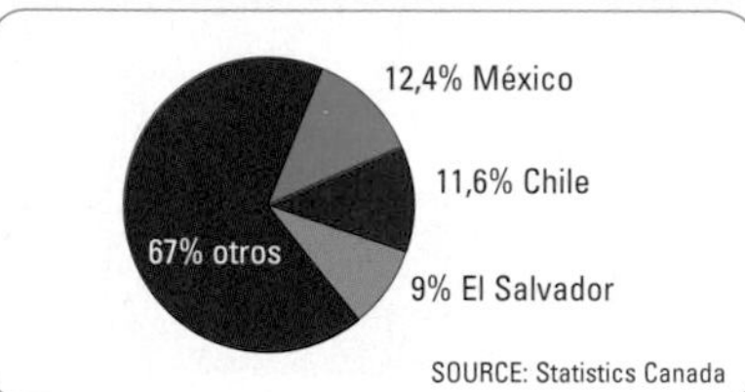

- **Ciudades con la mayor población hispana:** Montreal, Toronto, Vancouver

en cifras *in figures* población *population* mayor *largest* creció *grew* cada *each* niños *children* Se estima *It is estimated* va a ser *is going to be*

Mission District, en San Francisco

AK
HI
CANADÁ
Vancouver
Calgary
Ottawa
Montr
Toronto
San Francisco
Chicago
Nueva York
Las Vegas
EE. UU.
Los Ángeles
San Diego
Washington DC
San Antonio
Océano Atlántico
Miami
Golfo de México
MÉXICO
Mar Caribe

El Álamo, en San Antonio, Texas

recursos

WB pp. 9–10	VM pp. 249–250	I CD-ROM Lección 1	vistahigher learning.com

¡Increíble pero cierto!

La población hispana en los Estados Unidos creció° un 58% entre los años 1990 y 2000 (casi 13 millones de personas más). Hoy, uno de cada° seis niños° en los Estados Unidos es de origen hispano. Se estima° que en el año 2020 va a ser° uno de cada cuatro.

SOURCE: U.S. Census Bureau and The Associated Press

TEACHING OPTIONS

Heritage Speakers Ask heritage speakers to describe for the class the Hispanic celebrations that are held in the region where they come from. Ask them to tell the date when the celebration takes place, the event it commemorates, and some of the particulars of the celebration. Possible celebrations: **Cinco de Mayo, Día de la Raza, Día de los Muertos, Fiesta de San Juan, Carnaval**

Game Divide the class into groups of five students. Give groups five minutes to brainstorm place names (cities, states, lakes, rivers, montain ranges, and so forth) in the United States that have Spanish origins. One member of the group should take down the names in a numbered list. After five minutes, go over the names with the whole class, confirming the accuracy of each name. The team with the greatest number wins.

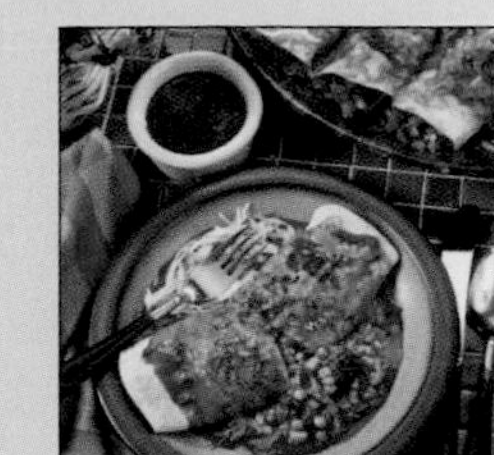

Comida° • La comida mexicana

La comida° mexicana es muy popular en los Estados Unidos. Los tacos, las enchiladas, las quesadillas y los frijoles son platos° mexicanos que frecuentemente forman parte de las comidas de muchos norteamericanos. También° son populares las variaciones de la comida mexicana en los Estados Unidos... el tex-mex y el cali-mex.

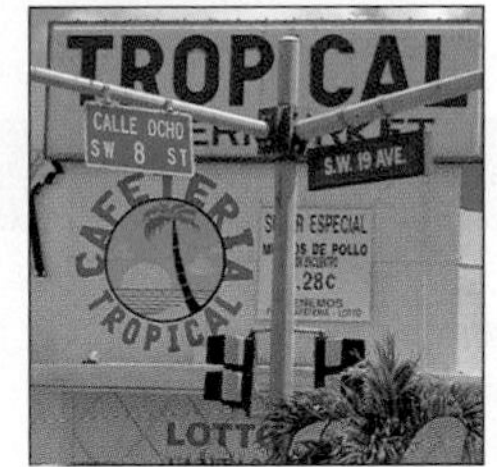

Lugares • La Pequeña Habana

La Pequeña Habana° es un barrio° de Miami, Florida, donde viven° muchos cubanoamericanos. Es un lugar° donde se encuentran° las costumbres° de la cultura cubana, los aromas y sabores° de su comida y la música salsa. La Pequeña Habana es una parte de Cuba en los Estados Unidos.

Costumbres • Desfile puertorriqueño

Cada junio desde° 1951 (mil novecientos cincuenta y uno), los puertorriqueños celebran su cultura con un desfile° en Nueva York. Es un gran espectáculo con carrozas° y música salsa, flamenco y hip-hop. Muchos espectadores llevan° la bandera° de Puerto Rico en su ropa° o pintada en la cara°.

Sociedad° • La influencia hispánica en Canadá

La presencia hispana en Canadá es importante en la cultura del país. En 1998 (mil novecientos noventa y ocho) se establecieron° los *Latin American Achievement Awards Canada*, para reconocer° los logros° de la comunidad en varios campos°. Dos figuras importantes de origen argentino son Alberto Manguel (novelista) y Sergio Marchi (Embajador° de Canadá en las Naciones Unidas°). Osvaldo Núñez es un político° de origen chileno. Hay grupos musicales que son parte de la cultura hispana en Canadá: Dominicanada, Bomba, Norteño y Rasca.

¿Qué aprendiste? Completa las frases con la información adecuada (*appropriate*).

1. Hay <u>39 millones</u> de personas de origen hispano en los Estados Unidos.
2. Los cuatro estados con las poblaciones hispanas más grandes son (en orden) <u>California</u>, Texas, <u>Nueva York</u> y Florida.
3. Toronto, Montreal y <u>Vancouver</u> son las tres ciudades con mayor población hispana del Canadá.
4. Las quesadillas y las enchiladas son platos <u>mexicanos</u>.
5. La Pequeña <u>Habana</u> es un barrio de Miami.
6. En Miami hay muchas personas de origen <u>cubano</u>.
7. Cada junio se celebra en Nueva York un gran desfile para personas de origen <u>puertorriqueño</u>.
8. Dominicanada es un <u>grupo musical</u> del Canadá.

Conexión Internet Investiga estos temas en el sitio **www.vistahigherlearning.com.**

1. Haz (*Make*) una lista de seis hispanos célebres de EE.UU. o Canadá. Explica (*Explain*) por qué (*why*) son célebres.
2. Escoge (*Choose*) seis lugares en los Estados Unidos con nombres hispanos y busca información sobre el origen y el significado (meaning) de cada nombre.

Comida *Food* platos *dishes* También *Also* La Pequeña Habana *Little Havana* barrio *neighborhood* viven *live* lugar *place* se encuentran *are found* costumbres *customs* sabores *flavors* Cada junio desde *Each June since* desfile *parade* con carrozas *with floats* llevan *wear* bandera *flag* ropa *clothing* cara *face* Sociedad *Society* se establecieron *were established* reconocer *to recognize* logros *achievements* campos *fields* Embajador *Ambassador* Naciones Unidas *United Nations* político *politician*

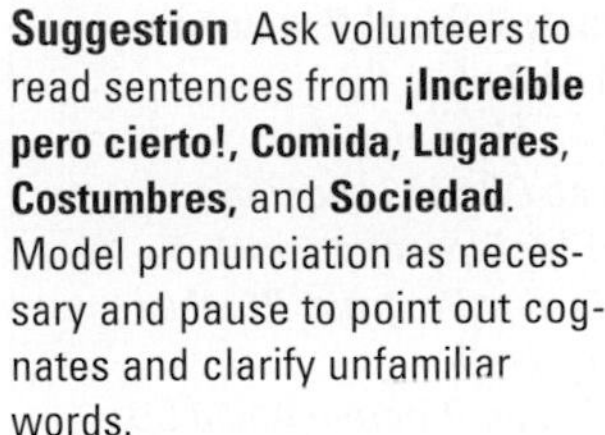

Suggestion Ask volunteers to read sentences from **¡Increíble pero cierto!, Comida, Lugares, Costumbres,** and **Sociedad**. Model pronunciation as necessary and pause to point out cognates and clarify unfamiliar words.

La comida mexicana Have students look at illustrated cookbooks or recipes to identify the ingredients and variations of the dishes mentioned in the paragraph.

La Pequeña Habana Many large cities in the United States have neighborhoods where people of Hispanic origin predominate. Encourage students to speak of neighborhoods they know.

Desfile puertorriqueño The Puerto Rican Parade takes place on the weekend nearest the feast day of St. John the Baptist (**San Juan Bautista**), the patron saint of San Juan, capital of Puerto Rico.

La influencia hispánica en Canadá Ask students to research the names and achievements of recipients of the Latin American Achievement Awards Canada. Have them share the information with the class.

Conexión Internet Students will find supporting Internet activities and links at **www.vistahigherlearning.com**.

TEACHING OPTIONS

Variación léxica Hispanic groups in the United States refer to themselves with various names. The most common of these terms, **hispano** and **latino**, refer to all people who come from Hispanic backgrounds, whatever the country of origin of their ancestors. **Puertorriqueño, cubanoamericano**, and **mexicoamericano** refer to Hispanics whose ancestors came from Puerto Rico, Cuba, and Mexico, respectively. Many Mexican Americans also refer to themselves as **chicanos**. This word has stronger socio-political connotations than **mexicoamericano**. Use of the word **chicano** implies identification with Mexican Americans' struggle for civil rights and equal opportunity in the United States. It also suggests an appreciation of the indigenous aspects which are an important part of Mexican and Mexican-American culture.

Instructional Resources
Vocabulary CD
Lab Manual, p. 6
Lab CD/MP3 ***Lección 1***
IRM: Tapescript, pp. 1–5
Testing Program: ***Pruebas****, pp. 1–12*
Testing Program Audio CD
Test Files CD-ROM

Suggestion Tell students that this is active vocabulary for which they are responsible and that it will appear on tests and exams.

Saludos

Hola.	*Hello; Hi.*
Buenos días.	*Good morning.*
Buenas tardes.	*Good afternoon.*
Buenas noches.	*Good evening; Good night.*

Despedidas

Adiós.	*Good-bye.*
Nos vemos.	*See you.*
Hasta luego.	*See you later.*
Hasta la vista.	*See you later.*
Hasta pronto.	*See you soon.*
Hasta mañana.	*See you tomorrow.*
Saludos a...	*Greetings to …*
Chau.	*Bye.*

¿Cómo está?

¿Cómo está usted?	*How are you?* (form.)
¿Cómo estás?	*How are you?* (fam.)
¿Qué hay de nuevo?	*What's new?*
¿Qué pasa?	*What's happening?; What's going on?*
¿Qué tal?	*How are you?; How is it going?*
(Muy) bien, gracias.	*(Very) well, thanks.*
Nada.	*Nothing.*
No muy bien.	*Not very well.*
Regular.	*So so; OK.*

Expresiones de cortesía

Con permiso.	*Pardon me; Excuse me.*
De nada.	*You're welcome.*
Lo siento.	*I'm sorry.*
(Muchas) gracias.	*Thank you (very much); Thanks (a lot).*
No hay de qué.	*You're welcome.*
Perdón.	*Pardon me; Excuse me.*
por favor	*please*

Títulos

señor (Sr.); don	*Mr.; sir*
señora (Sra.)	*Mrs.; ma'am*
señorita (Srta.)	*Miss*

Presentaciones

¿Cómo se llama usted?	*What's your name?* (form.)
¿Cómo te llamas (tú)?	*What's your name?* (fam.)
Me llamo...	*My name is …*
¿Y tú?	*And you?* (fam.)
¿Y usted?	*And you?* (form.)
Mucho gusto.	*Pleased to meet you.*
El gusto es mío.	*The pleasure is mine.*
Encantado/a.	*Delighted; Pleased to meet you.*
Igualmente.	*Likewise.*
Éste/Ésta es...	*This is …*
Le presento a...	*I would like to introduce* (name) *to you…* (form.)
Te presento a...	*I would like to introduce* (name) *to you…* (fam.)
nombre	*name*

¿De dónde es?

¿De dónde es usted?	*Where are you from?* (form.)
¿De dónde eres?	*Where are you from?* (fam.)
Soy de...	*I'm from …*

Palabras adicionales

¿cuánto(s)/a(s)?	*how much/many?*
¿de quién...?	*whose …?* (sing.)
¿de quiénes...?	*whose …?* (plural)
(no) hay	*there is (not); there are (not)*

Países

Ecuador	*Ecuador*
España	*Spain*
Estados Unidos (EE.UU.; E.U.)	*United States*
México	*Mexico*
Puerto Rico	*Puerto Rico*

Verbos

ser	*to be*

Sustantivos

el autobús	*bus*
la capital	*capital city*
el chico	*boy*
la chica	*girl*
la computadora	*computer*
la comunidad	*community*
el/la conductor(a)	*driver*
la conversación	*conversation*
la cosa	*thing*
el cuaderno	*notebook*
el día	*day*
el diario	*diary*
el diccionario	*dictionary*
la escuela	*school*
el/la estudiante	*student*
la foto(grafía)	*photograph*
la grabadora	*tape recorder*
el hombre	*man*
el/la joven	*youth; young person*
el lápiz	*pencil*
la lección	*lesson*
la maleta	*suitcase*
la mano	*hand*
la mujer	*woman*
la nacionalidad	*nationality*
el número	*number*
el país	*country*
la palabra	*word*
el/la pasajero/a	*passenger*
el problema	*problem*
el/la profesor(a)	*teacher*
el programa	*program*
el/la turista	*tourist*
el video	*video*

Numbers 0–30	*See page 14.*
Telling time	*See pages 22-23.*
Expresiones útiles	*See page 7.*

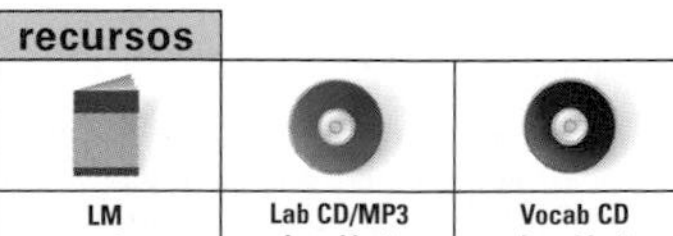

En la universidad 2

Communicative Goals

You will learn how to:

- **Talk about your classes and school life**
- **Discuss everyday activities**
- **Ask questions in Spanish**
- **Describe the location of people and things**

contextos

pages 36–39
- The classroom and academic life
- Days of the week
- Fields of study and academic subjects
- Class schedules

fotonovela

pages 40–43

Maite, Inés, Álex and Javier begin to get to know each other on the bus as they talk about their classes. Maite pretends to be a radio host and interviews the other students about their current classes. Álex and Javier discuss their favorite subjects.

estructura

pages 44–59
- Present tense of **-ar** verbs
- Forming questions in Spanish
- Present tense of **estar**
- Numbers 31-100

adelante

pages 60–65

Lectura: Read a brochure for a summer course in Madrid.
Escritura: Write a description of yourself.
Escuchar: Listen to a conversation between two students about their courses.
Proyecto: Make a poster advertising a year abroad in Spain.

panorama

pages 66–67

Featured country: España
- The University of Salamanca
- Linguistic regions of Spain
- The legendary **Museo del Prado**
- Spain's most popular dish

A PRIMERA VISTA

- **¿Hay dos chicas en la foto?**
- **¿Hay un libro o dos?**
- **¿Son turistas o estudiantes?**
- **¿Qué hora es, la una de la mañana o de la tarde?**

Lesson Goals

In **Lección 2** students will be introduced to the following:
- classroom- and university-related words
- names of academic courses and fields of study
- class schedules
- days of the week
- present tense of regular **–ar** verbs
- forming negative sentences
- forming questions
- the present tense of **estar**
- prepositions of location
- numbers 31–100
- using text formats to predict content
- brainstorming and organizing ideas for writing
- writing descriptions of themselves
- listening for cognates
- creating a poster for a "Year Abroad" program in Spain
- cultural and historical information about Spain

A primera vista Have students look at the photo. Say: **Es una foto de dos jóvenes en la universidad.** Then ask: **¿Qué son los jóvenes? (Son estudiantes.) ¿Qué hay en la mano del chico? (Hay un diccionario/libro.)**

INSTRUCTIONAL RESOURCES

Workbook/Video Manual: WB Activities, pp. 11–22
Laboratory Manual: Lab Activities, pp. 7–12
Workbook/Video Manual: Video Activities, pp. 215–216; pp. 251–252
Instructor's Resource Manual: **Hojas de actividades**, p. 163; **Vocabulario adicional**, p. 179; **¡Inténtalo!** & **Práctica** Answers, pp. 199–200; **Fotonovela** Translations, pp. 139–140; Textbook CD Tapescript, p. 86; Lab CDs Tapescript, pp. 6–10; **Fotonovela** Videoscript, p. 104; **Panorama cultural** Videoscript, p. 128
Info Gap Activities Booklet, pp. 5–8
Overhead Transparencies: #7, #8, #13, #14, #15
Lab Audio CD/MP3 **Lección 2**
Panorama cultural DVD/Video
Fotonovela DVD/Video
Testing Program, pp. 13–24
Testing Program Audio CD
Test Files CD-ROM
Companion website
Presentations CD-ROM
Textbook CD
Vocabulary CD
Interactive CD-ROM
Video CD-ROM
Web-SAM

Section Goals

In **Contextos**, students will learn and practice:

- names for people, places, and things at the university
- names of academic courses

Instructional Resources
Transparency #13
Textbook CD
Vocabulary CD
WB/VM: Workbook, pp. 11–12
Lab Manual, p. 7
Lab CD/MP3 ***Lección 2***
IRM: ***Vocab. adicional****, p. 179;*
Práctica *Answers, pp. 199–200;*
Tapescript, pp. 6–10; p. 86
Interactive CD-ROM
Companion website:
www.vistahigherlearning.com
Presentations CD-ROM

Suggestions

- Introduce vocabulary for classroom objects such as **mesa, libro, pluma, lápiz, papel**. Hold up or point to an object and say: **Es un lápiz.** Ask questions that include **¿Hay/No hay... ?** and **¿Cuántos/as... ?**
- Using either objects in the classroom or **Transparency #13**, point to items and ask questions such as: **¿Qué es? ¿Es una mesa? ¿Es un reloj?** Vary by asking: **¿Qué hay en el escritorio? ¿Qué hay en la mesa? ¿Cuántas tizas hay en la pizarra? ¿Hay una pluma en el escritorio de ____?**

Note: At this point you may want to present **Vocabulario adicional: Más vocabulario para las clases**, from the IRM.

En la universidad

Más vocabulario

la biblioteca	*library*
la cafetería	*cafeteria*
la casa	*house; home*
el estadio	*stadium*
el laboratorio	*laboratory*
la librería	*bookstore*
la residencia estudiantil	*dormitory*
la universidad	*university; college*
el/la compañero/a de clase	*classmate*
el/la compañero/a de cuarto	*roommate*
la clase	*class*
el examen	*test; exam*
el horario	*schedule*
la prueba	*test; quiz*
el semestre	*semester*
la tarea	*homework*
el trimestre	*trimester; quarter*
la administración de empresas	*business administration*
el arte	*art*
la especialización	*major*
la biología	*biology*
las ciencias	*sciences*
la computación	*computer science*
la contabilidad	*accounting*
el curso	*course*
la economía	*economics*
el español	*Spanish*
la física	*physics*
la geografía	*geography*
la música	*music*

Variación léxica

pluma ⟷ bolígrafo
pizarra ⟷ tablero (*Col.*)

recursos

TEXT CD Lección 2	WB pp. 11–12	LM p. 7	Lab CD/MP3 Lección 2	I CD-ROM Lección 2	Vocab CD Lección 2

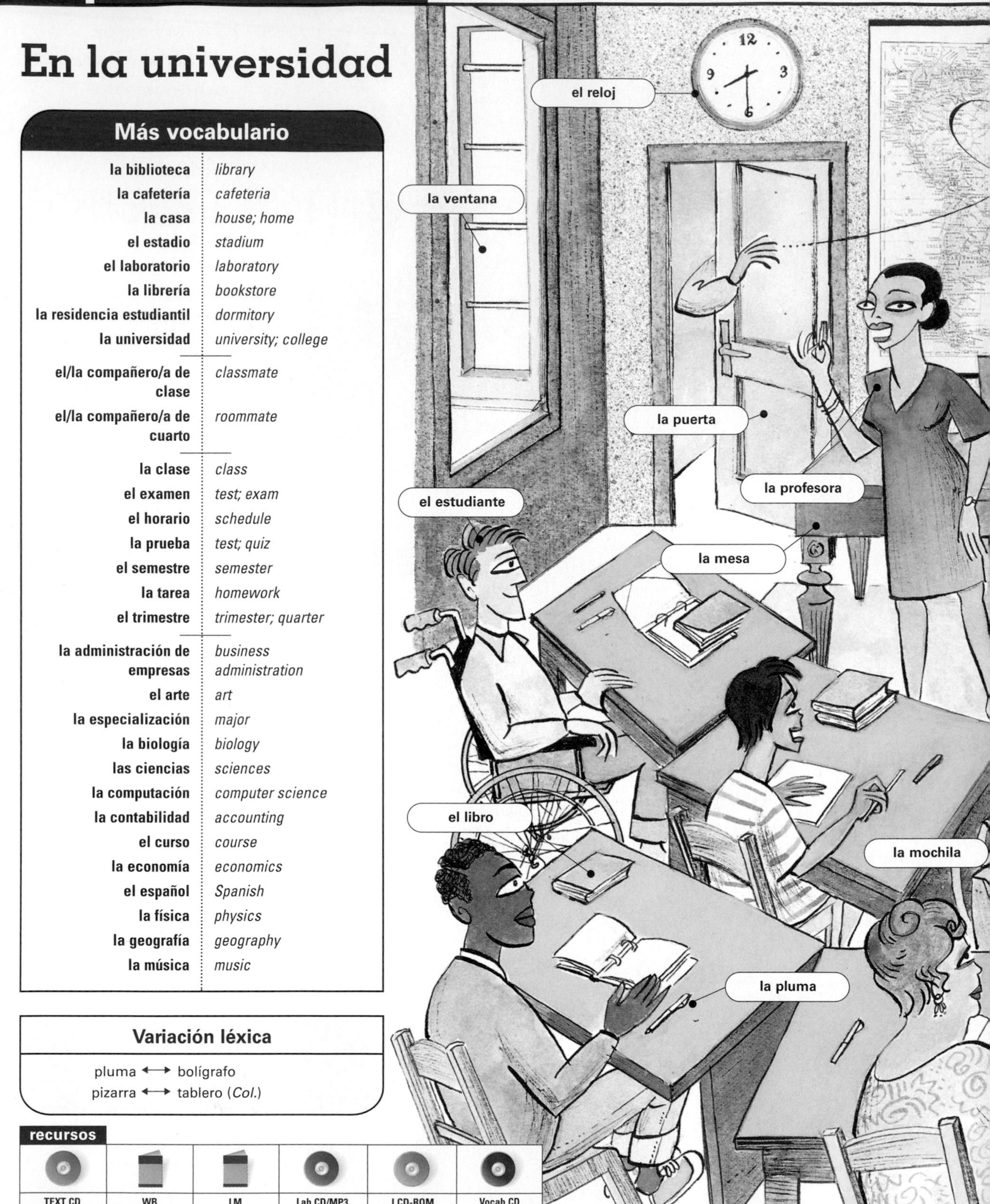

TEACHING OPTIONS

Variación léxica Ask heritage speakers to tell the class any other terms they use to talk about people, places, or things at the university. Ask them to tell where these terms are used. Possible responses: **el boli, la ciudad universitaria, el profe, el catedrático, la facultad, el profesorado, la asignatura, el gimnasio, el pizarrón, el salón de clases, el aula, el pupitre, el gis, el alumno**

Game Divide the class into teams. Then, in English, read aloud the name of an academic course and ask one of the teams to provide the Spanish equivalent. If the team provides the correct term, it gets a point. If not, the second team gets a chance at the same item. Alternate asking questions of the two teams until you have read all the course names. The team that has the most points at the end of the game wins.

Práctica

1 **Escuchar** Listen to Professor Morales talk about her Spanish classroom, then check the items she mentions.

puerta	✓	sillas	○
ventanas	✓	libros	✓
pizarra	✓	plumas	✓
borrador	○	mochilas	○
tiza	✓	papel	✓
escritorios	✓	reloj	✓

2 **Emparejar** Match each question with its most logical response. ¡Ojo! (*Careful!*) Two of the responses will not be used.

1. ¿Qué clase es? d
2. ¿Quiénes son? h
3. ¿Quién es? e
4. ¿De dónde es? c
5. ¿A qué hora es la clase de inglés? g
6. ¿Cuántos estudiantes hay? a

a. Hay veinticinco.
b. Es un reloj.
c. Es del Perú.
d. Es la clase de química.
e. Es el señor Bastos.
f. Mucho gusto.
g. Es a las nueve en punto.
h. Son los profesores.

3 **Identificar** Identify the word that does not fit in each group.

1. examen • grabadora • tarea • prueba grabadora
2. economía • matemáticas • biblioteca • contabilidad biblioteca
3. pizarra • tiza • borrador • librería librería
4. lápiz • cafetería • papel • cuaderno cafetería
5. veinte • diez • pluma • treinta pluma
6. conductor • laboratorio • autobús • pasajero laboratorio
7. humanidades • mesa • ciencias • lenguas extranjeras mesa
8. papelera • casa • residencia estudiantil • biblioteca papelera

4 **¿Qué clase es?** Use the clues to name the subject matter of each class.

modelo
los elementos, los átomos
Es la clase de química.

1. Abraham Lincoln, Winston Churchill Es la clase de historia.
2. Picasso, Leonardo da Vinci Es la clase de arte.
3. Freud, Jung Es la clase de psicología.
4. África, el océano Pacífico Es la clase de geografía.
5. la cultura de España, verbos Es la clase de español.
6. Hemingway, Shakespeare Es la clase de literatura.
7. geometría, trigonometría Es la clase de matemáticas.
8. las plantas, los animales Es la clase de biología.

1 Suggestion Have students check their answers by going over **Actividad 1** with the whole class.

1 Tapescript ¿Qué hay en mi clase de español? ¡Muchas cosas! Hay una puerta y cinco ventanas. Hay una pizarra con tiza. Hay muchos escritorios para los estudiantes. En los escritorios de los estudiantes hay libros y plumas. En la mesa de la profesora hay papel. Hay un mapa y un reloj en la clase también.
Textbook CD

2 Expansion Items b and f were not used. Ask the class to come up with questions or statements that would elicit these two items as responses.

3 Expansion Read the following as items 9 and 10: **9. pluma, lápiz, silla, tiza (silla); 10. ventana, estudiante, profesor, compañera de cuarto (ventana).**

4 Expansion Have the class brainstorm a list of famous people that they would associate with the following fields: **periodismo** (Ex: Dan Rather, Barbara Walters), **computación** (Ex: Bill Gates, Michael Dell), **humanidades** (Ex: Maya Angelou, Sandra Cisneros). Then have the class guess the field associated with each of the following people: Albert Einstein (**física**), Charles Darwin (**biología**), Alan Greenspan (**economía**).

TEACHING OPTIONS

Extra Practice Ask students what phrases or vocabulary words they associate with items such as the following: **1. la pizarra** (Ex: **la tiza, el borrador**), **2. la residencia estudiantil** (Ex: **el compañero de cuarto, la compañera de cuarto, el/la estudiante**), **3. el reloj** (Ex: **¿Qué hora es?, Son las..., Es la...**), **4. la biblioteca** (Ex: **los libros, los exámenes, las materias**).

Extra Practice On the board, write **¿Qué clases tomas?** and **Tomo...** . Explain the meaning of these phrases and ask your students to circulate around the classroom and imagine that they are meeting their classmates for the first time. Tell them to introduce themselves, find out where each person is from, and what classes he or she is taking. Follow up by asking individual students about what their classmates are taking.

Suggestions

- Write the following questions and answers on the board, explaining their meaning as you do so:
  —**¿Qué día es hoy?**
  —**Hoy es ____.**
  —**¿Qué día es mañana?** (Students learned **mañana** in **Lección 1.**)
  —**Mañana es ____.**
  —**¿Cuándo es la prueba?**
  —**Es el ____.**
  Then ask students the questions on the board.
- Tell students that Monday is traditionally the first day of the week in the Spanish-speaking world and usually appears as such on calendars.

5 Expansion Ask the class questions such as: **Mañana es viernes… ¿qué día fue ayer? (miércoles); Ayer fue domingo… ¿qué día es mañana? (martes)**

6 Suggestion Have the class review the list of **sustantivos** on page 34 and the numbers 0–30 on page 14 before doing this activity.

Los días de la semana

¿Qué día es hoy (today)?
Hoy es martes.
¿Cuándo (when) es el examen?
Es el viernes.

septiembre

lunes	martes	miércoles	jueves	viernes	sábado	domingo
	1	2	3	4	5	6
7	8	9	10			

¡LENGUA VIVA!

The days of the week are never capitalized in Spanish.

•••

Monday is considered the first day of the week in Spanish-speaking countries.

CONSÚLTALO

Note that September in Spanish is **septiembre**. To see all of the months of the year, go to **Contextos, Lección 5**, p. 138.

5 **¿Qué día es hoy?** Complete each statement with the correct day of the week.

1. Hoy es martes. Mañana es miércoles. Ayer fue lunes.
2. Ayer fue sábado. Mañana es lunes. Hoy es domingo.
3. Mañana es viernes. Hoy es jueves. Ayer fue miércoles.
4. Ayer fue domingo. Hoy es lunes. Mañana es martes.
5. Hoy es jueves. Ayer fue miércoles. Mañana es viernes.
6. Mañana es lunes. Hoy es domingo. Ayer fue sábado.

AYUDA

Ayer fue… *Yesterday was…*

6 **Analogías** Use these words to complete the analogies. Some words will not be used.

arte	día	martes	pizarra
biblioteca	domingo	matemáticas	profesor
catorce	estudiante	mujer	reloj

1. maleta ⟷ pasajero ⊜ mochila ⟷ estudiante
2. chico ⟷ chica ⊜ hombre ⟷ mujer
3. pluma ⟷ papel ⊜ tiza ⟷ pizarra
4. inglés ⟷ lengua ⊜ miércoles ⟷ día
5. papel ⟷ cuaderno ⊜ libro ⟷ biblioteca
6. quince ⟷ dieciséis ⊜ lunes ⟷ martes
7. Cervantes ⟷ literatura ⊜ Dalí ⟷ arte
8. autobús ⟷ conductor ⊜ clase ⟷ profesor
9. EE.UU. ⟷ mapa ⊜ hora ⟷ reloj
10. veinte ⟷ veintitrés ⊜ jueves ⟷ domingo

TEACHING OPTIONS

Heritage Speakers Have heritage speakers prepare a day-planner for the upcoming week. Tell them to list each day of the week and the things they expect to do each day, including classes, homework, tests, appointments, and social events. Tell them to include the time each activity takes place. Have them exchange their day-planners with a partner and check each other's work for errors.

Game Have the class play a chain-forming game in which the first student says a word in Spanish (e.g., **estudiante**). The next student has to think of a word that begins with the last letter of the first person's word (e.g., **español**). If a student can't think of a word, he or she is out of the game and it's the next student's turn. The last student left in the game is the winner.

Comunicación

¡ATENCIÓN!

Use **el** + [*day of the week*] when an activity occurs on a specific day and **los** + [*day of the week*] when an activity occurs regularly:

El lunes tengo un examen.
***On Monday** I have an exam.*

Los lunes y miércoles tomo biología.
***On Mondays and Wednesdays** I take biology.*

•••

Except for **sábados** and **domingos,** the singular and plural forms for days of the week are the same.

7 **Horario** Choose three classes to create your own class schedule, then discuss it with a classmate. Answers will vary.

materia	hora	días	profesor(a)
historia	9–10	lunes, miércoles	Ordóñez
biología	12–1	lunes, jueves	Dávila
periodismo	2–3	martes, jueves	Quiñones
matemáticas	2–3	miércoles, jueves	Jiménez
arte	12–1:30	lunes, miércoles	Molina

modelo

Estudiante 1: *Tomo (I take) biología los lunes y jueves con la profesora Dávila.*
Estudiante 2: *¿Sí? Yo no tomo biología. Yo tomo arte los lunes y miércoles con el profesor Molina.*

8 **La clase** First, look around your classroom to get a mental image, then close your eyes. Your partner will then use these words or other vocabulary to ask you questions about the classroom. After you have answered six questions, switch roles. Answers will vary.

modelo

Estudiante 1: *¿Cuántas ventanas hay?*
Estudiante 2: *Hay cuatro ventanas.*

escritorio	mochila	puerta
estudiante	pizarra	reloj
libro	profesor(a)	silla

9 **Nuevos amigos** During the first week of class, you meet a new student in the cafeteria. With a partner, prepare a conversation using these cues. Answers will vary.

Estudiante 1		Estudiante 2
Greet your new acquaintance.	→	Introduce yourself.
Find out about him or her.	→	Tell him or her about yourself.
Ask about your partner's class schedule.	→	Compare your schedule to your partner's.
Say nice to meet you and goodbye.	→	Say nice to meet you and goodbye.

7 Expansion Tell pairs to exchange schedules with another pair. Then have them repeat the activity with the new schedules, asking and answering questions in the third person. Ex: **—¿Qué clases toma ____?** **—Los lunes y jueves ____ toma biología.**

8 Expansion Repeat the exercise with campus-related vocabulary.

Successful Language Learning Remind the class that errors are a natural part of language learning. Point out that it is impossible to speak "perfectly" in any language. Emphasize that their spoken and written Spanish will improve if they make the effort to practice.

9 Suggestion Quickly review the basic greetings, courtesy expressions, and introductions taught in **Lección 1, Contextos,** pages 2–3.

TEACHING OPTIONS

Groups Have students do **Actividad 9** in groups, imagining that they are going to meet several new students in the cafeteria and find out about them. Have the groups prepare and present this activity as a skit in front of the class. Give the groups time to prepare and rehearse their skit, and tell them that they will be presenting it without a script or any other kind of notes.

Game Teach the class the word **con** (*with*). Then have your students write down a few simple sentences that describe their course schedules. Ex: **Los lunes, miércoles y viernes tomo español con la profesora Dávalos. Los martes y jueves tomo arte con el profesor Casas.** Then collect the descriptions and read them to the class. The class should try to guess who wrote each description.

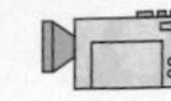

¿Qué clases tomas?

Maite, Inés, Javier y Álex hablan de las clases.

Section Goals

In **Fotonovela** students will:

- receive comprehensible input from free-flowing discourse
- learn functional phrases that preview lesson grammatical structures

Instructional Resources
WB/VM: Video Activities, pp. 215–216
***Fotonovela** DVD/Video (Start 00:06:10)*
Video CD-ROM
*IRM: **Fotonovela** Translations, pp. 139–140, Videoscript, p. 104*
Interactive CD-ROM

Video Recap: Lección 1
Before doing this **Fotonovela** section, review the previous one with this activity.

1. ¿Quiénes son Maite, Inés, Javier y Álex? (estudiantes)
2. ¿Cómo se llama el conductor? (don Francisco)
3. ¿Quiénes son del Ecuador? (don Francisco e Inés)
4. ¿De dónde es Maite? (España) ¿Y Álex? (México) ¿Y Javier? (Puerto Rico)

Video Synopsis While Álex writes an e-mail, Maite pretends to be a radio reporter and asks Inés and Javier a few questions about school. Álex is shocked that Javier doesn't like computers.

Suggestions

- Have students cover the **Expresiones útiles**. Then have them scan the captions under the video stills and find two phrases about classes and two phrases that express likes and dislikes.
- Ask a few basic questions that use the **Expresiones útiles.** Ex: **¿Qué clases tomas? ¿Te gusta la clase de _____?**

PERSONAJES

MAITE

INÉS

ÁLEX

JAVIER

ÁLEX Hola, Ricardo... Aquí estamos en la Mitad del Mundo. ¿Qué tal las clases en la UNAM?

MAITE Es exactamente como las fotos en los libros de geografía.

INÉS ¡Sí! ¿También tomas tú geografía?

MAITE Yo no. Yo tomo inglés y literatura. También tomo una clase de periodismo.

MAITE Muy buenos días. María Teresa Fuentes, de Radio Andina FM 93. Hoy estoy con estudiantes de la Universidad San Francisco de Quito. ¡A ver! La señorita que está cerca de la ventana... ¿Cómo te llamas y de dónde eres?

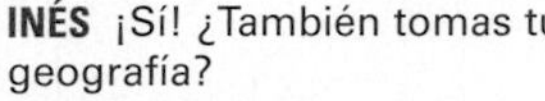

MAITE ¿En qué clase hay más chicos?

INÉS Bueno, eh... en la clase de historia.

MAITE ¿Y más chicas?

INÉS En la de sociología hay más chicas, casi un ochenta y cinco por ciento.

MAITE Y tú, joven, ¿cómo te llamas y de dónde eres?

JAVIER Me llamo Javier Gómez y soy de San Juan, Puerto Rico.

MAITE ¿Tomas muchas clases este semestre?

JAVIER Sí, tomo tres: historia y arte los lunes, miércoles y viernes y computación los martes y jueves.

MAITE ¿Te gustan las computadoras, Javier?

JAVIER No me gustan nada. Me gusta mucho más el arte... y sobre todo me gusta dibujar.

ÁLEX ¿Cómo que no? ¿No te gustan las computadoras?

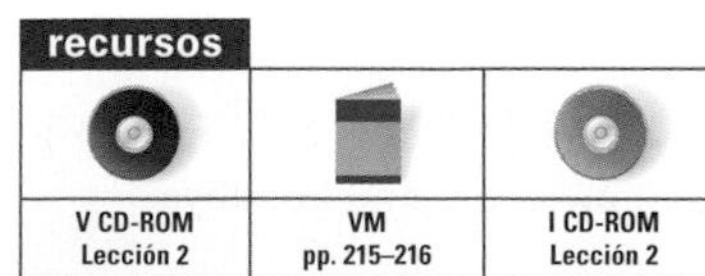

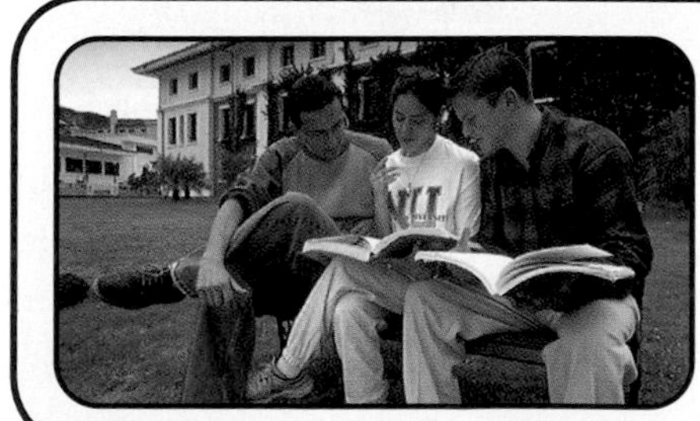

TEACHING OPTIONS

Video Tips General suggestions for using video clips in the classroom can be found on page IAE-12 of this Instructor's Annotated Edition.

¿Qué clases tomas? Play the **¿Qué clases tomas?** segment of this video module and have students give you a "play-by-play" description of the action. Write their descriptions on the board. After playing this segment of the video module, give the class a moment to read the descriptions you have written on the board. Then play the **¿Qué clases tomas?** segment a second time so students can add more details to the descriptions on the board, if necessary, or simply consolidate information. Finally, discuss the material on the board with the class and call attention to any incorrect information. Help your students prepare a brief plot summary.

Suggestion Have the class read through the entire **Fotonovela**, with volunteers playing the parts of Álex, Maite, Inés, and Javier.

Expresiones útiles Identify forms of **tomar** and **estar**. Point out question-forming devices and the accent marks over question words. Call attention to examples of numbers 31–100. Tell students that they will learn more about these concepts in **Estructura**. Point out that **gusta** is used when what is liked is singular, and **gustan** when what is liked is plural. A detailed discussion of the **gustar** construction (see **Estructura 7.4**) is unnecessary here.

INÉS Hola. Me llamo Inés Ayala Loor y soy del Ecuador... de Portoviejo.

MAITE Encantada. ¿Qué clases tomas en la universidad?

INÉS Tomo geografía, inglés, historia, sociología y arte.

MAITE Tomas muchas clases, ¿no?

INÉS Pues sí, me gusta estudiar mucho.

ÁLEX Pero si son muy interesantes, hombre.

JAVIER Sí, ¡muy interesantes!

Enfoque cultural La vida universitaria

Universities in Spanish-speaking countries differ from those in the United States. In most cases students enroll in programs that prepare them for a specific career, rather than choosing a major. The courses for these programs are standardized within each country, so students take few elective courses. The classes themselves are also taught differently. Most are conducted as lectures that meet one or two times weekly. Grades are often based on a scale of one to ten, where five is passing.

Expresiones útiles

Talking about classes

- ▶ **¿Qué tal las clases en la UNAM?** *How are classes going at UNAM?*
- ▶ **¿También tomas tú geografía?** *Are you also taking geography?*
- ▷ **No, tomo inglés y literatura.** *No, I'm taking English and literature.*

- ▶ **Tomas muchas clases, ¿no?** *You're taking lots of classes, aren't you?*
- ▷ **Pues sí.** *Well, yes.*

- ▶ **¿En qué clase hay más chicos?** *In which class are there more guys?*
- ▷ **En la clase de historia.** *In history class.*

Talking about likes/dislikes

- ▶ **¿Te gusta estudiar?** *Do you like to study?*
- ▷ **Sí, me gusta mucho. Pero también me gusta mirar la televisión.** *Yes, I like it a lot. But I also like to watch television.*
- ▶ **¿Te gusta la clase de sociología?** *Do you like sociology class?*
- ▷ **Sí, me gusta muchísimo.** *Yes, I like it very much.*

- ▶ **¿Te gustan las computadoras?** *Do you like computers?*
- ▷ **No, no me gustan nada.** *No, I don't like them at all.*

Talking about location

- ▶ **Aquí estamos en...** *Here we are at/in...*
- ▶ **¿Dónde está la señorita?** *Where is the young woman?*
- ▷ **Está cerca de la ventana.** *She's near the window.*

Expressing hesitation

- ▶ **A ver...** *Let's see...*
- ▶ **Bueno...** *Well...*

TEACHING OPTIONS

Enfoque cultural Draw students' attention to the first segment of the **Fotonovela**. Point out that when Álex asks how classes are going at the **UNAM**, he's referring to the **Universidad Nacional Autónoma de México**, located in Mexico City. The **UNAM** was founded in 1551. The university is a center of teaching and research in many disciplines, including accounting, architecture, medicine, philosophy and letters, psychology, and zoology. In addition to being an educational center, the university is famous for its spectacular architecture. The front exterior wall of the library, for example, features a monumental mosaic by Juan O'Gorman. Other buildings are adorned with murals by other important Mexican artists such as Diego Rivera and David Alfaro Siqueiros.

1 Suggestion Review the names of courses, pages 36–37, and the days of the week, page 38, before doing this activity.

2 Expansion Give these statements to the class as items 9–12: **9. Hay muchos chicos en mi clase de historia. (Inés) 10. Tomo tres clases... computación, historia y arte. (Javier) 11. Yo tomo tres clases... inglés, literatura y periodismo. (Maite) 12. ¿Yo? Soy de la capital de Puerto Rico. (Javier)**

3 Expansion Point out that one of the answers in the word bank will not be used. After your students complete this activity, have them write a sentence that includes the unused word (**sociología**).

4 Expansion Ask volunteers to present their conversation in front of the class.

The Affective Dimension Reassure students who seem anxious about speaking that perfect pronunciation isn't necessary for communication and that their pronunciation will improve with practice.

Reacciona a la fotonovela

1 **Escoger** Choose the answer that best completes each sentence.

1. Maite toma (*is taking*) c________ en la universidad.
   a. geografía, inglés y periodismo b. economía, periodismo y literatura
   c. periodismo, inglés y literatura
2. Inés toma sociología, geografía, a________.
   a. inglés, historia y arte b. periodismo, computación y arte
   c. historia, literatura y biología
3. Javier toma b________ clases este semestre.
   a. cuatro b. tres c. dos
4. Javier toma historia y c________ los c________.
   a. computación; martes y jueves b. arte; lunes, martes y miércoles
   c. arte; lunes, miércoles y viernes

2 **Identificar** Indicate which person would make each statement. The names may be used more than once.

1. Sí, me gusta estudiar. Inés
2. ¡Hola! ¿Te gustan las clases en la UNAM? Álex
3. ¿La clase de periodismo? Sí, me gusta mucho. Maite
4. Hay más chicas en la clase de sociología. Inés
5. Buenos días. Yo soy de Radio Andina FM 93. Maite
6. ¡Uf! ¡No me gustan las computadoras! Javier
7. Las computadoras son muy interesantes. Me gustan muchísimo. Álex
8. Me gusta dibujar en la clase de arte. Javier

INÉS

MAITE

JAVIER

ÁLEX

NOTA CULTURAL

Álex is a student at **la UNAM**, or **Universidad Nacional Autónoma de México** (*National Autonomous University of Mexico*). Founded in 1551, it is now one of the largest universities in the world, with an annual enrollment of over 250,000 students.

3 **Completar** These sentences are similar to things said in the **Fotonovela**. Complete each sentence with the correct word(s).

la sociología	el arte	la Universidad San Francisco de Quito
la clase de historia	geografía	la Mitad del Mundo

1. Maite, Javier, Inés y yo estamos en... la Mitad del Mundo
2. Hay fotos impresionantes de la Mitad del Mundo en los libros de... geografía
3. Me llamo Maite. Estoy aquí con estudiantes de... la Universidad San Francisco de Quito
4. Hay muchos chicos en... la clase de historia
5. No me gustan las computadoras. Me gusta más... el arte

NOTA CULTURAL

In the **Fotonovela,** Álex, Maite, Javier, and Inés visit **la Mitad del Mundo** (*Center of the World*), a monument north of Quito, Ecuador. It marks the line at which the equator divides the Earth's northern and southern hemispheres.

4 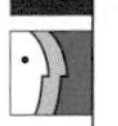 **Preguntas personales** Interview a classmate about his/her likes and dislikes of the university and university life. Answers will vary.

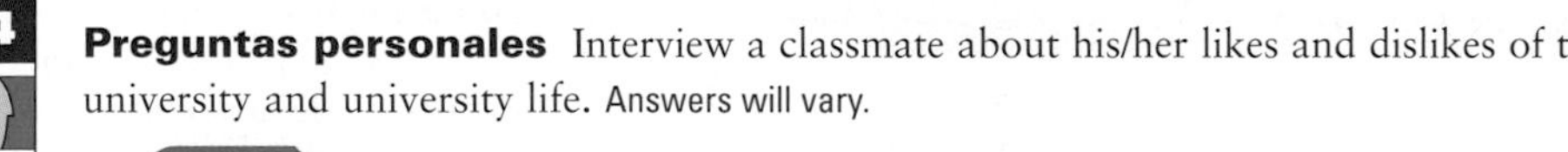

modelo

Estudiante 1: ¿Te gusta la cafetería?
Estudiante 2: No, no me gusta la cafetería. Pero me gusta la residencia estudiantil.
Estudiante 1: ¿Te gustan las computadoras?
Estudiante 2: Sí, me gustan mucho. Tomo una clase de computación.

TEACHING OPTIONS

Small Groups Have your students work in small groups to create a skit in which a radio reporter asks local university students where they are from, which classes they are taking, and which classes they like. Encourage your students to use the phrases in **Expresiones útiles** as much as possible. Have one or two groups present their skit to the class.

Extra Practice Have your students close their books and complete these statements with information from the **Fotonovela**. You may present the sentences orally or write them on the board. **1. Hoy estoy con dos _____ de la Universidad San Francisco de Quito. (estudiantes); 2. ¿En qué _____ hay más chicos? (clase); 3. ¿_____ te llamas y de _____ eres? (Cómo; dónde)**

Pronunciación

Spanish vowels

a **e** **i** **o** **u**

Spanish vowels are never silent; they are always pronounced in a short, crisp way without the glide sounds used in English.

Álex **clase** **nada** **encantada**

The letter **a** is pronounced like the *a* in *father*, but shorter.

el **ene** **mesa** **elefante**

The letter **e** is pronounced like the *e* in *they*, but shorter.

Inés **chica** **tiza** **señorita**

The letter **i** sounds like the *ee* in *beet*, but shorter.

hola **con** **libro** **don Francisco**

The letter **o** is pronounced like the *o* in *tone*, but shorter.

uno **regular** **saludos** **gusto**

The letter **u** sounds like the *oo* in *room*, but shorter.

Práctica Practice the vowels by saying the names of these places in Spain.

1. Madrid
2. Alicante
3. Tenerife
4. Toledo
5. Barcelona
6. Granada
7. Burgos
8. La Coruña

Oraciones Read the sentences aloud, focusing on the vowels.

1. Hola. Me llamo Ramiro Morgado.
2. Estudio arte en la Universidad de Salamanca.
3. Tomo también literatura y contabilidad.
4. Ay, tengo clase en cinco minutos. ¡Nos vemos!

Refranes Practice the vowels by reading these sayings aloud.

Del dicho al hecho hay un gran trecho.[1]

Cada loco con su tema.[2]

1 Easier said than done.
2 To each his own.

AYUDA

Although **ay** and **hay** are pronounced identically, they do not have the same meaning. **¡Ay!** is an exclamation expressing pain, shock, or affliction: *Oh, dear; Woe is me!* As you learned in **Lección 1**, **hay** is a verb form that means *there is, there are*. **Hay veinte libros.** (*There are twenty books.*)

recursos

TEXT CD Lección 2	LM p. 8	Lab CD/MP3 Lección 2	I CD-ROM Lección 2

Section Goal

In **Pronunciación** students will be introduced to the Spanish vowels and how they are pronounced.

Instructional Resources
Textbook CD
Lab Manual, p. 8
Lab CD/MP3 ***Lección 2***
IRM: Tapescript, pp. 6–10; p. 86
Interactive CD-ROM

Suggestions

- Point out that the drawings above the vowels on this page indicate the approximate position of the mouth as the vowels are pronounced.
- Model the pronunciation of each vowel and have students watch the shape of your mouth. Have them repeat the vowel after you. Then go through the example words.
- Pronounce a few of the example words and have the students write them on the board with their books closed.

Práctica/Oraciones/Refranes

These exercises are recorded on the Textbook CD. You may want to play the CD so students practice the pronunciation point by listening to Spanish spoken by speakers other than yourself.

TEACHING OPTIONS

Extra Practice Supply the class with the names of more places in Spain. Have your students spell each name aloud in Spanish, then ask them to pronounce each one. Avoid names that contain diphthongs. Ex: **Sevilla, Salamanca, Santander, Albacete, Gerona, Lugo, Badajoz, Tarragona, Logroño, Valladolid, Orense, Pamplona, Bilbao.**

Small Groups Have the class turn to the **Fotonovela**, pages 40–41, and work in groups of four to read all or part of the **Fotonovela** aloud, focusing on the correct pronunciation of the vowels. Circulate among the groups and model the correct pronunciation and intonation of words and phrases as needed.

Section Goals

In **Estructura 2.1** students will learn:

- the present tense of regular **–ar** verbs
- the formation of negative sentences

Instructional Resources

WB/VM: Workbook, pp. 13–14
Lab Manual, p. 9
Lab CD/MP3 ***Lección 2***
IRM: ***¡Inténtalo! & Práctica*** *Answers, pp. 199–200; Tapescript, pp. 6–10*
Interactive CD-ROM
Companion website: www.vistahigherlearning.com
Presentations CD-ROM

Suggestions

- Point out that students have been using verbs and verb constructions from the start: **¿Cómo te llamas?, hay, ser,** and so forth. Ask a student: **¿Qué clases tomas?** Model student answer as **Yo tomo...** Then ask another student: **¿Qué clases toma ____? Sí, toma ____.**
- Explain that because the verb endings mark the person speaking or spoken about, subject pronouns are usually optional in Spanish.
- Remind students that **vosotros/as** forms will not be actively practiced in **VISTAS**.

2.1 Present tense of –ar verbs

ANTE TODO In order to talk about activities, you need to use verbs. Verbs express actions or states of being. In English and Spanish, the infinitive is the base form of the verb. In English, the infinitive is preceded by the word *to*: *to study, to be*. The infinitive in Spanish is a one-word form and can be recognized by its endings: **–ar, –er,** or **–ir.** In this lesson, you will learn the forms of regular **–ar** verbs.

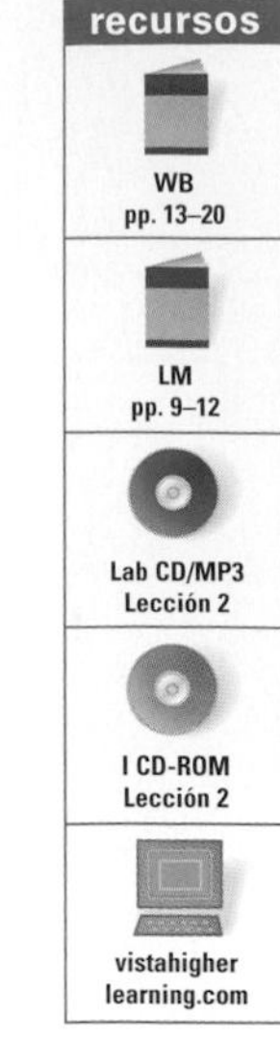

recursos
WB
pp. 13–20
LM
pp. 9–12
Lab CD/MP3
Lección 2
I CD-ROM
Lección 2
vistahigher
learning.com

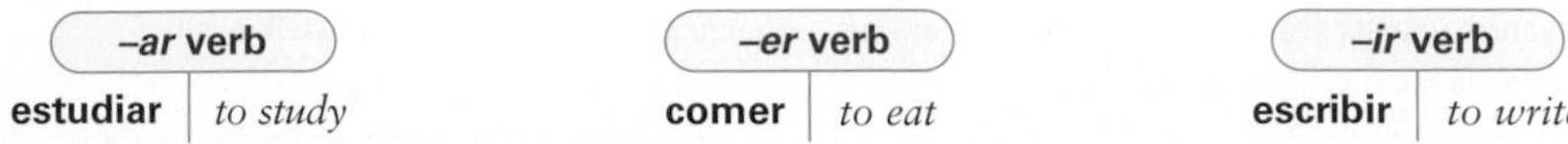

–ar verb		*–er* verb		*–ir* verb	
estudiar	*to study*	**comer**	*to eat*	**escribir**	*to write*

Present tense of *estudiar*

estudiar *(to study)*

SINGULAR FORMS	yo	estudi**o**	*I study*
	tú	estudi**as**	*you* (fam.) *study*
	Ud./él/ella	estudi**a**	*you* (form.) *study; he/she studies*
PLURAL FORMS	nosotros/as	estudi**amos**	*we study*
	vosotros/as	estudi**áis**	*you* (fam.) *study*
	Uds./ellos/ellas	estudi**an**	*you* (form.) *study; they study*

▶ To create the forms of most regular verbs in Spanish, you drop the infinitive endings (**–ar, –er, –ir**). You then add to the stem the endings that correspond to the different subject pronouns. The following diagram will help you visualize the process by which verb forms are created.

Conjugation of *–ar* verbs

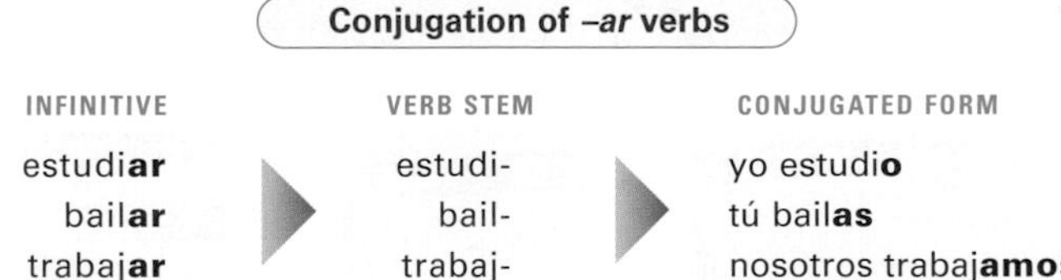

INFINITIVE	VERB STEM	CONJUGATED FORM
estudi**ar**	estudi-	yo estudi**o**
bail**ar**	bail-	tú bail**as**
trabaj**ar**	trabaj-	nosotros trabaj**amos**

TEACHING OPTIONS

Extra Practice Do a pattern practice drill. Write an infinitive from the list of common –**ar** verbs on page 45 on the board and ask individual students to provide conjugations for the different subject pronouns and/or names you suggest. Reverse activity by saying a conjugated form and asking students to give the appropriate subject pronoun.

Extra Practice Ask questions, using **estudiar, bailar,** and **trabajar.** Students should answer in complete sentences. Ask additional questions to get more information. Ex: —____, **¿trabajas? —Sí, trabajo. —¿Dónde trabajas? —Trabajo en ____. • —¿Quién baila los sábados? —Yo bailo los sábados. —¿Bailas merengue? • —¿Estudian ustedes mucho? —¿Quién estudia más? —¿Cuántas horas estudias los lunes? ¿Y los sábados?**

Common *–ar* verbs

bailar	*to dance*	**estudiar**	*to study*
buscar	*to look for*	**explicar**	*to explain*
caminar	*to walk*	**hablar**	*to talk; to speak*
cantar	*to sing*	**llegar**	*to arrive*
cenar	*to have dinner*	**llevar**	*to carry*
comprar	*to buy*	**mirar**	*to look (at); to watch*
contestar	*to answer*	**necesitar (+** ***inf.*****)**	*to need*
conversar	*to converse, to chat*	**practicar**	*to practice*
desayunar	*to have breakfast*	**preguntar**	*to ask (a question)*
descansar	*to rest*	**preparar**	*to prepare*
desear (+ ***inf.*****)**	*to desire; to wish*	**regresar**	*to return*
dibujar	*to draw*	**terminar**	*to end; to finish*
enseñar	*to teach*	**tomar**	*to take; to drink*
escuchar	*to listen (to)*	**trabajar**	*to work*
esperar (+ ***inf.*****)**	*to wait (for); to hope*	**viajar**	*to travel*

¡ATENCIÓN!

The Spanish verbs **buscar, escuchar, esperar,** and **mirar** do not need to be followed by prepositions as they do in English.

Busco la tarea.
I'm looking for the homework.

Escucho la música.
I'm listening to the music.

Espero el autobús.
I'm waiting for the bus.

Miro la pizarra.
I'm looking at the blackboard.

COMPARE & CONTRAST

Compare the verbs in the English sentences to the verb in the Spanish equivalent.

Paco **trabaja** en la cafetería.

1. *Paco works in the cafeteria.*
2. *Paco is working in the cafeteria.*
3. *Paco does work in the cafeteria.*

English uses three sets of forms to talk about the present: 1) the simple present (*Paco works*), 2) the present progressive (*Paco is working*), and 3) the emphatic present (*Paco does work*). In Spanish, the simple present can be used in all three cases.

In both Spanish and English, the present tense is also sometimes used to express future action.

Marina **viaja** a Madrid mañana.

1. *Marina travels to Madrid tomorrow.*
2. *Marina will travel to Madrid tomorrow.*
3. *Marina is traveling to Madrid tomorrow.*

▶ In Spanish, as in English, when two verbs are used together with no change of subject, the second verb is generally in the infinitive.

Deseo hablar con don Francisco.
I want to speak with don Francisco.

Necesitamos comprar cuadernos
We need to buy notebooks.

▶ To make a sentence negative in Spanish, the word **no** is placed before the conjugated verb. In this case, **no** means *not*.

Ellos **no** miran la televisión.
They don't watch television.

Alicia **no** desea bailar ahora.
Alicia doesn't want to dance now.

Suggestions

- Model pronunciation of each infinitive, having students repeat it after you. Then create sentences using **Me gusta...** and several infinitives. Ask students if they like to do some of the activities listed. (Ex: **¿Te gusta bailar?**)
- Model the **yo** form of several verbs, creating simple sentences about yourself (Ex: **Bailo con mis amigos.**) and asking students if they do the same activities (Ex: **¿Bailas mucho con tus amigos?**). Restate students' answers using the **él/ella** forms of the **–ar** verbs and then ask them to verify their classmates' answers.
  Ex: **¿____ baila mucho?**
  No, ____ no baila.
- Explain that the simple present tense in Spanish is the equivalent of the three present tense forms of English. Model sentences and give a few additional examples.
- Write additional examples of a conjugated verb followed by an infinitive on the board. Model additional sentences with **Me gusta..., ¿Te gusta...?,** and **Espero...** and infinitives.
- Explain that, when answering questions negatively, **no** must be used twice. Ask questions of students that will most likely result in negative answers.
  Ex: **—____, ¿bailas tango?**
  —No, no bailo tango.

TEACHING OPTIONS

Heritage Speakers Ask heritage speakers to come up with original sentences about the current semester/quarter that are true for them: what they study, if/where they work, television programs they like to watch, and any other activity that uses a verb found in this section. Ask comprehension questions of the rest of the class to verify the information.

Pairs Ask students to work with a partner to come up with ten original sentences, using verbs presented in this section. Point out that students may also use many of the vocabulary words from **Contextos** with these verbs. Pairs then share their sentences with the class to find out how many original sentences the class can come up with.

Suggestions

- Point out the lack of subject pronouns and the use of the double **no** in the photo captions.
- Model clarification/contrast sentences as well as those that show emphasis. Give a few additional statements in which you contrast and emphasize. Use **sí** to give further emphasis.
  Ex: —____, **¿te gusta bailar?**
  —No, no me gusta bailar.
  —____ **no baila. Yo sí bailo.**
- Point out the position of subjects and subject pronouns with regard to the verbs in affirmative and negative sentences.
- Ask brief questions about the **Fotonovela** characters using verbs from this lesson.
  Ex: **¿Qué clases toma Maite? ¿Dónde trabaja ella? ¿Qué estudia Javier?**

▶ Note that no subject pronouns were used in the Spanish conversation depicted above. Spanish speakers often omit them because the verb endings indicate who the subject is. In Spanish, subject pronouns are used for emphasis, clarification, or contrast, as in the examples below.

Clarification/Contrast

—¿Qué enseñan **ellos**?
What do they teach?

—**Ella** enseña arte y **él** enseña física.
She teaches art, and he teaches physics.

Emphasis

—¿Quién desea trabajar hoy?
Who wants to work today?

—**Yo** no deseo trabajar hoy.
I don't want to work today.

¡INTÉNTALO! Provide the present tense forms of these verbs. The first items have been done for you.

hablar

1. Yo hablo español.
2. Ellos hablan español.
3. Inés habla español.
4. Nosotras hablamos español.
5. Tú hablas español.
6. Los estudiantes hablan español.
7. Usted habla español.
8. Javier y yo hablamos español.

trabajar

1. Ustedes trabajan mucho.
2. Juanita y yo trabajamos mucho.
3. Nuestra profesora trabaja mucho.
4. Tú trabajas mucho.
5. Yo trabajo mucho.
6. Las chicas trabajan mucho.
7. Él trabaja mucho.
8. Tú y Álex trabajan mucho.

desear

1. Usted desea viajar.
2. Yo deseo viajar.
3. Nosotros deseamos viajar.
4. Lourdes y Luz desean viajar.
5. Tú deseas viajar.
6. Ella desea viajar.
7. Marco y yo deseamos viajar.
8. Ustedes desean viajar.

TEACHING OPTIONS

Video Show the video again to give students additional input containing verbs and verb forms. Stop the video where appropriate to discuss how certain verbs were used and to ask comprehension questions.

Game Divide the class into two teams. Indicate one team member at a time, alternating between teams. Give a verb in its infinitive form and name a subject pronoun. The team member should give the corresponding present tense verb form. Give a point per correct answer. Deduct a point for each wrong answer. The team with the most points at the end of play wins.

Práctica

1 Completar Complete the conversation with the appropriate forms of the verbs. Then act it out with a partner.

AYUDA

The Spanish **no** translates to both *no* and *not* in English. In negative answers to questions, you will need to use **no** twice:

¿Estudias geografía?
No, no estudio geografía

JUAN ¡Hola, Linda! ¿Qué tal las clases?

LINDA Bien. (1) Tomo (tomar) tres clases... química, biología y computación. Y tú, ¿cuántas clases (2) tomas (tomar)?

JUAN (3) Tomo (tomar) cuatro... sociología, biología, arte y literatura. Yo (4) tomo (tomar) biología a las cuatro con el doctor Cárdenas. ¿Y tú?

LINDA Lily, Alberto y yo (5) tomamos (tomar) biología a las diez, con la profesora Garza.

JUAN ¿(6) Estudian (estudiar) ustedes mucho?

LINDA Sí, porque hay muchos exámenes. Alberto y yo (7) estudiamos (estudiar) dos horas juntos todos los días (*together every day*).

JUAN ¿Lily no (8) estudia (estudiar) con ustedes?

LINDA Shhh... No, ella (9) estudia (estudiar) con su novio (*boyfriend*), Arturo.

2 Oraciones Form sentences using the words provided. Remember to conjugate the verbs and add any other necessary words.

1. Ustedes / practicar / vocabulario Ustedes practican el vocabulario.
2. (Yo) desear / practicar / verbos / hoy Deseo practicar los verbos hoy.
3. ¿Preparar (tú) / tarea? ¿Preparas la tarea?
4. clase de español / terminar / once La clase de español termina a las once.
5. ¿Qué / buscar / ustedes? ¿Qué buscan ustedes?
6. (Nosotros) buscar / pluma Buscamos una pluma.
7. (Yo) comprar / computadora Compro una computadora.
8. Mi (*My*) compañera de cuarto / regresar / lunes Mi compañera de cuarto regresa el lunes.
9. Ella / bailar / y / cantar / muy bien Ella baila y canta muy bien.
10. jóvenes / desear / descansar / ahora Los jóvenes desean descansar ahora.

3 Actividades Get together with a classmate and take turns asking each other if you do these activities.

bailar merengue	escuchar música rock	practicar el español
cantar bien	estudiar física	trabajar en la universidad
dibujar en clase	mirar la televisión	viajar a Europa

modelo

tomar el autobús
Estudiante 1: *¿Tomas el autobús?*
Estudiante 2: *Sí, tomo el autobús. / No, no tomo el autobús.*

1 Expansion Go over the answers quickly in class, then ask several pairs of students to act out the dialogue.

2 Suggestion Point out to students that they will need to conjugate the verbs and add missing articles and other words to complete these dehydrated sentences. Tell them that subject pronouns in parentheses are not included in the completed sentences. Model completion of the first sentence for the class.

3 Suggestion Before beginning the activity, give a two to three minute oral rapid-response drill. Give infinitives and call on students to give the conjugated form for the subjects you name.

3 Expansion Have students repeat the exercise by asking each other whether they like the activities listed. Ex: **¿Te gusta mirar la television?**

TEACHING OPTIONS

Pairs Have individual students write five dehydrated sentences and exchange them with a partner who will complete them. After pairs have completed their sentences, ask volunteers to share some of their dehydrated sentences. Write them on the board and have the whole class "rehydrate" them.

Extra Practice Prepare short descriptions of five easily recognizable people. Write their names on the board in random order. Then read your descriptions, having students match the description to the appropriate name. Ex: **Ella canta, baila y viaja mucho. (Jennifer López)**

Comunicación

4 

Describir With a partner, describe what you see in the pictures using the given verbs. Answers will vary.

modelo

enseñar
La profesora enseña química.

1. caminar, hablar, llevar

2. buscar, descansar, estudiar

3. dibujar, cantar, escuchar

4. llevar, tomar, viajar

5 

Charadas In groups of three students, play a game of charades using the verbs in the word bank. For example, if someone is studying, you say "**Estudias.**" The first person to guess correctly acts out the next charade. Answers will vary.

bailar	cantar	descansar	enseñar	mirar
caminar	conversar	dibujar	escuchar	preguntar

Síntesis

6 

Conversación Get together with a classmate and pretend that you are friends who have not seen each other on campus for a few days. Have a conversation in which you catch up on things. Mention how you're feeling, what classes you're taking, what days and times you have classes, and what classes you like and don't like. Answers will vary.

4 Suggestion Encourage students to offer additional descriptions of the drawings. Ex: **La profesora habla en clase. Hay números y letras en la pizarra y un libro en la mesa.** Ask volunteers to share their descriptions with the class.

5 Expansion You may want to split the class into two teams with volunteers from each team acting out the charades. Give points for correct guesses. Deduct points for incorrect guesses. The team with the most points at the end wins.

6 Suggestion Point out that, in addition to practicing **–ar** verbs, this activity recycles and reviews material from **Lección 1**: greetings, leave-takings, and telling time. Give students several minutes to plan their conversation before they begin speaking.

6 Expansion Have pairs of students present their conversations in front of the class.

TEACHING OPTIONS

Extra Practice Have students write a description of themselves made up of activities they like or don't like to do, using sentences containing **me gusta...** and **no me gusta...** . Collect the descriptions and read a few of them to the class. Have the class guess who wrote each description.

Game Play **Concentración**. Choose eight infinitives taught in this section, and write each one on a separate card. On another eight cards, draw or paste a picture that illustrates the action of each infinitive. Place the cards face-down in four rows of four. Play with even-numbered groups of students. In pairs, students select two cards. If the two cards match, the pair keeps them. If the cards don't match, students replace them in their original position. The pair with the most cards at the end wins.

2.2 Forming questions in Spanish

ANTE TODO There are three basic ways to ask questions in Spanish. Can you guess what they are by looking at the photos and photo captions on this page?

¿Dibujas mucho?
Las computadoras son muy interesantes, ¿no?
¿También tomas tú geografía?

CONSEJOS

With a partner, take turns saying the example statements and questions on this page out loud. With books closed, your partner should guess whether you are making a statement or asking a question. Make sure to raise the pitch of your voice at the end of the questions. Then take turns making up statements of your own and turning them into questions, using all three of the methods described on this page.

- One way to form a question is to raise the pitch of your voice at the end of a declarative sentence. When writing any question in Spanish, be sure to use an upside down question mark (**¿**) at the beginning and a regular question mark (**?**) at the end of the sentence.

Statement	Question
Ustedes trabajan los sábados. *You work on Saturdays.*	¿Ustedes trabajan los sábados? *Do you work on Saturdays?*
Miguel busca un mapa. *Miguel is looking for a map.*	¿Miguel busca un mapa? *Is Miguel looking for a map?*

- As in English, you can form a question by inverting the order of the subject and the verb of a declarative statement. The subject may even be placed at the end of the sentence.

Statement	Question
SUBJECT VERB **Ustedes trabajan** los sábados. *You work on Saturdays.*	VERB SUBJECT ¿**Trabajan ustedes** los sábados? *Do you work on Saturdays?*
SUBJECT VERB **Carlota regresa** a las seis. *Carlota returns at six.*	VERB SUBJECT ¿**Regresa** a las seis **Carlota**? *Does Carlota return at six?*

- Questions can also be formed by adding the tags **¿no?** or **¿verdad?** at the end of a statement.

Statement	Question
Ustedes trabajan los sábados. *You work on Saturdays.*	Ustedes trabajan los sábados, **¿verdad?** *You work on Saturdays, right?*
Carlota regresa a las seis. *Carlota returns at six.*	Carlota regresa a las seis, **¿no?** *Carlota returns at six, doesn't she?*

Section Goals

In **Estructura 2.2** students will be introduced to:
- forming questions in Spanish
- rising and falling intonation in questions and statements
- tag questions
- interrogative words

Instructional Resources
WB/VM: Workbook, pp. 15–16
Lab Manual, p. 10
Lab CD/MP3 ***Lección 2***
IRM: ***¡Inténtalo! & Práctica*** *Answers, pp. 199–200;*
Tapescript, pp. 6–10;
Hojas de actividades*, p. 163*
Interactive CD-ROM
Companion website: www.vistahigherlearning.com
Presentations CD-ROM

Suggestions

- Review questions such as: **¿Cómo te llamas? ¿Qué clases tomas?** Ask students to suggest others.
- Model the pronunciation and intonation of the various types of questions in the photo captions and example statements and questions. Point out that these types of questions signal a yes-no response.
- Explain that a more common way to form questions in Spanish is to invert the subject and verb.
- Explain that **¿no?** can only be used when the first part of the sentence does not include a negative statement. Use **¿verdad?** after a negative statement. Ex: **No trabajan hoy, ¿verdad?**
- Clarify that the inverted question mark does not necessarily appear at the beginning of the sentence.

TEACHING OPTIONS

Extra Practice/Pairs Write ten statements on the board. Have students convert the statements into questions by inverting subject/verb order. Students can work in pairs to write their questions. When they have finished, ask volunteers to present the questions to the class. Model rising intonation and inverting subject/verb order in the questions. Have the class pronounce the questions after you.

Extra Practice Using the same ten statements on the board from the previous activity, ask students to say them aloud using tag questions. Add a few negative statements to the statements on the board so that students will have to use **¿verdad?** as a tag question.

Suggestions
- Model pronunciation by asking questions. Ex: **¿Cómo estás? ¿Cuál es tu clase favorita?**
- Point out written accent marks on interrogative words.
- Point out that **¿qué?** and **¿cuál?** are not used interchangeably. The word **¿qué?** generally precedes a noun while **¿cuál?** is typically used with a verb. Compare and contrast the following: **¿Qué clase te gusta? ¿Cuál es tu clase favorita?** Write similar questions on the board but leave out the interrogative word. Ask students to tell whether **¿qué?** or **¿cuál?** is used for each.
- Point out **¿cuáles?** and **¿quiénes?** and give examples for each.
- Explain that the answer to the question **¿por qué?** is **porque**.
- Point out singular/plural and masculine/feminine variants for **¿cuánto/a?** and **¿cuántos/as?** Ex: **¿Cuánta tarea hay? ¿Cuántos libros hay?**
- Model pronunciation of example sentences, asking similar questions of students. Ex: ____, **¿dónde trabajas?** Ask other students to verify their classmates' answers. Ex: ____ **trabaja en** ____.

Question words

Interrogative words

¿Cómo?	*How?*	**¿De dónde?**	*From where?*
¿Cuál?, ¿Cuáles?	*Which?; Which one(s)?*	**¿Por qué?**	*Why?*
¿Cuándo?	*When?*	**¿Cuánto/a?**	*How much?*
¿Qué?	*What?; Which?*	**¿Cuántos/as?**	*How many?*
¿Dónde?	*Where?*	**¿Quién?**	*Who?*
¿Adónde?	*Where (to)?*	**¿Quiénes?**	*Who (plural)?*

▶ To ask a question that requires more than a simple *yes* or *no* answer, an interrogative word is used.

¿Cuál de ellos estudia en la biblioteca?
Which of them studies in the library?

¿Cuándo descansan ustedes?
When do you rest?

¿Cuántos estudiantes hablan español?
How many students speak Spanish?

¿Dónde trabaja Ricardo?
Where does Ricardo work?

¿Qué clases tomas?
What classes are you taking?

¿Adónde caminamos?
Where are we walking?

¿De dónde son Álex y Javier?
Where are Alex and Javier from?

¿Por qué necesitas hablar con ella?
Why do you need to talk to her?

¿Quién enseña la clase de arte?
Who teaches the art class?

¿Cuánta tarea hay?
How much homework is there?

CONSÚLTALO

¿Qué? and **¿cuál(es)?** You will learn more about the difference between **qué** and **cuál** in **Estructura 9.3**, pp. 284–285.

▶ When pronouncing this type of question, the pitch of your voice falls at the end of the sentence.

¿Cómo llegas a clase?
How do you get to class?

¿Por qué necesitas estudiar?
Why do you need to study?

▶ In Spanish **no** can mean both *no* and *not*. Therefore, when answering a yes/no question in the negative, you need to use **no** twice.

¿Caminan a la universidad?
Do you walk to the university

No, no caminamos a la universidad.
*No, we do **not** walk to the university.*

¡INTÉNTALO! Make questions out of these statements. Use intonation in column 1 and the tag **¿no?** in column 2. The first item has been done for you.

Statement	Intonation	Tag questions
1. Hablas inglés.	¿Hablas inglés?	Hablas inglés, ¿no?
2. Trabajamos mañana.	¿Trabajamos mañana?	Trabajamos mañana, ¿no?
3. Ustedes desean bailar.	¿Ustedes desean bailar?	Ustedes desean bailar, ¿no?
4. Raúl estudia mucho.	¿Raúl estudia mucho?	Raúl estudia mucho, ¿no?
5. Enseño a las nueve.	¿Enseño a las nueve?	Enseño a las nueve, ¿no?
6. Luz mira la televisión.	¿Luz mira la televisión?	Luz mira la televisión, ¿no?
7. Los chicos descansan.	¿Los chicos descansan?	Los chicos descansan, ¿no?
8. Él prepara la prueba.	¿Él prepara la prueba?	Él prepara la prueba, ¿no?

TEACHING OPTIONS

Video Show the video again to give students more input on forming questions. Stop the video where appropriate to discuss how certain questions, including tag questions, are formed. Have students focus on characters' rising and falling intonation in questions and statements.

Heritage Speakers Ask heritage speakers to give original statements and questions at random. Have the rest of the class determine whether each sentence is a statement or a question.
Pairs Give pairs of students five minutes to write original questions using as many interrogative words as they can. Can any group come up with questions using all interrogative words?

Práctica

1 **Preguntas** Change these sentences into questions by inverting the word order.

modelo

Ernesto habla con su compañero de clase.
¿Habla Ernesto con su compañero de clase? / ¿Habla con su compañero de clase Ernesto?

1. La profesora Cruz prepara la prueba.
   ¿Prepara la profesora Cruz la prueba? / ¿Prepara la prueba la profesora Cruz?
2. Sandra y yo necesitamos estudiar.
   ¿Necesitamos Sandra y yo estudiar? / ¿Necesitamos estudiar Sandra y yo?
3. Los chicos practican el vocabulario.
   ¿Practican los chicos el vocabulario? / ¿Practican el vocabulario los chicos?
4. Jaime termina la tarea.
   ¿Termina Jaime la tarea? / ¿Termina la tarea Jaime?
5. Tú trabajas en la biblioteca. ¿Trabajas tú en la biblioteca? / ¿Trabajas en la biblioteca tú?

¡ATENCIÓN!

Notice the difference between **¿por qué?**, which is written as two words and has an accent, and **porque**, which is written as one word without an accent:

¿por qué? *why?*
porque *because*

2 **Completar** Irene and Manolo are chatting in the library. Complete their conversation with the appropriate questions. Answers will vary.

IRENE Hola, Manolo. (1) ¿Cómo estás?/¿Qué tal?
MANOLO Bien, gracias. (2) ¿Y tú?
IRENE Muy bien. (3) ¿Qué hora es?
MANOLO Son las nueve.
IRENE (4) ¿Qué estudias?
MANOLO Estudio historia.
IRENE (5) ¿Por qué?
MANOLO Porque hay un examen mañana.
IRENE (6) ¿Te gusta la clase?
MANOLO Sí, me gusta mucho la clase.
IRENE (7) ¿Quién enseña la clase?
MANOLO El profesor Padilla enseña la clase.
IRENE (8) ¿Tomas psicología este semestre?
MANOLO No, no tomo psicología este semestre.
IRENE (9) ¿A qué hora regresas a la residencia?
MANOLO Regreso a la residencia a las once.
IRENE (10) ¿Deseas tomar una soda?
MANOLO No, no deseo tomar soda. ¡Deseo estudiar!

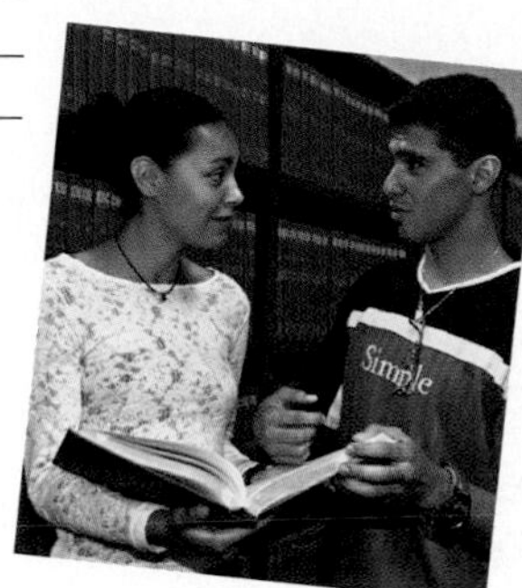

3 **Dos profesores** In pairs, create a dialogue, similar to the one in **Actividad 2**, between profesor Padilla and his colleague profesora Martínez. Use question words. Answers will vary.

modelo

Prof. Padilla: *¿Qué enseñas este semestre?*
Prof. Martínez: *Enseño dos cursos de sociología.*

1 Suggestion Ask students to give both ways of forming questions for each item. Explain that the last element in a question is emphatic, thus **¿Habla Ernesto con el Sr. Gómez?** and **¿Habla con el Sr. Gómez Ernesto?** have different emphases. In pairs, have students take turns making the statements and converting them into questions.

1 Expansion Have students add tag questions to the statements. Then have them convert the statements into negative sentences and add **¿verdad?**

2 Expansion Have pairs of students create a similar conversation, replacing the answers with items that are true for them. Then ask volunteer pairs to present their conversations to the class.

3 Suggestion To prepare students for the activity, have them brainstorm possible topics of conversation.

TEACHING OPTIONS

Heritage Speakers Ask students in the class to interview heritage speakers, whether in the class or outside. Students should prepare questions about who the person is, if he or she works and when/where, what he or she studies and why, and so forth. Have students present to the rest of the class the information they gather in the interviews.

Large Groups Divide the class into two groups. To each member of one group give a strip of paper with a question on it. Ex: **¿Cuántos estudiantes hay en la clase?** To each member of the other group give an answer. Ex: **Hay treinta estudiantes en la clase.** Have students find their partner. When you write the questions and answers, be careful that each question has only one possible answer.

4 Suggestions
- Because this is the first activity in which the **Hojas de actividades** (found in the IRM) are used, explain to students that they use the **Hojas** to complete the corresponding activity.
- Distribute the **Hojas de actividades** and explain that students must actively approach their classmates with their **Hoja** in hand. When they find someone who answers affirmatively, that student signs his or her name.

4 Expansion Ask students to say the name of someone who signed their **Hoja**. Then ask that student for more information. Ex: **¿Quién estudia computación? Ah, ¿sí? ____ estudia computación. ¿Dónde estudias computación, ____? ¿Quién es el profesor/la profesora?**

5 Expansion Play this with the entire class, selecting a few students to play the contestants and to "buzz in" their answers.

6 Suggestion Brainstorm ideas for interview questions and write them on the board, or have students prepare their questions as homework for an in-class interview session.

Comunicación

NATIONAL communication STANDARDS

4 

Encuesta Your instructor will give you a worksheet. Change the categories in the first column into questions, then use them to survey your classmates. Find at least one person for each category. Be prepared to report the results of your survey to the class. Answers will vary.

Categorías	Nombres
1. Estudiar computación	
2. Tomar una clase de psicología	
3. Dibujar bien	
4. Cantar bien	
5. Escuchar música clásica	
6. Escuchar jazz	
7. Hablar mucho en clase	
8. Desear viajar a España	

5 **Un juego** (*A game*) In groups of four or five, play a game of *Jeopardy.*® Each person has to write two clues. Then take turns reading the clues and guessing the questions. The person who guesses correctly reads the next clue. Answers will vary.

Es algo que...	**Es un lugar donde...**	**Es una persona que...**
It's something that...	*It's a place where...*	*It's a person that...*

modelo

Estudiante 1: Es un lugar donde estudiamos.
Estudiante 2: ¿Qué es la biblioteca?

Estudiante 1: Es algo que escuchamos.
Estudiante 2: ¿Qué es la música?

Estudiante 1: Es un director de España.
Estudiante 2: ¿Quién es Pedro Almodóvar?

NOTA CULTURAL

Pedro Almodóvar is an award-winning film director from Spain. His films are full of both humor and melodrama, and their controversial subject matter has often sparked great debate. His 1999 film **Todo sobre mi madre** (*All About My Mother*) received an Oscar for Best Foreign Film and Best Director at the Cannes Film Festival.

Síntesis

6 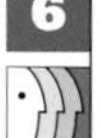

Entrevista Imagine that you are a reporter for the school newspaper. Write five questions about student life at your school and use them to interview two classmates. Be prepared to report your findings to the class. Answers will vary.

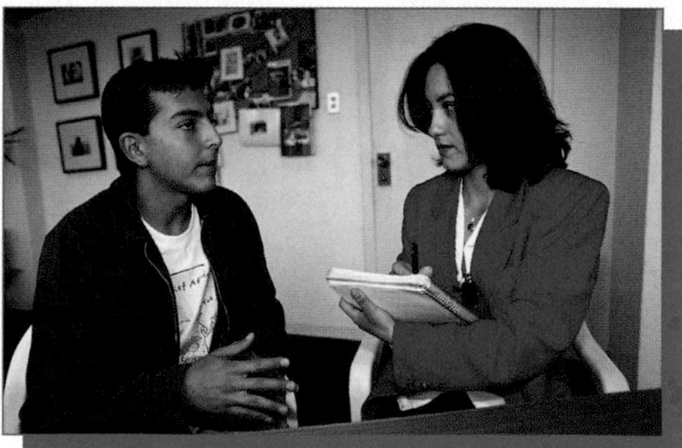

TEACHING OPTIONS

Extra Practice Have students go back to the **Fotonovela** on pages 40–41 and write as many questions as they can about what they see in the photos. Ask volunteers to share their questions as you write them on the board. Then call on individual students to answer them.

Extra Practice Prepare eight questions. Write their answers, but not the questions, on the board in random order. Then read your questions, having students match the question to the appropriate answer. Ex: **¿Cuándo es la clase de español? (Es los lunes, miércoles y viernes.)**

2.3 Present tense of estar

CONSÚLTALO

To review the forms of **ser**, see **Estructura 1.3**, pp. 17–19.

ANTE TODO In **Lección 1**, you learned how to conjugate and use the ver **ser** *(to be)*. You will now learn a second verb which means *to be*, the verb **estar**. Although **estar** ends in **–ar**, it does not follow the pattern of regular **–ar** verbs. The **yo** form (**estoy**) is irregular. Also, all forms have an accented **á** except the **yo** and **nosotros/as** forms.

Present tense of *estar*

estar *(to be)*

SINGULAR FORMS	yo	est**oy**	*I am*
	tú	est**ás**	*you* (fam.) *are*
	Ud./él/ella	est**á**	*you* (form.) *are; he/she is*
PLURAL FORMS	nosotros/as	est**amos**	*we are*
	vosotros/as	est**áis**	*you* (fam.) *are*
	Uds./ellos/ellas	est**án**	*you* (form.) *are; they are*

Hola, Ricardo...
Aquí estamos en la Mitad del Mundo.

María está en la biblioteca.

COMPARE & CONTRAST

In the following chart, compare the uses of the verb **estar** to those of the verb **ser**.

Uses of *estar*

Location
Estoy en casa
I am at home.

Inés **está** al lado de Javier.
Inés is next to Javier.

Health
Álex **está** enfermo hoy.
Álex is sick today.

Well-being
—¿Cómo **estás**, Maite?
How are you, Maite?

—**Estoy** muy bien, gracias.
I'm very well, thank you.

Uses of *ser*

Identity
Hola, **soy** Maite.
Hello, I'm Maite.

Occupation
Soy estudiante.
I'm a student.

Origins
—¿**Eres** de España?
Are you from Spain?

—Sí, **soy** de España.
Yes, I'm from Spain.

Time-telling
Son las cuatro.
It's four o'clock.

¡ATENCIÓN!

You use **la casa** to express *the house*, but **en casa** to express *at home.*

Section Goals

In **Estructura 2.3** students will be introduced to:
- the present tense of **estar**
- contrasts between **ser** and **estar**
- prepositions of location used with **estar**

Instructional Resources
Transparency #14
WB/VM: Workbook, pp. 17–18
Lab Manual, p. 11
*Lab CD/MP3 **Lección 2***
*IRM: **¡Inténtalo! & Práctica** Answers, pp. 199–200; Tapescript, pp. 6–10*
Interactive CD-ROM
Companion website: www.vistahigherlearning.com
Presentations CD-ROM

Suggestions

- Point out that only the **yo** and **nosotros/as** forms do not have a written accent.
- Emphasize that the principal distinction between **estar** and **ser** is that **estar** is generally used to express temporary conditions (**Álex está enfermo hoy.**) and **ser** is generally used to express inherent qualities (**Álex es inteligente.**).
- Students will learn to compare **ser** and **estar** formally in **Estructura 5.3**.

TEACHING OPTIONS

Extra Practice Give statements in English and have students say if they would use **ser** or **estar** in each. Ex: *I'm at home.* (**estar**) *I'm a student.* (**ser**) *I'm tired.* (**estar**) *I'm glad.* (**estar**) *I'm generous.* (**ser**)

Extra Practice Ask students where certain people are or probably are at this moment. Ex: **¿Dónde estás? (Estoy en la clase.) ¿Dónde está el presidente? (Está en Washington, D.C.)**

Heritage Speakers Ask heritage speakers whether they know of any instances where either **ser** or **estar** may be used. (They may point out more advanced uses, such as with certain adjectives: **Es aburrido.** vs. **Está aburrido.**) This may help to compare and contrast inherent vs. temporary conditions and qualities.

Suggestions

- Explain that prepositions typically indicate where one thing or person is in relation to another thing or person: *near, far, on, between, below.*
- Point out that **estar** in the eight model sentences indicates presence or existence in a place.
- Ask volunteers to read each of the captions for the video stills.
- Take a book or other object and place it in various locations in relation to your desk or a student's. Ask individual students about its location. Ex: **¿Dónde está el libro? ¿Está cerca o lejos del escritorio de ____? ¿Qué objeto está al lado/a la izquierda del libro?** Work through various locations, eliciting all of the prepositions of location.
- Ask where different students are in relation to one another. Ex: ____, **¿dónde está ____? Sí, está al lado (a la derecha/izquierda, delante, detrás) de ____.**

Prepositions often used with *estar*

al lado de	*next to; beside*	**delante de**	*in front of*
a la derecha de	*to the right of*	**detrás de**	*behind*
a la izquierda de	*to the left of*	**encima de**	*on top of*
en	*in; on*	**entre**	*between; among*
cerca de	*near*	**lejos de**	*far from*
con	*with*	**sin**	*without*
debajo de	*below*	**sobre**	*on; over*

▶ **Estar** is often used with certain prepositions to describe the location of a person or an object.

La clase **está al lado de** la biblioteca.
The class is next to the library.

Los libros **están encima del** escritorio.
The books are on top of the desk.

El laboratorio **está cerca de** la clase.
The lab is near the classroom.

Maribel **está delante de** José.
Maribel is in front of José.

El estadio no **está lejos de** la librería.
The stadium isn't far from the bookstore.

El mapa está **entre** la pizarra y la puerta.
The map is between the blackboard and the door.

Los estudiantes **están en** la clase.
The students are in class.

El libro **está sobre** la mesa.
The book is on the table.

¡A ver! La señorita que está cerca de la ventana...

Aquí estoy con cuatro estudiantes de la universidad... ¡Qué aventura!

¡INTÉNTALO! Provide the present tense forms of **estar**. The first item has been done for you.

1. Ustedes *están* en la clase.
2. José está en la biblioteca.
3. Yo estoy en el estadio.
4. Nosotras estamos en la cafetería.
5. Tú estás en el laboratorio.
6. Elena está en la librería.
7. Ellas están en la clase.
8. Ana y yo estamos en la clase.
9. Usted está en la biblioteca.
10. Javier y Maribel están en el estadio.
11. Nosotros estamos en la cafetería.
12. Yo estoy en el laboratorio.
13. Carmen y María están en la librería.
14. Tú estás en la clase.

TEACHING OPTIONS

Extra Practice Name well-known campus buildings and ask students to identify where they are in relation to other buildings. Model sample sentences so students will know how to answer. You may wish to write **la Facultad de** on the board and explain its meaning. Ex: **—¿Dónde está la biblioteca? —Está al lado de la Facultad de Química y detrás de la librería.**

TPR One student starts with a small beanbag or rubber ball. You call out another student identified only by his or her location with reference to other students. Ex: **Es la persona a la derecha de ____.** The student with the beanbag or ball has to throw it to the student identified. The latter student must then throw the object to the next person you identify.

Práctica

1

NOTA CULTURAL

In many Spanish-speaking countries, students attend the university in their home city. Because of this, they tend to live at home instead of in a college dormitory. However, students from small towns without universities typically study away from home.

Completar Daniela has just returned home from her classes at the local university. Complete this conversation with the appropriate forms of **ser** or **estar**.

MAMÁ Hola, Daniela. ¿Cómo (1) estás ?
DANIELA Hola, mamá. (2) Estoy bien. ¿Dónde (3) está papá? ¡Ya (*already*) (4) son las ocho de la noche!
MAMÁ No (5) está aquí. (6) Está en la oficina.
DANIELA Y Andrés y Margarita, ¿dónde (7) están ellos?
MAMÁ (8) Están en el restaurante La Palma con Martín.
DANIELA ¿Quién (9) es Martín?
MAMÁ (10) Es un compañero de clase. (11) Es de México.
DANIELA Ah. Y el restaurante La Palma, ¿dónde (12) está ?
MAMÁ (13) Está cerca de la Plaza Mayor, en San Modesto.
DANIELA Gracias, mamá. Voy (*I'm going*) al restaurante. ¡Hasta pronto!

2

Escoger Choose the preposition that best completes each sentence.

1. La pluma está (encima de / detrás de) la mesa. encima de
2. La ventana está (a la izquierda de / debajo de) la puerta. a la izquierda de
3. La pizarra está (debajo de / delante de) los estudiantes. delante de
4. Las sillas están (encima de / detrás de) los escritorios. detrás de
5. Los estudiantes llevan los libros (en / sobre) la mochila. en
6. La biblioteca está (sobre / al lado de) la residencia estudiantil. al lado de
7. España está (cerca de / lejos de) Puerto Rico. lejos de
8. Cuba está (cerca de / lejos de) los Estados Unidos. cerca de
9. Felipe trabaja (con / en) Ricardo en la cafetería. con

3

NOTA CULTURAL

Many universities in the Spanish-speaking world do not have a central campus bookstore. Students generally purchase their texts at designated commercial bookstores.

¿Dónde está...? Imagine that you are in the school bookstore and can't find various items. Ask the clerk (your partner) where the items in the drawing are located. Then switch roles. Answers will vary.

modelo

Estudiante 1: *¿Dónde están los diccionarios?*
Estudiante 2: *Los diccionarios están debajo de los libros de literatura.*

1 Suggestion Ask students to explain why they chose **ser** or **estar** in each case.

1 Expansion Ask two volunteers to present the conversation to the class.

2 Expansion Rework items 1 through 6, asking questions about items in the classroom or places at the university. Ex: **¿Qué objeto está encima de la mesa? ¿Dónde está la ventana?**

3 Suggestion Using **Transparency #14** or the drawing in the textbook, quickly have volunteers name the objects they see in the illustration.

3 Expansion Assign one student the role of **vendedor(a)** and another the role of **cliente/a**. Then name one of the items in the drawing and ask the participants to create a conversation as in the activity.

TEACHING OPTIONS

Extra Practice Use a large world map (one with Spanish labels is best), **Transparencies #1–#8**, and/or the maps on the inside covers of the textbook to ask students where countries and cities are in relation to each other on the map. Ex: **¿Bolivia está a la derecha del Brasil? ¿Uruguay está más cerca de Chile o del Ecuador? ¿Qué país está entre Colombia y Costa Rica? ¿Está Puerto Rico a la izquierda de la República Dominicana?**

Small Groups Have each group member think of a country or well-known location on campus and describe it with progressively more specific statements. After each statement, the other group members guess what country or location it is. Ex: **Es un país. Está en Europa. Esta cerca de España. Está a la izquierda de Italia y Suiza. Es Francia**.

4 Expansion After students have worked through the items, ask the same questions of selected individuals. Then expand on their answers by asking additional questions. Ex: **—¿Dónde estás los lunes a las diez de la mañana? —Estoy en la clase de español. —¿Dónde está la clase de español?**

5 Expansion Make copies of your campus map and distribute them to the class. Ask questions about where particular buildings are. Give yourself a starting point so that you can ask questions with as many prepositions as possible. Ex: **Estoy en la biblioteca. ¿Está lejos la librería?**

6 Expansion Call on students to share with the whole class the information they obtained.

Comunicación

NATIONAL communication STANDARDS

4 **¿Dónde estás...?** Get together with a partner and take turns asking each other where you are at these times. Answers will vary.

lunes / 10:00 a.m.
Estudiante 1: ¿Dónde estás los lunes a las diez de la mañana?
Estudiante 2: Estoy en la clase de español.

1. sábados / 6:00 a.m.
2. miércoles / 9:15 a.m.
3. lunes / 11:10 a.m.
4. jueves / 12:30 a.m.
5. viernes / 2:25 p.m.
6. martes / 3:50 p.m.
7. jueves / 5:45 p.m.
8. miércoles / 8:20 p.m.

5  **La ciudad universitaria** You are an exchange student at a Spanish university. Tell a classmate which buildings you are looking for and ask for their location relative to where you are. Answers will vary.

modelo

Estudiante 1: ¿La Facultad de Medicina está lejos?
Estudiante 2: No, está cerca. Está a la izquierda de la Facultad de Administración de Empresas.

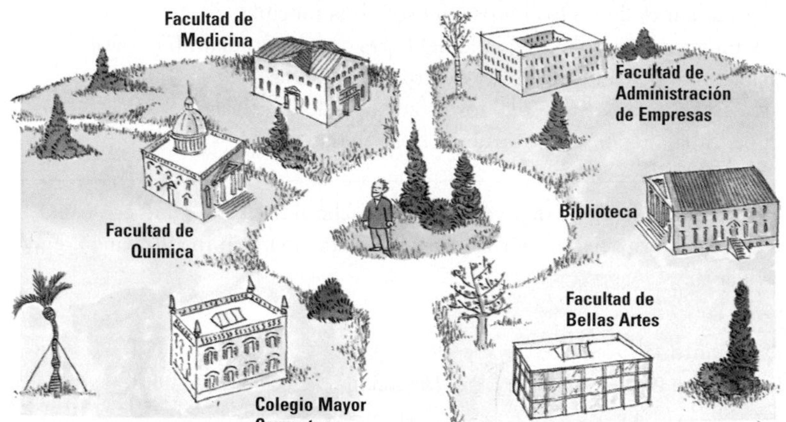

¡LENGUA VIVA!

La Facultad (*School*) de Filosofía y Letras includes departments, such as language, literature, philosophy, history, and linguistics. Fine Arts can be studied in **la Facultad de Bellas Artes.** In Spain the Business School is sometimes called **la Facultad de Ciencias Empresariales. Residencias estudiantiles** are referred to as **colegios mayores.**

6  **Entrevista** Use these questions to interview two classmates. Then switch roles. Answers will vary.

1. ¿Cómo estás?
2. ¿Dónde estamos ahora?
3. ¿Dónde está tu (*your*) compañero/a de cuarto ahora?
4. ¿Cuántos estudiantes hay en la clase de español?
5. ¿Quién(es) no está(n) en la clase hoy?
6. ¿A qué hora termina la clase hoy?
7. ¿Estudias mucho?
8. ¿Cuántas horas estudias para (*for*) una prueba?

TEACHING OPTIONS

Video Show the video again to give students more input containing **estar** and prepositions. Stop the video where appropriate to discuss how **estar** and prepositions were used and to ask comprehension questions.

Game Divide the class into two teams. Select a student from the first team to choose an item in the classroom and to write it down. Call on five students from the other team one at a time to ask questions in Spanish about where this item is. The first student can respond only with **sí, no, caliente** (*hot*), or **frío** (*cold*). If a team guesses the item within five tries, award it a point. If not, give the other team a point. The team with the most points wins.

2.4 Numbers 31–100

Los números 31 – 100

31	treinta y uno	**37**	treinta y siete	**50**	cincuenta
32	treinta y dos	**38**	treinta y ocho	**60**	sesenta
33	treinta y tres	**39**	treinta y nueve	**70**	setenta
34	treinta y cuatro	**40**	cuarenta	**80**	ochenta
35	treinta y cinco	**41**	cuarenta y uno	**90**	noventa
36	treinta y seis	**42**	cuarenta y dos	**100**	cien, ciento
			(and so on)		

- **Y** is used in most numbers from **31** through **99**.

Hay **ochenta y cinco** exámenes.
There are eighty-five exams.

Hay **cuarenta y dos** estudiantes.
There are forty-two students.

¿En qué clase hay más chicas?

En la de sociología... casi un ochenta y cinco por ciento.

- With numbers that end in **uno** (31, 41, etc.), **uno** becomes **un** before a masculine noun and **una** before a feminine noun.

Hay **treinta y un** chicos.
There are thirty-one guys.

Hay **treinta y una** chicas.
There are thirty-one girls.

- **Cien** is used before nouns and in counting. The words **un**, **una**, and **uno** are never used before **cien** in Spanish. **Ciento** is used for numbers over one hundred.

¿Cuántos libros hay? **Cientos.**
How many books are there? Hundreds.

Hay **cien** libros y **cien** sillas.
There are one hundred books and one hundred chairs.

¡INTÉNTALO! Provide the words for these numbers.

1. **56** cincuenta y seis
2. **31** treinta y uno
3. **84** ochenta y cuatro
4. **99** noventa y nueve
5. **43** cuarenta y tres
6. **68** sesenta y ocho
7. **72** setenta y dos
8. **35** treinta y cinco
9. **87** ochenta y siete
10. **59** cincuenta y nueve
11. **100** cien
12. **61** sesenta y uno
13. **96** noventa y seis
14. **74** setenta y cuatro
15. **42** cuarenta y dos

Section Goal

In **Estructura 2.4**, students will be introduced to numbers 31–100.

Instructional Resources
WB/VM: Workbook, pp. 19–20
Lab Manual, p. 12
Lab CD/MP3 ***Lección 2***
IRM: ***¡Inténtalo! & Práctica*** *Answers, pp. 199–200; Tapescript, pp. 6–10*
Info Gap Activities Booklet, pp. 5–8
Interactive CD-ROM
Companion website: www.vistahigherlearning.com
Presentations CD-ROM

Suggestions

- Review 0–30 by having the class count with you. When you reach 30, have individual students count through 39. Count 40 yourself and have students continue counting through 100.
- Write on the board numbers not included in the chart: 56, 68, 72, and so forth. Ask students to say the number in Spanish.
- Emphasize that from 31 to 99, numbers are written as three words (**treinta y nueve**).
- Remind students that **uno** changes into **un** and **una**, as in **veintiún** and **veintiuna**.
- Numbers 101 and greater are presented in **Lección 6**.

TEACHING OPTIONS

Extra Practice Do simple math problems (addition and subtraction) with numbers to 100. Include numbers 0–30 as well, for a well-balanced review. Remind students that **más** = *plus*, **menos** = *minus*, and **es/son** = *equals*.
Extra Practice Write the beginning of a series of numbers on the board and have students continue the sequence.
Ex: **5, 10, 15,...** or **3, 6, 9, 12,...**

Heritage Speakers Ask heritage speakers to give the house or apartment number where they live (they don't have to give the street name). Ask them to give the addresses in tens (**1471 = catorce setenta y uno**). Have volunteers write the numbers they say on the board.

1 Suggestion Point out that unlike some of their U.S. counterparts, college sports in the Hispanic world are not followed by the general public. Universities have sports teams, but their fans are usually limited to university students.

1 Expansion In pairs, have each student write three additional basketball scores and dictate them to his or her partner, who writes them down.

2 Suggestion Point out that when giving telephone numbers, the definite article **el** is used to refer to **el número: Es el noventa y uno,...**

2 Expansion Give actual phone numbers (yours, the department's, the bookstore's) as a dictation.

3 Expansion If individual departments or campus buildings have their own numbers, addresses, or mailstops, ask students to say them.

Práctica

1 Baloncesto Provide these basketball scores in Spanish.

1. Ohio State 76, Michigan 65 setenta y seis, sesenta y cinco
2. Florida 92, Florida State 84 noventa y dos, ochenta y cuatro
3. Stanford 58, UCLA 49 cincuenta y ocho, cuarenta y nueve
4. Purdue 81, Indiana 78 ochenta y uno, setenta y ocho
5. Princeton 67, Harvard 55 sesenta y siete, cincuenta y cinco
6. Duke 100, Virginia 91 cien, noventa y uno
7. Kansas 95, Colorado 53 noventa y cinco, cincuenta y tres
8. Texas 79, Oklahoma 47 setenta y nueve, cuarenta y siete
9. Army 86, Navy 71 ochenta y seis, setenta y uno
10. Kentucky 98, Tennessee 74 noventa y ocho, setenta y cuatro

NOTA CULTURAL

Basketball (**baloncesto** or **básquetbol**) is a popular sport in many Spanish-speaking countries. Spain, Puerto Rico, Argentina, and Mexico, for example, have national leagues and champion teams often go on to international competitions.

2 Números de teléfono What courses would you take if you were studying at a university in Spain? Take turns deciding and having your partner give you the phone number for enrollment information. Answers will vary.

modelo

Estudiante 1: Necesito tomar una clase de química.
Estudiante 2: El número del departamento es el noventa y uno, cuarenta y siete, uno, veintinueve, ochenta y siete.

NOTA CULTURAL

In Spanish-speaking countries, the number of digits in phone numbers may vary from four to seven; they are often said in pairs.

DIRECTORIO

Departamento	Número de teléfono
Administración de empresas	(91) 758-6562
Arte	(91) 944-1216
Biología	(91) 634-3211
Computación	(91) 472-2350
Contabilidad	(91) 419-7660
Economía	(91) 773-1382
Español	(91) 944-3915
Física	(91) 634-7148
Geografía	(91) 834-5238
Historia	(91) 834-3371
Literatura	(91) 552-6359
Psicología	(91) 564-8799
Química	(91) 471-2987
Sociología	(91) 837-2225

3 Números In pairs, take turns reading aloud telephone numbers at random from the list in **Actividad 2** without mentioning the associated department. Your partner must provide the department. Answers will vary.

modelo

Estudiante 1: (91) 564-8799.
Estudiante 2: Es el departamento de psicología.

TEACHING OPTIONS

Heritage Speakers Ask heritage speakers if they or members of their families say phone numbers in any particular manner other than the one presented.

Game Ask for two volunteers and station them at opposite ends of the board so neither one can see what the other is writing. Give a number from 0–100 for them to write on the board. If both students are correct, continue to give numbers until one writes an incorrect number. The winner continues on to play against another student.

Comunicación

4 **Precios** (*Prices*) With a partner, take turns asking how much the items in the ad cost.

AYUDA

una caja de *a box of*
un paquete de *a package of*

• • •

Note that in Spanish, a comma is used in place of a decimal point, which is the standard in the U.S.

U.S.	Spanish
$4.95	$4,95
$12.50	$12,50

Conversely, Spanish uses a period instead of a comma to indicate thousands.

U.S.	Spanish
1,500	1.500
50,000	50.000

modelo

Estudiante 1: *Deseo comprar papel. ¿Cuánto cuesta (How much does it cost)?*
Estudiante 2: *Un paquete cuesta (it costs) cuatro dólares y cuarenta y un centavos.*

5 **Entrevista** Find out the telephone numbers and e-mail addresses of four classmates.
Answers will vary.

AYUDA

arroba at (@)
punto *dot* (.)

modelo

Estudiante 1: *¿Cuál es tu (your) número de teléfono?*
Estudiante 2: *Es el 6-35-19-51.*
Estudiante 1: *¿Y tu dirección de correo electrónico?*
Estudiante 2: *Es jota-Smith-arroba-pe-ele-punto-e-de-u. (jsmith@pl.edu)*

Síntesis

6 **¿A qué distancia...?** Your instructor will give you and a partner incomplete charts that indicate the distances between Madrid and various locations. Fill in the missing information on your chart by asking your partner questions. Answers will vary.

modelo

Estudiante 1: *¿A qué distancia está Arganda del Rey?*
Estudiante 2: *Está a veintisiete kilómetros de Madrid.*

4 Suggestion Explain **¿cuánto cuesta...?** and present **dólares** and **centavos**.

4 Expansion Ask students how much they think common items (**un disco compacto, un video**) cost.

5 Suggestions

- Write your own e-mail address on the board as you pronounce it.
- Point out that **el correo electrónico** means e-mail.
- If students are reluctant to reveal their personal information, ask them to invent a phone number and e-mail address.
- Ask volunteers to share their phone numbers and e-mail addresses. Other students write them on the board.

6 Suggestions

- Divide the class into pairs and distribute the Info Gap Handouts from the Info Gap Activities Booklet that correspond to this activity. Explain that this type of activity is called an information-gap activity. In it, each partner has information that the other needs, and the way to get this information is by asking the partner questions.
- Point out and model **está a** [distance] **de...** to express distance.

Suggestion See the Info Gap Activities Booklet for an additional activity to practice the material presented in this section.

TEACHING OPTIONS

Small Groups In groups of three or four, have students think of a city or town within a 100-mile radius of your university city or town. They need to figure out how many miles away it is and what other cities or towns are nearby (**está cerca de...**). Then they get together with another group and read their descriptions. The other group has to guess which city or town is being described.

TPR Assign ten students a number from 0–100 and line them up in front of the class. Call out a number at random, and that student is to take a step forward. When two students have stepped forward, ask them to repeat their numbers. Then ask volunteers to add or subtract the two numbers given. Make sure the resulting sum is not greater than 100.

Section Goals

In **Lectura** students will:

- learn to use text formats to predict content
- read documents in Spanish

Instructional Resource
Companion website: www.vistahigherlearning.com

Estrategia Introduce the strategy. Point out that many documents have easily identifiable formats that can help readers predict content. Have students look at the document in the **Estrategia** box and ask them to name the recognizable elements:

- days of the week
- time
- classes

Ask what kind of document it is (a student's weekly schedule).

Cognados Have pairs of students scan **¡Español en Madrid!** and identify cognates and guess their meanings.

Examinar el texto Ask students what type of information is contained in **¡Español en Madrid!** (It's a brochure for a summer intensive Spanish language program.) Discuss elements of the recognizable format that helped them predict the content, such as headings, list of courses, course schedule with dates.

Lectura

Antes de leer

Estrategia

Predicting Content Through Formats

Recognizing the format of a document can help you to predict its content. For instance, invitations, greeting cards, and classified ads follow an easily identifiable format, which usually gives you a general idea of the information they contain. Look at the text and identify it based on its format.

	lunes	martes	miércoles	jueves	viernes
8:30	biología		biología		biología
9:00		historia		historia	
9:30	inglés		inglés		inglés
10:00					
10:30					
11:00					
12:00					
12:30					
1:00					
2:00	arte		arte		arte

If you guessed that this is a page from a student's schedule, you are correct. You can now infer that the document contains information about a student's weekly schedule, including days, times, and activities.

Cognados

With a classmate, make a list of the cognates in the text and guess their English meanings. What do cognates reveal about the content of the document?

Examinar el texto

Look at the format of the document entitled ***¡Español en Madrid!*** What type of text is it? What information do you expect to find in a document of this kind?

¡ESPAÑOL EN MADRID!

UAM

Programa de Cursos Intensivos de Español
Universidad Autónoma de Madrid

Madrid, la capital cultural de Europa, y la UAM te ofrecen cursos intensivos de verano° para aprender° español como nunca antes°.

Después de leer

Correspondencias

Provide the letter of each item in Column B that matches the words in Column A. Two items will not be used.

A	B
1. profesores f	a. (34) 91 523 4500
2. vivienda h	b. (34) 91 524 0210
3. Madrid d	c. 23 junio – 30 julio
4. número de teléfono a	d. capital cultural de Europa
5. Español 2B c	e. 16 junio – 22 julio
6. número de fax g	f. especializados en enseñar español como lengua extranjera
	g. (34) 91 523 4623
	h. familias españolas

TEACHING OPTIONS

Extra Practice Have students write as homework a weekly schedule (**horario semanal**) of a friend or family member. Ask them to label the days of the week in Spanish and add notes for that person's appointments and activities as well. In class, ask students questions about the schedules they wrote.
Ex: **¿Qué clase toma _____ hoy? ¿Trabaja _____ manaña?**
¿Cuántos días trabaja _____ esta semana?

Heritage Speakers Ask heritage speakers who have attended a university or institution of higher education in the Spanish-speaking world to describe what their schedule there was like, comparing and contrasting it with their schedule now. Invite them to make other comparisons between American or Canadian institutions of higher education and those in the Spanish-speaking world.

¿Dónde?
En el campus de la UAM, edificio° de la Facultad de Filosofía y Letras.

¿Quiénes son los profesores?
Son todos hablantes nativos del español y catedráticos° de la UAM especializados en enseñar el español como lengua extranjera.

¿Qué niveles se ofrecen?
Se ofrecen tres niveles° básicos:
1. Español Elemental, A, B y C
2. Español Intermedio, A y B
3. Español Avanzado, A y B

Viviendas
Para estudiantes extranjeros se ofrece vivienda° con familias españolas.

¿Cuándo?
Este verano desde° el 16 de junio hasta el 10 de agosto. Los cursos tienen una duración de 6 semanas.

Cursos	Empieza°	Termina
Español 1A	16 junio	22 julio
Español 1B	23 junio	30 julio
Español 1C	30 junio	10 agosto
Español 2A	16 junio	22 julio
Español 2B	23 junio	30 julio
Español 3A	16 junio	22 julio
Español 3B	23 junio	30 julio

Información
Para mayor información, sirvan comunicarse con la siguiente° oficina:

Universidad Autónoma de Madrid
Programa de Español como Lengua Extranjera
Ctra. Colmenar Viejo, Km. 15
28049 Madrid, ESPAÑA
Tel. (34) 91 523 4500
Fax (34) 91 523 4623
www.uam.es

verano *summer* **aprender** *to learn* **nunca antes** *never before* **edificio** *building* **catedráticos** *professors* **niveles** *levels* **vivienda** *housing* **desde** *from* **Empieza** *Begins* **siguiente** *following*

Correspondencias Go over the answers with the whole class or assign pairs of students to work together to check each other's answers.

¿Cierto o falso? Continue the activity with true/false statements such as these: **1. El campus de la UAM está en la Ciudad de México. (Falso; está en Madrid.) 2. Los cursos terminan en junio. (Falso; terminan en julio y agosto.) 3. Hay un curso de español intermedio. (Falso; hay dos cursos.) 4. Los cursos se ofrecen en el verano. (Cierto) 5. Hay una residencia estudiantil para los estudiantes extranjeros en el campus. (Falso; los estudiantes extranjeros viven con familias españolas.) 6. Hay un número en la universidad para más información. (Cierto) 7. Todos los profesores son hablantes nativos. (Cierto) 8. Los cursos tienen una duración de doce semanas. (Falso; tienen una duración de seis semanas.)**

¿Cierto o falso?

Indicate whether each statement is **cierto** (*true*) or **falso** (*false*). Then correct the false statements.

	Cierto	Falso
1. La Universidad Autónoma de Madrid ofrece (*offers*) cursos intensivos de italiano. Ofrece cursos intensivos de español.	❍	✓
2. La lengua nativa de los profesores del programa es el inglés. La lengua nativa de los profesores es el español.	❍	✓
3. Los cursos de español son en la Facultad de Ciencias. Son en el edificio de la Facultad de Filosofía y Letras.	❍	✓
4. Los estudiantes pueden vivir (*can live*) con familias españolas.	✓	❍
5. La universidad que ofrece los cursos intensivos está en Salamanca. Está en Madrid.	❍	✓
6. Español 3B termina en agosto. Termina en julio.	❍	✓
7. Si deseas información sobre (*about*) los cursos intensivos de español, es posible llamar al (34) 91 523 4500.	✓	❍
8. Español 1A empieza en julio. Empieza en junio.	❍	✓

TEACHING OPTIONS

Variación léxica Explain that in Spanish dates are usually written in the order of day/month/year rather than month/day/year, as they are in the United States and Canada. Someone from Mexico with a birthdate of July 5, 1986, therefore, would write his or her birthdate as 5/7/86. To avoid confusion, the month is often written with a roman numeral, 5/VII/86.

Pairs Provide students with magazines and newspapers in Spanish. Have pairs of students work together to look for documents in Spanish with easily recognizable formats, such as classified ads or advertisements in periodicals or on the Internet. Ask them to use cognates and other context clues to predict the content. Then have partners present their examples and findings to the class.

Section Goals

In **Escritura** students will:

- brainstorm and organize their ideas for writing
- write a description of themselves
- incorporate lesson vocabulary and structures

Estrategia Discuss information students might want to include in a self-description, recording their suggestions on the board in Spanish. Quickly review structures students will include in their writing, such as **me gusta** and **no me gusta** as well as the first person singular of several verbs, for example: **soy, estoy, tomo, trabajo, estudio**.

Tema Copy on the board the brief chat room description for Alicia Roberts, leaving blanks where her name, course of study, and university name appear. At the end, add the sentences **Me gusta** _____. and **No me gusta** _____. Model completing the description orally with your own information and then ask volunteers to complete it with their own information.

Escritura

Estrategia

Brainstorming

How do you find ideas to write about? In the early stages of writing, brainstorming can help you generate ideas on a specific topic. You should spend ten to fifteen minutes brainstorming and jotting down any ideas about the topic that occur to you. Whenever possible, try to write down your ideas in Spanish. Express your ideas in single words or phrases, and jot them down in any order. While brainstorming, don't worry about whether your ideas are good or bad. Selecting and organizing ideas should be the second stage of your writing. Remember that the more ideas you write down while you're brainstorming, the more options you'll have to choose from later when you start to organize your ideas.

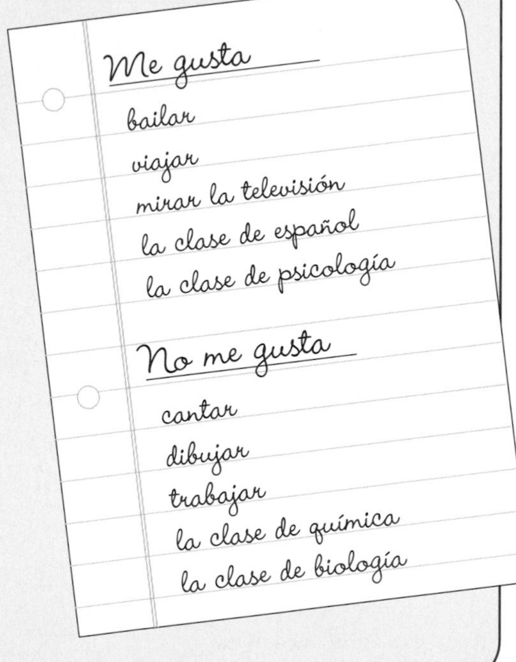

Tema

Una descripción

Write a description of yourself to post in a chat room on a website in order to meet Spanish-speaking people. Include this information in your description:

- Your name and where you are from, and a photo (optional) of yourself
- Your major and where you go to school
- The courses you are taking
- Where you work if you have a job
- Some of your likes and dislikes

¡Hola! Me llamo Alicia Roberts. Estudio matemáticas en la Universidad de Nueva York.

TEACHING OPTIONS

Proofreading Activity Copy the following sentences containing mistakes onto the board or a transparency as a proofreading activity to do with the whole class.

1. **¡Hola! Me llama Roberto García y estoy estudiante de lenguas extranjeras.**
2. **La biblioteca es al lado de la Facultad de Medicina, ¿sí?**
3. **Hay treinta y un centavo encima la mesa.**
4. **Sara, necesitas a estudiar más, si deseas a tomar la clase de psicología.**
5. **¿Te no gustas la clase de química, Carlos?**
6. **Los estudiantes escuchar la música rock en español sobre la mesa, ¿verdad?**
7. **¿Porque necesitas ciento dólares, Francisco?**
8. **¿Adónde son las tres chicas de España?**

Plan de escritura

1 Ideas y organización

Spend ten to fifteen minutes brainstorming information to put in your description. Then, on a separate sheet of paper, write the five points from the **Tema** section, leaving some blank space under each point. In a logical order, list under the corresponding points the ideas you just brainstormed. Eliminate ideas that don't pertain to the topic and add any missing information. Try to write your ideas in Spanish; doing so will make your first draft easier.

2 Primer borrador

Using the lists you prepared in **Ideas y organización,** write the first draft of your description.

3 Comentario

Exchange papers with a classmate and comment on each other's work, using these questions as a guide. Mention what you like about the person's writing, such as a certain description or style.

a. Does the description include all necessary information? Is any information extraneous?
b. Does the description include a sufficient number of details?
c. Are the ideas expressed clearly? Do they have the proper focus?
d. Do the ideas flow logically from one to another?
e. Do you have any other suggestions for making the description more interesting or complete?
f. Do you see any spelling or grammatical errors?

4 Redacción

Revise your first draft, keeping in mind your classmate's comments. Also incorporate any new ideas you may have. Before handing in the final version, use these suggestions to help you review your work:

a. Underline each verb and make sure that it agrees with its subject.
b. Check the gender and number of each noun and article.
c. Check your spelling and punctuation.

5 Evaluación y progreso

In groups, take turns reading your descriptions aloud. Point out the best three features of each description, then choose one to read aloud to the class. After your instructor has returned your paper, review the comments and corrections. On a separate sheet of paper, write the heading **Anotaciones para mejorar** (*Notes for improving*) **la escritura,** and list your most common errors so that you can avoid them in the future. Place this list and your corrected description in a folder labeled **Carpeta de trabajos.** This will become your writing portfolio, which you will use to review your progress.

Comentario

- Go over questions a–f with the whole class so peer readers understand their task. Then have pairs of students exchange descriptions.
- Have students read **Redacción** as homework. Ask them to rewrite their drafts incorporating the peer comments and following the directions in **Redacción**.

Evaluación y progreso
Divide the class into groups of five or six and give them time for each student to read his or her description. Then ask one member of each group to read his or her description aloud.

Writing Sample Here is an example of a well-written self-description.

¡Muy buenos días! Soy José Miguel Gutiérrez. Soy de Nogales, Arizona. Soy estudiante de computación en la Universidad de Arizona. Tomo cuatro clases este semestre. Tomo clases de computación, matemáticas, inglés y español. Me gusta estudiar, leer y trabajar, pero también me gusta bailar y cantar. También trabajo en la biblioteca. Trabajo los sábados de las ocho a las doce de la mañana.

EVALUATION: Descripción

Criteria	Scale
Content	1 2 3 4 5
Organization	1 2 3 4 5
Use of vocabulary	1 2 3 4 5
Grammatical accuracy	1 2 3 4 5

Scoring	
Excellent	18–20 points
Good	14–17 points
Satisfactory	10–13 points
Unsatisfactory	< 10 points

Section Goals

In **Escuchar** students will:

- listen for cognates in a short paragraph
- answer questions based on the content of a recorded conversation

Instructional Resources
Textbook CD
IRM: Tapescript, p. 86

Estrategia
Script 1. La democracia es una forma de gobierno. 2. A mí me gustan los conciertos, las obras de teatro y la danza.

Suggestion Invite students to look at the photo and describe what they see. Guide them to guess where they think Armando and Julia are and what they are talking about.

Ahora escucha
Script ARMANDO: ¡Hola, Julia! ¿Cómo estás?
JULIA: Bien. ¿Y tú, Armando?
A: Bien, gracias. ¿Qué tal tus clases?
J: Van bien.
A: ¿Tomas biología?
J: Este semestre no. Pero sí tomo astronomía y geología… los lunes, miércoles y viernes.
A: ¿Sólo dos? ¿Qué otras clases tomas?
J: Italiano y cálculo, los martes y jueves. ¿Y tú?
A: Los lunes, miércoles y viernes tomo antropología, filosofía y japonés. Los martes y jueves tomo italiano y cálculo.
J: ¿A qué hora es tu clase de italiano?
A: A las nueve, con la profesora Menotti.
J: Yo también tomo italiano los martes y jueves con la profesora Menotti, pero a las once.

Escuchar

Estrategia

Listening for cognates

You already know that cognates are words that have similar spellings and meanings in two or more languages: for example, *group* and **grupo** or *stereo* and **estéreo.** Listen for cognates to increase your comprehension of spoken Spanish.

To help you practice this strategy, you will now listen to two sentences. Make a list of all the cognates you hear.

Preparación

Based on the photograph, who do you think Armando and Julia are? What do you think they are talking about?

Ahora escucha 

Now you are going to hear Armando and Julia's conversation. Make a list of the cognates they use. Then complete the Spanish sentence with the topic of their conversation.

Armando	Julia
clases, biología	semestre, astronomía
antropología, filosofía	geología, italiano
japonés, italiano	cálculo, clase
cálculo, profesora	italiano, profesora

Based on your knowledge of cognates, decide whether the following statements are **cierto** or **falso**.

	Cierto	Falso
1. Armando y Julia hablan de la familia.	○	✓
2. Armando y Julia toman una clase de matemáticas.	✓	○
3. Julia toma clases de ciencias.	✓	○
4. Armando estudia lenguas extranjeras.	✓	○
5. Julia toma una clase de religión.	○	✓

Comprensión

Preguntas

Answer these questions about Armando and Julia's conversation.

1. ¿Qué clases toma Armando?
   Toma antropología, filosofía, japonés, italiano, y cálculo.
2. ¿Qué clases toma Julia?
   Toma astronomía, geología, italiano, y cálculo.

Seleccionar

Choose the answer that best completes each sentence.

1. Armando toma ___b___ clases en la universidad.
   a. cuatro b. cinco c. seis
2. Julia toma dos clases de ___c___.
   a. matemáticas b. lengua c. ciencia
3. Armando toma italiano y ___b___.
   a. astronomía b. japonés c. geología
4. Armando y Julia estudian ___c___ los martes y jueves.
   a. filosofía b. matemáticas c. italiano

Preguntas personales Answers will vary.

1. ¿Cuántas clases tomas tú este semestre?
2. ¿Qué clases tomas tú este semestre?
3. ¿Qué clases te gustan y qué clases no te gustan?

recursos

TEXT CD
Lección 2

Proyecto

Representa a una universidad

Imagine that you are enrolled in a university in Spain as part of a "Year Abroad" program. You're about to return home, and the Spanish university has asked you to be its goodwill ambassador. In this role, you will disseminate information about the university in Spain to your classmates.

1 Diseña un cartel

Create a vibrant and appealing poster that is intended to attract students to study in your program. Using the research tools found in **Recursos para la investigación,** select the institution you would like to represent. Make notes about programs and courses the university offers, and gather photographs that illustrate the school's appeal and the town or city where it is located. Then create your poster, which might include these elements:

- A simple, descriptive title
- A few lines inviting students to study at the university
- Photos of university locations and/or a campus map
- A summary of the courses offered
- Photos and a description of the town where the university is located

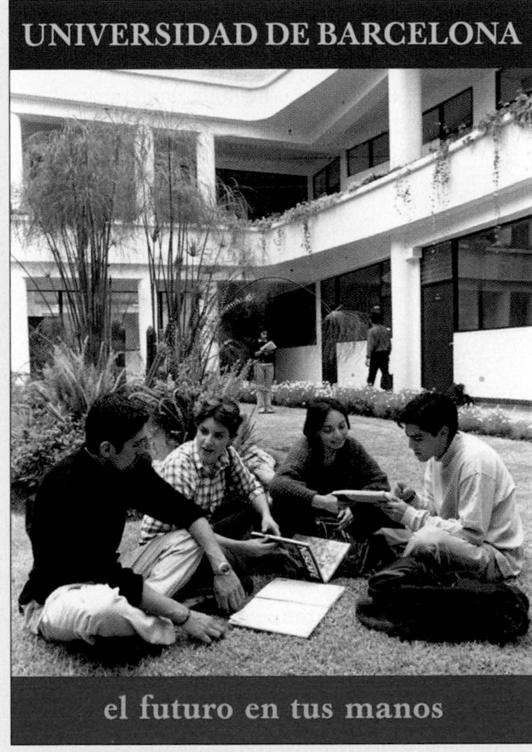

UNIVERSIDAD DE BARCELONA
el futuro en tus manos

2 Presenta la información

Give a brief presentation to your classmates about the Spanish university. Bring your poster and use it as a guide. Try to convince your classmates of the benefits of studying at this Spanish university.

recursos para la investigación

Internet Palabras clave: Spain, Spanish, university, universities

Comunidad Exchange students, faculty members, and residents in your community who are from Spain or have lived in Spain

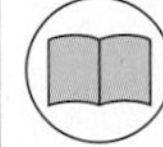
Biblioteca Encyclopedias, almanacs, guidebooks, travel magazines

Otros recursos Your school's International Studies Office, the Spanish embassy or consulates, and travel agencies

Section Goals

In **Proyecto** students will:

- create a poster for a "Year Abroad" program in Spain
- use Spanish as they research and interact with the wider world
- incorporate Spanish in an oral presentation

Suggestion Students might need a week to complete the project, so at the beginning of that time period, have them open their books to this page and glance over **Proyecto**. Explain that they are going to use their research skills to create a poster (**un cartel**) that tells about a "Year Abroad" program at a university in Spain.

Diseña un cartel

- Information on the Internet about Spanish universities will usually appear in Spanish. Tell students to use cognates and the formats of web pages to interpret what they find. Encourage them to try to decipher as much of the page as they can before looking at its translation, if available.
- Remind students to search in both Spanish and English for key words or phrases. Possible Spanish key words: **universidades españolas, estudiantes extranjeros, programa internacional, estudio internacional**

Presenta la información
Display posters around the classroom after students have given their presentations.

EVALUATION: Cartel

Criteria	Scale
Content	1 2 3 4
Comprehensibility	1 2 3 4
Organization	1 2 3 4
Accuracy	1 2 3 4
Visual appeal	1 2 3 4

Scoring	
Excellent	18–20 points
Good	14–17 points
Satisfactory	10–13 points
Unsatisfactory	< 10 points

2 panorama

Section Goal

In **Panorama**, students will receive comprehensible input by reading about the culture and economy of Spain.

Instructional Resources
Transparencies, #7, #8, #15
WB/VM: Workbook, pp. 21–22; Video Activities, pp. 251–252
***Panorama cultural** DVD/Video*
Interactive CD-ROM
IRM: Videoscript, p. 127
Companion website: www.vistahigherlearning.com
Presentations CD-ROM

Suggestion Project **Transparency #15** or have students use the map in their books to find the places mentioned. Explain that the Canary Islands are located in the Atlantic Ocean off the northwestern coast of Africa. Point out the photos that accompany the map on this page.

El país en cifras After **Idiomas** has been read, associate the regional languages with the larger map by asking questions such as: **¿Hablan catalán en Barcelona? ¿Qué idioma hablan en Madrid?** Point out that the names of languages may be capitalized as labels on maps, but are not capitalized when they appear in running text.

¡Increíble pero cierto! In addition to festivals related to economic and agricultural resources, Spain has many festivals rooted in its deep Catholic tradition. Among the most famous is **Semana Santa** (Holy Week) which is celebrated annually in Seville, and many other towns and cities, with great reverence and pageantry.

España

National Standards: connections, cultures

El país en cifras

- **Área:** 504.750 km² (kilómetros cuadrados) ó 194.884 millas cuadradas°, incluyendo las islas Baleares y las islas Canarias
- **Población:** 39.874.000
- **Capital:** Madrid—3.976.000
- **Ciudades principales:** Barcelona—2.729.000, Valencia—2.149.171, Sevilla—1.727.304, Zaragoza—827.730

SOURCE: Instituto Nacional de Estadística

- **Moneda°:** euro
- **Idiomas°:** español o castellano, catalán, gallego, valenciano, eusquera

Bandera de España

Españoles célebres

- **Miguel de Cervantes,** escritor° (1547–1616)
- **Pedro Almodóvar,** director de cine° (1949–)
- **Rosa Montero,** escritora y periodista° (1951–)
- **Pedro Duque,** astronauta (1963–)
- **Arantxa Sánchez Vicario,** tenista (1971–)

millas cuadradas *square miles* Moneda *Currency* Idiomas *Languages* escritor *writer* cine *film* periodista *reporter* pueblo *town* Cada año *Every year* Durante todo un día *All day long* miles *thousands* se tiran *throw at each other* varias toneladas *many tons*

El baile flamenco

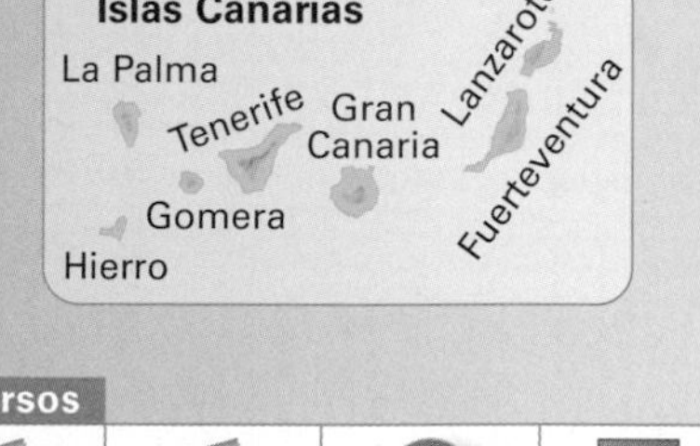

recursos

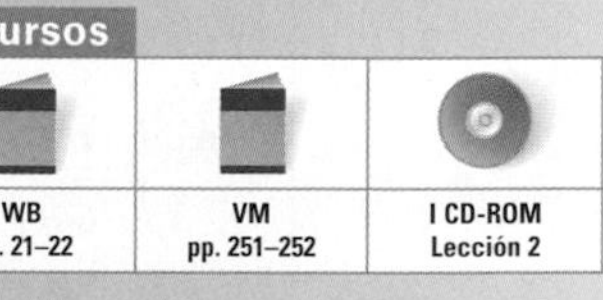

WB pp. 21–22	VM pp. 251–252	I CD-ROM Lección 2	vistahigher learning.com

¡Increíble pero cierto!

En Buñol, un pueblo° de Valencia, la producción de tomates es un recurso económico muy importante. Cada año° se celebra el festival de *La Tomatina*. Durante todo un día°, miles de personas se tiran° tomates. Llegan turistas de todo el país, y se usan varias toneladas° de tomates.

TEACHING OPTIONS

Heritage Speakers Paella, the national dish of Spain, is the ancestor of the popular Latin American dish, **arroz con pollo**. Ask heritage speakers if they know of any dishes traditional in their families that have their roots in Spanish cuisine. Invite them to describe the dish to the class.

Variación léxica Tell students that they may also see the word **eusquera** spelled **euskera** and **euskara**. The letter **k** is used in Spanish only in words of foreign origin. **Euskera,** or **euskara,** is the name of the Basque language in Basque, a language that linguists believe is unrelated to any other known language. **Euskera** is sometimes spelled **eusquera**, following the principles of Spanish orthography. The Spanish name for Basque is **vascuence** or **vasco**.

Lugares • La Universidad de Salamanca

La Universidad de Salamanca, fundada en 1218 (mil doscientos dieciocho), es la más antigua° de España. Más de 35.000 (treinta y cinco mil) estudiantes toman clases en la universidad. La universidad está en la ciudad de Salamanca, famosa por sus edificios° históricos, tales como° los puentes° romanos y las catedrales góticas.

Economía • La Unión Europea

Desde° 1992 (mil novecientos noventa y dos) España es miembro de la Unión Europea, un grupo de países europeos que trabaja para desarrollar° una política° económica y social común en Europa. La moneda de los países de la Unión Europea es el euro.

Las meninas, Diego Velázquez, 1656.

Artes • Velázquez y el Prado

El Prado, en Madrid, es uno de los museos más famosos del mundo°. En el Prado hay pinturas° importantes de Botticelli, del Greco, y de los españoles Goya y Velázquez. *Las Meninas* es la obra más conocida° de Diego Velázquez, pintor° oficial de la corte real° durante el siglo° XVII.

Comida • La paella

La paella es uno de los platos más típicos de España. Siempre se prepara° con arroz° y azafrán°, pero hay diferentes recetas°. La paella valenciana, por ejemplo, es de pollo° y conejo°, y la paella marinera es de mariscos°.

Una playa de Ibiza

¿Qué aprendiste? Completa las frases con la información adecuada.

1. La Unión Europea trabaja para desarrollar una política económica común en Europa.
2. El arroz y el azafrán son ingredientes básicos de la paella.
3. El Prado está en Madrid.
4. La universidad más antigua de España es la Universidad de Salamanca.
5. La ciudad de Salamanca es famosa por sus edificios históricos, tales como los puentes romanos.
6. El gallego es una de las lenguas oficiales de España.

Conexión Internet Investiga estos temas en el sitio **www.vistahigherlearning.com.**

1. Busca (*Look for*) información sobre la Universidad de Salamanca u otra universidad española. ¿Qué cursos ofrece (*does it offer*)? ¿Ofrece tu universidad cursos similares?
2. Busca información sobre un español o una española célebre (por ejemplo, un(a) político/a, un actor, una actriz, un(a) artista). ¿De qué parte de España es, y por qué es célebre?

más antigua *oldest* edificios *buildings* tales como *such as* puentes *bridges* Desde *Since* desarrollar *develop* política *policy* mundo *world* pinturas *paintings* más conocida *best-known* pintor *painter* corte real *royal court* siglo *century* Siempre se prepara *It is always prepared* arroz *rice* azafrán *saffron* recetas *recipes* pollo *chicken* conejo *rabbit* mariscos *seafood*

La Universidad de Salamanca The University of Salamanca hosts many programs for foreign students, and your campus foreign-study office may have brochures. One of the oldest universities in Europe, Salamanca is famous for its medieval buildings and student musical societies called **tunas**.

La Unión Europea Have students use the Internet, a newspaper, or a bank to learn the current exchange rate for euros on the international market.

Velázquez y el Prado Point out **la infanta Margarita**, the royal princess, with her attendants. The name **Las meninas** comes from the Portuguese word for "girls" used to refer to royal attendants. Reflected in the mirror are Margarita's parents, **los reyes Felipe IV y Mariana de Asturias**. Have students find Velázquez himself, standing paintbrush in hand, before an enormous canvas. You may wish to ask students to research the identity of the man in the doorway.

La paella Pairs can role-play a restaurant scene: the customer asks the waiter/waitress about the ingredients in the paella, then chooses **paella valenciana** or **paella marinera.**

Conexión Internet Students will find supporting Internet activities and links at **www.vistahigherlearning.com**.

TEACHING OPTIONS

Variación léxica Regional culture and languages have remained strong in Spain despite efforts made in the past to suppress them in the name of national unity. The language that has come to be called *Spanish*, **español,** is the language of the region of north central Spain called **Castilla**. Because Spain was unified under the Kingdom of Castile at the end of the Middle Ages, the language of Castile, **castellano**, became the principal language of government, business, and literature. Even today one is likely to hear Spanish referred to by Spanish speakers as **castellano** or **español**. Efforts to suppress the regional languages, though often harsh, were ineffective, and after the death of the dictator Francisco Franco and the return of power to regional governing bodies, the languages of Spain were given co-official status with Spanish in the regions where they are spoken.

Instructional Resources
Vocabulary CD
Lab Manual, p. 12
*Lab CD/MP3 **Lección 2***
IRM: Tapescript, pp. 6–10
*Testing Program: **Pruebas**, pp. 13–24*
Testing Program Audio CD
Test Files CD-ROM

La clase y la universidad

el borrador	*eraser*
la clase	*class*
el/la compañero/a de clase	*classmate*
el/la compañero/a de cuarto	*roommate*
el escritorio	*desk*
el/la estudiante	*student*
el libro	*book*
el mapa	*map*
la mesa	*table*
la mochila	*backpack*
el papel	*paper*
la papelera	*wastebasket*
la pizarra	*blackboard*
la pluma	*pen*
el/la profesor(a)	*teacher*
la puerta	*door*
el reloj	*clock; watch*
la silla	*seat*
la tiza	*chalk*
la ventana	*window*
la biblioteca	*library*
la cafetería	*cafeteria*
la casa	*house; home*
el estadio	*stadium*
el laboratorio	*laboratory*
la librería	*bookstore*
la residencia estudiantil	*dormitory*
la universidad	*university; college*
el curso, la materia	*course*
la especialización	*major*
el examen	*test; exam*
el horario	*schedule*
la prueba	*test; quiz*
el semestre	*semester*
la tarea	*homework*
el trimestre	*trimester; quarter*

recursos

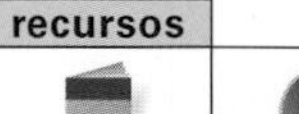	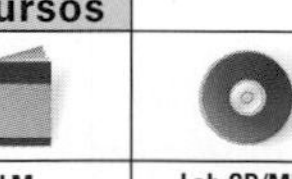	
LM p. 12	Lab CD/MP3 Lección 2	Vocab CD Lección 2

Las materias

la administración de empresas	*business administration*
el arte	*art*
la biología	*biology*
las ciencias	*sciences*
la computación	*computer science*
la contabilidad	*accounting*
la economía	*economics*
el español	*Spanish*
la física	*physics*
la geografía	*geography*
la historia	*history*
las humanidades	*humanities*
el inglés	*English*
las lenguas extranjeras	*foreign languages*
la literatura	*literature*
las matemáticas	*mathematics*
la música	*music*
el periodismo	*journalism*
la psicología	*psychology*
la química	*chemistry*
la sociología	*sociology*

Preposiciones

al lado de	*next to; beside*
a la derecha de	*to the right of*
a la izquierda de	*to the left of*
en	*in; on*
cerca de	*near*
con	*with*
debajo de	*below; under*
delante de	*in front of*
detrás de	*behind*
encima de	*on top of*
entre	*between; among*
lejos de	*far from*
sin	*without*
sobre	*on; over*

Palabras adicionales

¿Adónde?	*(to) Where?*
ahora	*now*
¿Cuál?, ¿Cuáles?	*Which?; Which one(s)?*
¿Por qué?	*Why?*
porque	*because*

Verbos

bailar	*to dance*
buscar	*to look for*
caminar	*to walk*
cantar	*to sing*
cenar	*to have dinner*
comprar	*to buy*
contestar	*to answer*
conversar	*to converse, to chat*
desayunar	*to have breakfast*
descansar	*to rest*
desear	*to wish; to desire*
dibujar	*to draw*
enseñar	*to teach*
escuchar la radio/música	*to listen (to) the radio/music*
esperar (+ *inf.*)	*to wait (for); to hope*
estar	*to be*
estudiar	*to study*
explicar	*to explain*
hablar	*to talk; to speak*
llegar	*to arrive*
llevar	*to carry*
mirar	*to look (at); to watch*
necesitar (+ *inf.*)	*to need*
practicar	*to practice*
preguntar	*to ask (a question)*
preparar	*to prepare*
regresar	*to return*
terminar	*to end; to finish*
tomar	*to take; to drink*
trabajar	*to work*
viajar	*to travel*

Los días de la semana

¿Cuándo?	*When?*
¿Qué día es hoy?	*What day is it?*
Hoy es…	*Today is …*
la semana	*week*
lunes	*Monday*
martes	*Tuesday*
miércoles	*Wednesday*
jueves	*Thursday*
viernes	*Friday*
sábado	*Saturday*
domingo	*Sunday*

Numbers 31–100	*See page 57.*
Expresiones útiles	*See page 41.*

La familia

3

Communicative Goals

You will learn how to:

- Talk about your family and friends
- Describe people and things
- Express ownership

Lesson Goals

In **Lección 3** students will be introduced to the following:

- terms for family relationships
- names of various professions
- descriptive adjectives
- possessive adjectives
- the present tense of common regular **–er** and **–ir** verbs
- the present tense of **tener** and **venir**
- context clues to unlock meaning of unfamiliar words
- using idea maps when writing
- how to write a friendly letter
- strategies for asking clarification in oral communication
- researching and creating a Spanish family tree
- cultural and historical information about Ecuador

A primera vista Here are some additional questions you can ask based on the photo: **¿Cuándo regresas a casa de tu familia? ¿Estudias lejos o cerca de la casa de tu familia? ¿De qué conversas con tu familia cuando regresas?**

A PRIMERA VISTA

- **¿Hay cuatro personas en la foto?**
- **¿Hay una mujer a la izquierda? ¿Y a la derecha?**
- **¿Está el hombre lejos de la mujer o al lado de ella?**
- **¿Conversan ellos? ¿Trabajan? ¿Viajan? ¿Caminan?**

INSTRUCTIONAL RESOURCES

Workbook/Video Manual: WB Activities, pp. 23–36
Laboratory Manual: Lab Activities, pp. 13–18
Workbook/Video Manual: Video Activities, pp. 217–218; pp. 253–254
Instructor's Resource Manual: **Hojas de actividades**, p. 164; **Vocabulario adicional**, pp. 180–181; **¡Inténtalo!** & **Práctica** Answers, p. 201; **Fotonovela** Translations, p. 140; Textbook CD Tapescript, p. 87; Lab CDs Tapescript, pp. 11–15; **Fotonovela** Videoscript, p. 105; **Panorama cultural** Videoscript, p. 128
Info Gap Activities Booklet, pp. 9–12
Overhead Transparencies: #5, #6, #16, #17, #18
Lab Audio CD/MP3 **Lección 3**
Panorama cultural DVD/Video
Fotonovela DVD/Video
Testing Program, pp. 25–36
Testing Program Audio CD
Test Files CD-ROM
Companion website
Presentations CD-ROM
Textbook CD
Vocabulary CD
Interactive CD-ROM
Video CD-ROM
Web-SAM

Section Goals

In **Contextos**, students will learn and practice
- terms for family relationships
- names of professions

Instructional Resources
Transparencies, #16, #17
Textbook CD
Vocabulary CD
WB/VM: Workbook, pp. 23–24
Lab Manual, p. 13
Lab CD/MP3 ***Lección 3***
IRM: ***Vocab. adicional****, p. 181;*
Práctica *Answers, p. 201;*
Tapescript, pp. 11–15; p. 87
Interactive CD-ROM
Companion website:
www.vistahigherlearning.com
Presentations CD-ROM

Suggestions

- Point out the meanings of plural family terms to students so they are aware that the masculine plural forms can refer to mixed groups of males and females:
  los hermanos *brothers; siblings; brothers and sisters*
  los primos *male cousins; male and female cousins*
  los sobrinos *nephews; nieces and nephews*
  los tíos *uncles; aunts and uncles*
- Introduce active lesson vocabulary. Ask: **¿Cómo se llama tu hermano?** Ask another student **¿Cómo se llama el hermano de ____?** Work your way through various family relationships.
- Project **Transparency #16.** Point out that the family tree is drawn from the point of view of José Miguel Pérez Santoro. Have students refer to the family tree to answer your questions about it. Ex: **¿Cómo se llama la madre de Víctor?**
- Discuss the pattern of Hispanic last names (**apellidos**). If your name follows this pattern, you may wish to use it as an example. Then ask volunteers to say what their names would be.
- You can find vocabulary on pets, should students inquire about it, in **Vocabulario adicional: Más vocabulario para hablar de la familia**, from the IRM.

La familia

Más vocabulario

los abuelos	*grandparents*
el/la bisabuelo/a	*great-grandfather/great-grandmother*
la familia	*family*
el/la gemelo/a	*twin*
el/la hermanastro/a	*stepbrother/stepsister*
el/la hijastro/a	*stepson/stepdaughter*
la madrastra	*stepmother*
el medio hermano/ la media hermana	*half-brother/ half-sister*
el padrastro	*stepfather*
los padres	*parents*
los parientes	*relatives*
el/la cuñado/a	*brother-in-law/ sister-in-law*
la nuera	*daughter-in-law*
el/la suegro/a	*father-in-law/ mother-in-law*
el yerno	*son-in-law*
el/la amigo/a	*friend*
el apellido	*last name*
la gente	*people*
el/la muchacho/a	*boy/girl*
el/la niño/a	*child*
el/la novio/a	*boyfriend/girlfriend*
la persona	*person*
el/la artista	*artist*
el/la ingeniero/a	*engineer*
el/la doctor(a), el/la médico/a	*doctor; physician*
el/la periodista	*journalist*
el/la programador(a)	*computer programmer*

Variación léxica

madre ⟷ mamá, mami (*colloquial*)
padre ⟷ papá, papi (*colloquial*)
muchacho/a ⟷ chico/a

recursos

TEXT CD Lección 3	WB pp. 23–24	LM p. 13	Lab CD/MP3 Lección 3	I CD-ROM Lección 3	Vocab CD Lección 3

La familia de José Miguel Pérez Santoro

Juan Santoro Sánchez
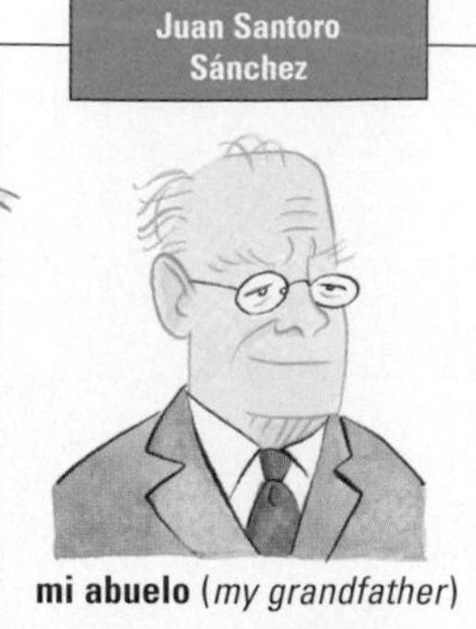
mi abuelo (*my grandfather*)

Ernesto Santoro González

mi tío (*uncle*)
hijo (*son*) **de Juan y Socorro**

Marina Gutiérrez de Santoro

mi tía (*aunt*)
esposa (*wife*) **de Ernesto**

Silvia Socorro Santoro Gutiérrez
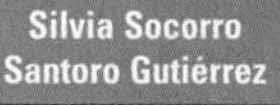

mi prima (*cousin*)
hija (*daughter*) **de Ernesto y Marina**

Héctor Manuel Santoro Gutiérrez

mi primo (*cousin*)
nieto (*grandson*) **de Juan y Socorro**

Carmen Santoro Gutiérrez

mi prima
hija de Ernesto y Marina

¡LENGUA VIVA!

In Spanish-speaking countries, it is common:
- for people to go by both first name and middle name, such as **José Miguel.**
- for people to have two last names: first the father's, then the mother's (the first last name of each parent) such as **Pérez Soto.**
- for wives sometimes to replace their second last name with their husband's first last name, preceded by **de: Mirta Santoro de Pérez.**

TEACHING OPTIONS

Extra Practice Draw your own family tree on a transparency or the board and label it with names. Ask students questions about it. Ex: **¿Es ____ mi tío o mi abuelo? ¿Cómo se llama mi madre? ____ es el primo de ____, ¿verdad? ¿____ es el sobrino o el hermano de ____? ¿Quién es el cuñado de ____?** Help them identify the relationships between members. Then invite them to ask you questions.

Variación léxica Ask heritage speakers to tell the class any other terms they use to refer to members of their families. These may include terms of endearment. Ask them to tell where these terms are used. Possible responses: **nene/nena, guagua, m'hijo/m'hija, chamaco/chamaca, chaval/chavala, cielo, cariño, corazón.**

Socorro González de Santoro

mi abuela (*my grandmother*)

Mirta Santoro de Pérez

mi madre (*mother*)
hija de Juan y Socorro

Rubén Ernesto Pérez Gómez

mi padre (*father*)
esposo de mi madre

José Miguel Pérez Santoro

hijo de Rubén y de Mirta

Beatriz Alicia Pérez de Morales

mi hermana (*sister*)

Felipe Morales Zapata

esposo (*husband*) de Beatriz Alicia

Víctor Miguel Morales Pérez

mi sobrino (*nephew*)
hermano (*brother*) de Anita

Anita Morales Pérez

mi sobrina (*niece*)
nieta (*granddaughter*) de mis padres

los hijos (*children*) de Beatriz Alicia y de Felipe

Práctica

1 Escuchar Listen to each statement made by José Miguel Pérez Santoro, then indicate whether it is **cierto** or **falso**, based on his family tree.

	Cierto	Falso		Cierto	Falso
1.	✓	○	6.	✓	○
2.	✓	○	7.	✓	○
3.	○	✓	8.	○	✓
4.	✓	○	9.	○	✓
5.	○	✓	10.	✓	○

2 Emparejar Provide the letter of the phrase that matches each description. Two items will not be used.

1. Mi hermano programa las computadoras. c
2. Son los padres de mi esposo. e
3. Son los hijos de mis (*my*) tíos. h
4. Mi tía trabaja en un hospital. a
5. Es el hijo de mi madrastra y el hijastro de mi padre. b
6. Es el esposo de mi hija. l
7. Es el hijo de mi hermana. k
8. Mi primo dibuja y pinta mucho. i
9. Mi hermanastra da (*gives*) clases en la universidad. j
10. Mi padre trabaja con planos (*blueprints*). d

a. Es médica.
b. Es mi hermanastro.
c. Es programador.
d. Es ingeniero.
e. Son mis suegros.
f. Es mi novio.
g. Es mi padrastro.
h. Son mis primos.
i. Es artista.
j. Es profesora.
k. Es mi sobrino.
l. Es mi yerno.

3 Definiciones Define these family terms in Spanish.

modelo
hijastro
Es el hijo de mi esposo/a, pero no es mi hijo.

1. abuela la madre de mi madre/padre
2. bisabuelo el abuelo de mi madre/padre
3. tío el hermano de mi madre/padre
4. parientes la familia extendida
5. suegra la madre de mi esposo/a
6. cuñado el esposo de mi hermana
7. nietos los hijos de mis hijos
8. yerno el esposo de mi hija
9. medio hermano el hijo de mi padre pero no de mi madre
10. hermanastro el hijo de mi madrastra/padrastro

1 Suggestion Have students correct the false statements by referring to José Miguel's family tree.

1 Tapescript 1. Beatriz Alicia es mi hermana. 2. Rubén es el abuelo de Víctor Miguel. 3. Silvia es mi sobrina. 4. Mirta y Rubén son los tíos de Héctor Manuel. 5. Anita es mi prima. 6. Ernesto es el hermano de mi madre. 7. Soy el tío de Anita. 8. Víctor Miguel es mi nieto. 9. Carmen, Beatriz Alicia y Marina son los nietos de Juan y Socorro. 10. El hijo de Juan y Socorro es el tío de Beatriz Alicia.
Textbook CD

The Affective Dimension Assure students that it isn't necessary to understand every word they hear. They may feel less anxious if they listen for general meaning.

2 Expansion After students finish, ask each one to provide a complete sentence combining elements from the numbered and lettered lists. Ex: **Los padres de mi esposo son mis suegros. Mis primos son los hijos de mis tíos**.

3 Expansion In pairs, have students write five definitions following the pattern of those in the activity.

TEACHING OPTIONS

Small Groups Have groups of three interview each other about their families, one conducting the interview, one answering, and one taking notes. At three-minute intervals have students switch roles until each has had each role. As a whole class, ask students questions about the families of other members of their group of three.

Game Have students state the relationship between people on José Miguel's family tree; their classmates will guess which person on the family tree they are describing. Ex: **Es la hermana de Ernesto y su padre es Juan. (Mirta) Héctor Manuel es su hermano y Beatriz Alicia es su prima. (Carmen o Silvia)** Take turns until each member of the class or group has had a chance to state a relationship.

4 Expansions
- Bring to class family-related photos. Prepare a fill-in-the-blank sentence for each. Talk about the photos, and ask volunteers to complete the sentences.
- Ask the class questions about the photos and captions. Ex: **¿Quién es artista? (Elena Vargas Soto es artista.) ¿Trabaja Irene? (Sí, es programadora.)**

4 **Escoger** Complete the description of each photo using words you have learned in **Contextos.** Some answers will vary.

1. La familia de Sara es muy grande.

2. Héctor y Lupita son novios.

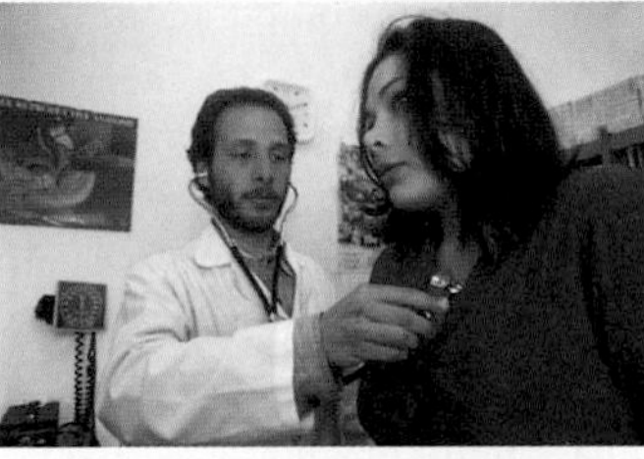

3. Alberto Díaz es médico.

4. Elena Vargas Soto es artista.

5. Los dos hermanos están en el parque.

6. Don Manuel es el abuelo de Martín.

7. Rubén camina con su hijo/padre.

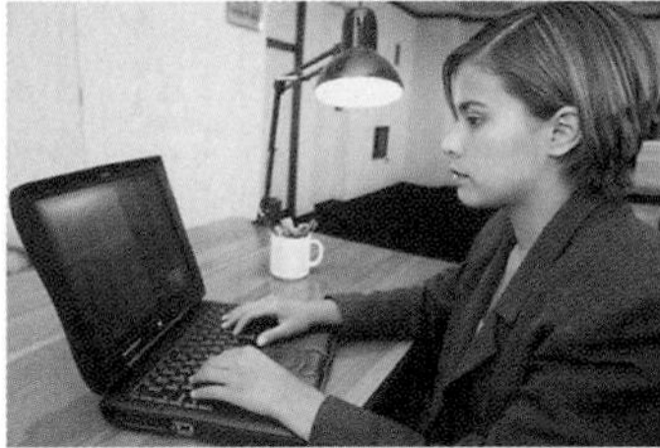

8. Irene es programadora.

NOTA CULTURAL

In the U.S., it is common for family members to live at great distances from one another. However, in Latin America and Spain, extended families tend to live near each other in the same neighborhood, town, city or region.

TEACHING OPTIONS

Extra Practice Ask students to bring in a family-related photo of their own and have them write a fill-in-the-blank sentence to go with it. Working in pairs, have them guess what is happening in each other's photo and complete the sentence.

Pairs Have pairs of students work together to create another sentence for each of the photos on this page. Ask one student to write sentences for the first four photos and the other student to write sentences for the remainder. When both have finished, ask them to exchange their sentences and correct each other's work.

Comunicación

5 **Una familia** With a classmate, identify the members in the family tree by asking questions about how each family member is related to Graciela Vargas García.

CONSÚLTALO

Cities and towns where family members are from can be seen in **Panorama** on p.100.

modelo

Estudiante 1: ¿Quién es Beatriz Pardo de Vargas?
Estudiante 2: Es la abuela de Graciela.

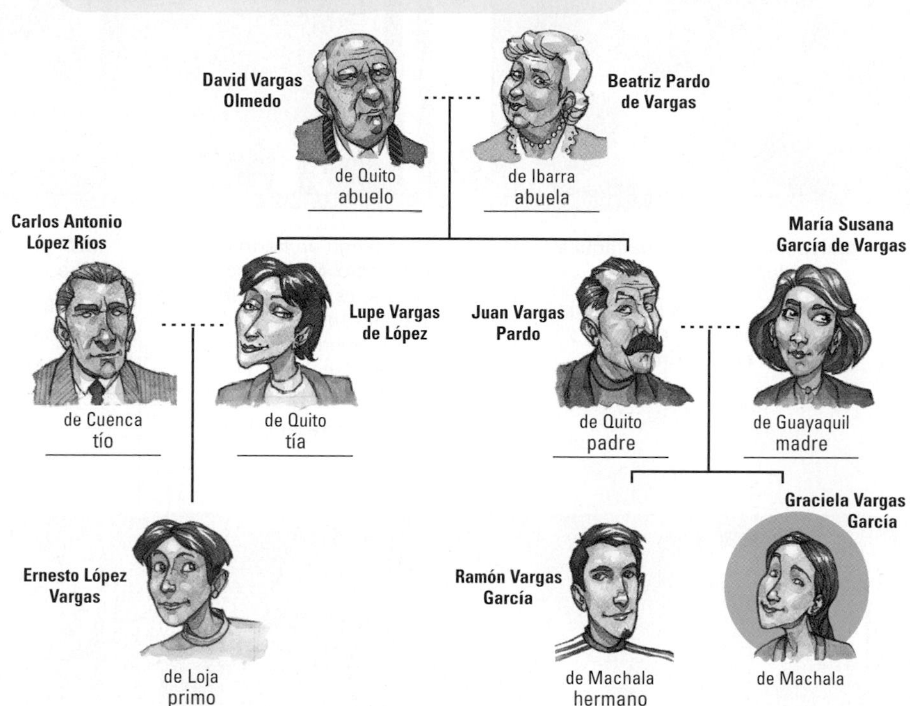

Now take turns asking each other these questions. Then invent three original questions.

1. ¿Cómo se llama el primo de Graciela? Se llama Ernesto López Vargas.
2. ¿Cómo se llama la hija de David y de Beatriz? Se llama Lupe Vargas de López.
3. ¿De dónde es María Susana? Es de Guayaquil.
4. ¿De dónde son Ramón y Graciela? Son de Machala.
5. ¿Cómo se llama el yerno de David y de Beatriz? Se llama Carlos Antonio López Ríos.
6. ¿De dónde es Carlos Antonio? Es de Cuenca.
7. ¿De dónde es Ernesto? Es de Loja.
8. ¿Cuáles son los apellidos del sobrino de Lupe? Son Vargas García.

6 **Preguntas personales** With a classmate, take turns asking each other these questions. Answers will vary.

AYUDA

tengo *I have*
tienes *you have*
tu *your* (sing.)
tus *your* (plural)
mi *my* (sing.)
mis *my* (plural)

1. ¿Cuántas personas hay en tu familia?
2. ¿Cómo se llaman tus padres? ¿De dónde son? ¿Dónde trabajan?
3. ¿Cuántos hermanos tienes? ¿Cómo se llaman? ¿Dónde estudian o trabajan?
4. ¿Cuántos primos tienes? ¿Cuáles son los apellidos de ellos? ¿Cuántos son niños y cuántos son adultos? ¿Hay más chicos o más chicas en tu familia?
5. ¿Eres tío/a? ¿Cómo se llaman tus sobrinos/as? ¿Dónde estudian o trabajan?
6. ¿Quién es tu pariente favorito?
7. ¿Tienes novio/a? ¿Tienes esposo/a? ¿Cómo se llama?

5 Suggestion Project **Transparency #17** to do this activity.

5 Expansion Model the pronunciation of the Ecuadorian cities mentioned. Ask students to locate each on the map of Ecuador, page 100. Ask students to say what they can tell about each city from the map.
Ex: **Guayaquil y Machala son ciudades de la costa del Pacífico. Quito, Loja y Cuenca son ciudades de la cordillera de los Andes. Quito es la capital del Ecuador.**

6 Expansions

- After modeling the activity with the whole class, have students circulate around the classroom asking their classmates these questions.
- Have pairs of students ask each other these questions, writing down the answers. After they have finished, ask students questions about their partner's answers.
  Ex: **¿Cuántas personas hay en la familia de ____? ¿Cómo se llaman los padres de ____? ¿De dónde son ellos? ¿Cuántos hermanos tiene ____?**

TEACHING OPTIONS

Extra Practice Ask students to draw their own family tree as homework. Have them label each position on the tree with the appropriate Spanish family term and the name of their family member. In class ask students questions about their families. Ex: **¿Cómo se llama tu prima? ¿Cómo es ella? ¿Ella es estudiante? ¿Cómo se llama tu madre? ¿Quién es tu cuñado?**

TPR Make a family tree using the whole class. Have each student write down the family designation you assign him or her on a note card or sheet of paper, then arrange students as in a family tree, with each one displaying the note card. Then, ask questions about relationships. Ex: **¿Quién es la madre de ____? ¿Cómo se llama el tío de ____?**

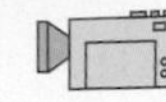

Section Goals

In **Fotonovela** students will:

- receive comprehensible input from free-flowing discourse
- learn functional phrases for talking about their families

Instructional Resources
WB/VM: Video Activities, pp. 217–218
***Fotonovela** DVD/Video (Start 00:12:14)*
Video CD-ROM
*IRM: **Fotonovela** Translations, p. 140, Videoscript, p. 105*
Interactive CD-ROM

Video Recap: Lección 2 Before doing this **Fotonovela** section, review the previous one with this activity.

1. ¿Quién estudia periodismo? (Maite)
2. ¿Quién toma cinco clases? (Inés)
3. ¿En qué clase de Inés hay más chicas? (sociología)
4. ¿Cuál es la opinión de Álex con respecto a las computadoras? (son muy interesantes)

Video Synopsis The bus trip continues. Maite, Inés, and Javier talk about their families. As they talk, Javier secretly sketches Inés. When Maite discovers what he is drawing, both he and Inés are embarrassed. Behind the wheel, Don Francisco wonders what is happening.

Suggestions

- Ask students to read the title, glance at the video stills, and predict what they think the episode will be about.
- Quickly review the predictions and confirm the correct one, asking a few questions to guide students in summarizing this episode.
- Work through the **Expresiones útiles** by asking students about their families. As you do, respond to the content of the responses and ask other students questions about their classmates' answers. Ex: **¿Cuántos hermanos tienes? (Sólo una hermana.)** Ask another student: **¿Cuántos hermanos tiene ____? (Sólo tiene una hermana.)**

¿Es grande tu familia?

NATIONAL STANDARDS communication cultures

Los chicos hablan de sus familias en el autobús.

PERSONAJES

MAITE

INÉS

DON FRANCISCO

ÁLEX

JAVIER

MAITE Inés, ¿tienes una familia grande?

INÉS Pues, sí... mis papás, mis abuelos, cuatro hermanas y muchos tíos y primos.

INÉS Sólo tengo un hermano mayor, Pablo. Su esposa, Francesca, es médica. No es ecuatoriana, es italiana. Sus papás viven en Roma, creo. Vienen de visita cada año. Ah... y Pablo es periodista.

MAITE ¡Qué interesante!

INÉS ¿Y tú, Javier? ¿Tienes hermanos?

JAVIER No, pero aquí tengo unas fotos de mi familia.

INÉS ¡Ah! ¡Qué bien! ¡A ver!

INÉS ¿Y cómo es él?

JAVIER Es muy simpático. Él es viejo pero es un hombre muy trabajador.

MAITE Oye, Javier, ¿qué dibujas?

JAVIER ¿Eh? ¿Quién? ¿Yo? ¡Nada!

MAITE ¡Venga! ¡No seas tonto!

MAITE Jaaavieeer... Oye, pero ¡qué bien dibujas!

JAVIER Este... pues... ¡Sí! ¡Gracias!

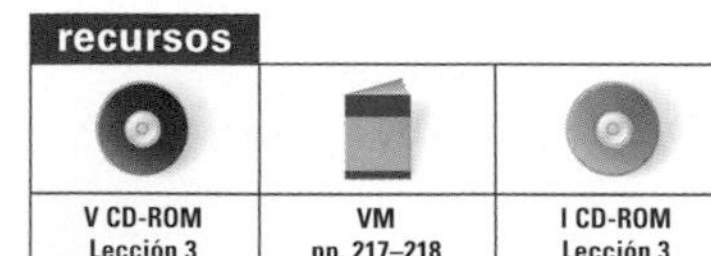

TEACHING OPTIONS

Video Tips General suggestions for using video clips in the classroom can be found on page IAE-12 of this Instructor's Annotated Edition.

¿Es grande tu familia? As an advance organizer before viewing the **¿Es grande tu familia?** segment of this video module, ask students to brainstorm a list of things that they think might happen in an episode in which the characters find out about each other's families. Then play the video segment once without sound and have the class create a plot summary based on visual clues. Afterward, show the video segment with sound and have the class correct any mistaken guesses and fill in any gaps in the plot summary they created.

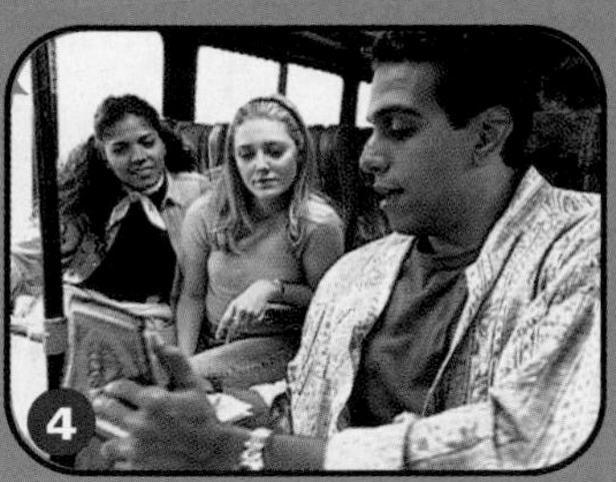

4

JAVIER ¡Aquí están!

INÉS ¡Qué alto es tu papá! Y tu mamá, ¡qué bonita!

5

JAVIER Mira, aquí estoy yo. Y éste es mi abuelo. Es el padre de mi mamá.

INÉS ¿Cuántos años tiene tu abuelo?

JAVIER Noventa y dos.

9

MAITE Álex, mira, ¿te gusta?

ÁLEX Sí, mucho. ¡Es muy bonito!

10

DON FRANCISCO Epa, ¿qué pasa con Inés y Javier?

Enfoque cultural La familia hispana

It is difficult to generalize about families in any culture, not just among Spanish speakers. There are many kinds of Hispanic families—large and small, close-knit and distant, loving and contentious. Traditionally, however, the family is one of the most important social institutions for Spanish speakers. Extended families, consisting of nuclear families and grandparents, aunts, and uncles, may reside in the same dwelling. Unmarried children often may live with their parents while attending college or working full-time.

Expresiones útiles

Talking about your family

▶ **¿Tienes una familia grande?**
Do you have a large family?
▷ **Sí... mis papás, mis abuelos, cuatro hermanas y muchos tíos.**
Yes... my parents, my grandparents, four sisters, and many (aunts and) uncles.
▷ **Sólo tengo un hermano mayor/menor.**
I only have one older/younger brother.

▶ **¿Tienes hermanos?**
Do you have siblings (brothers or sisters)?
▷ **No, soy hijo único.**
No, I'm an only (male) child.

▷ **Su esposa, Francesca, es médica.**
His wife, Francesca, is a doctor.
▷ **No es ecuatoriana, es italiana.**
She's not Ecuadorian; she's Italian.
▷ **Pablo es periodista.**
Pablo is a journalist.
▷ **Es el padre de mi mamá.**
He is my mother's father.

Describing people

▶ **¡Qué alto es tu papá!**
How tall your father is!
▶ **Y tu mamá, ¡qué bonita!**
And your mother, how pretty!

▶ **¿Cómo es tu abuelo?**
What is your grandfather like?
▷ **Es simpático.**
He's nice.
▷ **Es viejo.**
He's old.
▷ **Es un hombre muy trabajador.**
He's a very hard-working man.

Saying how old people are

▶ **¿Cuántos años tienes?**
How old are you?
▶ **¿Cuántos años tiene tu abuelo?**
How old is your grandfather?
▷ **Noventa y dos.**
Ninety-two.

Suggestion Ask students to read the **Fotonovela** conversation in groups of five. Ask one or two groups to present the script to the rest of the class.

Expresiones útiles Draw attention to the masculine, feminine, singular, and plural forms of descriptive adjectives and the present tense of **tener** in the video-still captions, **Expresiones útiles**, and as they occur in your conversation with the students. Point out that this material will be formally presented in **Estructura**. Correct students when they ask for correction, but do not expect them to be able to produce the forms correctly at this time.

TEACHING OPTIONS

Enfoque cultural The influence of Hispanic families frequently extends beyond the household. In the entertainment business, for instance, it is not unusual to find children following in the footsteps of their famous parents. Though theatrical families are not unheard of in the United States, Canada, or Great Britain, the phenomenon of children reaping the benefits of a parent's fame and connections is probably more frequent in the Spanish-speaking world. Students may recognize some of these stars of popular music whose parents were/are stars: Enrique Iglesias (Julio Iglesias), Christian Castro (Verónica Castro), Alejandro Fernández (Vicente Fernández).

1 Expansion Continue the activity with true/false statements such as these: **El padre de Javier es alto. (Cierto.) Javier tiene tres hermanos. (Falso; Javier no tiene hermanos.) Javier tiene unas fotos de su familia. (Cierto.) Inés es italiana. (Falso; Inés es del Ecuador.)**

2 Expansion Álex is the only student not associated with a statement. Ask the class to look at **Fotonovela** and **Expresiones útiles** on pages 74–75 and invent a statement for him. Remind students not to use his exact words. Ex: **¡Qué bonito! ¡Me gusta mucho!**

3 Expansion Have pairs who wrote about the same family exchange papers and compare their descriptions. Ask them to share the differences with the class.

4 Expansion Ask volunteers to share their partner's answers with the class.

Reacciona a la fotonovela

1 **¿Cierto o falso?** Indicate whether each sentence is **cierto** or **falso.** Correct the false statements.

	Cierto	Falso	
1. Inés tiene una familia grande.	✓	❍	
2. El hermano de Inés es médico.	❍	✓	Es periodista.
3. Francesca es de Italia.	✓	❍	
4. Javier tiene cuatro hermanos.	❍	✓	Javier no tiene hermanos.
5. El abuelo de Javier tiene ochenta años.	❍	✓	Tiene noventa y dos años.
6. Javier habla del padre de su (*his*) padre.	❍	✓	Javier habla del padre de su madre.

2 **Identificar** Indicate which person would make each statement. The names may be used more than once. **¡Ojo!** One name will not be used.

1. ¡Tengo una familia grande! ¡Tengo un hermano, cuatro hermanas y muchos primos! Inés
2. Mi abuelo tiene mucha energía. Trabaja mucho. Javier
3. ¿Es tu mamá? ¡Es muy bonita! Inés
4. Oye, chico… ¿qué dibujas? Maite
5. ¿Fotos de mi familia? ¡Tengo muchas! Javier
6. Mmm… Inés y Javier… ¿qué pasa con ellos? don Francisco
7. ¡Dibujas muy bien! Eres un artista excelente. Maite
8. Mmm… ¿Yo? ¡No dibujo nada! Javier

ÁLEX

JAVIER

INÉS

MAITE

DON FRANCISCO

3 **Escribir** In pairs, choose don Francisco, Álex, or Maite and write a brief description of his or her family. Be creative! Answers will vary.

MAITE

Maite es de España
¿Cómo es su familia?

ÁLEX

Álex es de México.
¿Cómo es su familia?

DON FRANCISCO

Don Francisco es del Ecuador.
¿Cómo es su familia?

4 **Conversar** With a partner, use these questions to talk about your families. Answers will vary.

1. ¿Cuántos años tienes?
2. ¿Tienes una familia grande?
3. ¿Tienes hermanos o hermanas?
4. ¿Cuántos años tiene tu abuelo (tu hermana, tu primo, etc.)?
5. ¿De dónde son tus padres?

AYUDA

Yo tengo… años.
Mi abuelo tiene… años.

TEACHING OPTIONS

Extra Practice Ask volunteers to ad-lib the **Fotonovela** episode for the class. Assure them that it is not necessary to memorize the **Fotonovela** or stick strictly to its content. They should try to get the general meaning across with the vocabulary and expressions they know, and they should also feel free to be creative. Give them time to prepare.

Variación léxica Clarify that in Spanish the adjective **americano/a** applies to all inhabitants of North and South America, not just citizens of the United States. In Spanish, residents of the United States are usually referred to with the adjective **norteamericano/a** or, more formally, with the adjective **estadounidense**.

Pronunciación

Diphthongs and linking

hermano **niña** **cuñado**

In Spanish, **a**, **e**, and **o** are considered strong vowels. The weak vowels are **i** and **u**.

ruido **parientes** **periodista**

A diphthong is a combination of two weak vowels or of a strong vowel and a weak vowel. Diphthongs are pronounced as a single syllable.

mi hijo **una clase excelente**

Two identical vowel sounds that appear together are pronounced like one long vowel.

la abuela

con Natalia **sus sobrinos** **las sillas**

Two identical consonants together sound like a single consonant.

es ingeniera **mis abuelos** **sus hijos**

A consonant at the end of a word is linked with the vowel at the beginning of the next word.

mi hermano **su esposa** **nuestro amigo**

A vowel at the end of a word is linked with the vowel at the beginning of the next word.

Práctica Say these words aloud, focusing on the diphthongs.

1. historia
2. nieto
3. parientes
4. novia
5. residencia
6. prueba
7. puerta
8. ciencias
9. lenguas
10. estudiar
11. izquierda
12. ecuatoriano

Oraciones Read these sentences aloud to practice diphthongs and linking words.

1. Hola. Me llamo Anita Amaral. Soy del Ecuador.
2. Somos seis en mi familia.
3. Tengo dos hermanos y una hermana.
4. Mi papá es del Ecuador y mi mamá es de España.

Refranes Read these sayings aloud to practice diphthongs and linking sounds.

Cuando una puerta se cierra, otra se abre.[1]

Hablando del rey de Roma, por la puerta se asoma.[2]

1 When one door closes, another opens.
2 Speak of the devil and he will appear.

recursos

TEXT CD	LM	Lab CD/MP3	I CD-ROM
Lección 3	p. 14	Lección 3	Lección 3

TEACHING OPTIONS

Heritage Speakers Ask heritage speakers if they know of other **refranes**. Write each **refrán** on the board and have the student who volunteered it explain what it means. Ex: **A quien Dios no le dio hijos, el diablo le da sobrinos. Más sabe el diablo por viejo que por diablo.**

Extra Practice Here are additional sentences to use for extra practice with diphthongs and linking: **Los estudiantes extranjeros hablan inglés. Mi abuela Ana tiene ochenta años. Juan y Enrique son hermanos. ¿Tu esposa aprende una lengua extranjera? Tengo un examen en la clase de español hoy.**

Section Goals

In **Pronunciación** students will be introduced to

- the strong and weak vowels
- common diphthongs
- linking in pronunciation

Instructional Resources
Textbook CD
Lab Manual, p. 14
Lab CD/MP3 ***Lección 3***
IRM: Tapescript, pp. 11–15; p. 87
Interactive CD-ROM

Suggestions

- Write **hermano, niña**, and **cuñado** on the board. Ask students to identify the strong and weak vowels.
- Pronounce **ruido, parientes,** and **periodista**, and have students identify the diphthong in each word. Point out that the strong vowels (**a, e, o**) do not combine with each other to form diphthongs. When two strong vowels come together, they are in different syllables.
- Point out that the letter **h** is silent.
- Pronounce **mi hermano** and **su esposa** and ask volunteers to write them on the board. Point out that the resulting linked vowels form a diphthong and are pronounced as one syllable.
- Follow the same procedure with **es ingeniera** and **mis abuelos**. You may want to introduce linking involving the other final consonants (**l, n, r, z**). Ex: **Son hermanos. El hermano mayor está aquí. ¿Cuál es tu hermana?**
- Ask students to provide words they learned in **Lecciones 1** and **2** and **Contextos** and **Fotonovela** of this lesson that exemplify each point.

Práctica/Oraciones/Refranes

These exercises are recorded on the Textbook CD. You may want to play the CD so students practice the pronunciation point by listening to Spanish spoken by speakers other than yourself.

Section Goals

In **Estructura 3.1**, students will learn:

- forms, agreement, and position of adjectives ending in **–o/–a**, **–e**, or a consonant
- high-frequency descriptive adjectives and some adjectives of nationality

Instructional Resources

WB/VM: Workbook, pp. 25–26
Lab Manual, p. 15
Lab CD/MP3 ***Lección 3***
IRM: ***Vocab. adicional****, pp. 180–181;* ***¡Inténtalo!*** *&* ***Práctica*** *Answers, p. 201; Tapescript, pp. 11–15*
Info Gap Activities Booklet, pp. 9–10
Interactive CD-ROM
Companion website: www.vistahigherlearning.com
Presentations CD-ROM

Suggestions

- Write these adjectives on the board: **ecuatoriana, alto, bonito, viejo, trabajador**. Ask volunteers to tell what each means and say whether it is masculine or feminine. Model one of the adjectives in a sentence and ask volunteers to use the others in sentences. Correct any agreement errors.
- Work through the discussion of adjective forms point by point, writing examples on the board. Test comprehension as you proceed by asking volunteers to supply the correct form of adjectives for nouns you suggest. Remind students that grammatical gender doesn't necessarily reflect the actual gender.

3.1 Descriptive adjectives

recursos: WB pp. 25–32 | LM pp. 15–18 | Lab CD/MP3 Lección 3 | I CD-ROM Lección 3 | vistahigherlearning.com

ANTE TODO Adjectives are words that describe people, places, and things. In Spanish, descriptive adjectives are often used with the verb **ser** to point out the characteristics or qualities of nouns or pronouns, such as nationality, size, color, shape, personality, and appearance.

NOUN	ADJECTIVE	PRONOUN	ADJECTIVE
El abuelo de Maite es **alto.**		**Él** es muy **simpático** también.	

Forms and agreement of adjectives

COMPARE & CONTRAST

In English, the forms of descriptive adjectives do not change to reflect the gender (masculine/feminine) and number (singular/plural) of the noun or pronoun they describe.

*Juan is **nice**.* *Elena is **nice**.* *They are **nice**.*

In Spanish, the forms of descriptive adjectives agree in gender and/or number with the nouns or pronouns they describe.

Juan es simpátic**o.** Elena es simpátic**a.** Ellos son simpátic**os.**

▶ Adjectives that end in **–o** have four different forms. The feminine singular is formed by changing the **–o** to **–a.** The plural is formed by adding **–s** to the singular forms.

Masculine		Feminine	
SINGULAR	PLURAL	SINGULAR	PLURAL
el muchach**o** alt**o**	los muchach**os** alt**os**	la muchach**a** alt**a**	las muchach**as** alt**as**

Mi abuelo es muy simpático.

¡Qué alto es tu papá! Y tu mamá, ¡qué bonita!

▶ Adjectives that end in **–e** or a consonant have the same masculine and feminine forms.

Masculine		Feminine	
SINGULAR	PLURAL	SINGULAR	PLURAL
el muchacho inteligent**e**	los muchachos inteligent**es**	la muchacha inteligent**e**	las muchachas inteligent**es**
el examen difíci**l**	los exámenes difíci**les**	la clase difíci**l**	las clases difíci**les**

TEACHING OPTIONS

Extra Practice Have pairs of students write sentences using adjectives such as **inteligente, alto, joven**. When they have finished, ask volunteers to dictate their sentences to you to write on the board. After you have written a sentence and corrected any errors, ask volunteers to suggest a sentence that uses the antonym of the adjective.

Heritage Speakers Have heritage speakers create short conversations in which they use as many of the descriptive adjectives as they can. Ask them to read their conversations to the class. Conversations may also be assigned to pairs of heritage speakers.

▶ Adjectives that end in **-or** are variable in both gender and number.

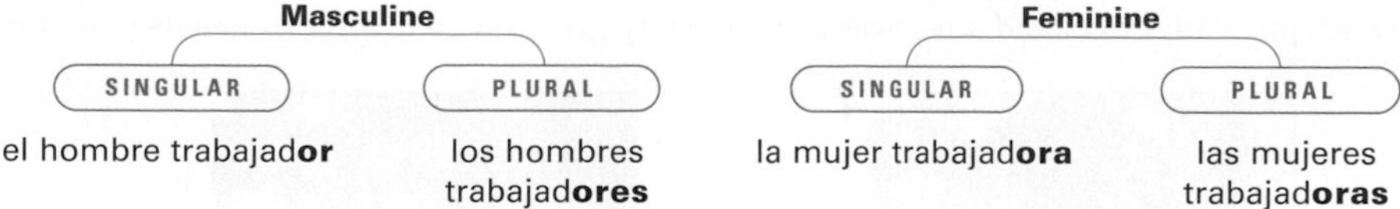

el hombre trabajad**or** | los hombres trabajad**ores** | la mujer trabajad**ora** | las mujeres trabajad**oras**

▶ Adjectives that refer to nouns of different genders use the masculine plural form.

Manuel es alt**o**. Lola es alt**a**. Manuel y Lola son alt**os**.

AYUDA

Remember to be aware of cognates, that is words that share similar spellings and meanings in Spanish and English.

A cognate can be a noun like **profesor** or a descriptive adjective like **interesante**.

Common adjectives

alto/a	*tall*	**gordo/a**	*fat*	**moreno/a**	*brunet(te)*
antipático/a	*unpleasant*	**grande**	*big; large*	**mucho/a**	*much; many; a lot of*
bajo/a	*short (in height)*	**guapo/a**	*handsome; good-looking*	**pelirrojo/a**	*red-haired*
bonito/a	*pretty*	**importante**	*important*	**pequeño/a**	*small*
bueno/a	*good*	**inteligente**	*intelligent*	**rubio/a**	*blond(e)*
delgado/a	*thin; slender*	**interesante**	*interesting*	**simpático/a**	*nice; likeable*
difícil	*hard; difficult*	**joven**	*young*	**tonto/a**	*silly; foolish*
fácil	*easy*	**malo/a**	*bad*	**trabajador(a)**	*hard-working*
feo/a	*ugly*	**mismo/a**	*same*	**viejo/a**	*old*

Adjectives of nationality

¡ATENCIÓN!

Unlike in English, Spanish adjectives of nationality are **not** capitalized. Proper names of countries, however, are capitalized.

México **Canadá**
China **Perú**

• • •

Note that adjectives of nationality which carry an accent mark on the last syllable, drop it in the feminine and plural forms.

inglés → **inglesa**
alemán → **alemanes**

▶ Adjectives of nationality are formed like other descriptive adjectives. Adjectives of nationality that end in **-o** form the feminine by changing the **-o** to **-a.**

chin**o** → chin**a** mexican**o** → mexican**a**

The plural is formed by adding an **-s** to the masculine or feminine form.

chin**o** → chin**os** mexican**a** → mexican**as**

▶ Adjectives of nationality that end in **-e** have only two forms, singular and plural.

canadiens**e** → canadiens**es** estadounidens**e** → estadounidens**es**

▶ Adjectives of nationality that end in a consonant form the feminine by adding **-a.**

alemá**n** → alema**na** españo**l** → españo**la**
japoné**s** → japone**sa** inglé**s** → ingle**sa**

Some adjectives of nationality

alemán, alemana	*German*	**inglés, inglesa**	*English*
canadiense	*Canadian*	**italiano/a**	*Italian*
chino/a	*Chinese*	**japonés, japonesa**	*Japanese*
ecuatoriano/a	*Ecuadorian*	**mexicano/a**	*Mexican*
español(a)	*Spanish*	**norteamericano/a**	*(North) American*
estadounidense	*from the U. S.*	**puertorriqueño/a**	*Puerto Rican*
francés, francesa	*French*	**ruso/a**	*Russian*

Suggestions

- Use pictures and the names of celebrities to teach descriptive adjectives in semantic pairs. Use either/or questions, yes/no questions, or a combination. Ex: **¿Michael Jordan es alto o bajo? (Es alto.) ¿Cindy Crawford es fea? (No, es bonita.) ¿Los candidatos son inteligentes o tontos? (Son inteligentes.)**
- Use pictures and the names of celebrities to practice adjectives of nationality. Ex: **Tony Blair, ¿es canadiense? (No, es inglés.) Madeleine Albright, ¿es francesa? (No, es norteamericana.)**
- Point out that adjectives with an accent mark on the last syllable are spelled without it when they add another syllable to form the feminine or the plural. Ex: **irlandés, irlandesa, irlandeses, irlandesas.**
- Point out that adjectives of nationality can be used as nouns as well as adjectives. Ex: **La chica ecuatoriana es guapa. La ecuatoriana es guapa.** Like adjectives, nouns of nationality are not capitalized in Spanish.
- At this point you may want to present **Vocabulario adicional: Más adjetivos de nacionalidad** and **Más vocabulario para hablar de la familia,** from the IRM.
- Add the nationalities of students and celebrities not on the list. When you introduce another nationality, write one of its forms on the board and ask what the other forms would be. Ex: **¿Los chicos del grupo *The Cardigans* son suecos? (Sí, son suecos.) ¿Cuáles son las formas singulares de *suecos*? (*sueco/sueca*)**

TEACHING OPTIONS

Extra Practice Write on the board the Spanish country name corresponding to each adjective of nationality that students have learned. Practice the adjectives by indicating a student, saying the country, and having the student come up with the corresponding adjective.

Heritage Speakers Ask heritage speakers to tell what countries their families have come from.

Game Divide the class into two teams. Indicate one team member at a time, alternating between teams. Give a certain form of an adjective and name another form which the team member should give. Ex: **ecuatorianos;** feminine singular (**ecuatoriana**). Give a point per correct answer. Deduct a point for each wrong answer. The team with the most points at the end of play wins.

Suggestions

- After describing each grammar point, practice it by asking questions like the following.

  Descriptive adjectives
  ¿Tienes amigos inteligentes? ¿Tienes amigas guapas? ¿Tomas clases difíciles? ¿Tienes compañeros trabajadores? ¿Tienes profesores simpáticos o antipáticos?

  Adjectives of quantity
  ¿Cuántos hermanos tienes? ¿Cuántas personas hay en la clase de español? ¿Cuántos amigos españoles tienes? ¿Cuántas materias estudias?

  Bueno/a* and *malo/a
  ¿Tus amigos son buenos estudiantes? ¿Tienes un buen diccionario? ¿Hoy es un mal día? ¿Tu novio es una persona mala?

  ***Grande* ¿Vives en una residencia grande o pequeña? ¿Estudias en una universidad grande o pequeña?**

- Ask short questions about the **Fotonovela** characters using adjectives from this lesson. Ex: **¿Son estadounidenses los cuatro estudiantes? ¿Es simpático o antipático el conductor? ¿Las dos muchachas son altas?**

Position of adjectives

▶ Descriptive adjectives and adjectives of nationality generally follow the nouns they modify.

El chico **rubio** es de España.
The blond boy is from Spain.

La mujer **española** habla inglés.
The Spanish woman speaks English.

▶ Unlike descriptive adjectives, adjectives of quantity are placed before the modified noun.

Hay **muchos** libros en la biblioteca.
There are many books in the library.

Hablo con **dos** turistas puertorriqueños.
I am talking with two Puerto Rican tourists.

▶ **Bueno/a** and **malo/a** can be placed before or after a noun. When placed before a masculine singular noun, the forms are shortened: **bueno → buen; malo → mal.**

Joaquín es un **buen** amigo.
Joaquín es un amigo **bueno.** → *Joaquín is a good friend.*

Hoy es un **mal** día.
Hoy es un día **malo.** → *Today is a bad day.*

▶ When **grande** appears before a singular noun, it is shortened to **gran,** and the meaning of the word changes: **gran** = *great* and **grande** = *big, large.*

Don Francisco es un **gran** hombre.
Don Francisco is a great man.

La familia de Inés es **grande**.
Inés' family is large.

¡LENGUA VIVA!

Like **bueno** and **grande**, **santo** is also shortened before masculine nouns (unless they begin with **To-** or **Do-**): **San Francisco, San José, Santo Tomás. Santa** is used with the names of female saints: **Santa Bárbara, Santa Clara**.

¡INTÉNTALO! Provide the appropriate forms of the adjectives. The first item in each group has been done for you.

simpático

1. Mi hermano es simpático.
2. La profesora Martínez es simpática.
3. Rosa y Teresa son simpáticas.
4. Nosotros somos simpáticos.

español

1. Luis es español.
2. Mis primas son españolas.
3. Rafael y yo somos españoles.
4. Mi tía es española.

difícil

1. Clara es difícil.
2. El periodista es difícil.
3. Ellas son difíciles.
4. Los turistas son difíciles.

guapo

1. Su esposo es guapo.
2. Mis sobrinas son guapas.
3. Los padres de ella son guapos.
4. Marta es guapa.

TEACHING OPTIONS

Video Show the video again to give students more input with descriptive adjectives. Stop the video where appropriate to discuss how certain adjectives were used.

Game Give pairs of students three minutes to jot down as many cities as they can that have **san, santo,** or **santa** as part of the name. After three minutes, go through the names with the whole class. The pair with the most names wins.

Extra Practice To reinforce adjective agreement, create sentences that follow the pattern of the sentences in **¡Inténtalo!** Say the sentence, have students repeat it, then say a different subject, varying the gender and number. Have students then say the sentence with the new subject, changing adjectives and verbs as necessary.

Práctica

1 **Emparejar** Find the words in column B that are the opposite of the words in column A. One word in B will not be used, and another will be used twice.

A		B
1. guapo	d	a. delgado
2. moreno	f	b. pequeño
3. alto	h	c. malo
4. gordo	a	d. feo
5. joven	e	e. viejo
6. grande	b	f. rubio
7. simpático	g	g. antipático
8. bonito	d	h. bajo

2 **Completar** Indicate the nationalities of the following people by selecting the correct adjectives and changing their forms when necessary.

1. Una persona del Ecuador es ecuatoriana.
2. Carlos Fuentes es un gran escritor (*writer*) de México; es mexicano.
3. Los habitantes de Vancouver son canadienses.
4. Armani es un diseñador de modas (*fashion designer*) italiano.
5. Gérard Depardieu es un actor francés.
6. Tony Blair y Margaret Thatcher son ingleses.
7. Claudia Schiffer y Boris Becker son alemanes.
8. Los habitantes de Puerto Rico son puertorriqueños.

NOTA CULTURAL

Carlos Fuentes (1928–) is one of Mexico's best known living writers. His novel, ***La muerte*** (*death*) ***de Artemio Cruz***, explores the psyche of a Mexican revolutionary.

3 **Describir** Look at the drawing and describe each family member using as many adjectives as possible. Some answers will vary.

1. Susana Romero Barcos es delgada, rubia.
2. Tomás Romero Barcos es pelirrojo, inteligente.
3. Los dos hermanos son jóvenes.
4. Josefina Barcos de Romero es alta, bonita, rubia.
5. Carlos Romero Sandoval es bajo, gordo.
6. Alberto Romero Pereda es viejo, bajo.
7. Tomás y su (*his*) padre son pelirrojos.
8. Susana y su (*her*) madre son altas, delgadas.

1 Expansions
- Ask volunteers to create sentences describing famous people, using an adjective from column A and its opposite from B. Ex: **Tom Cruise no es gordo, es delgado. Cristina Saralegui no es morena, es rubia.**
- Have students describe Jorge and Marcos using as many of the antonyms as they can. Ex: **Jorge es muy simpático, pero Marcos es antipático.**

2 Expansion Ask pairs of students to write four more statements modeled on the activity. Have them leave a space where the adjectives of nationality should go. Ask each pair to exchange its sentences with another pair, who will fill in the adjectives of nationality.

3 Expansions
- Have students say what each person in the drawing is not. Ex: **Susana Romero Barcos no es vieja. Tomás Romero Barcos no es moreno.**
- Have students ask each other questions about the family relationships shown in the illustration. Ex: **—¿Tomás Romero Barcos es el hijo de Alberto Romero Pereda? —No, Tomás es el hijo de Carlos Romero Sandoval.**

TEACHING OPTIONS

Extra Practice Have students write short descriptions of themselves. Tell them to mention where they are from and what they are studying, as well as describing their personalities and what they look like. Collect the descriptions and read a few of them to the class. Have the class guess who wrote each description.

Extra Practice Prepare short descriptions of five easily recognizable people. Write their names on the board in random order. Then read your descriptions as a dictation, having students copy your description and match the description to the appropriate name. Ex: **Ella es joven, morena, atlética e inteligente. (Serena Williams)**

4 Expansion Have small groups brainstorm a list of famous people, places, and things not in the activity. Ask them to include some plural items. Then ask the groups to exchange lists and describe the people, places, and things on the lists they receive.

5 Suggestion Have students divide a sheet of paper into two columns, labeling one **Yo** and the other **Mi novio/a ideal** or **Mi esposo/a ideal**. Have them brainstorm Spanish adjectives for each column. Ask them to rank each adjective in the second column in terms of its importance to them.

5 Expansion Ask small groups to write a personal ad describing a fictional person and his or her ideal mate. Have groups exchange and respond to each other's ads.

6 Suggestion Divide the class into pairs and distribute the Info Gap Handouts from the Info Gap Activities Booklet that correspond to this activity. Give the students ten minutes to complete this activity.

6 Expansions

- Ask questions based on the artwork. Ex: **¿Es alto el abuelo? ¿Es delgado el hijo menor?**
- Have volunteers take turns stating the differences. Then have them invent their own stories based on these families.

Comunicación

4 **¿Cómo es?** With a partner, take turns describing each item on the list. Tell your partner whether you agree (**Estoy de acuerdo.**) or disagree (**No estoy de acuerdo.**) with the descriptions. Answers will vary.

modelo

San Francisco
Estudiante 1: *San Francisco es una ciudad muy bonita.*
Estudiante 2: *No estoy de acuerdo. Es muy fea.*

1. Nueva York
2. Jim Carrey
3. Celine Dion
4. El presidente de los Estados Unidos
5. Steven Spielberg
6. La primera dama (*first lady*) de los Estados Unidos
7. El/La profesor(a) de español
8. Los Ángeles
9. Mi universidad
10. Mi clase de español

AYUDA

Here are some tips to help you complete the descriptions:

- **Jim Carrey es actor de cine.**
- **Celine Dion es cantante.**
- **Steven Spielberg es director de cine.**

5 **Anuncio personal** Write a personal ad that describes yourself and your ideal boyfriend, girlfriend, or mate. Then compare your ad with a classmate's. How are you similar and how are you different? Are you looking for the same things in a boyfriend, girlfriend, or mate? Answers will vary.

SOY ALTA, morena y bonita. Soy ecuatoriana, de Quito. Estudio arte en la universidad. Busco un chico similar. Mi novio ideal es alto, moreno, inteligente y muy simpático.

AYUDA

casado/a *married*
divorciado/a *divorced*
soltero/a *single; unmarried*

These words and others like them are presented in **Contextos, Lección 9, p. 272.**

Síntesis

6   **Diferencias** Your instructor will give you and a partner each a drawing of a family. Find the six differences between your picture and your partner's. Answers will vary.

modelo

Estudiante 1: *La madre es rubia.*
Estudiante 2: *No, la madre es morena.*

TEACHING OPTIONS

Heritage Speakers Ask heritage speakers to write descriptions of their extended families. Ask them to share their finished descriptions with the rest of the class. Encourage them to illustrate the descriptions with a few family photos, if they are available, or with photocopies of photos.

Extra Practice Have students collect several interesting pictures of people from magazines or newspapers. Have them prepare a description of one of the pictures ahead of time. Invite them to show the pictures to the class and then give their descriptions orally. The class will guess which of the pictures is being described.

3.2 Possessive adjectives

ANTE TODO Possessive adjectives, like descriptive adjectives, are words that are used to qualify people, places, or things. Possessive adjectives express the quality of ownership or possession.

Forms of possessive adjectives

SINGULAR FORMS	PLURAL FORMS	
mi	**mis**	*my*
tu	**tus**	*your* (fam.)
su	**sus**	*his, her, its, your* (form.)
nuestro/a	**nuestros/as**	*our*
vuestro/a	**vuestros/as**	*your* (fam.)
su	**sus**	*their, your* (form.)

COMPARE & CONTRAST

In English, possessive adjectives are invariable; that is, they do not agree in gender and number with the nouns they modify. Spanish possessive adjectives, however, do agree in number with the nouns they modify.

my cousin	*my cousins*	*my aunt*	*my aunts*
mi primo	**mis** primos	**mi** tía	**mis** tías

The forms **nuestro** and **vuestro** agree in both gender and number with the nouns they modify.

nuestr**o** prim**o** — nuestr**os** prim**os** — nuestr**a** tía — nuestr**as** tías

▶ Possessive adjectives are always placed before the nouns they modify.

—¿Está **tu novio** aquí?
Is your boyfriend here?

—No, **mi novio** está en la biblioteca.
No, my boyfriend is in the library.

CONSEJOS

Look at the context, focusing on nouns and pronouns, to help you determine the meaning of **su(s)**.

▶ Because **su** and **sus** have multiple meanings (*your, his, her, their, its*), you can avoid confusion by using this construction instead: [*article*] + [*noun*] + **de** + [*subject pronoun*].

sus parientes 

los parientes **de él/ella** — *his/her relatives*
los parientes **de Ud./Uds.** — *your relatives*
los parientes **de ellos/ellas** — *their relatives*

¡INTÉNTALO! Provide the appropriate form of each possessive adjective. The first item in each column has been done for you.

1. Es ___mi___ (*my*) libro.
2. ___Mi___ (*My*) familia es ecuatoriana.
3. ___Tu___ (*Your,* fam.) esposo es italiano.
4. ___Nuestro___ (*Our*) profesor es español.
5. Es ___su___ (*her*) reloj.
6. Es ___tu___ (*your,* fam.) mochila.
7. Es ___su___ (*your,* form.) maleta.
8. ___Su___ (*Their*) sobrina es alemana.

1. ___Sus___ (*Her*) primos son franceses.
2. ___Nuestros___ (*Our*) primos son canadienses.
3. Son ___sus___ (*their*) lápices.
4. ___Sus___ (*Their*) nietos son japoneses.
5. Son ___nuestras___ (*our*) plumas.
6. Son ___mis___ (*my*) papeles.
7. ___Mis___ (*My*) amigas son inglesas.
8. Son ___sus___ (*his*) cuadernos.

Section Goals

In **Estructura 3.2** students will be introduced to:
- possessive adjectives
- ways of clarifying **su(s)** when referent is ambiguous

Instructional Resources
WB/VM: Workbook, pp. 27–28
Lab Manual, p. 16
Lab CD/MP3 ***Lección 3***
IRM: ***¡Inténtalo!*** *&* ***Práctica*** *Answers, p. 201;*
Tapescript, pp. 11–15
Interactive CD-ROM
Companion website: www.vistahigherlearning.com
Presentations CD-ROM

Suggestions
- Introduce the concept of possessive adjectives. Ask volunteers questions, such as: **¿Es simpática tu madre? ¿Cómo es tu profesor(a) favorito/a?**
- List the possessive adjectives on the board. Use each with a noun to illustrate agreement. Point out that all possessive adjectives agree in number with the noun they modify but that only **nuestro/a** and **vuestro/a** show gender. Point out that **tú** (subject) has an accent mark; **tu** (possessive) does not.
- Ask students to give the plural or singular of possessive adjectives with nouns. Say: **Da el plural: mi profesor, nuestra clase**. Say: **Da el singular: mis manos, nuestras abuelas.**
- Write **su familia** and **sus amigos** on the board and ask the class to tell you the possible meanings. Then ask for volunteers to supply the equivalent clarifying phrases.

TEACHING OPTIONS

Video Replay the video segment, having students focus on possessive adjectives. Ask them to write down each one they hear, with the noun it modifies. Afterward, ask the class to describe the families of Inés and Javier. Remind them to use definite articles and **de** if necessary to avoid confusion with the possessive **su**.

Small Groups Give small groups three minutes to brainstorm how many words they can associate with the phrases **nuestro país, nuestro estado, nuestra universidad,** and **nuestra clase de español**. Have them model their responses on **En nuestra clase hay** ____ and **Nuestro país es** ____. Have the groups share their associations with the rest of the class.

1 Expansions
- Have students replace the nouns with nouns of a different number and gender. Then have them say each new sentence, changing the possessives as necessary.
- Have students respond to the question in item 8.

2 Expansions
- Replace the subject pronouns in parentheses with others and have the class provide new answers. Then have groups of students provide new nouns and the corresponding answers.
- Give the class sentences such as **Es su libro** and have volunteers rephrase them with **su(s)** or a clarifying prepositional phrase.

3 Suggestions
- Before doing the activity, quickly review **estar** by writing the present-tense forms on the board.
- Remind students that **estar** is used to indicate location.

3 Expansion Ask questions about objects that are in the classroom. Ex: **¿Dónde está mi escritorio? ¿Dónde está el libro de ____? ¿Dónde están las plumas de ____? ¿Dónde están tus lápices?**

Práctica

1 **La familia de Manolo** Complete each sentence with the correct possessive adjective. Use the subject of each sentence as a guide.

1. Me llamo Manolo, y __mi__ (nuestro, mi, sus) hermano es Federico.
2. __Nuestra__ (Nuestra, Sus, Mis) madre Silvia es profesora y enseña química.
3. Ella admira mucho a __sus__ (tu, nuestro, sus) estudiantes porque trabajan mucho.
4. Yo estudio en la misma universidad, pero no tomo clases con __mi__ (mi, nuestras, tus) madre.
5. Federico trabaja en una oficina con __nuestro__ (mis, tu, nuestro) padre.
6. __Su__ (Mi, Su, Tu) oficina está en el centro de Quito.
7. Javier y Óscar son __mis__ (mis, mi, sus) tíos de Guayaquil.
8. ¿Y tú? ¿Cómo es __tu__ (mi, su, tu) familia?

2 **Clarificar** Clarify each sentence with a prepositional phrase. Follow the model.

modelo
Su hermana es muy bonita. (ella)
La hermana de ella es muy bonita.

1. Su casa es muy grande. (ellos) La casa de ellos es muy grande.
2. ¿Cómo se llama su hermano? (ellas) ¿Cómo se llama el hermano de ellas?
3. Sus padres trabajan en el centro. (ella) Los padres de ella trabajan en el centro.
4. Sus abuelos son muy simpáticos. (él) Los abuelos de él son muy simpáticos.
5. Maribel es su prima. (ella) Maribel es la prima de ella.
6. Su primo lee los libros. (ellos) El primo de ellos lee los libros.

3 **¿Dónde está?** With a partner, imagine that you can't remember where you put some of the belongings you see in the pictures. Your partner will help you by reminding you where your things are. Take turns playing each role. Answers will vary.

CONSÚLTALO
For a list of useful prepositions for this exercise, refer to the table: *Prepositions often used with* ***estar***, in **Estructura 2.3**, p. 54.

modelo
Estudiante 1: *¿Dónde está mi mochila?*
Estudiante 2: *Tu mochila está encima del escritorio.*

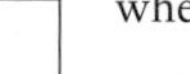

1.

2.

3.

4.
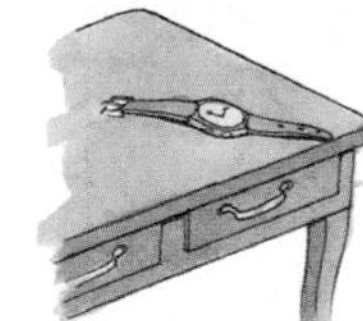

5.

6.

TEACHING OPTIONS

Extra Practice Ask students a few questions about the members of their immediate and extended families. Ex: **¿Cómo son tus padres? ¿Cómo se llama tu tío favorito? ¿Es el hermano de tu madre o de tu padre? ¿Tienes muchos primos? ¿Cómo se llaman tus primos? ¿De dónde son tus abuelos? ¿Hablas mucho con tus abuelos?**

Heritage Speakers Ask heritage speakers to write a paragraph about a favorite relative. Ask them to include the characteristics that make that relative their favorite. Have them explain what they have learned from their relative.

Comunicación

4 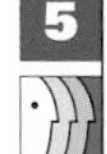 **Describir** Get together with a partner and take turns describing the people and places on the list. Answers will vary.

modelo

La biblioteca de su universidad

La biblioteca de nuestra universidad es muy grande. Hay muchos libros en la biblioteca. Mis amigos y yo estudiamos en la biblioteca.

1. Tu profesor favorito
2. Tu profesora favorita
3. Su clase de español
4. La librería de su universidad
5. Tus padres
6. Tus abuelos
7. Tu mejor (*best*) amigo
8. Tu mejor amiga
9. Su universidad
10. Tu país de origen

5 **Una familia** In small groups, each student pretends to be a different member of the family pictured and shares that person's private thoughts about the others in the family. Make two positive comments and two negative ones. Answers will vary.

modelo

Estudiante 1: *Mi hijo Roberto es muy trabajador. Estudia mucho y termina su tarea.*

Estudiante 2: *Nuestra familia es difícil. Mis padres no escuchan mis opiniones.*

Síntesis

6  **Describe a tu familia** Get together with two classmates and describe your family to them in several sentences (**Mi padre es alto y moreno. Mi madre es delgada y muy bonita. Mis hermanos son...**). They will work together to try to repeat your description (**Su padre es alto y moreno. Su madre...**). If they forget any details, they will ask you questions (**¿Es alto tu hermano?**). Alternate roles until all of you have described your families. Answers will vary.

4 Suggestion Ask students to suggest a few other details to add to the **modelo**. Then tell them to work in pairs, taking turns describing three or four of the items.

5 Suggestions
- Quickly review the descriptive adjectives on page 79. You can do this by saying an adjective and having volunteers give its opposite (**palabra opuesta**).
- Explain the activity to the class. Have students give names to the people in the photo following Hispanic naming conventions.

5 Expansion Ask a couple of groups to perform the activity for the class.

6 Suggestions
- Review the family vocabulary on pages 70–71.
- Explain that the class will divide into groups of three. One student will describe his or her own family (using **mi**), and then the other two will describe the first student's family to one another (using **su**) and ask for clarification as necessary (using **tu**). Before beginning, ask students to list the family members they plan to describe.

TEACHING OPTIONS

Extra Practice Have students work in small groups to prepare a description of a famous person, such as a politician, a movie star, or a sports figure, and his or her extended family. Tell them to feel free to invent family members as necessary. Have groups present their descriptions to the rest of the class.

Heritage Speakers Ask heritage speakers to describe their home country (**país de origen**) for the whole class. As they are giving their descriptions, ask them questions that elicit more information. Also, clarify for the class any unfamiliar words and expressions they may use.

Section Goals

In **Estructura 3.3** students will learn:

- the present-tense forms of regular **–er/–ir** verbs
- some high-frequency regular **–er/–ir** verbs

Instructional Resources
WB/VM: Workbook, pp. 29–30
Lab Manual, p. 17
*Lab CD/MP3 **Lección 3***
*IRM: **¡Inténtalo! & Práctica** Answers, p. 201;*
Tapescript, pp. 11–15;
***Hojas de actividades,** p. 164*
Info Gap Activities Booklet, pp. 11–12
Interactive CD-ROM
Companion website: www.vistahigherlearning.com
Presentations CD-ROM

Suggestions

- Write **trabajo** on the board and ask for the corresponding subject pronoun. (**yo**) Continue until you have the entire paradigm. Underline the endings, pointing out the characteristic vowel (**–a–**) where it appears and the personal endings.
- Ask questions and make statements that use the verb **comer** to elicit all the present-tense forms. Ex: **¿Comes en la cafetería o en un restaurante? Yo no como en la cafetería. ¿Come ____ en casa o en un bar?** As you elicit responses, write just the verbs on the board until you have the complete conjugation. Do the same with **escribir**. Ex: **¿Quién escribe muchas cartas? ¿A quién escribes?** When you have a complete paradigm of both verbs, write the paradigm of **trabajar** alongside. Help students identify the ending that is the same in all three conjugations. **yo** = (**–o**)

3.3 Present tense of –er and –ir verbs

ANTE TODO In **Lección 2,** you learned how to form the present tense of regular **–ar** verbs. You also learned about the importance of verb forms, which change to show who is performing the action. The chart below shows the forms of verbs from two other important verb groups, **–er** verbs, and **–ir** verbs.

CONSÚLTALO

To review the conjugation of **–ar** verbs, see **Estructura 2.1**, p. 44.

Present tense of *–er*, and *–ir* verbs

		comer *(to eat)*	**escribir** *(to write)*
SINGULAR FORMS	yo	com**o**	escrib**o**
	tú	com**es**	escrib**es**
	Ud./él/ella	com**e**	escrib**e**
PLURAL FORMS	nosotros/as	com**emos**	escrib**imos**
	vosotros/as	com**éis**	escrib**ís**
	Uds./ellos/ellas	com**en**	escrib**en**

▶ **–Er** and **–ir** verbs have very similar endings. Study the preceding chart to detect the patterns that make it easier for you to use them to communicate in Spanish.

CONSEJOS

Here are some tips on learning Spanish verbs:
1) Learn to identify the stem of each verb, to which all endings attach.
2) Memorize the endings that go with each verb and verb tense.
3) As often as possible, practice using different forms of each verb in speech and writing.
4) Devote extra time to learning irregular verbs, such as **ser** and **estar**.

Inés y Javier comen.

▶ Like **–ar** verbs, the **yo** forms of **–er** and **–ir** verbs end in **–o.**

Yo com**o**. Yo escrib**o**.

▶ Except for the **yo** form, all of the verb endings for **–er** verbs begin with **–e.**

–es	**–emos**	**–en**
–e	**–éis**	

▶ **–Er** and **–ir** verbs have the exact same endings, except in the **nosotros/as** and **vosotros/as** forms.

nosotros ◀ com**emos** / escrib**imos**

vosotros ◀ com**éis** / escrib**ís**

TEACHING OPTIONS

Heritage Speakers Have heritage speakers write ten statements about themselves, their family, and people that they know using ten different **–er/–ir** verbs introduced on pages 86–87.

Game Divide the class into two teams. Announce an infinitive and a subject pronoun (Ex: **creer/yo**) and have the first member of Team A give the appropriate conjugated form of the verb. If the team member answers correctly, his or her team gets one point. If he or she does not know the answer, give the first member of Team B the same infinitive and pronoun. If he or she does not know the answer, say the correct verb form and move on to the next team member of Team A. The team with the most points at the end of play wins.

Common *–er* and *–ir* verbs

–er verbs		–ir verbs	
aprender (a + *inf.*)	*to learn*	**abrir**	*to open*
beber	*to drink*	**asistir (a)**	*to attend*
comer	*to eat*	**compartir**	*to share*
comprender	*to understand*	**decidir (+ *inf.*)**	*to decide*
correr	*to run*	**describir**	*to describe*
creer (en)	*to believe (in)*	**escribir**	*to write*
deber (+ *inf.*)	*should; must; ought to*	**recibir**	*to receive*
leer	*to read*	**vivir**	*to live*

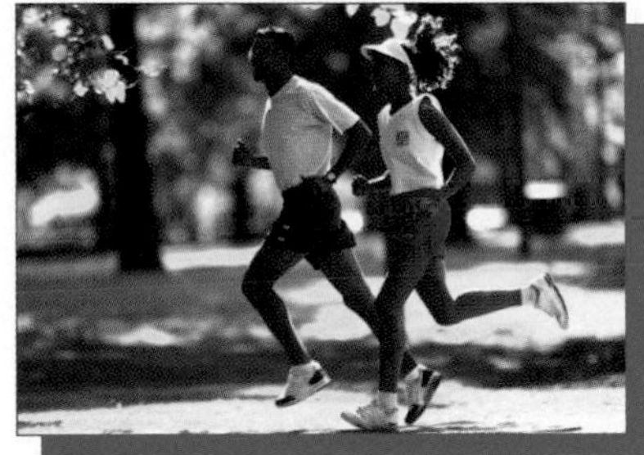
Ellos **corren** en el parque.

Él **escribe** una carta.

¡INTÉNTALO! Provide the appropriate present tense forms of these verbs. The first item in each column has been done for you.

correr

1. Graciela *corre*.
2. Tú corres.
3. Yo corro.
4. Sara y Ana corren.
5. Usted corre.
6. Ustedes corren.
7. La gente corre.
8. Marcos y yo corremos.

abrir

1. Ellos *abren* la puerta.
2. Carolina abre la maleta.
3. Yo abro las ventanas.
4. Nosotras abrimos los libros.
5. Usted abre el cuaderno.
6. Tú abres la ventana.
7. Ustedes abren las maletas.
8. Los muchachos abren los cuadernos.

aprender

1. Él *aprende* español.
2. Maribel y yo aprendemos inglés.
3. Tú aprendes japonés.
4. Tú y tu hermanastra aprenden francés.
5. Mi hijo aprende chino.
6. Yo aprendo alemán.
7. Usted aprende inglés.
8. Nosotros aprendemos italiano.

Suggestions

- Point out the characteristic vowel (–e–) of **–er** verbs. Then help students see that all the present-tense endings of regular **–er/–ir** verbs are the same except for the **nosotros/as** and **vosotros/as** forms.
- Reinforce **–er/–ir** endings and introduce the verbs by asking the whole class questions. First ask a series of questions with a single verb until you have elicited all of its present-tense forms. Have students answer with complete sentences. Ex: **¿Aprenden ustedes historia en nuestra clase? ¿Aprendes álgebra en tu clase de matemáticas? ¿Qué aprenden ____ y ____ en la clase de computación? Aprendo mucho cuando leo, ¿verdad?** Then, ask questions using all the verbs at random.
- Ask questions that spin off of the photos. Ex: **¿Quiénes corren en el parque en esta foto? ¿Quiénes de ustedes corren? ¿Dónde corren? ¿A quién creen que escribe el muchacho? ¿Escribe a su novia? ¿Escribe a su mamá? ¿Ustedes escriben a sus mamás? ¿Escriben a sus novios/as?**
- Ask students to come up with a list of things they routinely do in Spanish class or in any of their other classes. Encourage them to use as many of the **–er/–ir** verbs that they can.

TEACHING OPTIONS

Video Play the video and have students listen for **–er/–ir** verbs. Have them write down those they hear. Afterward, write the verbs on the board. Ask their meanings. Have students write original sentences using each verb.

Extra Practice Have students answer questions like the following about their Spanish class. Have them answer in complete sentences. **Ustedes estudian mucho para la clase de español, ¿verdad? Deben estudiar más, ¿no? Leen las lecciones, ¿no? Escriben mucho en clase, ¿verdad? Abren los libros, ¿no? Asisten al laboratorio de lenguas, ¿verdad? Comen sándwiches en la clase, ¿verdad? Beben café, ¿no? Comprenden el libro, ¿no?** Pairs may ask each other these questions by changing the verbs to the singular.

1 Expansions
- Working with the whole class, come up with the questions that would elicit the statements in this activity. Ex: **¿Dónde viven tú y tu familia? ¿Cuántos libros tienes? ¿Por qué tienes muchos libros? ¿Cómo es tu hermano Alfredo? ¿Cuándo asiste Alfredo a sus clases? ¿Cuándo corren ustedes? ¿Cuánto comen tus padres? ¿Cuánto deben comer tus padres?**
- Have small groups describe the family pictured here. Ask the groups to invent each person's name, using Hispanic naming conventions, and include his or her physical description, place of origin, and the family relationship to the other people in the photo.

2 Expansion Have pairs create two original dehydrated sentences for another pair to write out.

3 Expansion Write these words on the board for students to add to the activity: **aprender historia japonesa, escribir más cartas, comer más sushi, describir su viaje**.

Práctica

1 **Completar** Complete Susana's sentences about her family with the correct forms of the verbs in parentheses. One of the verbs will remain in the infinitive.

1. Mi familia y yo ___vivimos___ (vivir) en Guayaquil.
2. Tengo muchos libros. Me gusta ___leer___ (leer).
3. Mi hermano Alfredo es muy inteligente. Alfredo ___asiste___ (asistir) a clases los lunes, miércoles y viernes.
4. Los martes y jueves Alfredo y yo ___corremos___ (correr).
5. Mis padres ___comen___ (comer) mucho.
6. Yo ___creo___ (creer) que (*that*) mis padres deben comer menos (*less*).

2 **Oraciones** Juan is talking about what he and his friends do after school. Form complete sentences.

modelo

Yo / correr / amigos / lunes y miércoles
Yo corro con mis amigos los lunes y miércoles.

1. Manuela / asistir / clase / yoga Manuela asiste a la clase de yoga.
2. Eugenio / abrir / correo electrónico (*e-mail*) Eugenio abre su correo electrónico.
3. Isabel y yo / leer / biblioteca Isabel y yo leemos en la biblioteca.
4. Sofía y Roberto / aprender / hablar / inglés Sofía y Roberto aprenden a hablar inglés.
5. Tú / comer / cafetería / universidad Tú comes en la cafetería de la universidad.
6. Mi novia y yo / compartir / libro de historia Mi novia y yo compartimos el libro de historia.

3 **Consejos** Mario teaches Japanese at a university in Quito and is spending a year in Tokyo with his family. In pairs, use the words below to say what he and/or his family members are doing or should do to adjust to life in Japan. Then, create one more sentence using a verb not in the list. Answers will vary.

modelo

recibir libros / deber practicar japonés
Estudiante 1: *Mario y su esposa reciben muchos libros en japonés.*
Estudiante 2: *Los hijos deben practicar japonés.*

aprender japonés	decidir explorar el país
asistir a clases	escribir listas de palabras en japonés
beber sake	leer novelas japonesas
deber comer cosas nuevas	vivir con una familia japonesa
¿?	¿?

TEACHING OPTIONS

Pairs Have pairs of students play the roles of interviewer and movie star. Students can review previous lesson vocabulary lists in preparation. Give pairs sufficient time to plan and practice. When all pairs have completed the activity, ask a few of them to introduce their characters and perform the interview for the whole class.

Heritage Speakers Have heritage speakers brainstorm a list of things that a study-abroad student in a Spanish-speaking country might want to do. Have them base their list on **Actividad 3** using as many **–er/–ir** verbs as they can. Then have the rest of the class write full sentences based on the list.

Comunicación

4

Entrevista Get together with a classmate and use these questions to interview each other. Be prepared to report the results of your interviews to the class. Answers will vary.

1. ¿Dónde comes al mediodía? ¿Comes mucho?
2. ¿Debes comer más (*more*) o menos (*less*)?
3. ¿Cuándo asistes a tus clases?
4. ¿Cuál es tu clase favorita? ¿Por qué?
5. ¿Dónde vives?
6. ¿Con quién vives?
7. ¿Qué cursos debes tomar el próximo (*next*) semestre?
8. ¿Lees el periódico (*newspaper*)? ¿Qué periódico lees y cuándo?
9. ¿Recibes muchas cartas (*letters*)? ¿De quién(es)?
10. ¿Escribes poemas?

5

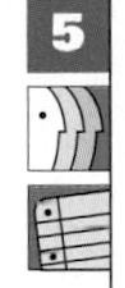

Encuesta Your instructor will give you a worksheet. Walk around the class and ask a different classmate each question about his/her familiy members. Be prepared to report the results of your survey to the class. Answers will vary.

Actividades	Miembros de la familia
1. Vivir en una casa	Los padres de Juan.
2. Beber café	
3. Correr todos los días (*every day*)	
4. Comer mucho en restaurantes	
5. Recibir mucho correo electrónico (*e-mail*)	
6. Comprender tres lenguas	
7. Deber estudiar más (*more*)	
8. Leer muchos libros	

Síntesis

6

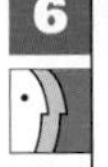

Horario Your instructor will give you and a partner incomplete versions of Alicia's schedule. Fill in the missing information on the schedule by talking to your partner. Be prepared to reconstruct Alicia's complete schedule with the class. Answers will vary.

modelo

Estudiante 1: A las ocho, Alicia corre.
Estudiante 2: ¡Ah, sí! (*Writes down information*)
Estudiante 2: A las nueve, ella ...

4 Suggestions
- Tell students that after one of them has interviewed his or her partner, they should switch roles.
- This activity is also suited to a group of three students, one of whom acts as note taker. They should switch roles at the end of each interview until all three have played all three roles.

5 Suggestions
- Model one or two of the questions. Then distribute the **Hojas de actividades**.
- The activity can also be done by pairs. Have students change the heading of the second column to **¿Sí o no?**

5 Expansion Go through the survey (**encuesta**) to find out how many students perform each activity. Record the results on the board. Ask: **¿Quiénes viven en una casa?**

6 Suggestion Divide the class into pairs and distribute the Info Gap Handouts from the Info Gap Activities Booklet that correspond to this activity. Give the students ten minutes to complete this activity.

6 Expansions
- Ask questions based on Alicia's schedule. Ex: **¿Qué hace Alicia a las nueve? (Ella desayuna.)**
- Have volunteers take turns reading aloud Alicia's schedule. Then have them write their own schedules using as many **–er/–ir** verbs as they can.

TEACHING OPTIONS

Small Groups Have small groups talk about their favorite classes and teachers. They should describe the classes and the teachers and indicate why they like them. They should also mention what days and times they attend each class. A few volunteers may present a summary of their conversation.

Extra Practice Here are four sentences containing **–er/–ir** verbs to use as a dictation. Read each twice, pausing after the second time for students to write. **1. Mi hermana Juana y yo asistimos a la Universidad de Quito. 2. Ella vive en la casa de mis padres y yo vivo en una residencia. 3. Juana es estudiante de letras y lee mucho. 4. Yo estudio computación y aprendo a programar computadoras.**

Section Goals

In **Estructura 3.4** students will:

- learn the present tense forms of **tener** and **venir**
- learn several common expressions with **tener**

Instructional Resources
WB/VM: Workbook, pp. 31–32
Lab Manual, p. 18
Lab CD/MP3 ***Lección 3***
IRM: ***¡Inténtalo!*** *&* ***Práctica*** *Answers, p. 201;*
Tapescript, pp. 11–15
Interactive CD-ROM
Companion website: www.vistahigherlearning.com
Presentations CD-ROM

Suggestions

- Model **tener** with the whole class by asking volunteers questions such as: **¿Tienes una familia grande? ¿Tienes hermanos? ¿Cuántos tíos tiene ____? ¿Tienes muchos primos?** Point out that students have been using forms of **tener** since the beginning of the lesson.
- Point out that the **yo** form of **tener** is irregular and ends in **–go**. Begin a paradigm for **tener** by writing **tengo** on the board. Ask volunteers questions that elicit **tengo** such as: **Tengo una pluma, ¿quién tiene un lápiz?**
- Write **tienes, tiene, tienen,** in the paradigm. Point out that in the **tú, Ud.**, and **Uds.** forms, the **–e–** of the verb stem changes to **–ie–**.
- Write **tenemos** in the paradigm and point out that this form is regular.
- Follow the same procedure to present **venir**. Have students give you the **nosotros** forms of **beber** and **escribir** for comparison.

3.4 Present tense of tener and venir

NATIONAL
comparisons
STANDARDS

ANTE TODO The verbs **tener** (*to have*) and **venir** (*to come*) are among the most frequently used in Spanish. Because most of their forms are irregular, you will have to learn each one individually.

tener **and** ***venir***

		tener	venir
SINGULAR FORMS	yo	ten**go**	ven**go**
	tú	tien**es**	vien**es**
	Ud./él/ella	tien**e**	vien**e**
PLURAL FORMS	nosotros/as	ten**emos**	ven**imos**
	vosotros/as	ten**éis**	ven**ís**
	Uds./ellos/ellas	tien**en**	vien**en**

▶ The endings are the same as those of regular **–er** and **–ir** verbs, except for the **yo** forms, which are irregular: **tengo, vengo.**

▶ In the **tú, Ud.,** and **Uds.** forms, the **e** of the stem changes to **ie** as shown below.

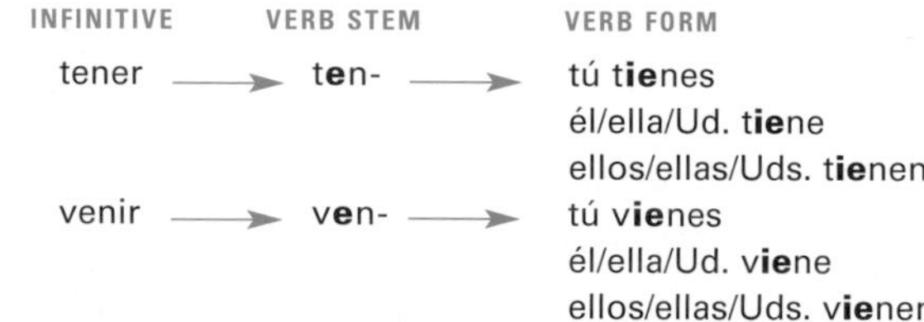

INFINITIVE	VERB STEM	VERB FORM
tener →	ten- →	tú t**ie**nes él/ella/Ud. t**ie**ne ellos/ellas/Uds. t**ie**nen
venir →	ven- →	tú v**ie**nes él/ella/Ud. v**ie**ne ellos/ellas/Uds. v**ie**nen

CONSEJOS

Use what you already know about regular **–er** and **–ir** verbs to identify the irregularities in **tener** and **venir**:
1) Which verb forms use a regular stem? Which use an irregular stem?
2) Which verb forms use the regular endings? Which use irregular endings?

¿Tienes hermanos?

Sí, tengo cuatro hermanas y un hermano mayor.

▶ The **nosotros** and **vosotros** forms are the only ones which are regular. Compare them to the forms of **comer** and **escribir** that you learned on page 86.

	tener	comer	venir	escribir
nosotros/as	ten**emos**	com**emos**	ven**imos**	escrib**imos**
vosotros/as	ten**éis**	com**éis**	ven**ís**	escrib**ís**

TEACHING OPTIONS

Heritage Speakers Have heritage speakers work in pairs to invent a short conversation in which they use forms of **tener, venir,** and other **–ir/–er** verbs they know. Tell them their conversations should involve the family and should include some descriptions of family members. Have pairs present their conversations to the whole class.

Extra Practice Use sentences such as the following for further practice with the conjugation of **tener** and **venir**. First write a sentence on the board and have students say it. Then say a new subject and have students repeat the sentence, substituting the new subject and making all necessary changes. **Yo tengo una familia grande. (Ernesto y yo, Ud., Tú, Ellos) Claudia y Pilar vienen a la clase de historia. (Nosotras, Ernesto, Uds., Tú)**

Expressions with *tener*

tener… años	*to be… years old*	**tener (mucha) prisa**	*to be in a (big) hurry*
tener (mucho) calor	*to be (very) hot*	**tener razón**	*to be right*
tener (mucho) cuidado	*to be (very) careful*	**no tener razón**	*to be wrong*
tener (mucho) frío	*to be (very) cold*	**tener (mucha) sed**	*to be (very) thirsty*
tener (mucha) hambre	*to be (very) hungry*	**tener (mucho) sueño**	*to be (very) sleepy*
tener (mucho) miedo (de)	*to be (very) afraid/ scared (of)*	**tener (mucha) suerte**	*to be (very) lucky*

▶ In certain idiomatic or set expressions in Spanish, you use the construction **tener** + [*noun*] to express *to be* + [*adjective*]. The chart above contains a list of the most common expressions with **tener.**

—¿**Tienen** hambre ustedes?
Are you hungry?

—Sí, y **tenemos** sed también.
Yes, and we're thirsty, too.

▶ To express an obligation, use **tener que** (*to have to*) + [*infinitive*].

—¿Qué **tienes que** estudiar hoy?
What do you have to study today?

—**Tengo que** estudiar biología.
I have to study biology.

▶ To ask people if they feel like doing something, use **tener ganas de** (*to feel like*) + [*infinitive*].

—¿**Tienes ganas de** comer?
Do you feel like eating?

—No, **tengo ganas de** dormir.
No, I feel like sleeping.

LAciudad.COM
Usted tiene que visitarnos.

¡INTÉNTALO! Provide the appropriate forms of **tener** and **venir**. The first item in each column has been done for you.

tener

1. Ellos __tienen__ dos hermanos.
2. Yo __tengo__ una hermana.
3. El artista __tiene__ tres primos.
4. Nosotros __tenemos__ diez tíos.
5. Eva y Diana __tienen__ un sobrino.
6. Usted __tiene__ cinco nietos.
7. Tú __tienes__ dos hermanastras.
8. Ustedes __tienen__ cuatro hijos.
9. Ella __tiene__ una hija.

venir

1. Mis padres __vienen__ de México.
2. Tú __vienes__ de España.
3. Nosotras __venimos__ de Cuba.
4. Pepe __viene__ de Italia.
5. Yo __vengo__ de Francia.
6. Ustedes __vienen__ del Canadá.
7. Alfonso y yo __venimos__ de Portugal.
8. Ellos __vienen__ de Alemania.
9. Usted __viene__ de Venezuela.

Suggestions

- Remind the class that Spanish uses **tener** + [*noun*] in many cases where English uses *to be* + [*adjective*].
- Model the use of the expressions by talking about yourself and asking students questions about themselves. Ex: **Tengo ____ años. Y tú, ¿cuántos años tienes? Esta mañana tengo frío. ¿Tienen frío ustedes? Y tú, ____, ¿tienes frío también o tienes calor? Yo no tengo sueño esta mañana. Me gusta enseñar por la mañana.**
- Present **tener que** + [*infinitive*] and **tener ganas de** + [*infinitive*] together. Go around the class asking questions that use the expressions, having students answer in complete sentences. Ex: ____, **¿tienes que estudiar más para la clase de español?**

TEACHING OPTIONS

Small Groups Have groups of three write nine sentences, each of which uses a different expression with **tener**, including **tener que** + [*infinitive*] and **tener ganas de** + [*infinitive*]. Ask volunteers to write some of their group's best sentences on the board. Work with the whole class to read the sentences and correct any errors.

Variación léxica Point out that **tener que** + [*infinitive*] not only expresses obligation, but also need. **Tengo que estudiar más** can mean either *I have to (am obligated to) study more* or *I need to study more.* Another way of expressing need is with the regular **–ar** verb **necesitar** + [*infinitive*]. Ex: **Necesito estudiar más.** This can also be said with **deber** + [*infinitive*]. Ex: **Debo estudiar más.**

Práctica

1 **Emparejar** Find the phrase in column B that matches best with the phrase in column A. One phrase in column B will not be used.

A		B
1. el Polo Norte	c	a. tener calor
2. una sauna	a	b. tener sed
3. la comida salada (*salty food*)	b	c. tener frío
4. una persona muy inteligente	d	d. tener razón
5. un abuelo	g	e. tener ganas de
6. una dieta	f	f. tener hambre
		g. tener 75 años

2 **Completar** Complete the sentences with the forms of **tener** or **venir.**

1. Hoy nosotros <u>tenemos</u> una reunión familiar (*family reunion*).
2. Yo <u>vengo</u> en autobús de la Universidad de Quito.
3. Todos mis parientes <u>vienen</u>, excepto mi tío Manolo y su esposa.
4. Ellos no <u>tienen</u> ganas de venir porque viven en Portoviejo.
5. Mi prima Susana y su novio no <u>vienen</u> hasta las ocho porque ella <u>tiene</u> que trabajar.
6. En las fiestas, mi hermana siempre <u>viene</u> muy tarde.
7. Nosotros <u>tenemos</u> mucha suerte porque las reuniones son divertidas (*fun*).
8. Mi madre cree que mis sobrinos son muy simpáticos. Creo que ella <u>tiene</u> razón.

3 **Describir** Look at the drawings and describe what people are doing using an expression with **tener.**

1. Tiene (mucha) prisa.

2. Tiene (mucho) calor.

3. Tiene veintiún años.

4. Tienen (mucha) hambre.

5. Tienen (mucho) frío.

6. Tiene (mucha) sed.

1 Suggestion Go over the activity with the class, reading a statement in Column A and having volunteers give the corresponding phrase in Column B. **Tener ganas de** doesn't match any items in Column A. Help students think of a word or phrase that would match it. Ex: **comer una pizza, asistir a un concierto**

1 Expansion Have pairs of students write sentences by combining elements from the two columns. Ex: **Sonia está en el Polo Norte y tiene mucho frío. José es una persona muy inteligente pero no tiene razón.**

2 Expansion Have students answer questions based on the completed activity. Ex: **¿Qué tienen ellos hoy? ¿Cómo viene el narrador a la reunión? ¿Quién no viene?**

3 Suggestion Before doing this activity with the whole class, have students identify which picture is referred to in each of the following statements. (Have them answer: **La(s) persona(s) del dibujo número ____.**) Ask: **¿Quién bebe Coca-Cola?** (6), **¿Quién asiste a una fiesta?** (3), **¿Quiénes comen pizza?** (4), **¿Quiénes esperan el autobús?** (5), **¿Quién corre a la oficina?** (1), **¿Quién hace ejercicio en una bicicleta?** (2)

3 Expansion Orally give students situations to elicit a response with a **tener** expression. Ex: **Pedro come mucho. ¿Por qué? (Porque tiene hambre.)**

TEACHING OPTIONS

Extra Practice Create sentences with **tener** and **venir** such as these: **1. Paula y Luis no tienen hambre, pero yo sí ____ mucha hambre. 2. Mis padres vienen del Ecuador, pero mis hermanos y yo ____ de los Estados Unidos. 3. ¿Tienes frío, Marta? Pues, Carlos y yo ____ calor. 4. Enrique viene de la residencia. ¿De dónde ____ tú, Angélica? 5. ¿Ustedes tienen que trabajar hoy? Yo no ____ que trabajar.**

TPR Assign gestures to each expression with **tener**. Ex: **tener calor:** *wipe brow,* **tener cuidado:** *look around suspiciously,* **tener frío:** *wrap arms around oneself and shiver,* **tener miedo:** *hold hand over mouth in fear.* Have students stand. Say an expression at random (**Tienes sueño**) and point at a student who should perform the appropriate gesture. Vary by pointing to more than one student (**Ustedes tienen hambre**).

Comunicación

4 **¿Sí o no?** Using complete sentences, indicate whether these statements apply to you.
Answers will vary.

1. Mi padre tiene 50 años.
2. Mis amigos vienen a mi casa todos los días (*every day*).
3. Vengo a la universidad los martes.
4. Tengo hambre.
5. Tengo dos computadoras.
6. Tengo sed.
7. Tengo que estudiar los domingos.
8. Tengo una familia grande.

Now interview a classmate by transforming each statement into a question. Be prepared to report the results of your interview to the class. Answers will vary.

modelo

Estudiante 1: *¿Tiene tu padre 50 años?*
Estudiante 2: *No, no tiene 50 años. Tiene 65.*

5 **Preguntas** Get together with a classmate and ask each other the following questions.
Answers will vary.

1. ¿Tienes que estudiar hoy?
2. ¿Cuántos años tienes? ¿Y tus hermanos/as?
3. ¿Cuándo vienes a la clase de español?
4. ¿Cuándo vienen tus amigos a tu casa, apartamento o residencia estudiantil?
5. ¿De qué tienes miedo? ¿Por qué?
6. ¿Qué tienes ganas de hacer esta noche (*tonight*)?

6 **Conversación** Use an expression with **tener** to hint at what's on your mind. Your partner will ask questions to find out why you feel that way. If your partner cannot guess what's on your mind after three attempts, tell him/her. Then switch roles.
Answers will vary.

modelo

Estudiante 1: *Tengo miedo.*
Estudiante 2: *¿Tienes que hablar en público?*
Estudiante 1: *No.*
Estudiante 2: *¿Tienes un examen hoy?*
Estudiante 1: *Sí, y no tengo tiempo para estudiar.*

Síntesis

7 **Minidrama** Act out this situation with a partner: you are introducing your boyfriend/girlfriend to your extended family. To avoid any surprises before you go, talk about who is coming and what each family member is like. Switch roles.
Answers will vary.

4 Suggestion Give students three minutes to read and answer the questions. Have them rephrase any statement that does not apply to them so that it does. Ex: **Mi padre tiene 80 años.** Then read the **modelo** and make clear the transformations involved.

5 Suggestion Remind students that each partner should both ask and answer all the questions. Ask volunteers to summarize the responses. Record these responses on the board as a survey (**encuesta**) about the class's characteristics.

6 Suggestion Give an expression with **tener**. (Ex: **Tengo mucha prisa.**) Encourage students to guess the reason using **tener** and **venir**. If they guess incorrectly, give them more specific clues. Ex: **Tengo mucho que hacer hoy. Es un día especial. (Viene un amigo.)**

6 Expansion In pairs, have students use **tener** and **venir** to invent a conversation between the characters in the drawing.

7 Suggestion Before doing **Síntesis**, have students quickly refamiliarize themselves with the following material: family vocabulary on pages 70–71; descriptive adjectives on pages 78–80; possessive adjectives on page 83; and the forms of **tener** and **venir** on page 90.

TEACHING OPTIONS

Small Groups Have small groups prepare skits in which one person takes a few friends to a family reunion. The introducer should make polite introductions and tell the people he or she is introducing a few facts about each other. All the people involved should attempt to make small talk.

Game Give pairs of students five minutes to write a conversation in which they use as many of the expressions with **tener** as they can in a logical manner. After the time is up ask pairs the number of **tener** expressions they used in their conversations. Have the top three or four perform their conversations before the whole class.

Section Goals

In **Lectura** students will:
- learn to use context clues in reading
- read context-rich selections about Hispanic families

Instructional Resource
Companion website: www.vistahigherlearning.com

Estrategia Tell students that they can often infer the meaning of an unfamiliar Spanish word by looking at the word's context and by using their common sense. Five types of context clues are:
- synonyms
- antonyms
- clarifications
- definitions
- additional details

Have students read the sentence **Ayer fui a ver a mi tía abuela, la hermana de mi abuela** from the letter. Point out that the meaning of **tía abuela** can be inferred from its similarity to the known word **abuela** and from the clarification that follows in the letter.

Examinar el texto Have students read Paragraph 1 silently. Point out the phrase **salgo a pasear** and ask a volunteer to explain how the context might give clues to the meaning. Afterward, point out that **salgo** is the first-person singular form of **salir** (*to go out*). Tell students they will learn all the forms of **salir** in **Lección 4**.

Examinar el formato Guide students to see that the photos and captions reveal that the paragraphs are about several different families.

Lectura

Antes de leer

Estrategia
Guessing meaning from context

As you read in Spanish, you'll often come across words you haven't learned. You can guess what they mean by looking at the surrounding words and sentences. Look at the following text and guess what **tía abuela** means, based on the context.

¡Hola, Claudia!
¿Qué hay de nuevo?
¿Sabes qué? Ayer fui a ver a mi tía abuela, la hermana de mi abuela. Tiene 85 años pero es muy independiente. Vive en un apartamento en Quito con su prima Lorena, quien también tiene 85 años.

If you guessed *great-aunt*, you are correct, and you can conclude from this word and the format clues that this is a letter about someone's visit with his or her great-aunt.

Examinar el texto

Quickly read through the paragraphs and find two or three words you don't know. Using the context as your guide, guess what these words mean. Then glance at the paragraphs where these words appear and try to predict what the paragraphs are about.

Examinar el formato

Look at the format of the reading. What clues do the captions, photos, and layout give you about its content?

recursos

vistahigherlearning.com

Gente • • • Las familias

1. Me llamo Armando y tengo setenta años pero no me considero viejo. Tengo seis nietas y un nieto. Vivo con mi hija y tengo la oportunidad de pasar mucho tiempo con ella y con mi nieto. Por las tardes salgo a pasear° por el parque con mi nieto y por la noche le leo cuentos°.

Armando. Tiene seis nietas y un nieto.

2. Mi prima Victoria y yo nos llevamos muy bien. Estudiamos juntas° en la universidad y compartimos un apartamento. Ella es muy inteligente y me ayuda con los estudios. Además, es muy simpática y generosa. Si no tengo dinero°, ¡ella me lo presta!

Diana. Vive con su prima.

3. Me llamo Ramona y soy paraguaya, aunque ahora vivo en los Estados Unidos. Tengo tres hijos, uno de nueve años, uno de doce y el mayor de quince. Es difícil a veces, pero mi esposo y yo tratamos° de ayudarlos y comprenderlos siempre.

Ramona. Sus hijos son muy importantes para ella.

TEACHING OPTIONS

Heritage Speakers Ask heritage speakers to use the paragraphs in **Gente... Las familias** as models for writing paragraphs about themselves and their families. Have them read their paragraphs to the class.

Extra Practice Use the following sentences, each of which contains an unfamiliar word or phrase, to practice using context clues. **1. Mi tío Daniel es maestro en una escuela secundaria; enseña ciencias. 2. No, mi sobrina no es antipática, ¡es un cariño! 3. Por favor, ¿tienes un boli o un lápiz con que escribir tu número de teléfono?**

4. Tengo mucha suerte. Aunque° mis padres están divorciados, tengo una familia muy unida. Tengo dos hermanos y dos hermanas. Me gusta hablar y salir a fiestas con ellos. Ahora tengo novio en la universidad y él no conoce a mis hermanos. ¡Espero que se lleven bien!

Ana María. Su familia es muy unida.

5. Antes quería° tener hermanos pero ya no es tan importante. Ser hijo único tiene muchas ventajas°: no tengo que compartir mis cosas con hermanos, no hay discusiones° y, como soy nieto único también, ¡mis abuelos piensan que soy perfecto!

Fernando. Es hijo único.

6. Como soy joven todavía°, no tengo ni esposa ni hijos. Pero tengo un sobrino, el hijo de mi hermano, que es muy especial para mí. Se llama Benjamín y tiene diez años. Es un muchacho muy simpático. Siempre tiene hambre y por lo tanto vamos frecuentemente a comer hamburguesas. Nos gusta también ir al cine° a ver películas de acción. Hablamos de todo. ¡Creo que ser tío es mejor que ser padre!

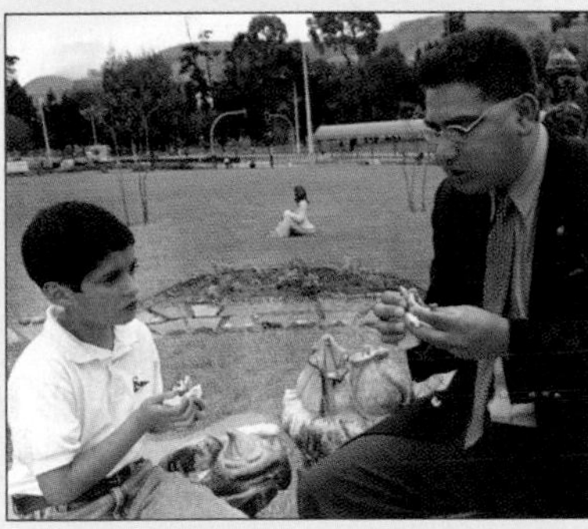
Santiago. Ser tío es divertido.

salgo a pasear *I go take a walk* **cuentos** *stories* **juntas** *together* **dinero** *money* **tratamos** *we try* **Aunque** *Although* **quería** *I wanted* **ventajas** *advantages* **discusiones** *arguments* **todavía** *still* **ir al cine** *go to the movies*

Después de leer

Emparejar

Glance at the paragraphs and see how the words and phrases in column A are used in context. Then find their definitions in column B.

A		B
1. me lo presta	d	a. the oldest
2. nos llevamos bien	h	b. movies
3. no conoce	g	c. the youngest
4. películas	b	d. loans it to me
5. mejor que	j	e. borrows it from me
6. el mayor	a	f. we see each other
		g. doesn't know
		h. we get along
		i. portraits
		j. better than

Seleccionar

Choose the sentence that best summarizes each paragraph.

1. Párrafo 1 a
   a. Me gusta mucho ser abuelo.
   b. No hablo mucho con mi nieto.
   c. No tengo nietos.
2. Párrafo 2 c
   a. Mi prima es antipática.
   b. Mi prima no es muy trabajadora.
   c. Mi prima y yo somos muy buenas amigas.
3. Párrafo 3 a
   a. Tener hijos es un gran sacrificio pero es muy bonito también.
   b. No comprendo a mis hijos.
   c. Mi esposo y yo no tenemos hijos.
4. Párrafo 4 c
   a. No hablo mucho con mis hermanos.
   b. Comparto mis cosas con mis hermanos.
   c. Mis hermanos y yo somos como (*like*) amigos.
5. Párrafo 5 a
   a. Me gusta ser hijo único.
   b. Tengo hermanos y hermanas.
   c. Vivo con mis abuelos.
6. Párrafo 6 b
   a. Mi sobrino tiene diez años.
   b. Me gusta mucho ser tío.
   c. Mi esposa y yo no tenemos hijos.

Emparejar If students have trouble inferring the meaning of any item, help them identify the corresponding context clues. **1. me lo presta (si no tengo dinero) 2. nos llevamos bien (compartimos un apartamento) 3. no conoce (ahora tengo novio en la universidad) 4. películas (cine) 5. mejor que (ser tío, ser padre) 6. el mayor (de quince)**

Seleccionar You might wish to ask students these listening comprehension questions. **1. ¿Cuántos años tiene Armando? (setenta) 2. ¿Con quién vive Armando? (con su hija) 3. ¿Con quién comparte una apartamento Diana? (con Victoria) 4. ¿Cómo es Victoria? (inteligente, simpática y generosa) 5. ¿De dónde es Ramona? (Es de Paraguay.) 6. ¿En qué país vive Ramona ahora? (en los Estados Unidos) 7. ¿Cómo es la familia de Ana María? (muy unida) 8. ¿Ana María tiene novio? (Sí, tiene novio.) 9. ¿Qué tiene muchas ventajas para Fernando? (ser hijo único) 10. ¿Qué piensan los abuelos de Fernando? (que es perfecto) 11. ¿Cómo se llama el sobrino de Santiago? (Benjamín) 12. ¿Qué tiene Benjamín siempre? (hambre)**

Suggestion Encourage students to record unfamiliar words and phrases that they learn in **Lectura** in their portfolios (**carpetas**).

TEACHING OPTIONS

Pairs Have pairs of students work together to read aloud several paragraphs and write a question about each. When they have finished, ask them to exchange their questions with another pair who can work together to answer them.

Extra Practice Have partners check their work in **Emparejar** by locating in the paragraphs the words and phrases which enabled them to infer the meanings of the target words and phrases.

Extra Practice Give students true or false statements about the paragraphs in **Lectura**. Ex: **Armando es muy joven. (Falso. Tiene 70 años.)**

Section Goals

In **Escritura** students will:

- learn to write a friendly letter in Spanish
- integrate vocabulary and structures taught in **Lección 3** and before

Estrategia Have students create their idea maps in Spanish. Some students may find it helpful to create their idea maps with note cards. They can write each detail that would be contained in a circle on a separate card to facilitate rearrangement.

Tema Introduce students to the common salutations (**saludos**) and closings (**despedidas**) used in friendly letters in Spanish. Point out that the salutation **Estimado/a** is more formal than **Querido/a**, which is rather familiar. Also point out that **Un abrazo** is less familiar in Spanish than its translation *a hug* would be in English.

Escritura

Estrategia

Using idea maps

How do you organize ideas for a first draft? Often, the organization of ideas represents the most challenging part of the process. Idea maps are useful for organizing pertinent information. Here is an example of an idea map you can use:

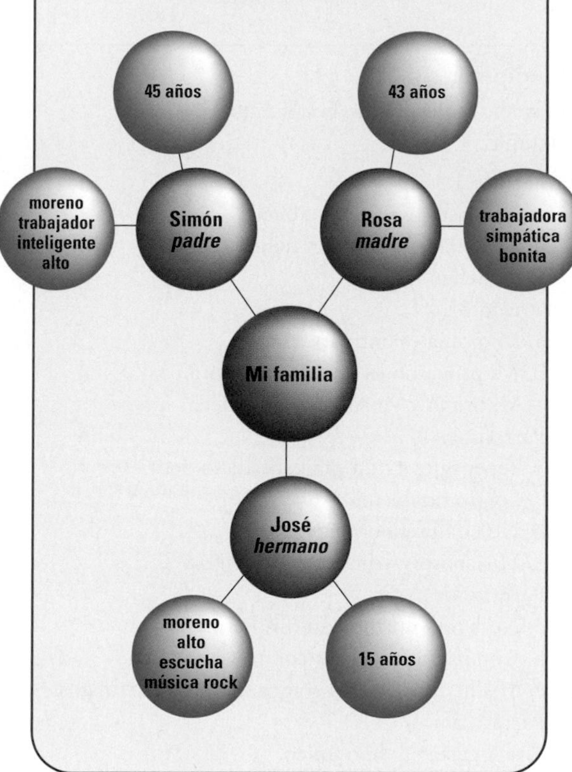

Tema

Escribir una carta

A friend you met in a chat room for Spanish speakers wants to know about your family. Using some of the verbs and adjectives you have learned in this lesson, write a brief letter describing your family or an imaginary family, including:

- Names and relationships
- Physical characteristics
- Hobbies and interests

Here are some useful expressions for letter writing in Spanish:

Salutations

Estimado/a Julio/Julia	*Dear Julio/Julia*
Querido/a Miguel/Ana María	*Dear Miguel/Ana María*

Closings

Un abrazo,	*A hug,*
Abrazos,	*Hugs,*
Cariños,	*Much love,*
¡Hasta pronto!	*See you soon!*
¡Hasta la próxima semana!	*See you next week!*

TEACHING OPTIONS

Proofreading Activity Copy as many of the following sentences containing mistakes onto the board or a transparency as you think appropriate for a proofreading activity to do with the whole class.

1. **Mis hermana Paula es una persona muy simpático y inteligente.**
2. **Ella es estudiante y asista a clases en una grande universidad.**
3. **Viva en una residencia estudiantil y lea muchos libros.**
4. **Tiene cinco clase y tiene de estudiar mucho.**
5. **A ella le gusta más tu clase de literatura inglésa.**

Plan de escritura

1 Ideas y organización

Create an idea map by filling out the first subsections with the names of your family members, then filling in as much information as possible about each one in Spanish.

2 Primer borrador

Using the idea map you prepared in **Ideas y organización,** write the first draft of the letter to your keypal.

3 Comentario

Exchange papers with a classmate and comment on each other's work, using the questions below as a guide. Begin by mentioning one or two points that you like about the person's letter, such as the adjectives used or the variety of **–ar, –er,** and **–ir** verbs.

a. Does the document contain all the elements of a letter?
b. Does the letter include sufficient details about each family member? Are any details extraneous?
c. Is the letter organized in a logical fashion? Does each paragraph transition logically to the next?
d. Do you have suggestions for making the letter more interesting or complete?
e. Do you see spelling or grammatical errors?

4 Redacción

Revise your first draft, keeping in mind your classmate's comments. Also incorporate any new ideas or information you may have. Before handing in the final version, review your work using these guidelines:

a. Underline each verb and make sure it agrees with the subject.
b. Check the gender and number of each article, noun, and adjective.
c. Check your spelling and punctuation.

5 Evaluación y progreso

Swap letters with a classmate. Then read the letter and point out the two things you like best about it. After your instructor returns your paper, review the comments and corrections. Note the most important issues on your **Anotaciones para mejorar la escritura** list in your **Carpeta de trabajos.**

Comentario
- Go over each of the guide questions with the whole class so peer readers understand their task. Then have pairs of students exchange letters. Allow five minutes for reading and comments. Allow five minutes for discussing comments.
- Have students read **Redacción** as homework. Ask them to rewrite their drafts, incorporating the peer comments and following the directions in **Redacción**.

Evaluación y progreso Give the class five minutes to exchange and read the final drafts of their classmates' letters. Then have them hand them in to you.

Writing Sample Here is a sample of a letter that would constitute superior writing achievement.

Querida Pilar,

Me llamo Francisco. Tengo veintiún años. Soy alto, moreno y delgado. También soy inteligente y trabajador.

Soy de los Estados Unidos. Mis padres también son de los Estados Unidos, pero mis abuelos, los padres de mi papá, son mexicanos. Vienen de visita cada año. No tengo una familia muy grande. Tengo sólo un hermano mayor y una hermana menor, pero tengo muchos tíos y primos.

Soy estudiante en la Universidad de Texas en Austin. Me gusta mucho la clase de matemáticas.

¿Y tú, Pilar? ¿Cómo eres? ¿Qué materias estudias? ¿Te gusta la universidad? ¿Cómo es tu familia?

¡Hasta pronto!
Francisco

EVALUATION: Carta

Criteria	Scale
Appropriate salutations/closings	1 2 3 4 5
Appropriate details	1 2 3 4 5
Organization	1 2 3 4 5
Accuracy	1 2 3 4 5

Scoring	
Excellent	18–20 points
Good	14–17 points
Satisfactory	10–13 points
Unsatisfactory	< 10 points

Section Goals

In **Escuchar** students will:
- listen to and summarize a short paragraph
- learn strategies for asking for clarification in oral communication
- answer questions based on the content of a recorded conversation

Instructional Resources
Textbook CD
IRM: Tapescript, p. 87

Estrategia
Script La familia de María Dolores es muy grande. Tiene dos hermanos y tres hermanas. Su familia vive en España. Pero la familia de Alberto es muy pequeña. No tiene hermanos ni hermanas. Alberto y sus padres viven en el Ecuador.

Suggestion Have students look at the photo and describe what they see. Guide them to guess where they think Cristina and Laura are and what they are talking about.

Ahora escucha
Script LAURA: ¿Qué hay de nuevo, Cristina?
CRISTINA: No mucho... sólo problemas con mi novio.
L: ¿Perdón?
C: No hay mucho de nuevo... sólo problemas con mi novio, Rafael.
L: ¿Qué les pasa?
C: Bueno, Rafael es alto y moreno... es muy guapo. Y es buena gente. Es inteligente también... pero es que no lo encuentro muy interesante.
L: ¿Cómo?
C: No es muy interesante. Sólo habla del fútbol y del béisbol. No me gusta hablar del fútbol las veinticuatro horas al día. No comprendo a los muchachos. ¿Cómo es tu novio, Laura?
L: Esteban es muy simpático. Es un poco gordo pero creo que es muy guapo. También es muy trabajador.
C: ¿Es interesante?
L: Sí. Hablamos dos o tres horas cada día. Hablamos de muchas cosas... las clases, los amigos... de todo.
C: ¡Qué bien! Siempre tengo mala suerte con los novios.

Escuchar

Estrategia

Asking for repetition/ Replaying the recording

Sometimes it is difficult to understand what people say, especially in a noisy environment. During a conversation, you can ask someone to repeat by saying **¿Cómo?** (*What?*) or **¿Perdón?** (*Pardon me?*). In class, you can ask your teacher to repeat by saying **Repita, por favor** (*Repeat, please*). If you don't understand a recorded activity, you can simply replay it.

To help you practice this strategy, you will listen to a short paragraph. Ask your professor to repeat it or replay the recording, and then summarize what you heard.

Preparación

Based on the photograph, where do you think Cristina and Laura are? What do you think Laura is saying to Cristina?

Ahora escucha 

Now you are going to hear Laura and Cristina's conversation. Use **R** to indicate which adjectives describe Cristina's boyfriend, Rafael. Use **E** for adjectives that describe Laura's boyfriend, Esteban. Some adjectives will not be used.

____ **rubio**	E **interesante**
____ **feo**	____ **antipático**
R **alto**	R **inteligente**
E **trabajador**	R **moreno**
E **un poco gordo**	____ **viejo**

Comprensión

Identificar

Which person would make each statement: Cristina or Laura?

	Cristina	Laura
1. Mi novio habla sólo de fútbol y de béisbol.	✓	❍
2. Tengo un novio muy interesante y simpático.	❍	✓
3. Mi novio es alto y moreno.	✓	❍
4. Mi novio trabaja mucho.	❍	✓
5. Mi amiga no tiene buena suerte con los muchachos.	❍	✓
6. El novio de mi amiga es un poco gordo, pero guapo.	✓	❍

¿Cierto o falso?

Indicate whether each sentence is **cierto** or **falso,** then correct the false statements.

	Cierto	Falso
1. Esteban es un chico interesante y simpático.	✓	❍
2. Laura tiene mala suerte con los chicos. Cristina tiene mala suerte con los chicos.	❍	✓
3. Rafael es muy interesante. Esteban es muy interesante.	❍	✓
4. Laura y su novio hablan de muchas cosas.	✓	❍

Proyecto

Describe a tu familia

Imagine that you have just returned from a summer exchange program in Ecuador. Your Spanish instructor has asked you to give a short presentation about the Ecuadorian family you stayed with.

1 Haz un árbol genealógico

Create an illustrated family tree of your Ecuadorian family. Using the research tools found in **Recursos para la investigación,** collect photographs of the family members, as well as photographs and short descriptions of the cities in Ecuador where they live. Your family tree might include these elements:

- A simple, yet descriptive title
- A format that clearly shows the relationships between the family members
- Photographs of the family members
- The names of the family members, using Hispanic conventions for the way names are written
- The names and photographs of the cities where the family members live
- Three or four adjectives that describe each family member

2 Presenta la información

Using your family tree as a guide, give a brief presentation to the class about your Ecuadorian family. Make your descriptions of the family members and where they live as interesting as you can. Leave your classmates wanting to go to Ecuador and experience the country and its people.

recursos para la investigación

	**Internet** Palabras clave: Ecuador, Ecuadorian, cities, geography, map(s)		**Comunidad** Exchange students, faculty members, and residents in your community who are from Ecuador or have lived in Ecuador
	**Biblioteca** Newspapers, magazines, travel magazines		**Otros recursos** Your school's International Studies Office, the Ecuadorian embassy or consulates, Ecuadorian travel agencies

Section Goals

In **Proyecto** students will:
- use Spanish as they carry out research and to interact with the wider world
- have the opportunity to make a presentation in Spanish
- create a family tree

Suggestion Students might need a week to complete the project, so at the beginning of that time period, have them read through **Proyecto**. Explain that they are going to carry out research on the cities and people of Ecuador. Tell them that they will make a family tree for an imaginary Ecuadorian family and present the family tree to the class.

Haz un árbol genealógico
Students may use newspaper or magazine photos for their family tree. Encourage them to be creative.

Presenta la información
- In preparation for their presentations, students may practice before a small group of friends who can critique the presentation.
- Rather than having all presentations on the same day, set aside sufficient class time to do a few at a time until all students have had a chance to present.

EVALUATION: Descripción

Criteria	Scale
Content	1 2 3 4
Comprehensibility	1 2 3 4
Organization	1 2 3 4
Accuracy	1 2 3 4
Use of visuals	1 2 3 4

Scoring	
Excellent	18–20 points
Good	14–17 points
Satisfactory	10–13 points
Unsatisfactory	< 10 points

Section Goal
In **Panorama**, students will receive comprehensible input by reading about the geography and culture of Ecuador.

Instructional Resources
Transparencies, #5, #6, #18
WB/VM: Workbook, pp. 33–34; Video Activities, pp. 253–254
***Panorama cultural** DVD/Video*
Interactive CD-ROM
IRM: Videoscript, p. 128
Companion website: www.vistahigherlearning.com
Presentations CD-ROM

Suggestion Have students look at the map of Ecuador or project **Transparency #18**. Then have them look at the call-out photos and read the captions. Encourage students to mention anything they may know about Ecuador.

El país en cifras
- Ask students to glance at the headings. Establish the kind of information contained in each and clarify unfamiliar words. Point out that every word in the headings has an English cognate.
- Ask volunteers to read the sections. After each section, ask other students questions about the content. Point out that where hundreds, thousands, and millions are separated by commas in English, most Spanish-speaking countries use periods. Model the pronunciation of the numbers.
- Point out that in September 2000 the U.S. dollar became the official currency of Ecuador.

¡Increíble pero cierto!
Mt. St. Helens in Washington and Cotopaxi in Ecuador are just two of a chain of volcanoes that stretches along the entire Pacific coast of North and South America, from Mt. McKinley in Alaska to Monte Sarmiento in Tierra del Fuego of southern Chile.

Ecuador

El país en cifras

- **Área:** 283.560 km² (109.483 millas²), *incluyendo las islas Galápagos, aproximadamente el área de Colorado*
- **Población:** 13.798.000
- **Capital:** Quito — 1.832.000
- **Ciudades principales:** Guayaquil — 2.359.000, Cuenca — 247.000, Machala — 191.000, Portoviejo — 164.000

SOURCE: Population Division, UN Secretariat

- **Moneda:** dólar estadounidense
- **Idiomas:** español (oficial), quichua

La lengua° oficial del Ecuador es el español, pero también se hablan° otras° lenguas en el país. Aproximadamente unos 4.000.000 de ecuatorianos hablan lenguas indígenas; la mayoría° de ellos habla quichua. El quichua es el dialecto ecuatoriano del quechua, la lengua de los incas.

Los indígenas del Ecuador hablan quichua.

Bandera del Ecuador

Indígenas del Amazonas

La ciudad de Quito y la Cordillera de los Andes

Catedral de Guayaquil

Ecuatorianos célebres
- **Francisco Eugenio De Santa Cruz y Espejo,** médico, periodista y patriota (1747–1795)
- **Juan León Mera,** novelista (1832–1894)
- **Eduardo Kingman,** pintor° (1913–1998)
- **Rosalía Arteaga,** abogada°, política y ex-vicepresidenta (1956–)

lengua *language* se hablan *are spoken* otras *other* mayoría *majority* pintor *painter* abogada *lawyer* sur *south* mundo *world* pies *feet* dos veces más alto *twice as tall*

recursos

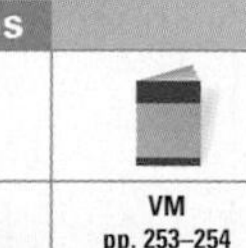
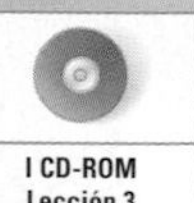
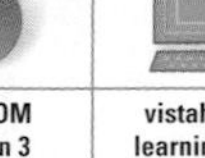

WB pp. 33–34	VM pp. 253–254	I CD-ROM Lección 3	vistahigher learning.com

¡Increíble pero cierto!

El volcán Cotopaxi, situado a unos 60 kilómetros al sur° de Quito, es considerado el volcán activo más alto del mundo°. Tiene una altura de 5.897 metros (19.340 pies°). Es dos veces más alto° que el monte St. Helens (2.550 metros o 9.215 pies) en el estado de Washington.

TEACHING OPTIONS

Heritage Speakers If a heritage speaker has visited Ecuador, ask him or her to prepare a short presentation about his or her experiences there. If possible, the presentation should be illustrated with photos and articles of the country.

Variación léxica Remind students that **km²** is the abbreviation for **kilómetros cuadrados** and that **millas²** is the abbreviation for **millas cuadradas**. Ask a volunteer to explain why **kilómetros** takes **cuadrados** and **millas** takes **cuadradas**.

Lugares • Las islas Galápagos

Muchas personas vienen de lejos a visitar las islas Galápagos porque son un verdadero tesoro° ecológico. Aquí Charles Darwin estudió° las especies que inspiraron° sus ideas sobre la evolución. Como las islas están lejos del continente, sus plantas y animales son únicos. Las islas son famosas por sus tortugas° gigantes.

Artes • Oswaldo Guayasamín

Oswaldo Guayasamín fue° uno de los artistas latinoamericanos más famosos del mundo. Fue escultor° y muralista. Su expresivo estilo viene del cubismo y sus temas preferidos son la injusticia y la pobreza° sufridas° por los indígenas de su país.

Madre y niño en azul, 1986, Oswaldo Guayasamín

Deportes • El *trekking*

El sistema montañoso de los Andes cruza° y divide el Ecuador en varias regiones. La Sierra, que tiene volcanes, grandes valles y una variedad increíble de plantas y animales, es perfecta para el *trekking*. Muchos turistas visitan el Ecuador cada° año para hacer° *trekking* y escalar montañas°.

Lugares • Latitud 0

Hay un monumento en el Ecuador, a unos 22 kilómetros (14 millas) de Quito, donde los visitantes están en el hemisferio norte y el hemisferio sur a la misma vez°. Este monumento se llama la Mitad del Mundo°, y es un destino turístico muy popular.

Explosión del volcán Tungurahua en 1999

¿Qué aprendiste? Completa las frases con la información correcta.

1. La ciudad más grande (*biggest*) del Ecuador es __Guayaquil__.
2. La capital del Ecuador es __Quito__.
3. Unos 4.000.000 de ecuatorianos hablan __quichua__.
4. Darwin estudió el proceso de la evolución en __las islas Galápagos__.
5. Dos temas del arte de __Guayasamín__ son la pobreza y la __injusticia__.
6. Un destino turístico muy popular es __la Mitad del Mundo__.
7. La Sierra es un lugar perfecto para el __trekking__.
8. El volcán __Cotopaxi__ es el volcán activo más alto del mundo.

Conexión Internet Investiga estos temas en el sitio **www.vistahigherlearning.com.**

1. Busca información sobre una ciudad del Ecuador. ¿Te gustaría (*would you like*) visitar la ciudad? ¿Por qué?
2. Haz una lista de tres animales o plantas que viven sólo en las islas Galápagos. ¿Dónde hay animales o plantas similares?

verdadero tesoro *true treasure* **estudió** *studied* **inspiraron** *inspired* **tortugas** *tortoises* **fue** *was* **escultor** *sculptor* **pobreza** *poverty* **sufridas** *suffered* **cruza** *crosses* **cada** *every* **hacer** *to do* **escalar montañas** *to climb mountains* **a la misma vez** *at the same time* **Mitad del Mundo** *Equatorial Line Monument (lit. Midpoint of the World)*

Las islas Galápagos Show magazine and book articles that give an idea of the Galapagos Islands. (See *National Geographic en Español*, April 1999, pages 2–41 as a source of dramatic photography.)

Oswaldo Guayasamín (1919–1999) The name **Guayasamín** means *white bird* in Quichua. The artist took this name out of solidarity with his Incan ancestors. Bring reproductions of some of Guayasamín's work to class. Show a variety of his often disturbing paintings and encourage students to talk about what the artist's social and political stance might be.

El *trekking* *Trekking* is one of several English words that have been accepted into Spanish. These words name phenomena whose popularity originated in the English-speaking world. Some words like these enter Spanish without much change: **camping, marketing**. Others are changed to match Spanish spelling patterns, as **líder** (*leader*) or **mítin** (*meeting*).

Latitud 0 Bring in a globe and have students find Ecuador and point out its location on the equator.

Conexión Internet Students will find supporting Internet activities and links at **www.vistahigherlearning.com**.

TEACHING OPTIONS

Variación léxica A word that the Quichua language has contributed to English is *jerky* (salted, dried meat), which comes from the Quichua word **charqui**. The Quichua-speaking peoples of the Andean highlands had perfected techniques for "freeze-drying" both vegetable tubers and meat before the first Spaniards arrived in the region. Freeze-dried potatoes, called **chuño**, are a staple in the diet of the inhabitants of the Andes.

In Ecuador and throughout the rest of South America, **charqui** is the word used to name meat preserved by drying. **Charqui** is an important component in the national cuisines of South America, and in Argentina, Uruguay, and Brazil its production is a major industry. In other parts of the Spanish-speaking world you may hear the terms **tasajo** or **carne seca** used instead of **charqui**.

Instructional Resources
Vocabulary CD
Lab Manual, p. 18
Lab CD/MP3 ***Lección 3***
IRM: Tapescript, pp. 11–15
Testing Program: ***Pruebas****,*
pp. 25–36
Testing Program Audio CD
Test Files CD-ROM

La familia

el/la abuelo/a	*grandfather/ grandmother*
los abuelos	*grandparents*
el apellido	*last name*
el/la bisabuelo/a	*great-grandfather/ great-grandmother*
el/la cuñado/a	*brother-in-law/ sister-in-law*
el/la esposo/a	*husband; wife; spouse*
la familia	*family*
el/la gemelo/a	*twin*
el/la hermanastro/a	*stepbrother/ stepsister*
el/la hermano/a	*brother/sister*
el/la hijastro/a	*stepson/ stepdaughter*
el/la hijo/a	*son/daughter*
los hijos	*children*
la madrastra	*stepmother*
la madre	*mother*
el/la medio/a hermano/a	*half-brother/ half-sister*
el/la nieto/a	*grandson/ granddaughter*
la nuera	*daughter-in-law*
el padrastro	*stepfather*
el padre	*father*
los padres	*parents*
los parientes	*relatives*
el/la primo/a	*cousin*
el/la sobrino/a	*nephew/niece*
el/la suegro/a	*father-in-law/ mother-in-law*
el/la tío/a	*uncle/aunt*
el yerno	*son-in-law*

recursos

LM p. 18	Lab CD/MP3 Lección 3	Vocab CD Lección 3

Otras personas

el/la amigo/a	*friend*
la gente	*people*
el/la muchacho/a	*boy/girl*
el/la niño/a	*child*
el/la novio/a	*boyfriend/girlfriend*
la persona	*person*

Profesiones

el/la artista	*artist*
el/la doctor(a), el/la médico/a	*doctor; physician*
el/la ingeniero/a	*engineer*
el/la periodista	*journalist*
el/la programador(a)	*computer programmer*

Adjetivos

alto/a	*tall*
antipático/a	*unpleasant*
bajo/a	*short (in height)*
bonito/a	*pretty*
buen, bueno/a	*good*
delgado/a	*thin; slender*
difícil	*difficult; hard*
fácil	*easy*
feo/a	*ugly*
gordo/a	*fat*
gran, grande	*big*
guapo/a	*handsome; good-looking*
importante	*important*
inteligente	*intelligent*
interesante	*interesting*
joven	*young*
mal, malo/a	*bad*
mismo/a	*same*
moreno/a	*brunet(te)*
mucho/a	*much; many; a lot of*
pelirrojo/a	*red-hair*
pequeño/a	*small*
rubio/a	*blond(e)*
simpático/a	*nice; likeable*
tonto/a	*silly; foolish*
trabajador(a)	*hard-working*
viejo/a	*old*

Nacionalidades

alemán, alemana	*German*
canadiense	*Canadian*
chino/a	*Chinese*
ecuatoriano/a	*Ecuadorian*
español(a)	*Spanish*
estadounidense	*from the U. S.*
francés, francesa	*French*
inglés, inglesa	*English*
italiano/a	*Italian*
japonés, japonesa	*Japanese*
mexicano/a	*Mexican*
norteamericano/a	*(North) American*
puertorriqueño/a	*Puerto Rican*
ruso/a	*Russian*

Verbos

abrir	*to open*
aprender (a + ***inf.*****)**	*to learn*
asistir (a)	*to attend*
beber	*to drink*
comer	*to eat*
compartir	*to share*
comprender	*to understand*
correr	*to run*
creer (en)	*to believe (in)*
deber (+ ***inf.*****)**	*should; must*
decidir (+ ***inf.*****)**	*to decide*
describir	*to describe*
escribir	*to write*
leer	*to read*
recibir	*to receive*
tener	*to have*
venir	*to come*
vivir	*to live*

Possessive adjectives	*See page 83.*
Expressions with ***tener***	*See page 91.*
Expresiones útiles	*See page 75.*

Los pasatiempos 4

Communicative Goals

You will learn how to:

- Talk about pastimes, weekend activities, and sports
- Make plans and invitations

contextos

pages 104–107
- Pastimes
- Sports
- Places in the city

fotonovela

pages 108–111

Don Francisco informs the students that they have an hour of free time. Inés and Javier decide to take a walk through the city. Maite and Álex go to a park where they are involved in a minor accident. On their way back, Álex invites Maite to go running.

estructura

pages 112–125
- Present tense of **ir**
- Stem-changing verbs: **e→ie; o→ue**
- Stem-changing verbs: **e→i**
- Verbs with irregular **yo** forms

adelante

pages 126–131

Lectura: Read about popular sports in Latin America.
Escritura: Write a pamphlet about activities in your community.
Escuchar: Listen to a conversation about pastimes.
Proyecto: Create a radio broadcast about sporting events.

panorama

pages 132–133

Featured country: México
- México D.F.: the largest city in the world
- The legacy of the Aztec civilization
- Frida Kahlo and Diego Rivera

A PRIMERA VISTA
- ¿Qué son estas personas, atletas o artistas?
- ¿En qué tienen interés, en el fútbol o el tenis?
- ¿Son viejos? ¿Son delgados?
- ¿Tienen frío o calor?

Lesson Goals

In **Lección 4** students will be introduced to the following:
- names of sports and other pastimes
- names of places in a city
- present tense of **ir**
- the contraction **al**
- **ir a** + [*infinitive*]
- present tense of common stem-changing verbs
- verbs with irregular **yo** forms
- predicting content by surveying graphic elements
- using a Spanish-English dictionary
- writing a pamphlet that lists events
- listening for the gist
- writing and delivering a radio sports broadcast
- cultural, historical, and geographic information about Mexico

A primera vista Here are some additional questions you can ask based on the photo: **¿Te gusta el fútbol? ¿Crees que son importantes los pasatiempos? ¿Trabajas mucho los sábados y domingos? ¿Bailas? ¿Lees? ¿Escuchas música?**

INSTRUCTIONAL RESOURCES

Workbook/Video Manual: WB Activities, pp. 37–48
Laboratory Manual: Lab Activities, pp. 19–24
Workbook/Video Manual: Video Activities, pp. 219–220; pp. 255–256
Instructor's Resource Manual: **Hojas de actividades**, p. 165; **Vocabulario adicional**, p. 182; **¡Inténtalo!** & **Práctica** Answers, pp. 202–203; **Fotonovela** Translations, pp. 140–141; Textbook CD Tapescript, p. 88; Lab CDs Tapescript, pp. 16–19; **Fotonovela** Videoscript, p. 106; **Panorama cultural** Videoscript, p. 129
Info Gap Activities Booklet, pp. 13–16
Overhead Transparencies: #1, #2, #19, #20, #21
Lab Audio CD/MP3 **Lección 4**
Panorama cultural DVD/Video
Fotonovela DVD/Video
Testing Program, pp. 37–48
Testing Program Audio CD
Test Files CD-ROM
Companion website
Presentations CD-ROM
Textbook CD
Vocabulary CD
Interactive CD-ROM
Video CD-ROM
Web-SAM

Section Goals

In **Contextos**, students will learn and practice:

- names of sports, pastimes, and other activities
- names of places in a city

Instructional Resources
Transparencies, #19, #20
Textbook CD
Vocabulary CD
WB/VM: Workbook, pp. 37–38
Lab Manual, p. 19
Lab CD/MP3 ***Lección 4***
IRM: ***Vocab. adicional,*** *p. 182;* ***Práctica*** *Answers, pp. 202–203; Tapescript, pp. 16–19; p. 88*
Interactive CD-ROM
Companion website: www.vistahigherlearning.com
Presentations CD-ROM

Suggestions

- Beginning in English, ask volunteers about sports they may enjoy. Ask: **Who likes to play a sport?** Write **practicar un deporte** on the board and explain what it means. To a student who answers, ask: **¿Qué deportes practicas?** Offer some cognates as suggestions: **¿Practicas el béisbol? ¿el vóleibol? ¿el tenis? ¿el golf?** After the student has answered, ask another student: **¿Qué deporte practica ____?**
- Project **Transparency #19.** Have students refer to the scene to answer your true-false questions about it. Ex: **¿Cierto o falso? Dos hombres juegan al baloncesto.** (**Cierto.**) **Una chica nada en la piscina.** (**Falso. Es un chico.**) Next, give names of famous athletes and ask students which sport each one is associated with. Ex: **¿Qué deporte practica Pedro Martínez?**
- Point out that except for the **nosotros/as** and **vosotros/as** forms, all present tense forms of **esquiar** carry an accent over the **i**: **esquío, esquías, esquía, esquían.**

Note: At this point you may want to present **Vocabulario adicional: Más vocabulario para el fin de semana**, from the IRM.

Los pasatiempos

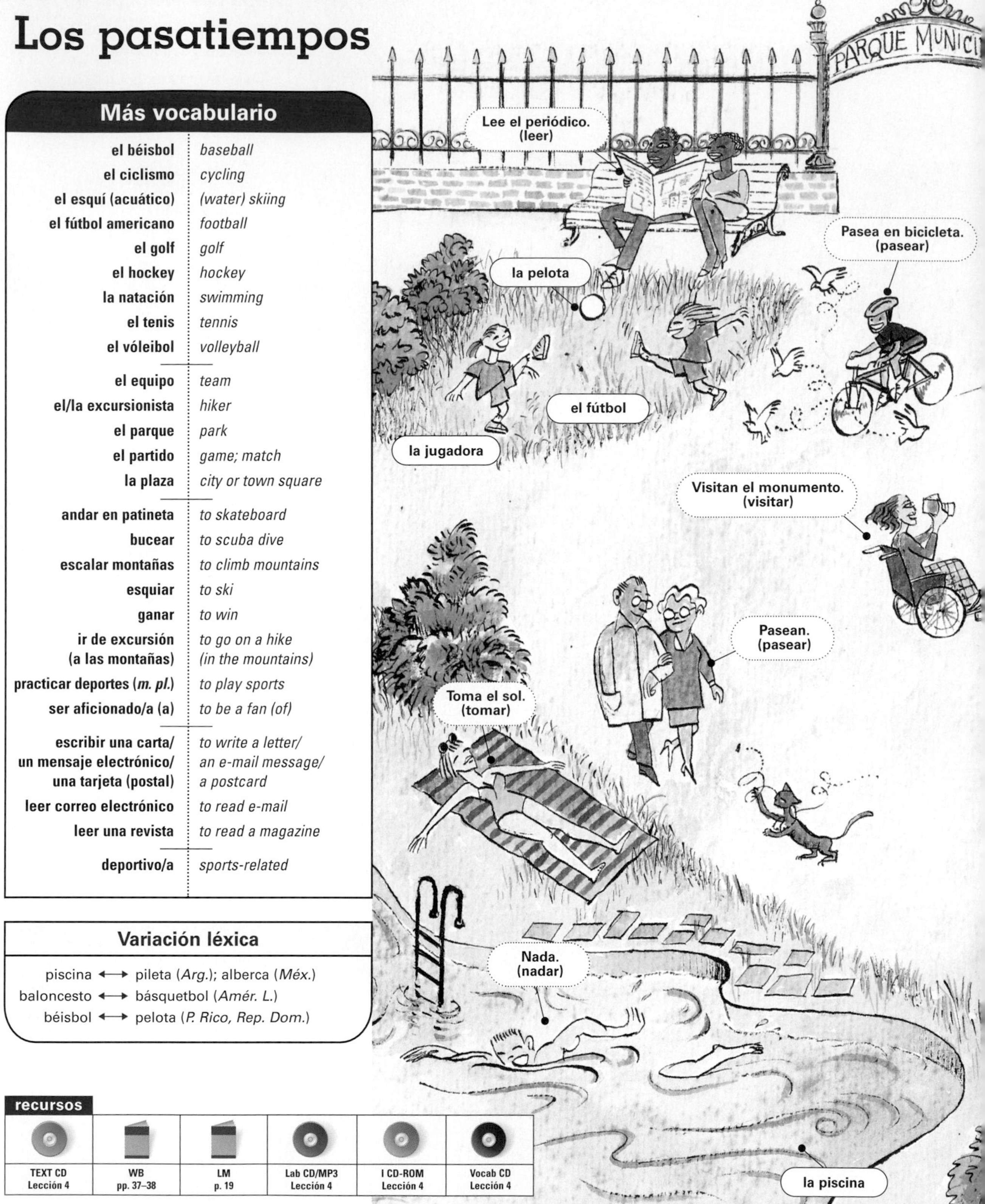

Más vocabulario

el béisbol	*baseball*
el ciclismo	*cycling*
el esquí (acuático)	*(water) skiing*
el fútbol americano	*football*
el golf	*golf*
el hockey	*hockey*
la natación	*swimming*
el tenis	*tennis*
el vóleibol	*volleyball*
el equipo	*team*
el/la excursionista	*hiker*
el parque	*park*
el partido	*game; match*
la plaza	*city or town square*
andar en patineta	*to skateboard*
bucear	*to scuba dive*
escalar montañas	*to climb mountains*
esquiar	*to ski*
ganar	*to win*
ir de excursión (a las montañas)	*to go on a hike (in the mountains)*
practicar deportes (*m. pl.*)	*to play sports*
ser aficionado/a (a)	*to be a fan (of)*
escribir una carta/ un mensaje electrónico/ una tarjeta (postal)	*to write a letter/ an e-mail message/ a postcard*
leer correo electrónico	*to read e-mail*
leer una revista	*to read a magazine*
deportivo/a	*sports-related*

Variación léxica

piscina ⟷ pileta (*Arg.*); alberca (*Méx.*)
baloncesto ⟷ básquetbol (*Amér. L.*)
béisbol ⟷ pelota (*P. Rico, Rep. Dom.*)

recursos

TEXT CD Lección 4	WB pp. 37–38	LM p. 19	Lab CD/MP3 Lección 4	I CD-ROM Lección 4	Vocab CD Lección 4

TEACHING OPTIONS

Game Have students work in pairs. Ask each to write down in Spanish his or her three favorite sports or leisure activities. In turn, each student shares his or her information with the other, who must remember what his or her partner has said without writing it down. With the whole class, ask students to report their partner's activities. The partner confirms whether all three reported activities were correct or not.

Variación léxica Point out that many sports in Spanish are referred to by names derived from English (**básquetbol, béisbol, fútbol**), including many in **Más vocabulario**: **el golf, el hockey, el vóleibol**. Ask students to guess the meaning of the following activities (be sure to use Spanish pronunciation): **el footing** (*jogging*), **el camping**, **el surf**(ing), **el windsurf**.

Práctica

1 **Escuchar** Indicate the letter of the activity in Column B that best corresponds to each statement you hear. Two items in Column B will not be used.

A	B
1. b	a. Leer correo electrónico
2. d	b. Tomar el sol
3. f	c. Pasear en bicicleta
4. c	d. Ir a un partido de fútbol americano
5. g	e. Escribir una tarjeta postal
6. h	f. Practicar muchos deportes
	g. Nadar
	h. Ir de excursión a las montañas

2 **¿Cierto o falso?** Indicate whether each statement is **cierto** or **falso** based on the illustration.

	Cierto	Falso
1. Un hombre nada en la piscina.	✓	❍
2. Un hombre lee una revista.	❍	✓
3. Un chico pasea en bicicleta.	✓	❍
4. Hay un partido de baloncesto en el parque.	✓	❍
5. Dos muchachos esquían.	❍	✓
6. Dos mujeres practican el golf.	❍	✓
7. Una mujer y dos niños visitan un monumento.	✓	❍
8. Un hombre bucea.	❍	✓
9. Hay un excursionista.	❍	✓
10. Una mujer toma el sol.	✓	❍

3 **Clasificar** Fill in the chart below with as many terms from **Contextos** as you can.
Answers will vary.

Actividades	Deportes	Personas

1 Suggestion Have students check their answers by going over **Actividad 1** with the whole class.

1 Tapescript 1. No me gusta nadar pero paso mucho tiempo al lado de la piscina. 2. Alicia y yo vamos al estadio a las cuatro. Creemos que nuestro equipo va a ganar. 3. Me gusta patinar en línea, esquiar y practicar el tenis. 4. El ciclismo es mi deporte favorito. 5. Me gusta mucho la natación. Paso mucho tiempo en la piscina. 6. Mi hermana es una gran excursionista.
Textbook CD

2 Expansion Ask students to write three additional true-false sentences based on the drawing. Ask volunteers to read their sentences aloud. The rest of the class indicates whether the statements are true or false.

3 Expansion Ask students to provide complete sentences based on the categories. You may wish to cue them to create different responses. Ex: **¿Qué es la natación? (La natación es un deporte.) ¿Dónde nadan las personas? (Nadan en una piscina.)**

TEACHING OPTIONS

Extra Practice Narrate a brief series of activities you want or need to do. Students have to guess the place to which you will have to go. Ex: **Necesito estudiar en un lugar tranquilo. También deseo leer una revista y unos periódicos. ¿Adónde voy?** (Write on board and explain meaning of **voy**.) (**la biblioteca**)

Game Play a modified version of Twenty Questions. Ask a volunteer to think of a sport, activity, person, or place (the item must come from the vocabulary drawing or list). Other students get one chance each to ask a yes-no question until someone guesses the item correctly. Limit attempts to ten questions per item. You may want to write some phrases on the board to cue students' questions.

4 Suggestions
- Project **Transparency #20** and ask brief yes-no questions to review vocabulary in **En el centro** and **Más vocabulario**. Ex: **¿Hay muchas diversiones en el centro? No tienen tiempo libre los fines de semana, ¿verdad? ¿Pasan ustedes los ratos libres en el museo?**
- Explain that **tiempo** is the generic word for *time*. Remind students to use **hora** when asking for the time: **¿Qué hora es?**

4 Expansions
- Read each item aloud and ask individuals to respond. After each answer is given, ask a different student to verify whether the answer is correct, using a complete sentence. Do the first verification yourself to model possible student responses. Ex: **—Tomamos una limonada. —Es un café/restaurante. —Sí. En un café/restaurante tomamos una limonada.**
- Have students work in pairs to convert items into a yes-no question. Ex: **¿Tomamos una limonada en el café? (Sí.) ¿Vemos una película en el restaurante? (No.)** Have students take turns answering questions.

5 Suggestion Review the forms of **gustar** that students learned in **Lección 2**. Ex: **Me gusta(n)** ____; **Te gusta(n)** ____.

5 Expansion Working with the same partner, have students create original questions and responses, modeled after those in the activity. Then have volunteers share their mini-conversation with the class.

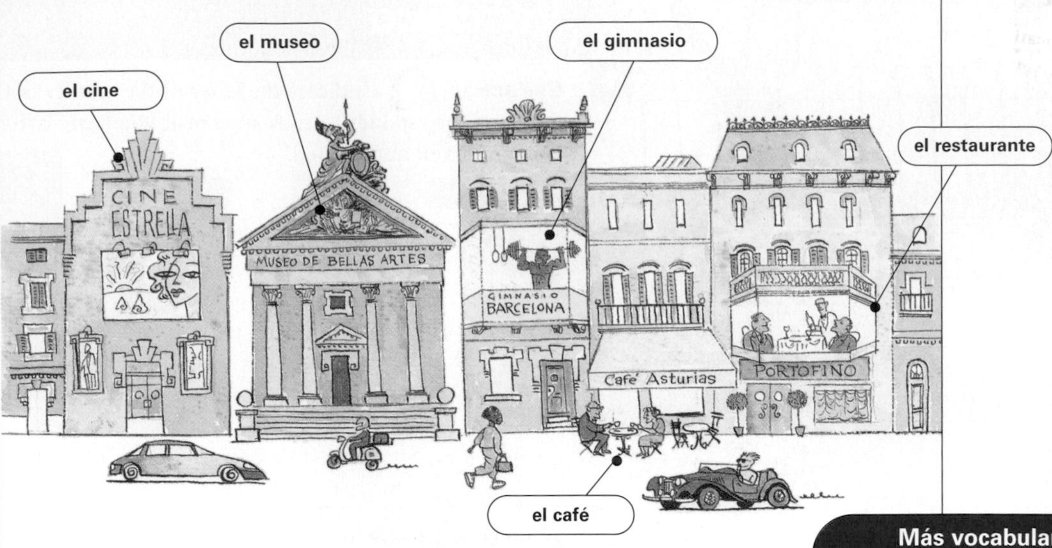

En el centro

Más vocabulario

la diversión	*fun activity; entertainment; recreation*
el fin de semana	*weekend*
el pasatiempo	*pastime; hobby*
los ratos libres	*spare (free) time*
el tiempo libre	*free time*
la iglesia	*church*
el lugar	*place*
pasar tiempo	*to spend time*
pasear por la ciudad/el pueblo	*to walk around the city/the town*
ver películas (*f. pl.*)	*to see movies*
favorito/a	*favorite*

4 Identificar Identify the place where these activities would take place.

modelo
Esquiamos.
Es una montaña.

1. Tomamos una limonada. Es un café./Es un restaurante.
2. Vemos una película. Es un cine.
3. Nadamos y tomamos el sol. Es una piscina./Es un parque.
4. Hay muchos monumentos. Es un parque./Es una ciudad.
5. Comemos tacos y fajitas. Es un restaurante.
6. Miramos pinturas (*paintings*) de Diego Rivera y Frida Kahlo. Es un museo.
7. Hay mucho tráfico. Es una ciudad./Es el centro.
8. Practicamos deportes. Es un gimnasio./Es un parque.

5 Entrevista In pairs, take turns asking each other and answering the questions.

1. ¿Hay un café cerca de la universidad? ¿Dónde está? Answers will vary.
2. ¿Cuál es tu restaurante favorito?
3. ¿Te gusta viajar y visitar monumentos? ¿Por qué?
4. ¿Te gusta ir al cine los fines de semana?
5. ¿Cuáles son tus películas favoritas?
6. ¿Te gusta practicar deportes?
7. ¿Cuáles son tus deportes favoritos? ¿Por qué?
8. ¿Cuáles son tus pasatiempos favoritos?

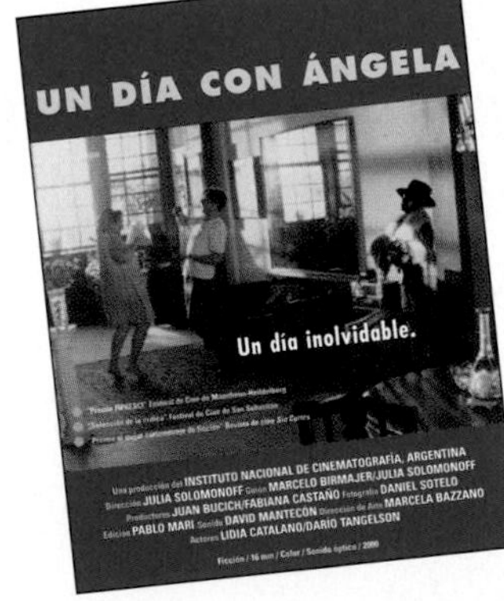

CONSÚLTALO
To review expressions with **gustar**, see **Lección 2, Expresiones útiles**, p. 41.

TEACHING OPTIONS

Extra Practice Give students five minutes to jot down the description of a typical weekend for them: what they do, where they go, with whom they spend their time. Circulate among the class to help out with unfamiliar vocabulary. Then have volunteers share their information with the others. The class decides whether they are representative of the "typical" student.

Game Play a game of continuous narration. Ex: One student begins with: **Es sábado por la mañana y voy [al café].** The next student then describes what he or she is doing there: **Estoy en el café y tomo una Coca-Cola.** Students should feel free to move the narration to other locales. You may need to write certain words and phrases on the board to aid them: **voy a/al..., luego, después**. See how long the class can continue the narration.

Comunicación

6 **Preguntar** Ask a classmate what he or she does in the places mentioned below. Your classmate will respond using verbs from the word bank. Answers will vary.

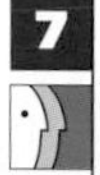

beber	leer	patinar
correr	mirar	practicar
escalar	nadar	tomar
escribir	pasear	visitar

modelo

un pueblo interesante
Estudiante 1: *¿Qué haces (do you do) cuando estás en un pueblo interesante?*
Estudiante 2: *Paseo por el pueblo y busco lugares bonitos.*

1. una biblioteca
2. un estadio
3. una plaza
4. una piscina
5. las montañas
6. un parque
7. un café
8. un museo

7 **Conversación** Using the words and expressions provided, work with a partner to prepare a short conversation about your pastimes. Answers will vary.

¿a qué hora?	¿cuándo?	¿qué?
¿cómo?	¿dónde?	¿con quién(es)?

modelo

Estudiante 1: *¿Cuándo patinas en línea?*
Estudiante 2: *Patino en línea los domingos. Y tú, ¿patinas en línea?*
Estudiante 1: *No, no me gusta patinar en línea. Me gusta practicar el béisbol.*

8 **Pasatiempos** In pairs, tell each other what pastimes three of your friends and family members enjoy. Be prepared to share with the class any pastimes you noticed they have in common. Answers will vary.

modelo

Estudiante 1: *Mi hermana pasea mucho en bicicleta. Pero mis padres practican la natación. Mi hermano no nada, pero visita muchos museos.*
Estudiante 2: *Mi primo lee muchas revistas, pero no practica muchos deportes. Mis tíos esquían y practican el golf...*

6 Suggestion Quickly review some of the verbs listed. Make sure students understand the meaning of **¿Qué haces... ?** and that they will use it throughout the activity.

6 Expansions
- Ask additional questions and have volunteers answer. Ex: **¿Qué haces en la residencia estudiantil (el apartamento, la casa)?** Suggested places: **la casa de un amigo/una amiga, el centro de la ciudad, el gimnasio**.
- Have students share their responses with the class. Then have them create a table based on the responses. Ex: **En la biblioteca: yo (leo, bailo, trabajo en la computadora)**

7 Suggestion Remind students of the forms of **gustar** that they learned in **Lección 2 Expresiones útiles**, page 41.

7 Expansion After students have asked and answered questions, ask volunteers to report their partner's activities back to the class. The partner should verify whether the information is correct.

8 Expansions
- Ask volunteers to share any pastimes they and their partners, friends, and families have in common. Ask for a show of hands to find out which activities are most popular and where they do them. What are the general tendencies of the class?
- In pairs, have students write sentences about the pastimes of a famous person. Then have them work with another pair who will guess who is the famous person being described.

TEACHING OPTIONS

Extra Practice On a sheet of paper, students write down six activities they like to do. Then they circulate around the room trying to find other students who also like to do those activities (**¿Te gusta... ?**). Once a student finds someone that shares a particular activity in common, he or she asks that student to sign his or her name (**Firma aquí, por favor.**). How many signatures can each student collect?

Game On a slip of paper, each student writes down the one activity that best describes him or her without writing down his or her name. Collect the slips of paper and mix them up in a hat. Pull out each slip of paper and read the activity. The rest of the class has to guess who the student is. If a particular activity best describes more than one student, ask them to elaborate: With whom do they do the activity? Where? When?

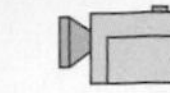

Section Goals

In **Fotonovela** students will:

- receive comprehensible input from free-flowing discourse
- learn functional phrases for making invitations and plans, talking about pastimes, and apologizing

Instructional Resources
WB/VM: Video Activities, pp. 219–220
***Fotonovela** DVD/Video (Start 00:17:00)*
Video CD-ROM
*IRM: **Fotonovela** Translations, pp. 140–141, Videoscript, p. 106*
Interactive CD-ROM

Video Recap: Lección 3
Before doing this **Fotonovela** section, review the previous one with this activity.

1. ____ tiene una familia grande. (Inés)
2. El ____ de Javier es viejo y trabajador. (abuelo)
3. ____ no tiene hermanos. (Javier)
4. Inés tiene ____ hermanas. (cuatro)

Video Synopsis The travelers have an hour to explore the city before checking into the cabins. Javier and Inés decide to stroll around the city. Álex and Maite go to the park. While Maite writes postcards, Álex and a young man play soccer. A stray ball hits Maite. Álex and Maite return to the bus, and Álex invites her to go running with him that evening.

Suggestions

- Have students quickly glance over the **Fotonovela** and make a list of the cognates they find. Then, have them guess what this episode is about.
- Have students tell you a few expressions used to talk about pastimes. Then ask a few questions. Ex: **¿Eres aficionado/a a un deporte? ¿Te gusta el fútbol?**

¡Vamos al parque!

Los estudiantes pasean por la ciudad y hablan de sus pasatiempos.

PERSONAJES

DON FRANCISCO

JAVIER

INÉS

ÁLEX

MAITE

JOVEN

1

DON FRANCISCO Tienen una hora libre. Pueden explorar la ciudad, si quieren. Tenemos que ir a las cabañas a las cuatro.

2

JAVIER Inés, ¿quieres ir a pasear por la ciudad?

INÉS Sí, vamos.

3

ÁLEX ¿Por qué no vamos al parque, Maite? Podemos hablar y tomar el sol.

MAITE ¡Buena idea! También quiero escribir unas postales.

6

ÁLEX ¡Maite!

MAITE ¡Dios mío!

7

JOVEN Mil perdones. Lo siento muchísimo.

MAITE ¡No es nada! Estoy bien.

8

ÁLEX Ya son las dos y treinta. Debemos regresar al autobús, ¿no?

MAITE Tienes razón.

ÁLEX Oye, Maite, ¿qué vas a hacer esta noche?

MAITE No tengo planes. ¿Por qué?

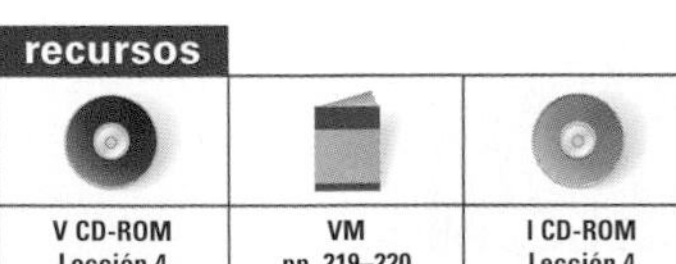

TEACHING OPTIONS

Video Tips General suggestions for using video clips in the classroom can be found on page IAE-12 of this Instructor's Annotated Edition.

¡Vamos al parque! Play the last half of the **¡Vamos al parque!** segment of this video module and have the class give you a description of what they saw. Write their observations on the board, pointing out any incorrect information. Repeat this process to allow the class to pick up more details of the plot. Then ask students to use the information they have accumulated to guess what happened at the beginning of the **¡Vamos al parque!** segment. Write their guesses on the board. Then play the entire video module and, through discussion, help the class summarize the plot.

4

MAITE ¿Eres aficionado a los deportes, Álex?

ÁLEX Sí, me gusta mucho el fútbol. Me gusta también nadar, correr e ir de excursión a las montañas.

MAITE Yo también corro mucho.

5

ÁLEX Oye, Maite, ¿por qué no jugamos al fútbol con él?

MAITE Mmm... no quiero. Voy a terminar de escribir unas postales.

9

ÁLEX Eh, este... a veces salgo a correr por la noche. ¿Quieres venir a correr conmigo?

MAITE Sí, vamos. ¿A qué hora?

ÁLEX ¿A las seis?

MAITE Perfecto.

10

DON FRANCISCO Esta noche van a correr. ¡Y yo no tengo energía para pasear!

Enfoque cultural El fútbol

Soccer, or **fútbol,** is the most popular spectator sport and the most widely played team game in the world. It is also the most popular sport in the Spanish-speaking world. People of all ages can be seen playing soccer in public parks and streets, and each country has a professional league with its own stars. Juan Ramón Riquelme from Argentina, Marcelo Salas from Chile, and Francisco Palencia from Mexico are among the most famous contemporary Hispanic soccer players.

Expresiones útiles

Making invitations

- ▶ **¿Por qué no vamos al parque?**
  Why don't we go to the park?
- ▷ **¡Buena idea!**
  Good idea!
- ▶ **¿Por qué no jugamos al fútbol?**
  Why don't we play soccer?
- ▷ **Mmm... no quiero.**
  Hmm... I don't want to.
- ▷ **Lo siento, pero no puedo.**
  I'm sorry, but I can't.
- ▶ **¿Quieres ir a pasear por la ciudad conmigo?**
  Do you want to walk around the city with me?
- ▷ **Sí, vamos.**
  Yes, let's go.
- ▷ **Sí, si tenemos tiempo.**
  Yes, if we have time.

Making plans

- ▶ **¿Qué vas a hacer esta noche?**
  What are you going to do tonight?
- ▷ **No tengo planes.**
  I don't have any plans.
- ▷ **Voy a terminar de escribir unas postales.**
  I'm going to finish writing some postcards.

Talking about pastimes

- ▶ **¿Eres aficionado/a a los deportes?**
  Are you a sports fan?
- ▷ **Sí, me gustan todos los deportes.**
  Yes, I like all sports.
- ▷ **Sí, me gusta mucho el fútbol.**
  Yes, I like soccer a lot.
- ▶ **Me gusta también nadar, correr e ir de excursión a las montañas.**
  I also like to swim, run, and go hiking in the mountains.
- ▷ **Yo también corro mucho.**
  I also run a lot.

Apologizing

- ▶ **Mil perdones./Lo siento muchísimo.**
  I'm so sorry.

Suggestion Have the class read through the entire **Fotonovela**, with volunteers playing the parts of Don Francisco, Javier, Inés, Álex, Maite, and the **Joven**. Have students take turns playing the roles so that more students participate.

Expresiones útiles Point out the written accents in the words **¿qué?**, **¿por qué?**, and **también**. Explain that accents indicate a stressed syllable in a word (**también**) and that all question words have accent marks. Then mention that **voy**, **vas**, **va**, and **vamos** are present-tense forms of the verb **ir**. Point out that **ir a** is used with an infinitive to tell what is going to happen. Ask: **¿Qué vas a hacer esta noche? ¿Por qué no vamos al parque?** Explain that **quiero**, **quieres**, and **siento** are forms of **querer** and **sentir**, which undergo a stem change from **e** to **ie** in certain forms. Tell your students that they will learn more about these concepts in **Estructura**.

TEACHING OPTIONS

Enfoque cultural Tell the class that children—generally boys—in Spanish-speaking countries often take up soccer at a very early age, playing on pick-up soccer teams in their neighborhoods. Many people continue to participate as players or spectators in local soccer clubs through adulthood. Explain that nearly every town or city has its own club and that larger cities have professional clubs that may be well-known throughout the nation. Team rivalries can be fierce. Mention that excitement about soccer often rises to a fever pitch every four years during the **Copa Mundial** (*World Cup*), which is the sport's international championship. At that time top-notch professional players, who may be members of teams in other countries, form national teams to compete with other national teams. Spanish-speaking countries have competed regularly in the World Cup, which was first played in Uruguay in 1930.

1 Suggestion Have the class briefly go over the **Fotonovela** characters' likes and dislikes.

2 Expansion Tell the class to add the **Joven** to the list of possible answers. Then give these additional items to the class: **6. ¿Te gustan los deportes? (Maite) 7. ¡Ay, señorita! Lo siento mucho. (Joven) 8. Ay, no tengo mucha energía. (don Francisco)**

3 Expansions
- Give these additional questions to the class: **5. ¿A qué hora corren Álex y Maite esta noche? (a las seis) 6. ¿A qué hora tienen que ir a las cabañas los estudiantes? (a las cuatro)**
- Rephrase the questions as true-false statements. Have students correct the false statements. Ex: **Inés y Javier desean ir al parque. (Falso. Desean pasear por la ciudad.)**

4 Possible Response
E1: ¿Eres aficionada a los deportes?
E2: Sí, me gustan mucho.
E1: ¿Te gusta el fútbol?
E2: Sí, mucho. Me gusta también nadar y correr. Oye, ¿qué vas a hacer esta noche?
E1: No tengo planes.
E2: ¿Quieres ir a correr conmigo?
E1: Lo siento pero no me gusta correr. ¿Te gusta patinar en línea? ¿Por qué no vamos al parque a patinar?
E2: ¡Buena idea!

Reacciona a la fotonovela

1 Escoger Choose the answer that best completes each sentence.

1. Inés y Javier ___b___.
   a. toman el sol b. pasean por la ciudad c. corren por el parque
2. Álex desea ___a___ en el parque.
   a. hablar y tomar el sol b. hablar y leer el periódico c. nadar y tomar el sol
3. A Álex le gusta nadar, ___c___.
   a. jugar al fútbol y escribir postales b. escalar montañas y esquiar
   c. ir de excursión y correr
4. A Maite le gusta ___b___.
   a. nadar y correr b. correr y escribir postales c. correr y jugar al fútbol
5. Maite desea ___c___.
   a. ir de excursión b. jugar al fútbol c. ir al parque

2 Identificar Identify the person who would make each statement.

1. No me gusta practicar el fútbol pero me gusta correr. ___Maite___
2. ¿Por qué no vamos a pasear por la ciudad? ___Javier___
3. ¿Por qué no exploran ustedes la ciudad? Tienen tiempo. ___don Francisco___
4. ¿Por qué no corres conmigo esta noche? ___Álex___
5. No voy al parque. Prefiero estar con mi amigo. ___Inés___

JAVIER

INÉS

ÁLEX

MAITE

DON FRANCISCO

3 Preguntas Answer the questions using the information from the **Fotonovela.**

1. ¿Qué desean hacer Inés y Javier?
   Desean pasear por la ciudad.
2. ¿Qué desea hacer Álex en el parque?
   Desea jugar al fútbol.
3. ¿Qué desea hacer Maite en el parque?
   Maite desea escribir postales./Maite desea terminar de escribir unas postales.
4. ¿Qué deciden hacer Maite y Álex esta noche?
   Deciden ir a correr.

4 Conversación With a partner, prepare a conversation in which you talk about pastimes and invite each other to do some activity together. Use the following expressions:

Answers will vary.

- ¿Eres aficionado/a a...?
- ¿Te gusta...?
- ¿Qué vas a hacer esta noche?
- ¿Por qué no...?
- ¿Quieres... conmigo?

AYUDA

contigo *with you*
¿A qué hora? *(At) What time?*
¿Dónde? *Where?*
No puedo porque... *I can't because...*
Nos vemos a las siete. *See you at seven.*

TEACHING OPTIONS

Small Groups Have the class quickly glance at frames 4–9 of the **Fotonovela**. Then have students work in groups of three to ad-lib what transpires between Álex, Maite, and the **Joven**. Assure them that it is not necessary to follow the **Fotonovela** word for word. Students should be creative while getting the general meaning across with the vocabulary and expressions they know.

Extra Practice Have your students close their books and complete these statements with words from the **Fotonovela**. **1. _____ a terminar de escribir unas postales. (Voy) 2. ¡Mil _____! Lo siento muchísimo. (perdones) 3. Inés, ¿_____ ir a pasear por la ciudad? (quieres) 4. ¿Por qué no _____ al parque, Maite? (vamos) 5. Maite, ¿qué vas a _____ esta noche? (hacer)**

Pronunciación

Word stress and accent marks

pe-lí-cu-la **e-di-fi-cio** **ver** **yo**

Every Spanish syllable contains at least one vowel. When two vowels (two weak vowels or one strong and one weak) are joined in the same syllable they form a **diphthong.** A **monosyllable** is a word formed by a single syllable.

bi-blio-te-ca **vi-si-tar** **par-que** **fút-bol**

The syllable of a Spanish word that is pronounced most emphatically is the "stressed" syllable.

pe-lo-ta **pis-ci-na** **ra-tos** **ha-blan**

Words that end in **n, s,** or a **vowel** are usually stressed on the next to last syllable.

na-ta-ción **pa-pá** **in-glés** **Jo-sé**

If words that end in **n, s,** or a **vowel** are stressed on the last syllable, they must carry an accent mark on the stressed syllable.

bai-lar **es-pa-ñol** **u-ni-ver-si-dad** **tra-ba-ja-dor**

Words that do *not* end in **n, s,** or a **vowel** are usually stressed on the last syllable.

béis-bol **lá-piz** **ár-bol** **Gó-mez**

If words that do *not* end in **n, s,** or a **vowel** are stressed on the next to last syllable, they must carry an accent mark on the stressed syllable.

En la unión está la fuerza.[2]

Práctica Pronounce each word, stressing the correct syllable. Then give the word stress rule for each word.

1. profesor
2. Puebla
3. ¿Cuántos?
4. Mazatlán
5. examen
6. ¿Cómo?
7. niños
8. Guadalajara
9. programador
10. México
11. están
12. geografía

Oraciones Read the conversation aloud to practice word stress.

MARINA Hola, Carlos. ¿Qué tal?
CARLOS Bien. Oye, ¿a qué hora es el partido de fútbol?
MARINA Creo que es a las siete.
CARLOS ¿Quieres ir?
MARINA Lo siento, pero no puedo. Tengo que estudiar biología.

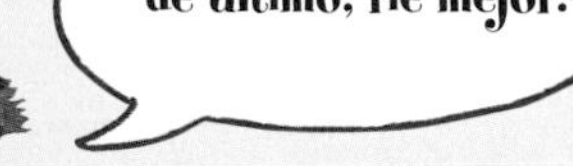

Quien ríe de último, ríe mejor.[1]

Refranes Read these sayings aloud to practice word stress.

1 He who laughs last, laughs longest.
2 United we stand.

recursos

TEXT CD	LM	Lab CD/MP3	I CD-ROM
Lección 4	p. 20	Lección 4	Lección 4

Section Goals

In **Pronunciación** students will be introduced to

- the concept of word stress
- diphthongs and monosyllables
- accent marks

Instructional Resources
Textbook CD
Lab Manual, p. 20
Lab CD/MP3 ***Lección 4***
IRM: Tapescript, pp. 16–19; p. 88
Interactive CD-ROM

Suggestions

- Write **película**, **edificio**, **ver**, and **yo** on the board. Model their pronunciation. Ask the class to identify the diphthongs and the monosyllables.
- Write **biblioteca**, **visitar**, and **parque** on the board. Model their pronunciation, then ask which syllables are stressed.
- As you go through each point in the explanation, write the example words on the board, pronounce them, and have students repeat. Then, ask students to provide words they learned in **Lecciones 1–3** and **Contextos** and **Fotonovela** of this lesson that exemplify each point.

Práctica/Oraciones/Refranes These exercises are recorded on the Textbook CD. You may want to play the CD so students practice the pronunciation point by listening to Spanish spoken by speakers other than yourself.

TEACHING OPTIONS

Extra Practice Write on the board or an overhead transparency a list of Mexican place names, then have the class pronounce each name, paying particular attention to word stress. Ex: **Campeche, Durango, Culiacán, Tepic, Chichén Itzá, Zacatecas, Colima, Nayarit, San Luis Potosí, Sonora, Puebla, Morelos, Veracruz, Toluca, Guanajuato, Pachuca, El Tajín, Chetumal**. Model pronunciation as necessary.

Small Groups On the board, write a list of words that the class already knows. Then have the class work in small groups to come up with the word stress rule that applies to each word. Ex: **Inés, lápiz, equipo, pluma, Javier, chicas, comer, Álex, mujer, tenis, hombre, libros, papel, parque, béisbol, excursión, deportes, fútbol, pasear, esquí**.

Section Goals

In **Estructura 4.1**, students will learn:
- the present tense of **ir**
- the contraction **al**
- **ir a** + *[infinitive]* to express future events
- **vamos a** to express *Let's* . . .

Instructional Resources
WB/VM: Workbook, pp. 39–40
Lab Manual, p. 21
*Lab CD/MP3 **Lección 4***
*IRM: **¡Inténtalo! & Práctica** Answers, pp. 202–203; Tapescript, pp. 16–19;*
***Hojas de actividades**, p. 165*
Info Gap Activities Booklet, pp. 13–14
Interactive CD-ROM
Companion website: www.vistahigherlearning.com
Presentations CD-ROM

Suggestions

- Write your next day's schedule on the board, mixing infinitives with nouns. Ex: **8:00—la biblioteca; 12:00—comer**. Explain what you are going to do using the verb **ir**. Ask volunteers questions about their schedules using forms of **ir**.
- Ask individuals questions about their future plans using **ir**. Ex: **¿Adónde vas el sábado? ¿Cuándo vas a viajar a México?** Point out the difference in usage between **dónde** and **adónde**. Ex: **¿Dónde está la casa de los Franco? ¿Adónde va José Franco?**
- After you have presented the use of **ir** to express the idea of *let's*, ask volunteers to respond to your prompts with suggestions of things to do. Ex: **Tengo hambre. (Vamos a la cafetería.) Quiero ver una buena película. (Vamos al cine.)**

4.1 Present tense of ir

ANTE TODO The verb **ir** (*to go*) is irregular in the present tense. Note that, except for the **yo** form (**voy**) and the lack of a written accent on the **vosotros** form (**vais**), the endings are the same as those for **–ar** verbs.

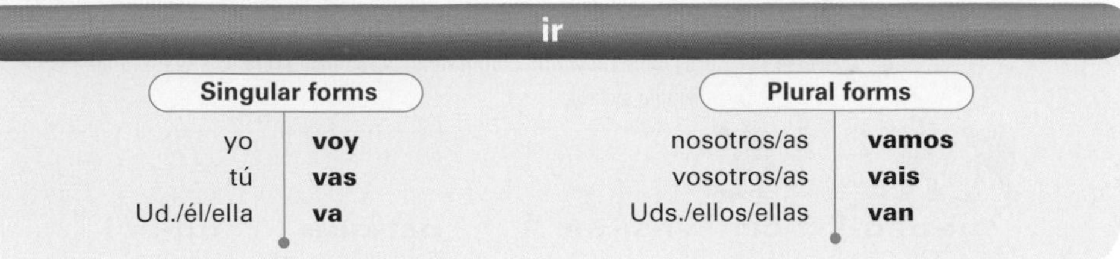

ir

Singular forms		Plural forms	
yo	**voy**	nosotros/as	**vamos**
tú	**vas**	vosotros/as	**vais**
Ud./él/ella	**va**	Uds./ellos/ellas	**van**

▶ **Ir** is often used with the preposition **a** (*to*). If **a** is followed by the definite article **el**, they combine to form the contraction **al**. If **a** is followed by the other definite articles (**la, las, los**), there is no contraction.

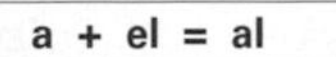

Voy **al** parque con Juan.
I'm going to the park with Juan.

Los excursionistas van **a las** montañas.
The hikers are going to the mountains.

▶ The construction **ir a** + *[infinitive]* is used to talk about actions that are going to happen in the future. It is equivalent to the English *to be going to* + *[infinitive]*.

Va a leer el periódico.
He is going to read the newspaper.

Van a pasear por el pueblo.
They are going to walk around town.

Voy a escribir unas postales.

Álex y Maite van a volver al autobús.

▶ **Vamos a** + *[infinitive]* can also express the idea of *let's (do something)*.

Vamos a pasear.
Let's take a stroll.

¡**Vamos a** ver!
Let's see!

¡INTÉNTALO! Provide the present tense forms of **ir**. The first item has been done for you.

1. Ellos van.
2. Yo voy.
3. Tu novio va.
4. Adela va.
5. Mi prima y yo vamos.
6. Tú vas.
7. Ustedes van.
8. Nosotros vamos.
9. Usted va.
10. Nosotras vamos.
11. Miguel va.
12. Ellos van.

recursos
WB pp. 39–46
LM pp. 21–24
Lab CD/MP3 Lección 4
I CD-ROM Lección 4
vistahigherlearning.com

CONSÚLTALO
To review the contraction **de** + **el**, see **Estructura 1.3**, pp. 18-19.

¡ATENCIÓN!
Remember to use **adónde** instead of **dónde** when asking a question that contains a form of the verb **ir**:
¿Adónde vas?
(To) Where are you going?

TEACHING OPTIONS

TPR Invent gestures to pantomime activities mentioned in **Lección 4**. Ex: **poner la televisión** (press the button on a remote control), **patinar** (skate), **nadar** (move arms as if swimming). Signal individuals to gesture appropriately as you cue activities with **Vamos a**. . . . Keep the pace brisk.
Heritage Speakers Have heritage speakers make a list of public or commercial places where people go in their home country that do not exist here. Have them write these names on the board and explain their meaning to the class.
Extra Practice To provide oral practice with the verb **ir**, provide prompts similar to those in **¡Inténtalo!** Say the subject and the verb, have students repeat it, then say a different subject, varying the gender and number. Have students then say the phrase with the new subject, changing the verb as necessary.

Práctica

1

CONSEJOS

Remember that to avoid repetition, you can drop subject pronouns (**tú**, **nosotros**, etc.) when they are the subject of a sentence.

¿Adónde van? Everyone in your neighborhood is dashing off to various places. Say where they are going.

1. la señora Castillo / el centro La señora Castillo va al centro.
2. las hermanas Gómez / la piscina Las hermanas Gómez van a la piscina.
3. tu tío y tu papá / el partido de fútbol Tu tío y tu papá van al partido de fútbol.
4. yo / el Museo de Arte Moderno (Yo) Voy al Museo de Arte Moderno.
5. nosotros / el restaurante Miramar (Nosotros) Vamos al restaurante Miramar.

2

¿Qué van a hacer? These sentences describe what several students in a college hiking club are doing today. Use **ir a** + [*infinitive*] to say that they are also going to do the same activities tomorrow.

modelo

Martín y Rodolfo nadan en la piscina.
Van a nadar en la piscina mañana también.

1. Sara lee una revista. Va a leer una revista mañana también.
2. Yo practico deportes. Voy a practicar deportes mañana también.
3. Ustedes van de excursión. Van a ir de excursión mañana también.
4. El presidente del club patina. Va a patinar mañana también.
5. Tú tomas el sol. Vas a tomar el sol mañana también.
6. Paseamos con nuestros amigos. Vamos a pasear con nuestros amigos mañana también.

3

Preguntas With a partner, take turns asking and answering questions about where the people are going and what they are going to do there. Some answers will vary.

modelo

Estudiante 1: *¿Adónde va Estela?*
Estudiante 2: *Va a la Librería Sol.*
Estudiante 1: *Va a comprar un libro.*

1. Álex y Miguel ¿Adónde van Álex y Miguel? Van al parque. Van a ...

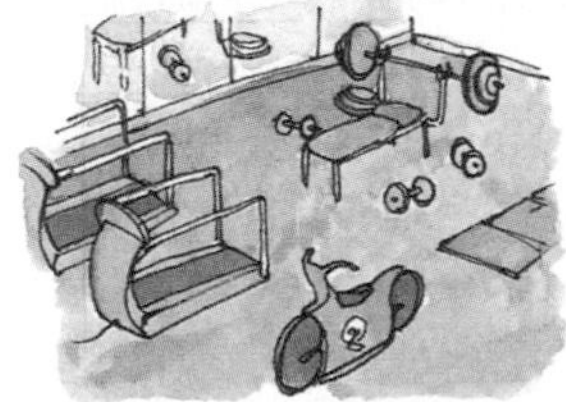

2. mi amigo ¿Adónde va mi amigo? Va al gimnasio. Va a ...

3. tú ¿Adónde vas? Voy al partido de tenis. Voy a ...

NOTA CULTURAL

The **Estadio Azteca** in Mexico City is the largest stadium in the Spanish-speaking world. It has a seating capacity of 106,000.

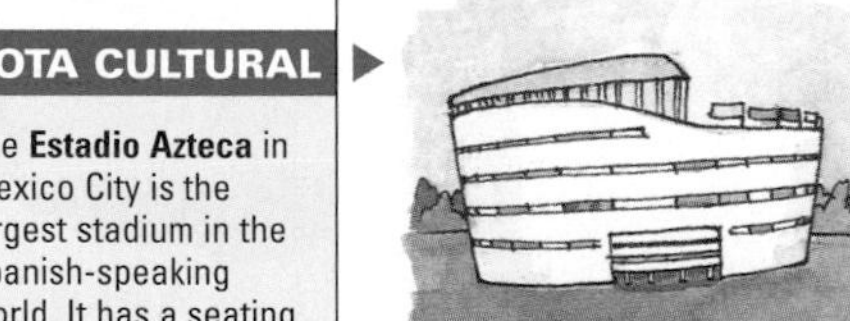

4. los estudiantes ¿Adónde van los estudiantes? Van al estadio. Van a ...

5. profesora Torres ¿Adónde va la profesora Torres? Va a la Biblioteca Nacional. Va a ...

6. Uds. ¿Adónde van Uds.? Vamos a la piscina. Vamos a ...

1 Suggestion Using pictures of people dressed for a particular activity, describe them to the class using the verb **ir**. Ex: Showing a picture of a basketball player, say: **Va al gimnasio.**

Consejos Reiterate the information, explaining that the personal endings on verbs make personal pronouns unnecessary except for emphasis.

1 Expansion Once you have done the activity, extend each answer with **pero** and a different name or pronoun, and have students complete the sentence. Ex: **La señora Castillo va al centro, pero el señor Castillo... (va al trabajo).**

2 Expansions

- Use the same pictures you used for **Actividad 1** to describe what the people are going to do. Ex: **Va a jugar al baloncesto.**
- Have students answer questions about tomorrow's activities. Ex: **¿Qué van a hacer tus amigos mañana? ¿Qué va a hacer tu compañero/a mañana?**

3 Expansion Have students work with a partner to write logic problems using **ir a** + [*infinitive*]. Ex: **Pilar, Guadalupe, Salvador y Manuel van a hacer diferentes cosas hoy. Salvador va a nadar y Manuel va a comer, pero no en la casa. Guadalupe y Pilar van a ver una película. ¿Adónde van?** Then have pairs exchange papers and solve one another's problem.

TEACHING OPTIONS

Heritage Speakers Ask heritage speakers to write six sentences with **ir** indicating places they go on weekends either by themselves or with friends and family. Ex: **Mi familia y yo vamos a visitar a mi abuela los domingos.**

Game Divide the class into four-member teams. Each team will write a description of tomorrow's events for a well-known fictional character. Teams take turns reading and/or writing the description on the board without giving the name of the character. The other teams guess the identity of the character. Each correct guess earns a point for the team while the team that is able to fool the others receives two points. The team with the most points wins. Ex: **Mañana va a dormir de día. Va a caminar de noche. Va a buscar una muchacha bonita. La muchacha va a tener miedo. (Es Drácula.)**

Comunicación

4 **Situaciones** Work with a partner and say where you and your friends go in the following situations. Answers will vary.

1. Cuando deseo descansar...
2. Cuando mi novio/a tiene que estudiar...
3. Si mis compañeros de clase necesitan practicar el español...
4. Si deseo hablar con unos amigos...
5. Cuando tengo dinero (*money*)...
6. Cuando mis amigos y yo tenemos hambre...
7. Si tengo tiempo libre...
8. Cuando mis amigos desean esquiar...
9. Si estoy de vacaciones...
10. Si quiero leer...

5  **Encuesta** Your instructor will give you a worksheet. Walk around the class and ask your classmates if they are going to do these activities today. Find one person to answer **Sí** and one to answer **No** for each item and note their names on the worksheet in the appropriate column. Be prepared to report your findings to the class. Answers will vary.

Tú: *¿Vas a leer el periódico hoy?*
Ana: *Sí, voy a leer el periódico hoy.*
Luis: *No, no voy a leer el periódico hoy.*

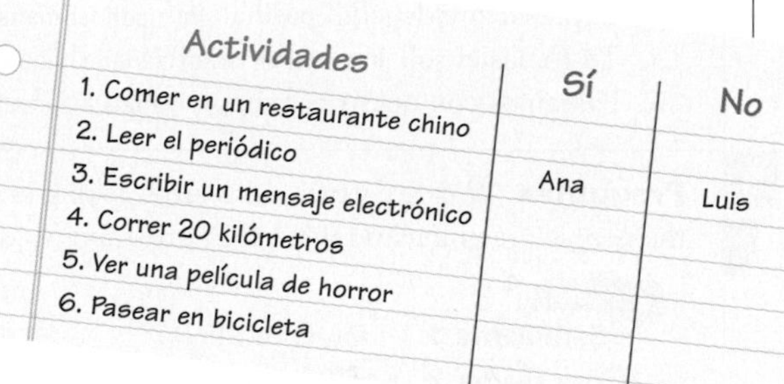

Actividades
Sí
No
1. Comer en un restaurante chino
2. Leer el periódico
Ana
Luis
3. Escribir un mensaje electrónico
4. Correr 20 kilómetros
5. Ver una película de horror
6. Pasear en bicicleta

6 **Entrevista** Interview two classmates to find out where they are going and what they are going to do on their next vacation. Answers will vary.

modelo

Estudiante 1: *¿Adónde vas de vacaciones (for vacation)?*
Estudiante 2: *Voy a Guadalajara con mis amigos.*
Estudiante 1: *¿Y qué van a hacer (to do) ustedes en Guadalajara?*
Estudiante 2: *Vamos a visitar unos monumentos y museos.*

Síntesis

7  **El fin de semana** Create a schedule with your activities for this weekend.

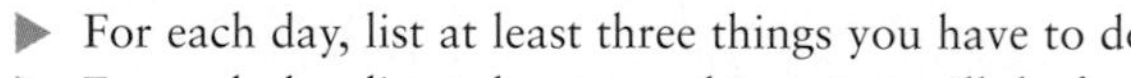

- For each day, list at least three things you have to do.
- For each day, list at least two things you will do for fun.
- Tell a classmate what your weekend schedule is like. He or she will write down what you say.
- Switch roles to see if you have any plans in common.
- Take turns asking each other to participate in some of the activities you listed.

Answers will vary.

4 Expansion Have students convert the dependent clause to its negative form and create a new independent clause. Ex: **Cuando no deseo descansar, voy al gimnasio.**

5 Suggestion Model turning the first phrase into a question. Ex: **¿Vas a comer en un restaurante chino hoy?** Then distribute the **Hojas de actividades** from the IRM that correspond to this activity. Give students five minutes to fill out the surveys.

5 Expansion After collecting the surveys, ask individuals about their plans. Ex: If someone's name appears by **mirar la televisión**, ask him or her: **¿Qué programa vas a mirar hoy?**

6 Suggestion Have each student use an idea map to brainstorm a trip he or she would like to take. Write **lugar** in the central circle and in surrounding circles write: **visitar, deportes, otras actividades, comida, compañeros/as**.

7 Suggestions
- Brainstorm useful expressions with your students before beginning the activity. Ex: **—¿Quieres jugar al tenis conmigo? —Lo siento, pero no puedo./Sí, vamos.**
- Have students make two columns on a sheet of paper. The first one should be headed **El fin de semana tengo que...** and the other **El fin de semana deseo...** Give students a few minutes to brainstorm about their activities for the weekend.

Suggestion See the Info Gap Activities Booklet for an additional activity to practice the material presented in this section.

TEACHING OPTIONS

Pairs Divide the class into pairs. Have the members of each pair take turns reading a time which you write on the board and making a suggestion of something to do. Ex: Write: **12:00**. **E1: Son las doce en punto. E2: Vamos a la cafetería.** Write: **12:45. E2: Es la una menos quince. E1: Vamos a la biblioteca.**

Game Divide the class into groups of three. Each group has a piece of paper to write the answers on. Name a category. Ex: **lugares públicos**. The first group member will write one answer and pass the paper to the next person. The paper will continue to circulate for two minutes. The group with the most words wins.

Video Show the video again to give students more input containing the verb **ir**. Stop the video where appropriate to discuss how **ir** is used to express different ideas.

4.2 Stem-changing verbs: e→ie, o→ue

NATIONAL
comparisons
STANDARDS

CONSÚLTALO

To review the present tense of regular **–ar** verbs, see **Estructura 2.1**, p. 44.

•••

To review the present tense of regular **–er** and **–ir** verbs, see **Estructura 3.3**, p. 86.

ANTE TODO Stem-changing verbs deviate from the normal pattern of regular verbs. In stem-changing verbs, the stressed vowel of the stem changes when the verb is conjugated.

INFINITIVE	VERB STEM	STEM CHANGE	CONJUGATED FORM
empezar	empez-	empi**e**z-	empi**e**zo
volver	volv-	vu**e**lv-	vu**e**lvo

▶ In many verbs, such as **empezar** *(to begin)*, the stem vowel changes from **e** to **ie**. Note that the **nosotros/as** and **vosotros/as** forms don't have a stem change.

empezar (e:ie)

Singular forms		Plural forms	
yo	emp**ie**zo	nosotros/as	empezamos
tú	emp**ie**zas	vosotros/as	empezáis
Ud./él/ella	emp**ie**za	Uds./ellos/ellas	emp**ie**zan

Álex y Maite vuelven al autobús.

Álex empieza a enviar mensajes.

▶ In many other verbs, such as **volver** *(to return)*, the stem vowel changes from **o** to **ue**. The **nosotros/as** and **vosotros/as** forms have no stem change.

volver (o:ue)

Singular forms		Plural forms	
yo	v**ue**lvo	nosotros/as	volvemos
tú	v**ue**lves	vosotros/as	volvéis
Ud./él/ella	v**ue**lve	Uds./ellos/ellas	v**ue**lven

▶ To help you identify stem-changing verbs, they will appear as follows throughout the text:

empezar (e:ie), volver (o:ue)

Section Goals

In **Estructura 4.2** students will be introduced to:

- present tense of stem-changing verbs: **e → ie**; **o → ue**
- common stem-changing verbs

Instructional Resources
WB/VM: Workbook, pp. 41–42
Lab Manual, p. 22
Lab CD/MP3 ***Lección 4***
IRM: ***¡Inténtalo!*** *&* ***Práctica*** *Answers, pp. 202–203; Tapescript, pp. 16–19*
Info Gap Activities Booklet, pp. 15–16
Interactive CD-ROM
Companion website: www.vistahigherlearning.com
Presentations CD-ROM

Suggestions

- Take a survey of students' habits. Ask: **¿Quiénes empiezan las clases a las ocho?** Make a chart on the board. Ask: **¿Quiénes vuelven a casa a las seis?** Then summarize the chart. Ex: **Tú vuelves a casa a las siete, pero Amanda vuelve a las seis. Nosotros volvemos a las cinco.**
- Copy the forms of **empezar** and **volver** on the board. Reiterate that the personal endings for the present tense of all the verbs listed in **Estructura 4.2** are the same as those for the present tense of regular **–ar**, **–er**, and **–ir** verbs.
- Explain that an easy way to remember which forms of these verbs have stem changes is to think of them as boot verbs. Draw a line around the stem-changing forms in each paradigm to show the boot-like shape.

TEACHING OPTIONS

Extra Practice Write a pattern sentence on the board, Ex: **Ella empieza una carta**. Have students copy the model and then dictate a list of different subjects. Ex: **Maite, nosotras, don Francisco**. Have students write down the subjects and supply the correct verb form. Ask volunteers to read their answers aloud.

Heritage Speakers Ask heritage speakers to work in pairs to conduct a mock interview with a Spanish-speaking celebrity such as Ricky Martin, Arantxa Sánchez-Vicario, Luis Miguel, and so forth, in which they use the verbs **empezar**, **volver**, **querer**, and **recordar**. Ask them to present their interview for the class and have students write down the forms of **empezar**, **volver**, **querer**, and **recordar** that they hear.

Suggestions

- Write **e:ie** and **o:ue** on the board and explain that some very common verbs have these types of stem changes. Point out that all the verbs listed are conjugated like **empezar** or **volver**. Model the pronunciation of the verbs and ask students a few questions using verbs of each type, having them answer in complete sentences. Ex: **¿A qué hora cierra la biblioteca? ¿Duermen los estudiantes tarde, por lo general? ¿Qué piensan hacer este fin de semana? ¿Quién quiere comer en un restaurante esta noche?**
- Point out the structure **jugar al** used with sports. Practice it by asking students about the sports they play. Have them answer in complete sentences. Ex: ____, **¿te gusta jugar al fútbol? Y tú,** ____, **¿juegas al fútbol? ¿Prefieres jugar al fútbol o ver un partido en el estadio? ¿Cuántos juegan al tenis? ¿Qué prefieres,** ____, **jugar al tenis o jugar al fútbol?**
- Prepare "dehydrated" sentences such as these: **Maite / empezar / la lección; Uds. / mostrar / los trabajos; Nosotros / jugar / al fútbol.** Write them on the board one at a time, and have students "hydrate" them.

Common stem-changing verbs

e:ie		o:ue	
cerrar	*to close*	**almorzar**	*to have lunch*
comenzar (a+*inf.*)	*to begin*	**contar**	*to count; to tell*
empezar (a+*inf.*)	*to begin*	**dormir**	*to sleep*
entender	*to understand*	**encontrar**	*to find*
pensar (+*inf.*)	*to think*	**mostrar**	*to show*
perder	*to lose; to miss*	**poder (+*inf.*)**	*to be able; can*
preferir (+*inf.*)	*to prefer*	**recordar**	*to remember*
querer (+*inf.*)	*to want; to love*	**volver**	*to return*

¡LENGUA VIVA!

The verb **perder** can mean *to lose* or *to miss*, in the sense of "to miss a train":

Siempre pierdo mis llaves.
I always lose my keys.

Es importante no perder el autobús.
It's important not to miss the bus.

▶ **Jugar** (*to play* a sport or game), is the only Spanish verb that has a **u:ue** stem change. **Jugar** is followed by **a** + [*definite article*] when the name of a sport or game is mentioned.

Oye, Maite,
¿por qué no jugamos al fútbol?

Álex y el joven juegan al fútbol.

▶ **Comenzar** and **empezar** require the preposition **a** when they are followed by an infinitive.

Comenzan a jugar a las siete.
They begin playing at seven.

Ana **empieza a** escribir una postal.
Ana starts to write a postcard.

▶ **Pensar** + [*infinitive*] means *to plan* or *to intend to do something*. **Pensar en** means *to think about someone* or *something*.

¿**Piensan** ir al gimnasio?
Are you planning to go to the gym?

¿**En** qué **piensas**?
What are you thinking about?

¡INTÉNTALO! Provide the present tense forms of these verbs. The first item in each column has been done for you.

cerrar (e:ie)

1. Ustedes cierran.
2. Tú cierras.
3. Nosotras cerramos.
4. Mi hermano cierra.
5. Yo cierro.
6. Usted cierra.
7. Los chicos cierran.
8. Ella cierra.

dormir (o:ue)

1. Mi abuela no duerme.
2. Yo no duermo.
3. Tú no duermes.
4. Mis hijos no duermen.
5. Usted no duerme.
6. Nosotros no dormimos.
7. Él no duerme.
8. Ustedes no duermen.

TEACHING OPTIONS

Extra Practice For additional drills of stem-changing verbs with the whole class or with students who need extra practice, do **¡Inténtalo!** orally using infinitives other than **cerrar** and **dormir**. Keep the pace rapid.

Large Group Arrange all the classroom chairs in a circle and use a small ball or paper wadded into a ball for this activity. Begin by naming the infinitive of a common stem-changing verb. Then name a pronoun. Ex: **querer / tú**. Then throw the paper ball to a student. The student catches the ball and says the appropriate form of the verb (**quieres**). Then he or she names a different pronoun and throws the ball to another student who must catch it and give the appropriate form of the verb. Continue until all subject pronouns have been covered, and then begin again with another infinitive.

Práctica

1 **Completar** Complete this conversation with the appropriate forms of the verbs. Then act it out with a partner.

PABLO Óscar, voy al centro ahora.
ÓSCAR ¿A qué hora (1) piensas (pensar) volver? El partido de fútbol (2) empieza (empezar) a las dos.
PABLO (3) Vuelvo (Volver) a la una. (4) Quiero (querer) ver el partido.
ÓSCAR (5) ¿Recuerdas (Recordar) que (*that*) nuestro equipo es muy bueno? (6) ¡Puede (poder) ganar!
PABLO No, (7) pienso (pensar) que va a (8) perder (perder). Los jugadores de Guadalajara son salvajes (*wild*) cuando (9) juegan (jugar).

2 **Preferencias** With a partner, take turns asking and answering questions about what these people want to do, using the cues provided.

NOTA CULTURAL

Dominó (*dominoes*) is a popular pastime throughout Colombia, Venezuela, Central America, and the Spanish-speaking countries of the Caribbean. It's played by young and old alike, primarily at family gatherings and among friends, but sometimes also competitively.

modelo

Guillermo: estudiar / pasear en bicicleta.
Estudiante 1: *¿Quiere estudiar Guillermo?*
Estudiante 2: *No, prefiere pasear en bicicleta.*

1. tú: trabajar / dormir
¿Quieres trabajar? No, prefiero dormir.
2. Uds.: mirar la televisión / jugar al dominó
¿Quieren Uds. mirar la televisión? No, preferimos jugar al dominó.
3. tus amigos: ir de excursión / descansar
¿Quieren ir de excursión tus amigos? No, mis amigos prefieren descansar.
4. tú: comer en la cafetería / ir a un restaurante
¿Quieres comer en la cafetería? No, prefiero ir a un restaurante.
5. Elisa: ver una película / leer una revista
¿Quiere ver una película Elisa? No, (Elisa) prefiere leer una revista.
6. María y su hermana: tomar el sol / practicar el esquí acuático
¿Quieren tomar el sol María y su hermana? No, (María y su hermana) prefieren practicar el esquí acuático.

3 **Describir** Use a verb from the list to describe what these people are doing.

almorzar cerrar contar dormir encontrar mostrar

1. Las niñas Las niñas duermen.

2. Yo (Yo) Cierro la ventana.

3. Nosotros (Nosotros) Almorzamos.

4. Tú (Tú) Encuentras una maleta.

5. Pedro Pedro muestra una foto.

6. Teresa Teresa cuenta.

1 Suggestion Divide the class into pairs and give them three minutes to act out the conversation. Then have partners switch roles.

1 Expansions
- Supply students with short-answer prompts based on the conversation. Ask students to give the questions that would have elicited the answers. Ex: **A las dos. (¿A qué hora empieza el partido de fútbol?) Porque no quiere perderse el partido. (¿Por qué vuelve Pablo a la una?)**
- Ask questions using **pensar** + [*infinitive*]; **pensar en**, and **perder** (in both senses). Ex: **¿Qué piensas hacer mañana? ¿En qué piensas ahora? ¿Cuándo pierdes las cosas?**

2 Suggestion Model the activity by reading the **modelo** and giving other examples in the **yo** form before assigning the activity to pairs. Ex: **¿Quiero descansar en casa? No, prefiero enseñar la clase.**

2 Expansion Have students ask one another questions of their own using the same pattern. Ex: **—¿Quieres jugar al baloncesto? —No, prefiero jugar al tenis.**

3 Expansion Bring in photos or magazine pictures to extend this activity. Choose pictures that lend themselves to being described by the common stem-changing verbs.

TEACHING OPTIONS

TPR Brainstorm gestures to go with each of the stem-changing verbs. Have students mime the activity you mention. Tell them that only male students should respond to **él/ellos** and only females to **ella/ellas**. Everyone should respond to **nosotros**.
Game Arrange students in rows of five or six (depending on whether you use **vosotros**), one behind the other. The first person in the row has a piece of paper. Call out the infinitive of a stem-changing verb. The first person writes the **yo** form and passes the paper to the student behind. That student writes the **tú** form and passes the paper on. There is to be no talking. The last person in the row holds up the paper to show the team has finished. The first team to finish the conjugation correctly gets a point. Have students rotate positions in their row before calling out another verb.

4 Suggestion Model the activity for the whole class by asking questions about a famous person. Ex: **¿Qué deporte practica Tiger Woods? ¿Con qué frecuencia juega al golf?** Write the answers on the board.

4 Expansion After tallying results on the board, ask students to graph them. Have them refer to **Lectura,** pages 126–127, for models.

5 Suggestion Model the activity for the whole class by choosing two events from the program that you would watch and asking the class to react.

5 Expansion Have students personalize the activity by choosing their favorite programs from the list. Compare and contrast students' reasons for their choices.

6 Suggestion Divide the class into pairs and distribute the Info Gap Handouts from the Info Gap Activities Booklet that correspond to this activity. Give students ten minutes to complete the activity.

6 Expansions
- Ask questions based on the artwork. Ex: **¿Dónde empiezan el día? (en el café) ¿Qué pueden hacer en la plaza mayor? (pueden pasear)**
- Have volunteers take turns completing the information in the puzzle. Then have students invent their own stories, using stem-changing verbs, about what happens to the same group of tourists.

Comunicación

NATIONAL communication STANDARDS

4 **Frecuencia** In pairs, use the verbs from the list and other stem-changing verbs you know to create sentences telling your partner which activities you do daily (**todos los días**), which you do once a month (**una vez al mes**), and which you do once a year (**una vez al año**). Then switch roles. Answers will vary.

Estudiante 1: *Yo recuerdo a mi familia todos los días.*
Estudiante 2: *Yo pierdo uno de mis libros una vez al año.*

cerrar	perder
dormir	poder
empezar	preferir
encontrar	querer
jugar	recordar
¿?	¿?

todos los días	una vez al mes	una vez al año

5 **En la televisión** Read the television listings for Saturday. In pairs, write a conversation between two siblings arguing about what to watch. Be creative and be prepared to act out your conversation for the class. Answers will vary.

modelo

Hermano: *Quiero ver la Copa Mundial.*
Hermana: *¡No! Prefiero ver...*

	13:00	14:00	15:00	16:00	17:00	18:00	19:00	20:00	21:00	22:00	23:00
7	Copa Mundial (*World Cup*) de fútbol			El tiempo libre		Fútbol internacional: Copa América: México-Argentina				Torneo de Natación	
8	Abierto (*Open*) Mexicano de Tenis: Alejandro Hernández (México) vs. Jacobo Díaz (España). Semifinales			Campeonato (*Championship*) de baloncesto Los Correcaminos de Tampico vs. los Santos de San Luis				Aficionados al buceo		Cozumel: Aventuras	
12	Gente famosa		Amigos	Médicos jóvenes			Película: **El centro de la ciudad**		Película: **Terror en la plaza mayor**		
13	El padrastro		Periodistas en peligro (*danger*)				El esquí acuático			Patinaje Artístico	
17	Biografías: La artista Frida Kahlo			Música de la semana			Entrevista del día: Miguel Indurain y su pasión por el ciclismo			Cine de la noche: **Los excursionistas perdidos** ***(lost)***	

NOTA CULTURAL

Miguel Indurain is a famous cyclist from Spain who has won the Tour de France bicycle race five times.

Very few cyclists have won this difficult race five times. Lance Armstrong of the U.S. achieved this in 2003.

Síntesis

6  **Situación** Your instructor will give you and your partner a partially illustrated itinerary of a city tour. Complete the itineraries by asking each other questions using the verbs in the captions and vocabulary you have learned. Answers will vary.

Estudiante 1: *Por la mañana, empiezan en el café.*
Estudiante 2: *Y luego ...*

TEACHING OPTIONS

Small Groups Have students choose their favorite leisure activity or sport and work together in groups of three with other students who have chosen that same activity. Have each group write six true sentences about the activity they have chosen, using a stem-changing verb in each.

Heritage Speakers Ask heritage speakers to describe sports preferences in their home communities, especially ones that are not widely known in the United States, such as **jai-alai**. How do the sports preferences in their home community compare to those of the class or with those graphed in **Lectura**, pages 126–127?

4.3 Stem-changing verbs: e→i

ANTE TODO You've already seen that many verbs in Spanish change their stem vowel when conjugated. There is a third kind of stem-vowel change in some verbs, such as **pedir** (*to ask for; to request*). In these verbs, the stressed vowel in the stem changes from **e** to **i**, as shown in the diagram.

INFINITIVE	VERB STEM	STEM CHANGE	CONJUGATED FORM
pedir	ped-	pid-	pido

▶ As with other stem-changing verbs you have learned, there is no stem change in the **nosotros/as** or **vosotros/as** forms in the present tense.

pedir (e:i)

Singular forms		Plural forms	
yo	pido	nosotros/as	pedimos
tú	pides	vosotros/as	pedís
Ud./él/ella	pide	Uds./ellos/ellas	piden

▶ To help you identify verbs with the **e:i** stem change, they will appear as follows throughout the text:

pedir (e:i)

▶ The following are the most common **e:i** stem-changing verbs:

conseguir	**decir**	**repetir**	**seguir**
to get; to obtain	*to say; to tell*	*to repeat*	*to follow; to continue; to keep (doing something)*

Pido favores cuando es necesario.
I ask for favors when it's necessary.

Javier **dice** la verdad.
Javier is telling the truth.

Sigue esperando.
He keeps waiting.

Consiguen ver buenas películas.
They get to see good movies.

▶ The **yo** forms of **seguir** and **conseguir** have a spelling change as well as the stem change **e→i**.

Sigo su plan.
I'm following their plan.

Consigo novelas en la librería.
I get novels at the bookstore.

¡LENGUA VIVA!

As you learned in **Lección 2, preguntar** *means to ask a question.* **Pedir,** however, means *to ask for something*:
Ella me pregunta cuántos años tengo.
She asks me how old I am.
Él me pide ayuda.
He asks me for help.

¡ATENCIÓN!

While **decir** follows the stem-change pattern of **e** to **i**, its **yo** form is irregular: **yo digo.** You will learn other verbs whose **yo** forms end in **–go** in **Estructura 4.4**, pp. 122–123.

•••

Here are some common expressions with **decir**:
decir la verdad
to tell the truth
decir mentiras
to tell lies
decir que
to say that
decir la respuesta
to say the answer

¡INTÉNTALO! Provide the correct forms of the verbs.

repetir (e:i)
1. Arturo y Eva repiten.
2. Yo repito.
3. Nosotros repetimos.
4. Julia repite.
5. Sofía y yo repetimos.
6. Tú repites.

decir (e:i)
1. Yo digo.
2. Él dice.
3. Tú dices.
4. Usted dice.
5. Ellas dicen.
6. Nosotros decimos.

seguir (e: i)
1. Yo sigo.
2. Nosotros seguimos.
3. Tú sigues.
4. Los chicos siguen.
5. Usted sigue.
6. Anita sigue.

Section Goal

In **Estructura 4.3** students will learn the present tense of stem-changing verbs: **e → i**.

Instructional Resources
WB/VM: Workbook, pp. 43–44
Lab Manual, p. 23
Lab CD/MP3 ***Lección 4***
IRM: ***¡Inténtalo!*** *&* ***Práctica*** *Answers, pp. 202–203; Tapescript, pp. 16–19*
Interactive CD-ROM
Companion website: www.vistahigherlearning.com
Presentations CD-ROM

Suggestions
- Take a survey of students' habits. Make a chart on the board. Ask questions like: **¿Quiénes piden Coca-Cola?** Then summarize the chart.
- Ask for volunteers to answer questions using **conseguir, decir, pedir, repetir,** and **seguir.**
- Reiterate that the personal endings for the present tense of all the verbs listed are the same as those for the present tense of regular **–ir** verbs.
- Point out the spelling changes in the **yo** forms of **seguir → sigo** and **conseguir → consigo.**
- Prepare "dehydrated" sentences, write them on the board one at a time, and have students "hydrate" them. Ex: **Tú / pedir / café; Ustedes / repetir / la pregunta; Nosotros / decir / la respuesta.**
- For additional drills with stem-changing verbs, do the **¡Inténtalo!** activity orally using other infinitives such as **conseguir, impedir, pedir,** and **servir.** Keep the pace rapid.

¡Atención! Since they are active vocabulary, go over the common expressions used with **decir.** In pairs, have students practice the different expressions by asking each other questions. Ex: **¿En qué circunstancias dices mentiras?**

Note: Students will learn more about **decir** with indirect object pronouns in **Estructura 6.2.**

TEACHING OPTIONS

Game Divide the class into two teams. Announce an infinitive and a subject pronoun (Ex: **decir / yo**). Have the first member of Team A give the appropriate conjugated form of the verb. If the team member answers correctly, Team A gets one point. If not, give the first member of Team B the same example. If he or she does not know the answer, give the correct verb form and move on. The team with the most points wins.

Extra Practice Bring in magazine pictures or photos of parks and city centers where people are doing fun activities. In teams, have students describe the photos using as many stem-changing verbs from **Estructura 4.2** and **4.3** as they can. Give points for the teams who use the most stem-changing verbs.

1 Suggestion Have students use **conseguir, decir, pedir, repetir,** and **seguir** to write original sentences using their own family members as subjects. Then have them exchange papers with a partner for peer-editing.

Nota cultural Have students research **El bosque de Chapultepec** in the library or on the Internet and bring to class a photo of the park and one new fact they learned about it.

2 Suggestion Before beginning the activity, ask students to brainstorm their choices for the sentences. Then model the activity. Ex: **Mis amigos piden muchos favores.**

2 Expansion In pairs, have students create three or four true-false statements based on this activity using stem-changing verbs from **Estructura 4.2** and **4.3**. Then, have pairs share their statements with another pair who must decide if they are true or false.

3 Suggestion Ask students to keep a record of their partner's responses. Take a class poll to see what percentage of students guessed their partner's statements correctly.

Práctica

1 **Completar** Complete these sentences with the correct form of the verb provided.

1. Cuando mi familia pasea por la ciudad, mi madre siempre va al café y ___pide___ (pedir) una soda.
2. Pero mi padre ___dice___ (decir) que perdemos mucho tiempo. Tiene prisa por llegar al bosque de Chapultepec.
3. Mi padre tiene suerte, porque él siempre ___consigue___ (conseguir) lo que (*that which*) desea.
4. Cuando llegamos al parque, mis hermanos y yo ___seguimos___ (seguir) conversando (*talking*) con nuestros padres.
5. Mis padres siempre ___repiten___ (repetir) la misma cosa: "Nosotros tomamos el sol aquí sin ustedes."
6. Yo siempre ___pido___ (pedir) permiso para volver a casa un poco más tarde porque me gusta mucho el parque.

NOTA CULTURAL

A popular weekend destination for residents and tourists, **El bosque de Chapultepec** is a beautiful park located in Mexico City. It occupies over 1.5 square miles and includes lakes, wooded areas, several museums, and a botanical garden.

2 **Combinar** Combine words from the columns to create sentences about yourself and people you know. Answers will vary.

A	B
Yo	(no) pedir muchos favores
Mi compañero/a de cuarto	nunca (*never*) pedir perdón
Mi mejor (*best*) amigo/a	nunca seguir las instrucciones
Mi familia	siempre seguir las instrucciones
Mis amigos/as	conseguir libros en Internet
Mis amigos y yo	repetir el vocabulario
Mis padres	(no) decir mentiras
Mi hermano/a	
Mi profesor(a) de español	

3 **Opiniones** Work in pairs to guess how your partner completed the sentences from **Actividad 2**. If you guess incorrectly, your partner must supply the correct answer. Switch roles. Answers will vary.

modelo

Estudiante 1: En mi opinión, tus padres consiguen libros en Internet.
Estudiante 2: ¡No! Mi hermana consigue libros en Internet.

CONSÚLTALO

To review possessive adjectives, see **Estructura 3.2**, p. 83.

TEACHING OPTIONS

Game In groups, have students write two brief stories: one should be a true story and the other should be fictional. Then, have them share their stories with another group who must decide whether their classmates **dicen la verdad o dicen mentiras**. Take a class poll to uncover the best liars.

Small Groups Explain to students that movie titles for English-language films are not usually directly translated into Spanish. Bring in a list of movie titles in Spanish. In groups, have students guess the movies based on the Spanish titles.

Comunicación

4 **Las películas** Use these questions to interview a classmate. Answers will vary.

1. ¿Prefieres las películas románticas, las películas de acción o las películas de horror? ¿Por qué?
2. ¿Dónde consigues información sobre (*about*) una película?
3. ¿Dónde consigues las entradas (*tickets*) para una película?
4. Para decidir qué películas vas a ver, ¿sigues las recomendaciones de los críticos? ¿Qué dicen los críticos en general?
5. ¿Qué cines en tu comunidad muestran las mejores (*best*) películas?
6. ¿Vas a ver una película esta semana? ¿A qué hora empieza la película?

Síntesis

5 **El cine** In pairs, first scan the ad and jot down all the stem-changing verbs. Then answer the questions. Be prepared to share your answers with the class. Answers will vary.

1. ¿Qué palabras indican que *Un mundo azul oscuro (Dark Blue World)* es una película dramática?
2. ¿Cuántas personas hay en el póster?
3. ¿Cómo son las personas del póster? ¿Qué relación tienen?
4. ¿Te gustan las películas como ésta (*this one*)?
5. Describe tu película favorita con los verbos de la **Lección 4.**

NOMINADA POR LA ACADEMIA CHECA A LOS OSCAR
JUGAR CON EL AMOR PUEDE RESULTAR PELIGROSO.
ALGUIEN PUEDE PERDERLO TODO
Y VOLVER A EMPEZAR DE NUEVO.
DEL PRODUCTOR Y DIRECTOR GANADOR DEL OSCAR POR "KOLYA"
UN MUNDO AZUL OSCURO
DARK BLUE WORLD
CONSEGUIR LO QUE QUIERES PUEDE COSTARTE
MUCHO MÁS DE LO QUE PIENSAS

4 Suggestions

- Have students report to the class what their partner said. After the presentation, encourage them to ask each other questions.
- Take a class poll to find out students' film genre and local movie theater preferences.

5 Suggestions

- Write the stem-changing verbs from the ad on the board. Have students conjugate the verbs using different subjects.
- In pairs, have students use the verbs from the ad to write a dramatic dialogue.
- Go over student responses to item 5.

TEACHING OPTIONS

Small Groups First, have students talk about how they would advertise fun activities in town. Then, have them create a poster similar to the movie poster using stem-changing verbs from **Estructura 4.2** and **4.3**.

Heritage Speakers Ask heritage speakers to talk about popular Spanish-language films. Brainstorm with the class a list of questions about the films using stem-changing verbs from **Estructura 4.2** and **4.3**. Have students ask the heritage speakers the questions. Ex: **¿Dónde conseguimos la película aquí? ¿Dices que es tu película favorita? ¿Prefieres películas en español o en inglés?**

NATIONAL comparisons STANDARDS

Section Goal
In **Estructura 4.4** students will learn verbs with irregular **yo** forms.

Instructional Resources
WB/VM: Workbook, pp. 45–46
Lab Manual, p. 24
Lab CD/MP3 ***Lección 4***
IRM: ***¡Inténtalo! & Práctica*** *Answers, pp. 202–203; Tapescript, pp. 16–19*
Interactive CD-ROM
Companion website: www.vistahigherlearning.com
Presentations CD-ROM

Suggestions
- Quickly review the present tense of **tener**, pointing out the **–go** ending of the **yo** form.
- Ask questions and make statements that elicit the **yo** forms of the verbs. Ex: **¿Haces la tarea en casa o en la biblioteca? (Hago la tarea en la biblioteca.) ¿Traes un diccionario a la clase? (Sí, traigo un diccionario a la clase.)** As you elicit responses, write just the verbs on the board until you have listed all the irregular **yo** forms.
- Go over the different uses of **salir** as outlined. Then model an additional example of each usage.

Successful Language Learning Point out that students should learn the verbs with irregular **yo** forms thoroughly because these will often be used in conversation.

4.4 Verbs with irregular yo forms

ANTE TODO In Spanish, several verbs have irregular **yo** forms in the present tense. You have already seen three verbs with the **–go** ending in the **yo** form: **decir → digo**, **tener → tengo**, and **venir → vengo**. Now you will learn several more.

Verbs with irregular *yo* forms

	hacer *(to do; to make)*	**poner** *(to put; to place)*	**salir** *(to leave)*	**suponer** *(to suppose)*	**traer** *(to bring)*
SINGULAR FORMS	**hago**	**pongo**	**salgo**	**supongo**	**traigo**
	haces	pones	sales	supones	traes
	hace	pone	sale	supone	trae
PLURAL FORMS	hacemos	ponemos	salimos	suponemos	traemos
	hacéis	ponéis	salís	suponéis	traéis
	hacen	ponen	salen	suponen	traen

▶ The verbs **hacer**, **poner**, **salir**, **suponer**, and **traer** have **yo** forms that end in **–go**. The other forms are regular.

A veces salgo a correr por la noche.

Nunca salgo a correr, no hago ejercicio, pero sí tengo energía... ¡para leer el periódico y tomar un café!

▶ **Poner** can also mean *to turn on* a household appliance.

Carlos **pone** la radio.
Carlos turns on the radio.

María **pone** la televisión.
María turns on the television.

▶ **Salir de** is used to indicate that someone is leaving a particular place.

Hoy **salgo del** hospital.
Today I leave the hospital.

Sale de la clase a las cuatro.
He leaves class at four.

▶ **Salir para** is used to indicate someone's destination.

Mañana **salgo para** México.
Tomorrow I leave for Mexico.

Hoy **salen para** España.
Today they leave for Spain.

▶ **Salir con** means *to leave with someone* or *something*, or *to date someone*.

Alberto **sale con** su mochila.
Alberto is leaving with his backpack.

Margarita **sale con** Guillermo.
Margarita is going out with Guillermo.

Hoy voy a **salir con** mi hermana.
Today I'm going out with my sister.

Mi primo **sale con** una chica muy bonita.
My cousin is going out with a very pretty girl.

TEACHING OPTIONS

TPR Use the verbs with irregular **yo** forms in different sentences. Students will mime what you are saying. Ex: **Hago la tarea.** (Students mime writing their homework.) **Pongo la radio.** (They mime turning on a radio.)

Game Divide the class into teams of three. Each team has a piece of paper. Call out an infinitive and a person. Ex: **traer / primera persona plural**. Each team has to compose a sentence with each person writing one part. The first team member writes a subject (Ex: **nosotras**). The second writes the correct form of the verb (Ex: **traemos**). The third gives a direct or indirect object (Ex: **el libro**). The first team to write a logical and correct sentence wins. Team members should rotate positions each time a new verb is given.

The verbs ver and oír

▶ The verb **ver** (*to see*) has an irregular **yo** form. The other forms of **ver** are regular.

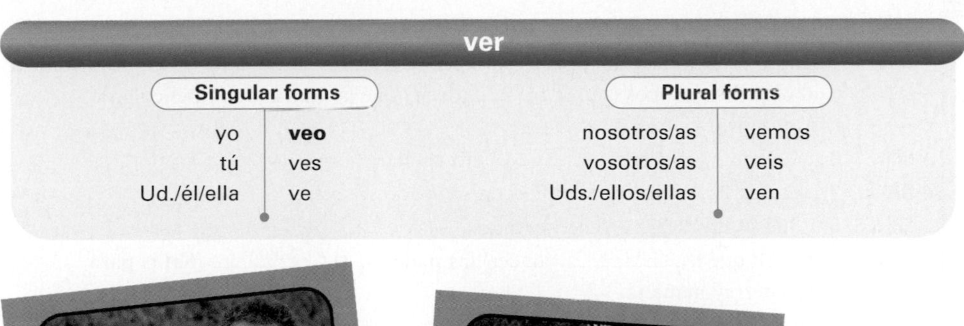

ver			
Singular forms		**Plural forms**	
yo	**veo**	nosotros/as	vemos
tú	ves	vosotros/as	veis
Ud./él/ella	ve	Uds./ellos/ellas	ven

Oye, ¿por qué no jugamos al fútbol?
Maite ve la pelota.

▶ The verb **oír** (*to hear*) has an irregular **yo** form and the spelling change **i→y** in the **tú, usted, él, ella, ustedes, ellos,** and **ellas** forms. The **nosotros/as** and **vosotros/as** forms have an accent mark.

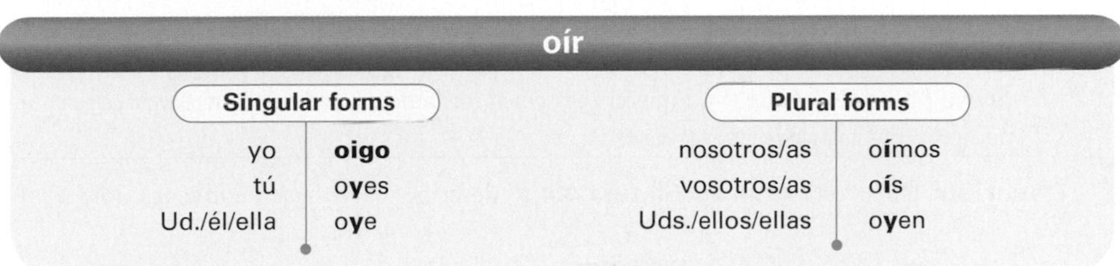

oír			
Singular forms		**Plural forms**	
yo	**oigo**	nosotros/as	**oí**mos
tú	o**y**es	vosotros/as	**oí**s
Ud./él/ella	o**y**e	Uds./ellos/ellas	o**y**en

Oigo a unas personas en la otra sala.
I hear some people in the other room.

¿**Oyes** música latina?
Do you hear Latin music?

¡INTÉNTALO! Provide the appropriate forms of these verbs. The first item has been done for you.

1. salir	Isabel sale	Nosotros salimos	Yo salgo
2. ver	Yo veo	Uds. ven	Tú ves
3. poner	Rita y yo ponemos	Yo pongo	Los niños ponen
4. hacer	Yo hago	Tú haces	Ud. hace
5. oír	Él oye	Nosotros oímos	Yo oigo
6. traer	Ellas traen	Yo traigo	Tú traes
7. suponer	Yo supongo	Mi amigo supone	Nosotras suponemos

Suggestions

- Point out that **oír** is irregular in all forms except **nosotros** and **vosotros**. Write a model sentence on the board. Ex: **Ustedes oyen el programa de radio todos los viernes**. Then change the subject, and have students give the new sentence. Ex: **tú (Tú oyes el programa de radio todos los viernes.)**
- Call out different forms of the verbs in **Estructura 4.4** and have volunteers say the infinitive. Ex: **oyen (oír)**. Keep the pace rapid.
- Explain the difference between **escuchar** (*to listen*) and **oír** (*to hear*). Ex: **Escucho la radio. No oigo el perro.**

TEACHING OPTIONS

Extra Practice For oral practice, call out subject pronouns and have students respond with the correct form of **ver** or **oír**. Reverse the drill by starting with forms of **ver** and **oír** and asking students to give the corresponding subject pronouns.

Pairs In pairs, have students create and then ask each other questions about their habits. Ex: **¿Sales a comer a restaurantes con tus amigos? ¿Ves la televisión en español? ¿Supones que una clase de matemáticas es muy difícil? ¿Haces ejercicio por la mañana?** Have students record their partner's answers and be prepared to share the information with the class.

1 Suggestion Quickly review the new verbs with irregular **yo** forms. Then, ask pairs to complete and act out the conversation, then switch roles.

1 Expansion Ask questions about the conversation. **¿Qué hace David hoy? ¿Qué hace Diana? ¿Por qué tienen que hacer las maletas Andrés y Javier? ¿Por qué pone Ernesto la televisión?**

2 Suggestion Model the activity by completing the **modelo** orally. Ask volunteers to say aloud each complete sentence.

2 Expansion Change the subjects of the dehydrated sentences in the activity and have students write or say aloud the new sentences.

3 Expansion Use magazine pictures which elicit the target verbs to extend the activity. Encourage students to add further descriptions if they can.

Práctica

1 Completar Complete this conversation with the appropriate forms of the verbs. Then act it out with a partner.

ERNESTO David, ¿qué (1) haces (hacer) hoy?

DAVID Ahora estudio biología, pero esta noche (2) salgo (salir) con Luisa. Vamos al cine. Los críticos (3) dicen (decir) que la nueva (*new*) película de Almodóvar es buena.

ERNESTO ¿Y Diana? ¿Qué (4) hace (hacer) ella?

DAVID (5) Sale (Salir) a comer con sus padres.

ERNESTO ¿Qué (6) hacen (hacer) Andrés y Javier?

DAVID Tienen que (7) hacer (hacer) las maletas. (8) Salen (Salir) para Monterrey mañana.

ERNESTO Pues, ¿qué (9) hago (hacer) yo?

DAVID (10) Supongo (Suponer) que puedes estudiar o (11) ver (ver) la televisión.

ERNESTO No quiero estudiar. Mejor (12) pongo (poner) el televisor. Mi programa favorito empieza en unos minutos.

2 Oraciones Form sentences using the cues provided and verbs from **Estructura 4.4**.

modelo

Tú / ______ / cosas / en / su lugar / antes de (*before*) / salir

Tú pones las cosas en su lugar antes de salir.

1. Mis amigos / ______ / conmigo / centro Mis amigos salen conmigo al centro.
2. Tú / ______ / cámara Tú traes una cámara.
3. Alberto / ______ / música del café Pasatiempos Alberto oye la música del café Pasatiempos.
4. Yo / no / ______ / muchas películas Yo no veo muchas películas.
5. domingo / nosotros / ______ / mucha / tarea El domingo, nosotros hacemos mucha tarea.
6. Si / yo / ______ / que / yo / querer / ir / cine / mis amigos / ir / también Si yo digo que quiero ir al cine, mis amigos van también.

3 Describir Use a verb from **Estructura 4.4** to describe what these people are doing.

1. Fernán Fernán pone la mochila en el escritorio.

2. Los aficionados Los aficionados salen del estadio.

3. Yo Yo traigo una cámara.

4. Nosotros Nosotros vemos el monumento.

5. La señora Vargas La señora Vargas no oye bien.

6. El estudiante El estudiante hace su tarea.

TEACHING OPTIONS

Pairs Have students write three sentences in each of which they use one of the target verbs from **Estructura 4.4**. Then ask them to copy their sentences onto a sheet of paper in "dehydrated" form, following the model of the sentences in **Actividad 2**. Students exchange their sentences with a partner, who writes the complete sentences on the paper. Finally, have partners check each other's work.

Extra Practice Have students use five of the target verbs from **Estructura 4.4** to write sentences about habits or likes they have that they think are somewhat unusual. Ex: **Traigo doce bolígrafos en la mochila. Hago la tarea en un café del centro. No pongo la televisión hasta las diez de la noche.**

Comunicación

4 **Preguntas** Get together with a classmate and ask each other these questions. Answers will vary.

1. ¿Qué traes a clase?
2. ¿Quiénes traen un diccionario a clase? ¿Por qué traen un diccionario?
3. ¿A qué hora sales de tu residencia o de tu casa por la mañana? ¿A qué hora sale tu compañero/a de cuarto o tu esposo/a?
4. ¿Dónde pones tus libros cuando regresas de clase? ¿Siempre (*Always*) pones tus cosas en su lugar?
5. ¿Pones fotos de tu familia en tu casa? ¿Quiénes son las personas que están en las fotos?
6. ¿Oyes la radio cuando estudias?
7. ¿En qué circunstancias dices mentiras?
8. ¿Haces mucha tarea los fines de semana?
9. ¿Sales con tus amigos los fines de semana? ¿A qué hora? ¿Qué hacen?
10. ¿Te gusta ver deportes en la televisión o prefieres ver otros programas? ¿Cuáles?

5 **Charadas** In groups, play a game of charades. Each person should think of two phrases using the verbs **hacer, poner, salir, oír, traer,** or **ver**. The first person to guess correctly acts out the next charade. Answers will vary.

6 **Entrevista** You are doing a market research report on lifestyles. Interview a classmate to find out when he or she goes out with the following people and what they do for entertainment. Answers will vary.

- los amigos
- el/la novio/a
- el/la esposo/a
- la familia

Síntesis

7 **Situación** Imagine that you are speaking with your roommate. With a partner, prepare a conversation using these cues. Answer will vary.

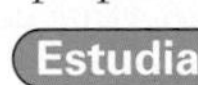

Estudiante 1	Estudiante 2
Ask your partner what he or she is doing.	Tell your partner that you are watching TV.
Say what you suppose he or she is watching.	Say that you like the show _______. Ask if he or she wants to watch.
Say no, because you are going out with friends and tell where you are going.	Say you think it's a good idea, and ask what your partner and his or her friends are doing there.
Say what you are going to do, and ask your partner whether her or she wants to come along.	Say no and tell your partner what you prefer to do.

4 Suggestion Model the activity for the class by asking volunteers the first two items.

4 Expansion Ask students questions about their own and their classmate's responses to the activity questions. Ex: **¿Tu compañera trae un diccionario a clase? ¿Por qué?**

5 Suggestions
- Model the activity by doing a charade and having the class guess. Ex: **Pongo un lápiz en la mesa.** Then divide the class into groups of five to seven students.
- Ask each group to pick out the best **charada**. Then ask the students to present them to the whole class, having the other groups guess what activities they are miming.

6 Suggestion Model the activity for the class, giving a report on your own lifestyle. Ex: **Salgo al cine con mis amigas. Me gusta comer en restaurantes con mi esposo. En familia vemos deportes en la televisión.** Remind students that a market researcher and his or her interviewee would address each other with the **Ud.** form of verbs.

7 Possible Response
E1: ¿Qué haces?
E2: Veo la tele.
E1: Supongo que ves el programa *Amigos*.
E2: Sí. Me gusta el programa. ¿Quieres ver la tele conmigo?
E1: No puedo. Salgo con mis amigos a la plaza mayor.
E2: Buena idea. ¿Qué hacen en la plaza?
E1: Vamos a escuchar música y a pasear. ¿Quieres venir?
E2: No. Prefiero descansar.

TEACHING OPTIONS

Pairs Have pairs of students role-play the perfect date. Students should write their script first, then present it to the class. Encourage students to use descriptive adjectives as well as the new verbs learned in **Estructura 4.4**.

Heritage Speakers Ask heritage speakers to make an oral presentation to the class about social customs in their home community. Remind them to use familiar vocabulary and simple sentences.

Section Goals

In **Lectura** students will:

- learn the strategy of predicting content by surveying the graphic elements in reading matter
- read a magazine article containing graphs and charts

Instructional Resource
Companion website:
www.vistahigherlearning.com

Estrategia Tell students that they can infer a great deal of information about the content of an article by surveying the graphic elements included in it. When students survey an article for its graphic elements, they should look for such things as:

- headlines or headings
- bylines
- photos
- photo captions
- graphs and tables

Examinar el texto Give students two minutes to take a look at the visual clues in the article and write down on a sheet of paper all the ideas the clues suggest. Have pairs of students compare their lists and discuss similarities and differences.

Contestar Ask the whole class the four questions. 1. María Úrsula Echevarría is the author of the article. 2. The article is about sports in the Hispanic world. 3. The most popular sports 4. Hispanic countries in world soccer championships

Lectura

Antes de leer

Estrategia

Predicting content from visuals

When you are reading in Spanish, be sure to look for visual clues that will orient you as to the content and purpose of what you are reading. Photos and illustrations, for example, will often give you a good idea of the main points that the reading covers. You may also encounter very helpful visuals that are used to summarize large amounts of data in a way that is easy to comprehend; these include bar graphs, pie charts, flow charts, lists of percentages, and other sorts of diagrams.

Examinar el texto

Take a quick look at the visual elements of the magazine article in order to generate a list of ideas about its content. Then compare your list with a classmate's. Are your lists the same or are they different? Discuss your lists and make any changes needed to produce a final list of ideas.

Contestar

Read the list of ideas you wrote in **Examinar el texto,** and look again at the visual elements of the magazine article. Then answer these questions:

1. Who is the woman in the photo, and what is her role?
2. What is the article about?
3. What is the subject of the pie chart?
4. What is the subject of the bar graph?

por María Úrsula Echevarría

El fútbol es el deporte más popular en el mundo° hispano, según° una encuesta° reciente realizada entre jóvenes universitarios. Mucha gente practica este deporte y tiene un equipo de fútbol favorito. Cada cuatro años se realiza la Copa Mundial°. Argentina y Uruguay han ganado° este campeonato° más de una vez°. Los aficionados siguen los partidos de fútbol en casa por tele y en muchos otros lugares como los bares, los restaurantes, los estadios y los clubes deportivos. Los jóvenes juegan al fútbol con sus amigos en parques y gimnasios.

Países hispanos en campeonatos mundiales de fútbol (1930-2002)

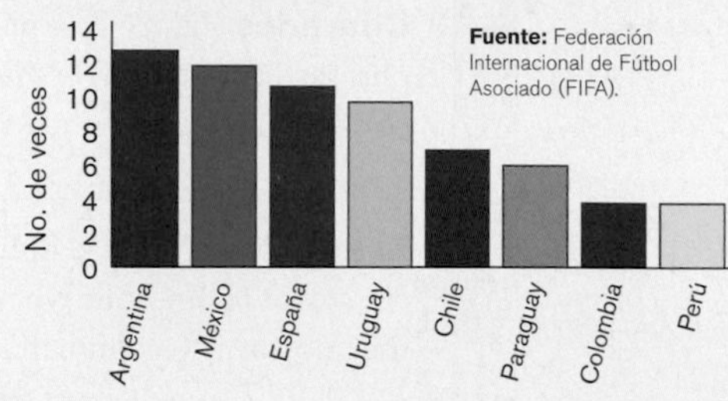

Pero, por supuesto°, en los países de habla hispana también hay otros deportes populares. ¿Qué deporte sigue al fútbol en estos países? Bueno, ¡depende del país y de otros factores!

Después de leer

Evaluación y predicción

Which of the following sports events would be most popular among the college students surveyed? Rate them from one (most popular) to five (least popular). Which would be the most popular at your college or university?
Answers will vary.

_________ 1. La Copa Mundial de Fútbol
_________ 2. Los Juegos Olímpicos
_________ 3. El torneo de tenis de Wimbledon
_________ 4. La Serie Mundial de Béisbol
_________ 5. El Tour de Francia

TEACHING OPTIONS

Variación léxica Remind students that the term **fútbol** in the Hispanic world refers to soccer. Remind them that in the English-speaking world outside of the United States and Canada, soccer is called football. The game called football here is called **fútbol americano** in the Spanish-speaking world.

Extra Practice Ask questions that require students to refer to the article. Model the use of the definite article with percentages. **¿Qué porcentaje prefiere el fútbol? (el 69 por ciento) ¿Qué porcentaje prefiere el vóleibol? (el 2 por ciento)**

No sólo el fútbol

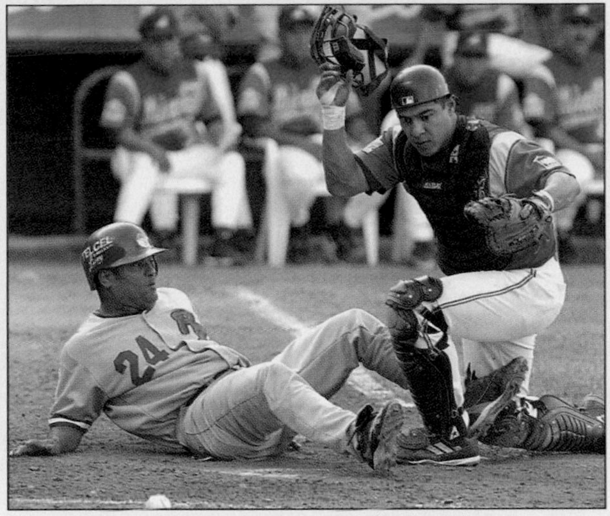

Donde el fútbol es más popular

En México el béisbol es el segundo° deporte más popular después° del fútbol. Pero en Argentina, después del fútbol, el rugby tiene mucha importancia. En Perú a la gente le gusta mucho ver partidos de vóleibol. ¿Y en España? Mucha gente prefiere el baloncesto, el tenis y el ciclismo.

En Colombia, por ejemplo, el béisbol es muy popular después del fútbol, aunque° esto varía según la región del país. En la costa del norte de Colombia, el béisbol es una pasión. Y el ciclismo también es un deporte que los colombianos siguen con mucho interés.

Donde el béisbol es más popular

En los países del Caribe, el béisbol es el deporte predominante. Éste es el caso en Puerto Rico, Cuba y la República Dominicana. Los niños empiezan a jugar cuando son muy pequeños. En Puerto Rico y la República Dominicana, la gente también quiere participar en otros deportes como el baloncesto, o ver los partidos en la tele. Y para los espectadores aficionados del Caribe, el boxeo es número dos.

Deportes más populares

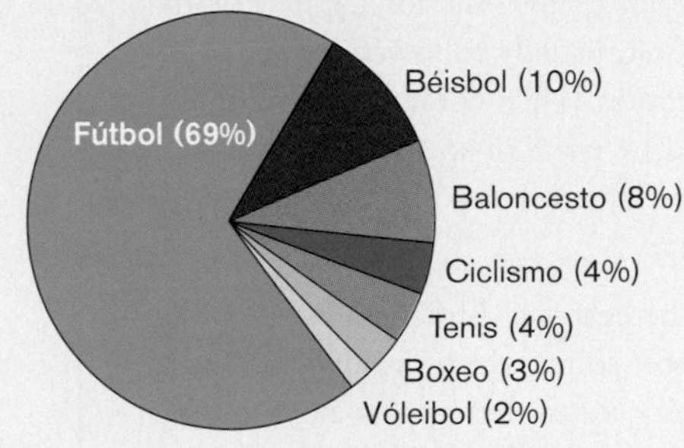

mundo *world* según *according to* encuesta *survey* se realiza la Copa Mundial *the World Cup is held* han ganado *have won* campeonato *championship* más de una vez *more than once* por supuesto *of course* segundo *second* después *after* aunque *although*

¿Cierto o falso?

Indicate whether each sentence is **cierto** or **falso,** then correct the false statements.

	Cierto	Falso
1. El vóleibol es el segundo deporte más popular en México. Es el béisbol.	❍	✓
2. En España a la gente le gustan varios deportes como el baloncesto y el ciclismo.	✓	❍
3. En la costa del norte de Colombia, el tenis es una pasión. El béisbol es una pasión.	❍	✓
4. En el Caribe el deporte más popular es el béisbol.	✓	❍

Preguntas

Answer these questions in Spanish. Answers will vary.

1. ¿Dónde ven los aficionados el fútbol? Y tú, ¿cómo ves tus deportes favoritos?
2. ¿Te gusta el fútbol? ¿Por qué?
3. ¿Miras la Copa Mundial en la televisión?
4. ¿Qué deportes miras en la televisión?
5. En tu opinión, ¿cuáles son los tres deportes más populares en tu universidad? ¿en tu comunidad? ¿en los Estados Unidos?
6. ¿Qué haces en tu tiempo libre?

Evaluación y predicción Write two headings on the board: **Entre los jóvenes del mundo hispano** and **Entre los jóvenes de nuestra universidad**. Ask students to raise their hands to respond to your questions about the ranking of each sporting event. Write down their reponses as you proceed. Ask: **¿Cuántos de ustedes creen que entre los jóvenes hispanos la Copa Mundial de Fútbol es el evento más popular? ¿Cuántos creen que los Juegos Olímpicos son el evento más popular?** Then ask: **Entre los jóvenes de nuestra universidad, ¿cuántos de ustedes creen que la Copa Mundial de Fútbol es el evento más popular?** Briefly discuss the differences indicated by student responses.

¿Cierto o falso? After students have corrected the false statements, have them provide a second sentence for each item. The new sentence should expand on the information in the item. Ex: **El fútbol es el deporte más popular en México.**

Preguntas Ask your students these additional questions. **7. ¿Cuál es el deporte más popular en el mundo hispano? (el fútbol) 8. ¿En qué países es el béisbol el deporte más popular? (en los países del Caribe) 9. ¿Pueden nombrar algunos jugadores hispanos de béisbol en los Estados Unidos?** (Answers will vary.) **10. ¿En qué país va a realizarse la próxima Copa Mundial de Fútbol? (Alemania 2006) 11. ¿Participan muchos países hispanos en campeonatos mundiales de fútbol? (sí)**

TEACHING OPTIONS

Pairs Have pairs work together to read the article aloud and write three questions about it. After they have finished, ask students to exchange their questions with another pair who can work together to answer them. Alternatively, you might pick pairs to read their questions to the class. Ask volunteers to answer them.

Heritage Speakers Ask heritage speakers to prepare a short presentation about soccer in their countries. Encourage them to include how popular the sport is, what the principal teams are, and whether their country has participated in a World Cup.

Section Goals

In **Escritura** students will:
- write a pamphlet listing sports events in their area
- integrate recreation-related vocabulary and structures taught in **Lección 4**

Estrategia Explain to students that when they look up a translation of an English word in a Spanish-English dictionary, they will frequently find more than one translation. They must decide which one best fits the context. Discuss the meanings of *racket* that might be found in an entry in a Spanish-English dictionary and the usefulness of the explanatory notes and abbreviations found in dictionary entries. Tell them that a good way of checking the meaning of a Spanish translation of an English word is to look the Spanish word up and see how it is translated into English.

Tema Discuss the three topics students may choose to write about. You may wish to introduce terms like **comité**, **guía de orientación**, **cámara de comercio**. Remind students of some of the common graphic features used in pamphlets: headings, times and places, brief descriptions of events, and prices.

Successful Language Learning Tell students that they should resist the temptation to look up every unknown word. Advise them to guess the word's meaning first based on context clues.

Escritura

Estrategia
Using a dictionary

A common mistake made by beginning language learners is to embrace the dictionary as the ultimate resource for reading, writing, and speaking. While it is true that the dictionary is a useful tool that can provide valuable information about vocabulary, using the dictionary correctly requires that you understand the elements of each entry.

If you glance at a Spanish-English dictionary, you will notice that its format is similar to that of an English dictionary. The word is listed first, usually followed by its pronunciation. Then come the definitions, organized by parts of speech. Sometimes the most frequently used definitions are listed first.

To find the best word for your needs, you should refer to the abbreviations and the explanatory notes that appear next to the entries. For example, imagine that you are writing about your pastimes. You want to write, "I want to buy a new racket for my match tomorrow," but you don't know the Spanish word for "racket." In the dictionary, you may find an entry like this:

racket s 1. alboroto; 2. raqueta (*dep.*)

The abbreviation key at the front of the dictionary says that *s* corresponds to **sustantivo** *(noun)*. Then, the first word you see is **alboroto.** The definition of **alboroto** is *noise* or *racket*, so **alboroto** is probably not the word you're looking for. The second word is **raqueta,** followed by the abbreviation *dep.*, which stands for **deportes.** This indicates that the word **raqueta** is the best choice for your needs.

Tema

Escribir un folleto.

Choose one topic.

1. You are the head of the Homecoming Committee at your school this year. Create a pamphlet that lists events for Friday night, Saturday, and Sunday. Include a brief description of each event and its time and location. Include activities for different age groups, since some alumni will bring their families.
2. You are on the Freshman Student Orientation Committee and are in charge of creating a pamphlet for new students describing the sports offered at your school. Write the flyer and include activities for both men and women.
3. You work for the Chamber of Commerce in your community. It is your job to market your community to potential residents. Write a brief pamphlet that describes the recreational opportunities your community provides, the areas where the activities take place, and the costs, if any. Be sure to include activities that will appeal to singles as well as couples and families; you should include activities for all age groups and for both men and women.

TEACHING OPTIONS

Proofreading Activity Copy the following sentences containing errors on the board or project on a transparency as a proofreading activity to do with the whole class. **1. Ernesto, ¿queres ir a el parque esta tarde? 2. Sí, me gustan el parque, porque yo juego al fútball. 3. Vamos almorzar y tomas el sol. 4. Vamos a ver si los muchachos jugan a fútbol. 5. ¡Ay, Ernesto! ¡Sólo pensas en el futbol! 6. ¡No es verdad! También salo para correr y ir de excursion. 7. Sí, veyo que eres un gran aficionado a los desportes. 8. Graciela, ¿nunca pensas haser un poco de ejercicio? 9. No, no haso ejercício nunca.**

1 Ideas y organización

Brainstorm the different types of activities included in the pamphlet, creating an idea map to organize them. Refer to a Spanish-English dictionary for words you don't know, but remember to consider each entry carefully before making a choice.

2 Primer borrador

Using your idea map from **Ideas y organización,** write the first draft of your pamphlet.

3 Comentario

Exchange papers with a classmate and comment on each other's work using these questions as a guide. Begin by mentioning one or two points that you like about your classmate's pamphlet, such as the activities listed for Homecoming, the description of the sports at your school, or the description of the recreational activities in your community.

a. Does the document contain all the required information?
b. Is any important information omitted? Is there any extraneous information that should be deleted?
c. Does the document include an appropriate variety of activities?
d. Is the document organized in a logical fashion?
e. Do you see errors in spelling, grammar, or word usage?
f. What other suggestions do you have for improving the document?

4 Redacción

Revise your first draft, keeping in mind your classmate's comments. Also, incorporate any new ideas or information you may have. Before handing in the final version, review your work using these guidelines:

a. Underline each verb and make sure it agrees with its subject. Double check stem-changing verbs and verbs with irregular **yo** forms.
b. Check the gender and number of each article, noun, and adjective.
c. Check your spelling and punctuation.
d. Consult your **Anotaciones para mejorar la escritura** to avoid repetition of previous errors.

5 Evaluación y progreso

Exchange papers with a new partner. Read his or her pamphlet and note any words and expressions that are new to you so that you can look them up in your dictionary later. After your instructor returns your paper, review the comments and corrections. Note the most important issues in your **Anotaciones para mejorar la escritura** in your **Carpeta.** If you have repeated a previous mistake, highlight it in your **Anotaciones.**

Comentario

- Go over guide questions a–f with the whole class. Then have students exchange their pamphlets. Allow five minutes for reading and comments.
- Have students read **Redacción** as homework. Ask them to rewrite their drafts, incorporating the peer comments and following the directions in **Redacción**.

Evaluación y progreso Give the class five minutes to exchange their final drafts, read them, and copy down unfamiliar words. Then students hand their pamphlets in.

Writing Sample Here is a sample pamphlet that would constitute superior writing achievement.

Las diversiones en nuestra ciudad

Usted puede encontrar la diversión que quiere en nuestra comunidad.

Estadio Sol—¿Es usted aficionado al fútbol? Usted y su familia pueden ver partidos de fútbol los sábados y domingos.

Museo de Arte—¿Le gusta el arte? Usted puede venir a ver las pinturas de los grandes artistas en nuestro museo.

Parque Central—Es un lugar bueno para pasear, patinar, conversar con los amigos, practicar baloncesto y también tomar el sol.

También hay restaurantes, cafés y cines en nuestra ciudad. Nuestra ciudad es un buen lugar para vivir.

EVALUATION: Folleto

Criteria	Scale
Appropriate details	1 2 3 4
Organization	1 2 3 4
Use of vocabulary	1 2 3 4
Grammatical accuracy	1 2 3 4
Mechanics	1 2 3 4

Scoring	
Excellent	18–20 points
Good	14–17 points
Satisfactory	10–13 points
Unsatisfactory	< 10 points

Section Goals

In **Escuchar** students will:
- listen to and summarize a short paragraph
- learn the strategy of listening for the gist
- answer questions based on the content of a recorded conversation

Instructional Resources
Textbook CD
IRM: Tapescript, p. 88

Estrategia
Script Buenas tardes y bienvenidos a la clase de español. En esta clase van a escuchar, escribir y conversar en cada clase, y ustedes también deben estudiar y practicar todos los días. Ahora encuentran el español difícil, pero cuando termine el curso van a comprender y comunicarse bien en español.

Suggestion Have students look at the photo and describe what they see. Guide them in saying what José is like and guessing what his favorite pastimes might be.

Ahora escucha
Script JOSÉ: No me gusta practicar deportes, pero sí tengo muchos pasatiempos. Me gusta mucho escribir y recibir correo electrónico. Me gusta también ir con mis amigos a mi café favorito. Siempre duermo una siesta por la tarde. A veces voy a ver un partido de béisbol. Me gusta mucho ver películas de acción pero mi novia prefiere las de romance… y por lo tanto veo muchas películas de romance.
ANABELA: Todos mis parientes dicen que soy demasiado activa. Soy aficionada a los deportes, pero también estudio mucho y necesito diversión. Aunque prefiero practicar el ciclismo, me gustan mucho la natación, el tenis, el golf... bueno, en realidad todos los deportes. No, eso no es cierto—no juego al baloncesto porque no soy alta. Para mis vacaciones quiero esquiar o escalar la montaña—depende si nieva. Suena divertido, ¿no?

Escuchar

Estrategia
Listening for the gist

Listening for the general idea, or gist, can help you follow what someone is saying even if you can't hear or understand some of the words. When you listen for the gist, you simply try to capture the essence of what you hear without focusing on individual words.

 To help you practice this strategy, you will listen to a paragraph made up of three sentences. Jot down a brief summary of what you hear.

Preparación

Based on the photo, what do you think José is like? Do you and José have similar interests?

Ahora escucha 

You will hear first José talking, then Anabela. As you listen, check off each person's favorite activities.

Pasatiempos favoritos de José

1. ___✔___ leer el correo electrónico
2. ______ jugar al béisbol
3. ___✔___ ver películas de acción
4. ___✔___ ir al café
5. ___✔___ ir a partidos de béisbol
6. ______ ver películas románticas
7. ___✔___ dormir la siesta
8. ___✔___ escribir mensajes electrónicos

Pasatiempos favoritos de Anabela

9. ___✔___ esquiar
10. ___✔___ nadar
11. ___✔___ practicar el ciclismo
12. ___✔___ jugar al golf
13. ______ jugar al baloncesto
14. ______ ir a ver partidos de tenis
15. ___✔___ escalar montañas
16. ______ estudiar

Comprensión

Preguntas

1. Who participates in more sports-related activities? Anabela
2. Who believes it's important to get enough rest? José
3. What sport does José like to watch? baseball
4. Why doesn't Anabela play basketball? Anabela says she is too short to play basketball.
5. What kind of movies does José's girlfriend prefer? She prefers romantic movies.
6. What is Anabela's favorite sport? cycling

Seleccionar

Which person do these statements best describe?

1. Le gusta practicar deportes. Anabela
2. Prefiere las películas de acción. José
3. Le gustan las computadoras. José
4. Le gusta nadar. Anabela
5. Siempre duerme una siesta por la tarde. José
6. Quiere ir de vacaciones a las montañas. Anabela

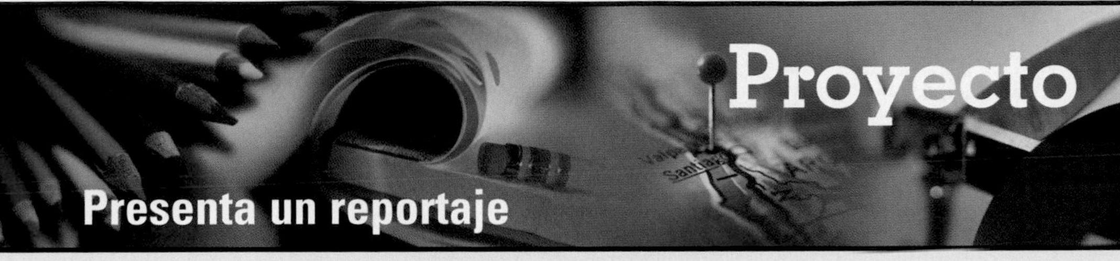

Proyecto

Presenta un reportaje

Imagine that you are a sports announcer for a large radio station in Mexico City. Your boss has asked you to deliver a new weekly broadcast, a guide to weekend sporting events.

1 Prepara el reportaje

Prepare a radio broadcast of the **Guía de eventos deportivos del fin de semana.** Using the research tools found in **Recursos para la investigación,** find out about the sports that are typically played in Mexico City. Then create your radio broadcast, which might include the following elements:

- A greeting to your listeners in which you introduce yourself and your program
- A list of the various sports events your listeners can attend or participate in
- The day and time each event is going to take place
- A brief, creative sign-off

2 Presenta la información

You may present your radio broadcast live or audiotape it so that it can be replayed for your class. You may want to greet your listeners as **radioyentes** and introduce yourself as **reportero/a** [your name]. Make your broadcast as appealing as possible so that your listeners will want to stay tuned.

recursos para la investigación

Internet Palabras clave: sports, pastimes, Mexico, Mexico City

Comunidad Exchange students, faculty members, and residents of your community who are from or have lived in Mexico City

Biblioteca Newspapers, sports magazines, travel magazines, travel guides

Otros recursos Sports programs on Spanish-language television stations

Section Goals

In **Proyecto** students will:
- use Spanish to carry out research and to interact with the wider world
- write and deliver a guide to weekend sporting events
- learn about sports in Mexico City

Suggestion Students might need a week to complete the project, so at the beginning of that time period, have them open their books to this page and look over **Proyecto**. Explain that they are going to research the most popular sports played in Mexico City and deliver the radio broadcast of a guide to weekend sporting events. Encourage students to talk about the kind of things they typically hear in a broadcast guide to sporting events.

Prepara el reportaje
- Students who have not heard a Spanish-language sports broadcast may need help with greetings and sign-offs. Possible greeting: **Buenas tardes, estimados radioyentes. Hoy es viernes, el ___, y su reportero es ___.** Possible sign-off: **Y por ahora, estimados radioyentes, eso es todo. Hasta el próximo viernes.**
- Remind students that they should address their radio audience with **Uds.** forms.

Presenta la información
Assign a number of broadcasts spread over several class meetings rather than having them all on the same day.

EVALUATION: Reportaje

Criteria	Scale
Use of vocabulary	1 2 3 4
Comprehensibility	1 2 3 4
Organization	1 2 3 4
Grammatical accuracy	1 2 3 4
Audience appeal	1 2 3 4

Scoring	
Excellent	18–20 points
Good	14–17 points
Satisfactory	10–13 points
Unsatisfactory	< 10 points

Section Goals

In **Panorama**, students will read about:

- the geography, history, and culture of Mexico
- Mexico's relationship with the United States

Instructional Resources
Transparencies, #1, #2, #21
WB/VM: Workbook, pp. 47–48; Video Activities, pp. 255–256
***Panorama cultural** DVD/Video*
Interactive CD-ROM
IRM: Videoscript, p. 128
Companion website: www.vistahigherlearning.com
Presentations CD-ROM

Suggestion Have students look at the map of Mexico or project **Transparency #21**. Ask questions about the locations of cities and natural features of Mexico. Ex: **¿Dónde está la capital? (en el centro del país)**

El país en cifras Because students will learn numbers over 100 in **Lección 6**, be sure to read aloud the numbers and dates in this section. Expand with questions related to section content. Ex: After **Área**, ask: **¿Qué ciudad mexicana está en la frontera con El Paso, Texas? (Ciudad Juárez)** Ask students if they can name other sister cities (**ciudades hermanas**) on the Mexico-U.S. border. (Tijuana/San Diego, Calexico/Mexicali, Laredo/Nuevo Laredo, Piedras Negras/Eagle Pass, Matamoros/Brownsville). Follow the same procedure with other sections.

¡Increíble pero cierto!
Streets in the ever-expanding Mexico City are also named for bodies of water, scientists, philosophers, professions, zodiac signs, and colors.

México

National Standards: connections, cultures

El país en cifras

- **Área:** 1.972.550 km² (761.603 millas²), casi° tres veces° el área de Texas.

La situación geográfica de México, al sur° de los Estados Unidos, ha influido° en la economía y la sociedad de los dos países. Una de las consecuencias es la emigración de la población mexicana al país vecino°. Hoy día, más de 20 millones de personas de descendencia mexicana viven en los Estados Unidos.

- **Población:** 80.073.000
- **Capital:** México, D.F.—18.934.000
- **Ciudades principales:** Guadalajara—3.889.000, Monterrey—3.502.000, Puebla—1.888.000, Ciudad Juárez—1.226.000

SOURCE: Population Division, UN Secretariat

- **Moneda:** peso mexicano
- **Idiomas:** español (oficial), náhuatl, idiomas mayas

La bandera de México

Mexicanos célebres

- **Benito Juárez,** héroe nacional (1806–1872)
- **Octavio Paz,** poeta (1914–1998)
- **Elena Poniatowska,** periodista y escritora (1933–)
- **Julio César Chávez,** boxeador (1962–)

casi *almost* veces *times* sur *south* ha influido en *has influenced* vecino *neighboring* vecindario *neighborhood* calles *streets* ha elegido *has chosen* Atún *tuna* cortas *short* nunca *never*

Un delfín en Baja California

ESTADOS UNIDOS
Ciudad Juárez
Golfo de California
Baja California
Río Grande
Río Bravo del Norte
Sierra Madre Oriental
Sierra Madre Occidental
Monterrey
Océano Pacífico
Puerto Vallarta
Guadalajara
Ciudad de México
Puebla
Acapulco
MÉXICO
ESTADOS UNIDOS
OCÉANO ATLÁNTICO
OCÉANO PACÍFICO
AMÉRICA DEL SUR

Autorretrato con mono (*Self-portrait with monkey*), 1938, Frida Kahlo

Ruinas aztecas en México D.F.

Saltador en Acapulco

recursos

WB pp. 47–48	VM pp. 255–256	I CD-ROM Lección 4	vistahigher learning.com

¡Increíble pero cierto!

En la Ciudad de México cada vecindario° nombra sus calles° en honor a un tema especial. Un vecindario ha elegido° la literatura, y tiene calles llamadas *Dickens, Dante* y *Shakespeare.* En otro están las calles del *Atún°* y del *Cilantro.* Irónicamente, las calles del *Amor* y la *Felicidad* son cortas°, mientras que la calle del *Trabajo* nunca° termina.

TEACHING OPTIONS

Heritage Speakers Mexico is a large and diverse nation, with many regions and regional cultures. Have heritage speakers who have visited Mexico describe the region which they visited in a short oral report to the class. Encourage them to include information about the cities, art, history, geography, customs, and cuisine of the region.

Small Groups Many of the dishes that distinguish Mexican cuisine have pre-Hispanic origins. To these native dishes have been added elements of Spanish and French cuisines, making Mexican food, like Mexican civilization, a dynamic mix of ingredients. Have groups of students look through Mexican cookbooks to find some striking examples of Mexican cuisine and describe them to the class.

Ciudades • México D.F.

La Ciudad de México, fundada° en 1525 (mil quinientos veinticinco), también se llama el D.F. o Distrito Federal. Muchos turistas e inmigrantes vienen a la ciudad porque es el centro cultural y económico del país. El crecimiento° de la población es de los más altos° del mundo. El D.F. tiene una población mayor que las de Nueva York, Madrid o París.

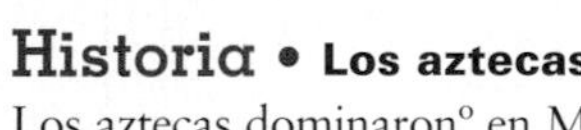

Artes • Diego Rivera y Frida Kahlo

Frida Kahlo y Diego Rivera eran° artistas mexicanos muy famosos. Casados° en 1929 (mil novecientos veintinueve), los dos se interesaron° en las condiciones sociales de la gente indígena de su país. Puedes ver algunas de sus obras° en el Museo de Arte Moderno de la Ciudad de México.

Historia • Los aztecas

Los aztecas dominaron° en México del siglo° XIV hasta el siglo XVI . Sus canales, puentes° y pirámides con templos religiosos eran° muy importantes. El imperio azteca terminó° cuando llegaron° los conquistadores en 1519 (mil quinientos diecinueve), pero la presencia azteca sigue hoy. La Ciudad de México está situada en la capital azteca de Tenochtitlán, y muchos turistas van a visitar sus ruinas°.

Golfo de México

Península de Yucatán

Mérida

Cancún

Bahía de Campeche

Veracruz

Istmo de Tehuantepec

BELICE

GUATEMALA

Comida • Las tortillas

La base de la comida mexicana es la tortilla, que se hace° con maíz° y con harina°. Los tacos, las enchiladas y las quesadillas se hacen con tortillas y son tan populares en México como en los Estados Unidos. Puedes conseguir tortillas muy buenas en muchos restaurantes mexicanos.

¿Qué aprendiste? Responde a las preguntas *(questions)* con una frase completa.

1. ¿Qué lenguas hablan los mexicanos? Los mexicanos hablan español, náhuatl e idiomas mayas.
2. ¿Cómo es la población del D.F. en comparación a otras ciudades? La población del D.F. es mayor.
3. ¿En qué se interesaron Kahlo y Rivera? Se interesaron en las condiciones sociales de la gente indígena de su país.
4. Nombra algunas *(some)* de las estructuras de la arquitectura azteca. Muchos canales, puentes y pirámides con templos religiosos.
5. ¿Dónde está situada la capital de México? Está situada en la capital azteca, Tenochtitlán.
6. ¿Por qué es importante la tortilla? Es la base de la comida mexicana.

Conexión Internet Investiga estos temas en el sitio **www.vistahigherlearning.com.**

1. Busca información sobre dos lugares de México. ¿Te gustaría (*Would you like*) vivir allí? ¿Por qué?
2. Busca información sobre dos artistas mexicanos. ¿Cómo se llaman sus obras (*works*) más famosas?

fundada *founded* crecimiento *growth* más altos *highest* eran *were* casados *married* se interesaron *were interested in* obras *works* dominaron *dominated* siglo *century* puentes *bridges* eran *were* terminó *ended* llegaron *arrived* ruinas *ruins* se hace *is made* maíz *corn* harina *flour*

México D.F. Mexicans seldom refer to their capital as **Ciudad de México**, but simply as **México**, or less frequently as **la capital**.

Diego Rivera y Frida Kahlo Show students reproductions of paintings by Kahlo and Rivera. Point out their distinctive styles and their specifically Mexican subjects.

Los aztecas Have students look at the image of an eagle holding a snake as the bird perches on a nopal cactus which appears on the Mexican flag. This image recalls an Aztec legend which declared that a great city would be built on the place where the nomadic Aztecs saw an eagle atop a cactus devouring a snake. That place grew into Mexico City.

Las tortillas Have students talk about Mexican dishes they have tried and Mexican restaurants they know. Inform them that certain dishes they might assume are Mexican (e.g., burritos) actually aren't originally Mexican at all. Ask what other food vocabulary they already know in Spanish. Ex: **arroz con pollo**.

Conexión Internet Students will find supporting Internet activities and links at **www.vistahigherlearning.com**.

TEACHING OPTIONS

Variación léxica Over 52 languages are spoken by indigenous communities in Mexico today. Not all of these languages have a written form. The speakers of Mayan languages are the most numerous non-Spanish speakers in Mexico. Náhuatl, the language of the Aztecs, is still spoken by many, and a number of Náhuatl words have entered Mexican Spanish. A few have also entered other languages. Mexican Spanish words derived from Náhuatl include **aguacate** (*avocado*), **guajolote** (*turkey*), **cacahuate** (*peanut*), **ejote** (*green bean*), **chile** (*chili pepper*), and **elote** (*corn*). Two words Náhuatl has given to other world languages are *tomato* and *chocolate*, products native to Mexico and brought to Europe only in the sixteenth century.

Instructional Resources
Vocabulary CD
Lab Manual, p. 24
Lab CD/MP3 ***Lección 4***
IRM: Tapescript, pp. 16–19
Testing Program: ***Pruebas****,*
pp. 37–48
Testing Program Audio CD
Test Files CD-ROM

Pasatiempos

andar en patineta	*to skateboard*
bucear	*to scuba dive*
escalar montañas (*f. pl.*)	*to climb mountains*
escribir una carta	*to write a letter*
escribir un mensaje electrónico	*to write an e-mail message*
escribir una (tarjeta) postal	*to write a postcard*
esquiar	*to ski*
ganar	*to win*
ir de excursión (a las montañas)	*to go on a hike (in the mountains)*
leer correo electrónico	*to read e-mail*
leer un periódico	*to read a newspaper*
leer una revista	*to read a magazine*
nadar	*to swim*
pasar tiempo	*to spend time*
pasear	*to take a walk; to stroll*
pasear en bicicleta	*to ride a bicycle*
pasear por la ciudad/el pueblo	*to walk around the city/the town*
patinar (en línea)	*to skate (in-line)*
practicar deportes (*m. pl.*)	*to play sports*
ser aficionado/a (a)	*to be a fan (of)*
tomar el sol	*to sunbathe*
ver películas (*f. pl.*)	*to see movies*
visitar monumentos (*m. pl.*)	*to visit monuments*
la diversión	*fun activity; entertainment; recreation*
el/la excursionista	*hiker*
el fin de semana	*weekend*
el pasatiempo	*pastime; hobby*
los ratos libres	*spare (free) time*
el tiempo libre	*free time*

Deportes

el baloncesto	*basketball*
el béisbol	*baseball*
el ciclismo	*cycling*
el equipo	*team*
el esquí (acuático)	*(water) skiing*
el fútbol	*soccer*
el fútbol americano	*football*
el golf	*golf*
el hockey	*hockey*
el/la jugador(a)	*player*
la natación	*swimming*
el partido	*game; match*
la pelota	*ball*
el tenis	*tennis*
el vóleibol	*volleyball*

Adjetivos

deportivo/a	*sports-related*
favorito/a	*favorite*

Lugares

el café	*café*
el centro	*downtown*
el cine	*movie theater*
el gimnasio	*gymnasium*
la iglesia	*church*
el lugar	*place*
el museo	*museum*
el parque	*park*
la piscina	*swimming pool*
la plaza	*city or town square*
el restaurante	*restaurant*

Verbos

almorzar (o:ue)	*to have lunch*
cerrar (e:ie)	*to close*
comenzar (e:ie)	*to begin*
conseguir (e:i)	*to get; to obtain*
contar (o:ue)	*to count; to tell*
decir (e:i)	*to say; to tell*
dormir (o:ue)	*to sleep*
empezar (e:ie)	*to begin*
encontrar (o:ue)	*to find*
entender (e:ie)	*to understand*
hacer	*to do; to make*
ir	*to go*
jugar (u:ue)	*to play*
mostrar (o:ue)	*to show*
oír	*to hear*
pedir (e:i)	*to ask for; to request*
pensar (e:ie)	*to think*
pensar (*+ inf.*)	*to intend*
pensar en	*to think about*
perder (e:ie)	*to lose; to miss*
poder (o:ue)	*to be able to; can*
poner	*to put; to place*
preferir (e:ie)	*to prefer*
querer (e:ie)	*to want; to love*
recordar (o:ue)	*to remember*
repetir (e:i)	*to repeat*
salir	*to leave*
seguir (e:i)	*to follow; to continue*
suponer	*to suppose*
traer	*to bring*
ver	*to see*
volver (o:ue)	*to return*

***Decir* expressions**	*See page 119.*
Expresiones útiles	*See page 109.*

recursos

LM p. 24	Lab CD/MP3 Lección 4	Vocab CD Lección 4

Las vacaciones

5

Communicative Goals

You will learn how to:

- Discuss and plan a vacation
- Describe a hotel
- Talk about how you feel
- Talk about the seasons and the weather

A PRIMERA VISTA

- ¿Dónde está la pareja: en una piscina o en el mar?
- ¿Son viejos o jóvenes?
- ¿Nadan o toman el sol?

contextos

pages 136–141

- Travel and vacation
- Months of the year
- Seasons and weather
- Ordinal numbers

fotonovela

pages 142–145

After arriving in Otavalo, the students and Don Francisco check into the hotel where they will be staying. Inés and Javier then decide to explore more of the city, while Maite and Álex decide to rest before their afternoon run.

estructura

pages 146–159

- **Estar** with conditions and emotions
- The present progressive
- **Ser** and **estar**
- Direct object nouns and pronouns

adelante

pages 160–165

Lectura: Read a hotel brochure from Puerto Rico.
Escritura: Write a travel brochure for a hotel.
Escuchar: Listen to a weather report.
Proyecto: Create a web page about Puerto Rico.

panorama

pages 166–167

Featured Country: Puerto Rico

- The Spanish fortress of El Morro
- The origins of "Salsa"
- U.S. – Puerto Rico relations

Lesson Goals

In **Lección 5** students will be introduced to the following:

- terms for traveling and vacations
- seasons and months of the year
- weather expressions
- ordinal numbers (1st–10th)
- **estar** with conditions and emotions
- adjectives for conditions and emotions
- present progressive of regular and irregular verbs
- comparison of the uses of **ser** and **estar**
- direct object nouns and pronouns
- personal **a**
- scanning to find specific information
- making an outline
- writing a brochure for a hotel or resort
- listening for key words
- designing a travel website
- cultural, geographic, and historical information about Puerto Rico

A primera vista Here are some additional questions you can ask based on the photo: **¿Dónde te gusta pasar tus ratos libres? ¿Qué haces en tus ratos libres? ¿Te gusta nadar? ¿Puedes nadar en una piscina todo el año?**

INSTRUCTIONAL RESOURCES

Workbook/Video Manual: WB Activities, pp. 49–58
Laboratory Manual: Lab Activities, pp. 25–30
Workbook/Video Manual: Video Activities, pp. 221–222; pp. 257–258
Instructor's Resource Manual: **Hojas de actividades**, p. 166; **Vocabulario adicional**, p. 183; **¡Inténtalo!** & **Práctica** Answers, pp. 204–205; **Fotonovela** Translations, p. 141; Textbook CD Tapescript, p. 89; Lab CDs Tapescript, pp. 20–24; **Fotonovela** Videoscript, p. 107; **Panorama cultural** Videoscript, p. 129
Info Gap Activities Booklet, pp. 17–20
Overhead Transparencies: #3, #4, #22, #23, #24, #25, #26, #27
Lab Audio CD/MP3 **Lección 5**
Panorama cultural DVD/Video
Fotonovela DVD/Video
Testing Program, pp. 49–60
Testing Program Audio CD
Test Files CD-ROM
Companion website
Presentations CD-ROM
Textbook CD
Vocabulary CD
Interactive CD-ROM
Video CD-ROM
Web-SAM

Section Goals

In **Contextos**, students will learn and practice:

- travel- and vacation-related vocabulary
- seasons and months of the year
- weather expressions
- ordinal numbers

Instructional Resources
Transparencies, #22, #23, #24
Textbook CD
Vocabulary CD
WB/VM: Workbook, pp. 49–50
Lab Manual, p. 25
Lab CD/MP3 ***Lección 5***
IRM: ***Hojas de actividades,*** *p. 166;* ***Vocab. adicional,*** *p. 183;* ***Práctica*** *Answers, pp. 204–205; Tapescript, pp. 20–24; p. 89*
Info Gap Activities Booklet, pp. 17–18
Interactive CD-ROM
Companion website: www.vistahigherlearning.com
Presentations CD-ROM

Suggestions

- Ask: **¿A quién le gusta mucho viajar? ¿Cómo prefieres viajar?** Introduce cognates as suggestions: **¿Te gusta viajar en auto?** Write each term on the board as you say it. Ask: **¿Adónde te gusta viajar? ¿A México?** Ask other students about their classmates' statements: **¿Adónde le gusta viajar a ____? ¿Cómo puede ____ viajar a ____?**
- Give students two minutes to review the four scenes. Then project **Transparency #22**. Ask questions about the four scenes. Ex: **¿Quién trabaja en una agencia de viajes? (el/la agente de viajes) ¿Quiénes trabajan en un hotel? (el botones, el/la empleado/a)**

Note: At this point you may want to present **Vocabulario adicional: Más vocabulario para las vacaciones**, from the IRM.

Las vacaciones

Más vocabulario

la cabaña	*cabin*
la cama	*bed*
la habitación individual, doble	*single, double room*
el piso	*floor (of a building)*
la planta baja	*ground floor*
el campo	*countryside*
el paisaje	*landscape*
el equipaje	*luggage*
la estación de autobuses, del metro, de tren	*bus, subway, train station*
la llegada	*arrival*
el pasaje (de ida y vuelta)	*(round-trip) ticket*
la salida	*departure; exit*
acampar	*to camp*
estar de vacaciones	*to be on vacation*
hacer las maletas	*to pack (one's suitcases)*
hacer una excursión	*to go on a hike, to go on a tour*
hacer turismo (m.)	*to go sightseeing*
hacer un viaje	*to take a trip*
ir de compras	*to go shopping*
ir de pesca	*to go fishing*
ir de vacaciones	*to go on vacation*
ir en autobús (m.), auto(móvil) (m.), avión (m.), barco (m), motocicleta (f.), taxi (m.)	*to go by bus, car, plane, boat, motorcycle, taxi*

Variación léxica

automóvil ⟷ coche (*Esp.*), carro (*Amér. L.*)
autobús ⟷ camión (*Méx.*), guagua (*P. Rico*)
motocicleta ⟷ moto (*coloquial*)

recursos

TEXT CD Lección 5	WB pp. 49–50	LM pp. 25	Lab CD/MP3 Lección 5	I CD-ROM Lección 5	Vocab CD Lección 5

En la agencia de viajes

En el hotel

TEACHING OPTIONS

Extra Practice Ask questions about the people, places, and activities in **Contextos**. Ex: **¿Qué actividades pueden hacer los turistas en una playa? ¿Pueden nadar? ¿tomar el sol? ¿sacar fotos?** Then expand questions to ask students what they specifically do at these places. ____, **¿qué haces tú cuando vas a la playa?** Students should respond in complete sentences.

Variación léxica Point out that these are just some of the different Spanish names for vehicles. Ask heritage speakers in class if they are familiar with other terms. While some of these terms are mutually understood in different regions (**el coche, el carro, el auto, el automóvil**), others are specific to a region and may not be understood by others (**la guagua, el camión**). Stress that the feminine article **la** is used with the abbreviation **moto**.

Práctica

1 **Escuchar** Indicate who would probably make each statement you hear. Each answer is used twice.

a. el agente de viajes
b. la inspectora de aduanas
c. un empleado del hotel

1. a
2. a
3. c
4. b
5. c
6. b

2 **Escoger** Choose the best answer for each sentence.

1. Un huésped es una persona que __b__.
   a. hace una excursión
   b. está en un hotel
   c. pesca en el mar
2. Abrimos la puerta con __a__.
   a. una llave
   b. una cabaña
   c. una llegada
3. Enrique tiene __b__ en las montañas.
   a. un pasaporte
   b. una cabaña
   c. un pasaje
4. Antes de (*Before*) ir de vacaciones hay que __c__.
   a. pescar
   b. ir en tren
   c. hacer las maletas
5. A veces (*Sometimes*) es necesario __b__ en un aeropuerto internacional.
   a. hacer turismo
   b. pasar por la aduana
   c. pescar
6. Me gusta mucho ir al campo. __a__ es increíble.
   a. El paisaje
   b. El pasaje
   c. El equipaje

3 **Analogías** Complete the analogies using the words below.

auto	botones	llegada	pasaporte
avión	huésped	mar	sacar

1. acampar → campo = pescar → mar
2. aduana → inspector = hotel → botones
3. llave → habitación = pasaje → avión
4. estudiante → libro = turista → pasaporte
5. aeropuerto → viajero = hotel → huésped
6. maleta → hacer = foto → sacar

1 Suggestion Have students check their answers as you go over **Actividad 1** with the class.

1 Tapescript 1. ¡Deben ir a Puerto Rico! Allí hay unas playas muy hermosas y pueden acampar. 2. Deben llamarme el lunes para confirmar la reservación. 3. Muy bien, señor… aquí tiene la llave de su habitación. 4. Lo siento, pero tengo que abrir sus maletas. 5. Su habitación está en el piso once, señora. 6. Necesito ver su pasaporte y sus maletas, por favor.
Textbook CD

2 Expansion Ask a volunteer to help you model making statements similar to item 1. Say: **Un turista es una persona que… (va de vacaciones).** Then ask volunteers to do the same with **un agente de viajes, un botones, un inspector de aduanas, un empleado de hotel**.

3 Suggestion Present these items using the following formula: ***Acampar* tiene la misma relación con *campo* que *pescar* tiene con… (*mar*).**

3 Expansion Ask volunteers to explain the relationship between each pair of words in the analogy. Ex: **El campo es un lugar donde las personas acampan. El mar es un lugar donde las personas pescan.**

TEACHING OPTIONS

Small Groups Have students work in groups of three to write a riddle about one of the people or objects in the **Contextos** illustrations. The group must come up with at least three descriptions of their subject. Then one of the group members reads the description to the class and asks **¿Qué soy?** Ex: **Soy un pequeño libro. Tengo una foto de una persona. Soy necesario si un viajero quiere viajar a otro país. ¿Qué soy? (Soy un pasaporte.)**

Large Groups Split the class into two evenly-numbered groups. Hand out cards at random to the members of each group. One type of card should contain a verb or verb phrase (Ex: **confirmar una reservación**). The other will contain a related noun (Ex: **el agente de viajes**). The people within the groups must find their partner.

Suggestions

- Project **Transparency #23** and have students look over the seasons and months of the year. Call out the names of holidays or campus events and ask students to say the month or season in which they occur.
- Introduce weather-related vocabulary by discussing the weather in your area today. Write the expressions on the board. Ex: **Hoy hace sol.**
- Project **Transparency #24** and use magazine pictures to cover as many weather conditions as possible from this page. Begin describing one of the pictures using one of the weather expressions. Then, ask volunteers further questions that elicit other expressions. Point out the use of **mucho/a** before nouns and **muy** before adjectives in these expressions.
- Review the shortened forms **buen** and **mal** and their use before **tiempo**.
- Use pictures that include human beings to illustrate the distinction between **tener calor/frío** and **hacer calor/frío**.

Successful Language Learning Remind students that the weather expressions are used very frequently in conversation and that they should make a special effort to learn them.

Las estaciones y los meses del año

el invierno: **diciembre, enero, febrero**

la primavera: **marzo, abril, mayo**

el verano: **junio, julio, agosto**

el otoño: **septiembre, octubre, noviembre**

—¿Cuál es la fecha de hoy? *What is today's date?*
—Es el primero de octubre. *It's the first of October.*
—Es el diez de noviembre. *It's November 10th.*

¡ATENCIÓN!

The names of the months are not capitalized in Spanish.

• • •

You use **primero** to indicate that it's the first day of the month. You use cardinal numbers to talk about other dates: **el dos, el dieciséis, el treinta.**

El tiempo

—¿Qué tiempo hace? *How's the weather?*
—Hace buen/mal tiempo. *The weather is good/bad.*

Hace (mucho) calor.
It's (very) hot.

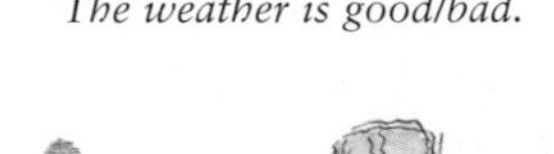

Hace (mucho) frío.
It's (very) cold.

Llueve.
It's raining.

Nieva.
It's snowing.

¡ATENCIÓN!

Llover (o:ue) (*to rain*) and **nevar (e:ie)** (*to snow*) are stem-changing verbs that are usually used in their third person singular forms: **llueve, nieva**.

It is also very common to say:

Está lloviendo. (*It's raining*).

Está nevando. (*It's snowing*).

See **Estructura 5.2**, p.148.

Más vocabulario

Está (muy) nublado.	*It's (very) cloudy.*
Hace fresco.	*It's cool.*
Hace (mucho) sol.	*It's (very) sunny.*
Hace (mucho) viento.	*It's (very) windy.*
Hay (mucha) niebla.	*It's (very) foggy.*

TEACHING OPTIONS

Pairs Have pairs of students work together to create sentences for each of the drawings on this page. Ask one student to write sentences for the first four drawings and the other to write sentences for the next four. When each has finished, ask them to exchange their sentences and correct their partner's work.

Extra Practice Create a number of cloze sentences about the weather that require the verb forms **hace, hay,** and **está** to be completed. Ex: **San Juan (está) en Puerto Rico. (Hace) mucho calor. No (está) muy nublado cuando (hace) sol. Cuando llueve sí (está) nublado, pero no (hay) niebla.**

4 **El Hotel Regis** Label the floors of the hotel.

communication NATIONAL STANDARDS

Números ordinales

primer, primero/a	*first*
segundo/a	*second*
tercer, tercero/a	*third*
cuarto/a	*fourth*
quinto/a	*fifth*
sexto/a	*sixth*
séptimo/a	*seventh*
octavo/a	*eighth*
noveno/a	*ninth*
décimo/a	*tenth*

a. séptimo piso
b. sexto piso
c. quinto piso
d. cuarto piso
e. tercer piso
f. segundo piso
g. primer piso
h. planta baja

5 **Contestar** Look at the illustration of the months and seasons on the previous page and, with a classmate, answer these questions.

¡ATENCIÓN!

Primero and **tercero** are shortened to **primer** and **tercer** before a masculine, singular noun: **el primer mes, el tercer piso.**

modelo

Estudiante 1: *¿Cuál es el primer mes de la primavera?*
Estudiante 2: *marzo*

1. ¿Cuál es el primer mes del invierno? diciembre
2. ¿Cuál es el segundo mes de la primavera? abril
3. ¿Cuál es el tercer mes del otoño? noviembre
4. ¿Cuál es el primer mes del año? enero
5. ¿Cuál es el quinto mes del año? mayo
6. ¿Cuál es el octavo mes del año? agosto
7. ¿Cuál es el décimo mes del año? octubre
8. ¿Cuál es el segundo mes del verano? julio
9. ¿Cuál es el tercer mes del invierno? febrero
10. ¿Cuál es la cuarta estación del año? el otoño

6 **Las estaciones** Name the season that applies to the description. Some answers may vary.

1. Las clases terminan. primavera
2. Vamos a la playa. verano
3. Acampamos. verano
4. Nieva mucho. invierno
5. Las clases empiezan. otoño
6. Hace mucho calor. verano
7. Llueve mucho. primavera
8. Esquiamos. invierno
9. El entrenamiento (*training*) de béisbol primavera
10 Día de acción de gracias (*Thanksgiving*) otoño

7 **¿Cuál es la fecha?** Give the dates for the following holidays.

modelo

el día de San Valentín
Es el 14 de febrero.

1. el día de San Patricio 17 de marzo
2 el día de Halloween 31 de octubre
3. el primer día de verano 20-23 de junio
4. el nuevo año primero de enero
5. mi cumpleaños (*birthday*) Answers will vary.
6. mi fiesta favorita Answers will vary.

4 Suggestion Point out that for numbers greater than ten, ordinal numbers do exist, though Spanish speakers rarely use them. They tend to use the cardinal numbers instead: **Está en el piso veintiuno.**

4 Expansion Ask students questions about ordinal numbers in their lives. Ex: **La clase de español, ¿en qué piso está? ¿En qué piso vives? ¿En qué piso está mi oficina?**

5 Suggestion Review seasons and months of the year. Have students close their books while you ask questions. Ex: **¿En qué estación estamos? ¿Qué estación tiene los meses de junio, julio y agosto?** Point out that the names of the months, like the names of days, are not capitalized.

5 Expansion Ask a student which month his or her birthday is in. Ask another student to give the season the first student's birthday falls in.

6 Suggestion Ask volunteers to name or describe events, situations, or holidays that are important to them or their families. Have the class name the season that applies.

7 Suggestion Bring in any kind of calendar from a Spanish-language publication (calendar of events, academic calendar, etc.). Ask students to name the important events and their scheduled dates.

TEACHING OPTIONS

TPR/Game Ask ten volunteers to line up facing the class. Make sure students know the starting point and what number in line they are. At random, call out ordinal numbers. The student to which each ordinal number corresponds has until the count of three to take a step forward. If they don't, they sit down and the order changes for the rest of the students further down the line. Who will the last student(s) standing be?

Small Groups Have students form groups of two to four. Hand out cards that contain the name of a holiday or other annual event. The group must come up with at least three sentences to describe the holiday or occasion *without mentioning its name.* They can, however, mention the season of the year. The other groups must first guess the month and day on which the event takes place, then name the holiday or event itself.

8 Suggestion Review weather expressions by asking students about current weather conditions around the world. Ex: **¿Hace calor en Alaska hoy? ¿Nieva en Puerto Rico?**

8 Expansion Use the alternate choices in the exercise to ask students weather-related questions. Ex: **No nieva en Cancún. ¿Dónde nieva?**

9 Suggestion Point out that **clima** is masculine, not feminine.

9 Expansion Ask students questions that compare and contrast the weather conditions presented in the activity or on the weather page of a Spanish-language newspaper. Ex: **Cuando la temperatura está a 85 grados en Buenos Aires, ¿a cuánto está en Tokio?**

10 Suggestion Model the activity by completing the first two sentences about yourself.

8 **Seleccionar** Paco is talking about his family and friends. Choose the word or phrase that best completes each sentence.

1. A mis padres les gusta ir a Cancún porque (hace sol, nieva). hace sol
2. Mi primo de Kansas dice que durante (*during*) un tornado, hace mucho (sol, viento). viento
3. Mis amigos van a esquiar si (nieva, está nublado). nieva
4. Tomo el sol cuando (hace calor, hay niebla). hace calor
5. Nosotros vamos a ver una película si hace (buen, mal) tiempo. mal
6. Mi hermana prefiere correr cuando (hace mucho calor, hace fresco). hace fresco
7. Mis tíos van de excursión si hace (buen, mal) tiempo. buen
8. Mi padre no quiere jugar al golf si (hace fresco, llueve). llueve
9. Cuando hace mucho (sol, frío) no salgo de casa y tomo chocolate caliente (*hot*). frío
10. Hoy mi sobrino va al parque porque (llueve, hace buen tiempo). hace buen tiempo

NOTA CULTURAL

Cancún, at the tip of Mexico's Yucatán Peninsula, is a popular tourist destination for foreigners and Mexicans alike. It offers beautiful beaches and excellent opportunities for snorkeling, diving, and sailing.

9 **El clima** With a partner, take turns asking and answering questions about the weather and temperatures in these cities. Answers will vary.

modelo

Estudiante 1: ¿Qué tiempo hace hoy en Nueva York?
Estudiante 2: Hace frío y hace viento.
Estudiante 1: ¿Cuál es la temperatura máxima?
Estudiante 2: Treinta y un grados (*degrees*).
Estudiante 1: ¿Y la temperatura mínima?
Estudiante 2: Diez grados.

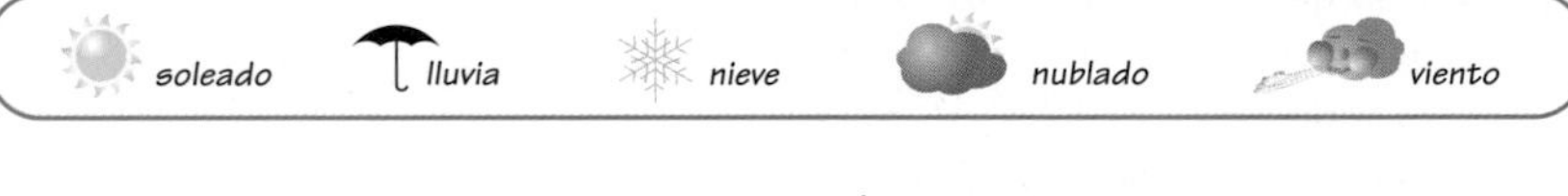

Nueva York	Miami	Chicago	París	Madrid	Tokio
Máx. 31°	Máx. 84°	Máx. 23°	Máx. 38°	Máx. 42°	Máx. 49°
Mín. 10°	Mín. 62°	Mín. 5°	Mín. 26°	Mín. 27°	Mín. 34°

Montreal	México D.F.	Cozumel	Caracas	Quito	Buenos Aires
Máx. 18°	Máx. 76°	Máx. 91°	Máx. 80°	Máx. 60°	Máx. 85°
Mín. 2°	Mín. 41°	Mín. 73°	Mín. 72°	Mín. 51°	Mín. 59°

NOTA CULTURAL

In most Spanish-speaking countries, temperatures are given in degrees Celsius. Do you know how to convert between **grados centígrados** and **grados Fahrenheit**?

degrees C. × 9 ÷ 5 + 32 = degrees F.

degrees F. - 32 × 5 ÷ 9 = degrees C.

10 **Completar** Complete these sentences with your own ideas. Answers will vary.

1. Cuando hace sol, yo...
2. Cuando llueve, mis amigos y yo...
3. Cuando hace calor, mi familia...
4. Cuando hay niebla, la gente...
5. Cuando hace frío, yo...
6. Cuando hace mal tiempo, mis amigos...
7. Cuando nieva, muchas personas...
8. Cuando está nublado, mis amigos y yo...
9. Cuando hace fresco, mis padres...
10. Cuando hace buen tiempo, mis amigos...

TEACHING OPTIONS

TPR Have volunteers mime situations that elicit weather-related vocabulary from the class. Ex: a shiver might elicit **hace frío** or a hand wiping a forehead might elicit **hace calor**.

Heritage Speakers Have heritage speakers write ten typical weather-dependent activities that they take part in when they are in their home communities. Refer them to **Actividad 10** as a model. When they have finished, invite them to share their summaries with the rest of the class.

Comunicación

11 **Preguntas personales** In pairs, ask each other the following questions.
Answers will vary.

1. ¿Cuál es la fecha de hoy?
2. ¿Qué estación es?
3. ¿Te gusta esta estación? ¿Por qué?
4. ¿Qué estación prefieres? ¿Por qué?
5. ¿Prefieres el mar o las montañas? ¿La playa o el campo? ¿Por qué?
6. Cuando estás de vacaciones, ¿qué haces?
7. Cuando haces turismo, ¿qué te gusta hacer y ver?
8. ¿Piensas ir de vacaciones este verano? ¿Adónde quieres ir? ¿Por qué?
9. ¿Qué deseas ver y dónde quieres visitar?
10. ¿Cómo te gusta viajar ... en avión, en motocicleta ...?

12 **Encuesta** Your instructor will give you a worksheet. How does the weather affect what you do? Walk around the class and ask your classmates what they prefer or like to do in the following weather conditions. Note their responses on your worksheet. Make sure to personalize your survey by adding a few original questions to the list. Be prepared to report your findings to the class.
Answers will vary.

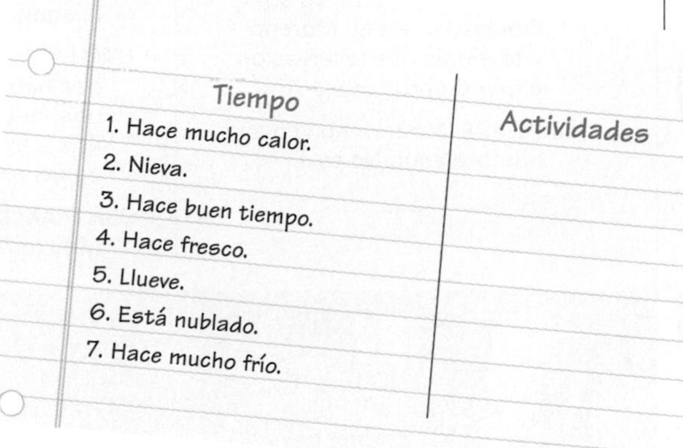

Tiempo
Actividades
1. Hace mucho calor.
2. Nieva.
3. Hace buen tiempo.
4. Hace fresco.
5. Llueve.
6. Está nublado.
7. Hace mucho frío.

CONSÚLTALO

Calor and **frío** can apply to both weather and people. **Hacer** is used to describe weather conditions or climate (**Hace frío en Santiago.** *It's cold in Santiago.*). **Tener** is used to refer to people (**El viajero tiene frío.** *The traveler is cold.*). See **Estructura 3.4** p. 91.

13 **Minidrama** With two or three classmates, prepare and act out a skit about people who are on vacation or are planning a vacation. The skit should take place in one of the areas mentioned below. Answers will vary.

1. Una agencia de viajes
2. Una casa
3. Un aeropuerto, una estación de tren o una estación de autobuses
4. Un hotel
5. El campo o la playa

Síntesis

14    **Un viaje** You are planning a trip to Mexico and have many questions about your itinerary on which your partner, a travel agent, will advise you. Your instructor will give you and your partner each a sheet with different instructions for acting out the roles.

11 Expansion Have students write the answers to questions 3–10 on a sheet of paper anonymously. Collect the sheets, shuffle them, and redistribute them for pairs to guess who wrote what.

12 Suggestion Model the activity by asking volunteers what they enjoy doing in hot weather. Ex: **Cuando hace calor, ¿qué haces? (Nado.)** Then distribute the **Hojas de actividades** from the IRM.

13 Suggestion With the whole class, brainstorm a list of people and topics that may be encountered in each situation and write it on the board.

13 Expansion Have students judge the skits in categories such as most original, funniest, most realistic, etc.

14 Suggestion Divide the class into pairs and distribute the Info Gap Handouts from the Info Gap Activities Booklet that correspond to this activity. Give the students ten minutes to complete this activity.

14 Expansion Have pairs put together the ideal itinerary for someone else traveling to Mexico, like a classmate, a relative, someone famous, or even **el/la profesor(a)**.

TEACHING OPTIONS

Pairs Tell students they are part of a scientific expedition to Antarctica (**la Antártida**). Have them write a letter back home about the weather conditions and their activities there. Begin the letter for them by writing **Queridos amigos** on the board.
Game Have each student draw a Bingo card with 25 squares (five rows of five). Tell them to write **GRATIS** (*free*) in the center square and the name of a different city in each of the other squares. Have them exchange cards. Call out different weather expressions. Ex: **Hace viento.** Students who think this description fits a city or cities on their board should mark the square with the weather condition. In order to win, a student must have marked five squares in a row and be able to give the weather condition for each one. Ex: **Hace mucho viento en Chicago.**

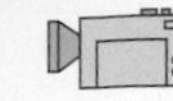

Section Goals

In **Fotonovela** students will:

- receive comprehensible input from free-flowing discourse
- learn functional phrases for talking to hotel personnel and describing a hotel room

Instructional Resources
WB/VM: Video Activities, pp. 221–222
***Fotonovela** DVD/Video (Start 00:22:28)*
Video CD-ROM
*IRM: **Fotonovela** Translations, p. 141, Videoscript, p. 107*
Interactive CD-ROM

Video Recap: Lección 4
Before doing this **Fotonovela** section, review the previous one with this activity.

1. ¿Qué van a hacer Inés y Javier en su hora libre? (van a pasear por la ciudad)
2. ¿Adónde van Maite y Álex? (van al parque)
3. ¿Por qué no quiere Maite jugar al fútbol? (prefiere escribir unas postales)
4. ¿Qué van a hacer Maite y Álex a las seis? (van a correr)

Video Synopsis The travelers check in at a hotel. Álex and Javier drop by the girls' cabin. Inés and Javier decide to explore the city further. Álex and Maite decide to stay behind. Maite notices that Javier and Inés spend lots of time together.

Suggestions

- Have the class glance over the **Fotonovela** and list words and phrases related to tourism and to making and responding to invitations.
- Ask various individuals how they are today, including the adjectives **cansado/a** and **aburrido/a**.
- Write **describir** on the board. Model the pronunciation and have the class guess its meaning. Ask the class to describe the perfect hotel. Ex: **¿Quién quiere describir una habitación de hotel perfecta?**
- Explain to students that video stills 2 and 3 present the numbers 101–103 for recognition only. They will formally learn numbers 101 and higher in **Estructura 6.1**.

Tenemos una reservación.

NATIONAL STANDARDS: communication, cultures

Don Francisco y los estudiantes llegan al hotel.

PERSONAJES

MAITE

INÉS

DON FRANCISCO

ÁLEX

JAVIER

EMPLEADA

BOTONES

1

EMPLEADA ¿En qué puedo servirles?

DON FRANCISCO Mire, yo soy Francisco Castillo Moreno y tenemos una reservación a mi nombre.

EMPLEADA Mmm... no veo su nombre aquí. No está.

2

DON FRANCISCO ¿Está segura, señorita? Quizás la reservación está a nombre de la agencia de viajes, Ecuatur.

EMPLEADA Pues sí, aquí está... dos habitaciones dobles y una individual, de la ciento uno a la ciento tres,... todas en las primeras cabañas.

DON FRANCISCO Gracias, señorita. Muy amable.

3

BOTONES Bueno, la habitación ciento dos... Por favor.

6

INÉS Oigan, yo estoy aburrida. ¿Quieren hacer algo?

JAVIER ¿Por qué no vamos a explorar la ciudad un poco más?

INÉS ¡Excelente idea! ¡Vamos!

7

MAITE No, yo no voy. Estoy cansada y quiero descansar un poco porque a las seis voy a correr con Álex.

ÁLEX Y yo quiero escribir un mensaje electrónico antes de ir a correr.

8

JAVIER Pues nosotros estamos listos, ¿verdad, Inés?

INÉS Sí, vamos.

MAITE Adiós.

INÉS & JAVIER ¡Chau!

recursos

V CD-ROM Lección 5	VM pp. 221–222	I CD-ROM Lección 5

TEACHING OPTIONS

Video Tips General suggestions for using video clips in the classroom can be found on page IAE-12 of this Instructor's Annotated Edition.

Tenemos una reservación As a method of setting expectations before viewing the **Tenemos una reservación** segment of this video module, ask students to brainstorm a list of things that might happen in a video episode in which the characters check into a hotel and decide how to spend the rest of the day. Then play the **Tenemos una reservación** segment once without sound and have the class create a plot summary based on visual clues. Afterward, show the video segment with sound and have the class correct any mistaken guesses and fill in any gaps.

4

ÁLEX Hola, chicas. ¿Qué están haciendo?

MAITE Estamos descansando.

5

JAVIER Oigan, no están nada mal las cabañas, ¿verdad?

INÉS Y todo está muy limpio y ordenado.

ÁLEX Sí, es excelente.

MAITE Y las camas son tan cómodas.

9

ÁLEX Bueno, nos vemos a las seis.

MAITE Sí, hasta luego.

ÁLEX Adiós.

10

MAITE ¿Inés y Javier? Juntos otra vez.

Enfoque cultural El alojamiento

There are many different types of lodging **(alojamiento)** for travelers in Hispanic countries. In major cities there are traditional hotels, but a more economical choice is a youth hostel, or **albergue juvenil,** where people can stay in a large, barracks-type room for a very low fee. Another option is an inn, or **hostal,** usually a privately owned residence. A unique type of lodging in Spain is a **parador,** which is usually a converted castle, palace, or villa that has been preserved and emphasizes the culture and cuisine of the region.

Expresiones útiles

Talking to hotel personnel

- ▶ **¿En qué puedo servirles?**
  How can I help you?
- ▷ **Tenemos una reservación a mi nombre.**
  We have a reservation in my name.
- ▶ **Mmm... no veo su nombre. No está.**
  I don't see your name. It's not here.
- ▷ **¿Está seguro/a? Quizás/Tal vez está a nombre de Ecuatur.**
  Are you sure? Maybe it's under the name of Ecuatur.
- ▶ **Aquí está... dos habitaciones dobles y una individual.**
  Here it is, two double rooms and one single.
- ▶ **Aquí tienen las llaves.**
  Here are your keys.
- ▷ **Gracias, señorita. Muy amable.**
  Thank you, miss. You're very kind.
- ▶ **¿Dónde pongo las maletas?**
  Where do I put the suitcases?
- ▷ **Allí, encima de la cama.**
  There, on the bed.

Describing a hotel

- ▶ **No están nada mal las cabañas.**
  The cabins aren't bad at all.
- ▶ **Todo está muy limpio y ordenado.**
  Everything is very clean and orderly.
- ▶ **Es excelente/estupendo/fabuloso/fenomenal.**
  It's excellent/stupendous/fabulous/great.
- ▶ **Es increíble/magnífico/maravilloso/perfecto.**
  It's incredible/magnificent/marvelous/perfect.
- ▶ **Las camas son tan cómodas.**
  The beds are so comfortable.

Talking about how you feel

- ▶ **Estoy un poco aburrido/a/cansado/a.**
  I'm a little bored/tired.

Suggestion Work through the scenes that correspond to video stills 1–3 with the whole class, asking volunteers to play each part. Have students work together in groups of four to read scenes 4–10 aloud.

Expresiones útiles Remind the class that **estoy**, **está**, and **están** are present tense forms of the verb **estar**, which is often used with adjectives that describe conditions and emotions. Remind students that **es** and **son** are present tense forms of the verb **ser**, which is often used to describe the characteristics of people and things and to make generalizations. Draw students' attention to video still 4 of the **Fotonovela**. Point out that **están haciendo** and **estamos descansando** are examples of the present progressive, which is used to emphasize that an action is in progress. Tell your students that they will learn more about these concepts in **Estructura**.

TEACHING OPTIONS

Enfoque cultural Point out to the class that a private residence that serves as an inn is sometimes called **una pensión**. Mention also that through exchange programs (**programas de intercambio**), many students travel to Spanish-speaking countries and live with host families. Tell the class that for long-term visits, travelers often save money by renting an apartment (**apartamento** or **departamento**) and cooking for themselves. In addition, encourage students to think critically about this information by discussing which type of lodging they would prefer if they were traveling to a Spanish-speaking country, and why.

1 Expansion To expand on the information contained in the items, have students create a follow-up sentence for each one, based on the **Fotonovela.**

2 Expansion Give these statements to the class as items 6–8: **6. Yo no voy. Necesito descansar. (Maite) 7. Ah, sí. Aquí tienen ustedes las llaves. (Empleada) 8. Bueno, aquí estamos... ésta es su habitación. (Botones)**

3 Expansion After students have determined the correct order, have pairs write sentences to describe what happens chronologically between items.

4 Possible Response
E1: ¿Puede llevar mis maletas a mi habitación?
E2: Sí, señorita.
E1: El hotel es excelente. Me gusta muchísimo. Todo está muy limpio.
E2: Sí, es un hotel maravilloso. Bueno, aquí estamos... la habitación sesenta y nueve, una habitación individual en el sexto piso.
E1: ¿Está usted seguro? Creo que tengo la habitación número noventa y seis.
E2: No, señorita. Usted tiene la habitación sesenta y nueve. ¿Dónde pongo las maletas?
E1: Puede ponerlas encima de la cama. Gracias.
E2: De nada. Adiós, señorita.

Reacciona a la fotonovela

1 Completar Complete these sentences with the correct term from the word bank.

aburrida	cansada	habitaciones individuales
la agencia de viajes	descansar	hacer las maletas
las camas	habitaciones dobles	las maletas

1. La reservación para el hotel está a nombre de la agencia de viajes.
2. Los estudiantes tienen dos habitaciones dobles.
3. Maite va a descansar porque está cansada.
4. El botones lleva las maletas a las habitaciones.
5. Las habitaciones son buenas y las camas son cómodas.

2 Identificar Identify the person who would make each statement.

1. Antes de correr voy a trabajar en la computadora un poco. Álex
2. Estoy aburrido. Tengo ganas de explorar la ciudad. ¿Vienes tú también? Javier
3. Lo siento mucho, señor, pero su nombre no está en la lista. Empleada
4. Creo que la reservación está a mi nombre, señorita. Don Francisco
5. Oye, el hotel es maravilloso, ¿no? Las habitaciones están muy limpias. Inés

EMPLEADA

ÁLEX

DON FRANCISCO

JAVIER

INÉS

¡ATENCIÓN!

The meanings of some adjectives, such as **aburrido,** change depending on whether they are used with **ser** or **estar.** See **Estructura 5.3**, pp. 152–153.

3 Ordenar Place these events in correct order.

a. Las chicas descansan en su habitación. 3
b. Javier e Inés deciden ir a explorar la ciudad. 5
c. Don Francisco habla con la empleada del hotel. 1
d. Javier, Maite, Inés y Álex hablan en la habitación de las chicas. 4
e. El botones pone (*puts*) las maletas en la cama. 2

4 Conversar With a partner use these cues to create a conversation between a bellhop and a hotel guest in Spain.

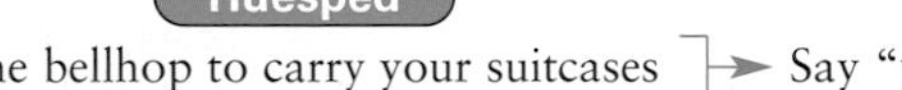

Huésped	Botones
Ask the bellhop to carry your suitcases to your room.	Say "yes, sir/ma'am/miss."
Comment that the hotel is excellent and that everything is very clean.	Agree, then point out the guest's room, a single room on the sixth floor.
Ask if the bellhop is sure. You think you have room 96.	Confirm that the guest has room 69. Ask where you should put the suitcases.
Tell the bellhop to put them on the bed and thank him or her.	Say "you're welcome" and "goodbye."

NOTA CULTURAL

You might have difficulty finding a hotel room in parts of Spain during the month of August. As in many other European countries, a large portion of the population goes on vacation for the entire month. Many shops and offices close. Life resumes its usual pace in September.

TEACHING OPTIONS

Extra Practice Give your students some true-false items about the **Fotonovela**. Have them correct the false items. Ex: **1. Maite quiere ir a explorar la ciudad. (Falso. Maite quiere descansar.) 2. Álex y Maite van a correr a las seis. (Cierto.) 3. Las reservaciones están a nombre de Ecuatur. (Cierto.) 4. Inés no quiere explorar la ciudad porque está cansada. (Falso. Está aburrida y quiere explorar.)**

Small Groups Have students work in groups of four to prepare a skit to present to the class. In the skit two friends check into a hotel, have a bellhop carry their suitcases to their rooms, and decide what to do for the rest of the day. Have students decide what city they are visiting, describe the hotel and their rooms, and explain what activities they want to do while they are visiting the city.

Pronunciación

Spanish b and v

bueno **vóleibol** **biblioteca** **vivir**

There is no difference in pronunciation between the Spanish letters **b** and **v**. However, each letter can be pronounced two different ways, depending on which letters appear next to them.

bonito **viajar** **también** **investigar**

B and **v** are pronounced like the English hard *b* when they appear either as the first letter of a word, at the beginning of a phrase, or after **m** or **n**.

deber **novio** **abril** **cerveza**

In all other positions, **b** and **v** have a softer pronunciation, which has no equivalent in English. Unlike the hard **b**, which is produced by tightly closing the lips and stopping the flow of air, the soft **b** is produced by keeping the lips slightly open.

bola **vela** **Caribe** **declive**

In both pronunciations, there is no difference in sound between **b** and **v**. The English *v* sound, produced by friction between the upper teeth and lower lip, does not exist in Spanish. Instead, the soft **b** comes from friction between the two lips.

Verónica y su esposo cantan boleros.

When **b** or **v** begins a word, its pronunciation depends on the previous word. At the beginning of a phrase or after a word that ends in **m** or **n**, it is pronounced as a hard **b**.

Benito es de Boquerón pero vive en Victoria.

Words that begin with **b** or **v** are pronounced with a soft **b** if they appear immediately after a word that ends in a vowel or any consonant other than **m** or **n**.

Práctica Read these words aloud to practice the **b** and the **v**.

1. hablamos	4. van	7. doble	10. cabaña
2. trabajar	5. contabilidad	8. novia	11. llave
3. botones	6. bien	9. béisbol	12. invierno

Oraciones Read these sentences aloud to practice the **b** and the **v**.

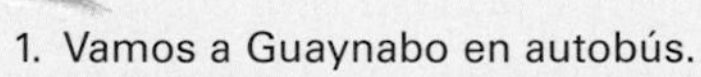

1. Vamos a Guaynabo en autobús.
2. Voy de vacaciones a la Isla Culebra.
3. Tengo una habitación individual en el octavo piso.
4. Víctor y Eva van en avión al Caribe.
5. La planta baja es bonita también.
6. ¿Qué vamos a ver en Bayamón?
7. Beatriz, la novia de Víctor, es de Arecibo, Puerto Rico.

Refranes Read these sayings aloud to practice the **b** and the **v**.

No hay mal que por bien no venga.[1]

Hombre prevenido vale por dos.[2]

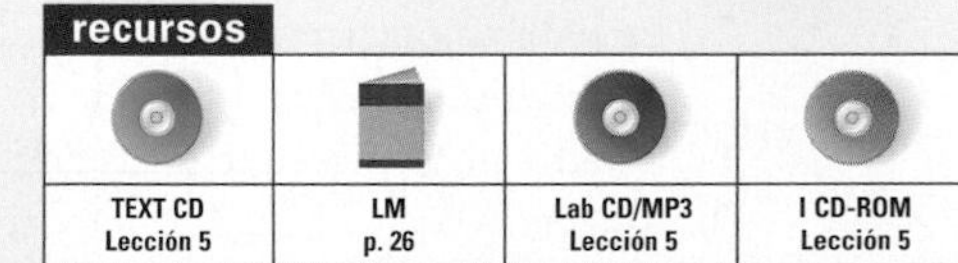

recursos
TEXT CD Lección 5
LM p. 26
Lab CD/MP3 Lección 5
I CD-ROM Lección 5

1 Every cloud has a silver lining.
2 An ounce of prevention equals a pound of cure.

Section Goal

In **Pronunciación** students will be introduced to the pronunciation of **b** and **v**.

Instructional Resources
Textbook CD
Lab Manual, p. 26
Lab CD/MP3 ***Lección 5***
IRM: Tapescript, pp. 20–24; p. 89
Interactive CD-ROM

Suggestions

- Emphasize that **b (alta)** and **v (baja)** are pronounced identically in Spanish but that, depending on the letter's position in a word, each is pronounced two ways. Pronounce **vóleibol** and **vivir** several times, asking students to listen for the difference between the initial and medial sounds represented by **b** and **v**.
- Explain the cases in which **b** and **v** are pronounced like English **b** in *boy* and model the pronunciation of **bonito, viajar, también**, and **investigar**.
- Point out that before **b** or **v**, **n** is usually pronounced **m**.
- Explain that in all other positions, **b** and **v** are fricatives. Pronounce **deber, novio, abril**, and **cerveza** as students watch your lips.
- Remind the class that Spanish has no sound like the English **v**. Pronounce **vida, vacaciones, avión, automóvil**.
- Explain that the same rules apply in connected speech. Practice with phrases like **de vacaciones, de ida y vuelta**.

Práctica/Oraciones/Refranes These exercises are recorded on the Textbook CD. You may want to play the CD so students practice the pronunciation point by listening to Spanish spoken by speakers other than yourself.

TEACHING OPTIONS

Extra Practice Write some additional proverbs on the board and have the class practice saying each one. Ex: **Más vale que sobre y no que falte.** (*Better too much than too little.*) **No sólo de pan vive el hombre.** (*Man doesn't live by bread alone.*) **A caballo regalado no se le ve el colmillo.** (*Don't look a gift horse in the mouth.*)

Small Groups Have students work in small groups and take turns reading aloud sentences from the **Fotonovela** on pages 142–143, focusing on the correct pronunciation of **b** and **v**. If a group member gets stuck on a word that contains **b** or **v**, the rest of the group should supply the rule that explains how it should be pronounced.

Section Goals

In **Estructura 5.1**, students will learn:

- to use **estar** to describe conditions and emotions
- adjectives that describe conditions and emotions

Instructional Resources
WB/VM: Workbook, pp. 51–52
Lab Manual, p. 27
Lab CD/MP3 ***Lección 5***
IRM: ***¡Inténtalo!*** *&* ***Práctica*** *Answers, pp. 204–205; Tapescript, pp. 20–24*
Interactive CD-ROM
Companion website: www.vistahigherlearning.com
Presentations CD-ROM

Suggestions

- Ask students to find examples of **estar** used with adjectives in the **Fotonovela**.
- Draw attention to the caption for video still 5 and compare the use of **estar** in the first two sentences with the use of **ser** in the third.
- Use TPR to practice the adjectives. Have the class stand and signal a student. Say: ____**, estás enojado/a.** (Student will make an angry face.) Continue signaling individuals until you have introduced most of the adjectives. Then vary the procedure by indicating more than one student. Keep the pace rapid so the drill seems like a game.

5.1 Estar with conditions and emotions

NATIONAL
comparisons
STANDARDS

ANTE TODO As you learned in **Lecciones 1** and **2**, the verb **estar** is used to talk about how you feel and to say where people, places, and things are located. **Estar** is also used with adjectives to talk about certain emotional and physical conditions.

▶ **Estar** is used with adjectives to describe the physical condition of places and things.

La habitación **está** sucia.
The room is dirty.

La puerta **está** cerrada.
The door is closed.

▶ **Estar** is also used with adjectives to describe how people feel, both mentally and physically.

Estoy aburrida. ¿Quieren hacer algo?

No, estoy cansada.

recursos
WB pp. 51–56
LM pp. 27–30
Lab CD/MP3 Lección 5
I CD-ROM Lección 5
vistahigherlearning.com

CONSÚLTALO

To review the present tense of **ser**, see **Estructura 1.3**, p. 18.

• • •

To review the present tense of **estar**, see **Estructura 2.3**, p. 53.

Adjectives that describe emotions and conditions

abierto/a	*open*	**contento/a**	*happy; content*	**listo/a**	*ready*
aburrido/a	*bored; boring*	**desordenado/a**	*disorderly*	**nervioso/a**	*nervous*
alegre	*happy; joyful*	**enamorado/a (de)**	*in love (with)*	**ocupado/a**	*busy*
avergonzado/a	*embarrassed*	**enojado/a**	*mad; angry*	**ordenado/a**	*orderly*
cansado/a	*tired*	**equivocado/a**	*wrong*	**preocupado/a (por)**	*worried (about)*
cerrado/a	*closed*	**feliz**	*happy*	**seguro/a**	*sure*
cómodo/a	*comfortable*	**limpio/a**	*clean*	**sucio/a**	*dirty*
confundido/a	*confused*			**triste**	*sad*

¡ATENCIÓN!

Two important expressions with **estar** that you can use to talk about conditions and emotions are **estar de buen humor** (*to be in a good mood*) and **estar de mal humor** (*to be in a bad mood*).

¡INTÉNTALO! Provide the present tense forms of **estar**, and choose which adjective best completes the sentence. The first item has been done for you.

1. La biblioteca *está* (cerrada / nerviosa) los domingos por la noche. *cerrada*
2. Nosotros estamos muy (ocupados / equivocados) todos los lunes. ocupados
3. Ellas están (alegres / confundidas) porque tienen tiempo libre. alegres
4. Javier está (enamorado / ordenado) de Maribel. enamorado
5. Diana está (enojada / limpia) con su novio. enojada
6. Yo estoy (nerviosa / abierta) por el viaje. nerviosa
7. La habitación siempre está (ordenada / segura) cuando vienen sus padres. ordenada
8. Ustedes no comprenden; están (equivocados / tristes). equivocados
9. Marina y yo estamos (preocupados / aburridos) por el examen. preocupados
10. Usted está muy (cansado / sucio) los lunes por la mañana. cansado

TEACHING OPTIONS

TPR Call out a sentence using an adjective and have students mime the emotion or show the condition. Ex: **Sus libros están abiertos.** (Students show their open books.) **Ustedes están alegres.** (Students act happy.) Next, call on volunteers to act out an emotion or condition and have the class tell what's going on. Ex: A student pretends to cry. (**Carlos está triste.**)

Video Show the **Fotonovela** video again and ask comprehension questions using **estar** and adjectives expressing emotions or conditions. Ex: **¿Cómo está la cabaña? (Todo está muy limpio y ordenado.) ¿Está cansado Javier? (No, no está cansado.) ¿Quién está cansado? (Maite está cansada.)**

Práctica

1 **¿Cómo están?** Complete Martín's statements about how he and other people are feeling. In the first blank, fill in the correct form of **estar**. In the second blank, fill in the adjective that best fits the context. Some answers may vary.

AYUDA

Make sure that you have agreement between:

- Subjects and verbs in person and number
- Nouns and adjectives in gender and number

Ell**os** no est**án** enferm**os**.
They are not sick.

1. Yo __estoy__ un poco __nervioso__ porque tengo un examen mañana.
2. Mi hermana Patricia __está__ muy __contenta__ porque mañana va a hacer una excursión al campo.
3. Mis hermanos Juan y José salen de la casa a las cinco de la mañana. Por la noche, siempre __están__ muy __cansados__.
4. Mi amigo Ramiro __está__ __enamorado__; su novia se llama Adela.
5. Mi papá y sus colegas __están__ muy __ocupados__ hoy. ¡Hay mucho trabajo!
6. Patricia y yo __estamos__ un poco __preocupados__ por ellos porque trabajan mucho.
7. Mi amiga Mónica __está__ un poco __triste/enojada__ porque su novio no puede salir esta noche.
8. Esta clase no es muy interesante. ¿Tú __estás__ __aburrido__ también?

2 **Describir** Describe the following people and places. Answers will vary.

1. Anabela
Está contenta.

2. Juan y Luisa
Están enojados.

3. la habitación de Teresa
Está ordenada/limpia.

4. la habitación de César
Está desordenada/sucia.

Comunicación

NATIONAL communication STANDARDS

3 **Situaciones** With a partner, use **estar** to talk about how you feel in these situations. Answers will vary.

1. Cuando hace sol...
2. Cuando tomas un examen...
3. Cuando estás de vacaciones...
4. Cuando tienes mucho trabajo...
5. Cuando viajas en avión...
6. Cuando estás con la familia...
7. Cuando estás en la clase de español...
8. Cuando ves una película con tu actor/actriz favorito/a...

1 Suggestion Have a volunteer model the first sentence by supplying the correct form of **estar** and an appropriate adjective. Ask the student to explain his or her choices.

1 Expansion Have students write five more sentences missing **estar** and an adjective like those in the activity. Then have them exchange papers and complete one another's sentences.

2 Expansions

- Have students write a sentence explaining why the people feel the way they do and why the rooms are the way they are.
- Have students pretend they are Anabela, Juan, or Luisa and give a short oral presentation describing who they are and how they feel today.

3 Suggestion Have partners alternate asking and answering questions until each has answered all items.

3 Expansion Ask students to keep a record of their partner's responses. Take a classroom poll to see what percentage of students felt a particular way for each situation.

TEACHING OPTIONS

Pairs Have students write a list of four questions using different conjugations of **estar** and four adjectives that have an opposite from the list on page 146. Students ask partners their questions. They respond negatively, then use the opposite adjective in an affirmative statement. Ex: **¿Está abierta la biblioteca? (No, no está abierta. Está cerrada.)**

Heritage Speakers Ask heritage speakers to work with a partner to play with word associations. Student A calls out an adjective. Student B calls out all the words that come to mind. After partners have each taken several turns, have them choose one set of associations to include in a poem or haiku.

Section Goals

In **Estructura** 5.2, students will learn:

- the present progressive of regular and irregular verbs
- the present progressive versus the simple present tense in Spanish

Instructional Resources
Transparency #25
WB/VM: Workbook, p. 53
Lab Manual, p. 28
Lab CD/MP3 ***Lección 5***
IRM: ***¡Inténtalo! & Práctica*** *Answers, pp. 204–205;*
Tapescript, pp. 20–24
Info Gap Activities Booklet, pp. 19–20
Interactive CD-ROM
Companion website: www.vistahigherlearning.com
Presentations CD-ROM

Suggestions

- Have students read the caption under video still 4 on page 143. Focus attention on **estar** + [*present participle*] to express what is going on at the moment. Then have students use the present progressive to describe what is happening in the rest of the **Fotonovela** episode.
- To elicit the present progressive, use regular verbs to ask questions about things students are not doing. Ex: **¿Estás comiendo pizza? (No, no estoy comiendo pizza.)**
- Explain the formation of the present progressive of regular verbs, writing examples on the board.
- Use pictures to elicit sentences with the present progressive. Ex: **¿Qué está haciendo el hombre alto? (Está sacando fotos.)** Continue until most students have had an opportunity to respond, and include present participles ending in **–yendo** as well as those with stem changes.

5.2 The present progressive

NATIONAL
comparisons
STANDARDS

ANTE TODO Both Spanish and English use the present progressive. In both languages, it consists of the present tense of the verb *to be* and the present participle (the *-ing* form of the verb in English).

Estoy escuchando.	Carlos **está corriendo**.	Ella **está escribiendo** una carta.
I am listening.	*Carlos is running.*	*She is writing a letter.*

Hola, chicas. ¿Qué están haciendo?

Estamos descansando.

▶ The present progressive is formed with the present tense of **estar** and the present participle of the main verb.

FORM OF ESTAR	+ PRESENT PARTICIPLE	FORM OF ESTAR	+ PRESENT PARTICIPLE
Estoy	**pescando.**	**Estamos**	**comiendo.**
I am	*fishing.*	*We are*	*eating.*

▶ The present participle of regular **–ar**, **–er**, and **–ir** verbs is formed as follows:

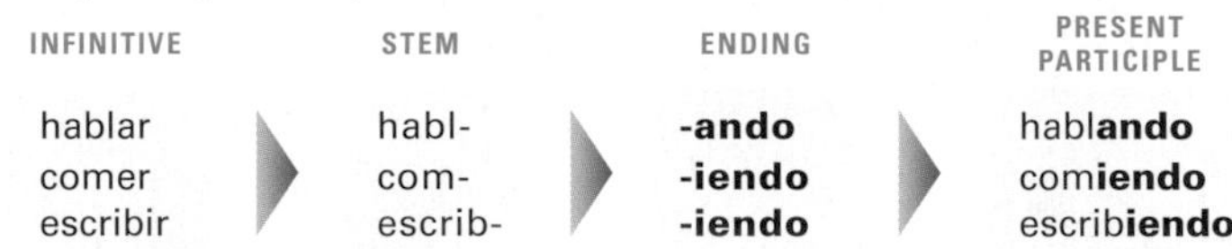

INFINITIVE	STEM	ENDING	PRESENT PARTICIPLE
hablar	habl-	**-ando**	habl**ando**
comer	com-	**-iendo**	com**iendo**
escribir	escrib-	**-iendo**	escrib**iendo**

¡ATENCIÓN!

When the stem of an **–er** or **–ir** verb ends in a vowel, the present participle ends in **–yendo.**

leer → le → leyendo
oír → o → oyendo
traer → tra → trayendo

▶ **Ir**, **poder**, and **venir** have irregular present participles (**yendo**, **pudiendo**, **viniendo**), but these verbs are rarely used in the present progressive. Several other verbs have irregular present participles that you will need to learn.

▶ **–Ir** stem-changing verbs have a stem change in the present participle.

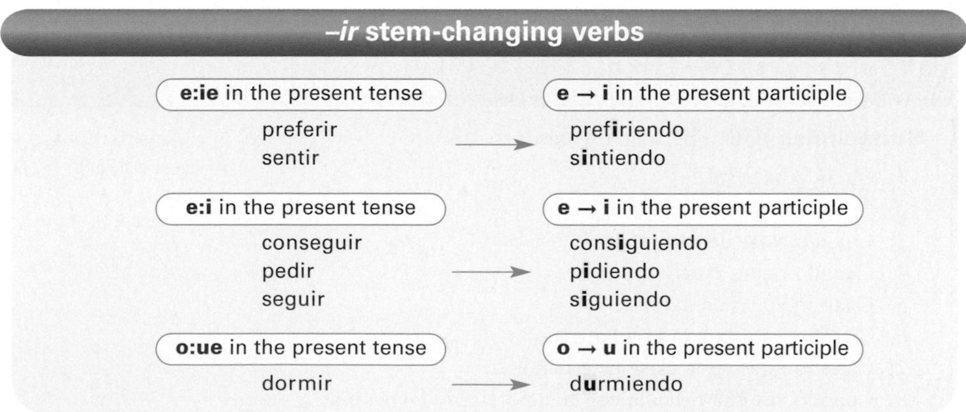

***–ir* stem-changing verbs**

e:ie in the present tense		**e → i** in the present participle
preferir sentir	→	pref**i**riendo s**i**ntiendo
e:i in the present tense		**e → i** in the present participle
conseguir pedir seguir	→	cons**i**guiendo p**i**diendo s**i**guiendo
o:ue in the present tense		**o → u** in the present participle
dormir	→	d**u**rmiendo

TEACHING OPTIONS

Large Groups Divide the class into three groups. Appoint leaders and give them a list of verbs. Leaders call out a verb and a subject (**seguir / yo**), then toss a ball or a piece of paper wadded into a ball to someone in the group. That student says the appropriate present progressive form of the verb (**estoy siguiendo**) and tosses the ball back. Leaders should call out all verbs on the list and toss the ball to every member of the group.

Extra Practice Mime an action. Ask students what you are doing. Students respond using the present progressive. Ex: Pick up a newspaper and pretend to read it. Ask: _____, **¿qué estoy haciendo? (Está leyendo el periódico.)** Also ask leading questions that may require either affirmative or negative answers depending on what you mime. **Y ahora, ¿estoy haciendo las maletas? (No, está bebiendo café.)**

COMPARE & CONTRAST

The use of the present progressive is much more restricted in Spanish than in English. In Spanish, the present progressive is mainly used to emphasize that an action is in progress at the time of speaking.

Inés **está escuchando** música latina **ahora mismo**.
Inés is listening to Latin music right now.

Álex y su amigo **todavía están jugando** al fútbol.
Álex and his friend are still playing soccer.

In English, the present progressive is often used to talk about situations and actions that occur over an extended period of time or in the future. In Spanish, the simple present tense is often used instead.

Javier **estudia** computación este semestre.
Javier is studying computer science this semester.

Inés y Maite **salen** mañana para los Estados Unidos.
Inés and Maite are leaving tomorrow for the United States.

Estamos pensando en lo mismo:
su Futuro
Su asesor para ganar
FIDUCOLOMBIA
Sociedad Fiduciaria S.A.

¡INTÉNTALO! Create complete sentences by putting the verbs in the present progressive. The first item has been done for you.

1. Mis amigos / descansar en la playa *Mis amigos están descansando en la playa.*
2. Nosotros / practicar deportes Estamos practicando deportes.
3. Carmen / comer en casa Carmen está comiendo en casa.
4. Nuestro equipo / ganar el partido Nuestro equipo está ganando el partido.
5. Yo / leer el periódico Estoy leyendo el periódico.
6. Él / pensar en comprar una bicicleta Está pensando en comprar una bicicleta.
7. Ustedes / jugar a las cartas Ustedes están jugando a las cartas.
8. José y Francisco / dormir José y Francisco están durmiendo.
9. Marisa / leer correo electrónico Marisa está leyendo correo electrónico.
10. Yo / preparar sándwiches Estoy preparando sándwiches.
11. Carlos / tomar fotos Carlos está tomando fotos.
12. ¿dormir / tú? ¿Estás durmiendo?

Suggestions

- Discuss each point in the **Compare & Contrast** box.
- Point out that the present progressive is rarely used with the verbs **ir, poder,** and **venir** since they already imply an action in progress.
- Write the following statements on the board. Ask students if they would use the present or the present progressive in Spanish for each item. 1. I'm going on vacation tomorrow. 2. She's packing her suitcase right now. 3. They are sightseeing in Madrid this week. 4. Roberto is still working. Then ask students to translate the items. **(1. Voy de vacaciones mañana. 2. Está haciendo la maleta ahora mismo. 3. Hacen turismo en Madrid esta semana. 4. Roberto todavía está trabajando.)**
- Have students rewrite the sentences in the **¡Inténtalo!** activity using the simple present. Ask volunteers to explain how the sentences change depending on whether the verb is in the present progressive or the simple present.

TEACHING OPTIONS

Pairs Have students write eight sentences in Spanish modeled after the examples in the **Compare & Contrast** box. There should be two sentences modeled after each example. Ask students to replace the verbs with blanks. Then, have students exchange their sentences with a partner for completion.

Extra Practice Ask students to find five photos from a magazine or create five drawings of people performing different activities. Have them write one sentence telling what the people in the photo/drawing are doing and one describing how they feel. Ex: **Juan está trabajando. Está cansado.**

1 Expansion Ask students comprehension questions that elicit the present progressive. Ex: **¿Quién está buscando información? (Marta y José Luis están buscando información.) ¿Qué información están buscando? (Están buscando información sobre San Juan.)**

2 Suggestion Before starting the activity, project **Transparency #25** and ask students questions about each drawing to elicit a description of what they see. Ex: **¿Quién está en el dibujo número 5? (Samuel está en el dibujo.) ¿Dónde está Samuel? (Está en la playa.) ¿Qué más ven en la foto? (Vemos una silla y el mar.)**

2 Expansion In pairs, have students describe five photos from their most recent vacation. Have them tell their partner where they are, what the weather is like, and what they are doing in the picture.

3 Expansion Have students choose five more celebrities and write what they are doing right now.

Práctica

1 Completar Alfredo's Spanish class is preparing to travel to Puerto Rico. Use the present progressive of the verb in parentheses to complete Alfredo's description of what everyone is doing.

1. Yo _estoy investigando_ (investigar) la situación política de la isla (*island*).
2. La esposa del profesor _está haciendo_ (hacer) las maletas.
3. Marta y José Luis _están buscando_ (buscar) información sobre San Juan en Internet.
4. Enrique y yo _estamos leyendo_ (leer) un correo electrónico de nuestro amigo puertorriqueño.
5. Javier _está aprendiendo_ (aprender) mucho sobre la cultura puertorriqueña.
6. Y tú _estás practicando_ (practicar) tu español, ¿verdad?

2 ¿Qué están haciendo? María and her friends are vacationing at a resort in San Juan, Puerto Rico. Complete her description of what everyone is doing right now.

CONSÚLTALO

For more information about Puerto Rico, see **Panorama**, pp. 166–167.

1. Yo
estoy escribiendo una carta.

2. Javier
está buceando en el mar.

3. Alejandro y Rebeca
están jugando a las cartas.

4. Celia y yo
estamos tomando el sol.

5. Samuel
está escuchando música.

6. Lorenzo
está durmiendo.

3 Personajes famosos Say what these celebrities are doing right now, using the cues provided. Answers will vary.

modelo

Serena Williams está jugando al tenis ahora mismo.

A		B	
John Grisham	Mikhail Baryshnikov	bailar	hablar
Sarah McLachlan	Picabo Street	cantar	hacer
James Cameron	Regis Philbin	correr	jugar
Venus Williams	¿?	escribir	¿?
Tiger Woods	¿?	esquiar	¿?

AYUDA

John Grisham - **novelas**
Sarah McLachlan - **canciones**
James Cameron - **cine**
Venus Williams - **tenis**
Tiger Woods - **golf**
Mikhail Baryshnikov - **ballet**
Picabo Street - **esquí**
Regis Philbin - **televisión**

TEACHING OPTIONS

Heritage Speakers Have students bring in photos (photocopies or magazine illustrations will also do) from a vacation. Ask them to describe the photos to a partner. Students should explain who is in the photo, what they are doing, and where they are. After students have practiced with a partner, have them present their descriptions to the class.

Game Student A mimes an action and states what he or she is doing. Student B states what the first student is doing, mimes the action, and then mimes a different action and states what he or she is doing. Students continue to add actions to the chain until it breaks. A new chain begins with the student following the breakdown. After five minutes of play, the group of students comprising the longest chain wins.

Comunicación

4 **Un amigo preguntón** You have a friend who calls you at all hours to see what you're doing. What do you tell him/her if he/she calls you at the following times?

Answers will vary.

modelo

8:00 a.m.
Estoy desayunando.

1. 5:00 a.m.	2. 9:30 a.m.	3. 11:00 a.m.	4. 12:00 p.m.
5. 2:00 p.m.	6. 5:00 p.m.	7. 9:00 p.m.	8. 11:30 p.m.

5 **Describir** Work with a partner and use the present progressive to describe what's going on in this Spanish beach scene. Answers will vary.

NOTA CULTURAL

Drawn by its warm climate and attractive coasts, more tourists flock to Spain annually than to practically any other country in the world. In the summer months, the arrival of tourists makes the country's population swell to over twice its year-round population.

6 **Conversar** Imagine that you and a classmate are each babysitting a group of children. With a partner, prepare a telephone conversation using these cues. Be creative and add further comments about the evening.

Estudiante 1	Estudiante 2
Say hello and ask what the kids are doing.	Say hello and tell your partner that two of your kids are doing their homework. Then ask what the kids at his/her house are doing.
Tell your partner that two of your kids are running and dancing in the house.	Tell your partner that one of the kids is reading.
Tell your partner that you are tired and that the other two are watching TV and eating pizza.	Tell your partner that one of the kids is sleeping.
Tell your partner that you have to go because the kids are playing soccer in the house.	Say goodbye and good luck (**¡Buena suerte!**)

Síntesis

7 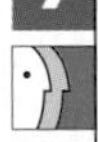 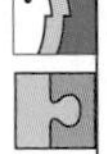 **¿Qué están haciendo?** A group of classmates is traveling to San Juan, Puerto Rico for a week-long Spanish immersion program. The participants are running late before the flight, and you and your partner must locate them. Your instructor will give you and your partner different handouts that will help you do this.

4 Suggestions
- Have students outline their daily activities and what time they do them before beginning the activity.
- Remind students to use **a la(s)** when expressing time.
- Convert **Actividad 1** into a pair activity. Ex: **E1: ¡Hola Andrés! Son las ocho de la mañana. ¿Qué estás haciendo? E2: Estoy desayunando.**

5 Suggestion Project **Transparency #25** and have students do the activity with their books closed.

5 Expansion In pairs, have students write a conversation between two or more of the persons in the drawing. Conversations should consist of at least three exchanges.

6 Suggestion Before beginning their conversation, have students brainstorm two lists: one with verbs that describe what children do at home and the other with adjectives that describe how each of the babysitters feels.

6 Expansion Ask pairs to tell each other what the parents of the two sets of children are doing. Ex: **Los padres de los niños buenos están visitando el museo. Los padres de los niños malos están en una fiesta.**

7 Suggestion Divide the class into pairs and distribute the Info Gap Handouts from the Info Gap Activities Booklet that correspond to this activity. Give the students ten minutes to complete this activity.

7 Expansion Have students work in pairs to say what each program participant is doing in flight. Ex: **Pedro está leyendo una novela.**

TEACHING OPTIONS

Video Show the video again, pausing after each exchange. Ask students to describe what each person in the shot is doing right at that moment.

TPR Write sentences with the present progressive on strips of paper. Call on a volunteer to pick a strip out of a hat to act out. The class tries to guess what the sentence is. Ex: **Yo estoy durmiendo en la cama.**

Pairs Ask students to write five sentences using the present progressive. Students should try to make their sentences as complex as possible. Have students dictate their sentences to their partners. After both partners have finished dictating their sentences, have them exchange papers for correction.

Section Goal

In **Estructura 5.3** students will review and compare the uses of **ser** and **estar**.

Instructional Resources
Transparency #26
WB/VM: Workbook, pp. 54–55
Lab Manual, p. 29
Lab CD/MP3 ***Lección 5***
IRM: ***¡Inténtalo! & Práctica*** *Answers, pp. 204–205; Tapescript, pp. 20–24*
Interactive CD-ROM
Companion website: www.vistahigherlearning.com
Presentations CD-ROM

Suggestions

- Have pairs brainstorm as many uses of **ser** with examples as they can. Compile a list on the board, and repeat for **estar**. Ask students where there might be some confusion about which verb to use.
- On the board or an overhead transparency, write in a single column one example of each use of **ser** and **estar**. Ex: **1. Álex es de México.** In a second column, write in random order each of the uses of **ser** and **estar** taught so far. Ex: **g. place of origin.** Call on individuals to match each example with the corresponding use.
- Write sentences with **ser** and **estar** on the board, but omitting the verb. Ask students to supply the correct form of **ser** or **estar**. Ex: **Mi casa ____ lejos de aquí. (estar, location; está)** If either **ser** or **estar** could be used, ask students to explain how the meaning of the sentence would change.

The Affective Dimension

If students feel anxious that Spanish has two verbs that mean *to be*, reassure them that they will soon feel more comfortable with this concept. Point out that Spanish speakers express rich shades of meaning by the way they use **ser** and **estar**.

5.3 Ser and estar

NATIONAL
comparisons
STANDARDS

ANTE TODO You have already learned that **ser** and **estar** both mean *to be* but are used for different purposes. The following charts summarize the key differences in usage between **ser** and **estar**.

¡ATENCIÓN!
Note that **de** is generally used after **ser** to express not only origin (**Es de Buenos Aires.**) and possession (**Es la pluma de Maite.**), but also what material something is made of (**La bicicleta es de metal.**).

Uses of *ser*	
1. Nationality and place of origin	Martín **es** argentino. **Es** de Buenos Aires.
2. Profession or occupation	Adela **es** agente de viajes. Francisco **es** médico.
3. Characteristics of people and things	José y Clara **son** simpáticos. El clima de Puerto Rico **es** agradable.
4. Generalizations	¡**Es** fabuloso viajar! **Es** difícil estudiar a la una de la mañana.
5. Possession	**Es** la pluma de Maite. **Son** las llaves de don Francisco.
6. What something is made of	La bicicleta **es** de metal. Los pasajes **son** de papel.
7. Time and date	Hoy **es** martes. **Son** las dos. Hoy **es** el primero de julio.
8. Where or when an event takes place	El partido **es** en el estadio Santa Fe. La conferencia **es** a las siete.

Soy Francisco Castillo Moreno. Yo soy de la agencia Ecuatur.

Su nombre no está en mi lista.

Uses of *estar*	
1. Location or spatial relationships	El aeropuerto **está** lejos de la ciudad. Tu habitación **está** en el tercer piso.
2. Health	¿Cómo **estás**? **Estoy** bien, gracias.
3. Physical states and conditions	El profesor **está** ocupado. Las ventanas **están** abiertas.
4. Emotional states	Marisa **está** feliz hoy. **Estoy** muy enojado con Javier.
5. Certain weather expressions	**Está** lloviendo. **Está** nublado.
6. Ongoing actions (progressive tenses)	**Estamos** estudiando para un examen. Ana **está** leyendo una novela.

TEACHING OPTIONS

Extra Practice Call out sentences containing forms of **ser** or **estar**. Ask students to identify the use of the verb.

Heritage Speakers Ask heritage speakers to write a postcard home about their vacation in Puerto Rico, incorporating as many of the uses of **ser** and **estar** as they can.

Game Divide the class into teams. Call out a purpose for either **ser** or **estar**. The first member of each team runs to the board and writes a sample sentence. If the sentence of the team finishing first is correct, the team gets a point. If not, check the next team, and so on. Practice all purposes for each verb, making sure each team member has had at least two turns, then tally the points to see which team wins.

Ser and *estar* with adjectives

- With many descriptive adjectives, **ser** and **estar** can both be used, but the meaning will change.

Juan **es** delgado. *Juan is thin.*	Ana **es** nerviosa. *Ana is a nervous person.*
Juan **está** más delgado hoy. *Juan looks thinner today.*	Ana **está** nerviosa por el examen. *Ana is nervous because of the exam.*

- In the examples above, the statements with **ser** are general observations about the inherent qualities of Juan and Ana. The statements with **estar** describe conditions that are variable.

- Here are some adjectives that change in meaning when used with **ser** and **estar**.

With *ser*	With *estar*
El chico **es listo**. *The boy is **smart**.*	El chico **está listo**. *The boy is **ready**.*
La profesora **es mala**. *The professor is **bad**.*	La profesora **está mala**. *The professor is **sick**.*
Jaime **es aburrido**. *Jaime is **boring**.*	Jaime **está aburrido**. *Jaime is **bored**.*
Las peras **son verdes**. *The pears are **green**.*	Las peras **están verdes**. *The pears are **not ripe**.*
El gato **es muy vivo.** *The cat is very **lively**.*	El gato **está vivo.** *The cat is **alive**.*
El puente **es seguro.** *The bridge is **safe**.*	Él no **está seguro.** *He's **not sure**.*

¡INTÉNTALO! Form complete sentences by using the correct form of **ser** or **estar**, the correct form of each adjective, and any other necessary words. The first item has been done for you.

1. Alejandra / cansado
   Alejandra está cansada.
2. Ellos / pelirrojo
   Ellos son pelirrojos.
3. Carmen / alto
   Carmen es alta.
4. Yo / la clase de español
   Estoy en la clase de español.
5. Película / a las once
   La película es a las once.
6. Hoy / viernes
   Hoy es viernes.
7. Nosotras / enojado
   Nosotras estamos enojadas.
8. Antonio / médico
   Antonio es médico.
9. Romeo y Julieta / enamorado
   Romeo y Julieta están enamorados.
10. Libros / de Ana
    Los libros son de Ana.
11. Marisa y Juan / estudiando
    Marisa y Juan están estudiando.
12. Partido de baloncesto / gimnasio
    El partido de baloncesto es en el gimnasio.

Suggestions

- Ask students if they notice any context clues in the examples that would help them choose between **ser** and **estar**.
- Write sentences like the following on the board: 1. Pilar is worried because she has a test tomorrow. **(Pilar está preocupada porque tiene una prueba mañana.)** 2. The bellman is very busy right now. **(El botones está muy ocupado ahora.)** 3. The beach is beautiful. **(La playa es hermosa.)** 4. Juan is very handsome today. **(Juan está muy guapo hoy.)** Have students translate the sentences into Spanish and ask them why they chose either **ser** or **estar** for their translation.
- Ask students questions like these to practice the different meanings of adjectives depending on whether they are used with **ser** or **estar**. **1. Manuel es un muchacho muy inteligente. ¿Está listo o es listo? 2. No me gusta la clase de física. ¿Está aburrida o es aburrida? 3. No sé si Carlos tiene 50 ó 51 años. ¿No estoy seguro/a o no soy seguro/a? 4. ¿El color del taxi es verde o está verde? 5. El profesor no enseña muy bien. ¿Está malo o es malo?**

TEACHING OPTIONS

Extra Practice Have students write sentences illustrating the contrasting meanings of adjectives that change meaning when used with **ser** or **estar**. Have students trade sentences for peer-editing before going over them with the class.
Video Show the **Fotonovela** video again. Have students jot down every time they hear a form of **ser** or **estar**. Discuss each use of **ser** and **estar** in the **Fotonovela**.

Pairs Tell students to imagine that they are to interview a celebrity visiting their hometown. Ask them to write questions employing at least ten different uses of **ser** and **estar**. Next, have them interview a partner, recording his or her answers. Students should then write a summary of their interviews.

1 Suggestion Before completing the activity, ask students to point out context clues that will help them determine whether to use **ser** or **estar**. For example, the word **hoy** in line 2 suggests that **guapo** is a physical state and not an inherent characteristic.

1 Expansion Have pairs write a continuation of the conversation and then present it to the class.

2 Suggestion Project **Transparency #26** and have students do the activity with their books closed after they've all read through the questions.

2 Expansion Bring in photos or magazine pictures that show many different people performing different activities. Have students use **ser** and **estar** to describe the scenes.

Práctica

1 **Completar** Complete this conversation with the appropriate forms of **ser** and **estar**.

EDUARDO ¡Hola, Ceci! ¿Cómo (1) estás?

CECILIA Hola, Eduardo. Bien, gracias. ¡Qué guapo (2) estás hoy!

EDUARDO Gracias. (3) Eres muy amable. Oye, ¿qué (4) estás haciendo? (5)¿ Estás ocupada?

CECILIA No, sólo le (6) estoy escribiendo una carta a mi prima Pilar.

EDUARDO ¿De dónde (7) es ella?

CECILIA Pilar (8) es del Ecuador. Su papá (9) es médico en Quito. Pero ahora Pilar y su familia (10) están de vacaciones en Ponce, Puerto Rico.

EDUARDO Y... ¿cómo (11) es Pilar?

CECILIA (12) Es muy lista. Y también (13) es alta, rubia y muy bonita.

2 **Describir** With a partner, describe the people in the drawing. Your descriptions should answer the questions. Answers will vary.

1. ¿Quiénes son las personas en el dibujo?
2. ¿Dónde están?
3. ¿Cómo son?
4. ¿Cómo están?
5. ¿Qué están haciendo?
6. ¿Qué estación es?
7. ¿Qué tiempo hace?
8. ¿Quiénes están de vacaciones?

TEACHING OPTIONS

Extra Practice Have students write a paragraph about a close friend, including the person's physical appearance, general disposition, place of birth, birthday, profession, and where the friend is now. Ask volunteers to share their paragraphs with the class.

Pairs Ask students to work with a partner to act out the following scenario. Student A is at the beach with some friends while Student B is at home. Student A calls Student B, trying to convince him or her to come to the beach. Students should try to employ as many uses of **ser** and **estar** in their scenario as possible. After acting out the scene once, have students switch roles.

Comunicación

3 **Describir** With a classmate, take turns describing the following people. First mention where each person is from. Then describe what each person is like, how each person is feeling, and what he or she is doing right now. Answers will vary.

modelo

tu compañero/a de cuarto

Mi compañera de cuarto es de San Juan, Puerto Rico. Es muy inteligente. Está cansada pero está estudiando porque tiene un examen.

1. tu mejor (*best*) amigo/a
2. tus padres
3. tu profesor(a) favorito/a
4. tu novio/a o esposo/a
5. tu primo/a favorito/a
6. tus abuelos

4 **Adivinar** Get together with a partner and describe a celebrity to him or her using these questions as a guide. Don't mention the celebrity's name. Can your partner guess who you are describing? Answers will vary.

1. ¿Cómo es?
2. ¿Cómo está?
3. ¿De dónde es?
4. ¿Dónde está?
5. ¿Qué está haciendo?
6. ¿Cuál es su profesión?

5 **En el aeropuerto** In small groups, take turns using **ser** and **estar** to describe this scene at Luis Muñoz Marín International Airport. What do the people in the picture look like? How are they feeling? What are they doing? Answers will vary.

NOTA CULTURAL

Luis Muñoz Marín International Airport in San Juan, Puerto Rico is a major transportation hub of the Caribbean. The airport connects the region with the rest of the world.

Síntesis

6 **Conversación** You and your partner are two of the characters in the drawing in **Actividad 5**. After boarding, you discover that you are sitting next to each other and must make conversation. Act out what you would say to your fellow passenger. Choose one of the pairs below or pick your own. Answers will vary.

1. Señor Villa y Elena
2. Señorita Esquivel y la señora Limón
3. Señora Villa y Luz
4. Emilio y Elena

TEACHING OPTIONS

Heritage Speakers Have heritage speakers write a television commercial for a vacation resort in the Spanish-speaking world. Ask them to employ as many uses of **ser** and **estar** as they can. If possible, after they've written their commercial, have them videotape it to show to the class.

TPR Call on a volunteer and whisper the name of a celebrity in his or her ear. The volunteer mimes actions, acts out characteristics, and uses props to elicit descriptions of the person. Ex: The volunteer points to the U.S. on a map. (**Es de los Estados Unidos.**) She then indicates a short man. (**Es un hombre bajo.**) She mimes riding a bicycle. (**Está paseando en bicicleta. ¿Es Lance Armstrong?**)

3 Suggestion Have students suggest names of celebrities to add to the list.

3 Expansion After pairs have practiced their descriptions, have them select two to present to the class.

4 Suggestion Assign the name of each student in the class to another student. Students circulate around the room asking the activity questions to determine the identity of the student assigned to each person. Students record the names of the students interviewed and their assigned students. After five minutes, see how many identities students were able to discover.

5 Suggestion Ask groups to choose a leader to moderate the activity, a secretary to record the group's description, and a proofreader to check that the written description is accurate. Then project **Transparency #26**. All students should take turns adding one sentence at a time to the group's description.

5 Expansion Have students pick one of the individuals pictured and write a one-paragraph description of that person, employing as many different uses of **ser** and **estar** as possible.

6 Suggestions
- Before starting, have students work in pairs to describe the character they will be playing to their partner.
- Make sure that students use **ser** and **estar**, the present progressive, and stem-changing verbs in their conversation, as well as vacation-, pastime-, and family-related vocabulary.

The Affective Dimension
Ask your students if they are more comfortable speaking Spanish with students they already know or students they don't know very well. Encourage them to consider pair and group activities as a cooperative venture in which group members support and encourage each other.

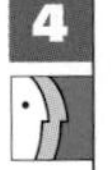
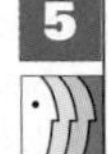

Section Goals

In **Estructura 5.4** students will study:
- direct object nouns
- the personal **a**
- direct object pronouns

Instructional Resources
WB/VM: Workbook, p. 56
Lab Manual, p. 30
Lab CD/MP3 ***Lección 5***
IRM: ***¡Inténtalo! & Práctica*** *Answers, pp. 204–205; Tapescript, pp. 20–24*
Interactive CD-ROM
Companion website: www.vistahigherlearning.com
Presentations CD-ROM

Suggestions
- Write these sentences on the board: **—¿Quién tiene el pasaporte? —Juan lo tiene.** Underline **pasaporte** and explain that it is a direct object. Then underline **lo** and explain that it is the masculine singular direct object pronoun. Translate both sentences. Follow the same procedure with these sentences: **—¿Quién hace turismo? —Simón lo hace. —¿Quién tiene la llave? —Pilar la tiene. —¿Quién escribe postales? —Jorge las escribe.**
- Ask individuals questions to elicit the personal **a**: **¿Tienes que esperar a tu novio con frecuencia? ¿Visitas a tu abuela los fines de semana? ¿Llamas a tu padre los sábados?**
- Continue by asking a series of questions to elicit third person direct object pronouns. Ask: **¿Quién ve el lápiz de Marcos? ¿Ves el libro de Daniela? ¿Quién quiere este diccionario? ¿Escuchas al profesor de matemáticas?**

5.4 Direct object nouns and pronouns

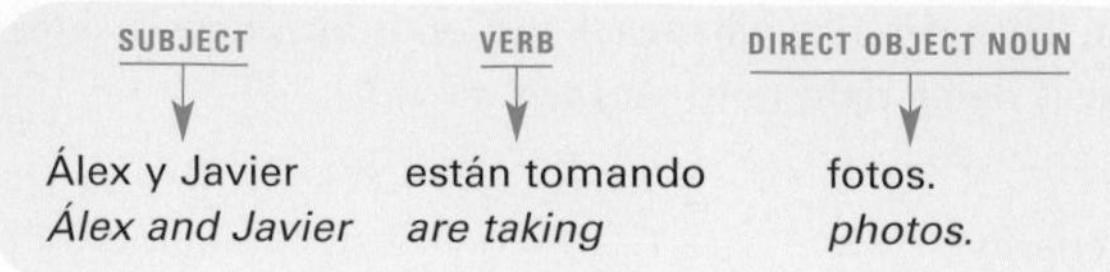

- A direct object noun receives the action of the verb directly and generally follows the verb. In the example above, the direct object noun answers the question *What are Javier and Álex taking?*

- When a direct object noun in Spanish is a person or a pet, it is preceded by the word **a**. This is called the personal **a**; there is no English equivalent for this construction.

Don Francisco visita **a** la señora Ramos.	Don Francisco visita el Hotel Prado.
Don Francisco is visiting Mrs. Ramos.	*Don Francisco is visiting the Hotel Prado.*

In the first sentence above, the personal **a** is required because the direct object is a person. In the second sentence, the personal **a** is not required because the direct object is a place, not a person.

¿Dónde pongo las maletas?
Puede ponerlas encima de la cama.

Hay muchos lugares interesantes por aquí. ¿Quieren ir a verlos?

Direct object pronouns

SINGULAR		PLURAL	
me	*me*	**nos**	*us*
te	*you* (fam.)	**os**	*you* (fam.)
lo	*you* (m., form.) *him; it* (m.)	**los**	*you* (m., form.) *them* (m.)
la	*you* (f., form.) *her; it* (f.)	**las**	*you* (f., form.) *them* (f.)

- Direct object pronouns are words that replace direct object nouns. Like English, Spanish sometimes uses a direct object pronoun to avoid repeating a noun already mentioned.

	DIRECT OBJECT		DIRECT OBJECT PRONOUN	
Maribel hace	las maletas.	Maribel	las	hace.
Felipe compra	el sombrero.	Felipe	lo	compra.
Vicky tiene	la llave.	Vicky	la	tiene.

TEACHING OPTIONS

TPR Call out a series of sentences with direct object nouns, some of which require the personal **a** and some of which do not. Have students raise their hands if the personal **a** is used.

Extra Practice Write six sentences on the board that have direct object nouns. Use two verbs in the simple present tense, two in the present progressive, and two using **ir a** + [*infinitive*]. Draw a line through the direct objects as students call them out. Have students state which pronouns to write to replace them. Now, draw an arrow from each pronoun to where it goes in the sentence as indicated by the students.

▶ In affirmative sentences, direct object pronouns generally appear before the conjugated verb. In negative sentences, the pronoun is placed between the word **no** and the verb.

Adela practica **el tenis**. Adela **lo** practica.	Adela no tiene **las llaves**. Adela **no las** tiene.
Carmen compra **los pasajes**. Carmen **los** compra.	Diego no hace **las maletas**. Diego **no las** hace.

▶ When the verb is an infinitive construction, such as **ir a** + [*infinitive*], the direct object pronoun can be placed before the conjugated form or attached to the infinitive.

Ellos van a escribir **unas postales**. — Ellos **las** van a escribir. / Ellos van a escribir**las**.

Lidia quiere ver **una película**. — Lidia **la** quiere ver. / Lidia quiere ver**la**.

▶ When the verb is in the present progressive, the direct object pronoun can be placed before the conjugated form or attached to the present participle.

Gerardo está leyendo **la lección**. — Gerardo **la** está leyendo. / Gerardo está leyéndo**la**.

Toni está mirando **el partido**. — Toni **lo** está mirando. / Toni está mirándo**lo.**

¡ATENCIÓN!

When a direct object pronoun is attached to the present participle, an accent mark is added to maintain the proper stress. To learn more about accents, see **Lección 4, Pronunciación,** p. 111, **Lección 10, Ortografía,** p. 305, and **Lección 11, Ortografía,** p. 337.

¡INTÉNTALO! Choose the correct response to each question. The first one has been done for you.

1. ¿Tienes el libro de español? c
   a. Sí, la tengo. b. No, no los tengo. c. Sí, lo tengo.
2. ¿Me puedes llevar al partido de baloncesto? b
   a. Sí, los puedo llevar. b. Sí, te puedo llevar. c. No, no las puedo llevar.
3. El artista quiere dibujarte con tu mamá, ¿no? b
   a. Sí, quiere dibujarlos mañana. b. Sí, nos quiere dibujar mañana.
   c. Sí, quiere dibujarte mañana.
4. ¿Quién tiene las llaves de nuestra habitación? a
   a. Yo no las tengo. b. Amalia los tiene, ¿no? c. Yo la tengo.
5. ¿Quién te lleva al aeropuerto? c
   a. Yo te llevo al aeropuerto. b. Rita los lleva al aeropuerto.
   c. Mónica me lleva al aeropuerto a las seis.
6. ¿Puedes oírme? a
   a. Sí, te puedo oír bien. b. No, no los oigo. c. Sí, las oigo bien.
7. ¿Estudia ella los verbos irregulares? c
   a. No, no la estudia. b. Sí, lo estudia. c. Sí, los estudia
8. ¿Practican ellos la pronunciación todos los días? b
   a. Sí, lo practican. b. Sí, la practican. c. No, no los practican.

Suggestions

- Elicit first and second person direct object pronouns by asking questions first of individual students and then groups of students. Ex: **¿Quién te invita a bailar con frecuencia? (Mi novio me invita a bailar con frecuencia.) ¿Quién te comprende? (Mi amigo me comprende.)**
- Questions directed at the class as a whole can elicit first person plural direct object pronouns. Ex: **¿Quiénes los llaman los fines de semana? (Nuestros padres nos llaman.) ¿Quiénes los esperan después de la clase? (Los amigos nos esperan.)**
- Use magazine pictures to practice the third person direct object pronouns with infinitives and the present progressive. Ex: **¿Quién está practicando tenis? (Pete Sampras lo está practicando. / Pete Sampras está practicándolo.) ¿Quién va a mirar la televisión? (El hombre con el pelo corto la va a mirar. / El hombre con el pelo corto va a mirarla.)**
- Point out that the direct object pronoun **los** refers to both masculine and mixed groups. **Las** refers only to feminine groups.

TEACHING OPTIONS

Extra Practice Make a list of 20 questions requiring direct object pronouns in the answer. Arrange students in two concentric circles. Students in the center circle ask questions from the list to those in the outer circle until you say stop (**¡Paren!**). The outer circle moves one person to the right and the questions begin again. Continue for five minutes, then have the students in the outer circle ask the questions.

Pairs Have students write ten sentences using direct object nouns. Their sentences should also include a mixture of verbs in the present progressive, simple present, and near future. Ask students to exchange their sentences with a partner, who will rewrite them using a direct object pronoun. Students should check their partner's work.

1 Suggestion Ask individual students to identify the direct object in each sentence before assigning the activity.

2 Expansion Ask questions using direct objects included and not included in the activity to elicit **Sí/No** answers. Ex: **¿Tiene Ramón reservaciones en el hotel? (Sí, las tiene.) ¿Tiene su mochila? (No, no la tiene.)**

3 Expansions
- Ask additional questions about the family's preparations, allowing students to decide who does what. Ex: **¿Quién compra una revista para leer en el avión? ¿Quién llama al taxi? ¿Quién practica el español?**
- Ask students true-false questions about who does what in the activity. Have them respond orally, correcting the false statements. Ex: **¿La señora Garza busca la cámara? (No, María la busca.)**

Práctica

1 Sustitución Professor Vega's class is planning a trip to Costa Rica. Describe their preparations by changing the direct object nouns into direct object pronouns.

modelo
La profesora Vega tiene su pasaporte.
La profesora Vega lo tiene.

1. Gustavo y Héctor confirman las reservaciones. Gustavo y Héctor las confirman.
2. Nosotros leemos los folletos (*brochures*). Nosotros los leemos.
3. Ana María estudia el mapa. Ana María lo estudia.
4. Yo aprendo los nombres de los monumentos de San José. Yo los aprendo.
5. Alicia escucha a la profesora. Alicia la escucha.
6. Miguel escribe las direcciones para ir al hotel. Miguel las escribe.
7. Esteban busca el pasaje. Esteban lo busca.
8. Nosotros planeamos una excursión. Nosotros la planeamos.

¡LENGUA VIVA!

There are many Spanish words that correspond to *ticket*. **Billete** and **pasaje** usually refer to a ticket for travel, such as an airplane ticket. **Entrada** refers to a ticket to an event, such as a concert or a movie. **Boleto** can be used in either case.

2 Vacaciones Ramón is going to San Juan, Puerto Rico with his friends, Javier and Marcos. Express his thoughts more succinctly using direct object pronouns.

modelo
Quiero hacer una excursión.
Quiero hacerla./La quiero hacer.

1. Voy a hacer mi maleta. Voy a hacerla./La voy a hacer.
2. Necesitamos llevar los pasaportes. Necesitamos llevarlos./Los necesitamos llevar.
3. Marcos está pidiendo el folleto turístico. Marcos está pidiéndolo./Marcos lo está pidiendo.
4. Javier debe llamar a sus padres. Javier debe llamarlos./Javier los debe llamar.
5. Ellos esperan visitar el Viejo San Juan. Ellos esperan visitarlo./Ellos lo esperan visitar.
6. Puedo llamar a Javier por la mañana. Puedo llamarlo./Lo puedo llamar.
7. Prefiero traer mi cámara. Prefiero traerla./La prefiero traer.
8. No queremos perder nuestras reservaciones de hotel. No queremos perderlas./No las queremos perder.

NOTA CULTURAL

Because Puerto Rico is a U.S. territory, passengers traveling there from the U.S. mainland do not need passports or visas. Passengers traveling to Puerto Rico from a foreign country, however, must meet travel requirements identical to those required for travel to the U.S. mainland. Puerto Ricans are U.S. citizens and can therefore travel to the U.S. mainland without any travel documents.

3 ¿Quién? The Garza family is preparing to go on a vacation to Puerto Rico. Based on the clues, answer the question. Use direct object pronouns in your answers.

modelo
¿Quién hace las reservaciones para el hotel? (El Sr. Garza)
El Sr. Garza las hace.

1. ¿Quién compra los pasajes para el vuelo (*flight*)? (La Sra. Garza)
   La Sra. Garza los compra.
2. ¿Quién tiene que hacer las maletas de los niños? (María)
   María tiene que hacerlas./María las tiene que hacer.
3. ¿Quiénes buscan los pasaportes? (Antonio y María)
   Antonio y María los buscan.
4. ¿Quién va a confirmar las reservaciones para el hotel? (La Sra. Garza)
   La Sra. Garza va a confirmarlas./La Sra. Garza las va a confirmar.
5. ¿Quién busca la cámara? (María)
   María la busca.
6. ¿Quién compra un mapa de Puerto Rico? (Antonio) Antonio lo compra.

TEACHING OPTIONS

Pairs Have students take turns asking each other who they know who does the following activities: **leer revistas, practicar el ciclismo, ganar siempre los partidos, visitar a sus padres durante las vacaciones, leer el periódico, escribir cartas, escuchar a sus profesores, practicar la natación.** Ex: **—¿Quién lee revistas? —Yo las leo.**

Heritage Speakers Have heritage speakers create a dialogue between a travel agent and client. The client would like to go to Puerto Rico and wants to know what he or she needs for the trip, how to prepare for it, and what to do once there. Have partners take turns playing both roles, choosing one of their role-plays to present to the class.

Comunicación

4 **Entrevista** Interview a classmate using these questions. Be sure to use direct object pronouns in your responses. Answers will vary.

1. ¿Ves mucho la televisión?
2. ¿Cúando vas a ver tu programa favorito?
3. ¿Quién prepara la comida (*food*) en tu casa?
4. ¿Te visita mucho tu familia?
5. ¿Visitas mucho a tus abuelos?
6. ¿Nos entienden nuestros padres a nosotros?
7. ¿Cuándo ves a tus amigos/as?
8. ¿Cuándo te llaman tus amigos/as?

5 **En el aeropuerto** Get together with a partner and take turns asking each other questions about the drawing. Use the word bank and direct object pronouns. Answers will vary.

modelo

Estudiante 1: *¿Quién está leyendo el libro?*
Estudiante 2: *Susana está leyéndolo.*

buscar	confirmar	escribir	leer	tener	vender
comprar	encontrar	escuchar	llevar	traer	¿?

Síntesis

6 **Adivinanzas** Play a guessing game in which you describe a person, place, or thing and your partner guesses who or what it is. Then switch roles. Each of you should give at least five descriptions. Answers will vary.

modelo

Estudiante 1: *Lo uso para (I use it to) escribir en mi cuaderno. Es amarillo y no es muy grande. ¿Qué es?*
Estudiante 2: *¿Es un lápiz?*
Estudiante 1: *¡Sí!*

4 Suggestion Ask students to take notes on their partner's answers. After the interviews, have them review answers in groups and report the most common answers to the class.

4 Expansion Have students write five more questions like the ones in the activity, then continue their interviews.

5 Suggestion Before assigning the activity, ask individual students to identify different objects in the picture that might be used as direct objects in questions and answers.

6 Expansion Have pairs write out five additional riddles like that in **Actividad 6**. Have them present their riddles for the rest of the class to answer.

TEACHING OPTIONS

Game Play a game of **20 Preguntas** with the class. Divide the class into two teams. Think of an object in the room. Alternate calling on teams to ask questions. Once a team knows the answer, the team captain should raise his or her hand. If right, the team gets a point. If wrong, the team loses a point. Play until one team has earned five points.

Pairs Have students create five questions that include the direct object pronouns **me**, **te**, and **nos**. Then have them ask their partners the questions on their list. Ex: **—¿Quién te llama mucho? —Mi novia me llama mucho. —¿Quién nos escucha cuando hacemos preguntas en español? —El/La profesor(a) y los estudiantes nos escuchan.**

Section Goals

In **Lectura** students will:

- learn the strategy of scanning to find specific information in reading matter
- read a brochure about eco-tourism in Puerto Rico

Instructional Resource
Companion website: www.vistahigherlearning.com

Estrategia Explain to students that a good way to get an idea of what an article or other text is about is to scan it before reading. Scanning means running one's eyes over a text in search of specific information that can be used to infer the content of the text. Explain that scanning a text before reading it is a good way to improve Spanish reading comprehension.

The Affective Dimension Point out to students that becoming familiar with cognates will help them feel less overwhelmed when they encounter new Spanish texts.

Examinar el texto Do the activity orally with the whole class. Some cognates that give a clue to the content of the text are: **turismo ecológico, hotel, aire acondicionado, perfecto, Parque Nacional Foresta, Museo de Arte Nativo, Reserva, Biosfera, Santuario**. These clues should tell a reader scanning the text that it is about a hotel promoting eco-tourism.

Preguntas Ask the questions orally of the whole class. Possible responses: 1. travel brochure 2. Puerto Rico 3. photos of beautiful tropical beaches, bays, and forests; the document is trying to attract the reader 4. Hotel La Cabaña in Lajas, Puerto Rico; attract guests

Lectura

Antes de leer

Estrategia
Scanning

Scanning involves glancing over a document in search of specific information. For example, you can scan a document to identify its format, to find cognates, to locate visual clues about the document's content, or to find specific facts. Scanning allows you to learn a great deal about a text without having to read it word for word.

Examinar el texto

Scan the reading selection for cognates and write a few of them down.

1. ____________ 4. ____________
2. ____________ 5. ____________
3. ____________ 6. ____________

Based on the cognates you found, what do you think this document is about?

____

Preguntas

Read the following questions. Then scan the document again to look for answers to the questions.

1. What is the format of the reading selection?
____
2. Which place is the document about?
____
3. What are some of the visual cues this document provides? What do they tell you about the content of the document?
____
4. Who produced the document, and what do you think it is for?
____

recursos

vistahigher learning.com

Turismo ecológico en Puerto Rico

Hotel La Cabaña
~ Lajas, Puerto Rico ~

Habitaciones

- 40 individuales
- 15 dobles
- Teléfono / TV / Cable
- Aire acondicionado
- Restaurante (Bar)
- Piscina
- Área de juegos
- Cajero automático°

El hotel está situado en Playa Grande, un pequeño pueblo de pescadores del mar Caribe. Es el lugar perfecto para el viajero que viene de vacaciones. Las playas son seguras y limpias, ideales para tomar el sol, descansar, tomar fotografías y nadar. Está abierto los 365 días del año. Hay una rebaja° especial para estudiantes universitarios.

DIRECCIÓN: Playa Grande 406, Lajas, PR 00667, cerca del Parque Nacional Foresta.

Cajero automático *ATM* rebaja *discount*

TEACHING OPTIONS

Heritage Speakers Ask heritage speakers of Puerto Rican descent who have lived on or visited the island to prepare a short presentation about the climate, geography, or people of Puerto Rico. Ask them to illustrate their presentations with photos they have taken or illustrations from magazines, if possible.

Small Groups Have five students work together to brainstorm a list of what would constitute an ideal tropical vacation for them. Each student should contribute at least one idea. Opinions will vary. Ask the group to designate one student to take notes and another to present the information to the class. When each group has its list, ask the designated presenter to share the information with the rest of the class. How do the groups differ? How are they similar?

Atracciones cercanas

Playa Grande ¿Busca la playa perfecta? Playa Grande es la playa que está buscando. Usted puede ir de pesca, sacar fotos, nadar y pasear en bicicleta. Playa Grande es un paraíso para el turista que quiere practicar deportes acuáticos. El lugar es bonito e interesante y usted tiene muchas oportunidades para descansar y disfrutar en familia.

Valle Niebla Ir de excursión, tomar café, montar a caballo, caminar, acampar, hacer picnic. Más de 100 lugares para acampar.

Bahía Fosforescente Sacar fotos, pescar, salidas de noche, excursión en barco. Una maravillosa experiencia con peces° fosforescentes.

Arrecifes de Coral Sacar fotos, bucear, explorar. Es un lugar único en el Caribe.

Playa Vieja Tomar el sol, pasear en bicicleta, jugar a las cartas, escuchar música. Ideal para la familia.

Parque Nacional Foresta Sacar fotos, visitar el Museo de Arte Nativo. Reserva Mundial de la Biosfera.

Santuario de las Aves Sacar fotos, observar aves°, seguir rutas de excursión.

peces *fish* aves *birds*

Después de leer

Listas

Which of the amenities of the Hotel La Cabaña would most interest these potential guests? Explain your choices.
Answers will vary.

1. Dos padres con un hijo de seis años y una hija de ocho años
____
2. Un hombre y una mujer en su luna de miel (*honeymoon*)
____
3. Una persona en un viaje de negocios (*business trip*)
____

Conversaciones

With a partner, take turns asking each other the following questions.

1. ¿Quieres visitar el Hotel La Cabaña? ¿Por qué?
2. Tienes tiempo de visitar sólo tres de las atracciones turísticas que están cerca del hotel. ¿Cuáles vas a visitar? ¿Por qué?
3. ¿Qué prefieres hacer en Valle Niebla? ¿En Playa Vieja? ¿En el Parque Nacional Foresta?

Situaciones

You have just arrived at the Hotel La Cabaña. Your classmate is the concierge. Use the phrases below to express your interests and ask him or her for suggestions about where to go.

1. montar a caballo
2. bucear
3. pasear en bicicleta
4. pescar
5. observar aves

Contestar

Answer the following questions.

1. ¿Quieres visitar Puerto Rico? Explica tu respuesta.
____
2. ¿Adónde quieres ir de vacaciones el verano que viene? Explica tu respuesta.
____

Listas
- Ask the following comprehension questions. **1. ¿El Hotel La Cabaña está situado cerca de qué mar? (el mar Caribe) 2. ¿Qué playa es un paraíso para el turista? (la Playa Grande) 3. ¿Dónde puede una persona ver peces fosforescentes? (en la Bahía Fosforescente)**
- Encourage discussion on each of the items by asking questions such as: **En su/tu opinión, ¿qué tipo de atracciones buscan los padres con hijos de seis y ocho años? ¿Qué esperan de un hotel? Y una pareja en su luna de miel, ¿qué tipo de atracciones espera encontrar en un hotel? En su/tu opinión, ¿qué busca una persona en un viaje de negocios?**

Conversaciones With the whole class, question various individuals about what their partner said. **¿Por qué (no) quiere ____ visitar el Hotel La Cabaña? ¿Qué atracciones quiere ver?** Ask other students: **Y tú, ¿quieres visitar el Parque Nacional o prefieres visitar un lugar diferente?**

Situaciones Give students a couple of minutes to review **Más vocabulario** on page 136 and **Expresiones útiles** on page 143. Add activities such as **sacar fotos, correr, nadar, ir de excursión.**

Contestar Have volunteers explain how the reading selection influenced their choice of vacation destination for next summer.

TEACHING OPTIONS

Pairs Have pairs of students work together to read the brochure aloud and write three questions about it. After they have finished, ask pairs to exchange their questions with another pair that can work together to answer them. Alternatively, you might pick pairs to read their questions to the class. Ask volunteers to answer them.

Extra Practice To practice scanning written material to infer its content, bring in short, simple Spanish-language magazine or newspaper articles you have read. Have pairs or small groups scan the articles to determine what they are about. Have them write down all the clues that help them. When each group has come to a decision, ask it to present its findings to the class. Confirm the accuracy of the inferences.

Section Goals
In **Escritura** students will:
- write a brochure for a hotel or resort
- integrate travel-related vocabulary and structures taught in **Lección 5**

Estrategia Explain that outlines are a great way for a writer to think about what a piece of writing will be like before actually expending much time and effort on writing. An outline is also a great way of keeping a writer on track while writing and helps him or her keep the whole writing project in mind as he or she is focusing attention on a specific part.

Tema Discuss the hotel or resort brochure students are to write. Go over the list of information that they might include. You might indicate a specific number of the points that should be included in the brochure. Tell students that the brochure for **Hotel La Cabaña** in **Lectura**, pages 160–161, can serve as a model for their writing. Remind them that they are writing with the purpose of attracting guests to the hotel or resort. Suggest that, as they begin to think about writing, students should brainstorm as many details as they can remember about the hotel they are going to describe. Tell them to do this in Spanish.

Suggestion If students write each of the individual items of their brainstorm lists on index cards, they can arrange and rearrange them into different idea maps as they plan their hotel or resort brochure.

Escritura

Estrategia
Making an outline

When we write to share information, an outline can serve to separate topics and subtopics, providing a framework for the presentation of data. Consider the following excerpt from an outline of the tourist brochure on pages 160–161.

IV. Descripción del sitio (con foto)
  A. Playa Grande
    1. Playas seguras y limpias
    2. Ideal para tomar el sol, descansar, tomar fotografías, nadar
  B. El hotel
    1. Abierto los 365 días del año
    2. Rebaja para estudiantes universitarios

Mapa de ideas

Idea maps can be used to create outlines. The major sections of an idea map correspond to the Roman numerals in an outline. The minor idea map sections correspond to the outline's capital letters, and so on. Consider the idea map that led to the outline above.

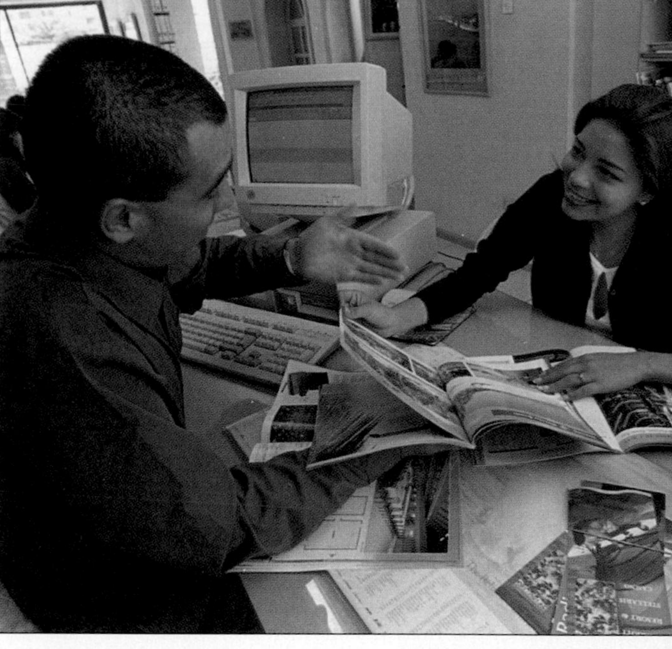

Tema

Escribir un folleto

Write a tourist brochure for a hotel or resort you have visited. If you wish, you may write about an imaginary hotel or resort. You may want to include some of the following information in your brochure:

- The name of the hotel or resort
- Phone and fax numbers that tourists can use to make contact
- The address of a website that tourists can consult
- An e-mail address that tourists can use to request information
- A description of the exterior of the hotel or resort
- A description of the interior of the hotel or resort, including facilities and amenities
- A description of the area around the hotel or resort, including its climate
- A listing of scenic natural attractions that are near the hotel or resort
- A listing of nearby cultural attractions
- A listing of recreational activities that tourists can pursue in the vicinity of the hotel or resort

TEACHING OPTIONS

Proofreading Activity Copy on the board or onto a transparency the following items containing errors as a proofreading activity to do with the whole class.

1. **¿Cuál es la fecha del primero día de inbierno?**
2. **César, tu habitación es muy sucia! ¿No lo prefieres limpia?**
3. **Maribel, ¿es buscando las llaves? Yo los tengo aquí.**
4. **Nuestras habitaciones son en el tercero piso del hotel.**
5. **Este hotel está muy viejo y las camas están muy incómodas.**
6. **La primer puerta a la izquierda está su habitación, señorita**
7. **Soy muy contento aprender sobre el ecotrismo. Voy a estudiar lo en mi clase de economía.**

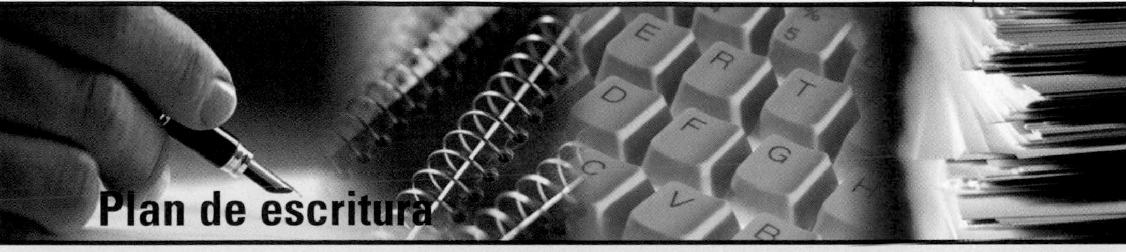

Plan de escritura

1 Ideas y organización

Which aspects of your vacation spot are the most attractive to prospective guests? Jot down your ideas based on your recollections or on the "perfect getaway." Then, organize your ideas in an outline, using only Spanish words and expressions. Remember to use a dictionary as a last resort.

2 Primer borrador

Using the outline you prepared in **Ideas y organización,** write the first draft of your brochure.

3 Comentario

Exchange papers with a classmate and comment on your partner's brochure, using these questions as a guide. Begin by mentioning one or two points that you like about the person's brochure, such as the description of the hotel or the location.

a. Would the brochure influence you to visit this hotel or resort?
b. Does the brochure provide all the required information?
c. Is the brochure organized in a logical fashion?
d. Do you have any suggestions for making the brochure more exciting?
e. Do you see any spelling or grammatical errors?

4 Redacción

Revise your first draft, keeping in mind your classmate's comments. Also incorporate any new ideas or information you may have. Before handing in the final version, review your work using these guidelines:

a. Underline each verb and make sure it agrees with the subject. Double check stem-changing verbs and verbs with irregular **yo** forms.
b. Check the gender and number of each article, noun, and adjective.
c. Check your spelling and punctuation, and consult your **Anotaciones para mejorar la escritura** to avoid repetition of previous errors.

5 Evaluación y progreso

Swap brochures with a classmate. After you have read the brochure, write a response in Spanish in which you:

- name the three aspects of the resort that appeal to you most or least.
- formulate two questions to clarify or expand on the information contained in the brochure.
- request a room for yourself and a companion in the near future.

After your instructor returns your paper, review the comments and corrections. Note the most important issues on your **Anotaciones para mejorar la escritura** list in your **Carpeta de trabajos.**

Comentario

- Go over guide questions a–e with the whole class. Then have students exchange their brochures. Allow five minutes for reading and comments.
- Have students read **Redacción** as homework. Ask them to rewrite their drafts, incorporating the peer comments and following the directions in **Redacción**.

Evaluación y progreso Give the class five minutes to exchange their final drafts, read them, and write their responses in Spanish. Then students hand their brochures in.

Writing Sample Here is a writing sample that would constitute superior achievement.

Bienvenidos al
Hotel Playa Bonita
Teléfono: 617.983.9322
Fax: 617.983.9344
Internet: www.playabonita.com

El Hotel Playa Bonita está muy cerca de San Francisco de Macorís, una pequeña ciudad situada en la costa del mar Caribe.

Nuestra atracción más famosa es Playa Bonita. En Playa Bonita usted puede nadar, pescar, montar a caballo, pasear en bicicleta, sacar fotos, tomar el sol o, si usted quiere, sólo descansar.

Nuestras habitaciones son bonitas, limpias y muy cómodas. También tenemos cabañas más cerca del mar.

Usted también puede ir de excursión al cercano Parque Nacional Buena Vista. O puede visitar el Museo de Arte Nativo en San Francisco de Macorís. Sólo hay que viajar quince minutos en autobús para llegar a sus puertas.

EVALUATION: Folleto

Criteria	Scale
Appropriate details	1 2 3 4 5
Organization	1 2 3 4 5
Use of vocabulary	1 2 3 4 5
Grammatical accuracy	1 2 3 4 5

Scoring	
Excellent	18–20 points
Good	14–17 points
Satisfactory	10–13 points
Unsatisfactory	< 10 points

Section Goals

In **Escuchar** students will:
- learn the strategy of listening for key words
- listen to a short paragraph and note the key words
- answer questions based on the content of a recorded conversation

Instructional Resources
Textbook CD
IRM: Tapescript, p. 89

Estrategia
Script Aquí está la foto de mis vacaciones en la playa. Ya lo sé; no debo pasar el tiempo tomando el sol. Es que vivo en una ciudad donde llueve casi todo el año y mis actividades favoritas son bucear, pescar en el mar y nadar.

Suggestion Have students look at the drawing and describe what they see. Guide them in saying what Hernán Jiménez is like and what he is doing.

Ahora escucha
Script Buenos días, queridos televidentes, les saluda el meteorólogo Hernán Jiménez, con el pronóstico del tiempo para nuestra bella isla.

Hoy, 17 de octubre, a las diez de la mañana, la temperatura en Santo Domingo es de 26 grados. Hace sol con viento del este a 10 kilómetros por hora.

En la tarde, va a estar un poco nublado con la posibilidad de lluvia. La temperatura máxima del día va a ser de 30 grados. Es una buena mañana para ir a la playa.

En las montañas hace bastante frío ahora y hay niebla, especialmente en el área de San Francisco de Macorís. La temperatura mínima de estas 24 horas va a ser de 18 grados. Va a llover casi todo el día. ¡No es buen día para excursiones a las montañas!

Hasta el noticiero del mediodía, me despido de ustedes. ¡Que les vaya bien!

Escuchar

Estrategia
Listening for key words

By listening for key words or phrases, you can identify the subject and main ideas of what you hear, as well as some of the details.

To practice this strategy, you will now listen to a short paragraph. As you listen, jot down the key words that help you identify the subject of the paragraph and its main ideas.

Preparación

Based on the illustration, who is Hernán Jiménez, and what is he doing? What keywords might you listen for to help you understand what he is saying?

Ahora escucha 

Now you are going to listen to a weather report by Hernán Jiménez. Note which phrases are correct according to the key words and phrases you hear.

Santo Domingo
1. hace sol ✔
2. va a hacer frío
3. una mañana de mal tiempo
4. va a estar nublado ✔
5. buena tarde para tomar el sol
6. buena mañana para la playa ✔

San Francisco de Macorís
1. hace frío ✔
2. hace sol
3. va a nevar
4. va a llover ✔
5. hay niebla ✔
6. buen día para excursiones

recursos
TEXT CD
Lección 5

Comprensión

¿Cierto o falso?

Indicate whether each statement is **cierto** or **falso,** based on the weather report. Correct the false statements.

1. Según (*According to*) el meteorólogo, la temperatura en Santo Domingo es de 26 grados.
   Cierto.
2. La temperatura máxima en Santo Domingo hoy va a ser de 30 grados.
   Cierto.
3. Está lloviendo ahora en Santo Domingo.
   Falso. Hace sol.
4. En San Francisco de Macorís la temperatura mínima de hoy va a ser de 20 grados.
   Falso. La temperatura mínima va a ser de 18 grados.
5. Va a llover mucho hoy en San Francisco de Macorís.
   Cierto.

Preguntas

In Spanish, answer these questions about the weather report.

1. ¿Hace viento en Santo Domingo ahora?
   Sí, hace viento en Santo Domingo.
2. ¿Hay niebla en Santo Domingo ahora? No, no hay niebla ahora en Santo Domingo. Hay niebla en San Francisco de Macorís.
3. ¿Está nevando ahora en San Francisco de Macorís?
   No, no está nevando ahora en San Francisco de Macorís.
4. ¿Qué tiempo hace en San Francisco de Macorís?
   Hace frío y hay niebla.

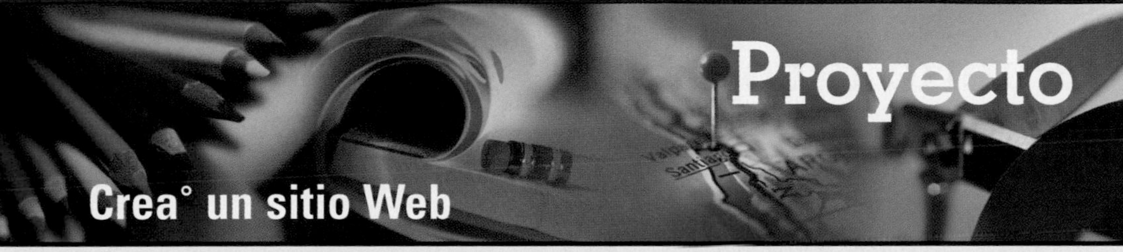

Crea° un sitio Web

Imagine that a travel agency has hired you to develop a web page to promote a travel package to Puerto Rico. The web page is intended to market the tour and inform potential travelers about the specifics.

1 Diseña° un sitio Web

Create a real or simulated website to tell potential customers about the merits of the tour. You will want to create a general home page for your site, as well as links to pages that describe the details. Use the research tools found in **Recursos para la investigación** to identify the sites the tour will visit, where the travelers will stay, and the activities they will be able to participate in. You might include the following elements:

- A home page with a general description of the tour and links to pages that supply the details
- A page describing the means of transportation
- A page describing hotels and other accomodations, including images if possible
- A page about the locations to be visited, including images if possible
- A page describing activities available to travelers, including images if possible

dirección: www.puertorico.com buscar imprimir

Excursión por la isla del encanto: Puerto Rico

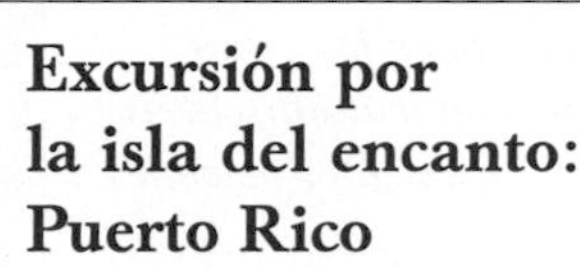

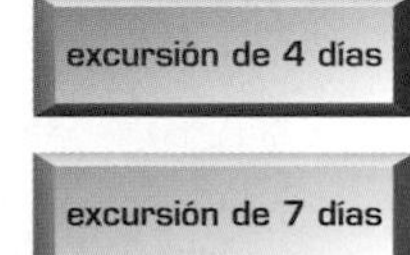

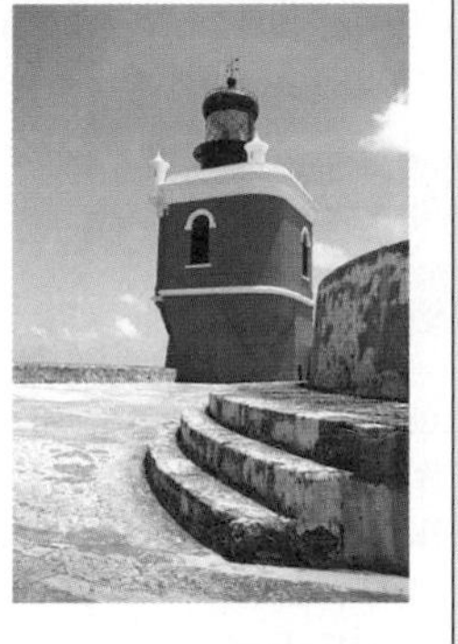

Agencia de Viajes El Morro
Tel: 787-234-5678
Fax: 787-876-5432

2 Presenta la información

Acting as the web page designer, present your work to the travel agency that hired you. Explain all the information that you have included and the images you have chosen. Answer any questions the agency executives may have about the website.

recursos para la investigación

Internet Palabras clave: Puerto Rico, vacations, hotels, transportation

Comunidad Students and faculty members who are from Puerto Rico or who have traveled to Puerto Rico

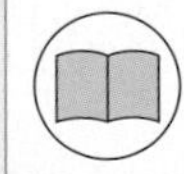

Biblioteca Guidebooks, travel magazines

Otros recursos Brochures from travel agencies

Crea *Create* Diseña *Design*

Section Goals

In **Proyecto** students will:

- use Spanish to carry out research on travel destinations and to interact with the wider world
- design a website advertising a tour to Puerto Rico
- learn about attractions in Puerto Rico

Suggestion Students might need a week to complete the project, so at the beginning of that time period, have them open their books to this page and look over **Proyecto**.

Diseña un sitio Web

- Students may create web page "frames" by drawing a navigation bar on the long side of a sheet of letter paper and photocopying it for each "web page" they create.
- Encourage students to come up with addresses for their websites.
- Teach students some Spanish terms related to the Internet, such as: **navegar en la red** (*to surf the web*), **página principal** (*home page*), **hacer clic** (*to click*), **pasar a la próxima página** (*to go to the next page*).
- Encourage students to use photos from magazines or their own drawings as visuals.

Presenta la información
Encourage the audience to assume the roles of travel agency executives and ask questions of the website presenter.

EVALUATION: Sitio Web

Criteria	Scale
Content	1 2 3 4
Organization	1 2 3 4
Accuracy	1 2 3 4
Creativity	1 2 3 4
Oral presentation	1 2 3 4

Scoring	
Excellent	18–20 points
Good	14–17 points
Satisfactory	10–13 points
Unsatisfactory	< 10 points

Section Goal

In **Panorama**, students will read about the geography, history, and culture of Puerto Rico.

Instructional Resources
Transparencies, #3, #4, #27
WB/VM: Workbook, pp. 57–58; Video Activities, pp. 257–258
***Panorama cultural** DVD/Video*
Interactive CD-ROM
IRM: Videoscript, p. 129
Companion website: www.vistahigherlearning.com
Presentations CD-ROM

Suggestion Have students look at the map of Puerto Rico or project **Transparency #27**. Discuss Puerto Rico's location in relation to the U.S. mainland and the other Caribbean islands. Encourage students to describe what they see in the photos.

El país en cifras After reading **Puertorriqueños célebres**, ask volunteers who are familiar with these individuals to tell a little more about each. You might also mention novelist Rosario Ferrer, whose *House on the Lagoon* ***(La casa de la laguna)*** gives a fictional portrait of a large part of Puerto Rican history.

¡Increíble pero cierto! The Río Camuy caves are actually a series of karstic sinkholes, formed by water sinking into and eroding limestone. Another significant cave in this system is Clara Cave, located in the Río Camuy Cave Park. The entrance of the 170-foot-high cave resembles the façade of a cathedral.

Puerto Rico

NATIONAL STANDARDS connections cultures

El país en cifras

- **Área:** 8.959 km^2 (3.459 $millas^2$) *menor° que el área de Connecticut*
- **Población:** 3.930.000

Puerto Rico es una de las islas más densamente pobladas° del mundo. Cerca de la mitad° de la población vive en San Juan, la capital.

- **Capital:** San Juan—1.410.000

SOURCE: Population Division, UN Secretariat

- **Ciudades principales:** Arecibo—100.000, Bayamón—222.815, Fajardo—40.000, Mayagüez—100.371, Ponce—187.749
- **Moneda:** dólar estadounidense
- **Idiomas:** español (oficial); inglés (oficial)

Aproximadamente la cuarta parte de la población puertorriqueña habla inglés. Pero, en las zonas turísticas este porcentaje es mucho más alto. El uso del inglés es obligatorio para documentos federales.

Bandera de Puerto Rico

Puertorriqueños célebres

- **Raúl Julia,** actor (1940–1994)
- **Roberto Clemente,** beisbolista (1934–1972)
- **Luis Rafael Sánchez,** escritor (1936–)
- **Ricky Martin,** cantante y actor (1971–)
- **Rita Moreno,** actriz, cantante, bailarina (1931–)

menor *less* pobladas *populated* mitad *half* río subterráneo *underground river* más largo *longest* sistema de cuevas *cave system* bóveda *vault* fortaleza *fort* caber *fit*

Plaza de Arecibo

Hoteles en El Condado, San Juan

Océano Atlántico
San Juan
Bayamón
Arecibo
Río Grande de Añasco
Mayagüez
Cordillera Central
Ponce
Sierra de Cayey
Mar Caribe

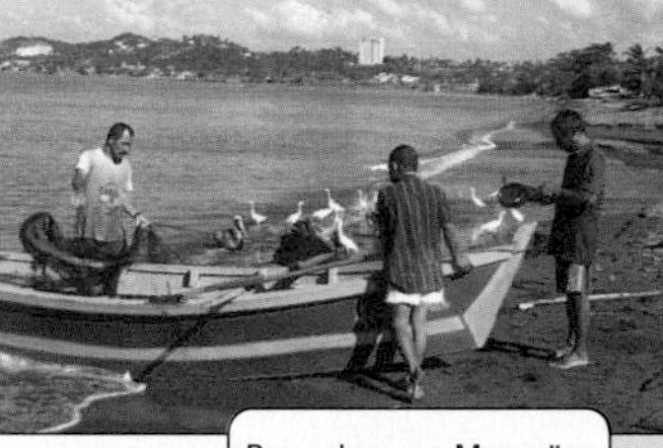
Pescadores en Mayagüez

Parque de Bombas, Ponce

OCÉANO ATLÁNTICO
PUERTO RIC
OCÉANO PACÍFICO

recursos

WB pp. 57–58	VM pp. 257–258	I CD-ROM Lección 5	vistahigherlearning.com

¡Increíble pero cierto!

El río *Camuy* es el tercer río subterráneo° más largo° del mundo y tiene el sistema de cuevas° más grande en el hemisferio occidental. La *Cueva de los Tres Pueblos* es una gigantesca bóveda°, tan grande que toda la fortaleza° del Morro puede caber° en su interior.

TEACHING OPTIONS

Heritage Speakers Encourage heritage speakers of Puerto Rican descent who have lived on the island or visited it to write a short description of their impressions. Ask them to describe people they knew or met, places they saw, and experiences they had. Ask them to think about what the most important thing they would tell a person from the mainland unfamiliar with the island would be and try to express it.

Worth Noting Baseball is a popular sport in Puerto Rico, home of the Winter League. Roberto Clemente, a player with the Pittsburgh Pirates who died tragically in a plane crash, was the first Latino to be inducted into the Baseball Hall of Fame.

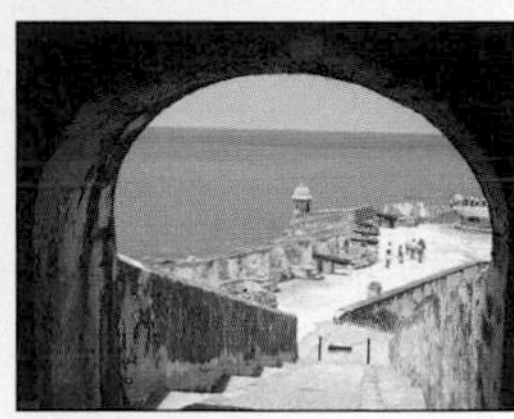

Lugares • El Morro

El Morro es una fortaleza que protegía° la bahía° de San Juan entre los años 1500 (mil quinientos) y 1900 (mil novecientos). Hoy día muchos turistas visitan este lugar, que ahora es un museo. Es el sitio más fotografiado de Puerto Rico. La arquitectura de la fortaleza es impresionante. Tiene misteriosos túneles, oscuras mazmorras° y vistas fabulosas de la bahía.

Artes • Salsa

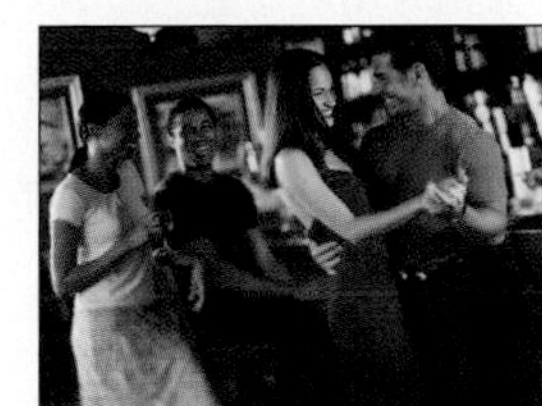

Este estilo musical, de orígenes puertorriqueños y cubanos, nació° en la ciudad de Nueva York. Dos de los músicos de salsa más famosos son Tito Puente y Willie Colón, los dos de Nueva York. Las estrellas° de la salsa en Puerto Rico son Felipe Rodríguez y Héctor Lavoe. Hoy, Puerto Rico es el centro universal de la salsa; el Gran Combo de Puerto Rico es una de las orquestas de salsa más famosas.

Isla de Culebra
Fajardo
Isla de Vieques

Ciencias • El Observatorio de Arecibo

El Observatorio de Arecibo tiene el radiotelescopio más grande del mundo. Gracias al telescopio los científicos° pueden estudiar la atmósfera de la Tierra° y la Luna°, fenómenos celestiales como los quasares y pulsares y escuchar emisiones de radio de otras galaxias, buscando inteligencia extraterrestre.

Historia • Relación con los Estados Unidos

Puerto Rico pasó a ser° parte de los Estados Unidos después de° la Guerra° de 1898 (mil ochocientos noventa y ocho) y se hizo° un estado libre asociado en 1952 (mil novecientos cincuenta y dos) . Los puertorriqueños, ciudadanos° estadounidenses desde° 1917 (mil novecientos diecisiete), tienen representación en el Congreso pero no votan en las elecciones presidenciales y no pagan impuestos° federales. Hay un debate entre los puertorriqueños: ¿debe la isla seguir como estado libre asociado, hacerse un estado como los otros o hacerse independiente?

¿Qué aprendiste? Responde a las preguntas con una frase completa.

1. ¿Cuál es la moneda de Puerto Rico? La moneda de Puerto Rico es el dólar estadounidense.
2. ¿Qué idiomas se hablan (*are spoken*) en Puerto Rico? Se hablan español e inglés en Puerto Rico.
3. ¿Cuál es el sitio más fotografiado de Puerto Rico? El Morro es el sitio más fotografiado de Puerto Rico.
4. ¿Qué es el Gran Combo? Es una orquesta de Puerto Rico.
5. ¿Qué hacen los científicos en el Observatorio de Arecibo? Los científicos estudian la atmósfera de la Tierra y la Luna y escuchan emisiones de otras galaxias.

Conexión Internet Investiga estos temas en el sitio **www.vistahigherlearning.com.**

1. Describe a dos puertorriqueños famosos. ¿Cómo son? ¿Qué hacen? ¿Dónde viven? ¿Por qué son célebres?
2. Busca información sobre lugares buenos para el ecoturismo en Puerto Rico. Luego presenta un informe a la clase.

protegía *protected* bahía *bay* mazmorras *dungeons* nació *was born* estrellas *stars* científicos *scientists* Tierra *Earth* Luna *Moon* pasó a ser *became* después de *after* Guerra *War* se hizo *became* ciudadanos *citizens* desde *since* pagan impuestos *pay taxes*

El Morro Remind students that at the time **El Morro** was built, piracy was a major concern for Spain and its Caribbean colonies. If possible, show other photos of **El Morro**, San Juan Bay, and **El Viejo San Juan**.

Salsa With students, listen to **salsa** or **merengue** from the Dominican Republic, and **rumba** or **mambo** from Cuba. Encourage them to identify common elements in the music (strong percussion patterns rooted in African traditions, alternating structure of soloist and ensemble, incorporation of Western instruments and musical vocabulary). Then, have them point out contrasts.

El Observatorio de Arecibo The Arecibo Ionospheric Observatory has the world's most sensitive radio telescope. It can detect objects up to 13 billion light years away. The telescope dish is 1,000 feet in diameter and covers 20 acres. The dish is made of about 40,000 aluminum mesh panels.

Relación con los Estados Unidos Point out that only Puerto Ricans living on the island vote in plebiscites on the question of the island's political relationship to the United States.

Conexión Internet Students will find supporting Internet activities and links at **www.vistahigherlearning.com**.

TEACHING OPTIONS

Variación léxica When the first Spanish colonists arrived on the island they were to name Puerto Rico, they found it inhabited by the Taínos, who called the island **Borinquen**. Puerto Ricans still use that name to refer to the island, and they frequently call themselves **borinqueños** or **boricuas**. The Puerto Rican national anthem is ***La borinqueña.*** Some other Taíno words that have entered Spanish (and English) are **huracán**, **hamaca**, **canoa**, and **iguana**. **Juracán** was the name of the Taíno god of the winds whose anger stirred up the great storms that periodically devastated the island. The hammock, of course, was the device the Taínos slept in, and canoes were the boats made of great hollowed-out logs with which they paddled between islands. The Taíno language also survives in many Puerto Rican place names: Arecibo, Bayamón, Guayama, Sierra de Cayey, Yauco, and Coamo.

Instructional Resources
Vocabulary CD
Lab Manual, p. 30
*Lab CD/MP3 **Lección 5***
IRM: Tapescript, pp. 20–24
*Testing Program: **Pruebas**, pp. 49–60*
Testing Program Audio CD
Test Files CD-ROM

Los viajes y las vacaciones

acampar	*to camp*
confirmar una reservación	*to confirm a reservation*
estar de vacaciones (*f. pl.*)	*to be on vacation*
hacer las maletas	*to pack (one's suitcases)*
hacer turismo (*m.*)	*to go sightseeing*
hacer un viaje	*to take a trip*
hacer una excursión	*to go on a hike; to go on a tour*
ir de compras (*f. pl.*)	*to go shopping*
ir de pesca (*f.*)	*to go fishing*
ir de vacaciones	*to go on vacation*
ir en autobús (*m.*), auto(móvil)(*m.*), avión (*m.*), barco (*m.*), motocicleta (*f.*), taxi (*m.*),	*to go by bus, car, plane, boat, motor-cycle, taxi*
jugar a las cartas	*to play cards*
montar a caballo (*m.*)	*to ride a horse*
pasar por la aduana	*to go through customs*
pescar	*to fish*
sacar/tomar fotos (*f. pl.*)	*to take photos*
el/la agente de viajes	*travel agent*
el/la inspector(a) de aduanas	*customs inspector*
el/la viajero/a	*traveler*
el aeropuerto	*airport*
la agencia de viajes	*travel agency*
la cabaña	*cabin*
el campo	*countryside*
el equipaje	*luggage*
la estación de autobuses, del metro, de tren	*bus, subway, train station*
la llegada	*arrival*
el mar	*sea*
el océano	*ocean*
el paisaje	*landscape*
el pasaje (de ida y vuelta)	*(round-trip) ticket*
el pasaporte	*passport*
la playa	*beach*
la salida	*departure; exit*

El hotel

el ascensor	*elevator*
el/la botones	*bellhop*
la cama	*bed*
el/la empleado/a	*employee*
la habitación individual, doble	*single, double room*
el hotel	*hotel*
el/la huésped	*guest*
la llave	*key*
el piso	*floor (of a building)*
la planta baja	*ground floor*

Adjetivos

abierto/a	*open*
aburrido/a	*bored; boring*
alegre	*happy; joyful*
amable	*nice; friendly*
avergonzado/a	*embarrassed*
cansado/a	*tired*
cerrado/a	*closed*
cómodo/a	*comfortable*
confundido	*confused*
contento/a	*happy; content*
desordenado/a	*disorderly*
enamorado/a (de)	*in love (with)*
enojado/a	*mad; angry*
equivocado/a	*wrong*
feliz	*happy*
limpio/a	*clean*
listo/a	*ready; smart*
nervioso/a	*nervous*
ocupado/a	*busy*
ordenado/a	*orderly*
preocupado/a (por)	*worried (about)*
seguro/a	*sure/safe*
sucio/a	*dirty*
triste	*sad*

Los números ordinales

primer, primero/a	*first*
segundo/a	*second*
tercer, tercero/a	*third*
cuarto/a	*fourth*
quinto/a	*fifth*
sexto/a	*sixth*
séptimo/a	*seventh*
octavo/a	*eighth*
noveno/a	*ninth*
décimo/a	*tenth*

Palabras adicionales

ahora mismo	*right now*
el año	*year*
¿Cuál es la fecha (de hoy)?	*What is the date (today)?*
de buen/mal humor	*in a good/bad mood*
la estación	*season*
el mes	*month*
todavía	*yet; still*

Seasons, months, and dates	*See page 138.*
Weather Expressions	*See page 138.*
Direct object pronouns	*See page 156.*
Expresiones útiles	*See page 143.*

recursos

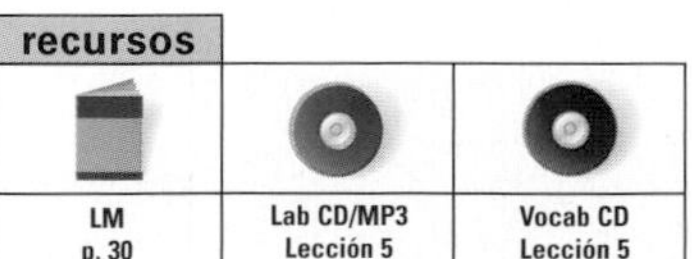

LM p. 30	Lab CD/MP3 Lección 5	Vocab CD Lección 5

¡De compras!

6

Communicative Goals

You will learn how to:

- Talk about and describe clothing
- Express preferences in a store
- Negotiate and pay for items you buy

A PRIMERA VISTA

- *¿Está comprando algo la mujer?*
- *¿Está buscando una maleta?*
- *¿Es delgada? ¿Es guapa o fea?*
- *¿Tiene el pelo largo o corto?*

Lesson Goals

In **Lección 6** students will be introduced to the following:

- terms for clothing and shopping
- colors
- numbers 101 and higher
- indirect object pronouns
- preterite tense of regular verbs
- demonstrative adjectives and pronouns
- skimming a text
- how to report an interview
- writing a report
- listening for linguistic cues
- writing and presenting a business plan
- cultural, geographic, economic, and historical information about Cuba

A primera vista Here are some additional questions you can ask based on the photo: **¿Te gusta ir de compras? ¿Por qué? ¿Estás de buen humor cuando vas de compras? ¿Qué compras cuando estás de vacaciones? ¿Estás pensando salir de vacaciones en el verano?**

INSTRUCTIONAL RESOURCES

Workbook/Video Manual: WB Activities, pp. 59–72
Laboratory Manual: Lab Activities, pp. 31–36
Workbook/Video Manual: Video Activities, pp. 223–224; pp. 259–260
Instructor's Resource Manual: **Vocabulario adicional**, p. 184; **¡Inténtalo!** & **Práctica** Answers, pp. 206–207; **Fotonovela** Translations, pp. 141–142; Textbook CD Tapescript, p. 90; Lab CDs Tapescript, pp. 25–29; **Fotonovela** Videoscript, p. 108; **Panorama cultural** Videoscript, p. 130
Info Gap Activities Booklet, pp. 21–24
Overhead Transparencies: #3, #4, #28, #29, #30
Lab Audio CD/MP3 **Lección 6**
Panorama cultural DVD/Video
Fotonovela DVD/Video
Testing Program, pp. 61–72; pp. 241–251
Testing Program Audio CD
Test Files CD-ROM
Companion website
Presentations CD-ROM
Textbook CD
Vocabulary CD
Interactive CD-ROM
Video CD-ROM
Web-SAM

Section Goals

In **Contextos**, students will learn and practice:

- clothing vocabulary
- vocabulary to use while shopping
- colors

Instructional Resources
Transparencies, #28, #29
Textbook CD
Vocabulary CD
WB/VM: Workbook, pp. 59–60
Lab Manual, p. 31
Lab CD/MP3 ***Lección 6***
IRM: ***Vocab. adicional****, p. 184;*
Práctica *Answers, pp. 206–207;*
Tapescript, pp. 25–29; p. 90
Interactive CD-ROM
Companion website:
www.vistahigherlearning.com
Presentations CD-ROM

Suggestions

- Ask volunteers about shopping preferences and habits. Say: **¿Qué te gusta comprar? ¿Discos compactos? ¿Programas para la computadora? ¿Ropa?** (point to your own clothing) **¿Adónde vas para comprar esas cosas? ¿Cuánto dinero gastas** (mime reaching in your pocket and paying for something) **normalmente?** Ask another student: **¿Adónde va de compras ____? Sí, va a ____. ¿Y qué compra allí? Sí, compra ____.**
- Project **Transparency #28**. Have students guess the meanings of **damas** and **caballeros**. Have them refer to the scene to answer your true-false questions about it. Ex: **El hombre paga con tarjeta de crédito. (Cierto) No venden zapatos en la tienda. (Falso) Se puede regatear en el almacén. (Falso)** Use as many clothing items and verbs from **Más vocabulario** as you can.

Note: At this point you may want to present **Vocabulario adicional: Más vocabulario para ir de compras**, from the IRM.

¡De compras!

Más vocabulario

el abrigo	*coat*
el almacén	*department store*
el calcetín	*sock*
el cinturón	*belt*
las gafas (de sol), las gafas (oscuras)	*(sun)glasses*
los guantes	*gloves*
el impermeable	*raincoat*
los lentes de contacto	*contact lenses*
los lentes (de sol)	*(sun)glasses*
la ropa	*clothing; clothes*
la ropa interior	*underwear*
la sandalia	*sandal*
el vestido	*dress*
los zapatos de tenis	*tennis shoes; sneakers*
el centro comercial	*shopping mall*
el mercado (al aire libre)	*(open-air) market*
el precio (fijo)	*(fixed; set) price*
la rebaja	*sale*
la tienda	*shop; store*
costar (o:ue)	*to cost*
gastar	*to spend (money)*
pagar	*to pay*
regatear	*to bargain*
vender	*to sell*
hacer juego (con)	*to match (with)*
llevar	*to wear; to take*
usar	*to wear; to use*

Variación léxica

calcetines ⟷ medias (*Amér. L.*)
cinturón ⟷ correa (*Col., Venez.*)
gafas/lentes ⟷ espejuelos (*Cuba, P.R.*), anteojos (*Arg., Chile*)
zapatos de tenis ⟷ zapatillas de deporte (*Esp.*), zapatillas (*Arg., Perú*)

recursos

TEXT CD Lección 6	WB pp. 59–60	LM p. 31	Lab CD/MP3 Lección 6	I CD-ROM Lección 6	Vocab CD Lección 6

TEACHING OPTIONS

Small Groups In groups of three or four, students close their books and make a list of as many of the articles of clothing that appear in the store scene as they can. Then have all groups call out their lists as you write down the items on the board. Did the groups remember all of the items pictured in the drawing?

Variación léxica Point out that terms for clothing vary widely throughout the Spanish-speaking world. For the most part, Spanish speakers of different regions can mutually understand each other when talking about clothing. Other variations include **los bluejeans = los vaqueros, los jeans; zapatos de tenis = los tenis; los pantalones = el pantalón; el suéter = el pulóver, el jersey; la chaqueta = la chamarra.**

Práctica

1 **Escuchar** Listen to Juanita and Vicente talk about what they're packing for their vacations. Indicate who is packing each item. If both are packing an item, write both names. If neither is packing an item, write an X.

1. abrigo Vicente
2. zapatos de tenis Juanita, Vicente
3. impermeable X
4. chaqueta Vicente
5. sandalias Juanita
6. bluejeans Juanita, Vicente
7. gafas de sol Vicente
8. camisetas Juanita, Vicente
9. traje de baño Juanita
10. botas Vicente
11. pantalones cortos Juanita
12. suéter Vicente

2 **Completar** Anita is talking about going shopping. Complete each sentence with the correct word(s) adding definite or indefinite articles when necessary.

caja	medias	tarjeta de crédito
centro comercial	par	traje de baño
dependientas	ropa	vendedores

1. Hoy voy a ir de compras al nuevo centro comercial.
2. Voy a ir a la tienda de ropa para mujeres. Siempre hay muchas rebajas y las dependientas son muy simpáticas.
3. Necesito comprarme un par de zapatos.
4. Y tengo que comprarme un traje de baño nuevo porque el sábado voy a la playa con mis amigos.
5. También voy a comprar unas medias para mi mamá.
6. Voy a pagar todo (*everything*) en la caja.
7. Pero hoy no tengo dinero. Voy a tener que usar mi tarjeta de crédito.
8. Mañana voy al mercado al aire libre. Me gusta regatear con los vendedores.

3 **Escoger** Choose the item in each group that does not belong.

1. almacén • centro comercial • mercado • sombrero sombrero
2. camisa • camiseta • blusa • botas botas
3. bluejeans • bolsa • falda • pantalones bolsa
4. abrigo • suéter • corbata • chaqueta corbata
5. mercado • tienda • almacén • cartera cartera
6. pagar • llevar • hacer juego (con) • usar pagar
7. botas • sandalias • zapatos • traje traje
8. vender • regatear • ropa interior • gastar ropa interior

1 Suggestion Have students check their answers by going over **Actividad 1** with the class.

1 Tapescript JUANITA: Hola. Me llamo Juanita. Mi familia y yo salimos de vacaciones mañana y estoy haciendo mis maletas. Para nuestra excursión al campo ya tengo bluejeans, camisetas y zapatos de tenis. También vamos a la playa… ¡no puedo esperar! Para ir a la playa necesito un traje de baño, pantalones cortos y sandalias. ¿Qué más necesito? Creo que es todo.
VICENTE: Buenos días. Soy Vicente. Estoy haciendo mis maletas porque mi familia y yo vamos a las montañas a esquiar. Los primeros dos días vamos a hacer una excursión por las montañas. Necesito zapatos de tenis, camisetas, una chaqueta y bluejeans. El tercer día vamos a esquiar. Necesito un abrigo, un suéter y botas… y gafas de sol.
Textbook CD

1 Expansion Have students indicate where these two are going: **¿Por qué necesita llevar sandalias Juanita?**

2 Expansion Ask pairs to write three additional fill-in-the-blank sentences based on Anita's shopping. Ask volunteers to read their sentences aloud. The rest of the class provides the correct answers.

3 Expansion Go over answers quickly in class. After each answer, indicate why a particular item doesn't belong. Ex: **1. El sombrero. No puedes ir de compras a un sombrero.**

TEACHING OPTIONS

Extra Practice Suggest a vacation spot and then ask students at random what clothing they need to take. Make it a continuing narration whereby the next student must say all of the items of clothing that came before and add one. Ex: **Vas a la playa. ¿Qué vas a llevar? E1: Voy a llevar un traje de baño. E2: Voy a llevar un traje de baño y lentes de sol.**

TPR Play a game of Simon Says (**Simón dice…**). Write on the board **levántense** and **siéntense** and explain that they mean stand up and sit down, respectively. Then start by saying: **Simón dice… los que llevan bluejeans, levántense.** Students wearing blue jeans stand up and remain standing until further instruction. Work through various articles of clothing. Be sure to give instructions without saying **Simón dice…** once in a while.

Suggestion Project **Transparency #29** and review the color words. Point to a drawing and say: **¿De qué color es esta camiseta?** After you go through several colors, ask: **Si mezclo el rojo y el azul, ¿qué color resulta? (el morado) Y si yo mezclo el amarillo y el rojo, ¿qué color resulta? (el anaranjado)** Then point to objects in the classroom and clothes you and students are wearing to elicit color words. Point out that color words are adjectives and agree with the nouns they modify.

4 Suggestion Before beginning the activity, ask several brief comprehension questions. Ex: **¿Quién lleva una camiseta roja? Sí, ____ lleva una camiseta roja. ¿Son baratos o caros los trajes de Armani?**

4 Expansion Show magazine pictures of various products (cars, computers, etc.) and ask students: **¿Es cara esta computadora o es barata? Sí, es barata.**

5 Expansion Point to various students in the class and ask others what color of clothing each is wearing. Ex: ____, **¿de qué color es la falda de ____? Sí, es ____.**

Los colores

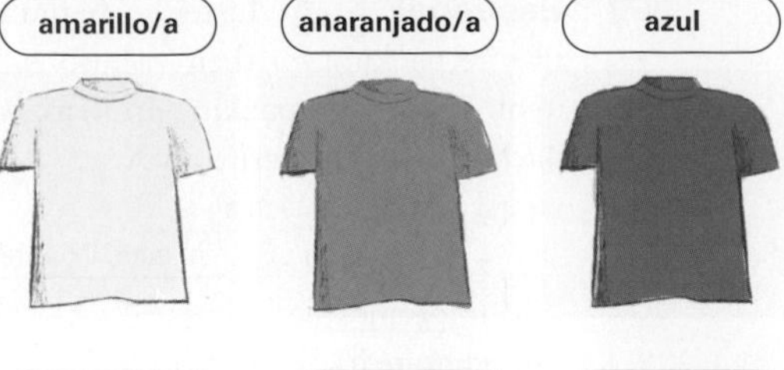

¡LENGUA VIVA!

The names of colors vary throughout the Spanish-speaking world. For example, in some countries, **anaranjado/a** may be referred to as **naranja**, **morado/a** as **púrpura**, and **rojo/a** as **colorado**.

Other terms that will prove helpful include **claro** (*light*) and **oscuro** (*dark*): **azul claro, azul oscuro.**

Adjetivos

barato/a	*cheap*
bueno/a	*good*
cada	*each*
caro/a	*expensive*
corto/a	*short (in length)*
elegante	*elegant*
hermoso/a	*beautiful*
largo/a	*long (in length)*
loco/a	*crazy*
nuevo/a	*new*
otro/a	*other; another*
pobre	*poor*
rico/a	*rich*

4 **Contrastes** Complete each phrase with the opposite of the underlined word.

1. una corbata barata • unas camisas... caras
2. unas vendedoras malas • unos dependientes... buenos
3. un vestido corto • una falda... larga
4. un hombre muy pobre • una mujer muy... rica
5. una cartera nueva • un cinturón... viejo
6. unos trajes hermosos • unos bluejeans... feos
7. un impermeable caro • unos suéteres... baratos
8. unos calcetines blancos • unas medias... negras

CONSÚLTALO

Like other adjectives you have seen, colors must agree in gender and number with the nouns they modify. Ex: **las camisas verdes, el vestido amarillo.** For a review of descriptive adjectives, see **Estructura 3.1** pp.78-79.

5 **Preguntas** Answer these questions with a classmate.

1. ¿De qué color es la rosa de Texas? Es amarilla.
2. ¿De qué color es la bandera (*flag*) del Canadá? Es roja y blanca.
3. ¿De qué color es la casa donde vive el presidente de los EE.UU.? Es blanca.
4. ¿De qué color es el océano Atlántico? Es azul.
5. ¿De qué color es la nieve? Es blanca.
6. ¿De qué color es el café? Es marrón./Es café.
7. ¿De qué color es el dólar de los EE.UU.? Es verde y blanco.
8. ¿De qué color es la cebra (*zebra*)? Es negra y blanca.

TEACHING OPTIONS

Pairs In pairs, students spend a few minutes creating a physical description of a well-known TV or cartoon character. Then they read their descriptions while the rest of the class guesses who the character is. Ex: **Soy bajo y un poco gordo. Llevo pantalones cortos azules y una camiseta anaranjada. Tengo el pelo amarillo. También soy amarillo. ¿Quién soy? (Bart Simpson)**

Game Play **Concentración**. On eight cards, write descriptions of clothing, including colors (Ex: **unos pantalones negros**). On another eight cards, draw pictures that match the descriptions. Place the cards face-down in four rows of four. In pairs, students select two cards. If the two cards match, the pair keeps them. If the two cards don't match, students replace them in their original position. The pair with the most cards at the end wins.

Comunicación

6 

Las maletas With a classmate, answer these questions about the drawings.

CONSÚLTALO

To review weather, see **Lección 5, Contextos**, p. 138.

1. ¿Qué ropa hay al lado de la maleta de Carmela?
   Hay una camiseta, unos pantalones cortos y un traje de baño.
2. ¿Qué hay en la maleta?
   Hay un sombrero y un par de sandalias.
3. ¿De qué color son las sandalias?
   Las sandalias son rojas.
4. ¿Adónde va Carmela?
   Va a la playa.
5. ¿Qué tiempo va a hacer?
   Va a hacer sol./ Va a hacer calor.

NOTA CULTURAL

Bariloche is a popular spot for skiing in South America. Located in Argentina's Patagonia region, the town is also known for its chocolate factories and its dramatic scenery with beautiful lakes, mountains, and forests.

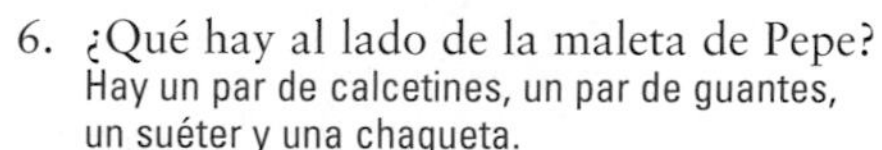

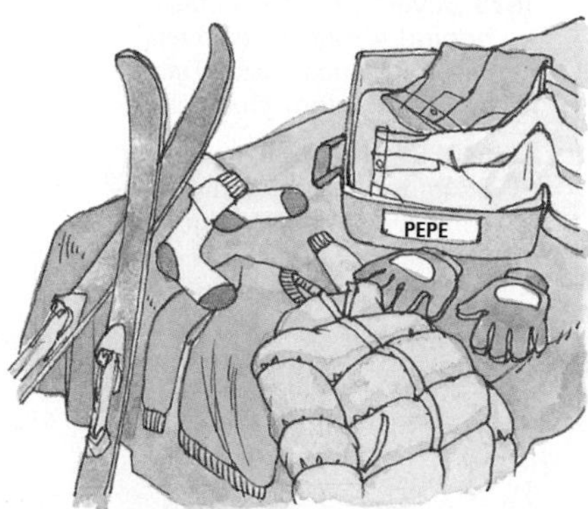

6. ¿Qué hay al lado de la maleta de Pepe?
   Hay un par de calcetines, un par de guantes, un suéter y una chaqueta.
7. ¿Qué hay en la maleta?
   Hay dos pares de pantalones.
8. ¿De qué color es el suéter?
   El suéter es rosado.
9. ¿Qué va a hacer Pepe en Bariloche?
   Va a esquiar.
10. ¿Qué tiempo va a hacer?
    Va a hacer frío./ Va a nevar.

7

¿Adónde van? Imagine that you are going on a vacation with two classmates. Get together with your classmates and decide where you're going. Then draw three suitcases and write in each one what clothing each person is taking. Present your drawings to the rest of the class, answering these questions. Answers will vary.

- ¿Adónde van?
- ¿Qué tiempo va a hacer allí?
- ¿Qué van a hacer allí?
- ¿Qué hay en sus maletas?
- ¿De qué color es la ropa que llevan?

8

Preferencias Use these questions to interview a classmate. Then switch roles. Answers will vary.

1. ¿Adónde vas a comprar ropa? ¿Por qué?
2. ¿Qué tipo de ropa prefieres? ¿Por qué?
3. ¿Cuáles son tus colores favoritos?
4. En tu opinión, ¿es importante comprar ropa nueva frecuentemente? ¿Por qué?
5. ¿Gastas mucho dinero en ropa cada mes? ¿Buscas rebajas?
6. ¿Regateas cuando compras ropa? ¿Usas una tarjeta de crédito?

6 Expansion Ask volunteers what kind of clothing they take with them when they visit the following places at the following times: **Seattle en la primavera, la Florida en el verano, Minnesota en el invierno, San Francisco en el otoño.**

7 Suggestion Assign groups and have them discuss where they are going the day before you do this activity in class.

7 Expansion Have students guess where the groups are going, based on the content of the suitcases. Facilitate guessing by asking the questions listed on the page.

8 Expansion Students report the findings of their interviews to the class. Ex: ____ **va a The Gap para comprar ropa porque allí la ropa no es cara. Prefiere la ropa informal...**

TEACHING OPTIONS

Extra Practice Students write a paragraph about the next vacation they plan to take and what clothing they plan to take with them. If students don't have a vacation planned, ask them to invent one. They should also include what kind of weather they expect at their destination and any weather-specific clothing they will need. Ask volunteers to share their paragraphs with the class.

Extra Practice Students write descriptions of the one article of clothing or complete outfit that best describes them without indicating who they are. Collect the papers and read the descriptions aloud. The rest of the class has to guess who each student is based on his or her defining article or outfit.

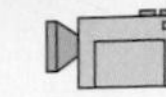

Section Goals

In **Fotonovela** students will:
- receive comprehensible input from free-flowing discourse
- learn functional phrases involving clothing and how much things cost

Instructional Resources
WB/VM: Video Activities, pp. 223–224
***Fotonovela** DVD/Video (Start 00:28:03)*
Video CD-ROM
*IRM: **Fotonovela** Translations, pp. 141–142, Videoscript, p. 108*
Interactive CD-ROM

Video Recap: Lección 5
Before doing this **Fotonovela** section, review the previous one with this activity.
1. ¿Qué pasa cuando llegan al hotel? (la empleada no encuentra la reservación)
2. ¿Qué piensan Javier, Inés, Maite y Álex de las cabañas? (no están nada mal; son muy limpias y ordenadas)
3. ¿Por qué quiere Maite descansar? (a las seis va a correr con Álex)
4. ¿Qué está pensando Maite cuando los demás salen de la habitación? (Inés y Javier están juntos otra vez)

Video Synopsis Inés and Javier go to an open-air market. Inés browses the market and eventually buys a purse for her sister, as well as a shirt and a hat for herself. Javier buys a sweater for the hike in the mountains.

Suggestions
- Have students scan the **Fotonovela** captions for vocabulary related to clothing or colors.
- Bring color photographs from magazines and ask the class questions about what the people in the photographs are wearing. Ex: **¿Qué lleva la señorita? ¿De qué color es?**
- Point out the clothing that a few individual students are wearing and ask them some questions about it. Ex: **Me gusta esa camisa azul. ¿Es de algodón? ¿Dónde la compraste?**
- Point out that in September 2000 the U.S. dollar became the official currency of Ecuador.

¡Qué ropa más bonita!

Javier e Inés van de compras al mercado.

PERSONAJES

INÉS

JAVIER

EL VENDEDOR

1

INÉS Javier, ¡qué ropa más bonita! A mí me gusta esa camisa blanca y azul. Debe ser de algodón. ¿Te gusta?

JAVIER Yo prefiero la camisa de la izquierda... la gris con rayas rojas. Hace juego con mis botas marrones.

2

INÉS Está bien, Javier. Mira, necesito comprarle un regalo a mi hermana Graciela. Acaba de empezar un nuevo trabajo...

JAVIER ¿Tal vez una bolsa?

3

VENDEDOR Esas bolsas son típicas de las montañas. ¿Le gusta?

INÉS Sí. Quiero comprarle una a mi hermana.

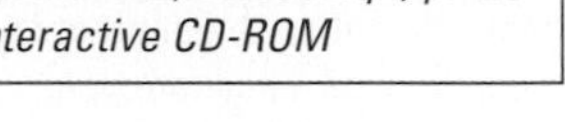

6

VENDEDOR Buenas tardes, joven. ¿Le puedo servir en algo?

JAVIER Sí. Voy a ir de excursión a las montañas y necesito un buen suéter.

VENDEDOR ¿Qué talla usa usted?

JAVIER Uso talla grande.

7

VENDEDOR Éstos son de talla grande.

JAVIER ¿Qué precio tiene ése?

VENDEDOR ¿Le gusta este suéter? Le cuesta ciento cincuenta mil sucres.

JAVIER Quiero comprarlo, pero, señor, no soy rico. ¿Ciento veinte mil sucres?

8

VENDEDOR Bueno, para usted... sólo ciento treinta mil sucres.

JAVIER Está bien, señor.

recursos

V CD-ROM Lección 6	VM pp. 223–224	I CD-ROM Lección 6

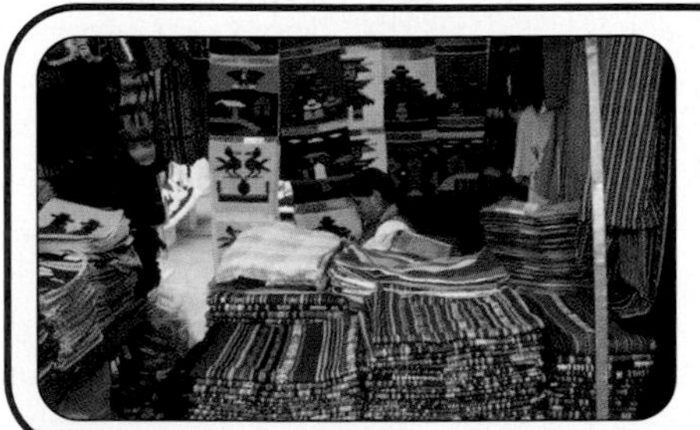

TEACHING OPTIONS

Video Tips General suggestions for using video clips in the classroom can be found on page IAE-12 of this Instructor's Annotated Edition.

¡Qué ropa más bonita! Photocopy the videoscript and opaque out 7–10 words with white correction fluid in order to create a master for a cloze activity. Hand out photocopies of the master to your students and have them fill in the missing words as they watch the **¡Qué ropa más bonita!** segment of this video module. You may want to show the segment twice or more if your students experience difficulties with this activity. You may also want your students to share their pages in small groups and help each other fill in any gaps.

INÉS Me gusta aquélla. ¿Cuánto cuesta?

VENDEDOR Ésa cuesta ciento sesenta mil sucres. ¡Es de muy buena calidad!

INÉS Uy, demasiado cara. Quizás otro día.

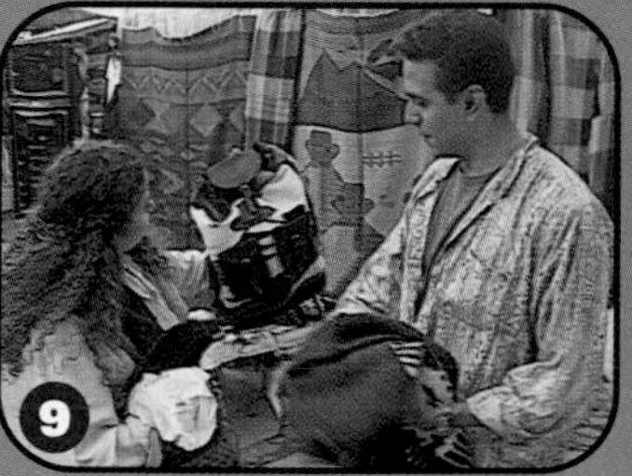

JAVIER Acabo de comprarme un suéter. Y tú, ¿qué compraste?

INÉS Compré esta bolsa para mi hermana.

INÉS También compré una camisa y un sombrero. ¿Qué tal me veo?

JAVIER ¡Guapa, muy guapa!

Expresiones útiles

Talking about clothing

- ▶ **¡Qué ropa más bonita!**
  What nice clothing!
- ▶ **Me gusta esta/esa camisa blanca de rayas negras.**
  I like this/that white shirt with black stripes.
- ▶ **Está de moda.**
  It's in fashion.
- ▶ **Debe ser de algodón/lana/seda.**
  It must be cotton/wool/silk.
- ▶ **Es de cuadros/lunares/rayas.**
  It's plaid/polka-dotted/striped.
- ▶ **Me gusta este/ese suéter.**
  I like this/that sweater.
- ▶ **Es de muy buena calidad.**
  It's very good quality.
- ▶ **¿Qué talla lleva/usa usted?**
  What size do you wear?
- ▷ **Llevo/Uso talla grande.**
  I wear a large.
- ▶ **¿Qué número calza usted?**
  What (shoe) size do you wear?
- ▷ **Calzo el treinta y seis.**
  I wear a size thirty-six.

Talking about how much things cost

- ▶ **¿Cuánto cuesta?**
  How much does it cost?
- ▷ **Sólo cuesta noventa mil sucres.**
  It only costs ninety thousand sucres.
- ▷ **Demasiado caro/a.**
  Too expensive.
- ▷ **Es una ganga.**
  It's a bargain.

Saying what you bought

- ▶ **¿Qué compró Ud./él/ella?**
  What did you (form.)/he/she buy?
- ▷ **Compré esta bolsa para mi hermana.**
  I bought this purse for my sister.
- ▶ **¿Qué compraste?**
  What did you buy?
- ▷ **Acabo de comprarme un sombrero.**
  I have just bought myself a hat.

Enfoque cultural Mercados al aire libre

Open-air markets, or **mercados al aire libre,** are an important part of the commerce and culture of many Hispanic countries. Fresh fruits and vegetables, tapestries, clothing, pottery and crafts are commonly seen among the vendors' wares. One of the most famous is the market in Otavalo, Ecuador, which has taken place every Saturday since pre-Incan times. Another popular market is **El Rastro** in Madrid, held every Sunday, where tourists can buy antiques and many other goods.

Suggestion Have students work in pairs to read the parts of Inés and Javier as they arrive at the market (frames 1–2), Inés bargaining with the vendor (frames 3–5), and Javier bargaining with the vendor (frames 6–8). Ask for volunteers to read their segment for the class.

Expresiones útiles Point out the verb forms **compré, compraste,** and **compró.** Tell the class that these are forms of the verb **comprar** in the preterite tense, and that the preterite is used to tell what happened in the past. Tell the class that **este, esta, ese,** and **esa** are examples of demonstrative adjectives, which are used to single out particular nouns. Also point out that the **me** in **Acabo de comprarme un sombrero** is an indirect object pronoun, used to tell for whom the hat was bought. Tell your students that they will learn more about these concepts in **Estructura.**

TEACHING OPTIONS

Enfoque cultural Tell the class that in many open-air markets in the Spanish-speaking world, customers are expected to engage in good-natured bargaining (**regateo**) with the sellers. Bargaining is not just a way of arriving at a price that is agreeable to both buyer and seller, it is a means of social interchange. Both participants enjoy the exchange. Point out that many stores and some open-air markets, however, charge a **precio fijo** (*fixed price*) for each item and do not allow bargaining. Also, point out to the class that consumers in Spanish-speaking countries, like their counterparts in the United States, may purchase goods in many different ways. Some prefer to visit open-air markets, small specialty shops, supermarkets, department stores, shopping centers, or malls, while others prefer the convenience of Internet shopping.

Reacciona a la fotonovela

1 **¿Cierto o falso?** Indicate whether each sentence is **cierto** or **falso**. Correct the false statements.

	Cierto	Falso
1. A Inés le gusta la camisa verde y amarilla. A Inés le gusta la camisa blanca y azul.	❍	✓
2. Javier necesita comprarle un regalo a su hermana. Inés necesita comprarle un regalo a su hermana.	❍	✓
3. Las bolsas en el mercado son típicas de las montañas.	✓	❍
4. Javier busca un traje de baño. Javier busca un suéter.	❍	✓
5. Inés compró un sombrero, un suéter y una bolsa. Inés compró una bolsa, una camisa y un sombrero.	❍	✓
6. Javier regatea con el vendedor.	✓	❍

2 **Identificar** Provide the name of the person who would make each statement. The names may be used more than once.

1. ¿Te gusta el sombrero que compré? Inés
2. Estos suéteres son de talla grande. ¿Qué talla usa usted? el vendedor
3. ¿Por qué no compras una bolsa para Graciela? Javier
4. Creo que mis botas hacen juego con la camisa. Javier
5. Estas bolsas son excelentes, de muy buena calidad. el vendedor
6. Creo que las blusas aquí son de algodón. Inés

INÉS

JAVIER

EL VENDEDOR

3 **Contestar** Answer the questions using the information in the **Fotonovela.**

1. Inés quiere comprarle un regalo a su hermana. ¿Por qué? Inés quiere comprarle un regalo a su hermana porque ella acaba de empezar un nuevo trabajo.
2. ¿Cuánto cuesta la bolsa de las montañas? La bolsa de las montañas cuesta ciento cincuenta mil sucres.
3. ¿Por qué necesita Javier un buen suéter? Javier necesita un buen suéter porque va de excursión a las montañas.
4. ¿Cuál es el precio final del suéter? El precio final del suéter es ciento treinta mil sucres.
5. ¿Qué compra Inés en el mercado? Inés compra una bolsa, una camisa y un sombrero.
6. ¿Qué talla usa Javier? Javier usa talla grande.

CONSEJOS

When discussing prices, it's important to keep in mind singular and plural forms of verbs.

La **camisa cuesta** diez dólares.

Las **botas cuestan** sesenta dólares.

El **precio** de las botas **es** sesenta dólares.

Los **precios** de la ropa **son** altos.

4 **Conversar** With a partner, role-play a conversation between a customer and a sales person in an open-air market. Answers will vary.

Cliente/a	Vendedor(a)
Say good afternoon.	Greet the customer and ask what he/she would like.
Explain that you are looking for a particular item of clothing.	Show him/her some items and ask what he/she prefers.
Discuss colors and sizes.	Discuss colors and sizes.
Ask for the price and begin bargaining.	Tell him/her a price. Negotiate a price.
Settle on a price and purchase the item.	Accept a price and say thank you.

NATIONAL communication STANDARDS

AYUDA

¿Qué desea? *What would you like?*

Estoy buscando... *I'm looking for...*

Prefiero el/la rojo/a. *I prefer the red one.*

¿Cuánto cuesta? *How much does it cost?*

Es demasiado. *It's too much.*

1 Expansion Once all statements are corrected, ask pairs to identify the characters and their lines from the **Fotonovela** episode that act each one out. Have pairs play out the scenes for the class.

2 Expansion Give these additional items to the class: **7. Pero, señor… no traigo mucho dinero. (Javier) 8. Señor, para usted… ochenta mil sucres. (vendedor) 9. Me gusta mucho esta camisa blanca de algodón. (Inés)**

3 Expansion Have pairs write two additional questions. Then in groups of four, pairs take turns asking, answering, and correcting each other's questions. Call on volunteers to share their questions with the rest of the class.

4 Possible Response
E1: Buenas tardes.
E2: Buenas tardes. ¿Le puedo servir en algo?
E1: Necesito una camisa.
E2: Pues, tengo estas camisas de algodón y estas camisas de seda. Son de muy buena calidad. ¿Cuál prefiere usted?
E1: Busco una camisa blanca o azul de algodón. Uso talla mediana.
E2: Las camisas de algodón son de talla mediana. Tengo esta camisa azul de algodón.
E1: Quiero comprarla, pero no soy rico/a. ¿Cuánto cuesta?
E2: Veinte dólares. Pero para usted... sólo quince dólares.
E1: Muy bien. La compro, pero sólo tengo diez dólares.
E2: Está bien. Muchas gracias, y adiós.

Successful Language Learning Tell your students to devote extra effort and attention to **Actividad 4**. This activity sums up the vocabulary and functional phrases that the students have learned earlier in the lesson. In addition, this activity explores a real-life situation that travelers might encounter when visiting a Spanish-speaking country.

TEACHING OPTIONS

Extra Practice Have the class answer questions about **Fotonovela**. Ex: **1. ¿Quién necesita una bolsa nueva para su trabajo? (Graciela, la hermana de Inés) 2. ¿Quién cree que las bolsas son demasiado caras? (Inés) 3. ¿De qué color son las botas de Javier? (marrón) 4. ¿Quién acaba de comprarse un suéter? (Javier)**

Small Groups Have the class work in small groups to write statements about the **Fotonovela**. Ask each group to exchange its statements with another group. Each group will then write out the question that would have elicited each statement. Ex: G1: **Graciela acaba de empezar un nuevo trabajo.** G2: **¿Quién acaba de empezar un nuevo trabajo?**

Pronunciación

The consonants d and t

¿Dónde? **vender** **nadar** **verdad**

Like **b** and **v**, the Spanish **d** can also have a hard sound or a soft sound, depending on which letters appear next to it.

Don **dinero** **tienda** **falda**

At the beginning of a phrase and after **n** or **l**, the letter **d** is pronounced with a hard sound. This sound is similar to the English *d* in *dog*, but a little softer and duller. The tongue should touch the back of the upper teeth, not the roof of the mouth.

medias **verde** **vestido** **huésped**

In all other positions, **d** has a soft sound. It is similar to the English *th* in *there*, but a little softer.

Don Diego no tiene el diccionario.

When **d** begins a word, its pronunciation depends on the previous word. At the beginning of a phrase or after a word that ends in **n** or **l**, it is pronounced as a hard **d**.

Doña Dolores es de la capital.

Words that begin with **d** are pronounced with a soft **d** if they appear immediately after a word that ends in a vowel or any consonant other than **n** or **l**.

traje **pantalones** **tarjeta** **tienda**

When pronouncing the Spanish **t**, the tongue should touch the back of the upper teeth, not the roof of the mouth. Unlike the English *t*, no air is expelled from the mouth.

Práctica Read these phrases aloud to practice the **d** and the **t**.

1. Hasta pronto.
2. De nada.
3. Mucho gusto.
4. Lo siento.
5. No hay de qué.
6. ¿De dónde es usted?
7. ¡Todos a bordo!
8. No puedo.
9. Es estupendo.
10. No tengo computadora.
11. ¿Cuándo vienen?
12. Son las tres y media.

Oraciones Read these sentences aloud to practice the **d** and the **t**.

1. Don Teodoro tiene una tienda en un almacén en La Habana.
2. Don Teodoro vende muchos trajes, vestidos y zapatos todos los días.
3. Un día un turista, Federico Machado, entra en la tienda para comprar un par de botas.
4. Federico regatea con don Teodoro y compra las botas y también un par de sandalias.

Refranes Read these sayings aloud to practice the **d** and the **t**.

En la variedad está el gusto.[1]

Aunque la mona se vista de seda, mona se queda.[2]

1 Variety is the spice of life.
2 You can't make a silk purse out of a sow's ear.

recursos

TEXT CD Lección 6	LM p. 32	Lab CD/MP3 Lección 6	I CD-ROM Lección 6

Section Goal

In **Pronunciación** students will be introduced to the pronunciation of the letters **d** and **t**.

Instructional Resources
Textbook CD
Lab Manual, p. 32
*Lab CD/MP3 **Lección 6***
IRM: Tapescript, pp. 25–29; p. 90
Interactive CD-ROM

Suggestions

- Say that **d** has a hard sound at the beginning of a phrase or after **n** or **l**. Write **don, dinero, tienda,** and **falda** on the board and have the class pronounce them.
- Explain that **d** has a soft sound in all other situations. Pronounce the words **medias, verde, vestido,** and **huésped** and have the class repeat.
- Point out that within phrases, **d** at the beginning of a word has a hard or soft sound depending on the last sound of the word that precedes it, according to the same rules described above for **d** at the beginning of a phrase. Read the example sentences aloud and have the class repeat.
- Explain that **t** is pronounced with the tongue at the back of the upper teeth and that, unlike English, no air is expelled from the mouth. Pronounce **traje, pantalones, tarjeta,** and **tienda** and have the class repeat. Then pronounce pairs of similar-sounding Spanish and English words, having students focus on the difference between the sounds of **t: ti/tea; tal/tall; todo/toad; tema/tame, tela/tell.**

Práctica/Oraciones/Refranes

These exercises are recorded on the Textbook CD. You may want to play the CD so students practice the pronunciation point by listening to Spanish spoken by speakers other than yourself.

TEACHING OPTIONS

Extra Practice Write some additional proverbs on the board and have the class practice saying each one. Ex: **De tal padre, tal hijo.** (Like father, like son.) **El que tiene tejado de cristal no tira piedras al vecino.** (People who live in glass houses shouldn't throw stones.) **Cuatro ojos ven más que dos.** (Two heads are better than one.)

Extra Practice Write on the board the names of these famous Cuban literary figures: José Martí, Julián del Casal, Gertrudis Gómez de Avellaneda, and Dulce María Loynaz. Say the names aloud and have the class repeat after you. Then ask the class to explain the pronunciation of each **d** and **t** in these names.

Section Goals

In **Estructura 6.1** students will learn:

- to count from 101 on
- punctuation and agreement rules pertaining to numbers

Instructional Resources
WB/VM: Workbook, pp. 61–62
Lab Manual, p. 33
Lab CD/MP3 ***Lección 6***
IRM: ***¡Inténtalo! & Práctica***
Answers, pp. 206–207;
Tapescript, pp. 25–29
Interactive CD-ROM
Companion website:
www.vistahigherlearning.com
Presentations CD-ROM

Suggestions

- Review numbers 0–100 by asking students questions that call for a number in the answer. Ex: **¿Cuántos estudiantes hay en la clase? ¿Cuántos años tienen? Ana tiene trece lápices y yo tengo cuarenta. ¿Cuántos lápices tenemos?**
- Write the following on the board: **cuatrocientos estudiantes, novecientas personas, dos mil libros, once millones de viajeros.** Help students deduce the meanings of the numbers.
- Write numbers on the board and call on individuals to read them.
- To practice agreement, write numbers from 101 to 999 followed by various nouns and have students read them.

Successful Language Learning Explain to students that to count from 101–199, **ciento** is used followed by 1–99, which they already know. Therefore 101 is **ciento uno**, 102 is **ciento dos**, 103 is **ciento tres**, and so forth up to 199, which is **ciento noventa y nueve**. They can use the same strategy after **doscientos/as, trescientos/as**, etc.

6.1 Numbers 101 and higher

NATIONAL
comparisons
STANDARDS

Numbers 101 and higher

101	ciento uno	**1.000**	mil
200	doscientos/as	**1.100**	mil cien
300	trescientos/as	**2.000**	dos mil
400	cuatrocientos/as	**5.000**	cinco mil
500	quinientos/as	**100.000**	cien mil
600	seiscientos/as	**200.000**	doscientos mil
700	setecientos/as	**550.000**	quinientos cincuenta mil
800	ochocientos/as	**1.000.000**	un millón (de)
900	novecientos/as	**8.000.000**	ocho millones (de)

▶ As shown in the preceding chart, Spanish uses a period to indicate thousands and millions, rather than a comma as used in English.

▶ The numbers 200 through 999 agree in gender with the nouns they modify.

324 bolsas	605 sombreros
trescientas veinticuatro bolsas	seiscientos cinco sombreros

La bolsa cuesta ciento sesenta mil sucres.

▶ The word **mil**, which can mean *a thousand* and *one thousand*, is not usually used in the plural form when referring to numbers. **Un millón** (*a million* or *one million*), has the plural form **millones** in which the accent is dropped.

1.000 zapatos	25.000 faldas	2.000.000 de clientes
mil zapatos	veinticinco mil faldas	dos millones de clientes

▶ To express a more complex number, string together its component parts.

55.422
cincuenta y cinco mil cuatrocientos veintidós

¡INTÉNTALO! Give the Spanish equivalent of each number. The first item has been done for you.

1. **102** *ciento dos*
2. **5.000.000** cinco millones
3. **2001** dos mil uno
4. **1776** mil setecientos setenta y seis
5. **345** trescientos cuarenta y cinco
6. **550.300** quinientos cincuenta mil trescientos
7. **235** doscientos treinta y cinco
8. **1999** mil novecientos noventa y nueve
9. **113** ciento trece
10. **205** doscientos cinco
11. **17.123** diecisiete mil ciento veintitrés
12. **497** cuatrocientos noventa y siete

recursos

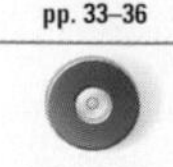
WB pp. 61–68

LM pp. 33–36

Lab CD/MP3 Lección 6

I CD-ROM Lección 6

vistahigher learning.com

¡LENGUA VIVA!

In Spanish, the years of dates (**fechas**) are not expressed as pairs of 2-digit numbers as they are in English (1979, *nineteen seventy-nine*): **1776, mil setecientos setenta y seis; 1945, mil novecientos cuarenta y cinco; 2001, dos mil uno.**

¡ATENCIÓN!

When **millón** or **millones** is used before a noun, the word **de** is placed between the two:

1.000.000 de hombres = un millón de hombres

12.000.000 de aviones = doce millones de aviones

•••

See **Estructura 2.4**, p. 57 to review the difference between **cien** and **ciento:**

100.000 = cien mil

2.101 = dos mil ciento uno

TEACHING OPTIONS

Game Ask students to stand up to create a number chain. The first student states the number 25. The next student says 50. Students continue the chain, using multiples of 25. If a student misses the next number in sequence, he or she must sit down. Continue play until only one student is left standing. If a challenge is required to break a tie, play the game with multiples of 30.

Pairs Ask students to create a list of nine items containing: both masculine and feminine nouns, three numerals in the hundreds, three in the thousands, and three in the millions. Once lists are completed, have students exchange them and read the items off their partner's list aloud. Partners should listen for the correct number and any agreement errors. Ex: **204 personas (doscientas cuatro personas)**

Práctica

1 **Completar** Complete the following sequences of numbers.

1. 50, 150, 250 ... 1.050 trescientos cincuenta, cuatrocientos cincuenta, quinientos cincuenta, seiscientos cincuenta, setecientos cincuenta, ochocientos cincuenta, novecientos cincuenta
2. 5.000, 20.000, 35.000 ... 95.000 cincuenta mil, sesenta y cinco mil, ochenta mil
3. 100.000, 200.000, 300.000 ... 1.000.000 cuatrocientos mil, quinientos mil, seiscientos mil, setecientos mil, ochocientos mil, novecientos mil
4. 100.000.000, 90.000.000, 80.000.000 ... 0 setenta millones, sesenta millones, cincuenta millones, cuarenta millones, treinta millones, veinte millones, diez millones

2 **Resolver** Read the math problems aloud and solve them.

+ más
− menos
= son

modelo

200 + 300 =
Doscientos más trescientos son quinientos.

1. 1000 + 753 = Mil más setecientos cincuenta y tres son mil setecientos cincuenta y tres.
2. 1.000.000 – 30.000 = Un millón menos treinta mil son novecientos setenta mil.
3. 10.000 + 555 = Diez mil más quinientos cincuenta y cinco son diez mil quinientos cincuenta y cinco.
4. 150 + 150 = Ciento cincuenta más ciento cincuenta son trescientos.
5. 100.000 + 205.000 = Cien mil más doscientos cinco mil son trescientos cinco mil.
6. 29.000 – 10.000 = Veintinueve mil menos diez mil son diecinueve mil.

Comunicación

3 **En la librería** In pairs look at the ad and answer the questions.

¡ATENCIÓN!

Note this difference between Spanish and English:
mil millones
a billion (1,000,000,000)
un billón
a trillion
(1,000,000,000,000)

¡Librería TU ACENTO tiene rebajas en toda la tienda!

Puedes comprar libros populares como:

El planeta rojo, 154 pesos, 210 páginas
Un billón de pesos y dónde lo gastan, 130 pesos, 455 páginas
Misterio en el almacén, 268 pesos, 379 páginas
Historia de la Segunda Guerra Mundial, 1939–1945, 324 pesos, 802 páginas
El béisbol: Pasión en La Habana, 249 pesos, 101 páginas
El loco del impermeable, 247 pesos, 290 páginas

1. ¿Qué libro tiene más páginas? ¿Cuántas tiene?
Historia de la Segunda Guerra Mundial, 1939–1945; 802 páginas
2. ¿Qué libro tiene menos (*least*) páginas? ¿Cuántas tiene?
El béisbol: Pasión en La Habana; 101 páginas
3. ¿Qué libro tiene una fecha en su título? ¿Cuál es la fecha?
Historia de la Segunda Guerra Mundial, 1939–1945
4. ¿Qué libro es más caro? ¿Cuánto cuesta?
Historia de la Segunda Guerra Mundial, 1939–1945; 324 pesos
5. ¿Qué libro es menos caro? ¿Cuánto cuesta?
Un billón de pesos y dónde lo gastan; 130 pesos
6. ¿Qué libro quieren ustedes comprar en la librería *Tu acento*? ¿Por qué?
Answers will vary
7. ¿Cuál es su libro favorito? ¿Cuántas páginas tiene?
Answers will vary

1 Suggestion Practice listening comprehension by having students read numbers from the activity to a partner, who writes them down.

1 Expansion Have pairs write three new number sequences like those in the activity. Then have them exchange their papers with another pair.

2 Expansion Have pairs convert one of the problems into a word problem. Ex: **Tengo doscientos dólares. Mi hermana tiene trescientos. ¿Cuántos dólares tenemos?**

3 Suggestion Ask questions about the ad before assigning the activity. Ex: **¿Dónde hay rebajas? (Hay rebajas en la librería *Tu acento*.) ¿Qué tipos de libros venden? (Venden libros de historia, de ciencia y de deportes.) ¿Cuánto cuestan los libros? (Cuestan entre 130 y 324 pesos.)**

3 Expansion Have small groups write a newspaper ad for a local business, incorporating numbers 101 and higher.

TEACHING OPTIONS

Heritage Speakers Ask heritage speakers to create a worksheet consisting of five math word problems for their classmates to complete. Have them read the problems to the class or a group of students, who, in turn, will solve the problems. They should also include an answer key to accompany their problems.

Large Groups Divide the class into groups of ten. Each person in each group is given a flashcard with a number 0–9. If one group is smaller, give the extra numbers to the group to distribute as necessary. Call out a number in which none of the digits is repeated. Students arrange themselves, showing their flashcard(s) to reflect the number you called out. Repeat with other numbers.

Section Goals

In **Estructura 6.2**, students will learn:

- to identify an indirect object noun
- how to use indirect object pronouns

Instructional Resources
WB/VM: Workbook, pp. 63–64
Lab Manual, p. 34
*Lab CD/MP3 **Lección 6***
*IRM: **¡Inténtalo! & Práctica** Answers, pp. 206–207; Tapescript, pp. 25–29*
Interactive CD-ROM
Companion website: www.vistahigherlearning.com
Presentations CD-ROM

Suggestions

- Write on the board: **Mi novio me escribe un mensaje electrónico.** Ask students what the direct object of the verb is. Then tell them that an indirect object is a noun or pronoun that answers the question *to or for whom or what?*
- Write the indirect object pronouns on the board. Ask how their forms differ from those of direct object pronouns.
- Ask volunteers to read aloud the video still captions, and have the class identify the indirect object pronoun in each. Have students identify the two indirect object nouns to which the pronoun refers.
- Point out that the redundant use of both an indirect object pronoun and an indirect object noun is common in Spanish and that, unlike in English, it is the indirect object noun that is optional, not the pronoun. Ex: **Ella le vende la ropa** is possible but **Ella vende la ropa a Elena** is less common.

6.2 Indirect object pronouns

ANTE TODO In **Lección 5**, you learned that a direct object is a noun or pronoun that receives the action of the verb directly. In contrast, indirect objects are nouns or pronouns that receive the action of the verb indirectly. Note the following example:

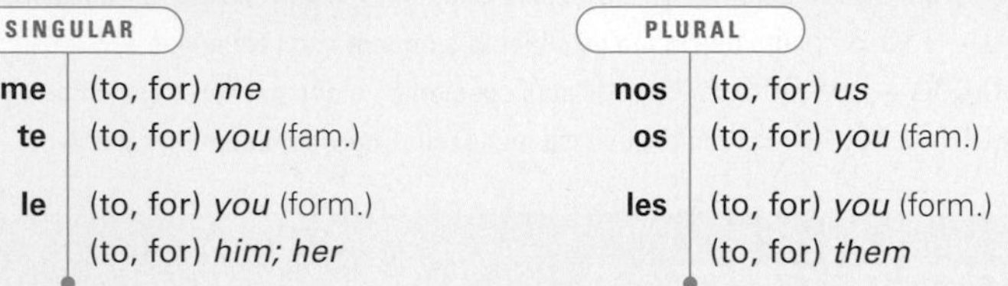

SUBJECT	I.O. PRONOUN	VERB	DIRECT OBJECT	INDIRECT OBJECT
Roberto	**le**	presta	cien pesos	**a Luisa**.
Roberto		*lends*	*100 pesos*	*to Luisa.*

An indirect object is a noun or pronoun that answers the question *to whom* or *for whom* an action is done. In the preceding example, the indirect object answers this question: **¿A quién le presta Roberto cien pesos?** *To whom does Roberto lend 100 pesos?*

Indirect object pronouns

SINGULAR		PLURAL	
me	(to, for) *me*	**nos**	(to, for) *us*
te	(to, for) *you* (fam.)	**os**	(to, for) *you* (fam.)
le	(to, for) *you* (form.) (to, for) *him; her*	**les**	(to, for) *you* (form.) (to, for) *them*

¡ATENCIÓN!
The forms of indirect object pronouns for the first and second persons (**me**, **te**, **nos**, **os**) are the same as the direct object pronouns.
Indirect object pronouns agree in number with the corresponding nouns, but not in gender.

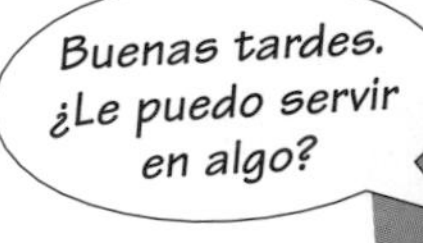

Buenas tardes.
¿Le puedo servir en algo?

Quiero comprarle una a mi hermana.

Using indirect object pronouns

▶ Spanish speakers commonly use both an indirect object pronoun and the noun to which it refers in the same sentence. This is done to emphasize and clarify to whom the pronoun refers.

Ella **le** (I.O. PRONOUN) vende la ropa a **Elena** (INDIRECT OBJECT).
Les (I.O. PRONOUN) prestamos el dinero a **Inés y Álex** (INDIRECT OBJECT).

▶ Indirect object pronouns are also used without the indirect object noun when the person for whom the action is being done is known.

Ana **le** presta la falda **a Elena**.
Ana lends her skirt to Elena.

También **le** presta unos bluejeans.
She also lends her a pair of blue jeans.

¡LENGUA VIVA!
There are many words used for jeans. Among them are **vaqueros**, **jeans**, **pantalones de mezclilla**, and **mahones**.

TEACHING OPTIONS

Extra Practice Write sentences like these on the board: **Ana te prepara unos tacos. Pablo no me escribe. Le presto dinero a Luisa. Les compramos unos regalos a los niños. María nos habla.** Ask students to come to the board and underline the direct objects and circle the indirect objects. If the indirect object is implied, have them write *I* next to the sentence.

Small Groups Have Student A "lend" an object to Student B and say: **Te presto mi...** Student B responds: **Me prestas tu...** Student C says: **Marcos le presta a Juana su...** Groups of three practice until everyone has begun the chain twice. Practice plural pronouns by having two groups join together and two students "lend" something to two other students.

- Indirect object pronouns are usually placed before the conjugated form of the verb. In negative sentences the pronoun is placed between **no** and the conjugated verb.

Martín **me** compra un regalo. *Martín buys me a gift.*	Eva **no me** escribe cartas. *Eva doesn't write me letters.*

¡ATENCIÓN!

When an indirect object pronoun is attached to a present participle, an accent mark is added to maintain the proper stress. For more information on accents, see **Pronunciación**, p. 111, **Ortografía**, p. 305, and p. 337.

- When a conjugated verb is followed by an infinitive or the present progressive, the indirect object pronoun may be placed before the conjugated verb or attached to the infinitive or present participle.

Él no quiere **pagarte**. *He does not want to pay you.*	Él está **escribiéndole** una postal a ella. *He is writing a postcard to her.*
Él no **te** quiere pagar. *He does not want to pay you.*	Él **le** está escribiendo una postal a ella. *He is writing a postcard to her.*

- Because the indirect object pronouns **le** and **les** have multiple meanings, Spanish speakers often clarify to whom the pronouns refer with the preposition **a** + [*pronoun*] or **a** + [*noun*].

UNCLARIFIED STATEMENTS	CLARIFIED STATEMENTS
Yo **le** compro un abrigo.	Yo **le** compro un abrigo **a él/ella/usted.**
Ella **le** describe un libro.	Ella **le** describe un libro **a Juan.**

UNCLARIFIED STATEMENTS	CLARIFIED STATEMENTS
Él **les** vende unos sombreros.	Él **les** vende unos sombreros a **ellos/ellas/ustedes.**
Ellos **les** hablan muy claro.	Ellos **les** hablan muy claro **a los clientes.**

- The irregular verb **dar** (*to give*), as well as **decir**, are often used with indirect object pronouns.

dar

Singular forms		Plural forms	
yo	**doy**	nosotros/as	**damos**
tú	**das**	vosotros/as	**dais**
Ud./él/ella	**da**	Uds./ellos/ellas	**dan**

¡ATENCIÓN!

Here are some common expressions with **dar**:
dar consejos *to give advice*
dar un regalo *to give a present*
dar una fiesta *to throw a party*

Mi abuela **me da** muchos regalos. *My grandmother gives me lots of gifts.*	**Te digo** la verdad. *I'm telling you the truth.*
Voy a **darle** consejos. *I'm going to give her advice.*	No **les digo** mentiras a mis padres. *I don't tell lies to my parents.*

CONSÚLTALO

Remember that **decir** is a stem-changing verb (**e:i**) with an irregular **yo** form: **digo**. To review the present tense of **decir**, see **Estructura 4.3**, p. 119.

¡INTÉNTALO! Use the cues in parentheses to provide the indirect object pronoun for the sentence. The first item has been done for you.

1. Juan __le__ quiere dar un regalo. (*to Elena*)
2. María __nos__ prepara un café. (*for us*)
3. Beatriz y Felipe __me__ escriben desde Cuba. (*to me*)
4. Marta y yo __les__ compramos unos guantes. (*for them*)
5. Los vendedores __te__ venden ropa. (*to you, fam. sing.*)
6. La dependienta __nos__ enseña los guantes. (*to us*)

Suggestions

- Point out that the position of indirect object pronouns in a sentence is the same as that of direct object pronouns.
- After going over the **¡Inténtalo!** orally with the class, ask students which items might require clarification (items 1 and 4). Ask them what they would add to each sentence in order to clarify **le** or **les**.
- As a comprehension check, have students write answers to these questions: **1. Necesitas comprar un regalo para tu mejor amigo. ¿Qué vas a comprarle? 2. ¿A quiénes les hablas todos los días? 3. ¿Quién te presta dinero cuando lo necesitas? 4. ¿Quién les está enseñando español a ustedes?**

TEACHING OPTIONS

Video Have students read along as you replay the **Fotonovela**. Ask them to note each time an indirect object pronoun is used. Point out that the pronouns used with the verb **gustar** are indirect objects because they answer the question *to whom?* Next, have students find each use of **le** and **les** and state to whom or what the pronouns refer.

Game Have students write a sentence with an indirect object pronoun. Each word is written on a separate slip of paper, then placed in an envelope. Students trade envelopes. After putting the sentences together, students write them down. Students continue trading envelopes and writing sentences. At the end of three minutes, the student with the most correctly deciphered sentences wins.

1 Suggestion Have students find the indirect object in each sentence and circle it.

1 Expansion Have students write four sentences about themselves modeled on those in the activity, leaving out the indirect object pronoun. Ex: **Yo ___ compro un regalo a mis padres. Mi tío ___ compra a mí una moto.** Then have them exchange papers and complete the sentences.

2 Expansion Have students convert three of their statements into questions for a partner using **¿Quién?, ¿A quién?,** and **¿Qué?** Ex: **¿Quién les vende la ropa? (el dependiente) ¿A quiénes les das regalos? (a mis primos) ¿Qué te explican tus padres? (los problemas)**

3 Suggestion Have students describe to a partner what they see in the photos. Ask them to describe not only the action, but also what the people look like physically and what they are wearing.

3 Expansion Divide the class into groups of four. Have each student pick a photo to present to the group as a verbal portrait. Each one should include an introductory sentence that sets the scene, followed by a body and conclusion. The verbal portrait should answer the questions *who, what, where, when,* and *why* with regard to what is seen in the photo. After everyone in the group has presented his or her photo, the group votes on which one to present to the class.

Práctica

1 **Completar** Fill in the correct pronouns to complete Mónica's description of her family's holiday shopping.

1. Juan y yo ___le___ damos una blusa a nuestra hermana Gisela.
2. Mi tía ___nos___ da a nosotros una mesa para la casa.
3. Gisela ___le___ da dos corbatas a su novio.
4. A mi mamá yo ___le___ doy un par de guantes negros.
5. A mi profesora ___le___ doy dos libros de José Martí.
6. Juan ___les___ da un regalo a mis padres.
7. Mis padres ___me___ dan a mí un traje nuevo.
8. Y a ti, yo ___te___ doy un regalo también. ¿Quieres verlo?

NOTA CULTURAL

Cuban writer and patriot **José Martí** (1853–1895) was born in **La Habana Vieja**, the old colonial center of Havana, Cuba. Founded by Spanish explorers in the early 1500s, Havana, along with San Juan, Puerto Rico, served as a major stopping point for the Spanish traveling to Mexico and South America in search of riches.

2 **Combinar** Use an item from each column and an indirect object pronoun to create logical sentences. Answers will vary.

modelo

Mis padres les dan regalos a mis primos.

A	B	C	D
Yo	comprar	correo electrónico	mí
El dependiente	dar	corbata	ustedes
El profesor Arce	decir	dinero en efectivo	clienta
La vendedora	escribir	ejercicio	la novia
Mis padres	explicar	problemas	mis primos
Tú	pagar	regalos	ti
Nosotros/as	prestar	ropa	nosotros
¿?	vender	¿?	¿?

3 **Describir** Describe what's happening in these photos based on the cues provided.

1. escribir / mensaje electrónico Álex le escribe un mensaje electrónico (a Ricardo).

2. mostrar / fotos Javier les muestra fotos (a Inés y Maite).

3. dar / documentos La Sra. Ramos le da los documentos (a Maite).

4. pedir / llaves Don Francisco le pide las llaves (a la empleada).

5. vender / suéter El vendedor le vende un suéter (a Javier).

6. comprar / bolsa Inés le compra una bolsa (a su hermana).

NOTA CULTURAL

Javier and Inés are shopping in the open-air market in Otavalo, Ecuador. **La Habana Vieja** (*Old Havana*), Cuba is the site of another well-known outdoor market. Located in the **Plaza de la Catedral**, it is a place where Cuban painters, artists, and sculptors sell their work, and other vendors offer handmade crafts and clothing.

TEACHING OPTIONS

Heritage Speakers Imagine that it's the holiday season. Ask heritage speakers to create a radio commercial for their favorite clothing store. Commercials should tell prospective customers what they can buy, for whom, and at what price.

Pairs Ask students to write five questions calling for an indirect object pronoun in the answer. Students ask their partners the questions, writing down their partner's answers. Students then review the questions and answers together to ensure that they were correct.

Comunicación

4 **Entrevista** Take turns with a classmate asking and answering questions using the word bank. Answers will vary.

modelo

escribir mensajes electrónicos
Estudiante 1: *¿A quién le escribes mensajes electrónicos?*
Estudiante 2: *Le escribo mensajes electrónicos a mi hermano.*

cantar canciones de amor (*love songs*)	escribir mensajes electrónicos
comprar ropa	pedir dinero
dar consejos	preparar comida (*food*) mexicana
decir mentiras	prestar dinero

5 **¡Somos ricos!** You and your classmates chipped in on a lottery ticket and you won! Now you want to spend money on your loved ones. In groups of three, discuss what each person is buying for family and friends. Answers will vary.

Estudiante 1: *Quiero comprarle un vestido de Carolina Herrera a mi madre.*
Estudiante 2: *Y yo voy a darles un carro nuevo a mis padres.*
Estudiante 3: *Voy a comprarles una casa a mis padres, pero a mis amigos no les voy a dar nada.*

NOTA CULTURAL

Carolina Herrera (1941–) is a Venezuelan fashion designer known worldwide for her elegant, understated designs. In the past two decades, she has become very successful and even has a fragrance line.

6 **Entrevista** Use these questions to interview a classmate. Answers will vary.

1. ¿Qué tiendas, almacenes o centros comerciales prefieres?
2. ¿A quién le compras regalos cuando hay rebajas?
3. ¿A quién le prestas dinero cuando esa persona lo necesita?
4. Quiero ir de compras. ¿Cuánto dinero me puedes prestar?
5. ¿Te dan tus padres su tarjeta de crédito cuando vas de compras?

Síntesis

7 **Minidrama** With two classmates, take turns playing the roles of two shoppers and a clerk in a clothing store. The shoppers should take turns talking about the articles of clothing they are looking for, for whom they are buying the clothes, and what they bought for the same people last year. The clerk should recommend several items based on the shoppers' descriptions. Answers will vary.

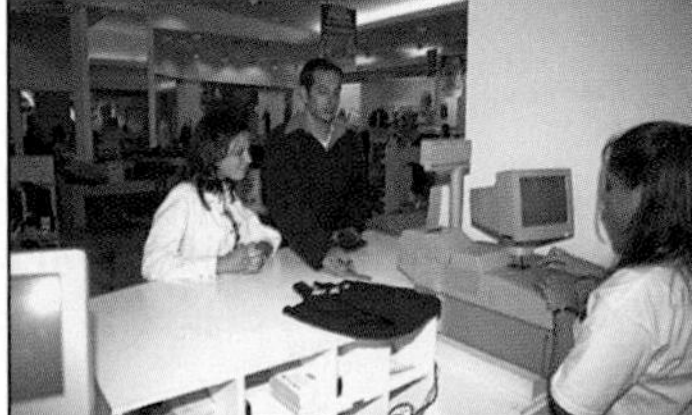

AYUDA

Here are some useful sentences in addition to the **Expresiones útiles** on p.175.

Me queda grande/pequeño.
It's big/small on me.

¿Tiene otro color?
Do you have another color?

¿Está en rebaja?
Is it on sale?

4 Expansion Give students five minutes to work in groups of three to brainstorm as many questions as they can using different forms of the verbs listed in the word bank. Invite two groups to come to the front of the class. Each group takes a turn asking the other its questions.

5 Expansion Have students research information about national lotteries in Spanish-speaking countries.

6 Expansion Take a class survey of the answers and write the results on the board.

7 Suggestions
- Have students rehearse their mini-dramas.
- Videotape the scenes in or outside of class.

TEACHING OPTIONS

Small Groups Have students write a conversation between two friends. One friend tries to convince the other to go shopping with him or her this weekend. The other friend explains that she can't and lists all the things she is going to do this weekend. Students should try to incorporate as many different indirect object pronouns in their conversations as possible.

Pairs Ask students to imagine they are going on an extended trip. Have them make a list of five things they are going to do (people they are going to write to, things they are going to buy for themselves or others, money they are going to borrow, etc.) before leaving. Ex: **Voy a comprarme unos zapatos nuevos.**

Section Goals

In **Estructura 6.3** students will learn:
- the preterite of regular verbs
- spelling changes in the preterite for verbs ending in **–car, –gar,** and **–zar**
- words commonly used with the preterite tense

Instructional Resources
WB/VM: Workbook, pp. 65–66
Lab Manual, p. 35
Lab CD/MP3 ***Lección 6***
IRM: ***¡Inténtalo! & Práctica*** *Answers, pp. 206–207; Tapescript, pp. 25–29*
Info Gap Activities Booklet, pp. 21–22
Interactive CD-ROM
Companion website: www.vistahigherlearning.com
Presentations CD-ROM

Suggestions
- Have students skim the captions for video stills 9 and 10 on page 175 and ask them what they mean. Guide students to see that these verbs describe actions that took place in the past.
- Introduce the preterite by describing some things you did yesterday, using the first-person preterite of known regular verbs. Use adverbs that signal the preterite (page 185) with your presentation. Ex: **Ayer compré una chaqueta nueva. Bueno, entré en el almacén y compré una de ellas. Y de repente, vi un sombrero. Decidí comprarlo también.** Each time you introduce a preterite form, write it on the board.
- After you have used several regular first-person preterites, expand by asking students questions. Ex: **Ayer compré un sombrero. Y tú, ____ , ¿qué compraste ayer? (Compré un libro.)** Ask other students about their classmates' answers. Ex: **¿Qué compró ____ ayer? (Compró un libro.)**

6.3 Preterite tense of regular verbs

NATIONAL
comparisons
STANDARDS

ANTE TODO In order to talk about events in the past, Spanish uses two simple tenses: the preterite and the imperfect. In this lesson, you will learn how to form the preterite tense, which is used to express actions or states completed in the past.

Preterite of regular *–ar, –er,* and *–ir* verbs

		–ar verbs **comprar**	*–er* verbs **vender**	*–ir* verbs **escribir**
SINGULAR FORMS	yo	compr**é** *I bought*	vend**í** *I sold*	escrib**í** *I wrote*
	tú	compr**aste**	vend**iste**	escrib**iste**
	Ud./él/ella	compr**ó**	vend**ió**	escrib**ió**
PLURAL FORMS	nosotros/as	compr**amos**	vend**imos**	escrib**imos**
	vosotros/as	compr**asteis**	vend**isteis**	escrib**isteis**
	Uds./ellos/ellas	compr**aron**	vend**ieron**	escrib**ieron**

¡ATENCIÓN!
The **yo** and **Ud./él/ella** forms of all three conjugations have written accents on the last syllable to show that it is stressed.

▶ As the preceding chart shows, the endings for regular **-er** and **-ir** verbs are identical in the preterite.

¿Qué compraste?

Compré esta bolsa.

▶ Note that the **nosotros/as** forms of regular **-ar** and **-ir** verbs in the preterite are identical to the present tense forms. Context will help you determine which tense is being used.

En invierno **compramos** la ropa en la tienda de la universidad.
In the winter, we buy clothing at the university store.

Anoche **compramos** unos zapatos de tenis y unas sandalias.
Last night we bought a pair of tennis shoes and a pair of sandals.

▶ **-Ar** and **-er** verbs that have a stem change in the present tense are regular in the preterite. They do *not* have a stem change.

	PRESENT	PRETERITE
cerrar (e:ie)	La tienda **cierra** a las seis.	La tienda **cerró** a las seis.
volver (o:ue)	Carlitos **vuelve** tarde.	Carlitos **volvió** tarde.
jugar (u:ue)	Él **juega** al fútbol.	Él **jugó** al fútbol.

¡ATENCIÓN!
-Ir verbs that have a stem change in the present tense also have a stem change in the preterite. You will learn about this in **Estructura 8.1**, p. 244.

TEACHING OPTIONS

Extra Practice For practice with discrimination between preterite forms, call out preterite forms of regular verbs and designate individuals to call out the corresponding subject pronoun. Ex: **comimos, creyeron, llegué, leíste, comenzamos, cerré, compraste, vendió.**

Pairs Have students tell their partners two things they did last week, two things their best friend did, and two things they did together. Each student then reports what his or her partner said to a member of another pair and listens to what that student reports.

Small Groups Give each group of five a list of verbs, including some with spelling changes. Student A chooses a verb from the list and gives the **yo** form. Student B gives the **tú** form, and so on. Students work their way down the list, alternating who begins the conjugation chain.

- Verbs that end in **-car**, **-gar**, and **-zar** have a spelling change in the first person singular (**yo** form) in the preterite.

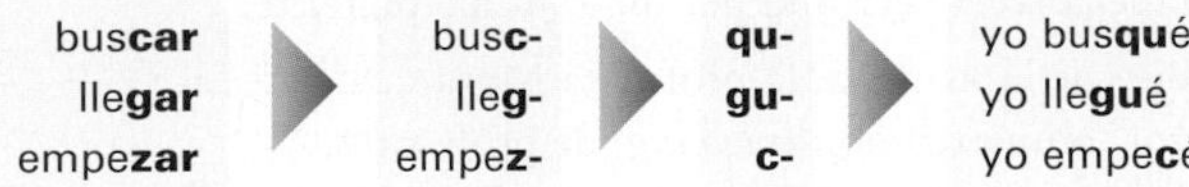

bus**car**	bus**c**-	**qu**-	yo bus**qué**
lle**gar**	lle**g**-	**gu**-	yo lle**gué**
empe**zar**	empe**z**-	**c**-	yo empe**cé**

- Except for the **yo** form, all other forms of **-car**, **-gar**, and **-zar** verbs are regular in the preterite.
- Three other verbs —**creer**, **leer**, and **oír** — have spelling changes in the preterite. The **i** of the verb endings of **creer**, **leer**, and **oír** carries an accent in the **yo, tú, nosotros/as,** and **vosotros/as** forms, and changes to **y** in the **Ud./él/ella** and **Uds./ellos/ellas** forms.

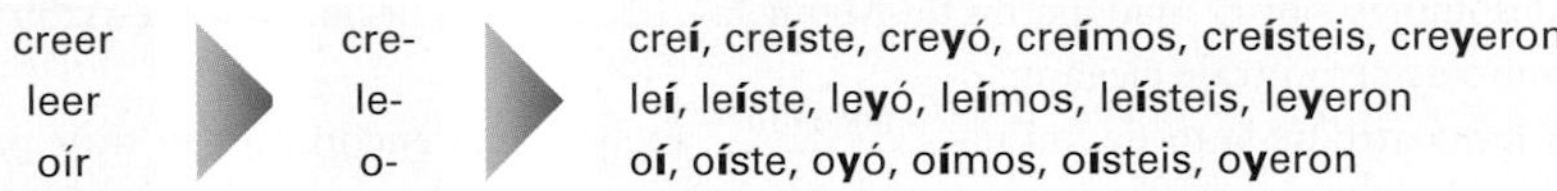

creer	cre-	cre**í**, cre**í**ste, cre**y**ó, cre**í**mos, cre**í**steis, cre**y**eron
leer	le-	le**í**, le**í**ste, le**y**ó, le**í**mos, le**í**steis, le**y**eron
oír	o-	o**í**, o**í**ste, o**y**ó, o**í**mos, o**í**steis, o**y**eron

- **Ver** is regular in the preterite, but none of its forms has an accent. **ver** → vi, viste, vio, vimos, visteis, vieron.

Words commonly used with the preterite

anoche	*last night*	**pasado/a (*adj.*)**	*last; past*
anteayer	*the day before yesterday*	**el año pasado**	*last year*
		la semana pasada	*last week*
ayer	*yesterday*	**una vez**	*once; one time*
de repente	*suddenly*	**dos veces**	*twice; two times*
desde... hasta...	*from... until...*	**ya**	*already*

Ayer llegué a Santiago de Cuba.
Yesterday I arrived in Santiago de Cuba.

Anoche oí un ruido extraño.
Last night I heard a strange noise.

- **Acabar de** + [*infinitive*] is used to say that something has just occurred. Note that **acabar** is in the present tense in this construction.

Acabo de comprar una falda.
I just bought a skirt.

Acabas de ir de compras.
You just went shopping.

¡INTÉNTALO! Provide the appropriate preterite forms of the verbs. The first item in each column has been done for you.

celebrar	comer	salir	comenzar
1. Elena celebró.	1. Los niños comieron.	1. Tú y yo salimos.	1. Ustedes comenzaron.
2. Yo celebré.	2. Tú comiste.	2. Ella salió.	2. Nosotras comenzamos.
3. Los chicos celebraron.	3. Usted comió.	3. Pablo y Elena salieron.	3. Yo comencé.
4. Emilio y yo celebramos.	4. Nosotros comimos.	4. Nosotros salimos.	4. Marcos comenzó.
5. Tú celebraste.	5. Yo comí.	5. Yo salí.	5. Tú comenzaste.

Suggestions

- Practice verbs with spelling changes in the preterite by asking students about things they read, heard, and saw yesterday. Ex: **¿Leíste el periódico ayer? ¿Quiénes vieron el pronóstico del tiempo? Yo oí que va a llover hoy. ¿Qué oyeron ustedes?**
- Use magazine pictures to demonstrate **acabar de**. Ex: **¿Quién acaba de ganar? (Tiger Woods acaba de ganar.) ¿Qué acaban de ver ellos? (Acaban de ver un fantasma.)**

TEACHING OPTIONS

Game Divide the class into teams of six, arranged in rows. Call out the infinitive of a verb. The first person writes the **yo** form on a sheet of paper and passes it to the second person, who writes the **tú** form. The third writes the **él/ella/Ud.** form, and so on. The sixth checks spelling. If all forms are correct, the team gets a point. Continue play, starting with a different person each time. The team with the most points after six rounds wins.

Extra Practice Have students write five things they did yesterday. Ask students questions about what they did to elicit as many different conjugations as possible. Ex: **Carlos, ¿leíste el periódico ayer? ¿Quién más leyó el periódico ayer?... Carlos y Ana, ustedes dos leyeron el periódico ayer, ¿verdad? Clase, ¿quiénes leyeron el periódico ayer?**

1 Expansion Ask questions about Andrea's weekend. Have students answer with complete sentences. Ex: **¿Quién asistió a una reunión? ¿Qué compraron los amigos?**

2 Suggestion After item 8 have pairs switch roles and repeat the activity.

2 Expansion Have students redo the activity, using **Uds.** as the subject of the questions and **nosotros** in the answers.

3 Suggestions
- Have students work with a partner to quickly review the preterite forms of the verbs in the activity.
- Divide the class into groups of four. Give students five minutes to see how many different sentences they can write. Have groups exchange their work with another group for peer editing. The group with the most sentences free of errors wins.

Práctica

1 **Completar** Andrea is talking about what happened last weekend. Complete each sentence by choosing the correct verb and putting it in the preterite.

1. El sábado a las diez de la mañana, la profesora Mora asistió (asistir, costar, usar) a una reunión (*meeting*) de profesores.
2. A la una, yo llegué (llegar, bucear, llevar) a la tienda con mis amigos.
3. Mis amigos y yo compramos (comprar, regatear, gastar) dos o tres cosas.
4. Yo compré (costar, comprar, escribir) unos pantalones negros y mi amigo Mateo compró (gastar, pasear, comprar) una camisa azul.
5. Después, nosotros comimos (llevar, vivir, comer) cerca de un mercado.
6. A las nueve, Pepe habló (hablar, pasear, nadar) con su novia por teléfono.
7. El sábado por la tarde, mi mamá les escribió (escribir, beber, vivir) una carta a nuestros parientes en Cuba.
8. El domingo por la mañana mi tía Manuela decidió (decidir, salir, escribir) comprarme un traje elegante.
9. A las cuatro de la tarde, mi tía encontró (beber, salir, encontrar) un traje para mí y después vimos (acabar, ver, salir) una película.

2 **Preguntas** Imagine that you have a pesky friend who keeps asking you questions. Respond that you already did or have just done what he/she asks.

modelo

leer la lección
Estudiante 1: *¿Leíste la lección?*
Estudiante 2: *Sí, ya la leí./Sí, acabo de leerla.*

1. escribir el correo electrónico
   —¿Escribiste el correo electrónico?
   —Sí, ya lo escribí./Acabo de escribirlo.
2. lavar (*to wash*) la ropa
   —¿Lavaste la ropa?
   —Sí, ya la lavé./Acabo de lavarla.
3. oír las noticias (*news*)
   —¿Oíste las noticias?
   —Sí, ya las oí./Acabo de oírlas.
4. comprar pantalones cortos
   —¿Compraste pantalones cortos?
   —Sí, ya los compré./Acabo de comprarlos.
5. practicar los verbos
   —¿Practicaste los verbos?
   —Sí, ya los practiqué./Acabo de practicarlos.
6. pagar la cuenta (*bill*)
   —¿Pagaste la cuenta?
   —Sí, ya la pagué./Acabo de pagarla.
7. empezar la composición
   —¿Empezaste la composición?
   —Sí, ya la empecé./Acabo de empezarla.
8. ver la película *Buena Vista Social Club*
   —¿Viste la película *Buena Vista Social Club*?
   —Sí, ya la vi./Acabo de verla.

NOTA CULTURAL

The **Buena Vista Social Club** is a musical phenomenon that has been taking the world by storm since the group's rise to stardom in the 1990s. A number of Cuban musicians, popular decades earlier but almost forgotten, recorded a Grammy-winning album of traditional Cuban music. Later, a film based on their comeback story was released, along with subsequent albums featuring not only the group's music, but also individual members' solo performances.

3 **Combinar** Combine words and phrases from each column to talk about what you and others did. Be sure to use the correct form of each verb. Answers will vary.

modelo

Mis amigos y yo llegamos tarde a clase una vez.

yo	ver televisión	anoche
mi compañero/a de cuarto	hablar con un(a) chico/a guapo/a	anteayer
mis amigos y yo	llevar un traje/vestido	ayer
mi mejor (*best*) amigo/a	comprar ropa nueva	la semana pasada
mis padres	leer un buen libro	el año pasado
el/la profesor(a) de español	llegar tarde a clase	una vez
el presidente de los Estados Unidos	gastar mucho dinero	dos veces
	compartir ropa	

TEACHING OPTIONS

Heritage Speakers Ask heritage speakers to imagine they have just visited an open-air market for the first time. Have them write a letter to a friend describing what they saw and did in the market. Then, ask students to exchange their letters with another person who will respond to them.

TPR Have groups of three students write out three sentences that use verbs in the preterite, with a verb from a different conjugation in each sentence. After they have finished writing, have each group mime its sentences for the class. When someone guesses the mimed action, the group writes its sentence on the board.

Comunicación

4 **Las vacaciones** Imagine that you took these photos on a vacation with friends. Get together with a partner and use the pictures to tell him or her about your trip. Answers will vary.

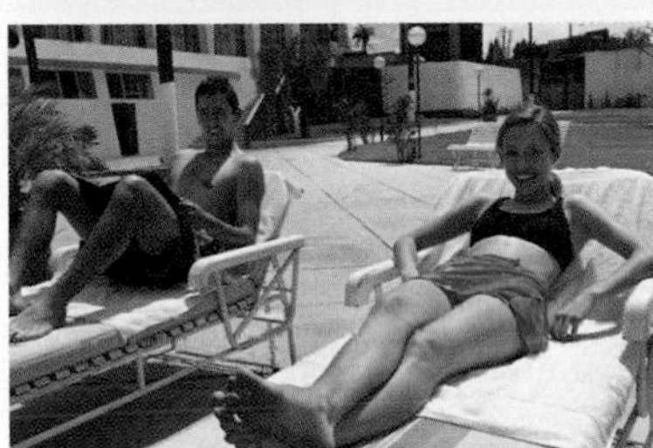

5 **El fin de semana** Your instructor will give you and your partner different incomplete charts about what four employees at **Almacén Gigante** did last weekend. After you fill out the chart based on each other's information, you will fill out the final column about your partner. Answers will vary.

Síntesis

6 **Conversación** Get together with a partner and have a conversation about what you did last week using verbs from the word bank. Don't forget to include school activities, shopping, and pastimes. Answers will vary.

acampar	comer	gastar	tomar
asistir	comprar	hablar	trabajar
bailar	correr	jugar	vender
beber	escribir	leer	ver
buscar	estudiar	oír	viajar

4 Suggestion Have students first state where they traveled and when. Then have them identify the people in the photos, stating their names and their relationship to them and describing their personality. Finally, students should tell what everyone did on the trip.

4 Expansion After completing the activity orally, have partners write a paragraph about their vacation, basing their account on the photos.

5 Suggestion Divide the class into pairs and distribute the Info Gap Handouts from the Info Gap Activities Booklet that correspond to this activity. Give the students ten minutes to complete this activity.

5 Expansion Have students tell the class about any activities that both their partner and one of the **Almacén Gigante** employees did. Ex: **La señora Zapata leyó un libro y mi compañero/a, _____, también. Los dos leyeron un libro.**

6 Suggestion Have volunteers rehearse their conversation, then present it to the class.

6 Expansion Have volunteers report orally to the class what their partners did last week.

TEACHING OPTIONS

Large Group Have students create a story chain about a student who had a very bad day. Begin the story by saying: **Ayer, Rigoberto pasó un día desastroso.** Call on a student at one corner of the class to continue the story by telling how Rigoberto began his day. The second person tells what happened next. Different students continue adding sentences until only one student remains. That person must conclude the story.

Extra Practice Have students make a "to do" list at the beginning of their day. Then, ask students to return to their list at the end of the day and write sentences stating which activities they completed. Ex: **limpiar mi habitación; No, no limpié mi habitación.**

Section Goal

In **Estructura 6.4** students will learn to use demonstrative adjectives and pronouns.

Instructional Resources
WB/VM: Workbook, pp. 67–68
Lab Manual, p. 36
Lab CD/MP3 ***Lección 6***
IRM: ***¡Inténtalo!*** *&* ***Práctica*** *Answers, pp. 206–207; Tapescript, pp. 25–29*
Info Gap Activities Booklet, pp. 23–24
Interactive CD-ROM
Companion website: www.vistahigherlearning.com
Presentations CD-ROM

Suggestions

- Point to the book on your desk. Say: **Este libro está en la mesa.** Point to a book on a student's desk. Say: **Ese libro está encima del escritorio de** ___. Then point to a book on the window ledge. Say: **Aquel libro está cerca de la ventana**. Follow the same procedure with **tiza, papeles,** and **plumas**.
- Point out that although the masculine singular forms **este** and **ese** do not end in **–o**, their plural forms end in **–os**: **estos, esos**.
- Hold up or point to objects and have students give the plural: **este libro, esta mochila, este traje, este zapato.** Repeat with forms of **ese** and **aquel** with other nouns.

6.4 Demonstrative adjectives and pronouns

NATIONAL
comparisons
STANDARDS

Demonstrative adjectives

ANTE TODO In Spanish, as in English, demonstrative adjectives are words that "demonstrate" or "point out" nouns. Demonstrative adjectives precede the nouns they modify and, like other Spanish adjectives you have studied, agree with them in gender and number. Observe these, then study the following chart.

esta camisa	**ese** vendedor	**aquellos** zapatos
this shirt	*that salesman*	*those shoes (over there)*

Demonstrative adjectives

Singular		Plural		
MASCULINE	FEMININE	MASCULINE	FEMININE	
este	**esta**	**estos**	**estas**	*this; these*
ese	**esa**	**esos**	**esas**	*that; those*
aquel	**aquella**	**aquellos**	**aquellas**	*that; those (over there)*

- There are three sets of demonstrative adjectives. To determine which one to use, you must establish the relationship between the speaker and the noun(s) being pointed out.
- The demonstrative adjectives **este, esta, estos,** and **estas** are used to point out nouns that are close to the speaker and the listener.

Me gustan estos zapatos.

- The demonstrative adjectives **ese, esa, esos,** and **esas** are used to point out nouns that are not close in space and time to the speaker. They may, however, be close to the listener.

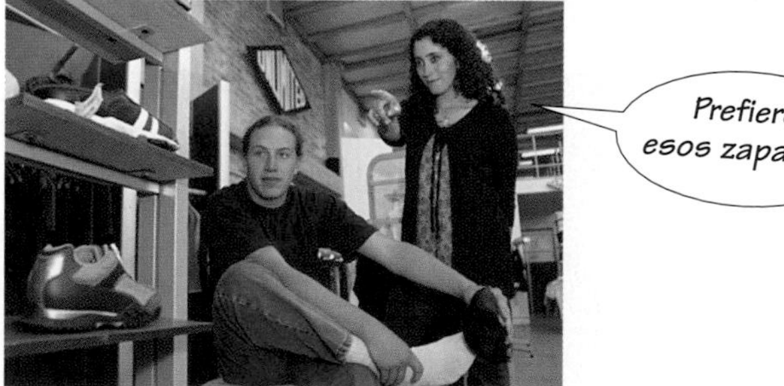
Prefiero esos zapatos.

TEACHING OPTIONS

Extra Practice Hold up one or two items of clothing or classroom objects. Have students write all three forms of the demonstrative pronouns that would apply. Ex: **estos zapatos, esos zapatos, aquellos zapatos.**

Pairs Refer students to **Contextos** on pages 170–171. Have them work with a partner to comment on the articles of clothing pictured. Ex: **Este suéter es bonito, ¿no? (No, ese suéter no es bonito. Es feo.)** or **Aquella camiseta es muy cara. (Sí, aquella camiseta es cara.)**

▶ The demonstrative adjectives **aquel, aquella, aquellos,** and **aquellas** are used to point out nouns that are far away from the speaker and the listener.

Aquel auto es de mi hermana.

Demonstrative pronouns

▶ Demonstrative pronouns are identical to their corresponding demonstrative adjectives, with the exception that they carry an accent mark on the stressed vowel.

—¿Quieres comprar **este suéter**?
Do you want to buy this sweater?

—No, no quiero **éste**. Quiero **ése**.
No, I don't want this one. I want that one.

—¿Vas a leer **estas revistas**?
Are you going to read these magazines?

—Sí, voy a leer **éstas**. También voy a leer **aquéllas**.
Yes, I'm going to read these. I'll also read those (over there).

Demonstrative pronouns

Singular		Plural	
MASCULINE	FEMININE	MASCULINE	FEMININE
éste	**ésta**	**éstos**	**éstas**
ése	**ésa**	**ésos**	**ésas**
aquél	**aquélla**	**aquéllos**	**aquéllas**

¡ATENCIÓN!

Like demonstrative adjectives, demonstrative pronouns agree in gender and number with the corresponding noun.

Este libro es de Pablito.

Éstos son de Juana.

▶ There are three neuter demonstrative pronouns: **esto**, **eso**, and **aquello**. These forms refer to unidentified or unspecified nouns, situations, ideas, and concepts. They do not change in gender or number and never carry an accent mark.

—¿Qué es **esto**?
What's this?

—**Eso** es interesante.
That's interesting.

—**Aquello** es bonito.
That's pretty.

¡INTÉNTALO! Provide the correct form of the demonstrative adjective for these nouns. The first item has been done for you.

1. la falda / este ___esta falda___
2. los estudiantes / este ___estos estudiantes___
3. los países / aquel ___aquellos países___
4. la ventana / ese ___esa ventana___
5. los periodistas / ese ___esos periodistas___
6. las empleadas / ese ___esas empleadas___
7. el chico / aquel ___aquel chico___
8. las sandalias / este ___estas sandalias___
9. el autobús / ese ___ese autobús___
10. las chicas / aquel ___aquellas chicas___

Suggestions

- Present the demonstrative pronouns by engaging students in short conversations about classroom objects and items of clothing. Ex: Pick up a student's backpack and ask him or her: **¿Es ésta mi mochila? (No, ésta es mi mochila.)** Turn to another student and ask about the same backpack: **¿Es ésa mi mochila? (No, ésa es la mochila de ___.)** Point to a pencil you have placed on the windowsill. Ask: **¿Es aquél tu lápiz? (No, aquél es su lápiz.)**
- To practice the neuter forms, write these expressions on the board: **¡Eso es fenomenal!**, **¡Esto es horrible!**, **¡Esto es estupendo!**, and **¿Qué es esto?** Then state situations and have students respond to them with one of the expressions. Situations: **Voy a cancelar el próximo examen. Voy a comprar un traje nuevo de color morado. La cafetería va a cerrar los lunes, miércoles y viernes. Aquí te tengo un regalo. Los coches están prohibidos en el campus.**
- Redo the **¡Inténtalo!** activity a second time, using demonstrative pronouns.

TEACHING OPTIONS

Small Groups Ask students to bring in fashion magazines. Have students work in groups of three to give their opinions about the clothing they see in the magazines. Students should tell which items they like and which they don't, using demonstrative adjectives and pronouns when giving their opinions.

Video Have students listen for the use of demonstrative pronouns as you replay the **Fotonovela**. Ask students to write each pronoun and the noun it refers to. Then, have students look at the transcript of the **Fotonovela** to see if they were correct.

1 Expansion Have students expand each sentence with a phrase that includes a demonstrative pronoun. Ex: **Aquellos sombreros son muy elegantes, pero éstos son más baratos.**

2 Suggestions
- Have students underline the nouns to which the demonstrative pronouns will refer.
- When you go over the activity, write each demonstrative pronoun on the board so students may verify that they have placed the accent marks correctly.

3 Expansions
- Divide the class into teams, then call out a color. The first team to find an object or article of clothing in the classroom and use the correct form of a demonstrative adjective or pronoun to express it gets one point. (Ex: **¡Aquella chaqueta es morada!**) Continue with other colors.
- Ask students to find a photo featuring different articles of clothing or to draw several articles of clothing. Have them write five statements like that of the **Estudiante 1** model in part one of this activity. Then have students exchange their statements and photo/drawing with a partner to write responses like that of the **Estudiante 2** model.

Práctica

1 Cambiar Make the singular sentences plural and the plural sentences singular.

modelo
Estas camisas son blancas.
Esta camisa es blanca.

1. Aquellos sombreros son muy elegantes. Aquel sombrero es muy elegante.
2. Ese abrigo es muy caro. Esos abrigos son muy caros.
3. Estos cinturones son hermosos. Este cinturón es hermoso.
4. Esos precios son muy buenos. Ese precio es muy bueno.
5. Estas faldas son muy cortas. Esta falda es muy corta.
6. ¿Quieres ir a aquel almacén? ¿Quieres ir a aquellos almacenes?
7. Esas blusas son baratas. Esa blusa es barata.
8. Esta corbata hace juego con mi traje. Estas corbatas hacen juego con mi traje.

2 Completar Here are some things people might say while shopping. Complete the sentences with the correct demonstrative pronouns.

1. No me gustan esos zapatos. Voy a comprar ___éstos___. (*these*)
2. ¿Vas a comprar ese traje o ___éste___? (*this one*)
3. Esta guayabera es bonita pero prefiero ___ésa___. (*that one*)
4. Estas corbatas rojas son muy bonitas pero ___ésas___ son fabulosas. (*those*)
5. Estos cinturones cuestan demasiado. Prefiero ___aquéllos___. (*those over there*)
6. ¿Te gustan esas botas o ___éstas___? (*these*)
7. Esa bolsa roja es bonita pero prefiero ___aquélla___. (*that one over there*)
8. No voy a comprar estas botas, voy a comprar ___aquéllas___. (*those over there*)
9. ¿Prefieres estos pantalones o ___ésos___? (*those*)
10. Me gusta este vestido pero voy a comprar ___ése___. (*that one*)
11. Me gusta ese almacén pero ___aquél___ es mejor (*better*). (*that one over there*)
12. Esa blusa es bonita pero cuesta demasiado. Voy a comprar ___ésta___. (*this one*)

NOTA CULTURAL

The **guayabera** is a men's shirt typically worn in some parts of the Caribbean. Never tucked in, it is casual wear, but variations exist for more formal occasions, such as weddings, parties, or the office.

3 Describir With your partner, look for two items in the classroom that are one of these colors: **amarillo, azul, blanco, marrón, negro, verde, rojo.** Take turns pointing them out to each other, first using demonstrative adjectives, and then demonstrative pronouns. Answers will vary.

modelo
azul
Estudiante 1: *Esta silla es azul. Aquella mochila es azul.*
Estudiante 2: *Ésta es azul. Aquélla es azul.*

Now use demonstrative adjectives and pronouns to discuss the colors of your classmates' clothing. One of you can ask a question about an article of clothing, using the wrong color. Your partner will correct you and point out that color somewhere else in the room.

modelo
Estudiante 1: *¿Esa camisa es negra?*
Estudiante 2: *No, ésa es azul. Aquélla es negra.*

TEACHING OPTIONS

Heritage Speakers Have students role-play a scene between friends out shopping for clothes. Student A tries to convince the friend that the clothes he or she wants to buy are not attractive. Student A suggests other items of clothing, but the friend does not agree. Students should use as many demonstrative adjectives and pronouns as possible.

Game Post pictures of different versions of the same object (Ex: sedan, sports car, all-terrain vehicle) on the board. Assign each a dollar figure. Team A guesses the price of each object, using demonstrative adjectives and pronouns. Team B either agrees or guesses a higher or lower price. The team that guesses the closest price, wins. Ex: **Este carro cuesta $20.000, ése cuesta $35.000 y aquél cuesta $18.000.**

Comunicación

4 **Conversación** With a classmate, use demonstrative adjectives and pronouns to ask each other questions about the people around you. Use words and expressions from the word bank and/or your own ideas. Answers will vary.

¿Cómo se llama...?	¿Cuántos años tiene(n)...?
¿Cómo es (son)...?	¿A qué hora...?
¿De quién es (son)...?	¿Cuándo...?
¿De dónde es (son)...?	¿Qué clases toma(n)...?

modelo

Estudiante 1: *¿Cómo se llama esa chica?*
Estudiante 2: *Se llama Rebeca.*
Estudiante 1: *¿A qué hora llegó aquel chico a la clase?*
Estudiante 2: *A las nueve.*

5 **En una tienda** Imagine that you and a classmate are in Madrid shopping at **Zara**. Study the floor plan, then have a conversation about what you see around you. Use demonstrative adjectives and pronouns as much as possible. Answers will vary.

modelo

Estudiante 1: *Me gusta este suéter azul.*
Estudiante 2: *Yo prefiero aquella chaqueta.*

NOTA CULTURAL

Zara is an international company based in Spain. It manufactures clothing and accessories for men, women, and children and also markets a popular fragrance line. While Zara makes both casual and sophisticated clothing, it is better known for its trendy, classy style that appeals to young professional women.

Síntesis

6   **Diferencias** Your instructor will give you and a partner each a drawing of a department store. They are almost identical, but not quite. Use demonstrative adjectives and pronouns to find seven differences.

modelo

Estudiante 1: *Aquellos lentes de sol son feos, ¿verdad?*
Estudiante 2: *No. Aquellos lentes de sol son hermosos.*

4 Suggestion Challenge both partners to ask a question for each item in the word bank and to ask at least one other question using an interrogative expression that is not included.

5 Expansion Divide students into groups of three to role-play a scene between a salesperson and two customers. The customers should ask about the different items of clothing pictured and the salesperson will answer. They talk about how the items fit and their cost. The customers then express their preferences and decide which items to buy.

6 Suggestion Divide the class into pairs and distribute the Info Gap Handouts from the Info Gap Activities Booklet that correspond to this activity. Give the students ten minutes to complete this activity.

6 Expansion Have pairs work together with another pair to compare the seven responses that confirmed the seven differences. Ex: **No. Aquellos lentes de sol no son feos. Aquéllos son hermosos**. Ask a few groups to share some of the sentences with the class.

TEACHING OPTIONS

Pairs Ask students to write a conversation between two people sitting at a busy sidewalk café in the city. They are watching the people who walk by, asking each other questions about what the passersby are doing, and making comments on their clothing. Students should use as many demonstrative adjectives and pronouns as possible in their conversations. Invite several pairs to present their conversation to the whole class.

Small Groups Ask students to bring in pictures of their families, a sports team, a group of friends, etc. Have them take turns asking about and identifying the people in the pictures.
Ex: **—¿Quién es aquella mujer? (¿Cuál?)**
—Aquélla con la camiseta roja. (Es mi...)

Section Goals

In **Lectura** students will:

- learn to skim a text
- use what they know about text format to predict a document's content
- read a text rich in cognates and recognizable format elements

Instructional Resource
Companion website:
www.vistahigherlearning.com

Estrategia Tell students that they can often predict the content of an unfamiliar document in Spanish by skimming it and looking for recognizable format elements.

Examinar el texto Have students skim the text at the top of the ad. Point out the cognate **Liquidación** and the series of percentages. Ask them to predict what type of document it is. (advertisement for a liquidation sale) Then ask students to scan the rest of the ad.

Buscar cognados Ask volunteers to point out cognates they notice.

Impresiones generales Ask students to sum up their general impression of the document by answering the three questions at the bottom.

Lectura

Antes de leer

Estrategia
Skimming

Skimming involves quickly reading through a document to absorb its general meaning. This allows you to understand the main ideas without having to read word for word. When you skim a text, you might want to look at its title and subtitles. You might also want to read the first sentence of each paragraph.

Examinar el texto

Look at the format of the reading selection. How is it organized? What does the organization of the document tell you about its content?

Buscar cognados

Scan the reading selection to locate at least five cognates. Based on the cognates, what do you think the reading selection is about?

1. ____________
2. ____________
3. ____________
4. ____________
5. ____________

The reading selection is about ____________.

Impresiones generales

Now skim the reading selection to understand its general meaning. Jot down your impressions. What new information did you learn about the document by skimming it? Based on all the information you now have, answer these questions.

1. Who produced this document?
2. What is its purpose?
3. Who is its intended audience?

¡Real° Liquidación° en Corona!

¡Grandes rebajas!

¡La rebaja está de moda en Corona!

SEÑORAS	CABALLEROS
Falda larga **ROPA BONITA** Algodón. De cuadros y rayas Talla mediana **Precio especial: $8.000**	**Pantalones** **OCÉANO** Colores blanco, azul y café Ahora: $11.550 **30% de rebaja**
Blusas de seda **BAMBÚ** Seda. De cuadros y de lunares Ahora: $21.000 **40% de rebaja**	**Zapatos** **COLOR** Italianos y franceses Números del 40 al 45 **Sólo $20.000 el par**
Sandalias de playa **GINO** Números del 35 al 38 Ahora: $12.000 el par **50% de rebaja**	**Chaqueta** **CASINO** Microfibra. Colores negro, blanco y gris Tallas P-M-G-XG **Ahora: $22.500**
Carteras **ELEGANCIA** Colores anaranjado, blanco, rosado y amarillo Ahora: $15.000 **50% de rebaja**	**Traje inglés** **GALES** Modelos originales Ahora: $105.000 **30% de rebaja**
Vestido de algodón **PANAMÁ** Colores blanco, azul y verde Ahora: $18.000 **30% de rebaja**	**Ropa interior** **ATLÁNTICO** Talla mediana Colores blanco, negro, gris **40% de rebaja**

Lunes a sábado de 9 a 21 horas.
Domingo de 10 a 14 horas.

TEACHING OPTIONS

Heritage Speakers Ask heritage speakers to create an ad for one or two items of clothing. Have them use the **¡Real Liquidación en Corona!** advertisement as a model. Have them share their ads with the class. Discuss the ads with the whole class.

Small Groups Have small groups of students work together to write a cloze paragraph about shopping for clothing, modeled on the **Completar** paragraph. Ask each group member to contribute two sentences to the paragraph. Then have the group make a clean copy, omitting several words or phrases, and writing the omitted words and phrases below the paragraph. Each group then exchanges its paragraph with another group, which, in turn, completes it. Finally, the groups that exchanged paragraphs get together to check and discuss the completed paragraphs.

¡Corona tiene las ofertas más locas del verano!

30% 40% 50%

La tienda más elegante de la ciudad con precios increíbles y con la tarjeta de crédito más conveniente del mercado.

JÓVENES	NIÑOS
Bluejeans chicos y chicas **PACOS** Americanos. Tradicional Ahora: $9.000 el par **30% de rebaja**	Vestido de niña **GIRASOL** Tallas de la 2 a la 12. De cuadros y rayas Ahora: $8.625 **30% de rebaja**
Suéteres **CARAMELO** Algodón y lana. Colores blanco, gris y negro Antes: $10.500 **Ahora: $6.825**	Pantalón deportivo de niño **MILÁN** Tallas de la 4 a la 16 Ahora: $13.500 **30% de rebaja**
Lentes de contacto **VISIÓN** Americanos. Colores azul, verde y morado Antes: $15.000 el par **Ahora $10.000**	Zapatos de tenis **ACUARIO** Números del 20 al 25 Ahora: $15.000 el par **30% de rebaja**
Trajes de baño chicos y chicas **SUBMARINO** Microfibra. Todas las tallas Ahora: $12.500 **50% de rebaja**	Pantalones cortos **MACARENA** Talla mediana Ahora: $15.000 **30% de rebaja**
Gafas de sol **VISIÓN** Origen canadiense Antes: $23.000 **Ahora: $14.950**	Camisetas de algodón **POLO** Antes: $15.000 Ahora: $7.500 **50% de rebaja**

Por la compra de $40.000, puede llevar un regalo gratis.

- Un hermoso cinturón de señora
- Un par de calcetines
- Una corbata de seda
- Una bolsa para la playa
- Una mochila
- Unas medias

real *royal* liquidación *clearance sale* antes *before*

Después de leer

Completar

Complete this paragraph about the reading selection with the correct forms of the words from the word bank.

almacén	hacer juego	tarjeta de crédito
caro	increíble	tienda
dinero	pantalones	verano
falda	rebaja	zapato

En este anuncio de periódico el almacén Corona anuncia la liquidación de verano con grandes rebajas en todos los departamentos. Con muy poco dinero usted puede equipar a toda su familia. Si no tiene dinero en efectivo, puede utilizar su tarjeta de crédito y pagar luego. Para el caballero con gustos refinados, hay zapatos importados de París y Roma. La señora elegante puede encontrar blusas de seda que hacen juego con todo tipo de pantalones/faldas o faldas/pantalones. Los precios de esta liquidación son realmente increíbles.

¿Cierto o falso?

Indicate whether each statement is **cierto** or **falso**. Correct the false statements.

1. Hay ropa de algodón para jóvenes.
   Cierto.
2. La ropa interior tiene una rebaja del 30%.
   Falso. Tiene una rebaja del 40%.
3. El almacén Corona tiene un departamento de zapatos.
   Cierto.
4. Normalmente las sandalias cuestan $22.000 el par.
   Falso. Normalmente cuestan $24.000.

Preguntas

Answer these questions in Spanish. Answer will vary.

1. Imagina que vas a ir a la tienda Corona. ¿Qué departamentos vas a visitar? ¿el departamento de ropa para señoras, el departamento de ropa para caballeros...?
2. ¿Qué vas a buscar en Corona?
3. ¿Hay tiendas similares a la tienda Corona en tu pueblo o ciudad? ¿Cómo se llaman? ¿Tienen muchas gangas?

Completar Have students quickly review the lesson vocabulary on pages 170–171 before they do this activity. Make sure that they understand the meaning of **dinero en efectivo** and **el caballero de gustos refinados.**

¿Cierto o falso? Present these as items 5–8. **5. Las camisetas Polo no tienen una rebaja grande. (Falso. Tienen una rebaja del 50%.) 6. Hay regalos con compras de $40.000. (Cierto.) 7. El almacén Corona está cerrado los domingos. (Falso. El almacén Corona está abierto de 10:00 a 14:00 los domingos.) 8. Se puede conseguir lentes de contacto verdes y morados en rebaja. (Cierto.)**

Preguntas Have small groups put together an ad for a store where they shop. Have them use the **Almacén Corona** ad as a model. If two or more groups chose the same store, compare their ads in a follow-up discussion with the class.

TEACHING OPTIONS

TPR Write items of clothing on slips of paper. Divide the class into two teams. Have a member of one team draw a slip. That team member mimes putting on the item of clothing. The other team guesses what it is. Give points for correct answers. The team with the most points wins.

Variación léxica Ask heritage speakers to tell the class phrases they use to ask the price of items. Ex: **¿Cuánto vale?**

Game Ask students to work in pairs to play a game of **Diez preguntas**. Partner A thinks of an item of clothing. Partner B asks questions and guesses the name of the item. Partner A keeps track of the number of questions and guesses. Allow partners to ask a total of ten questions and attempt to guess three times before moving on to the next item. The pair with the fewest questions overall wins.

Section Goals

In **Escritura** students will:

- conduct an interview
- integrate vocabulary and structures taught in **Lección 6** into a written report
- report on an interview

Estrategia Model how to answer questions in an interview by playing the role of an interviewee. Have students be interviewers, asking you the questions on this page. Allow recording so students can transcribe the interview. Then choose volunteers to report orally on the interview, either transcribing the interview verbatim, summarizing it, or summarizing it and quoting you occasionally.

Tema Tell students that they may interview another member of their class or they may interview a Spanish-speaking student they know. Encourage them to take notes as they conduct the interview or tape record it. They might want to work with a classmate they are not going to interview to brainstorm the questions. Introduce terms such as **entrevista, entrevistar, diálogo,** and **citas** as you present the activity.

Escritura

Estrategia

How to report an interview

There are several ways to prepare a written report about an interview. For example, you can transcribe the interview verbatim, you can simply summarize it, or you can summarize it but quote the speakers occasionally. In any event, the report should begin with an interesting title and a brief introduction, which may include the five W's (*what, where, when, who, why*) and the H (*how*) of the interview. The report should end with an interesting conclusion. Note that when you transcribe dialogue in Spanish, you should pay careful attention to format and punctuation.

Writing dialogue in Spanish

- If you need to transcribe an interview verbatim, you can use speakers' names to indicate a change of speaker.

CARMELA ¿Qué compraste? ¿Encontraste muchas gangas?

ROBERTO Sí, muchas. Compré un suéter, una camisa y dos corbatas. Y tú, ¿qué compraste?

CARMELA Una blusa y una falda muy bonitas. ¿Cuánto costó tu camisa?

ROBERTO Sólo diez dólares. ¿Cuánto costó tu blusa?

CARMELA Veinte dólares.

- You can also use a dash (*raya*) to mark the beginning of each speaker's words.

—¿Qué compraste?
—Un suéter y una camisa muy bonitos. Y tú, ¿encontraste muchas gangas?
—Sí... compré dos blusas, tres camisetas y un par de zapatos.
—¡A ver!

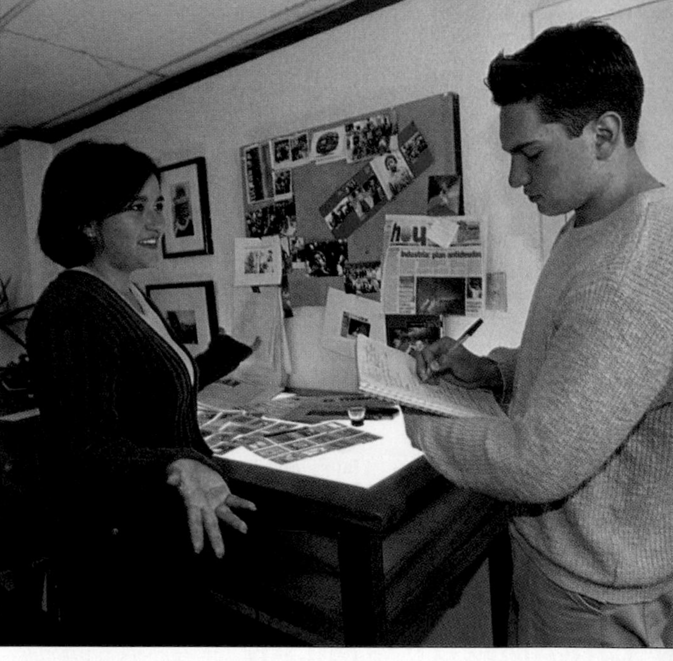

Tema

Escribe un informe

Write a report for the school newspaper about an interview you conducted with a student about his or her shopping habits and clothing preferences. First, brainstorm a list of interview questions. Then conduct the interview using the questions below as a guide, but feel free to ask other questions as they occur to you.

Examples of questions:

- ¿Cuándo vas de compras?
- ¿Adónde vas de compras?
- ¿Con quién vas de compras?
- ¿Qué tiendas, almacenes o centros comerciales prefieres?
- ¿Compras ropa de catálogos o por Internet?
- ¿Prefieres comprar ropa cara o barata? ¿Por qué? ¿Te gusta buscar gangas?
- ¿Qué ropa llevas cuando vas a clase?
- ¿Qué ropa llevas cuando sales a bailar?
- ¿Qué ropa llevas cuando practicas un deporte?
- ¿Cuáles son tus colores favoritos? ¿Compras mucha ropa de esos colores?
- ¿Les das ropa a tu familia o a tus amigos/as?

TEACHING OPTIONS

Proofreading Activity Copy the following interview questions and answers containing mistakes onto the board or a transparency as a proofreading activity to do with the whole class.

1. **Este blusa me costó veinte dólores y esta veinticinco.**
2. **Luis no creó que los pantalones cuestaron sólo treinta dólares.**
3. **Ayer buscé gangas en el almacén Corona pero no encuentré nada interestante.**
4. **¿Cuál prefieres, éste sombrero elegante pero caro o aquello sombrero barato?**
5. **No compré me nada ayer pero pensé comprar un par de bluejeans hoy.**
6. **El dependiente quiere le vender los zapatos caros pero mi tío busca aquéllas en rebaja.**

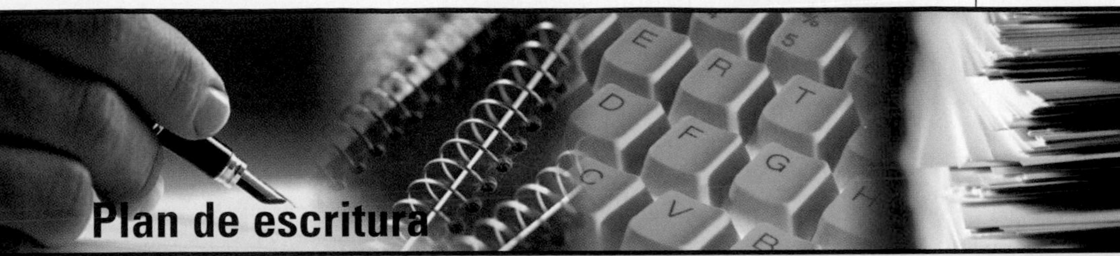

Plan de escritura

1 Ideas y organización

First, brainstorm a title for the report as well as ideas for how to introduce and present the information. Then use an idea map to help you organize your ideas, taking into account the variety of question words your interview answers. Finally, develop an outline for your report, organizing the interview questions in a logical order.

2 Primer borrador

Using your idea map and outline from **Ideas y organización,** write the rough draft of your report. Be sure that you have included an interesting introduction and conclusion.

3 Comentario

Exchange papers with a classmate and comment on each other's work using the questions below as a guide. Begin by mentioning one or two points that you like about the person's report, such as the title, the introduction, the conclusion, or the questions the interviewer asked.

a. Does the title capture your interest?
b. Are the introduction and conclusion adequate?
c. Is the report organized in a logical fashion?
d. Do you have suggestions for making the report more interesting?
e. Do you see spelling or grammatical errors?

4 Redacción

Revise your first draft, keeping in mind your classmate's comments. Also incorporate any new ideas or information you may have. Before handing in the final version, review your work using these guidelines:

a. Underline each verb and make sure that it agrees with the subject and that you have used the correct tense.
b. Check the gender and number of each article, noun, and adjective.
c. Circle the object pronouns and verify that you have used the correct form.
d. Check your spelling and punctuation, consulting your **Anotaciones para mejorar la escritura.**

5 Evaluación y progreso

Working in groups of four, share your papers. Give the title "best" or "most" to each paper on the basis of its strongest points. For example, "best use of Spanish," "most interesting questions," etc. After your instructor returns your paper, review the comments and corrections. Note the most important issues on your **Anotaciones para mejorar la escritura** list in your **carpeta.**

Comentario

- Go over questions a–e with the whole class so peer readers understand their task. Then have pairs of students exchange reports. Allow five minutes for reading and comments.
- Have students prepare **Redacción** as homework. Ask them to rewrite their drafts incorporating the peer comments and following the directions in **Redacción**.

Evaluación y progreso Give groups fifteen minutes to exchange and comment on the final drafts of their reports. Then have students hand them in.

Writing Sample Here is a sample report on an interview that would constitute superior writing achievement.

¡Cómo conseguir una ganga!

Roberto Álvarez habló con Gloria Becerra sobre cómo buscar las gangas. Vamos a ver cómo Gloria encuentra gangas fabulosas.

RA: Gloria, tú compras muchas cosas a precios muy bajos. ¿Cómo lo haces?

GB: Voy a los mercados al aire libre y a las tiendas de centros comerciales.
RA: ¿Te gusta regatear?
GB: Sí, me gusta mucho. Y voy a las tiendas cuando hay liquidaciones. Siempre hay gangas.
RA: ¿Cómo sabes de las liquidaciones?
GB: Voy de compras muchas veces por mes. También leo el periódico y escucho la radio.
RA: Gracias, Gloria. ¿Puedo ir de compras contigo?
GB: ¡Sí, vamos!

Después de esta entrevista, el periodista salió para el centro comercial Soles con Gloria Becerra. ¡Veamos las rebajas!

EVALUATION: Informe

Criteria	Scale
Content	1 2 3 4 5
Organization	1 2 3 4 5
Accuracy	1 2 3 4 5
Creativity	1 2 3 4 5

Scoring	
Excellent	18–20 points
Good	14–17 points
Satisfactory	10–13 points
Unsatisfactory	< 10 points

Section Goals

In **Escuchar** students will:
- listen for specific linguistic cues in oral sentences
- answer questions based on a recorded conversation

Instructional Resources
Textbook CD
IRM: Tapescript, p. 90

Estrategia
Script 1. Acabamos de pasear por la ciudad y encontramos unos monumentos fenomenales. 2. Estoy haciendo las maletas. 3. Carmen y Alejandro decidieron ir a un restaurante. 4. Mi familia y yo vamos a ir a la playa.

Suggestion Ask students to look at the photo of Marisol and Alicia and predict what they are talking about.

Ahora escucha
Script MARISOL: Oye, Alicia, ¿qué estás haciendo?
ALICIA: Estudiando no más. ¿Qué hay de nuevo?
M: Acabo de comprarme esos pantalones que andaba buscando.
A: ¿Los encontraste en el centro comercial? ¿Y cuánto te costaron?
M: Míralos. ¿Te gustan? En el almacén Melo tienen tremenda rebaja. Como estaban baratos me compré una blusa también. Es de cuadros pero creo que hace juego con los pantalones por el color rojo. ¿Qué piensas?
A: Es de los mismos colores que la falda y la blusa que llevaste cuando fuimos al cine anoche. La verdad es que te quedan muy bien esos colores. ¿No encontraste unos zapatos y un cinturón para completar el juego?
M: No lo digas ni de chiste. Mi tarjeta de crédito está que no aguanta más. Y trabajé poco la semana pasada. ¡Acabo de gastar todo el dinero para la semana!
A: ¡Ay, chica! Fui al centro comercial el mes pasado y encontré unos zapatos muy, pero muy de moda. Muy caros... pero buenos. No me los compré porque no los tenían en mi número. Voy a comprarlos cuando lleguen más.... el vendedor me va a llamar.
M: Ajá... ¿Y va a invitarte a salir con él?
A: ¡Ay! ¡No seas así! Ven, vamos al café. Te ves muy bien y no hay que gastar eso aquí.
M: De acuerdo. Vamos.

Escuchar

Estrategia

Listening for linguistic cues

You can enhance your listening comprehension by listening for specific linguistic cues. For example, if you listen for the endings of conjugated verbs, or for familiar constructions, such as **acabar de** + [*infinitive*] or **ir a** + [*infinitive*], you can find out whether an event already took place, is taking place now, or will take place in the future. Verb endings also give clues about who is participating in the action.

To practice listening for linguistic cues, you will now listen to four sentences. As you listen, note whether each sentence refers to a past, present, or future action. Also jot down the subject of each sentence.

Preparación

Based on the photograph at right, what do you think Marisol has recently done? What do you think Marisol and Alicia are talking about? What else can you guess about their conversation from the visual clues in the photograph?

Ahora escucha 

Now you are going to hear Marisol and Alicia's conversation. Make a list of the clothing items that each person mentions. Then put a check mark after the item if the person actually purchased it.

Marisol	Alicia
1. pantalones ✓	1. falda
2. blusa ✓	2. blusa
3. ______	3. zapatos
4. ______	4. cinturón

recursos
TEXT CD
Lección 6

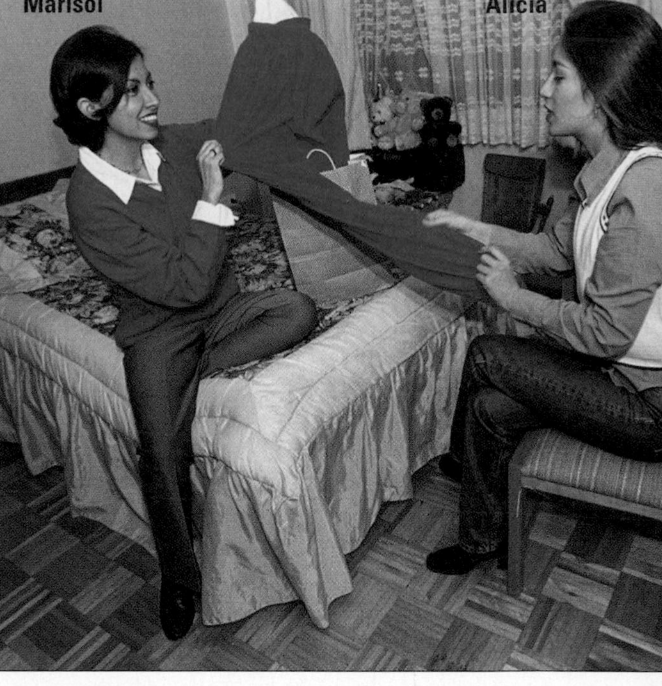

Comprensión

¿Cierto o falso?

Indicate whether each statement is **cierto** or **falso**. Then correct the false statements.

1. Marisol y Alicia acaban de ir de compras juntas (*together*). Falso. Marisol acaba de ir de compras.
2. Marisol va a comprar unos pantalones y una blusa mañana. Falso. Marisol ya los compró.
3. Marisol compró una blusa de cuadros. Cierto.
4. Alicia compró unos zapatos nuevos hoy. Falso. Alicia va a comp unos zapatos nuev
5. Alicia y Marisol van a ir al café. Cierto.
6. Marisol gastó todo el dinero de la semana en ropa nueva. Cierto.

Preguntas

Discuss the following questions with a classmate. Be sure to explain your answers. Answers will vary.

1. ¿Crees que Alicia y Marisol son buenas amigas? ¿Por qué?
2. ¿Cuál de las dos estudiantes es más ahorradora (*frugal*)? ¿Por qué?
3. ¿Crees que a Alicia le gusta la ropa que Marisol compró?
4. ¿Crees que la moda es importante para Alicia? ¿Para Marisol? ¿Por qué?
5. ¿Es importante para ti estar a la moda? ¿Por qué?

Proyecto

Prepara un plan de negocios°

Imagine that you are opening a store in Miami that will cater to customers of Cuban heritage. In order to get a start-up loan, you have to write and present your business plan to the bank.

1 Prepara el plan

Develop a business plan to present your idea to your banker. Using the research tools found in **Recursos para la investigación,** choose a location in Miami for your store. You should also choose the products you are going to sell and select a name that will appeal to your clientele. Your business plan might include these elements:

- The name and location of the store
- A visual presentation of your products
- The prices of your products and your expected profits
- An explanation of why you think your store will be successful

2 Presenta la información

You are meeting with your banker to summarize your business plan. Greet him or her in a formal, businesslike manner. Explain your business plan to the banker. You may want to show photographs or drawings of products and explain why the products will sell. Ask your banker for his or her reaction to your plan.

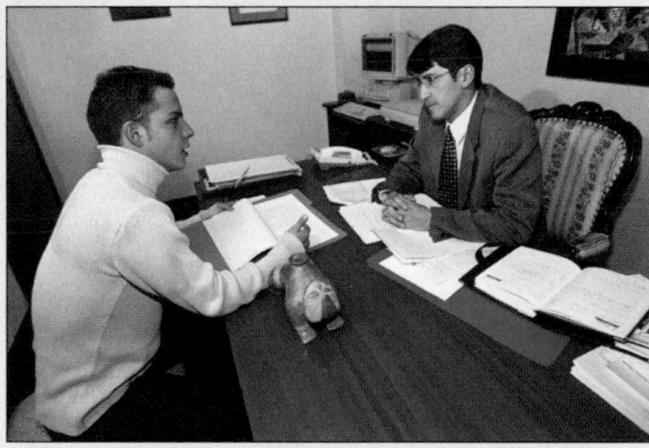

recursos para la investigación

 **Internet** Palabras clave: Miami, Cuban, stores, business	 **Comunidad** Students, faculty members, and residents of your community who are of Cuban heritage or who are from Miami
 **Biblioteca** Almanacs, newspapers, magazines	 **Otros recursos** Maps of Cuba or books about Cuba that may suggest a name for the store

negocios *business*

Section Goals

In **Proyecto** students will:

- use Spanish as they carry out research and interact with the wider world
- write and present a business plan for a store in Miami to cater to Cuban customers

Suggestion Students might need a week to complete the project, so at the beginning of that time period, have them open their books to this page and glance over **Proyecto**. Explain that they are going to write a business plan (**plan de negocios**) to acquire a bank loan (**préstamo bancario**) and present the plan to the bank.

Prepara el plan

- Students may acquire templates for business plans from local offices of the Small Business Administration or SCORE (Service Corps of Retired Executives), or download them from business-related sites on the Internet.
- Remind students that they should address business contacts with **Uds.** forms.

EVALUATION: Plan de negocios

Criteria	Scale
Content	1 2 3 4
Organization	1 2 3 4
Accuracy	1 2 3 4
Oral presentation	1 2 3 4
Creativity	1 2 3 4

Scoring	
Excellent	18–20 points
Good	14–17 points
Satisfactory	10–13 points
Unsatisfactory	< 10 points

Section Goal

In **Panorama,** students will read about the geography, culture, and economy of Cuba.

Instructional Resources
Transparencies, #3, #4, #30
WB/VM: Workbook, pp. 69–70;
Video Activities, pp. 259–260
***Panorama cultural** DVD/Video*
Interactive CD-ROM
IRM: Videoscript, p. 129
Companion website:
www.vistahigherlearning.com
Presentations CD-ROM

Suggestion Ask students to look at the map or project **Transparency #30.** Ask volunteers to read the captions on each call-out. Then discuss the call-out photos with the class.

The Affective Dimension
Some students may have strong feelings about Cuba. Ask your students to discuss their feelings.

El país en cifras

- After reading about **La Habana Vieja**, if possible, show students illustrations of this part of the city. See *National Geographic en Español,* June 1999, pages 36–45 for dramatic photos.
- Draw attention to the design and colors of the Cuban flag. Compare the Cuban flag to the Puerto Rican flag (page 166). Explain that Puerto Rico and Cuba, the last Spanish colonies in the western hemisphere, both gained their independence from Spain in 1898 in part through the intervention of the United States.

¡Increíble pero cierto! Due to the patterns of evolution and adaptation common to islands, Cuba has many examples of unique flora and fauna. Students may wish to research other examples.

Cuba

El país en cifras

- **Área:** 110.860 km^2 (42.803 millas^2), *aproximadamente el área de Pensilvania*
- **Población:** 11.369.000
- **Capital:** La Habana—2.306.000

La Habana Vieja fue declarada° Patrimonio° Cultural de la Humanidad por la UNESCO en 1982. Este distrito es uno de los lugares más fascinantes de Cuba. En La Plaza de Armas, se puede visitar el majestuoso Palacio de Capitanes Generales, que ahora es un museo. En la calle° Obispo, frecuentada por el autor Ernest Hemingway, hay hermosos cafés, clubes nocturnos y tiendas elegantes.

- **Ciudades principales:** Santiago de Cuba—446.000; Camagüey—294.000; Holguín—242.000; Guantánamo—208.000

SOURCE: Population Division, UN Secretariat

- **Moneda:** peso cubano
- **Idiomas:** español (oficial)

Bandera de Cuba

Cubanos célebres

- **Carlos Finlay,** doctor y científico (1833–1915)
- **José Martí,** político y poeta (1853–1895)
- **Fidel Castro,** primer ministro, comandante en jefe° de las fuerzas armadas (1926–)
- **Zoé Valdés,** escritora (1959–)

recursos

WB pp. 69–70	VM pp. 259–260	I CD-ROM Lección 6	vistahigher learning.com

fue declarada *was declared* Patrimonio *Heritage* calle *street* comandante en jefe *commander in chief* liviano *light* colibrí abeja *hummingbird bee* ave *bird* mundo *world* miden *measure* pesan *weigh*

¡Increíble pero cierto!

Pequeño y liviano°, el colibrí abeja° de Cuba es una de las 320 especies de colibrí, y es también el ave° más pequeña del mundo°. Menores que muchos insectos, estas aves minúsculas miden° 5 centímetros y pesan° sólo 1,95 gramos.

TEACHING OPTIONS

Variación léxica An item of clothing that you will see everywhere if you visit Cuba (or any of the other countries bordering the Caribbean) is the **guayabera**. A loose-fitting, short-sleeved shirt made of natural fibers, the **guayabera** is perfect for hot, humid climates. **Guayaberas** generally have large pockets and may be decorated with embroidery. They are worn open at the neck and never tucked in.

Extra Practice Introduce students to two stanzas of José Martí's poem **"Versos sencillos."** Some students may recognize these as verses from the song **"Guantanamera."**

Yo soy un hombre sincero
de donde crece la palma;
y, antes de morirme, quiero
echar mis versos del alma.

Yo vengo de todas partes,
y hacia todas partes voy;
arte soy entre las artes;
en los montes monte soy.

Baile • Ballet Nacional de Cuba

La bailarina Alicia Alonso fundó el Ballet Nacional de Cuba en 1948, después de° convertirse en una estrella° internacional en el Ballet de Nueva York y en Broadway. El Ballet Nacional de Cuba es famoso en todo el mundo por su creatividad y perfección técnica.

Economía • La caña de azúcar y el tabaco

La caña de azúcar° es el producto agrícola más cultivado° de la isla y su exportación es muy importante para la economía del país. El tabaco, que se usa para fabricar los famosos puros° cubanos, es otro cultivo de mucha importancia.

Historia • Los taínos

Los taínos eran° una de las tres tribus indígenas que vivían° en la isla cuando llegaron los españoles en el siglo XV. Los taínos también vivían en Puerto Rico, la República Dominicana, Haití, Trinidad, Jamaica y en partes de las Bahamas y la Florida.

Música • Celia Cruz

La cantante Celia Cruz (1924-2003) es considerada la reina° de la música salsa. Su carrera empezó en Cuba en los años cincuenta. Aunque° Celia Cruz salió de Cuba en 1960, siempre cantó en español. Su forma de cantar atrae a oyentes° de todo el mundo. Ganó un *Grammy* en 1990.

¿Qué aprendiste? Responde a las preguntas con una frase completa.

1. ¿Quién es el líder del gobierno de Cuba? El líder de Cuba es Fidel Castro.
2. ¿Qué autor está asociado con la Habana Vieja? Ernest Hemingway está asociado con la Habana Vieja.
3. ¿Por qué es famoso el Ballet Nacional de Cuba? Es famoso por su creatividad y perfección técnica.
4. ¿Cuáles son los dos cultivos más importantes para la economía cubana? Los cultivos más importantes son la caña de azúcar y el tabaco.
5. ¿Qué fabrican los cubanos con la planta del tabaco? Los cubanos fabrican puros.
6. ¿Quiénes son los taínos ? Son una tribu indígena.
7. ¿Cuándo empezó Celia Cruz su carrera musical? Empezó su carrera en los años cincuenta.

Conexión Internet Investiga estos temas en el sitio **www.vistahigherlearning.com.**

1. Busca información sobre un(a) cubano/a célebre. ¿Por qué es célebre? ¿Qué hace? ¿Todavía vive en Cuba?
2. Busca información sobre una de las ciudades principales de Cuba. ¿Qué atracciones hay en esta ciudad?

después de *after* estrella *star* caña de azúcar *sugar cane* cultivado *grown* puros *cigars* eran *were* vivían *lived* reina *queen* Aunque *Although* atrae a oyentes *attracts listeners*

Ballet Nacional de Cuba Although the **Ballet Nacional de Cuba** specializes in classical dance, Cuban popular dances (**habanera, mambo, rumba**) have gained worldwide popularity. Students can interview parents or others to see what they remember about Cuban dances.

La caña de azúcar y el tabaco The collapse of the Soviet bloc and the end of subsidies that sustained its economy dealt Cuba a blow. Since 1990, Cuba has been in **el período especial en tiempo de paz**. Government planners have decided to develop tourism, formerly seen as bourgeois and corrupting, as a means of gaining badly-needed foreign currency.

Los taínos The Taínos had a deep understanding of the use of native plants for medicinal purposes. Traditional Taíno healing arts have been preserved and handed down across generations in Cuba. Today, ethnobotanists are exploring this traditional knowledge as they search for modern medical resources.

Celia Cruz Bring in some of Celia Cruz's music for students to hear. Read song titles and make predictions about songs before listening to them, then confirm and revise predictions.

Conexión Internet Students will find supporting Internet activities and links at **www.vistahigherlearning.com**.

TEACHING OPTIONS

Variación léxica Some Cuban songs mention beings with names that don't sound Spanish, such as **Obatalá, Eleggúa,** and **Babaluayé**. These are divinities (**orichas**) of the Afro-Cuban religion, which has its origins in Yoruba-speaking West Africa. Forcibly converted to Catholicism upon their arrival in Cuba, Africans developed a syncretized religion in which they worshiped the gods they had brought from Africa in the form of Catholic saints. Babaluayé, for instance, is worshiped as **San Lázaro**. Obatalá is **Nuestra Señora de las Mercedes**. Cuban popular music is deeply rooted in the songs and dances with which Afro-Cubans expressed their devotion to the **orichas.** It is not surprising then that these gods should be so frequently invoked in this music.

Instructional Resources
Vocabulary CD
Lab Manual, p. 36
Lab CD/MP3 ***Lección 6***
IRM: Tapescript, pp. 25–29
Testing Program: ***Pruebas****, pp. 61–72;* ***Exámenes****, pp. 241–251*
Testing Program Audio CD
Test Files CD-ROM

La ropa

el abrigo	*coat*
los bluejeans	*jeans*
la blusa	*blouse*
la bolsa	*purse; bag*
la bota	*boot*
el calcetín	*sock*
la camisa	*shirt*
la camiseta	*t-shirt*
la cartera	*wallet*
la chaqueta	*jacket*
el cinturón	*belt*
la corbata	*tie*
la falda	*skirt*
las gafas (de sol), las gafas (oscuras)	*(sun)glasses*
los guantes	*gloves*
el impermeable	*raincoat*
los lentes de contacto	*contact lenses*
los lentes (de sol)	*(sun)glasses*
las medias	*pantyhose; stockings*
los pantalones	*pants*
los pantalones cortos	*shorts*
la ropa	*clothing; clothes*
la ropa interior	*underwear*
la sandalia	*sandal*
el sombrero	*hat*
el suéter	*sweater*
el traje	*suit*
el traje (de baño)	*(bathing) suit*
el vestido	*dress*
los zapatos de tenis	*tennis shoes, sneakers*

Ir de compras

el almacén	*department store*
la caja	*cash register*
el centro comercial	*shopping mall*
el/la cliente/a	*customer*
el/la dependiente/a	*clerk*
el dinero	*money*
(en) efectivo	*cash*
el mercado (al aire libre)	*(open-air) market*
un par de zapatos	*a pair of (shoes)*
el precio (fijo)	*(fixed; set) price*
la rebaja	*sale*
el regalo	*gift*
la tarjeta de crédito	*credit card*
la tienda	*shop; store*
el/la vendedor(a)	*salesperson*
costar (o:ue)	*to cost*
gastar	*to spend (money)*
hacer juego (con)	*to match (with)*
llevar	*to wear; to take*
pagar	*to pay*
regatear	*to bargain*
usar	*to wear; to use*
vender	*to sell*

Adjetivos

barato/a	*cheap*
bueno/a	*good*
cada	*each*
caro/a	*expensive*
corto/a	*short (in length)*
elegante	*elegant*
hermoso/a	*beautiful*
largo/a	*long (in length)*
loco/a	*crazy*
nuevo/a	*new*
otro/a	*other; another*
pobre	*poor*
rico/a	*rich*

Los colores

el color	*color*
amarillo/a	*yellow*
anaranjado/a	*orange*
azul	*blue*
blanco/a	*white*
gris	*gray*
marrón, café	*brown*
morado/a	*purple*
negro/a	*black*
rojo/a	*red*
rosado/a	*pink*
verde	*green*

Palabras adicionales

acabar de (+ inf.)	*to have just done something*
anoche	*last night*
anteayer	*the day before yesterday*
ayer	*yesterday*
de repente	*suddenly*
desde	*from*
dos veces	*twice; two times*
hasta	*until*
pasado/a (*adj.*)	*last; past*
el año pasado	*last year*
la semana pasada	*last week*
prestar	*to lend; to loan*
una vez	*once; one time*
ya	*already*

Numbers 101 and higher	*See page 178.*
Indirect object pronouns	*See page 180.*
***Dar* expressions**	*See page 181.*
Demonstrative adjectives and pronouns	*See page 188.*
Expresiones útiles	*See page 175.*

recursos

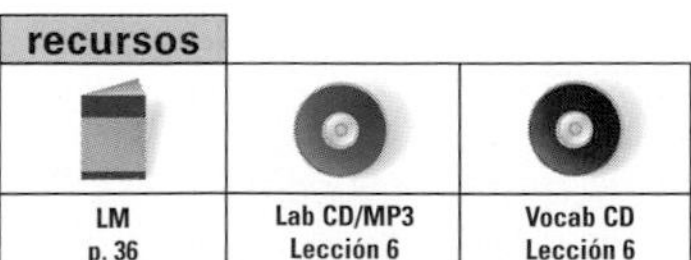

La rutina diaria

7

Communicative Goals

You will learn how to:

- Describe your daily routine
- Talk about personal hygiene
- Reassure someone

contextos

pages 202–205
- Daily routine
- Personal hygiene
- Time expressions

fotonovela

pages 206–209
Javier and Álex talk about their plans for the following morning. Javier explains that he doesn't like to wake up early because he usually stays up late. Álex promises to wake him up after his morning run.

estructura

pages 210–223
- Reflexive verbs
- Indefinite and negative words
- Preterite of **ser** and **ir**
- **Gustar** and verbs like **gustar**

adelante

pages 224–229
Lectura: Read an e-mail from Guillermo.
Escritura: Describe someone's daily routine.
Escuchar: Listen to an interview with a famous actor.
Proyecto: Create a travel itinerary.

panorama

pages 230–231
Featured Country: Perú
- Lima: capital of Perú
- The ruins of Machu Picchu
- Llamas and alpacas
- The mysterious Nazca lines

A PRIMERA VISTA

- **¿Está ella en casa o en una tienda?**
- **¿Es la blusa que lleva de rayas o lunares?**
- **¿Está contenta o enojada?**
- **¿De qué color son los ojos de ella? ¿Y el pelo?**

Lesson Goals

In **Lección 7** students will be introduced to the following:
- terms for daily routines
- reflexive verbs
- adverbs of time
- indefinite and negative words
- preterite of **ser** and **ir**
- forms of **gustar** and verbs like **gustar**
- predicting content from the title
- sequencing events
- writing a description of a place
- listening for background information
- writing a tour itinerary
- cultural, geographic, and historical information about Peru

A primera vista Here are some additional questions you can ask based on the photo: **¿Con quién vives? ¿Qué le dices antes de salir de casa? ¿Qué tipo de ropa llevas para ir a tus clases? ¿Les prestas esta ropa a tus amigos/as? ¿Qué ropa usaste en el verano? ¿Y en el invierno?**

INSTRUCTIONAL RESOURCES

Workbook/Video Manual: WB Activities, pp. 73–84
Laboratory Manual: Lab Activities, pp. 37–42
Workbook/Video Manual: Video Activities, pp. 225–226; pp. 261–262
Instructor's Resource Manual: **Hojas de actividades**, p. 167; **Vocabulario adicional**, p. 185; **¡Inténtalo!** & **Práctica** Answers, pp. 208–209; **Fotonovela** Translations, p. 142; Textbook CD Tapescript, p. 91; Lab CDs Tapescript, pp. 30–34; **Fotonovela** Videoscript, p. 109; **Panorama cultural** Videoscript, p. 130
Info Gap Activities Booklet, pp. 25–28
Overhead Transparencies: #5, #6, #31, #32
Lab Audio CD/MP3 **Lección 7**
Panorama cultural DVD/Video
Fotonovela DVD/Video
Testing Program, pp. 73–84
Testing Program Audio CD
Test Files CD-ROM
Companion website
Presentations CD-ROM
Textbook CD
Vocabulary CD
Interactive CD-ROM
Video CD-ROM
Web-SAM

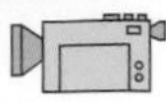

Section Goals

In **Fotonovela** students will:

- receive comprehensible input from free-flowing discourse
- learn functional phrases that preview lesson grammatical structures

Instructional Resources
WB/VM: Video Activities, pp. 225–226
***Fotonovela** DVD/Video (Start 00:34:37)*
Video CD-ROM
*IRM: **Fotonovela** Translations, p. 142, Videoscript, p. 109*
Interactive CD-ROM

Video Recap: Lección 6
Before doing this **Fotonovela** section, review the previous one with this activity.

1. ¿Qué está buscando Inés en el mercado? (un regalo para su hermana Graciela)
2. ¿Qué necesita Javier para su excursión a las montañas? (un suéter)
3. ¿Por qué le da el vendedor un buen precio a Javier? (Javier regatea)
4. ¿Qué compró Inés en el mercado? (una bolsa, una camisa y un sombrero)

Video Synopsis Javier returns from the market and shows Álex the sweater he bought. Álex and Javier discuss the fact that they have to get up early the next day. Álex, an early riser, agrees to wake Javier up after his morning run. Don Francisco comes by to remind them that the bus will leave at 8:30 a.m. tomorrow.

Suggestions

- Have your students skim the **Fotonovela** for the gist and write down their impressions. Ask for a few volunteers to share their impressions with the class.
- Write **Describe tu rutina diaria** on the board and have the class guess its meaning. Then use it to ask individual students to talk about their daily routines.

¡Jamás me levanto temprano!

National Standards: communication, cultures

Álex y Javier hablan de sus rutinas diarias.

PERSONAJES

DON FRANCISCO

ÁLEX

JAVIER

JAVIER Hola, Álex. ¿Qué estás haciendo?

ÁLEX Nada... sólo estoy leyendo mi correo electrónico. ¿Adónde fueron?

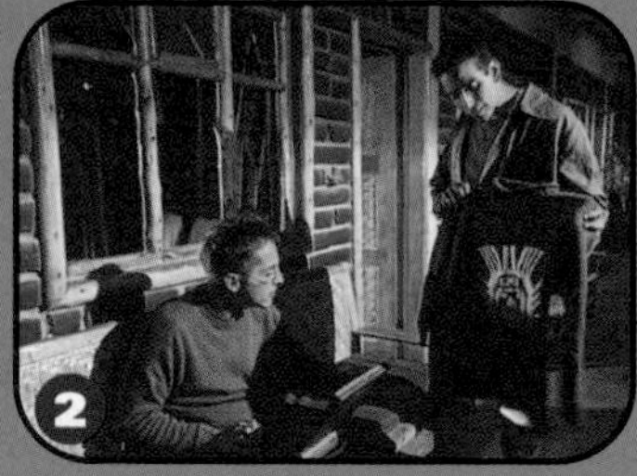

JAVIER Inés y yo fuimos a un mercado. Fue muy divertido. Mira, compré este suéter. Me encanta. No fue barato pero es chévere, ¿no?

ÁLEX Sí, es ideal para las montañas.

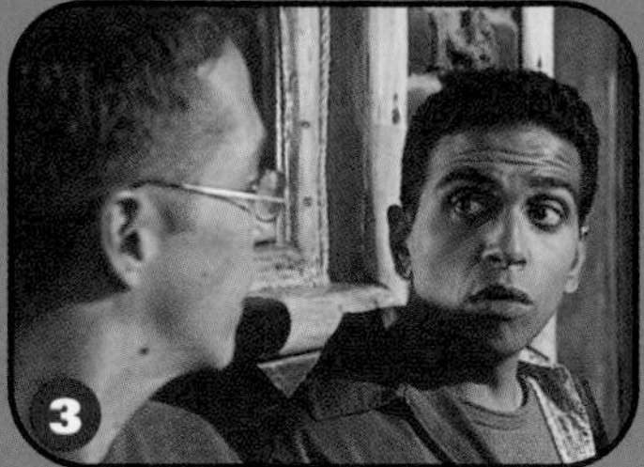

JAVIER ¡Qué interesantes son los mercados al aire libre! Me gustaría volver pero ya es tarde. Oye, Álex, sabes que mañana tenemos que levantarnos temprano.

ÁLEX Ningún problema.

JAVIER ¡Increíble! ¡Álex, el superhombre!

ÁLEX Oye, Javier, ¿por qué no puedes levantarte temprano?

JAVIER Es que por la noche no quiero dormir, sino dibujar y escuchar música. Por eso es difícil despertarme por la mañana.

JAVIER El autobús no sale hasta las ocho y media. ¿Vas a levantarte mañana a las seis también?

ÁLEX No, pero tengo que levantarme a las siete menos cuarto porque voy a correr.

JAVIER Ah, ya... ¿Puedes despertarme después de correr?

ÁLEX Éste es el plan para mañana. Me levanto a las siete menos cuarto y corro por treinta minutos. Vuelvo, me ducho, me visto y a las siete y media te despierto. ¿De acuerdo?

JAVIER ¡Absolutamente ninguna objeción!

recursos

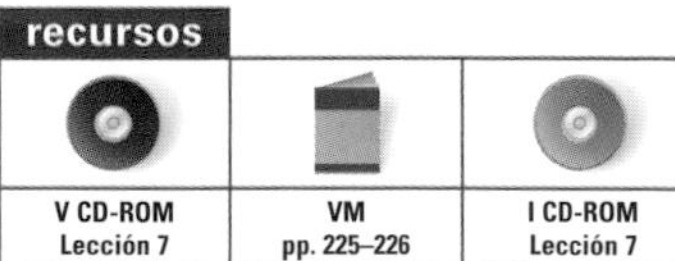

V CD-ROM Lección 7	VM pp. 225–226	I CD-ROM Lección 7

TEACHING OPTIONS

Video Tips General suggestions for using video clips in the classroom can be found on page IAE-12 of this Instructor's Annotated Edition.

¡Jamás me levanto temprano! Play the **¡Jamás me levanto temprano!** segment of this video module for the first time and have your students jot down notes on what they see and hear. Then have them work in groups of three to compare notes and prepare a brief plot summary. Play the segment again. Have students return to their groups to refine their summaries. Finally, discuss the plot with the entire class and correct any errors of fact or sequencing.

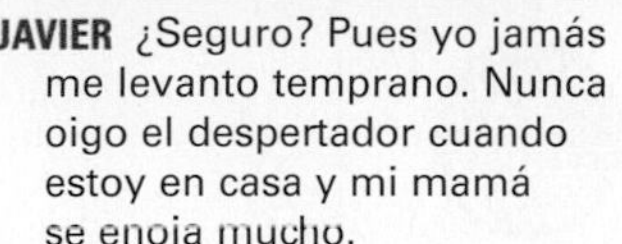

JAVIER ¿Seguro? Pues yo jamás me levanto temprano. Nunca oigo el despertador cuando estoy en casa y mi mamá se enoja mucho.

ÁLEX Tranquilo, Javier. Yo tengo una solución.

ÁLEX Cuando estoy en casa en la Ciudad de México, siempre me despierto a las seis en punto. Me ducho en cinco minutos y luego me cepillo los dientes. Después me afeito, me visto y ¡listo! ¡Me voy!

DON FRANCISCO Hola, chicos. Mañana salimos temprano, a las ocho y media... ni un minuto antes ni un minuto después.

ÁLEX No se preocupe, don Francisco. Todo está bajo control.

DON FRANCISCO Bueno, pues, hasta mañana.

DON FRANCISCO ¡Ay, los estudiantes! Siempre se acuestan tarde. ¡Qué vida!

Enfoque cultural El horario de la vida diaria

En algunos países hispanos, el horario de la vida diaria es muy diferente al de EE.UU. En estos países, muchas personas trabajan de las ocho de la mañana a las dos de la tarde. A las dos salen del trabajo para ir a almorzar. Vuelven a las cuatro y salen a las seis de la tarde. Muchos utilizan esas dos horas para almorzar en casa con sus familias y, a veces (*sometimes*), dormir una siesta. También, frecuentemente la gente cena más tarde que en los EE.UU.

Expresiones útiles

Telling where you went

- **¿Adónde fuiste/fue usted?** *Where did you go?*
- **Fui a un mercado.** *I went to a market.*
- **¿Adónde fueron ustedes?** *Where did you go?*
- **Fuimos a un mercado. Fue muy divertido.** *We went to a market. It was a lot of fun.*

Talking about morning routines

- **(Jamás) me levanto temprano/tarde.** *I (never) get up early/late.*
- **Nunca oigo el despertador.** *I never hear the alarm clock.*
- **Es difícil/fácil despertarme.** *It's hard/easy to wake up.*
- **Cuando estoy en casa, siempre me despierto a las seis en punto.** *When I'm home, I always wake up at six on the dot.*
- **Me ducho y luego me cepillo los dientes.** *I take a shower and then I brush my teeth.*
- **Después me afeito y me visto.** *Afterwards, I shave and get dressed.*

Reassuring someone

- **Ningún problema.** *No problem.*
- **No te preocupes.** *(fam.)*/ **No se preocupe.** *(form.)* *Don't worry.*
- **Todo está bajo control.** *Everything is under control.*
- **Tranquilo.** *Don't worry.; Be cool.*

Additional vocabulary

- **sino** *but (rather)*

Suggestion Have students get together in groups of three to act out the episode. Have one or two groups present it to the class.

Expresiones útiles Draw the class's attention to the verb forms **fui, fuiste, fue,** and **fuimos**. Explain that these are forms of the verbs **ir** and **ser** in the preterite tense. The context always makes clear which is meant. Then point out the phrases **me levanto, me despierto, me ducho, me cepillo, me afeito,** and **No te preocupes**. Tell the class that these are forms of the reflexive verbs **levantarse, despertarse, ducharse, cepillarse, afeitarse,** and **preocuparse**. Also, point out the words **siempre, nunca, jamás,** and **ningún**. Explain that **siempre** is called an indefinite word and that the other three are called negative words. Tell your students that they will learn more about all of these concepts in **Estructura.**

TEACHING OPTIONS

Enfoque cultural The two-hour "lunch" break (2:00 p.m. to 4:00 p.m.), which includes the day's largest meal and a period of rest afterward, is observed in many Spanish-speaking countries as the **siesta**. Explain to the class that although the **siesta** is part of the daily routine of many people in Spanish-speaking countries, the observance of this tradition is not universal. For example, when Spain entered the European Union, many Spanish businesspeople began to adjust their work schedules to mirror those of their counterparts in other European countries. Ask your students to discuss the custom of the **siesta** and its impact on businesses and on individual workers. Ask them if they think the **siesta** should be incorporated into the schedules of businesses in the United States, and why.

Reacciona a la fotonovela

1 **¿Cierto o falso?** Indica si las siguientes oraciones (*sentences*) son **ciertas** o **falsas.** Corrige (*Correct*) las frases falsas.

1. Álex está mirando la televisión.
   Falso. Álex está leyendo su correo electrónico.
2. El suéter que Javier acaba de comprar es caro pero es muy bonito.
   Cierto.
3. Javier cree que el mercado es aburrido y no quiere volver.
   Falso. Javier piensa que el mercado es muy interesante.
4. El autobús va a salir mañana a las siete y media en punto.
   Falso. El autobús sale mañana a las ocho y media en punto.
5. A Javier le gusta mucho dibujar y escuchar música por la noche.
   Cierto.

¡LENGUA VIVA!

Remember that **en punto** means *on the dot.* If the group were instead leaving at *around seven thirty,* you would say **a eso de las siete y media.**

2 **Identificar** Identifica quién puede decir las siguientes frases. Puedes usar cada nombre más de una vez.

1. ¡Ay, los estudiantes nunca se acuestan temprano! don Francisco
2. ¿El despertador? ¡Jamás lo oigo por la mañana! Javier
3. Es fácil despertarme temprano. Y sólo necesito cinco minutos para ducharme. Álex
4. Mañana vamos a salir a las ocho y media. Javier, don Francisco
5. Acabo de ir a un mercado fabuloso. Javier
6. No se preocupe. Tenemos todo bajo control para mañana. Álex

DON FRANCISCO

JAVIER

ÁLEX

3 **Ordenar** Ordena correctamente los planes que tiene Álex.

a. Me visto. 5
b. Corro por media hora. 2
c. Despierto a Javier a las siete y media. 6
d. Vuelvo a la habitación. 3
e. Me levanto a las siete menos cuarto. 1
f. Me ducho. 4

4 **Mi rutina** En parejas (*pairs*), hablen de sus rutinas de la mañana y de la noche. Indiquen a qué horas hacen las actividades más importantes. Answers will vary.

modelo

Estudiante 1: ¿Prefieres levantarte temprano o tarde?
Estudiante 2: Prefiero levantarme tarde... muy tarde.

Estudiante 1: ¿A qué hora te levantas durante la semana?
Estudiante 2: A las once. ¿Y tú?

CONSÚLTALO

To review telling time in Spanish, see **Estructura 1.4**, pp. 22–23.

1 Expansion Give these additional items to the class: **6. Javier siempre se despierta temprano. (Falso. Álex siempre se despierta temprano.) 7. Don Francisco cree que los estudiantes siempre se acuestan temprano. (Falso. Don Francisco cree que los estudiantes siempre se acuestan tarde.)**

2 Expansion Give these additional items to the class: **7. Quiero volver al mercado pero no hay tiempo. (Javier) 8. Cuando estoy en casa, siempre me despierto muy temprano. (Álex)**

3 Suggestion Have your students quickly glance over the caption to video still 8, page 206, before doing this activity.

3 Expansion Ask pairs to imagine another character's plans for the following day and list them using the **yo** form of the verbs as in the activity. Then have pairs share their lists with the class.

4 Suggestion Encourage students to use as many reflexive infinitives from **Contextos** as they can. They will learn to conjugate them formally in **Estructura 7.1**.

4 Possible Response
E1: ¿Prefieres levantarte tarde o temprano?
E2: Prefiero levantarme tarde... muy tarde.
E1: ¿A qué hora te levantas durante la semana?
E2: A las siete. ¿Y tú?
E1: Siempre me levanto muy temprano... a las cinco y media.
E2: Y ¿a qué hora te acuestas?
E1: Siempre me acuesto temprano, a las diez o a las once. ¿Y tú?
E2: Yo prefiero acostarme a las doce.

TEACHING OPTIONS

Extra Practice Have your students close their books. Then use the sentences from **Actividad 3**, in the correct order, as a dictation activity. Read each sentence twice slowly to give students an opportunity to write. Then read them again at normal speed, without pausing, to allow students to correct any errors or fill in any gaps.

Small Groups Have your students get together in groups of three to discuss and compare their daily routines. Tell your students to use as many of the words and expressions they have learned so far in this lesson as they can. Then ask for a few volunteers to describe the daily routine of one of their group members.

NATIONAL
comparisons
STANDARDS

Pronunciación

The consonants **r** and **rr**

ropa **rutina** **rico** **Ramón**

In Spanish, **r** has a strong trilled sound at the beginning of a word. No English words have a trill, but English speakers often produce a trill when they imitate the sound of a motor.

gustar **durante** **primero** **crema**

In any other position, **r** has a weak sound similar to the English *tt* in *better* or the English *dd* in *ladder*. In contrast to English, the tongue touches the roof of the mouth behind the teeth.

pizarra **corro** **marrón** **aburrido**

The letter **rr**, which only appears between vowels, always has a strong trilled sound.

caro **carro** **pero** **perro**

Between vowels, the difference between the strong trilled **rr** and the weak **r** is very important, as a mispronunciation could lead to confusion between two different words.

Práctica Lee las palabras en voz alta, prestando (*paying*) atención a la pronunciación de la **r** y la **rr**.

1. Perú
2. Rosa
3. borrador
4. madre
5. comprar
6. favor
7. rubio
8. reloj
9. Arequipa
10. tarde
11. cerrar
12. despertador

Oraciones Lee las oraciones en voz alta, prestando atención a la pronunciación de la **r** y la **rr**.

1. Ramón Robles Ruiz es programador. Su esposa Rosaura es artista.
2. A Rosaura Robles le encanta regatear en el mercado.
3. Ramón nunca regatea... le aburre regatear.
4. Rosaura siempre compra cosas baratas.
5. Ramón no es rico pero prefiere comprar cosas muy caras.
6. ¡El martes Ramón compró un carro nuevo!

Refranes Lee en voz alta los refranes, prestando atención a la **r** y a la **rr**.

Perro que ladra no muerde.[1]

No se ganó Zamora en una hora.2

1 A dog's bark is worse than its bite.
2 Rome wasn't built in a day.

recursos

TEXT CD Lección 7	LM p. 38	Lab CD/MP3 Lección 7	I CD-ROM Lección 7

Section Goal

In **Pronunciación** students will be introduced to the pronunciation of the letters **r** and **rr**.

Instructional Resources
Textbook CD
Lab Manual, p. 38
Lab CD/MP3 ***Lección 7***
IRM: Tapescript, pp. 30–34; p. 91
Interactive CD-ROM

Suggestions

- Explain that **r** is trilled at the beginning of a word, and that there are no words that have a trill in American English. Model the pronunciation of **ropa, rutina, rico**, and **Ramón** and have the class repeat.
- Point out that in any other position, **r** is pronounced like the *tt* in American English *better*. Write the words **gustar, durante, primero,** and **crema** on the board and ask for a volunteer to pronounce each word.
- Point out that **rr** always has a strong trilled sound and that it only appears between vowels. Pronounce the words **pizarra, corro, marrón,** and **aburrido** and have the class repeat.
- Have your students close their books. To help students discriminate between **r** and **rr**, pronounce the minimal pairs **caro/carro** and **pero/perro**. Write each word on the board as you pronounce it. Then pronounce each pair several times in random order, pausing after each for students to say which you pronounced. Ex: **caro, carro, caro, carro, carro, carro.**

Práctica/Oraciones/Refranes

These exercises are recorded on the Textbook CD. You may want to play the CD so students practice the pronunciation point by listening to Spanish spoken by speakers other than yourself.

TEACHING OPTIONS

Extra Practice Write the names of a few Peruvian cities on the board and ask for a volunteer to pronounce each name. Ex: Huaraz, Cajamarca, Trujillo, Puerto Maldonado, Cerro de Pasco, Piura. Then write the names of a few Peruvian literary figures on the board and repeat the process. Ex: Ricardo Palma, Ciro Alegría, Mario Vargas Llosa, César Vallejo.

Small Groups Have students work in small groups and take turns reading aloud sentences from the **Fotonovela** on pages 206–207, focusing on the correct pronunciation of **r** and **rr**.

Section Goals

In **Estructura 7.1** students will learn:
- the conjugation of reflexive verbs
- common reflexive verbs

Instructional Resources
WB/VM: Workbook, pp. 75–76
Lab Manual, p. 39
Lab CD/MP3 ***Lección 7***
IRM: ***¡Inténtalo!*** *&* ***Práctica*** *Answers, pp. 208–209; Tapescript, pp. 30–34*
Info Gap Activities Booklet, pp. 25–26
Interactive CD-ROM
Companion website: www.vistahigherlearning.com
Presentations CD-ROM

Suggestions

- Model the first-person reflexive by talking about yourself. Ex: **Me levanto muy temprano. Me levanto a las cinco de la mañana.**
- Model the second person by asking questions with a verb you have already used in the first person. Ex: **Y tú, ____ , ¿a qué hora te levantas? (Me levanto a las ocho.)**
- Introduce the third person by making statements and asking questions about what a student has told you. Ex: ____ **se levanta muy tarde, ¿no? (Sí, se levanta muy tarde.)**
- Write the paradigm of **lavarse** on the board and model its pronunciation.
- Use magazine pictures to clarify meanings between third-person singular and third-person plural forms. Ex: **Se lava las manos** and **Se lavan las manos.**

7.1 Reflexive verbs

ANTE TODO A reflexive verb is used to indicate that the subject does something to or for himself or herself. In other words, it "reflects" the action of the verb back to the subject. Reflexive verbs always use reflexive pronouns.

SUBJECT	REFLEXIVE VERB
Joaquín	**se ducha** por la mañana.

Reflexive verbs

lavarse *(to wash oneself)*

SINGULAR FORMS	yo	**me lavo**	*I wash (myself)*
	tú	**te lavas**	*you wash (yourself)*
	Ud.	**se lava**	*you wash (yourself)*
	él / ella	**se lava**	*he/she washes (himself/herself)*
PLURAL FORMS	nosotros/as	**nos lavamos**	*we wash (ourselves)*
	vosotros/as	**os laváis**	*you wash (yourselves)*
	Uds.	**se lavan**	*you wash (yourselves)*
	ellos/ellas	**se lavan**	*they wash (themselves)*

- The pronoun **se** attached to an infinitive identifies the verb as reflexive: **lavarse.**
- When a reflexive verb is conjugated, the reflexive pronoun agrees with the subject.

Me afeito. **Te despiertas** a las siete.

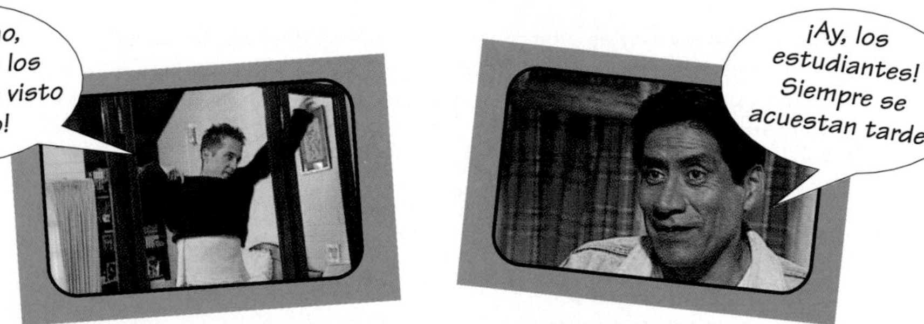

Me ducho, me cepillo los dientes, me visto y ¡listo!
¡Ay, los estudiantes! Siempre se acuestan tarde.

- Like object pronouns, reflexive pronouns generally appear before a conjugated verb. With infinitives and present participles, they may be placed before the conjugated verb or attached to the infinitive or present participle.

Ellos **se** van a vestir.
Ellos van a vestir**se**.
They are going to get dressed.

Nos estamos lavando las manos.
Estamos lavándo**nos** las manos.
We are washing our hands.

recursos
WB pp. 75–82
LM pp. 39–42
Lab CD/MP3 Lección 7
I CD-ROM Lección 7
vistahigherlearning.com

¡ATENCIÓN!
Except for **se**, reflexive pronouns have the same forms as direct and indirect object pronouns.
...
Se is used for both singular and plural subjects —there is no individual plural form:
Pablo **se** lava.
Ellos **se** lavan.

¡ATENCIÓN!
When a reflexive pronoun is attached to a present participle, an accent mark is added to maintain the original stress:
bañando → bañ**á**ndo**se**
afeitando → afeit**á**ndo**se**

TEACHING OPTIONS

Extra Practice To provide oral practice with reflexive verbs, create sentences that follow the pattern of the sentences in the examples. Say the sentence, have students repeat it, then say a different subject, varying the gender and number. Have students then say the sentence with the new subject, changing pronouns and verbs as necessary.

Heritage Speakers Have heritage speakers describe daily routines in their home communities. Encourage them to use their own linguistic variation of words presented in this lesson. Ex: **regarse (e:ie)**, **pintarse**. Have heritage speakers work together to compare and contrast activities as well as lexical variations.

Common reflexive verbs

acordarse (de) (o:ue)	*to remember*	**llamarse**	*to be called; to be named*
acostarse (o:ue)	*to go to bed*	**maquillarse**	*to put on makeup*
afeitarse	*to shave*	**peinarse**	*to comb one's hair*
bañarse	*to bathe; to take a bath*	**ponerse**	*to put on*
cepillarse	*to brush*	**ponerse** (+ *adj.*)	*to become (+ adj.)*
despedirse (de) (e:i)	*to say good-bye (to)*	**preocuparse (por)**	*to worry (about)*
despertarse (e:ie)	*to wake up*	**probarse** (o:ue)	*to try on*
dormirse (o:ue)	*to go to sleep; to fall asleep*	**quedarse**	*to stay; to remain*
ducharse	*to shower; to take a shower*	**quitarse**	*to take off*
		secarse	*to dry (oneself)*
enojarse (con)	*to get angry (with)*	**sentarse** (e:ie)	*to sit down*
irse	*to go away; to leave*	**sentirse** (e:ie)	*to feel*
lavarse	*to wash (oneself)*	**vestirse** (e:i)	*to get dressed*
levantarse	*to get up*		

AYUDA

You have already learned several adjectives that can be used with **ponerse** when it means *to become*: **alegre, cómodo/a, contento/a, elegante, guapo/a, nervioso/a, rojo/a,** and **triste.**

¡ATENCIÓN!

Because you learned how to form the preterite of non-reflexive regular verbs in **Estructura 6.3**, you also know how to form the preterite of the common reflexive verbs in the list, with the exception of the stem-changing **–ir** verbs, **irse** and **ponerse**. You will learn more preterite forms such as those of the verb **ir** (**Estructura 7.3**), stem-changing **–ir** verbs (**Estructura 8.1**) and **poner** (**Estructura 9.1**).

COMPARE & CONTRAST

Unlike English, a number of verbs in Spanish can be reflexive or non-reflexive. If the verb acts upon the subject, the reflexive form is used. If the verb acts upon something other than the subject, the non-reflexive form is used. Compare these sentences.

Lola **lava** los platos.

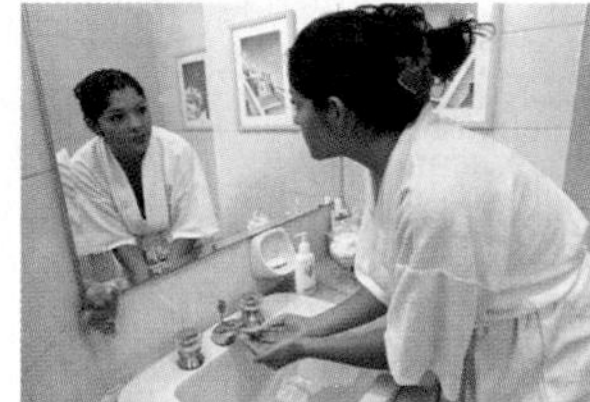

Lola **se lava** la cara.

As the preceding sentences show, reflexive verbs sometimes have different meanings than their non-reflexive counterparts. For example, **lavar** means *to wash*, while **lavarse** means *to wash oneself, to wash up*.

¡ATENCIÓN!

Parts of the body or clothing are generally not referred to with possessives, but with the definite article.

La niña se quitó **los** zapatos.

Necesito cepillarme **los** dientes.

¡INTÉNTALO!

Indica el presente de los verbos reflexivos que siguen. El primero de cada columna ya está conjugado.

despertarse

1. Mis hermanos *se despiertan* tarde.
2. Tú te despiertas tarde.
3. Nosotros nos despertamos tarde.
4. Benito se despierta tarde.
5. Yo me despierto tarde.
6. Ustedes se despiertan tarde.
7. Ella se despierta tarde.
8. Adriana y yo nos despertamos tarde.
9. Ellos se despiertan tarde.

ponerse

1. Él *se pone* una chaqueta.
2. Yo me pongo una chaqueta.
3. Usted se pone una chaqueta.
4. Nosotras nos ponemos una chaqueta.
5. Las niñas se ponen una chaqueta.
6. Tú te pones una chaqueta.
7. El botones se pone una chaqueta.
8. Beatriz y Gil se ponen una chaqueta.
9. Ustedes se ponen una chaqueta.

Suggestions

- Go through the list of common reflexive verbs asking students closed-answer questions. Ex: **¿Te acuerdas de tu primer día en la universidad? (Sí, me acuerdo.) ¿Los niños pequeños se acuestan tarde o temprano? (Los niños pequeños se acuestan temprano.)**
- To practice reflexive verbs in the preterite and periphrastic future (**ir a** + [*infinitive*]), talk and ask questions about what you and your students did yesterday and plan to do tomorrow. Ex: **Ayer me levanté a las seis. Pero el sábado me voy a levantar a las nueve.**
- Compare and contrast reflexive and non-reflexive verbs by giving examples. Ex: **Me ducho por la mañana. Nunca ducho al gato. Me pongo un suéter. Pongo la radio.**
- Ask volunteers to translate sentences such as: *He wakes the children at seven. He wakes up at seven.*

TEACHING OPTIONS

TPR Model gestures for a few of the reflexive verbs. Ex: **acordarse** (tap side of head), **acostarse** (lay head on folded hands). Have students stand. Begin by practicing as a class using only the **nosotros** form, saying an expression at random (**Nos lavamos la cara.**). Then vary the verb forms and point to a student who should perform an appropriate gesture. Keep the pace rapid. Vary by pointing to more than one student (**Ustedes se peinan.**).

Pairs Have students write a short account of their own daily routine. Then have pairs compare and contrast their routines using a Venn Diagram (see **Lección 9, Escritura**). Have the pair write one of their names in the left circle and one in the right circle, writing **Los/Las dos** where the circles overlap. Then have them list their activities in the appropriate location. Remember verbs under **Los/Las dos** should be in the first-person plural.

1 Suggestion Before assigning the activity, review reflexive verbs by comparing and contrasting weekday and weekend routines. Ex: **¿Te levantas tarde o temprano los sábados? ¿Te acuestas tarde o temprano los domingos?**

1 Expansion To practice the formal register, pose certain situations to the students and have them tell you what you are going to do. Ex: **Hace frío y nieva, pero necesito salir. (Usted va a ponerse el abrigo.) Acabo de levantarme. (Usted va a lavarse la cara.)**

2 Suggestion Before assigning the activity, review reflexive and non-reflexive verbs by asking questions using both forms. Ex: **¿Cuándo nos lavamos? (Nos lavamos todos los días.) ¿Cuándo lavamos el coche? (Lavamos el coche los fines de semana.)**

2 Expansion Have students write five sentences contrasting reflexive and non-reflexive forms of a common verb. Ex: **Me despierto a las siete. Despierto a mi compañero de cuarto a las ocho.**

3 Expansions
- Repeat the activity as a pattern drill, supplying different subjects for each drawing. Ex: **Número uno, yo. (Me quito los zapatos.) Número cinco, nosotras. (Nosotras nos maquillamos.)**
- Repeat the activity changing the verb to the preterite. Ex: **El joven se quitó los zapatos.**

Práctica

1 **Nuestra rutina** La familia de Blanca sigue la misma rutina todos los días. Según (*According to*) Blanca, ¿qué hacen ellos?

modelo
mamá / despertarse a las 5:00
Mamá se despierta a las cinco.

1. Roberto y yo / levantarse a las 7:00 Roberto y yo nos levantamos a las siete.
2. papá / ducharse primero y / luego afeitarse Papá se ducha primero y luego se afeita.
3. yo / lavarse la cara y / vestirse antes de tomar café Yo me lavo la cara y me visto antes de tomar café.
4. mamá / peinarse y / luego maquillarse Mamá se peina y luego se maquilla.
5. todos / sentarse a la mesa para comer Todos nos sentamos a la mesa para comer.
6. Roberto / cepillarse los dientes después de comer Roberto se cepilla los dientes después de comer.
7. yo / ponerse el abrigo antes de salir Yo me pongo el abrigo antes de salir.
8. nosotros / despedirse de mamá Nosotros nos despedimos de mamá.

NOTA CULTURAL

Como en los EE.UU., **tomar café** en el desayuno es muy común en los países hispanos.

En muchas familias, los niños toman café con leche (*coffee with milk*) en el desayuno antes de ir a la escuela.

El café en los países hispanos generalmente es más fuerte que en los EE.UU., y el descafeinado (*decaffeinated*) no es muy popular.

2 **La fiesta elegante** Selecciona el verbo apropiado y completa las frases con la forma correcta.

1. Tú __lavas__ (lavar / lavarse) el auto antes de ir a la fiesta.
2. Nosotros no __nos acordamos__ (acordar / acordarse) de comprar regalos.
3. Para llegar a tiempo, Raúl y Marta __acuestan__ (acostar / acostarse) a los niños antes de irse.
4. Yo __me siento__ (sentir / sentirse) bien hoy.
5. Mis amigos siempre __se visten__ (vestir / vestirse) con ropa muy cara.
6. ¿__Se prueban__ (probar / probarse) ustedes la ropa antes de comprarla?
7. Usted __se preocupa__ (preocupar / preocuparse) mucho por sus amigos, ¿no?
8. En general, __me afeito__ (afeitar / afeitarse) yo mismo, pero hoy el barbero me (*barber*) __afeita__ (afeitar / afeitarse).

¡LENGUA VIVA!

In Spain a car is called a **coche** while in many parts of Latin America it is known as a **carro.** Although you'll be understood using any of these terms, using **auto (automóvil)** will surely get you where you want to go.

3 **Describir** Mira los dibujos y describe lo que estas personas hacen. Some answers may vary.

1. El joven se quita los zapatos.

2. Carmen se duerme.

3. Juan se pone la camiseta.

4. Ellos se despiden.

5. Estrella se maquilla.

6. Toni se enoja con el perro.

TEACHING OPTIONS

Game Each group of four writes the daily routine of a celebrity. Groups take turns reading their descriptions aloud without giving the celebrity's name. Groups that guess the subject win a point while a group able to fool the class gets two points.

Extra Practice Have students figure out the morning schedule of the Ramírez family. Say: **El señor Ramírez se afeita antes que Alberto, pero después que Rafael. La señora Ramírez es la primera en ducharse y Montse es la última. Lolita se peina cuando su padre sale del cuarto de baño y antes que uno de sus hermanos. Nuria se maquilla después que Lolita, pero no inmediatamente después. (Primero se ducha la señora Ramírez. Después se afeita Rafael seguido por el señor Ramírez. Despúes se peina Lolita. Alberto se afeita y después Nuria se maquilla. Finalmente Montse se ducha.)**

Comunicación

4 **Preguntas personales** En parejas, túrnense (*take turns*) para hacerse estas preguntas.
Answers will vary.

1. ¿A qué hora te levantas durante la semana?
2. ¿A qué hora te levantas los fines de semana?
3. ¿Prefieres levantarte tarde o temprano? ¿Por qué?
4. ¿Te enojas frecuentemente con tus amigos?
5. ¿Te preocupas fácilmente? ¿Qué te preocupa?
6. ¿Qué cosas te ponen contento/a?
7. ¿Qué haces cuando te sientes triste?
8. ¿Y cuando te sientes alegre?
9. ¿Te acuestas tarde o temprano durante la semana?
10. ¿A qué hora te acuestas los fines de semana?

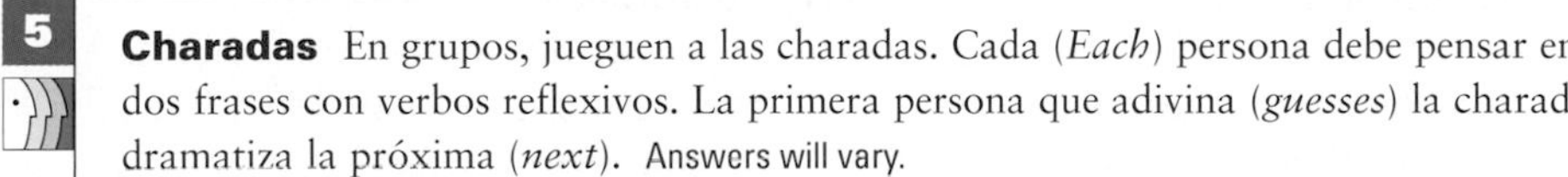

5 **Charadas** En grupos, jueguen a las charadas. Cada (*Each*) persona debe pensar en dos frases con verbos reflexivos. La primera persona que adivina (*guesses*) la charada dramatiza la próxima (*next*). Answers will vary.

6 **Debate** En grupos, discutan (*discuss*) este tema (*topic*): ¿Quiénes necesitan más tiempo para arreglarse (*to get ready*) antes de salir, los hombres o las mujeres? Hagan una lista de las razones (*reasons*) que tienen para defender sus ideas e informen a la clase.
Answers will vary.

Síntesis

7 **La familia ocupada** Tú y tu compañero/a asisten a un programa de verano en Lima, Perú. Viven con la familia Ramos. Tu profesor(a) te va a dar la rutina incompleta que la familia sigue en las mañanas. Trabaja con tu compañero/a para completarla.
Answers will vary.

modelo

Estudiante 1: ¿Qué hace el señor Ramos a las seis y cuarto?
Estudiante 2: El señor Ramos se levanta.

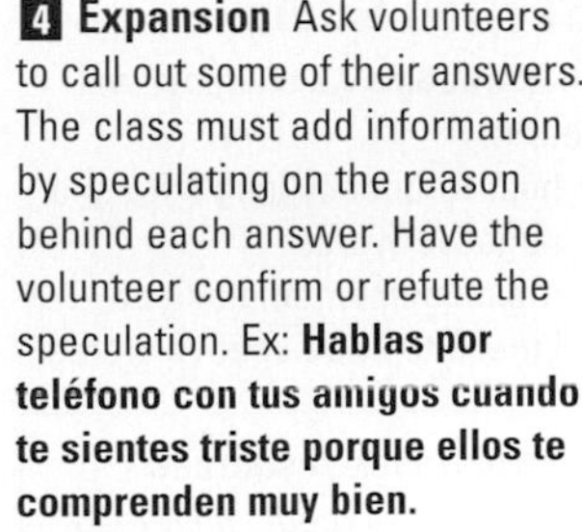

4 Expansion Ask volunteers to call out some of their answers. The class must add information by speculating on the reason behind each answer. Have the volunteer confirm or refute the speculation. Ex: **Hablas por teléfono con tus amigos cuando te sientes triste porque ellos te comprenden muy bien.**

5 Expansion Ask each group to present their best **charada** to the class.

6 Suggestion Before assigning groups, go over some of the things men and women do to get ready to go out. Ex: **Las mujeres se maquillan. Los hombres se afeitan.** Then ask students to indicate their opinion on the question and divide the class into groups accordingly.

7 Suggestion Divide the class into pairs and distribute the Info Gap Handouts from the Info Gap Activities Booklet that correspond to this activity. Give the students ten minutes to complete this activity.

7 Expansion Ask groups of four to imagine they all live in the same house and have them put together a message board to reflect their different schedules.

TEACHING OPTIONS

Game Divide the class into groups of three. Each member should tell his or her group about the strangest, funniest, or most exciting thing that he or she has done. The group chooses one account and writes it on a slip of paper. For each group's turn, you read the description aloud. The class has two minutes to ask group members questions to find out who did the activity. The groups that guess win one point; a group that is able to fool the class wins two points.

Extra Practice Prepare descriptions of five celebrities, using reflexives. Write their names randomly on the board. Then read the descriptions as a dictation, having students match each to a name. Ex: **Su deporte es el tenis, pero no juega en competiciones ahora. Se pone nervioso en los torneos y se enoja con frecuencia. (John McEnroe)**

Section Goals

In **Estructura 7.2** students will learn:

- high-frequency indefinite and negative words
- the placement and use of indefinite and negative words

Instructional Resources
WB/VM: Workbook, pp. 77–78
Lab Manual, p. 40
Lab CD/MP3 ***Lección 7***
IRM: ***¡Inténtalo! & Práctica*** *Answers, pp. 208–209; Tapescript, pp. 30–34;* ***Hojas de actividades****, p. 167*
Interactive CD-ROM
Companion website: www.vistahigherlearning.com
Presentations CD-ROM

Suggestions

- Write **alguien** and **nadie** on the board and ask questions about what students are wearing today. Ex: **Hoy alguien lleva una camiseta de Puerto Rico. ¿Quién es? ¿Alguien lleva pantalones anaranjados? No, nadie los lleva.**
- Use magazine pictures to compare and contrast indefinite and negative words. Ex: **La señora de la foto tiene algo en las manos. ¿El señor tiene algo en las manos también? No, el señor no tiene nada en las manos.**
- Ask volunteers questions about their activities since the last class, reiterating the answers by using the targeted structures. Ex: **¿Quién compró algo nuevo? Sólo dos personas. Nadie más compró algo nuevo. Los otros no compraron nada nuevo. Yo no compré nada nuevo tampoco.**
- Give further examples to consolidate the information presented in **¡Atención!** Ex: **¿Buscas a algún compañero? No, no busco a ningún compañero.**
- Point out that **uno/a(s)** can be used as an indefinite pronoun. Ex: **¿Tienes un lápiz? Sí, tengo uno.**

7.2 Indefinite and negative words

ANTE TODO Indefinite words refer to people and things that are not specific, for example, *someone* or *something*. Negative words deny the existence of people and things or contradict statements, for instance, *no one* or *nothing*. As the following chart shows, Spanish indefinite words have corresponding negative words, which are opposite in meaning.

Indefinite and negative words

Indefinite words		Negative words	
algo	*something; anything*	**nada**	*nothing; not anything*
alguien	*someone; somebody; anyone*	**nadie**	*no one; nobody; not anyone*
alguno/a(s), algún	*some; any*	**ninguno/a, ningún**	*no; none; not any*
o... o	*either... or*	**ni... ni**	*neither... nor*
siempre	*always*	**nunca, jamás**	*never, not ever*
también	*also; too*	**tampoco**	*neither; not either*

▶ There are two ways to form negative sentences in Spanish: 1) You can place the negative word before the verb, or 2) you can place **no** before the verb and the negative word after the verb.

Nadie se levanta temprano.
No one gets up early.

No se levanta nadie temprano.
No one gets up early.

Ellos **nunca se enojan**.
They never get angry.

Ellos **no se enojan nunca**.
They never get angry.

Yo siempre me despierto a las seis en punto. ¿Y tú?

Pues yo jamás me levanto temprano. Nunca oigo el despertador.

▶ Because they refer to people, **alguien** and **nadie** are often used with the personal **a**. The personal **a** is also used before **alguno/a, algunos/as,** and **ninguno/a** when these words refer to people and they are the direct object of the verb.

—Perdón, señor, ¿busca Ud. **a alguien**?
—No, gracias, señorita, no busco **a nadie**.

—Tomás, ¿buscas **a alguno** de tus hermanos?
—No, mamá, no busco **a ninguno**.

¡ATENCIÓN!

Before a masculine, singular noun, **alguno** and **ninguno** are shortened to **algún** and **ningún**.

—¿Tienen ustedes algún amigo peruano?
—No, no tenemos ningún amigo peruano.

•••

Alguno/a, algunos/as are not always used in the same way English uses *some* or *any*. Often, **algún** is used where ***a*** would be used in English.

¿Tienes algún libro que hable de los incas?
Do you have ***a*** *book that talks about the Incas?*

TEACHING OPTIONS

Extra Practice Write sentences like the following on the board and have the students complete them with an indefinite or negative word. Ex: **Los vegetarianos no comen carne ____ (nunca). Las madres ____ (siempre) se preocupan por sus hijos. En las fiestas ella no es sociable, ____ (ni) baila ____ (ni) habla con ____ (nadie).**

Pairs Have students practice by taking turns giving one-word indefinite and negative word prompts and having the other respond in full sentences. Ex: **E1: siempre. E2: Siempre le mando un mensaje electrónico a mi madre por la mañana. E1: tampoco E2: Yo no me levanto temprano tampoco.**

COMPARE & CONTRAST

In English, it is incorrect to use more than one negative word in a sentence. In Spanish, however, sentences frequently contain two or more negative words. Compare the following Spanish and English sentences.

Nunca le escribo a **nadie**.
*I **never** write to **anyone**.*

No me preocupo por **nada nunca**.
*I do **not ever** worry about **anything**.*

As the preceding sentences show, once an English sentence contains one negative word (for example, *not* or *never*), no other negative word may be used. Instead, indefinite (or affirmative) words are used. In Spanish, however, once a sentence is negative, no other affirmative (that is, indefinite) word may be used. Instead, all indefinite ideas must be expressed in the negative.

▶ Although in Spanish **pero** and **sino** both mean *but*, they are not interchangeable. **Sino** is used when the first part of a sentence is negative and the second part contradicts it. In this context, **sino** means *but rather* or *on the contrary*. In all other cases, **pero** is used to mean *but*.

Los estudiantes no se acuestan temprano **sino** tarde.
*The students don't go to bed early, **but rather** late.*

Las toallas son caras, **pero** bonitas.
*The towels are expensive, **but** beautiful.*

María no habla francés **sino** español.
*María doesn't speak French, **but rather** Spanish.*

José es inteligente, **pero** no saca buenas notas.
*José is intelligent **but** doesn't get good grades.*

¡INTÉNTALO! Cambia las siguientes frases para que sean negativas. La primera frase se da *(is given)* como ejemplo.

1. Siempre se viste bien.
   Nunca se viste bien.
   No se viste bien nunca.
2. Alguien se ducha.
   Nadie se ducha.
   No se ducha nadie.
3. Ellas van también.
   Ellas tampoco van.
   Ellas no van tampoco.
4. Alguien se pone nervioso.
   Nadie se pone nervioso.
   No se pone nervioso nadie.
5. Tú siempre te lavas las manos.
   Tú nunca / jamás te lavas las manos.
   Tú no te lavas las manos nunca / jamás.
6. Voy a traer algo.
   No voy a traer nada.
7. Juan se afeita también.
   Juan tampoco se afeita.
   Juan no se afeita tampoco.
8. Mis amigos viven en una residencia o en casa.
   Mis amigos no viven ni en una residencia ni en casa.
9. La profesora hace algo en su escritorio.
   La profesora no hace nada en su escritorio.
10. Tú y yo vamos al mercado.
    Ni tú ni yo vamos al mercado.
11. Tienen un espejo en su casa.
    No tienen ningún espejo en su casa.
12. Algunos niños se ponen el abrigo.
    Ningún niño se pone el abrigo.

Suggestions

- Reiterate that there is no limit to the number of negative words that can be strung together in a sentence in Spanish. Ex: **No hablo con nadie nunca de ningún problema, ni con mi familia ni con mis amigos.**
- Elicit negative responses by asking questions whose answers will clearly be negative. Ex: **¿Alguien lleva zapatos de lunares? (No, nadie lleva zapatos de lunares.) ¿Alguien tiene una moto en la mochila? (No, nadie tiene una moto en la mochila.)**
- Give examples of **pero** and **sino** using the seating of the students. Ex: ___ **se sienta al lado de** ___ **, pero no al lado de** ___ **. No se sienta a la izquierda de** ___ **, sino a la derecha.** ___ **no se sienta al lado de la ventana, pero está cerca de la puerta.**

TEACHING OPTIONS

Video Show the video again to give students more input containing indefinite and negative words. Stop the video where appropriate to discuss how these words are used.

Small Groups Give small groups five minutes to write a description of **un(a) señor(a) muy, pero muy antipático/a**. Tell students to use as many indefinite and negative words as possible to describe what makes this person so unpleasant.

1 Suggestion Ask a volunteer to change the **modelo** so that **sino** would be the correct choice. Ex: **Muchos estudiantes no viven en la residencia estudiantil, sino en apartamentos.**

1 Expansion Have pairs create four sentences, two with **sino** and two with **pero**. Have them "dehydrate" their sentences as in the **modelo** and exchange them with another pair who will write the complete sentences.

2 Suggestions

- Review indefinite and negative words by using them in short sentences and asking volunteers to contradict your statement. Ex: **Veo a alguien en la puerta. (No, usted no ve a nadie en la puerta.) Nunca vengo a clase con el libro. (No, usted siempre viene a clase con el libro.)**
- Display a magazine picture that shows a group of people involved in a specific activity. Then talk about the picture, modeling the types of constructions required in **Actividad 2**. Ex: **Todos trabajan en la oficina, pero sólo algunos tienen computadora.**

2 Expansion After students have dramatized the conversation in pairs, ask them to summarize it. **Ana María no encontró ningún regalo para Eliana. Tampoco vio a ninguna amiga en el centro comercial.**

Práctica

1 **¿Pero o sino?** Forma frases sobre los estudiantes usando **pero** o **sino.**

modelo

Muchos estudiantes viven en residencias estudiantiles / muchos de ellos quieren vivir fuera del campus.

Muchos estudiantes viven en residencias estudiantiles, pero muchos de ellos quieren vivir fuera del campus.

1. Marcos nunca se despierta temprano / siempre llega puntual a clase.
   Marcos nunca se despierta temprano, pero siempre llega puntual a clase.
2. Lisa y Katarina no se acuestan temprano / muy tarde.
   Lisa y Katarina no se acuestan temprano sino muy tarde.
3. Alfonso es inteligente / algunas veces es antipático.
   Alfonso es inteligente, pero algunas veces es antipático.
4. Los directores de la residencia no son ecuatorianos / peruanos.
   Los directores de la residencia no son ecuatorianos sino peruanos.
5. No nos acordamos de comprar champú / compramos jabón.
   No nos acordamos de comprar champú, pero compramos jabón.
6. Emilia no es estudiante / profesora.
   Emilia no es estudiante sino profesora.
7. No quiero levantarme / tengo que ir a clase.
   No quiero levantarme, pero tengo que ir a clase.
8. Miguel no se afeita por la mañana / por la noche.
   Miguel no se afeita por la mañana sino por la noche.

2 **Completar** Completa esta conversación. Usa expresiones negativas en tus respuestas. Luego, dramatiza la conversación con un(a) compañero/a. Answers will vary.

AURELIO Ana María, ¿encontraste algún regalo para Eliana?
ANA MARÍA (1) No, no encontré ningún regalo/nada para Eliana.
AURELIO ¿Viste a algunas amigas en el centro comercial?
ANA MARÍA (2) No, no vi a ninguna amiga/ninguna/nadie en el centro comercial.
AURELIO ¿Me llamó alguien?
ANA MARÍA (3) No, nadie te llamó./No, no te llamó nadie.
AURELIO ¿Quieres ir al teatro o al cine esta noche?
ANA MARÍA (4) No, no quiero ir ni al teatro ni al cine.
AURELIO ¿No quieres salir a comer?
ANA MARÍA (5) No, no quiero salir a comer (tampoco).
AURELIO ¿Hay algo interesante en la televisión esta noche?
ANA MARÍA (6) No, no hay nada interesante en la televisión.
AURELIO ¿Tienes algún problema?
ANA MARÍA (7) No, no tengo ningún problema/ninguno.

TEACHING OPTIONS

Extra Practice Have students bring pairs of photos or magazine pictures to class, such as two photos of different family members, to compare and contrast. Divide the class into groups of three and have each student present his or her pictures to the group. Ex: **Éste es mi tío Ignacio. Siempre viene a casa los domingos. Ésta es mi tía Yolanda. Vive en Lima y por eso nunca viene a casa.**

Extra Practice To provide oral practice with indefinite and negative words, create prompts that follow the pattern of the sentences in **Actividad 1** and **Actividad 2**. Say the first part of the sentence, then have students repeat it and finish the sentence. Ex: ___ **no se viste de azul hoy, sino** ___ **(de verde).** ___ **no llegó puntualmente a clase hoy, sino** ___ **(tarde).**

Comunicación

3 **Opiniones** Completa estas frases de una manera lógica. Luego, compara tus respuestas con las de un(a) compañero/a. Answers will vary.

1. Mi habitación es ________ pero ________.
2. Mis padres no son ________ sino ________.
3. Mi compañero/a es ________ pero ________.
4. Por la noche me gusta ________ pero ________.
5. Un(a) profesor(a) ideal no es ________ sino ________.
6. Mis amigos son ________ pero ________.

4 **Quejas *(Complaints)*** En parejas hagan (*make*) una lista de cinco quejas comunes (*common*) que tienen los estudiantes. Usen expresiones negativas. Answers will vary.

modelo

Nadie me entiende.

Ahora hagan (*make*) una lista de cinco quejas que los padres tienen de sus hijos.

modelo

Nunca limpian sus habitaciones.

5 **Anuncios *(Ads)*** En parejas, lean el anuncio y respondan a las preguntas. Answers will vary.

1. ¿Es el anuncio positivo o negativo? ¿Por qué? Answers will vary.
2. ¿Cuáles son las palabras indefinidas en el anuncio? algún, siempre, algo
3. Escriban el texto del anuncio cambiando todo por expresiones negativas. ¿No buscas ningún producto especial? ¡Nunca hay nada para nadie en las tiendas García!
4. Ahora preparen su propio (*own*) anuncio usando expresiones afirmativas y negativas para compartir con la clase.

¿Buscas algún producto especial?
¡Siempre hay algo para todos en las tiendas García!

¡LENGUA VIVA!

When companies decide to advertise in foreign markets, they must be very careful not to rely on literal translations, since false cognates and unintended interpretations can become real problems.

Síntesis

6 **Encuesta** Tu profesor(a) te va a dar una hoja de actividades para hacer una encuesta. Circula por la clase y pídeles a tus compañeros que comparen las actividades que hacen durante la semana con las que hacen durante los fines de semana. Escribe las respuestas. Answers will vary.

3 Suggestion Before assigning the activity, give some personal examples using different subjects. Ex: **Mi hijo es inteligente, pero no le gusta estudiar. Mi amiga no es norteamericana, sino española.**

4 Expansion Divide the class into all-male and all-female groups. Then have each group make two different lists: **Quejas que tienen los hombres de las mujeres** and **Quejas que tienen las mujeres de los hombres**. After five minutes, compare and contrast the answers and perceptions.

5 Expansion Have pairs work with another pair to combine the best aspects of each of their individual ads. Then have them present the "fused" ads to the class.

6 Suggestion Distribute the **Hojas de actividades** from the IRM that correspond to this activity.

6 Expansion Have students write five sentences using the information obtained through the **encuesta**. Ex: **Nadie va a la biblioteca durante el fin de semana, pero muchos vamos durante la semana. No estudiamos los sábados sino los domingos.**

TEACHING OPTIONS

Large Group Write the names of four vacation spots on four slips of paper and post them in different corners of the room. Ask students to pick their vacation preference by going to one of the corners. Then, have each group produce five reasons for their choice as well as one complaint about each of the other places.

Extra Practice Have students complete the following cloze activity using **pero, sino,** and **tampoco: Yo me levanto temprano y hago mi tarea, ___ (pero) mi compañera de apartamento prefiere hacerla por la noche y acostarse muy tarde. Ella no tiene exámenes este semestre ___ (sino) proyectos. Yo no tengo exámenes ___ (tampoco). Sólo tengo mucha, mucha tarea.**

Section Goal

In **Estructura 7.3** students will learn the preterite of **ser** and **ir**.

Instructional Resources
WB/VM: Workbook, p. 79
Lab Manual, p. 41
Lab CD/MP3 ***Lección 7***
IRM: ***¡Inténtalo! & Práctica*** *Answers, pp. 208–209; Tapescript, pp. 30–34*
Interactive CD-ROM
Companion website: www.vistahigherlearning.com
Presentations CD-ROM

Suggestions

- Ask volunteers to answer questions such as: **¿Fuiste al cine el sábado pasado? ¿Cómo fue la película? ¿Fueron tus amigos y tú a alguna fiesta durante el fin de semana? ¿Fue agradable la fiesta? ¿Quiénes fueron?**
- Contrast the preterite of **ser** and **ir** by saying pairs of sentences. Ex: **Anteayer fue sábado. Fui al supermercado el sábado. Ayer fue domingo. No fui al supermercado ayer. ¿Fueron ustedes al partido de fútbol el sábado? ¿Fue divertido el partido?** Point out that although the preterite forms of **ser** and **ir** are identical, there is rarely any confusion because context makes the meaning clear.

7.3 Preterite of ser and ir

NATIONAL
comparisons
STANDARDS

ANTE TODO In **Lección 6**, you learned how to form the preterite tense of regular **-ar**, **-er**, and **-ir** verbs. The following chart contains the preterite forms of **ser** (*to be*) and **ir** (*to go*). Since these forms are irregular, you will need to memorize them.

Preterite of *ser* and *ir*

		ser (*to be*)	**ir** (*to go*)
SINGULAR FORMS	yo	**fui**	**fui**
	tú	**fuiste**	**fuiste**
	Ud./él/ella	**fue**	**fue**
PLURAL FORMS	nosotros/as	**fuimos**	**fuimos**
	vosotros/as	**fuisteis**	**fuisteis**
	Uds./ellos/ellas	**fueron**	**fueron**

¡ATENCIÓN!

Note that, whereas regular **-er** and **-ir** verbs have accent marks in the **yo** and **Ud.** forms of the preterite, **ser** and **ir** do not.

▶ Since the preterite forms of **ser** and **ir** are identical, context clarifies which of the two verbs is being used.

Él **fue** a comprar champú y jabón.
He went to buy shampoo and soap.

—¿Cómo **fue** la película anoche?
How was the movie last night?

¿Adónde fueron Uds.?

Inés y yo fuimos a un mercado. Fue muy divertido.

¡INTÉNTALO! Completa las siguientes frases usando el pretérito de **ser** e **ir**. La primera frase de cada columna se da (*is given*) como ejemplo.

ir

1. Los viajeros __fueron__ a Perú.
2. Patricia __fue__ a Cuzco.
3. Tú __fuiste__ a Iquitos.
4. Gregorio y yo __fuimos__ a Lima.
5. Yo __fui__ a Trujillo.
6. Ustedes __fueron__ a Arequipa.
7. Mi padre __fue__ a Lima.
8. Nosotras __fuimos__ a Cuzco.
9. Él __fue__ a Machu Picchu.
10. Usted __fue__ a Nazca.

ser

1. Usted __fue__ muy amable.
2. Yo __fui__ muy cordial.
3. Ellos __fueron__ muy simpáticos.
4. Nosotros __fuimos__ muy desagradables.
5. Ella __fue__ muy antipática.
6. Tú __fuiste__ muy chistoso.
7. Ustedes __fueron__ muy cordiales.
8. La gente __fue__ muy agradable.
9. Tomás y yo __fuimos__ muy corteses.
10. Los profesores __fueron__ muy buenos.

TEACHING OPTIONS

Video Play the video segment and have students listen for preterite forms of **ser** and **ir**. Stop the video with each example to illustrate how context makes the meaning of the verb clear.

Pairs Have pairs of students solve this logic problem. **"Las vacaciones" Mis compañeros de casa, Julia y Fernando, y yo fuimos de vacaciones durante el mes de julio a Puerto Rico, a Chile y a México. Julia fue a un viaje de esquí, pero Fernando y yo fuimos a lugares donde hace sol. El viaje de Fernando fue desagradable porque hubo** (*there was*) **un huracán y fue imposible nadar en el Pacífico durante esos días. Por suerte, mi viaje fue muy agradable. ¿Adónde fui? (A Puerto Rico)**

Práctica

1 **Completar** Completa estas conversaciones con la forma correcta del pretérito de **ser** o **ir**. Indica el infinitivo de cada forma verbal.

Conversación 1

RAÚL ¿Adónde (1) fueron/ir ustedes de vacaciones?
PILAR (2) Fuimos/ir al Perú.
RAÚL ¿Cómo (3) fue/ser el viaje?
PILAR ¡(4) Fue/ser estupendo! Machu Picchu y la Plaza de Armas son increíbles.
RAÚL ¿(5) Fue/ser caro el viaje?
PILAR No, el precio (6) fue/ser muy bajo, sólo costó tres mil dólares.

Conversación 2

ISABEL Tina y Vicente (7) fueron/ser novios, ¿no?
LUCÍA Sí, pero ahora no. Anoche Tina (8) fue/ir a comer con Gregorio y la semana pasada ellos (9) fueron/ir al partido de fútbol.
ISABEL ¿Ah sí? Javier y yo (10) fuimos/ir al partido y no los vimos.

NOTA CULTURAL

La **Plaza de Armas** en Lima, Perú, es la plaza más famosa de la ciudad.
Es un sitio turístico muy popular. En la plaza está el palacio municipal. También hay jardines de rosas (*rose gardens*), una fuente (*fountain*), y una catedral.

2 **Descripciones** Forma frases con los siguientes elementos. Usa el pretérito. Answers will vary.

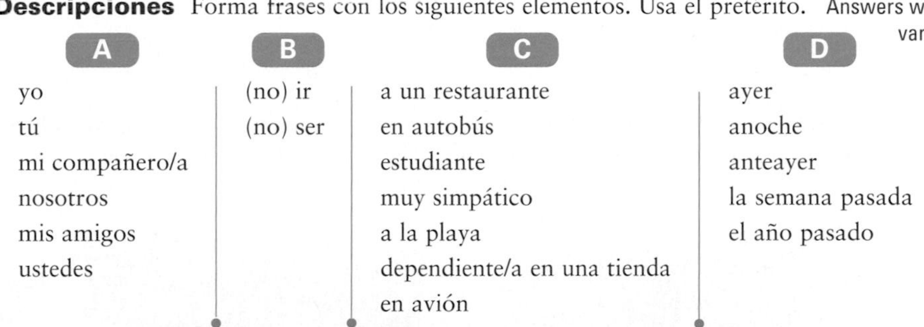

A	B	C	D
yo	(no) ir	a un restaurante	ayer
tú	(no) ser	en autobús	anoche
mi compañero/a		estudiante	anteayer
nosotros		muy simpático	la semana pasada
mis amigos		a la playa	el año pasado
ustedes		dependiente/a en una tienda	
		en avión	

Comunicación

3 **Preguntas** En parejas, túrnense (*take turns*) para hacerse estas preguntas. Answers will vary.

1. ¿Adónde fuiste de vacaciones este año? ¿Con quién fuiste?
2. ¿Cómo fueron tus vacaciones?
3. ¿Fuiste de compras esta semana? ¿Adónde? ¿Qué compraste?
4. ¿Fuiste al cine la semana pasada? ¿Fueron tus amigos también?
5. ¿Qué película viste? ¿Cómo fue?
6. ¿Fuiste a la cafetería hoy? ¿A qué hora?
7. ¿Adónde fuiste durante el fin de semana? ¿Por qué?
8. ¿Quién fue tu profesor(a) favorito/a el semestre pasado? ¿Por qué?

4 **El viaje** En parejas, escriban un diálogo de un(a) viajero/a hablando con el/la agente de viajes sobre un viaje que tomó recientemente. Tienen cinco minutos para escribirlo. La pareja con más usos del pretérito de **ser** e **ir** y con menos errores gana. Answers will vary.

modelo

Agente: *¿Cómo fue el viaje?*
Viajero: *El viaje fue maravilloso/horrible...*

1 Suggestion Before assigning the activity, write these cloze sentences on the board and ask volunteers to fill in the blanks. Ex: **¿Cómo ____ (fueron) los guías turísticos durante tu viaje? ¿Quién ____ (fue) con Marcela al baile?**

1 Expansion Ask small groups to write four questions based on the conversations. They should not write the answers. Groups then exchange papers and answer the questions they receive. Have them confirm their answers with the group who wrote the questions.

2 Expansion Ask a volunteer to say one of his or her sentences aloud. Point to another student, and call out an interrogative word in order to cue a question. Ex: **E1: No fui a un restaurante.** Say: **¿Adónde? E2: ¿Adónde fuiste?**

3 Expansion Have pairs team up to form groups of four. Each student should report three things about his or her partner to the group.

4 Expansion Ask pairs to write a similar conversation within a different context. Ex: **Un día horrible**.

TEACHING OPTIONS

Pairs Have groups of students role-play a TV interview with astronauts who have just returned from a long stay on Mars. Have students review previous lesson vocabulary lists as necessary in preparation. Give groups sufficient time to plan and practice their skits. When all groups have completed the activity, ask a few of them to perform their role-play for the whole class.

Heritage Speakers Ask heritage speakers to write a brief essay about their first experiences learning English. Have them read their accounts to the class, making sure to note new vocabulary on the board.

Section Goals

In **Estructura 7.4** students will learn:

- all forms of **gustar**
- other verbs that follow the pattern of **gustar**

Instructional Resources
WB/VM: Workbook, pp. 80–82
Lab Manual, p. 42
Lab CD/MP3 ***Lección 7***
IRM: ***¡Inténtalo! & Práctica*** *Answers, pp. 208–209; Tapescript, pp. 30–34*
Info Gap Activities Booklet, pp. 27–28
Interactive CD-ROM
Companion website: www.vistahigherlearning.com
Presentations CD-ROM

Suggestions

- Use realia to compare different products using the verb **gustar**. Ex: (with clothing) **Me gustan estos pantalones, pero no me gustan estos zapatos.** Then ask volunteers questions using different indirect object pronouns. Ex: _____ **, ¿te gusta este suéter?** _____ **, ¿le gusta a** _____ **este suéter?**
- Write the headings **Gustos** and **Disgustos** on the board. Have the class brainstorm a list of likes and dislikes among the college population including music artists, movies, clothes, or hobbies. Use the lists to form statements and questions illustrating the use of the verb **gustar**. Use different indirect object pronouns. Ex: **A los estudiantes universitarios no les gustan los Beatles. A mis amigos y a mí, sí nos gustan los Beatles. A los estudiantes no les gustan las películas infantiles.**

7.4 Gustar and verbs like gustar

ANTE TODO In **Lección 2**, you learned that the expressions **me gusta(n)** and **te gusta(n)** express the English concepts of *I like* and *you like.* You will now learn more about the verb **gustar** and other similar verbs. Observe the following examples.

Me gusta ese champú. 
ENGLISH EQUIVALENT *I like that shampoo.*
LITERAL MEANING *That shampoo is pleasing to me.*

¿**Te gustaron** las clases? 
ENGLISH EQUIVALENT *Did you like the classes?*
LITERAL MEANING *Were the classes pleasing to you?*

▶ As the examples show, the construction **me gusta(n)** does not have a direct equivalent in English. The literal meaning of this construction is *to be pleasing to (someone),* and it requires the use of an indirect object pronoun.

INDIRECT OBJECT PRONOUN		SUBJECT	SUBJECT		DIRECT OBJECT
Me	**gusta**	ese champú.	*I*	*like*	*that shampoo.*

▶ In the diagram above, observe how in the Spanish sentence the object being liked **(ese champú)** is really the subject of the sentence. The person who likes the object, in turn, is an indirect object because it answers the question: *To whom is the shampoo pleasing?*

¿No te gustan las computadoras?

Me gustan mucho los parques.

▶ The forms most commonly used with **gustar** and similar verbs are the third person (singular and plural). When the object or person being liked is singular, the singular form **(gusta)** is used. When two or more objects or persons are being liked, the plural form **(gustan)** is used. Observe the following diagram:

SINGULAR	me, te, le	gusta gustó	la película el concierto
PLURAL	nos, os, les	gustan gustaron	las vacaciones los museos de Lima

▶ To express what someone likes or does not like to do, **gustar** is followed by an infinitive. The singular form of **gustar** is used even if there is more than one infinitive.

No **nos gusta comer** a las nueve.
We don't like to eat at nine o'clock.

Les gusta cantar y **bailar** en las fiestas.
They like to sing and dance at parties.

TEACHING OPTIONS

Heritage Speakers Have heritage speakers compare and contrast activities they like to do with activities their parents/grandparents like to do. Encourage them to use the verb **gustar** and others that follow the same pattern, referring them to the list of verbs on page 221.

Game Divide the class into small groups. Give a prompt including subject and object. Ex: **ella/películas de horror.** Groups will have one minute to construct a sentence using **gustar** or one of the verbs that follow the pattern of **gustar**. Then one member from each group will write the sentence on the board. Award one point to each team for every correct response.

¡ATENCIÓN!

Mí (*me*) has an accent mark to distinguish it from the possessive adjective **mi** (*my*).

- The construction **a** + [*pronoun*] (**a mí, a ti, a Ud., a él,** etc.) is used to clarify or to emphasize who is pleased.

A ella le gustan las toallas verdes, pero **a él** no le gustan.
She likes green towels, but he doesn't like them.

A ti te gusta cenar en casa, pero **a mí** no me gusta.
You like to eat dinner at home, but I don't like to.

- The construction **a** + [*noun*] can also be used before the indirect object pronoun to clarify or to emphasize who is pleased.

A los turistas les gustó mucho Machu Picchu.
The tourists liked Machu Picchu a lot.

A Juanita le gustaron mucho los mercados al aire libre.
Juanita liked the open-air markets a lot.

- Other verbs in Spanish are used in the same way as **gustar**. Here is a list of the most common ones.

Verbs like *gustar*

aburrir	*to bore*	**importar**	*to be important to; to matter*
encantar	*to like very much; to love* (inanimate objects)	**interesar**	*to be interesting to; to interest*
faltar	*to lack; to need*	**molestar**	*to bother; to annoy*
fascinar	*to fascinate*	**quedar**	*to be left over; to fit* (clothing)

¡ATENCIÓN!

Faltar expresses what is lacking or missing. Ex: **Me falta una página.** *I'm missing one page.*

Quedar expresses how much of something is left. Ex: **Nos quedan tres pesos.** *We have three pesos left.*

• • •

Quedar means *to fit.* It's also used to tell *how something looks* (on someone).

Ex: **Estos zapatos me quedan bien.** *These shoes fit me well.*

Esa camisa te queda muy bien. *That shirt looks good on you.*

¡INTÉNTALO! Indica el pronombre del objeto indirecto y la forma del tiempo presente adecuados en cada frase. La primera frase de cada columna se da (*is given*) como ejemplo.

gustar

1. A él ___le gusta___ viajar.
2. A mí ___me gusta___ bailar.
3. A nosotras ___nos gusta___ cantar.
4. A ustedes ___les gusta___ leer.
5. A ti ___te gusta___ correr.
6. A Pedro ___le gusta___ gritar.
7. A mis padres ___les gusta___ caminar.
8. A usted ___le gusta___ jugar tenis.
9. A mi esposo y a mí ___nos gusta___ dormir.
10. A Alberto ___le gusta___ dibujar.
11. A todos ___nos/les gusta___ opinar.
12. A Pili no ___le gusta___ ir de compras.

encantar

1. A ellos ___les encantan___ los deportes.
2. A ti ___te encantan___ las películas.
3. A usted ___le encantan___ los viajes.
4. A mí ___me encantan___ las revistas.
5. A Jorge y a Luis ___les encantan___ los perros.
6. A nosotros ___nos encantan___ las vacaciones.
7. A ustedes ___les encantan___ las fiestas.
8. A Marcela ___le encantan___ los libros.
9. A mis amigos ___les encantan___ los museos.
10. A ella ___le encanta___ el ciclismo.
11. A Pedro ___le encanta___ el limón.
12. A ti y a mí ___nos encanta___ el baile.

Suggestions

- Use the lists of **Gustos** and **Disgustos** previously generated by the students to ask questions using different forms of **gustar**.
- Write a model sentence on the board such as those found in the examples. Ex: **A Carlos le gusta la comida argentina.** Then change the noun and ask volunteers to say the new sentence. Ex: **A nosotros (A nosotros nos gusta la comida argentina.)**
- Give examples of other common Spanish verbs that follow the pattern of **gustar**. Ex: **A mí me encantan las lenguas, pero me aburren las matemáticas. ¿Qué les interesa a ustedes? ¿Qué les aburre?**

TEACHING OPTIONS

Large Group Have the class sit in a circle. Student A begins by saying **Me gusta** and an activity he or she enjoys. Ex: **Me gusta correr.** Student B reports what student A said and adds his or her own favorite activity. **A Frank le gusta correr. A mí me gusta bailar.** Student C reports the preferences of the first two students and adds his or her own, and so forth. This activity may be used with any verb that follows the pattern of **gustar**.

Extra Practice Use this as a dictation. **1. A todos en mi familia nos encanta viajar. 2. Nos gusta viajar en avión, pero nos molestan los aviones pequeños. 3. A mi hijo le interesan las culturas latinoamericanas, a mi esposo le encantan los países de Asia y a mí me fascina Europa. 4. Todavía nos quedan muchos lugares por visitar y nos falta el tiempo necesario.**

1 Suggestion Before assigning the activity, have students underline the subject in each sentence.

1 Expansion Have students use the verbs in the activity to write a paragraph describing their own musical tastes.

2 Expansion Show students magazine pictures of people enjoying or not enjoying what they're doing. Ask them to form additional sentences with **gustar** or verbs that follow its pattern.

3 Expansion Have students call out the two additional sentences they created. After everyone has had a turn, ask the class how many similar or identical sentences they heard and what they were.

Práctica

1 **Completar** Completa las frases con todos los elementos necesarios.

1. __A__ Adela __le gustan__ (gustar) las canciones (*songs*) de Enrique Iglesias.
2. A __mí__ me __gusta__ (gustar) más la música de Shakira.
3. A mis amigos __les encanta__ (encantar) la música de Maná.
4. __A__ Juan y Rafael no les __molesta__ (molestar) la música alta (*loud*).
5. __A__ nosotros __nos fascinan__ (fascinar) los grupos de pop latino.
6. Creo que a Elena __le interesa__ (interesar) más la música clásica.
7. A __mí__ me __aburre__ (aburrir) la música clásica.
8. ¿A __ti__ te __falta__ (faltar) dinero para el concierto de Carlos Santana?
9. Sí. Sólo __me quedan__ (quedar) cinco dólares.
10. ¿Cuánto dinero te __queda__ (quedar) a __ti__?

NOTA CULTURAL

Ahora la música latina es popular en los EE.UU. gracias a artistas como **Shakira**, de nacionalidad colombiana, y **Enrique Iglesias**, español. Pero hay artistas famosos como **Carlos Santana** y **Gloria Estefan** que difundieron (*spread*) la música latina por todo el mundo (*world*) en los años 60, 70, 80 y 90.

2 **Describir** Mira los dibujos y describe lo que está pasando. Usa los siguientes verbos.

aburrir	faltar	molestar
encantar	interesar	quedar

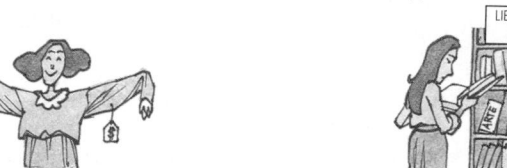

1. A Ramón le molesta el despertador.
2. A nosotros nos encanta esquiar.
3. A ti no te queda bien este vestido. A ti te queda mal/grande este vestido.
4. A Sara le interesan los libros de arte moderno.

3 **Gustos** Forma frases con los elementos de las columnas A, B y C. Después, inventa dos frases originales con los mismos verbos.

modelo

A ti te interesan las ruinas de Machu Picchu.

A	B	C
yo	aburrir	despertarse temprano
tú	encantar	mirarse en el espejo
mi mejor amigo/a	faltar	la música rock
mis amigos y yo	gustar	las pantuflas rosadas
Bart y Homer Simpson	interesar	la pasta de dientes con menta (*mint*)
Shakira	molestar	las ruinas de Machu Picchu
Antonio Banderas		los zapatos caros

TEACHING OPTIONS

Heritage Speakers Ask heritage speakers to talk about the music they like to listen to and don't like to listen to. Ask them to explain why they like it or don't like it. Ask if some music is good for dancing and some for listening, and so forth. Have them bring in an example for the class to listen to.

Extra Practice Write sentences like these on the board. Have students copy them and draw a face (☺/☹) next to each to indicate the feelings expressed in each sentence. Ex: **Me encantan las enchiladas verdes. (☺) 1. Me aburren las matemáticas. 2. Me fascina la ópera italiana. 3. Me falta dinero para comprar un auto. 4. Me queda pequeño el sombrero. 5. Me molestan los niños. 6. Me interesa la ecología.**

Comunicación

4 **Preguntas** En parejas, túrnense para hacer y contestar estas preguntas. Answers will vary.

1. ¿Te gusta levantarte temprano o tarde? ¿Por qué? ¿Y tu compañero/a de cuarto?
2. ¿Te gusta acostarte temprano o tarde? ¿Y tu compañero/a de cuarto?
3. ¿Te gusta dormir la siesta?
4. ¿Te gusta acampar o prefieres quedarte en un hotel cuando estás de vacaciones?
5. ¿Qué te gusta hacer en el verano?
6. ¿Qué te gusta más de esta universidad? ¿Qué te molesta?
7. ¿Te interesan más las ciencias o las humanidades? ¿Por qué?
8. ¿Qué cosas te molestan?

NOTA CULTURAL

La siesta (un descanso de dos o tres horas) no es hoy tan común como antes.
Cuando España entró en la Unión Europea, muchas empresas (*businesses*) redujeron (*reduced*) la siesta.

5 **Completar** Completa estas frases de una manera lógica. Answers will vary.

1. A mi novio/a le fascina(n)...
2. A mi mejor (*best*) amigo/a no le interesa(n)...
3. A mis padres les importa(n)...
4. A nosotros nos molesta(n)...
5. A mis hermanos les aburre(n)...
6. A mi compañero/a de cuarto le aburre(n)...
7. A los turistas les interesa(n)...
8. A los jugadores profesionales les encanta(n)...
9. A nuestro/a profesor(a) le molesta(n)...

6  

La residencia Tú y tu compañero/a de clase son los directores de una residencia estudiantil en Perú. Su profesor(a) les va a dar a cada uno de ustedes las descripciones de cinco estudiantes. Con la información tienen que escoger (*choose*) quiénes van a ser compañeros de cuarto. Después, completen la lista.

Síntesis

7 **Situación** Trabajen en parejas para representar los papeles (*roles*) de un(a) cliente/a y un(a) dependiente/a. Usen las instrucciones como guía. Answers will vary.

Dependiente/a	Cliente/a
Saluda al/a la cliente/a y pregúntale cómo lo/la puedes ayudar.	Saluda al/a la dependiente/a y dile (*tell him/her*) qué quieres comprar y qué colores prefieres.
Pregúntale si le interesan los estilos modernos y empieza a enseñarle la ropa.	Explícale que los estilos modernos te interesan. Escoge (*choose*) las cosas que te interesan.
Habla de los gustos del/de la cliente/a.	Habla de la ropa ((no) me queda(n) bien/mal, me encanta(n)...).
Da opiniones favorables al/a la cliente/a (las botas te quedan fantásticas...).	Decide cuáles son las cosas que te gustan y qué vas a comprar.

4 Expansion Take a class survey of the answers and write the results on the board. Ask volunteers to use verbs like **gustar** to summarize them.

5 Suggestion For items that start with **A mi(s)...** , have pairs compare their answers and then report to the class: first answers in common, then answers that differed. Ex: **A mis padres les importan los estudios, pero a los padres de ____ les importa más el dinero.**

6 Suggestion Divide the class into pairs and distribute the Info Gap Handouts from the Info Gap Activities Booklet that correspond to this activity. Give the students ten minutes to complete this activity.

6 Expansions
- Have pairs compare their matches by walking around the classroom until they have all compared their answers with one another.
- Have pairs choose one of the students and write her want ad looking for a suitable roommate.

7 Expansion Ask pairs to perform their conversation for the class or have them videotape it outside of class.

TEACHING OPTIONS

Pairs Have pairs prepare short TV commercials in which they use the target verbs presented in **Estructura 7.4** to sell a particular product. Group three pairs together so that each pair presents its skit to four other students.

Game Give groups of students five minutes to write a description of social life during a specific historical period such as the French Revolution or prehistoric times using as many of the target verbs presented in **Estructura 7.4** as possible. After the time is up ask groups the number of these verbs they used in their descriptions. Have the top three read their descriptions for the class. Students vote for the best description.

Section Goals

In **Lectura** students will:

- learn the strategy of predicting content from the title
- read an e-mail in Spanish

Instructional Resource
Companion website: www.vistahigherlearning.com

Estrategia Tell students that they can often predict the content of a newspaper article from its headline. Display or make up several cognate-rich headlines from Spanish newspapers, for example: **Decenas de miles recuerdan la explosión atómica en Hiroshima; Lanzamiento de musicahoy.net, sitio para profesionales y aficionados a la música; Anuncian el descubrimiento de nueve planetas**. Ask students to predict the content of each article.

Compartir Have students discuss how they are able to tell what the content will be by looking at the format of the text.

Cognados Discuss how scanning the text for cognates can help you predict the content of a text.

Lectura

Antes de leer

Estrategia

Predicting content from the title

Prediction is an invaluable strategy in reading for comprehension. We can usually predict the content of a newspaper article from its headline, for example. More often than not, we decide whether or not to read the article based on its headline. Predicting content from the title will help you increase your reading comprehension in Spanish.

Examinar el texto

Lee el título de la lectura y haz tres predicciones sobre el contenido. Escribe tus predicciones en una hoja de papel.

Compartir

Comparte tus ideas con un(a) compañero/a de clase.

Cognados

Haz una lista de seis cognados que encuentres en la lectura.

1. ______________________.
2. ______________________.
3. ______________________.
4. ______________________.
5. ______________________.
6. ______________________.

¿Qué te dicen los cognados sobre el tema de la lectura?

recursos

vistahigher learning.com

¡Qué día!

Anterior ▾ Siguiente ▾ Responder Responder a todos

Fecha: Lunes, 10 de mayo
De: Guillermo Zamora
Asunto: ¡Qué día!
Para: Lupe; Marcos; Sandra; Jorge

Hola chicos:

La semana pasada me di cuenta° de que necesito organizar mejor mi rutina... pero especialmente necesito prepararme mejor para los exámenes. Me falta mucha disciplina, me molesta no tener control de mi tiempo y nunca deseo repetir los eventos de esta semana.

El miércoles pasé todo el día y toda la noche estudiando para el examen de biología del jueves por la mañana. Me aburre la biología y no empecé a estudiar hasta el día antes del examen. El jueves a las 8, después de no dormir en toda la noche, fui exhausto al examen. Fue difícil, pero afortunadamente° me acordé de todo el material. Esa noche me acosté temprano y dormí mucho.

Me desperté a las 9, y fue extraño° ver a mi compañero de

TEACHING OPTIONS

Extra Practice Ask students to go through the selection and find sentences with **gustar** or other verbs that follow its pattern (**aburrir, encantar**, etc.). Have them use third person pronouns to rewrite the sentences and talk about Guillermo and Andrés. Ex: **A Guillermo le aburre la biología.** Encourage students to say more about the characters and what happens to them by creating additional sentences of the **gustar** type.

Heritage Speakers Ask heritage speakers if they use e-mail regularly to keep in touch with friends and family in their home country. Ask them if they've ever used Spanish-language versions of popular web-based e-mail applications. Have them share with the class the ones they like best.

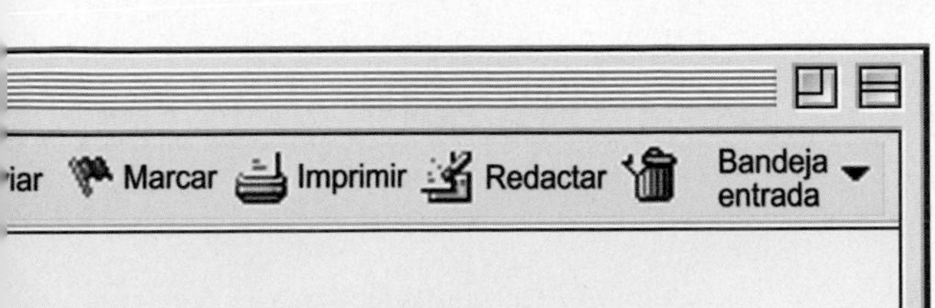

cuarto, Andrés, preparándose para ir a dormir. Nunca hablamos mucho y no comenté nada. Fui al baño a cepillarme los dientes para ir a clase. ¿Y Andrés? Él se acostó. "¡Qué extraño es este chico!," pensé.

Mi clase es a las 10, y fue necesario hacer las cosas rápido. Todo empezó a ir mal... eso pasa siempre cuando uno tiene prisa. Cuando busqué mis cosas para el baño, no las encontré. Entonces me duché sin jabón, me cepillé los dientes sin cepillo de dientes y me peiné con las manos. Tampoco encontré ropa limpia, y usé la sucia. Rápido, tomé mis libros. ¿Y Andrés? Roncando°... ¡a las 9:50!

Cuando salí corriendo para la clase, la prisa no me permitió ver el campus desierto. Cuando llegué a la clase, no vi a nadie. No vi al profesor ni a los estudiantes. Por último miré mi reloj, y vi la hora. Las 10 en punto... ¡de la noche!

¡Dormí 24 horas!

Guillermo

me di cuenta *I realized* **afortunadamente** *fortunately* **extraño** *strange* **Roncando** *snoring*

Después de leer

Seleccionar

Selecciona la respuesta (*answer*) correcta.

1. ¿Quién es el/la narrador(a)? _c_.
   a. Andrés
   b. una profesora
   c. Guillermo
2. ¿Qué le molesta al narrador? _b_.
   a. Le molestan los exámenes de biología.
   b. Le molesta no tener control de su tiempo.
   c. Le molesta mucho organizar su rutina.
3. ¿Por qué está exhausto? _c_.
   a. Porque fue a una fiesta la noche anterior.
   b. Porque no le gusta la biología.
   c. Porque pasó la noche anterior estudiando.
4. ¿Por qué no hay nadie en clase? _a_.
   a. Porque es de noche.
   b. Porque todos están de vacaciones.
   c. Porque el profesor canceló la clase.
5. ¿Cómo es la relación de Guillermo y Andrés? _b_
   a. Son buenos amigos.
   b. No hablan mucho.
   c. Tienen una buena relación.

Ordenar

Ordena los sucesos de la narración. Utiliza los números del 1 al 9.

a. Toma el examen de biología. _2_
b. No encuentra la bolsa para el baño. _5_
c. Andrés se duerme. _7_
d. Pasa todo el día y toda la noche estudiando para un examen. _1_
e. Se ducha sin jabón. _6_
f. Se acuesta temprano. _3_
g. Vuelve a su cuarto a las 10 de la noche. _9_
h. Se despierta a las 9 y su compañero de cuarto se prepara para dormir. _4_
i. Va a clase y no hay nadie. _8_

Contestar

Contesta estas preguntas. Answers will vary.

1. ¿Cómo es tu rutina diaria? ¿Muy organizada?
2. ¿Cuándo empiezas a estudiar para los exámenes?
3. ¿Tienes compañero/a de cuarto? ¿Son amigos/as?
4. Para comunicarte con tus amigos/as, ¿prefieres el teléfono o el correo electrónico? ¿Por qué?

Seleccionar Before beginning the activity, have students summarize the reading selection by listing all the verbs in the preterite. Then, have them use these verbs to talk about Guillermo's day.

Ordenar
- Before beginning, ask a volunteer to summarize in Spanish, using the third-person and present tense, the first two sentences of the reading selection.
- As writing practice, have students use the sentence in each item as the topic sentence of a short paragraph about Guillermo or Andrés.

Contestar Have students work in small groups to tell each other about a day when everything turned out wrong due to a miscalculation. Have groups vote for the most unusual story to share with the class.

TEACHING OPTIONS

Extra Practice Have pairs reconstruct Guillermo's confusing day graphically by means of one or more timelines (or other graphic representation). They should compare what Guillermo assumed was going on with what was actually occurring.

Pairs Have pairs of students work together to read the selection and write two questions about each paragraph. When they have finished, have them exchange their questions with another pair who can work together to answer them.

Section Goals

In **Escritura** students will:

- learn adverbial expressions of time to clarify transitions
- write a composition with an introduction, body, and conclusion in Spanish

Estrategia Discuss the importance of having an introduction (**introducción**), body (**parte principal**), and a conclusion (**conclusión**) in a narrative (**narración**). Then, with the entire class, read through the list of adverbs and adverbial phrases in the **Adverbios** box. Have volunteers create a sentence for each adverb or adverbial phrase listed.

Tema Read through the list of possible places with the students and have them choose the one in which they want to set their composition. Have groups of students who have chosen the same location get together and brainstorm ideas about how their daily routines would change in that place.

Note: This is the first time students will see these instructions entirely in Spanish. Remind them that much of what they will read in Spanish in **Plan de escritura** they already have seen several times in English. Go over **Ideas y organización** and **Primer borrador** with the class. Ask students to identify cognates that help them understand the instructions.

Escritura

Estrategia

Sequencing events

Paying strict attention to sequencing in a narrative will ensure that your writing flows logically from one part to the next. Of course, every composition should have an introduction, a body, and a conclusion.

The introduction presents the subject, the setting, the situation, and the people involved. The main part, or the body, describes the events and people's reactions to these events. The conclusion brings the narrative to a close.

Adverbs and adverbial phrases are sometimes used as transitions between the introduction, the body, and the conclusion. Here is a list of commonly used adverbs in Spanish:

Adverbios	
además; también	*in addition; also*
al principio; en un principio	*at first*
antes (de)	*before*
después	*then*
después (de)	*after*
entonces; luego	*then*
más tarde	*later*
primero	*first*
pronto	*soon*
por fin, finalmente	*finally*
al final	*finally*

Tema

Escribe tu rutina

Imagina tu rutina diaria en uno de estos lugares:

- una isla desierta
- el Polo Norte
- un crucero (*cruise ship*) transatlántico
- un desierto

Escribe una composición en la que describes tu rutina diaria en uno de estos lugares, o en algún otro lugar interesante de tu propia° invención. Mientras planeas tu composición, considera cómo cambian algunos de los elementos más básicos de tu rutina diaria en el lugar que escogiste.° Por ejemplo, ¿dónde te acuestas en el Polo Norte?, ¿cómo te duchas en el desierto?

Usa el presente de los verbos reflexivos que conoces e incluye algunos de los adverbios de esta página para organizar la secuencia de tus actividades. Piensa también en la información que debes incluir en cada sección de la narración. Por ejemplo, la introducción puede dar una descripción del lugar y de las personas que están allí, y la conclusión puede dar tus opiniones acerca del° lugar y de tu vida diaria allí.

tu propia *your own* escogiste *chose* acerca de *about*

TEACHING OPTIONS

Proofreading Activity Copy the following items containing mistakes onto the board or a transparency as a proofreading activity to do with the whole class.

1. **Por la mañana, Joaquín siempre ducha se pero no baña se nunca.**
2. **Abro el refrigerador, sino allí no encuentro algo de comer.**
3. **En la residencia nadie no se levanta o se acuesta temprano.**
4. **Anoche fuí al centro para ver una película de aventuras, pero no me gusté nada.**
5. **A Miriam no le gusta las matematicas pero sí las lenguas estranjeras.**
6. **Alfredo se fue a abrir la puerta pero no vio nadie allí.**

Plan de escritura

1 **Ideas y organización**

Utiliza adverbios para planear la secuencia de tu composición.

1. **Primero** 2. **Después** 3. **Entonces** 4. **Más tarde** 5. **Al final**

Al finalizar la secuencia de eventos, escribe unas notas sobre la introducción de tu narración. Recuerda las seis preguntas principales: **¿qué?, ¿quién?, ¿cuándo?, ¿dónde?, ¿cómo?** y **¿por qué?**.

2 **Primer borrador**

Utiliza tus notas de **Ideas y organización** para escribir el primer borrador.

3 **Comentario**

Intercambia° tu composición con la de un(a) compañero/a. Lee su borrador y reflexiona sobre los aspectos mejor escritos°, por ejemplo, los adverbios que conectan las diferentes partes de su composición. Compartan sus impresiones mutuamente. Utiliza estas preguntas para evaluar el trabajo de tu compañero/a:

a. ¿Tiene una introducción con toda la información importante?
b. ¿Es lógica la secuencia de eventos?
c. ¿Tienes sugerencias° para hacer la composición más interesante?
d. ¿Notas algún error de gramática o de ortografía°?

4 **Redacción**

Revisa° el primer borrador según las indicaciones de tu compañero/a. Incorpora nuevas ideas y/o más información para ampliar° tu composición y hacerla más interesante. Utiliza esta guía antes de escribir tu copia final:

a. Subraya° cada verbo para comprobar° la concordancia° con el sujeto y el uso del tiempo correcto. ¡Cuidado con los verbos reflexivos!
b. Revisa la concordancia entre los sustantivos, los artículos y los adjetivos.
c. Comprueba el uso correcto de los pronombres.
d. Revisa la ortografía y la puntuación.

5 **Evaluación y progreso**

Intercambia tu composición con la de otro/a compañero/a. Lee su trabajo y en otra hoja de papel dibuja las escenas que describe utilizando los adverbios que introducen la narración. Tu compañero/a puede usar tus dibujos para presentar la composición a la clase. Cuando tu profesor(a) te devuelva° el trabajo, anota los errores más importantes en **Anotaciones para mejorar la escritura** en tu **Carpeta de trabajos.**

Intercambia *Exchange* mejor escritos *best-written* sugerencias *suggestions* ortografía *spelling* Revisa *Check* ampliar *expand* Subraya *Underline* comprobar *verify* concordancia *agreement* devuelva *returns*

Comentario
- Go over guide questions a–d with the whole class so peer readers understand their task. Then have pairs of students exchange lists. Allow five minutes for reading and comments.
- Go over **Redacción** in class, making sure everyone understands the instructions. Ask students to rewrite their drafts, incorporating peer comments and following the directions in **Redacción**. Tell them to prepare a clean copy of their final draft to hand in.

Evaluación y progreso Give the class five minutes to exchange compositions and draw scenes. Then have students hand in their compositions.

Writing Sample Here is a sample composition that would constitute superior writing achievement.

En la isla más bonita

Esta isla es muy pequeña. De aquí sólo veo el océano, océano y más océano. Llegué aquí en un barco y no tengo planes para irme. Nadie vive en este lugar. Bueno, yo vivo aquí, pero yo soy la única.

Aquí me levanto cuando quiero levantarme. Como cuando quiero comer, y me acuesto cuando quiero acostarme. No tengo que asistir a las clases ni ir a trabajar. ¡Qué vida!

Todas las mañanas me ducho bajo una ducha especial. Sólo como frutas. Camino por la isla. Cada día es una aventura. Siempre veo algo nuevo. Hoy vi unos animales estupendos.

Me gusta mucho esta isla desierta. Quiero quedarme aquí mucho tiempo. Algún día tengo que volver a mi vida normal, pero por ahora la vida en esta isla es ¡la gran vida!

EVALUATION: Descripción

Criteria	Scale
Content	1 2 3 4 5
Organization	1 2 3 4 5
Use of vocabulary	1 2 3 4 5
Grammatical accuracy	1 2 3 4 5

Scoring	
Excellent	18–20 points
Good	14–17 points
Satisfactory	10–13 points
Unsatisfactory	< 10 points

Section Goal
In **Escuchar** students will learn the strategy of listening for background information.

Instructional Resources
Textbook CD
IRM: Tapescript, p. 91

Estrategia
Script ¿Te puedes creer los precios de la ropa que venden en el mercado al aire libre? Tienen unos bluejeans muy buenos que cuestan 52 soles. Y claro, puedes regatear y los consigues todavía más baratos. Vi unos iguales en el centro comercial y son mucho más caros. ¡Cuestan 97 soles!

Suggestion Read the directions with the students, then have them identify the photo situation.

Ahora escucha
Script CAROLINA: Buenas tardes, queridos televidentes, y bienvenidos a "Carolina al mediodía". Tenemos el gran placer de conversar hoy con Julián Larrea, un joven actor de extraordinario talento. Bienvenido, Julián. Ya sabes que tienes muchas admiradoras entre nuestro público y más que todo quieren saber los detalles de tu vida.
JULIÁN: Buenas, Carolina, y saludos a todos. No sé qué decirles; en realidad en mi vida hay rutina, como en la vida de todos.
C: No puede ser. Me imagino que tu vida es mucho más exótica que la mía. Bueno, para comenzar, ¿a qué hora te levantas?
J: Normalmente me levanto todos los días a la misma hora, también cuando estoy de viaje filmando una película. Siempre me despierto a las 5:30. Antes de ducharme y vestirme, siempre me gusta tomar un café mientras escucho un poco de música clásica. Así medito, escribo un poco y pienso sobre el día.
C: Cuando no estás filmando, ¿te quedas en casa durante el día?
J: Pues, en esos momentos, uso el tiempo libre para sentarme en casa a escribir. Pero sí tengo una rutina diaria de ejercicio. Corro unas cinco millas diarias y si hace mal tiempo voy al gimnasio.
C: Veo que eres una persona activa. Te mantienes en muy buena forma. ¿Qué más nos puedes decir de tu vida?
J: Bueno, no puedo negar que me encanta viajar. ¡Y la elegancia de algunos hoteles es increíble! Estuve en un hotel en Londres que tiene una ducha del tamaño de un cuarto normal.
C: Ya vemos que tu vida no es nada aburrida.
Qué gusto hablar contigo hoy, Julián.
J: El placer es mío. Gracias por la invitación, Carolina.

Escuchar

Estrategia
Using background information

Once you discern the topic of a conversation, take a minute to think about what you already know about the subject. Using this background information will help you guess the meaning of unknown words or linguistic structures.

To help you practice this strategy, you will now listen to a short paragraph. Jot down the subject of the paragraph, and then use your knowledge of the subject to listen for and write down the paragraph's main points.

Preparación

Según la foto, ¿dónde están Carolina y Julián? Piensa en lo que sabes de este tipo de situación. ¿De qué van a hablar?

Ahora escucha 

Ahora escucha la entrevista entre Carolina y Julián, teniendo en cuenta (*taking into account*) lo que sabes sobre este tipo de situación. Elige la información que completa correctamente cada oración.

1. Julián es __c__.
   a. político
   b. deportista profesional
   c. artista de cine
2. El público de Julián quiere saber de __b__.
   a. sus películas
   b. su vida
   c. su novia
3. Julián habla de __a__.
   a. sus viajes y sus rutinas
   b. sus parientes y amigos
   c. sus comidas favoritas
4. Julián __b__.
   a. se levanta y se acuesta a diferentes horas todos los días
   b. tiene una rutina diaria
   c. no quiere hablar de su vida

Comprensión

¿Cierto o falso?
Indica si las siguientes oraciones son **ciertas** o **falsas** según la información que Julián da en la entrevista.

1. Es difícil despertarme; generalmente duermo hasta las diez. __Falsa__
2. Pienso que mi vida no es más interesante que las vidas de ustedes. __Cierta__
3. Me gusta tener tiempo para pensar y meditar. __Cierta__
4. Nunca hago mucho ejercicio; no soy una persona activa. __Falsa__
5. Me fascinan las actividades tranquilas, como escribir y escuchar música clásica. __Cierta__
6. Los viajes me parecen aburridos. __Falsa__

Preguntas Answers will vary.
1. ¿Qué tiene Julián en común con otras personas de su misma profesión?
2. ¿Te parece que Julián siempre fue rico? ¿Por qué?
3. ¿Qué piensas de Julián como persona?

recursos

TEXT CD
Lección 7

Proyecto

Crea un itinerario de viaje

Tú y un grupo de estudiantes están planeando un viaje a Perú para ver las famosas ruinas incas de Machu Picchu. Individualmente o en grupos, planea un itinerario de viaje, incluyendo un programa° diario de actividades.

Investiga el país, la historia del imperio° inca y de la ciudad antigua de Machu Picchu. Busca información práctica y turística para planear la excursión y también investiga las costumbres y la rutina diaria de los peruanos. Considera si algunos aspectos de la rutina diaria de tu grupo van a cambiar° durante el viaje. Por ejemplo, ¿cómo deben vestirse para una excursión a los Andes?

1 Prepara el itinerario

Haz un folleto para presentar el itinerario de cada día de viaje e indica la hora para cada actividad. Incluye tiempo para la rutina diaria de tu grupo: cuidado personal, comidas y tiempo libre. Considera también:

- Restaurantes y comidas°
- Transporte: horarios de autobuses, trenes y aviones
- Hoteles: reservaciones, horas de registro°
- Información turística: horario de museos, de parques y de otros lugares turísticos
- Costumbres y rutinas locales
- Fotos y gráficas: elementos visuales para crear interés en el viaje
- Historia, descripciones y otra información interesante y útil para el grupo

PERÚ

Tierra de los Incas

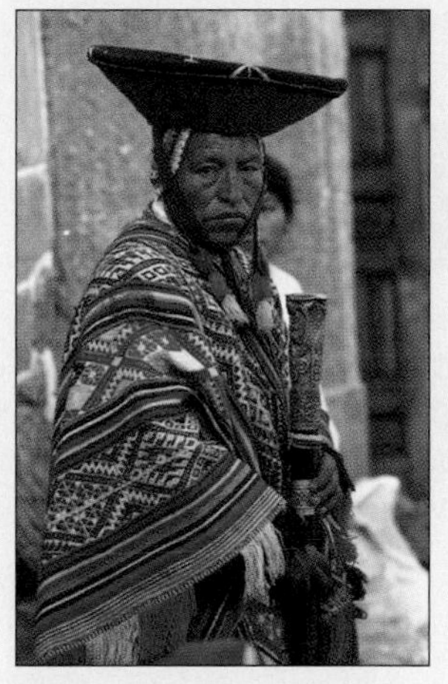

Agencia IncaTour

Cuzco, Perú

2 Presenta la información

Usa tu folleto para presentar el itinerario a la clase. Describe el país, la historia inca de Machu Picchu y también las actividades programadas para el viaje, mostrando fotos y respondiendo a las preguntas de tus compañeros.

recursos para la investigación

Internet Palabras clave: Perú, fotos de Machu Picchu, turismo, ciudades

Comunidad Estudiantes o profesores que son del Perú o que vivieron o viajaron allí, peruanos que viven en la comunidad

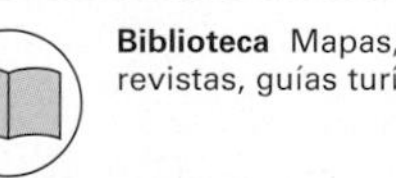

Biblioteca Mapas, almanaques, revistas, guías turísticas

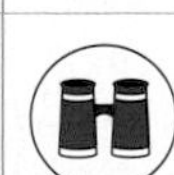

Otros recursos Folletos turísticos o revistas viejas que puedes recortar°

programa *schedule* imperio *empire* cambiar *to change* comidas *meals* registro *check-in* recortar *to cut up*

Section Goals

In **Proyecto** students will:

- learn about Peru, its history, its geography, and its people
- use Spanish as they research and interact with the wider world
- write and present a brochure for a group tour of Peru

Suggestion Students might need a week to complete the project, so at the beginning of that time period, have them open their books to this page and glance over **Proyecto**. Explain that they are going to use their research skills to prepare an itinerary for a tour of Peru that includes an excursion to Machu Picchu, the ancient city of the Incas. Tell them they will be writing a brochure that includes an itinerary, which they will present to the class. Encourage students to brainstorm what types of information they want to feature in their brochures.

Prepara el itinerario

- Students may search for information on Machu Picchu on the Internet.
- A trip from Lima to Cuzco, Peru, a starting point for most excursions to Machu Picchu, takes travelers from sea level to approximately 11,000 feet in altitude. Remind students to add information in their brochures about Peru's geography and how to dress appropriately.

EVALUATION: Itinerario

Criteria	Scale
Content	1 2 3 4
Organization	1 2 3 4
Accuracy	1 2 3 4
Visual appeal	1 2 3 4
Oral presentation	1 2 3 4

Scoring	
Excellent	18–20 points
Good	14–17 points
Satisfactory	10–13 points
Unsatisfactory	< 10 points

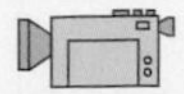

Section Goal

In **Panorama**, students will read about the geography, culture, and history of Peru.

Instructional Resources
Transparencies, #5, #6, #32
WB/VM: Workbook, pp. 83–84; Video Activities, pp. 261–262
***Panorama cultural** DVD/Video*
Interactive CD-ROM
IRM: Videoscript, p. 130
Companion website: www.vistahigherlearning.com
Presentations CD-ROM

Suggestion Have students look at the map of Peru or project **Transparency #32**. Ask them to find the **Río Amazonas** and the **Cordillera de los Andes**, and to speculate about the types of climate found in Peru. As a mountainous country near the equator, climate varies according to elevation and ranges from tropical to arctic. Point out that well over half of the territory of Peru lies within the Amazon Basin. Encourage students to tell what they know about Peru.

El país en cifras After each section, ask students questions about the content of what has been read. Point out that Iquitos, Peru's port city on the Amazon River, is a destination for ships that travel 2,300 miles up the Amazon from the Atlantic Ocean.

¡Increíble pero cierto!
In recent years, the **El Niño** weather phenomenon has caused flooding in the deserts of southern Peru. The Peruvian government is currently taking steps to preserve the **Líneas de Nazca** from further deterioration due to floods in the hope that scientists will someday discover more about their origins and meaning.

Perú

El país en cifras

- **Área:** 1.285.220 km^2 (496.224 millas^2), *un poco menos que el área de Alaska*
- **Población:** 27.804.000
- **Capital:** Lima —8.185.000
- **Ciudades principales:** Arequipa —764.000, Trujillo —643.000, Chiclayo —527.000, Callao —442.000, Iquitos —348.000

SOURCE: Population Division, UN Secretariat

Iquitos es un puerto muy importante en el río Amazonas. Desde Iquitos se envían° muchos productos a otros lugares, incluyendo goma°, nueces°, madera°, arroz°, café y tabaco. Iquitos es también un destino popular para los ecoturistas que visitan la selva°.

- **Moneda:** nuevo sol
- **Idiomas:** español (oficial), quechua (oficial), aimará

Bandera del Perú

Peruanos célebres

- **Clorinda Matto de Turner,** escritora (1854–1901)
- **César Vallejo,** poeta (1892–1938)
- **Javier Pérez de Cuéllar,** diplomático (1920–)
- **Mario Vargas Llosa,** novelista (1936–)

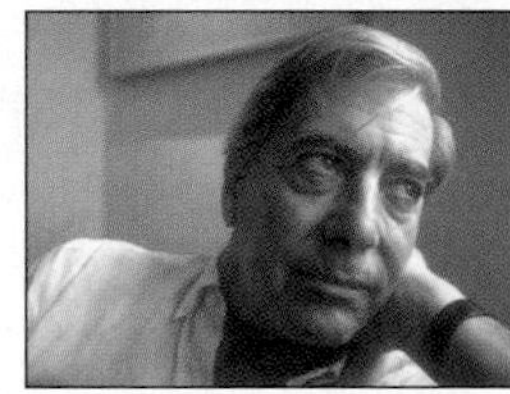

Mario Vargas Llosa

se envían *are shipped* goma *rubber* nueces *nuts* madera *timber* arroz *rice* selva *jungle* grabó *engraved* tamaño *size*

Bailando marinera norteña en Trujillo

Calle en la ciudad de Iquitos

Fuente de la Justicia en Lima

Mercado indígena en Cuzco

ECUADOR
COLOMBIA
Río Putumayo
Río Napo
Río Tigre
Río Amazonas
Iquitos
Río Pastaza
Río Marañón
Cordillera Oriental de los Andes
Río Huallaga
Chiclayo
Río Ucayali
Trujillo
Cordillera Central de los Andes
Río Urubamba
Callao
Lima
Cordillera Occidental de los Andes
Machu Picchu
Cuzco
Lago Titicaca
Océano Pacífico
Arequipa
ESTADOS UNIDOS
OCÉANO ATLÁNTICO
OCÉANO PACÍFICO
PERÚ
AMÉRICA DEL SUR

recursos

WB pp. 83–84	VM pp. 261-262	I CD-ROM Lección 7	vistahigher learning.com

¡Increíble pero cierto!

Hace más de dos mil años la civilización nazca de Perú grabó° más de 2.000 km de líneas en el desierto. Los dibujos sólo son descifrables desde el aire. Uno de ellos es un cóndor del tamaño° de un estadio. Las Líneas de Nazca son uno de los grandes misterios de la humanidad.

TEACHING OPTIONS

Heritage Speakers Ask heritage speakers from Peru or who have visited Peru to make a short presentation to the class about their impressions. Encourage them to speak of the region they are from or have visited and how it differs from other regions in this vast country. If they have photographs, ask them to bring them to class to illustrate their talk.

TPR Invite students to take turns guiding the class on tours of Peru's waterways: one student gives directions, and the others follow by tracing the route on their map of Peru. For example: **Comenzamos en el río Amazonas, pasando por Iquitos hasta llegar al río Ucayali.**

Lugares • Lima

Lima es una ciudad moderna y antigua° a la vez°. La Iglesia de San Francisco es notable por la influencia de la arquitectura árabe. También son fascinantes las exhibiciones sobre los incas en el Museo del Oro del Perú y en el Museo Nacional de Antropología y Arqueología. Barranco, el barrio° bohemio de la ciudad, es famoso por su ambiente cultural y sus bares y restaurantes.

RASIL

Historia • Los incas

Antes del siglo° XVI, los incas desarrollaron° sistemas avanzados de comunicaciones y de contabilidad y construyeron° acueductos, calles° y templos. A 80 kilómetros al noroeste de Cuzco está Machu Picchu, una ciudad antigua del imperio inca. Está a una altitud de 2.350 metros (7.710 pies), entre dos cimas° de los Andes. Cuando los conquistadores españoles llegaron a Perú, nunca encontraron a Machu Picchu. En 1911, el arqueólogo norteamericano Hiram Bingham la descubrió. Todavía no se sabe° ni cómo se construyó una ciudad a esa altura, ni por qué los incas la abandonaron.

Artes • La música andina

Machu Picchu aún no existía° cuando se originó la música cautivadora° de las antiguas culturas indígenas de los Andes. Las influencias española y africana le prestaron a esta música sus ritmos de hoy. Dos tipos de flauta°, la quena y la antara, producen esta música tan particular. En las décadas de los sesenta y los setenta se popularizó un movimiento para preservar la música andina, y hasta° Simon y Garfunkel la incorporaron en su repertorio con la canción° "El cóndor pasa".

Economía • Llamas y alpacas

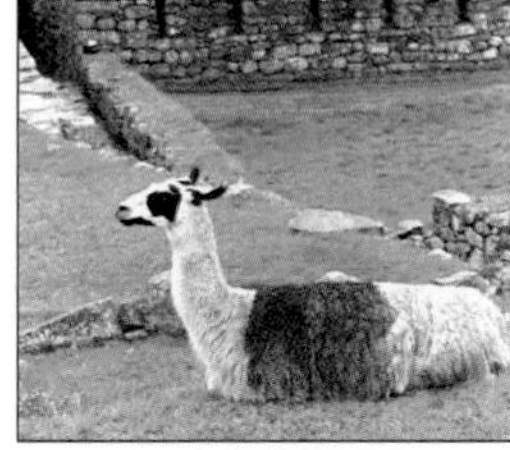

El Perú se conoce° por sus llamas, alpacas, guanacos y vicuñas, todos animales mamíferos° parientes del camello. Estos animales todavía son de enorme importancia para la economía del país. Dan lana° para hacer ropa, mantas°, bolsas y artículos turísticos. La llama se usa también para la carga y el transporte.

OLIVIA

¿Qué aprendiste? Responde a las preguntas con una frase completa.

1. ¿Qué productos envía Iquitos a otros lugares? Iquitos envía goma, nueces, madera, arroz, café y tabaco.
2. ¿Cuáles son las lenguas oficiales del Perú? Las lenguas oficiales del Perú son el español y el quechua.
3. ¿Por qué es notable la Iglesia de San Francisco en Lima? Es notable por la influencia de la arquitectura árabe.
4. ¿Por qué los conquistadores españoles no encontraron la ciudad de Machu Picchu? No la encontraron porque está entre dos cimas.
5. ¿Qué son la quena y la antara? Son dos tipos de flauta.
6. ¿Qué hacen los peruanos con la lana de sus llamas y alpacas? Hacen ropa, mantas, bolsas y artículos turísticos.

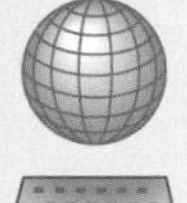

Conexión Internet Investiga estos temas en el sitio **www.vistahigherlearning.com.**

1. Investiga la cultura incaica. ¿Cuáles son algunos de los aspectos interesantes de su cultura?
2. Busca información sobre dos artistas, escritores o músicos peruanos, y presenta un breve informe a tu clase.

antigua *old* a la vez *at the same time* barrio *neighborhood* siglo *century* desarrollaron *developed* construyeron *built* calles *roads* cimas *summits* no se sabe *it is not known* no existía *didn't exist* cautivadora *captivating* flauta *flute* hasta *even* canción *song* se conoce *is known* mamíferos *mammalian* lana *wool* mantas *blankets*

Lima Lima is rich in colonial architecture. (*Américas*, October 2000, pages 16–23, has many photos of colonial Lima.) It is also the home of the University of San Marcos, established in 1551, the oldest university in South America.

Los incas Another invention of the Incas were the **quipus**, clusters of knotted strings that were a means of keeping records and sending messages. A **quipu** consisted of a series of small cords with knots in them attached to a larger cord. A cord's color, place, size, and the knots in it all had significance.

La música andina Ancient tombs, belonging to pre-Columbian cultures like the Nasca and Moche and predating even the Incan civilization, have yielded instruments and other artifacts indicating that the precursors of Andean music go back at least as far as two millenia.

Llamas y alpacas Of the camel-like animals of the Andes, only the sturdy llama has been domesticated as a pack animal. Its long, thick coat also provides fiber that is woven into a coarser grade of cloth. The more delicate alpaca and vicuña are raised only for their beautiful coats, used to create extremely high-quality cloth. The guanaco has never been domesticated.

Conexión Internet Students will find supporting Internet activities and links at **www.vistahigherlearning.com**.

TEACHING OPTIONS

Variación léxica Some of the most familiar words to have entered Spanish from the Quechua language are the names of animals native to the Andean region, such as **el cóndor, la llama, el puma,** and **la vicuña**. These words later passed from Spanish to a number of European languages, including English. **La alpaca** comes not from Quechua, the language of the Incas and their descendants, who inhabit most of the Andean region, but from Aymara, the language of native American people who live near Lake Titicaca on the Peruvian-Bolivian border. Most students are probably familiar with the traditional Quechua tune, ***El cóndor pasa***, popularized in a version by Simon and Garfunkel.

Instructional Resources
Vocabulary CD
Lab Manual, p. 42
Lab CD/MP3 ***Lección 7***
IRM: Tapescript, pp. 30–34
Testing Program: ***Pruebas,*** *pp. 73–84*
Testing Program Audio CD
Test Files CD-ROM

Los verbos reflexivos

acordarse (de) (o:ue)	*to remember*
acostarse (o:ue)	*to go to bed*
afeitarse	*to shave*
bañarse	*to bathe; take a bath*
cepillarse el pelo	*to brush one's hair*
cepillarse los dientes	*to brush one's teeth*
despedirse (de) (e:i)	*to say good-bye (to)*
despertarse (e:ie)	*to wake up*
dormirse (o:ue)	*to go to sleep; to fall asleep*
ducharse	*to shower; to take a shower*
enojarse (con)	*to get angry (with)*
irse	*to go away; to leave*
lavarse la cara	*to wash one's face*
lavarse las manos	*to wash one's hands*
levantarse	*to get up*
llamarse	*to be called; to be named*
maquillarse	*to put on makeup*
peinarse	*to comb one's hair*
ponerse	*to put on*
ponerse (+ *adj.*)	*to become (+ adj.)*
preocuparse (por)	*to worry (about)*
probarse (o:ue)	*to try on*
quedarse	*to stay; to remain*
quitarse	*to take off*
secarse	*to dry (oneself)*
sentarse (e:ie)	*to sit down*
sentirse (e:ie)	*to feel*
vestirse (e:i)	*to get dressed*

Palabras de secuencia

antes (de)	*before*
después (de)	*afterwards; then*
después de	*after*
durante	*during*
entonces	*then*
luego	*then*
más tarde	*later*
por último	*finally*

Palabras afirmativas y negativas

algo	*something; anything*
alguien	*someone; somebody; anyone*
alguno/a(s), algún	*some; any*
jamás	*never; not ever*
nada	*nothing; not anything*
nadie	*no one; nobody; not anyone*
ni... ni	*neither... nor*
ninguno/a, ningún	*no; none; not any*
nunca	*never; not ever*
o... o	*either... or*
siempre	*always*
también	*also; too*
tampoco	*neither; not either*

En el baño

el baño, el cuarto de baño	*bathroom*
el champú	*shampoo*
la crema de afeitar	*shaving cream*
la ducha	*shower*
el espejo	*mirror*
el inodoro	*toilet*
el jabón	*soap*
el lavabo	*sink*
el maquillaje	*makeup*
la pasta de dientes	*toothpaste*
la toalla	*towel*

Gustar y verbos similares

aburrir	*to bore*
encantar	*to like very much; to love (inanimate objects)*
faltar	*to lack; to need*
fascinar	*to fascinate*
gustar	*to be pleasing to; to like*
importar	*to be important to; to matter*
interesar	*to be interesting to; to interest*
molestar	*to bother; to annoy*
quedar	*to be left over; to fit (clothing)*

Palabras adicionales

el despertador	*alarm clock*
las pantuflas	*slippers*
la rutina diaria	*daily routine*
por la mañana	*in the morning*
por la noche	*at night*
por la tarde	*in the afternoon; in the evening*

Expresiones útiles	*See page 207.*

recursos

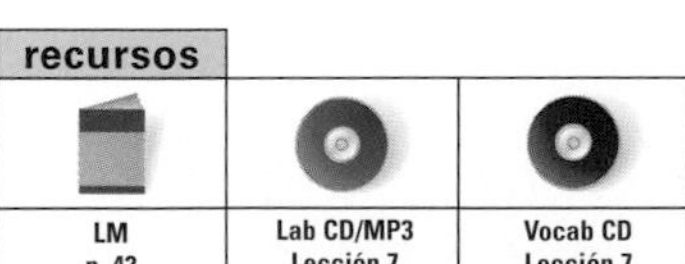

LM p. 42	Lab CD/MP3 Lección 7	Vocab CD Lección 7

La comida

8

Communicative Goals

You will learn how to:

- Order food in a restaurant
- Talk about and describe food

A PRIMERA VISTA

- ¿Están ellos en un restaurante?
- ¿Qué hacen? ¿Es parte de su rutina diaria?
- ¿Les gusta la comida?
- ¿Lleva él una camisa de cuadros o de rayas?

Lesson Goals

In **Lección 8** students will be introduced to the following:

- food terms
- meal-related words
- preterite of stem-changing verbs
- double object pronouns
- converting **le** and **les** to **se** with double object pronouns
- uses of **saber** and **conocer**
- more uses of personal **a**
- comparatives and superlatives
- reading for the main idea
- expressing and supporting opinions
- writing a restaurant review
- taking notes while listening
- planning a new restaurant and designing its menu
- cultural, geographic, and historical information about Guatemala

A primera vista Here are some additional questions you can ask based on the photo: **¿Siempre comes algo cuando te despiertas por la mañana? ¿Dónde comes? ¿Fuiste a algún lugar especial para comer el año pasado? ¿Adónde fuiste y quién fue? ¿Dónde te encanta comer? ¿Por qué? ¿Qué ropa te pones para salir a comer en una ocasión especial? ¿Qué más haces antes de salir?**

INSTRUCTIONAL RESOURCES

Workbook/Video Manual: WB Activities, pp. 85–96
Laboratory Manual: Lab Activities, pp. 43–48
Workbook/Video Manual: Video Activities, pp. 227–228; pp. 263–264
Instructor's Resource Manual: **Hojas de actividades**, p. 168; **Vocabulario adicional**, p. 186; **¡Inténtalo!** & **Práctica** Answers, pp. 210–211; **Fotonovela** Translations, pp. 142–143; Textbook CD Tapescript, p. 92; Lab CDs Tapescript, pp. 35–39; **Fotonovela** Videoscript, pp. 110–111; **Panorama cultural** Videoscript, p. 131
Info Gap Activities Booklet, pp. 29–32
Overhead Transparencies: #3, #4, #33, #34, #35
Lab Audio CD/MP3 **Lección 8**
Panorama cultural DVD/Video
Fotonovela DVD/Video
Testing Program, pp. 85–96
Testing Program Audio CD
Test Files CD-ROM
Companion website
Presentations CD-ROM
Textbook CD
Vocabulary CD
Interactive CD-ROM
Video CD-ROM
Web-SAM

Section Goals

In **Contextos** students will learn and practice:

- food names
- meal-related vocabulary

Instructional Resources

Transparencies, #33, #34
Textbook CD
Vocabulary CD
WB/VM: Workbook, pp. 85–86
Lab Manual, p. 43
Lab CD/MP3 ***Lección 8***
IRM: ***Vocab. adicional****, p. 186;*
Práctica *Answers, pp. 210–211;*
Tapescript, pp. 35–39; p. 92
Info Gap Activities Booklet, pp. 29–30
Interactive CD-ROM
Companion website: www.vistahigherlearning.com
Presentations CD-ROM

Suggestions

- Tell what you are going to have for lunch, writing food vocabulary on the board. Say: **Tengo hambre y voy a preparar una hamburguesa. ¿Qué ingredientes necesito? Pues, carne de res molida, queso, tomates, lechuga y mayonesa. También voy a preparar una ensalada. ¿Con qué ingredientes preparo la ensalada? A ver, lechuga, tomates, zanahorias,...**
- Project **Transparency #33.** Ask: **¿Sí o no? ¿Hay bananas en el dibujo del mercado? (Sí.) ¿Qué otras frutas hay? Y, ¿hay cerveza? (No.)** Next mention typical dishes and ask students to tell what ingredients are used to make them. Suggestions: **una ensalada verde, una ensalada de fruta, un sándwich.**
- Ask students what some of their favorite foods are. Ex: **Y a ti, _____, ¿qué te gusta comer?**

La comida

Más vocabulario

el/la camarero/a	*waiter*
la comida	*food; meal*
el/la dueño/a	*owner; landlord*
los entremeses	*hors d'oeuvres*
el menú	*menu*
el plato (principal)	*(main) dish*
la sección de (no) fumar	*(non) smoking section*
el agua (mineral)	*(mineral) water*
la bebida	*drink*
la cerveza	*beer*
la leche	*milk*
el ajo	*garlic*
las arvejas	*peas*
los cereales	*cereal; grain*
los frijoles	*beans*
el melocotón	*peach*
las papas/patatas (fritas)	*(fried) potatoes; French fries*
el pollo (asado)	*(roast) chicken*
el queso	*cheese*
la sandía	*watermelon*
el sándwich	*sandwich*
el yogur	*yogurt*
el aceite	*oil*
la margarina	*margarine*
la mayonesa	*mayonnaise*
el refresco	*soft drink*
el vinagre	*vinegar*
delicioso/a	*delicious*
rico/a	*tasty; delicious*
sabroso/a	*tasty; delicious*

Variación léxica

camarones ⟷ gambas (*Esp.*)
camarero ⟷ mesero (*Amér. L.*), mesonero (*Ven.*), mozo (*Arg., Chile, Urug., Perú*)
refresco ⟷ gaseosa (*Amér. C., Amér. S.*)

recursos

TEXT CD Lección 8	WB pp. 85–86	LM p. 43	Lab CD/MP3 Lección 8	I CD-ROM Lección 8	Vocab CD Lección 8

TEACHING OPTIONS

Extra Practice To review vocabulary for colors, ask students what colors the following food items are: **las bananas (amarillas), las uvas (verdes o moradas), las zanahorias (anaranjadas), los tomates (rojos), los frijoles (blancos, marrones, rojos o negros).**

Variación léxica Point out that food vocabulary varies from region to region in the Spanish-speaking world. When the Spanish visited the New World, they introduced many foods unknown to the indigenous peoples, and likewise they took back many food items previously unknown in Europe. Also point out the different names for fruits and vegetables in **¡Lengua viva!** on page 235.

¡LENGUA VIVA!

Many fruits and vegetables have a variety of names:

arveja ↔ guisante, chícharo
banana ↔ banano, plátano, guineo
champiñón ↔ seta, hongo
frijol ↔ habichuela
maíz ↔ choclo, elote
papa ↔ patata
tomate ↔ jitomate

Práctica

1 Escuchar Indica si las frases que vas a escuchar son **ciertas** o **falsas**, según el dibujo. Después, corrige (*correct*) las frases falsas.

1. Cierta
2. Falsa El hombre compra una naranja.
3. Cierta
4. Falsa El pollo es una carne y la zanahoria es una verdura.
5. Cierta
6. Falsa El hombre y la mujer no compran vinagre.
7. Falsa La naranja es una fruta.
8. Falsa La chuleta de cerdo es una carne.
9. Falsa El limón es una fruta y el jamón es una carne.
10. Cierta

2 Identificar Identifica la palabra que no está relacionada con su grupo.

1. champiñón • cebolla • banana • zanahoria banana
2. camarones • ajo • atún • salmón ajo
3. aceite • leche • refresco • agua mineral aceite
4. jamón • chuleta de cerdo • vinagre • carne de res vinagre
5. cerveza • lechuga • arvejas • frijoles cerveza
6. carne • pescado • mariscos • camarero camarero
7. pollo • naranja • limón • melocotón pollo
8. maíz • queso • tomate • champiñón queso
9. rico • sabroso • menú • delicioso menú
10. pescado • mariscos • salmón • bebida bebida

3 Completar Completa las frases con las palabras más lógicas.

1. ¡Me gusta mucho este plato! Es _b_.
   a. feo b. sabroso c. antipático
2. Camarero, ¿puedo ver el _c_, por favor?
   a. aceite b. maíz c. menú
3. A Elena no le gusta la _a_ pero le gusta mucho la fruta.
   a. carne b. uva c. naranja
4. Carlos y yo bebemos siempre agua _b_.
   a. cómodo b. mineral c. principal
5. Antes de su plato principal, Maribel comió _b_.
   a. cereales b. entremeses c. cerveza
6. El plato del día es _a_.
   a. el pollo asado b. la mayonesa c. el ajo
7. Margarita es vegetariana. Ella come _a_.
   a. frijoles b. chuletas c. jamón
8. Mi hermana le sirve _c_ a su niña.
   a. ajo b. vinagre c. yogur

1 Suggestion Have students check their answers by going over **Actividad 1** with the whole class.

1 Tapescript 1. La langosta está cerca de los camarones. 2. El hombre compra una pera. 3. La lechuga es una verdura. 4. El pollo y la zanahoria son carnes. 5. La cebolla está cerca del maíz. 6. El hombre y la mujer compran vinagre. 7. La naranja es una verdura. 8. La chuleta de cerdo es pescado. 9. El limón y el jamón son frutas. 10. El pavo está cerca del pollo.
Textbook CD

1 Expansion Have students write three additional true-false statements based on the drawing. Ask volunteers to read their statements aloud. The rest of the class indicates whether the statements are true or false, correcting the false statements.

2 Expansion Have students indicate why a particular item doesn't belong. Ex: **El champiñón, la cebolla y la zanahoria son verduras. La banana es una fruta.**

3 Expansion Give additional statements, which students must complete. Ex: **Un vegetariano no come ____. (carne) El atún y el salmón son tipos de ____. (pescado)**

TEACHING OPTIONS

Game Play **Concentración**. On eight cards, write names of food items. On another eight cards, draw or paste a picture that matches each food item. Place the cards face-down in four rows of four. In pairs, students select two cards. If the two cards match, the pair keeps them. If the two cards don't match, students replace them in their original positions. The group with the most cards at the end wins.

Game Play a modified version of Twenty Questions. Ask a volunteer to think of a food item from the vocabulary drawing or list. Other students get one chance each to ask a yes-no question until someone guesses the item correctly. Limit attempts to ten questions per item. You may want to write some phrases on the board to cue students' questions. Ex: **¿Es una fruta? ¿Es roja?**

Suggestions

- Involve the class in a conversation about meals. Say: **Por lo general, desayuno sólo café con leche y pan tostado, pero cuando tengo mucha hambre desayuno dos huevos y una salchicha también. ____, ¿qué desayunas tú?**
- Project **Transparency #34**. Say: **Mira el desayuno aquí. ¿Qué desayuna esta persona?** Then continue to **el almuerzo** and **la cena.** Have students identify the food items and participate in a conversation about their eating habits. Get them to talk about what, when, and where they eat. Say: **Yo siempre desayuno en casa, pero casi nunca almuerzo en casa. ¿A qué hora almuerzan ustedes por lo general?**
- Ask students to tell you their favorite foods to eat for each of the three meals. Ex: ____, **¿qué te gusta desayunar?** Introduce additional items such as **los espaguetis, la pasta, la pizza.**

Nota cultural Point out that in Spanish-speaking countries **el almuerzo** usually is the main meal of the day, consists of several courses, and is enjoyed at a leisurely pace. **La cena** is typically much lighter than **el almuerzo**.

Note: At this point you may want to present **Vocabulario adicional: Más vocabulario relacionado con la comida**, from the IRM.

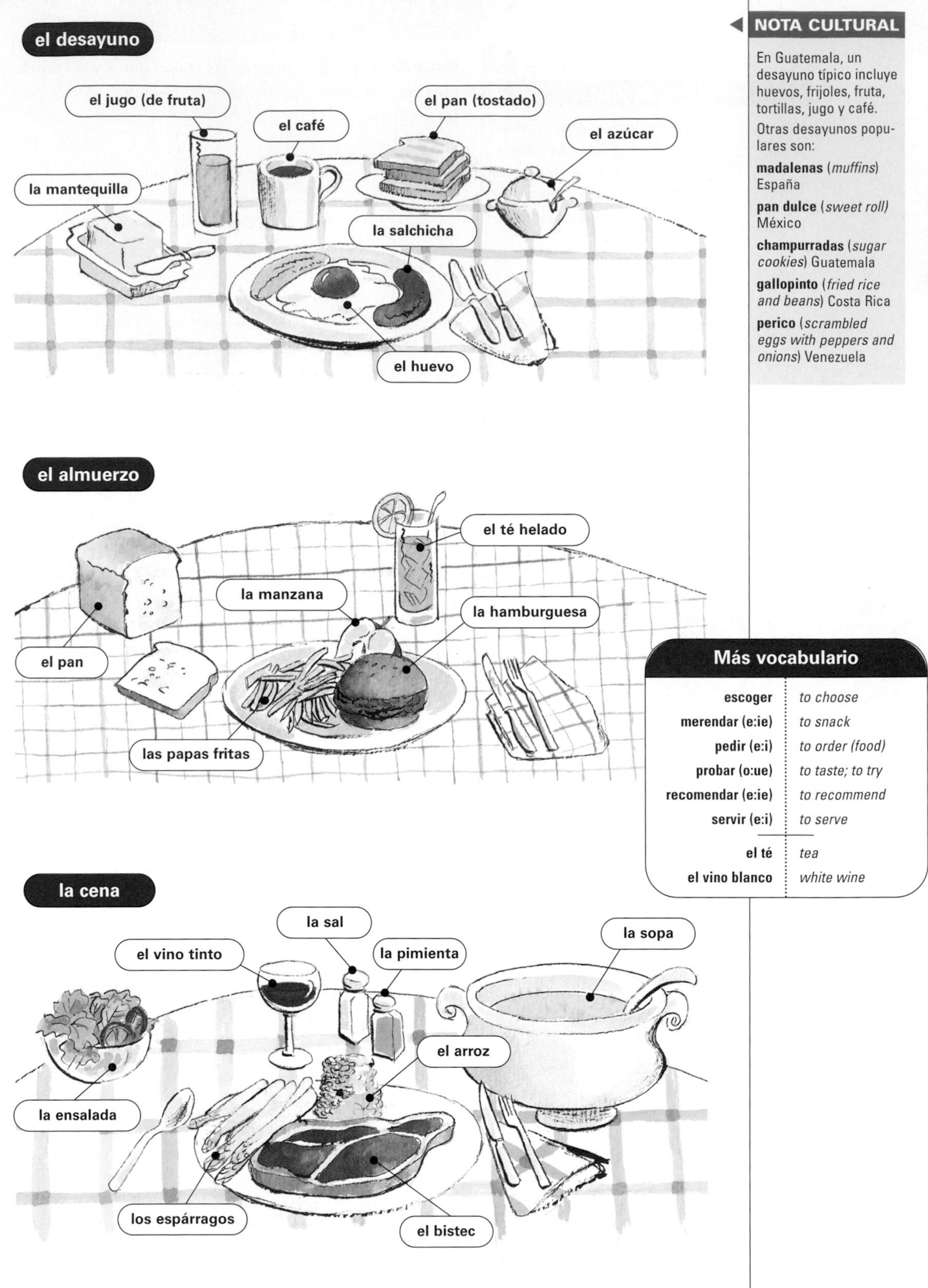

NOTA CULTURAL

En Guatemala, un desayuno típico incluye huevos, frijoles, fruta, tortillas, jugo y café. Otras desayunos populares son:

madalenas (*muffins*) España

pan dulce (*sweet roll*) México

champurradas (*sugar cookies*) Guatemala

gallopinto (*fried rice and beans*) Costa Rica

perico (*scrambled eggs with peppers and onions*) Venezuela

Más vocabulario

escoger	*to choose*
merendar (e:ie)	*to snack*
pedir (e:i)	*to order (food)*
probar (o:ue)	*to taste; to try*
recomendar (e:ie)	*to recommend*
servir (e:i)	*to serve*
el té	*tea*
el vino blanco	*white wine*

TEACHING OPTIONS

Small Groups In groups of three or four, students create a menu for a special occasion. Ask them what they are going to serve for **el primer plato, el plato principal**, and to drink. Write **el postre** on the board and explain that it means *dessert*. Explain that in Spanish-speaking countries fresh fruit and cheese are common as dessert, but you may also want to give **el pastel** (*pie, cake*) and **el helado** (*ice cream*). Students present their menu to the class.

Extra Practice Prepare descriptions of five to seven different meals, with a mix of breakfasts, lunches, and dinners. Have students write down what you say as a dictation and then guess the meal each describes.

4 **Completar** Trabaja con un(a) compañero/a de clase para relacionar cada producto con el grupo alimenticio (*food group*) correcto.

modelo

La carne es del grupo uno.

el aceite	las bananas	los cereales	la leche
el arroz	el café	los espárragos	el pescado
el azúcar	la carne	los frijoles	el vino

1. La leche y el queso son del grupo cuatro.
2. Los frijoles son del grupo ocho.
3. El pescado y el pollo son del grupo tres.
4. El aceite es del grupo cinco.
5. El azúcar es del grupo dos.
6. Las manzanas y las bananas son del grupo siete.
7. El café es del grupo seis.
8. Los cereales son del grupo diez.
9. Los espárragos y los tomates son del grupo nueve.
10. El pan y el arroz son del grupo diez.

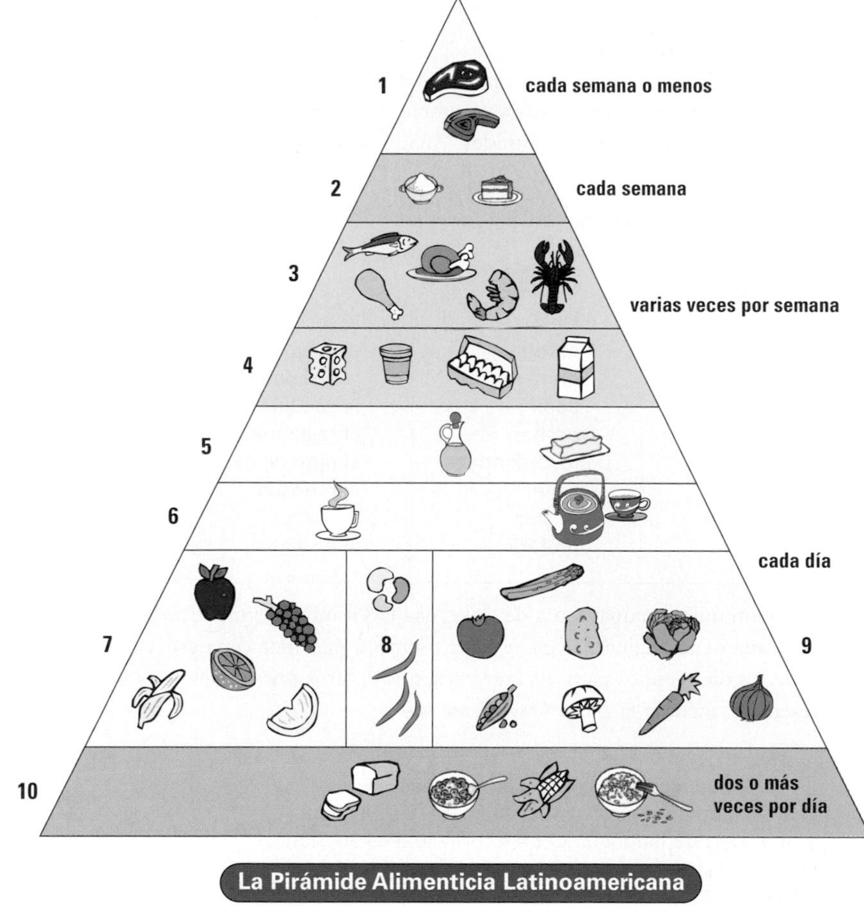

La Pirámide Alimenticia Latinoamericana

4 Suggestion Ask students to compare foods at the base of the pyramid with those at the top. (The foods at the bottom of the pyramid are essential dietary requirements. As one moves closer to the top, the food items become less essential to daily requirements but help to balance out a diet.)

4 Expansions

- Ask additional questions about the **pirámide alimenticia.** Ask: **¿Qué se debe comer varias veces por semana? ¿Qué se debe comer todos los días? ¿Cuáles son los productos que aparecen en el grupo cuatro? ¿y en el grupo siete?** Get students to talk about what they eat. **¿Comen ustedes carne sólo una vez a la semana o menos? ¿Qué comidas comen ustedes dos o más veces al día? ¿Toman café todos los días?**
- Ask students if they know which food groups and food products comprise the food pyramid used in this country. If you can get a copy of one, bring it to class and compare similarities and differences between the dietary requirements among cultures.

TEACHING OPTIONS

Heritage Speakers Ask heritage speakers to talk about food items or dishes unique to their country of origin that are not typically found in this country. Have them describe what the item looks and tastes like. If the item is a dish, they should briefly describe how to prepare it if they know how to do so.

Extra Practice Have students draw food pyramids based not on what they should eat but on what they actually do eat as part of their diet. Encourage them to include drawings or magazine cutouts to enhance the visual presentation. Then have students present their pyramids to the class.

5 Expansion Have students create three additional true-false statements that their partner must answer. Then ask volunteers to present their sentences for the rest of the class to answer.

6 Expansion Ask individual students what people in the activity logically do. Point out that there are many possible answers to your questions. Ex: **¿Qué hace la camarera en el restaurante? ¿Qué hace el dueño?**

Nota cultural Ask students if they know of any essential components of the diet of this country. Ask them if there are any essentials in their personal diets they can't live without.

7 Suggestion Emphasize the fact that students must include at least one item from each group in the **pirámide alimenticia**.

7 Expansion Ask students why they chose their food items—because they are personal preferences, for their health benefits, or because they went with other foods. Ex: **¿Por qué escogiste espárragos? ¿Te gustan mucho? ¿Son saludables? Van bien con el pescado, ¿verdad?**

5 **¿Cierto o falso?** Consulta la Pirámide Alimenticia Latinoamericana de la página 237 e indica si las frases son **ciertas** o **falsas**. Si la frase es falsa, escribe las comidas que sí están en el grupo indicado.

modelo

El queso está en el grupo diez.
Falso. En ese grupo están el maíz, el pan y el arroz.

1. La manzana, la banana, el limón y las arvejas están en el grupo siete.
Falsa. En ese grupo están la manzana, las uvas, la banana, la naranja y el limón.
2. En el grupo cuatro están los huevos, la leche y el aceite.
Falsa. En ese grupo están los huevos, la leche, el queso y el yogur.
3. El azúcar está en el grupo dos.
Cierta.
4. En el grupo diez están el pan, el arroz y el maíz.
Cierta.
5. El pollo está en el grupo uno.
Falsa. En ese grupo están el bistec y la chuleta de cerdo.
6. En el grupo nueve están la lechuga, el tomate, las arvejas, la naranja, la papa, los espárragos y la cebolla. Falsa. En ese grupo están la lechuga, el tomate, las arvejas, la zanahoria, la papa, los espárragos, la cebolla y el champiñón.
7. En el grupo seis están el café y el té.
Cierta.
8. En el grupo cinco está el arroz.
Falsa. En ese grupo está el aceite y la mantequilla.
9. En el grupo tres están el pescado, el yogur y el bistec.
Falsa. En ese grupo están el pescado, el pollo, el pavo, los camarones y la langosta.
10. En el grupo ocho está la cerveza.
Falsa. En ese grupo están los frijoles.

6 **Combinar** Combina palabras de cada columna, en cualquier (*any*) orden, para formar diez frases lógicas sobre las comidas. Añade otras palabras si es necesario.
Answers will vary.

modelo

La camarera nos sirve la ensalada.

A	B	C
El/La camarero/a	almorzar	la sección de no fumar
El/La dueño/a	escoger	el desayuno
Mi familia	merendar	la ensalada
Mi novio/a	pedir	la sandía
Mis amigos y yo	probar	el restaurante
Mis padres	recomendar	el jugo de naranja
Mi hermano/a	servir	el refresco
El/La médico/a	gustar	el plato
Yo	preferir	el arroz

NOTA CULTURAL

El arroz es un alimento básico en el Caribe, Centroamérica y México. Aparece frecuentemente como acompañante de un plato principal y se sirve con frijoles muchas veces. Un plato muy popular en varios países es el **arroz con pollo** *(chicken and rice casserole)*.

7 **Un menú** Con un(a) compañero/a de clase, usa la Pirámide Alimenticia Latinoamericana de la página 237 para crear un menú para una cena especial. Incluye alimentos de los diez grupos para los entremeses, los platos principales y las bebidas. Luego presenta el menú a la clase. Answers will vary.

modelo

La cena especial que voy a preparar es deliciosa. Primero, hay dos entremeses: una ensalada César y una sopa de langosta. El plato principal es salmón con una salsa de ajo y espárragos. También voy a servir arroz...

TEACHING OPTIONS

Extra Practice To review and practice the preterite along with food vocabulary, have students write a paragraph in which they describe what they ate up to this point today. Students should also indicate whether this meal or collection of meals represents a typical day for them. If not, they should explain why.

Small Groups In groups of two or three, students role-play a situation in a restaurant. One or two students play the customers and the other plays the **camarero/a**. Offer the following sentences on the board as suggested phrases: **¿Están listos para pedir?, ¿Qué nos recomienda usted?, ¿Me trae ____, por favor?, ¿Y para empezar?, A sus órdenes, La especialidad de la casa.**

Comunicación

8 **Conversación** En grupos, contesten las siguientes preguntas. Answers will vary.

1. ¿Meriendas mucho durante el día? ¿Qué comes? ¿A qué hora?
2. ¿Qué comidas te gustan más para la cena?
3. ¿A qué hora, dónde y con quién almuerzas?
4. ¿Cuáles son las comidas más (*most*) típicas de tu almuerzo?
5. ¿Desayunas? ¿Qué comes y bebes por la mañana?
6. ¿Qué comida deseas probar?
7. ¿Comes cada día comidas de los diferentes grupos de la pirámide alimenticia? ¿Cuáles son las comidas y bebidas más frecuentes en tu dieta?
8. ¿Qué comida recomiendas a tus amigos? ¿Por qué?
9. ¿Eres vegetariano/a? ¿Crees que ser vegetariano/a es una buena idea? ¿Por qué?
10. ¿Te gusta cocinar (*cook*)? ¿Qué comidas preparas para tus amigos? ¿Para tu familia?

¡LENGUA VIVA!

In addition to **beber**, the verb **tomar** is often used to express *to drink.*

9 **Describir** Con dos compañeros/as de clase, describe las dos fotos, contestando las siguientes preguntas. Answers will vary.

- ¿Quiénes están en las fotos?
- ¿Dónde están?
- ¿Qué hora es?
- ¿Qué comen y qué beben?

10 **Crucigrama *(Crossword puzzle)*** Tu profesor(a) les va a dar a ti y a tu compañero/a un crucigrama incompleto. Tú tienes las palabras que necesita tu compañero/a y él/ella tiene las palabras que tú necesitas. Tienen que darse pistas *(clues)* para completarlo. No pueden decir la palabra necesaria; deben utilizar definiciones, ejemplos y frases incompletas.

modelo

13 vertical: Es un condimento que normalmente viene con la sal.

10 horizontal: Es una fruta amarilla.

8 Expansion Ask the same questions of individual students. Ask other students to restate what their classmates answered.

¡Lengua viva! Explain that students already know several uses of **tomar (tomar clases, tomar fotos, tomar el sol)**. Explain that **tomar** with beverages is common in all Spanish-speaking countries. Ex: **¿Quieres tomar un café?**

9 Expansion Using magazine pictures that show people in eating situations, have students describe what's going on: who the people are, what they're eating and drinking, and so forth.

10 Suggestion Divide the class into pairs and distribute the Info Gap Handouts from the Info Gap Activities Booklet that correspond to this activity. Give the students ten minutes to complete this activity.

10 Expansion Have groups create another type of word puzzle, such as a word-find, to share with the class. It should contain additional food- and meal-related vocabulary.

TEACHING OPTIONS

Small Groups In groups of two to four, students prepare brief skits that have something to do with food. The skits may involve being in a market, in a restaurant, in a café, inviting people over for dinner, and so forth. Videotape the skits and play them back for the class to select the most creative one.

Game Play a game of continuous narration. One student begins with: **Voy a preparar** (*name of dish*) **y voy al mercado. Necesito comprar...** and names one food item. The next student then repeats the entire narration, adding another food item. Continue on through various students. When the possibilities for that particular dish are used up, have another student begin with another dish, repeating the process.

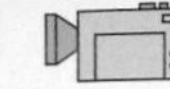

Section Goals

In **Fotonovela** students will:

- receive comprehensible input from free-flowing discourse
- learn functional phrases that preview lesson grammatical structures

Instructional Resources
WB/VM: Video Activities, pp. 227–228
***Fotonovela** DVD/Video (Start 00:39:36)*
Video CD-ROM
*IRM: **Fotonovela** Translations, pp. 142–143, Videoscript, pp. 110–111*
Interactive CD-ROM

Video Recap: Lección 7
Before doing this **Fotonovela** section, review the previous one with this activity.
1. ¿Qué no hace Javier jamás? (jamás se levanta temprano)
2. ¿Qué hace Javier por la noche? (dibuja y escucha música)
3. ¿Qué va a hacer Álex por Javier? (va a despertarlo)
4. ¿Qué hace Álex por la mañana? (se levanta, corre, se ducha y se viste)

Video Synopsis Don Francisco takes the travelers to the **Restaurante El Cráter** for lunch. The owner of the restaurant, Doña Rita, welcomes the group and makes recommendations about what to order. After the food is served, Don Francisco and Doña Rita plan a surprise birthday party for Maite.

Suggestions

- Have the class predict the content of the **Fotonovela** based on its title and the video stills.
- Quickly review the predictions and ask students a few questions to help them summarize this episode.
- Ask students about their favorite restaurants, using the active vocabulary in **Expresiones útiles.** Ex: **¿Conoces un buen restaurante en esta ciudad? ¿Cómo se llama? Cuando vas a ____, ¿qué pides? ¿Qué tal la comida en ____?**

¿Qué tal la comida?

NATIONAL STANDARDS communication cultures

Don Francisco y los estudiantes van al restaurante El Cráter.

PERSONAJES

MAITE

INÉS

DON FRANCISCO

ÁLEX

JAVIER

DOÑA RITA

CAMARERO

1

JAVIER ¿Sabes dónde estamos?

INÉS Mmm, no sé. Oiga, don Francisco, ¿sabe usted dónde estamos?

DON FRANCISCO Estamos cerca de Cotacachi.

2

ÁLEX ¿Dónde vamos a almorzar, don Francisco? ¿Conoce un buen restaurante en Cotacachi?

DON FRANCISCO Pues, conozco a doña Rita Perales, la dueña del mejor restaurante de la ciudad, el restaurante El Cráter.

3

DOÑA RITA Hombre, don Paco, ¿Usted por aquí?

DON FRANCISCO Sí, doña Rita... y hoy le traigo clientes. Le presento a Maite, Inés, Álex y Javier. Los llevo a las montañas para ir de excursión.

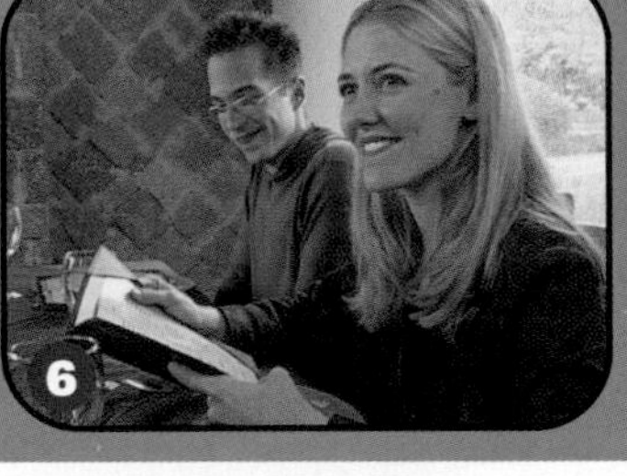
6

MAITE Voy a tomar un caldo de patas y un lomo a la plancha.

JAVIER Para mí las tortillas de maíz y el ceviche de camarón.

ÁLEX Yo también quisiera las tortillas de maíz y el ceviche.

INÉS Voy a pedir caldo de patas y lomo a la plancha.

7

DON FRANCISCO Yo quiero tortillas de maíz y una fuente de fritada, por favor.

DOÑA RITA Y de tomar, les recomiendo el jugo de piña, frutilla y mora. ¿Se lo traigo a todos?

TODOS Sí, perfecto.

8

CAMARERO ¿Qué plato pidió usted?

MAITE Un caldo de patas y lomo a la plancha.

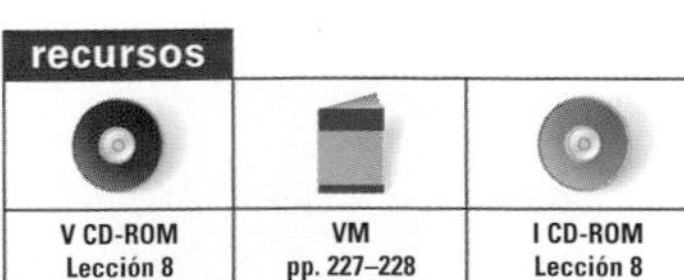

recursos
V CD-ROM
Lección 8
VM
pp. 227–228
I CD-ROM
Lección 8

TEACHING OPTIONS

Video Tips General suggestions for using video clips in the classroom can be found on page IAE-12 of this Instructor's Annotated Edition.
¿Qué tal la comida? Play the first half of the **¿Qué tal la comida?** segment of this video module and have the class give you a description of what they see. Write their observations on the board, pointing out any incorrect information. Repeat this process to allow the class to pick up more details of the plot. Then ask your students to use the information they have accumulated to guess what happens in the rest of the segment. Write their guesses on the board. Then play the entire segment and, through discussion, help the class summarize the plot.

DOÑA RITA ¡Bienvenidos al restaurante El Cráter! Están en muy buenas manos... don Francisco es el mejor conductor del país. Y no hay nada más bonito que nuestras montañas. Pero si van a ir de excursión deben comer bien. Vengan chicos, por aquí.

JAVIER ¿Qué nos recomienda Ud.?

DOÑA RITA Bueno, las tortillas de maíz son riquísimas. La especialidad de la casa es el caldo de patas... ¡tienen que probarlo! El lomo a la plancha es un poquito más caro que el caldo pero es sabrosísimo. También les recomiendo el ceviche y la fuente de fritada.

DOÑA RITA ¿Qué tal la comida? ¿Rica?

JAVIER Rica, no. ¡Riquísima!

ÁLEX Sí. ¡Y nos la sirvieron tan rápidamente!

MAITE Una comida deliciosa, gracias.

DON FRANCISCO Hoy es el cumpleaños de Maite...

DOÑA RITA ¡Ah! Tenemos unos pasteles que están como para chuparse los dedos...

Enfoque cultural La comida hispana

La cocina (*cuisine*) hispana es una combinación de comidas e ingredientes de varias regiones. La carne de res, la papa, el maíz y el chile, por ejemplo, son característicos de los países andinos. Los frijoles, el arroz, la caña de azúcar y la banana son productos típicos de los países del Caribe. La cocina española incorpora pescados y carnes cocinados (*cooked*) con condimentos como el ajo y la cebolla. La comida típica de Centroamérica es similar a la mexicana y consta de (*consists of*) carne, pescados, chile, tortillas y salsas.

Expresiones útiles

Finding out where you are

▶ **¿Sabe Ud./Sabes dónde estamos?**
Do you know where we are?
▷ **Estamos cerca de Cotacachi.**
We're near Cotacachi.

Talking about people and places you're familiar with

▶ **¿Conoce usted/Conoces un buen restaurante en Cotacachi?**
Do you know a good restaurant in Cotacachi?
▷ **Sí, conozco varios.**
Yes, I know several.
▶ **¿Conoce/Conoces a doña Rita?**
Do you know doña Rita?

Ordering food

▶ **¿Qué le puedo traer?**
What can I bring you?
▷ **Voy a tomar/pedir un caldo de patas y un lomo a la plancha.**
I am going to have/to order the beef soup and grilled flank steak.
▷ **Para mí las tortillas de maíz y el ceviche de camarón, por favor.**
Corn tortillas and lemon-marinated shrimp for me, please.
▷ **Yo también quisiera...**
I also would like...
▷ **Y de tomar, el jugo de piña, frutilla y mora.**
And pineapple/strawberry/blackberry juice to drink.
▶ **¿Qué plato pidió usted?**
What did you order?
▷ **Yo pedí un caldo de patas.**
I ordered the beef soup.

Talking about the food at a restaurant

▶ **¿Qué tal la comida?**
How is the food?
▷ **Muy rica, gracias.**
Very tasty, thanks.
▷ **¡Riquísima!**
Extremely delicious!

Suggestion Have the class read through the entire **Fotonovela**, with volunteers playing the parts of Don Francisco, Javier, Inés, Álex, Maite, Doña Rita, and the **Camarero**. Have students take turns playing the roles so that more students participate.

Expresiones útiles Point out some of the unfamiliar structures, which will be taught in detail in **Estructura**. Draw attention to the verb **pidió**. Explain that this is a form of the verb **pedir**, which has a stem change in the third-person forms of the preterite. Have the class read the caption for video still 5, and explain that **más caro que** is an example of a comparison. Point out that in caption 9, **nos la** is an example of an indirect object pronoun and a direct object pronoun used together. Tell your students that they will learn more about these concepts in **Estructura**.

TEACHING OPTIONS

Enfoque cultural Point out that meal times in Spanish-speaking countries differ from country to country. Breakfast (**el desayuno**) is often eaten between the hours of 7 and 9 in the morning, while lunch (**el almuerzo**) is usually eaten around 2 or 3 p.m. Late in the afternoon, some families have a snack (**merienda**) to tide them over until the last meal of the day (**la cena**), which is typically not very large and is served between 8 and 11 in the evening. Your students might also be interested to know that it is customary for family members to remain at the dinner table after the meal is over for an after-meal chat, **la sobremesa**. Tell students that in Spanish-speaking countries it is not common for people to eat their meals on the run and separately from other members of the family.

1 Suggestion Ask your students these questions before having them complete this activity: **¿Qué es El Cráter? ¿Quién es doña Rita? ¿Cuáles son algunas de las comidas del menú?**

2 Suggestion Have your students close their books. Then read each item aloud and have the class guess who would have made each statement.

2 Expansion Give the class these additional items: **7. Les van a gustar muchísimo nuestras montañas. (doña Rita) 8. ¿Les gustó la comida? (doña Rita) 9. Para mí, las tortillas de maíz y la fuente de fritada. (don Francisco)**

3 Suggestion Change the questions' focus by rephrasing them. Ex: **¿Qué es El Cráter? (Es el restaurante donde comieron don Francisco y los estudiantes.)**

4 Possible Responses
Conversation 1:
E1: Oye, María, ¿conoces un buen restaurante en esta ciudad?
E2: Sí... el restaurante El Pescador sirve comida sabrosísima.
E1: ¿Por qué no vamos a El Pescador esta noche?
E2: ¿A qué hora?
E1: ¿A las ocho?
E2: Perfecto.
E1: Está bien. Nos vemos a las ocho.
E2: Adiós.
Conversation 2:
E1: ¿Qué le puedo traer?
E2: Bueno, ¿cuáles son las especialidades de la casa?
E1: La especialidad de la casa es el lomo a la plancha. También, le recomiendo el caldo de patas.
E2: Mmm... voy a pedir los camarones y el lomo a la plancha. De tomar, voy a pedir el jugo de piña.
E1: Gracias, señor.

Reacciona a la fotonovela

1 Escoger Escoge la respuesta (*answer*) que completa mejor (*best*) cada oración.

1. Don Francisco lleva a los estudiantes a __c__ al restaurante de una amiga.
   a. cenar b. desayunar c. almorzar
2. Doña Rita es __b__.
   a. la hermana de don Francisco b. la dueña del restaurante
   c. una camarera que trabaja en El Cráter
3. Doña Rita les recomienda a los viajeros __a__.
   a. el caldo de patas y el lomo a la plancha
   b. el bistec, las verduras frescas y el vino tinto c. unos pasteles (*cakes*)
4. Inés va a pedir __c__.
   a. las tortillas de maíz y una fuente de fritada (*mixed grill*)
   b. el ceviche de camarón y el caldo de patas
   c. el caldo de patas y el lomo a la plancha

NOTA CULTURAL

El **ceviche** es un plato típico de Suramérica. Se prepara con jugo de limón, cebolla, chiles y pescado crudo *(raw)* o mariscos.

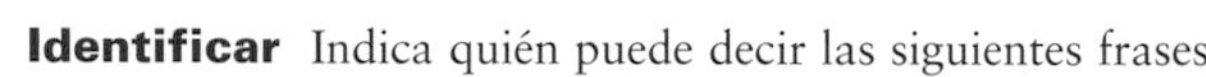

2 Identificar Indica quién puede decir las siguientes frases.

1. No me gusta esperar en los restaurantes. ¡Qué bueno que nos sirvieron rápidamente! Álex
2. Les recomiendo la especialidad de la casa. doña Rita
3. ¡Maite y yo pedimos los mismos platos! Inés
4. Disculpe, señora... ¿qué platos recomienda usted? Javier
5. Yo conozco a una señora que tiene un restaurante excelente. Les va a gustar mucho. don Francisco
6. Hoy es mi cumpleaños (*birthday*). Maite

ÁLEX

INÉS

DOÑA RITA

MAITE

DON FRANCISCO

JAVIER

3 Preguntas Contesta las siguientes preguntas sobre la **Fotonovela.**

1. ¿Dónde comieron don Francisco y los estudiantes?
   Comieron en el restaurante de doña Rita/El Cráter.
2. ¿Cuál es la especialidad de El Cráter?
   La especialidad de la casa es el caldo de patas.
3. ¿Qué pidió Javier? ¿Y Álex? ¿Qué tomaron todos? Javier pidió tortillas de maíz y el ceviche. Álex también pidió las tortillas de maíz y el ceviche. Todos tomaron jugo.
4. ¿Qué tal los pasteles en El Cráter?
   Los pasteles en El Cráter son sabrosísimos.

4 En el restaurante Answers will vary.

1. Prepara con un(a) compañero/a una conversación en la que le preguntas si conoce algún buen restaurante en tu comunidad. Tu compañero/a responde que él/ella sí conoce un restaurante que sirve una comida deliciosa. Lo/La invitas a cenar y tu compañero/a acepta. Determinan la hora para verse en el restaurante y se despiden (*say goodbye*).
2. Trabaja con un(a) compañero/a para representar los papeles (*roles*) de un(a) cliente/a y un(a) camarero/a en un restaurante. El/La camarero/a te pregunta qué te puede servir y tú preguntas cuál es la especialidad de la casa. El/La camarero/a te dice cuál es la especialidad y te recomienda algunos platos del menú. Tú pides entremeses, un plato principal y escoges una bebida. El/La camarero/a te da las gracias y luego te sirve la comida.

CONSÚLTALO

To review indefinite words like **algún**, see **Estructura 7.2**, p. 214.

TEACHING OPTIONS

Extra Practice Ask your students these questions about the **Fotonovela**. Ex: **¿En qué ciudad está el restaurante El Cráter? (Cotacachi) ¿Qué pidió Javier en el restaurante? (tortillas de maíz, ceviche de camarón) ¿Qué pidió don Francisco? (tortillas de maíz, fuente de fritada) ¿Cuándo es el cumpleaños de Maite? (hoy)**

Small Groups Have your students work in groups to prepare a skit in which a family goes to a restaurant, is seated by a waitperson, examines the menu, and orders dinner. Each family member should ask a few questions about the menu and then order an entree and a drink. Have one or two groups perform the skit in front of the class.

Pronunciación

ll, ñ, c, and z

pollo	llave	ella	cebolla

Most Spanish speakers pronounce the letter **ll** like the *y* in *yes.*

mañana	señor	baño	niña

The letter ***ñ*** is pronounced much like the *ny* in *canyon.*

café	colombiano	cuando	rico

Before **a**, **o**, or **u**, the Spanish **c** is pronounced like the *c* in *car.*

cereales	delicioso	conducir	conocer

Before **e** or **i**, the Spanish **c** is pronounced like the *s* in *sit*. (In parts of Spain, **c** before **e** or **i** is pronounced like the *th* in *think.*)

zeta	zanahoria	almuerzo	cerveza

The Spanish **z** is pronounced like the *s* in *sit.* (In parts of Spain, **z** is pronounced like the *th* in *think.*)

Práctica Lee las palabras en voz alta.

1. mantequilla
2. cuñado
3. aceite
4. manzana
5. español
6. cepillo
7. zapato
8. azúcar
9. quince
10. compañera
11. almorzar
12. calle

Oraciones Lee las oraciones en voz alta.

1. Mi compañero de cuarto se llama Toño Núñez. Su familia es de la ciudad de Guatemala y de Quetzaltenango.
2. Dice que la comida de su mamá es deliciosa, especialmente su pollo al champiñón y sus tortillas de maíz.
3. Creo que Toño tiene razón porque hoy cené en su casa y quiero volver mañana para cenar allí otra vez.

Refranes Lee los refranes en voz alta.

Las apariencias engañan.[1]

Panza llena, corazón contento.[2]

1 Looks can be deceiving.
2 A full belly makes a happy heart.

recursos

TEXT CD Lección 8	LM p. 44	Lab CD/MP3 Lección 8	I CD-ROM Lección 8

Section Goal

In **Pronunciación** students will be introduced to the pronunciation of the letters **ll**, **ñ**, **c**, and **z**.

Instructional Resources
Textbook CD
Lab Manual, p. 44
Lab CD/MP3 ***Lección 8***
IRM: Tapescript, pp. 35–39; p. 92
Interactive CD-ROM

Suggestions

- Point out that the Spanish letter **ll** is usually pronounced like the English *y* in *you.*
- Ask the class how the letter **ñ** is pronounced (like the *ny* in *canyon*).
- Tell the class that **c** is pronounced like the English *c* in *car* before **a**, **o**, or **u**.
- Ask the class how most Spanish speakers pronounce the letter **c** when it appears before **e** or **i** (like the English *s* in *some*). Then point out that **c** before **e** or **i** is pronounced like the English *th* in *think* in some parts of Spain.
- Explain that the Spanish **z** is usually pronounced like the English *s* in *some.* Mention that in parts of Spain, **z** is pronounced like the English *th* in *think.*
- As you explain the pronunciation of these sounds, write a few of the example words on the board and have students pronounce them.

Práctica/Oraciones/Refranes
These exercises are recorded on the Textbook CD. You may want to play the CD so students practice the pronunciation point by listening to Spanish spoken by speakers other than yourself.

TEACHING OPTIONS

Extra Practice Write the names of a few distinguished Guatemalans on the board and ask for a volunteer to pronounce each one. Ex: Luis Cardoza y Aragón (writer), Carlos Mérida (painter), Enrique Gómez Carrillo (writer), José Milla (writer), Alonso de la Paz (sculptor). Repeat the process with a few city names: Villanueva, Zacapa, Escuintla, Cobán.

Pairs Have the class work in pairs to practice the pronunciation of the sentences given in **Actividad 2 (Identificar)** on page 242. Encourage your students to help their partner if they have trouble pronouncing a particular word. Circulate around the class and model correct pronunciation as needed, focusing on the letters **ll**, **ñ**, **c**, and **z**.

Section Goal

In **Estructura 8.1**, students will be introduced to the preterite of stem-changing verbs.

Instructional Resources
WB/VM: Workbook, pp. 87–88
Lab Manual, p. 45
Lab CD/MP3 ***Lección 8***
IRM: ***¡Inténtalo!*** *&* ***Práctica*** *Answers, pp. 210–211;*
Tapescript, pp. 35–39
Interactive CD-ROM
Companion website: www.vistahigherlearning.com
Presentations CD-ROM

Suggestions

- Review present tense forms of **–ir** stem-changing verbs like **pedir** and **dormir**. Also review formation of the preterite of regular **–ir** verbs using **escribir** and **recibir**.
- Give model sentences that use these verbs in the preterite, emphasizing third-person forms. Ex: **Me dormí temprano anoche, pero mi compañero de cuarto se durmió muy tarde.**
- Point out that **morir** means *to die* and offer sample sentences using third-person preterite forms of the verb. Ex: **No tengo bisabuelos. Ya murieron.**
- Other **–ir** verbs that change their stem vowel in the preterite are **conseguir, despedirse, divertirse, pedir, preferir, repetir, seguir, sentir, sugerir, vestirse**.

8.1 Preterite of stem-changing verbs

NATIONAL
comparisons
STANDARDS

recursos
WB pp. 87–94
LM pp. 45–48
Lab CD/MP3 Lección 8
I CD-ROM Lección 8
vistahigherlearning.com

ANTE TODO As you learned in **Lección 6**, **–ar** and **–er** stem-changing verbs have no stem change in the preterite. **–Ir** stem-changing verbs, however, do have a stem change. Study the following charts and observe where the stem changes occur.

Preterite of *–ir* stem-changing verbs

		servir *(to serve)*	**dormir** *(to sleep)*
SINGULAR FORMS	yo	serví	dormí
	tú	serviste	dormiste
	Ud./él/ella	s**i**rvió	d**u**rmió
PLURAL FORMS	nosotros/as	servimos	dormimos
	vosotros/as	servisteis	dormisteis
	Uds./ellos/ellas	s**i**rvieron	d**u**rmieron

▶ Stem-changing **–ir** verbs, in the preterite only, have a stem change in the third-person singular and plural forms. The stem change consists of either **e** to **i** or **o** to **u**.

(e → i) pedir: p**i**dió, p**i**dieron (o → u) morir (*to die*): m**u**rió, m**u**rieron

Perdón, ¿quiénes pidieron las tortillas de maíz?

¿Y qué plato pidió usted?

¡INTÉNTALO! Cambia los infinitivos al pretérito.

1. Yo ___serví___. (servir, dormir, pedir, preferir, repetir, seguir)
   dormí, pedí, preferí, repetí, seguí
2. Usted __________. (morir, conseguir, pedir, sentirse, despedirse, vestirse)
   murió, consiguió, pidió, se sintió, se despidió, se vistió
3. Tú __________. (conseguir, servir, morir, pedir, dormir, repetir)
   conseguiste, serviste, moriste, pediste, dormiste, repetiste
4. Ellas __________. (repetir, dormir, seguir, preferir, morir, servir)
   repitieron, durmieron, siguieron, prefirieron, murieron, sirvieron
5. Nosotros __________. (seguir, preferir, servir, vestirse, despedirse, dormirse)
   seguimos, preferimos, servimos, nos vestimos, nos despedimos, nos dormimos
6. Ustedes __________. (sentirse, vestirse, conseguir, pedir, despedirse, dormirse)
   se sintieron, se vistieron, consiguieron, pidieron, se despidieron, se durmieron
7. Él __________. (dormir, morir, preferir, repetir, seguir, pedir)
   durmió, murió, prefirió, repitió, siguió, pidió

TEACHING OPTIONS

Extra Practice Do a pattern practice drill. Write a stem-changing **–ir** verb on the board and ask individual students to provide preterite forms for the different subject pronouns and/or names you call out. Ex: **seguir/Miguel (siguió)**. Reverse the activity by calling out a conjugated form and asking students to give the appropriate subject pronoun. Ex: **pidieron (ellos, ellas, Uds.)**.

Pairs Ask students to work in pairs to come up with ten original sentences in which they use third-person preterite forms of stem-changing **–ir** verbs. Point out that students should try to use many of the vocabulary items from **Contextos** in their sentences. Pairs then share their sentences with the rest of the class.

Práctica

NOTA CULTURAL

El horario de las comidas en España es muy distinto al de los EE.UU. El desayuno es muy ligero (*light*). La hora de la comida, o el almuerzo, es entre las 2 y las 3 de la tarde. Es la comida más importante del día. Mucha gente come una merienda o tapas por la tarde. La cena, normalmente ligera, suele ser entre las 9 y 11 de la noche.

1 **Completar** Completa las siguientes frases para describir lo que pasó anoche en el restaurante El Famoso.

1. Paula y Humberto Suárez llegaron al restaurante El Famoso a las ocho y siguieron (seguir) al camarero a una mesa en la sección de no fumar.
2. El señor Suárez pidió (pedir) una chuleta de cerdo. La señora Suárez decidió probar los camarones.
3. Para tomar, los dos pidieron (pedir) vino tinto.
4. El camarero repitió (repetir) el pedido (*the order*) para confirmarlo.
5. La comida tardó mucho (*took a long time*) en llegar y los señores Suárez se durmieron (dormirse) esperando la comida.
6. A las nueve el camarero les sirvió (servir) la comida.
7. Después de comer la chuleta de cerdo, el señor Suárez se sintió (sentirse) muy mal.
8. De repente, el señor Suárez se murió (morir).
9. Pobre señor Suárez... ¿por qué no pidió (pedir) los camarones?

2 **El camarero loco** En el restaurante La Hermosa trabaja un camarero muy loco que siempre comete muchos errores. Indica lo que los clientes pidieron y lo que el camarero les sirvió.

modelo

Armando / papas fritas

Armando pidió papas fritas, pero el camarero le sirvió maíz.

1. Nosotros / jugo de naranja Nosotros pedimos jugo de naranja, pero el camarero nos sirvió papas.
2. Beatriz / queso Beatriz pidió queso, pero el camarero le sirvió uvas.
3. Tú / arroz Tú pediste arroz, pero el camarero te sirvió arvejas/sopa.

4. Elena y Alejandro /atún Elena y Alejandro pidieron atún, pero el camarero les sirvió camarones (mariscos).
5. Usted / agua mineral Ud. pidió agua mineral, pero el camarero le sirvió vino tinto.
6. Yo / hamburguesa Yo pedí una hamburguesa, pero el camarero me sirvió zanahorias.

1 Expansion Ask students to work in pairs to come up with an alternate ending to the narration, using stem-changing **–ir** verbs in the preterite. Pairs then share their endings with the class. The class can vote on the most original ending.

2 Expansion In pairs, students redo the activity, this time role-playing the customer and the waiter. Model the possible interaction between the students. Ex: **E1: Perdón, pero pedí papas fritas y usted me sirvió maíz. E2: ¡Ay perdón! Le traigo papas fritas enseguida.** Students take turns playing the role of the customer and waiter.

TEACHING OPTIONS

Video Show the video again to give students more input with stem-changing **–ir** verbs in the preterite. Have them write down all the stem-changing forms (third person singular and plural) they hear. Stop the video where appropriate to discuss how certain verbs were used and to ask comprehension questions. Ex: **¿Qué pidió Maite? ¿Cómo sirvieron la comida?**

Extra Practice Prepare descriptions of five easily recognizable people in which you use the stem-changing forms of **–ir** verbs in the preterite. Write their names on the board in random order. Then read your descriptions, having students match the description to the appropriate name. Ex: **Murió en un accidente de avión en 1999.** (John F. Kennedy, Jr.)

3 Expansion Have students share their sentences with the class. Ask other students comprehension questions based on what was said.

4 Expansion To practice the formal register, have students ask you the same questions.

5 Expansion Have groups present their description to the class in the form of a narration.

Consúltalo In addition to pointing out words and expressions that may signal the preterite, remind students about transition words that help to move the flow of a narration. Ex: **primero, después, luego, también**.

Comunicación

3 **El almuerzo** Completa las oraciones de César de una manera lógica. Answers will vary.

modelo

Mi compañero de cuarto se despertó temprano, pero yo...

Mi compañero de cuarto se despertó temprano, pero yo me desperté tarde.

1. Yo llegué al restaurante a tiempo, pero mis amigos...
2. Beatriz pidió la ensalada de frutas, pero yo...
3. Yolanda les recomendó el bistec, pero Eva y Paco...
4. Nosotros preferimos las papas fritas, pero Yolanda...
5. El camarero sirvió la carne, pero yo...
6. Beatriz y yo pedimos café, pero Yolanda y Paco...
7. Eva se sintió enferma, pero Paco y yo...
8. Nosotros repetimos el postre, pero Eva...
9. Ellos salieron tarde, pero yo...
10. Yo me dormí temprano, pero mi compañero de cuarto...

NOTA CULTURAL

Hay cerca de 4.000 variedades de **papa**. Los incas del Perú fueron los primeros en cultivar papas en el año 200 a.C. Las utilizaron para curar heridas (*injuries*), prevenir enfermedades (*diseases*) y ayudar con la digestión.

4 **Entrevista** Trabajen en parejas y túrnense para entrevistar a su compañero/a. Answers will vary.

1. ¿Te acostaste tarde o temprano anoche? ¿A qué hora te dormiste? ¿Dormiste bien?
2. ¿A qué hora te despertaste esta mañana? Y ¿a qué hora te levantaste?
3. ¿A qué hora vas a acostarte esta noche?
4. ¿Qué almorzaste ayer? ¿Quién te sirvió el almuerzo?
5. ¿Qué cenaste ayer?
6. ¿Cenaste en un restaurante recientemente? ¿Con quién?
7. ¿Qué pediste en el restaurante? ¿Qué pidieron los demás?
8. ¿Se durmió alguien en alguna de tus clases la semana pasada? ¿En qué clase?

Síntesis

5 **Describir** En grupos, estudien la foto y las preguntas que siguen. Luego, describan la cena romántica de Eduardo y Rosa. Answers will vary.

- ¿Adónde salieron a cenar?
- ¿Qué pidieron?
- ¿Les sirvieron la comida rápidamente?
- ¿Les gustó la comida?
- ¿Cuánto costó?
- ¿Van a volver a este restaurante en el futuro?
- ¿Recomiendas el restaurante?

CONSÚLTALO

To review words commonly associated with the preterite such as **anoche**, see **Estructura 6.3**, p.185.

TEACHING OPTIONS

Pairs In pairs, students take turns telling each other about a memorable experience in a restaurant, whether it was a date, whether they were with family or friends, and so forth. Students should be encouraged to take notes as their partner narrates. Then have students reveal what their partner told them.

Extra Practice Using magazine pictures that show restaurant scenes, have students describe them in the past tense, using the preterite. Write on the board some stem-changing –**ir** verbs that might apply to what's going on in the pictures.

8.2 Double object pronouns

ANTE TODO In **Lecciones 5** and **6**, you learned that direct and indirect object pronouns replace nouns and that they often refer to nouns that have already been referenced. You will now learn how to use direct and indirect object pronouns together. Observe the following diagram.

Indirect Object Pronouns			Direct Object Pronouns	
me	nos	+	lo	los
te	os		la	las
le (se)	les (se)			

▶ When direct and indirect object pronouns are used together, the indirect object pronoun always precedes the direct object pronoun.

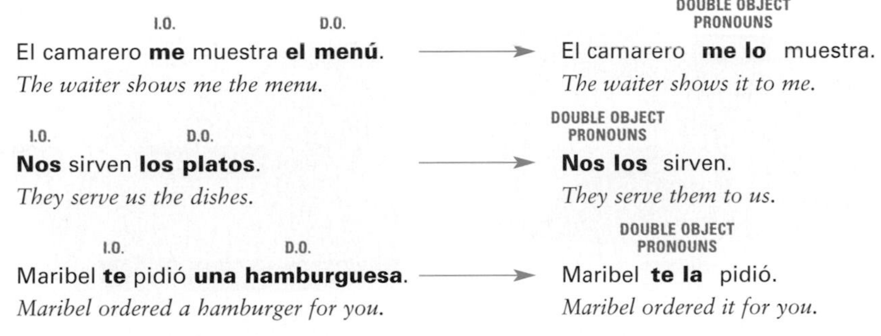

I.O. / D.O.		DOUBLE OBJECT PRONOUNS
El camarero **me** muestra **el menú**. *The waiter shows me the menu.*	→	El camarero **me lo** muestra. *The waiter shows it to me.*
Nos sirven **los platos**. *They serve us the dishes.*	→	**Nos los** sirven. *They serve them to us.*
Maribel **te** pidió **una hamburguesa**. *Maribel ordered a hamburger for you.*	→	Maribel **te la** pidió. *Maribel ordered it for you.*

Y de tomar, les recomiendo el jugo de piña... ¿Se lo traigo a todos?

▶ In Spanish, two pronouns that begin with the letter **l** cannot be used together. Therefore, the indirect object pronouns **le** and **les** always change to **se** when they are used with **lo, los, la,** and **las**.

I.O. / D.O.		DOUBLE OBJECT PRONOUNS
Le escribí **la carta**. *I wrote him the letter.*	→	**Se la** escribí. *I wrote it to him.*
Les sirvió **los entremeses**. *He served them the hors d'oeuvres.*	→	**Se los** sirvió. *He served them to them.*

Section Goals

In **Estructura 8.2** students will be introduced to:

- the use of double object pronouns
- converting **le** and **les** into **se** when used with third-person direct object pronouns

Instructional Resources
WB/VM: Workbook, pp. 89–90
Lab Manual, p. 46
Lab CD/MP3 ***Lección 8***
IRM: ***¡Inténtalo!*** *&* ***Práctica*** *Answers, pp. 210–211; Tapescript, pp. 35–39*
Info Gap Activities Booklet, pp. 31–32
Interactive CD-ROM
Companion website: www.vistahigherlearning.com
Presentations CD-ROM

Suggestions

- Briefly review direct object pronouns (**Estructura 5.4**) and indirect object pronouns (**Estructura 6.2**). Give sentences and have students convert objects into object pronouns. Ex: **Sara escribió la carta. (Sara la escribió.) Mis padres escribieron una carta. (yo) (Mis padres me escribieron una carta.)**
- Model additional examples for the students, asking them to make the conversion with **se.** Ex: **Le pedí papas fritas. (Se las pedí.) Les servimos café. (Se lo servimos.)**

TEACHING OPTIONS

Extra Practice Write six sentences on the board for students to express using double object pronouns. Ex: **Rita les sirvió la cena a los viajeros. (Rita se la sirvió.)**
Pairs In pairs, students write five sentences that contain both direct and indirect objects (not pronouns). Their partners must express the sentences using double object pronouns.

Video Show the video again to give students more input containing double object pronouns. Stop the video where appropriate to discuss how double object pronouns were used and to ask comprehension questions.

Suggestions

- Ask students questions to which they respond with third-person double object pronouns. Ex: **¿Le recomiendas el ceviche a ____ ? (Sí, se lo recomiendo.) ¿Les traes sándwiches a tus compañeros? (Sí, se los traigo.)**
- Practice pronoun placement with infinitives and present participles by giving sentences that show one method of pronoun placement and asking students to restate them another way. Ex: **Se lo voy a mandar. (Voy a mandárselo.)**

▶ Because **se** has multiple meanings, Spanish speakers often clarify to whom the pronoun refers by adding **a usted, a él, a ella, a ustedes, a ellos,** or **a ellas.**

¿El sombrero? Carlos **se** lo vendió **a ella.**
The hat? Carlos sold it to her.

¿Las verduras? Ellos **se** las compran a **usted.**
The vegetables? They buy them for you.

▶ Double object pronouns are placed before a conjugated verb. With infinitives and present participles, they may be placed before the conjugated verb or attached to the end of the infinitive or present participle.

DOUBLE OBJECT PRONOUNS	DOUBLE OBJECT PRONOUNS
Te lo voy a mostrar.	Voy a mostrár**telo**.
Nos las están sirviendo.	Están sirviéndo**noslas**.

¿Qué tal la comida, rica?

Sí. ¡Y nos la sirvieron tan rápidamente!

▶ As you can see above, when double object pronouns are attached to an infinitive or a present participle, an accent mark is added to maintain the original stress.

¡INTÉNTALO! Escribe el pronombre de objeto directo o indirecto que falta en cada frase.

Objeto directo

1. ¿La ensalada? El camarero nos ___la___ sirvió.
2. ¿El salmón? La dueña me___lo___ recomienda.
3. ¿La comida? Voy a preparárte___la___.
4. ¿Las bebidas? Estamos pidiéndose___las___.
5. ¿Los refrescos? Te ___los___ puedo traer ahora.
6. ¿Los platos de arroz? Van a servírnos___los___ después.

Objeto indirecto

1. ¿Puedes traerme tu plato? No, no ___te___ lo puedo traer.
2. ¿Quieres mostrarle la carta? Sí, voy a mostrár___se___la ahora.
3. ¿Les serviste la carne? No, no ___se___ la serví.
4. ¿Vas a leerle el menú? No, no ___se___ lo voy a leer.
5. ¿Me recomiendas la langosta? Sí, ___te___ la recomiendo.
6. ¿Cuándo vas a prepararnos la cena? ___Se___ la voy a preparar en una hora.

TEACHING OPTIONS

Pairs Have students create five dehydrated sentences for their partner to complete. They should include the following elements: subject / action / direct object / indirect object (name or pronoun). Ex: **Carlos / escribe / carta / Marta**. Their partner should "hydrate" this particular sentence as follows: **Carlos se la escribe (a Marta).**

Large Groups Split the class into two groups. Give cards that contain verbs that can take a direct object to one group. The other group gets cards containing nouns. Then select one member from each group to stand up and show his or her card. Another student converts the two elements into a sentence using double object pronouns: **mostrar / el libro →** [Name of student] **se lo va a mostrar**. Be sure each sentence makes sense.

Práctica

1 **Responder** Imagínate que trabajas de camarero/a en un restaurante. Responde a las órdenes de estos clientes usando pronombres.

AYUDA

Here are some other useful expressions:
ahora mismo *right now*
inmediatamente *immediately*
¡A la orden! *At your service!*
¡Ya voy! *I'm on my way!*

modelo
Sra. Gómez: Una ensalada, por favor.
Sí, señora. Enseguida (Right away) se la traigo.

1. Sr. López: La mantequilla, por favor. Sí, señor. Enseguida se la traigo.
2. Srta. Rivas: Los camarones, por favor. Sí, señorita. Enseguida se los traigo.
3. Sra. Lugones: El pollo asado, por favor. Sí, señora. Enseguida se lo traigo.
4. Tus compañeros/as de cuarto: Café, por favor. Sí, chicos. Enseguida se lo traigo.
5. Tu profesor(a) de español: Papas fritas, por favor. Sí, profesor(a). Enseguida se las traigo.
6. Dra. González: La chuleta de cerdo, por favor. Sí, doctora. Enseguida se la traigo.
7. Tus padres: Los champiñones, por favor. Sí, señores. Enseguida se los traigo.
8. Dr. Torres: La cuenta (*check*), por favor. Sí, doctor. Enseguida se la traigo.

2 **¿Quién?** La señora Cevallos está planeando una cena. Se pregunta cómo va a resolver ciertas situaciones. En parejas, túrnense (*take turns*) para decir lo que ella está pensando. Cambien los sustantivos (*nouns*) subrayados por pronombres de objeto directo y hagan (*make*) los otros cambios necesarios.

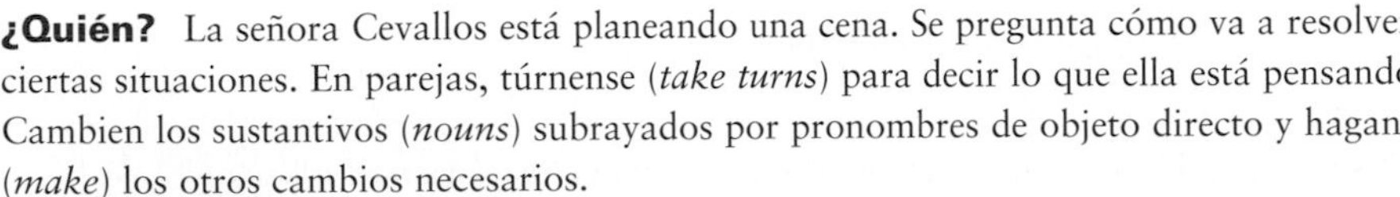

modelo
¡No tengo carne! ¿Quién va a traerme la <u>carne</u> del supermercado? (Mi esposo)
Mi esposo va a traérmela./Mi esposo me la va a traer.

1. ¡Las invitaciones! ¿Quién les manda <u>las invitaciones</u> a los invitados (*guests*)? (Mi hija) Mi hija se las manda.
2. No tengo tiempo de ir a la bodega. ¿Quién me puede comprar <u>el vino</u>? (Mi hijo) Mi hijo puede comprármelo./Mi hijo me lo puede comprar.
3. ¡Ay! No tengo suficientes platos. ¿Quién puede prestarme <u>los platos</u> que necesito? (Mi mamá) Mi mamá puede prestármelos./Mi mamá me los puede prestar.
4. Nos falta mantequilla. ¿Quién nos trae <u>la mantequilla</u>? (Mi cuñada) Mi cuñada nos la trae.
5. ¡Los postres (*desserts*)! ¿Quién está preparándonos <u>los postres</u>? (Silvia y Renata) Silvia y Renata están preparándonoslos./Silvia y Renata nos los están preparando.
6. No hay suficientes sillas. ¿Quiénes nos traen <u>las sillas</u> que faltan? (Héctor y Lorena) Héctor y Lorena nos las traen.
7. No tengo tiempo de pedirle el azúcar a Mónica. ¿Quién puede pedirle <u>el azúcar</u>? (Mi hijo) Mi hijo puede pedírselo./Mi hijo se lo puede pedir.
8. ¿Quién va a servirles <u>la cena</u> a los invitados? (Mis hijos) Mis hijos van a servírsela./Mis hijos se la van a servir.

NOTA CULTURAL

Los vinos de Chile son conocidos internacionalmente. **Concha y Toro** es el productor y exportador más grande de vinos de Chile. Las zonas más productivas de vino están al norte de Santiago, en el Valle Central.

1 Expansion Do the activity with the whole class, selecting a student to play the role of customer and another to play the role of waiter for each item.

Ayuda Model the helpful phrases in sentences. Point out that **ahora mismo, inmediatamente,** and **ya** can replace **enseguida** in the **modelo** for **Actividad 1.**

2 Expansions
- Change the subjects in parentheses for students to use different forms of the verbs.
- Use magazine pictures and ask students who is doing what to or for whom in the pictures. Ex: **La señora les muestra la casa a los jóvenes. Se la muestra a los jóvenes.**

TEACHING OPTIONS

Heritage Speakers Ask heritage speakers to talk about a favorite gift they received. Write **regalar** on the board and explain that it means *to give (a gift)*. Students should talk about what they received, who gave it to them (**regalar**), why, and so forth. Ask the rest of the class comprehension questions.

Game Play **Concentración**. Write sentences that use double object pronouns on each of eight cards. On another eight cards, draw or paste a picture that matches each description. Place the cards face-down in four rows of four. In pairs, students select two cards. If the two cards match, the pair keeps them. If they don't match, students replace them in their original position. The group with the most cards at the end wins.

3 Suggestion Continue the **modelo** exchange by asking: **¿Cuándo nos lo enseña? (Nos lo enseña los lunes, miércoles, jueves y viernes.)**

3 Expansion Ask questions of individual students. Then ask them why they answered as they did. Students answer using double object pronouns. Ex: **¿Quién te enseña español? (Usted me lo enseña.) ¿Por qué? (Usted me lo enseña porque es profesora de español.)**

4 Expansion Ask the questions of individual students. Then verify class comprehension by asking other students to repeat the information given.

5 Suggestion Divide the class into pairs and distribute the Info Gap Handouts from the Info Gap Activities Booklet that correspond to this activity. Give the students ten minutes to complete this activity.

5 Expansion With a different partner, ask pairs to make a list of the gifts they each received for their last birthday or other occasion. Then have them point to each item on their list and, using double object pronouns, tell their partner who bought it for them. Ex: (for **zapatos nuevos**) **Me los compró mi prima.**

Comunicación

NATIONAL communication STANDARDS

3 **Contestar** Trabajen en parejas. Túrnense para hacer preguntas usando las palabras interrogativas **¿Quién?** o **¿Cuándo?** y para responderlas. Sigan el modelo. Answers will vary.

modelo

nos enseña español
Estudiante 1: *¿Quién nos enseña español?*
Estudiante 2: *La profesora Camacho nos lo enseña.*

1. te puede explicar (*explain*) la tarea cuando no la entiendes
2. les vende el almuerzo a los estudiantes
3. vas a comprarme boletos (*tickets*) para un concierto
4. te escribe mensajes electrónicos
5. nos prepara los entremeses
6. me vas a prestar tu computadora
7. te compró esa bebida
8. nos va a recomendar el menú de la cafetería
9. le enseñó español al/a la profesor(a)
10. me vas a mostrar tu casa o apartamento

4  **Preguntas** Hazle estas preguntas a un(a) compañero/a. Answers will vary.

modelo

Estudiante 1: *¿Les prestas tu casa a tus amigos/as? ¿Por qué?*
Estudiante 2: *No, no se la presto a mis amigos porque no son muy responsables.*

1. ¿Me prestas tu coche (*car*)? ¿Ya le prestaste tu coche a otro/a amigo/a?
2. ¿Quién te presta dinero cuando lo necesitas?
3. ¿Les prestas dinero a tus amigos/as? ¿Por qué?
4. ¿Nos compras el almuerzo a mí y a los otros compañeros de clase?
5. ¿Les mandas correo electrónico a tus amigos? ¿Y a tu familia?
6. ¿Les das regalos a tus amigos? ¿Cuándo?
7. ¿Quién te va a preparar la cena esta noche?
8. ¿Quién te va a preparar el desayuno mañana?

Síntesis

5  **Regalos de Navidad** Tu profesor(a) te va a dar a ti y a un(a) compañero/a una parte de la lista de los regalos de Navidad (*Christmas gifts*) que Berta pidió y los regalos que sus parientes le compraron. Conversen para completar sus listas. Answers will vary.

Estudiante 1: *¿Qué le pidió Berta a su mamá?*
Estudiante 2: *Le pidió una computadora.*
Estudiante 2: *¿Se la compró?*
Estudiante 1: *Sí, se la compró.*

NOTA CULTURAL

Las fiestas navideñas (*Christmas season*) en los países hispanos duran hasta enero. En muchos lugares celebran **la Navidad** (*Christmas*), pero no se dan los regalos hasta el seis de enero, que es **el Día de los Reyes Magos** (*Three Kings' Day or Epiphany*).

TEACHING OPTIONS

Heritage Speakers Ask heritage speakers if they or their families celebrate **el Día de los Reyes Magos** (Epiphany, January 6). Ask them to expand on the information given in the **Nota cultural** sidebar and to tell whether **el Día de los Reyes** is more important for them than **la Navidad**.

Large Groups Divide the class in half. To each member of one half of the class give a strip of paper with a question on it. Ex: **¿Te compró ese suéter tu novia?** To each member of the other half of the class give the answer to one of the questions. Ex: **Sí, ella me lo compró.** Students must find their partner. Take care not to create sentences that can have more than one match.

8.3 Saber and conocer

ANTE TODO Spanish has two verbs that mean *to know*: **saber** and **conocer.** They cannot be used interchangeably. Note that all forms of **saber** and **conocer** are regular in the present tense except their **yo** forms.

Saber and conocer

		saber *(to know)*	**conocer** *(to know)*
SINGULAR FORMS	yo	**sé**	**conozco**
	tú	**sabes**	**conoces**
	Ud./él/ella	**sabe**	**conoce**
PLURAL FORMS	nosotros/as	**sabemos**	**conocemos**
	vosotros/as	**sabéis**	**conocéis**
	Uds./ellos/ellas	**saben**	**conocen**

¡ATENCIÓN!

Saber + [*adjective*] is used to explain how something *tastes.*
Ex: **Sabe muy dulce/bien/amargo.**
(It tastes very sweet/nice/bitter).
Saber + **a** means *to taste like.*
Ex: **Sabe a ajo.**
(*It tastes like garlic.*)
No sabe a nada.
(*It doesn't taste like anything.*)

▶ **Saber** means *to know a fact or piece(s) of information* or *to know how to do something.*

No **sé** tu número de teléfono.
I don't know your telephone number.

Mi hermana **sabe** hablar francés.
My sister knows how to speak French.

▶ **Conocer** means *to know* or *be familiar/acquainted* with a person, place, or thing.

¿**Conoces** la ciudad de Nueva York?
Do you know New York City?

No **conozco** a tu amigo Esteban.
I don't know your friend Esteban.

▶ When the direct object of **conocer** is a person or pet, the personal **a** is used.

¿Conoces los restaurantes de Tegucigalpa? *but* ¿Conoces **a** Rigoberta Menchú?

¡ATENCIÓN!

The following verbs are also conjugated like **conocer**:
conducir *to drive*
ofrecer *to offer*
parecer *to seem*
traducir *to translate*

¡INTÉNTALO! Escribe las formas apropiadas de los siguientes verbos.

saber

1. José no *sabe* la hora.
2. Sara y yo sabemos jugar al tenis.
3. ¿Por qué no sabes tú estos verbos?
4. Mis padres saben hablar japonés.
5. Yo sé a qué hora es la clase.
6. Usted no sabe dónde vivo.
7. Mi hermano no sabe nadar.
8. Nosotros sabemos muchas cosas.
9. Carlos nunca sabe qué hora es.
10. Yo sé dónde comer bien.

verbos como **conocer**

1. Usted y yo *conocemos* (conocer) bien Miami.
2. Mi compañero conduce (conducir) muy mal.
3. Esta clase parece (parecer) muy buena.
4. Ellos siempre me ofrecen (ofrecer) ayuda.
5. Yo traduzco (traducir) del chino al inglés.
6. Ana, ¿conoces (conocer) los poemas de Mistral?
7. Luis, pareces (parecer) triste.
8. Ustedes conducen (conducir) con cuidado.
9. Yo siempre les ofrezco (ofrecer) café a mis amigos.
10. Nadie me conoce (conocer) bien.

Section Goals

In **Estructura 8.3** students will learn:
- the uses of **saber** and **conocer**
- more uses of the personal **a**

Instructional Resources
WB/VM: Workbook, p. 91
Lab Manual, p. 47
Lab CD/MP3 ***Lección 8***
IRM: ***¡Inténtalo!*** *&* ***Práctica*** *Answers, pp. 210–211; Tapescript, pp. 35–39*
Interactive CD-ROM
Companion website: www.vistahigherlearning.com
Presentations CD-ROM

Suggestion Model **saber** by asking several questions with it. Ex: ____, **¿sabes mi número de teléfono? ¿Sabes dónde está la biblioteca?** Next write **conocer** on the board and ask questions such as: ____, **¿conoces a esta persona? ¿Me conoces a mí?** Ask students further questions using both verbs and help them infer the difference in use between the two.

¡Atención! Point out the **yo** forms of the verbs listed in the second **¡Atención!** sidebar.

TEACHING OPTIONS

Video Show the video again to give students more input with **saber** and **conocer**. Stop the video where appropriate to discuss how **saber** and **conocer** were used and to ask comprehension questions.

Extra Practice Call out several sentences in English which use *to know*. Have students say whether they would use **saber** or **conocer** to translate it. Ex: I know the answer to that question. (**saber**) He doesn't know the president. (**conocer**)

1 Expansion Make statements that use **saber** and **conocer** to describe famous people. Students have to guess who you are. Ex: **Sé jugar al tenis muy bien. También conozco muy bien a Venus Williams porque es mi hermana. ¿Quién soy? (Serena Williams)**

2 Expansion In pairs, have students create three original questions using the verbs **conocer, conducir, ofrecer,** and **saber**, which their partner answers in complete sentences. Call on volunteers to present their questions to the entire class for other volunteers to answer.

3 Suggestion In pairs, have students write down their partner's responses and summarize them aloud for the class.

3 Expansion Ask students questions about what certain celebrities know how to do or whom they know. Ex: **Brad Pitt, ¿conoce a Jennifer Aniston? (Sí, la conoce.) Sammy Sosa, ¿sabe jugar al béisbol? (Sí, sabe jugarlo.)**

Práctica

CONSÚLTALO

Locate the Guatemalan cities mentioned here, in **Panorama**, p. 266.

1 Completar Completa las frases con la forma apropiada de **saber** o **conocer.**

1. Mi hermana mayor ___sabe___ conducir, pero yo no___sé___.
2. —¿___Conoces___ a Carla, mi sobrina? —No, no la ___conozco___.
3. —¿___Saben___ ustedes el número de Marta? —Nosotras no lo ___sabemos___.
4. —Nosotros no ___conocemos___ Guatemala. —Ah, ¿no? Yo ___conozco___ bien las ciudades de Escuintla, Mazatenango, Quetzaltenango y Antigua.
5. —Todavía no ___conozco___ a tu novio. —Sí, ya lo ___sé___. Mañana te lo presento.
6. Yo ___sé___ esquiar, pero Tino y Luis son pequeños y no ___saben___.
7. Roberto ___conoce___ bien el Popol Vuh, el libro sagrado de los mayas, y también ___sabe___ leer los jeroglíficos de los templos mayas.

2 Emparejar Escoge la oracion de la lista A que corresponde con la de la lista B y escribe la forma correcta de los verbos en la lista B.

A

1. María del Carmen tiene mucha sed. b
2. ¿Puedes traducir el menú? No entiendo francés. d
3. ¿Sabes cuándo sirven los entremeses? a
4. Gloria, tú no tienes automóvil para ir a la fiesta, ¿verdad? f
5. Aquel camarero es el hijastro de mi cuñada María José. c
6. ¿De dónde es el dueño del restaurante? ¿Es francés? e

B

a. No lo sé, pero ___parece___ (parecer) que van a servirlos pronto.
b. Con gusto le ___ofrezco___ (ofrecer) una bebida.
c. ¿Ah, sí? Pues, no lo ___conozco___ (conocer). ¡Qué guapo!
d. Sí, te lo ___traduzco___ (traducir). Me gusta mucho practicar el francés.
e. No___sé___ (saber). No me acuerdo, pero conozco a su esposa. Es de Guatemala.
f. No, pero ___conduzco___ (conducir) el de mis padres.

3 Combinar Combina las columnas A, B y C para hacer oraciones completas.

Answers will vary.

modelo

No conozco a Stephen King. / Stephen King conoce a Meg Ryan.

A	B	C
Katie Couric	(no) conocer	Cameron Diaz
Bill Gates	(no) saber	Andy García
Shakira y Enrique Iglesias		cantar
Mike Myers		el lago de Atitlán en Guatemala
Stephen King		hablar dos lenguas extranjeras
Salma Hayek		hacer reír (*laugh*) a la gente
yo		preparar buenas comidas
tú		escribir novelas de horror
tu compañero/a		programar computadoras
nosotras		muchas personas importantes

TEACHING OPTIONS

Extra Practice Have students write down three things they know how to do well (**saber** + [*infinitive*] + **bien**). Collect the papers and read the sentences. The rest of the class tries to guess who wrote the sentences. This same activity could also be done with **conocer**.

Extra Practice Students write down six things they know how to do. Then they circulate around the room, asking their classmates if they know how to do those things as well. Ex: **Sé tocar el piano. ¿Sabes tocar el piano tú también?** When they find someone that answers **sí**, they ask that person to sign next to the activity (**Firma aquí, por favor.**). Have students try to get signatures for all their activities.

Comunicación

4 **Preguntas** Con un(a) compañero/a, háganse y respondan a las siguientes preguntas. Answers will vary.

1. ¿Qué restaurantes buenos conoces? ¿Vas mucho a comer a restaurantes?
2. En tu familia, ¿quién sabe cantar? ¿Tu opinión es objetiva?
3. ¿Conoces a algún artista hispano?
4. ¿Sabes usar bien Internet? ¿Te parece fácil o difícil?
5. ¿Sabes escuchar cuando alguien te habla de sus problemas?
6. ¿Conoces a algún (alguna) chef famoso/a? ¿Qué tipo de comida prepara?
7. ¿Conoces a algún (alguna) escritor(a) famoso/a?
8. ¿Sabes si ofrecen cursos de administración de empresas en la universidad?

AYUDA

Whereas in English we make contrasts by using *do/does*, in Spanish it is common to use **sí/no**.
Yo no lo conozco, pero mi novio **sí lo conoce**.
I don't know him, but my boyfriend **does**.

5 **Entrevista** Hazle preguntas a un(a) compañero/a sobre los siguientes temas. Utiliza los verbos **saber** y **conocer**. Answers will vary.

actividades	deportes	recetas (*recipes*)
ciudades	lenguas	restaurantes
compras	países	viajes

modelo

Estudiante 1: ¿Conoces un buen restaurante argentino?
Estudiante 2: Sí, conozco La parrilla ardiente.
Estudiante 1: ¿Sabes cocinar comida argentina?
Estudiante 2: Sí, sé preparar un buen asado.

NOTA CULTURAL

El **asado** es la barbacoa (*barbecue*) argentina. Un asado típico consiste en chorizos y otras carnes a la parrilla (*grill*). Según los argentinos, el secreto de un buen asado es el corte (*cut*) de la carne y el control del fuego (*fire*).

Síntesis

6 **Anuncio** En grupos, lean el anuncio (*advertisement*). Después, contesten las preguntas. Answers will vary.

1. Busquen ejemplos de los verbos **saber** y **conocer**.
2. ¿Qué saben del Centro Comercial Oviedo?
3. ¿Qué pueden hacer en el Centro Comercial Oviedo?
4. ¿Conocen otros centros comerciales como éste? ¿Cómo se llaman? ¿Dónde están?
5. ¿Conocen algún centro comercial en otro país? ¿Cómo es?

Él sabe dónde comer lo que más le gusta
Él sabe cómo jugar cuatro horas seguidas
Él sabe dónde está su regalo de cumpleaños
Él sabe dónde divertirse
... y usted sabe dónde puede encontrar un poco de todo. ¿Conoce algún otro lugar como éste?
Oviedo
Centro Comercial
Sabe lo que te gusta

NOTA CULTURAL

Los centros comerciales son muy populares en los países hispanos y en casi todas las principales ciudades hay varios. El Centro Sambil en Caracas, Venezuela, es el centro comercial más grande de Suramérica. Además de muchísimas tiendas, tiene una terraza con restaurantes, cafés y una vista espectacular de la ciudad.

4 Expansion Ask these questions of the whole class. Ask students who answer in the affirmative for additional information. Ex: **¿Quién conoce un buen restaurante? ¿Cuál es? ¿Por qué es tan bueno?**

5 Expansion Write on the board the topics listed. Then have students call out the names of the cities, recipes, etc. that their partner mentioned and write them under their respective topic. Have students divide up into groups accordingly and share additional information about what they know using **saber** and **conocer**.

6 Suggestion Before assigning groups, ask general questions about the ad. Ex: **¿De quién es el anuncio? ¿Qué venden?**

6 Expansion Have students generate their own poster using two examples each of **conocer** and **saber**.

TEACHING OPTIONS

Pairs Ask students to individually write brief paragraphs in which they use the verbs presented in this section. Then they exchange their papers with a partner. Students should help each other to make the paragraphs as error-free as possible. Collect the papers for grading.

Extra Practice Ask individual students questions that are most likely not true for them. When students give a negative answer, they should indicate someone else who *would* answer in the affirmative. Ex: _____, **¿conoces a Martin Sheen? No, no lo conozco, pero Rob Lowe sí lo conoce.**

8.4 Comparisons and superlatives

ANTE TODO Spanish and English use comparisons to indicate which of two people or things has a lesser, equal, or greater degree of a quality. Both languages also use superlatives to express the highest or lowest degree of a quality.

Comparisons

menos interesante	más grande	tan sabroso como
less interesting	*bigger*	*as delicious as*

Superlatives

la/el mejor	la/el peor	la más alta
the best	*the worst*	*the tallest*

Comparisons of inequality

▶ Comparisons of inequality are formed by placing **más** (*more*) or **menos** (*less*) before adjectives, adverbs, and nouns and **que** (*than*) after them.

más/menos + [*adjective* / *adverb* / *noun*] + **que**

adjectives

Los bistecs son **más caros que** el pollo.
Steaks are more expensive than chicken.

Estas uvas son **menos sabrosas que** esa pera.
These grapes are less tasty than that pear.

adverbs

Me acuesto **más tarde que** tú.
I go to bed later than you (do).

Mi hermano se despierta **menos temprano que** yo.
My brother wakes up less early than I (do).

nouns

Juan prepara **más platos que** José.
Juan prepares more dishes than José (does).

Susana come **menos carne que** Enrique.
Susana eats less meat than Enrique (does).

Tengo más hambre que un elefante.

El lomo a la plancha es un poquito más caro pero es sabrosísimo.

▶ With verbs, the following construction is used to make comparisons of inequality:

[*verb*] + **más/menos que**

Mis hermanos **comen más que** yo.
My brothers eat more than I (do).

Arturo **duerme menos que** su padre.
Arturo sleeps less than his father (does).

¡ATENCIÓN!

Note that while English has a comparative form for short adjectives (*taller*), such forms do not exist in Spanish (**más** alto).

• • •

When the comparison involves a numerical expression, **de** is used before the number instead of **que**.

Hay más **de** cincuenta naranjas.

Llego en menos **de** diez minutos.

Section Goals

In **Estructura 8.4** students will be introduced to:
- comparisons of inequality
- comparisons of equality
- superlatives
- irregular comparative and superlative words

Instructional Resources
WB/VM: Workbook, pp. 92–94
Lab Manual, p. 48
Lab CD/MP3 ***Lección 8***
IRM: ***¡Inténtalo! & Práctica*** *Answers, pp. 210–211; Tapescript, pp. 35–39;* ***Hojas de actividades****, p. 168*
Interactive CD-ROM
Companion website: www.vistahigherlearning.com
Presentations CD-ROM

Suggestions

- Write **más** + [*adjective*] + **que** and **menos** + [*adjective*] + **que** on the board, explaining their meaning. Illustrate with examples. Ex: **Esta clase es más grande que la clase de la tarde. La clase de la tarde es menos trabajadora que ésta.**
- Practice the structures by asking volunteers questions about classroom objects. **El lápiz de ____, ¿es más largo que el lápiz de ____? (No, es menos largo que el lápiz de ____.)**
- Point out that **que** and what follows it are optional if the items being compared are evident. Ex: **Los bistecs son más caros (que el pollo).**

TEACHING OPTIONS

Extra Practice Ask students questions that make comparisons of inequality using adjectives, adverbs, and nouns. Ex: **¿Qué es más sabroso que una ensalada de frutas? ¿Quién se despierta más tarde que tú? ¿Quién tiene más libros que yo?** Then ask questions that use verbs in their construction. Ex: **¿Quién habla más que yo en la clase?**

Heritage Speakers Ask heritage speakers to give four to five sentences in which they compare themselves to members of their families. Make sure that the comparisons are ones of inequality. Ask other students in the class to report what the heritage speakers said to verify comprehension.

Comparisons of equality

The following construction is used to make comparisons of equality.

tan + [*adjective* / *adverb*] + **como**

tanto/a(s) + [*singular noun* / *plural noun*] + **como**

¡ATENCIÓN!

Note that **tanto** acts as an adjective and therefore agrees in number and gender with the noun it modifies: **tantas cosas**.

• • •

Tan and **tanto** can also be used for emphasis, rather than to compare, with these meanings: **tan** *so*, **tanto** *so much*, **tantos/as** *so many*.

¡Tu almuerzo es **tan** grande!
*Your lunch is **so** big!*

¡Comes **tanto**!
*You eat **so much**!*

¡Comes **tantas** manzanas!
*You eat **so many** apples!*

¿Qué tal tu ceviche?

La comida es tan rica como en España.

Este plato es **tan delicioso como** aquél.
This dish is as delicious as that one (is).

Ustedes probaron **tantos platos como** ellos.
You tried as many dishes as they did.

▶ Comparisons of equality with verbs are formed by placing **tanto como** after the verb. Note that in this construction **tanto** does not change in number or gender.

[*verb*] + **tanto como**

No **duermo tanto como** mi tía.
I don't sleep as much as my aunt (does).

Estudiamos tanto como ustedes.
We study as much as you (do).

Superlatives

¡ATENCIÓN!

While **más** alone means *more*, after **el** or **la** (or **los** or **las**), it means *most*.

▶ The following construction is used to form superlatives. Note that the noun is always preceded by a definite article and that **de** is equivalent to the English *in* or *of*.

el/la/los/las + [*noun*] + **más/menos** + [*adjective*] + **de**

Es **el café más rico del** país.
It's the most delicious coffee in the country.

Es el menú **menos caro de** todos éstos.
It is the least expensive menu of all of these.

▶ The noun in a superlative construction can be omitted if the person, place, or thing referred to is clear.

¿El restaurante El Cráter?
Es **el más elegante** de la ciudad.
The El Cráter restaurant?
It's the most elegant (one) in the city.

Recomiendo el pollo asado.
Es **el más sabroso** del menú.
I recommend the roast chicken.
It's the most delicious on the menu.

Suggestions

- Practice by asking the class questions, the responses to which require comparisons of equality. Ex: **¿Quién es tan guapa como Jennifer López? ¿Quién tiene tanto dinero como Tiger Woods?**
- Ask questions that involve comparisons with yourself. Ex: **¿Quién es tan alto/a como yo? ¿Quién se acostó tan tarde como yo?**
- Involve the class in a conversation about themselves and classroom objects. Ex: ____, **¿por qué tienes tantas plumas?** ____, **¡tu mochila es tan grande! Puedes llevar muchos libros, ¿no? ¿Quién más tiene una mochila tan grande?**
- Practice superlative questions by asking student opinions. Ex: **¿Cuál es la clase más difícil de esta universidad? ¿Y la más fácil?**

TEACHING OPTIONS

Extra Practice Have students write three original comparative or superlative sentences that describe themselves. Ex: **Soy el jugador más bajo del equipo de baloncesto.** Then collect the papers and read the sentences aloud. See if the rest of the class can guess who wrote each description.

Game Divide the class into two groups, A and B. Place the names of 20 famous people into a hat. Select a member from each group to draw a name. The student from group A then has ten seconds to compare those two famous people. If the student has made a logical comparison, team A gets a point. Then it's team B's turn to make a different comparison. The team with the most points at the end wins.

Suggestions

- Ask questions and give examples to practice irregular comparative and superlative forms. Ex: **¿Quién es el menor de tu familia? ¿Ah, sí? ¿Cuántos hermanos mayores tienes?**
- Practice the differences between **grande—mayor** and **pequeño/a—menor** when referring to age by having two students stand. Ask **E1: ____ , ¿cuántos años tienes? (E1: Tengo dieciocho años.)** Then ask **E2: Y tú, ____ , ¿cuántos años tienes? (E2: Tengo diecinueve años.)** Now ask the class: **¿Quién es mayor? ¿Y quién es más grande?**

Irregular comparisons and superlatives

Irregular comparative and superlative forms

Adjective		Comparative form		Superlative form	
bueno/a	*good*	**mejor**	*better*	**el/la mejor**	*(the) best*
malo/a	*bad*	**peor**	*worse*	**el/la peor**	*(the) worst*
grande	*big*	**mayor**	*bigger*	**el/la mayor**	*(the) biggest*
pequeño/a	*small*	**menor**	*smaller*	**el/la menor**	*(the) smallest*
joven	*young*	**menor**	*younger*	**el/la menor**	*(the) youngest*
viejo/a	*old*	**mayor**	*older*	**el/la mayor**	*(the) eldest*

Inés, ¿tienes hermanos?
Sí, tengo un hermano mayor.

¿Adónde vamos a almorzar, don F?
Pues, conozco el mejor restaurante de la ciudad, el restaurante El Cráter.

▶ When **grande** and **pequeño/a** refer to age, the irregular comparative and superlative forms, **mayor** and **menor**, are used. However, when these adjectives refer to size, the regular forms, **más grande** and **más pequeño/a**, are used.

Isabel es **la mayor** de su familia.
Isabel is the eldest in her family.

Yo soy **menor** que tú.
I'm younger than you.

Tu ensalada es **más grande** que ésa.
Your salad is bigger than that one.

Pedí **el plato más pequeño** del menú.
I ordered the smallest dish on the menu.

CONSÚLTALO

To review how descriptive adjectives like **bueno**, **malo**, and **grande** shorten before nouns, see **Estructura 3.1**, p. 80.

▶ The adverbs **bien** and **mal** have the same irregular comparative forms as the adjectives **bueno/a** and **malo/a**.

Julio nada **mejor** que los otros chicos.
Julio swims better than the other boys.

Ellas cantan **peor** que las otras chicas.
They sing worse than the other girls.

ESTAR A LA ÚLTIMA
EN LIBROS
TE COSTARÁ MUY POCO
www.alcoste.com
Los más vendidos al mejor precio

TEACHING OPTIONS

Large Groups Divide students into groups of six. Give cards with adjectives listed at the top of this page to one group. Give cards with the corresponding irregular comparative form to another group. Students must find their partner. To avoid confusion, make duplicate cards of **mayor** and **menor**.

Extra Practice Ask students questions with superlatives about things and places at your university, in your city or town, in the class, and so forth. Include a good mix of regular and irregular superlative forms. Ex: **¿Cuál es el edificio más grande del campus? ¿Cuál es la peor clase de la universidad?**

Absolute superlatives

▶ In Spanish the absolute superlative is equivalent to *extremely, exceptionally, super,* or *very* before an adjective or adverb. You encountered an absolute superlative when you learned how to say **Me gusta(n) muchísimo...**

▶ To form the absolute superlative of most adjectives and adverbs, drop the final vowel, if there is one, and add **-ísimo/a(s).**

malo → mal- → malísimo

¡El bistec está **malísimo**!
The steak is very bad!

mucho → much- → muchísimo

Comes **muchísimo**.
You eat a lot (very, very much).

difícil + -ísimo → dificilísimo

Esta prueba es **dificilísima**.
This quiz is exceptionally difficult.

fácil + ísimo → facilísimo

Los exámenes son **facilísimos**.
The tests are extremely easy.

▶ Adjectives and adverbs whose stem ends in **c, g,** or **z** change spelling to **qu, gu,** and **c** in the absolute superlative.

rico → riquísimo **largo → larguísimo** **feliz → felicísimo**

▶ Adjectives that end in **-n** or **-r** normally form the absolute superlative by adding **-císimo.**

joven + -císimo → jovencísimo **trabajador + -císimo → trabajadorcísimo**

¡INTÉNTALO! Escribe el equivalente de las palabras en inglés.

Comparativos

1. (*than*) Ernesto mira más televisión __que__ Alberto.
2. (*less*) Tú eres __menos__ simpático que Federico.
3. (*as much*) La camarera sirve __tanta__ carne como pescado.
4. (*more*) Conozco __más__ restaurantes que tú.
5. (*as much as*) No estudio __tanto como__ tú.
6. (*as*) ¿Sabes jugar al tenis tan bien __como__ tu hermana?
7. (*as many*) ¿Puedes beber __tantos__ refrescos como yo?
8. (*as*) Mis amigos parecen __tan__ simpáticos como ustedes.

Superlativos

1. (*the most intelligent*) Marisa es __la más inteligente__ de todas.
2. (*the least boring*) Ricardo y Tomás son __los menos aburridos__ de la fiesta.
3. (*the worst*) Miguel y Antonio son __los peores__ estudiantes de la clase.
4. (*the oldest*) Mi profesor de biología es __el mayor__ de la universidad.
5. (*extremely delicious*) El pollo de este supermercado es __riquísimo__.
6. (*the youngest*) Carlos es __el menor__ de mis hermanos.
7. (*the best*) Este plato es __el mejor__ del restaurante.
8. (*extremely tall*) Sara es __altísima__.

Suggestions

- Use magazine pictures to compare and contrast absolute superlatives. Ex: **Este edificio parece modernísimo, pero éste no. Parece viejísimo.**
- Ask volunteers to identify people you describe using absolute superlatives. Ex: **Es riquísima. (Oprah Winfrey) Es graciosísimo. (Robin Williams)**

TEACHING OPTIONS

Extra Practice Give ten comparative and superlative sentences orally to practice listening comprehension. Dictate the sentences, then give students about 30 seconds per sentence to write the direct opposite. Ask volunteers to present their opposite sentences. Ex: **Ernesto mira más televisión que Alberto. (Alberto mira menos televisión que Ernesto.)**

Heritage Speakers Ask heritage speakers to discuss whether absolute superlatives are common in their culture or not (some regions and countries use them less frequently than others). Also have them discuss under what circumstances absolute superlatives are most frequently used, such as when talking about food, people, events, and so forth.

1 Suggestion Quickly review the use of **de** before numerals in comparisons.

1 Expansions

- Ask two students a question, then have another student compare them. Ex: **¿Cuántas horas de televisión miras cada día? ¿Y tú, ____? ____, haz una comparación.**
- Ask several pairs of students different types of questions for comparison later. Ex: **¿Cuáles prefieres, las películas de aventuras o los dramas? ¿Estudias más para la clase de español o para la clase de matemáticas?**

2 Expansion Turn the activity statements into questions and ask them of students. Have them make up answers that involve comparisons. Ex: **¿Cómo es Mario?**

3 Suggestion Distribute the **Hojas de actividades** from the IRM that correspond to this activity.

3 Expansion In pairs, have students select a member of their family or a close friend and describe him or her using comparatives and superlatives. Ask volunteers to share their description with the class.

Práctica

1

Escoger De las palabras que están entre paréntesis, escoge la correcta para comparar a dos hermanas muy diferentes. Haz (*Make*) las adaptaciones necesarias.

1. Lucila es más alta y más bonita ___que___ Tita. (de, más, menos, que)
2. Tita es más delgada porque come ___más___ verduras que su hermana. (de, más, menos, que)
3. Lucila es más ___simpática___ que Tita porque es alegre. (listo, simpático, bajo)
4. A Tita le gusta comer en casa. Va a ___menos___ restaurantes que su hermana. (más, menos, que) Es tímida, pero activa. Hace ___más___ ejercicio que su hermana. (más, tanto, menos) Todos los días toma más ___de___ cinco vasos de agua mineral. (que, tan, de)
5. Lucila come muchas papas fritas y se preocupa ___menos___ que Tita por comer frutas. (de, más, menos) ¡Son ___tan___ diferentes!, pero se llevan bien. (como, tan, tanto)

2

Emparejar Completa las oraciones (*sentences*) de la columna A con información de la columna B para comparar a Mario y a Luis, los novios de Lucila y Tita.

A

1. Mario es ___tan interesante___ como Luis.
2. Mario viaja tanto ___como___ Luis.
3. Luis escoge ___tantas___ clases de cocina (*cooking*) como Mario.
4. Luis habla ___francés___ tan bien como Mario.
5. Mario tiene tantos ___amigos extranjeros___ como Luis.
6. ¡Qué casualidad (*coincidence*)! Mario y Luis también son hermanos, pero no hay tanta ___diferencia___ entre ellos como entre Lucila y Tita.

B

tantas
diferencia
tan interesante
amigos extranjeros
como
francés

3

Completar Tu profesor(a) va a darte (*to give you*) una hoja de actividades con descripciones de José Valenzuela Carranza y Ana Orozco Hoffman. Completa las oraciones acerca de (*about*) Ana, José y sus familias con las palabras de la lista.

atlética	del	mejor	peor
altísima	la	menor	periodista
bajo	más	guapísimo	trabajadorcísimo
de	mayor	Orozco	Valenzuela

1. José es el ___menor___ y el más ___bajo___ de su familia. Es ___guapísimo___ y ___trabajadorcísimo___. Es el mejor ___periodista___ de la ciudad y el ___peor___ jugador de baloncesto.
2. Ana es la más ___atlética___ y ___la___ mejor jugadora de baloncesto del estado. Es la ___mayor___ de sus hermanos y es ___altísima___. Estudió la profesión ___más___ difícil ___de___ todas.
3. Jorge es el ___mejor___ jugador de juegos electrónicos de su familia.
4. Mauricio es el menor de la familia ___Orozco___.
5. El abuelo es el ___mayor___ de todos los miembros de la familia Valenzuela.
6. Fifí es la perra más antipática ___del___ mundo.

TEACHING OPTIONS

Extra Practice Using magazine pictures or your own drawings, show a family whose members vary widely in different aspects: age (write a number on each person that indicates how old he or she is), height, weight, and so forth. Ask students to make comparisons about that family. Give names to each family member so that they are easier to identify.

Large Groups Divide the class into two groups. Survey each group to get information about various topics. Ex: **¿Cuántos hacen ejercicio todos los días? ¿Cuántos van al cine cada fin de semana? ¿Cuántos comen comida rápida tres veces a la semana?** Ask for a show of hands and tally the number of hands. Then have students make comparisons between the two groups based on the information given.

Comunicación

4 **Intercambiar** En parejas, hagan comparaciones sobre diferentes cosas. Pueden usar las sugerencias de la lista u otras ideas. Answers will vary.

AYUDA

You can use the following adjectives in your comparisons:
bonito/a
caro/a
elegante
interesante
inteligente

modelo

Estudiante 1: Los pollos de Pollitos del Corral son los mejores del mundo.
Estudiante 2: Pues yo creo que los pollos de Rostipollos son tan buenos como los pollos de Pollitos del Corral.
Estudiante 1: Mmm... no tienen tanta mantequilla como los pollos de Pollitos del Corral. Tienes razón. Son sabrosísimos.

restaurantes en tu ciudad/pueblo
cafés en tu ciudad/pueblo
tiendas en tu ciudad/pueblo

periódicos en tu ciudad/pueblo
revistas favoritas
libros favoritos

comidas favoritas
los profesores
los cursos que toman

5 **Conversar** En grupos, túrnense (*take turns*) para hacer comparaciones entre ustedes mismos (*yourselves*) y una persona de cada categoría de la lista. Answers will vary.

- una persona de tu familia
- un(a) amigo/a especial
- un(a) persona famosa

Síntesis

6 **La familia López** En grupos, túrnense para hablar de Sara, Sabrina, Cristina, Ricardo y David y hacer comparaciones entre ellos. Answers will vary.

modelo

Estudiante 1: Sara es tan alta como Sabrina.
Estudiante 2: Sí, pero David es el más alto de la familia.
Estudiante 3: En mi opinión, él es guapísimo, también.

4 Expansion Ask pairs of volunteers to present one of their conversations to the class. Then survey the class to see with which of the students the class agrees more.

5 Suggestion Model the activity by making a few comparisons between yourself and some celebrity.

5 Expansion Ask a volunteer to share his or her comparisons. Then make comparisons between yourself and the student or yourself and the person the student mentioned. Continue to do this with different students, asking them to make similar comparisons as well.

6 Expansion Have students create a drawing of a family similar to the one on this page. Tell them not to let anyone see their drawings. Then pair students up and have them describe their drawings to one another. Each student must draw the family described by his or her partner.

TEACHING OPTIONS

Extra Practice As a listening comprehension activity, prepare short descriptions of five easily recognizable people in which you compare them to other recognizable people. Write their names on the board in random order. Then read your descriptions, having students match the description to the appropriate name. Ex: **Esta persona es más famosa que Enrique Iglesias pero es tan guapa como él. (Ricky Martin)**

TPR Give the same types of objects to different students but in different numbers. For example, hand out three books to one student, one book to another, and four to another. Then call on individuals to make comparisons between the students based on the number of objects they have.

Section Goals

In **Lectura** students will:

- learn to identify the main idea in a text
- read a content-rich menu and restaurant review

Instructional Resource
Companion website:
www.vistahigherlearning.com

Estrategia Tell students that recognizing the main idea of a text will help them unlock the meaning of unfamiliar words and phrases they come across while reading. Tell them to check the title first. The main idea is often expressed in the title. Tell them to read the topic sentence of each paragraph before they read the full text, so they will get a sense of the main idea.

Examinar el texto First, have students scan the menu. Ask how the title and subheadings help predict the content. Ask volunteers to state the meaning of each category of food served. Then have students scan the newspaper article. Ask them how the title and the format (the box with ratings) of the text give clues to the content.

Identificar la idea principal Ask students to read the column heading and the title of the article and predict the subject of the article and the author's purpose. Then have students read the topic sentence of the first paragraph and state the main idea. Finally, have them read the entire paragraph.

Lectura

Antes de leer

Estrategia

Reading for the main idea

As you know, you can learn a great deal about a reading selection by looking at the format and looking for cognates, titles and subtitles. You can skim to get the gist of the reading selection and scan it for specific information. Reading for the main idea is another useful strategy; it involves locating the topic sentences of each paragraph to determine the author's purpose for writing a particular piece. Topic sentences can provide clues about the content of each paragraph, as well as the general organization of the reading. Your choice of which reading strategies to use will depend on the style and format of each reading selection.

Examinar el texto

En esta sección tenemos dos textos diferentes. ¿Qué estrategias puedes usar para leer la crítica culinaria? ¿Cuáles son las apropiadas para familiarizarte con el menú? Utiliza las estrategias más eficaces° para cada texto. ¿Qué tienen en común? ¿Qué tipo de comida sirven en el restaurante?

Identificar la idea principal

Lee la primera frase de cada párrafo de la crítica culinaria del restaurante **La feria del maíz.** Apunta° el tema principal de cada párrafo. Luego lee todo el primer párrafo. ¿Crees que el restaurante le gustó al/a la autor(a) de la crítica culinaria? ¿Por qué? Ahora lee la crítica entera. En tu opinión, ¿cuál es la idea principal de la crítica? ¿Por qué la escribió el/la autor(a)? Compara tus opiniones con las de un(a) compañero/a.

recursos

vistahigher learning.com

eficaces *efficient* Apunta *Jot down*

M E N Ú

Entremeses

Tortilla servida con
• Ajiaceite (chile, aceite) • Ajicomino (chile, comino)

Pan tostado servido con
• Queso frito a la pimienta • Salsa de ajo y mayonesa

Sopas

• Tomate • Cebolla • Verduras • Pollo y huevo
• Carne de res • Mariscos

Entradas

Tomaticán
(tomate, papas, maíz, chile, arvejas, zanahorias y verduras)

Tamales
(maíz, azúcar, ajo, cebolla)

Frijoles enchilados
(frijoles negros, carne de cerdo o de res, arroz, chile)

Chilaquil
(tortilla de maíz, queso, hierbas y chile)

Tacos
(tortillas, pollo, verduras y mole)

Cóctel de mariscos
(camarones, langostas, vinagre, sal, pimienta, aceite)

Postres

• Plátanos caribeños • Cóctel de frutas al ron
• Uvate (uvas, azúcar de caña y ron) • Flan napolitano
• Helado de piña y naranja • Pastel de yogur

Después de leer

Preguntas

En parejas, contesten las siguientes preguntas sobre la crítica culinaria de **La feria del maíz.**

1. ¿Quién es el dueño y chef de **La feria del maíz**? Ernesto Sandoval
2. ¿Qué tipo de comida se sirve en el restaurante? tradicional
3. ¿Cuál es el problema con el servicio? Se necesitan más camareros.
4. ¿Cómo es el ambiente del restaurante? agradable
5. ¿Qué comidas probó el autor de la crítica culinaria? las tortillas, el ajiaceite, la sopa de mariscos, los tamales, los tacos de pollo y el flan
6. ¿Quieren probar ustedes el restaurante **La feria del maíz**? ¿Por qué? Answers will vary.

TEACHING OPTIONS

Heritage Speakers Ask heritage speakers to create a dinner menu featuring their favorite dishes, including lists of ingredients similar to those in the menu above. Have heritage speakers make copies of their menus, distribute them, and answer questions from classmates about how dishes are prepared or unfamiliar vocabulary.

Heritage Speakers Ask a heritage speaker who has visited Guatemala and dined in restaurants or cafés to prepare a short presentation about his or her experiences there. Of particular interest would be a comparison and contrast of city vs. small-town restaurants. If possible, the presentation should be illustrated with menus from the restaurants, advertisements, or photos of and articles about the country.

23F

Gastronomía

La feria del maíz

Sobresaliente°. En el nuevo restaurante **La feria del maíz** va a encontrar la perfecta combinación entre la comida tradicional y el encanto de la vieja ciudad de Antigua. Ernesto Sandoval, antiguo jefe de cocina° del famoso restaurante **El fogón**, está teniendo mucho éxito° en su nueva aventura culinaria.

El gerente°, el experimentado José Sierra, controla a la perfección la calidad del servicio. El camarero que me atendió esa noche fue muy amable en todo momento. Sólo hay que comentar que, debido al éxito inmediato de **La feria del maíz**, se necesitan más camareros para atender a los clientes de una forma más eficaz. En esta ocasión, el mesero tardó unos veinte minutos en traerme la bebida.

La feria del maíz
13 calle 4-41 Zona 1
La Antigua, Guatemala
2329912

lunes a sábado
10:30am-11:30pm
domingo 10:00am-10:00pm

Comida 🍴🍴🍴🍴🍴
Servicio 🍴🍴🍴
Ambiente 🍴🍴🍴🍴
Precio 🍴🍴🍴

Afortunadamente, no me importó mucho la espera entre plato y plato, pues el ambiente es tan agradable que me sentí como en casa. El restaurante mantiene el estilo colonial de Antigua. Por dentro°, el estilo es elegante y rústico a la vez. Cuando el tiempo lo permite, se puede comer también en el patio, donde hay muchas flores.

El servicio de camareros y el ambiente agradable del local pasan a un segundo plano cuando llega la comida, de una calidad extraordinaria. Las tortillas de casa se sirven con un ajiaceite delicioso. La sopa de mariscos es excelente, y los tamales, pues, tengo que confesar que son mejores que los de mi abuelita. También recomiendo los tacos de pollo, servidos con un mole buenísimo. De postre, don Ernesto me preparó su especialidad, un flan napolitano sabrosísimo.

Los precios pueden parecer altos° para una comida tradicional, pero, la calidad de los productos con que se cocinan los platos y el exquisito ambiente de **La feria del maíz** le garantizan° una experiencia inolvidable.

Bebidas

• Cerveza negra • Chilate (bebida de maíz, chile y cacao)
• Jugos de fruta • Agua mineral • Té helado
• Vino tinto/blanco • Ron

Sobresaliente *Outstanding* **jefe de cocina** *head chef* **éxito** *success* **gerente** *manager* **Por dentro** *Inside* **altos** *high* **garantizan** *guarantee*

Un(a) guía turístico/a

Tú eres un(a) guía turístico/a en Guatemala. Estás en el restaurante **La feria del maíz** con un grupo de turistas norteamericanos. Ellos no hablan español y quieren pedir de comer, pero necesitan tu ayuda. Lee nuevamente el menú e indica qué error comete cada turista.

1. La señora Johnson es diabética y no puede comer azúcar. Pide sopa de verdura y tamales. No pide nada de postre.
   No debe pedir los tamales porque tienen azúcar.
2. Los señores Petit son vegeterianos y piden sopa de tomate, frijoles enchilados y plátanos caribeños.
   No deben pedir los frijoles enchilados porque tienen carne.
3. El señor Smith, que es alérgico al chocolate, pide tortilla servida con ajiaceite, chilaquil y chilate para beber.
   No debe pedir chilate porque tiene cacao.
4. La adorable hija del señor Smith tiene sólo cuatro años y le gustan mucho las verduras y las frutas naturales. Su papá le pide tomaticán y un cóctel de frutas.
   No debe pedir el cóctel de frutas porque tiene ron.
5. La señorita Jackson está a dieta y pide uvate, flan napolitano y helado.
   No debe pedir postres porque está a dieta.

Preguntas

- Have students quickly review the article before answering the questions. Suggest that pairs take turns answering them. The student who does not answer a question should find the line of text that contains the answer.
- Expand the activity with these questions. **7. ¿Cómo fue el mesero que atendió al crítico? (Fue muy amable, pero estaba muy ocupado con otros clientes del restaurante.) 8. ¿Cuál fue la opinión del crítico con respecto a la comida? (La encontró toda de muy alta calidad.) 9. ¿Cómo son los precios de La feria del maíz? (Son altos, pero la calidad de la comida los justifica.)**

Un(a) guía turístico/a Ask pairs to work together to check the menu and state why each customer should not order the item(s) he or she has selected.

The Affective Dimension A source of discomfort in travel can be unfamiliar foods. Tell students that by learning about the foods of a country they are going to visit they can make that part of their visit even more enjoyable.

TEACHING OPTIONS

Extra Practice Ask students to review the items in **Un(a) guía turistico/a**, write a conversation, and act out the scene involving a tour guide eating lunch in a Guatemalan restaurant with several tourists. Have them work in groups of eight to assign the following roles: **mesero, guía turístico/a, la señora Johnson, los señores Petit, el señor Smith, la hija del señor Smith,** and **la señorita Jackson**. Each group can perform for the class.

Variación léxica Tell students that the adjective of place or nationality (**gentilicio**) for Guatemala is **guatemalteco/a**. Guatemalans often use a more colloquial term, **chapín**, as a synonym for **guatemalteco/a**.

Heritage Speakers Ask heritage speakers to describe restaurant etiquette in Spanish-speaking countries. Have them discuss how to order, call a food server, ask for the check, tip, and so forth.

Section Goals

In **Escritura** students will:

- learn to express and support opinions
- integrate in written form vocabulary and structures taught in **Lección 8**
- write a restaurant review

Estrategia Explain to students that when they write a restaurant review it is helpful to have some way of organizing the details required to support the rating. Have groups of three or four students write a list of questions in Spanish that readers of restaurant reviews might ask and use these to create a rating sheet. Tell them to refer to the list of questions on this page as a guide. Encourage students to leave space for comments in each category so they can record details that support their opinions. Suggest they fill out the rating sheet during the various stages of the meal.

Tema Go over the directions with the class, explaining that each student will rate (**puntuar**) a local restaurant and write a review of a meal there, including a recommendation for future restaurant-goers.

Escritura

Estrategia

Expressing and supporting opinions

Written reviews are just one of the many kinds of writing which require you to state your opinions. In order to convince your reader to take your opinions seriously, it is important to support them as thoroughly as possible. Details, facts, examples, and other forms of evidence are necessary. In a restaurant review, for example, it is not enough just to rate the food, service and atmosphere. Readers will want details about the dishes you ordered, the kind of service you received, and the type of atmosphere you encountered. If you were writing a concert or album review, what kinds of details might your readers expect to find?

It is easier to include details that support your opinions if you plan ahead. Before going to a place or event that you are planning to review, write a list of questions that your readers might ask. Decide which aspects of the experience you are going to rate and list the details that will help you decide upon a rating. You can then organize these lists into a questionnaire and a rating sheet. Bring these forms with you to help you make your opinions and to remind you of the kinds of information you need to gather in order to support those opinions. Later, these forms will help you organize your review into logical categories. They can also provide the details and other evidence you need to convince your readers of your opinions.

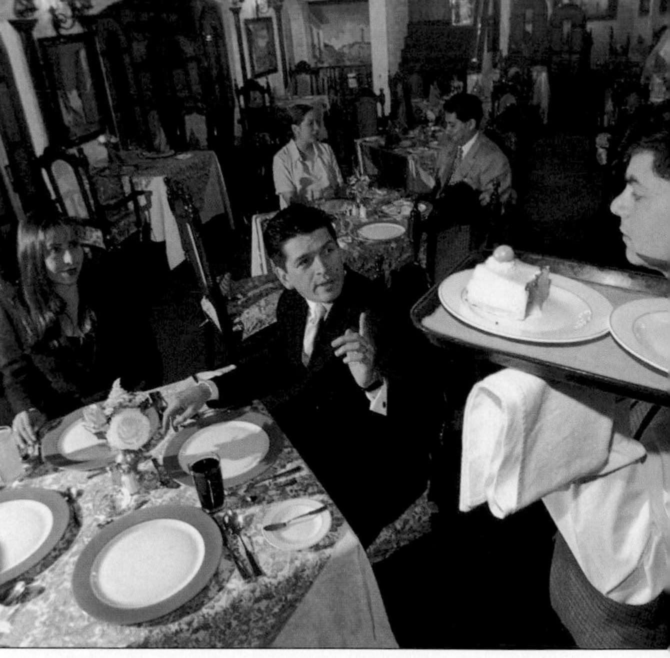

Tema

Escribir una crítica

Escribe una crítica culinaria° sobre un restaurante local para el periódico de la universidad. Clasifica el restaurante dándole de una a cinco estrellas° y anota tus recomendaciones para futuros clientes del restaurante. Incluye tus opiniones acerca de°:

- La comida
  ¿Qué tipo de comida es? ¿Qué tipo de ingredientes usan? ¿Es de buena calidad°? ¿Cuál es el mejor plato? ¿Y el peor? ¿Quién es el chef?
- El servicio
  ¿Hay que esperar mucho para conseguir una mesa? ¿Tiene el/la camarero/a un buen conocimiento del menú? ¿Atienden a los clientes con rapidez° y cortesía?
- El ambiente
  ¿Cómo es la decoración del restaurante? ¿Es el ambiente° informal o elegante? ¿Hay música o algún tipo de entretenimiento°? ¿Hay un bar? ¿Un patio?
- Información práctica
  ¿Cómo son los precios? ¿Se aceptan tarjetas de crédito? ¿Cuál es la dirección° y el número de teléfono? ¿Quién es el dueño? ¿El gerente?

crítica culinaria *restaurant review* estrellas *stars* acerca de *about* calidad *quality* rapidez *speed* ambiente *atmosphere* entretenimiento *entertainment* dirección *address*

TEACHING OPTIONS

Proofreading Activity Copy the following sentences containing mistakes onto the board or a transparency as a proofreading activity to do with the whole class.

1. **El Dr. Cavazos pedió un plato de tomaticán, pero el mesero lo servió a mí.**
2. **El tomaticán no es para mi. Puede usted servirlelo al doctor Cavazos.**
3. **No conozco qué pedir de postre. Me recomienda usted un postre ricísimo?**
4. **¿Sabes un buen restaurante por aquí? Sí, el restaurante Eldorado es el más bueno de la ciudad.**
5. **¡Ay, entre ti y mí, el restaurante Eldorado es el peor de la ciudad!**
6. **Pedí una sopa de res bien caliente, ¡pero la me servieron fría!**

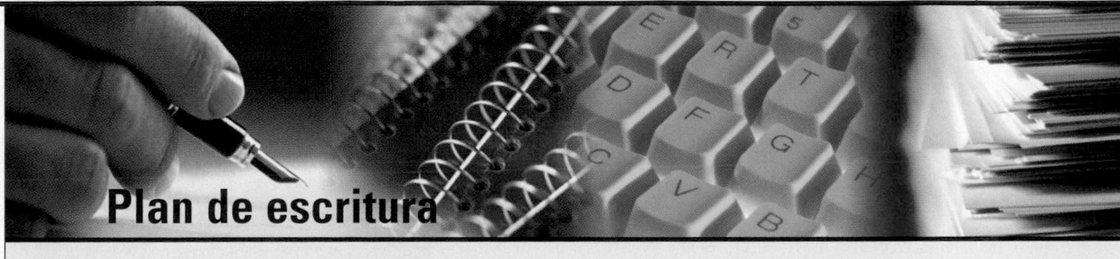

Plan de escritura

1 Ideas y organización

Usa un mapa de ideas para organizar tus comentarios sobre el **¿qué?, ¿quién?, ¿cuándo?, ¿dónde?, ¿cómo?** y **¿por qué?** de tu visita al restaurante y tu evaluación. Recuerda que tu artículo debe tener un título interesante para captar el interés del lector°. Utiliza un esquema° para organizar las diferentes partes de tu composición.

2 Primer borrador

Utilizando tus notas de **Ideas y organización,** escribe el primer borrador de tu artículo. Intenta° usar el diccionario como último recurso.

3 Comentario

Intercambia° tu composición con la de un(a) compañero/a. Lee su borrador y anota los aspectos mejor escritos° de su crítica, por ejemplo cómo expresa su opinión acerca de la comida. Utiliza estas preguntas para evaluar el trabajo de tu compañero/a:

1. ¿Es interesante el título del artículo?
2. ¿Incluye toda la información pertinente?
3. ¿Está bien organizado el artículo?
4. ¿Apoya° el/la autor(a) su opinión con detalles específicos?
5. ¿Hay errores gramaticales u ortográficos?

4 Redacción

Revisa° el primer borrador según las indicaciones de tu compañero/a. Incorpora nuevas ideas y/o más información para reforzar tu opinión. Utiliza esta guía para hacer la última revisión antes de escribir tu copia final.

1. Subraya° cada verbo para comprobar su concordancia con el sujeto. ¡Cuidado con el pretérito!
2. Revisa la concordancia entre los sustantivos, los artículos y los adjetivos.
3. Comprueba° el uso correcto de los pronombres.
4. Consulta tus **Anotaciones para mejorar la escritura** antes de revisar la ortografía y la puntuación.

5 Evaluación y progreso

Comprueba si hay un(a) compañero/a en la clase que conoce el restaurante evaluado en tu artículo y viceversa. Intercambien sus reportajes y después responde a estas preguntas.

- ¿Estás de acuerdo con la evaluación de tu compañero/a?
- ¿Qué impresiones del restaurante fueron similares o diferentes?

Lee los comentarios y las correcciones de tu profesor(a). Anota los errores más básicos en tu lista **Anotaciones para mejorar la escritura** en tu **Carpeta de trabajos**.

lector *reader* esquema *outline* Intenta *Try to* Intercambia *Exchange* escritos *written* Apoya *support*
Revisa *Check* Subraya *Underline* Comprueba *Verify*

Comentario

- Go over guide questions 1–5 with the class and allow five minutes for peer review.
- Have students prepare **Redacción** as homework.

Evaluación y progreso Give the class five minutes to compare final drafts.

Writing Sample Here is an example restaurant review that would constitute superior writing achievement.

La Paz ya no es sobresaliente

La Paz
444 Avenida de los Ángeles

martes a domingo
11:00 am – 11:00 pm
cerrado los lunes

Desafortunadamente, ya no puedo dar cinco estrellas al restaurante que antes fue uno de los mejores de esta ciudad.

El antiguo dueño del restaurante La Paz lo vendió el mes pasado. Parece que el nuevo dueño cambió no sólo el ambiente sino también el menú. Por fuera, parece una casa ordinaria. Por dentro, tiene muchas mesas y es difícil caminar por entre ellas. Ya no hay mesas en el patio.

Hay pocos platos en el menú. Pedí sopa de verduras y pollo con salsa verde. Esperé mucho tiempo por la comida porque no hay suficientes meseros. Cuando me sirvieron la sopa, estaba fría. No sé cuáles son los ingredientes de la salsa, pero no me gustó nada. Sólo sirven flan de postre y no es muy sabroso.

No hay duda de que necesitan hacer mucho para mejorar este restaurante. Voy a esperar tres meses para ver si lo consiguen.

EVALUATION: Crítica culinaria

Criteria	Scale
Content	1 2 3 4 5
Organization	1 2 3 4 5
Use of details to support opinions	1 2 3 4 5
Accuracy	1 2 3 4 5

Scoring	
Excellent	18–20 points
Good	14–17 points
Satisfactory	10–13 points
Unsatisfactory	< 10 points

Section Goals

In **Escuchar** students will:

- use the strategy of jotting down notes
- listen to a short paragraph and write down its main points
- answer questions based on a recorded interview

Instructional Resources
Textbook CD
IRM: Tapescript, p. 92

Estrategia
Script Sandra está avergonzada. Ayer fue a sus clases sin peinarse ni maquillarse. ¡Y la ropa que llevaba! ¡Una camiseta vieja con unos pantalones morados y unas sandalias rosadas! Hablé con ella y me contó que tiene muchos problemas. Salió muy mal en el examen, su abuela está enferma y también su novio se enojó con ella anteayer.

Suggestion Invite students to look at the photo and predict who they think Ramón Acevedo is and what he is going to talk about.

Ahora escucha
Script Bienvenidos a "La hora de la cocina". Hoy vamos a preparar un menú de Guatemala: pavo relleno, verduras en escabeche y un rico dulce de leche. Bueno, vamos a comenzar con el pavo relleno. Necesitan los siguientes ingredientes para servir de diez a doce personas: 1 pavo de 6 kilos, 500 gramos de carne de cerdo, 250 gramos de papas, 250 gramos de zanahorias, pimienta, sal, ajo, consomé, aceite y margarina.
Vamos a comenzar con el relleno. Hay que picar la carne de cerdo y las verduras en pedazos de un centímetro o menos. Ponemos a freír la carne con el ajo. Ponemos las papas a cocinar en un poco de agua. En otra sartén, vamos a freír las zanahorias en aceite, y añadimos las papas cocinadas, pimienta y consomé.
Bueno, ya están las verduras. Las revolvemos con la carne. Ahora, vamos a preparar el pavo. Tenemos que lavarlo bien. Le ponemos sal y pimienta por dentro y le ponemos el relleno. Hay que ponerle sal y pimienta por fuera, untarlo con margarina y cubrirlo con papel de aluminio. Ya estamos listos para ponerlo en el horno a 325 grados por unas 4 horas, más o menos. Les recomiendo un vino blanco para acompañar este plato. ¡Delicioso! Regresaremos en unos minutos después de los siguientes anuncios importantes. ¡No se vayan! Vamos a preparar unas sabrosas verduras en escabeche.

Escuchar

Estrategia

Jotting down notes as you listen

Jotting down notes while you listen to a conversation in Spanish can help you keep track of the important points or details. It will help you to focus actively on comprehension rather than on remembering what you have heard.

 To practice this strategy, you will now listen to a paragraph. Jot down the main points you hear.

Preparación

Según° la foto, ¿quién es Ramón Acevedo? ¿Sobre qué crees que va a hablar?

Ahora escucha 

Ahora escucha a Ramón Acevedo. Toma apuntes° de las instrucciones que él da en los espacios en blanco.

Ingredientes del relleno

carne de cerdo
ajo
papas
zanahorias
aceite
pimienta
consomé

Poner dentro del pavo

sal
pimienta
relleno

Instrucciones para cocinar°

untarlo° con margarina
cubrir° con papel de aluminio
poner en el horno° a 325 grados
por cuatro horas

Según *According to* **apuntes** *notes* **cocinar** *to cook* **untarlo** *baste it* **cubrir** *cover* **horno** *oven*

En Guatemala, el pavo relleno es un plato popular para celebrar la Navidad y el Año Nuevo.

Comprensión

Seleccionar

Usa tus apuntes para seleccionar la respuesta correcta para cada oración.

1. Ramón Acevedo prepara un menú ideal para c.
   a. una familia de tres personas b. una chica y su novio
   c. una familia de once
2. Este plato es perfecto para la persona a la que le gustan b.
   a. los mariscos y la langosta
   b. la carne de cerdo y las papas
   c. los espárragos y los frijoles
3. Este plato es ideal para el/la cocinero/a que a.
   a. tiene mucho tiempo b. tiene mucha prisa
   c. no tiene horno

Preguntas

Con dos o tres compañeros, respondan a las preguntas.
Answers will vary.

1. ¿Es similar el plato que prepara Ramón Acevedo a algún plato que ustedes comen? ¿En qué es similar? ¿En qué es distinto?
2. Escriban una variación de la receta de Ramón Acevedo. Usen ingredientes interesantes. ¿Es mejor su receta que la del señor Acevedo? ¿Por qué?

recursos

TEXT CD
Lección 8

Proyecto

Crea un nuevo restaurante guatemalteco

Imagina que vas a abrir un restaurante en la capital de Guatemala. Necesitas decidir qué vas a servir y a qué precio, y dónde vas a abrir el restaurante.

1 Diseña° el menú

El menú contiene información muy importante para la creación de tu nuevo negocio°. Usa los **Recursos para la investigación** para investigar cuáles son las comidas típicas y populares de Guatemala y para saber cuál es la moneda del país para ponerles precio a las comidas del restaurante. El menú puede incluir esta información:

- el nombre del restaurante
- la dirección del restaurante, tomando en cuenta° el diseño de la capital y la organización de sus calles y avenidas
- las comidas típicas de Guatemala que vas a servir (incluye platos principales, ensaladas, postres y bebidas)
- los precios de los platos en moneda guatemalteca

Palabras útiles

el postre	*dessert*
el flan	*baked custard*
el pastel	*cake; pie*
el helado	*ice cream*
el dulce	*sweet; candy*
la galleta	*cookie*

2 Presenta la información

Con tres o cuatro compañeros/as habla del plan que tienes para tu restaurante. Muéstrales° el menú que diseñaste. Háblales° de la comida que vas a servir. Pregúntales qué platos piensan que son los más sabrosos.

recursos para la investigación

 **Internet** Palabras clave: Guatemala, recetas°, cambio de moneda°, Ciudad de Guatemala	 **Comunidad** Estudiantes o profesores que son de Guatemala o que viajaron a Guatemala, guatemaltecos que viven en la comunidad
 **Biblioteca** Guías turísticas, periódicos con datos de cambio de moneda, almanaques	 **Otros recursos** Libros de cocina° de Centroamérica

Diseña *Design* negocio *business* tomando en cuenta *taking into account* Muéstrales *Show them* Háblales *Talk to them* recetas *recipes* cambio de moneda *currency exchange* libros de cocina *cookbooks*

Section Goals

In **Proyecto** students will:
- plan for a restaurant opening in Guatemala City
- design a menu
- integrate vocabulary and structures taught in **Lección 8**

Suggestion Students might need a week to complete the project, so at the beginning of that time period, have them open their books to this page and glance over **Proyecto**. Explain that they are going to plan to open a Guatemalan restaurant and design its menu.

Diseña el menú
- Provide students with several menus written in Spanish and English. Ask them to discuss the good and bad points of the design features of each, integrating what works well into their menus.
- Students can search for recipes or information on Guatemalan dishes on the Internet by using the key words and phrases **comidas típicas de Guatemala, recetas guatemaltecas**, or **recetas chapinas.**

Presenta la información
- Have students present their menus and plans in small groups.
- Encourage students to bring in dishes they have prepared.

EVALUATION: Plan/Menú

Criteria	Scale
Content	1 2 3 4
Organization	1 2 3 4
Accuracy	1 2 3 4
Oral presentation	1 2 3 4
Creativity	1 2 3 4

Scoring	
Excellent	18–20 points
Good	14–17 points
Satisfactory	10–13 points
Unsatisfactory	< 10 points

Section Goal

In **Panorama**, students will read about the geography and culture of Guatemala.

Instructional Resources
Transparencies, #3, #4, #35
WB/VM: Workbook, pp. 95–96; Video Activities, pp. 263–264
***Panorama cultural** DVD/Video*
Interactive CD-ROM
IRM: Videoscript, p. 130
Companion website: www.vistahigherlearning.com
Presentations CD-ROM

Suggestion Have students use the map in their books or project **Transparency #35**. Point out that Guatemala has three main climatic regions: the tropical Pacific and Caribbean coasts, the highlands (southwest), and jungle lowlands (north). Ask volunteers to read aloud the names of the cities, mountains, and rivers of Guatemala. Point out that indigenous languages are the source of many place names.

El país en cifras As you read about the languages of Guatemala, you might point out that there are many Guatemalans who are monolingual in either Spanish or a Mayan language. Many are bilingual, speaking an indigenous language and Spanish. When students look at the Guatemalan flag, point out that the quetzal is featured prominently in the shield in the center.

¡Increíble pero cierto! Guatemala is internationally renowned for the incredible wealth and diversity of its textile arts. Each village has a traditional "signature" weaving style that allows those in the know to quickly identify where each beautiful piece comes from.

Guatemala

NATIONAL STANDARDS connections cultures

El país en cifras

- **Área:** 108.890 km² (42.042 millas²), *un poco más pequeño que Tennessee*
- **Población:** 11.995.000
- **Capital:** la Ciudad de Guatemala—3.491.000
- **Ciudades principales:** Quetzaltenango—101.000, Escuintla—68.000, Mazatenango—42.000, Puerto Barrios—39.000

SOURCE: Population Division, UN Secretariat

- **Moneda:** quetzal
- **Idiomas:** español (oficial), lenguas mayas

El español es la lengua de un 60 por ciento° de la población; el otro 40 por ciento tiene una de las lenguas mayas (cakchiquel, quiché y kekchícomo entre otras) como lengua materna. Una palabra que las lenguas mayas tienen en común es ixim*, que significa maíz, un cultivo° de mucha importancia en estas culturas.*

Bandera de Guatemala

Guatemaltecos célebres

- **Carlos Mérida,** pintor (1891–1984)
- **Miguel Ángel Asturias,** escritor (1899–1974)
- **Margarita Carrera,** poeta y ensayista (1929–)
- **Rigoberta Menchú Tum,** activista (1959–)

por ciento *percent* cultivo *crop* telas *fabrics* tinte *dye* aplastados *crushed* hace... destiñan *keeps the colors from running*

ESTADOS UNIDOS
OCÉANO ATLÁNTICO
GUATEMALA
OCÉANO PACÍFICO
AMÉRICA DEL SUR

Vista de una calle céntrica en la Ciudad de Guatemala

Mujeres indígenas limpiando cebollas

MÉXICO
Sierra de Lacandón
Río Usumacinta
Lago Petén Itzá
Río de la Pasión
Lago de Izabal
Sierra de las Minas
Río Motagua
Quetzaltenango
Sierra Madre
Lago de Atitlán
Guatemala
Antigua Guatemala
Mazatenango
Escuintla
EL SALVADOR
Océano Pacífico

Iglesia de la Merced en Antigua Guatemala

recursos

WB pp. 95–96	VM pp. 263–264	I CD-ROM Lección 8	vista learni

¡Increíble pero cierto!

¿Qué ingrediente secreto se encuentra en las telas° tradicionales de Guatemala? ¡El mosquito! El excepcional tinte° de estas telas es producto de una combinación de flores y de mosquitos aplastados°. El insecto hace que los colores no se destiñan°. Quizás es por ésto que los artesanos representan la figura del mosquito en muchas de sus telas.

TEACHING OPTIONS

Worth Noting Although the indigenous population of Guatemala is Mayan, many place names in southwestern Guatemala are in Nahuatl, the language of the Aztecs of central Mexico. How did this happen? In the sixteenth century, Guatemala was conquered by Spaniards who came from the Valley of Mexico after having overthrown the Aztec rulers there. These conquistadors were accompanied by large numbers of Nahuatl-speaking allies, and it was these allies who renamed the captured Mayan strongholds with Nahuatl names. The suffix **–tenango**, which appears in many of these names, means "place with a wall," that is, a fortified place. **Quetzaltenango**, then, means fortified place of the quetzal bird; **Mazatenango** means fortified place of the deer.

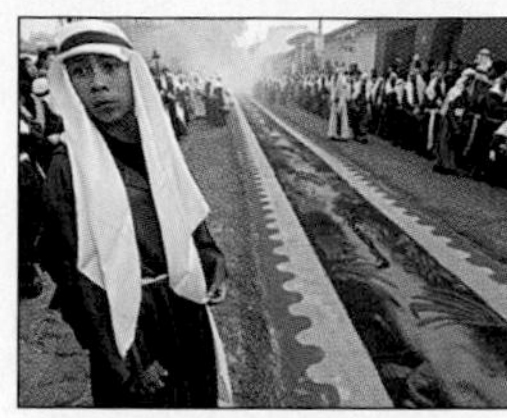

Ciudades • La Antigua Guatemala

La Antigua Guatemala fue fundada en 1543. Fue una capital de gran importancia hasta 1773, cuando un terremoto° la destruyó. La Antigua Guatemala conserva el carácter original de su arquitectura y hoy es uno de los centros turísticos del país. Su celebración de la Semana Santa° es, para muchas personas, la más importante del hemisferio.

Naturaleza • El quetzal

El quetzal simbolizó la libertad para los antiguos° mayas porque creían° que este pájaro° no podía vivir en cautividad°. Hoy el quetzal es el símbolo nacional. El pájaro da su nombre a la moneda nacional y aparece en los billetes° del país. Desafortunadamente, está en peligro° de extinción. Para su protección, el gobierno mantiene una reserva biológica especial.

Historia • Los mayas

Desde 1500 a.C. hasta 900 d.C. los mayas habitaron gran parte de lo que ahora es Guatemala. Su civilización fue muy avanzada. Fueron arquitectos y constructores de pirámides, templos y observatorios; descubrieron° y usaron el cero antes que los europeos, e inventaron un calendario complejo° y preciso.

Artesanía • La ropa tradicional

La ropa tradicional de los guatemaltecos se llama *huipil* y muestra el amor de la cultura maya por la naturaleza. Ellos se inspiran en las flores, plantas y animales para hacer sus diseños°. Es de colores vivos° y tiene formas geométricas. El diseño y los colores de cada *huipil* indican el pueblo de origen y a veces el sexo y la edad° de la persona que lo lleva.

¿Qué aprendiste? Responde a las preguntas con una frase completa.

1. ¿Qué significa la palabra *ixim*?
   La palabra *ixim* significa maíz.
2. ¿Quién es Rigoberta Menchú?
   Rigoberta Menchú es una activista de Guatemala.
3. ¿Qué pájaro representa a Guatemala?
   El quetzal representa a Guatemala.
4. ¿Qué simbolizó el quetzal para los mayas?
   El quetzal simbolizó la libertad para los mayas.
5. ¿Cuál es la moneda nacional de Guatemala?
   La moneda nacional de Guatemala es el quetzal.
6. ¿De qué fueron arquitectos los mayas?
   Los mayas fueron arquitectos de pirámides, templos y observatorios.
7. ¿Qué celebración de la Antigua Guatemala es la más importante del hemisferio para muchas personas? La celebración de la Semana Santa de la Antigua Guatemala es la más importante del hemisferio.
8. ¿Qué descubrieron los mayas antes que los europeos? Los mayas descubrieron el cero antes que los europeos.
9. ¿Qué muestra la ropa tradicional de los guatemaltecos? La ropa muestra el amor a la naturaleza.
10. ¿Qué indica un *huipil* con su diseño y sus colores? Con su diseño y colores, un *huipil* indica el pueblo de origen, el sexo y la edad de la persona.

Conexión Internet Investiga estos temas en el sitio **www.vistahigherlearning.com.**

1. Busca información sobre Rigoberta Menchú. ¿De dónde es? ¿Qué libros publicó? ¿Por qué es famosa?
2. Estudia un sitio arqueológico en Guatemala para aprender más sobre los mayas, y prepara un breve informe para tu clase.

terremoto *earthquake* Semana Santa *Holy Week* antiguos *ancient* creían *they believed* pájaro *bird* cautividad *captivity* los billetes *bills* peligro *danger* descubrieron *discovered* complejo *complex* diseños *designs* vivos *bright* edad *age*

Mar Caribe

Golfo de Honduras

erto rios

NDURAS

La Antigua Guatemala Students can use tour books and the Internet to learn more about **Semana Santa** celebrations in this Guatemalan city, usually referred to simply as Antigua. Encourage short presentations to the class.

El quetzal Recent conservation efforts in Guatemala, Costa Rica, and other Central American nations have focused on preserving the cloud forests (**bosque nuboso**) that are home to the quetzal.

Los mayas Today ethnobotanists are working with Mayan traditional healers to learn about medicinal uses of plants of the region.

La ropa tradicional Many indigenous Guatemalans still wear traditional garb richly decorated with embroidery. The **huipil** is a long, sleeveless tunic worn by women. A distinctively woven **faja**, or waist sash, identifies the town or village each woman comes from.

Conexión Internet Students will find supporting Internet activities and links at **www.vistahigherlearning.com**.

TEACHING OPTIONS

Worth Noting Spanish is a second language for more than 40% of Guatemalans. Students may be interested to learn that Guatemala has many bilingual education programs, where native languages are used in addition to Spanish for instructional purposes. There are also many government-sponsored Spanish as a Second Language (SSL) programs, offered through schools and radio or television. Speakers of Guatemala's indigenous languages often encounter problems similar to those found by other learners of Spanish: difficulty with agreement of number and gender.

Instructional Resources
Vocabulary CD
Lab Manual, p. 48
*Lab CD/MP3 **Lección 8***
IRM: Tapescript, pp. 35–39
*Testing Program: **Pruebas**, pp. 85–96*
Testing Program Audio CD
Test Files CD-ROM

Las comidas

el/la camarero/a	*waiter*
la comida	*food; meal*
el/la dueño/a	*owner; landlord*
el menú	*menu*
la sección de (no) fumar	*(non) smoking section*
el almuerzo	*lunch*
la cena	*dinner*
el desayuno	*breakfast*
los entremeses	*hors d'oeuvres*
el plato (principal)	*(main) dish*
delicioso/a	*delicious*
rico/a	*tasty; delicious*
sabroso/a	*tasty; delicious*
escoger	*to choose*
merendar (e:ie)	*to snack*
pedir (e:i)	*to order (food)*
probar (o:ue)	*to taste; to try*
recomendar (e:ie)	*to recommend*
servir (e:i)	*to serve*

Las frutas

la banana	*banana*
las frutas	*fruits*
el limón	*lemon*
la manzana	*apple*
el melocotón	*peach*
la naranja	*orange*
la pera	*pear*
la sandía	*watermelon*
la uva	*grape*

Las verduras

las arvejas	*peas*
la cebolla	*onion*
el champiñón	*mushroom*
la ensalada	*salad*
los espárragos	*asparagus*
los frijoles	*beans*
la lechuga	*lettuce*
el maíz	*corn*
las papas/patatas (fritas)	*(fried) potatoes; French fries*
el tomate	*tomato*
las verduras	*vegetables*
la zanahoria	*carrot*

La carne y el pescado

el atún	*tuna*
el bistec	*steak*
los camarones	*shrimp*
la carne	*meat*
la carne de res	*beef*
la chuleta (de cerdo)	*(pork) chop*
la hamburguesa	*hamburger*
el jamón	*ham*
la langosta	*lobster*
los mariscos	*shellfish*
el pavo	*turkey*
el pescado	*fish*
el pollo (asado)	*(roast) chicken*
la salchicha	*sausage*
el salmón	*salmon*

Otras comidas

el aceite	*oil*
el ajo	*garlic*
el arroz	*rice*
el azúcar	*sugar*
los cereales	*cereal; grains*
el huevo	*egg*
la mantequilla	*butter*
la margarina	*margarine*
la mayonesa	*mayonnaise*
el pan (tostado)	*(toasted) bread*
la pimienta	*black pepper*
el queso	*cheese*
la sal	*salt*
el sándwich	*sandwich*
la sopa	*soup*
el vinagre	*vinegar*
el yogur	*yogurt*

Las bebidas

el agua (mineral)	*(mineral) water*
la bebida	*drink*
el café	*coffee*
la cerveza	*beer*
el jugo (de fruta)	*(fruit) juice*
la leche	*milk*
el refresco	*soft drink*
el té (helado)	*(iced) tea*
el vino (blanco/tinto)	*(white/red) wine*

Verbos

conducir	*to drive*
conocer	*to know; to be acquainted with*
ofrecer	*to offer*
parecer	*to seem*
saber	*to know; to know how*
traducir	*to translate*
morir (o:ue)	*to die*

Las comparaciones

como	*like; as*
más de (*+ number*)	*more than*
más… que	*more … than*
menos de (*+ number*)	*fewer than*
menos… que	*less … than*
tan… como	*as … as*
tantos/as… como	*as many… as*
tanto… como	*as much… as*
el/la mayor	*the eldest*
el/la mejor	*the best*
el/la menor	*the youngest*
el/la peor	*the worst*
mejor	*better*
peor	*worse*

Expresiones útiles	*See page 241.*

recursos

LM p. 48	Lab CD/MP3 Lección 8	Vocab CD Lección 8

Las fiestas

9

Communicative Goals

You will learn how to:

- Express congratulations
- Express gratitude
- Ask for and pay the bill at a restaurant

A PRIMERA VISTA

- ¿Se conocen ellas?
- ¿Cómo se sienten, alegres o tristes?
- ¿Está una de las chicas más contenta que la otra?
- ¿De qué color es su ropa, marrón o negra?

Lesson Goals

In **Lección 9** students will be introduced to the following:

- terms for parties and celebrations
- words for stages of life and interpersonal relations
- irregular preterites
- verbs that change meaning in the preterite
- uses of **¿qué?** and **¿cuál?**
- pronouns after prepositions
- recognizing word families
- using a Venn diagram to organize information
- writing a comparative analysis
- using context to infer the meaning of unfamiliar words
- writing an article about a Chilean festival
- cultural, geographic, and economic information about Chile

A primera vista Here are some additional questions you can ask based on the photo: **¿Fuiste a una fiesta importante el año pasado? ¿Cuál fue la ocasión? ¿Sirvieron comida en la fiesta? ¿Qué sirvieron? En tu opinión, ¿qué fiestas son las más divertidas? ¿Por qué? ¿Conoces algún buen lugar para hacer una fiesta? ¿Por qué es bueno?**

INSTRUCTIONAL RESOURCES

Workbook/Video Manual: WB Activities, pp. 97–108
Laboratory Manual: Lab Activities, pp. 49–54
Workbook/Video Manual: Video Activities, pp. 229–230; pp. 265–266
Instructor's Resource Manual: **Hojas de actividades**, pp. 169–170; **Vocabulario adicional**, p. 187; **¡Inténtalo!** & **Práctica** Answers, p. 212; **Fotonovela** Translations, pp. 143–144; Textbook CD Tapescript, p. 93; Lab CDs Tapescript, pp. 40–44; **Fotonovela** Videoscript, p. 112; **Panorama cultural** Videoscript, p. 131
Info Gap Activities Booklet, pp. 33–36
Overhead Transparencies: #5, #6, #36, #37
Lab Audio CD/MP3 **Lección 9**
Panorama cultural DVD/Video
Fotonovela DVD/Video
Testing Program, pp. 97–108; pp. 217–227
Testing Program Audio CD
Test Files CD-ROM
Companion website
Presentations CD-ROM
Textbook CD
Vocabulary CD
Interactive CD-ROM
Video CD-ROM
Web-SAM

Section Goals

In **Contextos**, students will learn and practice:
- vocabulary related to parties and celebrations
- vocabulary used to talk about stages of life and interpersonal relations

Instructional Resources
Transparency #36
Textbook CD
Vocabulary CD
WB/VM: Workbook, pp. 97–98
Lab Manual, p. 49
Lab CD/MP3 ***Lección 9***
IRM: ***Vocab. adicional****, p. 187;*
Práctica *Answers, p. 212;*
Tapescript, pp. 40–44; p. 93;
Hojas de actividades*, p. 169*
Interactive CD-ROM
Companion website:
www.vistahigherlearning.com
Presentations CD-ROM

Suggestions

- Ask volunteers if they went to a party recently. Say: **¿Quiénes de ustedes fueron a una fiesta el fin de semana pasado? ¿Ah, sí? ¿Qué tomaste allí? ¿Comiste algo? ¿Bailaste? ¿Escuchaste música?** Write **divertirse** on the board and explain what it means. Ask: **¿Te divertiste allí?** Also write **pasarlo bien** on the board and explain what it means. Say: **Ah, te divertiste mucho allí. Entonces, lo pasaste bien, ¿no? No lo pasaste mal.**
- Project **Transparency #36.** Have students respond to your true-false statements about the scene. Ex: **¿Cierto o falso? Es una fiesta de cumpleaños. (Cierto.) Muchas personas lo pasan mal en la fiesta. (Falso.)** Next, engage students in a conversation about what types of parties they like best and why. Say: **¿Qué tipo de fiesta te gusta más? ¿Te gusta recibir regalos? ¿Te gusta comer muchos dulces?**

Note: At this point you may want to present **Vocabulario adicional: Más vocabulario para las celebraciones**, from the IRM.

Las fiestas

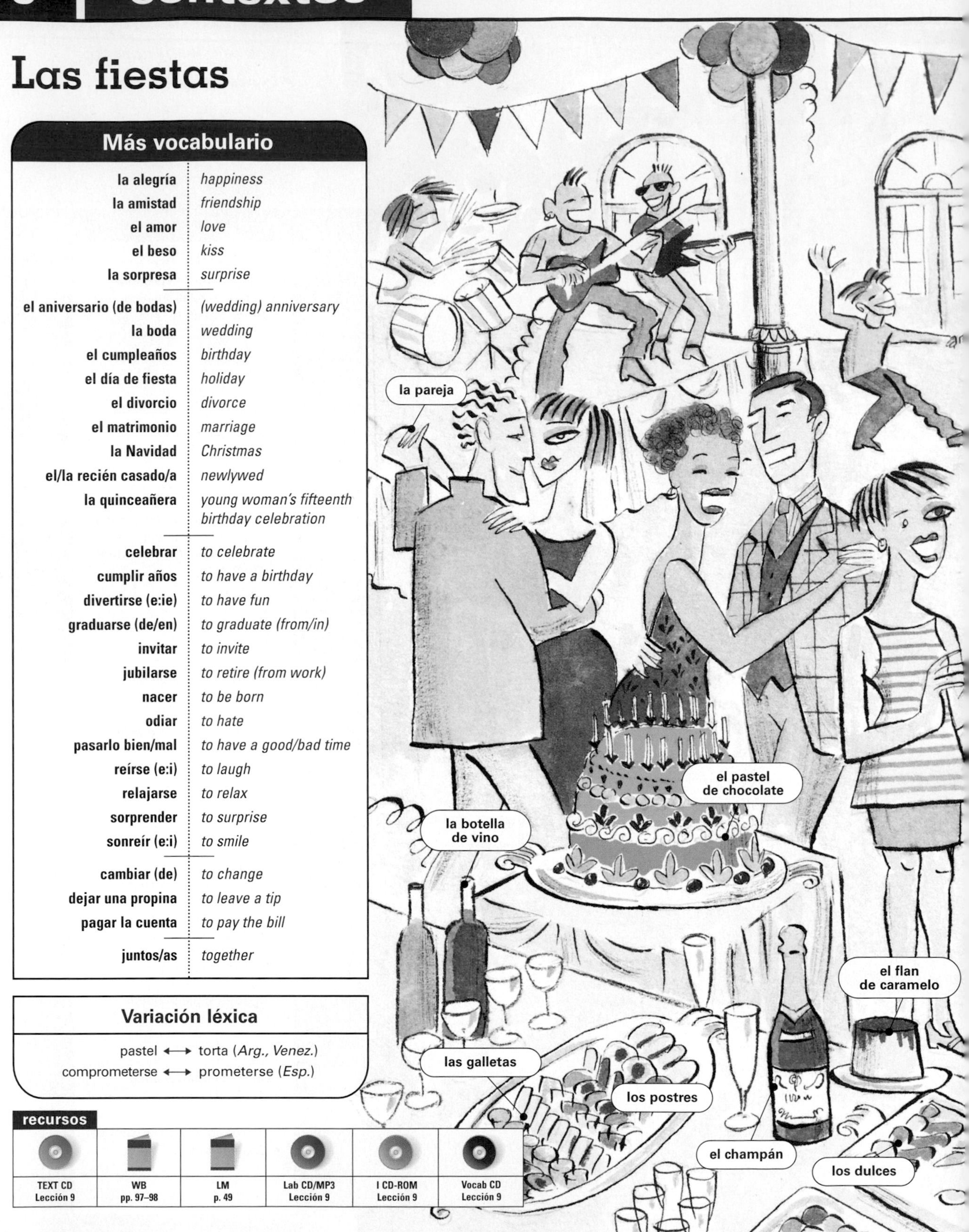

Más vocabulario

la alegría	*happiness*
la amistad	*friendship*
el amor	*love*
el beso	*kiss*
la sorpresa	*surprise*
el aniversario (de bodas)	*(wedding) anniversary*
la boda	*wedding*
el cumpleaños	*birthday*
el día de fiesta	*holiday*
el divorcio	*divorce*
el matrimonio	*marriage*
la Navidad	*Christmas*
el/la recién casado/a	*newlywed*
la quinceañera	*young woman's fifteenth birthday celebration*
celebrar	*to celebrate*
cumplir años	*to have a birthday*
divertirse (e:ie)	*to have fun*
graduarse (de/en)	*to graduate (from/in)*
invitar	*to invite*
jubilarse	*to retire (from work)*
nacer	*to be born*
odiar	*to hate*
pasarlo bien/mal	*to have a good/bad time*
reírse (e:i)	*to laugh*
relajarse	*to relax*
sorprender	*to surprise*
sonreír (e:i)	*to smile*
cambiar (de)	*to change*
dejar una propina	*to leave a tip*
pagar la cuenta	*to pay the bill*
juntos/as	*together*

Variación léxica

pastel ←→ torta (*Arg., Venez.*)
comprometerse ←→ prometerse (*Esp.*)

recursos

TEXT CD Lección 9	WB pp. 97–98	LM p. 49	Lab CD/MP3 Lección 9	I CD-ROM Lección 9	Vocab CD Lección 9

TEACHING OPTIONS

Extra Practice Ask students questions about birthdays and other celebrations and what days and months they fall on. Ask: ____, **¿cuándo es tu cumpleaños? (¿Qué día naciste?) ¿Estás casado/a? ¿Cuándo es tu aniversario de bodas?** Verify comprehension by asking other students to repeat. Then ask more general questions: **¿Cuándo es la Navidad?**

Worth Noting Point out that in addition to or instead of celebrating their birthday, many Hispanics celebrate their **día del santo**, or Saint's Day. This is the day that celebrates the saint for whom a person was named. In many Hispanic countries, the **día del santo** is just as important and significant in an individual's life as his or her **cumpleaños**.

Relaciones personales

casarse (con)	*to get married (to)*
comprometerse (con)	*to get engaged (to)*
divorciarse (de)	*to get divorced (from)*
enamorarse (de)	*to fall in love (with)*
llevarse bien/mal (con)	*to get along well/badly (with)*
romper (con)	*to break up (with)*
salir (con)	*to go out (with); to date*
separarse (de)	*to separate (from)*
tener una cita	*to have a date; to have an appointment*

Práctica

1 **Escuchar** Escucha la conversación e indica si las oraciones son **ciertas** o **falsas.**

1. A Silvia no le gusta mucho el chocolate. Falsa.
2. Silvia sabe que sus amigos le van a hacer una fiesta. Falsa.
3. Los amigos de Silvia le compraron un pastel de chocolate. Cierta.
4. Los amigos brindan por Silvia con refrescos. Falsa.
5. Silvia y sus amigos van a comer helado. Cierta.
6. Los amigos de Silvia le van a servir flan y galletas. Falsa.

2 **Emparejar** Indica la letra de la frase que mejor completa cada oración.

a. se jubiló	d. nos divertimos	g. se llevan bien
b. dejó una propina	e. nació	h. lo pasaron mal
c. sonrió	f. se casaron	i. tenemos una cita

1. María y sus compañeras de cuarto _g_. Son buenas amigas.
2. Pablo y yo _d_ en la fiesta. Bailamos y comimos mucho.
3. Manuel y Felipe _h_ en el cine. La película fue muy mala.
4. ¡Tengo una nueva sobrina! Ella _e_ ayer por la mañana.
5. Mi madre le _b_ muy grande al camarero.
6. Mi padre _a_ hace un año. Ahora no trabaja.
7. A Elena le gustan las galletas. Ella _c_ después de comérselas todas.
8. Jorge y yo _i_ esta noche. Vamos a ir a un restaurante muy elegante.
9. Jaime y Laura _f_ el septiembre pasado. La boda fue maravillosa.

3 **Definiciones** En parejas, definan las palabras y escriban una frase para cada ejemplo. Answers will vary. Suggested answers below.

modelo

romper (con) una pareja termina la relación
Marta rompió con su novio.

1. regalar dar un regalo
2. helado una comida fría y dulce
3. pareja dos personas enamoradas
4. invitado una persona que va a una fiesta
5. casarse ellos deciden estar juntos para siempre
6. quinceañera la fiesta de cumpleaños de una chica de 15 años
7. sorpresa la persona no sabe lo que va a pasar
8. pasarlo bien divertirse

1 Suggestion Have students check their answers by going over **Actividad 1** with the whole class.

1 Tapescript E1: ¿Estamos listos, amigos? E2: Creo que sí. Aquí tenemos el pastel y el helado… E3: De chocolate, espero. Ustedes saben cómo le encanta a Silvia el chocolate… E2: Por supuesto, el chocolate para Silvia. Bueno, un pastel de chocolate, el helado… E3: ¿El helado es de la cafetería o lo compraste cerca de la residencia estudiantil? E2: Lo compré en la tienda que está al lado de nuestra residencia. Es mejor que el helado de la cafetería. E1: Psstt… aquí viene Silvia… E1, E2, E3: ¡Sorpresa! ¡Sorpresa, Silvia! ¡Felicidades! E4: ¡Qué sorpresa! E3: ¿Y cuántos años cumples? E4: Dieciocho. ¡Gracias, amigos, muchas gracias! E1: Y ahora, ¡brindamos por nuestra amiga! E3: ¿Con qué brindamos? ¿Con el champán? E1: ¡Cómo no! ¡Por nuestra amiga Silvia, la más joven de todos nosotros! *Textbook CD*

2 Expansion Have students write three sentences based on the drawing on pages 270–271, leaving out a word or phrase from the vocabulary. In pairs, students complete their partner's sentence. Ex: **Dos personas ____ con champán. (brindan)**

3 Expansion Ask students personalized questions using verbs from the **Relaciones personales** box on this page. Ex: **¿Con quién te llevas muy bien? ¿Con quién te llevas mal?**

TEACHING OPTIONS

Heritage Speakers Ask heritage speakers about some Hispanic holidays or other celebrations that they or their families typically celebrate, such as **el Día de los Reyes Magos, el día del santo, la quinceañera, el Cinco de Mayo,** and **el Día de los Muertos**. Ask speakers to elaborate on what the celebrations are like: who attends, what they eat and drink, why those days are celebrated, and so forth.

Game Play **Concentración**. Write vocabulary items that pertain to parties and celebrations on each of eight cards. On another eight cards, draw or paste a picture that matches each description. Place the cards face-down in four rows of four. In pairs, students select two cards. If the two cards match, the pair keeps them. If the two cards don't match, students replace them in their original position. The pair with the most cards at the end wins.

Suggestion Engage students in a conversation about the stages in Sergio's life. Say: **Mira al bebé en el primer dibujo. ¡Qué contento está! ¿Qué hace en el segundo dibujo? Está paseando en un triciclo, ¿no? ¿Quiénes se acuerdan de su niñez?** Cover all the vocabulary in **Más vocabulario**.

4 Suggestion Before beginning, ask several true-false questions. Have students correct false statements. Ex: **Un soltero es un hombre que no está casado. (Cierto.) La vejez ocurre antes de la niñez. (Falso. La vejez ocurre después de la madurez.)**

4 Expansion Students create three original sentences that describe events mentioned in **Más vocabulario** on page 270. Then a partner has to name the event described. Ex: **Lourdes y Mario llevan diez años de casados. (el aniversario de bodas)**

5 Suggestion Explain that students are to give the opposite of the underlined words in their answers.

5 Expansion Have students use words and expressions with opposite meanings to share sentences about their family with a partner, who will then report the information to the class. Ex: **Mi abuelo se jubiló el año pasado, pero mi hermana mayor empezó a trabajar la semana pasada.**

Las etapas de la vida de Sergio

el nacimiento

la niñez

la adolescencia

la juventud

la madurez

la vejez

Más vocabulario

la edad	*age*
el estado civil	*marital status*
las etapas de la vida	*the stages of life*
la muerte	*death*
casado/a	*married*
divorciado/a	*divorced*
soltero/a	*single*
separado/a	*separated*
viudo/a	*widower/widow*

4 **Las etapas de la vida** Identifica las etapas de la vida que se describen (*are described*) en las siguientes (*following*) frases.

1. Mi abuela se jubiló y se mudó (*moved*) a Viña del Mar. la vejez
2. Mi padre trabaja para una compañía grande en Santiago. la madurez
3. ¿Viste a mi nuevo sobrino en el hospital? Es precioso y ¡tan pequeño! el nacimiento
4. Mi abuelo murió este año. la muerte
5. Mi hermana se enamoró de un chico nuevo en la escuela. la adolescencia
6. Mi hermana pequeña juega con muñecas (*dolls*). la niñez

NOTA CULTURAL

Viña del Mar es una ciudad en la costa de Chile, situada al oeste de Santiago. Tiene playas hermosas, excelentes hoteles, casinos y buenos restaurantes. Cada año en Viña del Mar se celebra el famosísimo Festival Internacional de la Canción (*song*).

5  **Cambiar** Tu hermano menor no entiende nada de las etapas de la vida. En parejas, túrnense (*take turns*) para decir que las afirmaciones son falsas y corríjanlas (*correct them*) cambiando las expresiones subrayadas (*underlined*).

modelo

Estudiante 1: La niñez es cuando trabajamos mucho.
Estudiante 2: No, te equivocas (*you're wrong*). La madurez es cuando trabajamos mucho.

1. El nacimiento es el fin de la vida. La muerte
2. La juventud es la etapa cuando nos jubilamos. La vejez
3. A los sesenta y cinco años, muchas personas comienzan a trabajar. se jubilan
4. Julián y nuestra prima se divorcian mañana. se casan
5. Mamá odia a su hermana. quiere / se lleva bien con
6. El abuelo murió, por eso la abuela es separada. viuda
7. Cuando te gradúas de la universidad, estás en la etapa de la adolescencia. la juventud
8. Mi tío nunca se casó, es viudo. soltero

AYUDA

Other ways to contradict someone:
No es verdad. *It's not true.*
Creo que no. *I don't think so.*
¡Claro que no! *Of course not!*
¡Qué va! *No way!*

TEACHING OPTIONS

Small Groups In groups of two to four, students perform a skit whose content describes and/or displays a particular stage of life (youth, old age, etc.) or marital status (married, single, divorced). The rest of the class has to try to figure out what the group is displaying.

Game Play a modified version of Twenty Questions. Ask a volunteer to think of a famous person. Other students get one chance each to ask a yes-no question until someone guesses the item correctly. Limit attempts to ten questions per famous person. Point out that students can narrow down their selection by using vocabulary about the stages of life and marital status.

Comunicación

6 **Una fiesta** Trabaja con dos compañeros/as para planear una fiesta. Recuerda incluir la siguiente información. Answers will vary.

1. ¿Qué tipo de fiesta es? ¿Dónde va a ser? ¿Cuándo va a ser?
2. ¿A quiénes van a invitar?
3. ¿Qué van a comer? ¿Quiénes van a llevar o a preparar la comida?
4. ¿Qué van a beber? ¿Quiénes van a llevar las bebidas?
5. ¿Qué van a hacer todos durante la fiesta?

7 **Encuesta** Tu profesor(a) va a darte una hoja de actividades. Haz las preguntas de la hoja a dos o tres compañeros/as de clase para saber qué actitudes tienen en sus relaciones personales. Luego comparte los resultados de la encuesta (*survey*) con la clase y comenta tus conclusiones. Answers will vary.

Preguntas	Nombres	Actitudes
1. ¿Te importa la amistad? ¿Por qué?		
2. ¿Es mejor tener un(a) buen(a) amigo/a o muchos/as amigos/as?		
3. ¿Cuáles son las características que buscas en tus amigos/as?		
4. ¿Tienes novio/a? ¿A qué edad es posible enamorarse?		
5. ¿Deben las parejas hacer todo juntos? ¿Deben tener las mismas opiniones? ¿Por qué?		

¡LENGUA VIVA!

While a **buen(a) amigo/a** is a *good friend*, the term **amigo/a íntimo/a** refers to a *close friend*, or a very good friend, without any romantic overtones.

8 **Minidrama** En parejas, consulten la ilustración en la página 272, y luego, usando las palabras de la lista, preparen un minidrama para representar (*to act out*) las etapas de la vida de Sergio. Pueden ser creativos e inventar más información sobre su vida.

amor	celebrar	enamorarse	romper
boda	comprometerse	graduarse	salir
cambiar	cumpleaños	jubilarse	separarse
casarse	divorciarse	nacer	tener una cita

6 Expansions
- Ask volunteer groups to talk to the class about the party they have just planned.
- Have students make invitations for their party. Ask the class to judge which invitation is the cleverest, funniest, most elegant, and so forth.

7 Suggestion Distribute the **Hojas de actividades.** Give students eight minutes to ask other group members the questions.

7 Expansion Take a survey of the attitudes found in the entire class. Ex: **¿Quiénes creen que es más importante tener un buen amigo que muchos amigos? ¿Quiénes creen que es más importante tener muchos amigos que un buen amigo?**

8 Expansion After all skits have been presented, have the class vote on the most original, funniest, truest to life, and so forth.

TEACHING OPTIONS

Extra Practice Using magazine pictures, display images that pertain to parties or celebrations, stages of life, or interpersonal relations. Have students describe the pictures and make guesses about who the people are, how they are feeling, and so forth.

Extra Practice As a listening comprehension activity, prepare short descriptions of five easily recognizable people. Use as much active lesson vocabulary as possible. Write their names on the board in random order. Then read your descriptions, having students match the description to the appropriate name.

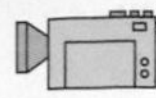

Section Goals

In **Fotonovela** students will:
- receive comprehensible input from free-flowing discourse
- learn functional phrases that preview lesson grammatical structures

Instructional Resources
WB/VM: Video Activities, pp. 229–230
***Fotonovela** DVD/Video (Start 00:47:00)*
Video CD-ROM
*IRM: **Fotonovela** Translations, pp. 143–144, Videoscript, p. 112*
Interactive CD-ROM

Video Recap: Lección 8
Before doing this **Fotonovela** section, review the previous one with this activity.
1. ¿Quién es doña Rita Perales? (la dueña del restaurante El Cráter)
2. ¿Qué platos sirven en El Cráter? (tortillas de maíz, caldo de patas, lomo a la plancha, ceviche, fuente de fritada, pasteles)
3. ¿Qué opinión tienen los estudiantes de la comida? (es riquísima)
4. ¿Cuál es la ocasión especial ese día? (el cumpleaños de Maite)

Video Synopsis While the travelers are looking at the dessert menu, Doña Rita and the waiter bring in some flan, a cake, and some wine to celebrate Maite's birthday. The group leaves Doña Rita a nice tip, thanks her, and says good-bye.

Suggestions
- Have students read the first line of dialogue in each **Fotonovela** segment and then make an educated guess about what happens in this episode.
- Quickly review the guesses your students made about the **Fotonovela**, and guide the class to a correct summary of the plot.

¡Feliz cumpleaños, Maite!

NATIONAL STANDARDS communication cultures

Don Francisco y los estudiantes celebran el cumpleaños de Maite en el restaurante El Cráter.

PERSONAJES

MAITE

INÉS

DON FRANCISCO

ÁLEX

JAVIER

DOÑA RITA

CAMARERO

1

INÉS A mí me encantan los dulces. Maite, ¿tú qué vas a pedir?

MAITE Ay, no sé. Todo parece tan delicioso. Quizás el pastel de chocolate.

2

JAVIER Para mí el pastel de chocolate con helado. Me encanta el chocolate. Y tú, Álex, ¿qué vas a pedir?

ÁLEX Generalmente prefiero la fruta, pero hoy creo que voy a probar el pastel de chocolate.

DON FRANCISCO Yo siempre tomo un flan y un café.

3

DOÑA RITA & CAMARERO ¡Feliz cumpleaños, Maite!

INÉS ¿Hoy es tu cumpleaños, Maite?

MAITE Sí, el 22 de junio. Y parece que vamos a celebrarlo.

TODOS MENOS MAITE ¡Felicidades!

6

ÁLEX Yo también acabo de cumplir los veintitrés años.

MAITE ¿Cuándo?

ÁLEX El cuatro de mayo.

7

DOÑA RITA Aquí tienen un flan, pastel de chocolate con helado... y una botella de vino para dar alegría.

MAITE ¡Qué sorpresa! ¡No sé qué decir! Muchísimas gracias.

8

DON FRANCISCO El conductor no puede tomar vino. Doña Rita, gracias por todo. ¿Puede traernos la cuenta?

DOÑA RITA Enseguida, Paco.

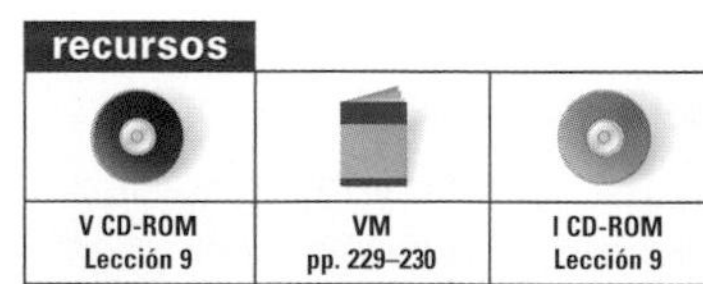
recursos

V CD-ROM Lección 9	VM pp. 229–230	I CD-ROM Lección 9

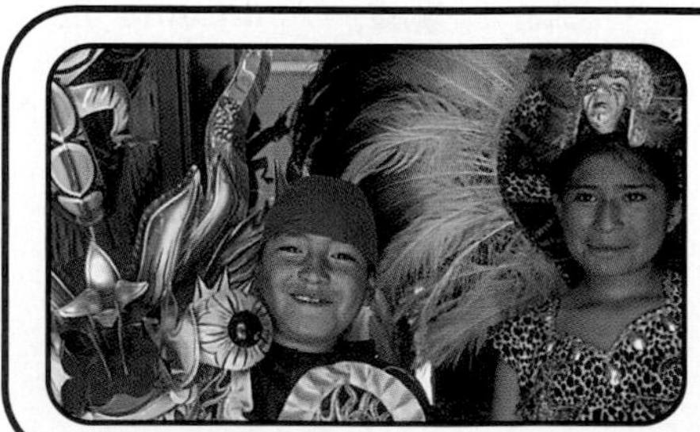

TEACHING OPTIONS

Video Tips General suggestions for using video clips in the classroom can be found on page IAE-12 of this Instructor's Annotated Edition.
¡Feliz cumpleaños, Maite! Ask your students to brainstorm a list of things that might happen during a surprise birthday party. Then play the **¡Feliz cumpleaños, Maite!** segment of this video module once, asking your students to take notes about what they see and hear. After viewing this video segment, have students use their notes to tell you what happened in this episode. Then play the segment again to allow your students to refine their notes. Repeat the discussion process and lead the class to an accurate summary of the plot.

MAITE ¡Gracias! Pero, ¿quién le dijo que es mi cumpleaños?

DOÑA RITA Lo supe por don Francisco.

ÁLEX Ayer te lo pregunté, ¡y no quisiste decírmelo! ¿Eh? ¡Qué mala eres!

JAVIER ¿Cuántos años cumples?

MAITE Veintitrés.

INÉS Creo que debemos dejar una buena propina. ¿Qué les parece?

MAITE Sí, vamos a darle una buena propina a la señora Perales. Es simpatiquísima.

DON FRANCISCO Gracias una vez más. Siempre lo paso muy bien aquí.

MAITE Muchísimas gracias, señora Perales. Por la comida, por la sorpresa y por ser tan amable con nosotros.

Enfoque cultural Las celebraciones hispanas

Las celebraciones de la independencia, los carnavales y la Semana Santa son fiestas importantísimas en los países hispanos. Las fechas de Navidad y Noche Vieja (*New Year's Eve*) son, quizás, las más festejadas (*celebrated*). Otra celebración importante es el santo. Cada día del año tiene un santo asignado, y algunas personas que se llaman igual que el santo del día (*who have the same name as the day's saint*) lo celebran. El 19 de marzo, por ejemplo, los que se llaman José o Josefa celebran el día de San José.

Expresiones útiles

Celebrating a birthday party

- ▶ **¡Feliz cumpleaños!**
  Happy birthday!
- ▶ **¡Felicidades!/¡Felicitaciones!**
  Congratulations!
- ▶ **¿Quién le dijo que es mi cumpleaños?**
  Who told you (form.) *that it's my birthday?*
- ▷ **Lo supe por don Francisco.**
  I found out through don Francisco.
- ▶ **¿Cuántos años cumples/cumple Ud.?**
  How old are you now?
- ▷ **Veintitrés.**
  Twenty-three.

Asking for and getting the bill

- ▶ **¿Puede traernos la cuenta?**
  Can you bring us the bill?
- ▶ **La cuenta, por favor.**
  The bill, please.
- ▷ **Enseguida, señor/señora/señorita.**
  Right away, sir/ma'am/miss.

Expressing gratitude

- ▶ **¡(Muchas) gracias!**
  Thank you (very much)!
- ▶ **Muchísimas gracias.**
  Thank you very, very much.
- ▶ **Gracias por todo.**
  Thanks for everything.
- ▶ **Gracias una vez más.**
  Thanks again. (lit. Thanks one more time.)

Leaving a tip

- ▶ **Creo que debemos dejar una buena propina. ¿Qué les parece?**
  I think we should leave a good tip. What do you guys think?
- ▷ **Sí, vamos a darle una buena propina.**
  Yes, let's give her a good tip.

Suggestion Go through the **Fotonovela**, asking for volunteers to read the various parts.

Expresiones útiles Draw attention to the forms **dijo** and **supe**. Explain that these are irregular preterite forms of the verbs **decir** and **saber**. Point out the phrase **no quisiste decírmelo** under video still 5 of the **Fotonovela**. Explain that **quisiste** is an irregular preterite form of the verb **querer**. Tell the class that **no querer** in the preterite means *to refuse.* Tell your students that they will learn more about these concepts in **Estructura**.

TEACHING OPTIONS

Enfoque cultural Tell the class that many young girls eagerly anticipate their **quinceañera**, or fifteenth birthday party, which celebrates their transition into adulthood. The **quinceañera** is frequently a lavish event with live music, catered food, and a long list of guests, who include people of all ages, especially the girl's parents, grandparents, aunts, uncles, and not just friends of the girl's own age. You might want to mention that for young men, the coming-of-age party traditionally coincides with the eighteenth or twenty-first birthday. Tell the class that many other events are celebrated by families in the Spanish-speaking world, including weddings, anniversaries, and graduations. Ask heritage speakers if they are aware of any other specific celebrations or festivals in the Hispanic world.

1 Expansion Have students work in pairs or small groups to write a question that would have elicited each of these statements.

2 Suggestion Ask students these questions before doing this activity: **¿A quién le gusta mucho la fruta? (a Álex) ¿A quién le gusta muchísimo el chocolate? (a Javier) ¿Quién no puede tomar vino? (don Francisco)**

2 Expansion Give these additional items to your students: **7. ¡No me lo puedo creer! ¿Pastel de chocolate y flan para mí? (Maite) 8. ¿Mi cumpleaños? Es el cuatro de mayo. (Álex)**

3 Suggestion Have the class review the vocabulary items on pages 270–271 before doing this activity.

3 Expansion Have pairs create additional sentences with the leftover items from the word bank.

4 Possible Response
E1: ¡Feliz cumpleaños! ¿Cuántos años cumples hoy?
E2: ¡Muchas gracias! Cumplo diecinueve.
E3: Buenas tardes. ¿En qué les puedo servir?
E1: Quisiera el pastel de chocolate y un café, por favor.
E2: Voy a pedir un pastel de chocolate con helado, y de tomar, un café.
[LATER...]
E1: Señorita, ¿puede traernos la cuenta?
E3: Enseguida, señor.
E2: La camarera fue muy amable. Debemos dejarle una buena propina, ¿no crees?
E1: Sí. Y yo voy a pagar la cuenta, porque es tu cumpleaños.
E2: Yo te ayudo. Gracias por todo...

Reacciona a la fotonovela

1

Completar Completa las frases con la información correcta, según la fotonovela.

1. De postre, don Francisco siempre pide un café y un flan.
2. A Javier le encanta el chocolate.
3. Álex cumplió los veintitrés años el cuatro de mayo.
4. Hoy Álex quiere tomar algo diferente. De postre, quiere pedir un pastel de chocolate.
5. Los estudiantes le van a dejar una buena propina a doña Rita.

2

Identificar Identifica quién puede decir las siguientes frases.

1. Gracias, doña Rita, pero no puedo tomar vino. don Francisco
2. ¡Qué simpática es doña Rita! Fue tan amable conmigo. Maite
3. A mí me encantan los dulces y los pasteles, ¡especialmente si son de chocolate! Javier
4. Mi amigo acaba de informarme que hoy es el cumpleaños de Maite. doña Rita
5. ¿Tienen algún postre de fruta? Los postres de fruta son los mejores. Álex
6. Me parece una buena idea dejarle una buena propina a la dueña. ¿Qué piensan ustedes? Inés

JAVIER ÁLEX
INÉS MAITE
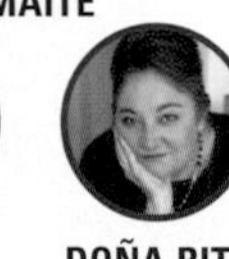
DON FRANCISCO DOÑA RITA

NOTA CULTURAL

En los países hispanos los camareros no dependen tanto de **las propinas** como en los EE.UU. Por eso, en estos países no es común dejar propina. Pero siempre es buena idea dejar una buena propina cuando el grupo es grande o el servicio es excepcional.

3

Completar Selecciona algunas de las opciones de la lista para completar las frases.

el amor	la cuenta	la galleta	la quinceañera
una botella de vino	día de fiesta	pedir	¡Qué sorpresa!
celebrar	el divorcio	un postre	una sorpresa

1. Maite no sabe que van a celebrar su cumpleaños porque es una sorpresa.
2. Cuando una pareja celebra su aniversario y quiere tomar algo especial, compra una botella de vino.
3. Después de una cena o un almuerzo, es normal pedir postre/la cuenta.
4. Inés y Maite no saben exactamente lo que van a pedir de postre.
5. Después de comer en un restaurante, tienes que pagar la cuenta.
6. Una pareja de enamorados nunca piensa en el divorcio.
7. Hoy no trabajamos porque es un día de fiesta.

CONSÚLTALO

Some Latin American countries mark a girl's fifteenth birthday by celebrating a **quinceañera,** a party in her honor in which she is "presented" to society. To read more, see **Lectura** p. 289.

4

Fiesta sorpresa Trabajen en grupos para representar una conversación en la que uno/a de ustedes está celebrando su cumpleaños en un restaurante.

- Una persona le desea feliz cumpleaños a su compañero/a y le pregunta cuántos años cumple.
- Cada persona del grupo le pide al/a la camarero/a un postre y algo de beber.
- Después de terminar los postres, una persona pide la cuenta.
- Otra persona habla de dejar una propina.
- Los amigos que no cumplen años dicen que quieren pagar la cuenta.
- El/la que cumple años les da las gracias por todo.

TEACHING OPTIONS

Extra Practice Ask volunteers to ad-lib the **Fotonovela** episode for the class. Assure them that it is not necessary to memorize the **Fotonovela** or stick strictly to its content. They should try to get the general meaning across with the vocabulary and expressions they know, and they should also feel free to be creative.

Pairs Have your students work in pairs to tell each other about celebrations in their families. Remind them to use as many expressions as possible from the **Expresiones útiles** on page 275, as well as the vocabulary on pages 270–271. Follow up by asking a few students to describe celebrations in their partner's family.

Pronunciación

The letters h, j, and g

helado **hombre** **hola** **hermosa**

The Spanish **h** is always silent.

José **jubilarse** **dejar** **pareja**

The letter **j** is pronounced much like the English *h* in *his.*

agencia **general** **Gil** **Gisela**

The letter **g** can be pronounced three different ways. Before **e** or **i**, the letter **g** is pronounced much like the English *h.*

Gustavo, gracias por llamar el domingo.

At the beginning of a phrase or after the letter **n**, the Spanish **g** is pronounced like the English *g* in *girl.*

Me gradué en agosto.

In any other position, the Spanish **g** has a somewhat softer sound.

Guerra **conseguir** **guantes** **agua**

In the combinations **gue** and **gui**, the **g** has a hard sound and the **u** is silent. In the combination **gua**, the **g** has a hard sound and the **u** is pronounced like the English *w.*

Práctica Lee las palabras en voz alta, prestando atención a la **h**, la **j** y la **g**.

1. hamburguesa	5. geografía	9. seguir	13. Jorge
2. jugar	6. magnífico	10. gracias	14. tengo
3. oreja	7. espejo	11. hijo	15. ahora
4. guapa	8. hago	12. galleta	16. guantes

Oraciones Lee las oraciones en voz alta, prestando atención a la **h**, la **j** y la **g**.

1. Hola. Me llamo Gustavo Hinojosa Lugones y vivo en Santiago de Chile.
2. Tengo una familia grande; somos tres hermanos y tres hermanas.
3. Voy a graduarme en mayo.
4. Para celebrar mi graduación mis padres van a regalarme un viaje a Egipto.
5. ¡Qué generosos son!

Refranes Lee los refranes en voz alta, prestando atención a la **h**, la **j** y la **g**.

A la larga, lo más dulce amarga.[1]
El hábito no hace al monje.[2]

1 Too much of a good thing.
2 The clothes don't make the man.

recursos

TEXT CD Lección 9	LM p. 50	Lab CD/MP3 Lección 9	I CD-ROM Lección 9

Section Goal

In **Pronunciación** students will be introduced to the pronunciation of **h**, **j**, and **g**.

Instructional Resources
Textbook CD
Lab Manual, p. 50
Lab CD/MP3 ***Lección 9***
IRM: Tapescript, pp. 40–44; p. 93
Interactive CD-ROM

Suggestions

- Ask the class how the Spanish **h** is pronounced. Ask volunteers to pronounce the example words.
- Explain that **j** is pronounced much like the English *h*.
- Draw attention to the fact that the letter **g** is pronounced like the English *h* before **e** or **i**. Write the example words on the board and ask volunteers to pronounce them.
- Point out that the letter **g** is pronounced like the English *g* in *good* at the beginning of a phrase or after the letter **n**.
- Explain that in any other position, particularly between vowels, **g** has a softer sound.
- Tell the class that in the combinations **gue** and **gui**, **g** has a hard sound and **u** is not pronounced. Explain that in the combinations **gua** and **guo**, the **u** sounds like the English *w*.

Práctica/Oraciones/Refranes
These exercises are recorded on the Textbook CD. You may want to play the CD so students practice the pronunciation point by listening to Spanish spoken by speakers other than yourself.

TEACHING OPTIONS

Extra Practice Write the names of these Chilean cities on the board and ask for a volunteer to pronounce each one: Santiago, Antofagasta, Rancagua, Coihaique. Repeat the process with the names of these Chilean writers: Alberto Blest Gana, Vicente Huidobro, Gabriela Mistral, Juan Modesto Castro.

Pairs Have your students work in pairs to read aloud the sentences in **Actividad 2, Identificar**, page 276. Encourage your students to help their partners if they have trouble pronouncing a particular word.

Section Goal

In **Estructura 9.1** students will be introduced to the irregular preterites of several common verbs.

Instructional Resources
WB/VM: Workbook, pp. 99–100
Lab Manual, p. 51
Lab CD/MP3 ***Lección 9***
IRM: ***¡Inténtalo! & Práctica*** *Answers, p. 212; Tapescript, pp. 40–44;* ***Hojas de actividades,*** *p. 170*
Interactive CD-ROM
Companion website: www.vistahigherlearning.com
Presentations CD-ROM

Suggestions

- Quickly review the present tense of a stem-changing verb such as **pedir**. Write the paradigm on the board and ask volunteers to point out the stem-changing forms.
- Work through the preterite paradigms of **tener**, **venir**, and **decir**, modeling the pronunciation.
- Use magazine pictures to ask about social events in the past. Ex: **¿Con quién vino este señor a la fiesta? (Vino con esa señora rubia.) ¿Qué se puso la señora López para ir a la boda? (Se puso un sombrero.)**

9.1 Irregular preterites

ANTE TODO You already know that the verbs **ir** and **ser** are irregular in the preterite. You will now learn other verbs whose preterite forms are also irregular.

recursos
WB pp. 99–104
LM pp. 51–54
Lab CD/MP3 Lección 9
I CD-ROM Lección 9
vistahigherlearning.com

Preterite of *tener, venir,* and *decir*

		tener (**u**-stem)	**venir** (**i**-stem)	**decir** (**j**-stem)
SINGULAR FORMS	yo	tuv**e**	vin**e**	dij**e**
	tú	tuv**iste**	vin**iste**	dij**iste**
	Ud./él/ella	tuv**o**	vin**o**	dij**o**
PLURAL FORMS	nosotros/as	tuv**imos**	vin**imos**	dij**imos**
	vosotros/as	tuv**isteis**	vin**isteis**	dij**isteis**
	Uds./ellos/ellas	tuv**ieron**	vin**ieron**	dij**eron**

▶ The following verbs observe similar stem-changes to **tener, venir,** and **decir**.

INFINITIVE	U-STEM	PRETERITE FORMS
poder	pud-	pude, pudiste, pudo, pudimos, pudisteis, pudieron
poner	pus-	puse, pusiste, puso, pusimos, pusisteis, pusieron
saber	sup-	supe, supiste, supo, supimos, supisteis, supieron
estar	estuv-	estuve, estuviste, estuvo, estuvimos, estuvisteis, estuvieron

INFINITIVE	I-STEM	PRETERITE FORMS
querer	quis-	quise, quisiste, quiso, quisimos, quisisteis, quisieron
hacer	hic-	hice, hiciste, hizo, hicimos, hicisteis, hicieron

INFINITIVE	J-STEM	PRETERITE FORMS
traer	traj-	traje, trajiste, trajo, trajimos, trajisteis, trajeron
conducir	conduj-	conduje, condujiste, condujo, condujimos, condujisteis, condujeron
traducir	traduj-	traduje, tradujiste, tradujo, tradujimos, tradujisteis, tradujeron

¡ATENCIÓN!
The endings of these verbs are the regular preterite endings of **–er/–ir** verbs, except for the **yo** and **Ud.** forms. Note that these two endings are unaccented.

¡ATENCIÓN!
Most verbs that end in **–cir** are **j**-stem verbs in the preterite. For example, **producir** → **produje, produjiste,** etc.

▶ Notice that the preterites with **j**-stems omit the letter **i** in the **ellos, ellas,** and **ustedes** form.

Mis amigos **trajeron** comida a la fiesta. Ellos **comieron** muchos dulces.

ORBITEL
$5.000
$10.000
$20.000
05
¿Dijiste larga distancia?
En tarjetas prepagadas ninguna te da más minutos para hablar

TEACHING OPTIONS

Extra Practice Do a pattern practice drill. Give an infinitive and ask individual students to provide conjugations for the different subject pronouns and/or names you suggest. Reverse activity by saying a conjugated form and asking students to give an appropriate subject pronoun.

Game Divide the class into two teams. Indicate one team member at a time, alternating between teams. Give a verb in its infinitive form and a subject pronoun. The team member should give the correct preterite form. Give a point per correct answer. Deduct a point for each wrong answer. The team with the most points at the end of play wins.

The preterite of *dar*

yo	d**i**	nosotros/as	d**imos**
tú	d**iste**	vosotros/as	d**isteis**
Ud./él/ella	d**io**	Uds./ellos/ellas	d**ieron**
SINGULAR FORMS		PLURAL FORMS	

▶ The endings for **dar** are the same as the regular preterite endings for **–er** and **–ir** verbs, except that there are no accent marks.

La camarera me **dio** el menú.
The waitress gave me the menu.

Le **di** a Juan algunos consejos.
I gave Juan some advice.

Los invitados le **dieron** un regalo.
The guests gave him/her a gift.

Nosotros **dimos** una gran fiesta.
We gave a great party.

▶ The preterite of **hay** (*inf.* **haber**) is **hubo** *(there was; there were)*.

CONSÚLTALO

Note that there are other ways to say *there was* or *there were* in Spanish. See **Estructura 10.1**, p. 306.

Doña Rita les dio una botella de vino a los viajeros.

Hubo una fiesta en el restaurante El Cráter.

¡INTÉNTALO! Escribe en cada espacio en blanco la forma correcta del pretérito del verbo que está entre paréntesis.

1. (querer) tú quisiste
2. (decir) usted dijo
3. (hacer) nosotras hicimos
4. (traer) yo traje
5. (conducir) ellas condujeron
6. (estar) ella estuvo
7. (tener) tú tuviste
8. (dar) ella y yo dimos
9. (traducir) yo traduje
10. (haber) ayer hubo
11. (saber) usted supo
12. (poner) ellos pusieron
13. (venir) yo vine
14. (poder) tú pudiste
15. (querer) ustedes quisieron
16. (estar) nosotras estuvimos
17. (decir) tú dijiste
18. (saber) ellos supieron
19. (hacer) él hizo
20. (poner) yo puse
21. (traer) nosotras trajimos
22. (tener) yo tuve
23. (dar) tú diste
24. (poder) ustedes pudieron

Suggestions

- Test comprehension by randomly calling out the infinitive of one of these verbs and a subject pronoun. Signal a student to give you the corresponding preterite form. Continue until you have covered a majority of the forms and given most of the class an opportunity to respond.
- Use the preterite forms of all these verbs by talking about what you did in the recent past and then asking students questions that involve them in a conversation about what they did in the recent past. You may want to avoid the preterite of **poder, saber,** and **querer** for the moment. Ex: **El sábado pasado tuve que ir a la fiesta de cumpleaños de mi sobrina. Cumplió siete años. Le di un bonito regalo. ____, ¿tuviste que ir a una fiesta el sábado? ¿No? Pues, ¿qué hiciste el sábado?**

TEACHING OPTIONS

Video Show the video again to give students more input containing irregular preterite forms. Stop the video where appropriate to discuss how certain verbs were used and to ask comprehension questions.

Extra Practice Have students write down six things they brought to class today. Then they walk around the room asking other students if they also brought those items (**¿Trajiste tus llaves a clase hoy?**). When they find a student that answers **sí,** they ask that student to sign his or her name next to that item (**Firma aquí, por favor.**). Can students get signatures for all the items they brought to class?

Práctica

1 Completar Completa estas frases con el pretérito de los verbos entre paréntesis.

1. El sábado ___hubo___ (haber) una fiesta sorpresa para Elsa en mi casa.
2. Sofía ___hizo___ (hacer) un pastel para la fiesta y Miguel ___trajo___ (traer) un flan.
3. Los amigos y parientes de Elsa ___vinieron___ (venir) y ___trajeron___ (traer) regalos.
4. El hermano de Elsa no ___vino___ (venir) porque ___tuvo___ (tener) que trabajar.
5. Su tía María Dolores tampoco ___pudo___ (poder) venir.
6. Cuando Elsa abrió la puerta, todos gritaron (*shouted*): "¡Feliz cumpleaños!" y su esposo le ___dio___ (dar) un beso.
7. Al final de la fiesta, todos ___dijeron___ (decir) que se divirtieron mucho.
8. La historia (*story*) le ___dio___ (dar) a Elsa tanta risa (*laughter*) que no ___pudo___ (poder) dejar de reírse durante toda la noche.

NOTA CULTURAL

El **flan** es un postre muy popular en los países de habla hispana. Se prepara con huevos y se sirve con salsa de caramelo. Existen variedades deliciosas como el flan de queso o el flan de coco.

2 Describir En parejas, usen verbos de la lista para describir lo que estas personas hicieron. Deben dar por lo menos dos frases por cada dibujo. Some answers will vary.

dar	hacer	tener	traer
estar	poner	traducir	venir

1. El señor López
El señor López le dio dinero a su hijo.

2. Norma
Norma puso el pavo en la mesa.

3. Anoche nosotros
Anoche nosotros tuvimos (hicimos/dimos) una fiesta de Navidad./Anoche nosotros estuvimos en una fiesta de Navidad.

4. Roberto y Elena
Roberto y Elena le trajeron/dieron un regalo a su amigo.

1 Expansions
- Ask individual students about the last time they threw a party. Ex: **La última vez que diste una fiesta, ¿quiénes estuvieron allí? ¿Fue alguien que no invitaste? ¿Qué llevaron los invitados?**
- Assign students to groups of three. Tell them they are going to write a narrative about a wedding. You will begin the story, then each student will add a sentence using a stem-changing verb in the preterite. Each group member should have at least two turns. Ex: **El domingo se casaron Carlos y Susana. Tuvieron una boda muy grande. (Vinieron muchos invitados. Hubo un pastel enorme y elegante.)**

2 Suggestion There are several possible answers other than those given in the annotations. Encourage the class to see how many sentences they can come up with to describe each drawing using the target verbs.

2 Expansion Using magazine pictures, show images similar to those in the activity. Students narrate what is happening in the images using irregular preterite verb forms.

TEACHING OPTIONS

Heritage Speakers Ask heritage speakers to talk about a party they once attended. They should include information on what kind of party it was, who was there, what people brought, what the guests did, and so forth. Verify comprehension by asking other students in the class to relate what was said.

Small Groups In groups of three or four, each student writes three sentences using irregular preterites. Two of the sentences must be true for them and the third must be false. The other members of the group have to guess which of the sentences is the false one. This can also be done with the whole class.

Comunicación

3 **Preguntas** En parejas, túrnense para hacerse y responder a estas preguntas.
Answers will vary.

1. ¿Fuiste a una fiesta de cumpleaños el año pasado? ¿De quién?
2. ¿Quiénes fueron a la fiesta?
3. ¿Quién condujo el carro?
4. ¿Cómo estuvo la fiesta?
5. ¿Quién llevó regalos, bebidas o comida? ¿Llevaste algo especial?
6. ¿Hubo comida? ¿Quién la hizo? ¿Hubo champán?
7. ¿Qué regalo diste tú? ¿Qué otros regalos dieron los invitados?
8. ¿Cuántos invitados hubo en la fiesta?
9. ¿Qué tipo de música hubo?
10. ¿Qué dijeron los invitados de la fiesta?

4 **Encuesta** Tu profesor(a) va a darte una hoja de actividades. Para cada una de las actividades de la lista, encuentra a alguien que hizo esa actividad en el tiempo indicado.
Answers will vary.

modelo

Traer dulces a clase
Estudiante 1: *¿Trajiste dulces a clase?*
Estudiante 2: *Sí, traje galletas y helado a la fiesta del fin del semestre.*

NOTA CULTURAL

Halloween es una fiesta que también se celebra en algunos países hispanos, como México, por su proximidad con los Estados Unidos, pero no es parte de la cultura hispana. Sin embargo, sí lo es el Día de todos los Santos (1 de noviembre) y el Día de los Muertos (2 de noviembre). Según la tradición mexicana, el Día de los Muertos los espíritus de los muertos regresan para visitar a los vivos. Muchas personas van al cementerio ese día y algunas pasan la noche allí. También es costumbre comer pan y dulces en forma de calaveras (*skulls*) y esqueletos (*skeletons*).

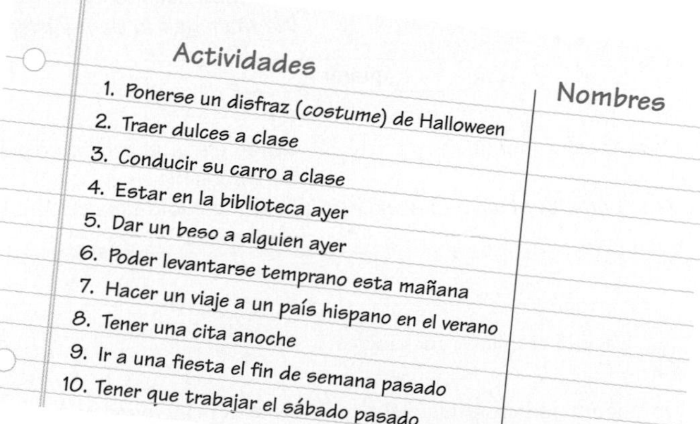

Actividades
Nombres
1. Ponerse un disfraz (costume) de Halloween
2. Traer dulces a clase
3. Conducir su carro a clase
4. Estar en la biblioteca ayer
5. Dar un beso a alguien ayer
6. Poder levantarse temprano esta mañana
7. Hacer un viaje a un país hispano en el verano
8. Tener una cita anoche
9. Ir a una fiesta el fin de semana pasado
10. Tener que trabajar el sábado pasado

Síntesis

5 **Conversación** En parejas, preparen una conversación en la que un(a) hermano/a va a visitar a su hermano/a para explicarle por qué no fue a su fiesta de graduación y para saber cómo estuvo la fiesta. Incluyan la siguiente información en la conversación:
Answers will vary.

- Cuál fue el menú
- Quiénes vinieron a la fiesta y quiénes no pudieron venir
- Quiénes prepararon la comida o trajeron algo
- Si él/ella tuvo que preparar algo
- Lo que la gente hizo antes y después de comer
- Cómo lo pasaron, bien o mal

3 Suggestion Instead of having students take turns, ask them to go through all the questions with their partner, writing down the information the partner gives them. Later, have them write a third-person description about their partner's experience.

3 Expansion To practice the formal register, call on different students to ask you the questions in the activity. Ex: **¿Fue a una fiesta de cumpleaños el año pasado? (Fui a una fiesta de cumpleaños anoche.)**

4 Suggestion Distribute the **Hojas de actividades**. Point out that to get information, students must form questions using the **tú** forms of the infinitives. Ex: **¿Trajiste dulces a clase?**

4 Expansion Write items 1–10 on the board and ask for a show of hands for each item. Ex: **¿Quién trajo dulces a clase?** Write tally marks next to each item to find out which activity was most popular.

5 Expansion Have pairs work in groups of four to write a paragraph combining the most interesting or unusual aspects of each pair's conversation. Ask a group representative to read the paragraph to the class, who will later vote for the most creative or funniest paragraph.

TEACHING OPTIONS

Extra Practice Ask students to write a brief composition on the **Fotonovela** from this lesson. Students should write about where the characters were, what they were doing, who ordered what, what they said to each other, and so forth. (Note: Students should stick to completed actions in the past [preterite]. The use of the imperfect for narrating a story will not be presented until **Lección 10.**)

Large Groups Divide the class in half. To each member of the first half give a strip of paper that has a question on it. Ex: **¿Quién me trajo el pastel de cumpleaños?** To each member of the second half give the answer to that question. Ex: **Marta te lo trajo.** Students must find their partner.

Section Goal

In **Estructura 9.2** students will be introduced to verbs that change meaning in the preterite tense.

Instructional Resources
WB/VM: Workbook, p. 101
Lab Manual, p. 52
*Lab CD/MP3 **Lección 9***
*IRM: **¡Inténtalo! & Práctica** Answers, p. 212; Tapescript, pp. 40–44*
Interactive CD-ROM
Companion website: www.vistahigherlearning.com
Presentations CD-ROM

Suggestions

- Introduce the preterite of **conocer**. Say: **Los conozco a ustedes muy bien ahora. Pero me acuerdo del día en que los conocí. ¿Ustedes se acuerdan del día en que nos conocimos?** Ask volunteers to compare and contrast the meanings of **conocer** in your example.
- Stress the meaning of **poder** in the preterite by giving both affirmative (*to manage; to succeed*) and negative (*to try and fail*) examples. Ex: **Pude leer todas sus composiciones anoche, pero no pude leer las composiciones de la otra clase.**
- Stress the meaning of **querer** in the preterite by giving both affirmative (*to try*) and negative (*to refuse*) examples. Ex: **Quisimos ver una película el sábado, pero no quise ver ninguna película violenta.**

9.2 Verbs that change meaning in the preterite

ANTE TODO The verbs **conocer, saber, poder,** and **querer** change meanings when used in the preterite. Because of this, each of them corresponds to more than one verb in English, depending on its tense.

Verbs that change meaning in the preterite

	Present	Preterite
conocer	*to know; to be acquainted with* **Conozco** a esa pareja. *I know that couple.*	*to meet* **Conocí** a esa pareja ayer. *I met that couple yesterday.*
saber	*to know information; to know how to do something* **Sabemos** la verdad. *We know the truth.*	*to find out; to learn* **Supimos** la verdad anoche. *We found out (learned) the truth last night.*
poder	*to be able; can* **Podemos** hacerlo. *We can do it.*	*to manage; to succeed (could and did)* **Pudimos** hacerlo ayer. *We managed to do it yesterday.*
querer	*to want; to love* **Quiero** ir a la fiesta pero tengo que trabajar. *I want to go the party, but I have to work.*	*to try* **Quise** evitar el accidente pero fue imposible. *I tried to avoid the accident but it was impossible.*

¡ATENCIÓN!

In the preterite, the verbs **poder** and **querer** have different meanings, depending on whether they are used in affirmative or negative sentences.

pude *I was able (to)*
no pude *I failed (to)*
quise *I tried (to)*
no quise *I refused (to)*

¡INTÉNTALO! Elige la respuesta más lógica.

1. Yo no hice lo que me pidieron mis padres. ¡Tengo mis principios! a
   a. No quise hacerlo. b. No supe hacerlo.
2. Hablamos por primera vez con Nuria y Ana en la boda. a
   a. Las conocimos en la boda. b. Las supimos en la boda.
3. Por fin hablé con mi hermano después de llamarlo siete veces. b
   a. No quise hablar con él. b. Pude hablar con él.
4. Josefina se acostó para relajarse. Se durmió inmediatamente. a
   a. Pudo relajarse. b. No pudo relajarse.
5. Después de mucho buscar, encontraste la definición en el diccionario. b
   a. No supiste la respuesta. b. Supiste la repuesta.
6. Las chicas fueron a la fiesta. Cantaron, bailaron mucho y hablaron con todos los invitados. a
   a. Ellas pudieron divertirse. b. Ellas no supieron divertirse.

TEACHING OPTIONS

Extra Practice Give sentences using **conocer, saber, poder,** and **querer** in the present tense that will be logical when converted into the preterite. Have students convert them and explain how the meanings of the sentences change. Ex: **Sé la fecha de la fiesta. Gustavo puede comprar un regalo bonito. Queremos conocer a los invitados. Felipe y Paula no quieren ir a la fiesta. No puedo hacer un flan.**

Heritage Speakers Ask heritage speakers to talk about one of the following situations in the past: (1) when they found out there was no Santa Claus (**saber**), (2) when they met their best friend (**conocer**), or (3) something they tried to do but couldn't (**querer/no poder**). Verify student comprehension by asking other students to relate what was said.

Práctica

1 **Carlos y Eva** Forma frases con los siguientes elementos. Usa el pretérito. Al final, inventa la razón del divorcio de Carlos y Eva.

1. Anoche / mi esposa y yo / saber / que / Carlos y Eva / divorciarse
   Anoche mi esposa y yo supimos que Carlos y Eva se divorciaron.
2. Los / conocer / viaje / Isla de Pascua
   Los conocimos en un viaje a la Isla de Pascua.
3. No / poder / hablar / mucho / con / ellos / ese / día
   No pudimos hablar mucho con ellos ese día.
4. Pero / ellos / ser / simpático / y / nosotros / hacer planes / vernos / con más / frecuencia
   Pero ellos fueron simpáticos y nosotros hicimos planes para vernos con más frecuencia.
5. Yo / poder / su / número / teléfono / encontrar / páginas / amarillo
   Yo pude encontrar su número de teléfono en las páginas amarillas.
6. (Yo) querer / llamar / les / ese día / pero / no / tener / tiempo.
   Quise llamarles ese día pero no tuve tiempo.
7. Cuando / los / llamar / nosotros / poder / hablar / Eva.
   Cuando los llamé, nosotros pudimos hablar con Eva.
8. Nosotros / saber / razón / divorcio / después / hablar / ella
   Nosotros supimos la razón del divorcio después de hablar con ella.

NOTA CULTURAL

La Isla de Pascua es un remoto territorio chileno situado en el océano Pacífico Sur. Sus inmensas estatuas son uno de los mayores misterios del mundo: nadie sabe cómo o por qué se construyeron. Para más información, véase **Panorama**, p. 295.

Comunicación

2 **Completar** Completa estas frases de una manera lógica. Answers will vary.

1. Ayer mi compañero/a de cuarto supo...
2. Esta mañana no pude...
3. Conocí a mi mejor amigo/a en...
4. Mis padres no quisieron...
5. Mi mejor amigo/a no pudo...
6. Mi novio/a y yo nos conocimos en...
7. La semana pasada supe...
8. Ayer mis amigos quisieron...

3 **Telenovela *(Soap opera)*** En parejas, escriban el diálogo para una escena de una telenovela. La escena trata de (*is about*) una situación amorosa entre tres personas: Mirta, Daniel y Raúl. Usen el pretérito de **conocer, poder, querer** y **saber** en su diálogo. Answers will vary.

Síntesis

4 **Conversación** En una hoja de papel, escribe dos listas: las cosas que hiciste durante el fin de semana y las cosas que quisiste hacer pero no pudiste. Luego, compara tu lista con la de un(a) compañero/a, y expliquen por qué no pudieron hacer esas cosas. Answers will vary.

1 Suggestion This activity can also be done in pairs.

1 Expansions
- In pairs, students create five similar dehydrated sentences for their partner to complete, using the verbs **conocer, saber, poder**, and **querer**. After pairs have completed this, ask volunteers to share some of their dehydrated sentences. Write them on the board and have the rest of the class "hydrate" them.
- Have pairs use preterite forms of **conocer, saber, poder**, and **querer** to role-play Carlos and Eva explaining their separate versions of the divorce to their friends.

2 Suggestion Before assigning the activity, share with the class some recent things you found out, tried to do but couldn't, or the names of people you met, inviting students to respond.

3 Suggestion Point out that unlike their U.S. counterparts, Hispanic soap operas run for a limited period of time, like a miniseries, and then end.

4 Expansion Have pairs repeat the activity, this time describing another person. Ask students to share their descriptions with the class, who will guess who is being described.

TEACHING OPTIONS

Video Show the video again to give students more input containing verbs that change meaning in the preterite. Stop the video where appropriate to discuss how certain verbs were used and to ask comprehension questions.

Pairs In pairs, students write three sentences using verbs that change meaning in the preterite. Two of the sentences must be true for them and the third must be false. Their partner has to guess which of the sentences is the false one.

Section Goals

In **Estructura 9.3** students will review:
- the uses of **¿qué?** and **¿cuál?**
- interrogative words and phrases

Instructional Resources
WB/VM: Workbook, pp. 102–103
Lab Manual, p. 53
*Lab CD/MP3 **Lección 9***
*IRM: **¡Inténtalo! & Práctica** Answers, p. 212; Tapescript, pp. 40–44*
Info Gap Activities Booklet, pp. 33–34
Interactive CD-ROM
Companion website: www.vistahigherlearning.com
Presentations CD-ROM

Suggestions

- Review the question words **¿qué?** and **¿cuál?** Write incomplete questions on the board and ask students which interrogative word best completes each sentence. Ex: **¿____ es tu número de teléfono? (Cuál) ¿____ es esto? (Qué)**
- Point out that while both question words mean *what?* or *which?*, **¿qué?** is used with a noun, whereas **¿cuál?** is used with a verb. Ex: **¿Qué clase te gusta más? ¿Cuál es tu clase favorita?**
- Review the chart of interrogative words and phrases. Ask students personalized questions using each of them and invite them to ask you questions. Ex: **¿Cuál es tu película favorita?** (***Como agua para chocolate***) **¿Qué director es su favorito? (Pedro Almodóvar)**

9.3 ¿Qué? and ¿cuál?

ANTE TODO You've already learned how to use interrogative words and phrases. As you know, **¿qué?** and **¿cuál?** or **¿cuáles?** mean *what?* or *which?* However, they are not interchangeable.

▶ **¿Qué?** is used to ask for a definition or an explanation.

¿Qué es el flan?
What is flan?

¿Qué estudias?
What do you study?

▶ **¿Cuál(es)?** is used when there is a choice among several possibilities.

¿Cuál de los dos prefieres, el vino o el champán?
Which of these (two) do you prefer, wine or champagne?

¿Cuáles son tus medias, las negras o las blancas?
Which ones are your socks, the black ones or the white ones?

▶ **¿Cuál?** cannot be used before a noun; in this case, **¿qué?** is used.

¿Qué sorpresa te dieron tus amigos?
What surprise did your friends give you?

¿Qué colores te gustan?
What colors do you like?

▶ **¿Qué?** used before a noun has the same meaning as **¿cuál?**

¿Qué regalo te gusta?
What (Which) gift do you like?

¿Qué dulces quieren ustedes?
What (Which) sweets do you want?

Review of interrogative words and phrases

¿a qué hora?	*at what time?*	**¿cuánto/a?**	*how much?*
¿adónde?	*(to) where?*	**¿cuántos/as?**	*how many?*
¿cómo?	*how?*	**¿de dónde?**	*from where?*
¿cuál(es)?	*what?; which?*	**¿dónde?**	*where?*
¿cuándo?	*when?*	**¿qué?**	*what?; which?*
		¿quién(es)?	*who?*

¡INTÉNTALO! Completa las preguntas con **¿qué?** o **¿cuál(es)?**, según el contexto.

1. ¿ Cuál de los dos te gusta más?
2. ¿ Cuál es tu teléfono?
3. ¿ Qué tipo de pastel pediste?
4. ¿ Qué es una quinceañera?
5. ¿ Qué haces ahora?
6. ¿ Cuáles son tus platos favoritos?
7. ¿ Qué bebidas te gustan más?
8. ¿ Qué es esto?
9. ¿ Cuál es el mejor?
10. ¿ Cuál es tu opinión?
11. ¿ Qué fiestas celebras tú?
12. ¿ Qué botella de vino prefieres?
13. ¿ Cuál es tu helado favorito?
14. ¿ Qué pones en la mesa?
15. ¿ Qué restaurante prefieres?
16. ¿ Qué estudiantes estudian más?
17. ¿ Qué quieres comer esta noche?
18. ¿ Cuál es la sorpresa mañana?
19. ¿ Qué postre prefieres?
20. ¿ Qué opinas?

TEACHING OPTIONS

Extra Practice Ask questions of individual students, using **¿qué?** and **¿cuál?** Make sure a portion of the questions are general and information-seeking in nature (**¿qué?**). Ex: **¿Qué es una guitarra? ¿Qué es un elefante?** This is also a good way for students to practice circumlocution (**Es algo que...**).

Extra Practice Students write one question using each of the interrogative words or phrases in the chart on this page. Then they ask those questions of a partner, who must answer in complete sentences.

Práctica

1 **Completar** Tu clase de español va a crear un sitio web. Completa estas frases con alguna(s) palabra(s) interrogativa(s). Luego, con un(a) compañero/a hagan y contesten las preguntas para obtener la información para el sitio web.

1. ¿ Cuál es la fecha de tu cumpleaños?
2. ¿ Dónde naciste?
3. ¿ Cuál es tu estado civil?
4. ¿ Cómo/Cuándo/Dónde te relajas?
5. ¿ Quién es tu mejor amigo/a?
6. ¿ Qué cosas te hacen reír?
7. ¿ Qué postres te gustan? ¿ Cuál te gusta más?
8. ¿ Qué problemas tuviste en la primera cita con alguien?

Comunicación

NATIONAL communication STANDARDS

2 **Una invitación** En parejas, lean esta invitación. Luego, túrnense para hacer y contestar preguntas con **qué** y **cuál** basadas en la información de la invitación. Answers will vary.

¡LENGUA VIVA!

The word **invitar** is not used exactly like *invite*. If you say **Te invito a un café**, it means that you are offering to buy that person a coffee.

modelo

Estudiante 1: ¿Cuál es el nombre del padre de la novia?
Estudiante 2: Su nombre es Fernando Sandoval Valera.

Fernando Sandoval Valera | *Lorenzo Vásquez Amaral*
Isabel Arzipe de Sandoval | *Elena Soto de Vásquez*

tienen el agrado de invitarlos
a la boda de sus hijos
María Luisa y José Antonio
La ceremonia religiosa tendrá lugar
el sábado 10 de junio a las dos de la tarde
en el Templo de Santo Domingo
(Calle Santo Domingo, 961).

Después de la ceremonia sírvanse pasar a la recepción en el salón de baile del Hotel Metrópoli (Sotero del Río, 465).

3 **Quinceañera** Trabaja con un(a) compañero/a. Uno de ustedes es el/la director(a) del salón de fiestas "Renacimiento". El/la otro/a es el padre/la madre de Ana María, quien quiere hacer la fiesta de quinceañera de su hija sin gastar más de $25 por invitado/a. Su profesor(a) va a darles la información necesaria para confirmar la reservación. Answers will vary.

modelo

Estudiante 1: ¿Cuánto cuestan los entremeses?
Estudiante 2: Depende. Puede escoger champiñones por 50 centavos o camarones por dos dólares.
Estudiante 1: ¡Uf! A mi hija le gustan los camarones, pero son muy caros.
Estudiante 2: Bueno, también puede escoger quesos por un dólar por invitado.

1 Expansion Conduct a conversation with the whole class to find consensus on some of the questions.

2 Expansions
- Ask students to share some of the questions they asked their partner, which other students answer in complete sentences.
- Have pairs design an invitation to a party, wedding, **quinceañera**, or other social event. Then have them answer questions from the class about their invitation without showing it. The class guesses what kind of social event is announced. Ex: **¿Dónde es el evento? (En el salón de baile "Cosmopolita") ¿A qué hora es? (A las ocho de la noche) ¿De quiénes es la invitación? (de los señores López Pujol) Es una quinceañera.** Finally, have pairs reveal their design to the class.

3 Suggestion Divide the class into pairs and distribute the Info Gap Handouts from the Info Gap Activities Booklet that correspond to this activity. Give the students ten minutes to complete this activity.

3 Expansion With the same partner or in small groups, have students prepare a **telenovela** skit with characters from the **quinceañera** invitation. Encourage students to use interrogative words as well as verbs that change meaning in the preterite.

TEACHING OPTIONS

Pairs In pairs, students prepare a skit between two friends talking. One of the friends is planning a surprise party (**fiesta sorpresa**) for a mutual friend. However, the other person reveals that he or she doesn't care all that much for the party honoree and tells why. The class can vote for the funniest or most original skit.

Game Play a game of *Jeopardy*®. Prepare five answers for each of six categories (30 questions in all), each in varying degrees of difficulty. Ask for three volunteers to play. Students must give their answers in the form of a question. You may also decrease the number of questions and have additional volunteers participate in the game.

Section Goals

In **Estructura 9.4** students will be introduced to:
- pronouns as objects of prepositions
- the pronoun-preposition combinations **conmigo** and **contigo**

Instructional Resources
WB/VM: Workbook, p. 104
Lab Manual, p. 54
*Lab CD/MP3 **Lección 9***
*IRM: **¡Inténtalo! & Práctica** Answers, p. 212; Tapescript, pp. 40–44*
Info Gap Activities Booklet, pp. 35–36
Interactive CD-ROM
Companion website: www.vistahigherlearning.com
Presentations CD-ROM

Suggestions

- Review the chart "Prepositions often used with **estar**" in **Estructura 2.3**. Use prepositional pronouns as you describe yourself and others in relation to people and things. Say: **¿Quién está delante de mí? Sí, ____ está delante de mí. ¿Y quién está detrás de ella? Sí, ____ está detrás de ella.**
- Ask students which pronouns they recognize and which are new. Ask the class to deduce the rules for pronouns after prepositions.

9.4 Pronouns after prepositions

ANTE TODO In Spanish, as in English, the object of a preposition is the noun or pronoun that follows a preposition. Observe the following diagram.

La sopa es para Alicia y para él.

Prepositional pronouns

	Singular		Plural	
preposition +	**mí**	*me*	**nosotros/as**	*us*
	ti	*you (fam.)*	**vosotros/as**	*you (fam.)*
	Ud.	*you (form.)*	**Uds.**	*you (form.)*
	él	*him*	**ellos**	*them (m.)*
	ella	*her*	**ellas**	*them (f.)*

▶ Note that, except for **mí** and **ti,** these pronouns are the same as the subject pronouns.

▶ The preposition **con** combines with **mí** and **ti** to form **conmigo** and **contigo,** respectively.

—¿Quieres venir **conmigo** a Concepción?
Do you want to come with me to Concepción?

—Sí, gracias, me gustaría ir **contigo.**
Yes, thanks, I would like to go with you.

▶ The preposition **entre** is followed by **tú** and **yo** instead of **ti** and **mí.**

Papá va a sentarse **entre tú y yo.**
Dad is going to sit between you and me.

¡ATENCIÓN!
Mí (*me*) has an accent mark to distinguish it from the possessive adjective **mi** (*my*).

CONSÚLTALO
For more prepositions, refer to **Estructura 2.3**, p. 54.

¡INTÉNTALO! Completa las siguientes frases con las preposiciones y los pronombres apropiados.

1. *(with him)* No quiero ir con él.
2. *(for her)* Las galletas son para ella.
3. *(for me)* Los mariscos son para mí.
4. *(with you,* pl. form.*)* Preferimos estar con ustedes.
5. *(with you,* fam.*)* Me gusta salir contigo.
6. *(with me)* ¿Por qué no quieres tener una cita conmigo?
7. *(for her)* La cuenta es para ella.
8. *(for them,* m.*)* La habitación es muy pequeña para ellos.
9. *(with them,* f.*)* Anoche celebré la Navidad con ellas.
10. *(for you,* fam.*)* Este beso es para ti.
11. *(with you,* fam.*)* Nunca me aburro contigo.
12. *(with you,* pl. form.*)* ¡Qué bien que vamos con ustedes!
13. *(for you,* fam.*)* Para ti la vida es muy fácil.
14. *(for them,* f.*)* Para ellas no hay sorpresas.

TEACHING OPTIONS

Extra Practice Describe someone in the classroom using prepositions of location, but don't indicate who that person is. Ex: **Esta persona está entre la ventana y ____. Y está enfrente de mí.** The rest of the class has to guess the person being described. Once students have this model, ask individuals to create similar descriptions so that their classmates may guess who is being described.

Game Divide the class into two groups. One student from the first group chooses an item that's in the classroom and writes it down. Call on five students from the other group one at a time to ask questions about where this item is. Ex: **¿Está cerca de mí?** The first student can respond with **sí, no, caliente,** or **frío**. If a team guesses the item within five tries, give them a point. If not, give the other team a point. The team with the most points wins.

Práctica

1 **Completar** David sale con sus amigos a comer. Para saber quién come qué, lee el mensaje electrónico que David le envió (*sent*) a Cecilia dos días después y completa el diálogo en el restaurante con los pronombres apropiados.

modelo

Camarero: *Los camarones en salsa verde, ¿para quién son?*
David: *Son para* ___ella___.

Para	Asunto

Hola, Cecilia:
¿Recuerdas la comida del viernes? Quiero repetir el menú en mi casa el miércoles. Ahora voy a escribir lo que comimos, luego me dices si falta algún plato. Yo pedí el filete de pescado y Maribel camarones en salsa verde. Tatiana pidió un plato grandísimo de machas a la parmesana. Diana y Silvia pidieron langostas, ¿te acuerdas? Y tú, ¿qué pediste? Ah, sí, un bistec grande con papas. Héctor también pidió un bistec, pero más pequeño. Miguel pidió pollo y vino tinto para todos. Y la profesora comió ensalada verde porque está a dieta. ¿Falta algo? Espero tu mensaje. Hasta pronto. David.

CAMARERO El filete de pescado, ¿para quién es?
DAVID Es para (1) ___mí___.
CAMARERO Aquí está. ¿Y las machas a la parmesana y las langostas?
DAVID Las machas son para (2) ___ella___.
SILVIA Y DIANA Las langostas son para (3) ___nosotras___.
CAMARERO Tengo un bistec grande...
DAVID Cecilia, es para (4) ___ti___, ¿no es cierto? (*Cecilia nods.*) Y el bistec más pequeño es para (5) ___él___.
CAMARERO ¿Y la botella de vino?
MIGUEL Es para todos (6) ___nosotros___, y el pollo es para (7) ___mí___.
CAMARERO (*a la profesora*) Entonces la ensalada verde es para (8) ___usted___.

NOTA CULTURAL

Las **machas a la parmesana** es un plato muy típico de Chile. Se prepara con machas, un tipo de almeja (*clam*) que se encuentra en Suramérica. Las machas a la parmesana se hacen con queso parmesano, limón, sal, pimienta y mantequilla, y luego se ponen en el horno (*oven*).

NATIONAL communication STANDARDS

Comunicación

2 **Compartir** Tu profesor(a) va a darte una hoja de actividades en la que hay un dibujo. En parejas, hagan preguntas para saber dónde está cada una de las personas en el dibujo. Ustedes tienen dos versiones diferentes de la ilustración. Al final (*end*) deben saber dónde está cada persona.

modelo

Estudiante 1: *¿Quién está al lado de Óscar?*
Estudiante 2: *Alfredo está al lado de él.*

Alfredo	Dolores	Graciela	Raúl
Sra. Blanco	Enrique	Leonor	Rubén
Carlos	Sra. Gómez	Óscar	Yolanda

AYUDA

Here are some other useful prepositions: **al lado de, debajo de, a la derecha de, a la izquierda de, cerca de, lejos de, delante de, detrás de, entre.**

1 Suggestion Remind students that they are to fill in the blanks with prepositional pronouns, not names of the characters in the conversation.

1 Expansion In small groups, have students play the roles of the people mentioned in the e-mail message. Ex: **E1: ¿Para quién son los camarones? E2: Son para mí. E1: ¿Y el bistec? E2: Es para él.**

2 Suggestion Divide the class into pairs and distribute the Info Gap Handouts from the Info Gap Activities Booklet that correspond to this activity. Give the students ten minutes to complete this activity.

2 Expansions
- Using both versions of the drawing as a guide, ask questions of the whole class to find out where the people are. Ex: **¿Quién sabe dónde está la señora Blanco?**
- Verify that all students labeled the characters correctly by suggesting changes to the drawing and using prepositions to ask about their new locations. Ex: **Yolanda y Carlos cambian de lugar. ¿Quién está al lado de Yolanda ahora? (Rubén)**

TEACHING OPTIONS

Video Show the video module again to give students more input containing prepositional pronouns. Stop the video where appropriate to discuss how certain pronouns were used and to ask comprehension questions.

Large Groups Give half of the class cards that contain an activity (Ex: **jugar al baloncesto**) and give the other half cards that contain a place (Ex: **el gimnasio**). Activity card students circulate around the room to find places that match their activities. Ex: **E1: Voy a jugar al baloncesto. ¿Puedo ir contigo? E2: Pues, yo voy al museo. No puedes ir conmigo.** or **Voy al gimnasio. Sí, puedes ir conmigo.**

Section Goals

In **Lectura** students will:

- learn to use word families to infer meaning in context
- read content-rich texts

Instructional Resource
Companion website:
www.vistahigherlearning.com

Estrategia Write **conocer** on the board, reminding students of the meaning *to know, be familiar with*. Next to it, write **conocimiento** and **conocido**. Tell students that recognizing the family relationship between a known word and unfamiliar words can help them infer the meaning of the words they don't yet know. Guide students to see that **conocimiento** is a noun meaning *knowledge, familiarity* and **conocido** is an adjective form of the verb meaning *known* or *well-known*.

Examinar el texto Have students scan the text for clues to its contents. Ask volunteers to tell what kind of text it is and how they know. Headlines (**titulares**), photos, and layout (**composición de la página**) reveal that it is the society news (**notas de sociedad**) in a newspaper.

Raíces Have students fill in the rest of the chart after they have read **Vida social**.

Lectura

Antes de leer

Estrategia
Recognizing word families

Recognizing root words can help you guess the meaning of words in context, ensuring better comprehension of a reading selection. Using this strategy will enrich your Spanish vocabulary as you will see below.

Examinar el texto

Familiarízate con el texto usando las estrategias de lectura más efectivas para ti. ¿Qué tipo de documento es? ¿De qué tratan° las cuatro secciones del documento? Explica tus respuestas.

Raíces°

Completa el siguiente cuadro° para ampliar tu vocabulario. Usa palabras de la lectura de esta lección y el vocabulario de las lecciones anteriores. ¿Qué significan las palabras que escribiste en el cuadro? Answers will vary.

modelo

Verbo	Sustantivos	Otras formas
agradecer	*agradecimiento/ gracias*	*agradecido*
1. estudiar	estudiante *student*	estudiado *studied*
2. celebrar *to celebrate*	celebración *celebration*	celebrado
3. bailar *to dance*	baile	bailable *danceable*
4. bautizar	bautismo *baptism*	bautizado *baptized*

¿De qué tratan...? *What are they about?*
Raíces *Roots* cuadro *chart*

Vida social

Matrimonio
Espinoza Álvarez-Reyes Salazar

El día sábado 12 de junio de 2004 a las 19 horas, se celebró el matrimonio de Silvia Reyes y Carlos Espinoza en la Catedral de Santiago. La ceremonia fue oficiada por el pastor Federico Salas y participaron los padres de los novios, el señor Jorge Espinoza y señora y el señor José Alfredo Reyes y señora. Después de la ceremonia, los padres de los recién casados ofrecieron una fiesta bailable en el restaurante Doña Mercedes.

Bautismo

José María recibió el bautismo el 26 de junio de 2004.

Sus padres, don Roberto Lagos Moreno y doña María Angélica Sánchez, compartieron la alegría de la fiesta con todos sus parientes y amigos. La ceremonia religiosa tuvo lugar° en la Catedral de Aguas Blancas. Después de la ceremonia, padres, parientes y amigos celebraron una fiesta en la residencia de la familia Lagos.

TEACHING OPTIONS

Heritage Speakers Ask heritage speakers to analyze the word **quinceañera** and tell what two words and which suffix it is made of. The suffix **–ero/a** indicates the word is an adjective. **Quinceañera** refers to both the party and the young woman. Then have them share what they know about the coming of age event for a 15-year-old girl celebrated throughout Latin America.

Extra Practice Here are some related words of which at least one form will be familiar to students. Guide them to recognize the relationship between words and meanings. **idea, ideal, idealismo, idealizar, idear, ideario, idealista • conservar, conservación, conserva, conservador • bueno, bondad, bondadoso, bonito • habla, hablador, hablar, hablante, hablado**

32B

Fiesta quinceañera

El doctor don Amador Larenas Fernández y la señora Felisa Vera de Larenas celebraron los quince años de su hija Ana Ester junto a sus parientes y amigos. La quinceañera° reside en la ciudad de Valparaíso y es estudiante del Colegio Francés. La fiesta de presentación en sociedad de la señorita Ana Ester fue el día viernes 4 de mayo a las 19 horas, en el Club Español. Entre los invitados especiales asistieron el alcalde° de la ciudad, don Pedro Castedo, y su esposa. La música estuvo a cargo de la Orquesta Americana. ¡Feliz cumpleaños le deseamos a la señorita Ana Ester en su fiesta bailable!

Expresión de gracias

Carmen Godoy Tapia

Agradecemos° sinceramente a todas las personas que nos acompañaron en el último adiós a nuestra apreciada esposa, madre, abuela y tía, la señora Carmen Godoy Tapia. El funeral tuvo lugar el día 28 de junio de 2004 en la ciudad de Viña del Mar. La vida de Carmen Godoy fue un ejemplo de trabajo, amistad, alegría y amor para todos nosotros. La familia agradece de todo corazón° su asistencia° al funeral a todos los parientes y amigos. Su esposo, hijos y familia.

tuvo lugar *took place* quinceañera *fifteen year-old girl* alcalde *mayor* Agradecemos *We thank* de todo corazón *sincerely* asistencia *attendance*

Después de leer

Corregir

Escribe estos comentarios otra vez para corregir la información errónea.

1. El alcalde y su esposa asistieron a la boda de Silvia y Carlos. El alcalde y su esposa asistieron a la fiesta de quinceañera de Ana Ester.
2. Todos los anuncios° describen eventos felices. Tres de los anuncios tratan de eventos felices. Uno trata de una muerte.
3. Ana Ester Larenas cumple dieciséis años. Ana Ester Larenas cumple quince años.
4. Roberto Lagos y María Angélica Sánchez son hermanos. Roberto Lagos y María Angélica Sánchez están casados/son esposos.
5. Carmen Godoy Tapia les dio las gracias a las personas que asistieron al funeral. La familia de Carmen Godoy Tapia les dio las gracias a las personas que asistieron al funeral.

Identificar

Escribe el nombre de la(s) persona(s) descrita(s)°.

1. Dejó viudo a su esposo en junio de 2004. Carmen Godoy Tapia
2. Sus padres y todos los invitados brindaron por él, pero él no entendió por qué. José María
3. El Club Español les presentó una cuenta considerable para pagar. don Amador Larenas Fernández y doña Felisa Vera de Larenas
4. Unió a los novios en santo matrimonio. el pastor Federico Salas
5. La celebración de su cumpleaños marcó el comienzo de su vida adulta. Ana Ester

Un anuncio

Trabaja con dos o tres compañeros/as de clase e inventen un anuncio breve sobre una celebración importante. Esta celebración puede ser una graduación, un matrimonio o una gran fiesta en la que ustedes participan. Incluyan la siguiente información.

1. Nombres de los participantes
2. La fecha, la hora y el lugar
3. Qué se celebra
4. Otros detalles de interés

anuncios *announcements* descritas *described*

Corregir Ask volunteers to correct each false statement and point out the location in the text where they found the correct answer.

Identificar
- If students have trouble inferring the meaning of any word or phrase, help them identify the corresponding context clues.
- Have pairs write one question for each of the five items and exchange them with another pair who answers the questions.

Un anuncio
- Provide students with examples of announcements from Spanish-language newspapers to analyze and use as models.
- Have heritage speakers work with students who are being exposed to Spanish for the first time. When students are finished writing, ask them to read their announcements aloud. Have students combine the articles to create their own **Vida social** page for a class newspaper.

TEACHING OPTIONS

Variación léxica Ask heritage speakers to share with the class other terms they use to refer to various types of celebrations. Possible responses: wedding: **matrimonio, boda, casamiento**; graduation: **graduación, promoción**; birthday: **cumpleaños, día del santo.**

Heritage Speakers If a heritage speaker has attended a wedding, baptism, funeral, or other similar celebration in a Spanish-speaking country, ask him or her to prepare a short presentation about the event.

Game Have students describe the people mentioned in the announcements they wrote for the above activity **Un anuncio**; their classmates will guess which person in the announcement they are describing. They may extend the game by giving clues about the event and having classmates guess the event.

Section Goals

In **Escritura** students will:

- create a Venn diagram to organize information
- learn words and phrases that signal similarity and difference
- write a comparative analysis

Estrategia Explain that a graphic organizer such as a Venn diagram is a great way to record information and visually organize details to be compared and contrasted in a comparative analysis. Draw a Venn diagram with the headings **Mi primer día de escuela secundaria, Mi primer día de universidad,** and subheadings **Diferencias** and **Similitudes**. Tell students they are going to complete a Venn diagram to compare their first day of high school and their first day of college. Discuss with the whole class how these events are alike and how they are different using some of the terms to signal similarities and differences.

Tema Explain to students that to write a comparative analysis, they will need to use words or phrases that signal similarities **(similitudes)** and differences **(diferencias)**. Model the pronunciation of the words and expressions under **Escribir una composición** with the whole class. Then have volunteers use them in sentences to express the similarities and differences listed in the Venn diagram.

Escritura

Estrategia

Planning and writing a comparative analysis

Writing any kind of comparative analysis requires careful planning. Venn diagrams are useful for organizing your ideas visually before comparing and contrasting people, places, objects, events, or issues. To create a Venn diagram, draw two circles that overlap and label the top of each circle. List the differences between the two elements in the outer rings of the two circles, then list their similarities where the two circles overlap. Review the following example.

Diferencias y similitudes

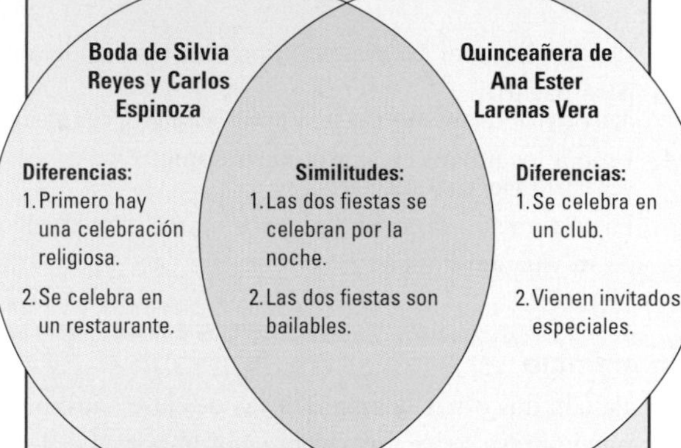

Boda de Silvia Reyes y Carlos Espinoza
Diferencias:
1. Primero hay una celebración religiosa.
2. Se celebra en un restaurante.
Similitudes:
1. Las dos fiestas se celebran por la noche.
2. Las dos fiestas son bailables.
Quinceañera de Ana Ester Larenas Vera
Diferencias:
1. Se celebra en un club.
2. Vienen invitados especiales.

La lista de palabras y expresiones a la derecha puede ayudarte a escribir este tipo de ensayo (*essay*).

Tema

Escribir una composición

Compara una celebración familiar (como una boda, una fiesta de cumpleaños o una graduación) a la que tú asististe recientemente, con otro tipo de celebración. Utiliza palabras y expresiones de la siguiente lista.

Para expresar similitudes

además; también	*in addition; also*
al igual que	*the same as*
como	*as; like*
de la misma manera	*in the same manner (way)*
del mismo modo	*in the same manner (way)*
tan + [*adjetivo*] + como	*as +* [adjective] *+ as*
tanto/a(s) + [*sustantivo*] + como	*as many/much +* [noun] *+ as*

Para expresar diferencias

a diferencia de	*unlike*
a pesar de	*in spite of*
aunque	*although*
en cambio	*on the other hand*
más/menos... que	*more/less . . . than*
no obstante	*nevertheless; however*
por otro lado	*on the other hand*
por el contrario	*on the other hand*
sin embargo	*nevertheless; however*

TEACHING OPTIONS

Proofreading Activity Copy on the board or onto a transparency the following items containing mistakes as a proofreading activity to do with the whole class.

1. **Concepción me deció que habió muchos invitados en su fiesta de cumpleaños.**
2. **¿Cuáles consejos siempre los dan a los recien casados?**
3. **Los invitados trajieron muchos regalos cuando venieron a la fiesta.**
4. **¿Cuál pensaste cuando sabiste las noticias de la boda?**
5. **Viné a la fiesta pero no pasé lo bien.**
6. **¿Qué me deces si te do un regalo bonito?**
7. **Me dijieron que Isabel rompió con Mario. ¿Cuál piensas tú?**

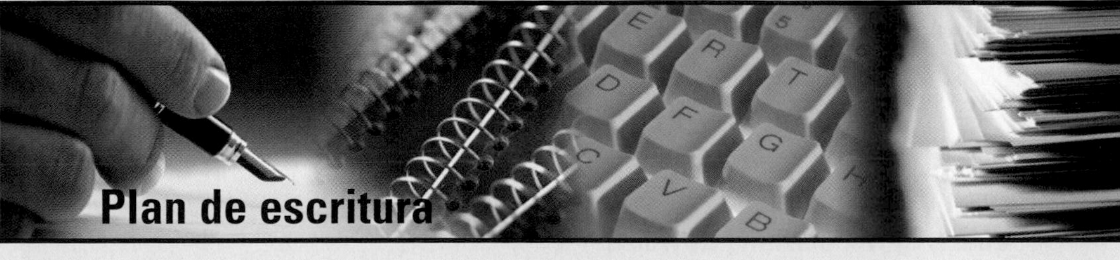

Plan de escritura

1 Ideas y organización
Toma unos minutos para decidir qué celebraciones vas a comparar. Utiliza un diagrama de Venn para anotar las similitudes y las diferencias entre las dos celebraciones.

2 Primer borrador
Utiliza tus notas de **Ideas y organización** para escribir el primer borrador de tu composición. Escribe todo lo que puedas sin consultar en ningún sitio. Después consulta el texto y tus apuntes° de clase. Usa el diccionario como último° recurso.

3 Comentario
Intercambia° tu composición con la de un(a) compañero/a. Lee su borrador y anota sus ideas en un diagrama de Venn. Compara tu diagrama de Venn con el diagrama que él/ella preparó antes. Después:

1. Ofrécele° algunas sugerencias para mejorar su composición. Si ves algunos errores gramaticales u ortográficos°, coméntaselos°.
2. Si él/ella tiene dificultad en realizar un diagrama de Venn basado en tu composición, debes cambiar la organización de la composición. Incorpora nuevas ideas y/o más información para ampliar° la comparación entre las celebraciones.

4 Redacción
Utiliza esta guía para hacer la última revisión antes de escribir tu copia final.

1. Subraya° cada verbo para comprobar° la concordancia° con el sujeto. ¡Cuidado con los verbos irregulares en el pretérito!
2. Revisa la concordancia entre los sustantivos y los adjetivos en cada oración.
3. Comprueba el uso correcto de los pronombres.
4. Revisa la ortografía y la puntuación otra vez con la ayuda de tus **Anotaciones para mejorar la escritura.**

5 Evaluación y progreso
Intercambia tu composición con la de otro/a compañero/a. Lee su composición y escribe una evaluación del contenido°. Utiliza las palabras y expresiones que aprendiste en la **Lección 9**. Cuando tu profesor(a) te devuelva el trabajo, lee sus comentarios y correcciones con cuidado. Anota tus errores más importantes en tu lista de **Anotaciones para mejorar la escritura** en tu **Carpeta de trabajos.**

apuntes *notes* último *last* Intercambia *Exchange* Ofrécele *Offer him/her* ortográficos *spelling* coméntaselos *comment on them* ampliar *expand* Subraya *Underline* comprobar *to check* concordancia *agreement* contenido *contents*

Comentario
- Go over items 1 and 2 with the whole class so peer readers understand their task. Then have pairs exchange compositions. Allow five minutes for reading and making a Venn diagram. Allow five minutes for comments.
- Have students prepare **Redacción** as homework. Ask them to rewrite their drafts incorporating the peer comments and following the directions in **Redacción**. Tell them to prepare a clean copy of their final draft to hand in.

Evaluación y progreso Give the class five minutes to exchange and comment on their final drafts. Then have them hand them in.

Writing Sample Here is a sample composition that would constitute superior writing achievement.

Dos celebraciones bonitas

En mi familia se celebraron dos eventos bonitos este año. Primero, en abril se celebró la boda de mi prima Juana. Después en noviembre se celebró la quinceañera de mi hermana Elena.

Las dos celebraciones tuvieron mucho en común. En las dos ocasiones se celebró una ceremonia religiosa. Hubo muchos parientes y amigos que vinieron a la quinceañera al igual que a la boda. ¡Todos bailamos en las fiestas!

Sin embargo, también hubo diferencias. La boda se celebró en una iglesia por la mañana. En cambio, la quinceañera se celebró en un club por la noche.

Me divertí en las dos celebraciones pero creo que me divertí más en la quinceañera.

EVALUATION: Composición

Criteria	Scale
Content	1 2 3 4
Organization	1 2 3 4
Use of comparisons/contrasts	1 2 3 4
Use of vocabulary	1 2 3 4
Accuracy	1 2 3 4

Scoring	
Excellent	18–20 points
Good	14–17 points
Satisfactory	10–13 points
Unsatisfactory	< 10 points

Section Goals

In **Escuchar** students will:

- use context to infer meaning of unfamiliar words
- answer questions based on a recorded conversation

Instructional Resources
Textbook CD
IRM: Tapescript, p. 93

Estrategia

Script Hoy mi sobrino Gabriel cumplió seis años. Antes de la fiesta, ayudé a mi hermana a decorar la sala con globos de todos los colores, pero ¡qué bulla después!, cuando los niños se pusieron a estallarlos todos. El pastel de cumpleaños estaba riquísimo y cuando Gabriel sopló las velas, apagó las seis. Los otros niños le regalaron un montón de juguetes, y nos divertimos mucho.

Suggestion Have students read the invitation and guess what Rosa and Josefina will be talking about in the recorded conversation.

Ahora escucha

Script JOSEFINA: Rosa, ¿te divertiste anoche en la fiesta?
ROSA: Sí, me divertí más en el aniversario que en la boda. ¡La fiesta estuvo fenomenal! Fue buena idea festejar el aniversario en un restaurante. Así todos pudieron relajarse.
J: En parte, yo lo disfruté porque son una pareja tan linda; qué dicha que estén tan enamorados después de diez años de matrimonio. Me gustaría tener una relación como la de ellos. Y también saberlo celebrar con tanta alegría. ¡Pero qué cantidad de comida y bebida!
R: Es verdad que Margarita y Roberto exageran un poco con sus fiestas, pero son de la clase de gente que le gusta celebrar los eventos de la vida. Y como tienen tantas amistades y dos familias tan grandes....
J: Oye, Rosa, hablando de familia, ¿llegaste a conocer al cuñado de Magali? Es soltero, ¿no? Quise bailar con él pero no me sacó a bailar.
R: Hablas de Rafael. Es muy bien parecido; ¡ese pelo...! Estuve hablando con él después del brindis. Me dijo que no le gusta ni el champán ni el vino; él finge tomar cuando brindan porque no lo soporta. No te sacó a bailar porque él y Susana estaban juntos en la fiesta.
J: De todos modos, aun sin Rafael, bailé toda la noche. Lo pasé muy, pero muy bien.

Escuchar

Estrategia

Guessing the meaning of words through context

When you hear an unfamiliar word, you can often guess its meaning by listening to the words and phrases around it.

To practice this strategy, you will now listen to a paragraph. Jot down the unfamiliar words that you hear. Then listen to the paragraph again and jot down the word or words that are the most useful clues to the meaning of each unfamiliar word.

Margarita Robles de García
y Roberto García Olmos

Piden su presencia en la celebración
del décimo aniversario de bodas
el día 13 de marzo de 2004
con una misa en la Iglesia Virgen del Coromoto
a las 6:30

seguida por cena y baile
en el restaurante El Campanero,
Calle Principal, Las Mercedes
a las 8:30

Preparación

Lee la invitación. ¿De qué crees que van a hablar Rosa y Josefina?

Ahora escucha 

Ahora escucha la conversación entre Josefina y Rosa. Cuando oigas una de las palabras de la columna A, usa el contexto para identificar el sinónimo o la definición en la columna B.

A	B
d festejar	a. conmemoración religiosa de una muerte
c dicha	b. tolera
h bien parecido	c. suerte
g finge (fingir)	d. celebrar
b soporta (soportar)	e. me divertí
e yo lo disfruté (disfrutar)	f. horror
	g. crea una ficción
	h. guapo

Comprensión

¿Cierto o falso?

Lee cada frase e indica si lo que dice es **cierto** o **falso**. Corrige las frases falsas.

1. No invitaron a mucha gente a la fiesta de Margarita y Roberto porque ellos no conocen a muchas personas. Falso. Fueron muchos invitados.
2. Algunos fueron a la fiesta con pareja y otros fueron sin compañero/a. Cierto.
3. Margarita y Roberto decidieron celebrar el décimo aniversario porque no tuvieron ninguna celebración en su matrimonio. Falso. Celebraron el segundo aniversario porque les gustan las fiestas.
4. A Rosa y a Josefina les parece interesante Rafael. Cierto.
5. Josefina se divirtió mucho en la fiesta porque bailó toda la noche con Rafael. Falso. Josefina se divirtió mucho pero bailó con otros, no con Rafael.

Preguntas Answers will vary.

1. ¿Son solteras Rosa y Josefina? ¿Cómo lo sabes?
2. ¿Tienen las chicas una amistad de mucho tiempo con la pareja que celebra su aniversario? ¿Cómo lo sabes?

Prepara un reportaje

Imagina que eres periodista en un día de fiesta en Chile. Vas a escribir un artículo o reportaje para describir ese día y las cosas que hiciste.

1 Escribe un artículo

Escribe un artículo de un día de fiesta o de una celebración que viste en Chile. Usa los **Recursos para la investigación** para obtener información sobre las fiestas nacionales, las celebraciones y los festivales de Chile. Elige° la celebración que más te interesa y busca información y fotos. El artículo puede incluir esta información:

- el nombre de la celebración
- cuándo fue
- cómo celebraron el día festivo, incluyendo la ropa especial que usaron, la comida, la música y el baile
- qué hiciste tú durante la celebración
- fotos de la celebración (en colores, si es posible)

2 Presenta la información

Presenta el artículo a la clase. Puedes fotocopiar el artículo para darles copias a tus compañeros/as. Habla del día festivo en el que participaste. Informa a tus compañeros/as qué se celebró en esta fiesta, que hizo la gente y que hiciste tú en particular. Quieres interesar a toda la clase en la celebración y por lo tanto° es importante explicarles los detalles° y presentarles fotos en colores.

recursos para la investigación

 **Internet** Palabras clave: Chile, festividad(es), festival(es), fiestas religiosas

 **Comunidad** Estudiantes o profesores que son de Chile o que viajaron a Chile, chilenos que viven en la comunidad

 **Biblioteca** Libros de cultura o de folklore, guías turísticas, revistas

 **Otros recursos** Videos turísticos de Chile

Elige *Choose* por lo tanto *therefore* detalles *details*

Section Goals

In **Proyecto** students will:
- pretend they are journalists in Chile
- investigate and write an article about a Chilean festival

Suggestion Students might need a week to complete the project, so at the beginning of that time period, have them open their books to this page and glance over **Proyecto**. Tell them that they are going to use their Spanish skills as they carry out research on festivals in Chile and write an article on a Chilean festival; for example, **Semana Santa** (Holy Week), which takes place in March or April, or **Día de la independencia** (Independence Day), which is September 18.

Escribe un artículo
- Provide students with examples of articles written in Spanish about festivals in Spanish-speaking countries.
- Students can search the Internet for information on Chilean festivals by using the Spanish key words and phrases **fiestas típicas de Chile, fiestas chilenas,** or **festivales chilenos.**

Presenta la información
- Have students present the articles as though they were at a live broadcast of the event.
- Do a few presentations at a time over several days.

EVALUATION: Artículo

Criteria	Scale
Content	1 2 3 4
Organization	1 2 3 4
Use of comparisons/contrasts	1 2 3 4
Visual appeal	1 2 3 4
Oral presentation	1 2 3 4

Scoring	
Excellent	18–20 points
Good	14–17 points
Satisfactory	10–13 points
Unsatisfactory	< 10 points

Section Goal

In **Panorama**, students will read about the geography, culture, and economy of Chile.

Instructional Resources
Transparencies, #5, #6, #37
WB/VM: Workbook, pp. 105–106; Video Activities, pp. 265–266
***Panorama cultural** DVD/Video*
Interactive CD-ROM
IRM: Videoscript, p. 131
Companion website: www.vistahigherlearning.com
Presentations CD-ROM

Suggestion Ask students to look at the map of Chile, or project **Transparency #37**, and to talk about the physical features of the country. Point out that Chile is 2,880 miles from north to south, but no more than 264 miles from east to west. Point out that Chile has a variety of climates.

El país en cifras After reading **Chilenos célebres,** give students more information about O'Higgins. They can probably guess correctly that his father was an Irish immigrant, but should also know that he is considered one of the founders of modern Latin America, along with Simón Bolívar and José de San Martín. These "founding fathers" are called **los próceres**.

¡Increíble pero cierto! Chile lies in a seismically active zone and has developed state-of-the-art seismic engineering in order to address architectural vulnerability and other issues that impact this earthquake-prone region.

Chile

El país en cifras

- **Área:** 756.950 km² (292.259 millas²), *dos veces el área de Montana*
- **Población:** 15.589.000 *Aproximadamente el 80 por ciento de la población es urbana, y la tercera parte° de los chilenos vive en la capital.*
- **Capital:** Santiago de Chile—5.720.000
- **Ciudades principales:** Concepción—356.000, Viña del Mar—326.000, Valparaíso—283.000, Temuco—246.000

SOURCE: Population Division, UN Secretariat

- **Moneda:** peso chileno
- **Idiomas:** español (oficial), mapuche

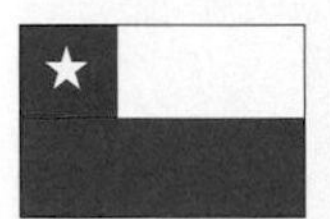

Bandera de Chile

Chilenos célebres

- **Bernardo O'Higgins,** militar° y héroe nacional (1778–1842)
- **Gabriela Mistral,** Premio Nobel de Literatura, 1945; poeta y diplomática (1889–1957)
- **Pablo Neruda,** Premio Nobel de Literatura, 1971; poeta (1904–1973)
- **Isabel Allende,** novelista (1942–)

Pablo Neruda

la tercera parte *a third* **militar** *soldier* **el terremoto** *earthquake* **heridas** *wounded* **hogar** *home*

PERÚ
Pampa del Tamarugal
Cordillera de los Andes
BOLIVIA
Océano Pacífico
Valparaíso
Viña del Mar
Santiago de Chile
Río Maipo
ARGENTINA
Concepción
Temuco
Lago Buenos Aires
Punta Arenas
Océano Atlántico
Estrecho de Magallanes
Isla Grande de Tierra del Fuego

Pescadores de Valparaíso

Palacio de la Moneda en Santiago

Una calle de Santiago

Una celebración en Temuco

Vista de la costa de Viña del Mar

recursos

WB	VM	I CD-ROM	vistahi learning
pp. 105–106	pp. 265–266	Lección 9	

¡Increíble pero cierto!

El terremoto° más grande de la historia tuvo lugar en Chile el 22 de mayo de 1960. Registró una intensidad récord de 9.5 en la escala de Richter. Murieron 2.000 personas, 3.000 resultaron heridas° y 2.000.000 perdieron su hogar°. La geografía del país se modificó notablemente.

TEACHING OPTIONS

Heritage Speakers Invite heritage speakers to prepare a poem by **Pablo Neruda** to read aloud for the class. Many of the **Odas elementales,** such as **"Oda a la alcachofa", "Oda al tomate",** and **"Oda a la cebolla",** are written in simple language. Prepare copies of the poem beforehand and go over unfamiliar vocabulary with the class.

Worth Noting Though Chile is the second smallest Spanish-speaking country in South America (only Ecuador is smaller), it has 2,800 miles of coastline. In the north is the Desert of Atacama, the driest region on earth. Some of the highest peaks in the Andes lie on Chile's border with Argentina. Chile's agricultural region is a valley the size of central California's. The southern archipelago is cool, foggy, and rainy, like the Alaska panhandle.

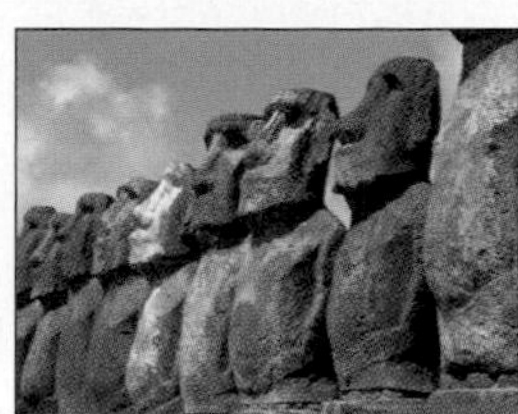

Lugares • La Isla de Pascua

La Isla de Pascua° recibió ese nombre porque los exploradores holandeses° llegaron a la isla por primera vez el día de Pascua de 1722. Ahora es parte del territorio de Chile. La Isla de Pascua es famosa por los *moai*, estatuas enormes que representan personas con rasgos° muy exagerados. Estas estatuas las construyeron los *rapa nui*, los antiguos habitantes de la zona. Todavía no se sabe mucho sobre los *rapa nui*, ni tampoco se sabe por qué decidieron abandonar la isla.

Deportes • Los deportes de invierno

Hay muchos lugares para practicar los deportes de invierno en Chile porque las montañas nevadas de los Andes ocupan gran parte del país. El Parque Nacional de Villarrica, por ejemplo, situado al pie de un volcán y junto a° un lago, es un sitio popular para el esquí y el *snowboard*. Para los que prefieren deportes más extremos, el centro de esquí Valle Nevado organiza excursiones del heli-esquí.

Ciencias • Astronomía

Los observatorios chilenos, situados en los Andes, son lugares excelentes para las observaciones astronómicas. Científicos° de todo el mundo van a Chile para estudiar las estrellas° y otros fenómenos de la galaxia. Hoy día Chile está construyendo nuevos observatorios y telescopios para mejorar las imágenes del universo.

Economía • El vino

La producción de vino comenzó en Chile en el siglo° XVI. Ahora la industria del vino constituye una parte importante de la actividad agrícola del país y la exportación de sus productos está subiendo° cada vez más. Los vinos chilenos reciben el aprecio internacional por su gran variedad, sus ricos y complejos sabores° y su precio moderado. Los más conocidos internacionalmente son los vinos de Aconcagua, de Santiago y de Huasco.

¿Qué aprendiste? Responde a las preguntas con una frase completa.

1. ¿Qué porcentaje (*percentage*) de la población chilena es urbana? El 80 por ciento de la población chilena es urbana.
2. ¿Qué son los *moai*? ¿Dónde están? Los *moai* son estatuas enormes. Están en la Isla de Pascua.
3. ¿Qué deporte extremo ofrece el centro de esquí Valle Nevado? Se practica el *heli-esquí*.
4. ¿Por qué van a Chile científicos de todo el mundo? Porque los observatorios chilenos son excelentes para las observaciones astronómicas.
5. ¿Cuándo comenzó la producción de vino en Chile? Comenzó en el siglo XVI.
6. ¿Por qué reciben los vinos chilenos el aprecio internacional? Lo reciben por su variedad, sus ricos y complejos sabores y su precio moderado.

Conexión Internet Investiga estos temas en el sitio **www.vistahigherlearning.com.**

1. Busca información sobre Pablo Neruda e Isabel Allende. ¿Dónde y cuándo nacieron? ¿Cuáles son algunas de sus obras (*works*)? ¿Cuáles son algunos de los temas de sus obras?
2. Busca información sobre sitios donde los chilenos y los turistas practican deportes de invierno en Chile. Selecciona un sitio y descríbeselo a tu clase.

La Isla de Pascua *Easter Island* holandeses *Dutch* rasgos *features* junto a *beside* Científicos *Scientists* estrellas *stars* siglo *century* subiendo *increasing* complejos sabores *complex flavors*

La Isla de Pascua With its vibrant Polynesian culture, Easter Island is unlike anywhere else in Chile. Located 2,000 miles from the nearest island and 4,000 from the Chilean coast, it is one of the most isolated places on earth. Until the 1960s, it was visited once a year by a Chilean warship bringing supplies. Now there are regular air connections to Santiago.

Los deportes de invierno Remind students that some of the highest mountains in South America lie along the border Chile shares with Argentina. In the south is the **Parque Nacional Torres del Paine**, a national park featuring ice caverns, deep glacial trenches, and other spectacular features.

Astronomía In 1962, the Cerro Tololo Inter-American Observatory was founded as a joint project between Chilean and American astronomers. Since that time, so many other major telescopes have been installed for research purposes that Chile can now claim to have the highest concentration of telescopes in the world.

El vino Invite students to research the wine-growing regions of Chile and to compare them to wine-growing regions in California, France, or other wine-producing areas.

Conexión Internet Students will find supporting Internet activities and links at **www.vistahigherlearning.com**.

TEACHING OPTIONS

Worth Noting The native Mapuche people of southern Chile are a small minority of the Chilean population today, but have maintained a strong cultural identity since the time of their first contact with Europeans. In fact, they resisted conquest so well that it was only in the late 19th century that the government of Chile could assert actual sovereignty over the region south of the river Bío-bío. However, the majority of Chileans are of European descent. Chilean Spanish is much less infused with indigenous lexical items than is the Spanish of countries such as Guatemala and Mexico, where the larger indigenous population has made a greater impact on the language.

Instructional Resources
Vocabulary CD
Lab Manual, p. 54
*Lab CD/MP3 **Lección 9***
IRM: Tapescript, pp. 40–44
*Testing Program: **Pruebas**, pp. 97–108; **Exámenes**, pp. 217–227*
Testing Program Audio CD
Test Files CD-ROM

Las celebraciones

el aniversario (de bodas)	*(wedding) anniversary*
la boda	*wedding*
el cumpleaños	*birthday*
el día de fiesta	*holiday*
la fiesta	*party*
el/la invitado/a	*guest*
la Navidad	*Christmas*
la quinceañera	*young woman's fifteenth birthday celebration*
la sorpresa	*surprise*
brindar	*to toast* (drink)
celebrar	*to celebrate*
cumplir años	*to have a birthday*
dejar una propina	*to leave a tip*
divertirse (e:ie)	*to have fun*
invitar	*to invite*
pagar la cuenta	*to pay the bill*
pasarlo bien/mal	*to have a good/bad time*
regalar	*to give* (a gift)
reírse (e:i)	*to laugh*
relajarse	*to relax*
sonreír (e:i)	*to smile*
sorprender	*to surprise*

Los postres y otras comidas

la botella (de vino)	*bottle (of wine)*
el champán	*champagne*
los dulces	*sweets; candy*
el flan (de caramelo)	*baked (caramel) custard*
la galleta	*cookie*
el helado	*ice cream*
el pastel (de chocolate)	*(chocolate) cake; pie*
el postre	*dessert*

Las relaciones personales

la amistad	*friendship*
el amor	*love*
el divorcio	*divorce*
el estado civil	*marital status*
el matrimonio	*marriage*
la pareja	(married) *couple; partner*
el/la recién casado/a	*newlywed*
casarse (con)	*to get married (to)*
comprometerse (con)	*to get engaged (to)*
divorciarse (de)	*to get divorced (from)*
enamorarse (de)	*to fall in love (with)*
llevarse bien/mal (con)	*to get along well/ badly (with)*
odiar	*to hate*
romper (con)	*to break up (with)*
salir (con)	*to go out (with); to date*
separarse (de)	*to separate (from)*
tener una cita	*to have a date; to have an appointment*
casado/a	*married*
divorciado/a	*divorced*
juntos/as	*together*
separado/a	*separated*
soltero/a	*single*
viudo/a	*widower/widow*

Las etapas de la vida

la adolescencia	*adolescence*
la edad	*age*
el estado civil	*marital status*
las etapas de la vida	*the stages of life*
la juventud	*youth*
la madurez	*maturity; middle age*
la muerte	*death*
el nacimiento	*birth*
la niñez	*childhood*
la vejez	*old age*
cambiar (de)	*to change*
graduarse (de/en)	*to graduate (from/in)*
jubilarse	*to retire (from work)*
nacer	*to be born*

Palabras adicionales

la alegría	*happiness*
el beso	*kiss*
conmigo	*with me*
contigo	*with you*

Expresiones útiles	*See page 275.*

recursos

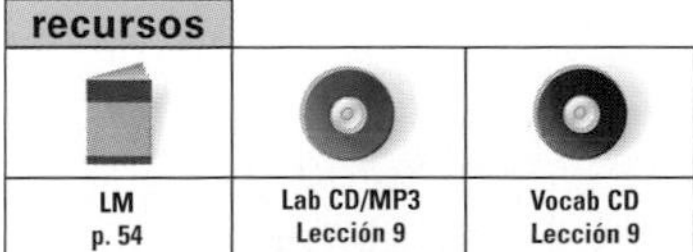

LM
p. 54
Lab CD/MP3
Lección 9
Vocab CD
Lección 9

En el consultorio 10

Communicative Goals

You will learn how to:

- Describe how you feel physically
- Talk about health and medical conditions

A PRIMERA VISTA

- **¿Cuál de ellas es la doctora? ¿La mujer de pelo largo o de pelo corto?**
- **¿En qué etapa de la vida está la doctora, la vejez o la madurez?**
- **¿Es una de ellas mayor que la otra o son aproximadamente de la misma edad?**

Lesson Goals

In **Lección 10** students will be introduced to the following:

- names of parts of the body
- health-related terms
- imperfect tense
- uses of the preterite and imperfect tenses
- impersonal constructions with **se**
- using **se** for unplanned events
- forming adverbs using [*adjective*] + **–mente**
- common adverbs and adverbial expressions
- activating background knowledge
- mastering the simple past tenses
- writing about an illness or accident
- listening for specific information
- writing and delivering a speech on the Costa Rican political or social system for a conference
- cultural, geographic, and economic information about Costa Rica

A primera vista Here are some additional questions you can ask based on the photo: **¿Cuándo conociste a tu médico/a? ¿Vas mucho a verlo/a? ¿Estuviste en su oficina la semana pasada? ¿El año pasado? ¿Cuándo? ¿Cuáles son las mejores comidas para sentirte bien? ¿Cuáles son las peores?**

INSTRUCTIONAL RESOURCES

Workbook/Video Manual: WB Activities, pp. 109–122
Laboratory Manual: Lab Activities, pp. 55–60
Workbook/Video Manual: Video Activities, pp. 231–232; pp. 267–268
Instructor's Resource Manual: **Vocabulario adicional**, p. 188; **¡Inténtalo!** & **Práctica** Answers, pp. 213–214; **Fotonovela** Translations, p. 144; Textbook CD Tapescript, p. 94; Lab CDs Tapescript, pp. 45–48; **Fotonovela** Videoscript, p. 113; **Panorama cultural** Videoscript, p. 132
Info Gap Activities Booklet, pp. 37–40
Overhead Transparencies: #3, #4, #38, #39
Lab Audio CD/MP3 **Lección 10**
Panorama cultural DVD/Video
Fotonovela DVD/Video
Testing Program, pp. 109–120
Testing Program Audio CD
Test Files CD-ROM
Companion website
Presentations CD-ROM
Textbook CD
Vocabulary CD
Interactive CD-ROM
Video CD-ROM
Web-SAM

Section Goals

In **Contextos**, students will learn and practice:

- names of parts of the body
- vocabulary for talking about illnesses and accidents
- vocabulary associated with medical visits

Instructional Resources
Transparency #38
Textbook CD
Vocabulary CD
WB/VM: Workbook, pp. 109–110
Lab Manual, p. 55
Lab CD/MP3 ***Lección 10***
IRM: ***Vocab. adicional****, p. 188;*
Práctica *Answers, pp. 213–214;*
Tapescript, pp. 45–48; p. 94
Info Gap Activities Booklet, pp. 37–38
Interactive CD-ROM
Companion website: www.vistahigherlearning.com
Presentations CD-ROM

Suggestions

- Using cognate vocabulary, pointing to parts of your body, and miming procedures, talk about a hospital visit, real or imaginary. Use the imperfect as input before it's presented in **Estructura 10.1.** Ex: **Recientemente fui al hospital. Me dolían la cabeza, la garganta, los ojos, la nariz... El médico me puso una inyección con antibióticos.** Ask comprehension questions and point to body parts. Ex: **¿Me dolía la nariz? ¿el brazo? ¿la cabeza?**
- Project **Transparency #38.** Have students refer to the scene and the vocabulary boxes as you give yes-no statements about the new vocabulary. Ex: **¿Sí o no? La enfermera le toma la temperatura a la paciente. (Sí.) La doctora le pone una inyección al hombre. (No.)** Then ask volunteers to describe what's going on in the scene, using as much of the new vocabulary as possible.

En el consultorio

Más vocabulario

la clínica	*clinic*
el consultorio	*doctor's office*
el/la dentista	*dentist*
el examen médico	*physical exam*
la farmacia	*pharmacy*
el hospital	*hospital*
la operación	*operation*
la sala de emergencia(s)	*emergency room*
el cuerpo	*body*
la muela	*molar*
el oído	*(sense of) hearing; inner ear*
el accidente	*accident*
la salud	*health*
el síntoma	*symptom*
caerse	*to fall (down)*
darse con	*to bump into; to run into*
doler (o:ue)	*to hurt*
enfermarse	*to get sick*
estar enfermo/a	*to be sick*
lastimarse (el pie)	*to injure (one's foot)*
poner una inyección	*to give an injection*
recetar	*to prescribe*
romperse (la pierna)	*to break (one's leg)*
sacar(se) una muela	*to have a tooth removed*
sufrir una enfermedad	*to suffer an illness*
torcerse (o:ue) (el tobillo)	*to sprain (one's ankle)*
toser	*to cough*

Variación léxica

gripe ⟷ gripa (*Col., Gua., Méx.*)
resfriado ⟷ catarro (*Cuba, Esp., Gua.*)
sala de emergencia(s) ⟷ sala de urgencias (*Arg., Esp., Méx.*)
romperse ⟷ quebrarse (*Arg., Gua.*)

Síntomas y condiciones médicas

el dolor (de cabeza)	*(head)ache; pain*
la gripe	*flu*
la infección	*infection*
el resfriado	*cold*
la tos	*cough*
congestionado/a	*congested; stuffed up*
embarazada	*pregnant*
grave	*grave; serious*
mareado/a	*dizzy; nauseated*
médico/a	*medical*
saludable	*healthy*
sano/a	*healthy*
ser alérgico/a (a)	*to be allergic (to)*
tener dolor (m.)	*to have pain*
tener fiebre	*to have a fever*

recursos

TEXT CD Lección 10	WB pp. 109–110	LM p. 55	Lab CD/MP3 Lección 10	I CD-ROM Lección 10	Vocab CD Lección 10

TEACHING OPTIONS

TPR Play a game of Simon Says (**Simón dice...**). Write **señalen** on the board and explain that it means *point.* Start by saying: **Simón dice... señalen la nariz.** Students are to touch their nose and keep their hand there until instructed to do otherwise. Work through various parts of the body. Be sure to give instructions without saying **Simón dice...** once in a while.

Variación léxica Point out differences in vocabulary related to health, as well as some false cognates students should be aware of. **Embarazada** means *pregnant*, not *embarrassed.* You may also want to present **constipado/a** and explain that it does not mean *constipated*, but rather *congested, stuffed up.*

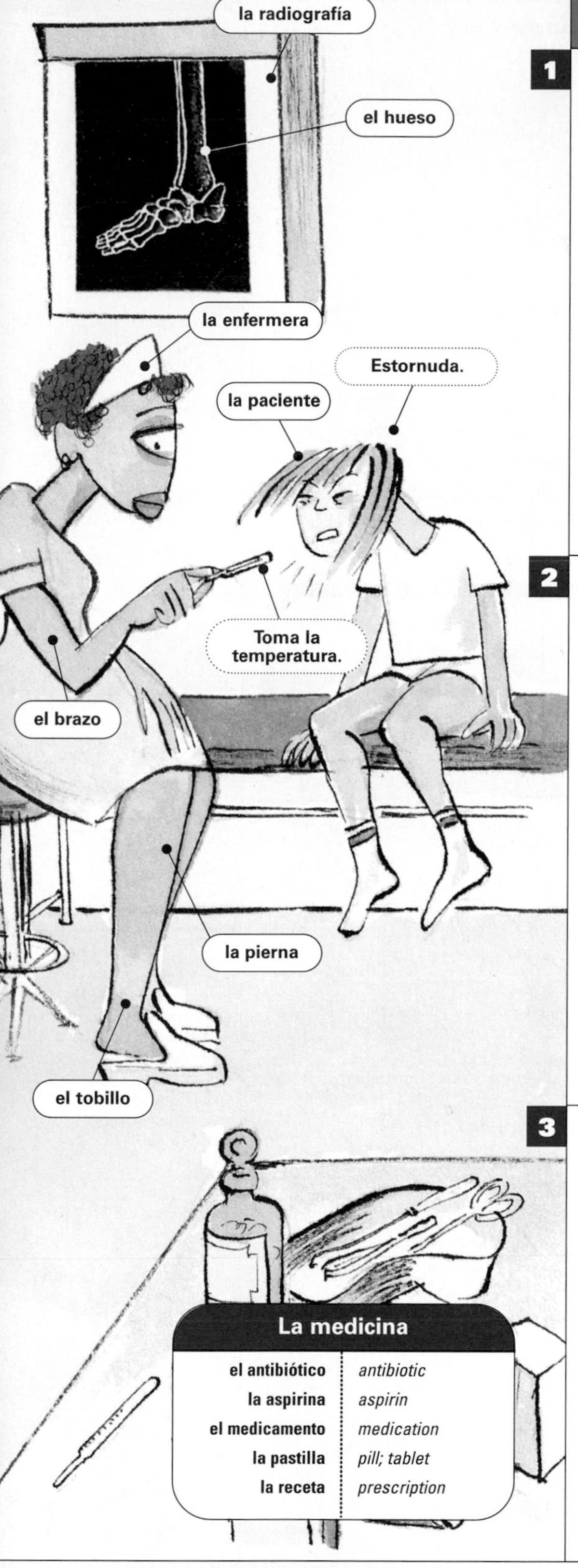

La medicina

el antibiótico	*antibiotic*
la aspirina	*aspirin*
el medicamento	*medication*
la pastilla	*pill; tablet*
la receta	*prescription*

Práctica

1 **Escuchar** Escucha las frases y selecciona la respuesta más adecuada.

a. Tengo dolor de cabeza y fiebre.
b. No fui a la clase porque estaba enfermo.
c. Me caí la semana pasada jugando al tenis.
d. Debes ir a la farmacia.
e. Porque tengo gripe.
f. Sí, tengo mucha tos por las noches.
g. Lo llevaron directamente a la sala de emergencia.
h. No sé. Todavía tienen que tomarme la temperatura.

1. c
2. e
3. g
4. d
5. f
6. h
7. a
8. b

2 **Completar** Completa las siguientes frases con una palabra de la misma familia de la palabra subrayada. Usa la forma correcta de cada palabra.

1. Cuando oyes algo, usas el ___oído___, que es uno de los cinco sentidos.
2. Cuando te enfermas, te sientes ___enfermo/a___ y necesitas ir al consultorio para ver a la ___enfermera___.
3. El médico examina tu salud durante tu ___examen médico___ anual.
4. ¿Alguien ___estornudó___? Creo que oí un estornudo (*sneeze*).
5. No puedo arrodillarme (*kneel down*) porque me lastimé la ___rodilla___ en un accidente de coche.
6. ¿Vas al ___consultorio___ para consultar al médico?
7. Si te rompes (*break*) un diente, vas al ___dentista___.
8. Si tienes una ___infección___ de garganta, tu garganta está infectada.

3 **Contestar** Mira el dibujo de las páginas 298 y 299 y contesta las preguntas. Answers will vary.

1. ¿Qué hace la doctora?
2. ¿Qué hay en la pared?
3. ¿Qué hace la enfermera?
4. ¿Qué hace el paciente?
5. ¿A quién le duele la garganta?
6. ¿Qué hace la paciente?
7. ¿Qué tiene la paciente?
8. ¿Quién toma la temperatura?

1 Suggestion Have students check their answers as you go over **Actividad 1** with the whole class.

1 Tapescript 1. ¿Cuándo te caíste? 2. ¿Por qué vas al médico? 3. ¿Adónde llevaron a Juan después del accidente? 4. ¿Adónde debo ir para conseguir estas pastillas? 5. ¿Tienes mucha tos? 6. ¿Tienes fiebre? 7. ¿Cuáles son sus síntomas, señor? 8. Ayer no te vi en la clase de biología. ¿Por qué? *Textbook CD*

2 Suggestion Have students say which part of speech the underlined word is and which part of speech the word they write on the blank is.

2 Expansion Have students write two additional sentences following the pattern of those in the activity. Their partner has to come up with the correct missing word.

3 Expansion Ask additional questions about the doctor's office scene for volunteers to answer. Ex: **¿Quiénes trabajan en el consultorio? (la médica/doctora, la enfermera) ¿Qué hace la chica? (Estornuda.)**

TEACHING OPTIONS

Game Play **Concentración**. On eight cards, write names for parts of the body or items found in a doctor's office. On another eight cards, draw or paste a picture that matches each description. Place the cards face-down in four rows of four. In pairs, students select two cards. If the two cards match, the pair keeps them. If the two cards don't match, students replace them in their original position. The group with the most cards at the end wins.

Heritage Speakers Ask heritage speakers to describe a visit they made to a doctor's office. Verify comprehension by having students relate what was said. On the board write any nonactive vocabulary that the native speakers may use, such as **auscultar los pulmones, sacar la lengua, tomar la presión arterial, la sangre,** and so forth.

4 Suggestion Point out that there are often several parts of the body that may be associated with each activity. Encourage students to list as many as they can.

4 Expansion Say parts of the body and ask pairs of students to associate them with as many activities as they can.

5 Expansions
- Write the three categories with their point totals on the board. Ask for a show of hands for those who fall into the different groups based on their point totals. Analyze the trends of the class—are your students healthy or unhealthy?
- Ask for volunteers from each of the three groups to explain whether they think the results of the survey are accurate or not. Ask them to give examples based on their own eating, exercise, and other health habits.

Note: At this point you may want to present **Vocabulario adicional: Más vocabulario para el consultorio**, from the IRM.

4

Asociaciones Trabajen en parejas para identificar las partes del cuerpo que ustedes asocian con las siguientes actividades. Sigan el modelo. Answers will vary.

modelo

nadar

Estudiante 1: Usamos los brazos para nadar.

Estudiante 2: Usamos las piernas también.

1. hablar por teléfono
2. tocar el piano
3. correr en el parque
4. escuchar música
5. ver una película
6. toser
7. llevar zapatos
8. comprar perfume
9. estudiar biología
10. comer lomo a la plancha

AYUDA

Remember that in Spanish, body parts are usually referred to with an article and not a possessive:
Me duelen los pies.
The idea of "my" is expressed by the indirect object pronoun **me.**

5

Cuestionario Contesta el cuestionario seleccionando las respuestas que reflejen mejor tus experiencias. Suma (*Add*) los puntos de cada respuesta y anota el resultado. Después, con el resto de la clase, compara y analiza los resultados del cuestionario y comenta lo que dicen de la salud y de los hábitos de todo el grupo. Answers will vary.

¿Tienes buena salud?

27-30 puntos	Salud y hábitos excelentes
23-26 puntos	Salud y hábitos buenos
22 puntos o menos	Salud y hábitos problemáticos

1. **¿Con qué frecuencia te enfermas? (resfriados, gripe, etc.)**
   Cuatro veces por año o más. (1 punto)
   Dos o tres veces por año. (2 puntos)
   Casi nunca. (3 puntos)
2. **¿Con qué frecuencia tienes dolores de estómago o problemas digestivos?**
   Con mucha frecuencia. (1 punto)
   A veces. (2 puntos)
   Casi nunca. (3 puntos)
3. **¿Con qué frecuencia sufres de dolores de cabeza?**
   Frecuentemente. (1 punto)
   A veces. (2 puntos)
   Casi nunca. (3 puntos)
4. **¿Comes verduras y frutas?**
   No, casi nunca como verduras ni frutas. (1 punto)
   Sí, a veces. (2 puntos)
   Sí, todos los días. (3 puntos)
5. **¿Eres alérgico/a a algo?**
   Sí, a muchas cosas. (1 punto)
   Sí, a algunas cosas. (2 puntos)
   No. (3 puntos)
6. **¿Haces ejercicios aeróbicos?**
   No, casi nunca hago ejercicios aeróbicos. (1 punto)
   Sí, a veces. (2 puntos)
   Sí, con frecuencia. (3 puntos)
7. **¿Con qué frecuencia te haces un examen médico?**
   Nunca o casi nunca. (1 punto)
   Cada dos años. (2 puntos)
   Cada año y/o antes de practicar un deporte. (3 puntos)
8. **¿Con qué frecuencia vas al dentista?**
   Nunca voy al dentista. (1 punto)
   Sólo cuando me duele una muela. (2 puntos)
   Por lo menos una vez por año. (3 puntos)
9. **¿Qué comes normalmente por la mañana?**
   No como nada por la mañana. (1 punto)
   Tomo una bebida dietética. (2 puntos)
   Como cereal y fruta. (3 puntos)
10. **¿Con qué frecuencia te sientes mareado/a?**
    Frecuentemente. (1 punto)
    A veces. (2 puntos)
    Casi nunca. (3 puntos)

NOTA CULTURAL

Al igual que (*just like*) en Costa Rica (ver **Panorama**, pp. 326-327), en España, México y Argentina los servicios médicos son gratis (*free*). En España, por ejemplo, se paga el servicio médico con fondos (*funds*) públicos.

TEACHING OPTIONS

Pairs In pairs, students interview each other using the questions from the realia piece in **Actividad 5**. However, students are not limited to the choices given for answers if they can make other statements that are true for them. Then have students present the results of their interview in class. Does the interviewer think that his or her partner is in great health, relatively good health, or poor health?

Game Play a modified version of Twenty Questions. Ask a volunteer to think of a part of the body. Other students get one chance each to ask a yes-no question until someone guesses the item correctly. Limit attempts to ten questions per item. You may want to write some phrases on the board to cue students' questions. Encourage students to guess by associating activities with various parts of the body.

Comunicación

6 **¿Qué le pasó?** Trabajen en un grupo de dos o tres personas. Hablen de lo que les pasó y de cómo se sienten las personas que aparecen en los dibujos. Answers will vary.

1. Adela

2. Francisco

3. Pilar

4. Pedro

5. Cristina

6. Félix

7 **Un accidente** Cuéntale (*Tell*) a la clase de un accidente o una enfermedad que tuviste. Incluye información que conteste las siguientes preguntas. Answers will vary.

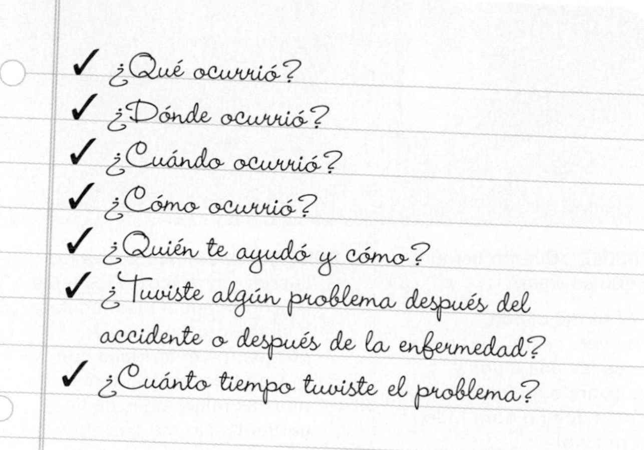

✓ ¿Qué ocurrió?
✓ ¿Dónde ocurrió?
✓ ¿Cuándo ocurrió?
✓ ¿Cómo ocurrió?
✓ ¿Quién te ayudó y cómo?
✓ ¿Tuviste algún problema después del accidente o después de la enfermedad?
✓ ¿Cuánto tiempo tuviste el problema?

8 **Crucigrama (*Crossword*)** Tu profesor(a) les va a dar a ti y a tu compañero/a un crucigrama incompleto. Tú tienes las palabras que necesita tu compañero/a y él/ella tiene las palabras que tú necesitas. Tienen que darse pistas (*clues*) para completarlo. No pueden decir la palabra necesaria; deben utilizar definiciones, ejemplos y frases incompletas.

modelo

10 horizontal: La usamos para hablar.
14 vertical: Es el médico que examina los dientes.

Successful Language Learning Tell your students to imagine situations in which they commonly see a doctor and to think about what they would say in Spanish in each of these situations.

6 Expansions
- Ask students to list the various possibilities of what happened to these people and how they feel. Have them name possible treatments for each.
- Bring in magazine pictures related to illness, medicine, and medical appointments. Have students describe what is going on in the images.

7 Suggestion Talk about an illness or accident you may have had.

7 Expansion To practice more verb forms, have students talk about an illness or accident that someone they know may have had.

8 Suggestion Divide the class into pairs and distribute the Info Gap Handouts from the Info Gap Activities Booklet that correspond to this activity. Give the students ten minutes to complete this activity.

8 Expansion Have pairs use words from the crossword to role-play a visit to a doctor's office. One partner can play the role of doctor and the other that of patient.

TEACHING OPTIONS

Small Groups Prepare four different descriptions of a fantastical beast or alien. Ex: **Tiene dos narices y tres ojos. Los ojos están encima de la cabeza,** and so forth. Read each description line by line to groups of three or four. Members of the group take turns drawing the description on the board. Did they get the description right?

Extra Practice Have students write physical descriptions of themselves. Students should use as much vocabulary from this lesson as they can. Collect the papers and read the descriptions aloud. The rest of the class has to guess who is being described. Write **Mido ____ pies y ____ pulgadas** on the board and explain what it means.

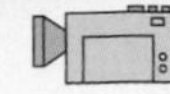

Section Goals

In **Fotonovela** students will:

- receive comprehensible input from free-flowing discourse
- learn functional phrases that preview lesson grammatical structures

Instructional Resources
WB/VM: Video Activities, pp. 231–232
***Fotonovela** DVD/Video (Start 00:52:19)*
Video CD-ROM
*IRM: **Fotonovela** Translations, p. 144, Videoscript, p. 113*
Interactive CD-ROM

Video Recap: Lección 9
Before doing this **Fotonovela** section, review the previous one with this activity.

1. ¿De quién fue el cumpleaños? (de Maite)
2. ¿Cómo supo doña Rita del cumpleaños? (se lo dijo don Francisco)
3. ¿Qué trajo doña Rita de comer para celebrar el cumpleaños? (flan, pastel de chocolate con helado y vino)
4. ¿Quién no tomó vino? ¿Por qué no? (don Francisco, porque es el conductor)

Video Synopsis While on the bus, Javier injures his foot. Don Francisco tells the group they are close to the clinic of a friend of his, Doctora Márquez. Doctora Márquez determines that Javier simply twisted his ankle. She prescribes some pain medication and sends Javier and Don Francisco on their way.

Suggestions

- Have your students scan the **Fotonovela** for words and expressions related to health care. Then have them predict what will happen in this episode.
- Review the predictions, asking a few questions that guide students in summarizing this episode.

¡Uf! ¡Qué dolor!

NATIONAL STANDARDS communication cultures

Don Francisco y Javier van a la clínica de la doctora Márquez.

PERSONAJES

INÉS

DON FRANCISCO

JAVIER

DRA. MÁRQUEZ

1

JAVIER Estoy aburrido... tengo ganas de dibujar. Con permiso.

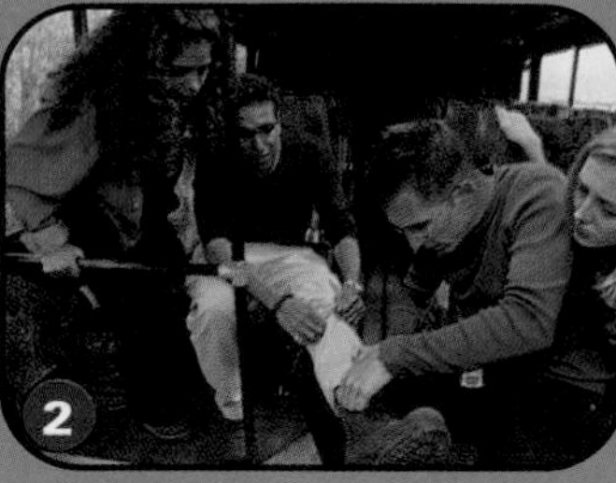

2

INÉS ¡Javier! ¿Qué te pasó?

JAVIER ¡Ay! ¡Uf! ¡Qué dolor! ¡Creo que me rompí el tobillo!

3

DON FRANCISCO No te preocupes, Javier. Estamos cerca de la clínica donde trabaja la doctora Márquez, mi amiga.

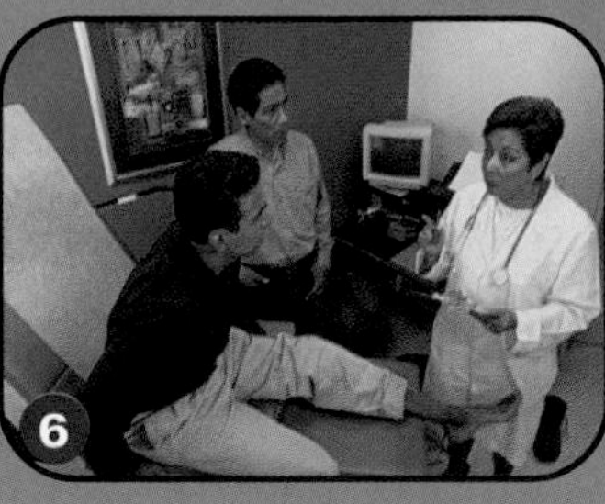

6

DRA. MÁRQUEZ ¿Cuánto tiempo hace que se cayó?

JAVIER Ya se me olvidó... déjeme ver... este... eran más o menos las dos o dos y media cuando me caí... o sea hace más de una hora. ¡Me duele mucho!

DRA. MÁRQUEZ Bueno, vamos a sacarle una radiografía. Queremos ver si se rompió uno de los huesos del pie.

7

DON FRANCISCO Sabes, Javier, cuando era chico yo les tenía mucho miedo a los médicos. Visitaba mucho al doctor porque me enfermaba con mucha frecuencia... tenía muchas infecciones de la garganta. No me gustaban las inyecciones ni las pastillas. Una vez me rompí la pierna jugando al fútbol...

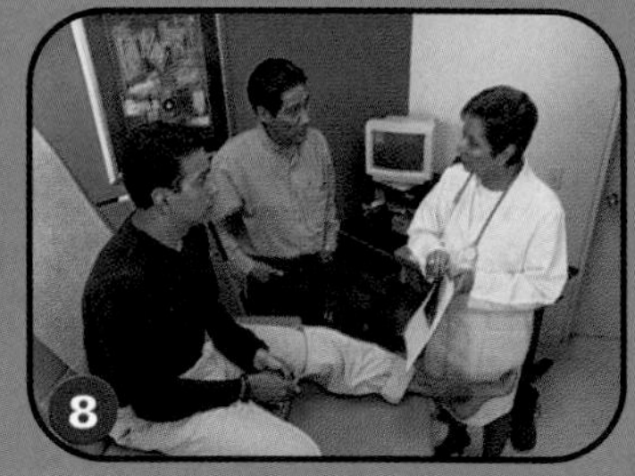

8

JAVIER ¡Doctora! ¿Qué dice? ¿Está roto el tobillo?

DRA. MÁRQUEZ Tranquilo, le tengo buenas noticias, Javier. No está roto el tobillo. Apenas está torcido.

recursos

V CD-ROM Lección 10	VM pp. 231–232	I CD-ROM Lección 10

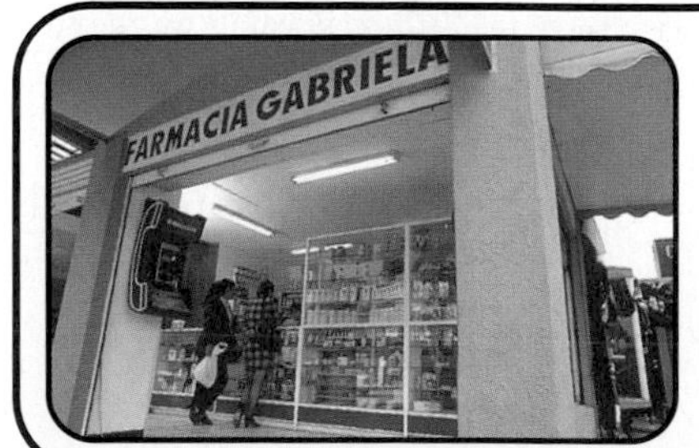

TEACHING OPTIONS

Video Tips General suggestions for using video clips in the classroom can be found on page IAE-12 of this Instructor's Annotated Edition.
¡Uf! ¡Qué dolor! Play the **¡Uf! ¡Qué dolor!** segment of this video module and have your students jot down key words that they hear. Then have them work in small groups to prepare a brief plot summary based on their lists of key words. Play the segment again and have students return to their groups to refine their summaries. Finally, discuss the plot of this episode with the entire class and correct any errors of fact or sequencing that students may have.

JAVIER ¿Tengo dolor? Sí, mucho. ¿Dónde? En el tobillo. ¿Tengo fiebre? No lo creo. ¿Estoy mareado? Un poco. ¿Soy alérgico a algún medicamento? No. ¿Embarazada? Definitivamente NO.

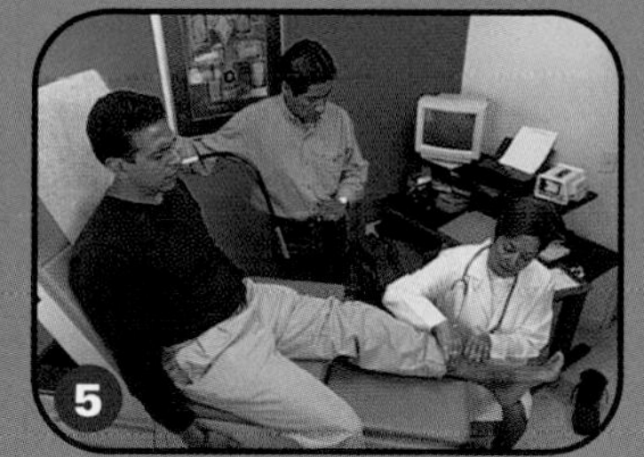

DRA. MÁRQUEZ ¿Cómo se lastimó el pie?

JAVIER Me caí cuando estaba en el autobús.

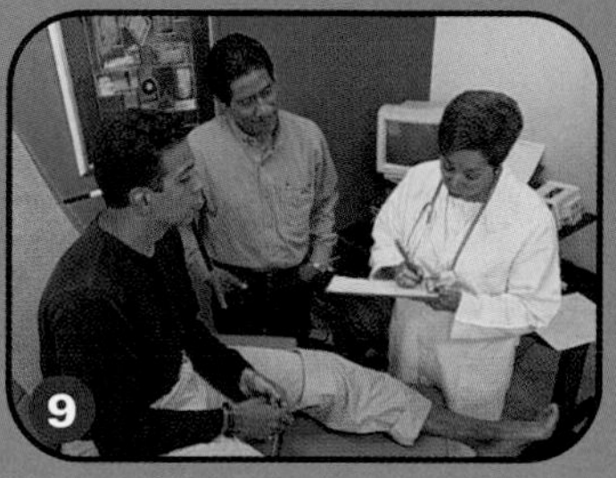

JAVIER Pero, ¿voy a poder ir de excursión con mis amigos?

DRA. MÁRQUEZ Creo que sí. Pero debe descansar y no caminar mucho durante un par de días. Le receto unas pastillas para el dolor.

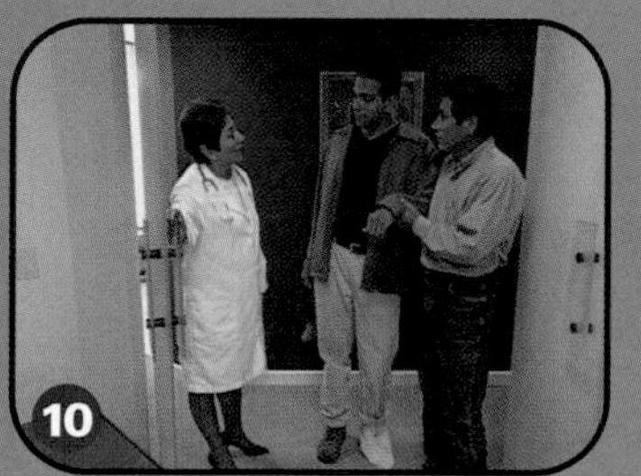

DRA. MÁRQUEZ Adiós, Francisco. Adiós, Javier. ¡Cuidado! ¡Buena suerte en las montañas!

Enfoque cultural La medicina en los países hispanos

Varios factores económicos y culturales hacen el sistema de sanidad de los países hispanos diferente del sistema estadounidense. En las farmacias, muchas veces las personas le consultan sus síntomas al farmacéutico y él mismo (*he himself*) les da el medicamento, sin necesidad de recetas médicas. La influencia de las culturas indígenas se refleja en la importancia que tienen los curanderos (*folk medicine practitioners*) en muchas regiones. Éstos combinan hierbas medicinales y elementos religiosos para curar las enfermedades.

Expresiones útiles

Discussing medical conditions

▶ **¿Cómo se lastimó el pie?**
How did you hurt your foot?
▷ **Me caí en el autobús.**
I fell when I was on the bus.

▶ **¿Te duele el tobillo?**
Does your ankle hurt? (fam.)
▶ **¿Le duele el tobillo?**
Does your ankle hurt? (form.)
▷ **Sí, (me duele) mucho.**
Yes, (it hurts) a lot.

▶ **¿Es usted alérgico/a a algún medicamento?**
Are you allergic to any medication?
▷ **Sí, soy alérgico/a a la penicilina.**
Yes, I'm allergic to penicillin.

▶ **¿Está roto el tobillo?**
Is my ankle broken?
▷ **No está roto. Apenas está torcido.**
It's not broken. It's just twisted.

▶ **¿Te enfermabas frecuentemente?**
Did you get sick frequently? (fam.)
▷ **Sí, me enfermaba frecuentemente.**
Yes, I used to get sick frequently.
▷ **Tenía muchas infecciones.**
I used to get a lot of infections.

Other expressions

▶ **hace** + [*period of time*] + **que** + [*present tense*]:
▶ **¿Cuánto tiempo hace que te duele?**
How long has it been hurting?
▷ **Hace una hora que me duele.**
It's been hurting for an hour.

▶ **hace** + [*period of time*] + **que** + [*preterite*]:
▶ **¿Cuánto tiempo hace que se cayó?**
How long ago did you fall?
▷ **Me caí hace más de una hora./Hace más de una hora que me caí.**
I fell more than an hour ago.

Suggestion Ask students to read the **Fotonovela** conversation in groups of four. Ask one or two groups to present the episode to the class.

Expresiones útiles Point out the verb forms **enfermaba, enfermabas,** and **tenía**. Explain that these are imperfect tense forms, used here to talk about habitual events in the past. Point out the adverb **frecuentemente** and tell the class that many adverbs end in **–mente**. In frame 6 of the **Fotonovela**, point out the phrase **se me olvidó** and inform the class that **se** constructions are often used to talk about unplanned events. Tell your students that they will learn more about these concepts in **Estructura**.

Successful Language Learning Tell your students that before traveling to a Spanish-speaking country, they should make a list of their allergies and medical needs and learn how to say them in Spanish.

TEACHING OPTIONS

Enfoque cultural Explain to the class that most Spanish-speaking countries, including Spain, Mexico, and Costa Rica, offer free health care to all citizens through systems of state-run hospitals and clinics. Point out that residents of large, cosmopolitan areas generally have access to a wide variety of medical specialists and to the latest advances in health care. The same cannot usually be said about people who live in rural areas. Although many residents of rural areas have access to doctors, hospitals, and public health clinics, some, either by necessity or by choice, seek medical assistance from **curanderos** (*folk medicine practitioners*) and **parteras** (*midwives*).

1 Expansion Give these additional items to the class: **6. Javier tiene el tobillo roto. (Falso. El tobillo no está roto. Está torcido.) 7. La doctora Márquez le receta un poco de penicilina. (Falso. Le receta unas pastillas para el dolor.)**

2 Expansion Give these additional items to the class: **7. Le voy a recetar unas pastillas para el dolor. (Dra. Márquez) 8. Cuando era niño no me gustaba mucho ir al doctor. (don Francisco)**

3 Suggestion Divide the class into small groups and distribute six strips of paper to each. Each strip should contain one of the sentences in the activity. Distribute the strips to each group in random order so that every member receives at least two sentences. Have groups put the sentences in correct order and then return them to a group representative, who will read them aloud.

4 Possible Response
E1: Buenos días. ¿Cómo se lastimó?
E2: Bueno, doctor, me caí en casa.
E1: ¿Y cuánto tiempo hace que se cayó?
E2: Hace más de dos horas. Creo que me rompí el dedo.
E1: ¿Ah, sí? ¿Le duele mucho?
E2: Me duele muchísimo, doctor. Y estoy mareada.
E1: Bueno, le voy a sacar una radiografía primero.
E2: ¿Está roto el dedo?
E1: No se preocupe, señorita. No está roto el dedo. Como le duele mucho, le receto unas pastillas para el dolor.
E2: Sí, doctor. Gracias.

The Affective Dimension Point out to your students that they are more likely to feel anxious about speaking Spanish during a medical emergency. Tell them to rehearse phrases that they might use in such a situation and to visualize themselves remaining calm.

Reacciona a la fotonovela

1

¿Cierto o falso? Decide si lo que dicen las siguientes frases sobre Javier es **cierto** o **falso**. Corrige las frases falsas.

	Cierto	Falso	
1. Está aburrido y tiene ganas de hacer algo creativo.	✓	❍	
2. Cree que se rompió la rodilla.	❍	✓	Cree que se rompió el tobillo.
3. Se lastimó cuando se cayó en el autobús.	✓	❍	
4. Es alérgico a dos medicamentos.	❍	✓	No es alérgico a ningún medicamento.
5. No está mareado pero sí tiene un poco de fiebre.	❍	✓	Está un poco mareado pero no tiene fiebre.

2

Identificar Identifica quién puede decir las siguientes frases.

1. Hace años me rompí la pierna cuando estaba jugando al fútbol. don Francisco
2. Hace más de una hora que me rompí la pierna. Me duele muchísimo. Javier
3. Tengo que sacarle una radiografía. No sé si se rompió uno de los huesos del pie. Dra. Márquez
4. No hay problema, vamos a ver a mi amiga, la doctora Márquez. don Francisco
5. Bueno, parece que el tobillo no está roto. Qué bueno, ¿no? Dra. Márquez
6. No sé si voy a poder ir de excursión con el grupo. Javier

DRA. MÁRQUEZ

DON FRANCISCO

JAVIER

3

Ordenar Pon los siguientes eventos en el orden correcto.

a. La doctora le saca una radiografía. 4
b. La doctora le receta unas pastillas para el dolor. 6
c. Javier se lastima el tobillo en el autobús. 2
d. Don Francisco le habla a Javier de cuando era chico. 5
e. Javier quiere dibujar un rato (*a while*). 1
f. Don Francisco lo lleva a una clínica. 3

4

En el consultorio Trabajen en parejas para representar los papeles (*roles*) de un(a) médico/a y su paciente. Usen las instrucciones como guía.

El/la médico/a	El/la paciente
Pregúntale al / a la paciente si le duele.	Te caíste en casa. Describe tu dolor.
Pregúntale cuánto tiempo hace que se cayó.	Describe la situación. Piensas que te rompiste el dedo.
Mira el dedo. Debes recomendar un tratamiento (*treatment*) al / a la paciente.	Debes hacer preguntas al / a la médico/a sobre el tratamiento (*treatment*).

AYUDA

Here are some useful expressions:
¿Cómo se lastimó...?
¿Le duele...?
¿Cuánto tiempo hace que...?
Tengo...
Estoy...
¿Es usted alérgico/a a algún medicamento?
Usted debe...

TEACHING OPTIONS

Heritage Speakers Ask heritage speakers in your class to prepare a poster that gives information about the health care system of their country of origin or other Spanish-speaking countries they have visited. You may want to display the posters in your classroom.

Extra Practice Ask your students a few questions about the **Fotonovela**. Ex: **1. ¿Quién se lastimó en el autobús? (Javier) 2. ¿Cómo se llama la amiga de don Francisco? (Dra. Márquez) 3. ¿Adónde lleva don Francisco a Javier? (a la clínica de la doctora Márquez) 4. ¿Quién tenía muchas infecciones de la garganta? (don Francisco)**

Ortografía

El acento y las sílabas fuertes

In Spanish, written accent marks are used on many words. Here is a review of some of the principles governing word stress and the use of written accents.

as-pi-ri-na **gri-pe** **to-man** **an-tes**

In Spanish, when a word ends in a vowel, **-n**, or **-s**, the spoken stress usually falls on the next-to-last syllable. Words of this type are very common and do not need a written accent.

a-sí **in-glés** **in-fec-ción** **hé-ro-e**

When a word ends in a vowel, **-n**, or **-s**, and the spoken stress does *not* fall on the next-to-last syllable, then a written accent is needed.

hos-pi-tal **na-riz** **re-ce-tar** **to-ser**

When a word ends in any consonant *other* than **-n** or **-s**, the spoken stress usually falls on the last syllable. Words of this type are very common and do not need a written accent.

lá-piz **fút-bol** **hués-ped** **sué-ter**

When a word ends in any consonant *other* than **-n** or **-s** and the spoken stress does *not* fall on the last syllable, then a written accent is needed.

far-ma-cia **bio-lo-gí-a** **su-cio** **frí-o**

Diphthongs (two weak vowels or a strong and weak vowel together) are normally pronounced as a single syllable. A written accent is needed when a diphthong is broken into two syllables.

sol **pan** **mar** **tos**

Spanish words of only one syllable do not usually carry a written accent (unless it is to distinguish meaning: **se** and **sé**.)

CONSÚLTALO

In Spanish, **a**, **e** and **o** are considered strong vowels while **i** and **u** are weak vowels. To review this concept, see **Lección 3, Pronunciación** p. 77.

Práctica Busca las palabras que necesitan acento escrito y escribe su forma correcta.

1. sal-mon salmón
2. ins-pec-tor
3. nu-me-ro número
4. fa-cil fácil
5. ju-go
6. a-bri-go
7. ra-pi-do rápido
8. sa-ba-do sábado
9. vez
10. me-nu menú
11. o-pe-ra-cion operación
12. im-per-me-a-ble
13. a-de-mas además
14. re-ga-te-ar
15. an-ti-pa-ti-co antipático
16. far-ma-cia
17. es-qui esquí
18. pen-sion pensión
19. pa-is país
20. per-don perdón

El ahorcado (*Hangman*) Juega al ahorcado para adivinar las palabras.

1. __ l __ __ __ __ a — Vas allí cuando estás enfermo. clínica
2. __ __ __ e __ c __ __ n — Se usa para poner una vacuna (*vaccination*). inyección
3. __ __ d __ o __ __ __ __ __ __ a — Ves los huesos. radiografía
4. __ __ __ i __ o — Trabaja en un hospital. médico
5. a __ __ __ b __ __ __ __ __ __ __ — Es una medicina. antibiótico

recursos

LM	Lab CD/MP3	I CD-ROM
p. 56	Lección 10	Lección 10

Section Goals

In **Ortografía** students will review:

- word stress
- the use of written accent marks

Instructional Resource
Interactive CD-ROM

Suggestions

- You may want to explain that all words in which the spoken stress falls on the antepenultimate syllable or one before will carry a written accent, regardless of the letter they end in.
- As you go through each point in the explanation, write the example words on the board, pronounce them, and have students repeat. Then, ask students to provide words they learned in previous lessons that exemplify each point.
- Make a list of unfamiliar words on the board, leaving out any written accent marks. Pronounce them, and ask students whether and where a written accent mark should be placed. Include words that carry a written accent mark as well as some that don't.
- Point out that **Ortografía** replaces **Pronunciación** in the Student Edition for **Lecciones 10–18**, but not in the Lab Manual. The **Recursos** box references the **Pronunciación** sections found in all lessons of the Lab Manual.

TEACHING OPTIONS

Extra Practice Have your students close their books. Then give them the sentences in **Actividad 1, ¿Cierto o falso?**, page 304 as a dictation. Say each sentence twice slowly and once at normal speed to give your students enough time to write. Then have them open their books and check their work.

Pairs Ask your students to work in pairs to explain why each word in the **Práctica** activity does or does not have a written accent mark. The same process can be followed with the words in the **El ahorcado** activity.

10.1 The imperfect tense

ANTE TODO In **Lección 8** you learned the preterite tense. You will now learn the imperfect, used to describe past activities in a different way.

The imperfect of regular verbs

		cantar	beber	escribir
SINGULAR FORMS	yo	cant**aba**	beb**ía**	escrib**ía**
	tú	cant**abas**	beb**ías**	escrib**ías**
	Ud./él/ella	cant**aba**	beb**ía**	escrib**ía**
PLURAL FORMS	nosotros/as	cant**ábamos**	beb**íamos**	escrib**íamos**
	vosotros/as	cant**abais**	beb**íais**	escrib**íais**
	Uds./ellos/ellas	cant**aban**	beb**ían**	escrib**ían**

Sabes, Javier, cuando era chico yo les tenía mucho miedo a los médicos.

De niño tenía que ir mucho a una clínica en San Juan. ¡No me gustaban nada las inyecciones!

▶ There are no stem changes in the imperfect.

entender (e: ie)	**Entendíamos** japonés. *We used to understand Japanese.*
servir (e:i)	El camarero les **servía** el café. *The waiter was serving them coffee.*
doler (o:ue)	A Javier le **dolía** el tobillo. *Javier's ankle was hurting.*

▶ The imperfect form of **hay** is **había** *(there was; there were; there used to be)*. Like **hay, había** can be followed by a singular or plural noun.

Había un solo médico en la sala.
There was only one doctor in the room.

Había dos pacientes allí.
There were two patients there.

Irregular verbs in the imperfect

		ir	ser	ver
SINGULAR FORMS	yo	iba	era	ve**ía**
	tú	ib**as**	er**as**	ve**ías**
	Ud./él/ella	iba	era	ve**ía**
PLURAL FORMS	nosotros/as	íb**amos**	ér**amos**	ve**íamos**
	vosotros/as	ib**ais**	er**ais**	ve**íais**
	Uds./ellos/ellas	ib**an**	er**an**	ve**ían**

recursos

WB pp. 111–120
LM pp. 57–60
Lab CD/MP3 Lección 10
I CD-ROM Lección 10
vistahigher learning.com

¡ATENCIÓN!

Note that the imperfect endings of **–er** and **–ir** verbs are the same. Also note that the **nosotros** form of **–ar** verbs always carries an accent mark on the first **a** of the ending. All forms of **–er** and **–ir** verbs in the imperfect carry an accent on the first **i** of the ending.

¡ATENCIÓN!

Ir, **ser**, and **ver** are the only verbs in Spanish that are irregular in the imperfect.

Section Goal

In **Estructura 10.1**, students will learn the imperfect tense.

Instructional Resources
WB/VM: Workbook, pp. 111–112
Lab Manual, p. 57
Lab CD/MP3 ***Lección 10***
IRM: ***¡Inténtalo! & Práctica*** *Answers, pp. 213–214; Tapescript, pp. 45–48*
Info Gap Activities Booklet, pp. 39–40
Interactive CD-ROM
Companion website: www.vistahigherlearning.com
Presentations CD-ROM

Suggestions

- Ask volunteers to answer questions about childhood illnesses and injuries. Ex: **Cuando eras niño/a, ¿te enfermabas con frecuencia? ¿Te rompiste la pierna alguna vez? ¿Tuviste sarampión** (*measles*)**?**
- Draw a horizontal line on the board and write under it: **cuando era chico/a**. Draw intersecting vertical lines on it at various points labeling them with the medical conditions described by volunteers. Ex: **Tuve sarampión. Me rompí el brazo. Estuve seis días en el hospital.**
- Explain to students that they can already express the past with the preterite tense, and now they are learning the imperfect tense, which they can use to express the past in a different way.
- As you work through the discussion of the imperfect, test comprehension by asking volunteers to supply the correct form of verbs for the subjects you suggest. Ex: **romper / nosotros (rompíamos)**
- Point out that **había** is impersonal and must be used whether followed by a singular or plural noun. Ex: **Había una enfermera. Había muchas enfermeras.**

TEACHING OPTIONS

Extra Practice To provide oral practice with the imperfect tense, change the pronouns in **¡Inténtalo!** on page 307. Have students give the appropriate forms for each infinitive listed.

Heritage Speakers Have heritage speakers compare and contrast cultural concepts of medical treatment in their home communities and the United States or Canada. Ask them to use the imperfect tense to describe how medical problems and emergencies were handled in their family.

CONSÚLTALO

You will learn more about the contrast between the preterite and the imperfect in **Estructura 10.2**, pp. 310–311.

Uses of the imperfect

▶ The imperfect is used to describe past events in a different way than the preterite. As a general rule, the imperfect is used to describe actions which are seen by the speaker as incomplete or "continuing," while the preterite is used to describe actions which have been completed. The imperfect expresses what was happening at a certain time or how things used to be. The preterite, in contrast, expresses a completed action.

—¿Qué te **pasó**? *What happened to you?*	—Me **torcí** el tobillo. *I sprained my ankle.*
—¿Dónde **vivías** de niño? *Where did you live as a child?*	—**Vivía** en San José. *I lived in San José.*

▶ The following words and expressions are often used with the imperfect because they express habitual or repeated actions: **de niño/a** (*as a child*), **todos los días** (*every day*), **mientras** (*while*).

Uses of the imperfect

1. Habitual or repeated actions	**Íbamos** al parque los domingos. *We used to go to the park on Sundays.*
2. Events or actions that were in progress	Yo **leía** mientras él **estudiaba**. *I was reading while he was studying.*
3. Physical characteristics	**Era** alto y guapo. *He was tall and handsome.*
4. Mental or emotional states	**Quería** mucho a su familia. *He loved his family very much.*
5. Time-telling	**Eran** las tres y media. *It was 3:30.*
6. Age	Los niños **tenían** seis años. *The children were six years old.*

¡INTÉNTALO! Indica la forma correcta de cada verbo en el imperfecto.

1. Yo hablaba (hablar, bailar, recetar, correr, comer, decidir, vivir)
   bailaba, recetaba, corría, comía, decidía, vivía
2. Tú ________ (nadar, encontrar, comprender, venir, ir, ser, ver)
   nadabas, encontrabas, comprendías, venías, ibas, eras, veías
3. Usted ________ (hacer, doler, asistir, ser, pasear, poder, ir)
   hacía, dolía, asistía, era, paseaba, podía, iba
4. Nosotras ________ (ser, tomar, ir, poner, seguir, ver, pensar)
   éramos, tomábamos, íbamos, poníamos, seguíamos, veíamos, pensábamos
5. Ellos ________ (salir, viajar, ir, querer, ser, pedir, empezar)
   salían, viajaban, iban, querían, eran, pedían, empezaban
6. Yo ________ (ver, estornudar, sufrir, ir, dar, ser, toser)
   veía, estornudaba, sufría, iba, daba, era, tosía

Suggestions

- Ask students to compare and contrast a home video with a snapshot in the family picture album. Then call their attention to the brief description of uses of the imperfect. Which actions would be best captured by a home video? (Continuing actions; incomplete actions; what was happening; how things used to be.) Which actions are best captured in a snapshot? (A completed action.)
- Ask students to answer questions about themselves in the past. Ex: **Y tú, ____ , ¿ibas al parque los domingos cuando eras niño/a? ¿Qué hacías mientras tu madre preparaba la comida? ¿Cómo eras de niño/a?**
- Ask questions about the **Fotonovela** characters using the imperfect.

Successful Language Learning
Ask students to think about what they used to do when they were younger and imagine how to say it in Spanish. This is good practice for real-life conversations because people often talk about their childhood when making new friends.

TEACHING OPTIONS

Video Show the video again to give students more input about the use of the imperfect. Stop the video at appropriate moments to contrast the use of preterite and imperfect tenses.

Game Divide the class into two teams. Indicate one team member at a time, alternating between teams. Give a certain infinitive and name a subject for which the team member should supply the correct form of the verb in the imperfect. Give a point per correct answer. Deduct a point for each wrong answer. The team with the most points at the end of play wins.

1 Suggestions
- Before assigning the activity, review the forms of the imperfect by calling out an infinitive and a series of subject pronouns. Ask volunteers to give the corresponding forms. Ex: **querer, Ud. (quería); yo (quería); nosotras (queríamos)**. Include irregular verbs.
- As a model, write the following sentences on the board and have volunteers supply the verb forms and then reorder the sentences. **No ____ (dormir) bien. (dormía/1); ____ (ser) la una de la mañana cuando llamé al doctor. (era/3); Me desperté a las once porque ____ (sentirse) mal. (me sentía/2)**

1 Expansion Have students write a conversation between Miguelito and his friends in which he relates what happened after the accident.

2 Expansion Ask students to identify the reason the imperfect was necessary in each sentence.

3 Expansion Write these sentences on the board, and have students complete them in pairs. **1. Fui al doctor porque ____. 2. Tuvo que ir al dentista porque ____. 3. El médico le dio unas pastillas porque ____. 4. La enfermera le tomó la temperatura porque ____.**

Práctica

1 Completar Primero, completa las frases con el imperfecto de los verbos. Luego, pon las oraciones en orden lógico y compáralas con las de un(a) compañero/a.

a. El doctor dijo que no __era__ (ser) nada grave. 7
b. El doctor __quería__ (querer) ver la nariz del niño. 6
c. Su mamá __estaba__ (estar) dibujando cuando Miguelito entró llorando. 3
d. Miguelito __tenía__ (tener) la nariz hinchada (*swollen*). Fueron al hospital. 4
e. Miguelito no __iba__ (ir) a jugar más. Ahora quería ir a casa a descansar. 8
f. Miguelito y sus amigos __jugaban__ (jugar) al béisbol en el patio. 2
g. __Eran__ (ser) las dos de la tarde. 1
h. Miguelito le dijo a la enfermera que __le dolía__ (dolerle) la nariz. 5

2 Transformar Forma oraciones completas. Usa las formas correctas del imperfecto y añade (*add*) todas las palabras necesarias.

1. Julieta y César / ser / paramédicos
   Julieta y César eran paramédicos.
2. trabajar / juntos y / llevarse / bien
   Trabajaban juntos y se llevaban muy bien.
3. cuando / haber / accidente, / siempre / analizar / situación / con cuidado
   Cuando había un accidente, siempre analizaban la situación con cuidado.
4. preocuparse / mucho / por / pacientes
   Se preocupaban mucho por los pacientes.
5. si / paciente / tener / mucho / dolor, / ponerle / inyección
   Si el paciente tenía mucho dolor, le ponían una inyección.

3 En la escuela de medicina Usa los verbos de la lista para completar las frases con las formas correctas del imperfecto. Algunos verbos se usan más de una vez.
Some answers will vary.

caerse	enfermarse	ir	querer	tener
comprender	estornudar	pensar	sentirse	tomar
doler	hacer	poder	ser	toser

1. Cuando Javier y Victoria __eran__ estudiantes de medicina, siempre __tenían__ que ir al médico.
2. Cada vez que él __tomaba__ un examen, a Javier le __dolía__ mucho la cabeza.
3. Cuando Victoria __hacía__ ejercicio aeróbico, siempre __se sentía__ mareada.
4. Todas las primaveras, Javier __estornudaba/tosía__ mucho porque es alérgico al polen.
5. Victoria también __se caía__ de su bicicleta en camino a clase.
6. Después de comer en la cafetería, a Victoria siempre le __dolía__ el estómago.
7. Javier __quería/pensaba__ ser médico para ayudar a los demás.
8. Pero no __comprendía__ por qué él __se enfermaba__ con tanta frecuencia.
9. Cuando Victoria __tenía__ fiebre, no __podía__ ni leer el termómetro.
10. Javier __tenía__ dolor de muelas, pero nunca __quería__ ir al dentista.
11. Victoria __tosía/estornudaba__ mucho cuando __se sentía__ congestionada.
12. Javier y Victoria __pensaban__ que nunca __iban__ a graduarse.

NOTA CULTURAL

En los países de habla hispana, los estudiantes generalmente eligen su carrera (*career*) universitaria cuando salen de la escuela secundaria. Por ejemplo, los que quieren ser médicos empiezan sus estudios de medicina cuando entran a la universidad. Los estudiantes de medicina tienen cerca de seis o siete años de estudios universitarios y después dos años más de especialización.

TEACHING OPTIONS

TPR Model gestures for physical or emotional states using the imperfect. Ex: **Me dolía la cabeza.** (furrow your brow and rub your forehead); **Tenía fiebre.** (fan yourself); and so forth. Have students stand. Say an expression at random (**Estornudabas**) and signal a student to perform the appropriate gesture. Keep the pace rapid. Vary by pointing to more than one student (**Ustedes se enfermaban.**).

Small Groups Have students write about a favorite or not-fondly-remembered doctor or dentist from the past. Refer them to **Actividad 2** for ideas. When they are finished, have them read each other's descriptions in groups of four.

Extra Practice Have students bring in video clips from popular movies. Choose three or four clips and have the students describe the events after viewing.

Comunicación

4 **Entrevista** Trabajen en parejas. Un(a) estudiante usa estas preguntas para entrevistar a su compañero/a. Luego compartan los resultados de la entrevista con la clase. Answers will vary.

1. Cuando eras estudiante de primaria, ¿te gustaban tus profesores/as?
2. ¿Veías mucha televisión cuando eras niño/a?
3. Cuando tenías diez años, ¿cuál era tu programa de televisión favorito?
4. Cuando eras niño/a, ¿qué hacía tu familia durante las vacaciones?
5. ¿Cuántos años tenías en 1996?
6. Cuando eras estudiante de secundaria, ¿qué hacías con tus amigos/as?
7. Cuando tenías quince años, ¿cuál era tu grupo musical favorito?
8. Antes de tomar esta clase, ¿sabías hablar español?

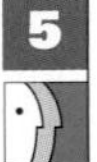

5 **Describir** En parejas, túrnense para describir cómo eran sus vidas cuando eran niños. Pueden usar las sugerencias de la lista u otras ideas. Luego informen a la clase sobre la vida del/de la compañero/a. Answers will vary.

modelo

De niña, mi familia y yo siempre íbamos a Tortuguero. Tomábamos un barco desde Limón, y por las noches mirábamos las tortugas (turtles) en la playa. Algunas veces teníamos suerte, porque las tortugas venían a poner (lay) huevos. Otras veces, volvíamos al hotel sin ver ninguna tortuga.

- Las vacaciones
- Ocasiones especiales
- Qué hacías durante el verano
- Celebraciones con tus amigos/as
- Celebraciones con tu familia
- Cómo era tu escuela
- Cómo eran tus amigos/as
- Los viajes que hacías
- A qué jugabas
- Qué hacías cuando te sentías enfermo/a

NOTA CULTURAL

El Parque Nacional Tortuguero está en la costa del Caribe, al norte de la ciudad de Limón, en Costa Rica. Varias especies de tortuga (*turtle*) utilizan las playas del parque para poner (*lay*) sus huevos. Esto ocurre de noche, y hay guías que llevan pequeños grupos de turistas a observar este fenómeno biológico.

Síntesis

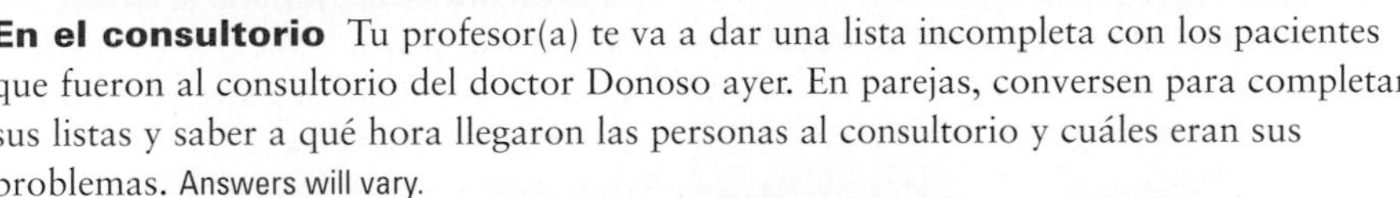

6 **En el consultorio** Tu profesor(a) te va a dar una lista incompleta con los pacientes que fueron al consultorio del doctor Donoso ayer. En parejas, conversen para completar sus listas y saber a qué hora llegaron las personas al consultorio y cuáles eran sus problemas. Answers will vary.

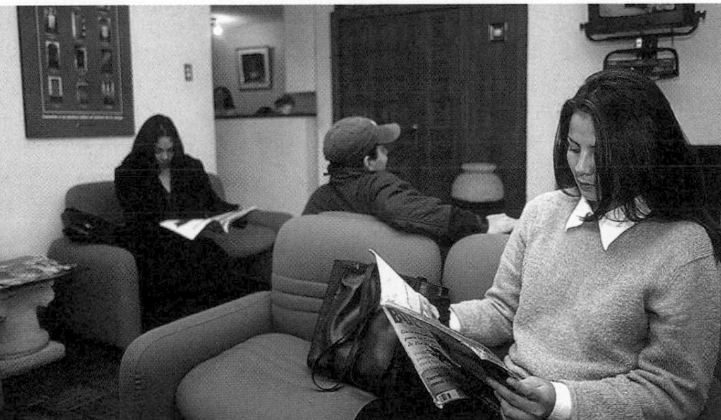

4 Suggestion Students should record the results of their interviews in a Venn diagram, which they can use to present the information to the class.

5 Suggestions
- Before students report to the class, divide the class into groups of four. After each report, the groups decide on a question for the presenter. Then have the groups take turns asking the student about his or her experience.
- Assign this activity as a short written composition.

6 Suggestion Divide the class into pairs and distribute the Info Gap Handouts from the Info Gap Activities Booklet that correspond to this activity. Give the students ten minutes to complete this activity.

6 Expansion Have pairs write Dr. Donoso's advice for three of the patients. Later, have them read the advice to the class and compare it with what other pairs wrote for the same patients.

TEACHING OPTIONS

Large Groups Label the four corners of the room **La Revolución Americana, Tiempos prehistóricos, El Imperio Romano,** and **El Japón de los samurai.** Have students go to the corner that best describes what historical period they would visit if they could. Each group should then discuss their reasons for choosing that period using the imperfect tense. A spokesperson will summarize the group response to the rest of the class.

Game Divide the class into groups of three. Each group should decide on a historical or fictional villain. When it is their turn, they will give the class one hint. The other groups are allowed three questions, which must be answered truthfully. At the end of the question/answer session, groups must guess the identity. Award one point for each correct guess and two to any group able to stump the class.

Section Goal

In **Estructura 10.2** students will compare and contrast the uses and meanings of the preterite and imperfect tenses.

Instructional Resources
WB/VM: Workbook, pp. 113–116
Lab Manual, p. 58
Lab CD/MP3 ***Lección 10***
IRM: ***¡Inténtalo! & Práctica*** *Answers, pp. 213–214; Tapescript, pp. 45–48*
Interactive CD-ROM
Companion website: www.vistahigherlearning.com
Presentations CD-ROM

Suggestions
- Have a volunteer read Javier's words in the caption of the left-hand video still on this page. Ask which verb is imperfect (**estaba**) and which is preterite (**Me caí**). Repeat for the right-hand video still showing Don Francisco (**jugaba/me rompí**).
- Give personalized examples as you contrast the preterite and the imperfect. Ex: **La semana pasada tuve que ir al dentista. Me dolía mucho la muela.**

10.2 The preterite and the imperfect

ANTE TODO Now that you have learned the forms of the preterite and the imperfect, you will learn more about how they are used. The preterite and the imperfect are not interchangeable. In Spanish, the choice between these two tenses depends on the context and on the point of view of the speaker.

Me caí cuando estaba en el autobús.

De niño jugaba mucho al fútbol. Una vez me rompí la pierna.

COMPARE & CONTRAST

Uses of the preterite

1. To express actions that are viewed by the speaker as completed

Don Francisco **se rompió** la pierna.
Don Francisco broke his leg.
Fueron a Buenos Aires ayer.
They went to Buenos Aires yesterday.

2. To express the beginning or end of a past action

La película **empezó** a las nueve.
The movie began at nine o'clock.
Ayer **terminé** el proyecto para la clase de química.
Yesterday I finished the project for chemistry class.

3. To narrate a series of past actions or events

La doctora me **miró** los oídos, me **hizo** unas preguntas y **escribió** la receta.
The doctor looked in my ears, asked me some questions, and wrote the prescription.
Me di con la mesa, **me caí** y **me lastimé** el pie.
I bumped into the table, I fell, and I injured my foot.

Uses of the imperfect

1. To describe an ongoing past action with no reference to its beginning or end

Don Francisco **esperaba** a Javier.
Don Francisco was waiting for Javier.
El médico **se preocupaba** por sus pacientes.
The doctor worried about his patients.

2. To express habitual past actions and events

Cuando **era** joven, **jugaba** al tenis.
When I was young, I used to play tennis.
De niño, don Francisco **se enfermaba** con mucha frecuencia.
As a child, Don Francisco used to get sick very frequently.

3. To describe physical and emotional states or characteristics.

La chica **quería** descansar. **Se sentía** mal y **tenía** dolor de cabeza.
The girl wanted to rest. She felt ill and had a headache.
Ellos **eran** altos y **tenían** ojos verdes.
They were tall and had green eyes.
Estábamos felices de ver a la familia.
We were happy to see the family.

AYUDA

These words and expressions, as well as similar ones, commonly occur with the preterite: **ayer, anteayer, una vez, dos veces, tres veces, el año pasado, de repente**.
They usually imply that an action has happened at a specific point in time. For a review, see **Estructura 6.3**, p. 185.

AYUDA

These words and expressions, as well as similar ones, commonly occur with the imperfect: **de niño/a, todos los días, mientras, siempre, con frecuencia, todas las semanas**. They usually express habitual or repeated actions in the past.

TEACHING OPTIONS

Extra Practice Write in English a simple, humorous retelling of a well-known fairy tale. Read it to the class, pausing after each verb in the past to ask the class whether the imperfect or preterite would be used in Spanish. Ex: Once upon a time there was a girl named Little Red Riding Hood. She wanted to take lunch to her ailing grandmother. She put a loaf of bread, a wedge of cheese, and a bottle of Beaujolais in a basket and set off through the woods. Meanwhile, farther down the path, a big, ugly, snaggle-toothed wolf was leaning against a tree, filing his nails . . .

Pairs On separate slips of paper, have students write six true statements, one for each of the uses of the preterite and imperfect in **Compare & Contrast**. Have them mix up the slips and exchange them with a partner, who will identify the preterite or imperfect use the sentence illustrates.

▶ The preterite and the imperfect often appear in the same sentence. In such cases the imperfect describes what *was happening*, while the preterite describes the action that "interrupted" the ongoing activity.

Miraba la tele cuando **sonó** el teléfono.
I was watching TV when the phone rang.

Maite **leía** el periódico cuando **llegó** Álex.
Maite was reading the newspaper when Álex arrived.

▶ You will also see the preterite and the imperfect together in narratives such as fiction, news, and retelling of events. In these cases the imperfect provides all of the background information, such as time, weather, and location, while the preterite indicates the specific events that occurred to advance the plot.

Eran las dos de la mañana y el detective ya no **podía** mantenerse despierto. **Se bajó** lentamente del coche, **estiró** las piernas y **levantó** los brazos hacia el cielo oscuro.
It was two in the morning, and the detective could no longer stay awake. He slowly stepped out of the car, stretched his legs, and raised his arms toward the dark sky.

La luna **estaba** llena y no **había** en el cielo ni una sola nube. De repente, el detective **escuchó** un grito espeluznante proveniente del parque.
The moon was full and there wasn't a single cloud in the sky. Suddenly, the detective heard a piercing scream coming from the park.

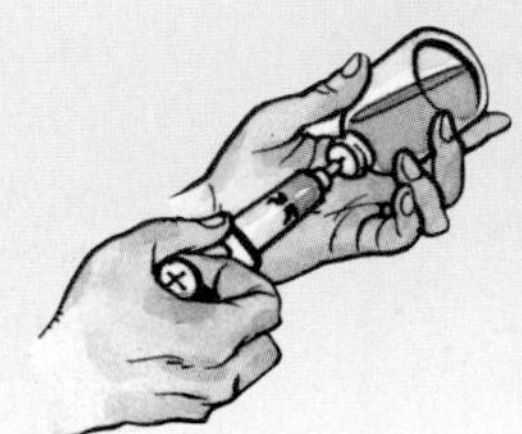

Un médico colombiano descubrió la vacuna contra la malaria

El doctor colombiano Manuel Elkin Patarroyo descubrió una vacuna contra la malaria. Esta enfermedad se erradicó hace décadas en muchas partes del mundo. Sin embargo, los casos de malaria empezaban a aumentar otra vez, justo cuando salió la vacuna de Patarroyo. En mayo de 1993, el doctor Patarroyo donó la vacuna, a nombre de Colombia, a la Organización Mundial de la Salud. Los grandes laboratorios farmacéuticos presionaron a la OMS porque querían la vacuna. Pero en 1995 las dos partes, el doctor Patarroyo y la OMS, ratificaron el pacto original.

¡INTÉNTALO! Elige el pretérito o el imperfecto para completar la historia. Explica por qué se usa ese tiempo verbal en cada ocasión. Answers will vary. Suggested answers.

1. __Eran__ (Fueron/Eran) las doce.
2. __Había__ (Hubo/Había) mucha gente en la calle.
3. A las doce y media, Tomás y yo __entramos__ (entramos/entrábamos) en el Restaurante Tárcoles.
4. Todos los días yo __almorzaba__ (almorcé/almorzaba) con Tomás al mediodía.
5. El camarero __llegó__ (llegó/llegaba) inmediatamente, para darnos el menú.
6. Nosotros __empezamos__ (empezamos/empezábamos) a leerlo.
7. Yo __pedí__ (pedí/pedía) el pescado.
8. De repente, el camarero __volvió__ (volvió/volvía) a nuestra mesa.
9. Y nos __dio__ (dio/daba) una mala noticia.
10. Desafortunadamente, no __tenían__ (tuvieron/tenían) más pescado.
11. Por eso Tomás y yo __decidimos__ (decidimos/decidíamos) comer en otro lugar.
12. __Llovía__ (Llovió/Llovía) muy fuerte cuando __salimos__ (salimos/salíamos) del café.
13. Así que __regresamos__ (regresamos/regresábamos) al Restaurante Tárcoles.
14. Esta vez, __pedí__ (pedí/pedía) el arroz con pollo.

Suggestions

- Give further examples from your own experience that contrast the imperfect and the preterite. Ex: **Quería ver la nueva película ____, pero anoche sólo pude ir a las diez de la noche. La película estaba buena, pero terminó muy tarde. Era la una cuando llegué a casa. Me acosté muy tarde y esta mañana, cuando me levanté, estaba cansadísimo/a.**
- Have students find the example of an interrupted action in the realia.
- Involve the class in a conversation about what they did in the past. Ask: ____, **¿paseabas en bicicleta cuando eras niño/a? ¿Te caíste alguna vez?** ____, **¿cuando eras niño/a iba tu familia de vacaciones todos los años? ¿Adónde iban?**
- After completing **¡Inténtalo!**, have students explain why the preterite or imperfect was used in each case. Then call on different students to create other sentences illustrating the same uses.

TEACHING OPTIONS

Pairs Ask students to narrate the most interesting, embarassing, exciting, or annoying thing that has happened to them recently. Tell them to describe what happened and how they felt, using preterite and imperfect verbs.

Heritage Speakers Ask heritage speakers to write a summary of what happened in the **Fotonovela**. Tell them that their summaries should first set the scene and establish background information about the characters, where they are, and what they were doing, then explain what happened.

1 Expansion Have volunteers explain why they chose the preterite or imperfect in each case. Ask them to point out any words or expressions that triggered one tense or the other.

2 Expansion Ask comprehension questions about the article. Ex: **¿Qué pasó ayer? ¿Dónde hubo un accidente? ¿Qué tiempo hacía? ¿Qué le pasó a la mujer que manejaba? ¿Y a su pasajero? ¿Qué hizo el conductor del autobús? ¿Qué les pasó a los pasajeros del autobús?**

3 Expansions

- After students have compared their sentences, ask them to report to the class on the most interesting things their partner said.
- Ask students to expand on one of their sentences, creating a paragraph about an imaginary or actual past experience.

Práctica

1 **Seleccionar** Utiliza el tiempo verbal adecuado, según (*according to*) el contexto.

1. La semana pasada, Manolo y Aurora _querían_ (querer) dar una fiesta. _Decidieron_ (Decidir) invitar a seis amigos y servirles mucha comida.
2. Manolo y Aurora _estaban_ (estar) preparando la comida cuando Elena _llamó_ (llamar). Como siempre, _tenía_ (tener) que estudiar para un examen.
3. A las seis, _volvió_ (volver) a sonar el teléfono. Su amigo Francisco tampoco _podía_ (poder) ir a la fiesta, porque _tenía_ (tener) fiebre. Manolo y Aurora _se sentían_ (sentirse) muy tristes, pero _tenían_ (tener) que preparar la comida.
4. Después de otros 15 minutos, _sonó_ (sonar) el teléfono. Sus amigos, los señores Vega, _estaban_ (estar) en camino (*en route*) al hospital: a su hijo le _dolía_ (doler) mucho el estómago. Sólo dos de los amigos _podían_ (poder) ir a la cena.
5. Por supuesto, _iban_ (ir) a tener demasiada comida. Finalmente, cinco minutos antes de las ocho, _llamaron_ (llamar) Ramón y Javier. Ellos _pensaban_ (pensar) que la fiesta _era_ (ser) la próxima semana.
6. Tristes, Manolo y Aurora _se sentaron_ (sentarse) a comer solos. Mientras _comían_ (comer) pronto _llegaron_ (llegar) a la conclusión de que _era_ (ser) mejor estar solos: ¡La comida _estaba_ (estar) malísima!

2 **Completar** Completa esta noticia con la forma correcta del pretérito o el imperfecto.

Un accidente trágico

Ayer temprano por la mañana (1) _hubo_ (haber) un trágico accidente en el centro de Buenos Aires cuando un autobús no (2) _vio_ (ver) venir un carro. La mujer que (3) _manejaba_ (manejar) el carro (4) _murió_ (morir) al instante y los paramédicos (5) _tuvieron_ (tener) que llevar al pasajero al hospital porque (6) _sufrió_ (sufrir) varias fracturas. El conductor del autobús (7) _dijo_ (decir) que no (8) _vio_ (ver) el carro hasta el último (*last*) momento porque (9) _había_ (haber) mucha niebla y (10) _estaba_ (estar) lloviendo. Él (11) _intentó_ (intentar) (*to attempt*) dar un viraje brusco (*to swerve*), pero (12) _perdió_ (perder) el control del autobús y no (13) _pudo_ (poder) evitar (*to avoid*) el accidente. Según nos informaron, no (14) _se lastimó_ (lastimarse) ningún pasajero del autobús.

CONSEJOS

Reading Spanish-language newspapers is a good way to practice verb tenses. You will find that both the imperfect and the preterite occur with great regularity. Many newsstands carry international papers, and many Spanish-language newspapers (such as Spain's *El País*, Mexico's *Reforma*, and Argentina's *Clarín*) are on the Web.

3 **Completar** Completa las frases de una manera lógica. Usa el pretérito o el imperfecto. En parejas, comparen sus respuestas. Answers will vary.

1. De niño/a, yo...
2. Yo conducía el coche mientras...
3. Anoche mi novio/a...
4. Ayer el/la profesor(a)...
5. La semana pasada un(a) amigo/a...
6. Con frecuencia mis padres...
7. Esta mañana en la cafetería...
8. Hablábamos con el doctor cuando...

TEACHING OPTIONS

Small Groups Have students work in groups of four to write a short article about an imaginary road trip they took last summer. Students should use the imperfect to set the scene and the preterite to narrate the events. Each student should contribute three sentences to the article. When finished, have students read their articles to the class.

Heritage Speakers Ask heritage speakers to write a brief narration of a well-known fairy tale such as Little Red Riding Hood (**Caperucita Roja**). Allow them to change details as they see fit, modernizing the story or setting it in another country, for example, but tell them to pay special attention to the use of preterite and imperfect verbs. Have them share their retellings with the class.

Comunicación

4 **Entrevista** Usa estas preguntas para entrevistar a un(a) compañero/a acerca de su primer(a) novio/a. Si quieres, puedes añadir (*to add*) otras preguntas. Answers will vary.

1. ¿Quién fue tu primer(a) novio/a?
2. ¿Cuántos años tenían ustedes cuando se conocieron?
3. ¿Cómo era él/ella?
4. ¿Qué le gustaba hacer? ¿Le interesaban los deportes?
5. ¿Por cuánto tiempo salieron ustedes?
6. ¿Qué hacían ustedes cuando salían?
7. ¿Pensaban casarse?
8. ¿Cuándo y por qué rompieron ustedes?

5 **La sala de emergencia** En parejas, miren la lista e inventen qué les pasó a estas personas que están en la sala de emergencias. Answers will vary.

modelo

Eran las tres de la tarde. Como todos los días, Pablo jugaba al fútbol con sus amigos. Estaba muy contento. De repente, se cayó y se rompió el brazo. Después fue a la sala de emergencias.

Paciente	Edad	Hora	Condición
1. Pablo Romero	9 años	15:20	hueso roto (el brazo)
2. Estela Rodríguez	45 años	15:25	tobillo torcido
3. Lupe Quintana	29 años	15:37	embarazada, dolores
4. Manuel López	52 años	15:45	infección de garganta
5. Marta Díaz	3 años	16:00	temperatura muy alta, fiebre
6. Roberto Salazar	32 años	16:06	dolor de muelas
7. Marco Brito	18 años	16:18	daño en el cuello, posible fractura
8. Ana María Ortiz	66 años	16:29	reacción alérgica a un medicamento

6 **Situación** Anoche alguien robó (*stole*) el examen de la **Lección 10** de la oficina de tu profesor(a) y tú tienes que averiguar (*to find out*) quién lo hizo. Pregúntales a tres compañeros dónde estaban, con quién estaban y qué hicieron entre las ocho y las doce de la noche. Answers will vary.

Síntesis

7 **La primera vez** En grupos, cuéntense cómo fue la primera vez que les pusieron una inyección, se rompieron un hueso, pasaron la noche en un hospital, estuvieron mareados/as, etc. Incluyan los siguientes puntos en su conversación: una descripción del día que hacía, sus edades, qué pasó y cómo se sentían. Answers will vary.

4 Suggestion Before the interviews, have students prepare a few notes to help them in their responses.

4 Expansion Have students write a summary of their partner's responses, omitting all names. Collect the summaries, then read them to the class. Have students guess who had the relationship described in the summary.

5 Expansion Have pairs share their answers with the class, but without mentioning the name of the character. The class must guess which one is being described.

6 Expansion Have students decide who in their group would be the most likely thief based on his or her responses. Ask the group to prepare a police report explaining why they believe their suspect is the culprit.

7 Suggestion Before assigning groups, have students list information they can include in their descriptions such as their age, the time, the date, what the weather was like, and so forth. Next have them list the events of the day in the order they happened.

7 Expansion Have students decide who in their group is most accident prone on the basis of his or her responses. Ask the group to prepare a doctor's account of his or her treatments in the emergency room.

TEACHING OPTIONS

Small Groups Have students write and perform a conversation for the class. Three customers are trying to explain to a gas station attendant what happened to them and why their vehicles need repair. Students should use the preterite and imperfect.

Game On your computer, create a short narrative in past time based on a well-known story. Double space between each sentence so the sentences may be easily cut apart into strips. Print two copies of the sentences and cut them apart. Then make a copy of the file and edit it, changing all preterites to imperfects and vice versa. Print out two copies of this version and cut the sentences apart. Into each of two bags put a complete set of each version of the story, mix the strips up, and challenge two groups to reconstruct the correct version of the story. The group that does so first wins.

Section Goals

In **Estructura 10.3** students will be introduced to:

- impersonal constructions with **se**
- using **se** for unplanned events

Instructional Resources
WB/VM: Workbook, pp. 117–118
Lab Manual, p. 59
Lab CD/MP3 ***Lección 10***
IRM: ***¡Inténtalo! & Práctica*** *Answers, pp. 213–214; Tapescript, pp. 45–48*
Interactive CD-ROM
Companion website: www.vistahigherlearning.com
Presentations CD-ROM

Suggestions

- Have students look at the three signs in the grammar explanation, and ask simple questions about the situations. Ex: **¿Podemos nadar en esta playa?**
- Test comprehension by asking questions based on similar **se** constructions. Ex: **¿Se habla español en Inglaterra? (No, se habla inglés.) ¿Dónde se filman las películas norteamericanas? (Se filman en Hollywood.)**

10.3 Constructions with se

ANTE TODO In **Lección 7** you learned how to use **se** as the third person reflexive pronoun (**El se despierta. Ellos se visten. Ella se baña.**). **Se** can also be used to form constructions in which the person performing the action is not expressed or is de-emphasized.

Impersonal constructions with *se*

▶ In Spanish, verbs that are not reflexive can be used with **se** to form impersonal constructions. These are statements in which the person performing the action is not expressed or defined. In English, the passive voice or indefinite subjects *(you, they, one)* are used.

Se habla español en Costa Rica.
Spanish is spoken in Costa Rica.

Se hacen operaciones aquí.
They perform operations here.

Se puede leer en la sala de espera.
You can read in the waiting room.

Se necesitan medicinas enseguida.
They need medicine right away.

¡ATENCIÓN!
Note that the third person singular verb form is used with singular nouns and the third person plural form is used with plural nouns:
Se vende ropa.
Se venden camisas.

▶ You often see the impersonal **se** in signs, advertisements, and directions.

SE PROHÍBE NADAR

Se necesitan programadores
GRUPO TECNO
Tel. 778-34-34

ENTRADA
Se entra por la izquierda

Se for unplanned events

¿Cuánto tiempo hace que se cayó?
Ya se me olvidó.

Bueno, vamos a sacarle una radiografía para ver si se le rompió el hueso.

▶ **Se** is also used to form statements that describe accidental or unplanned events. In this construction, the person who performs the action is de-emphasized, so as to imply that the accident or unplanned event is not his or her direct responsibility. These statements are constructed using the following pattern.

se	+	[INDIRECT OBJECT PRONOUN]	+	[VERB]	+	[SUBJECT]
Se		me		cayó		la pluma.

TEACHING OPTIONS

TPR Use impersonal constructions with **se** to have students draw what you say. Ex: You say: **Se prohíbe entrar**, and students draw a door with a diagonal line through it. Other possible expressions could be: **Se sale por la derecha. Se permiten perros. Se prohíben botellas.**

Extra Practice Have students bring in common icons or international signs. They can find these on the Internet. Then pair students to write directions using **se** for each of the icons and signs. Ex: **Se prohíbe entrar. Se prohíbe pasar. Se habla español.**

▶ In this type of construction, what would normally be the direct object of the sentence becomes the subject, and it agrees with the verb, not with the indirect object pronoun.

I.O. PRONOUN
VERB
SUBJECT
Se
me, te, le
quedó
cayó
dañó
SINGULAR
la receta.
la taza.
el radio.
nos, os, les
rompieron
olvidaron
perdieron
PLURAL
las botellas.
las pastillas.
las llaves.

¡ATENCIÓN!

While Spanish has a verb for *to fall* (**caer**), there is no direct translation for *to drop*. **Dejar caer** (*let fall*) is often used to mean *to drop*.
Ex: **El médico dejó caer la aspirina.** (*The doctor dropped the aspirin*).

▶ The following verbs are the ones most frequently used with **se** to describe unplanned events.

Verbs commonly used with *se*

caer	*to fall; to drop*	**perder (e: ie)**	*to lose*
dañar	*to damage; to break down*	**quedar**	*to be left behind*
olvidar	*to forget*	**romper**	*to break*

Se me perdió el teléfono de la farmacia.
I lost the pharmacy's phone number.

Se nos olvidaron los pasajes.
We forgot the tickets.

▶ To clarify or emphasize who the person involved in the action is, this construction commonly begins with the preposition **a** + [*noun*] or **a** + [*prepositional pronoun*].

CONSÚLTALO

For an explanation of prepositional pronouns, refer to **Estructura 9.4**, p. 286.

Al paciente se le perdió la receta.
The patient lost his prescription.

A Diana se le olvidó ir al consultorio ayer.
Diana forgot to go to the doctor's office yesterday.

A mí se me cayeron los cuadernos.
I dropped the notebooks.

A ustedes se les quedaron los libros en casa.
You left the books at home.

¡INTÉNTALO! Completa las frases de la columna A con **se** impersonal y los verbos correspondientes en presente.

A

1. Se enseñan (enseñar) cinco lenguas en esta universidad.
2. Se come (comer) muy bien en El Cráter.
3. Se venden (vender) muchas camisetas allí.
4. Se sirven (servir) platos exquisitos cada noche.
5. Se necesita (necesitar) mucho dinero.
6. Se busca (buscar) secretaria.

Completa las frases de la columna B con **se** y los verbos en pretérito para expresar sucesos imprevistos.

B

1. Se me rompieron (*I broke*) las gafas.
2. Se te cayeron (*You* (fam.) *dropped*) las pastillas.
3. Se les perdió (*They lost*) la receta.
4. Se le quedó (*You* (form.) *left*) aquí la radiografía.
5. Se nos olvidó (*We forgot*) pagar la medicina.
6. Se les quedaron (*They left*) los antibióticos en la clínica.

Successful Language Learning
Tell your students that this construction has no exact equivalent in English. Tell them to examine the examples in the textbook and make up examples of their own in order to get a feel for how this construction works.

Suggestions

- Test comprehension by asking volunteers to change sentences from plural to singular and vice versa. Ex: **Se me perdieron las llaves. (Se me perdió la llave.)**
- Have students finish sentences using a construction with **se** to express an unplanned event. Ex: **Al doctor ____. (se le cayó el termómetro) A la profesora ____. (se le quedaron los papeles en casa)**
- Involve students in a conversation about unplanned events that happened to them recently. Say: **Se me olvidaron los lentes oscuros esta mañana. Y a ti, ____, ¿se te olvidó algo esta mañana? ¿Qué se te olvidó?** Continue with other verbs. Ex: **¿A quién se le perdió algo importante esta semana? ¿Qué se te perdió, ____?**

TEACHING OPTIONS

Video Show the video again to give students more input containing constructions with **se**. Have students write down as many of the examples of the construction as they can. After viewing the video, have students edit their lists and cross out any reflexive verbs that they mistakenly understood to be constructions with **se**.

Heritage Speakers Ask heritage speakers to write a fictional or true account of a day in which everything went wrong. Ask them to include as many constructions with **se** as possible. Have them read their accounts aloud to the class to give extra practice to their classmates.

1 Expansions
- Change the date from 1901 to 2002 and go through the exercise again orally.
- Have students work in pairs and, using constructions with **se**, write a description of a period in history such as the French or American Revolution, the Sixties, Prohibition, and so forth. Then have pairs form groups of six to read their descriptions aloud to their group.
- Have students use **se** constructions to compare cultural differences between Spanish-speaking countries and their own. Ex: **Aquí se habla inglés, pero en ____ se habla español.**

2 Suggestions
- Model the activity by asking volunteers to translate similar sentences. Ex: Nurse sought. **(Se busca enfermera.)** Used books bought. **(Se compran libros usados.)**
- Ask students to describe where these signs could be found locally.

3 Suggestion Have students work in pairs to brainstorm verbs that could be used to complete this activity.

3 Expansion Use magazine pictures to have students continue describing past events using constructions with **se**.

Práctica

1 **¿Cierto o falso?** Lee estas oraciones sobre la vida en 1901. Indica si lo que dice cada oración es **cierto** o **falso**. Luego corrige las oraciones falsas.

1. Se veía mucha televisión. Falso. No se veía televisión. Se leía mucho.
2. Se escribían muchos libros. Cierto.
3. Se viajaba mucho en tren. Cierto.
4. Se montaba a caballo. Cierto.
5. Se mandaba mucho correo electrónico. Falso. No se mandaba correo electrónico. Se mandaban muchas cartas y postales.
6. Se preparaban muchas comidas en casa. Cierto.
7. Se llevaban minifaldas. Falso. No se llevaban minifaldas. Se llevaban faldas largas.
8. Se pasaba mucho tiempo con la familia. Cierto.

2 **Traducir** Traduce estos letreros (*signs*) y anuncios (*ads*) al español.

1. Nurses needed Se necesitan enfermeros/as
2. Eating and drinking prohibited Se prohíbe comer y beber
3. Programmers sought Se buscan programadores
4. English is spoken Se habla inglés
5. Computers sold Se venden computadoras
6. No talking Se prohíbe hablar
7. Teacher needed Se necesita profesor / profesora
8. Books sold Se venden libros
9. Do not enter Se prohíbe entrar
10. Spanish is spoken Se habla español

3 **¿Qué pasó?** Mira los dibujos e indica lo que pasó en cada uno. Some answers will vary.

1. camarero / pastel

Al camarero se le cayó el pastel.

2. Sr. Álvarez / espejo

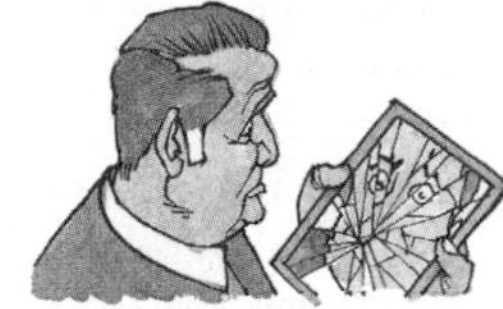

Al señor Álvarez se le rompió el espejo.

3. Arturo / tarea

A Arturo se le olvidó la tarea.

4. Sra. Domínguez / llaves

A la Sra. Domínguez se le perdieron las llaves.

5. Carla y Lupe / botellas de vino

A Carla y Lupe se les rompieron dos botellas de vino.

6. Juana / platos

A Juana se le rompieron los platos.

TEACHING OPTIONS

Extra Practice Have students imagine that they have just seen a movie about the future. Have them work in groups to prepare a description of the way of life portrayed in the movie using the imperfect tense and constructions with **se**. Ex: **No se necesitaba trabajar. Se usaban robots para hacer todo. Se viajaba por telepatía. No se comía nada sino en los fines de semana.**

Game Divide the class into groups of four. Have each group think of a famous place or public building and compose four signs that could be found on the premises. Groups will take turns reading their signs aloud. Each group that correctly identifies the place or building receives a point. Award two points to the group that is able to stump the rest of the class.

Comunicación

4 **Preguntas** Trabajen en parejas y usen estas preguntas para entrevistarse. Answers will vary.

1. ¿Qué comidas se sirven en tu restaurante favorito?
2. ¿Se te olvidó invitar a alguien a tu última fiesta o comida? ¿A quién?
3. ¿A qué hora se abre la cafetería de tu universidad?
4. ¿Alguna vez se te quedó algo importante en la casa? ¿Qué?
5. ¿Alguna vez se te perdió algo importante durante un viaje?
6. ¿Qué se vende en una farmacia?
7. ¿Sabes si en la farmacia se aceptan cheques?
8. ¿Alguna vez se te rompió algo muy caro? ¿Qué?

5 **Opiniones** En parejas, terminen cada oración con ideas originales. Después, comparen los resultados con la clase para ver qué pareja tuvo las mejores ideas. Answers will vary.

1. No se tiene que dejar propina cuando...
2. Antes de viajar, se debe...
3. Si se come bien, ...
4. Para tener una vida sana, se debe...
5. Se sirve la mejor comida en...
6. Se hablan muchas lenguas en...

Síntesis

6 **Anuncios** En grupos, preparen dos anuncios de televisión para presentar a la clase. Usen el imperfecto y por lo menos dos construcciones con **se** en cada uno. Answers will vary.

modelo

Se me cayeron unos libros en el pie y me dolía mucho. Pero ahora no, gracias a SuperAspirina 500. ¡Dos pastillas y se me fue el dolor! Se puede comprar SuperAspirina 500 en todas las farmacias Recetamax.

NOTA CULTURAL

En muchos países de Latinoamérica es posible conseguir medicinas en **las farmacias**, sin la receta de un médico. Comúnmente, los farmacéuticos (*pharmacists*) diagnostican el problema del/de la cliente/a y le venden el medicamento adecuado.

4 Suggestion Model a detailed answer by choosing among questions 4, 5, and 8, providing as many details as possible for the students. Ex: **Una vez cuando era adolescente se me rompió un plato muy caro de mi abuela. Pero ella no se enojó. Me dijo: No te preocupes por el plato. ¿Te lastimaste?**

4 Expansion Have each pair decide on the most unusual answer to the questions. Ask the student who gave it to describe the event to the class.

5 Expansion Have pairs write similar beginnings to three different statements using a **se** construction. Pairs exchange papers and finish each other's sentences. Afterwards, ask them to check one another's work.

6 Expansion After all the groups have presented their ads, have each group write a letter of complaint. Their letter should be directed to one of the other groups, claiming false advertising.

TEACHING OPTIONS

Extra Practice Write the following sentence fragments on the board and ask students to supply several logical endings using a construction with **se: 1. Cuando subía al avión, ____. (se le cayó la maleta; se le torció el pie) 2. Una vez, cuando comía en un restaurante elegante, ____. (se me rompió un vaso; me dio un dolor de estómago) 3. Ayer cuando venía a clase, ____. (se me descompuso la bicicleta; me caí y se me rompió el brazo) 4. Cuando era niño/a, ____. (siempre se me olvidaban las cosas; se me perdían siempre las cosas) 5. El otro día cuando lavaba los platos, ____. (se me rompieron tres vasos; se me terminó el detergente)**

Section Goals

In **Estructura 10.4** students will learn:

- the formation of adverbs using [*adjective*] + **–mente**
- common adverbs and adverbial expressions

Instructional Resources
WB/VM: Workbook, pp. 119–120
Lab Manual, p. 60
Lab CD/MP3 ***Lección 10***
IRM: ***¡Inténtalo!*** *&* ***Práctica*** *Answers, pp. 213–214;*
Tapescript, pp. 45–48
Interactive CD-ROM
Companion website:
www.vistahigherlearning.com
Presentations CD-ROM

Suggestions

- Use magazine pictures to review known adverbs. Ex: **Mira la foto que tengo *aquí*. *Hoy* esta chica se siente *bien*, pero *ayer* se sentía *mal*.** Write the adverbs on the board as you proceed.
- After presenting the formation of adverbs that end in **–mente**, ask volunteers to convert known adjectives into adverbs and then use them in a sentence. Ex: **cómodo/cómodamente: Alberto se sentó cómodamente en la silla.**

10.4 Adverbs

ANTE TODO Adverbs are words that describe how, when, and where actions take place. They can modify verbs, adjectives, and even other adverbs. In previous lessons, you have already learned many Spanish adverbs, such as the ones below.

bien	nunca	temprano
mal	hoy	ayer
muy	siempre	aquí

▶ The most common adverbs are those which end in **–mente.** These are equivalent to the English adverbs which end in *-ly.*

fácilmente *easily* **generalmente** *generally*
verdaderamente *truly, really* **simplemente** *simply*

▶ To form adverbs which end in **–mente,** add **–mente** to the feminine form of the adjective. If the adjective does not have a special feminine form, just add **–mente** to the standard form.

ADJECTIVE	FEMININE FORM	SUFFIX	ADVERB
seguro	segura	-mente	seguramente
fabuloso	fabulosa	-mente	fabulosamente
enorme		-mente	enormemente
feliz		-mente	felizmente

▶ Adverbs that end in **–mente** generally follow the verb, while adverbs that modify an adjective or another adverb precede the word they modify.

Javier dibuja **maravillosamente.**
Javier draws wonderfully.

Inés está **casi siempre** ocupada.
Inés is almost always busy.

¡ATENCIÓN!
When a sentence contains two or more adverbs in sequence, the suffix **–mente** is dropped from all but the last adverb.
Ex: **El médico nos habló simple y abiertamente.** *The doctor spoke to us simply and openly.*
• • •
Adjectives do not lose their accents when adding **–mente.**
Ex:
fácil → **fácilmente**
débil → **débilmente**

Common adverbs and adverbial expressions

a menudo	*often*	**así**	*like this; so*	**menos**	*less*
a tiempo	*on time*	**bastante**	*enough; rather*	**muchas veces**	*a lot; many times*
a veces	*sometimes*	**casi**	*almost*	**poco**	*little*
además (de)	*furthermore; besides*	**con frecuencia**	*frequently*	**por lo menos**	*at least*
apenas	*hardly; scarcely*	**de vez en cuando**	*from time to time*	**pronto**	*soon*
		despacio	*slowly*	**rápido**	*quickly*

¡ATENCIÓN!
Rápido functions as an adjective (**Ella tiene una computadora rápida.**) as well as an adverb (**Ella corre rápido.**). Note that as an adverb, **rápido** does not need to agree with any other word in the sentence. You can also use the adverb **rápidamente** (**Ella corre rápidamente**).

¡INTÉNTALO! Transforma los siguientes adjetivos en adverbios.

1. alegre alegremente
2. constante constantemente
3. gradual gradualmente
4. perfecto perfectamente
5. real realmente
6. frecuente frecuentemente
7. tranquilo tranquilamente
8. regular regularmente
9. maravilloso maravillosamente
10. normal normalmente
11. básico básicamente
12. afortunado afortunadamente

TEACHING OPTIONS

Heritage Speakers Have heritage speakers interview an older member of their home community about daily life when he or she was a young adult. Students should write a summary of the information, using at least eight of the common adverbs and adverbial expressions listed.

Extra Practice Have pairs of students write sentences using adverbs such as **nunca, hoy, lentamente,** and so forth. When they have finished, ask volunteers to dictate their sentences to you to write on the board. After you have written a sentence and corrected any errors, ask volunteers to suggest a sentence that uses the antonym of the adverb.

Práctica

1 **Escoger** Completa las oraciones con los adverbios adecuados.

1. La cita era para las dos pero llegamos ___tarde___. (mientras, nunca, tarde)
2. El problema fue que ___ayer___ se nos descompuso el despertador. (aquí, ayer, despacio)
3. La recepcionista no se enojó porque sabe que normalmente llego ___a tiempo___. (a veces, a tiempo, poco)
4. ___Por lo menos___ el doctor estaba listo. (por lo menos, muchas veces, casi)
5. ___Apenas___ tuvimos que esperar cinco minutos. (así, además, apenas)
6. El doctor dijo que nuestra hija Irene necesitaba cambiar su rutina diaria ___inmediatamente___. (temprano, menos, inmediatamente)
7. El doctor nos explicó ___bien___ las recomendaciones del Cirujano General (*Surgeon General*) sobre la salud de los jóvenes. (de vez en cuando, bien, apenas)
8. ___Afortunadamente___ nos dijo que Irene estaba bien, pero tenía que hacer más ejercicio y comer mejor. (bastante, afortunadamete, a menudo)

NOTA CULTURAL

La doctora Antonia Novello, de Puerto Rico, fue la primera mujer y la primera hispana en tomar el cargo de **Cirujana General** de los Estados Unidos (1990-1993).

Comunicación

2 **Aspirina** Lee el anuncio y responde a las preguntas con un(a) compañero/a.

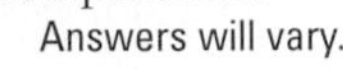

Answers will vary.

No Hay Tiempo Para el Dolor de Cabeza
Si tienes prisa, o simplemente quieres que tu dolor de cabeza se vaya muy pronto, piensa en Bayer. Se asimila mejor y actúa rápidamente. Ya no se puede perder tiempo por un dolor de cabeza.
ASPIRINA
Bayer
Siempre a tu lado.

1. ¿Cuáles son los adverbios que aparecen en el anuncio?
2. Según el anuncio, ¿cuáles son las ventajas (*advantages*) de este tipo de aspirina? ¿Cuáles son sus cualidades?
3. ¿Tienen ustedes muchos dolores de cabeza? ¿Qué toman para curarlos?
4. ¿Qué medicamentos ven con frecuencia en los anuncios de televisión? Escriban descripciones de varios de estos anuncios. Usen adverbios en sus descripciones.

1 Suggestion Review common adverbs and adverbial expressions by drawing a three-column chart on the board. Title the columns **¿Cómo?**, **¿Cuándo?**, and **¿Dónde?** Ask volunteers to call out adverbs for each column. Write the correct answers on the board. Ex: **¿Cómo? (a tiempo, lentamente, temprano) ¿Cuándo? (nunca, siempre, a menudo) ¿Dónde? (aquí, allí)**

2 Suggestion Before assigning the activity, ask some general questions about the ad. Ex: **¿Qué producto se vende? ¿Dónde se encuentra un anuncio de este tipo?**

2 Expansion Have pairs do a similar ad for a different pharmaceutical product. Collect the ads and read the descriptions aloud. The rest of the class will guess what product is being advertised.

TEACHING OPTIONS

Extra Practice Here are five sentences containing adverbs to use as a dictation. **1. A mi profesor de español siempre se le olvidan las cosas. 2. Con frecuencia se pone dos zapatos diferentes por la mañana. 3. De vez en cuando trae un calcetín negro y otro blanco. 4. De vez en cuando se le pierden los papeles. 5. Felizmente es un profesor excelente y siempre aprendemos mucho en su clase.**

Game Divide the class into groups of three. Each group should have a piece of paper or a transparency. Say the name of a historical figure and give groups three minutes to write down as many facts as they can about that person, using adverbs and adverbial expressions. At the end of each round, have groups project their answers or read them aloud. Award one point to the group with the most correct answers for each historical figure.

Section Goals

In **Lectura** students will:
- learn to activate background knowledge to understand a reading selection
- read a content-rich text on health care while traveling

Instructional Resource
Companion website:
www.vistahigherlearning.com

Estrategia Tell students that they will find it easier to understand the content of a reading selection on a particular topic by reviewing what they know about the subject before reading. Then ask students to brainstorm ways to stay healthy while traveling. Possible responses: don't drink the water, don't eat raw fruit or vegetables, pack personal medical supplies that may not be available at the destination.

Examinar el texto Students should mention that the text is an interview (**entrevista**) by a journalist (**periodista**) of an author (**autora**) whose book is about health care while traveling.

Conocimiento previo Have small groups write a paragraph summarizing ways to safeguard health while traveling. Their recommendations should be based on their collective experiences. Encourage them to draw on the experiences of people they know if no one in the group can relate personally to one of the situations mentioned in the items. Have groups share their paragraphs with the class.

The Affective Dimension Remind your students that they will probably feel less anxious about reading in Spanish if they follow the suggestions in the **Estrategia** sections, which are designed to reinforce and increase reading comprehension skills.

Lectura

Antes de leer

Estrategia
Activating background knowledge

Using what you already know about a particular subject will often help you better understand a reading selection. For example, if you read an article about a recent medical discovery, you might think about what you already know about health in order to understand unfamiliar words or concepts.

Examinar el texto

Utiliza las estrategias de lectura que tú consideras las más efectivas para hacer unas observaciones preliminares acerca del texto. Después trabajen en parejas para comparar sus observaciones acerca del texto. Luego contesten las siguientes preguntas:

- Analiza el formato del texto. ¿Qué tipo de texto es? ¿Dónde crees que se publicó este artículo?
- ¿Quiénes son Carla Baron y Tomás Monterrey?
- Mira la foto del libro. ¿Qué sugiere el título del libro sobre su contenido?

Conocimiento previo

Ahora piensen en su conocimiento previo° sobre el cuidado de la salud en los viajes. Consideren las siguientes preguntas:

- ¿Viajaste alguna vez a otro estado o a otro país?
- ¿Tuviste algunos problemas durante tus viajes con el agua, la comida o el clima del país?
- ¿Olvidaste poner en tu maleta algún medicamento que después necesitaste?
- Imagina que tu amigo/a se va de viaje. Dile por lo menos cinco cosas que debe hacer para prevenir cualquier problema de salud.

recursos

conocimiento previo *Background knowledge*

Libro de la semana

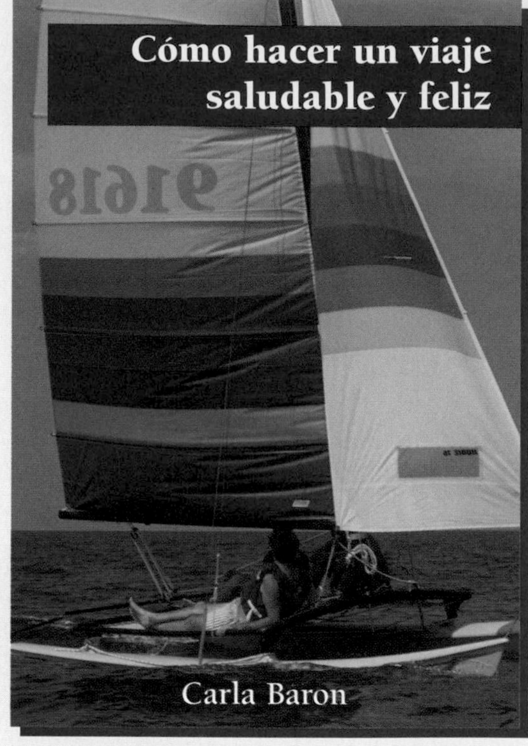

Después de leer

Correspondencias Busca las correspondencias entre los problemas y las recomendaciones.

Problemas

1. el agua _b_
2. el sol _d_
3. la comida _a_
4. la identificación _e_
5. el clima _c_

Recomendaciones

a. Hay que adaptarse a los ingredientes no familiares.
b. Toma sólo productos purificados (*purified*).
c. Es importante llevar ropa adecuada cuando viajas.
d. Lleva loción o crema con alta protección solar.
e. Lleva tu pasaporte.

TEACHING OPTIONS

Heritage Speakers Have pairs of heritage speakers interview each other about health problems they have encountered while traveling. First, have them brainstorm a list of pertinent questions, then have them take turns asking and answering them. After the interview each student writes a short paragraph about his or her own experience.

Small Groups Have groups of three select a country they would like to visit. Ask students to research what food and beverage precautions should be taken (**precauciones que se deben tomar**) by visitors to that country. Students should mention precautions such as not eating undercooked meat, uncooked seafood or vegetables, raw fruits, or unpasteurized dairy products, and not drinking tap water or drinks with ice or mixed with water.

Entrevista a Carla Baron

por Tomás Monterrey

Tomás: ¿Por qué escribió su libro *Cómo hacer un viaje saludable y feliz?*

Carla: Me encanta viajar, conocer otras culturas y escribir. Mi primer viaje lo hice cuando era estudiante universitaria. Todavía recuerdo el día en que llegamos a San Juan, Puerto Rico. Era el panorama ideal para unas vacaciones maravillosas, pero al llegar a la habitación del hotel, bebí mucha agua de la llave° y luego pedí un jugo de frutas con mucho hielo°. El clima en San Juan es tropical y yo tenía mucha sed y calor. Los síntomas llegaron en menos de media hora: pasé dos días con dolor de estómago y corriendo al cuarto de baño cada 10 minutos. Desde entonces, siempre que viajo sólo bebo agua mineral y llevo un pequeño bolso con medicinas necesarias como pastillas para el dolor y también bloqueador solar, una crema repelente de mosquitos y un desinfectante.

Tomás: ¿Son reales° las situaciones que se narran en su libro?

Carla: Sí, son reales y son mis propias° historias°. A menudo los autores crean caricaturas divertidas de un turista en dificultades. ¡En mi libro la turista en dificultades soy yo!

Tomás: ¿Qué recomendaciones puede encontrar el lector en su libro?

Carla: Bueno, mi libro es anecdótico y humorístico, pero el tema de la salud se trata° de manera seria. En general, se dan recomendaciones sobre ropa adecuada para cada sitio, consejos para protegerse del sol, y comidas y bebidas adecuadas para el turista que viaja al Caribe o a la América del Sur.

Tomás: ¿Tiene algún consejo para las personas que se enferman cuando viajan?

Carla: Muchas veces los turistas toman el avión sin saber nada acerca del país que van a visitar. Ponen toda su ropa en la maleta, toman el pasaporte, la cámara fotográfica y ¡a volar°! Es necesario tomar precauciones porque nuestro cuerpo necesita adaptarse al clima, al sol, a la humedad, al agua y a la comida. Se trata de° viajar, admirar las maravillas del mundo y regresar a casa con hermosos recuerdos. En resumen, el secreto es "prevenir en vez de° curar".

llave *faucet* hielo *ice* reales *true* propias *own* historias *stories* se trata *is treated* ¡a volar! *Off they go!* Se trata de *It's a question of* en vez de *instead of*

Correspondencias Ask students to work together in pairs to use cognates and context clues to match **Problemas** with **Recomendaciones**.

Seleccionar
- Have students check their work by locating the sections in the text where the answers can be found.
- Ask the questions of the whole class. Ask volunteers to answer orally or to write their answers on the board.

Seleccionar Selecciona la respuesta correcta.

1. El tema principal de este libro es __d__.
   a. Puerto Rico b. la salud y el agua c. otras culturas d. el cuidado de la salud en los viajes
2. Las situaciones narradas en el libro son __a__.
   a. autobiográficas b. inventadas c. ficticias
3. ¿Qué recomendaciones no vas a encontrar en este libro? __d__
   a. cómo vestirse adecuadamente
   b. cómo prevenir las quemaduras solares
   c. consejos sobre la comida y la bebida
   d. cómo dar propina en los países del Caribe o de América del Sur
4. En opinión de la Srta. Baron, __b__.
   a. es bueno tomar agua de la llave y beber jugo de frutas con mucho hielo
   b. es mejor tomar solamente agua embotellada (*bottled*)
   c. los minerales son buenos para el dolor abdominal
   d. es importante visitar el cuarto de baño cada 10 minutos
5. ¿Cuál de los siguientes productos no lleva la autora cuando viaja a otros países? __c__
   a. desinfectante
   b. crema repelente
   c. detergente
   d. pastillas medicinales

TEACHING OPTIONS

Pairs Ask pairs to use the items in **Correspondencias** on page 320 as a model. Have them work together to write additional possibilities for **Problemas** and **Recomendaciones**. Ex: **Problema: el dinero; Recomendación: lleva cheques de viajero o una tarjeta de crédito internacional**. When pairs have completed five more items, have them exchange their items with another pair who can match them.

Heritage Speakers Ask heritage speakers to prepare a short presentation of health tips for traveling in their countries. Students should include information on any immunizations that may be required; appropriate clothing, particularly for countries in which the seasons are opposite ours; spicy regional foods or dishes that may cause digestive problems; and so forth.

Section Goals

In **Escritura** students will:

- write a narrative using the preterite and the imperfect
- integrate lesson vocabulary structures in their narrative

Estrategia Write the following sentences on the board: **1. La enfermera le puso una inyección. 2. Cuando el médico estaba en la sala de emergencias, no había antibióticos para todos los pacientes. 3. Fue a sacarse una muela la semana pasada. 4. Mi abuelo tenía dolor en las rodillas y no podía caminar muy lejos.** Ask volunteers to explain why the preterite or imperfect tense was used in each case. Then have the class write down actions for their composition in the preterite or imperfect and compare their lists with those of a few classmates.

Tema Explain that the story or composition students are to write will be about something that occurred in the past. Encourage them to brainstorm as many details as possible about the event before they begin writing. Tell them that one way of organizing a narrative is by chronological order.

Successful Language Learning Remind your students to check for the correct use of the preterite and the imperfect whenever they write about the past in Spanish. Tell them they may find it helpful to memorize the summary of preterite versus imperfect in **Estrategia.**

Escritura

Estrategia

Mastering the simple past tenses

In Spanish, when you write about events that occurred in the past you will need to know when to use the preterite and when to use the imperfect tense. A good understanding of the uses of each tense will make it much easier to determine which one to use as you write.

Look at the following summary of the uses of the preterite and the imperfect and write your own example sentence for each of the rules described.

Preterite vs. imperfect

Preterite

1. Actions viewed as completed
   ____
2. Beginning or end of past actions
   ____
3. Series of past actions
   ____

Imperfect

1. Ongoing past actions
   ____
2. Habitual past actions
   ____
3. Mental, physical and emotional states and characteristics in the past
   ____

Get together with a few classmates to compare your example sentences. Then use these sentences and the chart as a guide to help you decide which tense to use as you are writing a story or other type of narration about the past.

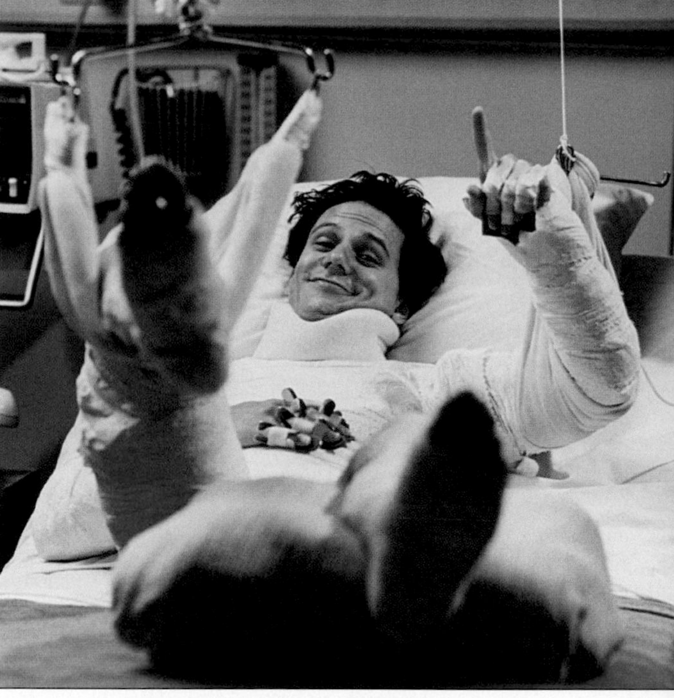

Tema

Escribir una historia

Escribe una historia acerca de una experiencia tuya° (o de otra persona) con una enfermedad, accidente o problema médico. Tu historia puede ser real o imaginaria y puede tratarse de un incidente divertido, humorístico o desastroso°. Incluye todos los detalles relevantes. Consulta la lista de sugerencias° con detalles que puedes incluir.

- Descripción del/de la paciente
  Nombre y apellidos
  Edad
  Características físicas
  Historial médico°
- Descripción de los síntomas
  Enfermedades
  Accidente
  Problemas médicos
- Descripción del tratamiento°
  Tratamientos
  Recetas
  Operaciones

tuya *of yours* desastroso *disastrous* sugerencias *suggestions*
Historial médico *medical history* tratamiento *treatment*

TEACHING OPTIONS

Proofreading Activity Copy the following sentences containing mistakes onto the board or a transparency as a proofreading activity to do with the whole class.

1. **¿Cuánto tiempo hace que te rompía la pierna? ¿Hace por menos un año?**
2. **Cuando fui niño, ía al médico con frecuencia.**
3. **Juan siempre tuvo un resfriado y le dolió la cabeza.**
4. **Lourdes caminó por el campus cuando se le caía las llaves.**
5. **Fue las diez de la mañana en punto cuando llegabamos a la clase.**
6. **¿Ustedes se les olvidaba la tarea ayer?**
7. **De niño casi cantabamos el himno nacional en la clase.**

1 **Ideas y organización**

Haz una lista de todos los detalles que quieres narrar. Escoge los detalles más interesantes para tu narración.

2 **Primer borrador**

Utilizando tus apuntes de **Ideas y organización** y tu lista de los usos del pretérito y el imperfecto, escribe el primer borrador de tu historia.

3 **Comentario**

Intercambia tu historia con la de un(a) compañero/a. Lee su borrador y reflexiona sobre las partes mejor escritas de su historia. Comparte tus impresiones. Utiliza esta guía para evaluar el trabajo de tu compañero/a:

1. ¿Son interesantes los detalles de la narración? ¿Necesita más detalles o menos detalles?
2. ¿Contiene redundancias la narración? ¿Cómo pueden eliminarse?
3. ¿Es lógica la secuencia de los eventos?
4. ¿Se usan correctamente el pretérito y el imperfecto?
5. ¿Notas errores de gramática o de ortografía?

4 **Redacción**

Revisa el primer borrador según las indicaciones de tu compañero/a. Si es necesario, incorpora nuevas ideas para enriquecer la narración de los eventos. Utiliza esta guía para hacer la última revisión antes de escribir tu copia final:

1. Subraya cada verbo para comprobar el uso correcto del pretérito y del imperfecto.
2. Revisa la concordancia entre el sujeto y el verbo de cada frase.
3. Revisa la concordancia entre los sustantivos y los adjetivos.
4. Revisa los pronombres para comprobar el uso correcto de cada uno.
5. Revisa la ortografía y la puntuación otra vez con la ayuda de tus **Anotaciones para mejorar la escritura.**

5 **Evaluación y progreso**

Reúnete° con tres compañeros/as. Doblen° la parte superior de cada composición para esconder° el nombre del/de la autor(a). Intercambien sus composiciones con las de otro grupo. Lean los trabajos del otro grupo e intenten determinar de quién es cada composición. Como último paso, lee con interés los comentarios y las correcciones de tu profesor(a), anotando los errores en las **Anotaciones para mejorar la escritura** en tu **Carpeta de trabajos.**

Reúnete *Get together* Doblen *Fold back* esconder *to hide*

Comentario
- Go over guide questions 1–5 with the whole class so peer readers understand their task. Then have pairs of students exchange compositions. Allow five minutes for reading and comments. Allow five minutes for discussing comments.
- Have students prepare **Redacción** as homework. Ask them to rewrite their drafts, incorporating the peer comments and following the directions in **Redacción**.

Evaluación y progreso Give the class five minutes to exchange and comment on the final drafts of their compositions. Then have students hand them in.

Writing Sample Here is a sample of a composition that would constitute superior writing achievement.

Tomás es uno de los mejores amigos de mis padres. Es un costarricense muy simpático de unos 45 años, alto y gordo. Tomás tiene una historia de problemas con alergias y sinusitis. El verano pasado hizo una excursión turística a las ruinas de Monte Albán, cerca de la ciudad de Oaxaca. Hacía mucho calor y pasó todo el día caminando por las ruinas. Luego, caminó por la ciudad. Había mucha contaminación por los coches y autobuses y empezó a toser muchísimo. Por la noche, Tomás se quejaba de dolor de cabeza, estaba mareado y cuando empezó a vomitar, su esposa llamó una ambulancia. En el hospital el médico le explicó que tenía sinusitis grave a causa de los contaminantes en el aire y del calor; le recetó unos antibióticos.

EVALUATION: Historia

Criteria	Scale
Content	1 2 3 4
Organization	1 2 3 4
Use of preterite and imperfect	1 2 3 4
Use of vocabulary	1 2 3 4
Accuracy and mechanics	1 2 3 4

Scoring	
Excellent	18–20 points
Good	14–17 points
Satisfactory	10–13 points
Unsatisfactory	< 10 points

Section Goals

In **Escuchar** students will:

- listen to a short paragraph and identify the topic
- answer questions based on the content of a recorded conversation

Instructional Resources
Textbook CD
IRM: Tapescript, p. 94

Estrategia
Script Ya sé que no pudiste venir a mi quinceañera. ¡Cuánto lo siento, Juanita! Vinieron muchos invitados, ¡creo que eran más de cien! Todos se divirtieron y yo lo pasé fenomenal. Llevé un traje largo y rosado con mucho encaje, y guantes y zapatos del mismo color. Mi tía Rosa, la madrina de la fiesta, me preparó el pastel. Me imagino que sabes que el pastel era de chocolate porque me fascina el chocolate. Me dieron muchos regalos. ¡Imagínate!, mis abuelos me regalaron un viaje para ir a visitarte.

Suggestion Have students look at the photo and guide them to see that Carlos Peña is talking to a health care provider about his illness.

Ahora Escucha
Script SRTA. MÉNDEZ: Consultorio del Dr. Aguilar. Buenos días.
CARLOS PEÑA: Buenos días, señorita. Habla Carlos Peña. Mire, no me siento nada bien.
M: ¿Qué tiene?
C: Tengo mucha tos. Apenas me deja dormir. Estoy muy congestionado y tengo un tremendo dolor de cabeza.
M: ¿Cuánto tiempo hace que se siente así?
C: Bueno, hace cinco días que me empezó a doler la garganta. Fue de mal en peor.
M: ¿Tiene fiebre?
C: Pues, en realidad, no lo sé. No me tomé la temperatura, pero creo que sí tengo fiebre porque tengo mucho frío y me duelen los huesos.
M: Pienso que usted tiene la gripe. Primero hay que verificar que no tiene una infección, pero creo que el doctor le va a recetar algo que va a ayudarle.
Le puedo dar una cita con el médico hoy a las tres de la tarde.
C: Excelente.
M: ¿Cómo me dijo que se llama?
C: Carlos Peña, señorita.
M: ¿Y su fecha de nacimiento y su teléfono, por favor?
C: 4 de octubre de 1983, y mi teléfono... seis cuarenta y tres, veinticinco, cincuenta y dos.
M: Muy bien. Hasta las tres.
C: Sí. Muchas gracias, señorita, y hasta luego.

Escuchar

Estrategia

Listening for specific information

You can listen for specific information effectively once you identify the subject of a conversation and use your background knowledge to predict what kinds of information you might hear.

To practice this strategy, you will listen to a paragraph from a letter Marta wrote to a friend about her fifteenth birthday celebration. Before you listen to the paragraph, use what you know about this type of party to predict the content of the letter. What kinds of details might Marta include in her description of the celebration? Now listen to the paragraph and jot down the specific information Marta relates. Then compare these details to the predictions you made about the letter.

Preparación

Mira la foto. ¿Con quién crees que está conversando Carlos Peña? ¿De qué están hablando?

Ahora escucha 

Ahora escucha la conversación de la señorita Méndez y Carlos Peña. Marca las frases donde se mencionan los síntomas de Carlos.

1. ____ Tiene infección en los ojos.
2. ____ Se lastimó el dedo.
3. ✔ No puede dormir.
4. ✔ Siente dolor en los huesos.
5. ____ Está mareado.
6. ✔ Está congestionado.
7. ____ Le duele el estómago.
8. ✔ Le duele la cabeza.
9. ____ Es alérgico a la aspirina.
10. ✔ Tiene tos.
11. ✔ Le duele la garganta.
12. ____ Se rompió la pierna.
13. ____ Tiene dolor de oído.
14. ✔ Tiene frío.

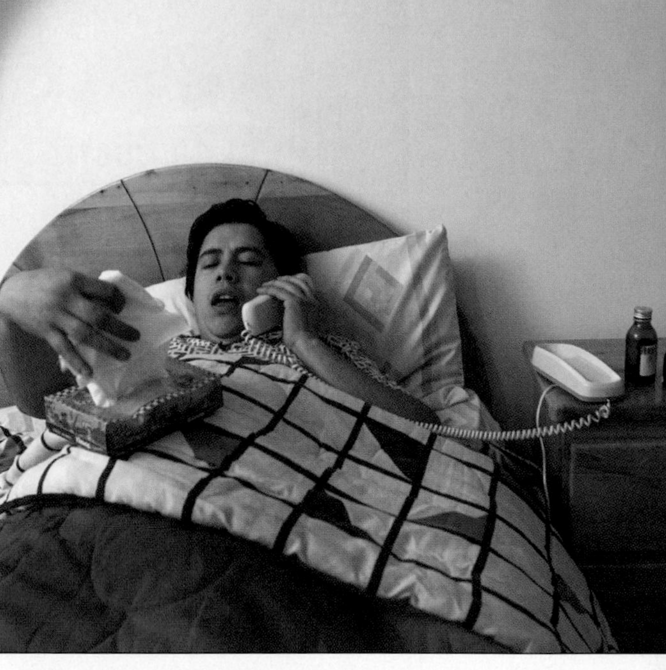

Comprensión

Preguntas

1. ¿Tiene fiebre Carlos? Carlos no sabe si tiene fiebre pero tiene mucho frío y le duelen los huesos.
2. ¿Cuánto tiempo hace que le duele la garganta a Carlos? Hace cinco días que le duele la garganta.
3. ¿Qué tiene que hacer el médico antes de recetarle algo a Carlos? Tiene que ver si tiene una infección.
4. ¿A qué hora es su cita con el médico? Es a las tres de la tarde.
5. Después de darle una cita con el médico, ¿qué otra información le pide a Carlos la señorita del consultorio? Le pide su nombre, su fecha de nacimiento y su número de teléfono.
6. En tu opinión, ¿qué tiene Carlos? ¿Gripe? ¿Un resfriado? ¿Alergias? Explica tu opinión. Answers will vary.

Diálogo

Con un(a) compañero/a, escribe el diálogo entre el Dr. Aguilar y Carlos Peña en el consultorio del médico. Usa la información del diálogo telefónico para pensar en lo que dice el médico mientras examina a Carlos. Imagina cómo responde Carlos y qué preguntas le hace al médico. ¿Cuál es el diagnóstico del médico?

Participa en una conferencia

Imagina que eres un conferenciante° preparando una conferencia° en la que vas a hablar sobre el sistema político y social costarricense.

1 Prepara la presentación

Prepara una presentación sobre dos o tres de los sistemas políticos y sociales de Costa Rica que más te interesan. Aquí tienes una lista de los posibles temas que puedes usar en tu presentación.

- El sistema de sanidad°: el seguro° médico, la eficacia del sistema, la repercusión económica
- El sistema educativo: la enseñanza pública, las universidades
- Las ayudas° sociales: las ayudas para las víctimas de los accidentes de trabajo, las ayudas a la maternidad
- El gobierno: la democracia, los partidos políticos
- El sistema jurídico°
- La defensa nacional y la eliminación del ejército

Usa los **Recursos para la investigación** para buscar información sobre los temas sociales que escojas para la conferencia.

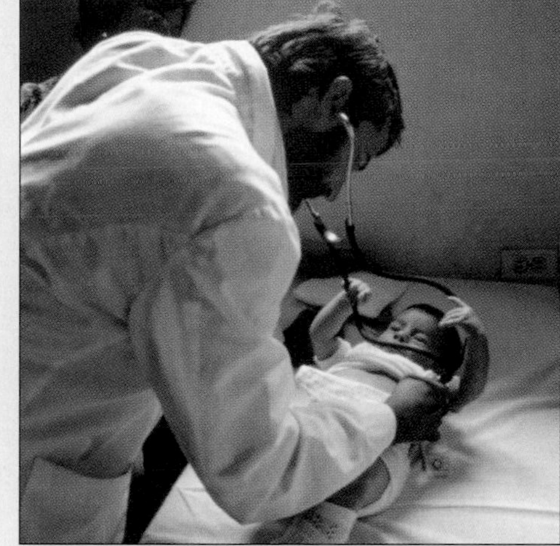

En los hospitales públicos de Costa Rica, como el Hospital de los Niños, los servicios médicos son gratuitos.

2 Presenta la información

Presenta tu información en la conferencia y pregúntales después a tus compañeros/as su opinión sobre los sistemas políticos y sociales de Costa Rica. ¿Qué tienen en común estos sistemas con los de los Estados Unidos? ¿En qué se diferencian los sistemas?

recursos para la investigación

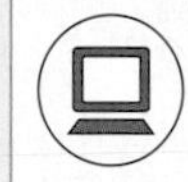

Internet Palabras clave: Costa Rica, San José, seguro médico, gobierno

Comunidad Estudiantes y profesores que son de Costa Rica o que lo conocen

Biblioteca Enciclopedias, libros sobre Costa Rica, libros sobre sistemas políticos y sociales

Otros recursos Embajadas o consulados costarricenses

conferenciante *lecturer* conferencia *lecture* sistema de sanidad *health care system* seguro *insurance* ayudas *assistance* jurídico *legal*

Section Goals

In **Proyecto** students will:
- use Spanish as they research and interact with the wider world
- write and deliver a speech on the Costa Rican political or social system as a speaker at a conference
- learn about Costa Rican political and social systems

Suggestion Students might need a week to complete the project, so at the beginning of that time period, have them open their books to this page and glance over **Proyecto**.

Prepara la presentación
- Explain to students that Costa Rica's political and social systems fall under **Ministerios** (Ministries), for example, **Ministerio de Salud** (Ministry of Health), **Ministerio de Educación** (Ministry of Education), and so forth.
- Have students work in groups of six to divide up the research. Then they can designate a group member or group members to give the speech.

Presenta la información
- Have students organize a mock conference (**conferencia simulada**) in which every group's representative or each student gives his or her speech in front of all the conference participants.
- In lieu of the standard presentation to a passive audience, invite students to guide an interactive question-and-answer session with their classmates.
- You may wish to set aside sufficient class time to do a few presentations at a time until all students have had a chance to present.

EVALUATION: Conferencia

Criteria	Scale
Content	1 2 3 4
Organization	1 2 3 4
Accuracy	1 2 3 4
Comprehensibility	1 2 3 4
Creativity	1 2 3 4

Scoring	
Excellent	18–20 points
Good	14–17 points
Satisfactory	10–13 points
Unsatisfactory	< 10 points

Section Goal
In **Panorama**, students will read about the geography and culture of Costa Rica.

Instructional Resources
Transparencies, #3, #4, #39
WB/VM: Workbook, pp. 121–122; Video Activities, pp. 267–268
***Panorama cultural** DVD/Video*
Interactive CD-ROM
IRM: Videoscript, p. 131
Companion website: www.vistahigherlearning.com
Presentations CD-ROM

Suggestion Have students look at the map of Costa Rica or project **Transparency #39.** Encourage them to mention the physical features that they notice. Discuss the images in the call-out photos.

El país en cifras After each section, ask students questions about the content. Ex: **¿Entre qué masas de agua está Costa Rica? ¿Las ciudades principales, en qué lado de la Cordillera Central están?** When reading about Costa Rica's population, point out that the country has over a 90% literacy rate, the best in Latin America. Point out that Óscar Arias received the Nobel Peace Prize for his work in resolving civil wars in the other Central American countries during the 1970s.

¡Increíble pero cierto! Costa Rica has one of the most longstanding democratic traditions in America. Although it has no army, it does have a national police force and a rural guard.

Costa Rica

El país en cifras

- **Área:** 51.100 km² (19.730 millas²), *aproximadamente el área de Virginia Occidental°*
- **Población:** 4.200.000

Costa Rica es el país de Centroamérica con la población más homogénea. El 98% de sus habitantes es blanco y mestizo°. Más del 50% de la población es de descendencia° española y un alto porcentaje tiene sus orígenes en otros países europeos.

- **Capital:** San José —1.037.000
- **Ciudades principales:** Alajuela —173.000, Cartago —119.000, Puntarenas —102.000, Heredia —73.000

SOURCE: Population Division, UN Secretariat

- **Moneda:** colón costarricense°
- **Idioma:** español (oficial)

Bandera de Costa Rica

Celebración del Viernes Santo

Cráter del Volcán Poás

NICARAGUA · Río San Juan · Río Tempisque · Cordillera de Guanacaste · Volcán Poás · Cordillera Central · Cordillera de Tilarán · Alajuela · Puntarenas · Heredia · Río Grande de Tárcoles · Volcán Irazú · San José · Cartago · Océano Pacífico

Edificio Metálico en San José

Costarricenses célebres

- **Carmen Lyra,** escritora (1888–1949)
- **Chavela Vargas,** cantante (1919–)
- **Óscar Arias Sánchez,** político (1949–)
- **Claudia Poll,** nadadora° olímpica (1972–)

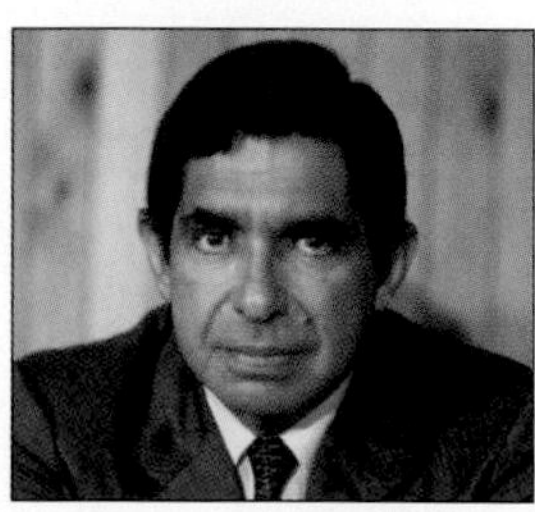

Óscar Arias recibió el Premio Nobel de la Paz en 1987.

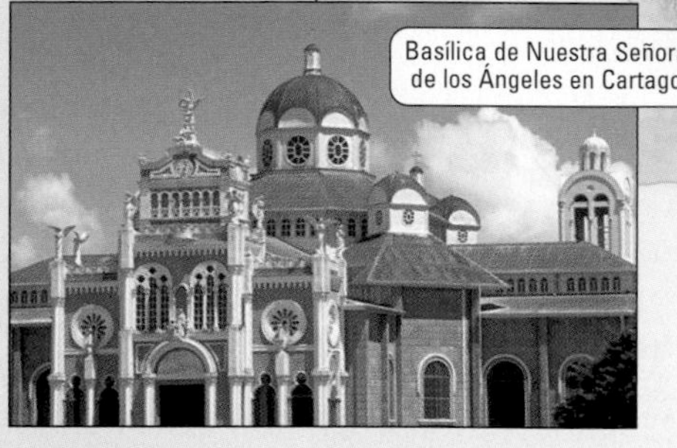

Basílica de Nuestra Señora de los Ángeles en Cartago

ESTADOS UNIDOS · OCÉANO ATLÁNTICO · COSTA RICA · OCÉANO PACÍFICO · AMÉRICA DEL SUR

recursos

WB pp. 121–122	VM pp. 267–268	I CD-ROM Lección 10	vistahigherlearning.com

Virginia Occidental *West Virginia* mestizo *of indigenous and white parentage* descendencia *descent* costarricense *Costa Rican* nadadora *swimmer* ejército *army* gastos *expenditures* cuartel *barracks*

¡Increíble pero cierto!

Costa Rica es el único país latinoamericano que no tiene ejército°. Sin gastos° militares, el gobierno puede poner más dinero en la educación y las artes. En la foto aparece el Museo Nacional de Costa Rica, antiguo cuartel del ejército.

TEACHING OPTIONS

Heritage Speakers Invite students of Costa Rican background or from other countries of Central America to share information about the national nicknames that Central Americans use for each other. Costa Ricans are called **ticos**, Nicaraguans are called **nicas**, and Guatemalans are called **chapines**.

Variación léxica If you visit Costa Rica, you may hear a few interesting colloquialisms such as these. **Pulpería** is the word for the *corner grocery store.* A gas station is called a **bomba**, literally a *pump.* A city block is called **cien metros**, literally *a hundred meters.*

Lugares • Los parques nacionales

Establecido° para la protección de los delicados ecosistemas de la región y su biodiversidad, el sistema de parques nacionales ocupa el 12% del territorio de Costa Rica. En los parques, los ecoturistas pueden ver hermosas cataratas°, montañas y una multitud de plantas exóticas. Algunos parques ofrecen también la oportunidad de ver quetzales, monos°, jaguares, armadillos y elegantes mariposas° en su hábitat natural.

Economía • Las plantaciones de café

Costa Rica fue el primer país centroamericano en desarrollar° la industria del café. En el siglo° XIX los costarricenses empezaron a exportar su delicioso café, de rico aroma, a Inglaterra°, lo cual contribuyó mucho a la prosperidad de la nación. Hoy día, más de 50.000 costarricenses trabajan en el cultivo de café. El café representa cerca del 15% de las exportaciones anuales del país.

Mar Caribe

Limón

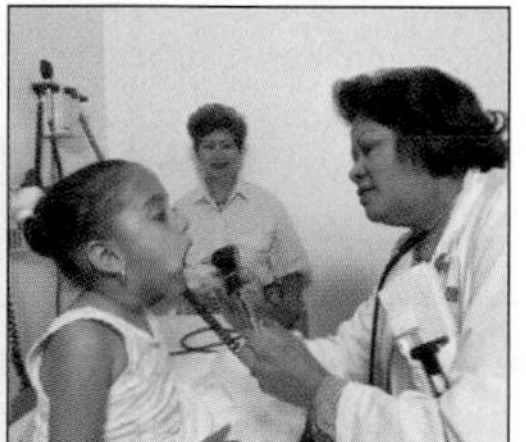

Sociedad • Una nación progresista

Un modelo de democracia y de estabilidad, Costa Rica es también uno de los países más progresistas del mundo°. Ofrece servicios médicos gratuitos° a todos sus ciudadanos° y también a los turistas. En 1870 Costa Rica eliminó la pena de muerte° y en 1948 eliminó el ejército° e hizo obligatoria y gratuita la educación para todos los costarricenses.

PANAMÁ

Bañistas en Limón

¿Qué aprendiste? Responde a las preguntas con una frase completa.

1. ¿Cómo se llama la capital de Costa Rica? La capital de Costa Rica se llama San José.
2. ¿Quién es Claudia Poll? Claudia Poll es una nadadora olímpica.
3. ¿Qué porcentaje del territorio de Costa Rica ocupan los parques nacionales? Los parques nacionales ocupan el 12% del territorio de Costa Rica.
4. ¿Qué hacen los parques nacionales? Los parques nacionales protegen los ecosistemas de la región y su biodiversidad.
5. ¿Qué pueden ver los turistas en los parques nacionales? En los parques nacionales, los turistas pueden ver cataratas, montañas y muchas plantas exóticas.
6. ¿Cuántos costarricenses trabajan en las plantaciones de café hoy día? Más de 50.000 costarricenses trabajan en las plantaciones de café hoy día.
7. ¿Cuándo eliminó Costa Rica la pena de muerte? Costa Rica eliminó la pena de muerte en 1870.

Conexión Internet Investiga estos temas en el sitio **www.vistahigherlearning.com.**

1. Busca información sobre Óscar Arias Sánchez. ¿Quién es? ¿Por qué se le considera (*is he considered*) un costarricense célebre?
2. Busca información sobre los artistas de Costa Rica. ¿Qué artista, escritor o cantante te interesa más? ¿Por qué?

Establecido *Established* cataratas *waterfalls* monos *monkeys* mariposas *butterflies* desarrollar *develop* siglo *century* Inglaterra *England* mundo *world* gratuitos *free* ciudadanos *citizens* pena de muerte *death penalty* ejército *army*

Los parques nacionales Costa Rica's system of national parks was begun in the 1960s. With the addition of buffer zones in which some logging and farming are allowed, the percentage of Costa Rica's territory protected by environmental legislation rose to 27%.

Las plantaciones de café Invite students to prepare a coffee-tasting session, where they sample the coffees of Central America. You may wish to compare them to South American or African coffees as well. Teach vocabulary to describe the flavors: **rico, amargo, fuerte,** and so forth.

Una nación progresista Because of its mild climate (in terms of weather *and* politics), Costa Rica has become a major destination for retired and expatriate Americans. Survey students to see how many have visited Costa Rica already, and how many know of friends or family who have visited or live there.

Conexión Internet Students will find supporting Internet activities and links at **www.vistahigherlearning.com.**

TEACHING OPTIONS

Worth Noting Costa Rica has three types of lands protected by ecological legislation: **parques nacionales, refugios silvestres,** and **reservas biológicas**. Costa Rica's most famous protected area is the **Reserva Biológica Bosque Nuboso Monteverde** (Monteverde Cloud Forest Biological Reserve), where over 400 different species of birds have been recorded. The town of Monteverde was founded by Quakers from the United States in 1951 who began dairy farming and cheese-making there. In order to protect the watershed, the settlers decided to preserve about a third of their property as a biological reserve. In 1972 this area was more than doubled, and this became the **Reserva Biológica**. Today Monteverde still has a cheese factory (**La Fábrica**) and its cheeses are sold throughout the country.

Instructional Resources
Vocabulary CD
Lab Manual, p. 60
Lab CD/MP3 ***Lección 10***
IRM: Tapescript, pp. 45–48
Testing Program: ***Pruebas,*** *pp. 109–120*
Testing Program Audio CD
Test Files CD-ROM

El cuerpo

la boca	*mouth*
el brazo	*arm*
la cabeza	*head*
el corazón	*heart*
el cuello	*neck*
el cuerpo	*body*
el dedo	*finger*
el estómago	*stomach*
la garganta	*throat*
el hueso	*bone*
la muela	*molar*
la nariz	*nose*
el oído	*(sense of) hearing; inner ear*
el ojo	*eye*
la oreja	*(outer) ear*
el pie	*foot*
la pierna	*leg*
la rodilla	*knee*
el tobillo	*ankle*

La salud

el accidente	*accident*
el antibiótico	*antibiotic*
la aspirina	*aspirin*
la clínica	*clinic*
el consultorio	*doctor's office*
el/la dentista	*dentist*
el/la doctor(a)	*doctor*
el dolor (de cabeza)	*(head)ache; pain*
el/la enfermero/a	*nurse*
el examen médico	*physical exam*
la farmacia	*pharmacy*
la gripe	*flu*
el hospital	*hospital*
la infección	*infection*
el medicamento	*medication*
la medicina	*medicine*
la operación	*operation*
el/la paciente	*patient*
la pastilla	*pill; tablet*
la radiografía	*X-ray*
la receta	*prescription*
el resfriado	*cold (illness)*
la sala de emergencia(s)	*emergency room*
la salud	*health*
el síntoma	*symptom*
la tos	*cough*

Verbos

caerse	*to fall (down)*
dañar	*to damage; to break down*
darse con	*to bump into; to run into*
doler (o:ue)	*to hurt*
enfermarse	*to get sick*
estar enfermo/a	*to be sick*
estornudar	*to sneeze*
lastimarse (el pie)	*to injure (one's foot)*
olvidar	*to forget*
poner una inyección	*to give an injection*
prohibir	*to prohibit*
recetar	*to prescribe*
romper	*to break*
romperse (la pierna)	*to break (one's leg)*
sacar(se) una muela	*to have a tooth removed*
ser alérgico/a (a)	*to be allergic (to)*
sufrir una enfermedad	*to suffer an illness*
tener dolor (*m.*)	*to have a pain*
tener fiebre	*to have a fever*
tomar la temperatura	*to take someone's temperature*
torcerse (o:ue) (el tobillo)	*to sprain (one's ankle)*
toser	*to cough*

Adjetivos

congestionado/a	*congested; stuffed-up*
embarazada	*pregnant*
grave	*grave; serious*
mareado/a	*dizzy; nauseated*
médico/a	*medical*
saludable	*healthy*
sano/a	*healthy*

Adverbios

a menudo	*often*
a tiempo	*on time*
a veces	*sometimes*
además (de)	*furthermore; besides*
apenas	*hardly; scarcely*
así	*like this; so*
bastante	*enough; rather*
casi	*almost*
con frecuencia	*frequently*
de niño/a	*as a child*
de vez en cuando	*from time to time*
despacio	*slowly*
menos	*less*
mientras	*while*
muchas veces	*a lot; many times*
poco	*little*
por lo menos	*at least*
pronto	*soon*
rápido	*quickly*
todos los días	*every day*

Expresiones útiles	*See page 303.*

recursos

LM p. 60	Lab CD/MP3 Lección 10	Vocab CD Lección 10

La tecnología 11

Communicative Goals

You will learn how to:

- Talk about using technology and electronic products
- Use common expressions on the telephone
- Talk about car trouble

A PRIMERA VISTA

- *¿Se llevan ellos bien o mal?*
- *¿Crees que hace mucho tiempo que se conocen?*
- *¿Son saludables?*
- *¿Qué partes del cuerpo se ven en la foto?*

Lesson Goals

In **Lección 11** students will be introduced to the following:

- terms related to home electronics and the Internet
- terms related to cars and their accessories
- familiar (**tú**) commands
- uses of **por** and **para**
- reciprocal reflexive verbs
- stressed possessive adjectives and pronouns
- recognizing borrowed words
- listing key words before writing
- giving instructions in an e-mail
- recognizing the genre of spoken discourse
- creating an advertisement for a cybercafé
- cultural, geographic, and historical information about Argentina

A primera vista Here are some additional questions you can ask based on the photo: **¿Te gustan las computadoras? ¿Para qué usas el correo electrónico? ¿Cómo se escribían tus padres cuando no existía el correo electrónico? ¿Se hablaban tus abuelos por teléfono con frecuencia? ¿Cuánto tiempo hace que sabes manejar? ¿Tienes carro?**

INSTRUCTIONAL RESOURCES

Workbook/Video Manual: WB Activities, pp. 123–134
Laboratory Manual: Lab Activities, pp. 61–66
Workbook/Video Manual: Video Activities, pp. 233–234; pp. 269–270
Instructor's Resource Manual: **Vocabulario adicional**, p. 189; **¡Inténtalo!** & **Práctica** Answers, pp. 215–216; **Fotonovela** Translations, pp. 144–145; Textbook CD Tapescript, p. 95; Lab CDs Tapescript, pp. 49–53; **Fotonovela** Videoscript, pp. 114–115; **Panorama cultural** Videoscript, p. 132
Info Gap Activities Booklet, pp. 41–44
Overhead Transparencies: #5, #6, #40, #41, #42
Lab Audio CD/MP3 **Lección 11**
Panorama cultural DVD/Video
Fotonovela DVD/Video
Testing Program, pp. 121–132
Testing Program Audio CD
Test Files CD-ROM
Companion website
Presentations CD-ROM
Textbook CD
Vocabulary CD
Interactive CD-ROM
Video CD-ROM
Web-SAM

Section Goals

In **Contextos**, students will learn and practice:

- vocabulary related to home electronics and the Internet
- terms related to cars and their accessories

Instructional Resources
Transparencies, #40, #41
Textbook CD
Vocabulary CD
WB/VM: Workbook, pp. 123–124
Lab Manual, p. 61
Lab CD/MP3 ***Lección 11***
IRM: ***Vocab. adicional****,*
p. 189; ***Práctica*** *Answers,*
pp. 215–216; Tapescript,
pp. 49–53; p. 95
Interactive CD-ROM
Companion website:
www.vistahigherlearning.com
Presentations CD-ROM

Suggestions

- Ask students about electronic items they may have. Ex: **¿Cuántos de ustedes tienen cámara digital? ¿Cuántos tienen un sitio web? ¿Cuántos tienen teléfono celular? ¿Cuántas veces al día lo usas?**
- Have students open their books to the drawing on pages 330–331 or project **Transparency #40**. Ask students questions to elicit computer vocabulary and involve them in a conversation about their computer use. Ex: **¿Es portátil la computadora? ¿Qué se usa para mover el cursor? ¿Quiénes navegan en la red? ¿Cuál es tu sitio web favorito?**
- Ask students about electronic items by giving true-false statements about associations. Ex: **El control remoto se usa con el televisor. (Cierto.)**

La tecnología

Más vocabulario

la calculadora	*calculator*
la cámara de video, digital	*video, digital camera*
el canal	*(TV) channel*
el cederrón	*CD-ROM*
la contestadora	*answering machine*
el estéreo	*stereo*
el ***fax***	*fax (machine)*
la televisión por cable	*cable television*
el tocadiscos compacto	*compact disc player*
el video(casete)	*video(cassette)*
el archivo	*file*
arroba	*@ symbol*
la dirección electrónica	*e-mail address*
Internet	*Internet*
la página principal	*home page*
el programa de computación	*software*
la red	*network; Web*
el sitio web	*website*
apagar	*to turn off*
borrar	*to erase*
descargar	*to download*
funcionar	*to work*
grabar	*to record*
guardar	*to save*
imprimir	*to print*
llamar	*to call*
navegar (en Internet)	*to surf (the Internet)*
poner, prender	*to turn on*
quemar	*to burn (a CD)*
sonar (o:ue)	*to ring*
descompuesto/a	*not working; out of order*
lento/a	*slow*
lleno/a	*full*

Variación léxica

computadora ⟷ ordenador (*Esp.*), computador (*Col.*)
descargar ⟷ bajar (*Esp., Col., Arg., Ven.*)

recursos

TEXT CD Lección 11	WB pp. 123–124	LM p. 61	Lab CD/MP3 Lección 11	I CD-ROM Lección 11	Vocab CD Lección 11

TEACHING OPTIONS

Extra Practice Students write down a list of six electronic or other technology items they have or use frequently. Then they circulate around the room asking others if they have those items too. When someone answers affirmatively, the student asks for his or her signature (**Firma aquí, por favor**). Students should try to get a different signature for each item.

Game Play **Concentración**. On eight cards, write names of electronic items. On another eight cards, draw or paste a picture that matches each of the first eight cards. Place the cards face-down in four rows of four. In pairs, students select two cards. If the two cards match, the pair keeps them. If the two cards don't match, students replace them in their original position. The group with the most cards at the end wins.

Práctica

1 **Escuchar** Escucha esta conversación entre dos amigas. Después completa las oraciones.

1. María y Ana están en __b__.
   a. una tienda b. un cibercafé c. un restaurante
2. El hijo de Ana le mandó __a__.
   a. unas fotos digitales b. un cederrón c. un disco compacto
3. A María le encantan __b__.
   a. los celulares b. las cámaras digitales c. los cibercafés
4. Ana prefiere guardar las fotos en __c__.
   a. la pantalla b. un archivo c. un cederrón
5. María quiere tomar un café y __c__.
   a. poner la computadora b. sacar fotos digitales
   c. navegar en Internet
6. Ana paga por el café y __a__.
   a. el uso de Internet b. la impresora c. el cederrón

2 **Oraciones** Escribe oraciones usando los elementos siguientes. Usa el pretérito y agrega (*add*) las palabras necesarias.

1. Yo / descargar / fotos digitales / Internet
   Yo descargué las fotos digitales por Internet.
2. Yo / apagar / televisor / diez / noche
   Yo apagué el televisor a las diez de la noche.
3. ¿Quién / poner / videocasetera?
   ¿Quién puso la videocasetera?
4. Daniel y su esposa / comprar / computadora portátil / ayer
   Daniel y su esposa compraron una computadora portátil ayer.
5. Sara y yo / ir / cibercafé / para / navegar en Internet
   Sara y yo fuimos al cibercafé para navegar en Internet.
6. Jaime / decidir / comprar / calculadora / nuevo
   Jaime decidió comprar una calculadora nueva.
7. Sandra / perder / control remoto
   Sandra perdió el control remoto.
8. David / poner / contestadora / y / acostarse
   David puso la contestadora y se acostó.
9. teléfono celular / sonar / pero / yo / no contestar
   El teléfono celular sonó pero yo no contesté.
10. Yo / sacar / fotos / cámara digital
    Yo saqué fotos con una cámara digital.

3 **Preguntas** Mira el dibujo de las páginas 330–331 y contesta las preguntas. Answers will vary.

1. ¿Qué tipo de café es?
2. ¿Cuántas impresoras hay? ¿Cuántos ratones?
3. ¿Por qué vinieron estas personas al café?
4. ¿Qué hace el camarero?
5. ¿Qué hace la mujer en la computadora? ¿Y el hombre?
6. ¿Qué máquinas están cerca del televisor?
7. ¿Dónde hay un cibercafé en tu ciudad?
8. ¿Por qué puedes tú necesitar un cibercafé?

TEACHING OPTIONS

Pairs Have pairs of students role-play one of the following situations taking place in a cybercafé: 1. One student plays an irate customer who claims to have been overcharged for brief Internet use. The second plays the cybercafé employee who insists on being paid the full amount, claiming that the customer spent quite a bit of time online. 2. One student plays a customer who has been waiting over an hour to use a computer and must ask another customer to log off and give him or her a chance. The second customer becomes annoyed at the request and the two must sort it all out.

Heritage Speakers Ask heritage speakers to tell about an experience with a visit to a cybercafé in a Spanish-speaking country: where they were, how much it cost, what the experience was like, etc. Ask other students to relate what was said.

1 Suggestion Have students check their answers by going over **Actividad 1** with the whole class.

1 Tapescript ANA: ¿María? ¿Qué haces aquí en el cibercafé? ¿No tienes Internet en casa?
MARÍA: Pues, sí, pero la computadora está descompuesta. Tengo que esperar unos días más.
A: Te entiendo. Me pasó lo mismo con la computadora portátil hace poco. Todavía no funciona bien . . . por eso vine aquí.
M: ¿Recibiste algún mensaje interesante?
A: Sí. Mi hijo está de vacaciones con unos amigos en Argentina. Tiene una cámara digital y me mandó unas fotos digitales.
M: ¡Qué bien! Me encantan las cámaras digitales. Normalmente imprimimos las fotos con nuestra impresora y no tenemos que ir a ninguna tienda. Es muy conveniente.
A: Claro que sí. También imprimo fotos, pero no voy a imprimirlas ahora. Prefiero guardarlas en un cederrón.
M: Buena idea. Ahí está mi café. Voy a navegar en Internet mientras tomo mi cafecito.
A: Bueno. Tengo que irme. Voy a pagar por el café y el uso de Internet. ¿No es muy caro, verdad?
M: Para nada, es muy barato. Hasta luego.
A: Chau. Nos vemos.
Textbook CD

2 Expansion In pairs, students create three similar dehydrated sentences for their partner to complete. Write some on the board and have the class "hydrate" them.

3 Expansion Have small groups discuss how they would design and run their own cybercafé. Encourage them to be creative with as many details as possible. What would they name it? Where would it be located? What would customers find there? How much would the services cost?

Suggestions

- Using cognate vocabulary, ask students about cars. Ex: **¿Cuántos de ustedes tienen carro? ¿Qué tipo de carro es? ¿Cuántas veces a la semana tienes que llenar el tanque? ¿Cuánto cuesta la gasolina ahora?**
- Project **Transparency #41**. Have students refer to the scene as you give true-false statements about it. Ex: **Un mecánico limpia el parabrisas. (Falso.)**

4 Suggestion Before beginning the activity, ask several brief yes-no questions to test comprehension. Ex: **¿Sí o no? Se usa el baúl para llenar el tanque. (No.)**

4 Expansion In pairs, students create three similar sentences for their partner to complete. Write some on the board and have the class complete them.

5 Expansion Ask groups to discuss car troubles they have had. Possible subjects are: a visit to the mechanic's, a car accident, getting a speeding ticket, etc. Write helpful vocabulary on the board. Ex: **ponerle una multa, exceder la velocidad máxima,** etc. Have each group pick the strangest or funniest story to share with the class.

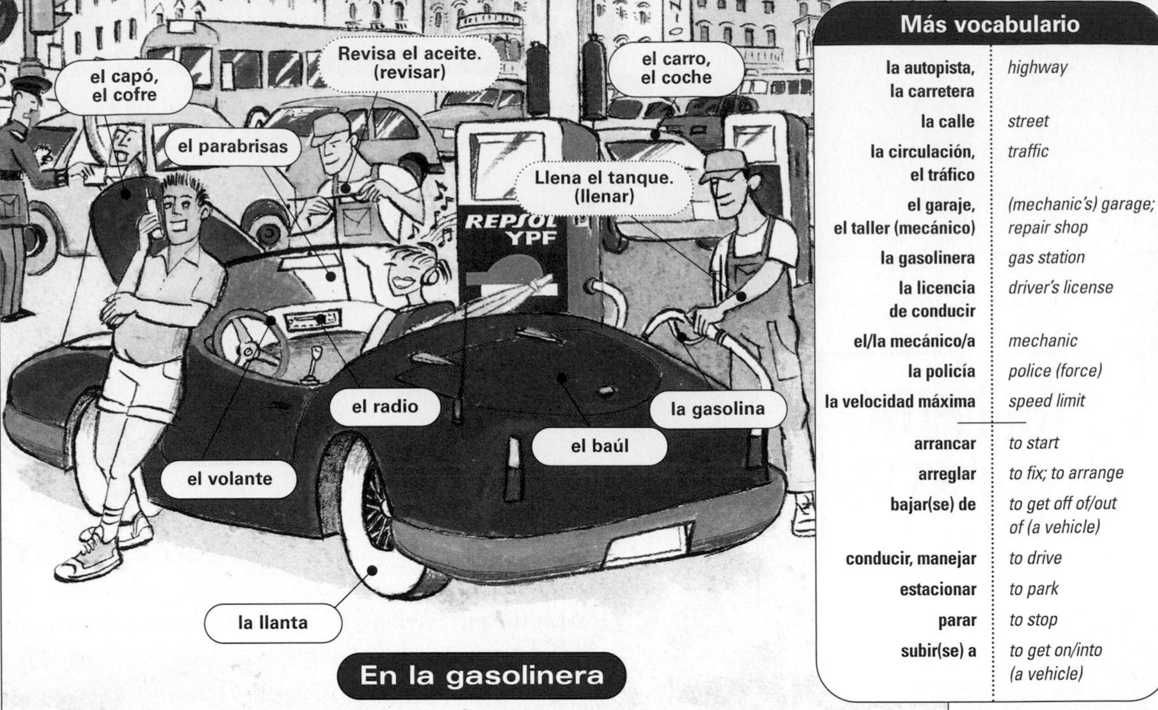

En la gasolinera

Más vocabulario

la autopista, la carretera	*highway*
la calle	*street*
la circulación, el tráfico	*traffic*
el garaje, el taller (mecánico)	*(mechanic's) garage; repair shop*
la gasolinera	*gas station*
la licencia de conducir	*driver's license*
el/la mecánico/a	*mechanic*
la policía	*police (force)*
la velocidad máxima	*speed limit*
arrancar	*to start*
arreglar	*to fix; to arrange*
bajar(se) de	*to get off of/out of (a vehicle)*
conducir, manejar	*to drive*
estacionar	*to park*
parar	*to stop*
subir(se) a	*to get on/into (a vehicle)*

4 Completar Completa las siguientes frases con las palabras correctas.

1. Para poder conducir legalmente necesitas... una licencia de conducir.
2. Puedes poner las maletas en... el baúl.
3. Si tu carro no funciona debes llevarlo a... un mecánico / un taller.
4. Para llenar el tanque de tu coche necesitas ir a... la gasolinera.
5. Antes de un viaje largo, es importante revisar... el aceite.
6. Otra palabra para autopista es... carretera.
7. Mientras hablas por teléfono celular, no es buena idea... conducir.
8. Otra palabra para coche es... carro.

¡LENGUA VIVA!

Aunque **carro** es el término que se usa en la mayoría de países hispanos, no es el único. En España, por ejemplo, se dice **coche**, y en Argentina, Chile y Uruguay se dice **auto**.

5 Conversación Completa la conversación con las formas correctas de las siguientes palabras.

el aceite	la gasolina	llenar	revisar	el taller
el baúl	las llantas	manejar	el parabrisas	el volante

EMPLEADO Bienvenido al (1) taller mecánico *Óscar*. ¿En qué le puedo servir?

JUAN Buenos días. Quiero (2) llenar el tanque y revisar (3) el aceite, por favor.

EMPLEADO Con mucho gusto. Si quiere, también le limpio (4) el parabrisas.

JUAN Sí, gracias. Está un poquito sucio. La próxima semana tengo que (5) manejar hasta Buenos Aires. ¿Puede cambiar (6) las llantas? Están gastadas (*worn*).

EMPLEADO Claro que sí, pero voy a tardar un par de horas.

JUAN Mejor regreso mañana. Ahora no tengo tiempo. ¿Cuánto le debo por (7) la gasolina?

EMPLEADO Sesenta pesos. Y veinticinco por (8) revisar y cambiar el aceite.

CONSÚLTALO

For more information about **Buenos Aires**, see **Panorama** p. 358.

TEACHING OPTIONS

Small Groups Draw a picture of a car on the board. Be sure to include identifiable parts of the car (windshield, steering wheel, tires, gas tank, trunk, hood). Make cards that contain the Spanish names for these items and place tape on the back of the cards. In groups of three or four, students try to place the cards on the corresponding part of the drawing.

Variación léxica Talk about word relationships. Ask students if they can explain why a trunk is called **maletera** in Peru (it's a place where one puts the **maletas**). Also explain that **cajuela** (*trunk* in Mexico) is a word that is related to others that have similar meanings: **caja** (*box*), **cajón** (*drawer*).

Comunicación

6

Preguntas Trabajen en grupos para contestar las siguientes preguntas. Después compartan sus respuestas con la clase. Answers will vary.

1. a. ¿Tienes un teléfono celular? ¿Para qué lo usas?
   b. ¿Qué utilizas más: el teléfono o el correo electrónico? ¿Por qué?
   c. En tu opinión, ¿cuáles son las ventajas (*advantages*) y desventajas de los diferentes modos de comunicación?
2. a. ¿Con qué frecuencia usas la computadora?
   b. ¿Para qué usas Internet?
   c. ¿Tienes tu propio sitio web? ¿Cómo es?
3. a. ¿Miras la televisión con frecuencia? ¿Qué programas ves?
   b. ¿Tienes televisión por cable? ¿Por qué?
   c. ¿Tienes una videocasetera? ¿Un reproductor de DVD? ¿Un reproductor de DVD en la computadora?
   d. ¿A través de (*By*) qué medio escuchas música? ¿Radio, estéreo, tocadiscos compacto o computadora?
4. a. ¿Tienes licencia de conducir?
   b. ¿Cuánto tiempo hace que la conseguiste?
   c. ¿Tienes carro? Descríbelo.
   d. ¿Llevas tu carro al taller? ¿Para qué?

NOTA CULTURAL

Algunos sitios web utilizan códigos para identificar su país de origen. Éstos son los códigos para algunos países hispanohablantes.

Argentina	.ar
Colombia	.co
México	.mx
España	.es
Venezuela	.ve

CONSÚLTALO

To review expressions like **hace...que**, see **Lección 10, Expresiones útiles**, p. 303.

7

Postal En parejas, lean la tarjeta postal. Después contesten las preguntas.

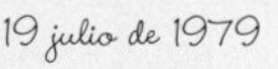

19 julio de 1979

Hola Paco,

¡Saludos! Estamos de viaje por unas semanas. La Costa del Sol es muy bonita. No hemos encontrado a tus amigos porque nunca están en casa cuando llamamos. El teléfono suena y suena y nadie contesta. Vamos a seguir llamando.

Sacamos muchas fotos muy divertidas. Cuando regresemos y las revelemos (*get them developed*), te las voy a enseñar. Las playas son preciosas y la gente muy amable. Hasta ahora (*until now*) el único problema fue que la oficina en la cual reservamos un carro perdió nuestros papeles y tuvimos que esperar mucho tiempo.

También tuvimos un pequeño problema con el hotel. La agencia de viajes nos reservó una habitación en un hotel que está muy lejos de todo. No podemos cambiarla, pero no me importa mucho. A pesar de eso, estamos contentos.

Tu hermana, Gabriela

Francisco Jiménez
San Lorenzo 3250
Rosario, Argentina 2000

1. ¿Cuáles son los problemas que ocurren en el viaje de Gabriela?
2. Con la tecnología de hoy, ¿existen los mismos problemas cuando se viaja? ¿Por qué?
3. Hagan una comparación entre la tecnología de los años 70 y 80 y la de hoy.
4. Imaginen que la hija de Gabriela escribe un correo electrónico sobre el mismo tema con fecha de hoy. Escriban ese correo, incorporando la tecnología de hoy (teléfonos celulares, Internet, cámaras digitales, etc.). Inventen nuevos problemas.

6 Expansion Write names of electronic communication devices on the board (**teléfono celular, fax, computadora,** and so forth). Then survey the class to find out how many people own or use these items. Analyze the trends of the class.

7 Suggestion Possible answers: **1. Gabriela no encuentra a los amigos de Paco porque nunca están en casa, tuvo que esperar mucho por el carro y su hotel estaba muy lejos de todo. 2. No existen los mismos problemas porque existen las contestadoras y los teléfonos celulares, se puede reservar un carro en Internet y se puede buscar información sobre un hotel en la red antes del viaje.**

7 Expansion Ask groups to write a postcard similar to the one in the activity, except that in theirs the problems encountered during the trip are a direct result of the existence of technology, not its absence.

Note: At this point you may want to present **Vocabulario adicional: Más vocabulario para el carro y la tecnología,** from the IRM.

TEACHING OPTIONS

Extra Practice Have students do an Internet research project on technology and technology terminology in the Spanish-speaking world. Suggest possible topics and sites where students may look for information. Have students write out their reports and present them to the class.

Small/Large Groups Stage a debate about the role of technology in today's world. Propose this debate topic: **La tecnología: ¿beneficio o no?** Divide each group in half, assigning each side a position. Allow groups time to plan their arguments before staging the debate. You may also divide the class into two large groups to have the debate with the entire class.

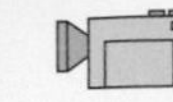

Section Goals

In **Fotonovela** students will:

- receive comprehensible input from free-flowing discourse
- learn functional phrases that preview lesson grammatical structures

Instructional Resources
WB/VM: Video Activities, pp. 233–234
***Fotonovela** DVD/Video (Start 00:58:05)*
Video CD-ROM
*IRM: **Fotonovela** Translations, pp. 144–145, Videoscript, pp. 114–115*
Interactive CD-ROM

Video Recap: Lección 10
Before doing this **Fotonovela** section, review the previous one with this activity.

1. ¿Qué le pasó a Javier en el autobús? (se lastimó el tobillo)
2. ¿Adónde llevó don Francisco a Javier? (a ver a su amiga, la doctora Márquez)
3. ¿Qué mostró la radiografía? (el tobillo de Javier estaba torcido)
4. ¿Qué le recetó la doctora a Javier? (unas pastillas para el dolor)

Video Synopsis On the way to Ibarra, the bus breaks down. Don Francisco can't locate the problem, but Inés, an experienced mechanic, diagnoses it as a burned-out alternator. Álex uses his cell phone to call Don Francisco's friend, Sr. Fonseca, who is a mechanic. Maite and Don Francisco praise Inés and Álex for saving the day.

Suggestions

- Have your students cover the **Fotonovela** dialogue and guess what happens in this episode based on the video stills only.
- Quickly review the guesses your students made. Ask them a few questions to guide them in summarizing this episode.

Tecnohombre, ¡mi héroe!

NATIONAL STANDARDS communication cultures

El autobús se daña.

PERSONAJES

MAITE

INÉS

DON FRANCISCO

ÁLEX

JAVIER

SR. FONSECA

ÁLEX ¿Bueno? ... Con él habla... Ah, ¿cómo estás? ... Aquí, yo muy bien. Vamos para Ibarra. ¿Sabes lo que pasó? Esta tarde íbamos para Ibarra cuando Javier tuvo un accidente en el autobús. Se cayó y tuvimos que llevarlo a una clínica.

JAVIER Episodio veintiuno: Tecnohombre y los superamigos suyos salvan el mundo una vez más.

INÉS Oh, Tecnohombre, ¡mi héroe!

MAITE ¡Qué cómicos! Un día de éstos, ya van a ver...

ÁLEX Van a ver quién es realmente Tecnohombre. Mis superamigos y yo nos hablamos todos los días por el teléfono Internet, trabajando para salvar el mundo. Pero ahora, con su permiso, quiero escribirle un mensaje electrónico a mi mamá y navegar en la red un ratito.

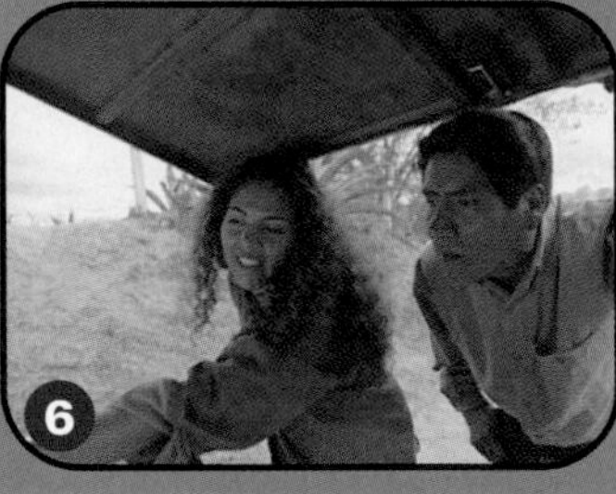

INÉS Pues... no sé... creo que es el alternador. A ver... sí... Mire, don Francisco... está quemado el alternador.

DON FRANCISCO Ah, sí. Pero aquí no podemos arreglarlo. Conozco a un mecánico pero está en Ibarra, a veinte kilómetros de aquí.

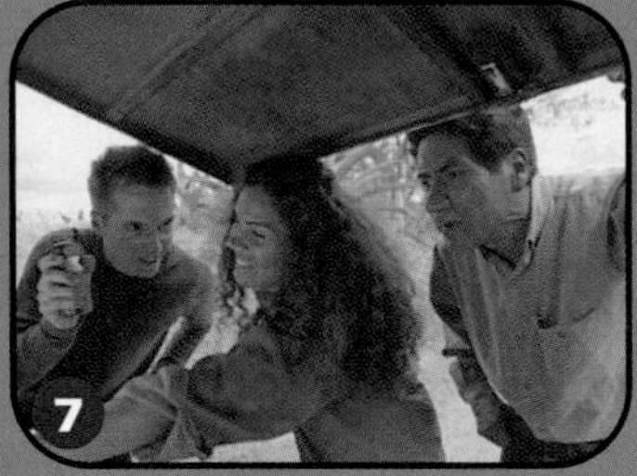

ÁLEX ¡Tecnohombre, a sus órdenes!

DON FRANCISCO ¡Eres la salvación, Álex! Llama al Sr. Fonseca al cinco, treinta y dos, cuarenta y siete, noventa y uno. Nos conocemos muy bien. Seguro que nos ayuda.

ÁLEX Buenas tardes. ¿Con el Sr. Fonseca por favor? ... Soy Álex Morales, cliente de Ecuatur. Le hablo de parte del señor Francisco Castillo... Es que íbamos para Ibarra y se nos dañó el autobús. ... Pensamos que es el... el alternador... Estamos a veinte kilómetros de la ciudad...

recursos

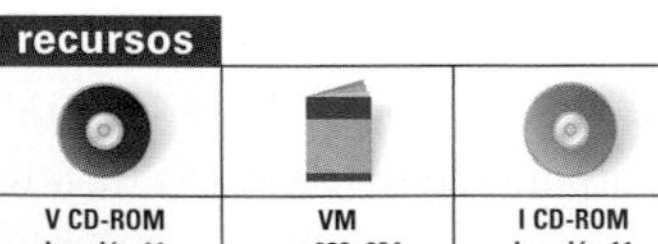

V CD-ROM Lección 11	VM pp. 233–234	I CD-ROM Lección 11

TEACHING OPTIONS

Video Tips General suggestions for using video clips in the classroom can be found on page IAE-12 of this Instructor's Annotated Edition.

Tecnohombre, ¡mi héroe! Make a photocopy of the videoscript and white out ten words to create a master for a cloze activity. Hand out photocopies of the master to your students and have them fill in the missing words as they watch the **Tecnohombre, ¡mi héroe!** video module. You may want to show the segment twice or more if your students experience difficulties with this activity. You may also want your students to share their pages in small groups and help each other fill in any gaps.

4

DON FRANCISCO Chicos, creo que tenemos un problema con el autobús. ¿Por qué no se bajan?

5

DON FRANCISCO Mmm, no veo el problema.

INÉS Cuando estaba en la escuela secundaria, trabajé en el taller de mi tío. Me enseñó mucho sobre mecánica. Por suerte, arreglé unos autobuses como éste.

DON FRANCISCO ¡No me digas! Bueno, ¿qué piensas?

9

SR. FONSECA Creo que va a ser mejor arreglar el autobús allí mismo. Tranquilo, enseguida salgo.

10

ÁLEX Buenas noticias. El señor Fonseca viene enseguida. Piensa que puede arreglar el autobús aquí mismo.

MAITE ¡La Mujer Mecánica y Tecnohombre, mis héroes!

DON FRANCISCO ¡Y los míos también!

Enfoque cultural El transporte en la ciudad

En las ciudades hispanas suele haber (*there is usually*) más transporte público que en las estadounidenses y sus habitantes dependen menos de los carros. En los países hispanos también es más frecuente el uso de carros pequeños y de motocicletas que gastan poca gasolina. En las ciudades españolas, por ejemplo, la gasolina es muy cara y también hay poco espacio para el estacionamiento (*parking*); por eso es tan frecuente el uso de vehículos pequeños y económicos.

Expresiones útiles

Talking on the telephone

- ▶ **Aló./¿Bueno?/Diga.**
  Hello.
- ▶ **¿Quién habla?**
  Who is speaking?
- ▶ **¿De parte de quién?**
  Who is calling?
- ▷ **Con él/ella habla.**
  This is he/she.
- ▷ **Le hablo de parte de Francisco Castillo.**
  I'm speaking to you on behalf of Francisco Castillo.
- ▶ **¿Puedo dejar un recado?**
  May I leave a message?
- ▷ **Está bien. Llamo más tarde.**
  That's fine. I'll call later.

Talking about bus or car problems

- ▶ **¿Qué pasó?**
  What happened?
- ▷ **Se nos dañó el autobús.**
  The bus broke down.
- ▷ **Se nos pinchó una llanta.**
  We had a flat tire.
- ▷ **Está quemado el alternador.**
  The alternator is burned out.

Saying how far away things are

- ▶ **Está a veinte kilómetros de aquí.**
  It's twenty kilometers from here.
- ▶ **Estamos a veinte millas de la ciudad.**
  We're twenty miles from the city.

Expressing surprise

- ▶ **¡No me digas!**
  You don't say! (fam.)
- ▶ **¡No me diga!**
  You don't say! (form.)

Offering assistance

- ▶ **A sus órdenes.**
  At your service.

Additional vocabulary

- ▶ **aquí mismo**
  right here

Suggestion Have the class read through the entire **Fotonovela**, with volunteers playing the various roles. Have students take turns playing the roles so that more of them participate.

Expresiones útiles Draw the attention of the class to the phrase **nos hablamos** in the caption of video still 3. Explain that this is a reciprocal reflexive construction that expresses a shared action between Álex and his friends. Point out the words **los míos** in the caption of video still 10 and tell the class that this is an example of a possessive pronoun. Tell your students that they will learn more about these concepts in **Estructura**.

TEACHING OPTIONS

Enfoque cultural Like anywhere else, large cities in the Spanish-speaking world often experience traffic gridlock. To address this problem, these cities have emphasized public transportation. Almost all of them have extensive public bus systems. Mexico City, with a population estimated at over 20 million, has been singled out for particular praise because of its **metro** (*subway*) system. The Mexico City metro, which is efficient and well maintained, costs very little to ride and provides transportation to approximately four million riders on its eleven lines each day. Though its 175 stations are notably attractive, two downtown stations are of more than transportation interest. The Insurgentes station is packed with market stalls of every type, and the Pino Suárez station, near the national palace, houses an Aztec pyramid, unearthed during the excavations when the metro was built.

1 Suggestion Read these items to the class as a true-false activity. Ask students to correct the false statements. Ex: **Álex quiere escribirle a su mamá y navegar en la red. (Cierto.)**

2 Expansion Give these additional items to the class: **6. El problema es el alternador, creo. (Inés) 7. Hola. ¿Está el señor Fonseca? (Álex) 8. Tengo ganas de navegar en la red. (Álex)**

3 Possible Response
E1: ¿Bueno? Taller Mendoza.
E2: Buenos días. Tengo un problema con mi carro.
E1: ¿Qué pasó? ¿Cuál es el problema exactamente?
E2: El carro no arranca cuando hace frío. No sé si es el alternador.
E1: Tengo que revisarlo. ¿Puede venir al taller?
E2: Creo que sí. ¿A qué hora debo pasar?
E1: Tengo tiempo esta tarde a las tres.
E2: Muy bien. Es buena hora para mí también.
E1: Nos vemos a las tres. Gracias, y hasta esta tarde.
E2: Hasta luego.

The Affective Dimension

Point out that talking on the phone can be more stressful than talking with someone in person because one doesn't see the other person's facial expressions or gestures. Remind your students that they don't need to understand every word, and that they should ask the other person to repeat if necessary.

Reacciona a la fotonovela

1 **Seleccionar** Selecciona las respuestas que completan correctamente las siguientes frases.

1. Álex quiere __b__.
   a. llamar a su mamá por teléfono celular b. escribirle a su mamá y navegar en la red c. hablar por teléfono Internet y navegar en la red
2. Se les dañó el autobús. Inés dice que __a__.
   a. el alternador está quemado b. se pinchó una llanta c. el taller está lejos
3. Álex llama al mecánico, el señor __c__.
   a. Castillo b. Ibarra c. Fonseca
4. Maite llama a Inés la "Mujer Mecánica" porque antes __a__.
   a. trabajaba en el taller de su tío b. arreglaba computadoras c. conocía a muchos mecánicos
5. El grupo está a __c__ de la ciudad.
   a. veinte millas b. veinte grados centígrados c. veinte kilómetros

2 **Identificar** Identifica quién puede decir las siguientes frases.

1. Gracias a mi tío tengo un poco de experiencia arreglando autobuses. Inés
2. Sé manejar un autobús pero no sé arreglarlo. ¿Por qué no llamamos a mi amigo? don Francisco
3. Sabes, admiro mucho a la Mujer Mecánica y a Tecnohombre. Maite
4. Aló... Sí, ¿de parte de quién? Álex
5. El nombre de Tecnohombre fue idea mía. ¡Qué cómico!, ¿no? Javier

3 **Problema mecánico** Trabajen en parejas para representar los papeles (*roles*) de un(a) mecánico/a y un(a) cliente/a que está llamando al taller porque su carro está descompuesto. Usen las instrucciones como guía.

Mecánico/a	Cliente/a
Contesta el teléfono con un saludo y el nombre del taller.	Saluda y explica que tu carro está descompuesto.
Pregunta qué tipo de problema tiene exactamente.	Explica que tu carro no arranca cuando hace frío.
Di que debe traer el carro al taller.	Pregunta cuándo puedes llevarlo.
Ofrece una hora para revisar el carro.	Acepta la hora que ofrece el/la mecánico/a.
Da las gracias y despídete.	Despídete y cuelga (*hang up*) el teléfono.

Ahora cambien los papeles y representen otra conversación. Ustedes son un(a) técnico/a y un(a) cliente/a. Usen estas ideas:

el celular no guarda mensajes	la impresora imprime muy lentamente
la computadora no descarga fotos	el reproductor de DVD está descompuesto

TEACHING OPTIONS

Extra Practice Have each student choose one of the **Fotonovela** characters and then prepare a five- to six-sentence summary of the day's events from that person's point of view. Have a few volunteers read their summaries to the class; the class will guess which character would have given each summary.

Small Groups Have the class work in small groups to write questions about the **Fotonovela**. Have each group hand its questions to another group, which will write the answers. Ex: **G1: ¿A quién llamó Álex? G2: Álex llamó al señor Fonseca, el mecánico.**

Ortografía

La acentuación de palabras similares

Although accent marks usually indicate which syllable in a word is stressed, they are also used to distinguish between words that have the same or similar spellings.

Él maneja el coche. **Sí, voy si quieres.**

Although one-syllable words do not usually carry written accents, some *do* have accent marks to distinguish them from words that have the same spelling but different meanings.

Sé cocinar. **Se baña.** **¿Tomas té?** **Te duermes.**

Sé (*I know*) and **té** (*tea*) have accent marks to distinguish them from the pronouns **se** and **te**.

para mí **mi cámara** **Tú lees.** **tu estéreo**

Mí (*Me*) and **tú** (*you*) have accent marks to distinguish them from the possessive adjectives **mi** and **tu**.

¿Por qué vas? **Voy porque quiero.**

Several words of more than one syllable also have accent marks to distinguish them from words that have the same or similar spellings.

Éste es rápido. **Este módem es rápido.**

Demonstrative pronouns have accent marks to distinguish them from demonstrative adjectives.

¿Cuándo fuiste? **Fui cuando me llamó.**
¿Dónde trabajas? **Voy al taller donde trabajo.**

Adverbs have accent marks when they are used to convey a question.

Práctica Marca los acentos en las palabras que los necesitan.

ANA Alo, soy Ana. ¿Que tal? Aló/¿Qué?
JUAN Hola, pero... ¿por que me llamas tan tarde? ¿por qué?
ANA Porque mañana tienes que llevarme a la universidad. Mi auto esta dañado. está
JUAN ¿Como se daño? ¿Cómo?/dañó
ANA Se daño el sabado. Un vecino (*neighbor*) choco con (*crashed into*) el. dañó/sábado/chocó/él

Crucigrama Utiliza las siguientes pistas (*clues*) para completar el crucigrama. ¡Ojo con los acentos!

Horizontales

1. Él _________ levanta.
4. No voy _________ no puedo.
7. Tú _________ acuestas.
9. ¿ _________ es el examen?
10. Quiero este video y _________.

Verticales

2. ¿Cómo _________ usted?
3. Eres _________ mi hermano.
5. ¿_________ tal?
6. Me gusta _________ suéter.
8. Navego _________ la red.

	[1]S	[2]E			[3]C				
		S		[4]P	O	R	[5]Q	U	[6]E
		[7]T	[8]E		M		U		S
[9]C	U	Á	N	D	O		[10]É	S	E

recursos

LM p. 62	Lab CD/MP3 Lección 11	I CD-ROM Lección 11

Section Goal

In **Ortografía** students will learn about the use of accent marks to distinguish between words that have the same or similar spellings.

Instructional Resource
Interactive CD-ROM

Suggestions

- As you go through each point in the explanation, pronounce the example sentences, as well as some of your own, and have students write them on the board.
- Write the example sentences, as well as some of your own, on the board without accent marks. Ask students where the written accents should go.
- Emphasize the difference in stress between **por qué** and **porque**.
- Ask students to provide words they learned in previous lessons that exemplify each point.
- Point out that **Ortografía** replaces **Pronunciación** in the Student Edition for **Lecciones 10–18**, but not in the Lab Manual. The **Recursos** box references the **Pronunciación** sections found in all lessons of the Lab Manual.

TEACHING OPTIONS

Small Groups Have your students work in groups to explain which words in the **Práctica** activity need written accents and why. If necessary, have your students quickly review the information about accents in the **Ortografía** section of **Lección 10**, page 305.

Extra Practice Write these sentences on the board or on a transparency without accent marks. **Esta es mi camara. Papa la trajo del Japon para mi. • ¿Donde encontraste mi mochila? ¡Pues, donde la dejaste, claro! • ¿Cuando visito Buenos Aires Mario? Se que Lourdes fue alli el año pasado, pero ¿cuando fue el? • ¿Me explicas por que llegas tarde? Porque mi coche esta descompuesto.**

11 estructura

Section Goals

In **Estructura 11.1**, students will learn:
- negative **tú** commands
- affirmative **tú** commands

Instructional Resources
WB/VM: Workbook, pp. 125–126
Lab Manual, p. 63
*Lab CD/MP3 **Lección 11***
*IRM: **¡Inténtalo!** & **Práctica** Answers, pp. 215–216; Tapescript, pp. 49–53*
Info Gap Activities Booklet, pp. 41–42
Interactive CD-ROM
Companion website: www.vistahigherlearning.com
Presentations CD-ROM

Suggestions
- Model the use of informal commands with simple examples using TPR and gestures. Ex: Point to a student and say: ____, **levántate. Gracias, ahora siéntate.** Give other commands using **camina, vuelve, toca,** and **corre**.
- Help students recognize that the affirmative **tú** command forms of regular verbs are the same as the third-person singular forms.
- Make clear to students that **tú** commands are spoken to people one addresses as **tú**.

11.1 Familiar commands

recursos
WB pp. 125–132
LM pp. 63–66
Lab CD/MP3 Lección 11
I CD-ROM Lección 11
vistahigherlearning.com

ANTE TODO In Spanish, the command forms are used to give orders or advice. You use **tú** commands when you want to give an order or advice to someone you normally address with the familiar **tú**.

Affirmative *tú* commands

Infinitive	Present tense *él/ella* form	Affirmative *tú* command
hablar	habla	**habla** (tú)
guardar	guarda	**guarda** (tú)
prender	prende	**prende** (tú)
volver	vuelve	**vuelve** (tú)
pedir	pide	**pide** (tú)
imprimir	imprime	**imprime** (tú)

▶ Affirmative **tú** commands usually have the same form as the **él/ella** form of the present indicative.

Guarda el documento antes de cerrarlo.
Save the document before closing it.

Imprime tu tarea para la clase de inglés.
Print your homework for English class.

▶ There are eight irregular affirmative **tú** commands.

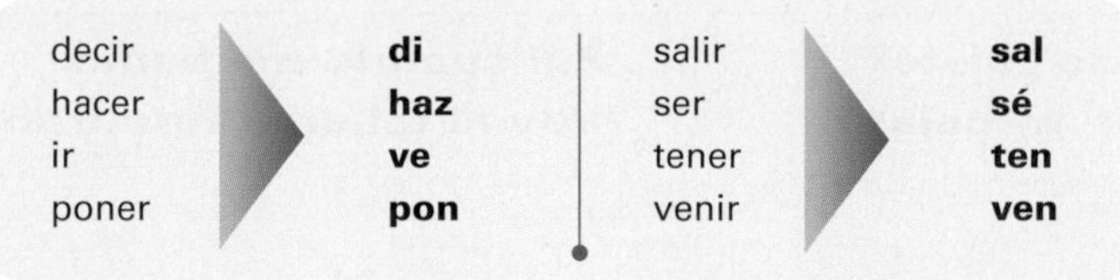

decir	**di**	salir	**sal**
hacer	**haz**	ser	**sé**
ir	**ve**	tener	**ten**
poner	**pon**	venir	**ven**

¡**Sal** de aquí ahora mismo!
Leave here at once!

Haz los ejercicios.
Do the exercises.

▶ Since **ir** and **ver** have the same **tú** command (**ve**), context will determine the meaning.

Ve al cibercafé con Yolanda.
Go to the cybercafé with Yolanda.

Ve ese programa... es muy interesante.
See that program... it's very interesting.

Apaga ese walkman y contesta el teléfono.

¡No me digas!

TEACHING OPTIONS

TPR Ask individual students to comply with a series of commands requiring them to perform actions or move around the room. While the student follows the command, the class writes it down as a volunteer writes it on the board. Be sure to use both affirmative and negative commands. Ex: **Recoge ese papel. Ponlo en la basura. Regresa a tu escritorio. No te sientes. Siéntate ahora.**

Pairs Ask students to imagine they are starting a computer club. Have them make a list of five things to do in order to get ready for the first meeting and five things not to do to make sure everything runs smoothly, using infinitives. Then have students take turns telling partners what to do or not do.

Negative *tú* commands

Infinitive	Present tense *yo* form	Negative *tú* command
hablar	hablo	**no hables** (tú)
guardar	guardo	**no guardes** (tú)
prender	prendo	**no prendas** (tú)
volver	vuelvo	**no vuelvas** (tú)
pedir	pido	**no pidas** (tú)

▶ The negative **tú** commands are formed by dropping the final **–o** of the **yo** form of the present tense. For **–ar** verbs, add **–es**. For **–er** and **–ir** verbs, add **–as**.

Héctor, **no pares** el carro en el medio de la calle.
Héctor, don't stop the car in the middle of the street.

No prendas la computadora todavía.
Don't turn on the computer yet.

▶ Verbs with irregular **yo** forms maintain the same irregularity in their negative **tú** commands. These verbs include **conducir, conocer, decir, hacer, ofrecer, oír, poner, salir, tener, traducir, traer, venir,** and **ver**.

No pongas aquel cederrón en la computadora portátil.
Don't put that CD-ROM in the laptop.

No conduzcas tan rápido.
Don't drive so fast.

▶ Note also that stem-changing verbs keep their stem changes in negative **tú** commands.

No p**ie**rdas tu licencia de conducir.
Don't lose your driver's license.

No v**ue**lvas a esa gasolinera.
Don't go back to that gas station.

No rep**i**tas las instrucciones.
Don't repeat the instructions.

▶ Verbs ending in **–car**, **–gar**, and **–zar** have a spelling change in the negative **tú** commands.

sa**car**	**c** → **qu**	no sa**qu**es
apa**gar**	**g** → **gu**	no apa**gu**es
almor**zar**	**z** → **c**	no almuer**c**es

▶ The following verbs have irregular negative **tú** commands.

Infinitive	Negative *tú* command
dar	**no des**
estar	**no estés**
ir	**no vayas**
saber	**no sepas**
ser	**no seas**

¡ATENCIÓN!

In affirmative commands, reflexive, indirect, and direct object pronouns are always attached to the end of the verb. In negative commands, these pronouns always precede the verb.

Bórralos. /No los borres.

Escríbeles un correo electrónico./**No les escribas** un correo electrónico.

•••

When a pronoun is attached to an affirmative command that has two or more syllables, an accent mark is added to maintain the original stress:

borra → bórralos
prende → préndela
imprime → imprímelo

¡INTÉNTALO! Indica los mandatos (*commands*) familiares afirmativos y negativos de estos verbos.

1. correr	Corre más rápido.	No corras más rápido.
2. llenar	Llena el tanque.	No llenes el tanque.
3. salir	Sal ahora.	No salgas ahora.
4. descargar	Descarga ese documento.	No descargues ese documento.
5. venir	Ven aquí.	No vengas aquí.
6. levantarse	Levántate temprano.	No te levantes temprano.
7. volver	Vuelve pronto.	No vuelvas pronto.
8. hacerlo	Hazlo ya.	No lo hagas ahora.

Suggestions

- Contrast the negative forms of **tú** commands by giving an affirmative command followed by a negative command. Ex: ____ **, camina a la puerta. No camines rápidamente.** Write the examples on the board as you go along.
- Test comprehension and practice negative **tú** commands by calling out the infinitives of a variety of regular verbs the students already know and asking individual students to convert them into negative commands. Ex: **toser: no tosas; pedir: no pidas; pensar: no pienses.**
- Ask volunteers to convert affirmative **tú** commands with reflexive and object pronouns into negative forms. Ex: **Imprímelo. (No lo imprimas.) Vete. (No te vayas.)**

TEACHING OPTIONS

Heritage Speakers Ask heritage speakers to look for an advertisement in a Spanish-language magazine or newspaper in which they find informal commands used. Have students bring a copy of the ad to class. Ask them to share it with the class and explain why they think informal commands were used instead of formal ones.

Extra Practice Have pairs imagine that they are in charge of a computer lab at a university in a Spanish-speaking country. Have them make a handout of four things students must do and four things they must not do while in the lab. Instruct them to use **tú** commands throughout. Then, write **Mandatos afirmativos** and **Mandatos negativos** on the board and ask individuals to write one of their commands in the appropriate column.

1 Expansion Continue this activity orally with the class, using regular verbs. Call out a negative command and designate individuals to make corresponding affirmative commands. Ex: **No sirvas la comida ahora. (Sirve la comida ahora.** or **Sírvela ahora.)**

2 Expansion Ask volunteers to role-play the conversation between Pedro and Marina.

3 Suggestion Review the vocabulary in the word bank by asking students to make associations with each word. Ex: **imprimir (documento), descargar (programa)**

Práctica

1 **Completar** Tu mejor amigo no entiende nada de tecnología y te pide ayuda. Completa los comentarios de tu amigo con el mandato de cada verbo.

1. No __vengas__ en una hora. __Ven__ ahora mismo. (venir)
2. __Haz__ tu tarea después. No la __hagas__ ahora. (hacer)
3. No __vayas__ a la tienda a comprar papel para la impresora. __Ve__ a la cafetería a comprarme algo de comer. (ir)
4. No __me digas__ que no sabes abrir un archivo. __Dime__ que el programa de computación funciona sin problemas. (decirme)
5. __Sé__ generoso con tu tiempo, y no __seas__ antipático si no entiendo fácilmente. (ser)
6. __Ten__ mucha paciencia y no __tengas__ prisa. (tener)
7. __Apaga__ tu teléfono celular, pero no __apagues__ la computadora. (apagar)

2 **Cambiar** Pedro y Marina no pueden ponerse de acuerdo (*agree*) cuando viajan en su carro. Cuando Pedro dice que algo es necesario, Marina expresa una opinión diferente. Usa la información entre paréntesis para formar las órdenes que Marina le da a Pedro.

modelo

Pedro: Necesito revisar el aceite del carro. (seguir hasta el próximo pueblo)
Marina: No revises el aceite del carro. Sigue hasta el próximo pueblo.

1. Necesito conducir más rápido. (parar el carro) No conduzcas más rápido. Para el carro.
2. Necesito poner el radio. (hablarme) No pongas el radio. Háblame.
3. Necesito almorzar ahora. (comer más tarde) No almuerces ahora. Come más tarde.
4. Necesito sacar los discos compactos. (manejar con cuidado) No saques... Maneja...
5. Necesito estacionar el carro en esta calle. (pensar en otra opción) No estaciones... Piensa...
6. Necesito volver a esa gasolinera. (arreglar el carro en un taller) No vuelvas... Arregla...
7. Necesito leer el mapa. (pedirle ayuda a aquella señora) No leas... Pídele...
8. Necesito dormir en el carro. (acostarse en una cama) No duermas... Acuéstate...

3 **Problemas** Tú y tu compañero/a trabajan en el centro de computadoras de la universidad. Muchos estudiantes están llamando con problemas. Denles órdenes para ayudarlos a resolverlos. Answers will vary; suggested answers below.

modelo

Problema: No veo nada en la pantalla.
Tu respuesta: Prende la pantalla de tu computadora.

apagar...	descargar...	guardar...	navegar...	quemar...
borrar...	funcionar...	imprimir...	prender...	grabar...

1. No me gusta este programa de computación. Descarga otro.
2. Tengo miedo de perder mi documento. Guárdalo.
3. Prefiero leer este sitio web en papel. Imprímelo.
4. Mi correo electrónico funciona muy lentamente. Borra los mensajes más viejos.
5. Busco información sobre los gauchos de Argentina. Navega en Internet.
6. Tengo demasiados archivos en mi computadora. Borra algunos archivos.
7. Mi computadora se congeló (*froze*). Apaga la computadora y luego préndela.
8. Quiero ver las fotos del cumpleaños de mi hermana. Descárgalas.

NOTA CULTURAL

Los gauchos (*nomadic cowboys*), conocidos por su habilidad (*skill*) para montar caballos y utilizar lazos, viven en la región más extensa de Argentina, la Patagonia. Esta región ocupa casi la mitad (*half*) de la superficie (*land area*) del país.

TEACHING OPTIONS

TPR Have pairs of students brainstorm a list of actions that can be mimed. Then have them give each other **tú** commands based on the actions. Call on several pairs to demonstrate their actions for the class. When a repertoire of mimable actions is established, do rapid-fire TPR with the whole class using these commands/actions.

Pairs Have students create three questions about technology, then work with a partner to ask and respond to the questions with affirmative and negative commands. If a student responds with a negative command, he or she must follow it with an affirmative command. Ex: **¿Debo apagar la computadora todos los días antes de acostarme? (No, no la apagues. Pero guarda todos tus documentos.)**

Comunicación

4 **Órdenes** Circula por la clase e intercambia órdenes negativas y afirmativas con tus compañeros/as. Debes seguir las órdenes que ellos te dan o reaccionar apropiadamente. Answers will vary.

modelo

Estudiante 1: Dame todo tu dinero.
Estudiante 2: No, no quiero dártelo. Muéstrame tu cuaderno.
Estudiante 1: Aquí está.
Estudiante 3: Ve a la pizarra y escribe tu nombre.
Estudiante 4: No quiero. Hazlo tú.

5 **Anuncios** Miren este anuncio (*ad*). Luego, en grupos pequeños, preparen tres anuncios adicionales para tres escuelas que compiten (*compete*) con ésta. Answers will vary.

INFORMÁTICA ARGENTINA
Toma nuestros cursos y aprende a usar la computadora
abre y lee tus archivos
imprime tus documentos
entra al campo de la tecnología
¡Ponte en contacto con nosotros llamando al 11-4-129-1508 HOY!

Síntesis

6 **¡Tanto que hacer!** Tu profesor(a) te va a dar una lista de diligencias (*errands*). Algunas las hiciste tú y algunas las hizo tu compañero/a. Las diligencias que ya hicieron tienen esta marca ✔. Pero quedan cuatro diligencias por hacer. Dale mandatos a tu compañero/a, y él/ella responde para confirmar si hay que hacerla o ya la hizo. Answers will vary.

modelo

Estudiante 1: Llena el tanque.
Estudiante 2: Ya llené el tanque. / ¡Oh, no! Tenemos que llenar el tanque.

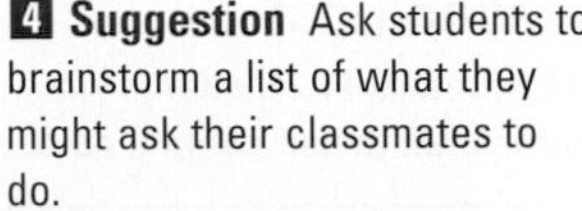

4 Suggestion Ask students to brainstorm a list of what they might ask their classmates to do.

4 Expansion Have volunteers report to the class what they were asked to do, what they did, and what they did not do.

5 Suggestion Ask comprehension questions about the ad. **¿Qué se anuncia? ¿Cómo puedes informarte? ¿Dónde se encuentra este tipo de anuncio?**

5 Expansion Post the finished ads in different places around the classroom. Have groups circulate and write one question for each poster. Then have group members ask their questions. Group answers should include a **tú** command.

6 Suggestions

- Divide the class into pairs and distribute the Info Gap Handouts from the Info Gap Activities Booklet that correspond to this activity. Give the students ten minutes to complete this activity.
- Ask volunteers to give examples of **tú** commands that college students usually give to their roommate. Ex: **Saca la basura. Apaga la tele. No te acuestes en el sofá.**

TEACHING OPTIONS

Pairs Have pairs prepare a conversation between two roommates, both of whom are hurrying to get ready for a party. Students should use affirmative and negative **tú** commands to tell each other what they have to do to arrive at the party on time. Ex: **E1: ¡Sal del baño ya! E2: ¡No me grites! E1: Pero tengo que maquillarme. E2: Maquíllate más tarde. Yo necesito ducharme.**

Extra Practice Review the verbs in **Contextos** and informal commands by stating a verb, then calling on a volunteer to make an affirmative command using that verb. Call on a second volunteer to counter with a negative command.

Section Goal

In **Estructura 11.2** students will learn when to use **por** and **para**.

Instructional Resources
WB/VM: Workbook, pp. 127–128
Lab Manual, p. 64
Lab CD/MP3 ***Lección 11***
IRM: ***¡Inténtalo! & Práctica*** *Answers, pp. 215–216; Tapescript, pp. 49–53*
Interactive CD-ROM
Companion website: www.vistahigherlearning.com
Presentations CD-ROM

Suggestions

- Have a volunteer read the caption of video still 3 on page 334. Focus on **. . . nos hablamos todos los días por el teléfono Internet, trabajando para salvar el mundo.** Point out **por** and **para**.
- Ask students to translate phrases requiring **por**. Ex: *talk by phone, send information by e-mail, walk across campus, walk along Bécquer Street, arrive in the afternoon/in the morning, be worried about the accident/about your friend, go 30 miles per hour, study for four hours.*

11.2 Por and para

NATIONAL
comparisons
STANDARDS

ANTE TODO Unlike English, Spanish has two words that mean *for*: **por** and **para.** These two prepositions are not interchangeable. Study the following charts to see how they are used.

Es para usted. Es un cliente de don Paco.

Álex habla por teléfono.

Por **is used to indicate...**

1. Motion or a general location *(around, through, along, by)*	La excursión nos llevó **por** el centro. *The tour took us through downtown.* Pasamos **por** el parque y **por** el río. *We passed by the park and along the river.*
2. Duration of an action *(for, during, in)*	Estuve en la Patagonia **por** un mes. *I was in Patagonia for a month.* Ana navegó la red **por** la tarde. *Ana surfed the net in the afternoon.*
3. Reason or motive for an action *(because of, on account of, on behalf of)*	Lo hizo **por** su familia. *She did it on behalf of her family.* Papá llegó a casa tarde **por** el tráfico. *Dad arrived home late because of the traffic.*
4. Object of a search *(for, in search of)*	Vengo **por** ti a las ocho. *I'm coming for you at eight.* Javier fue **por** su cámara digital. *Javier went in search of his digital camera.*
5. Means by which something is done *(by, by way of, by means of)*	Ellos viajan **por** la autopista. *They travel by (by way of) the highway.* ¿Hablaste con la policía **por** teléfono? *Did you talk to the police by (on the) phone?*
6. Exchange or substitution *(for, in exchange for)*	Le di dinero **por** la videocasetera. *I gave him money for the VCR.* Muchas gracias **por** el cederrón. *Thank you very much for the CD-ROM.*
7. Unit of measure *(per, by)*	José manejaba a 120 kilómetros **por** hora. *José was driving 120 kilometers per hour.*

¡ATENCIÓN!

Por is also used in several idiomatic expressions, including:
por aquí *around here*
por ejemplo *for example*
por eso *that's why; therefore*
por fin *finally*

¡ATENCIÓN!

Remember that when giving an exact time, **de** is used instead of **por** before **la mañana**, **la tarde**, etc.

La clase empieza a las nueve **de** la mañana.

• • •

In addition to **por**, **durante** is also commonly used to mean *for* when referring to time.

Esperé al mecánico **durante** cincuenta minutos.

TEACHING OPTIONS

TPR Call out a sentence, omitting either **por** or **para**. If students think **por** should be used in the sentence, they raise one hand. If they think **para** should be used, they raise two hands. Avoid cases where either **por** or **para** could be used. Ex: **Tengo que leer el capítulo 11 ____ mañana.** (two hands) **Jimena trabaja ____ la noche.** (one hand) **Estaba en Buenos Aires ____ el mes de marzo.** (one hand)

Game Divide the class into four or five teams, giving each team a large piece of paper. Call out a use of either **por** or **para**. Teams have one minute to write as many sentences as they can, employing that use. Check answers by having a volunteer read his or her team's sentences. Give a point for each correct sentence. Keep score on the board. The team with the most correct sentences wins.

Para is used to indicate...

1. Destination (*toward, in the direction of*)	Salimos **para** Córdoba el sábado. *We are leaving for Córdoba on Saturday.*
2. Deadline or a specific time in the future (*by, for*)	Él va a arreglar el carro **para** el viernes. *He will fix the car by Friday.*
3. Purpose or goal + [*infinitive*] (*in order to*)	Juan estudia **para** (ser) mecánico. *Juan is studying to be a mechanic.*
4. Purpose + [*noun*] (*for, used for*)	Es una llanta **para** el carro. *It's a tire for the car.*
5. The recipient of something (*for*)	Compré una impresora **para** mi hijo. *I bought a printer for my son.*
6. Comparison with others or an opinion (*for, considering*)	**Para** un joven, es demasiado serio. *For a young person, he is too serious.* **Para** mí, esta lección no es difícil. *For me, this lesson isn't difficult.*
7. In the employ of (*for*)	Sara trabaja **para** Telecom Argentina. *Sara works for Telecom Argentina.*

▶ In many cases it is grammatically correct to use either **por** or **para** in a sentence. The meaning of the sentence is different, however, depending on which preposition is used.

Caminé **por** el parque. *I walked through the park.*	Caminé **para** el parque. *I walked to (toward) the park.*
Trabajó **por** su padre. *He worked for (in place of) his father.*	Trabajó **para** su padre. *He worked for his father('s company).*

¡INTÉNTALO! Completa estas frases con las preposiciones **por** o **para**.

1. Fuimos al cibercafé ___por___ la tarde.
2. Necesitas un módem ___para___ navegar en la red.
3. Entraron ___por___ la puerta.
4. Quiero un pasaje ___para___ Buenos Aires.
5. ___Para___ arrancar el carro, necesito la llave.
6. Arreglé el televisor ___para___ mi amigo.
7. Estuvieron nerviosos ___por___ el examen.
8. ¿No hay una gasolinera ___por___ aquí?
9. Esta computadora es ___para___ Ud.
10. Juan está enfermo. Tengo que trabajar ___por___ él.
11. Estuvimos en Cancún ___por___ dos meses.
12. ___Para___ mí, el español es difícil.
13. Tengo que estudiar la lección ___para___ el lunes.
14. Voy a ir ___por___ la carretera.
15. Compré dulces ___para___ mi novia.
16. Compramos el auto ___por___ un buen precio.

Suggestions

- Create a matching activity for the uses of **para**. Write sentences exemplifying each use of **para** listed, but not in the order they are given in the text. Ex: **1. El señor López compró el Ferrari para Mariana. 2. Este autobús va para Corrientes. 3. Para don Francisco, conducir un autobús no es nada difícil. 4. Don Francisco trabaja para Ecuatur. 5. Estudia para llegar a ser ingeniero. 6. El baúl es para las maletas. 7. Tengo que pagar la multa para el lunes.** Call on individual students to match each sentence with its usage.
- Have students make two flashcards. On one they write **por** and on the other **para**. Call out one of the uses for either word. Students show the appropriate card. Then call on a volunteer to write a sentence illustrating that use on the board. The class determines whether the sentence is correct or not.
- Use magazine pictures to practice example sentences in which either **por** or **para** is correct. Ex: **Este señor hace la cena para su esposa. Los novios montan a caballo por el campo.**

TEACHING OPTIONS

Extra Practice Give each student in the class a strip of paper on which you have written one of the uses of **por** or **para**, or a sentence that is an example of one of the uses. Have students circulate around the room until they find the person who has the match for their use or sentence. After everyone has found a partner, the pairs read their sentences and uses to the class.

Pairs/Game Have students create cards for a memory game. There should be one card for each use of **por** and **para**, and one card with a sentence illustrating each use, for a total of 28 cards. When finished, students lay all the cards face down. Then, taking turns, students uncover two cards at a time, trying to match a use to a sentence. The student with the most matches wins.

1 Expansion Have students list the uses of **por** and **para** in the paragraph. Then ask them to work in pairs to add sentences to the paragraph, employing the remaining uses of **por** and **para**. (Remaining uses of **por**: reason or motive, object of search, means, unit of measure; remaining uses of **para**: destination, deadline, purpose + [*noun*], comparison, employment.)

2 Suggestions
- Model the activity by creating a sentence with an element from each column. Ask a volunteer to explain your choice of **por** or **para**. Possible sentences: **Fuimos al mercado para comprar frutas por la mañana. No fueron a Buenos Aires por tres días para divertirse.**
- Divide the class into groups of three. Groups should write as many sentences as they can by combining elements from each column in a given amount of time. The group with the most correct sentences wins.

3 Expansion Have students take turns with a partner to expand their descriptions to a short oral narrative. After each drawing has been described, ask students to pick two or three of their narratives and link them into a story.

Práctica

1 Completar Completa este párrafo con las preposiciones **por** o **para.**

El mes pasado mi esposo y yo hicimos un viaje a Buenos Aires y sólo pagamos dos mil dólares (1) por los pasajes. Estuvimos en Buenos Aires (2) por una semana y recorrimos toda la ciudad. Durante el día caminamos (3) por la plaza San Martín, el microcentro y el barrio de La Boca, donde viven muchos artistas. (4) Por la noche fuimos a una tanguería, que es una especie de teatro (5) para mirar a la gente bailar tango. Dos días después decidimos hacer una excursión (6) por las pampas (7) para ver el paisaje y un rodeo con gauchos. Alquilamos (*we rented*) un carro y manejamos (8) por todas partes y pasamos unos días muy agradables. El último *(last)* día que estuvimos en Buenos Aires fuimos a Galerías Pacífico (9) para comprar recuerdos (*souvenirs*) (10) para nuestros hijos y nietos. Compramos tantos regalos que tuvimos que pagar impuestos (*duties*) cuando pasamos (11) por la aduana al regresar.

2 Oraciones Crea frases originales con los elementos de las columnas. Une los elementos usando **por** o **para.** Answers will vary.

modelo

Fuimos a Mar del Plata por razones de salud para visitar a un especialista.

(No) fuimos al mercado	por/para	comprar frutas	por/para	¿?
(No) fuimos a las montañas	por/para	tres días	por/para	¿?
(No) fuiste a Mar del Plata	por/para	razones de salud	por/para	¿?
(No) fueron a Buenos Aires	por/para	tomar el sol	por/para	¿?

NOTA CULTURAL

Mar del Plata es un centro turístico en la costa de Argentina. La ciudad es conocida como "la perla del Atlántico" y todos los años muchos turistas visitan sus playas y casinos.

3 Describir Usa **por** o **para** y el tiempo presente para describir estos dibujos.

Answers will vary.

1. ____________ 2. ____________ 3. ____________

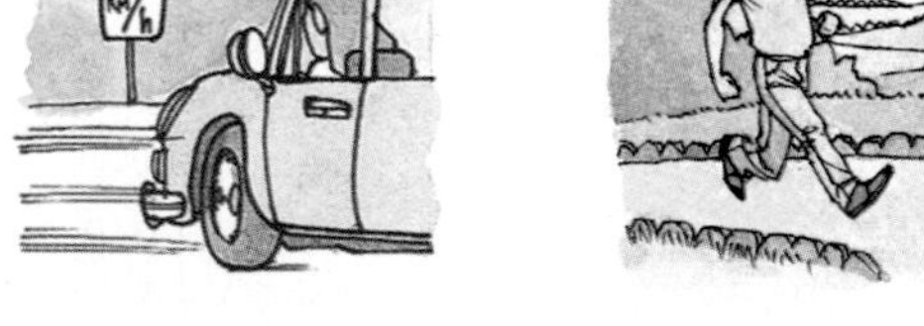

4. ____________ 5. ____________ 6. ____________

TEACHING OPTIONS

Large Group Have students create ten questions for a survey about the use of modern technology. Questions should include as many uses of **por** and **para** as possible. When finished, have students administer their survey to five different people in the room, then compile their results. Ex: **¿Por cuántos minutos al día hablas por teléfono celular?**

Heritage Speakers Ask heritage speakers to imagine they are explaining to a younger sibling how to maintain the family car and why certain types of maintenance are necessary. Students should employ as many different uses of **por** and **para** in their explanations as possible.

Comunicación

4 **Descripciones** Usa **por** o **para** y completa estas frases de una manera (*manner*) lógica. Luego, compara tus respuestas con las de un(a) compañero/a. Answers will vary.

1. En casa, hablo con mis amigos...
2. Mi padre/madre trabaja...
3. Ayer fui al taller...
4. Los miércoles tengo clases...
5. A veces voy a la biblioteca...
6. Esta noche tengo que estudiar...
7. Necesito... dólares...
8. Compré un regalo...
9. Mi mejor amigo/a estudia...
10. Necesito hacer la tarea...

5 **Situación** En parejas, dramaticen esta situación. Utilicen muchos ejemplos de **por** y **para**. Answers will vary.

Hijo/a	Padre/Madre
Pídele dinero a tu padre/madre.	Pregúntale a tu hijo/a para qué lo necesita.
Dile que quieres comprar un carro.	Pregúntale por qué necesita un carro.
Explica tres razones por las que necesitas un carro.	Explica por qué sus razones son buenas o malas.
Dile que por no tener un carro tu vida es muy difícil.	Decide si vas a darle el dinero y explica por qué.

Síntesis

6 **Una subasta (*auction*)** Cada estudiante debe traer a la clase un objeto o una foto del objeto para vender. En grupos, túrnense para ser el/la vendedor(a) y los postores (*bidders*). Para empezar, el/la vendedor(a) describe el objeto y explica para qué se usa y por qué alguien debe comprarlo. Answers will vary.

modelo

Vendedor(a): *Aquí tengo una videocasetera Sony. Pueden usar esta videocasetera para ver películas en su casa o para grabar sus programas favoritos. Sólo hace un año que la compré y todavía funciona perfectamente. ¿Quién ofrece $150.00 para empezar?*

Postor(a) 1: *$50.00 por la videocasetera.*

Vendedor(a): *¿Quién me ofrece $60.00? Es una ganga a este precio. Yo pagué $200.00 por ella.*

Postor(a) 2: *Ofrezco $60.00 por la videocasetera.*

4 Suggestion Model the activity by completing one of the sentence starters in two different ways.

4 Expansion Have students create new sentences, employing additional uses of **por** and **para**.

5 Suggestion Ask students about the car in the picture. Ex: **¿Te gusta este carro? ¿Cuánto se paga por un carro así? ¿A cuántas millas por hora corre este carro?**

5 Expansions
- Ask volunteers to role-play their conversation for the class.
- Showing a picture of an old used car, ask students to create a new conversation. The parents are offering to buy their son/daughter this car instead of the one shown in the activity.

6 Suggestions
- Before the bidding begins, display the items to be auctioned off and name them. Invite students to walk around with their group members and discuss what the items are, their purposes, and how much they will pay for them.
- Have groups prepare the opening statements for the items their members brought. Students then take turns opening up the bidding for the entire class. Non-group members may bid on each item. Group members bid to keep the bidding alive.

TEACHING OPTIONS

Small Groups Have students create a television advertisement for a car or piece of technological equipment. Students should: describe the item, why the customer should buy it, and how much it costs; explain that the item is on sale only until a certain date; and detail any possible trade-ins. Students should use **por** and **para** when possible in their ad.

Extra Practice For students still having trouble with distinguishing between **por** and **para**, have them create a mnemonic device, like a story or chant, for remembering the different uses. Ex: **Vine por la tarde y busqué por el parque, por el río y por el centro. Busqué por horas. Viajé por carro, por tren y por avión.** Do the same for **para**.

Section Goal

In **Estructura 11.3** students will learn the use of reciprocal reflexives.

Instructional Resources
WB/VM: Workbook, pp. 129–130
Lab Manual, p. 65
Lab CD/MP3 ***Lección 11***
IRM: ***¡Inténtalo! & Práctica*** *Answers, pp. 215–216; Tapescript, pp. 49–53*
Interactive CD-ROM
Companion website: www.vistahigherlearning.com
Presentations CD-ROM

Suggestions

- Ask a volunteer to explain what reflexive verbs are. Ask other students to provide examples. Review reflexive verbs and pronouns by asking students questions about their personal routine. Ex: **Yo me desperté a las seis de la mañana. Y tú, ____, ¿a qué hora te despertaste?**
- After going over the example sentences, ask students questions that contain or require reciprocal constructions. Ex: **¿Los estudiantes y los profesores siempre se saludan? ¿Se ven ustedes con frecuencia durante la semana? ¿Los candidatos siempre se respetan?**

11.3 Reciprocal reflexives

ANTE TODO In **Lección 7**, you learned that reflexive verbs indicate that the subject of a sentence does the action to itself. Reciprocal reflexives, on the other hand, express a shared or reciprocal action between two or more people or things. In this context, the pronoun means *(to) each other* or *(to) one another.*

Luis y Marta **se** miran en el espejo.
Luis and Marta look at themselves in the mirror.

Luis y Marta **se** miran.
Luis and Marta look at each other.

▶ Only the plural forms of the reflexive pronouns (**nos**, **os**, **se**) are used to express reciprocal actions because the action must involve more than one person or thing.

Cuando **nos vimos** en la calle, **nos abrazamos**.
When we saw each other on the street, we hugged one another.

Ustedes **se** van a **encontrar** en el cibercafé, ¿no?
You are meeting each other at the cybercafé, right?

Nos ayudamos cuando usamos la computadora.
We help each other when we use the computer.

Las amigas **se saludaron** y **se besaron**.
The friends greeted each other and kissed one another.

¡ATENCIÓN!

Here is a list of common verbs that can express reciprocal actions:

abrazar(se) *to hug; to embrace (each other)*
ayudar(se) *to help (each other)*
besar(se) *to kiss (each other)*
encontrar(se) *to meet (each other); run into (each other)*
saludar(se) *to greet (each other)*

¡INTÉNTALO! Indica el reflexivo recíproco adecuado y el presente o el pretérito de estos verbos.

El presente

1. (escribir) Los novios _se escriben_.
   Nosotros _nos escribimos_.
   Ana y Ernesto _se escriben_.
2. (escuchar) Mis tíos _se escuchan_.
   Nosotros _nos escuchamos_.
   Ellos _se escuchan_.
3. (ver) Nosotros _nos vemos_.
   Fernando y Tomás _se ven_.
   Ustedes _se ven_.
4. (llamar) Ellas _se llaman_.
   Mis hermanos _se llaman_.
   Pepa y yo _nos llamamos_.

El pretérito

1. (saludar) Nicolás y tú _se saludaron_.
   Nuestros vecinos _se saludaron_.
   Nosotros _nos saludamos_.
2. (hablar) Los amigos _se hablaron_.
   Elena y yo _nos hablamos_.
   Nosotras _nos hablamos_.
3. (conocer) Alberto y yo _nos conocimos_.
   Ustedes _se conocieron_.
   Ellos _se conocieron_.
4. (encontrar) Ana y Javier _se encontraron_.
   Los primos _se encontraron_.
   Mi hermana y yo _nos encontramos_.

TEACHING OPTIONS

Extra Practice Have students write sentences using the following verbs to describe what they and their significant other or best friend do together, or what their friends do together: **llamarse por teléfono, verse, decirse, ayudarse, encontrarse, reunirse.** Ex: **Mi amigo y yo siempre nos ayudamos.**

Pairs Have students write and perform a conversation in which they discuss two friends who are romantically involved, but have had a misunderstanding. Ask them to incorporate the following verbs: **conocerse, encontrarse, quererse, hablarse, enojarse, besarse, mirarse,** and **entenderse.**

Práctica

1 **Un amor recíproco** Describe a Laura y a Elián usando los verbos recíprocos.

modelo

Laura veía a Elián todos los días. Elián veía a Laura todos los días.
Laura y Elián *se veían todos los días.*

1. Laura conocía bien a Elián. Elián conocía bien a Laura.
   Laura y Elián se conocían bien.
2. Laura miraba a Elián con amor. Elián la miraba con amor también.
   Laura y Elián se miraban con amor.
3. Laura entendía bien a Elián. Elián entendía bien a Laura.
   Laura y Elián se entendían bien.
4. Laura hablaba con Elián todas las noches por teléfono. Elián hablaba con Laura todas las noches por teléfono.
   Laura y Elián se hablaban todas las noches por teléfono.
5. Laura ayudaba a Elián con sus problemas. Elián la ayudaba también con sus problemas.
   Laura y Elián se ayudaban con sus problemas.

2 **Describir** Mira los dibujos y describe lo que estas personas hicieron.

1. Las hermanas se abrazaron.

2. Ellos se besaron.

3. Gilberto y Mercedes no se miraron / no se hablaron / se enojaron.

4. Tú y yo nos saludamos / nos encontramos en la calle.

Comunicación

3 **Preguntas** En parejas, túrnense para hacerse estas preguntas. Answers will vary.

1. ¿Se vieron tú y tu mejor amigo/a ayer? ¿Cuándo se ven ustedes normalmente?
2. ¿Dónde se encuentran tú y tus amigos?
3. ¿Se ayudan tú y tu mejor amigo/a con sus problemas?
4. ¿Se entienden bien tú y tu novio/a?
5. ¿Dónde se conocieron tú y tu novio/a? ¿Cuánto tiempo hace que se conocen ustedes?
6. ¿Cuándo se dan regalos tú y tu novio/a?
7. ¿Se escriben tú y tus amigos por correo electrónico o prefieren llamarse por teléfono?
8. ¿Siempre se llevan bien tú y tu compañero/a de cuarto? Explica.

1 Suggestion Review conjugations of the imperfect tense before beginning the activity.

1 Expansions
- Have students expand upon the sentences to create a story about Laura and Elián falling in love.
- Have students rewrite the sentences, imagining that they are talking about themselves and their significant other, a close friend, or a relative.

2 Suggestion Have pairs choose a drawing and create the story of what the characters did leading up to the moment pictured and what they did after that. Ask pairs to share their stories and have the class vote for the most original or funniest one.

3 Suggestions
- Ask students to read through the questions and prepare short answers before talking to their partner.
- Encourage students to verify what they hear by paraphrasing or summarizing their partner's responses.

3 Expansion Have students ask follow-up questions after their partner has answered the original ones. Ex: **¿A qué hora se vieron ayer? ¿Dónde se vieron? ¿Por qué se vieron ayer? ¿Para qué se ven ustedes normalmente?**

TEACHING OPTIONS

Game Divide the class into groups of four to play a guessing game. Write a verb on the board. Groups have 20 seconds to come up with a famous couple or two famous people or entities that behave or feel that way toward each other. The verb may be in the present, imperfect, or preterite tense. Ex: **quererse— Romeo y Julieta se querían.** All groups with a correct answer earn a point.

TPR Call on a pair of volunteers to act out a reciprocal action. The class will guess the action, using the verb in a sentence.
Heritage Speakers Ask heritage speakers to summarize the action of their favorite love story, soap opera, or television drama. They should try to use as many reciprocal reflexives as possible in their summary.

Section Goals

In **Estructura 11.4** students will learn:

- the stressed possessive adjectives and pronouns
- placement of stressed possessive adjectives

Instructional Resources
WB/VM: Workbook, pp. 131–132
Lab Manual, p. 66
Lab CD/MP3 ***Lección 11***
IRM: ***¡Inténtalo!*** *&* ***Práctica*** *Answers, pp. 215–216;*
Tapescript, pp. 49–53
Info Gap Activities Booklet, pp. 43–44
Interactive CD-ROM
Companion website: www.vistahigherlearning.com
Presentations CD-ROM

Suggestions

- Ask a few questions that involve possessive adjectives and respond to student answers with statements that involve the stressed possessive pronouns. Write each stressed pronoun you introduce on the board as you say it. Ex: ____ , **¿es éste tu lápiz? (Sí.) Pues, este lápiz es tuyo,** ____ . Show your own pencil. **Éste es mi lápiz. Este lápiz es mío.**
- Write the masculine forms of the stressed possessive adjectives/pronouns on the board, and ask volunteers to give the feminine and plural forms. Emphasize that when a stressed possessive adjective is used, the word it modifies is preceded by an article.

11.4 Stressed possessive adjectives and pronouns

ANTE TODO In contrast to English, Spanish has two types of possessive adjectives: the unstressed (or short) forms you learned in **Lección 3** and the stressed (or long) forms. The stressed possessive adjectives are used for emphasis or to express the English phrases *of mine, of yours, of his,* and so on.

Stressed possessive adjectives

Masculine singular	Feminine singular	Masculine plural	Feminine plural	
mío	**mía**	**míos**	**mías**	*my; (of) mine*
tuyo	**tuya**	**tuyos**	**tuyas**	*your; (of) yours (fam.)*
suyo	**suya**	**suyos**	**suyas**	*your; (of) yours (form.); his; (of) his; her; (of) hers; its*
nuestro	**nuestra**	**nuestros**	**nuestras**	*our; (of) ours*
vuestro	**vuestra**	**vuestros**	**vuestras**	*your; (of) yours (fam.)*
suyo	**suya**	**suyos**	**suyas**	*your; (of) yours (form.); their; (of) theirs*

¡ATENCIÓN!

Used with **un/una**, these possessives are similar in meaning to the English expression *of mine/yours/etc.*

Juancho es un amigo mío.
Juancho is a friend of mine.

▶ Stressed possessive adjectives must agree in gender and number with the nouns they modify.

su impresora
her printer

nuestros televisores
our television sets

la impresora **suya**
her printer

los televisores **nuestros**
our television sets

▶ Stressed possessive adjectives are placed after the noun they modify, while unstressed possessive adjectives are placed before the noun.

Son **mis** llaves.
They are my keys.

Son las llaves **mías**.
They are my keys.

▶ A definite article, an indefinite article, or a demonstrative adjective usually precedes a noun modified by a stressed possessive adjective.

Me encantan	**unos** discos compactos **tuyos**.	*I love some of your CDs.*
	los discos compactos **tuyos**.	*I love your CDs.*
	estos discos compactos **tuyos**.	*I love these CDs of yours.*

▶ Since **suyo, suya, suyos,** and **suyas** have more than one meaning, you can avoid confusion by using the construction: [*article*] + [*noun*] + **de** + [*subject pronoun*].

el teclado **suyo**

el teclado **de él/ella**	*his/her keyboard*
el teclado **de usted**	*your keyboard*
el teclado **de ellos/ellas**	*their keyboard*
el teclado **de ustedes**	*your keyboard*

CONSÚLTALO

This is the same construction you learned in **Lección 3** for clarifying **su** and **sus**. To review unstressed possessive adjectives, see **Estructura 3.2**, p. 83.

TEACHING OPTIONS

TPR Place different objects and/or photos of objects in a large bag. Ask students to retrieve one item from the bag as you whisper a name or names of people in the classroom into the students' ears. The students then mime how to use the item and to whom the item belongs. The class makes guesses like the following: **Es el carro de ____ y de ____. Es el carro suyo.**

Extra Practice Refer students to the chart of possessive adjectives on this page. Call out a noun and subject, then ask students to tell you which adjective they would use. Ex: **discos compactos, ustedes (suyos)**

Possessive pronouns

- Possessive pronouns are used to replace a noun + [*possessive adjective*]. In Spanish, the possessive pronouns have the same forms as the stressed possessive adjectives, and they are preceded by a definite article.

la calculadora **nuestra**	**la nuestra**
el *fax* **tuyo**	**el tuyo**
los archivos **suyos**	**los suyos**

- A possessive pronoun agrees in number and gender with the noun it replaces.

—Aquí está **mi coche.** ¿Dónde está **el tuyo**?
Here's my car. Where is yours?

—**El mío** está en el taller de mi hermano.
Mine is at my brother's garage.

—¿Tienes **las revistas** de Carlos?
Do you have Carlos' magazines?

—No, pero tengo **las nuestras.**
No, but I have ours.

¡ATENCIÓN!

The definite article (**el/la**) is usually omitted when a stressed possessive follows the verb **ser**.

Perdone, ¿pero **es suya** esta cámara?

No, no **es mía**.

Episodio veintiuno: Tecnohombre y los superamigos suyos salvan el mundo una vez más.

La Mujer Mecánica y Tecnohombre, ¡mis héroes!
¡Y los míos también!

¡INTÉNTALO! Indica las formas tónicas (*stressed*) de estos adjetivos posesivos y los pronombres posesivos correspondientes.

		adjetivos	pronombres
1.	su videocasetera	la videocasetera suya	la suya
2.	mi televisor	el televisor mío	el mío
3.	nuestros discos compactos	los discos compactos nuestros	los nuestros
4.	tus calculadoras	las calculadoras tuyas	las tuyas
5.	su monitor	el monitor suyo	el suyo
6.	mis videos	los videos míos	los míos
7.	nuestra impresora	la impresora nuestra	la nuestra
8.	tu estéreo	el estéreo tuyo	el tuyo
9.	nuestro cederrón	el cederrón nuestro	el nuestro
10.	mi computadora	la computadora mía	la mía

Suggestions

- Use a balled-up piece of paper to practice possessives. Call out a sentence using an unstressed possessive adjective. Toss the balled-up piece of paper to a student who restates the sentence, using a stressed possessive adjective. That student, in turn, tosses the ball to another student, who states the sentence using a possessive pronoun and tosses the ball back to you. Ex: **Nuestra impresora es nueva. La impresora nuestra es nueva. La nuestra es nueva.**
- Ask students questions using unstressed possessive adjectives or the [*article*] + [*noun*] + **de** construction before a name, having them answer with a possessive pronoun. Ex: **Es tu cuaderno, ¿verdad? (Sí, es el mío.) Clase, ¿son éstos sus exámenes? (Sí, son los nuestros.) Ésta es la mochila negra de ____, ¿no? (No, no es la suya. La mochila roja es la suya.)**
- Point out that the function of the stressed possessives is to give emphasis. They are often used to point out contrasts. Ex: **¿Tu carro es azul? Pues, el carro mío es rojo. ¿Tu cámara digital no es buena? La mía es excelente.**

TEACHING OPTIONS

Video Replay the **Fotonovela**, having students listen for each use of an unstressed possessive adjective and write down the sentence in which it occurs. Next, have students rewrite those sentences using a stressed possessive adjective. Then, discuss how the use of stressed possessive adjectives affected the meaning or fluidity of the sentences.

Pairs Tell students that their laundry has gotten mixed up with their roommate's and since they are the same size and have the same tastes in clothing, they can't tell what belongs to whom. Have them ask each other questions about different articles of clothing. Ex: **—¿Son tuyos estos pantalones de rayas? —Sí, son míos. —Y ¿estos calcetines rojos son tuyos? —Sí, son míos, pero esta camisa grandísima no es mía.**

1 Expansion Have pairs write four sentences that use stressed possessive adjectives or pronouns. Have them "dehydrate" their sentences following the model of this activity and then exchange them with another pair that "rehydrates" them.

2 Expansion Have students continue the activity, using the following items: **la impresora, el teléfono celular, la videocasetera, el reproductor de DVD, la contestadora,** and **el *walkman*.**

3 Expansion Have students create conversations modeled after the ones in the activity and perform them for the class. Each one should consist of at least six lines and use as many stressed possessive adjectives and pronouns as possible.

Práctica

1 **Frases** Forma frases con las siguientes palabras. Usa el presente.

1. Un / amiga / suyo / vivir / Mendoza Una amiga suya vive en Mendoza.
2. ¿Me / prestar / calculadora / tuyo? ¿Me prestas la calculadora tuya?
3. El / coche / suyo / nunca / funcionar / bien El coche suyo nunca funciona bien.
4. No / nos / interesar / problemas / suyo No nos interesan los problemas suyos.
5. Yo / querer / cámara digital / mío / ahora mismo Yo quiero la cámara digital mía ahora mismo.
6. Un / amigos / nuestro / manejar / como / loco Unos amigos nuestros manejan como locos.

2 **¿Es suyo?** Un policía ha capturado al hombre que robó (*robbed*) en tu casa. Ahora quiere saber qué cosas son tuyas. Túrnate con un(a) compañero/a para hacer el papel del policía y usa las pistas (*clues*) para contestar las preguntas.

modelo

No/viejo
Policía: *Esta calculadora, ¿es suya?*
Estudiante: *No, no es mía. La mía era más vieja.*

1. Sí Este estéreo, ¿es suyo?/Sí, es mío.

2. Sí Esta computadora portátil, ¿es suya?/Sí, es mía.

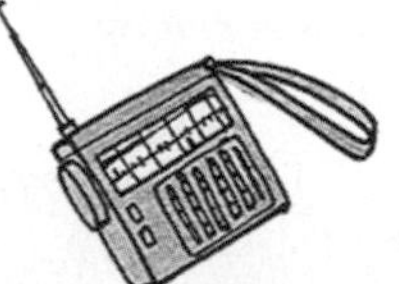

3. Sí Este radio, ¿es suyo?/ Sí, es mío.

4. No/grande Este televisor, ¿es suyo?/ No, no es mío. El mío era más grande.

5. No/pequeño Esta cámara de video, ¿es suya?/ No, no es mía. La mía era más pequeña.

6. No/de Shakira Estos discos compactos, ¿son suyos?/ No, no son míos. Los míos eran de Shakira.

NOTA CULTURAL

Hija de madre colombiana y padre libanés, **Shakira** se inspira en las dos culturas para crear su música. A los 15 años grabó un álbum que se encontró entre los favoritos de la música latina. En 2001, Shakira entró al mercado norteamericano con su álbum *Laundry Service* que incluye canciones en inglés y español.

3 **Conversaciones** Completa estas conversaciones con las formas adecuadas de los pronombres posesivos.

1. —La casa de los Ortiz estaba en la Avenida 9 de Julio. ¿Dónde estaba la casa de ustedes?
   —La nuestra estaba en la calle Bolívar.
2. —A Carmen le encanta su monitor nuevo.
   —¿Sí? A José no le gusta el suyo.
3. —Puse mis discos aquí. ¿Dónde pusiste los tuyos, Alfonso?
   —Puse los míos en el escritorio.
4. —Se me olvidó traer mis llaves. ¿Trajeron ustedes las suyas?
   —No, dejamos las nuestras en casa.
5. —Yo compré mi computadora en una tienda y Marta compró la suya en Internet. Y la tuya, ¿dónde la compraste?
   —La mía es de Cíbermax.

TEACHING OPTIONS

Large Groups Have students bring in a photo of their favorite car and tell them to imagine that everyone in town is picking up his or her car at the mechanic's shop at the same time. Have students role-play a scene between the mechanic and several customers. The mechanic tries to determine which car belongs to whom.

Pairs Have students make a wish list consisting of ten items, then give it to another pair. Students should decide who gets what on the list, justifying their claim. Ex: **La bicicleta nueva es mía. La necesito para ir a la universidad.** Students should try to use at least one possessive adjective or pronoun in their claims.

Comunicación

4 **Identificar** Trabajen en grupos. Cada estudiante da tres objetos. Pongan (*Put*) todos los objetos juntos. Luego, un(a) estudiante escoge uno o dos objetos y le pregunta a otro/a si esos objetos son suyos. Usen los adjetivos posesivos en sus preguntas.
Answers will vary.

modelo

Estudiante 1: Felipe, ¿son tuyos estos discos compactos?
Estudiante 2: Sí, son míos.
No, no son míos. Son los discos compactos de Bárbara.

5 **Comparar** Trabajen en parejas. Intenta (*Try to*) convencer a tu compañero/a de que algo que tú tienes es mejor que el que él/ella tiene. Pueden hablar de sus carros, estéreos, discos compactos, clases, horarios o trabajos. Answers will vary.

modelo

Estudiante 1: Mi computadora tiene una pantalla de quince pulgadas (*inches*). ¿Y la tuya?
Estudiante 2: La mía es mejor porque tiene una pantalla de diecisiete pulgadas.
Estudiante 1: Pues la mía...

Síntesis

6 **Inventos locos** En grupos pequeños, lean la descripción de este invento fantástico. Después diseñen su propio invento y expliquen por qué es mejor que el de los demás grupos. Utilicen los posesivos, **por** y **para** y el vocabulario de **Contextos**.

Nuestro celular tiene conexión a Internet, ¿y el tuyo?

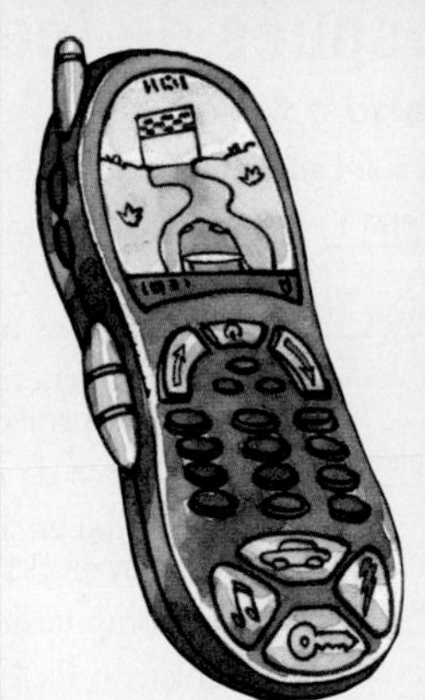

Este teléfono celular es mucho mejor que el tuyo por estas razones:

- El nuestro tiene capacidad para guardar un millón de mensajes electrónicos.
- El celular nuestro toma video.
- Da la temperatura.
- Funciona como control remoto para la tele.
- También arranca el coche y toca música como un *walkman*.

Sirve para todo.

Oferta: $45 dólares por mes (con un contrato mínimo de dos años)

Para más información, llama al 607-362-1990 o visita nuestro sitio web www.telefonoloco.com

4 Suggestion If students can't bring in three objects, have them either find photos of objects or draw them. Students should find one feminine, one masculine, and one plural object to do the activity.

5 Suggestion Before beginning the activity, have students make a list of objects to compare. Next have them brainstorm as many different qualities or features of those objects as they can. Finally, have them list adjectives or other descriptors that they might use to compare the objects they've chosen.

5 Expansion Have pairs who had a heated discussion perform it for the class.

6 Expansion Have students change their ad to market their product for television or radio.

Suggestion See the Info Gap Activities Booklet for an additional activity to practice the material presented in this section.

TEACHING OPTIONS

Large Group Ask each student to bring in a photo of an object. Tell students not to tell anyone what their object is, and place it in a large sack. Call students up one at a time to choose a photo from the sack. Students then circulate around the classroom, trying to find the owner of their photo. Ex: **¿Es tuyo este disco compacto? (No, no es mío.** or **Sí, es mío.)**

Heritage Speakers Have heritage speakers imagine that they are salespersons at a car dealership and they are writing a letter to a customer explaining why their cars are better than those of the other two dealerships in town. Students should compare several attributes of the cars and use stressed possessive adjectives and pronouns when appropriate.

Section Goals

In **Lectura** students will:
- learn to recognize borrowed words
- increase their reading comprehension in Spanish by using borrowed words to predict content
- read a content-rich text with borrowed words

Instructional Resource
Companion website: www.vistahigherlearning.com

Estrategia Tell students that recognizing words borrowed from English will help them understand unfamiliar texts.

Examinar el texto Ask students to scan the text for borrowed words. When they are finished, ask volunteers to tell what the text is about.

Buscar Model for the whole class the pronunciation of the borrowed words.

Predecir Discuss how borrowed words coupled with other context clues helped students predict content.

Lectura

Antes de leer

Estrategia
Recognizing borrowed words

One way languages grow is by borrowing words from each other. English words that relate to technology are often borrowed by Spanish and other languages throughout the world. Sometimes the words are modified slightly to fit the sounds of the languages that borrow them. When reading in Spanish, you can often increase your understanding by looking for words borrowed from English or other languages you know.

Examinar el texto

Mira brevemente° la selección. ¿De qué trata°? ¿Cómo lo sabes?

Buscar

Esta lectura contiene varias palabras tomadas° del inglés. Trabaja con un(a) compañero/a para encontrarlas. Internet, fax, Deep Blue

Predecir

Trabaja con un(a) compañero/a para contestar las siguientes preguntas. Answers will vary.

1. En la foto, ¿quiénes participan en el juego?
2. ¿Jugabas en una computadora cuando eras niño/a? ¿Juegas ahora?
3. ¿Cómo cambiaron las computadoras y la tecnología en los años 80? ¿En los años 90?
4. ¿Qué tipo de "inteligencia" tiene una computadora?
5. ¿Qué significa "inteligencia artificial" para ti?

brevemente *briefly* ¿De qué trata? *What is it about?* tomadas *taken*

Inteligencia y memoria: la inteligencia artificial

por **Alfonso Santamaría**

Una de las principales características de la película de ciencia ficción *2001: una odisea del espacio*, es la gran inteligencia de su protagonista no humano, la computadora HAL-9000. Para muchas personas, la genial película de Stanley Kubrick es una reflexión sobre la evolución de la inteligencia, desde que el hombre utilizó por primera vez un hueso como herramienta° hasta la llegada de la inteligencia artificial (I.A.).

Ahora que vivimos en el siglo XXI, un mundo en el que Internet y el *fax* son ya comunes, podemos preguntarnos: ¿consiguieron los científicos especialistas en I.A. crear una computadora como HAL? La respuesta es no. Hoy día no existe una computadora con las capacidades intelectuales de HAL porque todavía no existen *inteligencias*

herramienta *tool* sentido común *common sense* desarrollo *development* ajedrez *chess*

Después de leer

¿Cierto o falso?

Indica si cada frase es cierta o falsa. Corrige las frases falsas.

Cierta 1. La computadora HAL-9000 era muy inteligente.

Falsa 2. Deep Blue es un buen ejemplo de la inteligencia artificial general. Deep Blue es un buen ejemplo de la inteligencia artificial especializada.

Falsa 3. El maestro de ajedrez Garry Kasparov le ganó a Deep Blue en 1997. Deep Blue le ganó a Garry Kasparov en 1997.

Cierta 4. Las computadoras no tienen la creatividad de Mozart o Picasso.

Falsa 5. Hoy hay computadoras como HAL-9000. Las computadoras con la inteligencia de HAL-9000 son pura ciencia ficción.

TEACHING OPTIONS

Extra Practice Provide students with brief texts in Spanish on inflation, unemployment, or a topic that lends itself to numerical expressions, particularly percentages. Ask them to scan the text and write two or three corresponding questions, such as: **¿Cuánto subió la inflación este mes?** Have students exchange articles and questions with a partner and answer one another's questions.

Game Have students describe a type of new technology that has changed their lives; their classmates will guess what they are describing. Tell students to present the most general clues first, moving toward more specific clues: Ex: **Con esto puedo enviarles mensajes a mis amigos. Y los amigos míos pueden leerlos y responderme casi inmediatamente. (correo electrónico)**

artificiales generales que demuestren lo que llamamos "sentido común"°. Sin embargo, la I.A. está progresando mucho en el desarrollo° de las inteligencias especializadas. El ejemplo más famoso es Deep Blue, la computadora de IBM especializada en jugar al ajedrez°.

La idea de crear una máquina con capacidad para jugar al ajedrez se originó en 1950. En esa década, el científico Claude Shannon desarrolló una teoría que se convirtió en realidad en 1967, cuando apareció el primer programa que permitió a una computadora competir, aunque sin éxito°, en un campeonato° de ajedrez. Más de veinte años después, un grupo de expertos en I.A. fue al centro de investigación

Thomas J. Watson de Nueva York para desarrollar Deep Blue, la computadora que en 1997 derrotó° al campeón mundial de ajedrez, Garry Kasparov. Esta extraordinaria computadora pudo ganarle al maestro ruso de ajedrez porque estaba diseñada para procesar 200 millones de jugadas° por segundo. Además, Deep Blue guardaba en su memoria una recopilación de los movimientos de ajedrez más brillantes de toda la historia, entre ellos los que Kasparov efectuó en sus competiciones anteriores.

Para muchas personas la victoria de Deep Blue sobre Kasparov simbolizó la victoria de la inteligencia artificial sobre la del ser humano°. Debemos reconocer los grandes avances científicos en el área de las computadoras y las ventajas° que pueden traernos en un futuro, pero también tenemos que entender sus limitaciones. Las computadoras generan nuevos modelos con conocimientos° muy definidos, pero todavía no tienen sentido común: una computadora como Deep Blue puede ganar una partida° de ajedrez, pero no puede explicar la diferencia entre una reina° y un peón°. Tampoco puede crear algo nuevo y original a partir de lo establecido, como hicieron Mozart o Picasso.

Las inteligencias artificiales especializadas son una realidad. ¿Pero una inteligencia como la de HAL-9000? Pura ciencia ficción. ■

éxito *success* campeonato *championship* derrotó *defeated* jugadas *moves* la del ser humano *that of the human being* ventajas *advantages* conocimientos *knowledge* partida *match* reina *queen* peón *pawn*

¿Cierto o falso? If students have difficulty with any item, have them work in pairs to locate the source of that information in the text.

Preguntas As you go over the items with the class, have students jot down the correct answers in complete sentences. Then, assign each answer to a small group, who will use it as a topic sentence for a short paragraph that elaborates on the answer's idea based on the reading. This elaboration can be done orally and groups should later share their discussions with the class.

Conversar Ask students how the views expressed in the article might have influenced their answers to these questions.

Preguntas

Contesta las preguntas.

1. ¿Qué tipo de inteligencia se relaciona con HAL-9000? La inteligencia artificial general se relaciona con HAL-9000.
2. ¿Qué tipo de inteligencia tienen las computadoras como Deep Blue? Las computadoras como Deep Blue tienen una inteligencia especializada.
3. ¿Cuándo se originó la idea de crear una máquina para jugar al ajedrez? La idea de crear una máquina para jugar al ajedrez se originó en 1950.
4. ¿Qué compañía inventó Deep Blue? IBM inventó Deep Blue.
5. ¿Por qué Deep Blue le pudo ganar a Garry Kasparov? Deep Blue le ganó a Garry Kasparov porque podía procesar 200 millones de jugadas por segundo.

Conversar

En grupos pequeños, hablen de los siguientes temas. Answers will vary.

1. ¿Son las computadoras más inteligentes que los seres humanos?
2. ¿Para qué cosas son mejores las computadoras, y para qué cosas son mejores los seres humanos? ¿Por qué?
3. En el futuro, ¿van a tener las computadoras la inteligencia de los seres humanos? ¿Cuándo?

TEACHING OPTIONS

Small Groups Ask students to work in groups of six. Tell them to improvise and create a humorous story as a group. Ask one person in the group to start it off by giving an introductory sentence, such as: **Ayer estuvimos en el coche y ocurrió algo muy raro.** Others add sentences with additional details to complete the story. Encourage students to be creative and make the story as long as they wish.

Pairs Ask students to work together to create answers and corresponding questions. Have one partner create the answers to questions about artificial intelligence. The other partner develops the questions that relate to the answers. Then partners switch roles.

Section Goals

In **Escritura** students will:
- learn to prepare for writing by making a list of key words they plan to use as they write
- write an e-mail to a friend giving instructions for posting a personal ad on a website

Estrategia Discuss the importance of writing clear instructions and the need to be precise. Encourage students to rely primarily on vocabulary they already know when preparing their list of key words. They should consult the dictionary only if they need a word that they consider central to their writing. Explain that spending too much time looking through a dictionary could sidetrack them and make them lose the focus of the writing activity.

Tema Have students brainstorm and categorize a list of verbs and instructions that they may use in their e-mails. Ask a volunteer to record students' suggestions in a word map on the board. Tell students they will be composing their e-mails using affirmative and negative **tú** commands.

Escritura

Estrategia

Listing key words

Once you have determined the purpose for a piece of writing and identified your audience, it is helpful to make a list of key words you can use while writing. If you were to write a description of your campus, for example, you would probably need a list of prepositions that describe location, such as **en frente de, al lado de,** and **detrás de.** Likewise, a list of descriptive adjectives would be useful to you if you were writing about the people and places of your childhood.

By preparing a list of potential words ahead of time, you will find it easier to avoid using the dictionary while writing your first draft. You will probably also learn a few new words in Spanish while preparing your list of key words.

Listing useful vocabulary is also a valuable organizational strategy, since the act of brainstorming key words will help you to form ideas about your topic. In addition, a list of key words can help you avoid redundancy when you write.

If you were going to help someone write a personal ad, what words would be most helpful to you? Jot a few of them down and compare your list with a partner's. Did you choose the same words? Would you choose any different or additional words, based on what your partner wrote?

1. ______________________
2. ______________________
3. ______________________
4. ______________________
5. ______________________
6. ______________________

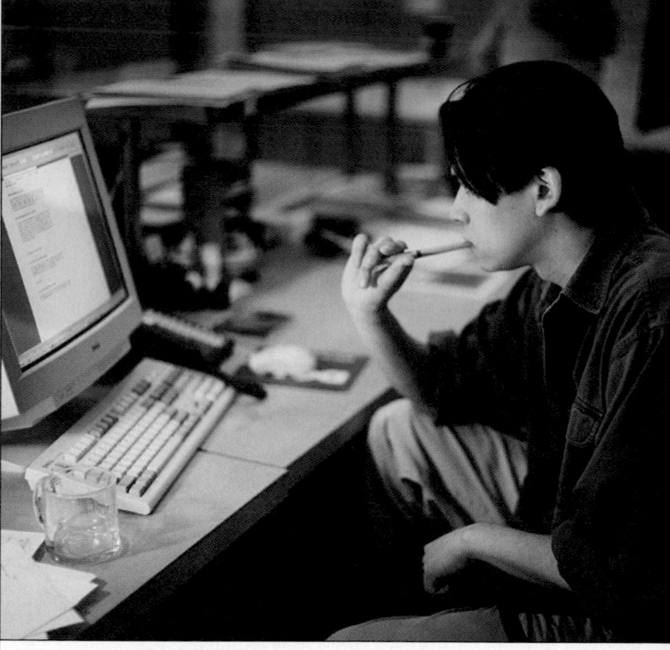

Tema

Escribir instrucciones

Un(a) amigo/a tuyo/a quiere escribir un anuncio° personal en un sitio web para citas románticas. Tú tienes experiencia con esto y vas a decirle qué debe decir y no decir en su perfil°.

Escríbele un correo en el que le explicas claramente° cómo hacerlo.

Cuando escribas tu correo considera la siguiente información:

- El nombre del sitio web
- Mandatos afirmativos que describen en detalle lo que tu amigo/a debe escribir
- Una descripción física, sus pasatiempos, sus actividades favoritas y otras cosas originales como el tipo de carro que tiene o su signo del zodiaco
- Su dirección electrónica, su número de teléfono celular, etc.
- Mandatos negativos sobre cosas que tu amigo/a no debe escribir en el anuncio

anuncio *ad* perfil *profile* claramente *clearly*

TEACHING OPTIONS

Proofreading Activity Copy the following items containing mistakes onto the board or a transparency as a proofreading activity to do with the whole class.

1. **David comía un sándwich, mientras buscó información en el Internet por un informe sobre la Argentina.**
2. **Siempre revisé mío correo electrónico por la mañana.**
3. **Pasa para mi apartamento y mira la mía computadora nueva.**
4. **De repente el carro suo se arrancaba.**
5. **Rita y Eugenia se habla para teléfono celular cada día.**
6. **¡Y al clímax del concierto sonaba un teléfono celular! ¡Qué disastre! Siempre apago mío.**

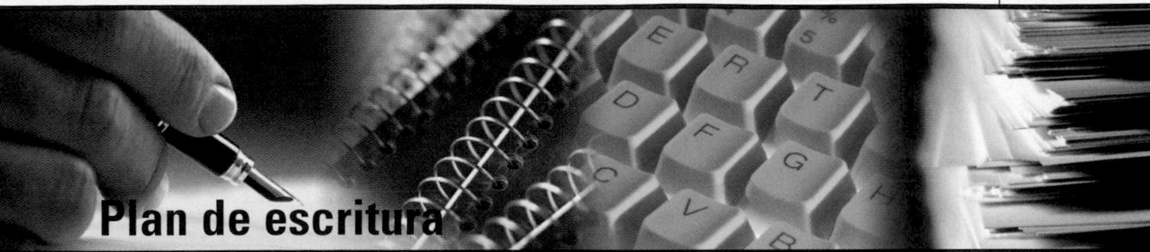

Plan de escritura

1 Ideas y organización

Apunta° las palabras y expresiones que quieres utilizar para las instrucciones, incluyendo la información importante para un anuncio personal. Si quieres, puedes basar tus instrucciones en un anuncio inventado por ti.

2 Primer borrador

Utilizando la lista de palabras clave° de **Ideas y organización,** escribe el primer borrador de las instrucciones. Utiliza el texto, los apuntes de clase y el diccionario solamente como último recurso°.

3 Comentario

Intercambia tus instrucciones con las de un(a) compañero/a. Comparte tus opiniones sobre el primer borrador utilizando estas preguntas como guía:

a. ¿Están claras las instrucciones o necesitan alguna clarificación?
b. ¿Hay suficientes detalles o hay demasiados?
c. ¿Hay errores de gramática, vocabulario o puntuación?
d. ¿Tienes otras sugerencias para mejorar las instrucciones?

4 Redacción

Revisa el primer borrador según las instrucciones de tu compañero/a. Utiliza la siguiente guía para hacer una última revisión antes de escribir tu versión final.

a. Mira las instrucciones. ¿Omitiste detalles importantes? ¿Incluiste demasiados detalles?
b. Subraya° todos los verbos. ¿Utilizaste la forma correcta de cada uno?
c. Revisa la ortografía y la puntuación una vez más con la ayuda de tus **Anotaciones para mejorar la escritura.**

5 Evaluación y progreso

Trabaja con un(a) compañero/a. Lee las instrucciones que escribió. Cuando recibas las correcciones y los comentarios de tu profesor(a), anota tus errores en las **Anotaciones para mejorar la escritura** en tu **Carpeta de trabajos.**

Apunta *Jot down* clave *key* recurso *resource* Subraya *Underline*

Comentario
- Go over guide questions a–d with the class. Then have pairs exchange e-mails. Allow five minutes for reading and comments.
- Have students follow the directions in **Redacción** as homework.

Evaluación y progreso Give the class ten minutes to carry out the activity. Then have students hand in their e-mails.

Writing Sample Here is a sample e-mail with instructions that would constitute superior writing achievement.

Esteban,
Para escribir el anuncio personal ideal, visita el sitio www.amor.com. Haz una descripción de tu apariencia física general, pero no des muchos detalles. Sólo da el color de los ojos y del pelo. Di que te gusta el fútbol y la natación, pero no digas que nunca lees. Explica que tienes un buen trabajo pero que tu carro es viejo porque esperas ir al Caribe el verano próximo. También escribe que viviste unos años en Buenos Aires, pero no escribas que debes viajar con frecuencia por tu trabajo. Ah, y no olvides mencionar que eres capricornio y por eso te gusta mucho ser sociable. Pon tu dirección electrónica en el anuncio, porque si no lo haces, ¡nadie te responde! Te deseo mucha suerte. Llámame o mándame un correo electrónico si tienes alguna pregunta. ¡Chau!

Víctor

EVALUATION: Instrucciones

Criteria	Scale
Content	1 2 3 4 5
Organization	1 2 3 4 5
Use of vocabulary	1 2 3 4 5
Grammatical accuracy	1 2 3 4 5

Scoring	
Excellent	18–20 points
Good	14–17 points
Satisfactory	10–13 points
Unsatisfactory	< 10 points

Section Goals
In **Escuchar** students will:
- practice recognizing the genre of two short examples of spoken discourse
- answer questions based on a broadcast advertisement for a computer store

Instructional Resources
Textbook CD
IRM: Tapescript, p. 95

Estrategia
Script 1. Buenos días. Hoy tenemos la gran oportunidad de conversar con el futbolista Carlos Roa del equipo argentino. Carlos, ¿qué opinas del partido que ganaron contra Chile?
2. Buenos días. Ésta es la residencia del arquitecto Rivera. No hay nadie en casa en estos momentos. Por favor, deje un mensaje y lo llamaré lo más pronto posible.

Suggestion Make sure students correctly identified the two genres in the **Estrategia** recording as **entrevista** and **mensaje de contestadora**. Then, have them look at the photo and describe what they see. Guide them to see that Ricardo Moreno is broadcasting from a radio studio.

Ahora escucha
Script Necesita, ¿navegar en Internet o imprimir documentos? ¿Descargar fotos o quemar un cederrón? Si usted está buscando una computadora y no está seguro del tipo de computadora que necesita, hable con nosotros. Le ayudamos a escoger la computadora más adecuada para usted. ¡Es facilísimo! Los dependientes de nuestra tienda de computación conocen los últimos avances en programas de computación, conexiones a Internet, computadoras portátiles, impresoras y más. También tenemos los mejores precios. Venga inmediatamente a Mundo de Computación en Paseo Las Américas para ver qué fácil es comprar la computadora perfecta. O visite nuestro sitio web en la dirección www.mundodecom.ar.

Escuchar

Estrategia
Recognizing the genre of spoken discourse

You will encounter many different genres of spoken discourse in Spanish. For example, you may hear a political speech, a radio interview, a commercial, a message on an answering machine, or a news broadcast. Try to identify the genre of what you hear so that you can activate your background knowledge about that type of discourse and identify the speakers' motives and intentions.

 To practice this strategy, you will now listen to two short selections. Identify the genre of each one.

Preparación
Mira la foto de Ricardo Moreno. ¿Puedes imaginarte qué tipo de discurso vas a oír?

Ahora escucha 
Mientras escuchas a Ricardo Moreno, responde a las preguntas.

1. ¿Qué tipo de discurso es? c
   a. las noticias° por radio o televisión
   b. una conversación entre amigos
   c. un anuncio° comercial
   d. una reseña° de una película
2. ¿De qué habla? c
   a. del tiempo
   b. de su vida
   c. de un producto o servicio
   d. de algo que oyó o vio
3. ¿Cuál es el propósito°? b
   a. informar
   b. vender
   c. relacionarse con alguien
   d. dar opiniones

Comprensión
Identificar
Indica si la siguiente información está incluida en el discurso; si está incluida, escribe los detalles que escuchaste.

	Sí	No
1. El anuncio describe un servicio. Venden computadoras y productos para computadoras.	✓	
2. Explica cómo está de salud.		✓
3. Informa sobre la variedad de productos. programas de computación, impresoras, computadoras portátiles	✓	
4. Pide tu opinión.		✓
5. Explica por qué es la mejor tienda. Tiene buenos precios.	✓	
6. Informa sobre el tiempo para mañana.		✓
7. Informa dónde se puede conseguir el servicio. en Mundo de Computación	✓	
8. Informa sobre las noticias del mundo.		✓

Haz un anuncio
Con tres o cuatro compañeros, hagan un anuncio comercial de algún producto. No se olviden de dar toda la información necesaria. Después presenten su anuncio a la clase.

noticias *news* anuncio *advertisement* reseña *review* propósito *purpose*

Proyecto

Promociona un nuevo cibercafé

Imagina que trabajas para una agencia de publicidad en Argentina. Tienes que crear un anuncio° para promocionar un nuevo cibercafé en Buenos Aires.

1 Diseña el anuncio

Crea un anuncio para una revista, teniendo en cuenta° el mercado argentino. Usa los **recursos para la investigación** para encontrar información sobre cibercafés en países hispanos. Investiga también el mercado argentino para poder explicar por qué es necesario un nuevo cibercafé en la capital. El anuncio debe:

- describir toda la tecnología que se ofrece a los clientes, incluyendo fotos o dibujos si es posible.
- explicar por qué este cibercafé es mejor que los que ya existen en Buenos Aires.
- hablar de los precios, de la zona donde está ubicado° y de otros servicios importantes que se ofrecen en el cibercafé.

2 Presenta la información

Usa el anuncio de revista como base para hacer un anuncio publicitario de radio. Puedes presentar el anuncio a tus compañeros/as en persona o lo puedes grabar para la clase. El anuncio debe animar° a tus compañeros/as a visitar el cibercafé.

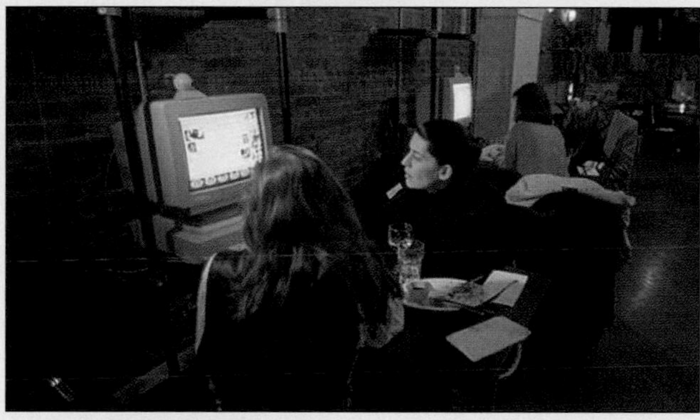

recursos para la investigación

Internet Palabras clave: cibercafé, Buenos Aires, Internet, tecnología

Comunidad Personas que conocen los nuevos adelantos° en Internet, o que han estado° en un cibercafé, estudiantes o profesores argentinos

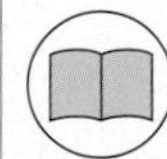
Biblioteca Revistas de Internet, periódicos

Otros recursos Anuncios de cibercafés en Internet

anuncio *ad* teniendo en cuenta *keeping in mind* está ubicado *is located* animar *encourage* adelantos *advances* han estado *have been*

Section Goals

In **Proyecto** students will:

- use Spanish as they research and interact with the wider world
- create a magazine advertisement for a cybercafé in Buenos Aires
- create a radio advertisement for the cybercafé

Suggestion Students might need a week to complete the project, so at the beginning of that time period, have them open their books to this page and glance over **Proyecto**. Tell them they are going to create an advertisement for a cybercafé that they will use to make a radio commercial.

Diseña el anuncio

- Bring in examples of advertisements for technology products in Spanish-language magazines for students to examine.
- Record some advertisements from your local Spanish-language radio station and play them for the class.

Presenta la información You may wish to set aside sufficient class time to do a few presentations at a time until all students have had a chance to present.

EVALUATION: Anuncio

Criteria	Scale
Content	1 2 3 4
Organization	1 2 3 4
Accuracy	1 2 3 4
Creativity	1 2 3 4
Oral presentation	1 2 3 4

Scoring	
Excellent	18–20 points
Good	14–17 points
Satisfactory	10–13 points
Unsatisfactory	< 10 points

Section Goal

In **Panorama**, students will read about the geography, history, and culture of Argentina.

Instructional Resources
Transparencies, #5, #6, #42
WB/VM: Workbook, pp. 133–134; Video Activities, pp. 269–270
***Panorama cultural** DVD/Video*
Interactive CD-ROM
IRM: Videoscript, p. 132
Companion website: www.vistahigherlearning.com
Presentations CD-ROM

Suggestions

- Have students look at the map of Argentina or project **Transparency #42**. Guide students to recognize Argentina's great size and the variety of topographical features, such as mountains (**los Andes**), vast plains (**las pampas**), and large rivers.
- Point out that Argentina is one of the largest beef producers in the world and that **gauchos** have played an important role in the culture of the country. **Bariloche** is an important winter recreation area. Remind students that June–August is winter in the southern hemisphere.

El país en cifras **Patagonia** is very sparsely populated, but **Buenos Aires** is a metropolis about the size of New York City. Invite students to mention anything they know about Argentina.

¡Increíble pero cierto! Under the leadership of General José de San Martín, Argentina won its independence from Spain on July 9, 1816. Like Simón Bolívar, San Martín is venerated as one of the great heroes of Latin America.

11 panorama

Argentina

El país en cifras

- **Área:** 2.780.400 km^2 (1.074.000 millas^2)
  Argentina es el país de habla española más grande del mundo. Su territorio es dos veces el tamaño° de Alaska.
- **Población:** 39.302.000
- **Capital:** Buenos Aires —12.439.000
  En Buenos Aires vive cerca del cuarenta por ciento de la población total del país. La ciudad es conocida° como el "París de Sudamérica" por el estilo parisino° de muchas de sus calles y edificios.

Buenos Aires

- **Ciudades principales:** Córdoba —1.458.000, Rosario —1.370.000, Mendoza —1.025.000

SOURCE: Population Division, UN Secretariat

- **Moneda:** peso argentino
- **Idiomas:** español (oficial), guaraní

Bandera de Argentina

Argentinos célebres

- **Jorge Luis Borges,** escritor (1899–1986)
- **María Eva Duarte de Perón ("Evita"),** primera dama° (1919–1952)
- **Mercedes Sosa,** cantante (1935–)
- **Gato Barbieri,** saxofonista (1935–)

tamaño *size* conocida *known* parisino *Parisian* primera dama *First Lady* ancha *wide* lado *side* mide *it measures* campo *field*

recursos

WB pp. 133–134	VM pp. 269–270	I CD-ROM Lección 11	vistahigher learning.com

¡Increíble pero cierto!

La Avenida 9 de Julio en Buenos Aires es la calle más ancha° del mundo. De lado° a lado mide° cerca de 140 metros, lo que es equivalente a un campo° y medio de fútbol. Su nombre conmemora el Día de la Independencia de Argentina.

TEACHING OPTIONS

Worth Noting The Argentinian cowboy, the **gaucho**, has played as significant a role in the folklore of Argentina as the cowboy of the Old West has played in that of the United States. Two classic works of Argentinian literature focus on the gaucho. ***El gaucho Martín Fierro***, an epic poem by José Hernández (1834–1886), celebrates the gaucho's fiercely independent way of life. Diego Sarmiento (1811–1888) subtitled his work ***Facundo: Civilización y barbarie***, and saw the nomadic, uneducated gauchos as hindrances in Argentina's pursuit of economic, social, and political progress.

Extra Practice Have students listen to a song on one of the many recordings by singer Mercedes Sosa. Then, have pairs work together to transcribe the lyrics. Invite volunteers to share their work with the class.

BRASIL

Historia • Inmigración europea

Se dice que Argentina es el país más "europeo" de toda la Latinoamérica, porque después del año 1880, una gran cantidad de inmigrantes dejó Europa para establecerse en este país. Las diferentes culturas de estos inmigrantes, que venían de Italia, Alemania, España e Inglaterra, han dejado una profunda huella° en la música, el cine, el arte y la arquitectura de la Argentina.

Artes • El tango

El tango, un baile con sonidos y ritmos de origen africano, italiano y español, es uno de los símbolos culturales más importantes de la Argentina. Se originó entre los porteños°, muchos de ellos inmigrantes, en la década de 1880. Se hizo popular en París y más tarde entre la clase alta de Argentina. En un principio°, el tango era un baile provocativo y violento, pero se hizo más romántico durante los años 30. Hoy día es popular en muchas partes del mundo°.

Lugares • Las cataratas de Iguazú

Entre las fronteras de la Argentina, el Paraguay y el Brasil, al norte de Buenos Aires y cerca de la confluencia° de los ríos Iguazú y Paraná, están las famosas cataratas° de Iguazú. Estas extensas cataratas tienen unos 70 m (230 pies) de altura° y, en época de lluvias, llegan a medir 4 km (2,5 mi) de ancho. Situadas en el Parque Nacional Iguazú, las cataratas son uno de los sitios turísticos más visitados de la América del Sur.

¿Qué aprendiste? Responde a las preguntas con una frase completa.

1. ¿Qué porcentaje de la población de la Argentina vive en la capital?
   Cerca del cuarenta por ciento de la población de la Argentina vive en la capital.
2. ¿Quién es Mercedes Sosa?
   Mercedes Sosa es una cantante argentina.
3. Se dice que la Argentina es el país más europeo de América Latina. ¿Por qué? Se dice que la Argentina es el país más europeo de la América Latina porque muchos inmigrantes europeos se establecieron allí.
4. ¿Qué tipo de baile es uno de los símbolos culturales más importantes de la Argentina?
   El tango es uno de los símbolos culturales más importantes de la Argentina.
5. ¿Dónde y cuándo se originó el tango?
   El tango se originó entre los porteños en la década de 1880.
6. ¿Cómo era el tango originalmente?
   El tango era un baile provocativo y violento.
7. ¿En qué parque nacional están las cataratas de Iguazú?
   Las cataratas de Iguazú están en el Parque Nacional Iguazú.

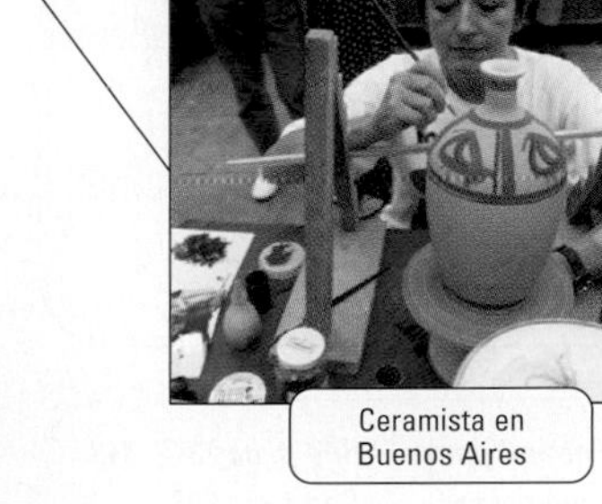

Ceramista en Buenos Aires

Conexión Internet Investiga estos temas en el sitio **www.vistahigherlearning.com.**

1. Busca información sobre el tango. ¿Te gustan los ritmos y sonidos del tango? ¿Por qué? ¿Se baila el tango en tu comunidad?
2. ¿Quiénes fueron Juan y Eva Perón y qué importancia tienen en la historia de la Argentina?

han dejado una profunda huella *have left a deep mark* porteños *people of Buenos Aires* En un principio *At first* mundo *world* confluencia *junction* cataratas *waterfalls* altura *height*

Inmigración europea Among the European immigrants who arrived in waves on Argentina's shores were thousands of Jews. An interesting chapter in the history of the **pampas** features Jewish **gauchos**. A generous pre-Zionist philanthropist purchased land for Jews who settled on the Argentine grasslands. At one time, the number of Yiddish-language newspapers in Argentina was second only to that in New York City.

El tango The great classic interpreter of tango was Carlos Gardel (1890–1935). If possible, bring in a recording of his version of a tango such as **"Cuesta abajo"** or **"Volver."** A modern exponent of tango was Astor Piazzola (1921–1992). His **tango nuevo** has found interpreters such as cellist Yo-Yo Ma and the Kronos Quartet.

Las cataratas de Iguazú In the **Guaraní** language, Iguazú means "big water." The falls are three times wider than Niagara and have been declared a World Heritage Site by UNESCO. Iguazú National Park was established in 1934 to protect and preserve this natural treasure.

Conexión Internet Students will find supporting Internet activities and links at **www.vistahigherlearning.com**.

TEACHING OPTIONS

Variación léxica Argentinians frequently use the word **¡che!** to get the attention of someone they are talking to. **Che** also serves as a kind of spoken exclamation point with which Argentinians pepper their speech. This is so noticeable to outsiders that Argentinians are often given the nickname **Che** in other parts of the Spanish-speaking world. Another notable feature of Argentinian Spanish is the existence, alongside **tú**, of **vos** as the second-person singular familiar pronoun. **Vos** is also heard in other parts of Latin America, and it is accompanied by corresponding verb forms in the present tense. Here are some equivalents: **vos contás / tú cuentas, vos pensás / tú piensas, vos sos / tú eres, vos ponés / tú pones, vos venís / tú vienes.**

Instructional Resources
Vocabulary CD
Lab Manual, p. 66
Lab CD/MP3 ***Lección 11***
IRM: Tapescript, pp. 49–53
Testing Program: ***Pruebas****, pp. 121–132*
Testing Program Audio CD
Test Files CD-ROM

La tecnología

la calculadora	*calculator*
la cámara digital, de video	*digital, video camera*
el canal	*(TV) channel*
el cibercafé	*cybercafé*
la contestadora	*answering machine*
el control remoto	*remote control*
el disco compacto	*compact disc*
el estéreo	*stereo*
el *fax*	*fax (machine)*
el radio	*radio (set)*
el teléfono (celular)	*(cell) telephone*
la televisión por cable	*cable television*
el televisor	*televison set*
el tocadiscos compacto	*compact disc player*
el video(casete)	*video(cassette)*
la videocasetera	*VCR*
el *walkman*	*walkman*
apagar	*to turn off*
funcionar	*to work*
llamar	*to call*
poner, prender	*to turn on*
sonar (o:ue)	*to ring*
descompuesto/a	*not working; out of order*
lento/a	*slow*
lleno/a	*full*

Verbos

abrazar(se)	*to hug; to embrace (each other)*
ayudar(se)	*to help (each other)*
besar(se)	*to kiss (each other)*
encontrar(se) (o:ue)	*to meet (each other); to run into (each other)*
saludar(se)	*to greet (each other)*

La computadora

el archivo	*file*
arroba	*@ symbol*
el cederrón	*CD-ROM*
la computadora (portátil)	*(portable) computer; (laptop)*
la dirección electrónica	*e-mail address*
el disco compacto	*compact disc*
la impresora	*printer*
Internet	*Internet*
el monitor	*(computer) monitor*
la página principal	*home page*
la pantalla	*screen*
el programa de computación	*software*
el ratón	*mouse*
la red	*network; Web*
el reproductor de DVD	*DVD player*
el sitio web	*website*
el teclado	*keyboard*
borrar	*to erase*
descargar	*to download*
grabar	*to record*
guardar	*to save*
imprimir	*to print*
navegar (en Internet)	*to surf (the Internet)*
quemar	*to burn (a CD)*

El carro

la autopista, la carretera	*highway*
el baúl	*trunk*
la calle	*street*
el capó, el cofre	*hood*
el carro, el coche	*car*
la circulación, el tráfico	*traffic*
el garaje, el taller (mecánico)	*garage; (mechanic's) repair shop*
la gasolina	*gasoline*
la gasolinera	*gas station*
la licencia de conducir	*driver's license*
la llanta	*tire*
el/la mecánico/a	*mechanic*
el parabrisas	*windshield*
la policía	*police (force)*
la velocidad máxima	*speed limit*
el volante	*steering wheel*
arrancar	*to start*
arreglar	*to fix; to arrange*
bajar(se) de	*to get off of/out of (a vehicle)*
conducir, manejar	*to drive*
estacionar	*to park*
llenar (el tanque)	*to fill (the tank)*
parar	*to stop*
revisar (el aceite)	*to check (the oil)*
subir(se) a	*to get on/into (a vehicle)*

Otras palabras y expresiones

por aquí	*around here*
por ejemplo	*for example*
por eso	*that's why; therefore*
por fin	*finally*

Por* and *para	*See pages 342–343.*
Stressed possessive adjectives and pronouns	*See page 348.*
Expresiones útiles	*See page 335.*

recursos

LM p. 66	Lab CD/MP3 Lección 11	Vocab CD Lección 11

La vivienda

12

Communicative Goals

You will learn how to:

- **Welcome people to your home**
- **Describe your house or apartment**
- **Talk about household chores**
- **Give instructions**

contextos

fotonovela

estructura

adelante

panorama

A PRIMERA VISTA

- **¿Está el chico en casa?**
- **¿Tiene una casa moderna o vieja?**
- **¿Tiene una computadora?**
- **¿Se va a vestir para ir al trabajo o al gimnasio?**

Lesson Goals

In **Lección 12** students will be introduced to the following:
- terms for parts of a house
- names of common household objects
- terms for household chores
- relative pronouns
- formal commands
- object pronouns with formal commands
- present subjunctive
- subjunctive with verbs and expressions of will and influence
- locating the main parts of a sentence
- using linking words
- writing a lease agreement
- using visual cues while listening
- writing a letter to a contractor describing a house to be built
- cultural and geographic information about Panama

A primera vista Here are some additional questions you can ask based on the photo: **¿Dónde vives? ¿Con quién vives? ¿Cómo es la casa tuya? ¿Qué haces en casa por la noche? ¿Qué haces los fines de semana? ¿Tienes una computadora en casa? ¿Qué otros productos tecnológicos tienes? ¿Cómo te vistes cuando estás en casa? ¿Comes en casa con mucha frecuencia? ¿Qué te gusta comer cuando estás en casa?**

INSTRUCTIONAL RESOURCES

Workbook/Video Manual: WB Activities, pp. 135–148
Laboratory Manual: Lab Activities, pp. 67–72
Workbook/Video Manual: Video Activities, pp. 235–236; pp. 271–272
Instructor's Resource Manual: **Vocabulario adicional**, p. 190; **¡Inténtalo!** & **Práctica** Answers, pp. 217–218; **Fotonovela** Translations, p. 145; Textbook CD Tapescript, p. 96; Lab CDs Tapescript, pp. 54–58; **Fotonovela** Videoscript, p. 116; **Panorama cultural** Videoscript, p. 133
Info Gap Activities Booklet, pp. 45–48
Overhead Transparencies: #3, #4, #43, #44, #45, #46
Lab Audio CD/MP3 **Lección 12**
Panorama cultural DVD/Video
Fotonovela DVD/Video
Testing Program, pp. 133–144; pp. 253–263
Testing Program Audio CD
Test Files CD-ROM
Companion website
Presentations CD-ROM
Textbook CD
Vocabulary CD
Interactive CD-ROM
Video CD-ROM
Web-SAM

Section Goals

In **Contextos**, students will learn and practice:

- names of rooms in a home
- names of common household objects
- terms for household chores

Instructional Resources
Transparencies, #43, #44
Textbook CD
Vocabulary CD
WB/VM: Workbook, pp. 135–136
Lab Manual, p. 67
Lab CD/MP3 ***Lección 12***
IRM: ***Vocab. adicional,*** *p. 190;* ***Práctica*** *Answers, pp. 217–218; Tapescript, pp. 54–58; p. 96*
Info Gap Activities Booklet, pp. 45–46
Interactive CD-ROM
Companion website: www.vistahigherlearning.com
Presentations CD-ROM

Suggestions

- Project **Transparency #43** and describe the house, naming the kinds of rooms and introducing those that aren't shown. Ex: **Ésta es la casa de los Hernández. Hay una sala grande, un dormitorio, una oficina, una cocina y un altillo. También hay un cuarto de baño, un sótano, un patio y un garaje, pero no vemos estos cuartos en la ilustración.**
- Project **Transparency #43**. Ask open-ended questions about the house and housework. Ex: **¿Dónde se pone la comida después de regresar del supermercado? ¿Qué se hace en la oficina?** Personalize questions, getting students to talk to you and one another about themselves and their living arrangements. _____, **¿vives en una residencia o en un apartamento? ¿Cuántos cuartos hay? Y tú,** _____, **¿vives en un apartamento con cinco cuartos?**

Note: At this point you may want to present **Vocabulario adicional: Más vocabulario para el hogar**, from the IRM.

La vivienda

Más vocabulario

las afueras	*suburbs; outskirts*
el alquiler	*rent (payment)*
el ama (*m., f.*) de casa	*housekeeper; caretaker*
el barrio	*neighborhood*
el edificio de apartamentos	*apartment building*
el/la vecino/a	*neighbor*
la vivienda	*housing*
el balcón	*balcony*
el cuarto	*room*
la entrada	*entrance*
la escalera	*stairs; stairway*
el garaje	*garage*
el jardín	*garden; yard*
el pasillo	*hallway*
el patio	*patio; yard*
el sótano	*basement; cellar*
la cafetera	*coffee maker*
el electrodoméstico	*electrical appliance*
el horno (de microondas)	*(microwave) oven*
la lavadora	*washing machine*
la luz	*light, electricity*
la secadora	*clothes dryer*
la tostadora	*toaster*
el cartel	*poster*
la mesita de noche	*night stand*
los muebles	*furniture*
alquilar	*to rent*
mudarse	*to move (from one house to another)*

Los quehaceres domésticos

arreglar	*to neaten; to straighten up*
barrer el suelo	*to sweep the floor*
cocinar	*to cook*
ensuciar	*to get (something) dirty*
hacer quehaceres domésticos	*to do household chores*
lavar (el suelo, los platos)	*to wash (the floor, the dishes)*
limpiar la casa	*to clean the house*
planchar la ropa	*to iron the clothes*
quitar la mesa	*to clear the table*

Variación léxica

alcoba, dormitorio ⟷ aposento (*Rep. Dom.*); recámara (*Méx.*)
apartamento ⟷ departamento (*Arg., Chile*); piso (*Esp.*)
lavar los platos ⟷ lavar/fregar los trastes (*Amér. C., Rep. Dom.*)

recursos

TEXT CD Lección 12	WB pp. 135–136	LM p. 67	Lab CD/MP3 Lección 12	I CD-ROM Lección 12	Vocab CD Lección 12

TEACHING OPTIONS

Extra Practice Ask students to complete these analogies.

1. **aspiradora :** ____ **(alfombra) :: lavadora : ropa (*aspiradora* es a** ____ **como *lavadora* es a *ropa*)**
2. **frío : calor :: congelador :** ____ **(horno)**
3. **cama : alcoba ::** ____ **(escritorio) : oficina**
4. **platos : cocina :: carro :** ____ **(garaje)**

Variación léxica Ask heritage speakers to tell the class any other terms they use to refer to rooms in a home. Ex: **alcoba, dormitorio = aposento** (D.R.), **recámara** (Mex.); **lavar los platos = fregar los trastes** (D.R.). Also ask heritage speakers to describe typical homes in Spanish-speaking countries.

Práctica

1 **Escuchar** Escucha la conversación y completa las frases.

1. Pedro va a limpiar primero la sala.
2. Paula va a comenzar en la cocina.
3. Pedro le recuerda (*reminds*) a Paula que debe hacer la cama en la alcoba de huéspedes.
4. Pedro va a planchar la ropa en el sótano.
5. Pedro también va a limpiar la oficina.
6. Ellos están limpiando la casa porque la madre de Pedro viene a visitarlos.

2 **Escoger** Escoge la letra de la respuesta correcta.

1. Cuando quieres salir al aire libre y estás en el tercer piso, vas b.
   a. al pasillo b. al balcón c. al sótano
2. Cuando quieres tener una lámpara y un despertador cerca de tu cama, puedes ponerlos en c.
   a. el barrio b. el cuadro c. la mesita de noche
3. Si no quieres vivir en el centro de la ciudad, puedes mudarte b.
   a. al alquiler b. a las afueras c. a la vivienda
4. Guardamos (*We keep*) los pantalones, las camisas y los zapatos en b.
   a. la secadora b. el armario c. el patio
5. Para subir de la planta baja al primer piso, usamos c.
   a. las entradas b. los carteles c. las escaleras
6. Ponemos cuadros y pinturas en a.
   a. las paredes b. los quehaceres c. los jardines

3 **Definiciones** En parejas, identifiquen cada cosa que se describe. Luego inventen sus propias descripciones de algunas palabras y expresiones de **Contextos**.

modelo

Estudiante 1: *Si vives en un apartamento, lo tienes que pagar cada mes.*
Estudiante 2: *el alquiler*

1. Es donde pones la cabeza cuando duermes. una almohada
2. Es el quehacer doméstico que haces después de comer. lavar los platos/quitar la mesa
3. Cubren (*They cover*) las ventanas y decoran la sala a la vez (*at the same time*). las cortinas
4. Algunos ejemplos de éstos son las cómodas, las mesitas y los sillones. los muebles
5. Son las personas que viven en tu barrio. los vecinos

1 Suggestion Help students check their answers by converting each sentence into a question and asking volunteers to give the correct response. Ex: **¿Qué es lo que va a limpiar Pedro primero? ¿Dónde va a comenzar Paula?**

1 Tapescript PEDRO: Paula, tenemos que limpiar toda la casa esta mañana. ¿Por dónde podemos empezar?
PAULA: Pienso empezar por la cocina. Voy a lavar los platos, sacar la basura y barrer el suelo.
PE: Pues, primero voy a limpiar la sala. Necesito pasar la aspiradora y sacudir los muebles.
PA: Después de la sala, ¿qué cuarto quieres limpiar?
PE: Después quiero limpiar la oficina.
PA: Entonces yo voy a limpiar la alcoba de huéspedes.
PE: Bueno. Debes hacer la cama en esa alcoba también.
PA: Ya lo sé. Ah, ¿puedes planchar la ropa en el sótano, Pedro?
PE: Sí... Espero que todo vaya bien durante la visita de mi madre.
PA: Sí. Pues yo espero que ella no venga hasta que todo esté limpio. ¡No nos queda mucho tiempo para terminar!
Textbook CD

2 Expansion Go over the answers by turning the statements into questions. Ex: **Cuando quieres salir al aire libre y estás en el tercer piso, ¿adónde vas?**

3 Suggestion Have pairs give each other words from **Contextos** for their partner to define. Ex: **Pasillo. (Lugar que sirve para pasar de un cuarto al otro.)**

TEACHING OPTIONS

Small Groups Have groups of three interview each other about their dream house, one conducting the interview, one answering, and one taking notes. At three-minute intervals have students switch roles until each has been interviewer, interviewee, and note-taker. Then pair up the groups and have them report to one another using their notes.

Game Ask students to bring in pictures of mansions, castles, or palaces. Divide the class into groups of three, and have each group write a description of the rest of the residence that isn't visible. Have each group read its description aloud. To determine the winner, ask the students to vote for the best description.

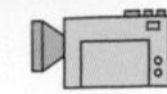

¡Les va a encantar la casa!

NATIONAL STANDARDS: communication, cultures

Don Francisco y los estudiantes llegan a Ibarra.

Section Goals

In **Fotonovela** students will:
- receive comprehensible input from free-flowing discourse
- learn functional phrases that preview lesson grammatical structures

Instructional Resources
WB/VM: Video Activities, pp. 235–236
***Fotonovela** DVD/Video (Start 01:04:59)*
Video CD-ROM
*IRM: **Fotonovela** Translations, p. 145, Videoscript, p. 116*
Interactive CD-ROM

Video Recap: Lección 11
Before doing this **Fotonovela** section, review the previous one with this activity.

1. ¿Qué hace Álex con sus amigos todos los días? (hablan por teléfono Internet)
2. ¿Por qué sabe Inés mucho de mecánica? (trabajó en el taller de su tío)
3. ¿Qué problema tiene el autobús? (el alternador está quemado)
4. ¿Quién es el señor Fonseca? (un mecánico de Ibarra, amigo de don Francisco)
5. ¿Cómo va a ayudar el señor Fonseca? (va a arreglar el autobús allí mismo)

Video Synopsis Don Francisco and the students go to the house where they will stay before their hike. The housekeeper shows the students around the house. Don Francisco tells the students to help with the chores, and he advises them that their guide for the hike will arrive at seven the next morning.

Suggestions

- Have your students guess what happens in this **Fotonovela** episode, based on its title and the video stills.
- Ask the class if this **Fotonovela** episode was what they expected, based on the predictions they made.

PERSONAJES

INÉS

DON FRANCISCO

ÁLEX

JAVIER

SRA. VIVES

1

SRA. VIVES ¡Hola, bienvenidos!

DON FRANCISCO Señora Vives, le presento a los chicos. Chicos, ésta es la señora Vives, el ama de casa.

2

SRA. VIVES Encantada. Síganme que quiero mostrarles la casa. ¡Les va a encantar!

3

SRA. VIVES Esta alcoba es para los chicos. Tienen dos camas, una mesita de noche, una cómoda... En el armario hay más mantas y almohadas por si las necesitan.

6

SRA. VIVES Ésta es la sala. El sofá y los sillones son muy cómodos. Pero, por favor, ¡no los ensucien!

7

SRA. VIVES Allí están la cocina y el comedor. Al fondo del pasillo hay un baño.

8

DON FRANCISCO Chicos, a ver... ¡atención! La señora Vives les va a preparar las comidas. Pero quiero que ustedes la ayuden con los quehaceres domésticos. Quiero que arreglen sus alcobas, que hagan las camas, que pongan la mesa... ¿entendido?

JAVIER No se preocupe... la vamos a ayudar en todo lo posible.

ÁLEX Sí, cuente con nosotros.

recursos

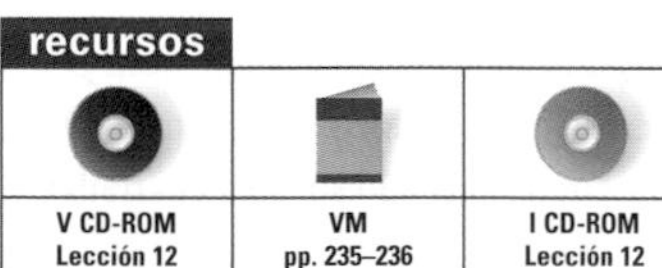

V CD-ROM Lección 12	VM pp. 235–236	I CD-ROM Lección 12

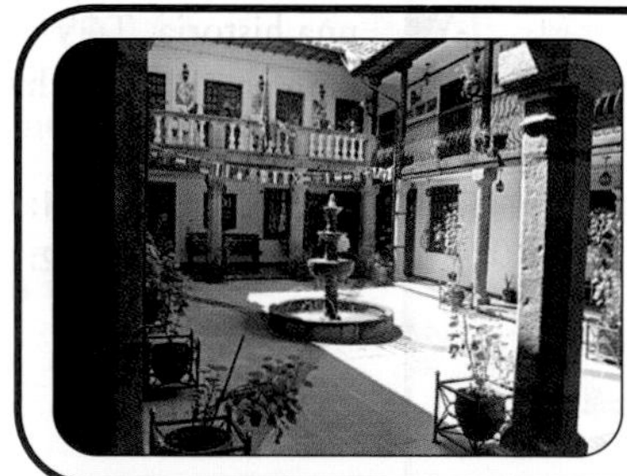

TEACHING OPTIONS

Video Tips General suggestions for using video clips in the classroom can be found on page IAE-12 of this Instructor's Annotated Edition.

¡Les va a encantar la casa! Play the last half of the **Lección 12** video episode, except the **Resumen** segment. Have your students summarize what they see and hear. Then, have the class predict what will happen in the first half of the video episode, based on their observations. Write their predictions on the board. Then play the entire episode, including the **Resumen**, and, through discussion, guide the class to a correct summary of the plot.

SRA. VIVES Javier, no ponga las maletas en la cama. Póngalas en el piso, por favor.

SRA. VIVES Tomen ustedes esta alcoba, chicas.

INÉS Insistimos en que nos deje ayudarla a preparar la comida.

SRA. VIVES No, chicos, no es para tanto, pero gracias por la oferta. Descansen un rato que seguramente están cansados.

ÁLEX Gracias. A mí me gustaría pasear por la ciudad.

INÉS Perdone, don Francisco, ¿a qué hora viene el guía mañana?

DON FRANCISCO ¿Martín? Viene temprano, a las siete de la mañana. Les aconsejo que se acuesten temprano esta noche. ¡Nada de televisión ni de conversaciones largas!

ESTUDIANTES ¡Ay, don Francisco!

Enfoque cultural Las viviendas

Del mismo modo que en los países hispanos era típico construir las ciudades en torno a una plaza central, también era frecuente construir las casas alrededor de un patio abierto central. Aunque esta arquitectura tradicional ya no es muy común, la importancia del patio sigue intacta en la cultura hispana. No es extraño ver crecer árboles de mangos y de aguacates en los patios de las casas de los países tropicales de Latinoamérica. En el sur de España, los geranios y otras flores alegran los balcones y terrazas de las viviendas.

Expresiones útiles

Welcoming people

- **¡Bienvenido(s)/a(s)!**
  Welcome!

Showing people around the house

- **Síganme... que quiero mostrarles la casa.**
  Follow me... I want to show you the house.
- **Esta alcoba es para los chicos.**
  This bedroom is for the guys.
- **Ésta es la sala.**
  This is the living room.
- **Allí están la cocina y el comedor.**
  The kitchen and dining room are over there.
- **Al fondo del pasillo hay un baño.**
  At the end of the hall there is a bathroom.

Telling people what to do

- **Quiero que la ayude(n) con los quehaceres domésticos.**
  I want you to help her with the household chores.
- **Quiero que arregle(n) su(s) alcoba(s).**
  I want you to straighten your room(s).
- **Quiero que haga(n) las camas.**
  I want you to make the beds.
- **Quiero que ponga(n) la mesa.**
  I want you to set the table.
- **Cuente con nosotros.**
  You can count on us.
- **Insistimos en que nos deje ayudarla a preparar la comida.**
  We insist that you let us help you make the food.
- **Le (Les) aconsejo que se acueste(n) temprano.**
  I recommend that you go to bed early.

Other expressions

- **No es para tanto.**
  It's not a big deal.
- **Gracias por la oferta.**
  Thanks for the offer.

Suggestion Have the class read through the entire **Fotonovela**, with volunteers playing the various parts. You may want to point out the form **gustaría** in the caption under video still 9. Explain to students that it is the conditional of **gustar** and that they will learn more about it in **Estructura 17.1**. Tell them that **me gustaría** means *I'd like*.

Expresiones útiles Point out that the verbs **Síganme** and **Cuente** are command forms. Have the class guess which is an **usted** command and which is an **ustedes** command. Then point out the sentences that begin with **Quiero que...** , **Insistimos en que...** , and **Le (les) aconsejo que....** Explain that these sentences are examples of the present subjunctive with verbs of will or influence. Write two or three of these sentences on the board. Point out that the main clause in each sentence contains a verb of will or influence, while the subordinate clause contains a verb in the present subjunctive. Tell your students that they will learn more about these concepts in **Estructura**.

The Affective Dimension Tell students that travelers in a foreign country may feel culture shock for a while. These feelings are normal and tend to diminish with time.

TEACHING OPTIONS

Enfoque cultural The "traditional" houses built around patios described here have ancient roots, going back to the style of houses built by the Romans. The traditional Spanish house made a very clear separation between the interior of the house, which was a private and protected space, and the street, which was public and exposed. Modern residents of large cities in Spanish-speaking countries often live in apartments, which may be rented but are sometimes owned by the occupants. Explain that the first floor (**planta baja**) of many multistory buildings is occupied by places of business, while the upper floors consist of apartments. Point out that it is not unusual for an apartment dweller in the United States or Canada to refer to his or her home as a house; explain that in Spanish-speaking countries, the word **casa** is often used in the same way.

1 Expansion Give these additional items to the class: **6. Álex quiere descansar. (Falso. Álex quiere pasear por la ciudad.) 7. Martín va a llegar mañana a las cuatro de la tarde. (Falso. Martín va a llegar a las siete de la mañana.)**

2 Suggestion Have the class skim the **Fotonovela** on pages 366–367 before they begin this activity.

2 Expansion Write these additional items on the board: **6. Ésta es la alcoba de las chicas. (Sra. Vives) 7. El guía va a llegar a las siete de la mañana. (don Francisco) 8. ¿Quieren descansar un rato? (Sra. Vives) 9. Chicos, les presento a la señora Vives. (don Francisco)**

3 Expansion Ask pairs to come up with lists of other household chores that can be done in each of the rooms. Have them share their answers with the class. Keep count of the items on their lists to find out which pair came up with the most correct possibilities.

4 Possible Response
E1: Quiero mostrarte mi casa. Ésta es la sala. Me gusta mirar la televisión allí. Aquí está la oficina. Allí hablo por teléfono y trabajo en la computadora. Éste es el garaje. Es donde tengo mis dos coches. Y aquí está la cocina, donde preparo las comidas. Quiero que me ayudes a sacudir los muebles y pasar la aspiradora.
E2: Está bien. Ahora quiero mostrarte mi apartamento....

Reacciona a la fotonovela

1 **¿Cierto o falso?** Indica si lo que dicen las siguientes frases es **cierto** o **falso**. Corrige las frases falsas.

	Cierto	Falso
1. Las alcobas de los estudiantes tienen dos camas, dos mesitas de noche y una cómoda. Tienen sólo una mesita de noche.	❍	✓
2. La señora Vives no quiere que Javier ponga las maletas en la cama.	✓	❍
3. El sofá y los sillones están en la sala.	✓	❍
4. Los estudiantes tienen que sacudir los muebles y sacar la basura. Tienen que arreglar las alcobas, hacer las camas y poner la mesa.	❍	✓
5. Los estudiantes van a preparar las comidas. La señora Vives va a preparar las comidas.	❍	✓

2 **Identificar** Identifica quién puede decir las siguientes frases.

1. Nos gustaría preparar la comida esta noche. ¿Le parece bien a usted? Inés
2. Miren, si quieren otra almohada o manta, hay más en el armario. Sra. Vives
3. Tranquilo, tranquilo, que nosotros vamos a ayudarla muchísimo. Javier
4. Tengo ganas de caminar un poco por la ciudad. Álex
5. No quiero que nadie mire la televisión esta noche. ¡Tenemos que levantarnos temprano mañana! don Francisco

3 **Completar** Los estudiantes y la señora Vives están haciendo los quehaceres. Adivina en qué cuarto está cada uno de ellos.

1. Inés limpia el congelador. Inés está en la cocina.
2. Javier limpia el escritorio. Javier está en la oficina.
3. Álex pasa la aspiradora debajo de la mesa y las sillas. Álex está en el comedor.
4. La señora Vives sacude el sillón. La señora Vives está en la sala.
5. Don Francisco no está haciendo nada. Él está dormido en el dormitorio/ la alcoba.

4 **Mi casa** Dibuja el plano (*floor plan*) de una casa o de un apartamento. Puede ser el plano de la casa o del apartamento donde vives o de donde te gustaría vivir. Después, trabajen en parejas y describan lo que se hace en cuatro de las habitaciones. Para terminar, pídanse (*ask for*) ayuda para hacer dos quehaceres domésticos. Pueden usar estas frases en su conversación. Answers will vary.

Quiero mostrarte...	Al fondo hay...
Ésta es (la cocina).	Quiero que me ayudes a (sacar la basura).
Allí yo (preparo la comida).	Por favor, ayúdame con...

TEACHING OPTIONS

TPR Have the class label various parts of the classroom with the names of rooms one would typically find in a house. Then have groups of three perform a skit in which the owner of the house is showing it to two inquisitive exchange students who are going to be spending the semester there. Give the groups time to prepare.

Game Have each of your students write a few sentences that one of the characters in this **Fotonovela** episode would say. They can look at the **Fotonovela** for ideas, but they shouldn't copy sentences from it word for word. Then have each student read his or her sentences to the class. The class will guess which character would say those sentences.

Ortografía

Las mayúsculas y las minúsculas

Here are some of the rules that govern the use of capital letters (**mayúsculas**) and lowercase letters (**minúsculas**) in Spanish.

Los estudiantes llegaron al aeropuerto a las dos. Luego fueron al hotel.

In both Spanish and English, the first letter of every sentence is capitalized.

Rubén Blades **Panamá** **Colón** **los Andes**

The first letter of all proper nouns (names of people, countries, cities, geographical features, etc.) is capitalized.

Cien años de soledad ***Don Quijote de la Mancha***
El País ***Muy Interesante***

The first letter of the first word in titles of books, films, and works of art is generally capitalized, as well as the first letter of any proper names. In newspaper and magazine titles, as well as other short titles, the initial letter of each word is often capitalized.

la señora Ramos **don Francisco**
el presidente **Sra. Vives**

Titles associated with people are *not* capitalized unless they appear as the first word in a sentence. Note, however, that the first letter of an abbreviated title is capitalized.

Último **Álex** **MENÚ** **PERDÓN**

Accent marks should be retained on capital letters. In practice, however, this rule is often ignored.

lunes **viernes** **marzo** **primavera**

The first letter of days, months, and seasons is not capitalized.

español **estadounidense** **japonés** **panameños**

The first letter of nationalities and languages is not capitalized.

ofesor Herrera, cierto que somos venenosas°?

Sí, Pepito. ¿Por qué lloras?

Práctica Corrige las mayúsculas y minúsculas incorrectas.

1. soy lourdes romero. Soy Colombiana.
   Soy Lourdes Romero. Soy colombiana.
2. éste Es mi Hermano álex.
   Éste es mi hermano Álex.
3. somos De panamá. Somos de Panamá.
4. ¿es ud. La sra. benavides?
   ¿Es Ud. la Sra. Benavides?
5. ud. Llegó el Lunes, ¿no?
   Ud. llegó el lunes, ¿no?

Palabras desordenadas Lee el diálogo de las serpientes. Ordena las letras para saber de qué palabras se trata. Después escribe las letras indicadas para descubrir por qué llora Pepito.

m n a a P á ◯ _ _ _ _ _
s t e m r a ◯ _ _ _ _ _
i g s l é n _ _ _ ◯ _ _
y a U r u g u _ _ _ ◯ _ _ _
r o ñ e s a _ _ _ _ _ ◯

¡ _orque _e acabo de morder° la _en_u_!

venenosas *venomous* morder *to bite*

Respuestas: Panamá, martes, inglés, Uruguay, señora. ¡Porque me acabo de morder la lengua!

recursos

LM p. 68	Lab CD/MP3 Lección 12	I CD-ROM Lección 12

Section Goal

In **Ortografía** students will learn about the rules for capitalization in Spanish.

Instructional Resource
Interactive CD-ROM

Suggestions

- Explain that in a few Spanish city and country names the definite article is considered part of the name, and is thus capitalized. Ex: **La Habana, La Coruña, La Haya, El Salvador**
- Spanish treatment of titles of books, film, and works of art differs from English. In Spanish, only the first word and any proper noun gets an initial capital. Spanish treatment of the names of newspapers and magazines is the same as in English. Tell students that ***El País*** is a newspaper and ***Muy Interesante*** is a magazine. All the items mentioned are italicized in print.
- After going through the explanation, write example titles, names, sentences, etc., all in lower case, on the board. Then, ask pairs to decide which letters should be capitalized.
- Point out that **Ortografía** replaces **Pronunciación** in the Student Edition for **Lecciones 10–18**, but not in the Lab Manual. The **Recursos** box references the **Pronunciación** sections found in all lessons of the Lab Manual.

TEACHING OPTIONS

Pairs Have your students work in pairs to circle all the capital letters in the **Enfoque cultural** on page 367. Then have them explain why each of these letters is capitalized. Afterward, have them look through the **Enfoque cultural** for examples of uncapitalized words discussed in **Ortografía**.

Extra Practice Give this sentence to the class as a dictation: **El doctor Guzmán, el amigo panameño de la señorita Rivera, llegó a Quito el lunes doce de mayo.** Tell the class to abbreviate all titles. To allow your students time to write, read the sentence twice slowly and once at full speed.

Section Goal

In **Estructura 12.1** students will learn the relative pronouns and their use.

Instructional Resources
WB/VM: Workbook, pp. 137–138
Lab Manual, p. 69
Lab CD/MP3 ***Lección 12***
IRM: ***¡Inténtalo! & Práctica*** *Answers, pp. 217–218; Tapescript, pp. 54–58*
Interactive CD-ROM
Companion website: www.vistahigherlearning.com
Presentations CD-ROM

Suggestions

- Have students open to the **Fotonovela** on pages 366–367. Ask open-ended questions about the situation and then rephrase the students' short answers into sentences using relative pronouns. Write your sentences on the board and underline the relative pronoun. Ex: **¿Quién va a preparar la comida? (la Sra. Vives) Sí, ella es la persona que va a preparar la comida. ¿Qué cuarto tiene un sofá y sillones cómodos? (la sala) Sí, la sala es el cuarto que tiene un sofá y sillones cómodos.**
- Compare and contrast the use of **que** and **quien** by writing some examples on the board. Ex: **Es la chica que vino con Carlos a mi fiesta. Es la chica a quien conocí en mi fiesta.** Have students deduce the rule.

12.1 Relative pronouns

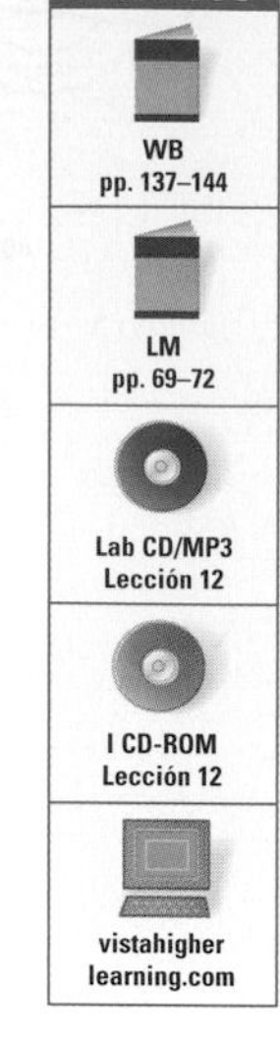

ANTE TODO In both English and Spanish, relative pronouns are used to combine two sentences or clauses that share a common element, such as a noun or pronoun. Study the following diagram.

Mis padres me regalaron **la aspiradora**.
My parents gave me the vacuum cleaner.

La aspiradora funciona muy bien.
The vacuum cleaner works really well.

La aspiradora **que** me regalaron mis padres funciona muy bien.
The vacuum cleaner that my parents gave me works really well.

Lourdes es muy inteligente.
Lourdes is very intelligent.

Lourdes estudia español.
Lourdes is studying Spanish.

Lourdes, **quien** estudia español, es muy inteligente.
Lourdes, who studies Spanish, is very intelligent.

Pueden usar las almohadas que están en el armario.

Chicos, ésta es la señora Vives, quien les va a mostrar la casa.

- Spanish has three frequently-used relative pronouns, as shown in the following list.

que	*that; which; who*
quien(es)	*who; whom; that*
lo que	*that which; what*

¡ATENCIÓN!
Interrogative words (**qué**, **quién**, etc.) always carry an accent. Relative pronouns, however, never carry a written accent.

- **Que** is the most frequently used relative pronoun. It can refer to things or to people. Unlike its English counterpart, *that*, **que** is never omitted.

¿Dónde está la cafetera **que** compré?
Where is the coffee maker (that) I bought?

El hombre **que** limpia es Pedro.
The man who is cleaning is Pedro.

- The relative pronoun **quien** refers only to people and is often used after a preposition or the personal **a.** Note that **quien** has only two forms: **quien** (singular) and **quienes** (plural).

¿Son las chicas **de quienes** me hablaste la semana pasada?
Are they the girls (that) you told me about last week?

Eva, **a quien** conocí anoche, es mi nueva vecina.
Eva, whom I met last night, is my new neighbor.

TEACHING OPTIONS

Extra Practice Write the following sentences on the board, and have students supply the correct relative pronoun:
1. Hay una escalera ____ (que) sube al primer piso.
2. Elena es la muchacha a ____ (quien) le presté la aspiradora.
3. ¿Dónde pusiste la ropa ____ (que) acabas de quitarte?
4. ¿Cuál es el señor a ____ (quien) le alquilas tu casa?
5. La cómoda ____ (que) compramos la semana pasada está en el dormitorio de mi hermana.

Heritage Speakers Have heritage speakers create descriptions of favorite gathering places in their home communities using complex sentences with relative pronouns. Possible sites might be the local parish, the town square, or a favorite park.

¡LENGUA VIVA!

In English, it is generally recommended that *who(m)* be used to refer to people, and that *that* and *which* be used to refer to things. In Spanish, however, it is perfectly acceptable to use **que** when referring to people.

▶ **Quien(es)** is occasionally used instead of **que** in clauses set off by commas.

Lola, **quien** es cubana, es médica.
Lola, who is Cuban, is a doctor.

Su tía, **que** es alemana, ya llegó.
His aunt, who is German, already arrived.

▶ Unlike **que** and **quien(es), lo que** doesn't refer to a specific noun. It refers to an idea, a situation, or a past event and means *what, that which,* or *the thing that.*

Este mercado tiene todo lo que Inés necesita.

A la señora Vives no le gustó lo que hizo Javier.

Lo que me molesta es el calor.
What bothers me is the heat.

Lo que quiero es una casa.
What I want is a house.

¡INTÉNTALO! Completa las siguientes oraciones con pronombres relativos.

1. Voy a utilizar los platos ___que___ me regaló mi abuela.
2. Ana comparte un apartamento con la chica a ___quien___ conocimos en la fiesta de Jorge.
3. Esta oficina tiene todo ___lo que___ necesitamos.
4. Puedes estudiar en el dormitorio ___que___ está a la derecha de la cocina.
5. Los señores ___que___ viven en esa casa acaban de llegar de Centroamérica.
6. Los niños a ___quienes___ viste en nuestro jardín son mis sobrinos.
7. La piscina ___que___ ves desde la ventana es la piscina de mis vecinos.
8. Fue Úrsula ___quien___ ayudó a mamá a limpiar el refrigerador.
9. Ya te dije que fue mi padre ___quien___ alquiló el apartamento.
10. ___Lo que___ te dijo Pablo no es cierto.
11. Tengo que sacudir los muebles ___que___ están en el altillo una vez al mes.
12. No entiendo por qué no lavaste los vasos ___que___ te dije.
13. La mujer a ___quien___ saludaste vive en las afueras.
14. ¿Sabes ___lo que___ necesita este dormitorio? ¡Unas cortinas!
15. No quiero volver a hacer ___lo que___ hice ayer.
16. No me gusta vivir con personas a ___quienes___ no conozco.

Suggestions

- Test comprehension as you proceed by asking volunteers to answer questions about students and objects in the classroom. Ex: **¿Cómo se llama la estudiante que se sienta detrás de ____? ¿Cómo se llaman los estudiantes a quienes acabo de hacer esta pregunta? ¿Dónde está la tarea que ustedes hicieron para hoy?**
- Line up four to five pictures. Ask questions that use relative pronouns or elicit them in student answers. Ex: **¿Quién está comiendo una hamburguesa? (El muchacho que está sentado en la playa está comiendo una hamburguesa.) ¿Quién sabe lo que está haciendo esta muchacha? (Está quitando la mesa.)**
- Ask students to make two short lists: **Lo que tengo en mi casa** and **Lo que quiero tener en mi casa**. Ask volunteers to read part of their lists to the class. Encourage a conversation by asking questions such as: **¿Es esto lo que tienes en tu casa? ¿Es un ____ lo que quieres tú?**

TEACHING OPTIONS

Video Show the video again to give students more input containing relative pronouns. Stop the video where appropriate to discuss how relative pronouns were used.

Game Ask students to bring in some interesting pictures from magazines or the Internet, but tell them not to show these photos to one another. Divide the class into groups of three. Each group should pick a picture. One student will write an accurate description of it, and the others will write imaginary descriptions. Tell them to use relative pronouns in the descriptions. Each group will read its three descriptions aloud without showing the picture. Give the rest of the class two minutes to ask questions about the descriptions before guessing which is the accurate description. Award one point for a correct guess and two points to the team able to fool the class.

1 Expansion Ask students to write their own completions to the sentences. Then ask several volunteers to read their sentences aloud.

2 Expansion Ask questions about the content of the activity. **¿Quiénes quieren comprar una casa? (Jaime y Tina) ¿Qué casa quieren comprar? (una casa que está en las afueras de la ciudad) ¿De quién era la casa? (de una artista famosa) ¿Cómo venden la casa? (con todos los muebles que tenía) ¿Qué tipo de alfombra tiene la sala? (una alfombra que la artista trajo de Kuwait)**

3 Suggestion Ask a volunteer to read the **modelo** aloud. Ask another volunteer to explain what word is replaced by the relative pronoun **que**.

3 Expansion Have pairs write two more sentences that contain relative pronouns and refer to Javier and Ana's new home.

Práctica

1 Combinar Combina elementos de la columna A y la columna B para formar oraciones lógicas.

A	B
1. Ése es el hombre __d__.	a. con quien bailaba es mi vecina
2. La mujer __a__.	b. que te compró Cecilia
3. No traje __e__.	c. quien canta mis canciones (*songs*) favoritas, es de Panamá
4. ¿Te gusta la tostadora __b__?	d. que arregló mi lavadora
5. ¿Cómo se llama el programa __g__?	e. lo que necesito para la clase de matemáticas
6. Rubén Blades, __c__.	f. que comiste en el restaurante
	g. que viste en la televisión anoche

NOTA CULTURAL

Rubén Blades es un cantante y actor panameño muy famoso. Ganador de cuatro premios Grammy, Rubén Blades es conocido por su propio estilo de música salsa que demuestra una conciencia social. Se graduó de la Universidad de Panamá y de la Escuela de Derecho de Harvard.

2 Completar Completa la historia sobre la casa que Jaime y Tina quieren comprar, usando los pronombres relativos **que, quien, quienes** o **lo que.**

1. Jaime y Tina son los chicos a __quienes__ conocí la semana pasada.
2. Quieren comprar una casa __que__ está en las afueras de la ciudad.
3. Es una casa __que__ era de una artista famosa.
4. La artista, a __quien__ yo conocía, murió el año pasado y no tenía hijos.
5. Ahora se vende la casa con todos los muebles __que__ ella tenía.
6. La sala tiene una alfombra __que__ ella trajo de Kuwait.
7. La casa tiene muchos estantes, __lo que__ a Tina le encanta.

3 Combinar Javier y Ana acaban de casarse y han comprado una casa y muchas otras cosas. Combina sus declaraciones para formar una sola oración con los pronombres relativos **que, quien(es)** y **lo que.**

modelo

Vamos a usar los vasos nuevos mañana. Los pusimos en el comedor.
Mañana vamos a usar los vasos nuevos que pusimos en el comedor.

1. Tenemos una cafetera nueva. Mi prima nos la regaló.
   Tenemos una cafetera nueva que mi prima nos regaló.
2. Tenemos una cómoda nueva. Es bueno porque no hay espacio en el armario.
   Tenemos una cómoda nueva, lo que es bueno porque no hay espacio en el armario.
3. Esos platos no nos costaron mucho. Están encima del horno.
   Esos platos que están encima del horno no nos costaron mucho.
4. Esas copas me las regaló mi amiga Amalia. Ella viene a visitarme mañana.
   Esas copas me las regaló mi amiga Amalia, quien viene a visitarme mañana.
5. La lavadora está casi nueva. Nos la regalaron mis suegros.
   La lavadora que nos regalaron mis suegros está casi nueva.
6. La vecina nos dio una manta de lana. Ella la compró en México.
   La vecina nos dio una manta de lana que compró en México.

TEACHING OPTIONS

Extra Practice Have students use relative pronouns to complete this paragraph. ____ **(Lo que) tenemos que hacer es buscar otro apartamento. El apartamento ____ (que) tenemos sólo tiene dos alcobas. Ayer hablamos con un compañero ____ (que) alquila una casa cerca de aquí. Buscamos algo similar a ____ (lo que) él tiene: tres alcobas, una cocina, una sala y dos cuartos de baño... ¡y un alquiler bajo! Nos dio el nombre de varios agentes a ____ (quienes) podemos contactar para más información.**

Pairs Ask students to write a description of a new household gadget, using relative pronouns. Their descriptions should include the purpose of the gadget and how it is used.

Comunicación

4 **Entrevista** En parejas, túrnense para hacerse las siguientes preguntas. Answers will vary.

1. ¿Qué es lo que más te gusta de vivir en las afueras o en la ciudad?
2. ¿Cómo son las personas que viven en tu barrio?
3. ¿Cuál es el quehacer doméstico que menos te gusta? ¿Y el que más te gusta?
4. ¿Quién es la persona que hace los quehaceres domésticos en tu casa?
5. ¿Quiénes son las personas con quienes más sales los fines de semana? ¿Quién es la persona a quien más llamas por teléfono?
6. ¿Cuál es el deporte que más te gusta? ¿Cuál es el que menos te gusta?
7. ¿Cuál es el barrio de tu ciudad que más te gusta y por qué?
8. ¿Quién es la persona a quien más llamas cuando tienes problemas?
9. ¿Quién es la persona a quien más admiras? ¿Por qué?
10. ¿Qué es lo que más te gusta de tu casa?
11. ¿Qué es lo que más te molesta de tus amigos?
12. ¿Qué es lo que menos te gusta de tu barrio?

5 **Adivinanza** En grupos, túrnense para describir distintas partes de una vivienda usando pronombres relativos. Los demás compañeros tienen que hacer preguntas hasta que adivinen (*guess*) la palabra. Answers will vary.

modelo

Estudiante 1: *Es lo que tenemos en el dormitorio.*
Estudiante 2: *¿Es el mueble que usamos para dormir?*
Estudiante 1: *No. Es lo que usamos para guardar la ropa.*
Estudiante 3: *Lo sé. Es la cómoda.*

Síntesis

6 **Definir** En parejas, definan las palabras. Usen los pronombres relativos **que, quien(es)** y **lo que.** Luego compartan sus definiciones con la clase. Answers will vary.

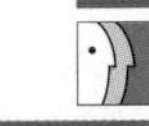

AYUDA

Remember that **de,** followed by the name of a material, means *made of.*
Es de algodón.
It's made of cotton.

• • •

Es un tipo de means *It's a kind/sort of...*
Es un tipo de flor.
It's a kind of flower.

modelo

lavadora *Es lo que se usa para lavar la ropa.*
pastel *Es un postre que comes en tu cumpleaños.*

alquiler	flan	patio	tenedor
amigos	guantes	postre	termómetro
aspiradora	jabón	sillón	vaso
enfermera	manta	sótano	vecino

4 Suggestion Have students take notes on the answers provided by their partners to use in expansion activities.

4 Expansions
- Have pairs team up to form groups of four. Each student will report on his or her partner, using the information obtained in the interview.
- Have pairs of students write four more questions modeled on the activity. Ask each pair to exchange its questions with another.

5 Expansion Have groups choose their three best **adivinanzas** and present them to the rest of the class.

6 Expansion Have pairs choose one of the items listed in the activity and develop a magazine ad. Their ad should include three sentences with relative pronouns.

TEACHING OPTIONS

Small Groups Have students bring in pictures of houses (exterior only). Have them work in groups of three to write a description of what they imagine the interiors to be like. Remind them to use relative pronouns in their descriptions.
Extra Practice For practice in listening comprehension, prepare short descriptions of five easily recognizable residences. Write their names on the board in random order. Then read your descriptions as a dictation, having students copy your description and match it to the appropriate name. Ex: **Es un castillo que está situado en una pequeña montaña cerca del Océano Pacífico de California. Lo construyó un norteamericano considerado bastante excéntrico. Es un sitio que visitan muchos turistas cada año.** (Hearst Castle)

Section Goals

In **Estructura 12.2** students will learn:

- formal commands
- use of object pronouns with formal commands

Instructional Resources
WB/VM: Workbook, pp. 139–140
Lab Manual, p. 70
Lab CD/MP3 ***Lección 12***
IRM: ***¡Inténtalo! & Práctica*** *Answers, pp. 217–218; Tapescript, pp. 54–58*
Info Gap Activities Booklet, pp. 47–48
Interactive CD-ROM
Companion website: www.vistahigherlearning.com
Presentations CD-ROM

Suggestions

- Model the use of formal commands with simple examples using TPR and gestures. Ex: **Levántense. Siéntense.** Then point to individual students. Ex: ____ **, levántese.** Give other commands using **salga/salgan, vuelva/vuelvan,** and **venga/vengan**.
- Write the following sentences on the board, contrasting their meaning with the examples in the text: **Habla con ellos. Come frutas y verduras. Lavan los platos ahora mismo. Beben menos té y café.**
- Consolidate by having volunteers give the command forms for other verbs, such as **alquilar, correr,** or **imprimir**.

12.2 Formal commands

ANTE TODO As you learned in **Lección 11**, the command forms are used to give orders or advice. Formal commands are used with people you address as **usted** or **ustedes.** Observe the following examples, then study the chart.

Hable con ellos, don Francisco.
Talk with them, don Francisco.

Coma frutas y verduras.
Eat fruits and vegetables.

Laven los platos ahora mismo.
Wash the dishes right now.

Beban menos té y café.
Drink less tea and coffee.

CONSEJOS

Learning these command forms will be very helpful since the same forms are used for the subjunctive, which you will begin learning in the next section.

Formal commands (*Ud.* and *Uds.*)

Infinitive	Present tense *yo* form	*Ud.* command	*Uds.* command
limpiar	limpi**o**	limpi**e**	limpi**en**
barrer	barr**o**	barr**a**	barr**an**
sacudir	sacud**o**	sacud**a**	sacud**an**
decir (e:i)	dig**o**	dig**a**	dig**an**
pensar (e:ie)	piens**o**	piens**e**	piens**en**
volver (o:ue)	vuelv**o**	vuelv**a**	vuelv**an**
servir (e:i)	sirv**o**	sirv**a**	sirv**an**

▶ The **Ud.** and **Uds.** commands, like the negative **tú** commands, are formed by dropping the final **-o** of the **yo** form of the present tense. For **-ar** verbs, add **-e** or **-en**. For **-er** and **-ir** verbs, add **-a** or **-an**.

No se preocupe...
La vamos a ayudar en
todo lo posible.

▶ Verbs with irregular **yo** forms maintain the same irregularity in their formal commands. These verbs include **conducir, conocer, decir, hacer, ofrecer, oír, poner, salir, tener, traducir, traer, venir,** and **ver.**

Oiga, don Francisco...
Listen, don Francisco...

¡Salga inmediatamente!
Leave immediately!

Ponga la mesa, por favor.
Set the table, please.

Hagan la cama antes de salir.
Make the bed before leaving.

▶ Note also that stem-changing verbs maintain their stem-changes in **Ud.** and **Uds.** commands.

e:ie	o:ue	e:i
No **pierda** la llave.	**Vuelva** temprano, joven.	**Sirva** la sopa, por favor.
Cierren la puerta.	**Duerman** bien, chicos.	**Repitan** las frases.

TEACHING OPTIONS

Video Replay the video segment, having students focus on formal commands. Ask them to write down each formal command that they hear. Then form groups of three and have students compare their lists.

TPR Have students stand. Using the verbs presented in the discussion of formal commands, give commands at random (Ex: **Barra el suelo. Lave los platos. Sacuda los muebles.**) and point to a student who should perform the appropriate gesture. Keep the pace rapid. Vary by calling out names of more than one student. (Ex: **Pongan la mesa. Hagan la cama.**)

CONSEJOS

These spelling changes are necessary to ensure that the words are pronounced correctly. See **Lección 8, Pronunciación**, p. 243, and **Lección 9, Pronunciación**, p. 277.

• • •

It may help you to study the following five series of syllables. Note that within each series, the consonant sound doesn't change.

ca que qui co cu
za ce ci zo zu
ga gue gui go gu
ja ge gi jo ju

▶ Verbs ending in **-car, -gar,** and **-zar** have a spelling change in the command forms.

sa**car**	**c → qu**	sa**qu**e, sa**qu**en
ju**gar**	**g → gu**	jue**gu**e, jue**gu**en
almor**zar**	**z → c**	almuer**c**e, almuer**c**en

▶ The following verbs have irregular formal commands.

Infinitive	*Ud.* command	*Uds.* command
dar	**dé**	**den**
estar	**esté**	**estén**
ir	**vaya**	**vayan**
saber	**sepa**	**sepan**
ser	**sea**	**sean**

▶ To make a formal command negative, simply place **no** before the verb.

No ponga las maletas en la cama.
Don't put the suitcases on the bed.

No ensucien los sillones.
Don't dirty the armchairs.

¡ATENCIÓN!

When a pronoun is attached to an affirmative command that has two or more syllables, an accent mark is added to maintain the original stress:

limpie → límpielo
lean → léanlo
diga → dígamelo
sacudan → sacúdanlos

▶ In affirmative commands, reflexive, indirect and direct object pronouns are always attached to the end of the verb.

Siénten**se**, por favor.
Síga**me,** Laura.

Acuésten**se** ahora.
Póngan**las** en el suelo, por favor.

▶ In negative commands, these pronouns always precede the verb.

No **se** preocupe.
No **me lo** dé.

No **los** ensucien.
No **nos las** traigan.

▶ **Ud.** and **Uds.** can be used with the command forms to strike a more formal tone. In such instances they follow the command form.

Muéstrele usted la foto a su amigo.
Show the photo to your friend.

Tomen ustedes esta alcoba.
Take this bedroom.

¡INTÉNTALO! Indica cuáles son los mandatos afirmativos y negativos correspondientes.

1. escucharlo (Ud.) Escúchelo. No lo escuche.
2. decírmelo (Uds.) Díganmelo. No me lo digan.
3. salir (Ud.) Salga. No salga.
4. servírnoslo (Uds.) Sírvannoslo. No nos lo sirvan.
5. barrerla (Ud.) Bárrala. No la barra.
6. hacerlo (Ud.) Hágalo. No lo haga.
7. ir (Uds.) Vayan. No vayan.
8. sentarse (Uds.) Siéntense. No se sienten.

Suggestions

- Ask volunteers to write formal command forms of other verbs with spelling changes on the board. Ex: **empezar (empiece); comenzar (comience); buscar (busque); pagar (pague); llegar (llegue).**
- Test comprehension as you proceed by asking volunteers to supply the correct form of other verbs you suggest.
- Point out that the accent mark on **dé** serves to distinguish the verb form from the preposition **de**.
- Point out that the affirmative answer for item 4 of **¡Inténtalo!** is spelled with a double **n**: **Sírvannoslo.**

TEACHING OPTIONS

Extra Practice Write a list of situations on the board using singular and plural forms. Ex: **La cocina está sucia. Mis amigos y yo tenemos hambre. Tenemos miedo.** Then have students write responses in the form of commands. (**Límpiela. Hagan la cena. No tengan miedo.**)

Heritage Speakers Ask heritage speakers to make a list of ten commands they would hear in their home communities that would probably not be heard elsewhere. Ex: **Sírvale el café al niño. Acuéstese después de almorzar.**

1 Expansions
- Ask volunteers to give more organization tips not included in the activity for Señora González.
- Have students work in pairs to formulate a list of instructions for the movers. Ex: **Tengan cuidado con los platos. No pongan los cuadros en una caja.** With the whole class, compare and contrast the commands the pairs have formulated.

2 Suggestion Before starting the activity, have volunteers describe the situation in each of the drawings. Have them identify who is speaking to whom.

2 Expansion Continue the exercise by using magazine pictures. Ex: **Tengan paciencia con los niños.**

Práctica

1 **Completar** La señora González quiere mudarse de casa. Ayúdala a organizarse. Indica el mandato formal de cada verbo.

1. ___Lea___ los anuncios (*ads*) del periódico y ___guárdelos___. (leer, guardar)
2. ___Vaya___ personalmente y ___vea___ las casas usted misma. (ir, ver)
3. Decida qué casa quiere y ___llame___ al agente. ___Pídale___ un contrato de alquiler. (llamar, pedirle)
4. ___Contrate___ un camión (*truck*) para ese día y ___pregúnteles___ la hora exacta de llegada. (contratar, preguntarles)
5. El día de la mudanza (*On moving day*) ___esté___ tranquila. ___Vuelva___ a revisar su lista para completar todo lo que tiene que hacer. (estar, volver)
6. Primero, ___dígales___ a todos en casa que usted va a estar ocupada. No ___les diga___ que usted va a hacerlo todo. (decirles, decirles)
7. ___Saque___ tiempo para hacer las maletas tranquilamente. No ___les haga___ las maletas a los niños más grandes. (sacar, hacerles)
8. No ___se preocupe___. ___Sepa___ que todo va a salir bien. (preocuparse, saber)

2 **¿Qué dicen?** Mira los dibujos y escribe un mandato lógico para cada uno. Usa palabras que aprendiste en **Contextos**. Answers will vary; suggested answers below.

1. ___Abran sus libros, por favor.___

2. ___Cierre la puerta. ¡Hace frío!___

3. ___Traiga usted la cuenta, por favor.___

4. ___La cocina está sucia. Bárranla, por favor.___

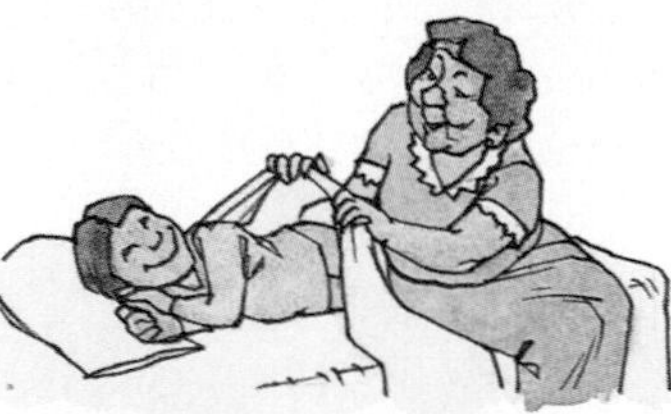

5. ___Duerma bien, niña.___

6. ___Arreglen el cuarto, por favor. Está desordenado.___

TEACHING OPTIONS

Small Groups Form small groups of students who have similar living arrangements, such as dormitories, at home, or in an apartment. Then have the groups make a list of suggestions for a newly arrived older resident. Ex: **No ponga usted la tele después de las diez. Saque la basura temprano. No estacione usted el carro en la calle. No invite a los amigos suyos a visitar después de las once.**

Extra Practice Here are five sentences to use as a dictation. Read each twice, pausing after the second time for students to write. **1. Saquen la basura a la calle. 2. Almuerce usted conmigo hoy. 3. Niños, jueguen en la calle. 4. Váyase inmediatamente. 5. Esté usted aquí a las diez.**

Comunicación

3 **Solucionar** Trabajen en parejas para presentar los siguientes problemas. Un(a) estudiante presenta los problemas de la columna A y el/la otro/a los de la columna B. Usen mandatos formales y túrnense para ofrecer soluciones. Answers will vary.

modelo

Estudiante 1: Vilma se torció un tobillo jugando al tenis. Es la tercera vez.
Estudiante 2: No juegue más al tenis. / Vaya a ver a un especialista.

A

1. Se me perdió el libro de español con todas mis notas.
2. A Vicente se le cayó la botella de vino para la cena.
3. ¿Cómo? ¿Se le olvidó traer el traje de baño a la playa?
4. Se nos quedaron los boletos en la casa. El avión sale en una hora.

B

1. Mis hijas no se levantan temprano. Siempre llegan tarde a la escuela.
2. A mi abuela le robaron las maletas. Era su primer día de vacaciones.
3. Nuestra casa es demasiado pequeña para nuestra familia.
4. Me preocupo constantemente por Roberto. Trabaja demasiado.

4 **Conversaciones** En parejas, escojan dos situaciones y preparen conversaciones para presentar a la clase. Usen mandatos formales. Answers will vary.

modelo

Lupita: Señor Ramírez, siento mucho llegar tan tarde. Mi niño se enfermó. ¿Qué debo hacer?
Sr. Ramírez: No se preocupe. Siéntese y descanse un poco.

SITUACIÓN 1 Profesor Rosado, no vine la semana pasada porque el equipo jugaba en Boquete. ¿Qué debo hacer para ponerme al día *(catch up)*?

SITUACIÓN 2 Los invitados de la boda llegan a las cuatro de la tarde, la mesa está sin poner y el champán sin servir. Los camareros apenas están llegando. ¿Qué deben hacer los camareros?

SITUACIÓN 3 Mi novio es un poco aburrido. No le gustan ni el cine, ni los deportes, ni salir a comer. Tampoco habla mucho. ¿Qué puedo hacer o qué le puedo decir?

SITUACIÓN 4 Tengo que preparar una presentación para mañana sobre el Canal de Panamá. ¿Por dónde comienzo?

NOTA CULTURAL

El 31 de diciembre de 1999, los Estados Unidos cedió control del **Canal de Panamá** al gobierno de Panamá, terminando así casi 100 años de administración estadounidense.

Síntesis

5 **Presentar** En grupos, preparen un anuncio (*ad*) de televisión para presentar a la clase. El anuncio debe tratar de (*be about*) un detergente, un electrodoméstico, o una agencia inmobiliaria (*real estate agency*). Usen mandatos, los pronombres relativos **(que, quien(es)** o **lo que)** y el **se** impersonal. Answers will vary.

modelo

Compre el lavaplatos Siglo XXI. Tiene todo lo que usted desea. Es el lavaplatos que mejor funciona. Venga a verlo ahora mismo... No pierda ni un minuto más. Se aceptan tarjetas de crédito.

3 Suggestion Ask volunteers to offer other suggestions for the problem in the **modelo**. Ex: **Tenga usted más cuidado. Compre nuevos zapatos de tenis.**

3 Expansion Ask pairs to pick their most humorous or unusual response to present to the class.

4 Expansion Have pairs write another scenario on a sheet of paper. Then ask them to exchange papers and give them two minutes to prepare another dialogue. Have them act out their dialogues for the authors.

5 Suggestion Divide the class into small groups. Have them choose a product or business and brainstorm positive attributes that they want to advertise.

5 Expansions

- Ask different groups to share their commercials with the class.
- Have groups videotape their ads outside of class. Encourage them to be as creative as possible.

The Affective Dimension Students may feel more comfortable speaking if they assume the personae of celebrity endorsers when presenting the television commercial.

Suggestion See the Info Gap Activities Booklet for an additional activity to practice the material presented in this section.

TEACHING OPTIONS

Heritage Speakers Have heritage speakers write a description of a household item commonly found in their homes, but not typically in other communities. Ex: **comal, molcajete, cafetera exprés, paellera,** and so forth. Have them read their descriptions to the class. Then, have them use formal commands to share with the class a recipe that calls for using one of the items described.

Pairs Have pairs of students write a series of commands for a famous sports figure. Ex: (John McEnroe) **No se enoje. Tenga paciencia. Escuche a los árbitros. No tire la raqueta.**

Section Goals

In **Estructura 12.3** students will learn:
- present subjunctive of regular verbs
- present subjunctive of stem-changing verbs
- irregular verbs in the present subjunctive

Instructional Resources
WB/VM: Workbook, pp. 141–142
Lab Manual, p. 71
Lab CD/MP3 ***Lección 12***
IRM: ***¡Inténtalo! & Práctica*** *Answers, pp. 217–218;*
Tapescript, pp. 54–58
Interactive CD-ROM
Companion website: www.vistahigherlearning.com
Presentations CD-ROM

Suggestions
- Write sentences such as the following on the board in two columns labeled *Indicative* and *Subjunctive.* Column 1: **Mi esposo lava los platos. Mi esposo barre el suelo. Mi esposo cocina.** Column 2: **Mi esposo quiere que yo lave los platos. Mi esposo quiere que yo barra el suelo. Mi esposo quiere que yo cocine.** Underline **yo lave**, asking students what the indicative form would be. Do the same for the other sentences.
- Check for understanding by asking volunteers to give subjunctive forms of other regular verbs from this lesson such as **planchar, barrer,** and **sacudir**.

12.3 The present subjunctive

ANTE TODO With the exception of commands, all of the verb forms you have been using have been in the indicative mood. The indicative is used to state facts and to express actions or states that the speaker considers to be real and definite. In contrast, the subjunctive mood expresses the speaker's attitudes toward events, as well as actions or states the speaker views as uncertain or hypothetical.

Quiero que ustedes ayuden con los quehaceres domésticos.

Insistimos en que nos deje ayudarla a preparar la comida.

Present subjunctive of regular verbs

		hablar	comer	escribir
SINGULAR FORMS	yo	habl**e**	com**a**	escrib**a**
	tú	habl**es**	com**as**	escrib**as**
	Ud./él/ella	habl**e**	com**a**	escrib**a**
PLURAL FORMS	nosotros/as	habl**emos**	com**amos**	escrib**amos**
	vosotros/as	habl**éis**	com**áis**	escrib**áis**
	Uds./ellos/ellas	habl**en**	com**an**	escrib**an**

¡LENGUA VIVA!
You may think that English has no subjunctive, but it does! It used to be very common but now survives mostly in set expressions such as *if I were you* and *be that as it may.*

▶ The present subjunctive is formed very much like **usted** and **ustedes** and *negative* **tú** commands. From the **yo** form of the present indicative, drop the **-o** ending, and replace it with the subjunctive endings.

INFINITIVE	PRESENT INDICATIVE	VERB STEM	PRESENT SUBJUNCTIVE
hablar	**hablo**	**habl-**	**hable**
comer	**como**	**com-**	**coma**
escribir	**escribo**	**escrib-**	**escriba**

▶ The present subjunctive endings are:

–ar verbs		*–er* and *–ir* verbs	
–e	**–emos**	**–a**	**–amos**
–es	**–éis**	**–as**	**–áis**
–e	**–en**	**–a**	**–an**

CONSEJOS
Note that, in the present subjunctive, **–ar** verbs use endings normally associated with present tense **–er** and **–ir** verbs. Likewise, **–er** and **–ir** verbs in the present subjunctive use endings normally associated with **–ar** verbs in the present tense. Note also that, in the present subjunctive, the **yo** form is the same as the **Ud./él/ella** form.

TEACHING OPTIONS

Large Group You will need a wadded piece of paper or a beanbag for this activity. Have students arrange their chairs in a circle. Then say an infinitive of a regular verb and a subject pronoun. Ex: **alquilar / nosotros**. Throw the paper to a student. He or she must provide the correct subjunctive form (**alquilemos**).

Extra Practice Create sentences that use the subjunctive. Say the sentence, and have students repeat. Then call out a different subject for the subordinate clause. Have students then say the sentence with the new subject, making all other necessary changes. Ex: **Quiero que ustedes trabajen mucho. Javier. (Quiero que Javier trabaje mucho.) Quiero que lleguen temprano. Nosotras. (Quiero que lleguemos temprano.)**

▶ Verbs with irregular **yo** forms show the same irregularity in all forms of the present subjunctive.

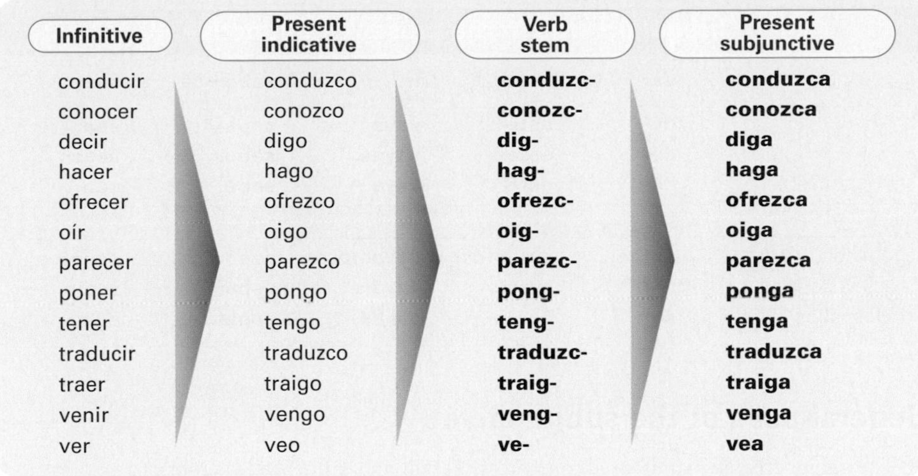

Infinitive	Present indicative	Verb stem	Present subjunctive
conducir	conduzco	**conduzc-**	**conduzca**
conocer	conozco	**conozc-**	**conozca**
decir	digo	**dig-**	**diga**
hacer	hago	**hag-**	**haga**
ofrecer	ofrezco	**ofrezc-**	**ofrezca**
oír	oigo	**oig-**	**oiga**
parecer	parezco	**parezc-**	**parezca**
poner	pongo	**pong-**	**ponga**
tener	tengo	**teng-**	**tenga**
traducir	traduzco	**traduzc-**	**traduzca**
traer	traigo	**traig-**	**traiga**
venir	vengo	**veng-**	**venga**
ver	veo	**ve-**	**vea**

▶ To maintain the **-c, -g,** and **-z** sounds, verbs ending in **-car, -gar,** and **-zar** have a spelling change in all forms of the present subjunctive.

sacar: sa**qu**e, sa**qu**es, sa**qu**e, sa**qu**emos, sa**qué**is, sa**qu**en
jugar: jue**gu**e, jue**gu**es, jue**gu**e, ju**gu**emos, ju**gu**éis, jue**gu**en
almorzar: almuer**c**e, almuer**c**es, almuer**c**e, almor**c**emos, almor**cé**is, almuer**c**en

Present subjunctive of stem-changing verbs

¡ATENCIÓN!

Note that stem-changing verbs and verbs that have a spelling change have the same ending as regular verbs in the present subjunctive.

▶ **-Ar** and **-er** stem-changing verbs have the same stem changes in the subjunctive as they do in the present indicative.

pensar (e:ie): p**ie**nse, p**ie**nses, p**ie**nse, pensemos, penséis, p**ie**nsen
mostrar (o:ue): m**ue**stre, m**ue**stres, m**ue**stre, mostremos, mostréis, m**ue**stren
entender (e:ie): ent**ie**nda, ent**ie**ndas, ent**ie**nda, entendamos, entendáis, ent**ie**ndan
volver (o:ue): v**ue**lva, v**ue**lvas, v**ue**lva, volvamos, volváis, v**ue**lvan

▶ **–Ir** stem-changing verbs have the same stem changes in the subjunctive as they do in the present indicative, but in addition, the **nosotros/as** and **vosotros/as** forms undergo a stem change. The unstressed **e** changes to **i,** while the unstressed **o** changes to **u.**

pedir (e:i): p**i**da, p**i**das, p**i**da, p**i**damos, p**i**dáis, p**i**dan
sentir (e:ie): s**ie**nta, s**ie**ntas, s**ie**nta, s**i**ntamos, s**i**ntáis, s**ie**ntan
dormir (o:ue): d**ue**rma, d**ue**rmas, d**ue**rma, d**u**rmamos, d**u**rmáis, d**ue**rman

Suggestions

- It may be helpful for students to be aware how English uses the subjunctive mood. Ex: *I wish she were here. I insisted that he take notes. I suggest you be there tomorrow. If it were me, I would be happy. Be that as it may . . . .*
- Emphasize the stem changes that occur in the **nosotros/as** and **vosotros/as** forms of **–ir** stem-changing verbs.

TEACHING OPTIONS

Pairs Have pairs of students role-play landlord/landlady and new resident. Students should refer to the **Fotonovela** as a model. Give pairs sufficient time to plan and practice. When all pairs have completed the activity, ask a few of them to introduce their characters and perform the conversation for the whole class.

Heritage Speakers Ask heritage speakers to compare male and female attitudes toward domestic life using the subjunctive. Ex: **Las mujeres quieren que los hombres... Los hombres insisten en que...** Their comparative study should reflect values in their communities.

Suggestions

- Give examples of sentences for one or two forms of each verb, using **Quiero que...** Ex: ____, **quiero que le des tu lápiz a ____. Quiero que ustedes estén en la clase a las ____ en punto. Quiero que mi hija vaya de compras conmigo esta tarde. Quiero que ustedes sepan todas las formas del subjuntivo.**
- Check understanding by writing on the board main clauses ending in **que** that require a subjunctive in the subordinate clause. Invite volunteers to suggest several endings for each, using verbs they have just gone over. Ex: **Es importante que... (aprendamos español, yo entienda la lección, los estudiantes traigan sus libros)**.
- Explain that whereas the word *that* is usually optional in English, **que** is required in Spanish.

Irregular verbs in the present subjunctive

▶ The following five verbs are irregular in the present subjunctive.

Irregular verbs in the present subjunctive

		dar	estar	ir	saber	ser
SINGULAR FORMS	yo	**dé**	**esté**	**vaya**	**sepa**	**sea**
	tú	**des**	**estés**	**vayas**	**sepas**	**seas**
	Ud./él/ella	**dé**	**esté**	**vaya**	**sepa**	**sea**
PLURAL FORMS	nosotros/as	**demos**	**estemos**	**vayamos**	**sepamos**	**seamos**
	vosotros/as	**deis**	**estéis**	**vayáis**	**sepáis**	**seáis**
	Uds./ellos/ellas	**den**	**estén**	**vayan**	**sepan**	**sean**

¡ATENCIÓN!

The subjunctive form of **hay** (*there is, there are*) is also irregular: **haya**.

General uses of the subjunctive

▶ The subjunctive is mainly used to express: 1) will and influence, 2) emotion, 3) doubt, disbelief, and denial, and 4) indefiniteness and nonexistence.

▶ The subjunctive is most often used in sentences that consist of a main clause and a subordinate clause. The main clause contains a verb or expression that triggers the use of the subjunctive. The conjunction **que** connects the subordinate clause to the main clause.

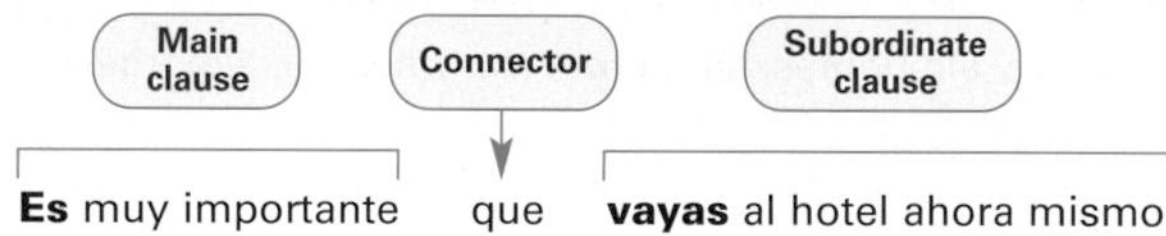
Main clause
Connector
Subordinate clause
Es muy importante
que
vayas al hotel ahora mismo.

▶ These impersonal expressions are always followed by clauses in the subjunctive:

Es bueno que... *It's good that...*	**Es mejor que...** *It's better that...*	**Es malo que...** *It's bad that...*
Es importante que... *It's important that...*	**Es necesario que...** *It's necessary that...*	**Es urgente que...** *It's urgent that...*

¡INTÉNTALO! Indica el presente de subjuntivo de los siguientes verbos.

1. (alquilar, beber, vivir) que yo alquile, beba, viva
2. (estudiar, aprender, asistir) que tú estudies, aprendas, asistas
3. (encontrar, poder, dormir) que él encuentre, pueda, duerma
4. (hacer, tener, venir) que nosotras hagamos, tengamos, vengamos
5. (dar, hablar, escribir) que ellos den, hablen, escriban
6. (pagar, empezar, buscar) que ustedes paguen, empiecen, busquen
7. (ser, ir, saber) que yo sea, vaya, sepa
8. (estar, dar, oír) que tú estés, des, oigas
9. (arreglar, leer, abrir) que nosotros arreglemos, leamos, abramos
10. (cantar, leer, vivir) que ellas canten, lean, vivan

TEACHING OPTIONS

Video Show the video module again to give students more comprehensible input that uses the present subjunctive. Stop the video where appropriate and ask students to say which of the four principal uses of the subjunctive (will and influence; emotion; doubt, disbelief, and denial; indefiniteness and nonexistence) is expressed in each instance.

Extra Practice Here are five sentences containing verbs in the present subjunctive to use as a dictation. Read each twice, pausing after the second time for students to write. **1. Es urgente que encontremos una casa nueva. 2. Es mejor que cada uno tenga su propia alcoba. 3. Necesitamos una casa que esté cerca de la universidad. 4. No es urgente que nos mudemos inmediatamente. 5. Pero sí es importante que empecemos a buscar la casa ya.**

Práctica

1 **Completar** Completa las oraciones conjugando los verbos entre paréntesis. Luego empareja las oraciones del primer grupo con las del segundo grupo.

A

1. Es mejor que cenemos en casa. (nosotros, cenar) b
2. Es importante que visites las casas colgantes de Cuenca. (tú, visitar) c
3. Señora, es urgente que le saque la muela. Parece que tiene una infección. (yo, sacar) e
4. Es malo que Ana les dé tantos dulces a los niños. (dar) a
5. Es necesario que lleguen a la una de la tarde. (Uds., llegar) f
6. Es importante que nos acostemos temprano. (nosotros, acostarse) d

NOTA CULTURAL

Las casas colgantes (*hanging*) de Cuenca, España, son muy famosas. Estas casas están situadas en un acantilado (*cliff*) y forman parte del paisaje (*landscape*) de la ciudad.

B

a. Es importante que coman más verduras. (ellos, comer)
b. No, es mejor que salgamos a comer. (nosotros, salir)
c. Y yo creo que es bueno que vaya a Madrid después. (yo, ir)
d. En mi opinión, no es necesario que durmamos tanto. (nosotros, dormir)
e. ¿Ah, sí? ¿Es necesario que me tome un antibiótico también? (yo, tomar)
f. Para llegar a tiempo, es necesario que almorcemos temprano. (nosotros, almorzar)

Comunicación

2 **Minidiálogos** En parejas, completen los minidiálogos con expresiones impersonales de una manera lógica. Answers will vary.

modelo

Miguelito: Mamá, no quiero arreglar mi cuarto.
Señora Casas: Es necesario que lo arregles. Y es importante que sacudas los muebles también.

1. **MIGUELITO** Mamá, no quiero estudiar. Quiero salir a jugar con mis amigos.
   SRA. CASAS ____________________
2. **MIGUELITO** Mamá, es que no me gustan las verduras. Prefiero comer pasteles.
   SRA. CASAS ____________________
3. **MIGUELITO** ¿Tengo que poner la mesa, mamá?
   SRA. CASAS ____________________
4. **MIGUELITO** No me siento bien, mamá. Me duele todo el cuerpo y tengo fiebre.
   SRA. CASAS ____________________

3 **Entrevista** Trabajen en parejas. Entrevístense usando estas preguntas. Expliquen sus respuestas. Answers will vary.

1. ¿Es importante que los niños ayuden con los quehaceres domésticos?
2. ¿Es urgente que los norteamericanos aprendan otras lenguas?
3. Si un(a) norteamericano/a quiere aprender francés, ¿es mejor que lo aprenda en Francia?
4. En su universidad, ¿es necesario que los estudiantes vivan en residencias estudiantiles?
5. ¿Es importante que todos los estudiantes asistan a la universidad?

1 Expansion After students have paired the sentences from each group, have them continue a couple of the short conversations with two more sentences using the subjunctive. Ex: **No es posible que encontremos un restaurante con mesas libres a las siete. Es mejor que salgamos ahora mismo para no tener ese problema.**

2 Expansions
- Ask volunteers to share their mini-dialogues with the rest of the class.
- Ask questions about Miguelito and Señora Casas using the subjunctive. Ex: **¿En qué insiste la señora Casas? (Insiste en que Miguelito arregle su cuarto; coma verduras; ponga la mesa.) ¿Qué quiere Miguelito? (Quiere salir a jugar; comer pasteles.)**

3 Expansion Ask students to report on their partner's answers using complete sentences and explanations. Ex: **¿Qué opina ____ sobre los quehaceres de los niños? ¿Cree que es importante que ayuden?**

TEACHING OPTIONS

Heritage Speakers Have heritage speakers write ten sentences comparing mainstream social practices with those of their cultural communities. Ex: **Aquí, es correcto que una señora le extienda la mano a un caballero. En nuestra cultura se considera mala educación que un caballero no le extienda la mano a una señora primero.**

Small Groups Divide the class into groups of four. Assign each group one of the following personal characteristics: **apariencia física; dinero; inteligencia; personalidad.** Have groups use the subjunctive to write sentences about the importance or unimportance of this trait for certain individuals. Ex: **Para ser "Miss Universo" es importante que una chica sea guapa.**

Section Goals

In **Estructura 12.4** students will learn:
- the subjunctive with verbs and expressions of will and influence
- common verbs of will and influence

Instructional Resources
Transparency #45
WB/VM: Workbook, pp. 143–144
Lab Manual, p. 72
Lab CD/MP3 ***Lección 12***
IRM: ***¡Inténtalo!*** *&* ***Práctica*** *Answers, pp. 217–218; Tapescript, pp. 54–58*
Interactive CD-ROM
Companion website: www.vistahigherlearning.com
Presentations CD-ROM

Suggestions

- Write the word **Recomendaciones** on the board. Ask volunteers for household tips and write them on the board in the infinitive with the student's name in parentheses. Ex: **Hacer todos los quehaceres los sábados** (Paul) **Lavar los platos en el lavaplatos** (Sara) When you have approximately ten suggestions, begin rephrasing them using verbs of will and influence with subordinate clauses. Ex: **Paul nos aconseja que hagamos todos los quehaceres los sábados. Sara recomienda que lavemos los platos en el lavaplatos.** After you have modeled several responses, ask volunteers to continue. Give them cues such as: **¿Qué sugiere ____ ?**
- Go through the lists of verbs of will and influence and impersonal expressions that generally take the subjunctive, giving examples of their use and asking volunteers for others.
- Have a volunteer read the advertisement for Dentabrit and explain what the subject of each clause is.

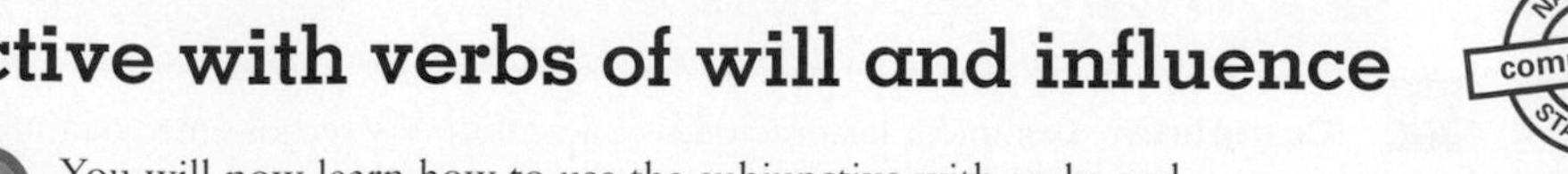

12.4 Subjunctive with verbs of will and influence

ANTE TODO You will now learn how to use the subjunctive with verbs and expressions of will and influence.

- Verbs of will and influence are often used when someone wants to affect the actions or behavior of other people.

Enrique **quiere** que salgamos a cenar.
Enrique wants us to go out to dinner.

Paola **prefiere** que cenemos en casa.
Paola prefers that we have dinner at home.

¡ATENCIÓN!
In English, constructions using the infinitive, such as *I want you to go*, are often used with verbs or expressions of will or influence. This is not the case in Spanish, where the subjunctive would be used in a subordinate clause.

- Here is a list of widely used verbs of will and influence.

Verbs of will and influence

aconsejar	*to advise*	**pedir** (e:i)	*to ask (for)*
desear	*to wish; to desire*	**preferir** (e:ie)	*to prefer*
importar	*to be important; to matter*	**prohibir**	*to prohibit*
		querer (e:ie)	*to want*
insistir (en)	*to insist (on)*	**recomendar** (e:ie)	*to recommend*
mandar	*to order*	**rogar** (o:ue)	*to beg; to plead*
necesitar	*to need*	**sugerir** (e:ie)	*to suggest*

- Some impersonal expressions, such as **es necesario que, es importante que, es mejor que,** and **es urgente que,** are considered expressions of will or influence.

- When the main clause contains an expression of will or influence, the subjunctive is required in the subordinate clause, provided that the two clauses have different subjects.

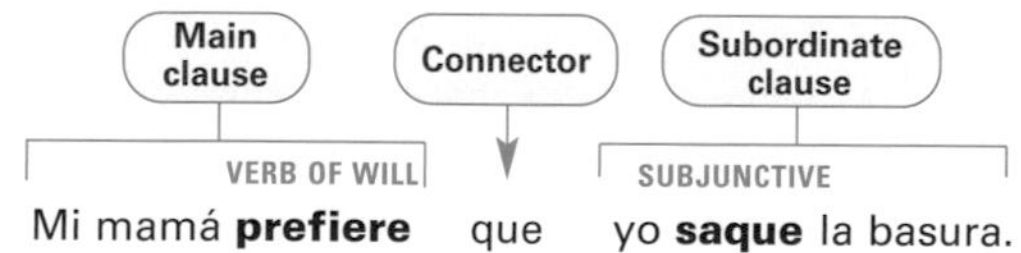

Mi mamá **prefiere** que yo **saque** la basura.

TEACHING OPTIONS

Small Groups Have groups of three write nine sentences, each of which uses a different verb of will and influence with the subjunctive. Ask volunteers to write some of their group's best sentences on the board. Work with the whole class to read the sentences and correct any errors.

Extra Practice Have students finish the following incomplete sentences. **1. Yo insisto en que mis amigos... 2. No quiero que mi familia... 3. Para mí es importante que el amor... 4. Prefiero que mi residencia... 5. Mi novio/a no quiere que yo... 6. Los profesores siempre recomiendan a los estudiantes que... 7. El doctor sugiere que nosotros... 8. Mi madre me ruega que... 9. El policía manda que los estudiantes... 10. El fotógrafo prefiere que nosotras...**

Quiero que arreglen sus alcobas, que hagan las camas, que pongan la mesa...

...y les aconsejo que se acuesten temprano esta noche.

▶ Indirect object pronouns are often used with the verbs **aconsejar, importar, mandar, pedir, prohibir, recomendar, rogar,** and **sugerir.**

Te aconsejo que estudies.
I advise you to study.

Les recomiendo que barran el suelo.
I recommend that you sweep the floor.

Le sugiero que vaya a casa.
I suggest that he go home.

Le ruego que no venga.
I beg him not to come.

▶ Note that all the forms of **prohibir** in the present tense carry a written accent, except for the **nosotros** form: **prohíbo, prohíbes, prohíbe, prohibimos, prohibís, prohíben.**

Ella les **prohíbe** que miren la televisión.
She prohibits them from watching television.

Nos **prohíben** que nademos en la piscina.
They prohibit that we swim in the swimming pool.

▶ The infinitive is used with words or expressions of will and influence, if there is no change of subject in the sentence.

No quiero **sacudir** los muebles.
I don't want to dust the furniture.

Es importante **sacar** la basura.
It's important to take out the trash.

Paco prefiere **descansar.**
Paco prefers to rest.

No es necesario **quitar** la mesa.
It's not necessary to clear the table.

¡INTÉNTALO! Completa cada oración con la forma correcta del verbo entre paréntesis.

1. Te sugiero que vayas (ir) con ella al supermercado.
2. Él necesita que yo le preste (prestar) dinero.
3. No queremos que tú hagas (hacer) nada especial para nosotros.
4. Mis papás quieren que yo limpie (limpiar) mi cuarto.
5. Nos piden que la ayudemos (ayudar) a preparar la comida.
6. Quieren que tú saques (sacar) la basura todos los días.
7. Quiero descansar (descansar) esta noche.
8. Es importante que ustedes limpien (limpiar) los estantes.
9. Su tía les manda que pongan (poner) la mesa.
10. Te aconsejo que no salgas (salir) con él.
11. Mi tío insiste en que mi prima haga (hacer) la cama.
12. Prefiero ir (ir) al cine.
13. Es necesario estudiar (estudiar).
14. Recomiendo que ustedes pasen (pasar) la aspiradora.

Suggestions

- Have a volunteer read aloud the examples in the captions to the video stills. Point out that in each example the subject of the verb in the main clause is different from the subject of the verb in the subordinate clause.
- Elicit indirect object pronouns with verbs of influence by making statements that give advice and asking students for advice. Ex: **Yo siempre les aconsejo a mis estudiantes que estudien mucho. ¿Qué me recomiendan ustedes a mí?** Continue: **1. Mi coche no arranca cuando hace mucho frío. ¿Qué me recomiendas, ____? 2. Mi apartamento está siempre desordenado. ¿Qué me aconsejan? 3. Voy a tener huéspedes este fin de semana. ¿Qué nos sugieren que hagamos?**
- Write the following sentences on the board: **Quiero que almuerces en la cafetería. Quiero almorzar en la cafetería.** Ask a volunteer to explain why an infinitive is used in the second sentence instead of the subjunctive.

TEACHING OPTIONS

Extra Practice Create sentences that follow the pattern of the sentences in **¡Inténtalo!** Say the sentence, have students repeat it, then give a different subject pronoun for the subordinate clause, varying the person and number. Have students then say the sentence with the new subject, changing pronouns and verbs as necessary.

TPR Have students stand. At random call out implied commands using statements with verbs of will or influence and actions that can be mimed. Ex: **Quiero que laves los platos. Insisto en que hagas la cama.** When you make a statement, point to a student to mime the action. Also use plural statements and point to more than one student. When you use negative statements, indicated students should do nothing. Keep the pace rapid.

1 Expansion Have pairs write a summary of the dialogue in the third person. Ask one or two volunteers to read their summaries to the class.

2 Suggestion Ask two volunteers to read the **modelo**. Then ask other volunteers to offer additional suggestions for Isabel.

2 Expansion Have students create two suggestions for each person. In the second they should use one of the impersonal expressions listed on page 382.

3 Expansion Have a conversation with the class about the information they learned in their interviews. Ask: **¿A quiénes siempre les dan consejos sus amigos? ¿Quiénes siempre les dan consejos a los amigos suyos? ¿Qué tipo de cosas aconsejan?**

Práctica

1 Completar Completa el diálogo con palabras de la lista.

cocina	haga	quiere	sea
comas	ponga	saber	ser
diga	prohíbe	sé	vaya

IRENE Tengo problemas con Vilma. Sé que debo hablar con ella. ¿Qué me recomiendas que le (1) diga ?

JULIA Pues, necesito (2) saber más antes de darte consejos.

IRENE Bueno, para empezar me (3) prohíbe que traiga dulces a la casa.

JULIA Pero chica, tiene razón. Es mejor que tú no (4) comas cosas dulces.

IRENE Sí, ya lo sé. Pero quiero que (5) sea más flexible. Además, insiste en que yo (6) haga todo en la casa.

JULIA Yo (7) sé que Vilma (8) cocina y hace los quehaceres todos los días.

IRENE Sí, pero siempre que hay fiesta me pide que (9) ponga los cubiertos y las copas en la mesa y que (10) vaya al sótano por las servilletas y los platos. ¡Es lo que más odio: ir al sótano!

JULIA Mujer, ¡Vilma sólo (11) quiere que ayudes en la casa!

2 Aconsejar En parejas, lean lo que dice cada persona. Luego den consejos lógicos usando verbos como **aconsejar, recomendar** y **prohibir.** Sus consejos deben ser diferentes de lo que la persona quiere hacer. Answers will vary.

modelo

Isabel: Quiero conseguir un comedor con los muebles más caros del mundo.
Consejo: *Te aconsejamos que consigas unos muebles menos caros.*

1. **DAVID** Pienso poner el cuadro del lago de Maracaibo en la cocina.
2. **SARA** Voy a ir a la gasolinera para comprar unas copas de cristal elegantes.
3. **SR. ALARCÓN** Insisto en comenzar a arreglar el jardín en marzo.
4. **SRA. VILLA** Quiero ver las tazas y los platos de la tienda El Ama de Casa Feliz.
5. **DOLORES** Voy a poner servilletas de tela (*cloth*) para los cuarenta invitados.
6. **SR. PARDO** Pienso poner todos mis muebles nuevos en el altillo.
7. **SRA. GONZÁLEZ** Hay una fiesta en mi casa esta noche pero no quiero arreglar la casa.
8. **CARLITOS** Hoy no tengo ganas de hacer las camas ni de quitar la mesa.

NOTA CULTURAL

En el **lago de Maracaibo**, en Venezuela, hay casas suspendidas sobre el agua que se llaman palafitos. Los palafitos son reminiscentes de la ciudad italiana de Venecia, de donde viene el nombre "Venezuela", que significa "pequeña Venecia".

3 Preguntas En parejas, túrnense para contestar las preguntas. Usen el subjuntivo. Answers will vary.

1. ¿Te dan consejos tus amigos/as? ¿Qué te aconsejan? ¿Aceptas sus consejos? ¿Por qué?
2. ¿Qué te sugieren tus profesores que hagas antes de terminar los cursos que tomas?
3. ¿Insisten tus amigos/as en que salgas mucho con ellos?
4. ¿Qué quieres que te regalen tu familia y tus amigos/as en tu cumpleaños?
5. ¿Qué le recomiendas tú a un(a) amigo/a que no quiere salir los sábados con su novio/a?
6. ¿Qué les aconsejas a los nuevos estudiantes de tu universidad?

TEACHING OPTIONS

Small Groups Have small groups prepare skits in which a group of roommates is discussing how to divide the household chores equitably. Give groups time to prepare and practice their skits before presenting them to the class.

Game Give pairs of students five minutes to write a conversation in which they use logically as many of the verbs of will and influence with the subjunctive as they can. After the time is up, ask pairs the number of subjunctive constructions using verbs of will and influence they used in their conversations. Have the top three or four perform their conversations for the whole class.

Comunicación

4 **Inventar** En parejas, preparen una lista de seis personas famosas. Un(a) estudiante da el nombre de una persona famosa y el/la otro/a le da un consejo. Answers will vary.

modelo

Estudiante 1: Judge Judy.
Estudiante 2: Le recomiendo que sea más simpática con la gente.
Estudiante 2: Leonardo DiCaprio.
Estudiante 1: Le aconsejo que haga más películas.

5 **Hablar** En parejas, miren la ilustración. Imaginen que Gerardo es su hermano y necesita ayuda para arreglar su casa y resolver sus problemas románticos y económicos. Usen expresiones impersonales y verbos como **aconsejar**, **sugerir** y **recomendar**. Answers will vary.

modelo

Es mejor que arregles el apartamento más a menudo.
Te aconsejo que no dejes para mañana lo que puedes hacer hoy.

Síntesis

6 **La doctora Salvamórez** Hernán tiene problemas con su novia y le escribe a la doctora Salvamórez, columnista del periódico *Panamá y su gente*. Ella responde a las cartas de personas con problemas románticos. En parejas, lean la carta de Hernán y después usen el subjuntivo para escribir los consejos de la doctora. Answers will vary.

Estimada doctora Salvamórez,

Mi novia nunca quiere que yo salga de casa. No le molesta que vengan mis amigos a visitarme. Pero insiste en que nosotros sólo miremos los programas de televisión que ella quiere. Necesita saber dónde estoy en cada momento, y yo necesito que ella me dé un poco de independencia. ¿Qué hago?

Hernán

4 Suggestion Ask volunteers to read the **modelo** aloud and provide other suggestions for Judge Judy and Leonardo DiCaprio.

4 Expansion Ask each pair to pick out their favorite response and share it with the class. Have everyone vote for the most clever, most shocking, or funniest suggestion.

5 Suggestion Before beginning the activity, project **Transparency #45** and ask volunteers to describe the drawing, naming everything they see and all the chores that need to be done.

5 Expansion Have students change partners and take turns playing the roles of Gerardo and one sibling giving him advice. Ex: **Te sugiero que pongas la pizza en la basura.**

6 Expansions

- Have pairs compare their responses in groups of four. Ask groups to choose which among all of the suggestions are the most likely to work for Hernán and have them share these with the class.
- Have pairs choose a famous couple in history or fiction. Ex: Romeo and Juliet or Napoleon and Josephine. Then have them write a letter from one of the couples to **doctora Salvamórez.** Finally, have them exchange their letters with another pair and write the corresponding responses from the doctor.

TEACHING OPTIONS

Heritage Speakers Have heritage speakers write a list of ten suggestions for other class members participating in an exchange program in their cultural communities. Their suggestions should focus on participating in daily life in their host family's home.

Large Group Write the names of famous historical figures on individual sticky notes and place them on the students' backs. The students should circulate around the room giving each other advice that will help them guess their "identity."

Section Goals

In **Lectura** students will:

- learn to locate the main parts of a sentence
- read a content-rich text with long sentences

Instructional Resource
Companion website: www.vistahigherlearning.com

Estrategia Tell students that if they have trouble reading long sentences in Spanish, they should pause to identify the main verb of the sentence and its subject. They should then reread the sentence in its entirety.

Examinar el texto Students should see from the layout (cover page with title, photo, and phone numbers; interior pages with an introduction and several headings followed by short paragraphs) that this is a brochure. Revealing cognates are: **información** (cover) and **residencia oficial del Presidente de Panamá** (introduction).

¿Probable o improbable? Ask volunteers to read aloud each item and give the answer. Have a volunteer rephrase the improbable statement so that it is probable.

Frases largas Ask pairs to suggest a couple of long sentences. Have them point out the main verb and subject.

Lectura

Antes de leer

Estrategia
Locating the main parts of a sentence

Did you know that a text written in Spanish is an average of 15% longer than the same text written in English? Because the Spanish language tends to use more words to express ideas, you will often encounter long sentences when reading in Spanish. Of course, the length of sentences varies with genre and with authors' individual styles. To help you understand long sentences, identify the main parts of the sentence before trying to read it in its entirety. First locate the main verb of the sentence, along with its subject, ignoring any words or phrases set off by commas. Then reread the sentence, adding details like direct and indirect objects, transitional words, and prepositional phrases.

Examinar el texto

Mira el formato de la lectura. ¿Qué tipo de documento es? ¿Qué cognados encuentras en la lectura? ¿Qué te dicen sobre el tema de la selección?

¿Probable o improbable?

Mira brevemente el texto e indica si las siguientes frases son probables o improbables.

1. Este folleto° es de interés turístico. probable
2. Describe un edificio moderno cubano. improbable
3. Incluye algunas explicaciones de arquitectura. probable
4. Espera atraer° a visitantes al lugar. probable

Frases largas

Mira el texto y busca algunas frases largas. Con un(a) compañero/a, identifiquen las partes principales de la frase y después examinen las descripciones adicionales. ¿Qué significan las frases?

folleto *brochure* atraer *to attract* épocas *time periods*

Bienvenidos al Palacio de Las Garzas

El palacio está abierto de martes a domingo.
Para más información,
llame al teléfono 507-226-7000.
También puede solicitar° un folleto
a la casilla° 3467,
Ciudad de Panamá, Panamá.

Después de leer

Ordenar

Pon los siguientes eventos en el orden cronológico adecuado.

__3__ El palacio se convirtió en residencia presidencial.
__2__ Durante diferentes épocas°, maestros, médicos y banqueros practicaron su profesión en el palacio.
__4__ El Dr. Belisario Porras ocupó el palacio por primera vez.
__1__ Los colonizadores construyeron el palacio.
__5__ Se renovó el palacio.
__6__ Los turistas pueden visitar el palacio de martes a domingo.

TEACHING OPTIONS

Heritage Speakers Ask heritage speakers to give a brief presentation about the official residence of the president of their home country. Tell them to include in their description recommendations to visitors about what rooms and objects are particularly noteworthy and should not be missed. If it is possible, they should illustrate their presentation with photographs or brochures.

Extra Practice Have students work in pairs to write ten suggestions, recommendations, or statements using the subjunctive for what their idea of a dream house **(la casa de mis sueños)** would be like. Ex: **Para mí es importante que haya una piscina de tamaño olímpico en la casa de mis sueños. Recomiendo que la cocina sea grande porque me gusta cocinar. Es necesario que tenga varias alcobas porque siempre tengo huéspedes.**

El Palacio de Las Garzas° es la residencia oficial del Presidente de Panamá desde 1903. Fue construido en 1673 para ser la casa de un gobernador español. Con el paso de los años fue almacén, escuela, hospital, aduana, banco y por último, palacio presidencial.

En la actualidad el edificio tiene tres pisos, pero los planos originales muestran una construcción de un piso con un gran patio en el centro. La restauración del palacio comenzó en el año 1922 y los trabajos fueron realizados por el arquitecto Villanueva-Myers y el pintor Roberto Lewis. El palacio, un monumento al estilo colonial, todavía conserva su elegancia y buen gusto, y es una de las principales atracciones turísticas del barrio Casco Viejo°.

Planta baja

El patio de las Garzas

Una antigua puerta de hierro° recibe a los visitantes. El patio interior todavía conserva los elementos originales de la construcción: piso de mármol°, columnas de perla gris y una magnífica fuente de agua en el centro. Aquí están las nueve garzas que le dan el nombre al palacio y que representan las nueve provincias de Panamá.

Primer piso

El salón Amarillo

Aquí el turista puede visitar una galería de cuarenta y un retratos° de gobernadores y personajes ilustres de Panamá. La principal atracción de este salón es el sillón presidencial, que se usa especialmente cuando hay cambio de presidente. Otros atractivos de esta área son el comedor de Los Tamarindos, que se destaca° por la elegancia de sus muebles y sus lámparas de cristal, y el patio andaluz, con sus coloridos mosaicos que representan la unión de la cultura indígena y la española.

El salón Dr. Belisario Porras

Este elegante y majestuoso salón es uno de los lugares más importantes del Palacio de Las Garzas. Lleva su nombre en honor al Dr. Belisario Porras, quien fue tres veces presidente de Panamá (1912–1916, 1918–1920 y 1920–1924).

Segundo piso

Es el área residencial del palacio y el visitante no tiene acceso a ella. Los armarios, las cómodas y los espejos de la alcoba fueron comprados en Italia y Francia por el presidente Porras, mientras que las alfombras, cortinas y frazadas° son originarias de España.

solicitar *request* casilla *post office box* Garzas *Herons*
Casco Viejo *Old Quarter* hierro *iron* mármol *marble* retratos *portraits*
se destaca *stands out* frazadas *blankets*

Ordenar Quickly go over the correct order by asking a volunteer to read the sentence he or she believes should be first, another volunteer to read the sentence that should be second, and so forth.

Preguntas Have students rewrite the questions as statements, incorporating the answers in them. Ex: **El comedor de Los Tamarindos es notable por sus muebles elegantes y sus lámparas de cristal.**

Conversación After groups have finished their conversations, encourage the whole class to talk about the three questions. Besides asking the questions in the text, ask: **¿En qué difiere el Palacio de Las Garzas de otras casas? ¿A quién no le gustaría vivir en el Palacio de Las Garzas? ¿Por qué? ¿Quién está de acuerdo?**

Preguntas

Contesta las preguntas.

1. ¿Qué sala es notable por sus muebles elegantes y sus lámparas de cristal? el comedor de Los Tamarindos
2. ¿En qué parte del palacio se encuentra la residencia del presidente? en el segundo piso
3. ¿Dónde empiezan los turistas su visita al palacio? en el patio de las Garzas
4. ¿En qué lugar se representa artísticamente la rica herencia cultural de Panamá? en el patio andaluz
5. ¿Qué salón honra la memoria de un gran panameño? el salón Dr. Belisario Porras
6. ¿Qué partes del palacio te gustaría más visitar? ¿Por qué? Explica tu respuesta. Answers will vary.

Conversación

En grupos de tres o cuatro estudiantes, hablen sobre lo siguiente: Answers will vary.

1. ¿Qué tiene en común el Palacio de Las Garzas con otras residencias presidenciales u otras casas muy grandes?
2. ¿Te gustaría vivir en el Palacio de Las Garzas? ¿Por qué?
3. Imagina que puedes diseñar tu palacio ideal. Describe los planos para cada piso del palacio.

TEACHING OPTIONS

Variación léxica Point out that **piso** is a multiple-meaning word that may mean *floor, flooring; apartment, flat;* or *story* (of a building). In Spanish, the **planta baja** of a building is its ground floor. The second story is called the **primer piso**; the third story is called the **segundo piso,** and so forth. The top floor in a building is called the **planta alta**. In the **Palacio de Las Garzas,** the **segundo piso** is also the **planta alta**.

Groups Ask students to work in groups of four or five to role-play a guided tour of the **Palacio de Las Garzas.** One group member plays the guide and the others play tourists. Encourage the guide to develop a script and the tourists to ask questions about the residence and its occupants. Give each group time to prepare and practice before performing their skit for the class.

Section Goals

In **Escritura** students will:
- learn to use linking words
- integrate **Lección 12** vocabulary and structures
- write a lease agreement

Estrategia Review the linking words. Point out that they are all words that students are familiar with. Ask volunteers to use a few of them in sentences.

Tema
- Review with students the details suggested for inclusion in the lease agreement. You may wish to present the following terms students can use in their agreements: **arrendatario** (*tenant*); **arrendador** (*landlord*); **propietario** (*owner*); **estipulaciones** (*stipulations*); **parte** (*party*); **de anticipación, de antelación** (*in advance*).
- Provide students with samples of legal documents in Spanish. (Many legal forms are downloadable from the Internet.) Go over the format of these documents with students, clarifying legal terminology as necessary.

Escritura

Estrategia

Using linking words

You can make your writing sound more sophisticated by using linking words to connect simple sentences or ideas and create more complex sentences. Consider the following passages, which illustrate this effect:

Without linking words

En la actualidad el edificio tiene tres pisos. Los planos originales muestran una construcción de un piso con un gran patio en el centro. La restauración del palacio comenzó en el año 1922. Los trabajos fueron realizados por el arquitecto Villanueva-Myers y el pintor Roberto Lewis.

With linking words

En la actualidad el edificio tiene tres pisos, pero los planos originales muestran una construcción de un piso con un gran patio en el centro. La restauración del palacio comenzó en el año 1922 y los trabajos fueron realizados por el arquitecto Villanueva-Myers y el pintor Roberto Lewis.

Linking words

cuando	*when*
mientras	*while*
pero	*but*
porque	*because*
pues	*since*
que	*that; who; which*
quien	*who*
sino	*but (rather)*
y	*and*
o	*or*

Tema

Escribir un contrato de arrendamiento

Eres el/la administrador(a)° de un edificio de apartamentos. Prepara un contrato de arrendamiento° para los nuevos inquilinos°. El contrato debe incluir los siguientes detalles:

- La dirección° del apartamento y del/de la administrador(a)
- Las fechas del contrato
- El precio del alquiler y el día que se debe pagar
- El precio del depósito
- Información y reglas° acerca de:
  - la basura
  - el correo
  - los animales domésticos
  - el ruido°
  - los servicios° de electricidad y agua
  - el uso de electrodomésticos
- Otros aspectos importantes de la vida comunitaria

administrador(a) *manager* contrato de arrendamiento *lease* inquilinos *tenants* dirección *address* reglas *rules* ruido *noise* servicios *utilities*

TEACHING OPTIONS

Proofreading Activity Copy the following sentences containing mistakes onto the board or a transparency as a proofreading activity to do with the whole class.

1. **El agente nos recomienda que buscamos una casa de las afueras, la que no me gusta nada.**
2. **Nuestros amigos Panameños acaban de encontrar en el centro lo qué buscaban.**
3. **¿Es ésta la casa de quien me hablaste el Lunes?**
4. **Es necesario que Uds. pasan al balcón para ver el océano pacífico.**
5. **Por favor, entran Uds. en la sala y observan que es grande.**
6. **Los martínez, quiénes conocieron ayer, son sus vecinos.**
7. **¿Sepan Uds. que el vecino del otro lado sea muy famoso?**

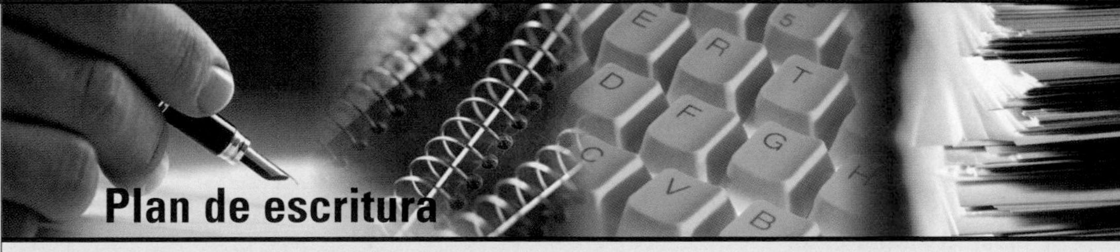

Plan de escritura

1 Ideas y organización

Después de pensar en el tema durante unos minutos, apunta tus ideas usando un mapa de ideas. Convierte el mapa en bosquejo° para asegurar la organización lógica de tu escrito.

2 Primer borrador

Utiliza tu bosquejo de **Ideas y organización** para escribir el primer borrador del contrato. Consulta tus apuntes de clase y las **Anotaciones para mejorar la escritura** en tu **Carpeta de trabajos** para no repetir errores previos.

3 Comentario

Intercambia el contrato con un(a) compañero/a. Lee su borrador y anota las partes mejor escritas de su composición, especialmente el uso de las palabras de enlace°. Compartan sus impresiones utilizando esta guía:

1. ¿Incluye toda la información pertinente?
2. ¿Hay una buena organización de los detalles específicos dentro del contrato?
3. ¿Emplea palabras de enlace para unir ideas y frases cortas?
4. ¿Qué sugerencias puedes darle al/a la escritor(a) para mejorar su documento?
5. ¿Ves errores gramaticales u ortográficos?

4 Redacción

Revisa el primer borrador según las indicaciones de tu compañero/a. Utiliza esta guía para hacer la última revisión antes de escribir tu versión final:

1. Utiliza palabras de enlace para unir las oraciones cortas.
2. Revisa la concordancia entre el sujeto y el verbo de cada oración.
3. Revisa la concordancia entre los sustantivos y los adjetivos.
4. Cuando es necesario, sustituye los sustantivos por pronombres u otro elemento gramatical para evitar la redundancia.
5. Consulta tus **Anotaciones para mejorar la escritura** antes de revisar la ortografía y la puntuación.

5 Evaluación y progreso

Trabaja con tres compañeros/as y lee sus trabajos. Después de escuchar atentamente las reglas de los "administradores", escoge las que, en tu opinión, garantizan una vida comunitaria tranquila°. Explica tu elección. No olvides leer atentamente los comentarios y las correcciones de tu profesor(a). Finalmente, anota los errores fundamentales en las **Anotaciones para mejorar la escritura** en tu **Carpeta de trabajos.**

bosquejo *outline* palabras de enlace *linking words* tranquila *calm; quiet*

Comentario

- Allow pairs five minutes for reading and commenting on their leases. Allow five minutes for discussing comments.
- Have students prepare **Redacción** for the next class.

Evaluación y progreso Give the class five minutes to exchange and comment on the final drafts of their leases. Then have them hand them in.

Writing Sample Here is an example of a lease that would constitute superior writing achievement.

Contrato de arrendamiento de vivienda

Arrendador: Don Fernando Cuevas

Arrendatarios: Don Rafael Calderón y doña Ana Ugarte de Calderón

OBJETO DEL CONTRATO: Don Fernando Cuevas, propietaro de los Apartamentos Las Brisas, Avenida Arenales 445, Colón, Panamá, alquila el apartamento 10 a los arrendatarios.

ESTIPULACIONES: La duración del contrato es de un año, comenzando el 15 de septiembre de 2004. El alquiler mensual es de $750,00, pagable el 15 de cada mes. Hay un depósito de $750,00. Los arrendatarios pagan por separado los gastos de electricidad y agua. Los lunes pasan para recoger la basura. No se permite ningún animal. Se prohíben ruidos después de las 10 de la noche.

En prueba de conformidad, ambas partes firman este contrato el primero de septiembre de 2004.

EVALUATION: Contrato

Criteria	Scale
Content	1 2 3 4
Organization	1 2 3 4
Use of vocabulary	1 2 3 4
Use of linking words	1 2 3 4
Grammatical accuracy	1 2 3 4

Scoring	
Excellent	18–20 points
Good	14–17 points
Satisfactory	10–13 points
Unsatisfactory	< 10 points

Section Goals

In **Escuchar** students will:

- use visual clues to help them understand an oral passage
- answer questions based on the content of a recorded conversation

Instructional Resources
Textbook CD
IRM: Tapescript, p. 96

Estrategia
Script En mi niñez lo pasé muy bien. Vivíamos en una pequeña casa en la isla Colón con vistas al mar. Pasaba las horas buceando alrededor de los arrecifes de coral. A veces me iba a pasear por las plantaciones de bananos o a visitar el pueblo de los indios guayamí. Otros días iba con mi hermano al mar en una pequeña lancha para pescar. Era una vida feliz y tranquila. Ahora vivo en la ciudad de Panamá. ¡Qué diferencia!

Suggestion Have students look at the drawing of a newspaper clipping. Ask them to describe what they see and read. Then have them guess the meaning of **Bienes raíces**.

Ahora escucha
Script ADRIANA: Mira, papá, tienen una sección especial de bienes raíces en el periódico. Felipe, mira esta casa... tiene un jardín enorme.
FELIPE: ¡Qué linda! ¡Uy, qué cara! ¿Qué piensa usted? ¿Debemos buscar una casa o un apartamento?
SR. NÚÑEZ: Bueno, hijos, hay muchas cosas que deben considerar. Primero, ¿les gustaría vivir en las afueras o en el centro de la ciudad?
F: Pues, señor Núñez, yo prefiero vivir en la ciudad. Así tenemos el teatro, los parques, los centros comerciales... todo cerca de casa. Sé que Adriana quiere vivir en las afueras porque es más tranquilo.
S: De todos modos van a necesitar un mínimo de dos alcobas, un baño, una sala grande... ¿Qué más?
A: Es importante que tengamos una oficina para mí y un patio para las plantas.

Escuchar

Estrategia

Using visual cues

Visual cues like illustrations and headings provide useful clues about what you will hear.

To practice this strategy, you will listen to a passage related to the following photo. Jot down the clues the photo gives you as you listen.

Preparación

Mira el dibujo. ¿Qué pistas te da para comprender la conversación que vas a escuchar? ¿Qué significa *bienes raíces*?

Ahora escucha 

Mira los anuncios de esta página y escucha la conversación entre el señor Núñez, Adriana y Felipe. Luego indica si cada descripción se refiere a la casa ideal de Adriana y Felipe, a la casa del anuncio° o al apartamento del anuncio.

Frases	La casa ideal	La casa del anuncio	El apartamento del anuncio
Es barato.	___	___	✔
Tiene cuatro alcobas.	___	✔	___
Tiene una oficina.	✔	___	___
Tiene un balcón.	___	___	✔
Tiene una cocina moderna.	___	✔	___
Tiene un jardín muy grande.	___	✔	___
Tiene un patio.	✔	___	___

18G

Bienes raíces

Se vende.
4 alcobas, 3 baños, cocina moderna, jardín con árboles frutales.
B/. 225.000

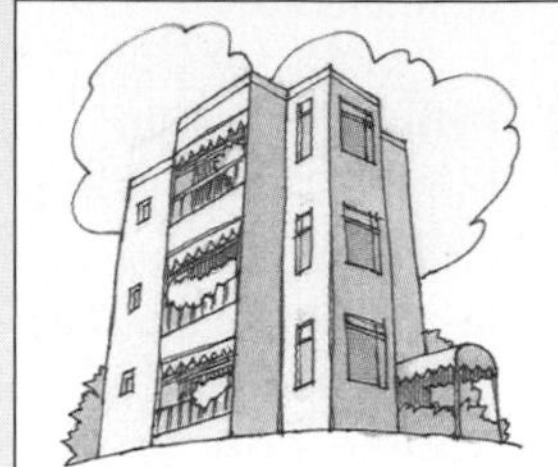

Se alquila.
2 alcobas, 1 baño.
Balcón. Urbanización Las Brisas. B/. 525

Comprensión

Preguntas

1. ¿Cuál es la relación entre el señor Núñez, Adriana y Felipe? ¿Cómo lo sabes? El Sr. Núñez es el padre de Adriana y Felipe es su esposo.
2. ¿Qué diferencia de opinión hay entre Adriana y Felipe sobre dónde quieren vivir? Felipe prefiere vivir en la ciudad, pero Adriana quiere vivir en las afueras.
3. Usa la información de los dibujos y la conversación para entender lo que dice Adriana al final. ¿Qué significa "todo a su debido tiempo"? Answers will vary.

Conversación En parejas, túrnense para hacer y responder a las preguntas. Answers will vary.

1. ¿Qué tienen en común el apartamento y la casa del anuncio con el lugar donde tú vives?
2. ¿Qué piensas de la recomendación del señor Núñez?
3. ¿Qué tipo de sugerencias te da tu familia sobre dónde vivir?
4. ¿Dónde prefieres vivir tú, en un apartamento o en una casa? Explica por qué.

anuncio *advertisement*

S: Como no tienen mucho dinero ahorrado, es mejor que alquilen un apartamento pequeño por un tiempo. Así pueden ahorrar su dinero para comprar la casa ideal. Miren este apartamento. Tiene un balcón precioso y está en un barrio muy seguro y bonito. Y el alquiler es muy razonable.

F: Adriana, me parece que tu padre tiene razón. Con un alquiler tan barato, podemos comprar muebles y también ahorrar dinero cada mes.
A: ¡Ay!, quiero mi casa. Pero, bueno, ¡todo a su debido tiempo!

Proyecto

Diseña una casa de vacaciones

Imagina que quieres construir° una casa de vacaciones en Panamá. Vas a decidir dónde quieres construir la casa y cómo va a ser.

1 Escribe una carta al contratista

Escribe una carta detallada° al contratista de obras°, explicando dónde vas a construir la casa, cómo va a ser y los muebles que quieres para la casa. Primero usa los **Recursos para la investigación** para decidir en qué ciudad o región de Panamá quieres construir la casa. Busca fotos del lugar que escojas. Comienza la carta con el encabezamiento° "Estimado/a Sr./Sra...." y concluye con "Atentamente" antes de tu firma°. Tu carta al contratista de obras puede incluir la siguiente información:

- una descripción de la ubicación° de la casa (selva°, isla, valle°, con vistas al mar, etc.)
- una explicación del tipo de casa que quieres (cuántos pisos, de madera°, de cemento, etc.)
- un plano° que tú dibujaste, incluyendo el nombre de cada cuarto de la casa
- una descripción de los muebles que debe llevar cada cuarto

2 Presenta la información a tus compañeros

Reúnete con 3 ó 4 compañeros/as. Prepara fotos y/o un mapa para mostrar dónde vas a construir la casa. Usa el plano para describirles la casa y todos los detalles especiales, incluyendo los muebles.

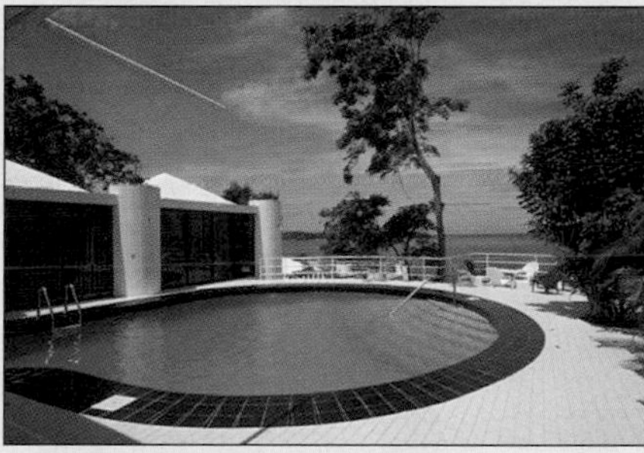

recursos para la investigación

Internet Palabras clave: Panamá, fotos, turismo, casas, bienes raíces

Comunidad Personas de Panamá, personas que saben de los estilos y materiales de construcción en Centroamérica

Biblioteca Mapas, enciclopedias, guías turísticas, revistas

Otros recursos revistas y folletos turísticos que se pueden recortar (*cut up*), anuncios de casas

construir *to build* detallada *detailed* contratista de obras *building contractor* encabezamiento *salutation* firma *signature* ubicación *location* selva *forest; jungle* valle *valley* madera *wood* plano *floor plan*

Section Goals

In **Proyecto** students will:

- use Spanish as they research and interact with the wider world
- write a letter to a contractor describing a house to be built

Suggestion Students might need a week to complete the project, so at the beginning of that time period, have them open their books to this page and glance over **Proyecto**. Tell them they are first going to write a letter to a contractor (**un contratista**) in Panama describing the type of vacation home they want to have built and its specifications.

Escribe una carta al contratista

- Provide samples of business letters in Spanish for students to use as models. Review the **saludo** (*salutation*), **cuerpo o texto de la carta** (*body of the letter*), and **despedida** (*closing*).
- Students may use freeware or shareware programs available on the Internet to design floor plans (**planos**).

Presenta la información a tus compañeros

- Students may be able to find a map of the area where they plan to build and create a transparency to be shown on an overhead projector.
- You may wish to set aside sufficient class time to do a few presentations at a time until all students have had a chance to present.

EVALUATION: Casa de vacaciones

Criteria	Scale
Content	1 2 3 4
Organization	1 2 3 4
Use of vocabulary	1 2 3 4
Use of linking words	1 2 3 4
Grammatical accuracy	1 2 3 4

Scoring	
Excellent	18–20 points
Good	14–17 points
Satisfactory	10–13 points
Unsatisfactory	< 10 points

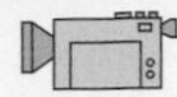

Section Goal

In **Panorama**, students will read about the geography and culture of Panama.

Instructional Resources
Transparencies, #3, #4, #46
WB/VM: Workbook, pp. 145–146; Video Activities, pp. 271–272
***Panorama cultural** DVD/Video*
Interactive CD-ROM
IRM: Videoscript, p. 132
Companion website: www.vistahigherlearning.com
Presentations CD-ROM

Suggestion Have students look at the map of Panama or project **Transparency #46** and discuss the physical features of the country. Point out the bodies of water that run along the coasts of Panama, and the canal that cuts through the isthmus **(istmo)**. Then, have students look at the call-out photos and read the captions. Point out that the Kuna people live on the San Blas islands in the Caribbean Sea.

El país en cifras Mention that the national currency, the balboa, is named for **Vasco Núñez de Balboa**, who explored the Isthmus of Panama in 1501. Tell students that **Chibcha** is a major indigenous language group, with dialects spoken by native people from central Colombia through eastern Nicaragua. After reading about the **Panameños célebres**, ask students to share what they know about the individuals listed and how they learned about them.

¡Increíble pero cierto! The opening of the Panama Canal not only dramatically reduced the distance ships had to travel to get from the Atlantic Ocean to the Pacific, it also provided a much safer route than the stormy, perilous route around Cape Horn and through the Straits of Magellan.

Panamá

El país en cifras

- **Área:** 78.200 km^2 (30.193 millas^2), *aproximadamente el área de Carolina del Sur*
- **Población:** 1.773.000
- **Capital:** La ciudad de Panamá —1.299.000
- **Ciudades principales:** Colón —138.000, David —125.000

SOURCE: Population Division, UN Secretariat

- **Moneda:** balboa; Es equivalente al dólar estadounidense.

En Panamá circulan los billetes de dólar estadounidense. El país centroamericano, sin embargo, acuña° sus propias monedas. "El peso" es una moneda grande equivalente a cincuenta centavos°. La moneda de cinco centavos es llamada frecuentemente "real".

- **Idiomas:** español (oficial), chibcha, inglés

La mayoría de los panameños es bilingüe. La lengua materna del 14% de los panameños es el inglés.

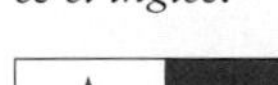

Bandera de Panamá

Panameños célebres

- **Rod Carew,** beisbolista (1945–)
- **Mireya Moscoso,** política (1947–)
- **Rubén Blades,** músico y político (1948–)

acuña *mints* centavos *cents* actualmente *currently* peaje *toll* promedio *average*

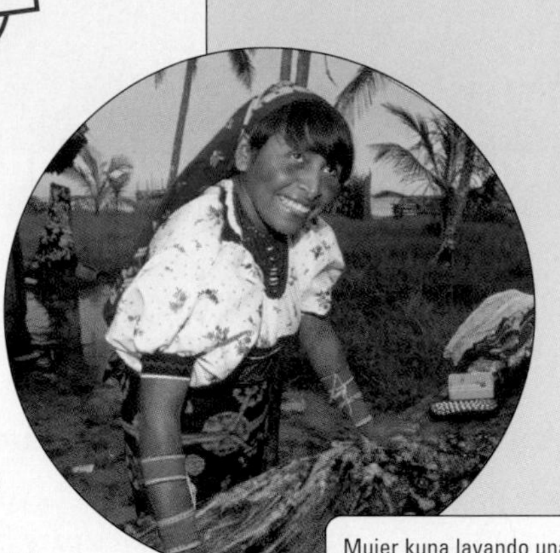

Mujer kuna lavando una mola

Un turista disfruta del bosque tropical colgado de un cable.

COSTA RICA
Lago Gatún
Canal de Panamá
Islas San Blas
Bocas del Toro
Mar Caribe
Colón
Cordillera de San Blas
Río Chepo
Serranía de Tabasarái
Ciudad de Panamá
David
Río Cobre
Isla del Rey
Océano Pacífico
Golfo de Panamá
Isla de Coiba
ESTADOS UNIDOS
OCÉANO ATLÁNTICO
PANAMÁ
AMÉRICA DEL SUR

Ruinas de un fuerte panameño

recursos

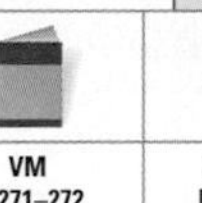			
WB pp. 145–146	VM p. 271–272	I CD-ROM Lección 12	vistahigher learning.com

¡Increíble pero cierto!

¿Conocías estos datos sobre el Canal de Panamá?

- Gracias al Canal de Panamá, el viaje en barco de Nueva York a Tokio es 3.000 millas más corto.
- Su construcción costó 639 millones de dólares.
- Actualmente° lo usan 38 barcos al día.
- El peaje° promedio° cuesta 40.000 dólares.

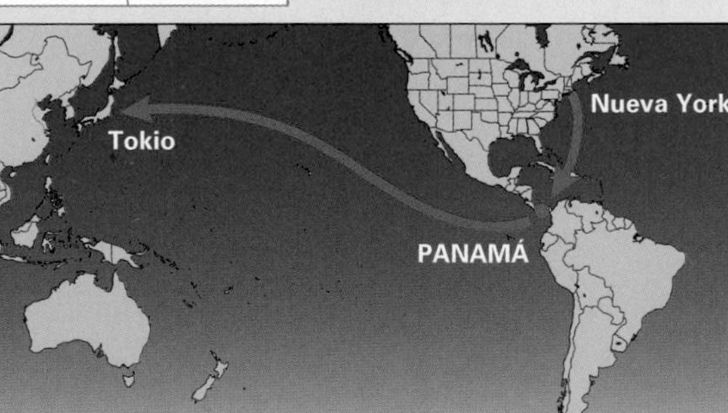

TEACHING OPTIONS

Heritage Speakers Invite Panamanian students or heritage speakers who have visited Panama to share information about language patterns there. Have these students talk about what languages they speak at home, what language is usually learned first, how English speakers acquire English, and so forth.

Extra Practice Rubén Blades changed the world of salsa music by introducing lyrics with social import into what had previously been simply dance music. If possible, bring in his recording ***Buscando América***, and have students listen to "**El Padre Antonio y su monaguillo Andrés,**" based on the story of Archbishop Romero of El Salvador. Or, listen to the story of "**Pedro Navaja**" on ***Siembra***, Blades's classic collaboration with Willie Colón. Have students write a summary of the song in English, or describe how Blades's salsa differs from traditional "romantic" salsa.

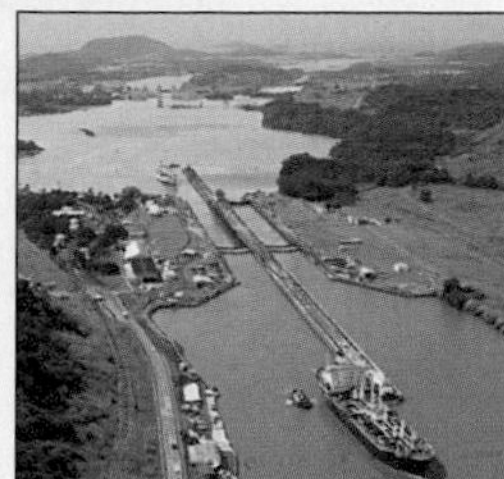

Lugares • El Canal de Panamá

El Canal de Panamá conecta el océano Pacífico con el océano Atlántico. Se empezó a construir en 1903 y se terminó diez años después. Es la fuente° principal de ingresos° del país, gracias al dinero que se recibe de los más de 12.000 buques° que pasan anualmente por el canal.

Artes • La mola

La mola es una forma de arte textil de los kunas, una tribu indígena que vive en las islas San Blas, en Panamá. Las molas se hacen con capas° y fragmentos de tela° de colores vivos°. Sus diseños son muchas veces abstractos, inspirados en las formas del coral. Las molas tradicionales son las más apreciadas y sus diseños son completamente geométricos. Antes sólo se usaban como ropa, pero hoy día también se usan para decorar las casas.

Deportes • El buceo

Panamá, cuyo° nombre significa "lugar de muchos peces°", es un sitio excelente para los aficionados del buceo, el buceo con esnórkel y la pesca. Las playas en los dos lados del istmo°, el mar Caribe a un lado y el océano Pacífico al otro, son muy variadas. Unas están destinadas al turismo y otras tienen un gran valor° ecológico, por la diversidad de su vida marina, abundante en arrecifes° de coral. En la playa Bluff, por ejemplo, se pueden observar cuatro especies de tortugas° en peligro° de extinción.

COLOMBIA

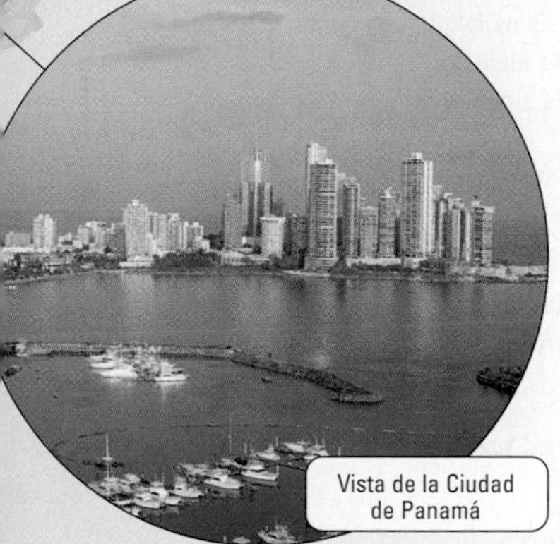

Vista de la Ciudad de Panamá

¿Qué aprendiste? Responde a las preguntas con una frase completa.

1. ¿Cuál es la lengua materna del catorce por ciento de los panameños?
   El inglés es la lengua materna del catorce por ciento de los panameños.
2. ¿A qué unidad monetaria (*monetary unit*) es equivalente el balboa?
   El balboa es equivalente al dólar estadounidense.
3. ¿Qué océanos une el Canal de Panamá?
   El Canal de Panamá une los océanos Atlántico y Pacífico.
4. ¿Quién es Rubén Blades?
   Rubén Blades es un músico y político panameño.
5. ¿Qué son las molas?
   Las molas son una forma de arte textil común entre los kunas.
6. ¿Cómo son los diseños de las molas?
   Sus diseños son abstractos.
7. ¿Para qué se usaban las molas antes?
   Las molas se usaban como ropa.
8. ¿Cómo son las playas de Panamá?
   Son muy variadas; unas están destinadas al turismo, otras tienen valor ecológico.
9. ¿Qué significa "Panamá"?
   "Panamá" significa "lugar de muchos peces".

Conexión Internet Investiga estos temas en el sitio **www.vistahigherlearning.com.**

1. Investiga la historia de las relaciones entre Panamá y los Estados Unidos y la decisión de devolver (*give back*) el Canal de Panamá. ¿Estás de acuerdo con la decisión? Explica tu opinión.
2. Investiga los kunas u otro grupo indígena de Panamá. ¿En qué partes del país viven? ¿Qué lenguas hablan? ¿Cómo es su cultura?

fuente *source* ingresos *income* buques *ships* capas *layers* tela *fabric* vivos *bright* cuyo *whose* peces *fish* istmo *isthmus* valor *value* arrecifes *reefs* tortugas *turtles* peligro *danger*

El Canal de Panamá The Panama Canal is a lake-and-lock type of canal, connecting the Atlantic and Pacific oceans at one of the lowest points on the Continental Divide. It is about 40 miles long and is one of the two most strategic waterways on earth (the Suez Canal is the other).

La mola The Kuna people originally lived on mainland Panama, but preferred to move to the San Blas islands, where they could maintain their way of life. Elaborate traditions accompany every life-cycle event in Kuna culture, and many of these ceremonies are depicted on the elaborate appliqué **molas**, which are the pride of the Kuna women.

El buceo An excellent place for diving in Panama is the **Parque Nacional Bastimentos**, in the **Archipiélago de Bocas del Toro**. In this nature reserve, turtles nest on some of the beaches. Its coral reefs are home to more than 200 species of tropical fish, in addition to lobsters and other sea life; manatees also inhabit these waters. The park is also known for its mangroves, which offer snorkelers another aquatic experience.

Conexión Internet Students will find supporting Internet activities and links at **www.vistahigherlearning.com**.

TEACHING OPTIONS

Worth Noting The Kuna people have a strong, rich oral tradition. During regular community meetings, ritual forms of speaking, including storytelling and speeches, are presented by community elders. It is only over the past decade that a written form of the Kuna language has been developed by outsiders. However, as Spanish—and even English—begin to encroach more and more into Kuna Yala (the Kuna name for their homeland), linguistic anthropologists have highlighted the urgency of recording and preserving the rich Kuna oral tradition, fearing that the traditional Kuna language and culture will begin to be diluted by outside influences.

Instructional Resources
Vocabulary CD
Lab Manual, p. 72
*Lab CD/MP3 **Lección 12***
IRM: Tapescript, pp. 54–58
*Testing Program: **Pruebas**, pp. 133–144; **Exámenes**, pp. 253–263*
Testing Program Audio CD
Test Files CD-ROM

Las viviendas

las afueras	*suburbs; outskirts*
el alquiler	*rent (payment)*
el ama (*m., f.*) de casa	*housekeeper; caretaker*
el barrio	*neighborhood*
el edificio de apartamentos	*apartment building*
el/la vecino/a	*neighbor*
la vivienda	*housing*
alquilar	*to rent*
mudarse	*to move (from one house to another)*

Los cuartos y otros lugares

la alcoba, el dormitorio	*bedroom*
el altillo	*attic*
el balcón	*balcony*
la cocina	*kitchen*
el comedor	*dining room*
el cuarto	*room*
la entrada	*entrance*
la escalera	*stairs; stairway*
el garaje	*garage*
el jardín	*garden; yard*
la oficina	*office*
el pasillo	*hallway*
el patio	*patio; yard*
la sala	*living room*
el sótano	*basement; cellar*

Los muebles y otras cosas

la alfombra	*carpet; rug*
la almohada	*pillow*
el armario	*closet*
el cartel	*poster*
la cómoda	*chest of drawers*
las cortinas	*curtains*
el cuadro	*picture*
el estante	*bookcase; bookshelves*
la lámpara	*lamp*
la luz	*light; electricity*
la manta	*blanket*
la mesita	*end table*
la mesita de noche	*night stand*
los muebles	*furniture*
la pared	*wall*
la pintura	*painting; picture*
el sillón	*armchair*
el sofá	*couch; sofa*

Los electrodomésticos

la cafetera	*coffee maker*
la cocina, la estufa	*stove*
el congelador	*freezer*
el electrodoméstico	*electric appliance*
el horno (de microondas)	*(microwave) oven*
la lavadora	*washing machine*
el lavaplatos	*dishwasher*
el refrigerador	*refrigerator*
la secadora	*clothes dryer*
la tostadora	*toaster*

La mesa

la copa	*wineglass; goblet*
la cuchara	*(table or large) spoon*
el cuchillo	*knife*
el plato	*plate*
la servilleta	*napkin*
la taza	*cup*
el tenedor	*fork*
el vaso	*glass*

Los quehaceres domésticos

arreglar	*to neaten; to straighten up*
barrer el suelo	*to sweep the floor*
cocinar	*to cook*
ensuciar	*to get (something) dirty*
hacer la cama	*to make the bed*
hacer quehaceres domésticos	*to do household chores*
lavar (el suelo, los platos)	*to wash (the floor, the dishes)*
limpiar la casa	*to clean the house*
pasar la aspiradora	*to vacuum*
planchar la ropa	*to iron the clothes*
poner la mesa	*to set the table*
quitar la mesa	*to clear the table*
sacar la basura	*to take out the trash*
sacudir los muebles	*to dust the furniture*

Verbos y expresiones verbales

aconsejar	*to advise*
insistir (en)	*to insist (on)*
mandar	*to order*
recomendar (e:ie)	*to recommend*
rogar (o:ue)	*to beg; to plead*
sugerir (e:ie)	*to suggest*
Es bueno que...	*It's good that...*
Es importante que...	*It's important that...*
Es malo que...	*It's bad that...*
Es mejor que...	*It's better that...*
Es necesario que...	*It's necessary that...*
Es urgente que...	*It's urgent that...*

Relative pronouns	*See page 370.*
Expresiones útiles	*See page 367.*

recursos

	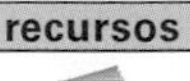	
LM p. 72	Lab CD/MP3 Lección 12	Vocab CD Lección 12

La naturaleza

13

Communicative Goals

You will learn how to:

- **Talk about and discuss the environment**
- **Express your beliefs and opinions about issues**

contextos

pages 396–399
- Nature
- The environment
- Recycling and conservation

fotonovela

pages 400–403

Don Francisco introduces the students to Martín, who will be their guide as they hike to the volcano. Martín takes the students to where they will be hiking and talks to them about what they will be seeing.

estructura

pages 404–415
- The subjunctive with verbs of emotion
- The subjunctive with doubt, disbelief, and denial
- The subjunctive with conjunctions

adelante

pages 416–421

Lectura: Read a poem.
Escritura: Write to a friend, newspaper, or magazine.
Escuchar: Listen to a speech about the environment.
Proyecto: Write a letter to a government official.

panorama

pages 422–423

Featured country: Colombia
- The gold museum
- Gabriel García Márquez
- Cartagena de Indias

A PRIMERA VISTA

- *¿Son estas personas excursionistas?*
- *¿Es importante que usen zapatos deportivos?*
- *¿Se llevan bien o mal?*
- *¿Se divierten o no?*

Lesson Goals

In **Lección 13** students will be introduced to the following:
- terms to describe nature and the environment
- conservation and recycling terms
- subjunctive with verbs and expressions of emotion
- subjunctive with verbs and expressions of doubt, disbelief, and denial
- expressions of certainty
- subjunctive with conjunctions
- when the infinitive follows a conjunction
- recognizing the purpose of a text
- considering audience and purpose when writing
- writing a persuasive letter or article
- using background knowledge and context to guess meaning
- writing a letter in the role of an environmental activist
- cultural, geographic, and historical information about Colombia

A primera vista Here are some additional questions you can ask based on the photo: **¿Vives en la ciudad? ¿En las afueras? ¿En el campo? ¿Te gusta pasar tiempo fuera de la casa? ¿Por qué? ¿Tienes algún pasatiempo? ¿Cuál? ¿Dónde lo practicas? ¿Puedes escalar montañas? ¿Te gusta acampar? ¿Dónde puedes hacer estas actividades? ¿Adónde prefieres ir de vacaciones?**

INSTRUCTIONAL RESOURCES

Workbook/Video Manual: WB Activities, pp. 149–158
Laboratory Manual: Lab Activities, pp. 73–77
Workbook/Video Manual: Video Activities, pp. 237–238; pp. 273–274
Instructor's Resource Manual: **Vocabulario adicional**, p. 191; **¡Inténtalo!** & **Práctica** Answers, p. 219; **Fotonovela** Translations, p. 146; Textbook CD Tapescript, p. 97; Lab CDs Tapescript, pp. 59–62; **Fotonovela** Videoscript, pp. 117–118; **Panorama cultural** Videoscript, p. 133
Info Gap Activities Booklet, pp. 49–52
Overhead Transparencies: #5, #6, #47, #48, #49
Lab Audio CD/MP3 **Lección 13**
Panorama cultural DVD/Video
Fotonovela DVD/Video
Testing Program, pp. 145–156
Testing Program Audio CD
Test Files CD-ROM
Companion website
Presentations CD-ROM
Textbook CD
Vocabulary CD
Interactive CD-ROM
Video CD-ROM
Web-SAM

Section Goals

In **Contextos** students will learn and practice:
- terms to describe nature
- conservation terms

Instructional Resources
Transparencies, #47, #48
Textbook CD
Vocabulary CD
WB/VM: Workbook, pp. 149–150
Lab Manual, p. 73
Lab CD/MP3 ***Lección 13***
IRM: ***Vocab. adicional****, p. 191;*
Práctica *Answers, p. 219;*
Tapescript, pp. 59–62; p. 97
Interactive CD-ROM
Companion website:
www.vistahigherlearning.com
Presentations CD-ROM

Suggestions

- Write the headings **la naturaleza** and **la conservación** on the board, asking students to guess what they mean. Then, have two volunteers come to the board and write down all the English words the class can brainstorm pertaining to nature and conservation. After the class has produced at least 15 words under each heading, have students look in their texts to see how many of their Spanish equivalents they can find.
- Project **Transparency #47.** Point to vocabulary items illustrated and ask volunteers to identify each item. Then begin a conversation by asking personalized questions that recycle the items already covered and introduce those in **Más vocabulario.** Ex: **¿Cuáles son los recursos naturales de nuestra región? ¿Adónde van ustedes para hacer un picnic? ¿Cuáles son los problemas de contaminación del medio ambiente de nuestra región?**

Note: At this point you may want to present **Vocabulario adicional: Más vocabulario para la naturaleza**, from the IRM.

La naturaleza

Más vocabulario

el animal	*animal*
el bosque (tropical)	*(tropical; rain) forest*
el desierto	*desert*
la naturaleza	*nature*
la planta	*plant*
la región	*region; area*
la selva, la jungla	*jungle*
la tierra	*land; soil*
el cielo	*sky*
la estrella	*star*
la luna	*moon*
el mundo	*world*
la conservación	*conservation*
la contaminación (del aire; del agua)	*(air; water) pollution*
la deforestación	*deforestation*
la ecología	*ecology*
el ecoturismo	*ecotourism*
la energía (nuclear; solar)	*(nuclear; solar) energy*
la extinción	*extinction*
la lluvia (ácida)	*(acid) rain*
el medio ambiente	*environment*
el peligro	*danger*
el recurso natural	*natural resource*
la solución	*solution*
el gobierno	*government*
la ley	*law*
la población	*population*
puro/a	*pure*

Variación léxica

césped ←→ pasto (*Perú*); grama (*Venez., Col.*); zacate (*Méx.*)

recursos

TEXT CD	WB	LM	Lab CD/MP3	I CD-ROM	Vocab CD
Lección 13	pp. 149–150	p. 73	Lección 13	Lección 13	Lección 13

el ave, el pájaro
el cráter
el volcán
el pez
la vaca
el árbol
el césped, la hierba
el perro
el gato

TEACHING OPTIONS

Variación léxica Tell students that they might see **hierba** spelled **yerba**. In either case, the pronunciation is the same. Ask heritage speakers what word is used for *grass* or *lawn* in their home country. Invite them also to think of other things found in nature that have more than one name. Ex: **culebra/serpiente/víbora** (*snake*); **piedra/roca** (*rock*); **bosque tropical/selva tropical** (*rain forest*).

Extra Practice Whisper a vocabulary word into a student's ear. That student should draw on the board a picture or pictures that explain the word. The class must guess the word, call it out, then spell it in Spanish as the volunteer writes it on the board.

Práctica

1 Escuchar Mientras escuchas las frases, anota los sustantivos (*nouns*) que se refieren a las plantas, los animales, la tierra y el cielo.

Plantas	Animales	Tierra	Cielo
flores	perro	valle	sol
hierba	gatos	volcán	nubes
árboles	vacas	bosque tropical	estrellas

2 Seleccionar Selecciona la palabra que no está relacionada con cada grupo.

1. estrella • gobierno • luna • sol gobierno
2. gatos • peces • perros • hierba hierba
3. contaminación • extinción • ecoturismo • deforestación ecoturismo
4. lago • río • mar • peligro • peligro
5. vaca • gato • pájaro • población población
6. conservación • lluvia ácida • ecología • recurso natural lluvia ácida
7. cielo • cráter • aire • nube cráter
8. desierto • solución • selva • bosque solución
9. nube • cielo • lluvia • piedra piedra
10. flor • césped • sendero • árbol sendero

3 Definir Trabaja con un(a) compañero/a para definir o describir cada palabra. Sigue el modelo. Answers will vary.

modelo

Estudiante 1: *¿Qué es el cielo?*
Estudiante 2: *El cielo está sobre la tierra y tiene nubes.*

1. la población
2. un valle
3. la lluvia
4. la naturaleza
5. un desierto
6. la extinción
7. la ecología
8. un sendero

4 Describir Trabajen en parejas para describir las siguientes fotos. Answers will vary.

1 Suggestion Check the answers orally with the whole class.

1 Tapescript 1. Mi novio siempre me compra flores para nuestro aniversario. 2. Cuando era pequeño jugaba con mi perro todo el tiempo. 3. Javier prefiere jugar al fútbol norteamericano sobre hierba natural. 4. Antes de las vacaciones, los estudiantes tomaban el sol en el parque. 5. No puedo visitarte porque soy alérgico a los gatos. 6. Durante la tormenta, las nubes grises cubrían toda la ciudad. 7. Cerca de la casa de mi hermana hay un valle donde siempre hay muchas vacas. 8. Algunas noches vamos al campo para ver las estrellas. 9. El Puracé es un volcán activo en los Andes colombianos. 10. Los árboles de los bosques tropicales contienen las curas para muchas enfermedades.
Textbook CD

2 Suggestion Have students give answers and state a category for each group. Ex: **1. Cosas que están en el cielo.**

3 Expansion Have pairs read their definitions aloud in random order for the class to guess which term is being described.

4 Suggestion Have pairs include the following in the descriptions: objects in the photos, the colors, what the weather is like, the time of day, the country where the photo was taken. Ask students to pick a description to present to the class.

4 Expansion Ask students to imagine the photos were taken on a recent vacation. Have them write a brief essay about their vacation, incorporating their descriptions.

TEACHING OPTIONS

TPR Make a series of true-false statements related to the lesson theme using the vocabulary. Tell students to remain seated if a statement is true and to stand if it is false. Ex: **A los gatos les gusta nadar en los lagos.** (Students stand.) **Los carros son responsables en parte de la contaminación del aire.** (Students remain seated.)

Game Have students fold a sheet of paper into 16 squares (four folds in half) and choose one vocabulary word to write in each square. Call out definitions for the vocabulary words. If students have the defined word, they mark their paper. The first student to mark four words in a row (across, down, or diagonally) calls out "**Loto.**" The student then reads his or her words to check if the definitions have been given.

Suggestion Involve students in a discussion about recycling and conservation. Project **Transparency #48** and ask volunteers to describe what is happening in the drawing. Ask: **¿Quién me quiere describir lo que se ve en la ilustración? ¿Qué hace la señora de la izquierda? (Recicla una lata de aluminio.)** Cover the active vocabulary, then guide the conversation toward students' own experiences and opinions. Ask questions like the following: **¿Tiene un buen programa de reciclaje nuestra ciudad? ¿Qué hacen ustedes para reducir la contaminación del medio ambiente? ¿Qué hace la universidad? ¿Cómo estamos afectados por la contaminación en nuestra ciudad/región? ¿Cuál es el mayor problema ecológico de nuestra región? ¿Qué evitan ustedes por razones ecológicas?**

5 Expansions

- Ask questions that require students to recycle the activity vocabulary. Ex: **¿Qué debemos hacer para mantener las calles limpias de basura? ¿Para qué trabajan los científicos? ¿Por qué es necesario que trabajemos para proteger el medio ambiente?**
- Have students write five more original sentences, using different forms of the verbs. Ask volunteers to share their sentences with the class.

Recicla la lata de aluminio. (reciclar)
el envase de plástico
Recoge la botella de vidrio. (recoger)

El reciclaje

Más vocabulario

cazar	*to hunt*
conservar	*to conserve*
contaminar	*to pollute*
controlar	*to control*
cuidar	*to take care of*
dejar de (+ *inf.*)	*to stop (doing something)*
desarrollar	*to develop*
descubrir	*to discover*
destruir	*to destroy*
estar afectado/a (por)	*to be affected (by)*
estar contaminado/a	*to be polluted*
evitar	*to avoid*
mejorar	*to improve*
proteger	*to protect*
reducir	*to reduce*
resolver (o:ue)	*to resolve; to solve*
respirar	*to breathe*

5 **Completar** Selecciona la palabra o la expresión adecuada para completar cada frase.

contaminar	se desarrollaron	resolver
controlan	descubrir	recoger
destruyen	están afectadas	cuidan
reciclamos	proteger	mejoramos

1. Si vemos basura en las calles, la debemos ___recoger___.
2. Los científicos trabajan para ___descubrir___ nuevas soluciones.
3. Es necesario que todos trabajemos juntos para ___resolver___ los problemas del medio ambiente.
4. Debemos ___proteger___ el medio ambiente porque hoy día está en peligro.
5. Muchas leyes nuevas ___controlan___ el número de árboles que se puede cortar (*cut down*).
6. Las primeras civilizaciones ___se desarrollaron___ cerca de los ríos y los mares.
7. Todas las personas del mundo ___están afectadas___ por la contaminación.
8. Los turistas deben tener cuidado de no ___contaminar___ las regiones que visitan.
9. Podemos conservar los recursos si ___reciclamos___ el aluminio, el vidrio y el plástico.
10. La lluvia ácida, la contaminación y la deforestación ___destruyen___ el medio ambiente.

TEACHING OPTIONS

Pairs Have pairs of students write each vocabulary word from this page on index cards. Pairs then shuffle the cards and take turns drawing from the stack. The student who draws a card then must make a comment about conservation or the environment, using the word he or she has drawn. One partner writes down the other partner's comment. After students finish the stack, call on volunteers to share their comments.

Small Groups Divide the class into groups of three or four. Have each group make a list of eight environmental problems in the region. Ask groups to trade lists. Have them write solutions to the problems on the list they receive, and then give the lists back to the original group. After reading the solutions, the original groups should give reasons why the solutions are good or not.

Comunicación

6 **¿Es importante?** Lee el siguiente párrafo y después contesta las preguntas con un(a) compañero/a. Some answers will vary.

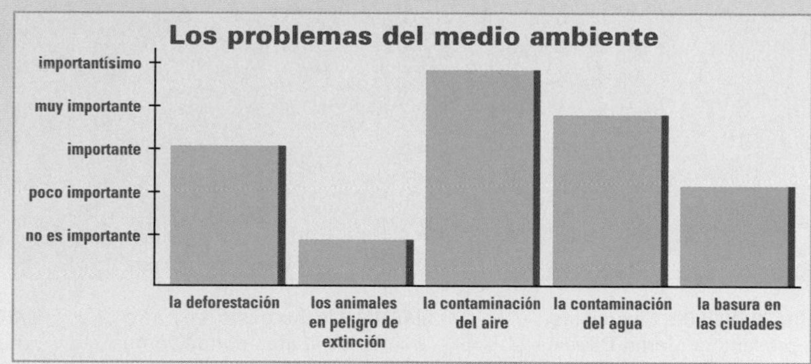

Para celebrar El día de la tierra, una estación de radio colombiana hizo una pequeña encuesta (*survey*) entre estudiantes universitarios, donde les preguntaron sobre los problemas del medio ambiente. Se les preguntó cuáles creían que eran los cinco problemas más importantes del medio ambiente. Ellos también tenían que decidir el orden de importancia de estos problemas, del uno al cinco.

Los resultados probaron (*proved*) que la mayoría de los estudiantes están preocupados por la contaminación del aire. Muchos mencionaron que no hay aire puro en las ciudades. El problema número dos para los estudiantes es que los ríos y los lagos están afectados por la contaminación. La deforestación quedó como el problema número tres, la basura en las ciudades el número cuatro y los animales en peligro de extinción el número cinco.

1. ¿Según la encuesta, qué problema consideran más grave? ¿Qué problema consideran menos grave? la contaminación del aire; los animales en peligro de extinción
2. ¿Cómo creen que se puede evitar o resolver el problema más importante?
3. ¿Es necesario resolver el problema menos importante? ¿Por qué?
4. ¿Consideran ustedes que existen los mismos problemas en su comunidad? Den algunos ejemplos.

7 **Situaciones** Trabajen en grupos pequeños para representar las siguientes situaciones. Answers will vary.

1. Un(a) representante de una agencia ambiental (*environmental*) habla con el/la presidente/a de una compañía industrial que está contaminando un río o el aire.
2. Un(a) guía de ecoturismo habla con un grupo sobre cómo disfrutar (*enjoy*) de la naturaleza y conservar el medio ambiente.
3. Un(a) representante de la universidad habla con un grupo de nuevos estudiantes sobre la campaña (*campaign*) ambiental de la universidad y trata de reclutar (*tries to recruit*) miembros para un club que trabaja para la protección del medio ambiente.

8 **Escribir una carta** Trabajen en parejas para escribir una carta a una empresa real o imaginaria que esté contaminando el medio ambiente. Expliquen las consecuencias que sus acciones van a tener para el medio ambiente. Sugiéranle algunas ideas para que solucionen el problema. Utilicen por lo menos diez palabras de **Contextos**.
Answers will vary.

6 Expansion Divide the class into groups of five to discuss follow-up questions 2–4. Groups should reach a consensus for each question, then report to the class.

7 Suggestion Divide the class into groups of three. Have each group choose a situation, but make sure that all situations are covered. Have students take turns playing each role. After groups have had time to prepare their situations, invite some of them to present them to the class.

8 Suggestions
- Remind students that a business letter in Spanish begins with a salutation such as **Estimado(s) señor(es)** and ends with a closing such as **Atentamente**.
- With the whole class, brainstorm a list of companies that are known to have had environmental problems. Ask the class to categorize the companies by what they produce and the problems they cause. Then divide the class into pairs and have them choose a company.

TEACHING OPTIONS

Heritage Speakers Ask heritage speakers to interview family members or people in their community about the environmental challenges in the region they come from. Encourage them to find out how the problems impact the land and the people. Have students report their findings to the class.

Large Groups Write environmental problems and possible solutions on separate index cards. Ex: **la destrucción de los bosques tropicales—limitar el número de árboles que se cortan; la contaminación de los ríos—reducir la cantidad de sustancias químicas vertidas en el agua**. Hand the cards out to students. Students with problem cards ask their classmates questions until they find a viable solution.

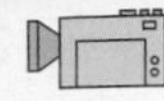

Section Goals
In **Fotonovela** students will:
- receive comprehensible input from free-flowing discourse
- learn functional phrases that preview lesson grammatical structures

Instructional Resources
WB/VM: Video Activities, pp. 237–238
***Fotonovela** DVD/Video (Start 01:10:38)*
Video CD-ROM
*IRM: **Fotonovela** Translations, p. 146, Videoscript, pp. 117–118*
Interactive CD-ROM

Video Recap: Lección 12
Before doing this **Fotonovela** section, review the previous one with this activity.
1. ¿Quién es la señora Vives? (el ama de casa)
2. ¿Qué muebles tiene la alcoba de los chicos? (dos camas, una mesita de noche, una cómoda, un armario)
3. ¿Qué quiere don Francisco que hagan los chicos? (quiere que ayuden a la señora Vives con los quehaceres domésticos)
4. ¿Por qué les aconseja don Francisco a los chicos que se acuesten temprano? (porque Martín, el guía, viene a las siete de la mañana)

Video Synopsis Don Francisco introduces the students to Martín, who will be their guide on the hike. Martín takes the students to the site of the hike, where they discuss the need for environmental protection.

Suggestions
- Have your students scan this **Fotonovela** episode and list words related to nature and the environment. Then have them predict what will happen in this episode. Write down their predictions.
- Quickly review the guesses your students made about the **Fotonovela**. Through discussion, guide the class to a correct summary of the plot.

¡Qué paisaje más hermoso!

NATIONAL STANDARDS communication cultures

Martín y los estudiantes visitan el sendero en las montañas.

PERSONAJES

MAITE

INÉS

DON FRANCISCO

ÁLEX

JAVIER

MARTÍN

1

DON FRANCISCO Chicos, les presento a Martín Dávalos, el guía de la excursión. Martín, nuestros pasajeros—Maite, Javier, Inés y Álex.

2

MARTÍN Mucho gusto. Voy a llevarlos al área donde vamos a ir de excursión mañana. ¿Qué les parece?

ESTUDIANTES ¡Sí! ¡Vamos!

3

MAITE ¡Qué paisaje más hermoso!

INÉS No creo que haya lugares más bonitos en el mundo.

6

JAVIER Entiendo que mañana vamos a cruzar un río. ¿Está contaminado?

MARTÍN En las montañas el río no parece estar afectado por la contaminación. Cerca de las ciudades, sin embargo, el río tiene bastante contaminación.

7

ÁLEX ¡Qué aire tan puro se respira aquí! No es como en la Ciudad de México... Tenemos un problema gravísimo de contaminación.

MARTÍN A menos que resuelvan ese problema, los habitantes van a sufrir muchas enfermedades en el futuro.

8

INÉS Creo que todos debemos hacer algo para proteger el medio ambiente.

MAITE Yo creo que todos los países deben establecer leyes que controlen el uso de automóviles.

recursos

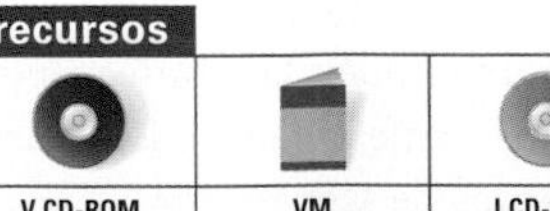

V CD-ROM Lección 13	VM pp. 237–238	I CD-ROM Lección 13

TEACHING OPTIONS

Video Tips General suggestions for using video clips in the classroom can be found on page IAE-12 of this Instructor's Annotated Edition.

¡Qué paisaje más hermoso! Play the video episode and have your students give you a "play-by-play" description of the action. Write their descriptions on the board. Then replay it, asking the class to list any key words they hear. Write some of their key words on the board. Finally, discuss the material on the board with the class and guide the class toward a correct summary of the plot.

MARTÍN Esperamos que ustedes se diviertan mucho, pero es necesario que cuiden la naturaleza.

JAVIER Se pueden tomar fotos, ¿verdad?

MARTÍN Sí, con tal de que no toques las flores o las plantas.

ÁLEX ¿Hay problemas de contaminación en esta región?

MARTÍN La contaminación es un problema en todo el mundo. Pero aquí tenemos un programa de reciclaje. Si ves por el sendero botellas, papeles o latas, recógelos.

JAVIER Pero Maite, ¿tú vas a dejar de usar tu carro en Madrid?

MAITE Pues voy a tener que usar el metro... Pero tú sabes que mi coche es tan pequeñito... casi no contamina nada.

INÉS ¡Ven, Javier!

JAVIER ¡¡Ya voy!!

Enfoque cultural El ecoturismo

La contaminación es un problema en todo el mundo, incluyendo los países hispanohablantes. Sin embargo (*However*), el ecoturismo enseña a los turistas y a los habitantes de las regiones turísticas la importancia de cuidar el medio ambiente. El ecoturismo es muy popular en los bosques tropicales de países como Costa Rica y Perú, donde hay animales y plantas que están en peligro de extinción. Gracias al ecoturismo, los dueños de las tiendas de estas zonas turísticas son sus mismos habitantes, lo cual evita que el turismo altere estas regiones.

Expresiones útiles

Talking about the environment

- ▶ **¿Hay problemas de contaminación en esta región?**
  Are there problems with pollution in this region/area?
- ▷ **La contaminación es un problema en todo el mundo.**
  Pollution is a problem throughout the world.

- ▶ **¿Está contaminado el río?**
  Is the river polluted?
- ▷ **En las montañas el río no parece estar afectado por la contaminación.**
  In the mountains, the river does not seem to be affected by pollution.
- ▷ **Cerca de las ciudades el río tiene bastante contaminación.**
  Near the cities, the river is pretty polluted.

- ▶ **¡Qué aire tan puro se respira aquí!**
  The air you breathe here is so pure!
- ▶ **Puedes tomar fotos, con tal de que no toques las plantas.**
  You can take pictures, provided that you don't touch the plants.
- ▶ **Es necesario que cuiden la naturaleza.**
  It's necessary that you take care of nature/respect the environment.
- ▶ **Tenemos un problema gravísimo de contaminación.**
  We have an extremely serious problem with pollution.
- ▶ **A menos que resuelvan el problema, los habitantes van a sufrir muchas enfermedades.**
  Unless they solve the problem, the inhabitants are going to suffer many illnesses.
- ▶ **Tenemos un programa de reciclaje.**
  We have a recycling program.
- ▶ **Si ves por el sendero botellas, papeles o latas, recógelos.**
  If you see bottles, papers, or cans along the trail, pick them up.

Suggestions

- Continue the conversation that you began in **Contextos** about the state of the environment in your area. Integrate **Expresiones útiles** into the conversation. Ex: **¿Cuál es el mayor problema de contaminación en esta región? ¿Qué creen ustedes que debemos hacer para proteger el medio ambiente?**
- Have the class work in groups to read through the entire **Fotonovela** aloud, with volunteers playing the various parts.

Expresiones útiles Have the class look at video still 3 of the **Fotonovela**. Explain that **No creo que haya lugares más bonitos en el mundo** is an example of the present subjunctive used with an expression of doubt. In video still 4, point out that **Esperamos que ustedes se diviertan mucho** is an example of the present subjunctive with a verb of emotion. Draw attention to **con tal de que no toques las flores** in video still 4 and **a menos que resuelvan ese problema** in video still 7; explain that **con tal de que** and **a menos que** are conjunctions that are always followed by the subjunctive. Tell your students that they will learn more about these concepts in **Estructura**.

TEACHING OPTIONS

Enfoque cultural Many governments in the Spanish-speaking world have established national parks and biological reserves to preserve their natural treasures. Costa Rica and Ecuador, of course, are famous for their protection of ecological treasures. But there are other famous examples. **El Yunque**, located near San Juan, Puerto Rico, also known as the **Bosque Nacional del Caribe**, preserves a tract of the Caribbean rain forest. **Parque Nacional Manu**, in Peru's Amazon basin, is famous for its brilliantly colored macaws, its jaguars, ocelots, otters, and alligators. **Parque Nacional Canaima**, in the Guiana Highlands of Venezuela, is home of the microecologies of the **tepuyes** and **Salto Ángel**, the highest waterfall in the world. **Parque Nacional Torres del Paine** in Chilean Patagonia contains some of the most spectacularly rugged crags in the southern Andes.

1 Expansion Have students use the subject of the sentence in each item to write new sentences that incorporate words from **Contextos**.

2 Expansion Have pairs come up with a response that Martín would give for each of the comments listed in the activity, with the exception of items 3 and 6.

3 Expansion Have pairs use the answers to the questions as if they were lines of dialogue, incorporating them into a conversation, different from the one in the episode, among the **Fotonovela** characters. Have pairs perform their conversation for the class.

4 Possible Response
E1: ¿Hay problemas de contaminación donde vives?
E2: Sí, tenemos un problema muy grave de contaminación de los ríos. Hay muchos papeles, botellas y latas en los ríos. En las montañas, los ríos no están afectados por la contaminación pero en las ciudades, sí. ¿En tu región hay problemas de contaminación?
E1: Sí, tenemos un problema gravísimo de contaminación del aire. ¡No se puede respirar aire puro! Esto causa enfermedades para los habitantes.
E2: Qué terrible. ¿Cómo podemos resolver los problemas de la contaminación?
E1: Bueno, nosotros tenemos un programa de reciclaje ahora. Reciclamos papeles, latas y botellas de vidrio y plástico. También algunas personas tratan de no usar el auto. Usan el metro o caminan al trabajo o a la universidad.

The Affective Dimension
Many students feel nervous when called on to give an answer or to read aloud. You can minimize this source of anxiety by asking for volunteers and by having students work in pairs or groups.

Reacciona a la fotonovela

1

Seleccionar Selecciona la respuesta más lógica para cada frase.

1. Martín va a llevar a los estudiantes al lugar donde van a __c__.
   a. contaminar el río b. bailar c. ir de excursión
2. El río está más afectado por la contaminación __b__.
   a. cerca de los bosques b. en las ciudades c. en las montañas
3. Martín quiere que los estudiantes __a__.
   a. limpien los senderos b. descubran nuevos senderos c. no usen sus autos
4. La naturaleza está formada por __c__.
   a. los ríos, las montañas y las leyes b. los animales, las latas y los ríos
   c. los lagos, los animales y las plantas
5. La contaminación del aire puede producir __b__.
   a. problemas del estómago b. enfermedades respiratorias c. enfermedades mentales

2

Identificar Identifica quién puede decir las siguientes frases. Puedes usar cada nombre más de una vez.

ÁLEX INÉS MAITE MARTÍN JAVIER

1. Es necesario que hagamos algo por el medio ambiente, ¿pero qué? Inés
2. En mi ciudad es imposible respirar aire limpio. ¡Está muy contaminado! Álex
3. En el futuro, a causa del problema de la contaminación, las personas van a tener problemas de salud. Martín
4. El metro es una excelente alternativa al coche. Maite
5. ¿Está limpio o contaminado el río? Javier
6. Es importante reciclar latas y botellas. Martín
7. De todos los lugares del mundo, me parece que éste es el mejor. Inés
8. Como todo el mundo usa automóviles, debemos establecer leyes para controlar cómo y cuándo usarlos. Maite

NOTA CULTURAL

En la capital de México existe la ley de "Hoy no circula" la cual controla el uso de **los automóviles**. Las personas no pueden manejar su carro un día a la semana. Por ejemplo, los automóviles con placas (*plates*) que terminan en 5 y 6 no pueden circular los lunes.

3

Preguntas Responde a las siguientes preguntas usando la información de **Fotonovela**.

1. Según Martín, ¿qué es necesario que hagan los estudiantes? ¿Qué no pueden hacer?
   Es necesario que cuiden la naturaleza. No pueden tocar las plantas ni las flores.
2. ¿Qué problemas del medio ambiente mencionan Martín y los estudiantes?
   Hay problemas de contaminación del aire y de los ríos.
3. ¿Qué cree Maite que deben hacer los países?
   Los países deben establecer leyes que controlen el uso de los automóviles.
4. ¿Qué cosas se pueden reciclar? Menciona tres.
   Se pueden reciclar las botellas, los papeles y las latas.
5. ¿Qué otro medio de transporte importante dice Maite que hay en Madrid?
   Dice que el metro es importante.

4

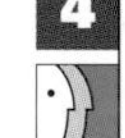

El medio ambiente En parejas, discutan algunos problemas ambientales y sus posibles soluciones. Usen las siguientes preguntas y frases en su conversación.
Answers will vary.

- ¿Hay problemas de contaminación donde vives?
- Tenemos un problema muy grave de contaminación de...
- ¿Cómo podemos resolver los problemas de la contaminación?

TEACHING OPTIONS

Extra Practice You may want to use the sentences in **Actividad 1** or **Actividad 2** on this page for a dictation activity. Have your students close their books, then read each sentence twice slowly and once at regular speed. Then have students open their books and correct any errors in their work.

Small Groups Have your students work in groups of three to write a short article about their environmental concerns for a local newsletter (**boletín informativo**). Their articles should include a description of a few environmental problems and some suggestions for solving them. When groups have finished, have them share their articles with the rest of the class.

Ortografía

Los signos de puntuación

In Spanish, as in English, punctuation marks are important because they help you express your ideas in a clear, organized way.

No podía ver las llaves. Las buscó por los estantes, las mesas, las sillas, el suelo; minutos después, decidió mirar por la ventana. Allí estaban...

The **punto y coma (;)**, the **tres puntos (...)**, and the **punto (.)** are used in very similar ways in Spanish and English.

Argentina, Brasil, Paraguay y Uruguay son miembros de Mercosur.

In Spanish, the **coma (,)** is not used before **y** or **o** in a series.

13,5% **29,2°** **3.000.000** **$2.999,99**

In numbers, Spanish uses a **coma** where English uses a decimal point and a **punto** where English uses a comma.

¿Dónde está? **¡Ven aquí!**

Questions in Spanish are preceded and followed by **signos de interrogación (¿ ?)**, and exclamations are preceded and followed by **signos de exclamación (¡ !)**.

Práctica Lee el párrafo e indica los signos de puntuación necesarios. Answers will vary.

Ayer recibí la invitación de boda de Marta mi amiga colombiana inmediatamente empecé a pensar en un posible regalo fui al almacén donde Marta y su novio tenían una lista de regalos había de todo copas cafeteras tostadoras finalmente decidí regalarles un perro ya sé que es un regalo extraño pero espero que les guste a los dos

¿Palabras de amor? El siguiente diálogo tiene diferentes significados (*meanings*) dependiendo de los signos de puntuación que utilices y el lugar donde los pongas. Intenta encontrar los diferentes significados. Answers will vary.

JULIÁN me quieres
MARISOL no puedo vivir sin ti
JULIÁN me quieres dejar
MARISOL no me parece mala idea
JULIÁN no eres feliz conmigo
MARISOL no soy feliz

recursos

LM p. 74	Lab CD/MP3 Lección 13	I CD-ROM Lección 13

Section Goal

In **Ortografía** students will learn the use of punctuation marks in Spanish.

Instructional Resource
Interactive CD-ROM

Suggestions

- Explain that ellipsis marks are used in Spanish to indicate omissions and hesitations, but that there is no space before or between the marks in Spanish. There is, however, a space after them.
- Model reading the numerical examples. Ex: **13,5% = trece coma cinco por ciento; 29,2° = veintinueve coma dos grados.** Write numbers on the board for translations into Spanish. Ex: 89.3%; 5,020,307; $13.50; 0.49%.
- Explain that the inverted question mark or exclamation point does not always come at the beginning of a sentence, but at the beginning of the part of the sentence where the question or exclamation begins. Ex: **—¿Cómo estás, Mirta? —¡Súper bien, Andrés! Y tú, ¿cómo estás? —No me siento bien y me duele la cabeza, ¡caramba!**
- Point out that **Ortografía** replaces **Pronunciación** in the Student Edition for **Lecciones 10–18**, but not in the Lab Manual. The **Recursos** box references the **Pronunciación** sections found in all lessons of the Lab Manual.

¿Palabras de amor? Two possibilities for punctuation:

J: ¿Me quieres?
M: ¡No puedo vivir sin ti!
J: ¿Me quieres dejar?
M: No. Me parece mala idea.
J: ¿No eres feliz conmigo?
M: No. Soy feliz.

J: ¿Me quieres?
M: No. Puedo vivir sin ti.
J: ¡Me quieres dejar!
M: No me parece mala idea.
J: ¿No eres feliz conmigo?
M: No soy feliz.

TEACHING OPTIONS

Pairs Have pairs write example sentences for each of the four punctuation rules explained in **Ortografía**. Then ask volunteers to write their sentences on the board.

Extra Practice Go over the **¿Palabras de amor?** dialogue and point out how it can be punctuated in different ways to express opposite meanings. Reinforce this by having your students work in pairs to dramatize the dialogue in both ways. Ask a few pairs to present the contrasting dialogues to the class.

Section Goals

In **Estructura 13.1** students will learn:

- to use the subjunctive with verbs and expressions of emotion
- common verbs and expressions of emotion

Instructional Resources

WB/VM: Workbook, pp. 151–152
Lab Manual, p. 75
Lab CD/MP3 ***Lección 13***
IRM: ***¡Inténtalo! & Práctica*** *Answers, p. 219; Tapescript, pp. 59–62*
Info Gap Activities Booklet, pp. 49–50
Interactive CD-ROM
Companion website: www.vistahigherlearning.com
Presentations CD-ROM

Suggestions

- Ask students to call out some of the verbs that trigger the subjunctive in subordinate clauses that follow them (see Verbs of will and influence in **Estructura 12.4**). Write them on the board and ask students to use some of them in sentences to review the conjugation of regular **–ar, –er,** and **–ir** verbs.
- Model the use of some common verbs and expressions of emotion. Ex: **Me molesta mucho que recojan la basura sólo una vez a la semana. Me sorprende que alguna gente no se interese por cuestiones del medio ambiente. Es ridículo que echemos tanto en la basura.** Then ask volunteers to use other verbs and expressions in sentences.

13.1 The subjunctive with verbs of emotion

NATIONAL comparisons STANDARDS

recursos

WB pp. 151–156
LM pp. 75–77
Lab CD/MP3 Lección 13
I CD-ROM Lección 13
vistahigherlearning.com

ANTE TODO In the previous lesson, you learned how to use the subjunctive with expressions of will and influence. You will now learn how to use the subjunctive with verbs and expressions of emotion.

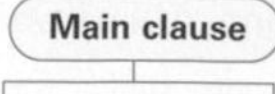

Main clause		Subordinate clause
Marta **espera**	que	yo **vaya** al lago este fin de semana.

▶ When the verb in the main clause of a sentence expresses an emotion or feeling such as hope, fear, joy, pity, surprise, etc., the subjunctive is required in the subordinate clause.

Nos alegramos de que te **gusten** las flores.
We are happy that you like the flowers.

Siento que tú no **puedas** venir mañana.
I'm sorry that you can't come tomorrow.

Temo que Ana no **pueda** ir mañana con nosotros.
I'm afraid that Ana won't be able to go with us tomorrow.

Le **sorprende** que Juan **sea** tan joven.
It surprises him that Juan is so young.

Esperamos que ustedes se diviertan mucho en la excursión.

Es triste que tengamos un problema grave de contaminación en la Ciudad de México.

Common verbs and expressions of emotion

alegrarse (de)	*to be happy*	**tener miedo (de)**	*to be afraid (of)*
esperar	*to hope; to wish*	**es extraño**	*it's strange*
gustar	*to be pleasing; to like*	**es una lástima**	*it's a shame*
molestar	*to bother*	**es ridículo**	*it's ridiculous*
sentir (e:ie)	*to be sorry; to regret*	**es terrible**	*it's terrible*
sorprender	*to surprise*	**es triste**	*it's sad*
temer	*to be afraid; to fear*	**ojalá (que)**	*I hope (that); I wish (that)*

CONSÚLTALO

Certain verbs of emotion like **gustar, molestar,** and **sorprender** require indirect object pronouns. For more examples, see **Estructura 7.4**, pp. 220–221.

Me molesta que la gente no **recicle** el plástico.
It bothers me that people don't recycle plastic.

Es triste que **tengamos** problemas con la deforestación.
It's sad that we have problems with deforestation.

TEACHING OPTIONS

Large Group Have students circulate around the room, interviewing their classmates about their hopes and fears for the future. Ex: **¿Qué deseas para el futuro? (Deseo que encontremos una solución al problema de la contaminación.) ¿Qué es lo que más temes? (Temo que destruyamos nuestro medio ambiente.)** Encourage students to use the common verbs and expressions of emotion in their responses.

Extra Practice Ask students to imagine that they have just finished watching a documentary about the effects of pollution. Have them write five responses to what they saw and heard, using different verbs or expressions of emotion in each sentence. Ex: **Me sorprende que el río esté contaminado.**

▶ As with expressions of will and influence, the infinitive, not the subjunctive, is used after an expression of emotion when there is no change of subject from the main clause to the subordinate clause. Compare these sentences.

Temo **llegar** tarde. *I'm afraid I'll arrive late.*	Temo que mi novio **llegue** tarde. *I'm afraid my boyfriend will arrive late.*

▶ The expression **ojalá (que)** means *I hope* or *I wish,* and it is always followed by the subjunctive. Note that the use of **que** with this expression is optional.

Ojalá (que) se conserven nuestros recursos naturales. *I hope (that) our natural resources will be conserved.*	**Ojalá (que) recojan** la basura hoy. *I hope (that) they collect the garbage today.*

Ojalá que
su aseguradora escuche sus necesidades con la misma atención.
COLMENA
salud - medicina
Con su familia, por su futuro.
Por fin usted se puede poner en manos de una compañía confiable.

¡INTÉNTALO! Completa las oraciones con las formas correctas de los verbos.

1. Ojalá que ellos descubran (descubrir) nuevas formas de energía.
2. Espero que Ana nos ayude (ayudar) a recoger la basura en la carretera.
3. Es una lástima que la gente no recicle (reciclar) más.
4. Esperamos proteger (proteger) el aire de nuestra comunidad.
5. Me alegro de que mis amigos quieran (querer) conservar la naturaleza.
6. A mis padres les gusta que nosotros participemos (participar) en programas de conservación.
7. Es malo contaminar (contaminar) el medio ambiente.
8. Espero que tú vengas (venir) a la reunión (*meeting*) del Club de Ecología.
9. Siento que nuestras ciudades estén (estar) afectadas por la contaminación.
10. Ojalá que yo pueda (poder) hacer algo para reducir la contaminación.

Suggestions

- Compare and contrast the use of the infinitive and the subjunctive with examples like the following: **Juan espera hacer algo para aliviar el problema de la contaminación ambiental. Juan espera que el gobierno haga algo para aliviar el problema de la contaminación ambiental.** Then proceed: **¿Es terrible no reciclar? ¿Es terrible que yo no recicle? ¿Les molesta sentarse aquí? ¿Les molesta que nos sentemos aquí?**
- Use a ball or balled-up piece of paper to expand on the **¡Inténtalo!** activity. Read the beginning of one of the sentences (the words before the blank) and toss the ball to one of your students, who should then complete the sentence in an original manner using the correct subjunctive form of a verb or an infinitive.

The Affective Dimension

Reassure students they will feel more comfortable with the subjunctive as they continue studying Spanish.

TEACHING OPTIONS

Extra Practice Have students look at the drawing for **Contextos** on pages 396–397. Ask them to imagine they are one of the people pictured. Then have them write five sentences about how they feel from the point of view of that person. Ex: **Espero que a Alicia le guste la comida. Ojalá Gustavo no pierda las llaves del carro esta vez. Es ridículo que llevemos el perro y el gato a un picnic.**

Pairs Have students write five sentences describing nature or the environment. Students then read their sentences to a partner who will respond to each one, expressing a feeling or hope. Ex: **Hay muchos animales que están en peligro de extinción. (Es terrible que haya muchos animales en peligro de extinción.)**

1 Suggestions
- Before starting the activity, have students read the items listed in the word bank. Ask volunteers to point out which verbs are in the subjunctive and which items trigger it.
- Ask individuals to explain why they chose the verb or expression they did.

1 Expansion Ask pairs to create an original conversation based on the one in the activity. Students should use the subjunctive at least six times. Call on pairs to perform their conversations for the class. Have the class vote for the funniest or most original one.

2 Suggestion Have volunteers look at the dehydrated sentences and name elements that could trigger the subjunctive in a following clause. Ex: **esperar, ojalá, molestarme**

Práctica

1 Completar Completa el diálogo con palabras de la lista. Compara tus respuestas con las de un(a) compañero/a.

Bogotá, Colombia

alegro	molesta	salga
encuentren	ojalá	tengo miedo de
estén	puedan	vayan
lleguen	reduzcan	visitar

OLGA Me alegro de que Adriana y Raquel (1) vayan a Colombia. ¿Van a estudiar?
SARA Sí. Es una lástima que (2) lleguen una semana tarde. Ojalá que la universidad las ayude a buscar casa. (3) Tengo miedo de que no consigan dónde vivir.
OLGA Me (4) molesta que seas tan pesimista, pero sí, yo también espero que (5) encuentren gente simpática y que hablen mucho español.
SARA Sí, ojalá. Van a hacer un estudio sobre la deforestación en las costas. Es triste que en tantos países los recursos naturales (6) estén en peligro.
OLGA Pues, me (7) alegro de que no se queden mucho en la capital por la contaminación. (8) Ojalá tengan tiempo de viajar por el país.
SARA Sí, espero que (9) puedan por lo menos ir a la costa. Sé que también esperan (10) visitar la Catedral de Sal de Zipaquirá.

NOTA CULTURAL

Los principales factores que determinan la temperatura de **Bogotá, Colombia** son su proximidad al ecuador y su altitud, 2.650 metros (8.660 pies) sobre el nivel (*level*) del mar. Con un promedio (*average*) de 14.5° C (58° F), Bogotá disfruta de un clima templado (*mild*) durante la mayor parte del año. Hay, sin embargo, variaciones considerables durante el día (18° C) y la noche (9° C).

2 Transformar Transforma los siguientes elementos en frases completas para formar un diálogo entre Juan y la madre de Raquel. Añade palabras si es necesario. Luego, con un(a) compañero/a, presenta el diálogo a la clase. Answers will vary.

1. Juan, / esperar / (tú) escribirle / Raquel. / Ser / tu / novia. / Ojalá / no / sentirse / sola Juan, espero que (tú) le escribas a Raquel. Es tu novia. Ojalá (que) no se sienta sola.
2. molestarme / (Ud.) decirme / lo que / tener / hacer. / Ahora / mismo / le / estar / escribiendo Me molesta que (Ud.) me diga lo que tengo que hacer. Ahora mismo le estoy escribiendo.
3. alegrarme / oírte / decir / eso. / Ser / terrible / estar / lejos / cuando / nadie / recordarte Me alegra oírte decir eso. Es terrible estar lejos cuando nadie te recuerda.
4. señora, / ¡yo / tener / miedo / (ella) no recordarme / mí! / Ser / triste / estar / sin / novia Señora, ¡yo tengo miedo que (ella) no me recuerde a mí! Es triste estar sin novia.
5. ser / ridículo / (tú) sentirte / así. / Tú / saber / ella / querer / casarse / contigo Es ridículo que te sientas así. Tú sabes que ella quiere casarse contigo.
6. ridículo / o / no, / sorprenderme / (todos) preocuparse / ella / y / (nadie) acordarse / mí Ridículo o no, me sorprende que todos se preocupen por ella y nadie se acuerde de mí.

TEACHING OPTIONS

Game Write each of the common verbs and expressions of emotion on slips of paper and put them in a box or bag. On separate strips write an equal number of infinitives and subject pronouns. Place these in a separate box or bag. Divide the class into two teams. One member of each team draws a slip of paper from each box and writes a sentence on the board using the sentence elements on both slips. If the sentence makes sense and the grammar is correct, that team gets a point. Play until every team member has had a chance to go to the board. The team with the most points at the end of play wins.

Pairs Have students tell a partner three things that bother him or her and three things he or she is happy about.

Comunicación

3 **Comentar** En parejas, túrnense para formar oraciones sobre su ciudad, sus clases, su gobierno o algún otro tema, usando expresiones como **me alegro de que, temo que** y **es extraño que.** Luego reaccionen a los comentarios de su compañero/a. Answers will vary.

modelo

Estudiante 1: *Me alegro de que vayan a limpiar el río.*
Estudiante 2: *Yo también. Me preocupa que el agua del río esté tan sucia.*

4 **Contestar** Lee el mensaje electrónico que Raquel le escribió a su novio Juan. Luego, en parejas, contesten el mensaje usando expresiones como **me sorprende que, me molesta que** y **es una lástima que.** Answers will vary.

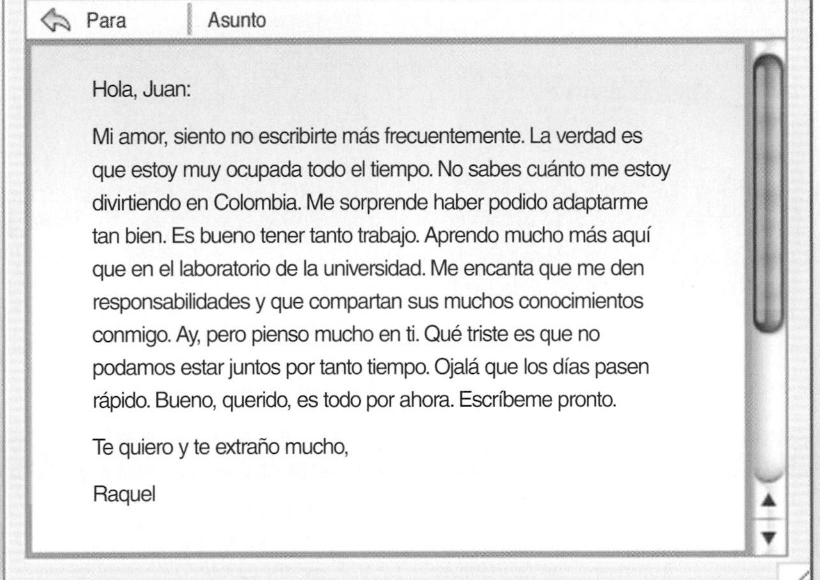
Para | Asunto

Hola, Juan:

Mi amor, siento no escribirte más frecuentemente. La verdad es que estoy muy ocupada todo el tiempo. No sabes cuánto me estoy divirtiendo en Colombia. Me sorprende haber podido adaptarme tan bien. Es bueno tener tanto trabajo. Aprendo mucho más aquí que en el laboratorio de la universidad. Me encanta que me den responsabilidades y que compartan sus muchos conocimientos conmigo. Ay, pero pienso mucho en ti. Qué triste es que no podamos estar juntos por tanto tiempo. Ojalá que los días pasen rápido. Bueno, querido, es todo por ahora. Escríbeme pronto.

Te quiero y te extraño mucho,

Raquel

AYUDA

Echar de menos (a alguien) and **extrañar (a alguien)**, are two ways of saying *to miss (someone)*.

Síntesis

5  **No te preocupes** Estás muy preocupado/a por los problemas del medio ambiente y le comentas a tu compañero/a todas tus preocupaciones. Él/ella va a darte la solución adecuada para tus preocupaciones. Su profesor(a) les va a dar una hoja distinta a cada uno con la información necesaria para completar la actividad. Answers will vary.

modelo

Estudiante 1: *Me molesta que las personas tiren basura en las calles.*
Estudiante 2: *Por eso es muy importante que los políticos hagan leyes para conservar las ciudades limpias.*

3 Suggestions

- Before starting the activity, have students divide a sheet of paper into four columns, with the following headings: **nuestra ciudad, las clases, el gobierno**, and another subject of their choosing. Ask them to brainstorm topics or issues for each column.
- Have groups write statements about these issues and then hand them off to another group for its reactions. The second group should write down their comments and exchange them with the first group.

4 Expansion In pairs, have students tell each other about a memorable e-mail that they've written. Using verbs and expressions of emotion, partners must respond to the e-mail as if they had received it. Wherever applicable, ask pairs to compare their partner's response with the one they actually received from the real recipient.

5 Suggestion Divide the class into pairs and distribute the Info Gap Handouts from the Info Gap Activities Booklet that correspond to this activity. Give the students ten minutes to complete this activity.

5 Expansion Have students work in groups of three to create a public service announcement. Groups should choose one of the ecological problems they mentioned in the activity, and include the proposed solutions for that problem in their announcement.

TEACHING OPTIONS

Small Groups Divide students into groups of three. Have students write three predictions about the future on separate pieces of paper and put them in a sack. Students take turns drawing predictions and reading them to the group. Group members respond with an appropriate expression of emotion. Ex: **Voy a ganar millones de dólares algún día. (Me alegro que vayas a ganar millones de dólares.)**

Heritage Speakers Ask heritage speakers to imagine that they are world leaders speaking at an environmental summit. Have students deliver a short speech to the class about some of the world's environmental problems and how they hope to solve them. Students should use as many verbs and expressions of emotion as possible.

Section Goals

In **Estructura 13.2** students will learn:

- to use the subjunctive with verbs and expressions of doubt, disbelief, and denial
- common verbs and expressions of doubt, disbelief, and denial
- expressions of certainty

Instructional Resources
WB/VM: Workbook, pp. 153–154
Lab Manual, p. 76
*Lab CD/MP3 **Lección 13***
*IRM: **¡Inténtalo!** & **Práctica** Answers, p. 219; Tapescript, pp. 59–62*
Interactive CD-ROM
Companion website: www.vistahigherlearning.com
Presentations CD-ROM

Suggestions

- Introduce a few of the expressions of doubt, disbelief, or denial by talking about a topic familiar to the whole class. Ex: **Dudo que el equipo de baloncesto vaya a ganar el partido este fin de semana. Es probable que el equipo contrario gane. No es cierto que el entrenador de nuestro equipo sea tan bueno como se dice.** As you introduce each expression of doubt, disbelief, or denial, write it on the board, making sure that everyone understands its meaning and recognizes the subjunctive verb in the subordinate clause.
- Ask volunteers to read the captions to the video stills, having them identify the phrase that triggers the subjunctive and the verb in the subjunctive.

13.2 The subjunctive with doubt, disbelief, and denial

ANTE TODO Just as the subjunctive is required with expressions of emotion, influence, and will, it is also used with expressions of doubt, disbelief, and denial.

Main clause		Subordinate clause
Dudan	que	su hijo les **diga** la verdad.

▶ The subjunctive is always used in a subordinate clause when there is a change of subject and the expression in the main clause implies negation or uncertainty.

No creo que haya lugares más bonitos en el mundo.

Dudo que el río esté contaminado aquí en las montañas.

▶ Here is a list of some common expressions of doubt, disbelief, or denial.

Expressions of doubt, disbelief, or denial

dudar	*to doubt*	**no es seguro**	*it's not certain*
negar (e:ie)	*to deny*	**no es verdad**	*it's not true*
no creer	*not to believe*	**es imposible**	*it's impossible*
no estar seguro/a (de)	*not to be sure*	**es improbable**	*it's improbable*
no es cierto	*it's not true; it's not certain*	**(no) es posible**	*it's (not) possible*
		(no) es probable	*it's (not) probable*

El gobierno **niega** que el agua **esté** contaminada.
The government denies that the water is contaminated.

Dudo que el gobierno **resuelva** el problema.
I doubt that the government will solve the problem.

Es probable que **haya** menos bosques y selvas en el futuro.
It's probable that there will be fewer forests and jungles in the future.

No es verdad que mi hermano **estudie** ecología.
It's not true that my brother studies ecology.

¡LENGUA VIVA!
In English, the expression *it is probable* indicates a fairly high degree of certainty. In Spanish, however, **es probable** implies uncertainty and therefore triggers the subjunctive in the subordinate clause: **Es muy probable que venga Elena.**

TEACHING OPTIONS

Extra Practice Write these statements on the board, then ask students to write their reactions using a different expression of doubt, disbelief, or denial for each. **Muchos tipos de peces viven en el desierto. El cielo se está cayendo. Plantas enormes crecen en la luna. Los carros pequeños no contaminan. No hay ningún animal en peligro de extinción.**

Pairs Ask students to write five absurd statements. Students react to their partner's statements with an expression of doubt, disbelief, or denial as their partner reads them aloud. Ex: **Unos hombres verdes vienen a visitarme todos los días. (No creo que unos hombres verdes vengan a visitarte todos los días.)**

▶ The indicative is used in a subordinate clause when there is no doubt or uncertainty in the main clause. Here is a list of some expressions of certainty.

Expressions of certainty

no dudar	*not to doubt*	**estar seguro/a (de)**	*to be sure*
no cabe duda de	*there is no doubt*	**es cierto**	*it's true; it's certain*
no hay duda de	*there is no doubt*	**es seguro**	*it's certain*
no negar (e:ie)	*not to deny*	**es verdad**	*it's true*
creer	*to believe*	**es obvio**	*it's obvious*

No negamos que **hay** demasiados carros en las carreteras.
We don't deny that there are too many cars on the highways.

Es verdad que Colombia **es** un país bonito.
It's true that Colombia is a beautiful country.

No hay duda de que el Amazonas **es** uno de los ríos más largos.
There is no doubt that the Amazon is one of the longest rivers.

Es obvio que los tigres **están** en peligro de extinción.
It's obvious that tigers are in danger of extinction.

▶ In affirmative sentences, the verb **creer** expresses belief or certainty, so it is followed by the indicative. In negative sentences, however, when doubt is implied, **creer** is followed by the subjunctive.

No creo que **haya** vida en el planeta Marte.
I don't believe that there is life on the planet Mars.

Creo que **debemos** usar exclusivamente la energía solar.
I believe we should use solar energy exclusively.

▶ The expressions **quizás** and **tal vez** are usually followed by the subjunctive because they imply doubt about something.

Quizás haga sol mañana.
Perhaps it will be sunny tomorrow.

Tal vez veamos la luna esta noche.
Perhaps we will see the moon tonight.

¡INTÉNTALO! Completa estas frases con la forma correcta del verbo.

1. Dudo que ellos trabajen (trabajar).
2. Es cierto que él come (comer) mucho.
3. Es imposible que ellos salgan (salir).
4. Es probable que ustedes ganen (ganar).
5. No creo que ella vuelva (volver).
6. Es posible que nosotros vayamos (ir).
7. Dudamos que tú recicles (reciclar).
8. Creo que ellos juegan (jugar) al fútbol.
9. No niego que ustedes estudian (estudiar).
10. Es posible que ella no venga (venir) a casa.
11. Es probable que ellos duerman (dormir).
12. Es posible que Marta llame (llamar).
13. Tal vez Juan no nos oiga (oír).
14. No es cierto que ellos nos ayuden (ayudar).
15. Es obvio que Luis se aburre (aburrirse).
16. Creo que Juana va (ir) a casarse.

Suggestions

- Have students respond to statements that elicit expressions of doubt, disbelief, or denial and expressions of certainty. Ex: **Terminan la nueva residencia antes del próximo trimestre. (Es seguro que la terminan antes del próximo trimestre.) La universidad va a tener un nuevo presidente pronto. (No es verdad que la universidad vaya a tener un nuevo presidente pronto.)**
- Have students change the items in **¡Inténtalo!**, making the affirmative verbs in the main clauses negative, and the negative ones affirmative, and making all corresponding changes. Item 1, then, becomes: **No dudo que ellos trabajan.**

TEACHING OPTIONS

TPR Call out a series of sentences, using either an expression of certainty or an expression of doubt, disbelief, or denial. Have students stand if they hear an expression of certainty or remain seated if they hear an expression of doubt. Ex: **Es cierto que algunos pájaros hablan.** (Students stand.)

Extra Practice Have students write sentences about three things of which they are certain and three things they doubt or can't believe. Students should use a different expression for each of their sentences. Have students share some of their sentences with the class.

1 Expansion Have pairs prepare another conversation between Raúl and his father using expressions of doubt, disbelief, and denial as well as expressions of certainty. This time, Raúl is explaining the advantages of the Internet to his reluctant father and trying to persuade him to use it. Have pairs act out the conversation for the class.

2 Expansions
- Continue the activity by making other false statements. Ex: **Voy a hacer una excursión a la Patagonia mañana. Mi abuela sólo come pasteles y cebollas.**
- Ask students to write down two true sentences and two false ones. Encourage them to write statements that are all relatively likely. Have partners read their sentences to each other in random order. Pairs must express whether they think their partner's statements are true or false by using sentences with expressions of doubt, disbelief, and denial or expressions of certainty. Ex: **Mañana tengo que ir al médico. (Dudo que tengas que ir al médico.)** The student who stumps his or her partner with all four statements wins. Have pairs share the most challenging sentences with the class.

Práctica

1 **Escoger** Escoge las respuestas correctas para completar el diálogo. Luego dramatiza el diálogo con un(a) compañero/a.

RAÚL Ustedes dudan que yo realmente (1) estudie (estudio/estudie). No niego que a veces me (2) divierto (divierto/divierta) demasiado, pero no cabe duda de que (3) tomo (tomo/tome) mis estudios en serio. Estoy seguro de que cuando me vean graduarme van a pensar de manera diferente. Creo que no (4) tienen (tienen/tengan) razón con sus críticas.

PAPÁ Es posible que tu mamá y yo no (5) tengamos (tenemos/tengamos) razón. Es cierto que a veces (6) dudamos (dudamos/dudemos) de ti. Pero no hay duda de que te (7) pasas (pasas/pases) toda la noche en Internet y oyendo música. No es nada seguro que (8) estés (estás/estés) estudiando.

RAÚL Es verdad que (9) uso (uso/use) mucho la computadora pero, ¡piensen! ¿No es posible que (10) sea (es/sea) para buscar información para mis clases? ¡No hay duda de que Internet (11) es (es/sea) el mejor recurso del mundo! Es obvio que ustedes (12) piensan (piensan/piensen) que no hago nada, pero no es cierto.

PAPÁ No dudo que esta conversación nos (13) va (va/vaya) a ayudar. Pero tal vez esta noche (14) puedas (puedes/puedas) trabajar sin música. ¿Está bien?

2 **Dudas** Carolina es una chica que siempre miente. Expresa tus dudas sobre lo que Carolina está diciendo ahora. Usa las expresiones entre paréntesis para tus respuestas.

modelo

El próximo año mi familia y yo vamos de vacaciones por diez meses. (dudar)

¡Ja! Dudo que vayan de vacaciones por ese tiempo. ¡Ustedes no son ricos!

1. Estoy escribiendo una novela en español. (no creer)
   No creo que estés escribiendo una novela en español.
2. Mi tía es la directora del *Sierra Club*. (no ser verdad)
   No es verdad que tu tía sea la directora del Sierra Club.
3. Dos profesores míos juegan para los Osos *(Bears)* de Chicago. (ser imposible)
   Es imposible que dos profesores tuyos jueguen para los Osos.
4. Mi mejor amiga conoce al chef Emeril. (no ser cierto)
   No es cierto que tu mejor amiga conozca al chef Emeril.
5. Mi padre es dueño del Centro Rockefeller. (no ser posible)
   No es posible que tu padre sea dueño del Centro Rockefeller.
6. Yo ya tengo un doctorado *(doctorate)* en lenguas. (ser improbable)
   Es improbable que tengas un doctorado en lenguas.

AYUDA

Some useful expressions to say that you don't believe someone:
¡Qué va!
¡Imposible!
¡No te creo!
¡Es mentira!

TEACHING OPTIONS

Large Groups Divide the class into groups of six to stage an environmental debate. Some groups should play the role of environmental advocates while others represent industrialists and big business. Have students take turns presenting a policy platform for the group they represent. When they are finished, opposing groups express their doubts, disbeliefs, and denials.

Heritage Speakers Ask heritage speakers to write an editorial about a current event or political issue in their community. In the body of their essay, students should include expressions of certainty as well as expressions of doubt, disbelief, or denial.

Comunicación

3 **Entrevista** En parejas, imaginen que trabajan para un periódico y que tienen que hacerle una entrevista a la conservacionista Mary Axtmann, la coordinadora del programa Ciudadanos Pro Bosque San Patricio, en Puerto Rico. Escriban seis preguntas para la entrevista después de leer las declaraciones de Mary Axtmann. Al final, inventen las respuestas de Axtmann. Answers will vary.

NOTA CULTURAL

La asociación de **Mary Axtmann** trabaja para la conservación del bosque San Patricio. También ofrece conferencias sobre temas ambientales, hace un censo anual de pájaros y tiene un grupo de guías voluntarios. La comunidad hace todo el trabajo; la asociación no recibe ninguna ayuda del gobierno.

Declaraciones de Mary Axtmann:

"...que el bosque es un recurso ecológico educativo para la comunidad."

"El bosque San Patricio es un pulmón (*lung*) que produce oxígeno para la ciudad."

"El bosque San Patricio está en medio de la ciudad de San Juan. Por eso digo que este bosque es una esmeralda (*emerald*) en un mar de concreto."

"El bosque pertenece (*belongs*) a la comunidad."

"Nosotros salvamos este bosque mediante la propuesta (*proposal*) y no la protesta."

4  **Adivinar** Escribe cinco oraciones sobre tu vida presente y futura. Cuatro deben ser falsas y sólo una debe ser cierta. Presenta tus oraciones al grupo. El grupo adivina *(guesses)* cuál es la oración cierta y expresa sus dudas sobre las oraciones falsas. Answers will vary.

modelo

Estudiante 1: *Quiero irme un año a la selva a trabajar.*
Estudiante 2: *Dudo que te guste vivir en la selva.*
Estudiante 3: *En cinco años voy a ser presidente de los Estados Unidos.*
Estudiante 2: *No creo que seas presidente de los Estados Unidos en cinco años. ¡Tal vez en treinta!*

AYUDA

Here are some useful verbs for talking about plans:

esperar → *to hope*
querer → *to want*
pretender → *to intend*
pensar → *to plan*

Note that **pretender** and *pretend* are false cognates. To say *to pretend*, use the verb **fingir.**

Síntesis

5  **Intercambiar** En grupos, escriban un párrafo sobre los problemas del medio ambiente en su estado o en su comunidad. Compartan su párrafo con otro grupo, que va a ofrecer opiniones y soluciones. Luego presenten su párrafo, con las opiniones y soluciones del otro grupo, a la clase. Answers will vary.

3 Suggestion Before starting, have the class brainstorm different topics that might be discussed with Mary Axtmann.

3 Expansion Ask pairs to act out their interviews for the class.

4 Suggestion Ask students to choose a secretary to write down the group members' true statements to present to the class.

5 Suggestion Assign students to groups of four. Ask group members to appoint a mediator to lead the discussion, a secretary to write the paragraph, a checker to proofread what was written, and a stenographer to take notes on the opinions and solutions of the other group.

5 Expansion Have students create a poster illustrating the environmental problems in their community and proposing possible solutions.

TEACHING OPTIONS

Small Groups Assign scenarios to groups of three. Have students take turns playing a reporter interviewing the other two about what is happening in each situation. The interviewees should use expressions of certainty or doubt, disbelief, and denial when responding to the reporter's questions. Possible scenarios: protest in favor of animal rights, a volcano about to erupt, a local ecological problem, a vacation in the mountains.

Game Divide the class into two teams. One team writes sentences with expressions of certainty while the other writes sentences with expressions of doubt, disbelief, or denial. Put all the sentences in a hat. Students take turns drawing sentences for their team and stating the opposite of what the sentence says. The team with the most sentences using the correct mood wins.

Section Goals

In **Estructura 13.3**, students will learn:

- conjunctions that require the subjunctive
- when the infinitive follows a conjunction
- conjunctions followed by the subjunctive or the indicative

Instructional Resources
WB/VM: Workbook, pp. 155–156
Lab Manual, p. 77
*Lab CD/MP3 **Lección 13***
*IRM: **¡Inténtalo!** & **Práctica** Answers, p. 219; Tapescript, pp. 59–62*
Info Gap Activities Booklet, pp. 51–52
Interactive CD-ROM
Companion website: www.vistahigherlearning.com
Presentations CD-ROM

Suggestions

- To introduce conjunctions that require the subjunctive, make a few statements about yourself. Ex: **Nunca llego a clase tarde a menos que tenga un problema con mi carro. Siempre leo mis mensajes electrónicos antes de que empiece mi primera clase. Camino a clase con tal de que no llueva.** Write each conjunction on the board as you go along.
- Have volunteers read the captions to the video stills. Help them identify the conjunctions in the sentences and the subjunctive verbs in the subordinate clauses.

13.3 The subjunctive with conjunctions

ANTE TODO In both Spanish and English, conjunctions are words or phrases that connect other words and clauses in sentences. Certain conjunctions commonly introduce adverbial clauses, which describe *how, why, when,* and *where* an action takes place.

Main clause	Conjunction	Adverbial clause
Vamos a visitar a Carlos	**antes de que**	**regrese** a California.

Se pueden tomar fotos, ¿verdad?
Sí, con tal de que no toques ni las flores ni las plantas.

A menos que resuelvan el problema de la contaminación, los habitantes van a sufrir muchas enfermedades en el futuro.

▶ The subjunctive is used to express a hypothetical situation, uncertainty as to whether an action or event will take place, or a condition that may or may not be fulfilled.

Voy a dejar un recado **en caso de que Gustavo me llame.**
I'm going to leave a message in case Gustavo calls me.

Voy al supermercado **para que tengas** algo de comer.
I'm going to the store so that you'll have something to eat.

▶ Here is a list of the conjunctions that always require the subjunctive.

Conjunctions that require the subjunctive

a menos que	*unless*	**en caso (de) que**	*in case (that)*
antes (de) que	*before*	**para que**	*so that*
con tal (de) que	*provided that*	**sin que**	*without*

Algunos animales van a morir **a menos que** haya leyes para protegerlos.
Some animals are going to die unless there are laws to protect them.

Ellos nos llevan a la selva **para que** veamos las plantas tropicales.
They are taking us to the jungle so that we may see the tropical plants.

¡ATENCIÓN!
Note that while you may use a gerund with the English equivalent of these conjunctions, in Spanish you must use the subjunctive.
Ex: **Lo hacemos sin que nos lo pidan.**
We do it without them (their) asking us.

▶ The infinitive is used after the prepositions **antes de, para,** and **sin** when there is no change of subject.

Te llamamos **antes de salir** de la casa.
We will call you before leaving the house.

Te llamamos mañana **antes de que salgas.**
We will call you tomorrow before you leave.

TEACHING OPTIONS

Extra Practice Write the following partial sentences on the board. Have students complete them with true or invented information about their own lives. **Voy a terminar los estudios con tal de que..., Necesito $500 en caso de que..., Puedo salir este sábado a menos que..., El mundo cambia sin que..., Debo... antes de que..., Mis padres... para que yo...**

Video Have students divide a sheet of paper into four sections, labeling them **voluntad, emoción, duda,** and **conjunción**. Replay the video. Have them listen for each use of the subjunctive, marking the example they hear in the appropriate section. Play the video again, then have students write a short summary that includes each use of the subjunctive.

Conjunctions with subjunctive or indicative

Voy a formar un club de ecología tan pronto como vuelva a España.

Cuando veo basura, la recojo.

Conjunctions used with subjunctive or indicative

cuando	*when*	**hasta que**	*until*
después de que	*after*	**tan pronto como**	*as soon as*
en cuanto	*as soon as*		

▶ With the conjunctions above, use the subjunctive in the subordinate clause if the main clause expresses a future action or command.

Vamos a resolver el problema **cuando desarrollemos** nuevas tecnologías.
We are going to solve the problem when we develop new technologies.

Después de que ustedes **tomen** sus refrescos, reciclen las botellas.
After you drink your soft drinks, recycle the bottles.

▶ With these conjunctions, the indicative is used in the subordinate clause if the verb in the main clause expresses an action that habitually happens, or that happened in the past.

Contaminan los ríos **cuando construyen** nuevos edificios.
They pollute the rivers when they build new buildings.

Contaminaron el río **cuando construyeron** ese edificio.
They polluted the river when they built that building.

¡INTÉNTALO! Completa las oraciones con las formas correctas de los verbos.

1. Voy a estudiar ecología cuando <u>vuelva</u> (volver) a la universidad.
2. No podemos evitar la lluvia ácida a menos que todos <u>trabajemos</u> (trabajar) juntos.
3. No podemos conducir sin <u>contaminar</u> (contaminar) el aire.
4. Siempre recogemos mucha basura cuando <u>vamos</u> (ir) al parque.
5. Elisa habló con el Presidente del Club de Ecología después de que <u>terminó</u> (terminar) la reunión.
6. Vamos de excursión para <u>observar</u> (observar) los animales y plantas.
7. La contaminación va a ser un problema muy serio hasta que nosotros <u>cambiemos</u> (cambiar) nuestros sistemas de producción y transporte.
8. El gobierno debe crear más parques nacionales antes de que los bosques y ríos <u>estén</u> (estar) completamente contaminados.
9. La gente recicla con tal de que no <u>sea</u> (ser) díficil.

Suggestions

- Write sentences that use **antes de** and **para** and ask volunteers to rewrite them so that they end with subordinate clauses instead of a preposition and an infinitive. Ex: **Voy a hablar con Paula antes de ir a clase. (...antes de que ella vaya a clase; ...antes de que Sergio le hable; ...antes de que ella compre esas botas.)**
- Have students circle the conjunctions that always require the subjunctive in the **¡Inténtalo!** activity as they complete it.

TEACHING OPTIONS

TPR Make several statements, some with conjunctions followed by the infinitive and some with conjunctions followed by the subjunctive. After each statement, hold up two flashcards, one with *I* for infinitive and one with *S* for subjunctive. Students point to the card that represents what they heard. Ex: **Juan habla despacio para que todos lo entiendan. (S) No necesitan un carro para ir a la universidad. (I)**

Extra Practice Have students use the following conjunctions to make statements about the environment: **para, para que, sin, sin que, antes de,** and **antes de que.** Ex: **Es importante empezar un programa de reciclaje antes de que tengamos demasiada basura. No es posible conservar los bosques a menos que se dejen de cortar tantos árboles.**

1 Expansions

- Ask students to write new endings for each sentence. Ex: **Voy a llevar a mis hijos al parque para que... (hagan más ejercicio/jueguen con sus amigos/pasen más tiempo fuera de la casa).**
- Ask pairs to write six original complex sentences like the ones in the activity about a trip they plan to take. Have them use one conjunction that requires the subjunctive in each sentence.

2 Suggestion As you go through the items, ask students which conjunctions require the subjunctive and which could be followed by the subjunctive or the indicative. For those that could take both, discuss which one students used and why.

2 Expansion Have students write more than one way to finish each sentence in the activity.

3 Expansion Have students create a fund-raising advertisement for one of these organizations for their local newspaper. Students should state the goals of the organization, how these goals are in the public interest, and where and how a donation can be made.

Práctica

1 Completar La señora Montero habla de una excursión que quiere hacer con su familia. Completa las oraciones con la forma correcta de cada verbo.

1. Voy a llevar a mis hijos al parque para que __aprendan__ (aprender) sobre la naturaleza.
2. Voy a pasar todo el día allí a menos que __haga__ (hacer) mucho frío.
3. En bicicleta podemos explorar el parque sin __caminar__ (caminar) demasiado.
4. Vamos a bajar al cráter con tal de que no se __prohíba__ (prohibir).
5. Siempre llevamos al perro cuando __vamos__ (ir) al parque.
6. No pensamos ir muy lejos en caso de que __llueva__ (llover).
7. Vamos a almorzar a la orilla (*shore*) del río cuando nosotros __terminemos__ (terminar) de preparar la comida.
8. Mis hijos van a dejar todo limpio antes de __salir__ (salir) del parque.

2 Oraciones Completa las siguientes oraciones de una manera lógica. Answers will vary.

1. No podemos controlar la contaminación del aire a menos que...
2. Voy a reciclar los productos de papel y de vidrio en cuanto...
3. Debemos comprar coches eléctricos tan pronto como...
4. Protegemos los animales en peligro de extinción para que...
5. Mis amigos y yo vamos a recoger la basura de la universidad después de que...
6. No podemos desarrollar nuevas fuentes (*sources*) de energía sin...
7. Hay que eliminar la contaminación del agua para...
8. No podemos proteger la naturaleza sin que...

3 Organizaciones En parejas, lean las descripciones de las organizaciones de conservación. Luego expresen en sus propias (*own*) palabras las opiniones de cada organización. Answers will vary.

Organización: Fundación Río Orinoco
Problema: La destrucción de los ríos
Solución: Programa para limpiar las orillas de los ríos y reducir la erosión y así proteger los ríos

Organización: Oficina de Turismo Internacional
Problema: Necesidad de mejorar la imagen del país en el mercado turístico internacional
Solución: Plan para promover el ecoturismo en los 33 parques nacionales, usando agencias de publicidad e implementando un plan agresivo de conservación

Organización: Asociación Nabusimake-Pico Colón
Problema: Un lugar turístico popular en la Sierra Nevada, Santa Marta, necesita mejor mantenimiento
Solución: Programa de voluntarios para limpiar y mejorar los senderos

AYUDA

Here are some expressions you can use as you do **Actividad 3:**

Se puede evitar... con tal de que...
Es necesario... para que...
Debemos prohibir... antes de que...
No es posible... sin que...
Vamos a... tan pronto como...
A menos que... no vamos a...

TEACHING OPTIONS

Pairs Ask students to imagine that unless some dramatic actions are taken, the world as we know it will end in five days. It is their responsibility as community leaders to give a speech warning people what will happen unless everyone takes action. Have students work with a partner to prepare a three-minute presentation for the class, using as many different conjunctions that require the subjunctive as possible.

Small Groups Divide the class into groups of four. The first student begins a sentence, the second picks a conjunction, and the third student finishes the sentence. The fourth student writes the sentence down. Students should take turns playing the different roles until they have created eight sentences.

Comunicación

4 

Preguntas En parejas, túrnense para hacerse las siguientes preguntas. Answers will vary.

1. ¿Qué haces cada noche antes de acostarte?
2. ¿Qué haces después de salir de la universidad?
3. ¿Qué hace tu familia para que puedas asistir a la universidad?
4. ¿Qué piensas hacer tan pronto como te gradúes?
5. ¿Qué quieres hacer mañana, a menos que haga mal tiempo?
6. ¿Qué haces en tus clases sin que los profesores lo sepan?

5 **Comparar** En parejas, comparen una actividad rutinaria que ustedes hacen con algo que van a hacer en el futuro. Usen palabras de la lista. Answers will vary.

antes de	después de que	hasta que	sin (que)
antes de que	en caso de que	para (que)	tan pronto como

modelo

Estudiante 1: *El sábado vamos al lago. Tan pronto como volvamos, vamos a estudiar para el examen.*
Estudiante 2: *Todos los sábados llevo a mi primo al parque para que juegue. Pero el sábado que viene, con tal de que no llueva, lo voy a llevar a las montañas.*

Síntesis

6 

Tres en raya (*Tic-Tac-Toe*) Formen dos equipos. Una persona comienza una frase y otra persona de su equipo la termina usando palabras de la gráfica. El primer equipo que forme tres oraciones seguidas *(in a row)* gana el tres en raya. Hay que usar la conjunción o la preposición y el verbo correctamente. Si no, ¡no cuenta! Answers will vary.

¡LENGUA VIVA!

Tic-tac-toe has various names in the Spanish-speaking world, including **tres en raya, tres en línea, ta-te-ti, gato, la vieja,** and **triqui-triqui.**

modelo

Equipo 1
Estudiante 1: *Dudo que podamos eliminar la deforestación...*
Estudiante 2: *sin que nos ayude el gobierno.*
Equipo 2
Estudiante 1: *Creo que podemos conservar nuestros recursos naturales...*
Estudiante 2: *con tal de que todos hagamos algo para ayudar.*

cuando	con tal de que	para que
antes de que	para	sin que
hasta que	en caso de que	antes de

4 Expansion When pairs have finished asking and answering the questions, work with the whole class, asking several individuals each of the questions and asking other students to react to their responses. Ex: ____ **hace aeróbicos antes de acostarse. ¿Quién más hace ejercicio? ¡Uf! Hacer ejercicio me parece excesivo. ¿Quiénes ven la tele? ¿Nadie lee un libro antes de acostarse?**

5 Suggestion Have partners compare the routines of other people they know and what they are going to do in the future. Have them do the same with celebrities, taking guesses about their routines.

6 Suggestion Have groups prepare tic-tac-toe cards like the one shown in the activity.

6 Expansion Regroup the students to do a second round of tic-tac-toe.

Suggestion See the Info Gap Activities Booklet for an additional activity to practice the material presented in this section.

TEACHING OPTIONS

Heritage Speakers Ask heritage speakers if they ever played tic-tac-toe when growing up. What did they call it? Was it one of the names listed in **¡Lengua viva!**? Ask them the names of other childhood games they played and to describe them. Are the games similar to those played by the native English speakers in the class?

Pairs Ask partners to interview each other about what they must do today for their future goals to become a reality. Students should state what their goals are, the necessary conditions to achieve them, and talk about obstacles they may encounter. Students should use as many conjunctions as possible in their interviews. Have pairs present their interviews to the class.

Section Goals

In **Lectura** students will:

- learn that recognizing the purpose of a text can help them to understand it
- read a poem

Instructional Resource
Companion website:
www.vistahigherlearning.com

Estrategia Tell students that recognizing the writer's purpose will help them comprehend an unfamiliar text.

Examinar el texto Have students scan the text, using the reading strategies they have learned to determine the author's purpose. Then have them work with a partner to answer the questions. Students should recognize that the text is a poem because it is divided into verses and stanzas.

Predicciones Tell pairs that where their predictions differ they should refer back to the text for resolution.

Determinar el propósito Tell students that as they read the poem they should try to express its message in their own words.

Lectura

Antes de leer

Estrategia

Recognizing the purpose of a text

When you are faced with an unfamiliar text, it is important to determine the writer's purpose. If you are reading an editorial in a newspaper, for example, you know that the journalist's objective is to persuade you of his or her point of view. Identifying the purpose of a text will help you better comprehend its meaning.

Examinar el texto

Utiliza las estrategias de lectura para familiarizarte con el texto. Después contesta las siguientes preguntas y compara tus respuestas con las de un(a) compañero/a.

- ¿De qué trata la lectura?°
- ¿Es una fábula°, un poema, un artículo de periódico...?
- ¿Cómo lo sabes?

Predicciones

Lee estas predicciones sobre la lectura e indica si estás de acuerdo° con ellas. Después compara tus opiniones con las de un(a) compañero/a.

1. La lectura trata del medio ambiente.
2. La autora se preocupa por la contaminación.
3. Habla de la naturaleza y de los seres humanos.
4. Tiene opiniones muy fuertes.

Determinar el propósito

Con un(a) compañero/a, hablen de los posibles propósitos° del texto. Consideren estas preguntas:

- ¿Qué te dice el género° del texto sobre los posibles propósitos del texto?
- ¿Piensas que el texto puede tener más de un propósito? ¿Por qué?

recursos

¿De qué trata la lectura? *What is the reading about?* fábula *fable* estás de acuerdo *you agree* propósitos *purposes* género *type*

Todos contra la contaminación

Gloria Fuertes

La escritora española Gloria Fuertes nació el 28 de julio de 1917 y murió en 1988. En 1950 publicó su primer libro de poesía y desde entonces escribió poemas para niños y para adultos. De 1960 a 1963 vivió en los Estados Unidos donde dio clases de literatura en varias universidades. A partir de los años setenta trabajó en programas para niños en Televisión Española.

TEACHING OPTIONS

Heritage Speakers Ask heritage speakers to retell in their own words or perform a dramatic reading of this poem or any other poem with which they are familiar. If possible, have them make copies of the text for the class.

Pairs Write slogans like the following on the board: **Conserve el medio ambiente, Prohibido contaminar, Este planeta es para generaciones futuras.** Have pairs of students brainstorm other slogans for bumper stickers to promote environmental causes. Ask pairs to share their work with the whole class.

Que los hombres no manchen° los ríos.
Que los hombres no manchen el mar.
Que los niños no maltraten° los árboles.
Que los hombres no ensucien la ciudad.

(No quererse es lo que más contamina,
sobre el barco o bajo la mina°).

Que los tigres no tengan garras°,
que los países no tengan guerras°.

Que los niños no maten pájaros,
que los gatos no maten ratones°
y sobre todo, que los hombres
no maten hombres.

manchen *pollute* maltraten *mistreat* mina *mine*
garras *claws* guerras *wars* ratones *mice*

Después de leer

¿Cierto o falso?

Indica si lo que se dice es **cierto** o **falso**. Corrige las afirmaciones falsas.

1. La autora cree que los hombres no manchan los ríos.
   Falso. La autora quiere que los hombres no manchen los ríos.
2. Ella piensa que las ciudades están limpias.
   Falso. La autora piensa que los hombres ensucian la ciudad.
3. Ella quiere que los países no tengan guerras.
   Cierto.
4. Según ella, es importante que los hombres no se maten.
   Cierto.
5. Dice que los gatos no matan los ratones.
   Falso. Quiere que los gatos no maten los ratones.

Contestar

Contesta estas preguntas. Answers will vary.

1. ¿Cuáles son tres de los problemas que menciona la poeta?
2. ¿Qué crees que quiere decir la poeta en los siguientes versos: "No quererse es lo que más contamina, sobre el barco o bajo la mina"?
3. ¿Tienen importancia las repeticiones en el poema? Explica por qué.
4. Explica qué significan para ti los últimos versos del poema.

Ser poeta

En grupos, un(a) estudiante asume el papel de la poeta de "Todos contra la contaminación". Los/Las otros/as estudiantes le hacen preguntas sobre las ideas y los sentimientos expresados en su poema.

Un grupo de poetas

El poema de Gloria Fuertes habla de algunos problemas del medio ambiente. En grupos pequeños escojan uno de los problemas mencionados y escriban un poema sobre ese tema. Altérnense para escribir un verso cada vez que sea su turno. Compartan su poema con la clase cuando lo terminen.

¿Cierto o falso? After the false statements have been identified and corrected, summarize the poem by having pairs rewrite them. Have them use the subjunctive after verbs and expressions of emotion, doubt, disbelief, and denial, as well as after conjunctions. Ex: **La autora duda que los hombres no manchen los ríos.**

Contestar Divide the class into groups of four to compare and debate individuals' answers to the questions. Assign a moderator to help the group reach as much consensus as possible on each question and then relate the group's opinions to the class.

Ser poeta Have groups act out their interviews in front of the class. After the role-play, encourage the rest of the class to ask additional questions or make additional comments.

Un grupo de poetas After groups have written and presented their poems to the class, re-assign groups so that each student in the new groups represents a different topic from the poem. Have these new groups write a second poem incorporating ideas about all the topics represented.

TEACHING OPTIONS

Extra Practice Ask students to look for other poems in Spanish. Have them check for poems written originally in Spanish as well as those that have been translated. Have them read the poem to the class.

Heritage Speakers Ask heritage speakers if they know of a traditional poem or song in Spanish significant to their community or have heard someone in their family reciting or singing one. If so, encourage them to bring copies of it to class and read it aloud. Ask them to explain its importance and whether it is passed on from one generation to the next.

Section Goals

In **Escritura** students will:

- learn about writer's audience and purpose
- integrate related vocabulary structures taught in **Lección 13**
- write a persuasive letter or article in Spanish

Estrategia Review the purpose and audience suggested, as well as questions 1–5, with the class. Then ask students to apply the answers to the questions to each of the scenarios listed in **Tema**. Students should discuss the purpose of their writing and how to determine their audience.

Tema If possible, provide students with samples of persuasive letters, such as letters to the editor, in Spanish. Ask students to identify the audience and the author's purpose for each letter.

The Affective Dimension After students have handed in their letters, ask them if the topics they chose interested them. Then discuss with them how their writing was influenced by their level of interest in the topic.

Escritura

Estrategia

Considering audience and purpose

Writing always has a specific purpose. During the planning stages, a writer must determine to whom he or she is addressing the piece, and what he or she wants to express to the reader. Once you have defined both your audience and your purpose, you will be able to decide which genre, vocabulary, and grammatical structures will best serve your literary composition.

Let's say you want to share your thoughts on local traffic problems. Your audience can be either the local government or the community. You could choose to write a newspaper article, a letter to the editor, or a letter to the city's governing board. But first you should ask yourself these questions:

1. Are you going to comment on traffic problems in general, or are you going to point out several specific problems?
2. Are you simply intending to register a complaint?
3. Are you simply intending to inform others and increase public awareness of the problems?
4. Are you hoping to persuade others to adopt your point of view?
5. Are you hoping to inspire others to take concrete actions?

The answers to these questions will help you establish the purpose of your writing and determine your audience. Of course, your writing can have more than one purpose. For example, you may intend for your writing to both inform others of a problem and inspire them to take action.

Tema

Escribir una carta o un artículo

Escoge uno de los siguientes temas. Luego decide si vas a escribir una carta a un(a) amigo/a, una carta a un periódico, un artículo de periódico o de revista, etc.

1. Escribe sobre los programas que existen para proteger la naturaleza en tu comunidad. ¿Funcionan bien? ¿Participan todos los vecinos de tu comunidad en los programas? ¿Tienes dudas sobre el futuro del medio ambiente en tu comunidad?
2. Describe uno de los atractivos naturales de tu región. ¿Te sientes optimista sobre el futuro de tu región? ¿Qué están haciendo el gobierno y los ciudadanos° de tu región para proteger la naturaleza? ¿Es necesario hacer más?
3. Escribe sobre algún programa para proteger el medio ambiente a nivel° nacional. ¿Es un programa del gobierno o de una empresa° privada°? ¿Cómo funciona? ¿Quiénes participan? ¿Tienes dudas sobre el programa? ¿Crees que debe cambiarse o mejorarse? ¿Cómo?

ciudadanos *citizens* nivel *level* empresa *company* privada *private*

TEACHING OPTIONS

Proofreading Activity Copy the following sentences containing mistakes onto the board or a transparency as a proofreading activity to do with the whole class.

1. **Por qué no crees que la situación es seria?**
2. **Es terrible que esa compañía sigue contaminando las lagunas, los ríos, y los océanos.**
3. **No debemos esperar hasta que nuestros hijos se enferman para que preocuparnos con la contaminación ambiental.**
4. **¡No deja esa basura en el suelo, recojela!**
5. **Ojalá podemos encontrar soluciones a este problema, no tenemos mucho tiempo.**
6. **Dudo que el gobierno deja que pasan estas cosas.**

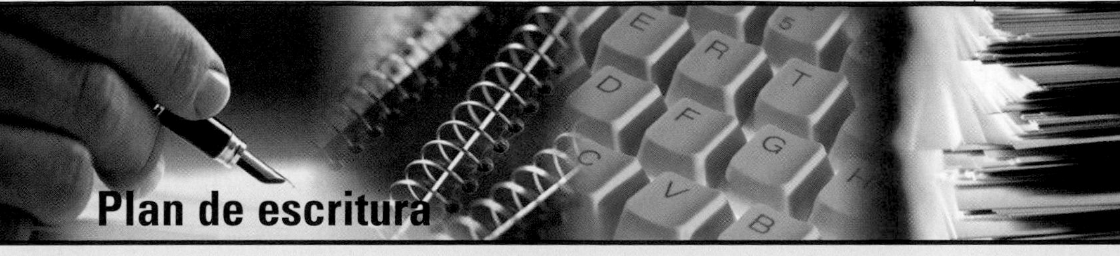

Plan de escritura

1 **Ideas y organización**

Toma unos minutos para contestar estas preguntas:

- ¿Cuál es el propósito° de tu composición?
- ¿Quién va a leer tu composición?
- Utiliza las estrategias de organización, como un mapa de ideas o un esquema°, para planear tu composición.

2 **Primer borrador**

Utilizando tus apuntes° de **Ideas y organización,** escribe el primer borrador. No debes consultar el texto, los apuntes de clase ni el diccionario.

3 **Comentario**

Intercambia el primer borrador con el de un(a) compañero/a. Lee su borrador y comparte tu análisis utilizando esta guía:

a. ¿Está claro el borrador? ¿Cuál es el propósito de la composición de tu compañero/a?
b. ¿Incluye toda la información pertinente?
c. ¿Está bien organizado el borrador?
d. ¿Es interesante?
e. ¿Hay errores gramaticales u ortográficos?

4 **Redacción**

Revisa el primer borrador según las indicaciones de tu compañero/a. Si tu compañero/a tuvo dificultad en determinar el propósito de tu composición, repasa la sección de **Ideas y organización** antes de revisar tu borrador. Usa esta guía para hacer una última revisión antes de escribir la versión final:

a. Subraya° cada verbo para comprobar° la concordancia° de los verbos y los sujetos.
b. Revisa la concordancia de los sustantivos y los adjetivos en cada oración.
c. Revisa los pronombres para comprobar el uso correcto de cada uno.
d. Revisa la ortografía y la puntuación otra vez con la ayuda de tus **Anotaciones para mejorar la escritura.**

5 **Evaluación y progreso**

Comparte tu versión final con dos compañeros/as de clase. Cada estudiante debe leer su versión en voz alta. Después los otros miembros del grupo deben hacerle preguntas o comentarios. El/La escritor(a) debe responder oralmente a cada pregunta o comentario. Lee con cuidado los comentarios que hace tu profesor(a) en tu trabajo y anota los errores más importantes en las **Anotaciones para mejorar la escritura** en tu **Carpeta de trabajos.**

propósito *purpose* esquema *outline* apuntes *notes* Subraya *Underline* comprobar *to check* concordancia *agreement*

EVALUATION: Una carta o un artículo

Criteria	Scale
Content	1 2 3 4
Organization	1 2 3 4
Use of vocabulary	1 2 3 4
Accuracy and mechanics	1 2 3 4
Creativity	1 2 3 4

Scoring	
Excellent	18–20 points
Good	14–17 points
Satisfactory	10–13 points
Unsatisfactory	< 10 points

Comentario

- Go over guide questions a–e with the whole class so peer readers understand their task. Then have pairs of students exchange drafts. Allow five minutes for reading and comments. Allow five minutes for discussing comments.
- Have students prepare **Redacción** as homework. Ask them to rewrite their drafts, incorporating the peer comments and following the directions in **Redacción**. Tell them to prepare a clean copy of their final draft to hand in.

Evaluación y progreso Give groups of three fifteen minutes to read aloud and comment on their letters or articles.

Writing Sample Here is a sample letter that would constitute superior writing achievement.

Carta al director

Señor Director:

Hace cuarenta años que vivo en esta comunidad. Es una comunidad muy bonita y agradable porque hay muchos parques y otros lugares donde la gente puede ir para ver la naturaleza. Espero que toda la comunidad esté de acuerdo cuando digo que es importante que cuidemos de nuestros parques.

Ahora me preocupo por el Parque Robles. Ayer hice una excursión allí, y lo encontré en condiciones desastrosas. ¡Por todo el sendero que sigue el río encontré basura! Por supuesto, la recogí. Pero siento mucho que los otros excursionistas no cuiden del parque.

Pronto ya no vamos a tener este bonito parque, a menos que hagamos algo. ¡Ya no podemos esperar más! Necesitamos que todos participen como voluntarios en un programa para mantener limpio el parque y proteger este tesoro.

Atentamente,
Linda Esquivel

Section Goals

In **Escuchar** students will:
- use background knowledge and context to guess the meaning of unknown words
- listen to a short speech

Instructional Resources
Textbook CD
IRM: Tapescript, p. 97

Estrategia
Script Es necesario que las casas del futuro sean construidas en barrios que tengan todos los recursos esenciales para la vida cotidiana: tiendas, centros comerciales, cines, restaurantes y parques, por ejemplo. El medio ambiente ya no soporta tantas autopistas llenas de coches y, por lo tanto, es importante que la gente pueda caminar para ir de compras o para ir a divertirse. Recomiendo que vivamos en casas con jardines compartidos para usar menos espacio y, más importante, para que los vecinos se conozcan.

Suggestion Have students look at the drawing and guess what it depicts.

Ahora escucha
Script Les vengo a hablar hoy porque aunque espero que el futuro sea color de rosa, temo que no sea así. Vivimos en esta tierra de preciosos recursos naturales —nuestros ríos de los cuales dependemos para el agua que nos da vida, el aire que respiramos, los árboles que nos protegen, los animales cuyas vidas están entrelazadas con nuestras vidas. Es una lástima que no apreciemos lo mucho que tenemos.
Es terrible que haya días con tanta contaminación del aire que nuestros ancianos se enferman y nuestros hijos no pueden respirar. La tala de árboles es un problema grave... hoy día, cuando llueve, el río Cauca se llena de tierra porque no hay árboles que aguanten la tierra. La contaminación del río está afectando gravemente la ecología de las playas de Barranquilla, una de nuestras joyas. Ojalá que me oigan y piensen bien en el futuro de nuestra comunidad. Espero que aprendamos a conservar la naturaleza y que podamos cuidar el patrimonio de nuestros hijos.

Escuchar

Estrategia
Using background knowledge/ Guessing meaning from context

Listening for the general idea, or gist, can help you follow what someone is saying even if you can't hear or understand some of the words. When you listen for the gist, you simply try to capture the essence of what you hear without focusing on individual words.

To practice these strategies, you will listen to a paragraph written by Jaime Urbinas, an urban planner. Before listening to the paragraph, write down what you think it will be about, based on Jaime Urbinas' profession. As you listen to the paragraph, jot down any words or expressions you don't know and use context clues to guess their meanings.

Preparación

Mira el dibujo. ¿Qué pistas° te da sobre el tema del discurso° de Soledad Morales?

Ahora escucha 

Vas a escuchar un discurso de Soledad Morales, una activista preocupada por el medio ambiente. Antes de escuchar, marca las palabras y frases que tú crees que ella va a usar en su discurso. Después marca las palabras y frases que escuchaste.

Palabras	Antes de escuchar	Después de escuchar
el futuro	______	✔
el cine	______	______
los recursos naturales	______	✔
el aire	______	✔
los ríos	______	✔
la contaminación	______	✔
las diversiones	______	______
la reciclaje	______	______

pistas *clues* discurso *speech* Subraya *Underline*

Comprensión

Escoger

Subraya° la definición correcta de cada palabra.

1. patrimonio (fatherland, heritage, acrimony) heritage
2. ancianos (elderly, ancient, antiques) elderly
3. entrelazadas (destined, interrupted, intertwined) intertwined
4. aguantar (to hold back, to destroy, to pollute) to hold back
5. apreciar (to value, to imitate, to consider) to value
6. tala (planting, cutting, watering) cutting

Ahora ustedes

Trabaja con un(a) compañero/a. Escriban seis recomendaciones que creen que la señora Morales va a darle al gobierno colombiano para mejorar los problemas del medio ambiente. Answers will vary.

1. ______
2. ______
3. ______
4. ______
5. ______
6. ______

recursos

TEXT CD
Lección 13

Proyecto

Protege el medio ambiente

Imagina que eres un(a) activista ambiental° en Colombia. Crees que es muy importante que se proteja la bella naturaleza del país.

1 Escribe una carta

Escribe una carta a un representante del gobierno colombiano para hablarle de tus preocupaciones, deseos y dudas sobre el futuro del medio ambiente en Colombia. Primero usa los **Recursos para la investigación** para informarte del paisaje y del medio ambiente de Colombia, incluyendo los problemas ambientales. Busca fotos que representen la información que encontraste. También investiga para obtener el nombre del representante del gobierno que está encargado° del medio ambiente. Sigue este orden en tu carta:

- Encabeza° la carta con "Estimado/a Sr./Sra. ..." y concluye con "Atentamente" antes de tu firma°.
- Explica lo que temes de los problemas ambientales, lo que esperas y tus dudas sobre el futuro.
- Explica lo que recomiendas para resolver algunos de los problemas.

2 Presenta la información

Lee la carta a tus compañeros/as. Muéstrales fotos del paisaje colombiano y fotos que muestren problemas ambientales, para ayudarlos a entender por qué tus preocupaciones y recomendaciones son urgentes e importantes.

Las tortugas marinas están en grave peligro de extinción.

recursos para la investigación

	**Internet** Palabras clave: Colombia, ecología, medio ambiente, contaminación, gobierno, Ministerio del Medio Ambiente, fotos		**Comunidad** Estudiantes o profesores que son de Colombia, personas de la comunidad que han viajado° a Colombia
	**Biblioteca** Revistas de organizaciones ambientales internacionales, periódicos		**Otros recursos** Comunicación con organizaciones ambientales internacionales por teléfono o correo electrónico

ambiental *environmental* encargado *in charge of* Encabeza *Write a salutation* firma *signature* han viajado *have traveled*

Section Goals

In **Proyecto** students will:
- use Spanish while researching and interacting with the wider world
- write a letter in the role of an environmental activist in Colombia

Suggestion Students might need a week to complete the project, so at the beginning of that time period, have them open their books to this page and glance over **Proyecto**. Tell them they are going to write a letter about protecting the environment to the official of the Colombian government in charge of environmental affairs.

Escribe una carta While the Internet can be a source of information on a wide range of topics, the reliability of such information is generally much more dubious than information gathered from printed sources. Tell students not to base all their research on Internet sources.

Presenta la información
- Students' presentations will be more interesting if they integrate visual aids such as posters, brochures, or music or audio recordings.
- You may wish to set aside sufficient class time to do a few presentations at a time until all students have had a chance to present.

EVALUATION: Una carta

Criteria	Scale
Content	1 2 3 4
Organization	1 2 3 4
Accuracy	1 2 3 4
Creativity	1 2 3 4
Oral presentation	1 2 3 4

Scoring	
Excellent	18–20 points
Good	14–17 points
Satisfactory	10–13 points
Unsatisfactory	< 10 points

Section Goal
In **Panorama**, students will read about the geography, history, and culture of Colombia.

Instructional Resources
Transparencies, #5, #6, #49
WB/VM: Workbook, pp. 157–158; Video Activities, pp. 273–274
***Panorama cultural** DVD/Video*
Interactive CD-ROM
IRM: Videoscript, p. 133
Companion website: www.vistahigherlearning.com
Presentations CD-ROM

Suggestion Have students look at the map of Colombia or project **Transparency #49** and talk about the physical features of the country. Point out the three parallel ranges of the Andes in the west, and the Amazon Basin in the east and south. After students look at the call-out photos and read the captions, point out that there are no major cities in the eastern half of the country. Ask students to suggest reasons for the lack of population there.

El país en cifras After reading the **Población** section, ask students what the impact might be of having 55% of the nation's territory unpopulated, and the sort of problems this might create for a national government. Remind students that **chibcha** is spoken as far north as Nicaragua. **Araucano** is a language spoken by indigenous people of the Andes.

¡Increíble pero cierto! In their desperation to uncover the gold from Lake Guatavita, Spaniards made several attempts to drain the lake. Around 1545, Hernán Pérez de Quesada set up a bucket brigade that lowered the water level by several meters, allowing gold to be gathered.

Colombia

El país en cifras

- **Área:** 1.138.910 km^2 (439.734 millas^2), *tres veces el área de Montana*
- **Población:** 43.821.000

De todos los países de habla hispana, sólo México tiene más habitantes° que Colombia. Casi toda la población colombiana vive en las áreas montañosas y la costa occidental° del país. Aproximadamente el 55% de la superficie° del país está sin poblar°.

- **Capital:** Santa Fe de Bogotá —6.547.000
- **Ciudades principales:** Cali —2.893.000, Medellín —3.070.000, Barranquilla —1.853.000, Cartagena —768.000

SOURCE: Population Division, UN Secretariat

Medellín

- **Moneda:** peso colombiano
- **Idiomas:** español (oficial)

Bandera de Colombia

Colombianos célebres

- **Edgar Negret,** escultor°, pintor (1920–)
- **Gabriel García Márquez,** escritor (1928–)
- **Juan Pablo Montoya,** automovilista (1975–)
- **Shakira,** cantante (1977–)

habitantes *inhabitants* occidental *western* superficie *surface* sin poblar *unpopulated* escultor *sculptor* dioses *gods* arrojaban *threw* cacique *chief* llevó *led* de oro *golden*

Baile típico de Barranquilla

Plaza Bolívar, Bogotá

Barranquilla
Cartagena
Mar Caribe
PANAMÁ
Sierra Nevada de Santa Marta
VENEZUELA
Cordillera Occidental de los Andes
Río Magdalena
ESTADOS UNIDOS
OCÉANO ATLÁNTICO
COLOMBIA
OCÉANO PACÍFICO
AMÉRICA DEL SUR
Medellín
Cordillera Central de los Andes
Río Meta
Bogotá
Cali
Volcán Nevado del Huila
Cordillera Oriental de los Andes
Océano Pacífico
ECUADOR
PERÚ

Cultivo de caña de azúcar cerca de Cali

recursos

WB pp. 157–158	VM pp. 273–274	I CD-ROM Lección 13	vistahigherlearning.com

¡Increíble pero cierto!

En el siglo XVI los exploradores españoles oyeron la leyenda de El Dorado. Esta leyenda cuenta que los indios, como parte de un ritual en honor a los dioses°, arrojaban° oro a la laguna de Guatavita y el cacique° se sumergía en sus aguas cubierto de oro. Aunque esto era cierto, muy pronto la exageración llevó° al mito de una ciudad de oro°.

Laguna de Guatavita

TEACHING OPTIONS

Heritage Speakers One of Colombia's contributions to Latin popular music is the dance form called the **cumbia**. The cumbia was born out of the fusion of musical elements contributed by each of Colombia's three main ethnic groups: Andean Indians, Africans, and Europeans. According to ethnomusicologists, the flutes and wind instruments characteristically used in the cumbia derive from Andean Indian music, the rhythms have their origin in African music, and the melodies are shaped by Spanish popular melodies. Cumbias are popular outside of Colombia, particularly in Mexico. Another Colombian dance form, this one native to the Caribbean coast, is the **vallenato**. In the vallenato, which is a fusion of African and European elements, the Andean element is missing. Encourage heritage speakers to bring examples of cumbias and vallenatos for the class to listen to and compare and contrast.

Lugares • El Museo del Oro

El famoso Museo del Oro° del Banco de la República fue fundado° en Bogotá en 1939 para preservar las piezas de orfebrería° de la época precolombina. En el museo, que tiene más de 30.000 piezas de oro, se pueden ver joyas°, ornamentos religiosos y figuras que sirvieron de ídolos. El cuidado con el que se hicieron los objetos de oro refleja la creencia° de las tribus indígenas de que el oro era la expresión física de la energía creadora° de los dioses°.

Literatura • Gabriel García Márquez (1928–)

Gabriel García Márquez, ganador del Premio Nobel de Literatura en 1982, es uno de los escritores contemporáneos más importantes del mundo. García Márquez publicó su primer cuento° en 1947, cuando era estudiante universitario. Su libro más conocido, *Cien años de soledad*, está escrito en el estilo° literario llamado "realismo mágico", un estilo que mezcla° la realidad con lo irreal y lo mítico°.

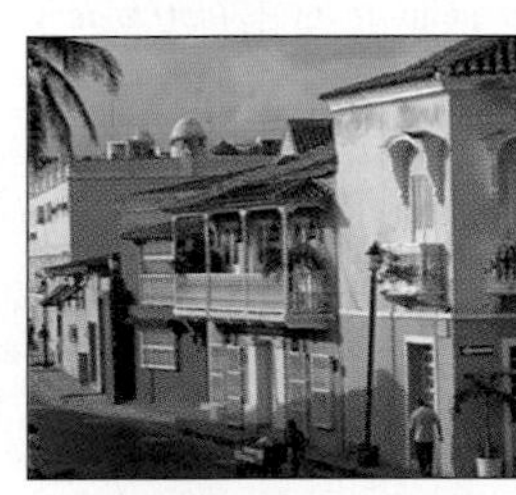

Historia • Cartagena de Indias

Los españoles fundaron la ciudad de Cartagena de Indias en 1533 y construyeron a su lado la fortaleza° más grande de las Américas, el Castillo de San Felipe de Barajas. En la ciudad de Cartagena se conservan° muchos edificios de la época colonial, como iglesias, monasterios, palacios y mansiones. Cartagena es conocida también por el Festival de Música del Caribe y su prestigioso Festival Internacional de Cine.

BRASIL

¿Qué aprendiste? Responde a las preguntas con una frase completa.

1. ¿Cuáles son las principales ciudades de Colombia? Las principales ciudades de Colombia son Santa Fe de Bogotá, Cali, Medellín y Barranquilla.
2. ¿Qué país de habla hispana tiene más habitantes que Colombia? México tiene más habitantes que Colombia.
3. ¿Quién es Edgar Negret? Edgar Negret es un escultor y pintor colombiano.
4. ¿Para qué fue fundado el Museo del Oro? El Museo del Oro fue fundado para preservar las piezas de orfebrería de la época precolombina.
5. ¿Qué tipos de objetos hay en el Museo del Oro? En el Museo del Oro hay joyas, ornamentos religiosos y figuras que sirvieron de ídolos.
6. ¿Quién ganó el Premio Nobel de Literatura en 1982? Gabriel García Márquez ganó el Premio Nobel de Literatura en 1982.
7. ¿Cuál es el libro más famoso de García Márquez? *Cien años de soledad* es el libro más famoso de García Márquez.
8. ¿Qué es el "realismo mágico"? El "realismo mágico" es un estilo literario que mezcla la realidad con lo irreal y lo mítico.
9. ¿Qué construyeron los españoles al lado de la ciudad de Cartagena de Indias? Los españoles construyeron el Castillo de San Felipe de Barajas al lado de Cartagena de Indias.
10. ¿Qué festivales internacionales se celebran en Cartagena? Se celebran el Festival Internacional de Cine y el Festival de Música del Caribe.

Conexión Internet Investiga estos temas en el sitio **www.vistahigherlearning.com.**

1. Busca información sobre las ciudades más grandes de Colombia. ¿Qué lugares de interés hay en estas ciudades? ¿Qué puede hacer un(a) turista en estas ciudades?
2. Busca información sobre pintores y escultores colombianos como Edgar Negret, Débora Arango o Fernando Botero. ¿Cuáles son algunas de sus obras más conocidas? ¿Cuáles son sus temas?

Oro *Gold* fundado *founded* orfebrería *goldsmithing* joyas *jewels* creencia *belief* creadora *creative* dioses *gods* cuento *story* estilo *style* mezcla *mixes* mítico *mythical* fortaleza *fortress* se conservan *are preserved*

El Museo del Oro In pre-Columbian times, the native peoples from different regions of Colombia developed distinct styles of working with gold. Some preferred to melt copper into the metal before working it, some pounded the gold, while others poured it into molds. If possible, bring photos of pre-Columbian gold work for the class to look at.

Gabriel García Márquez García Márquez was raised primarily by his maternal grandparents, who made a profound impression upon his life and his literature. His grandfather was a man of strong ideals and a military hero. His grandmother held fast to many superstitious folk beliefs, which she espoused as gospel. Both of these elements surface in García Márquez's magical realism.

Cartagena de Indias Because Cartagena de Indias was the point of departure for shipments of Andean gold to Spain, it was the frequent target of pirate attacks from the 16th through the 18th centuries. It was besieged on five occasions. The most famous siege was led by the English pirate Sir Francis Drake, in 1586. He held the city for 100 days, until the residents surrendered to him some 100,000 pieces of gold!

Conexión Internet Students will find supporting Internet activities and links at **www.vistahigherlearning.com**.

TEACHING OPTIONS

Worth Noting Colombia, like other mountainous countries near the equator, does not experience the four seasons that are known in parts of the United States and Canada. The average temperature of a given location does not vary much during the course of a year. Climate, however, changes dramatically with elevation, the higher altitudes being cooler than the low-lying ones. While the average temperature at sea level is 86°, 57° is the average temperature in Bogotá, the third highest capital in the world, behind La Paz, Bolivia, and Quito, Ecuador. When Colombians speak of **verano** or **invierno**, they are referring the the dry season **(verano)** and the rainy season **(invierno).** When these seasons occur varies from one part of the country to another. In the Andean region, the **verano**, or dry season, generally falls between December and March.

Instructional Resources
Vocabulary CD
Lab Manual, p. 77
Lab CD/MP3 ***Lección 13***
IRM: Tapescript, pp. 59–62
Testing Program: ***Pruebas****,*
pp. 145–156
Testing Program Audio CD
Test Files CD-ROM

La naturaleza

el árbol	*tree*
el bosque (tropical)	*(tropical; rain) forest*
el césped, la hierba	*grass*
el cielo	*sky*
el cráter	*crater*
el desierto	*desert*
la estrella	*star*
la flor	*flower*
el lago	*lake*
la luna	*moon*
el mundo	*world*
la naturaleza	*nature*
la nube	*cloud*
la piedra	*stone*
la planta	*plant*
la región	*region; area*
el río	*river*
la selva, la jungla	*jungle*
el sendero	*trail; trailhead*
el sol	*sun*
la tierra	*land; soil*
el valle	*valley*
el volcán	*volcano*

Los animales

el animal	*animal*
el ave, el pájaro	*bird*
el gato	*cat*
el perro	*dog*
el pez	*fish*
la vaca	*cow*

El medio ambiente

la conservación	*conservation*
la contaminación (del aire; del agua)	*(air; water) pollution*
la deforestación	*deforestation*
la ecología	*ecology*
el ecoturismo	*ecotourism*
la energía (nuclear, solar)	*(nuclear, solar) energy*
el envase	*container*
la extinción	*extinction*
el gobierno	*government*
la lata	*(tin) can*
la ley	*law*
la lluvia (ácida)	*(acid) rain*
el medio ambiente	*environment*
el peligro	*danger*
la población	*population*
el reciclaje	*recycling*
el recurso natural	*natural resource*
la solución	*solution*
cazar	*to hunt*
conservar	*to conserve*
contaminar	*to pollute*
controlar	*to control*
cuidar	*to take care of*
dejar de (+ *inf.*)	*to stop (doing something)*
desarrollar	*to develop*
descubrir	*to discover*
destruir	*to destroy*
estar afectado/a (por)	*to be affected (by)*
estar contaminado/a	*to be polluted*
evitar	*to avoid*
mejorar	*to improve*
proteger	*to protect*
reciclar	*to recycle*
recoger	*to pick up*
reducir	*to reduce*
resolver (o:ue)	*to resolve; to solve*
respirar	*to breathe*
de aluminio	*(made) of aluminum*
de plástico	*(made) of plastic*
de vidrio	*(made) of glass*
puro/a	*pure*

Las emociones

alegrarse (de)	*to be happy*
esperar	*to hope; to wish*
sentir (e:ie)	*to be sorry; to regret*
temer	*to fear*
es extraño	*it's strange*
es una lástima	*it's a shame*
es ridículo	*it's ridiculous*
es terrible	*it's terrible*
es triste	*it's sad*
ojalá (que)	*I hope (that); I wish (that)*

Las dudas y certezas

(no) dudar	*(not) to doubt*
(no) negar (e:ie)	*(not) to deny*
(no) creer	*(not) to believe*
es imposible	*it's impossible*
es improbable	*it's improbable*
es obvio	*it's obvious*
No cabe duda de	*There is no doubt that...*
No hay duda de	*There is no doubt that...*
(no) es posible	*it's (not) possible*
(no) es probable	*it's (not) probable*
(no) es cierto	*it's (not) certain*
(no) es verdad	*it's (not) true*
(no) es seguro	*it's (not) certain*

Conjunciones

a menos que	*unless*
antes (de) que	*before*
con tal (de) que	*provided (that)*
cuando	*when*
después de que	*after*
en caso (de) que	*in case (that)*
en cuanto	*as soon as*
hasta que	*until*
para que	*so that*
sin que	*without*
tan pronto como	*as soon as*

Expresiones útiles	*See page 401.*

recursos

LM p. 77	Lab CD/MP3 Lección 13	Vocab CD Lección 13

En la ciudad

14

Communicative Goals

You will learn how to:

- **Give advice to others**
- **Give and receive directions**
- **Discuss daily chores**

Lesson Goals

In **Lección 14** students will be introduced to the following:

- names of commercial establishments
- banking terminology
- citing locations
- subjunctive in adjective clauses
- **nosotros/as** commands
- forming regular past participles
- irregular past participles
- past participles as adjectives
- identifying a narrator's point of view
- avoiding redundancy
- writing an e-mail
- listening for specific information and linguistic cues
- writing and presenting a brochure for a model community in Venezuela
- cultural, geographic, economic, and historical information about Venezuela

A PRIMERA VISTA

- **¿Viven estas personas en un bosque, un pueblo o una ciudad?**
- **¿Dónde están, en una calle o en un sendero?**
- **¿Es limpio o sucio el lugar donde están?**
- **¿Es posible que estén afectadas por la contaminación?**

A primera vista Here are some additional questions you can ask based on the photo: **¿Vives en una ciudad? ¿Cuál? ¿Cómo es la vida en la ciudad? ¿Cómo es la vida en el campo? ¿Prefieres vivir ahí? ¿Por qué? ¿Es posible que no haya contaminación en una ciudad? ¿Cómo? ¿Qué responsabilidades tienen las personas que viven en una ciudad para proteger el medio ambiente?**

INSTRUCTIONAL RESOURCES

Workbook/Video Manual: WB Activities, pp. 159–168
Laboratory Manual: Lab Activities, pp. 79–83
Workbook/Video Manual: Video Activities, pp. 239–240; pp. 275–276
Instructor's Resource Manual: **Hojas de actividades**, p. 171; **Vocabulario adicional**, p. 192; **¡Inténtalo!** & **Práctica** Answers, p. 220; **Fotonovela** Translations, pp. 146–147; Textbook CD Tapescript, p. 98; Lab CDs Tapescript, pp. 63–66; **Fotonovela** Videoscript, pp. 119–120; **Panorama cultural** Videoscript, p. 134
Info Gap Activities Booklet, pp. 53–56
Overhead Transparencies: #5, #6, #50, #51, #52
Lab Audio CD/MP3 **Lección 14**
Panorama cultural DVD/Video
Fotonovela DVD/Video
Testing Program, pp. 157–168
Testing Program Audio CD
Test Files CD-ROM
Companion website
Presentations CD-ROM
Textbook CD
Vocabulary CD
Interactive CD-ROM
Video CD-ROM
Web-SAM

Section Goals

In **Contextos**, students will learn and practice:
- names of commercial establishments
- banking terminology
- citing locations

Instructional Resources
Transparencies, #50, #51
Textbook CD
Vocabulary CD
WB/VM: Workbook, pp. 159–160
Lab Manual, p. 79
Lab CD/MP3 ***Lección 14***
IRM: ***Vocab. adicional****, p. 192;* ***Práctica*** *Answers, p. 220; Tapescript, pp. 63–66; p. 98*
Interactive CD-ROM
Companion website: www.vistahigherlearning.com
Presentations CD-ROM

Suggestions
- Using realia or magazine pictures, ask volunteers to identify the items. Ex: **carne, zapato, pan**. As students give their answers, write the names of corresponding establishments on the board (**carnicería, zapatería, panadería**). Then present banking vocabulary by miming common transactions. Ex: **Cuando necesito dinero, voy al banco. Escribo un cheque y lo cobro.**
- Project **Transparency #50**. Have students refer to the picture to answer your questions about it. Ex: **¿Dónde queda el cajero automático? ¿Qué tienda queda entre la lavandería y la carnicería? ¿Qué establecimiento se encuentra encima del supermercado? Las dos señoras frente a la estatua, ¿de qué hablan? ¿Qué tipo de transacciones pueden hacerse en un banco?**

Successful Language Learning Ask students to imagine how they would use this vocabulary when traveling.

Note: At this point you may want to present **Vocabulario adicional: Más vocabulario para la ciudad**, from the IRM.

En la ciudad

Más vocabulario

la frutería	*fruit store*
la heladería	*ice cream shop*
la pastelería	*pastry shop*
la pescadería	*fish market*
la cuadra	*(city) block*
la dirección	*address*
la esquina	*corner*
el estacionamiento	*parking lot*
derecho	*straight (ahead)*
enfrente de	*opposite; facing*
hacia	*toward*
cruzar	*to cross*
doblar	*to turn*
hacer diligencias	*to run errands*
quedar	*to be located*
el cheque (de viajero)	*(traveler's) check*
la cuenta corriente	*checking account*
la cuenta de ahorros	*savings account*
ahorrar	*to save (money)*
cobrar	*to cash (a check)*
depositar	*to deposit*
firmar	*to sign*
llenar (un formulario)	*to fill out (a form)*
pagar a plazos	*to pay in installments*
pagar al contado, en efectivo	*to pay in cash*
pedir prestado	*to borrow*
pedir un préstamo	*to apply for a loan*
ser gratis	*to be free of charge*

Variación léxica

cuadra ⟷ manzana (*Esp.*)
direcciones ⟷ indicaciones (*Esp.*)
doblar ⟷ girar; virar; voltear
hacer diligencias ⟷ hacer mandados

recursos

TEXT CD Lección 14	WB pp. 159–160	LM p. 79	Lab CD/MP3 Lección 14	I CD-ROM Lección 14	Vocab CD Lección 14

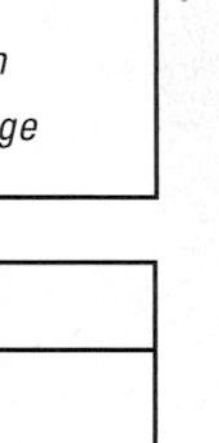

TEACHING OPTIONS

Heritage Speakers Have heritage speakers write about shopping and banking customs in their home communities. Have them mention such things as business hours and the prevalence of specialty shops compared to supermarkets or department stores. Encourage them to compare and contrast customs cross-generationally as well as cross-culturally.

Pairs Have students individually draw schematic maps of a couple of blocks around a city square, labeling every establishment and naming the streets. Then have them write a description of the location of each establishment and exchange it with a partner. They then use the partner's description to recreate the city map on which the description is based. Afterward, partners compare the two sets of maps.

Práctica

1 Escuchar Mira el dibujo de las páginas 426 y 427. Luego escucha las frases e indica si lo que dice cada una es **cierto** o **falso.**

	Cierto	Falso		Cierto	Falso
1.	❍	✓	6.	✓	❍
2.	✓	❍	7.	✓	❍
3.	❍	✓	8.	❍	✓
4.	✓	❍	9.	❍	✓
5.	❍	✓	10.	✓	❍

2 Seleccionar Selecciona los lugares de la lista en los que haces las siguientes diligencias.

banco	lavandería	pescadería
carnicería	joyería	salón de belleza
frutería	pastelería	zapatería

1. comprar galletas pastelería
2. comprar manzanas frutería
3. comprar un collar (*necklace*) joyería
4. cortarte (*to cut*) el pelo salón de belleza
5. lavar la ropa lavandería
6. comprar pescado pescadería
7. comprar pollo carnicería
8. comprar sandalias zapatería

3 Completar Llena los espacios en blanco con las palabras más adecuadas.

1. El banco me regaló un reloj. Fue gratis.
2. Me gusta ahorrar dinero, pero no me molesta gastarlo.
3. La cajera me dijo que tenía que firmar el cheque en el dorso (*on the back*) para cobrarlo.
4. Para pagar con un cheque, necesito tener dinero en mi cuenta corriente.
5. Mi madre va a un cajero automático para obtener dinero en efectivo cuando el banco está cerrado.
6. Cada viernes, Julio lleva su cheque al banco y lo cobra para tener dinero en efectivo.
7. Cada viernes Ana lleva su cheque al banco y lo deposita en su cuenta de ahorros.
8. Anoche en el restaurante, Marco pagó en efectivo/al contado en vez de usar una tarjeta de crédito.
9. Cuando viajas, es buena idea llevar cheques de viajero.
10. Para pedir un préstamo, Miguel y Susana tuvieron que llenar cuatro formularios.

1 Suggestion Help students check their answers by reading each statement in the tapescript to the class and asking volunteers to say whether it is true or false. Have students correct the false statements.

1 Tapescript 1. El supermercado queda al este de la plaza, al lado de la joyería. 2. La zapatería está al lado de la carnicería. 3. El banco queda al sur de la plaza. 4. Cuando sales de la zapatería, la lavandería está a su lado. 5. La carnicería está al lado del banco. 6. Cuando sales de la joyería, el cajero automático está a su lado. 7. No hay ninguna heladería cerca de la plaza. 8. La joyería está al oeste de la peluquería. 9. Hay una frutería al norte de la plaza. 10. No hay ninguna pastelería cerca de la plaza.
Textbook CD

2 Expansion After students finish, ask them what else could be bought in the establishments listed. Ex: **¿Qué más podemos comprar en la pastelería?**

3 Expansion Ask students to compare and contrast two different facets of banking. Ex: ATM vs. traditional tellers; credit card vs. check; savings account vs. checking account. Have them work in groups of three to make a list of **Ventajas** and **Desventajas**.

TEACHING OPTIONS

Game Play **Concentración**. On eight cards, write names of types of commercial establishments. On another eight cards, draw or paste a picture that matches each commercial establishment. Place the cards face-down in four rows of four. In pairs, students select two cards. If the two cards match, the pair keeps them. If the two cards don't match, students replace them in their original position. The group with the most cards at the end wins.

Pairs Have each student write a shopping list (**lista de la compra/lista del mandado**) with ten items. Have students include items found in different stores. Then have them exchange their shopping list with a partner. Using the shopping list received, each student tells his or her partner where to go to get each item. Ex: **unas botas nuevas → Para comprar unas botas nuevas, tienes que ir a la zapatería que queda en la calle ____.**

Suggestion Project **Transparency #51** and ask students questions about the picture to elicit active vocabulary. **¿Qué hace la señora en la ventanilla? Y la gente que espera detrás de ella, ¿qué hace?** When you have covered the vocabulary, involve students in a conversation about mail and the post office. Ex: **Necesito estampillas. ¿Dónde está la oficina de correos que está más cerca de aquí? A mí me parece que la carta es una forma de escritura en vías de extinción. Desde que uso el correo electrónico, casi nunca escribo cartas. ¿Quiénes todavía escriben cartas?**

4 Expansions
- After you have gone over the activity, have students practice the conversation with a partner.
- Have pairs create short conversations similar to the one presented in the activity, but set in a different place of business. Ex: **el salón de belleza, la pescadería.**

5 Suggestions
- Create a word bank of useful phrases on the board. Ask volunteers to suggest expressions and grammatical constructions that will help students develop their role-plays.
- Go over the new vocabulary once again by asking questions. Ex: **¿Cuándo pedimos un préstamo? ¿Los cheques son para una cuenta corriente o una cuenta de ahorros?**

¡LENGUA VIVA!
Note that **correo** can mean either *mail* or *post office*. Other ways to say *post office* are: **la oficina de correos** and **correos**.

4 **Conversación** Completa la conversación entre Juanita y el cartero con las palabras más adecuadas.

CARTERO Buenas tardes, ¿es usted la señorita Ramírez? Le traigo un (1) paquete.
JUANITA Sí, soy yo. ¿Quién lo envía?
CARTERO La Sra. Ramírez. Y también tiene dos (2) cartas.
JUANITA Ay, pero ¡ninguna es de mi novio! ¿No llegó nada de Manuel Fuentes?
CARTERO Sí, pero él echó la carta al (3) buzón sin poner un (4) sello en el sobre.
JUANITA Entonces, ¿qué recomienda usted que haga?
CARTERO Sugiero que vaya al (5) correo. Con tal de que pague el costo del sello, se le puede dar la carta sin ningún problema.
JUANITA Uy, otra diligencia, y no tengo mucho tiempo esta tarde para (6) hacer cola en el correo, pero voy enseguida. ¡Ojalá que sea una carta de amor!

¡LENGUA VIVA!
In Spanish, **Soy yo** means *That's me* or *It's me*. **¿Eres tú?/ ¿Es Ud.?** means *Is that you?*

5  **En el banco** Tú eres un(a) empleado/a de banco y tu compañero/a es un(a) estudiante universitario/a que necesita abrir una cuenta corriente. En parejas, hagan una lista de las palabras que pueden necesitar para esta conversación. Después lean las siguientes situaciones y modifiquen su lista original según la situación. Answers will vary.

- una pareja de recién casados quiere pedir un préstamo para comprar una casa
- una persona quiere información de los servicios que ofrece el banco
- un(a) estudiante va a estudiar al extranjero (*abroad*) y quiere saber qué tiene que hacer para llevar su dinero de una forma segura
- una persona acaba de ganar 50 millones de dólares en la lotería y quiere saber cómo invertirlos (*invest it*)

Ahora, escojan una de las cuatro situaciones y represéntenla para la clase.

TEACHING OPTIONS

Extra Practice Ask students to surf the Internet for banks in Spanish-speaking countries. Have them write a summary of services, rates, hours, and so forth offered by the bank.

Game Divide the class into two teams. They should sit in a row facing one another so that a person from team A is directly across from a person from team B. Begin with the first two students and work your way down the row. Say a word, and the first one to make an association with a different word wins a point for his or her team. Ex: You say: **correos**. The first person from team B answers: **sello; cartero; carta.** Team B wins three points.

Comunicación

6 **Diligencias** En parejas, decidan quién va a hacer cada diligencia y cuál es la manera más rápida de llegar a los diferentes lugares desde el campus. Answers will vary.

modelo

Cobrar unos cheques
Estudiante 1: *Yo voy a cobrar unos cheques. ¿Cómo llego al banco?*
Estudiante 2: *Conduce hacia el norte hasta cruzar la calle Oak. El banco queda en la esquina a la izquierda.*

1. Enviar un paquete
2. Comprar botas nuevas
3. Comprar un pastel de cumpleaños
4. Lavar unas camisas
5. Comprar helado
6. Cortarte (*to cut*) el pelo

¡ATENCIÓN!

Note these different meanings:
quedar *to be located; to be left over; to fit*
quedarse *to stay, to remain*

7 **El Hatillo** Trabajen en parejas para representar los papeles (*roles*) de un(a) turista que está perdido/a en El Hatillo y de un(a) residente de la ciudad que quiere ayudarlo/la. Answers will vary.

NOTA CULTURAL

El Hatillo es un pueblo cerca de Caracas popular por su arquitectura pintoresca, sus restaurantes y sus tiendas de artesanía.

modelo

Plaza Sucre, Café Primavera
Estudiante 1: *Perdón, ¿por dónde queda la Plaza Sucre?*
Estudiante 2: *Del Café Primavera, camine derecho por la calle Sucre hasta cruzar la calle Comercio...*

1. Plaza Bolívar, farmacia
2. Casa de la Cultura, Plaza Sucre
3. banco, terminal
4. estacionamiento (este), escuela
5. Plaza Sucre, estacionamiento (oeste)
6. joyería, banco
7. farmacia, joyería
8. zapatería, iglesia

8 **Direcciones** En grupos, escriban un minidrama en el que unos/as turistas están preguntando cómo llegar a diferentes sitios de la comunidad en la que ustedes viven. Answers will vary.

6 Suggestion Draw a map of your campus and nearby streets with local commerce, asking students to direct you. Ex: **¿En qué calle queda el banco más cercano? ¿Qué tienda se encuentra en la esquina de ____ y ____?**

7 Suggestions
- Go over the icons in the legend to the map, finding the places each represents.
- Explain that the task is to give directions to the first place from the second place. Ask students to find **Café Primavera** and **Plaza Sucre** on the map.

7 Expansion Ask students to research El Hatillo on the Internet.

8 Suggestions
- As a class, brainstorm different tourist sites in and around your area. Write them on the board.
- Using one of the sites listed on the board, model the activity by asking volunteers to give driving directions from campus.

TEACHING OPTIONS

Extra Practice Have pairs list the five best places for local college students. Ex: **la mejor pizza, el mejor corte de pelo,** and so forth. Then have them write directions to each place from campus. Expand to have students debate their choices.

Game Divide the class into groups of three. Each must write directions to a particular commercial establishment close to campus. The groups read their directions, and the other groups try to guess what errand they are running. Each group that guesses correctly wins a point.

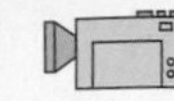

Section Goals

In **Fotonovela** students will:

- receive comprehensible input from free-flowing discourse
- learn functional phrases that preview lesson grammatical structures

Instructional Resources
WB/VM: Video Activities, pp. 239–240
***Fotonovela** DVD/Video (Start 01:16:02)*
Video CD-ROM
*IRM: **Fotonovela** Translations, pp. 146–147, Videoscript, pp. 119–120*
Interactive CD-ROM

Video Recap: Lección 13
Before doing this **Fotonovela** section, review the previous one with this activity.

1. ¿Adónde lleva Martín a los chicos? (al área donde van a ir de excursión)
2. ¿Qué dice él de la contaminación en la región? (es un problema en todo el mundo; tienen un programa de reciclaje)
3. ¿Qué dice Martín de la contaminación del río? (en las montañas no está contaminado; cerca de las ciudades tiene bastante contaminación)
4. ¿Qué va a hacer Maite para proteger el medio ambiente? (va a usar el metro)

Video Synopsis Don Francisco and Martín advise the students about things they need for the hike. Álex and Maite decide to go to the supermarket, the bank, and the post office. They get lost downtown, but a young man gives them directions. After finishing their errands, Álex and Maite return to the house.

Suggestions

- Ask students to predict what they would see and hear in an episode in which the main characters get lost while running errands. Then, ask them a few questions to help them summarize this episode.
- Ask for volunteers to list a few expressions that would be used to get directions. Then ask for volunteers to give you directions to a nearby location.

Estamos perdidos.

Maite y Álex hacen diligencias en el centro.

PERSONAJES

MAITE

INÉS

DON FRANCISCO

ÁLEX

JAVIER

MARTÍN

JOVEN

MARTÍN & DON FRANCISCO Buenas tardes.

JAVIER Hola. ¿Qué tal? Estamos conversando sobre la excursión de mañana.

DON FRANCISCO ¿Ya tienen todo lo que necesitan? A todos los excursionistas yo siempre les recomiendo llevar zapatos cómodos, una mochila, gafas oscuras y un suéter por si hace frío.

JAVIER Todo listo, don Francisco.

MARTÍN Les aconsejo que traigan algo de comer.

ÁLEX Mmm... no pensamos en eso.

MAITE ¡Deja de preocuparte tanto, Álex! Podemos comprar algo en el supermercado ahora mismo. ¿Vamos?

JOVEN ¡Hola! ¿Puedo ayudarte en algo?

MAITE Sí, estamos perdidos. ¿Hay un banco por aquí con cajero automático?

JOVEN Mmm... no hay ningún banco en esta calle que tenga cajero automático.

JOVEN Pero conozco uno en la calle Pedro Moncayo que sí tiene cajero automático. Cruzas esta calle y luego doblas a la izquierda. Sigues todo derecho y antes de que lleguen a la Joyería Crespo van a ver un letrero grande del Banco del Pacífico.

MAITE También buscamos un supermercado.

JOVEN Pues, allí mismo enfrente del banco hay un supermercado pequeño. Fácil, ¿no?

MAITE Creo que sí. Muchas gracias por su ayuda.

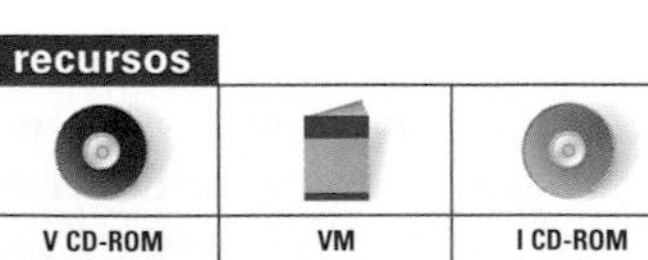

recursos		
V CD-ROM Lección 14	VM pp. 239–240	I CD-ROM Lección 14

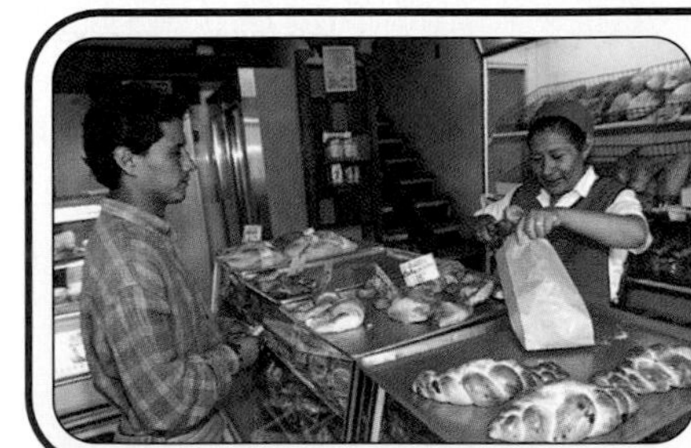

TEACHING OPTIONS

Video Tips General suggestions for using video clips in the classroom can be found on page IAE-12 of this Instructor's Annotated Edition.

Estamos perdidos Play the **Resumen** segment of this video module without sound and ask the class to summarize what they see. Ask them to predict the content of the main video episode based on what they see in the **Resumen**. Write their predictions on the board. Then play the main video episode and the **Resumen** with sound. Finally, through questions and discussion, lead the class to a correct summary of the plot.

ÁLEX ¡Excelente idea! En cuanto termine mi café te acompaño.

MAITE Necesito pasar por el banco y por el correo para mandar unas cartas.

ÁLEX Está bien.

ÁLEX ¿Necesitan algo del centro?

INÉS ¡Sí! Cuando vayan al correo, ¿pueden echar estas postales al buzón? Además necesito unas estampillas.

ÁLEX Por supuesto.

MAITE Ten, guapa, tus sellos.

INÉS Gracias, Maite. ¿Qué tal les fue en el centro?

MAITE ¡Súper bien! Fuimos al banco y al correo. Luego en el supermercado compramos comida para la excursión. Y antes de regresar, paramos en una heladería.

MAITE ¡Ah! Y otra cosa. Cuando llegamos al centro conocimos a un joven muy simpático que nos dio direcciones. Era muy amable... ¡y muy guapo!

Enfoque cultural Las tiendas especializadas

La popularidad de los supermercados está aumentando (*growing*) en los países hispanos, pero todavía muchas personas van a tiendas especializadas para comprar comidas como la carne, el pescado, el pan y los dulces. La pulpería, por ejemplo, es una tienda típica de las zonas rurales de algunos países de Latinoamérica. La gente va a una pulpería para tomar una bebida o comprar productos esenciales. Otra tienda típica de algunos países hispanos es la rosticería, donde se asan (*roast*) y se venden carnes para llevar (*takeout*).

Expresiones útiles

Giving advice

- ▶ **Les recomiendo/Hay que llevar zapatos cómodos.**
  I recommend that you/It's necessary to wear comfortable shoes.
- ▶ **Les aconsejo que traigan algo de comer.**
  I advise you to bring something to eat.

Talking about errands

- ▶ **Necesito pasar por el banco.**
  I need to go by the bank.
- ▷ **En cuanto termine mi café te acompaño.**
  As soon as I finish my coffee, I'll go with you.

Getting directions

- ▶ **Estamos perdidos.**
  We're lost.
- ▶ **¿Hay un banco por aquí con cajero automático?**
  Is there a bank around here with an ATM?
- ▷ **Crucen esta calle y luego doblen a la izquierda/derecha.**
  Cross this street and then turn to the left/right.
- ▷ **Sigan todo derecho.**
  Go straight ahead.
- ▷ **Antes de que lleguen a la joyería van a ver un letrero grande.**
  Before you get to the jewelry store, you're going to see a big sign.
- ▶ **¿Por dónde queda el supermercado?**
  Where is the supermarket?
- ▷ **Está a dos cuadras de aquí.**
  It's two blocks from here.
- ▷ **Queda en la calle Flores.**
  It's on Flores street.
- ▷ **Pues, allí mismo enfrente del banco hay un supermercado.**
  Well, right in front of the bank there is a supermarket.

Suggestion Ask for volunteers to read the various parts in the captions for video stills 1–5 of the **Fotonovela**. Then have the class work in groups of four to read aloud the captions for video stills 6–10.

Expresiones útiles Draw attention to the sentence **Estamos perdidos**. Tell the class that **perdidos** is a past participle of the verb **perder** and that it is used here as an adjective. Then point out the sentence in video still 6 **... no hay ningún banco en esta calle que tenga cajero automático.** Explain to students that its subordinate clause also functions as an adjective and, in this particular case, requires the subjunctive because the bank doesn't exist. Tell your students that they will learn more about these concepts in **Estructura**.

TEACHING OPTIONS

Enfoque cultural You might want to introduce the names of these additional specialty shops: **el estanco** (a place where tobacco products, postcards, and stamps are sold), **la perfumería** (perfume shop), **el quiosco** (a newsstand where newspapers and magazines are sold), and **la relojería** (a shop that specializes in clocks and watches). Then write a list of items on the board and ask your students where they would go to obtain each one. Ex: **carne, pescado, libros, helado, fruta, comida, tarjetas postales, relojes, revistas, periódicos, cigarros, un pastel, un préstamo.**

1 Expansion Give the class these additional items: **5. El joven llevó a Álex y a Maite al banco. (Falso. El joven les dio direcciones.) 6. Después de hacer sus diligencias, Maite y Álex fueron a una heladería. (Cierto.)**

2 Suggestion Have your students write these sentences on separate slips of paper so that they can rearrange them until they determine the correct order.

3 Expansion Have pairs come up with an additional situation and then make a list of the errands the **Fotonovela** characters need to run in order to complete it. Then have them read the list of errands aloud so the class can guess what the situation might be.

4 Possible Response
E1: Voy al supermercado y a la heladería. ¿Quieres ir conmigo?
E2: Sí, en cuanto termine mi almuerzo te acompaño.
E1: Necesito pasar por el banco porque necesito dinero.
E2: Yo también necesito ir al banco. ¿Hay un banco por aquí con cajero automático?
E1: Hay un cajero automático a tres cuadras de aquí. Queda en la calle Libertad.
E2: También necesito ir a la lavandería y al correo para mandar unas cartas.
E1: Ningún problema… el correo y la lavandería están cerca del banco.
E2: Oye, ¿qué vas a hacer esta noche?
E1: Voy a ir a la fiesta que celebran para un amigo. ¿Quieres venir?
E2: ¡Sí, gracias!

Reacciona a la fotonovela

1 **¿Cierto o falso?** Decide si lo que dicen las siguientes frases es **cierto** o **falso.** Corrige las frases falsas.

	Cierto	Falso	
1. Don Francisco insiste en que los excursionistas lleven una cámara.	❍	✓	Don Francisco recomienda que los excursionistas lleven zapatos cómodos, una mochila, gafas oscuras y un suéter.
2. Inés escribió unas postales y ahora necesita mandarlas por correo.	✓	❍	
3. El joven dice que el Banco del Atlántico tiene un cajero automático.	❍	✓	El Banco del Pacífico tiene un cajero automático.
4. Enfrente del banco hay una heladería.	❍	✓	Enfrente del banco hay un supermercado pequeño.

CONSÚLTALO

To review the use of verbs like **insistir**, see **Estructura 12.4**, p. 382.

2 **Ordenar** Pon los eventos de la **Fotonovela** en el orden correcto.

a. Un joven ayuda a Álex y a Maite a encontrar el banco porque están perdidos. 3
b. Álex y Maite comen un helado. 6
c. Inés les da unas postales a Maite y a Álex para echar al buzón. 2
d. Maite y Álex van al banco y al correo. 4
e. Álex termina su café. 1
f. Maite y Álex van al supermercado y compran comida. 5

3 **Otras diligencias** En parejas, hagan una lista de las diligencias que Maite, Álex, Inés y Javier necesitan hacer para completar las siguientes actividades.

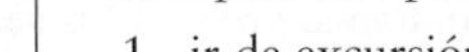

1. ir de excursión
2. pedir una beca (*scholarship*)
3. visitar una nueva ciudad
4. abrir una cuenta corriente
5. celebrar el cumpleaños de Maite
6. comprar una nueva computadora portátil

JAVIER MAITE ÁLEX

INÉS

4 **Conversación** Un(a) compañero/a y tú son vecinos/as. Uno/a de ustedes acaba de mudarse y necesita ayuda porque no conoce la ciudad. Los dos tienen que hacer algunas diligencias y deciden hacerlas juntos/as. Preparen una conversación breve incluyendo planes para ir a los siguientes lugares. Answers will vary.

modelo

Estudiante 1: Necesito lavar mi ropa. ¿Sabes dónde queda una lavandería?
Estudiante 2: Sí. Aquí a dos cuadras hay una. También tengo que lavar mi ropa. ¿Qué te parece si vamos juntos?

- un banco
- una lavandería
- un supermercado
- una heladería
- una panadería

AYUDA

primero *first*
luego *then*
¿Sabes dónde queda…? *Do you know where…is?*
¿Qué te parece? *What do you think?*
¡Cómo no! *But of course!*

TEACHING OPTIONS

Game Prepare several sets of directions that explain how to get to well-known places on campus or in your community, without mentioning the destinations by name. Read each set of directions aloud and ask the class to tell you where they would end up if they followed your directions.

Pairs Ask pairs to create a skit in which a tourist asks for directions in a Spanish-speaking country. Give the class sufficient time to prepare and rehearse the skits, then ask for a few volunteers to present their skits to the class.

Ortografía

Las abreviaturas

In Spanish, as in English, abbreviations are often used in order to save space and time while writing. Here are some of the most commonly used abbreviations in Spanish.

usted → **Ud.** **ustedes** → **Uds.**

As you have already learned, the subject pronouns **usted** and **ustedes** are often abbreviated.

don → **D.** **doña** → **Dña.** **doctor(a)** → **Dr(a).**
señor → **Sr.** **señora** → **Sra.** **señorita** → **Srta.**

These titles are frequently abbreviated.

centímetro → **cm** **metro** → **m** **kilómetro** → **km**
litro → **l** **gramo** → **g, gr** **kilogramo** → **kg**

The abbreviations for these units of measurement are often used, but without periods.

por ejemplo → **p. ej.** **página(s)** → **pág(s).**

These abbreviations are often seen in books.

Sra. Emilia F. Bazán
Cía. Romero, S.A.
3336
Calle Lozano, n.º 37
Caracas, Venezuela

derecha → **dcha.** **izquierda** → **izq., izqda.**
código postal → **C.P.** **número** → **n.º**

These abbreviations are often used in mailing addresses.

Banco → **Bco.** **Compañía** → **Cía.**
cuenta corriente → **c/c.** **Sociedad Anónima (*Inc.*)** → **S.A.**

These abbreviations are frequently used in the business world.

Práctica Escribe otra vez la siguiente información usando las abreviaturas adecuadas.

1. doña María Dña.
2. señora Pérez Sra.
3. Compañía Mexicana de Inversiones Cía.
4. usted Ud.
5. Banco de Santander Bco.
6. doctor Medina Dr.
7. Código Postal 03697 C.P.
8. cuenta corriente número 20-453 c/c., n.º

Emparejar En la tabla hay 9 abreviaturas. Empareja los cuadros necesarios para formarlas. S.A., Bco., cm, Dña., c/c., dcha., Srta., C.P., Ud.

S.	c.	C.	c	co.	U
B	c/	Sr	A.	D	dc
ta.	P.	ña.	ha.	m	d.

recursos

LM p. 80	Lab CD/MP3 Lección 14	I CD-ROM Lección 14

Section Goal

In **Ortografía** students will learn some common Spanish abbreviations.

Instructional Resource
Interactive CD-ROM

Suggestions

- Point out that the abbreviations **Ud.** and **Uds.** begin with a capital letter, though the spelled-out forms do not.
- Write **D., Dña., Dr., Dra., Sr., Sra.,** and **Srta.** on the board. Again, point out that the abbreviations begin with a capital letter, though the spelled-out forms do not.
- Point out that the period in **n.º** does not appear at the end of the abbreviation.
- Point out that **Ortografía** replaces **Pronunciación** in the Student Edition for **Lecciones 10–18**, but not in the Lab Manual. The **Recursos** box references the **Pronunciación** sections found in all lessons of the Lab Manual.

Successful Language Learning Tell students that the ability to recognize common abbreviations will make it easier for them to interpret written information in a Spanish-speaking country.

TEACHING OPTIONS

Pairs Have the class work in pairs to write an imaginary mailing address that uses as many abbreviations as possible. Then have a few pairs write their work on the board and ask for volunteers to read the addresses aloud.

Extra Practice Write a list of abbreviations on the board; each abbreviation should have one letter missing. Have the class fill in the missing letters and tell you what each abbreviation stands for. Ex: **U__., D__a., g__, Bc__., d__ha., p__gs., __zq., S.__.**

Section Goal

In **Estructura 14.1** students will learn the use of the subjunctive in adjective clauses.

Instructional Resources
WB/VM: Workbook, pp. 161–162
Lab Manual, p. 81
Lab CD/MP3 ***Lección 14***
IRM: ***¡Inténtalo! & Práctica*** *Answers, p. 220; Tapescript, pp. 63–66;* ***Hojas de actividades****, p. 171*
Info Gap Activities Booklet, pp. 53–54
Interactive CD-ROM
Companion website: www.vistahigherlearning.com
Presentations CD-ROM

Suggestions

- Use magazine pictures to compare and contrast the uses of the indicative and subjunctive in adjective clauses. Ex: **Esta casa tiene una fuente en el jardín. Yo busco una casa que tenga piscina. Este señor come insectos vivos. ¿Conocen a alguien que coma insectos vivos?**
- Ask volunteers to answer questions that describe their wishes. Ex: **¿Qué buscas en una casa? ¿Qué buscas en un(a) compañero/a de cuarto?**
- Ask volunteers to read the captions to the video stills and point out the subordinate adjective clause and its antecedent, then indicate the verb in the present subjunctive.

14.1 The subjunctive in adjective clauses

NATIONAL STANDARDS comparisons

ANTE TODO In **Lección 13**, you learned that the subjunctive is used in adverbial clauses after certain conjunctions. You will now learn how the subjunctive can be used in adjective clauses to express that the existence of someone or something is uncertain or indefinite.

¿Hay un banco por aquí que tenga cajero automático?

No hay ningún banco en esta calle que tenga cajero automático.

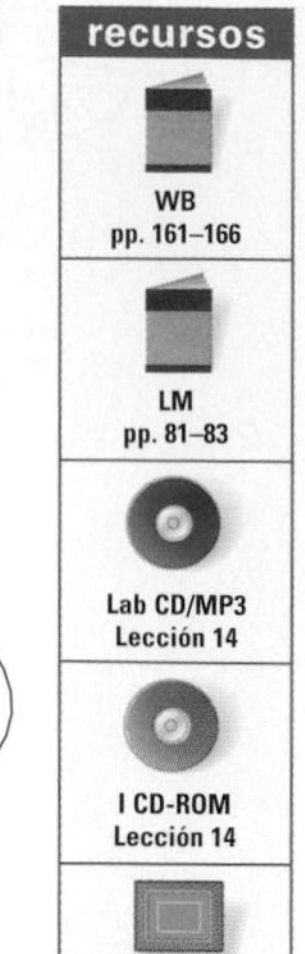

▶ The subjunctive is used in an adjective (or subordinate) clause that refers to a person, place, thing, or idea that either does not exist or whose existence is uncertain or indefinite. In the examples below, compare the differences in meaning between the statements using the indicative and those using the subjunctive.

¡ATENCIÓN!
Adjective clauses are subordinate clauses that modify a noun or pronoun in the main clause of a sentence. That noun or pronoun is called the *antecedent*.

Indicative	Subjunctive
Necesito **el libro** que **tiene** información sobre Venezuela. *I need **the book** that has information about Venezuela.*	Necesito **un libro** que **tenga** información sobre Venezuela. *I need **a book** that has information about Venezuela.*
Quiero vivir en **esta casa** que **tiene** jardín. *I want to live in **this house** that has a garden.*	Quiero vivir en **una casa** que **tenga** jardín. *I want to live in **a house** that has a garden.*
En mi barrio, hay **una heladería** que **vende** helado de mango. *In my neighborhood, **there's an ice cream store** that sells mango ice cream.*	En mi barrio no hay **ninguna heladería** que **venda** helado de mango. *In my neighborhood, **there are no ice cream stores** that sell mango ice cream.*

▶ When the adjective clause refers to a person, place, thing, or idea that is clearly known, certain, or definite, the indicative is used.

Quiero ir **al supermercado** que **vende** productos venezolanos.
I want to go to the supermarket that sells Venezuelan products.

Busco **al profesor** que **enseña** japonés.
I'm looking for the professor who teaches Japanese.

Conozco **a alguien** que **va** a esa peluquería.
I know someone who goes to that beauty salon.

Tengo **un amigo** que **vive** cerca de mi casa.
I have a friend who lives near my house.

TEACHING OPTIONS

Extra Practice To provide oral practice with adjective clauses in the subjunctive and indicative, create sentences that follow the pattern of the sentences in the examples. Say a sentence, have students repeat it, then change the main clause. Have students then say the sentence with the new clause, changing the subordinate clause as necessary. **Conozco una tienda donde venden helados riquísimos. → Busco una tienda donde...**

Heritage Speakers Have heritage speakers compare and contrast business establishments in their cultural communities and communities outside it. They should use both the indicative and the subjunctive, varying the verbs in the main clause as much as possible.

▶ The personal **a** is not used with direct objects that are hypothetical people. However, as you learned in **Lección 7**, **alguien** and **nadie** are always preceded by the personal **a** when they function as direct objects.

Necesitamos **un empleado** que **sepa** usar computadoras.
We need an employee who knows how to use computers.

Necesitamos **al empleado** que **sabe** usar computadoras.
We need the employee who knows how to use computers.

Buscamos **a alguien** que **pueda** cocinar.
We're looking for someone who can cook.

No conocemos **a nadie** que **pueda** cocinar.
We don't know anyone who can cook.

¡ATENCIÓN!

Here are some verbs which are commonly followed by adjective clauses in the subjunctive:

necesitar **encontrar**
querer **conocer**
buscar **haber**

▶ The subjunctive is commonly used in questions with adjective clauses when the speaker is trying to find out information about which he or she is uncertain. However, if the person who responds to the question knows the information, the indicative is used.

—¿Hay un parque que **esté** cerca de nuestro hotel?
Is there a park that's near our hotel?

—Sí, hay un parque que **está** muy cerca del hotel.
Yes, there's a park that's very near the hotel.

SECCIÓN
AMARILLA
Busque cualquier información que necesite.

¡INTÉNTALO!

Escoge entre el subjuntivo o el indicativo para completar cada oración.

1. Necesito una persona que ___pueda___ (puede/pueda) cantar bien.
2. Buscamos a alguien que ___tenga___ (tiene/tenga) paciencia.
3. ¿Hay restaurantes aquí que ___sirvan___ (sirven/sirvan) comida japonesa?
4. Tengo una amiga que ___saca___ (saca/saque) fotografías muy bonitas.
5. Hay una carnicería que ___está___ (está/esté) cerca de aquí.
6. No vemos ningún apartamento que nos ___interese___ (interesa/interese).
7. Conozco a un estudiante que ___come___ (come/coma) hamburguesas todos los días.
8. ¿Hay alguien que ___diga___ (dice/diga) la verdad?

Suggestions

- Ask closed-ended questions, repeating the answer using complete sentences and the subjunctive. Ex: ____, **¿conoces a alguien que sepa hablar japonés? (No.)** ____ **no conoce a nadie que sepa japonés, pero** ____ **conoce a una joven japonesa que estudia inglés.**
- Test comprehension as you proceed by asking volunteers to supply the correct form of verbs for adjective clauses you suggest. Ex: **Prefiero la playa donde** ____ **menos gente. (hay) Prefiero una playa donde** ____ **menos gente. (haya)**
- Suggest main clauses with the verbs in **¡Atención!** and ask students to write the adjective clause. Ex: **Necesito un coche que... ; Busco al señor que... ; No hay nadie que...**
- Ask a volunteer to read the realia and explain why the verb **necesite** is in the subjunctive.

TEACHING OPTIONS

Pairs Ask pairs to use the sentences from **¡Inténtalo!** and the unused verbs **(puede, tiene, sirven, saque, esté, interesa, coma, dice)** and rewrite the sentence, changing the main clause accordingly.

Extra Practice Ask students to describe the ideal community. Their descriptions should include only sentences in the subjunctive. Refer them to the verbs included in **¡Atención!** to help them develop their descriptions.

3 Expansion Ask students to expand their answers with a reason for their choice. Ex: **Paguemos en efectivo. Tenemos bastante dinero.**

4 Expansion Have groups bring in tourist information for another city in the Spanish-speaking world and repeat the activity. Encourage them to make copies of this information for the class. They should then present to the class their suggestions for what to do, using **nosotros/as** commands.

5 Suggestion Before beginning the activity, have students brainstorm different financial problems and solutions encountered by roommates sharing an apartment. Write their responses on the board.

5 Expansion Call on pairs to perform their **Situación** for the class.

Suggestion See the Info Gap Activities Booklet for an additional activity to practice the material presented in this section.

Comunicación

3 **Preguntar** Tú y tu compañero/a están de vacaciones en Caracas y se hacen sugerencias para resolver las situaciones que se presentan. Inventen mandatos afirmativos o negativos usando **nosotros/as.** Answers will vary.

modelo

Se nos olvidaron las tarjetas de crédito.
Paguemos en efectivo./No compremos más regalos.

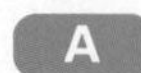

A	B
1. El museo está a sólo una cuadra de aquí.	1. Tenemos muchos cheques de viajero.
2. Tenemos hambre.	2. Tenemos prisa para llegar al cine.
3. Hay mucha cola en el cine.	3. Estamos cansados y queremos dormir.

4 **Decisiones** Trabajen en grupos pequeños. Ustedes están en Caracas por dos días. Lean esta página de una guía turística sobre la ciudad y decidan qué van a hacer hoy por la mañana, por la tarde y por la noche. Hagan oraciones con mandatos afirmativos o negativos usando **nosotros/as.** Answers will vary.

modelo

Visitemos el Museo de Arte Contemporáneo Sofía Imber esta tarde. Quiero ver las esculturas de Jesús Rafael Soto.

NOTA CULTURAL

El venezolano **Jesús Rafael Soto** (1923–) es un escultor y pintor moderno. Sus obras cinéticas (*kinetic works*) frecuentemente incluyen formas que brillan (*shimmer*) y vibran.

Guía de Caracas

MUSEOS
- **Museo de Arte Colonial** Avenida Panteón
- **Museo de Arte Contemporáneo Sofía Imber** Parque Central. Esculturas de Jesús Rafael Soto y pinturas de Miró, Chagall y Picasso.
- **Galería de Arte Nacional** Parque Central. Colección de más de 4000 obras de arte venezolano.

SITIOS DE INTERÉS
- **Plaza Bolívar**
- **Jardín Botánico** Avenida Interna UCV. De 8:00 a 5:00.
- **Parque del Este** Avenida Francisco de Miranda. Parque más grande de la ciudad con terrario.
- **Casa Natal de Simón Bolívar** Esquina de Sociedad de la avenida Universitaria. Casa colonial donde nació El Libertador.

RESTAURANTES
- **El Barquero** Avenida Luis Roche
- **Restaurante El Coyuco** Avenida Urdaneta
- **Restaurante Sorrento** Avenida Francisco Solano
- **Café Tonino** Avenida Andrés Bello

Síntesis

5 **Situación** Tú y un(a) compañero/a viven juntos en un apartamento y tienen problemas económicos. Describan los problemas y sugieran algunas soluciones. Hagan oraciones con mandatos afirmativos o negativos usando **nosotros/as.** Answers will vary.

modelo

Es importante que reduzcamos nuestros gastos (expenses). Hagamos un presupuesto (budget).

TEACHING OPTIONS

Video Show the video again to give students more input containing **nosotros/as** commands. Ask students to write down all the examples they hear in the dialogue. When the video has finished, review the lists as a class.

Pairs Have students develop a role-play in which two friends or a couple are deciding at which local restaurant to have dinner. Students should use **nosotros/as** commands as much as possible. Call on different pairs to perform their role-plays for the class.

14.3 Past participles used as adjectives

ANTE TODO In **Lección 5**, you learned about present participles (**estudiando**). Both Spanish and English have past participles. The past participles of English verbs often end in **-ed** (*to turn* ➤ *turned*), but many are also irregular (*to buy* ➤ *bought; to drive* ➤ *driven*).

¡ATENCIÓN!

The past participles of **-er** and **-ir** verbs whose stems end in **-a, -e,** or **-o** carry a written accent mark on the **i** of the **-ido** ending.

caer	**caído**
creer	**creído**
leer	**leído**
oír	**oído**
reír	**reído**
sonreír	**sonreído**
traer	**traído**

▶ In Spanish, regular **-ar** verbs form the past participle with **-ado.** Regular **-er** and **-ir** verbs form the past participle with **-ido.**

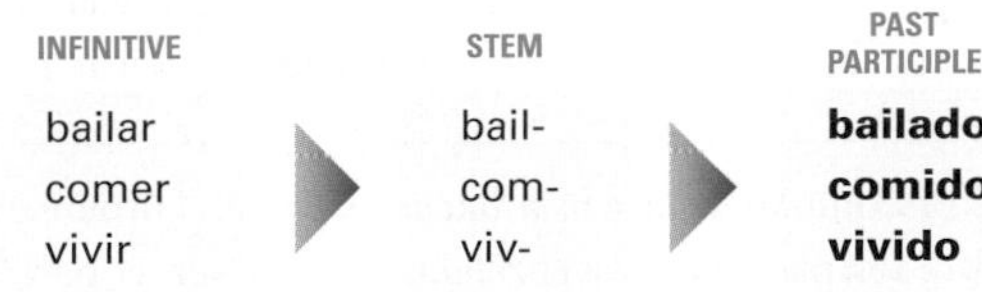

INFINITIVE	STEM	PAST PARTICIPLE
bailar	bail-	**bailado**
comer	com-	**comido**
vivir	viv-	**vivido**

Irregular past participles

abrir	**abierto**	morir	**muerto**
decir	**dicho**	poner	**puesto**
describir	**descrito**	resolver	**resuelto**
descubrir	**descubierto**	romper	**roto**
escribir	**escrito**	ver	**visto**
hacer	**hecho**	volver	**vuelto**

CONSEJOS

You already know several participles used as adjectives: **aburrido, interesado, nublado, perdido,** etc.

• • •

Note that all irregular past participles except **dicho** and **hecho** end in **-to.**

▶ In Spanish, as in English, past participles can be used as adjectives. They are often used with the verb **estar** to describe a condition or state that results from an action. Like other Spanish adjectives, they must agree in gender and number with the nouns they modify.

En la entrada hay algunos letreros **escritos** en español.
In the entrance, there are some signs written in Spanish.

Tenemos la mesa **puesta** y la cena **hecha.**
We have the table set and dinner made.

La joyería **está cerrada.**
The jewelry store is closed.

El cheque ya **está firmado.**
The check is already signed.

¡INTÉNTALO! Indica la forma correcta del participio pasado de estos verbos.

1. hablar hablado
2. beber bebido
3. decidir decidido
4. romper roto
5. escribir escrito
6. cantar cantado
7. oír oído
8. traer traído
9. correr corrido
10. leer leído
11. ver visto
12. hacer hecho
13. morir muerto
14. reír reído
15. mirar mirado
16. abrir abierto

Section Goals

In **Estructura 14.3** students will learn:

- to form regular past participles
- irregular past participles
- to use past participles as adjectives

Instructional Resources

WB/VM: Workbook, pp. 165–166
Lab Manual, p. 83
Lab CD/MP3 ***Lección 14***
IRM: ***¡Inténtalo!*** *&* ***Práctica*** *Answers, p. 220; Tapescript, pp. 63–66*
Interactive CD-ROM
Companion website: www.vistahigherlearning.com
Presentations CD-ROM

Suggestions

- Use magazine pictures to review some of the following regular past participles students have learned as adjectives: **aburrido, afectado, avergonzado, cansado, casado, cerrado, desordenado, enamorado, enojado, equivocado, mareado, ocupado, ordenado, preocupado.** As you review these forms, have students indicate the corresponding infinitives.
- Check for understanding by calling out known infinitives and asking volunteers to give their past participles. Ex: **mirar, comprender, cumplir**
- Practice irregular forms by asking students to finish incomplete sentences. Ex: **Esas piñatas son ____ en México. (hechas) La biblioteca está ____ toda la noche. (abierta)**

TEACHING OPTIONS

Extra Practice To provide oral practice with past participle agreement, create substitution drills. Ex: ***Felipe* está enojado. (Lupe/Los estudiantes/Mis hermanas/El profesor)** • ***El cheque* ya está firmado. (La carta/Las tarjetas/El artículo)** Say a sentence and have students repeat. Say a cue. Have students replace the subject of the original sentence with the cued subject and make any other necessary changes.

Game Divide the class into groups of five and have each team sit in a row. The first person in the row has a blank piece of paper. Have five infinitives in mind. Call out one of them. Allow the student with the paper ten seconds to write down the past participle of the infinitive and pass the paper to the next in row. The group with the most correct responses wins.

1 Expansion Have pairs make a list of new nouns of different gender and/or number, one for each item in the activity, to replace the original nouns being modified by past participles. They should double-check that the new sentences will make sense. Have them exchange their list with another pair, who should rewrite the sentences making all necessary changes, then return them to the first pair for correction.

2 Expansion Have students redo the activity using a negative response and a different past participle used as an adjective to provide a reason. Ex: **No, no están comprados porque el banco está cerrado hoy. No, no están confirmadas porque el teléfono del hotel está ocupado.**

3 Expansion In small groups, have students tell each other what they say when they brag like the **estudiante competitivo**, using past participles as adjectives. Then have a group representative share some of their sentences for the class to guess the person who said them.

Práctica

1 Completar Completa estas frases con la forma adecuada del participio pasado del verbo que está entre paréntesis.

1. Hoy mi peluquería favorita está cerrada (cerrar).
2. Por eso, voy al salón de belleza de la esquina que está abierto (abrir) todos los días.
3. Queda en la Plaza Bolívar, una plaza muy conocida (conocer).
4. Todos los productos y servicios de esta tienda están descritos (describir) en un catálogo.
5. El nombre del salón está escrito (escribir) en el letrero y en la acera (*sidewalk*).
6. Cuando esta diligencia esté hecha (hacer), necesito pasar por el banco.

NOTA CULTURAL

Simón Bolívar (1783–1830) es considerado el "libertador" de cinco países de Suramérica: Venezuela, Perú, Bolivia, Colombia y Ecuador. Su apellido se ve en nombres como Bolivia, Ciudad Bolívar, la Universidad Simón Bolívar, el bolívar (la moneda venezolana) y en los nombres de muchas plazas y monumentos.

2 Preparaciones Tú y tu compañero/a van a hacer un viaje. Túrnense para hacerse las siguientes preguntas sobre los preparativos *(preparations)*. Usen el participio pasado en sus respuestas.

modelo

Estudiante 1: *¿Firmaste el cheque de viajero?*
Estudiante 2: *Sí, el cheque de viajero ya está firmado.*

1. ¿Compraste los boletos para el avión? Sí, los boletos ya están comprados.
2. ¿Confirmaste las reservaciones para el hotel? Sí, las reservaciones ya están confirmadas.
3. ¿Firmaste tu pasaporte? Sí, mi pasaporte ya está firmado.
4. ¿Lavaste la ropa? Sí, la ropa ya está lavada.
5. ¿Resolviste el problema con el banco? Sí, el problema con el banco ya está resuelto.
6. ¿Pagaste todas las cuentas? Sí, las cuentas ya están pagadas.
7. ¿Hiciste todas las diligencias? Sí, todas las diligencias ya están hechas.
8. ¿Hiciste las maletas? Sí, las maletas ya están hechas.

3 El estudiante competitivo En parejas, túrnense para hacer el papel (*play the role*) de un(a) estudiante que es muy competitivo/a y siempre quiere ser mejor que los demás. Usen los participios pasados de los verbos subrayados. Answers will vary. Sample answers below.

modelo

Estudiante 1: *A veces se me daña la computadora.*
Estudiante 2: *Yo sé mucho de computadoras. Mi computadora nunca está dañada.*

1. Yo no hago la cama todos los días.
   Soy muy ordenado/a. Mi cama siempre está hecha.
2. Casi nunca resuelvo mis problemas.
   Soy muy eficiente. Mis problemas siempre están resueltos.
3. Nunca guardo mis documentos importantes.
   Soy muy organizado/a. Mis documentos importantes siempre están guardados.
4. Es difícil para mí terminar mis tareas.
   Soy muy responsable. Mis tareas siempre están terminadas.
5. Siempre se me olvida firmar mis tarjetas de crédito.
   Soy muy responsable. Todas mis tarjetas de crédito están firmadas.
6. Nunca pongo la mesa cuando ceno.
   Soy muy organizado/a. Mi mesa siempre está puesta.
7. No quiero escribir la composición para mañana.
   Soy muy buen estudiante. Mi composición ya está escrita.
8. Casi nunca lavo mi carro. Yo soy muy limpio/a. Mi carro siempre está lavado.

TEACHING OPTIONS

Heritage Speakers Have heritage speakers write a short description of their own hometown. Encourage them to use active vocabulary from **Contextos** and at least twelve past participles used as adjectives in their descriptions.

Extra Practice Write these sentences on the board. Have students copy them and draw a happy or sad face next to each to show the situations and/or feelings expressed. Ex: **Ni está la comida hecha ni está la mesa puesta.** ☹ **1. El reloj está descompuesto. 2. Con el dinero ahorrado en las compras, podemos ir al cine. 3. Todo el dinero está perdido. 4. Con el préstamo del banco tenemos resuelto nuestro problema. 5. Vamos a la pastelería de la esquina abierta recientemente.**

Comunicación

4 

Preguntas En parejas, túrnense para hacerse estas preguntas. Answers will vary.

1. ¿Dejas alguna luz prendida en tu casa por la noche?
2. ¿Está ordenado tu cuarto?
3. ¿Prefieres comprar libros usados o nuevos? ¿Por qué?
4. ¿Tienes mucho dinero ahorrado?
5. ¿Necesitas pedirles dinero prestado a tus padres?
6. ¿Estás preocupado/a por el medio ambiente?
7. ¿Qué haces cuando no estás preparado/a para una clase?
8. ¿Qué haces cuando estás perdido/a en una ciudad?

5

Describir Tú y un(a) compañero/a son agentes de policía y tienen que investigar un crimen. Miren el dibujo y describan lo que encontraron en la habitación del señor Villalonga. Usen el participio pasado en la descripción. Luego, comparen su descripción con la de otra pareja. Answers will vary.

modelo

La puerta del baño no estaba cerrada.

AYUDA

You may want to use the past participles of these verbs to describe the illustration:

abrir, desordenar *(to make untidy)*, **hacer, poner, tirar** *(to throw)*

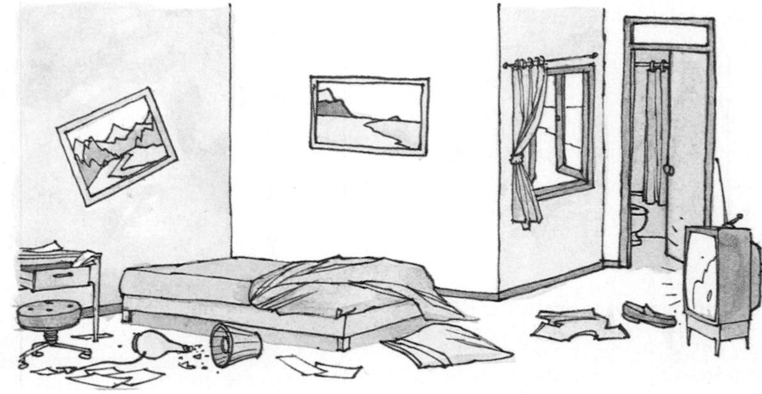

Síntesis

6 

Entre líneas En parejas, representen una conversación entre un empleado de banco y una clienta. Usen las primeras dos líneas para empezar y la última para terminar, pero inventen las líneas del medio (*middle*). Usen participios pasados. Answers will vary.

EMPLEADO Buenos días, señora Ibáñez. ¿En qué la puedo ayudar?
CLIENTA Tengo un problema con este banco. ¡Todavía no está resuelto!
...
CLIENTA ¡No vuelvo nunca a este banco!

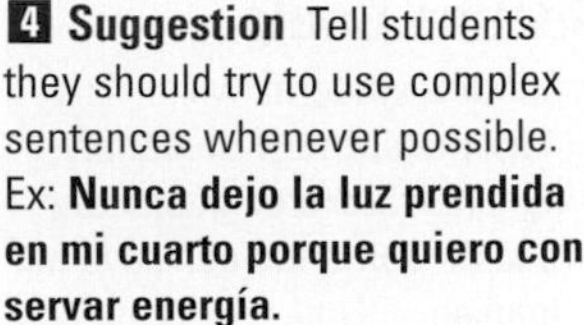

4 Suggestion Tell students they should try to use complex sentences whenever possible. Ex: **Nunca dejo la luz prendida en mi cuarto porque quiero conservar energía.**

4 Expansion Have one member of each pair write down the answers, choosing only one per question and mixing up his or her own with his or her partner's. Then have pairs exchange papers with another pair, who will read the list of answers and guess who from the first pair gave each answer. Have pairs work in groups of four to correct each other's guesses.

5 Suggestion Allow students a couple of minutes to take notes about the crime scene before assigning the activity to pairs.

5 Expansion Have students give their answers in round-robin format. Remind them that each contribution has to contain new information not already supplied by another pair.

6 Suggestion Have the class brainstorm a list of banking problems an individual might have. Write the list on the board.

6 Expansion Invite volunteers to perform their conversation for the class.

TEACHING OPTIONS

Pairs Have pairs make a promotional flyer for a new business in town. Their flyers should include at least three past participles used as adjectives. When they have finished, circulate the flyers in the class.

Game Divide the class into groups of three. Each group should think of a famous place or a historical monument. The other groups will take turns asking questions about the monument. Questions can only be answered with **sí/no** and each one should have a past participle used as an adjective. Ex: **¿Está abierto al público? ¿Es conocido solamente en este país?** The first group to guess the identity of the site wins a point.

Section Goals

In **Lectura** students will:

- learn the strategy of identifying a narrator's point of view
- read an authentic narrative in Spanish

Instructional Resource
Companion website: www.vistahigherlearning.com

Estrategia Tell students that recognizing the point of view from which a narrative is told will help them comprehend it. Write the following first sentences of two narratives on the board and ask students to identify the point of view.

Cristóbal Colón vio por primera vez el territorio de Venezuela el 1° de agosto de 1498 en su tercer viaje al Nuevo Mundo.

Muy pronto tuvimos que reconocer que no íbamos a solucionar el caso sin mucho trabajo.

Examinar el texto Ask students to read the first paragraph of **"Grandezas de la burocracia"** and determine whether the narrative is written from the first- or third-person point of view.

Seleccionar Have pairs work through this activity together. If they have difficulty answering any question, suggest one of the partners read aloud corresponding portions of the text.

Suggestion Point out the forms **permitiera, dignase,** and **estuviese** in the reading. Explain that they are forms of the past subjunctive, which will be presented in **Estructura 16.3**. Tell your students they can probably figure out the meaning of these words using context clues and the glosses.

Lectura

Antes de leer

Estrategia
Identifying point of view

You can understand a narrative more completely if you identify the point of view of the narrator. You can do this by simply asking yourself from whose perspective the story is being told. Some stories are narrated in the first person. That is, the narrator is a character in the story, and everything you read is filtered through that person's thoughts, emotions, and opinions. Other stories have an omniscient narrator who is not one of the story's characters and who reports the thoughts and actions of all the characters.

Examinar el texto

Lee brevemente el cuento. ¿De qué trata? ¿Cómo lo sabes? ¿Se narra en primera persona o tiene un narrador omnisciente? ¿Cómo lo sabes?

Seleccionar

Completa cada frase con la información adecuada.

1. Los personajes° son __a__.
   a. árabes b. franceses c. argentinos
2. Abderrahmán era __b__.
   a. el ingeniero más sabio de los árabes
   b. un califa importante
   c. supervisor de la construcción de la ciudad
3. El cuento° tiene que ver° con __a__.
   a. la construcción de una ciudad
   b. los problemas del califa con su esposa
   c. la burocracia en Bagdad
4. El supervisor de la construcción prometió terminar el proyecto dentro de __c__.
   a. diez años b. cuatro años c. un año

recursos

vistahigherlearning.com

personajes *characters* cuento *story*
tiene que ver con *has to do with*

Grandezas° de la burocracia

Marco Denevi

Marco Denevi nació en Buenos Aires, Argentina, en 1922 y murió en la misma ciudad en 1998. Su novela Rosaura a las diez *lo llevó a la fama en 1955. Escribió cuentos, novelas, obras teatrales y, a partir de 1980°, se dedicó a escribir periodismo político. La obra de Denevi, candidato al Premio Nobel de Literatura, se caracteriza por su ingenio° y sentido del humor.*

Después de leer

Completar

Completa cada frase con la información adecuada. Answers will va

1. Abderrahmán quería fundar ______.
2. Kamaru-l-Akmar prometió ______.
3. Después del primer año, Kamaru-l-Akmar pidió ______.
4. Abderrahmán se enojó porque ______.
5. Cuando Abderrahmán vio la ciudad, dijo que ______.
6. Mientras planeaban la futura ciudad, los ingenieros y arquitectos construyeron ______.

TEACHING OPTIONS

Heritage Speakers Ask heritage speakers if they have visited an **alcázar** (*fortress*) or a **mezquita** (*mosque*) in Spain or another Spanish-speaking country. Ask them to give a brief presentation on the features of either of these structures, what they saw, and where it is located. Ask them to display postcards, photos, or brochures as visual aids, if possible.

Pairs Have pairs of students work together to read **"Grandezas de la burocracia"** and write two questions about the selection. When they have finished, have them exchange their questions with another pair who can work together to answer them.

Cuentan que Abderrahmán decidió fundar° la ciudad más hermosa del mundo, para lo cual mandó llamar a una multitud de ingenieros, de arquitectos y de artistas a cuya cabeza estaba Kamaru-l-Akmar, el primero y el más sabio° de los ingenieros árabes.

Kamaru-l-Akmar prometió que en un año la ciudad estaría edificada°, con sus alcázares°, sus mezquitas° y jardines más bellos que los de Susa y Ecbatana y aun° que los de Bagdad. Pero solicitó al califa° que le permitiera construirla con entera libertad y fantasía y según sus propias ideas, y que no se dignase verla sino una vez que estuviese concluida°. Abderrahmán, sonriendo, accedió.

Al cabo del° primer año Kamaru-l-Akmar pidió otro año de prórroga°, que el califa gustosamente le concedió. Esto se repitió varias veces. Así transcurrieron° no menos de diez años. Hasta que Abderrahmán, encolerizado°, decidió ir a investigar.

Cuando llegó, una sonrisa le borró el ceño adusto°. ¡Es la más hermosa ciudad que han contemplado ojos mortales! —le dijo a Kamaru-l-Akmar—. ¿Por qué no me avisaste que estaba construida?

Kamaru-l-Akmar inclinó la frente° y no se atrevió° a confesar al califa que lo que estaba viendo eran los palacios y jardines que los ingenieros, arquitectos y demás artistas habían levantado para sí mismos mientras estudiaban los planes de la futura ciudad.

Así fue construida Zahara, a orillas del° Guadalquivir.

grandezas *grandeurs* a partir de 1980 *from 1980 on*
ingenio *creativity* fundar *to found* sabio *wise*
estaría edificada *would be built* alcázares *fortresses*
mezquitas *mosques* aun *even* califa *caliph (an Islamic leader)*
sino una vez que estuviese concluida *until it was finished*
Al cabo de *At the end of* prórroga *extension*
transcurrieron *passed* encolerizado *angry*
le borró el ceño adusto *wiped the stern frown off his face*
frente *forehead* no se atrevió *didn't dare* a orillas de *on the shores of*

Completar Have pairs work through this activity before you go over the answers orally with the whole class. Ask pairs to find the correct answer to each item in the text. If pairs have difficulty answering any question, suggest one of the partners read aloud corresponding portions of the text.

Contestar Ask volunteers to answer questions orally in class. Involve the whole class in discussing opinions of **el califa** and **Kamaru-l-Akmar** as well as the meaning of the word **burocracia**.

Diálogo Give students sufficient time to prepare and practice their dialogues. Ask volunteers to perform them for the whole class.

Contestar

Contesta estas preguntas.

1. Describe al califa y a Kamaru-l-Akmar. ¿Qué tipo de personas crees que son? Explica tu respuesta.
2. ¿Por qué el ingeniero no quiere que Abderrahmán vea la ciudad antes de que termine la construcción? Explica tu respuesta.
3. ¿Qué significa la palabra **burocracia**? Da algunos ejemplos.
4. ¿Por qué este cuento se llama *Grandezas de la burocracia*?
5. ¿Crees que el narrador de este cuento está a favor° o en contra de° la burocracia? Explica tu opinión.

Diálogo

Trabaja con un(a) compañero/a para preparar una conversación en tres partes, basándose en la lectura. Después presenten la conversación a la clase.

- Primera parte: El califa habla con el más sabio de los ingenieros sobre la ciudad que quiere fundar.
- Segunda parte: Kamaru-l-Akmar pide la séptima prórroga y explica por qué es necesaria. El califa se la concede pero no está muy contento.
- Tercera parte: Abderrahmán y Kamaru-l-Akmar visitan el lugar de construcción en el décimo año.

a favor de *in favor of* en contra de *against*

TEACHING OPTIONS

Heritage Speakers Have heritage speakers bring a map (in Spanish) of a city where they have lived or that they have visited. Have them describe important landmarks or points of interest. They should indicate the major highways, bridges, squares, and so forth, on the map as they describe the location of the points of interest and transportation routes.

TPR Have students work in pairs. One partner is blindfolded and the other gives directions to get from one place in the classroom to another. For example: **Te voy a decir cómo llegar de tu escritorio a la puerta del salón. Camina derecho cinco pasos. Da tres pasos a la izquierda y luego dobla a la derecha y camina cuatro pasos para que no choques con el escritorio. Estás cerca de la puerta. Sigue derecho dos pasos más. Allí está la puerta.**

Section Goals

In **Escritura** students will:
- learn to avoid redundancies
- integrate **Lección 14** vocabulary and structures
- write an e-mail in Spanish

Estrategia Have a volunteer write the paragraph labeled *Redundant* on the board as you dictate it. Ask another volunteer to read the second sentence and identify the redundancy (**redundancia**). Continue asking volunteers to point out the redundancies until everyone is satisfied with the revised paragraph.

Tema Brainstorm a list of Spanish-speaking cities where students might like to spend a week, especially considering that they must spend part of their time working on a literature assignment. Have the class suggest the types of sites they could visit during their stay and how they plan to divide up their time.

The Affective Dimension Students will feel less anxious about writing in Spanish if they follow the advice in the **Estrategia, Tema,** and **Plan de escritura** sections. These offer step-by-step support for the writing process.

Escritura

Estrategia

Avoiding redundancies

Redundancy is the needless repetition of words or ideas. To avoid redundancy with verbs and nouns, consult a Spanish language thesaurus (**Diccionario de sinónimos**). You can also avoid redundancy by using object pronouns, possessive adjectives, demonstrative adjectives and pronouns, and relative pronouns. Remember that in Spanish, subject pronouns are generally used only for clarification, emphasis, or contrast. Study the example below:

Redundant:

Susana quería visitar a su amiga. Susana estaba en la ciudad. Susana tomó el tren y perdió el mapa de la ciudad. Susana estaba perdida en la ciudad. Susana estaba nerviosa. Por fin, la amiga de Susana la llamó a Susana y le dio direcciones.

Improved:

Susana, quien estaba en la ciudad, quería visitar a su amiga. Tomó el tren y perdió el mapa. Estaba perdida y nerviosa. Por fin, su amiga la llamó y le dio direcciones.

Tema

Escribir un correo electrónico

Vas a visitar a un(a) amigo/a que vive en una ciudad que no conoces. Vas a pasar allí una semana y tienes que hacer también un trabajo para tu clase de literatura. Tienes planes de alquilar un carro pero no sabes cómo llegar del aeropuerto a la casa de tu amigo/a.

Escríbele a tu amigo/a un correo electrónico describiendo lo que te interesa hacer allí y dale sugerencias de actividades que pueden hacer juntos/as. No olvides mencionar lo que necesitas para hacer tu trabajo. Puedes basarte en una visita real o imaginaria.

Considera la siguiente lista de datos que puedes incluir en el correo electrónico:

- El nombre de la ciudad que vas a visitar
- Los lugares que más te interesa visitar
- Lo que necesitas para hacer tu trabajo:
  - acceso a Internet
  - direcciones para llegar a la biblioteca pública
  - tiempo para estar solo/a
  - libros para consultar
- Mandatos para las actividades que van a compartir

TEACHING OPTIONS

Proofreading Activity Copy the following dialogue containing mistakes onto the board or a transparency as a proofreading activity to do with the whole class.

1. **Queremos vivir en una parte de la ciudad que tiene muchos árboles y que queda cerca al centro.**
2. **¿Hay un restaurante en el centro que tiene comida vegetariana y que está abierta los lunes?**
3. **Cuando llegamos al centro esta tarde, buscamos un buen restaurante.**
4. **A ver si la tienda esta cerrado cuando llegamos.**
5. **En cuanto encontremos una tienda donde se venden gafas de sol, compremosnoslas.**

Plan de escritura

1 Ideas y organización
Después de pensar en el tema durante unos minutos, apunta tus ideas. Utiliza un mapa de ideas para organizar el borrador de tu correo electrónico.

2 Primer borrador
Utiliza tus notas de **Ideas y organización** para escribir el primer borrador de tu correo electrónico. Usa el diccionario solamente como último recurso y no te olvides de repasar° tu lista de **Anotaciones para mejorar la escritura** en tu **Carpeta de trabajos.**

3 Comentario
Intercambia tu composición con la de un(a) compañero/a. Lee su borrador y anota los aspectos mejor escritos. Compartan sus impresiones utilizando esta guía:

1. ¿Incluye toda la información pertinente?
2. ¿Está bien organizado?
3. ¿Hay alguna redundancia?
4. ¿Qué sugerencias puedes darle al/a la escritor(a) para mejorar su composición?
5. ¿Hay errores gramaticales u ortográficos?

4 Redacción
Revisa el primer borrador según las indicaciones de tu compañero/a. Incorpora nuevas ideas y/o más información si es necesario. Utiliza esta guía para hacer la última revisión antes de escribir la versión final del correo electrónico:

1. Subraya° el sujeto de cada oración. Si es necesario, usa pronombres u otro elemento gramatical para eliminar la redundancia.
2. Subraya dos veces cada verbo para comprobar la concordancia con el sujeto. ¡Cuidado con los verbos irregulares en el subjuntivo!
3. Revisa la concordancia entre los sustantivos y los adjetivos en cada oración.
4. Comprueba° el uso correcto de los pronombres.
5. Consulta tus **Anotaciones para mejorar la escritura** antes de revisar la ortografía y la puntuación.

5 Evaluación y progreso
Trabaja con dos o tres compañeros/as. Utilicen una parte de cada composición para formular una nueva redacción° y compártanla con la clase. Cuando tu profesor(a) te devuelva° tu trabajo, lee sus comentarios y correcciones y anota los errores de conceptos fundamentales en tu lista de **Anotaciones para mejorar la escritura** en tu **Carpeta de trabajos.**

repasar *review* Subraya *Underline* Comprueba *Check* redacción *version* devuelva *returns*

Comentario

- Go over guide questions 1–5 with the whole class so peer readers understand their task. Then have pairs of students exchange e-mails. Allow five minutes for reading and comments. Allow five minutes for discussing comments.
- Have students prepare **Redacción** for the next class. Ask them to rewrite their drafts, incorporating the peer comments and following the directions in **Redacción**.

Evaluación y progreso Give groups ten minutes to exchange their e-mails and create a new one to present to the class.

Writing Sample Here is a sample e-mail that would constitute superior writing achievement.

Hola Graciela,

Ya falta poco para mi semana contigo en Caracas. ¡Hay tantos lugares que deseo visitar! El primer día, visitemos El Hatillo y caminemos por sus calles para admirar la arquitectura. También en algún momento no conduzcamos y tomemos el metro para observar las obras de famosos artistas venezolanos en las estaciones. Para ir del aeropuerto a tu casa, voy a alquilar un carro, pero necesito que me des direcciones. También necesito escribir un trabajo para mi clase de literatura. No me molesta, porque creo que es la excusa perfecta para estar solo y leer en una de las bonitas playas cerca de Caracas descritas en mi guía. Uno de los días es importante que yo tenga acceso a Internet para escribirle a mi profesor. Puedo hacerlo en una biblioteca pública que también tenga una buena colección de novelas latinoamericanas. Sólo tienes que decirme dónde queda. Estoy contando los minutos. ¡Hasta muy pronto!

Pedro

EVALUATION: Correo electrónico

Criteria	Scale
Content	1 2 3 4 5
Organization	1 2 3 4 5
Use of vocabulary	1 2 3 4 5
Grammatical accuracy	1 2 3 4 5

Scoring	
Excellent	18–20 points
Good	14–17 points
Satisfactory	10–13 points
Unsatisfactory	< 10 points

Section Goals

In **Escuchar** students will:

- listen for specific information and linguistic cues
- answer questions based on a recorded conversation

Instructional Resources
Textbook CD
IRM: Tapescript, p. 98

Estrategia
Script Hace muchos años que los residentes de nuestra ciudad están preocupados por la contaminación del aire. El año pasado se mudaron más de cinco mil personas a nuestra ciudad. Hay cada año más carros en las calles y el problema de la contaminación va de mal en peor. Los estudiantes de la universidad de Puerto Ordaz piensan que este problema es importante; quieren desarrollar carros que usen menos gasolina para evitar más contaminación ambiental.

Suggestion Have students describe the photo. Guide them to guess who Eduardo and Alberto are and what they are doing.

Ahora escucha
Script ALBERTO: Demetrio me dijo que fue de compras con Carlos y Roberto a Macro. Y tú, Eduardo, ¿has ido?
EDUARDO: ¡Claro que sí, Alberto! Tienen las últimas modas. Me compré estos zapatos allí. ¡Carísimos!, pero me fascinan y, de ñapa, son cómodos.
A: Pues, ya acabé de estudiar para el examen de psicología. Creo que voy a ir esta tarde porque me siento muy fuera de la onda. ¡Soy el único que no ha ido a Macro! ¿Dónde queda?
E: Es por Sabana Grande. ¿Vas a ir por metro o en carro?
A: Es mejor ir por metro. Es muy difícil estacionar el carro en Sabana Grande. No me gusta manejarlo tampoco porque los frenos están malos.
E: Bueno, súbete al metro en la línea amarilla hasta Plaza Venezuela. Cuando salgas de la estación de metro dobla a la izquierda hacia Chacaíto. Sigue derecho por dos cuadras.
A: Ah, sí, enfrente de la joyería donde le compraste el anillo a Rebeca.
E: No, la joyería queda una cuadra hacia el sur. Pasa el Banco Mercantil y dobla a la derecha. Tan pronto como pases la pizzería Papagallo, vas a ver un letrero rojo grandísimo a mano izquierda que dice Macro.
A: Gracias, Eduardo. ¿No quieres ir? Así no me pierdo.
E: No, hoy no puedo. Tengo que estudiar y a las cuatro tengo una cita con Rebeca. Pero estoy seguro que vas a llegar lo más bien.

Escuchar

Estrategia

Listening for specific information/ Listening for linguistic cues

As you already know, you don't have to hear or understand every word when listening to Spanish. You can often get the facts you need by listening for specific pieces of information. You should also be aware of the linguistic structures you hear. For example, by listening for verb endings, you can ascertain whether the verbs describe past, present, or future actions, and they can also indicate who is performing the action.

To practice these strategies, you will listen to a short paragraph about an environmental issue. What environmental problem is being discussed? What is the cause of the problem? Has the problem been solved, or is the solution under development?

Preparación

Describe la foto. Según la foto, ¿qué información específica piensas que vas a oír en el diálogo?

Ahora escucha 

Lee estas frases y luego escucha la conversación entre Alberto y Eduardo. Indica si cada verbo se refiere a algo en el pasado, en el presente o en el futuro.

Acciones

1. Demetrio / comprar en Macro ___pasado___
2. Alberto / comprar en Macro ___futuro___
3. Alberto / estudiar psicología ___pasado___
4. carro / tener frenos malos ___presente___
5. Eduardo / comprar un anillo para Rebeca ___pasado___
6. Eduardo / estudiar ___futuro___

Comprensión

Descripciones

Marca las frases que describen correctamente a Alberto.

1. ___✔___ Es organizado en sus estudios.
2. ______ Compró unas flores para su novia.
3. ______ No le gusta tomar el metro.
4. ___✔___ No conoce bien la zona de Sabana Grande y Chacaíto.
5. ___✔___ No tiene buen sentido de la orientación°.
6. ___✔___ Le gusta ir a los lugares que están de moda.

Preguntas

1. ¿Por qué Alberto prefiere ir en metro a Macro?
   Porque es muy difícil estacionar el carro en Sabana Grande.
2. ¿Crees que Alberto y Eduardo viven en una ciudad grande o en un pueblo? ¿Cómo lo sabes?
   Viven en una ciudad grande porque tiene metro.
3. ¿Va Eduardo a acompañar a Alberto? ¿Por qué?
   No puede porque tiene que estudiar y tiene cita con Rebeca.

Conversación

En grupos pequeños, hablen de sus tiendas favoritas y de cómo llegar a ellas desde la universidad. ¿En qué lugares tienen la última moda? ¿Los mejores precios? ¿Hay buenas tiendas cerca de la universidad?

Answers will vary.

sentido de la orientación *sense of direction*

recursos

Proyecto

Promociona° una comunidad

Imagina que eres miembro de un grupo que está diseñando y promocionando una comunidad modelo en Venezuela.

1 Prepara un folleto

Crea un folleto° para hacer publicidad de una comunidad modelo que van a construir° en Venezuela. Usa los **Recursos para la investigación** para escoger el lugar ideal para el proyecto, considerando la geografía, el terreno, el clima, el acceso a ciudades grandes, los eventos culturales y los atractivos naturales. El folleto puede incluir la siguiente información:

- Un pequeño mapa de Venezuela que indica dónde está localizada la comunidad modelo
- Fotos de la zona
- Un mapa de la zona que muestra las tiendas y las atracciones principales del centro de la comunidad
- Una explicación de la ubicación° ideal de la comunidad, incluyendo clima, atractivos naturales y acceso a ciudades importantes
- Varios párrafos que expliquen las características de la comunidad, sus atracciones y las razones por las cuales va a ser una comunidad mejor que las otras

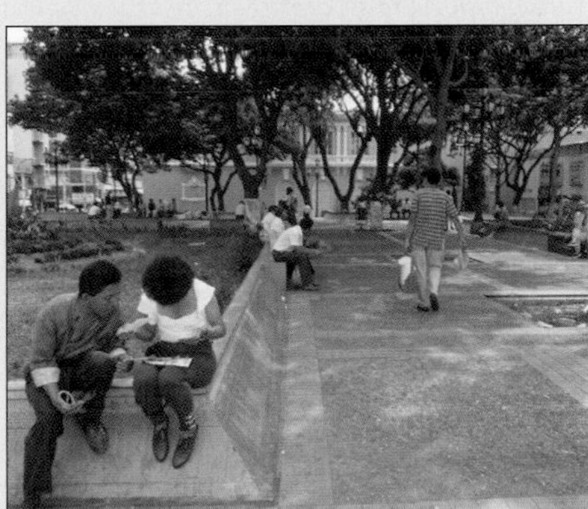

2 Presenta la información

Reúnete con tres o cuatro compañeros/as. Usa el folleto como guía para promocionar la comunidad con tus compañeros. La meta° de la presentación es mostrar que esta comunidad es única por su ubicación, atracciones y recursos.

Luego comparen las comunidades que han planeado. ¿Están en las mismas regiones geográficas o en lugares muy distintos? ¿Tienen las mismas atracciones culturales y naturales? ¿Qué ventajas especiales tiene cada una de sus comunidades?

recursos para la investigación

Internet Palabras clave: Venezuela, ciudad, ciudades, fotos, geografía, atractivos, arte, cultura, mapa

Comunidad Profesores, estudiantes o personas en la comunidad que son venezolanos o que han viajado° por Venezuela

Biblioteca Mapas, enciclopedias, revistas, guías turísticas

Otros recursos Investigar los recursos especiales que tienen las mejores comunidades

promociona *promote* **folleto** *brochure* **construir** *to build* **ubicación** *location* **meta** *goal* **han viajado** *have traveled*

Section Goals

In **Proyecto** students will:
- learn about Venezuela, its geography, culture, and people
- use Spanish as they do research and interact with the wider world
- write and present a brochure for a model community in Venezuela

Suggestion Students might need a week to complete the project, so at the beginning of that time period, have them open their books to this page and glance over **Proyecto**. Explain that they are going to use their research skills to prepare a brochure to promote a model community in Venezuela. Ask them to review the list of information to include and have them brainstorm what types of information they want to feature in their brochures.

Prepara un folleto
- Students may wish to interview local community designers or community developers to get first-hand information on what goes into developing a model community.
- You may wish to have students work in pairs, with one partner focusing on the residential areas and the other on the commercial areas of the community.

Presenta la información If you assigned partners, give them time to coordinate and practice their individual portions of the presentation.

EVALUATION: Folleto

Criteria	Scale
Content	1 2 3 4 5
Organization	1 2 3 4 5
Grammatical accuracy	1 2 3 4 5
Creativity	1 2 3 4 5

Scoring	
Excellent	18–20 points
Good	14–17 points
Satisfactory	10–13 points
Unsatisfactory	< 10 points

Section Goal
In **Panorama**, students will read about the history, geography, and economy of Venezuela.

Instructional Resources
Transparencies, #5, #6, #52
WB/VM: Workbook, pp. 167–168; Video Activities, pp. 275–276
***Panorama cultural** DVD/Video*
Interactive CD-ROM
IRM: Videoscript, p. 134
Companion website: www.vistahigherlearning.com
Presentations CD-ROM

Suggestion Have students look at the map of Venezuela or project **Transparency #52** and talk about the physical features of the country. Have students trace the **Río Orinoco** and notice the types of terrain it runs through (such as **Los Llanos** and the Amazon basin). Note that the principal cities are all located along the Caribbean coast.

El país en cifras Point out that the national currency is named for Simón Bolívar, the Latin American hero who played a central role in the struggle for independence from Spain. Point out that Bolívar's birthplace was Caracas. After reading about the **yanomami**, point out to students the vastness of Venezuela's jungle area, and remind them that various groups of indigenous people inhabit this largely undeveloped area.

¡Increíble pero cierto! Angel Falls is located in a rugged, inaccessible area of Venezuela, the Guiana Highlands, and is most easily viewed from the air. In fact, that is how the falls were first identified by Venezuelans in 1935. Subsequently, James C. Angel crash-landed a plane in the area, and made the first non-native exploration of this natural wonder.

Venezuela

El país en cifras

- **Área:** 912.050 km² (352.144 millas²), *aproximadamente dos veces el área de California*
- **Población:** 23.323.000
- **Capital:** Caracas —3.261.000
- **Ciudades principales:** Maracaibo —2.172.000, Valencia —2.320.000, Maracay —1.249.000, Barquisimeto —1.005.000

SOURCE: Population Division, UN Secretariat

- **Moneda:** bolívar
- **Idiomas:** español (oficial), arahuaco, caribe

El yanomami es uno de los idiomas indígenas que se habla en Venezuela. La cultura de los yanomami tiene su centro en el sur de Venezuela, en el bosque tropical. Son cazadores° y agricultores y viven en comunidades de hasta 400 miembros.

Bandera de Venezuela

Venezolanos célebres

- **Teresa Carreño,** compositora y pianista (1853–1917)
- **Rómulo Gallegos,** escritor y político (1884–1979)
- **Andrés Eloy Blanco,** poeta (1897–1955)
- **Baruj Benacerraf,** científico (1920–)

Baruj Benacerraf, junto con dos de sus colegas, recibió el Premio Nobel por sus investigaciones en el campo° de la inmunología y las enfermedades autoinmunes. Nacido en Caracas, Benacerraf también vivió en París y reside ahora en los Estados Unidos.

cazadores *hunters* campo *field* caída *drop* catarata *waterfall*

Vista central de Caracas

Maracaibo • Lago de Maracaibo • Valencia • Caracas • Cordillera Central de la Costa • Río Orinoco • COLOMBIA • Macizo de las Guayanas • GUYANA • BRASIL

Llanero de la zona central de Venezuela

Una piragua

ESTADOS UNIDOS • OCÉANO ATLÁNTICO • OCÉANO PACÍFICO • VENEZUELA

recursos

WB pp. 167–168	VM pp. 275–276	I CD-ROM Lección 14	vistahigherlearning.com

¡Increíble pero cierto!

Con una caída° de 979 m (3.212 pies) desde la meseta de Auyan Tepuy, Salto Ángel (*Angel Falls*), en Venezuela, es la catarata° más alta del mundo, ¡diecisiete veces más alta que las cataratas del Niágara! James C. Angel la descubrió en 1937. Los indígenas de la zona la denominan Churún Merú.

TEACHING OPTIONS

Variación léxica Venezuelan Spanish has a rich repertoire of regionalisms and colloquialisms. If your students go to Caracas, they are certainly going to hear the word **pana**, which means both **amigo** and **amiga**. Ex: **¡Eso es chévere, pana!** The Venezuelan equivalent of *guy* or *girl* is **chamo/a**. An inhabitant of the city of Caracas is a **caraqueño/a**. Some other words that are specific to Venezuela are **cambur** for **banana** and **caraota** for **frijol**.

Worth Noting Rómulo Gallegos's great novel, ***Doña Bárbara***, is set in the **Llanos** of Venezuela, a region known for its culture of cattle raising. The theme of the novel is one that has been explored by many Latin American writers, the struggle between **civilización y barbarie**.

Economía • El petróleo

La industria petrolera° es muy importante para la economía venezolana. La mayor concentración de petróleo se encuentra debajo del lago Maracaibo, el lago más grande de Suramérica. En 1976 se nacionalizaron las empresas° petroleras y pasaron a ser propiedad° del estado con el nombre de *Petróleos de Venezuela*. Este producto representa más del 70% de las exportaciones del país, siendo Estados Unidos su principal comprador°.

Actualidades • Caracas

El *boom* petrolero de los años cincuenta transformó a Caracas en una ciudad cosmopolita. Sus rascacielos° y excelentes sistemas de transporte la hacen una de las ciudades más modernas de Latinoamérica. El metro, construido en 1983, es uno de los más modernos del mundo y sus extensas carreteras y autopistas conectan la ciudad con el interior del país. El corazón de la ciudad es el Parque Central, una zona de centros comerciales, tiendas, restaurantes y clubes.

Historia • Simón Bolívar (1783-1830)

A finales del siglo° XVIII, Venezuela, al igual que otros países suramericanos, todavía estaba bajo el dominio de la corona° española. El general Simón Bolívar, nacido en Caracas, es llamado "El Libertador" porque fue el líder del movimiento independentista suramericano en el área que hoy es Venezuela, Colombia, Ecuador, Perú y Bolivia.

¿Qué aprendiste? Responde a las preguntas con una frase completa.

1. ¿Cuál es la moneda de Venezuela?
   La moneda de Venezuela es el bolívar.
2. ¿Quién fue Rómulo Gallegos?
   Rómulo Gallegos fue un escritor y político venezolano.
3. ¿Cuál es el lago más grande de Suramérica?
   El lago Maracaibo es el lago más grande de Suramérica.
4. ¿Cuál es el producto más exportado de Venezuela?
   El producto más exportado de Venezuela es el petróleo.
5. ¿Qué ocurrió en 1976 con las empresas petroleras?
   En 1976 las empresas petroleras se nacionalizaron.
6. ¿Cómo se llama la capital de Venezuela?
   La capital de Venezuela se llama Caracas.
7. ¿Qué hay en el Parque Central de Caracas?
   Hay centros comerciales, tiendas, restaurantes y clubes.
8. ¿Por qué es conocido Simón Bolívar como "El Libertador"?
   Simón Bolívar es conocido como "El Libertador" porque fue el líder del movimiento independentista suramericano.

Tejedor° en Los Aleros, aldea° en los Andes de Venezuela

Conexión Internet Investiga estos temas en el sitio **www.vistahigherlearning.com.**

1. Busca información sobre Simón Bolívar. ¿Cuáles son algunos de los episodios más importantes de su vida? ¿Crees que Bolívar fue un estadista (*statesman*) de primera categoría? ¿Por qué?
2. Prepara un plan para un viaje de ecoturismo por el Orinoco. ¿Qué quieres ver y hacer durante la excursión? ¿Por qué?

industria petrolera *oil industry* empresas *companies* propiedad *property* comprador *buyer* rascacielos *skyscrapers* siglo *century* corona *crown* tejedor *weaver* aldea *village*

El petróleo Students may be surprised to learn that Venezuela is among the world's top ten crude oil producers, with 73 billion barrels of proven petroleum reserves. Venezuela may have up to as much as 1.2 trillion barrels of extra-heavy oil, including bitumen.

Caracas Both Caracas and Houston are major urban areas fueled by oil booms. Students may find it interesting to compare how these cities have developed: Houston's urban development is limited only by the coastline, allowing it to sprawl in all other directions; Caracas is hemmed into a narrow valley by two ranges of mountains, leading to its dense development and its many high-rises.

Simón Bolívar The life of Simón Bolívar has inspired artists of every sort: from painters and sculptors to musicians and writers. In 1989, Colombian Nobel winner Gabriel García Márquez published ***El general en su laberinto***, his vision of Bolívar toward the end of his life, as he muses about his accomplishments and disappointments.

Conexión Internet Students will find supporting Internet activities and links at **www.vistahigherlearning.com**.

TEACHING OPTIONS

Worth Noting Tell students that the **Salto Ángel**, besides being the highest uninterrupted waterfall in the world, falls from the top of a **tepuy** (pl. **tepuyes**), a flat-topped, sandstone mountain with vertical sides. Because of the isolation that results from their great elevation and their vertical sides, the top of each tepuy has its own closed ecology, featuring plants and animals of different species that grow nowhere else on earth, including the tops of neighboring tepuyes. The chilly, damp climate atop a tepuy differs so markedly from the tropical climate at its base that species acclimatized to it cannot survive on the **sabana** below and vice versa. This ensures the isolation of the ecological system atop each tepuy.

Heritage Speakers Ask heritage speakers who come from Venezuela or have visited there to tell the class about their experience in the country.

Instructional Resources
Vocabulary CD
Lab Manual, p. 83
Lab CD/MP3 ***Lección 14***
IRM: Tapescript, pp. 63–66
Testing Program: ***Pruebas,*** *pp. 157–168*
Testing Program Audio CD
Test Files CD-ROM

En la ciudad

el banco	*bank*
la carnicería	*butcher shop*
el correo	*post office*
el estacionamiento	*parking lot*
la frutería	*fruit store*
la heladería	*ice cream shop*
la joyería	*jewelry store*
la lavandería	*laundromat*
la panadería	*bakery*
la pastelería	*pastry shop*
la peluquería, el salón de belleza	*beauty salon*
la pescadería	*fish market*
el supermercado	*supermarket*
la zapatería	*shoe store*
hacer cola	*to stand in line*
hacer diligencias	*to run errands*

En el correo

el cartero	*mail carrier*
el correo	*mail/post office*
el paquete	*package*
la estampilla, el sello	*stamp*
el sobre	*envelope*
echar (una carta) al buzón	*to put (a letter) in the mailbox; to mail*
enviar, mandar	*to send; to mail*

En el banco

el cajero automático	*ATM*
la cuenta corriente	*checking account*
la cuenta de ahorros	*savings account*
el cheque (de viajero)	*(traveler's) check*
ahorrar	*to save (money)*
cobrar	*to cash (a check)*
depositar	*to deposit*
firmar	*to sign*
llenar (un formulario)	*to fill out (a form)*
pagar a plazos	*to pay in installments*
pagar al contado, en efectivo	*to pay in cash*
pedir prestado	*to borrow*
pedir un préstamo	*to apply for a loan*
ser gratis	*to be free of charge*

Las direcciones

la cuadra	*(city) block*
la dirección	*address*
la esquina	*corner*
el letrero	*sign*
cruzar	*to cross*
dar direcciones	*to give directions*
doblar	*to turn*
estar perdido/a	*to be lost*
quedar	*to be located*
(al) este	*(to the) east*
(al) norte	*(to the) north*
(al) oeste	*(to the) west*
(al) sur	*(to the) south*
derecho	*straight (ahead)*
enfrente de	*opposite; facing*
hacia	*toward*

Past participles used as adjectives	*See page 441.*
Expresiones útiles	*See page 431.*

recursos

El bienestar

15

Communicative Goals

You will learn how to:

- **Talk about health, well-being, and nutrition**
- **Talk about physical activities**

contextos

pages 454–457

- Health and well-being
- Exercise and physical activity
- Nutrition

fotonovela

pages 458–461

The students and Martín go on their long-awaited hike. Don Francisco greets them when they return at the end of the day, and listens to their reactions to what they saw and experienced.

estructura

pages 462–471

- The present perfect
- The past perfect
- The present perfect subjunctive

adelante

pages 472–477

Lectura: Read a poem.
Escritura: Write a personal health plan.
Escuchar: Listen to a radio program about exercise.
Proyecto: Create a brochure for an adventure sports vacation in Bolivia.

panorama

pages 478–479

Featured Country: Bolivia

- Titicaca: The highest navigable lake in the world
- Andean music
- Tiahuanaco: City of the gods

A PRIMERA VISTA

- ¿Dónde están estas personas?
- ¿Practican deportes frecuentemente?
- ¿Son activos o sedentarios?
- ¿Es probable que les importe su salud?

Lesson Goals

In **Lección 15** students will be introduced to the following:

- terms for health and exercise
- nutrition terms
- present perfect
- past perfect
- present perfect subjunctive
- making inferences
- organizing information logically when writing
- writing a personal fitness plan
- listening for the gist and for cognates
- writing a brochure for adventure travel in Bolivia
- cultural, geographic, and historical information about Bolivia

A primera vista Here are some additional questions you can ask based on the photo: **¿Crees que tienes buena salud? ¿Cómo lo sabes? ¿Vas al gimnasio regularmente? ¿Usas tu carro para hacer diligencias, o caminas? ¿Qué haces cuando te sientes nervioso/a o cansado/a? ¿Es importante que desayunes todas las mañanas? ¿Qué comes durante el día? ¿Cuántas horas duermes cada noche? ¿Conoces algún programa que ofrezca buenas ideas para mejorar la salud? ¿Cuál?**

INSTRUCTIONAL RESOURCES

Workbook/Video Manual: WB Activities, pp. 169–180
Laboratory Manual: Lab Activities, pp. 85–89
Workbook/Video Manual: Video Activities, pp. 241–242; pp. 277–278
Instructor's Resource Manual: **Hojas de actividades**, p. 172; **Vocabulario adicional**, p. 193; **¡Inténtalo!** & **Práctica** Answers, p. 221; **Fotonovela** Translations, p. 147; Textbook CD Tapescript, p. 99; Lab CDs Tapescript, pp. 67–70; **Fotonovela** Videoscript, p. 121; **Panorama cultural** Videoscript, p. 134
Info Gap Activities Booklet, pp. 57–60
Overhead Transparencies: #5, #6, #53, #54, #55
Lab Audio CD/MP3 **Lección 15**
Panorama cultural DVD/Video
Fotonovela DVD/Video
Testing Program, pp. 169–180
Testing Program Audio CD
Test Files CD-ROM
Companion website
Presentations CD-ROM
Textbook CD
Vocabulary CD
Interactive CD-ROM
Video CD-ROM
Web-SAM

Section Goals

In **Contextos**, students will learn and practice:

- vocabulary used to talk about health and exercise
- vocabulary used to discuss nutrition and a healthy diet

Instructional Resources
Transparencies, #53, #54
Textbook CD
Vocabulary CD
WB/VM: Workbook, pp. 169–170
Lab Manual, p. 85
*Lab CD/MP3 **Lección 15***
*IRM: **Vocab. adicional**, p. 193; **Práctica** Answers, p. 221; Tapescript, pp. 67–70; p. 99*
Info Gap Activities Booklet, pp. 57–58
Interactive CD-ROM
Companion website: www.vistahigherlearning.com
Presentations CD-ROM

Suggestions

- Write **hacer ejercicios** on the board, then ask personalized questions such as the following, writing new vocabulary on the board: **¿Quiénes hacen ejercicios regularmente? ¿Hacen ejercicios aeróbicos? ¿Quiénes levantan pesas? ¿Quiénes no hacen ejercicios nunca?** Tell students that they are going to learn vocabulary related to exercise and nutrition.
- Project **Transparency #53.** Give the people in the transparency names and make statements and ask questions about their activities. Ex: **El señor Garza es teleadicto. Él no hace ejercicios. Ve televisión y come papitas fritas. ¿Es activo o sedentario? ¿Lleva una vida sana?** After you have gone over the active vocabulary, ask students personalized questions about their exercise habits. Ex: **¿Qué hacen para aliviar el estrés? ____, ¿qué haces para aliviar el estrés? ¿Creen que se puede hacer demasiada gimnasia? ¿Creen que es más importante ser flexible o ser fuerte?**
- Point out the *no smoking* sign at the top right of the drawing. Explain to students that the infinitive, instead of a command form, is often found on public signs to express prohibitions or instructions. Ex: **No fumar.**

El bienestar

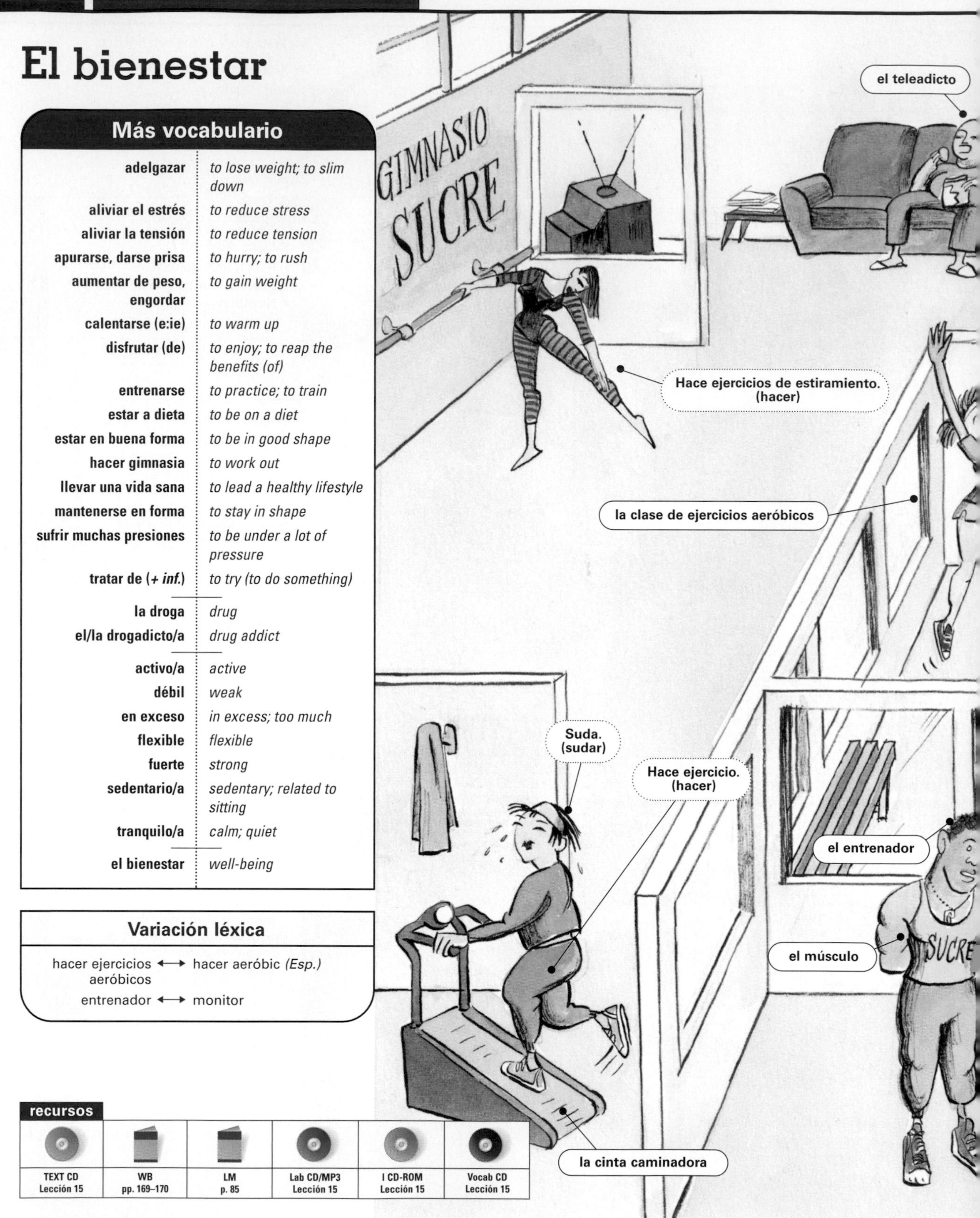

Más vocabulario

adelgazar	*to lose weight; to slim down*
aliviar el estrés	*to reduce stress*
aliviar la tensión	*to reduce tension*
apurarse, darse prisa	*to hurry; to rush*
aumentar de peso, engordar	*to gain weight*
calentarse (e:ie)	*to warm up*
disfrutar (de)	*to enjoy; to reap the benefits (of)*
entrenarse	*to practice; to train*
estar a dieta	*to be on a diet*
estar en buena forma	*to be in good shape*
hacer gimnasia	*to work out*
llevar una vida sana	*to lead a healthy lifestyle*
mantenerse en forma	*to stay in shape*
sufrir muchas presiones	*to be under a lot of pressure*
tratar de (+ *inf.*)	*to try (to do something)*
la droga	*drug*
el/la drogadicto/a	*drug addict*
activo/a	*active*
débil	*weak*
en exceso	*in excess; too much*
flexible	*flexible*
fuerte	*strong*
sedentario/a	*sedentary; related to sitting*
tranquilo/a	*calm; quiet*
el bienestar	*well-being*

Variación léxica

hacer ejercicios aeróbicos ⟷ hacer aeróbic *(Esp.)*
entrenador ⟷ monitor

recursos

TEXT CD Lección 15	WB pp. 169–170	LM p. 85	Lab CD/MP3 Lección 15	I CD-ROM Lección 15	Vocab CD Lección 15

TEACHING OPTIONS

TPR Ask students to stand. Call out commands based on the lesson vocabulary. Ex: **¡Levanten pesas! ¡Hagan ejercicios aeróbicos! ¡Apúrense! ¡Descansen!** Working with students, invent a gesture to mime each activity. When you have invented gestures to cover all the vocabulary, carry out a TPR activity with the class. Keep the pace rapid. Vary singular and plural commands.

Variación léxica Point out that the fitness movement began in the United States and spread to other parts of the world; hence, many of the terms related to fitness are borrowed from English. Ask heritage speakers if they can think of other fitness terms that may have been influenced by English.

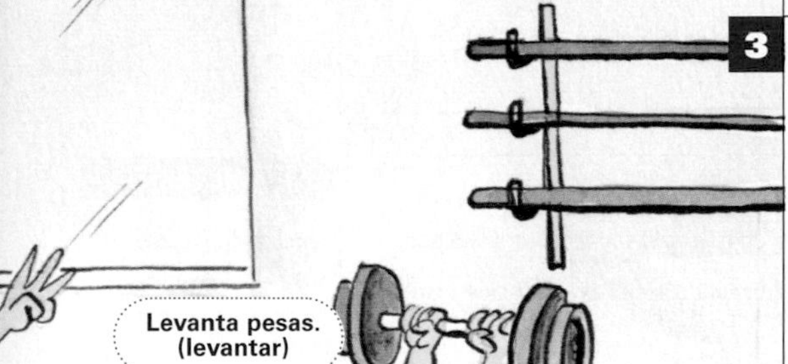

Práctica

1 Escuchar Mira el dibujo en las páginas 454 y 455. Luego escucha las frases e indica si lo que se dice en cada frase es **cierto** o **falso**.

	Cierto	Falso		Cierto	Falso
1.	❍	✓	6.	❍	✓
2.	❍	✓	7.	❍	✓
3.	✓	❍	8.	✓	❍
4.	✓	❍	9.	❍	✓
5.	✓	❍	10.	❍	✓

2 Identificar Identifica el opuesto (*opposite*) de cada palabra.

apurarse	fuerte
disfrutar	mantenerse en forma
engordar	sedentario
estar enfermo	sufrir muchas presiones
flexible	tranquilo

1. activo sedentario
2. adelgazar engordar
3. aliviar el estrés sufrir muchas presiones
4. débil fuerte
5. ir despacio apurarse
6. estar sano estar enfermo
7. nervioso tranquilo
8. ser teleadicto mantenerse en forma

3 Combinar Combina palabras de cada columna para formar diez frases lógicas sobre el bienestar.

1. David levanta pesas	j	a. aumentó de peso.
2. Estás en buena forma	f	b. estiramiento.
3. Felipe se lastimó	h	c. fuertes.
4. José y Rafael	g	d. presiones.
5. María y yo somos	c	e. porque quieren adelgazar.
6. Mi hermano	a	f. porque haces ejercicio.
7. Sara hace ejercicios de	b	g. sudan mucho en el gimnasio.
8. Mis primas están a dieta	e	h. un músculo de la pierna.
9. Para llevar una vida sana,	i	i. no se debe fumar.
10. Ellos sufren muchas	d	j. y corre mucho.

1 Suggestion Check answers by reading each item individually and asking volunteers to say whether the statement is true or false. Have students change the false statements to make them true.

1 Tapescript 1. Se puede fumar dentro del gimnasio. 2. El teleadicto está en buena forma. 3. Los músculos del entrenador son grandes. 4. La mujer que está corriendo también está sudando. 5. Se puede recibir un masaje en el Gimnasio Sucre. 6. Hay cuatro hombres en la clase de ejercicios aeróbicos. 7. El hombre que levanta pesas lleva una vida muy sedentaria. 8. La instructora de la clase de ejercicios aeróbicos lleva una vida muy activa. 9. El hombre que mira televisión está a dieta. 10. No hay nadie en el gimnasio que haga ejercicios de estiramiento.
Textbook CD

2 Expansion Have students use each pair of opposite terms in sentences illustrating their contrasting meanings. Ex: **José está muy nervioso porque no estudió para el examen. Roberto estudió por dos horas; por eso está tranquilo.**

3 Expansion Have students create their own original endings for each of the sentence fragments in the left column.

Successful Language Learning Mention that working out to a Spanish-language exercise program would be excellent listening practice.

Note: At this point you may want to present **Vocabulario adicional: Más vocabulario para el bienestar**, from the IRM.

TEACHING OPTIONS

Pairs Have pairs of students interview each other about what they do to stay in shape. Interviewers should also find out how often their partner does these things and when he or she did them over the past week. Ask students to write a brief report summarizing the interview.

Game Divide the class into groups of three. Ask a group to leave the room while the class chooses a vocabulary word or expression. When the group returns, they must try to guess it by asking the class yes or no questions. If the group guesses the word within ten questions, the group gets a point. Ex: **¿Es un lugar? ¿Describe a una persona? ¿Es una acción? ¿Es algo bueno para el bienestar?**

Suggestions

- Project **Transparency #54.** First, ask open-ended or yes/no questions that elicit the names of the foods depicted. Ex: **¿Qué es esto? (un huevo) Y esto al lado del queso, ¿son papas fritas?** Then ask students either/or questions to elicit the vocabulary in **La nutrición**. Ex: **¿La carne tiene proteínas o vitaminas? ¿Las bebidas alcohólicas tienen colesterol o no?** Continue asking for information or opinions. Ex: **¿Cuáles son algunas comidas que tienen colesterol? La cafeína, ¿creen que es una droga? ¿Por qué?**
- Point out that although English *alcohol* contains three syllables, Spanish **alcohol** is pronounced as two syllables.

4 Expansion After checking each item, ask students a personal question based on the information in that item, or have them comment on that information. Ex: **¿Comen ustedes comidas con mucha proteína después de hacer ejercicio? ¿Piensan que es buena idea comer comidas de todos los grupos alimenticios? ¿Por qué?**

Ayuda Present the vocabulary using the words in sentences that describe your eating or physical activity patterns.

5 Suggestion Have students discuss each question thoroughly before they move on to the next one. Also have them note opinions, ideas, and habits they have in common.

5 Expansion As students share their answers with the class, have a volunteer write down any common themes that stand out. Have a class discussion about these themes and their origins.

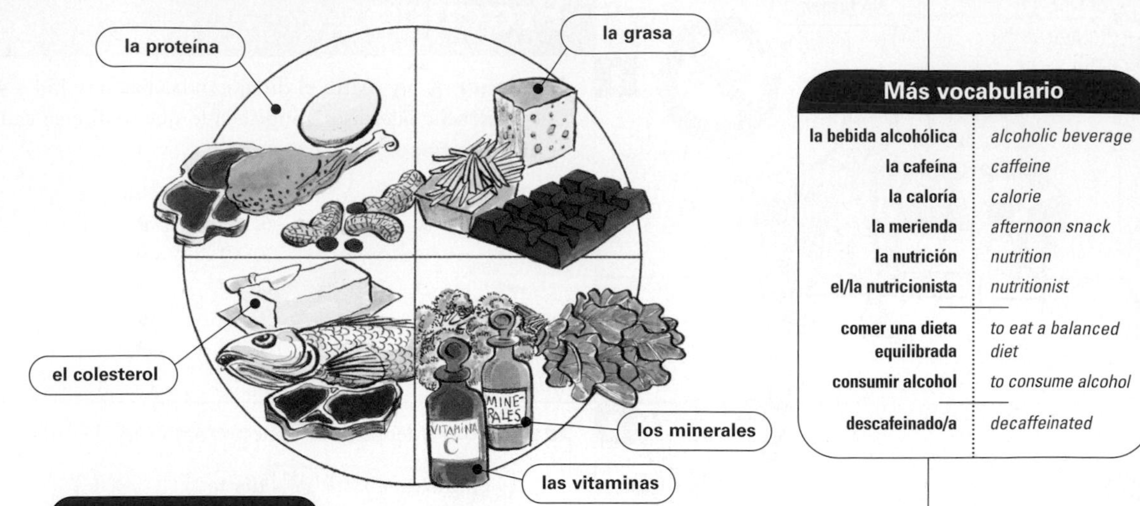

La nutrición

Más vocabulario

la bebida alcohólica	*alcoholic beverage*
la cafeína	*caffeine*
la caloría	*calorie*
la merienda	*afternoon snack*
la nutrición	*nutrition*
el/la nutricionista	*nutritionist*
comer una dieta equilibrada	*to eat a balanced diet*
consumir alcohol	*to consume alcohol*
descafeinado/a	*decaffeinated*

4 **Completar** Completa cada frase con la palabra adecuada.

1. Después de hacer ejercicio, como pollo o bistec porque contienen _b_.
   a. drogas b. proteínas c. grasa
2. Para _c_ es necesario consumir comidas de todos los grupos alimenticios (*nutrition groups*).
   a. aliviar el estrés b. correr c. comer una dieta equilibrada
3. Mis primas _a_ una buena comida.
   a. disfrutan de b. tratan de c. sudan
4. Mi entrenador no come chocolate ni papas fritas porque contienen _c_.
   a. dietas b. vitaminas c. mucha grasa
5. Mi padre no come mantequilla porque él necesita reducir _b_.
   a. la nutrición b. el colesterol c. el bienestar
6. Mi novio cuenta _c_ porque está a dieta.
   a. las pesas b. los músculos c. las calorías

CONSÚLTALO

To review what you have learned about nutrition and food groups, see **Contextos Lección 8**, pp. 234–237.

5 **La nutrición** En parejas, hablen de los tipos de comida que comen y las consecuencias que tienen para su salud. Luego compartan la información con la clase. Answers will vary.

1. ¿Cuántas comidas con mucha grasa comes regularmente? ¿Piensas que debes comer menos comidas de este tipo? ¿Por qué?
2. ¿Compras comidas con muchos minerales y vitaminas? ¿Necesitas consumir más comidas que los contienen? ¿Por qué?
3. ¿Tiene algún miembro de tu familia problemas con el colesterol? ¿Qué haces para evitar problemas con el colesterol?
4. ¿Eres vegetariano/a? ¿Conoces a alguien que sea vegetariano/a? ¿Qué piensas de la idea de no comer carne u otros productos animales? ¿Es posible comer una dieta equilibrada sin comer carne? Explica.
5. ¿Tomas cafeína en exceso? ¿Qué ventajas (*advantages*) y desventajas tiene la cafeína? Den ejemplos de productos que contienen cafeína y productos descafeinados.
6. ¿Llevas una vida sana? ¿Y tus amigos? ¿Crees que en general los estudiantes llevan una vida sana? ¿Por qué?

AYUDA

Some useful words:
sano = saludable
en general = por lo general
estricto
normalmente
muchas veces
a veces
de vez en cuando

TEACHING OPTIONS

Extra Practice Make a series of statements about healthy and unhealthy habits. Have students call out **bueno** if the habit is healthy and **malo** if it is not. Ex: **Antes de hacer ejercicio, siempre como comidas con mucha grasa. (malo) Consumo muy poco alcohol. (bueno)**

Heritage Speakers Ask heritage speakers to interview friends and relatives about their exercise and dietary habits. Have them also find out whether attitudes regarding diet and exercise are the same among their Spanish-speaking acquaintances as those among their English-speaking ones. Have students report their findings to the class.

Comunicación

6 **Un anuncio** En grupos de cuatro, imaginen que son dueños/as de un gimnasio con un equipo (*equipment*) moderno, entrenadores calificados y un(a) nutricionista. Preparen y presenten un anuncio para la televisión que hable del gimnasio y atraiga (*attracts*) a una gran variedad de nuevos clientes. No se olviden de presentar la siguiente información: Answers will vary.

- Las ventajas de estar en buena forma
- El equipo que tienen
- Los servicios y clases que ofrecen
- Las características únicas del gimnasio
- La dirección y el teléfono del gimnasio
- El precio para los socios (*members*) del gimnasio

7  **Recomendaciones para la salud** En parejas, imaginen que están preocupados con los malos hábitos de un(a) amigo/a suyo/a que no está bien últimamente (*lately*). Escriban y representen una conversación en la cual hablan de lo que está pasando en la vida de su amigo/a y los cambios que necesita hacer para llevar una vida sana. Answers will vary.

8 **El teleadicto** Con un(a) compañero/a, representen los papeles (*play the roles*) de un(a) nutricionista y un(a) teleadicto/a. La persona sedentaria habla de sus malos hábitos en las comidas y de que no hace ejercicio. También dice que toma demasiado café y que siente mucho estrés. El/La nutricionista le sugiere una dieta equilibrada con bebidas descafeinadas y una rutina para mantenerse en buena forma. El/La teleadicto/a le da las gracias por su ayuda. Answers will vary.

9   **El gimnasio perfecto** Tú y tu compañero/a quieren encontrar el gimnasio perfecto. Tú tienes el anuncio del gimnasio *Bienestar* y tu compañero tiene el del gimnasio *Músculos*. Hazle preguntas a tu compañero/a sobre las actividades que se ofrecen en el otro gimnasio. Tu profesor(a) le va a dar a cada uno de ustedes una hoja distinta con la información necesaria para completar la actividad.

Estudiante 1: *¿Se ofrecen clases para levantar pesas?*
Estudiante 2: *Sí, se ofrecen clases todos los lunes a las seis de la tarde para levantar pesas.*

6 Suggestions
- If possible, have students visit health clubs in your area to gather advertising brochures and/or fitness magazines to help them brainstorm ideas for their commercial.
- Have groups write their advertisement so that each student gets to speak for an equal amount of time.

7 Suggestions
- Suggest that students use expressions of doubt followed by the subjunctive or expressions of certainty. Review the verbs and expressions on pages 408–409 as necessary.
- Have students discuss at least five bad habits their friend has, explain why he or she has them, and what he or she did unsuccessfully to overcome them. Then, have students discuss possible ways of successfully overcoming each habit.

8 Suggestion Review the verbs and expressions of will and influence on pages 382–383 before doing the activity.

8 Expansion Have students conduct a follow-up interview which takes place one month after the initial meeting.

9 Suggestion Divide the class into pairs and distribute the Info Gap Handouts from the Info Gap Activities Booklet that correspond to this activity. Give the students ten minutes to complete this activity.

9 Expansions
- Have pairs work in groups of four to discuss which gym they personally would join and why.
- Have groups compare the gyms described in the activity with the campus gym and share their comparisons with the class.

TEACHING OPTIONS

Pairs Have students imagine that they are personal lifestyle consultants. Have them give their partner a set of ten guidelines on how to begin a comprehensive health program. Suggestions should be made regarding diet, aerobic exercise, strength training, flexibility training, and stress management. Have students switch roles.

Extra Practice Ask students to write down five personal goals for achieving or maintaining a healthy lifestyle. Then have them write a brief paragraph explaining why they want to attain these goals and how they plan to achieve them. Call on volunteers to share their goals with the class.

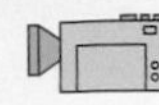

Section Goals

In **Fotonovela** students will:
- receive comprehensible input from free-flowing discourse
- learn functional phrases that preview lesson grammatical structures

Instructional Resources
WB/VM: Video Activities, pp. 241–242
***Fotonovela** DVD/Video (Start 01:22:23)*
Video CD-ROM
*IRM: **Fotonovela** Translations, p. 147, Videoscript, p. 121*
Interactive CD-ROM

Video Recap: Lección 14
Before doing this **Fotonovela** section, review the previous one with this activity.
1. ¿Qué recomienda don Francisco que lleven todos los excursionistas? (zapatos cómodos, una mochila, gafas oscuras y un suéter)
2. ¿Qué quiere Inés que Álex y Maite le compren en el centro? (unas estampillas/unos sellos)
3. ¿Por qué hablaron Maite y Álex con un joven? (porque estaban perdidos)
4. ¿Dónde estaba el supermercado? (enfrente del banco)

Video Synopsis Martín leads the students in some warm-up stretches before the hike. During the hike, the students chat, take pictures, and admire their surroundings. Afterward, they talk about the wonderful time they had. Don Francisco tells the group it's time to go back for dinner.

Suggestions

- Have students read only the first statement in each numbered frame of this **Fotonovela** episode. Then have them predict the content of the episode, based only on those sentences. Write down their predictions.
- Quickly review the predictions your students made about the **Fotonovela**. Through discussion, help the class summarize the plot.

¡Qué buena excursión!

NATIONAL STANDARDS communication cultures

Martín y los estudiantes van de excursión a las montañas.

PERSONAJES

MAITE

INÉS

DON FRANCISCO

ÁLEX

JAVIER

MARTÍN

1

MARTÍN Buenos días, don Francisco.

DON FRANCISCO ¡Hola, Martín!

MARTÍN Ya veo que han traído lo que necesitan. ¡Todos han venido muy bien equipados!

2

MARTÍN Muy bien. ¡Atención, chicos! Primero hagamos algunos ejercicios de estiramiento...

3

MARTÍN Es bueno que se hayan mantenido en buena forma. Entonces, jóvenes, ¿ya están listos?

JAVIER ¡Sí, listísimos! No puedo creer que finalmente haya llegado el gran día.

6

DON FRANCISCO ¡Hola! ¡Qué alegría verlos! ¿Cómo les fue en la excursión?

JAVIER Increíble, don Efe. Nunca había visto un paisaje tan espectacular. Es un lugar estupendo. Saqué mil fotos y tengo montones de escenas para dibujar.

7

MAITE Nunca había hecho una excursión. ¡Me encantó! Cuando vuelva a España, voy a tener mucho que contarle a mi familia.

8

INÉS Ha sido la mejor excursión de mi vida. Amigos, Martín, don Efe, mil gracias.

recursos

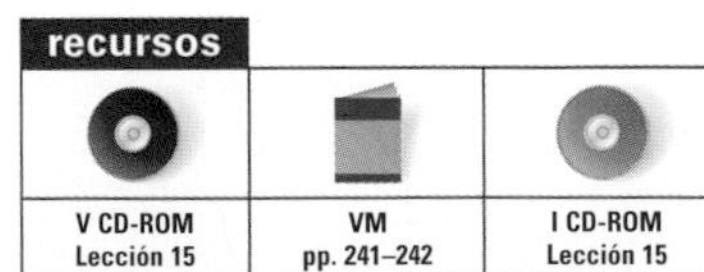

V CD-ROM Lección 15	VM pp. 241–242	I CD-ROM Lección 15

TEACHING OPTIONS

Video Tips General suggestions for using video clips in the classroom can be found on page IAE-12 of this Instructor's Annotated Edition.
¡Qué buena excursión! To introduce the class to this video episode, play only the **Resumen** segment and have your students tell you what they saw and heard. Then play the main video episode and have your students jot down notes about the plot. Next, have the class work in small groups to compare notes and prepare summaries of the main video episode. Ask one or two groups to read their summaries to the class. Finally, discuss the plot with the entire class and correct any errors of fact or sequencing.

MARTÍN ¡Fabuloso! ¡En marcha, pues!

DON FRANCISCO ¡Adiós! ¡Cuídense!

Martín y los estudiantes pasan ocho horas caminando en las montañas. Hablan, sacan fotos y disfrutan del paisaje. Se divierten muchísimo.

ÁLEX Sí, gracias, Martín. Gracias por todo.

MARTÍN No hay de qué. Ha sido un placer.

DON FRANCISCO Chicos, pues, es hora de volver. Creo que la señora Vives nos ha preparado una cena muy especial.

Enfoque cultural Para estar en buena forma

Cada país del mundo hispano tiene deportes populares diferentes. En Argentina, por ejemplo, se juega mucho al fútbol, en Venezuela se juega al béisbol y en Colombia y España hay muchos aficionados al ciclismo. Otro deporte conocido en el mundo hispano es el jai alai, que es un juego de pelota originario del País Vasco (España). Su nombre significa "día de fiesta" en vascuence y es un deporte que se practica también en México, en la Florida, en Rhode Island y en Connecticut (EE.UU.).

Expresiones útiles

Getting ready to start a hike

- ▶ **Ya veo que han traído lo que necesitan.**
  I see that you have brought what you need.
- ▶ **¡Todos han venido muy bien equipados!**
  Everyone has come very well equipped!
- ▶ **Primero hagamos algunos ejercicios de estiramiento.**
  First let's do some stretching exercises.
- ▶ **No puedo creer que finalmente haya llegado el gran día.**
  I can't believe that the big day has finally arrived.
- ▶ **¿(Están) listos?**
  (Are you) ready?
- ▷ **¡En marcha, pues!**
  Let's get going, then!

Talking about a hike

- ▶ **¿Cómo les fue en la excursión?**
  How did the hike go?
- ▷ **Nunca había visto un paisaje tan espectacular.**
  I had never seen such spectacular scenery.
- ▷ **Nunca había hecho una excursión. ¡Me encantó!**
  I had never gone on a hike before. I loved it!
- ▷ **Ha sido la mejor excursión de mi vida.**
  It's been the best hike of my life.

Courtesy expressions

- ▶ **Gracias por todo.**
  Thanks for everything.
- ▶ **Ha sido un placer.**
  It's been a pleasure.
- ▶ **¡Cuídense!**
  Take care!

Suggestion Have the class read through the entire **Fotonovela**, with volunteers playing the various parts.

Expresiones útiles Point out that **han traído, han venido,** and **Ha sido** are examples of the present perfect, which combines a present tense form of the verb **haber** with the past participle of another verb. Explain that **había visto** and **había hecho** are examples of the past perfect, which combines an imperfect tense form of **haber** with a past participle. Finally, draw attention to the sentence **No puedo creer que finalmente haya llegado el gran día.** Tell the class that **haya llegado** is an example of the present perfect subjunctive, which combines a present subjunctive form of **haber** with a past participle. Tell your students that they will learn more about these concepts in **Estructura**.

TEACHING OPTIONS

Enfoque cultural Magazines and newspapers in Spain and Latin America have picked up on the public's interest in health and often publish articles about cardiovascular fitness, maintaining a healthful diet, and avoiding stress. These topics are also frequently discussed on television and radio programs in Spain and Latin America, and on Spanish-language radio and television programs in the United States. Ask your students, especially heritage speakers, if they have read articles or tuned in to programming of this kind. Also, if you have copies of magazine or newspaper articles in Spanish about health or fitness, you may want to show them to the class.

1 Expansion Have the class work in pairs or small groups to write a question that would elicit each statement.

2 Expansions
- Give the class these additional items: **7. Bueno, chicos… hay que hacer unos ejercicios antes de empezar. (Martín) 8. ¿Qué tal les fue en la excursión? (don Francisco)**
- Have your students close their books, then give them these sentences as a dictation. Read each sentence twice slowly and then once at regular speed so that the class will have time to write.

3 Suggestion Ask your students a few questions using words from the word bank. Ex: **¿Comes mucha grasa? ¿Qué es un teleadicto? ¿Cómo te mantienes en forma? ¿Qué haces para mantenerte en forma?**

3 Expansion Have pairs write sentences using any leftover words from the word bank. Ask volunteers to share their sentences with the class.

Reacciona a la fotonovela

1 Seleccionar Selecciona la respuesta que mejor completa cada frase.

1. Antes de salir, Martín les recomienda a los estudiantes que hagan __a__.
   a. ejercicios de estiramiento b. ejercicios aeróbicos c. gimnasia
2. Los excursionistas hablaron, __c__ en las montañas.
   a. levantaron pesas y se divirtieron b. caminaron y dibujaron
   c. sacaron fotos y disfrutaron del paisaje
3. Inés dice que ha sido la mejor excursión __c__.
   a. del viaje b. del año c. de su vida
4. Cuando Maite vuelva a España, va a __b__.
   a. tener montones de escenas para dibujar b. tener mucho que contarle a su familia
   c. tener muchas fotos que enseñarle a su familia
5. La señora Vives les ha preparado __a__.
   a. una cena especial b. un día en las montañas muy especial
   c. una excursión espectacular

NOTA CULTURAL

En Latinoamérica hay muchos lugares populares para hacer **excursiones**. Cientos de personas viajan anualmente a México para escalar los volcanes Popocatépetl e Iztaccíhuatl.

En Centroamérica, el bosque Monteverde de Costa Rica y el Parque Internacional La Amistad de Panamá son muy famosos. En Suramérica la zona montañosa de los Andes es muy visitada.

2 Identificar Identifica quién puede decir las siguientes frases.

1. Oye, muchísimas gracias por el mejor día de mi vida. ¡Fue divertidísimo! Inés
2. Parece que están todos preparados, ¿no? ¡Perfecto! Bueno, ¡vamos! Martín
3. Cuando vea a mis papás y a mis hermanos voy a tener mucho que contarles. Maite
4. Debemos volver ahora para comer. ¡Vamos a tener una cena especial! don Francisco
5. El lugar fue fenomenal, uno de los más bonitos que he visto. ¡Qué bueno que traje mi cámara! Javier
6. ¡Gracias por todo, Martín! Álex/Maite/Inés/Javier

JAVIER

INÉS

ÁLEX

MAITE

DON FRANCISCO

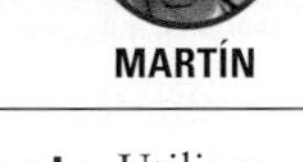

MARTÍN

3 Inventar En parejas, hagan descripciones de los personajes de la **fotonovela**. Utilicen las frases, la lista de palabras y otras expresiones que sepan. Answers will vary.

aliviar el estrés	hacer ejercicios de estiramiento	mantenerse en forma
bienestar	masaje	teleadicto/a
grasa	llevar una vida sana	vitamina

modelo

Martín es activo, flexible y fuerte.
Martín siempre hace ejercicios de estiramiento. Está en buena forma y lleva una vida muy sana…

1. A Javier le duelen los músculos después de hacer gimnasia.
2. Don Francisco a veces sufre presiones y estrés en su trabajo.
3. A Inés le encanta salir con amigos o leer un buen libro.
4. Álex trata de comer una dieta equilibrada.
5. Maite no es muy flexible.

TEACHING OPTIONS

Extra Practice Ask the class a few additional questions about the **Fotonovela**. Ex: **¿Qué hicieron Martín y los chicos antes de empezar la excursión? (Hicieron unos ejercicios de estiramiento.) ¿Qué hicieron los estudiantes durante la excursión? (Caminaron, hablaron, sacaron fotos y miraron el paisaje.)**

Pairs Have pairs prepare a television program in which a traveler is interviewed about a recent hiking trip. Give them time to prepare and rehearse; then ask for volunteers to present their programs to the class. Alternately, you may want the students to videotape their programs and play them for the class.

Ortografía

Las letras b y v

Since there is no difference in pronunciation between the Spanish letters **b** and **v**, spelling words that contain these letters can be tricky. Here are some tips.

nombre **blusa** **absoluto** **descubrir**

The letter **b** is always used before consonants.

bonita **botella** **buscar** **bienestar**

At the beginning of words, the letter **b** is usually used when it is followed by the letter combinations **-on, -or, -ot, -u, -ur, -us, -ien,** and **-ene.**

adelgazaba **disfrutaban** **ibas** **íbamos**

The letter **b** is used in the verb endings of the imperfect tense for **–ar** verbs and the verb **ir.**

voy **vamos** **estuvo** **tuvieron**

The letter **v** is used in the present tense forms of **ir** and in the preterite forms of **estar** and **tener.**

octavo **huevo** **activa** **grave**

The letter **v** is used in these noun and adjective endings: **-avo/a, -evo/a, -ivo/a, -ave, -eve.**

Práctica Completa las palabras con las letras **b** o **v**.

1. Una _v_ez me lastimé el _b_razo cuando esta_b_a _b_uceando.
2. Manuela se ol_v_idó sus li_b_ros en el auto_b_ús.
3. Ernesto tomó el _b_orrador y se puso todo _b_lanco de tiza.
4. Para tener una _v_ida sana y saluda_b_le necesitas tomar _v_itaminas.
5. En mi pue_b_lo hay un _b_ule_v_ar que tiene muchos ár_b_oles.

El ahorcado (*Hangman*) Juega al ahorcado para adivinar las palabras.

1. n u b e s — Están en el cielo. nubes
2. b u z ó n — Relacionado con el correo buzón
3. b o t e l l a — Está llena de líquido. botella
4. n i e v e — Fenómeno meteorológico nieve
5. v e n t a n a s — Los "ojos" de la casa ventanas

recursos

LM p. 86	Lab CD/MP3 Lección 15	I CD-ROM Lección 15

Section Goal

In **Ortografía** students will learn about the spelling of words that contain **b** and **v**.

Instructional Resource
Interactive CD-ROM

Suggestions

- Ask the class if **b** or **v** is used before a consonant. Then say the words **nombre, blusa, absoluto,** and **descubrir** and have volunteers write them on the board.
- Write the words **bonita, botella, buscar,** and **bienestar** on the board. Ask the class to explain why these words are spelled with **b**.
- Ask the class if **b** or **v** is used in the endings of **–ar** verbs and the verb **ir** in the imperfect tense. Then say the words **adelgazaba, disfrutaban, ibas,** and **íbamos** and ask for volunteers to write them on the board.
- Ask why the words **voy, vamos, estuvo,** and **tuvieron** are spelled with **v** and have volunteers write them on the board.
- Write the words **octavo, huevo, activa,** and **grave** on the board and ask the class to explain why these words are spelled with **v**.
- Point out that **Ortografía** replaces **Pronunciación** in the Student Edition for **Lecciones 10–18**, but not in the Lab Manual. The **Recursos** box references the **Pronunciación** sections found in all lessons of the Lab Manual.

TEACHING OPTIONS

Small Groups On the board, write the following sentences: **Doña __ioleta era muy acti__a y lle__aba una __ida muy sana. Siempre comía __ien y nunca toma__a __ino ni refrescos. Nunca fuma__a e i__a al gimnasio todos los días para hacer ejercicios aeró__icos.** Have your students work in groups to fill in the missing letters.

Pairs Have partners use **Vocabulario** at the back of the book to help them write five sentences that contain words with **b** and **v**. Encourage students to use as many of these words as they can. They should leave blanks in place of these letters, as in **Práctica**. Then have pairs exchange papers and complete the words.

Section Goal

In **Estructura 15.1** students will learn the use of the present perfect.

Instructional Resources
WB/VM: Workbook, pp. 171–172
Lab Manual, p. 87
Lab CD/MP3 ***Lección 15***
IRM: ***¡Inténtalo!*** *&* ***Práctica*** *Answers, p. 221; Tapescript, pp. 67–70*
Interactive CD-ROM
Companion website: www.vistahigherlearning.com
Presentations CD-ROM

Suggestions

- Have students turn to pages 458–459. Ask them to read the **Fotonovela** again and write down the past participles they find. Ask students if they are used as adjectives or as parts of verbs.
- Model the present perfect by making statements about what you and others in the class have done, or by asking students questions. Ex: **Yo he preparado una lección. Ustedes han leído la sección de Estructura, ¿verdad? ¿Quién no la ha leído?**

Consúltalo Tell students that while the present perfect is generally used in Spanish just as it is in English, the expression *to have just* done something is expressed in Spanish by **acabar de** + [*infinitive*]. Write the following sentences on the board and contrast them: **Acabo de venir del gimnasio. / He venido del gimnasio.**

15.1 The present perfect

NATIONAL
comparisons
STANDARDS

ANTE TODO In **Lección 14**, you learned how to form past participles. You will now learn how to form the present perfect indicative (**el pretérito perfecto de indicativo**), a compound tense that uses the past participle. The present perfect is used to talk about what someone *has done*. In Spanish, it is formed with the present tense of the auxiliary verb **haber** and a past participle.

Ya veo que han traído todo lo que necesitan.

Todos han venido muy bien equipados.

recursos

WB pp. 171–176

LM pp. 87–89

Lab CD/MP3 Lección 15

I CD-ROM Lección 15

vistahigher learning.com

Present indicative of *haber*

Singular forms		Plural forms	
yo	**he**	nosotros/as	**hemos**
tú	**has**	vosotros/as	**habéis**
Ud./él/ella	**ha**	Uds./ellos/ellas	**han**

Tú no **has aumentado de** peso.
You haven't gained weight.

¿**Ha asistido** Juan a la clase de ejercicios aeróbicos?
Has Juan attended the aerobics class?

Yo ya **he leído** esos libros.
I've already read those books.

Hemos conocido al entrenador.
We have met the trainer.

CONSÚLTALO

To review what you have learned about participles, see **Estructura 14.3**, p. 441.

▶ The past participle does not change in form when it is part of the present perfect tense; it only changes in form when it is used as an adjective.

Clara **ha abierto** las ventanas.
Clara has opened the windows.

Las ventanas están **abiertas.**
The windows are open.

Yo **he cerrado** la puerta del gimnasio.
I've closed the door to the gym.

La puerta del gimnasio está **cerrada.**
The door to the gym is closed.

CONSÚLTALO

Remember that the Spanish equivalent of the English *to have just (done something)* is **acabar de** + [*infinitive*]. Do not use the present perfect to express that English structure.
Juan acaba de llegar.
Juan has just arrived.
See **Estructura 6.3**, p. 185.

▶ In Spanish, the present perfect indicative is generally used just as it is used in English: to talk about what someone has done or what has occurred. It usually refers to the recent past.

He trabajado cuarenta horas esta semana.
I have worked forty hours this week.

¿Cuál es el último libro que **has leído**?
What is the last book that you have read?

TEACHING OPTIONS

Extra Practice Ask students what they have done over the past week to lead a healthy lifestyle. Ask follow-up questions to elicit a variety of different conjugations of the present perfect. Ex: **¿Qué han hecho esta semana pasada para llevar una vida sana? Y tú, ____, ¿qué has hecho? Clase, ¿qué ha hecho ____ esta semana?**

Pairs Ask students to tell their partner five things they have done in the past to stay in shape. Partners repeat back what the students have said, using the **tú** form of the present perfect. Ex: **He levantado pesas. (Muy bien. Has levantado pesas.)**

▶ In English, the auxiliary verb and the past participle are often separated. In Spanish, however, these two elements—**haber** and the past participle—cannot be separated by any word.

Siempre **hemos vivido** en Bolivia.
We have always lived in Bolivia.

Usted nunca **ha venido** a mi oficina.
You have never come to my office.

Creo que la señora Vives nos ha preparado una cena muy especial.

Gracias, Martín.
No hay de qué. Ha sido un placer.

▶ The word **no** and any object or reflexive pronouns are placed immediately before **haber.**

Yo **no he comido la merienda.**
I haven't eaten the snack.

¿Por qué **no la has comido**?
Why haven't you eaten it?

Susana ya **se ha entrenado**.
Susana has already practiced.

Ellos **no lo han terminado**.
They haven't finished it.

▶ Note that *to have* can be either a main verb or an auxiliary verb in English. As a main verb, it corresponds to **tener,** while as an auxiliary, it corresponds to **haber.**

Tengo muchos amigos.
I have a lot of friends.

He tenido mucho éxito.
I have had a lot of success.

▶ To form the present perfect of **hay,** use the third person singular of **haber (ha) + habido.**

Ha habido muchos problemas con el nuevo profesor.
There have been a lot of problems with the new professor.

Ha habido un accidente en la calle Central.
There has been an accident on Central Street.

¡INTÉNTALO! Indica el pretérito perfecto de indicativo de los siguientes verbos.

1. (disfrutar, comer, vivir) yo he disfrutado, he comido, he vivido
2. (traer, adelgazar, compartir) tú has traído, has adelgazado, has compartido
3. (venir, estar, correr) Ud. ha venido, ha estado, ha corrido
4. (leer, resolver, poner) ella ha leído, ha resuelto, ha puesto
5. (decir, romper, hacer) ellos han dicho, han roto, han hecho
6. (mantenerse, dormirse) nosotros nos hemos mantenido, nos hemos dormido
7. (estar, escribir, ver) yo he estado, he escrito, he visto
8. (vivir, correr, morir) él ha vivido, ha corrido, ha muerto

Suggestions

- Ask students questions in the present perfect with indirect and direct objects. Ex: ____, **¿has estudiado bien la lección? (Sí, la he estudiado bien.)** ____, **¿has entendido todo lo que te he dicho? (No, no lo he entendido todo.) ¿Todos me han entregado el trabajo de hoy? (Sí, todos se lo hemos entregado.)**
- Explain that although an adverb can never appear between **haber** and its past participle, it may appear in other positions in the sentence to change emphasis. Ex: **Hemos vivido siempre en Bolivia. Hemos vivido en Bolivia siempre.**
- Practice adverb placement by supplying an adverb for each item in **¡Inténtalo!** Ex: **siempre (siempre he disfrutado/he disfrutado siempre)**

TEACHING OPTIONS

Large Groups Divide the class into three groups. Have students write down five physical activities. Then have them ask each of their group members if they have ever done those activities and record their answers. Ex: **¿Has hecho ejercicios de estiramiento alguna vez? ¿Has levantado pesas? ¿Has hecho ejercicios en un gimnasio?**

Extra Practice Draw a time line on the board. On the far right of the line, write **el presente**. Just to the left of that point, write **el pasado muy reciente**. To the left of that, write **el pasado reciente**. Then to the far left, write **el pasado**. Make a statement using the preterite, the present perfect, or **acabar de** + [*infinitive*]. Have students indicate on the timeline when the action took place.

1 Expansion Have students write five original sentences using the present perfect to describe their past health and that of their friends and family members.

Ayuda Practice the expressions by using sentences that describe your and your students' lives. Ex: **He viajado a España un par de veces. ¿Quién ha viajado a España muchas veces?**

2 Expansions
- Ask students follow-up questions about their responses.
- Have partners elaborate on their responses by asking each other questions about what they have done. Ex: **—¿Has buceado? —Sí, he buceado varias veces. —¡Qué suerte! ¿Dónde has buceado, en el Caribe?**

3 Expansions
- Take a survey of the answers given and write the results on the board. Then ask volunteers to summarize the results. Ex: **Casi todos hemos dejado de tomar refrescos.**
- Ask students to give examples of the benefits of adopting some of the healthy habits listed. Ex: **Ahora puedo subir las escaleras hasta el quinto piso sin llegar cansado/a.**

Práctica

1 **Completar** Estas oraciones describen el bienestar o los problemas de unos estudiantes. Completa las oraciones con el pretérito perfecto de indicativo de los verbos de la lista.

adelgazar	comer	llevar
aumentar	hacer	sufrir

1. Luisa ___ha sufrido___ muchas presiones este año.
2. Juan y Raúl ___han aumentado___ de peso porque no hacen ejercicio.
3. Pero María y yo ___hemos adelgazado___ porque trabajamos en exceso y nos olvidamos de comer.
4. Desde siempre, yo ___he llevado___ una vida muy sana.
5. Pero tú y yo no ___hemos hecho___ gimnasia este semestre.

2 **¿Qué has hecho?** Indica si has hecho lo siguiente. Answers will vary.

modelo

Escalar una montaña

Sí, he escalado varias montañas./No, no he escalado nunca una montaña.

1. Jugar al baloncesto
2. Viajar a Bolivia
3. Conocer a una persona famosa
4. Levantar pesas
5. Comer un insecto
6. Recibir un masaje
7. Aprender un segundo idioma
8. Bailar salsa
9. Ver una película española
10. Escuchar música latina
11. Estar despierto 24 horas
12. Bucear

AYUDA

You may use some of these expressions in your answers:

una vez *once*
un par de veces *a couple of times*
algunas veces *a few times*
varias veces *several times*
muchas veces *many times, often*

3 **La vida sana** En parejas, túrnense para hacer preguntas sobre el tema de la vida sana. Sean creativos. Answers will vary.

modelo

Encontrar un gimnasio

Estudiante 1: *¿Has encontrado un buen gimnasio cerca de tu casa?*

Estudiante 2: *Yo no he encontrado un gimnasio pero sé que debo buscar uno.*

1. Tratar de estar en forma
2. Estar a dieta los últimos dos meses
3. Dejar de tomar refrescos
4. Hacerse una prueba del colesterol
5. Entrenarse cinco días a la semana
6. Cambiar de una vida sedentaria a una vida activa
7. Tomar vitaminas por las noches y por las mañanas
8. Hacer ejercicio para aliviar la tensión
9. Consumir mucha proteína
10. Dejar de fumar

TEACHING OPTIONS

Small Groups Divide the class into groups of four to write and perform skits in which one student plays a personal trainer, another plays a nutritionist, and the other two play clients. The personal trainer and nutritionist ask the clients whether they have done the things they have recommended. The clients explain what they have done and make excuses for what they haven't done.

Pairs Have students discuss with a classmate five things they have already done today. Ex: **He estudiado la lección para esta clase. He ido al gimnasio. He ido a una clase de ejercicios aeróbicos. He almorzado con unos amigos. He escrito una carta a mis abuelos. ¿Qué has hecho tú?**

Comunicación

4 **Descripción** En parejas, describan lo que ha(n) hecho y no ha(n) hecho la(s) persona(s) en cada dibujo. Usen la imaginación. Answers will vary.

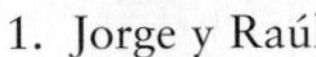

1. Jorge y Raúl

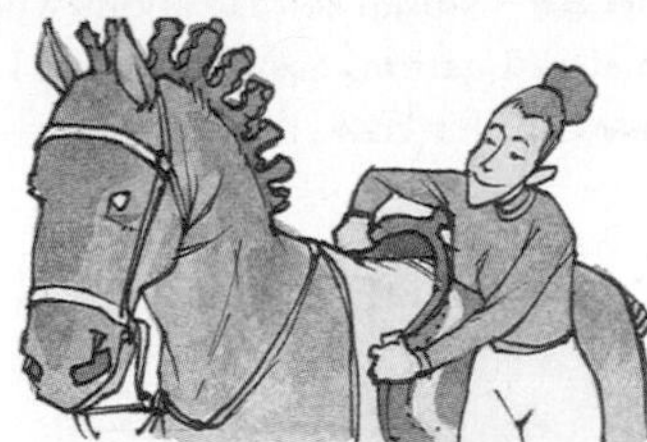

2. Luisa

3. Jacobo

4. Natalia y Diego

5. Ricardo

6. Carmen

5 **Describir** En parejas, identifiquen a una persona que lleva una vida muy sana. Puede ser una persona que conocen o un personaje que aparece en una película o programa de televisión. Entre los dos, escriban una descripción de lo que esta persona ha hecho para llevar una vida sana. Answers will vary.

modelo

Pedro Penzini Fleury siempre ha hecho todo lo posible para mantenerse en forma. Él...

NOTA CULTURAL

El doctor venezolano **Pedro Penzini Fleury** tiene un programa popular de radio sobre la importancia del bienestar en la vida diaria. También tiene una columna en el periódico.

Síntesis

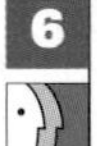

6 **Situación** Trabajen en parejas para representar los papeles de un(a) enfermero/a de la universidad y un(a) estudiante. El/La enfermero/a de la clínica de la universidad está conversando con el/la estudiante que no se siente nada bien. El/La enfermero/a debe averiguar de dónde viene el problema e investigar los hábitos del/de la estudiante. El/La estudiante le explica lo que ha hecho en los últimos meses y cómo se ha sentido. Luego el/la enfermero/a le da recomendaciones al/a la estudiante de cómo llevar una vida más sana. Answers will vary.

4 Suggestion Before beginning the activity, ask volunteers to describe the people in each drawing and how they feel.

5 Suggestion Have pairs describe eight different things their chosen person has done that exemplifies a healthy lifestyle. Remind them to include introductory and concluding statements in their description.

5 Expansion Have students choose someone who is the exact opposite of the healthy person they chose earlier and write a description of what that person has done that exemplifies an unhealthy lifestyle.

6 Expansion While pairs are performing their role-plays for the class, stop the action after the patient has described his or her symptoms and what he or she has done in the last few months. Ask the audience to make a diagnosis. Then have the players finish their presentation.

TEACHING OPTIONS

Game Have students write three important things they have done over the past year on a slip of paper and put it in a box. Ex: **Este año he creado un sitio web.** Have students draw a paper from the box, then circulate around the room, asking students if they have done the activities listed, until they find the person who wrote the slip of paper. The first person to find a match wins.

Heritage Speakers Have heritage speakers interview someone who has immigrated from a Spanish-speaking country to the United States or Canada to find out how that person's life has changed since moving. Students should find out how the interviewee's physical activity and diet have changed. Have students present their findings in a brief written report.

Section Goal

In **Estructura 15.2** students will learn the use of the past perfect tense.

Instructional Resources
WB/VM: Workbook, pp. 173–174
Lab Manual, p. 88
Lab CD/MP3 ***Lección 15***
IRM: ***Hojas de actividades,*** *p. 172;* ***¡Inténtalo! & Práctica*** *Answers, p. 221; Tapescript, pp. 67–70*
Info Gap Activities Booklet, pp. 59–60
Interactive CD-ROM
Companion website: www.vistahigherlearning.com
Presentations CD-ROM

Suggestions

- Introduce the past perfect tense by making statements about the past that are true for you. Write examples of the past perfect on the board as you use them. Ex: **Esta mañana vine a la universidad en la bicicleta de mi hijo. Nunca antes había venido en bicicleta. Por lo general, vengo en carro. Muchas veces antes había caminado y también había venido en autobús cuando tenía prisa, pero nunca en bicicleta.**
- Check for comprehension of **ya** by contrasting it with **nunca**. Ex: **Antes del semestre pasado, nunca había enseñado este curso, pero ya había enseñado otros cursos de español.**

Successful Language Learning Tell your students to imagine how they might use the past perfect to tell someone about their lives.

15.2 The past perfect

NATIONAL
comparisons
STANDARDS

ANTE TODO The past perfect indicative (**el pretérito pluscuamperfecto de indicativo**) is used to talk about what someone *had done* or what *had occurred* before another past action, event, or state. Like the present perfect, the past perfect uses a form of **haber**—in this case, the imperfect—plus the past participle.

Nunca había visto un paisaje tan espectacular.

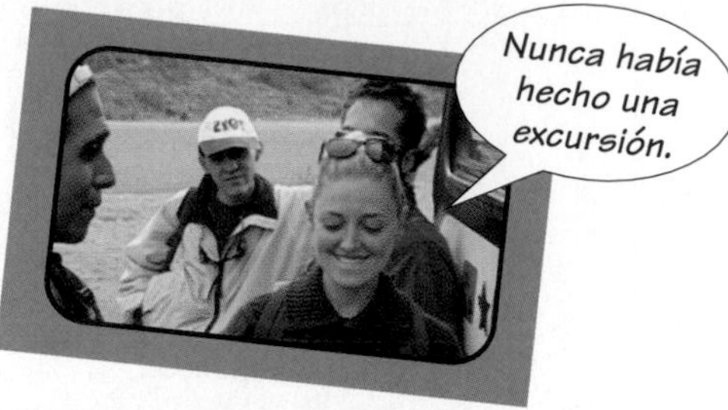
Nunca había hecho una excursión.

Past perfect indicative

		cerrar	perder	asistir
SINGULAR FORMS	yo	**había** cerrado	**había** perdido	**había** asistido
	tú	**habías** cerrado	**habías** perdido	**habías** asistido
	Ud./él/ella	**había** cerrado	**había** perdido	**había** asistido
PLURAL FORMS	nosotros/as	**habíamos** cerrado	**habíamos** perdido	**habíamos** asistido
	vosotros/as	**habíais** cerrado	**habíais** perdido	**habíais** asistido
	Uds./ellos/ellas	**habían** cerrado	**habían** perdido	**habían** asistido

Antes de 2003, **había vivido** en La Paz.
Before 2003, I had lived in La Paz.

Cuando llegamos, Luis ya **había salido.**
When we arrived, Luis had already left.

▶ The past perfect is often used with the word **ya** (*already*) to indicate that an action, event, or state had already occurred before another. Remember that, unlike its English equivalent, **ya** cannot be placed between **haber** and the past participle.

Ella **ya había salido** cuando llamaron.
She had already left when they called.

Cuando llegué, Raúl **ya se había acostado.**
When I arrived, Raúl had already gone to bed.

¡ATENCIÓN!

The past perfect is often used in conjunction with **antes de** + [*noun*] or **antes de** + [*infinitive*] to describe when the action(s) occurred.

Antes de este año, nunca había estudiado español.
Before this year, I had never studied Spanish.

Luis me había llamado antes de venir.
Luis had called me before he came.

¡INTÉNTALO! Indica el pretérito pluscuamperfecto de indicativo de cada verbo.

1. Nosotros ya <u>habíamos cenado</u> (cenar) cuando nos llamaron.
2. Antes de tomar esta clase, yo no <u>había estudiado</u> (estudiar) nunca el español.
3. Antes de ir a México, ellos nunca <u>habían ido</u> (ir) a otro país.
4. Eduardo nunca <u>se había entrenado</u> (entrenarse) tanto en invierno.
5. Tú siempre <u>habías llevado</u> (llevar) una vida sana antes del año pasado.
6. Antes de conocerte, yo ya te <u>había visto</u> (ver) muchas veces.

TEACHING OPTIONS

Extra Practice Have students write sentences, using the past perfect and each of the following twice: **antes de** + [*infinitive*], **antes de que** + [*conjugated verb*], the preterite, and the imperfect. Have students peer edit their work before sharing their sentences with the class. Ex: **Nuestros bisabuelos ya habían muerto cuando éramos niños.**

TPR Make a series of statements about the past, using two different verbs. After making a statement, call out the infinitive of one of the verbs. If that action occurred before the other one, have students raise one finger. If it occurred after the other action, have them raise two fingers. Ex: **Tomás ya había bajado de la montaña cuando empezó a nevar. Empezar.** (two fingers)

Práctica

1 Completar Completa los minidiálogos con las formas correctas del pretérito pluscuamperfecto de indicativo.

1. **SARA** Antes de cumplir los 15 años, ¿ habías estudiado (estudiar) tú otra lengua?
   JOSÉ Sí, había tomado (tomar) clases de inglés y de italiano.
2. **DOLORES** Antes de ir a Argentina, ¿ habían probado (probar) tú y tu familia el mate?
   TOMÁS Sí, ya habíamos tomado (tomar) mate muchas veces.
3. **ANTONIO** Antes de este año, ¿ había corrido (correr) usted en un maratón?
   SRA. VERA No, nunca lo había hecho (hacer).
4. **SOFÍA** Antes de su enfermedad, ¿ había sufrido (sufrir) muchas presiones tu tío?
   IRENE Sí... y él nunca se había mantenido (mantenerse) en buena forma.

NOTA CULTURAL

La yerba mate, una bebida similar al té, es muy popular en Argentina, Uruguay y Paraguay. Se dice que controla el estrés, la obesidad, y que estimula el sistema inmunológico. Tradicionalmente, se toma en una calabaza (*gourd*) con una bombilla filtrante (*tea-filtering straw*).

2 Quehaceres Indica lo que ya había hecho cada miembro de la familia antes de la llegada de la madre, la señora Ferrer. Answers will vary.

3 Tu vida Indica si ya habías hecho las siguientes cosas antes de cumplir los 16 años. Answers will vary.

1. Hacer un viaje en avión
2. Escalar una montaña
3. Escribir un poema
4. Leer una novela
5. Enamorarte
6. Tomar clases de aeróbicos
7. Montar a caballo
8. Ir de pesca
9. Manejar un carro
10. Navegar en la red

1 Expansions
- Have students pick one of the interchanges and expand upon it to create a conversation with six lines.
- Have students create an original conversation like the ones in the activity. Call on volunteers to perform them for the class.

2 Expansion Divide the class into groups of six. Have each person in a group choose the role of one of the family members. Tell students that they are cleaning the house because they want to surprise Señora Ferrer for Mother's Day. Have students ask each other questions about what they've already done and what still needs to be done.

3 Suggestion Ask students questions to elicit the answers for the activity. Ex: **¿Quién había hecho un viaje en avión antes de cumplir los 16 años?** Ask follow-up questions to elicit other conjugations of the past perfect. Ex: **Entonces clase, ¿quiénes habían hecho un viaje en avión antes de cumplir los 16 años? (Ana y Rosa habían hecho...)**

TEACHING OPTIONS

Pairs Have students imagine they have joined a gym for the first time and are telling a friend about their new experiences. Ask students to tell their partner five things they had never done before going to a gym. Ex: **Nunca había sudado tanto antes de empezar a ir al gimnasio.**

Extra Practice Ask students to write six things they had already done before the following birthdays: **los tres años, los siete años, los 13 años, los 16 años, los 18 años, los 21 años.** Ex: **Antes de los tres años ya había caminado.**

4 Suggestion Distribute the **Hojas de actividades** from the IRM that correspond to this activity.

4 Expansion Call on volunteers to read their sentences aloud for the class to react to them. Then make statements about your own life and have students react to them.

5 Suggestion Before beginning the activity, survey the class to find out who exercises regularly and/or carefully watches what he or she eats. Ask these students to use the past perfect to say what they had done in their life prior to starting their fitness or diet program. Ex: **Había comido pastel de chocolate todos los días.**

5 Expansion Have groups create an ad for a different type of health-related business, for instance a vegetarian restaurant.

Suggestion See the Info Gap Activities Booklet for an additional activity to practice the material presented in this section.

Comunicación

NATIONAL communication STANDARDS

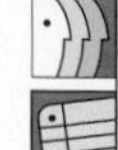

4 **Lo dudo** Tu profesor(a) va a darte una hoja de actividades. Escribe cinco oraciones, algunas ciertas y algunas falsas, de cosas que habías hecho antes de venir a la universidad. Luego, en grupos, túrnense para leer sus oraciones. Cada miembro del grupo debe decir "es cierto" o "lo dudo" después de cada una. Escribe la reacción de cada compañero/a en la columna apropiada. ¿Quién obtuvo más respuestas ciertas? Answers will vary.

Oraciones	Miguel	Ana	Beatriz
1. Cuando tenía 10 años, ya había manejado el carro de mi papá.	Lo dudo.	Es cierto.	Lo dudo.
2.			
3.			
4.			
5.			

Síntesis

NATIONAL communication STANDARDS

5 **Gimnasio Olímpico** En parejas, lean el anuncio y contesten las preguntas.

Hasta el año pasado, siempre había mirado la tele sentado en el sofá durante mis ratos libres. ¡Era un sedentario y un teleadicto! Jamás había practicado ningún deporte y había aumentado mucho de peso.
Este año, he empezado a comer una dieta más sana y voy al gimnasio todos los días. He comenzado a ser una persona muy activa y he adelgazado. Disfruto de una vida sana y ... ¡Me siento muy feliz!
Manténgase en forma.
¡Acabo de descubrir una nueva vida!
¡Venga al Gimnasio Olímpico hoy mismo!

1. Identifiquen los elementos del pretérito pluscuamperfecto de indicativo en el anuncio. había mirado; había practicado; había aumentado.
2. ¿Cómo era la vida del hombre cuando llevaba una vida sedentaria? ¿Cómo es ahora? Answers will vary.
3. ¿Se identifican ustedes con algunos de los hábitos, presentes o pasados, de este hombre? ¿Con cuáles? Answers will vary.
4. ¿Qué les recomienda el hombre del anuncio a los lectores? ¿Creen que les da buenos consejos? Answers will vary.

TEACHING OPTIONS

Small Groups Divide students into groups of three. Student A begins a sentence with **antes de que** + [*conjugated verb*]. Student B finishes the sentence with a verb in the past perfect. Student C writes the sentence down. Have students alternate their roles until they've created nine sentences. Then, have all group members check the sentences before sharing them with the class.

Large Groups Divide the class into groups of six for a game of "one-upmanship." The first student states something he or she had done before a certain event in his or her past. The second student tells what the first one had done, then counters with something even more outrageous that he or she had done, and so on, until everyone has participated. Ex: _____ **había..., pero yo había...**

15.3 The present perfect subjunctive

ANTE TODO The present perfect subjunctive (**el pretérito perfecto de subjuntivo**), like the present perfect indicative, is used to talk about what *has happened.* The present perfect subjunctive is formed using the present subjunctive of the auxiliary verb **haber** and a past participle.

Present perfect indicative			Present perfect subjunctive		
	PRESENT INDICATIVE OF HABER	PAST PARTICIPLE		PRESENT SUBJUNCTIVE OF HABER	PAST PARTICIPLE
yo	**he**	**hablado**	**yo**	**haya**	**hablado**

Present perfect subjunctive

		cerrar	perder	asistir
SINGULAR FORMS	yo	**haya** cerrado	**haya** perdido	**haya** asistido
	tú	**hayas** cerrado	**hayas** perdido	**hayas** asistido
	Ud./él/ella	**haya** cerrado	**haya** perdido	**haya** asistido
PLURAL FORMS	nosotros/as	**hayamos** cerrado	**hayamos** perdido	**hayamos** asistido
	vosotros/as	**hayáis** cerrado	**hayáis** perdido	**hayáis** asistido
	Uds./ellos/ellas	**hayan** cerrado	**hayan** perdido	**hayan** asistido

¡ATENCIÓN!

The perfect forms are often used with **ya** (*already*). Remember that **ya** must come either before or after **haber** and the participle, which are never separated in Spanish.

Dudo que Enrique **ya** lo **haya hecho.**

Dudo que Enrique lo **haya hecho ya.**

•••

In Spanish the present perfect subjunctive is used for a recent action.

No creo que lo **hayas dicho** bien.
I don't think you said it right.

Espero que él **haya llegado.**
I hope he arrived.

▶ The same conditions which trigger the use of the present subjunctive apply to the present perfect subjunctive.

Present subjunctive	Present perfect subjunctive
Espero que **duermas** bien. *I hope that you sleep well.*	Espero que **hayas dormido** bien. *I hope that you have slept well.*
No creo que **aumente** de peso. *I don't think he will gain weight.*	No creo que **haya aumentado** de peso. *I don't think he has gained weight.*

▶ The action expressed by the present perfect subjunctive is seen as occurring before the action expressed in the main clause.

Me alegro de que ustedes **se hayan reído** tanto esta tarde.
I'm glad that you have laughed so much this afternoon.

Dudo que ella **se haya divertido** mucho con su suegra.
I doubt that she has enjoyed herself much with her mother-in-law.

¡INTÉNTALO! Indica el pretérito perfecto de subjuntivo de los verbos entre paréntesis.

1. Me gusta que ustedes __hayan dicho__ (decir) la verdad.
2. No creo que tú __hayas comido__ (comer) tanto.
3. Es imposible que usted __haya podido__ (poder) hacer tal (*such a*) cosa.
4. Me alegro de que tú y yo __hayamos merendado__ (merendar) juntas.
5. Es posible que yo __haya adelgazado__ (adelgazar) un poco esta semana.
6. Espero que __haya habido__ (haber) suficiente comida en la celebración.

Section Goal

In **Estructura 15.3** students will learn the use of the present perfect subjunctive.

Instructional Resources
WB/VM: Workbook, pp. 175–176
Lab Manual, p. 89
Lab CD/MP3 ***Lección 15***
IRM: ***¡Inténtalo! & Práctica*** *Answers, p. 221; Tapescript, pp. 67–70*
Interactive CD-ROM
Companion website: www.vistahigherlearning.com
Presentations CD-ROM

Suggestions

- Ask a volunteer to tell you something he or she has done this week. Respond with a comment using the present perfect subjunctive. Ex: **Me alegro de que hayas levantado pesas. ¡Ay, no exageres chico/a! ¡Dudo que hayas trabajado tanto!** Write present perfect subjunctive forms on the board as you say them.
- Ask volunteers to tell you what they have done during the past week. Again, comment on their statements in ways that trigger the present perfect subjunctive, but this time elicit peer comments that use the present perfect subjunctive.

TEACHING OPTIONS

Extra Practice Ask students to write their reactions to the following statements: **1. Ángela ha dejado de fumar. 2. Roberto ya ha estudiado ocho horas hoy. 3. Todos los teleadictos han seguido una dieta balanceada. 4. No he preparado la prueba para mañana. 5. Mi marido y yo hemos estado enfermos.** Ex: **Martín ha perdido cinco kilos. Es bueno que Martín haya perdido cinco kilos.**

Small Groups Divide the class into groups of three. Have students take turns telling the group three wishes they hope to have fulfilled by the end of the day. Ex: **Espero que mi compañero haya limpiado el apartamento.**

1 Suggestion Call on volunteers to read each completed sentence to the class. Then call on different students to point out the verb or expression triggering the subjunctive.

1 Expansion After students have read each completed item, ask them the following comprehension questions. **1. ¿Por qué crees que Julio se ha sentido mal? 2. ¿Ha cambiado Lourdes de trabajo, según la persona que habla? 3. ¿Por qué están Nuria y su amiga tristes? 4. ¿Qué ha hecho Samuel? ¿Por qué? 5. ¿Qué es increíble? ¿Por qué? 6. ¿Cuántos años tiene la abuela? ¿Ha llevado una vida sana?**

2 Suggestions
- Working with the entire class, elicit descriptions of what each of the characters depicted is like and how he or she got that way.
- Have students write their comments and then exchange them with a partner for peer editing. Students should make sure their partner's sentences are logical and grammatically correct.

2 Expansion Call on a student to read one of his or her comments, omitting any character's name. Have the class indicate which person is being described.

Práctica

1 Completar Laura está preocupada por su familia y sus amigos/as. Completa las oraciones con la forma correcta del pretérito perfecto de subjuntivo de los verbos entre paréntesis.

1. ¡Qué lástima que Julio _se haya sentido_ (sentirse) tan mal en la competencia! Dudo que _se haya entrenado_ (entrenarse) lo suficiente.
2. No creo que Lourdes y su amiga _se hayan ido_ (irse) de ese trabajo donde siempre tienen tantos problemas. Espero que Lourdes _haya aprendido_ (aprender) a aliviar el estrés.
3. Es triste que Nuria y yo _hayamos perdido_ (perder) el partido. Esperamos que los entrenadores del gimnasio nos _hayan preparado_ (preparar) un buen programa para ponernos en forma.
4. No estoy segura de que Samuel _haya llevado_ (llevar) una vida sana. Es bueno que él _haya decidido_ (decidir) mejorar su dieta.
5. Me preocupa mucho que Ana y Rosa _hayan fumado_ (fumar) tanto de jóvenes (*as young people*). Es increíble que ellas no _se hayan enfermado_ (enfermarse).
6. Me alegro de que mi abuela _haya disfrutado_ (disfrutar) de buena salud toda su vida. Es increíble que ella _haya cumplido_ (cumplir) noventa años.

2 Describir Haz dos comentarios sobre la(s) persona(s) que hay en cada dibujo usando frases como **no creo que, dudo que, es probable que, me alegro de que, espero que** y **siento que.** Usa el pretérito perfecto de subjuntivo. Answers will vary.

CONSÚLTALO

To review verbs of will and influence, see **Estructura 12.4**, p. 382. To review expressions of doubt, disbelief, and denial, see **Estructura 13.2**, p. 408.

modelo

Es probable que Javier haya levantado pesas por muchos años.
Me alegro de que Javier se haya mantenido en forma.

Javier

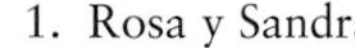
1. Rosa y Sandra

2. Roberto

3. Mariela

4. Lorena y su amigo

5. señora Matos

6. Sonia y René

TEACHING OPTIONS

Pairs Have students tell their partner three true things and three untrue things they have done this past year. Partners respond with an expression of doubt and the present perfect subjunctive to those things they believe are false and an expression of certainty and the present perfect indicative to those they believe are true.

Video Replay the video for students. Each time they hear the present perfect indicative, have them raise one hand. Each time they hear the past perfect indicative, have them raise two hands. Each time they hear the present perfect subjunctive, have them stand.

Comunicación

3 **¿Sí o no?** En parejas, comenten estas afirmaciones (*statements*) usando las expresiones de la lista. Answers will vary.

Dudo que...	Es imposible que...	Me alegro de que (no)...
Es bueno que (no)...	Espero que (no)...	No creo que...

modelo

Estudiante 1: Ya llegó el fin del año escolar.
Estudiante 2: Es imposible que haya llegado el fin del año escolar.

1. Recibí una A en la clase de español.
2. Tu mejor amigo aumentó de peso recientemente.
3. Madonna dio un concierto ayer con Plácido Domingo.
4. Mis padres ganaron un millón de dólares.
5. He aprendido a hablar japonés.
6. Nuestro/a profesor(a) vino aquí de Bolivia.
7. Salí anoche con...
8. El año pasado mi familia y yo fuimos de excursión a...

4 **Viaje por Bolivia** Imaginen que sus amigos, Luis y Julia, están viajando por Bolivia y que les han mandado postales a ustedes. En grupos, lean las postales y conversen de lo que les ha escrito Luis. Usen frases como **dudo que, espero que, me alegro de que, temo que, siento que** y **es posible que.** Answers will vary.

NOTA CULTURAL

Aimará es una de las lenguas oficiales de Bolivia, como el español y el quechua. Casi la mitad (*half*) de la población del país habla lenguas indígenas.

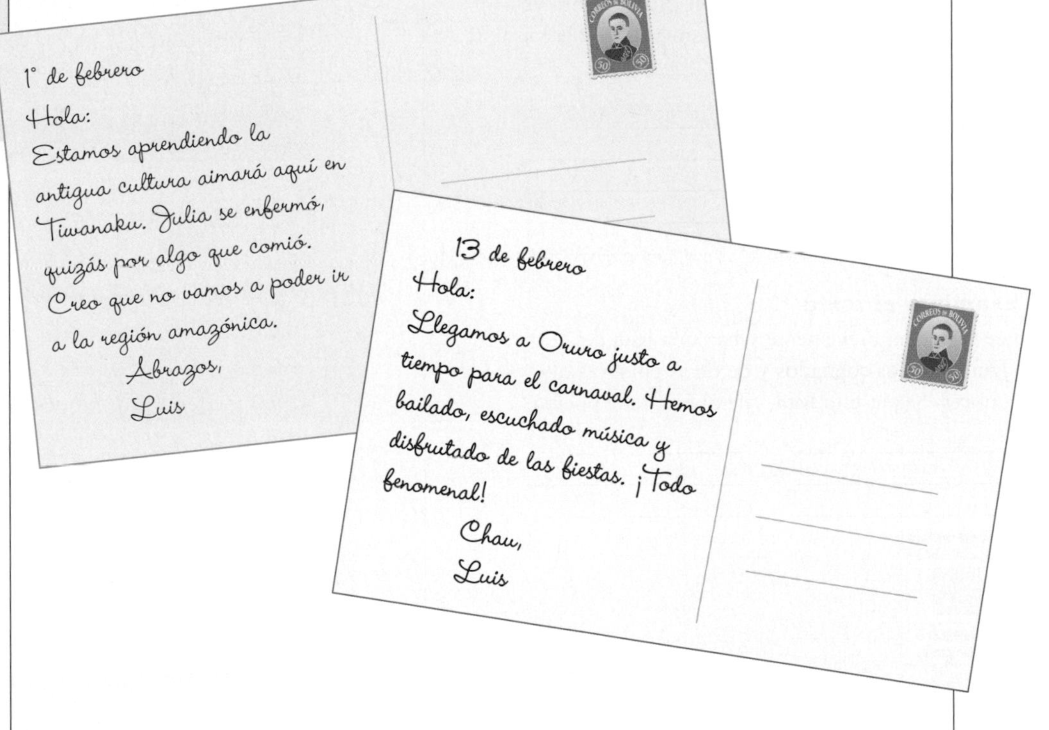

1° de febrero
Hola:
Estamos aprendiendo la antigua cultura aimará aquí en Tiwanaku. Julia se enfermó, quizás por algo que comió. Creo que no vamos a poder ir a la región amazónica.
Abrazos,
Luis
13 de febrero
Hola:
Llegamos a Oruro justo a tiempo para el carnaval. Hemos bailado, escuchado música y disfrutado de las fiestas. ¡Todo fenomenal!
Chau,
Luis

3 Suggestions
- Before dividing the class into pairs, go over the expressions in the word bank and ask two volunteers to read the **modelo**. Then offer one more possible response.
- Remind students to take turns reading statements and responding to them so that both partners generate half the responses.

3 Expansions
- Assign pairs to groups of four. Have them compare their answers and then form new responses to each statement.
- Ask pairs to write four additional statements about what they have done and have a second pair respond to them. Ex: **Nosotros hemos viajado a la luna. (Es imposible que ustedes hayan viajado a la luna.)**

4 Suggestions
- Have students read the postcards silently to themselves. Ask them to note the verbs expressing actions to which they might react.
- Call on volunteers to read Luis's postcards aloud to the class. Allow pairs five minutes to write as many reactions to them as they can. Have students exchange their written reactions with another pair for correction. After the corrected statements are returned, call on students to share some of them with the class.

4 Expansion Ask students to imagine they are Luis's close friends. Have them write a response to each of his postcards. They should react to what Luis wrote, ask questions about what he had done before Julia became ill or before they went to the carnival festivities, and talk about what they have done while Luis has been away.

TEACHING OPTIONS

Small Groups Have students describe to groups of three or four the last time they went to the gym or engaged in an outdoor sports activity. Each group member will react appropriately using the present perfect subjunctive. Ex: **La última vez que fui al gimnasio, asistí a tres clases de aeróbicos. (No creo que hayas asistido a tres clases. Es demasiado ejercicio.)**

Pairs Have students imagine they are having a follow-up session with a nutritionist. Students should talk about five things they have done to change their diet. The nutritionist will respond appropriately using the present perfect subjunctive. Have students switch roles.

Section Goals

In **Lectura** students will:
- learn to make inferences and draw conclusions to understand a text
- read a content-rich poem and practice inferential reading

Instructional Resource
Companion website: www.vistahigherlearning.com

Estrategia
- Introduce the term **pista** before you discuss the strategy.
- Tell students that poets do not generally spell out everything for their readers. Explain that they will need to look for clues in the poem to infer information left unstated and draw conclusions that will help them comprehend what the poet is implying.

El título Ask pairs to brainstorm a list of things that one *does* have the opportunity to choose in life. Later, have them work in groups of four to compare their lists and pick out two examples to share with the class.

Examinar el texto After students have scanned the text, have them work in pairs and share their lists of cognates and other clues they can use to predict what the poem is about.

Lectura

Antes de leer

Estrategia
Making inferences

For dramatic effect and to achieve a smoother writing style, authors often do not explicitly supply the reader with all the details of a story or poem. Clues in the text can help you infer those things the writer chooses not to state in a direct manner. You simply "read between the lines" to fill in the missing information and draw conclusions. To practice making inferences, read the following statement:

A Liliana le encanta ir al gimnasio. Hace años que empezó a levantar pesas.

Based on this statement alone, what inferences can you draw about Liliana?

El título

Sin leer el texto del poema, lee el título. Piensa en las cosas de la vida que una persona no escoge. Haz una lista.

____
____
____
____
____

Examinar el texto

Lee el poema brevemente y haz una lista de algunos de los cognados y de otras palabras que conoces. Según esta lista, ¿de qué trata el poema?

_______________ _______________
_______________ _______________
_______________ _______________

recursos

vistahigher learning.com

Uno no escoge

Gioconda Belli

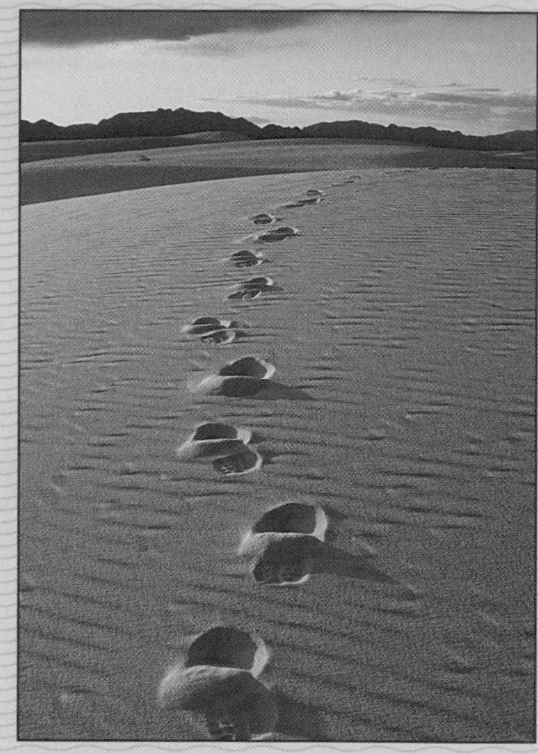

La escritora nicaragüense Gioconda Belli nació en Managua en 1948. Durante la lucha° de revolución de su país, Belli vivió en México en donde escribió su novela Línea de fuego. *Con esta novela ganó el premio Las Américas en 1978. La obra de Belli rompe con las estructuras tradicionales y expresa la urgencia de un cambio social en su país.*

TEACHING OPTIONS

Pairs Remind students that they can appreciate the lyrical nature of poetry by reading a poem aloud. Have partners read **"Uno no escoge"** to each other. Tell them to pay close attention to how the lines are punctuated and the stanzas arranged.

Small Groups First, have students work in pairs to name a few reasons why someone would go into exile. Then, have pairs work in groups of four to compare their ideas. Have them guess Gioconda Belli's reasons for going into exile, and ask a few volunteers to research the topic and share the information in the following class.

Uno no escoge el país donde nace;
pero ama el país donde ha nacido.

Uno no escoge el tiempo para venir al mundo;
pero debe dejar huella° de su tiempo.

Nadie puede evadir su responsabilidad.

Nadie puede taparse° los ojos, los oídos,
enmudecer° y cortarse° las manos.

Todos tenemos un deber de amor que cumplir,
una historia que nacer
una meta° que alcanzar°

No escogimos el momento para venir al mundo:
Ahora podemos hacer el mundo
en que nacerá° y crecerá°
la semilla° que trajimos con nosotros.

lucha *fight* **dejar huella** *leave a mark* **taparse** *to cover up* **enmudecer** *to fall silent* **cortarse** *to cut* **meta** *goal* **alcanzar** *to reach* **nacerá** *will be born* **crecerá** *will grow* **la semilla** *seed*

Después de leer

¿Cierto o falso?

Indica si estos comentarios sobre el texto son **ciertos** o **falsos.**

	Cierto	Falso
1. Podemos escoger el país donde nacemos.	❍	✓
2. No es necesario hacer algo importante en la vida.	❍	✓
3. Debemos ser responsables.	✓	❍
4. No debemos dejar de ver, escuchar y saber lo que pasa en el mundo.	✓	❍
5. Debemos ignorar el amor.	❍	✓
6. Cada persona tiene importancia en el mundo.	✓	❍

Inferencias

Contesta estas preguntas.

1. ¿Cuál es el tema principal del poema?
2. ¿Estás de acuerdo con las ideas de la poeta?
3. ¿Por qué crees que escribió el poema?
4. Después de leer, ¿has cambiado tu opinión sobre el significado del título? ¿Qué piensas ahora?

Analizar

El poema está compuesto de seis partes. Con un(a) compañero/a, traten de escribir el significado de cada una de las partes. Después, compartan sus ideas con la clase.

Preguntas

Contesta estas preguntas.

1. ¿Cuáles son tus metas personales?
2. ¿Tienes muchas responsabilidades? ¿Cuáles son?
3. ¿Crees que lo que haga una persona puede cambiar el mundo? ¿Por qué?
4. ¿Crees que Gioconda Belli es una líder en cuestiones de bienestar social en su país? Explica tu respuesta.

¿Cierto o falso? Have pairs correct the false statements. Then, have them locate the lines in the poem that corroborate each one. Have pairs read these lines aloud to ensure that everyone in the class chose the same ones. Have students solve any discrepancies.

Inferencias Much of the poem's message lies in ideas that are not explicitly stated. Have groups discuss these implied ideas and develop them as a collection of explicit statements. Ask students to imagine how they would be expressed if included in the poem as additional lines. Then, have each group rewrite a longer version of the poem incorporating the new statements.

Analizar Have each student come up with a title for his or her favorite section of the poem. Then, in groups of four, have them compare their titles and explain why they apply well to aspects of their own life. Once all students have had a chance to speak, have them work individually to write a short poem about themselves based on one of the titles.

Preguntas Have small groups choose a respected politician, media celebrity, or other philanthropist who has done admirable work for a humanitarian cause. Have them answer items 1–3 as if they were this person.

TEACHING OPTIONS

Heritage Speakers Ask heritage speakers to share with the class what they might know of Nicaragua and its history. Have them work with other students in the class to validate the poem's message in light of historical and political events in this Central American nation.

Pairs Encourage pairs of students to visit a library or surf the Internet and bring in another example of Belli's poetry. Ask them to point out for the class any similarities they found between it and **"Uno no escoge."** Ask each student to say which poem he or she prefers personally and share with the class his or her reasons.

Section Goals

In **Escritura** students will:

- learn to organize information logically
- integrate **Lección 15** vocabulary and structures
- write a personal fitness plan in Spanish

Estrategia Have students brainstorm details of maintaining a personal fitness plan that includes nutrition, exercise, and stress reduction. Then have a volunteer tell about his or her plan, and guide students in organizing the information in three different ways: chronologically, sequentially, and in order of importance.

Tema Review the three suggested categories of details to include. Then, have volunteers make up questions or use the ones on this page to interview you regarding your personal fitness plan.

Successful Language Learning Point out to your students that this strategy will help them write better in both Spanish and English.

Escritura

Estrategia

Organizing information logically

Many times a written piece may require you to include a great deal of information. You might want to organize your information in one of three different ways:

- Chronologically (e.g., events in the history of a country)
- Sequentially (e.g., steps in a recipe)
- In order of importance

Organizing your information in this manner will make both your writing and your message clearer to your readers. If you were writing a piece on weight reduction, for example, you would need to organize your ideas about two general areas: eating right and exercise. You would need to decide which of the two is more important according to your purpose in writing the piece. If your main idea is that eating right is the key to losing weight, you might want to start your piece with a discussion of good eating habits. You might want to discuss the following aspects of eating right in order of their importance:

- Quantities of food
- Selecting appropriate foods from the food pyramid
- Healthful recipes
- Percentage of fat in each meal
- Calorie count
- Percentage of carbohydrates in each meal
- Frequency of meals

You would then complete the piece by following the same process to discuss the various aspects of the importance of getting exercise.

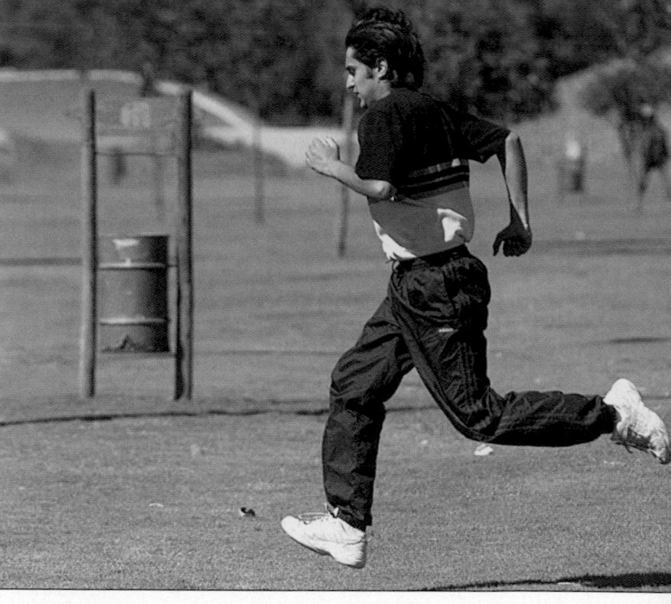

Tema

Escribir un plan personal de bienestar

Desarrolla un plan personal para mejorar tu bienestar, tanto físico como emocional. Tu plan debe describir:

1. Lo que has hecho para mejorar tu bienestar y llevar una vida sana
2. Lo que no has podido hacer todavía
3. Las actividades que debes hacer en los próximos meses

Considera también la siguiente lista de preguntas.

La nutrición

- ¿Comes una dieta equilibrada?
- ¿Consumes suficientes vitaminas y minerales? ¿Consumes demasiada grasa?
- ¿Quieres aumentar de peso o adelgazar?
- ¿Qué puedes hacer para mejorar tu dieta?

El ejercicio

- ¿Haces ejercicio? ¿Con qué frecuencia?
- ¿Vas al gimnasio? ¿Qué tipo de ejercicios haces allí?
- ¿Practicas algún deporte?
- ¿Qué puedes hacer para mejorar tu bienestar físico?

El estrés

- ¿Sufres muchas presiones?
- ¿Qué actividades o problemas te causan estrés?
- ¿Qué haces (o debes hacer) para aliviar el estrés y sentirte más tranquilo/a?
- ¿Qué puedes hacer para mejorar tu bienestar emocional?

TEACHING OPTIONS

Proofreading Activity Copy the following sentences containing mistakes onto the board or a transparency as a proofreading activity to do with the whole class.

1. **¿Tu padre ha tenidos problemas con el colesterol? Espero que ha dejado de comer comidas grasosas.**
2. **Ya tengo trabajado cuarenta horas esta semana y todavía no tengo terminado.**
3. **Guillermo ha un plan para aliviar el estrés. Había sufrido mucho del estrés recientemente.**
4. **Me alegro que has dejado de fumar y por fin has empezado a llevar una vida sana.**
5. **El gimnasio ya ha cerrado antes de que he llegado.**

Plan de escritura

1 Ideas y organización

Antes de escribir, piensa y anota lo que has hecho hasta ahora, lo que no has hecho, y lo que todavía tienes que hacer para conseguir tus objetivos. Organiza en orden cronológico tus planes para el futuro, según la importancia de cada actividad.

2 Primer borrador

Utiliza tus apuntes de **Ideas y organización** para escribir el primer borrador de tu plan personal. Haz todo lo que puedas sin la ayuda del texto o del diccionario.

3 Comentario

Intercambia° tu plan personal con el de un(a) compañero/a y lee su borrador. Comparte tus opiniones sobre el documento, utilizando estas preguntas como guía:

a. ¿Incluye toda la información pertinente?
b. ¿Está organizada la información de una manera lógica?
c. ¿Se puede mejorar la organización de las ideas?
d. ¿Hay errores gramaticales u ortográficos°?
e. ¿Qué otras sugerencias puedes darle al/a la escritor(a) para mejorar el documento?

4 Redacción

Revisa el primer borrador según las indicaciones de tu compañero/a. Antes de escribir la versión final, revisa tu trabajo según la siguiente guía:

a. Subraya° cada verbo para comprobar° el uso correcto de los tiempos verbales y del subjuntivo. ¡Cuidado con los verbos irregulares!
b. Revisa la concordancia° entre los verbos y los sujetos.
c. Revisa la concordancia entre los sustantivos y los artículos definidos e indefinidos.
d. Revisa la concordancia entre los sustantivos y los adjetivos.
e. Revisa los pronombres para comprobar el uso correcto de cada uno.
f. Consulta tus **Anotaciones para mejorar la escritura** para evitar la repetición de errores previos.

5 Evaluación y progreso

Comparte tu descripción con tres estudiantes. Compilen las mejores ideas de cada estudiante en un nuevo plan de bienestar para presentar a la clase. Cuando recibas los comentarios y las correcciones de tu profesor(a), anota tus errores en las **Anotaciones para mejorar la escritura** en tu **Carpeta de trabajos.**

Intercambia *Exchange* ortográficos *spelling* Subraya *Underline* comprobar *to check* concordancia *agreement*

Comentario

- Go over guide questions a–e with the whole class so peer readers understand their task. Then have pairs of students exchange fitness plans.
- Have students prepare **Redacción** as homework.

Evaluación y progreso Give students five minutes to compare final drafts.

Writing Sample Here is a sample fitness plan that would constitute superior writing achievement.

Mi plan personal de bienestar

Problema: ¡He notado que es muy difícil comer cosas que no contengan azúcar! En los últimos meses he comido mucho azúcar y como resultado he aumentado de peso. Además, no siempre me siento bien. Creo que es por la cantidad de azúcar que como y la cafeína que consumo.

Solución: Voy a dejar de comer azúcar y voy a consumir menos cafeína. Ahora tengo muchas recetas para comidas sin azúcar. Trataré de reducir la cantidad de cafeína al tomar solamente una taza de café cada día.

Problema: Soy teleadicto y llevo una vida sedentaria. En el pasado, nunca había asistido a clases de ejercicios aeróbicos. Tampoco caminaba más de una o dos veces por semana. Eso no es suficiente si uno quiere adelgazar.

Solución: En los próximos seis meses voy a ir al gimnasio tres o cuatro veces por semana para participar en las clases de ejercicios aeróbicos.

Ahora que tengo un perro, tengo que caminar cada día. Trataré de caminar por lo menos 20 minutos, dos veces al día. Además, pienso levantar pesas y usar mi bicicleta.

¡Pronto llevaré una vida más sana!

EVALUATION: Plan personal de bienestar

Criteria	Scale
Content	1 2 3 4
Organization	1 2 3 4
Use of vocabulary	1 2 3 4
Accuracy and mechanics	1 2 3 4
Creativity	1 2 3 4

Scoring	
Excellent	18–20 points
Good	14–17 points
Satisfactory	10–13 points
Unsatisfactory	< 10 points

Section Goals

In **Escuchar** students will:

- listen for the gist and for cognates
- answer questions about a radio program

Instructional Resources
Textbook CD
IRM: Tapescript, p. 99

Estrategia
Script Cuando nos casamos le prometí a Magdalena que no íbamos a residir con su familia por más de un año. Y si Dios quiere, ¡así va a ser! Magdalena y yo encontramos un condominio absolutamente perfecto. Hoy pasamos por el banco para pedir el préstamo hipotecario. ¡Espero que no haya problema con el chequeo del crédito!

Suggestion Have students describe what they see.

Ahora escucha
Script Buenos días, radioyentes, y bienvenidos a "Tu bienestar". Les habla Ofelia Cortez de Bauer. Hoy vamos a hablar de la importancia de estar en buena forma. Primero quiero que entiendan que estar en buena forma no es sólo cosa de estar delgado o ser fuerte. Para mantenerse en forma deben tener tres objetivos: condicionar el sistema cardiopulmonar, aumentar la fuerza muscular y mejorar la flexibilidad. Cada persona tiene sus propios objetivos, y también sus propias limitaciones físicas, y debe diseñar su programa con un monitor de acuerdo con éstos. Pero óiganme bien, ¡lo más importante es tener una rutina variada, con ejercicios que les gusten —porque de otro modo no lo van a hacer! Mi rutina personal es la siguiente. Dos días por semana voy a la clase de ejercicios aeróbicos, claro con un buen calentamiento al comienzo. Tres días por semana corro en el parque, o si hace mal tiempo, uso una caminadora en el gimnasio. Luego levanto pesas y termino haciendo estiramientos de los músculos. Los fines de semana me mantengo activa pero hago una variedad de cosas de acuerdo a lo que quiere hacer la familia. A veces practico la natación; otras, vamos de excursión al campo, por ejemplo. Como les había dicho la semana pasada, como unas 1.600 calorías al día, mayormente alimentos con poca grasa y sin sal. Disfruto mucho del bienestar que estos hábitos me producen. Ahora iremos a unos anuncios de nuestros patrocinadores. Cuando regresemos, voy a contestar sus preguntas acerca del ejercicio, la dieta o el bienestar en general. El teléfono es el 43.89.76. No se vayan. Ya regresamos con mucha más información.

Escuchar

Estrategia
Listening for the gist/ Listening for cognates

Combining these two strategies is an easy way to get a good sense of what you hear. When you listen for the gist, you get the general idea of what you're hearing, which allows you to interpret cognates and other words in a meaningful context. Similarly, the cognates give you information about the details of the story that you might not have understood when listening for the gist.

To practice these strategies, you will listen to a short paragraph. Write down the gist of what you hear and jot down a few cognates. Based on the gist and the cognates, what conclusions can you draw about what you heard?

Preparación

Mira la foto. ¿Qué pistas° te da de lo que vas a oír?

Ahora escucha 

Escucha lo que dice Ofelia Cortez de Bauer. Anota algunos de los cognados que escuchas y también la idea general del discurso°.

____
____
____
____

Idea general: ____________________

Ahora contesta las siguientes preguntas.

1. ¿Cuál es el género° del discurso?
2. ¿Cuál es el tema?
3. ¿Cuál es el propósito°?

pistas *clues* discurso *speech* género *genre* propósito *purpose*
público *audience* debía haber incluido *should have included*

Comprensión

¿Cierto o falso?

Indica si lo que dicen las siguentes frases es **cierto** o **falso**. Corrige las oraciones que son falsas.

	Cierto	Falso
1. La señora Bauer habla de la importancia de estar en buena forma y de hacer ejercicio.	✓	❍
2. Según ella, lo más importante es que lleves el programa sugerido por los expertos. Lo más importante es que lleves un programa variado que te guste.	❍	✓
3. La señora Bauer participa en actividades individuales y de grupo.	✓	❍
4. El único objetivo del tipo de programa que ella sugiere es adelgazar. Los objetivos de su programa son: condicionar el sistema cardiopulmonar, aumentar la fuerza muscular y mejorar la flexibilidad.	❍	✓

Preguntas Answers will vary.

1. Imagina que el programa de radio sigue. Según las pistas que ella dio, ¿qué vas a oír en la segunda parte?
2. ¿A qué tipo de público° le interesa el tema del que habla la señora Bauer?
3. ¿Sigues los consejos de la señora Bauer? Explica tu respuesta.
4. ¿Qué piensas de los consejos que ella da? ¿Hay otra información que ella debía haber incluido°?

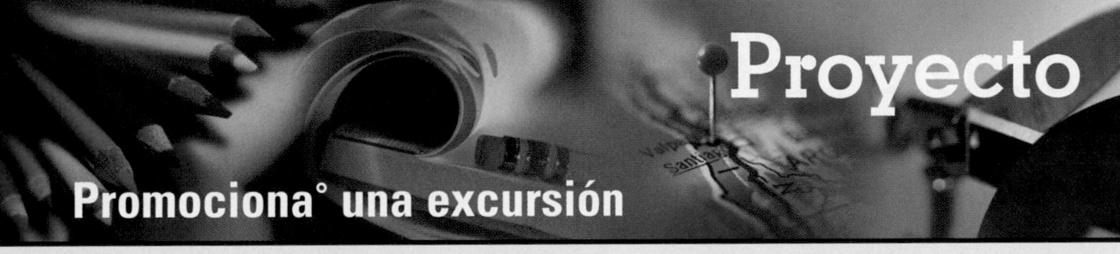

Promociona° una excursión

Estás a cargo de° promocionar una excursión por Bolivia. Este viaje no es como ningún otro porque combina el ejercicio con el turismo y la aventura, y es sólo para personas que estén en buena forma.

1 Prepara un folleto

Crea un folleto° llamativo° para vender la idea de este tipo de excursión. Usa los **Recursos para la investigación** para identificar los lugares que van a visitar en Bolivia y lo que van a hacer en cada uno de esos lugares. El folleto puede incluir lo siguiente:

- Fotos y descripciones de los lugares que van a visitar
- Descripciones de las actividades que van a hacer en cada lugar, con enfoque° en las actividades deportivas y de aventura
- Una explicación de las comidas y de otros aspectos de la excursión que son importantes para la salud
- Una advertencia° de que las personas que participan deben estar en buena forma
- Una explicación del examen médico que los viajeros necesitan hacerse antes del viaje
- El costo del viaje

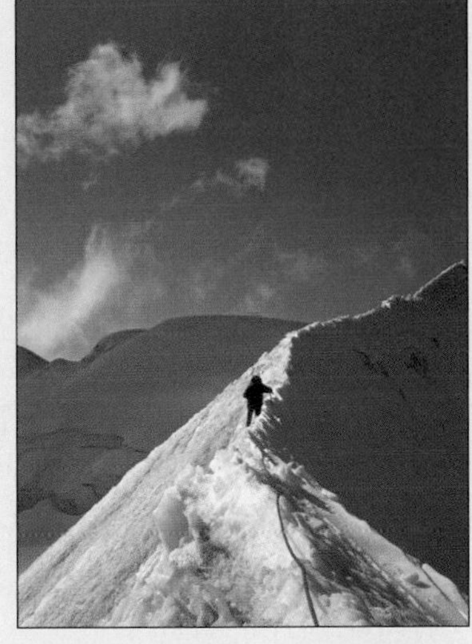

2 Presenta la información

Usa el folleto para crear un anuncio° publicitario informativo. Explica los aspectos especiales de esta excursión, incluyendo las aventuras y las actividades deportivas que se ofrecen. Puedes presentar el anuncio informativo en vivo° o filmarlo en video para después presentarlo a la clase.

En grupos pequeños, comparen las excursiones que han planeado. ¿Qué tienen en común? ¿En qué se diferencian?

recursos para la investigación

Internet Palabras clave: Bolivia, turismo, fotos, excursiones

Comunidad Profesores, estudiantes o personas de la comunidad que son de Bolivia o que han viajado por Bolivia

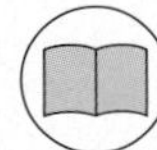
Biblioteca Guías turísticas, revistas, mapas, enciclopedias

Otros recursos Mapa topográfico, folletos de agencias de viajes

Promociona *Promote* a cargo de *in charge of* folleto *brochure* llamativo *eye-catching* enfoque *focus* advertencia *warning* anuncio *commercial; announcement* en vivo *live*

Section Goals

In **Proyecto** students will:
- use Spanish as they research and interact with the wider world
- write and design a brochure promoting adventure travel in Bolivia
- learn about what Bolivia has to offer the adventure traveler

Suggestion Students might need a week to complete the project, so at the beginning of that time period, have them open their books to this page and glance over **Proyecto**. Explain that they are going to use their research skills to prepare a brochure for adventure travel in Bolivia. Discuss the inherent risk (**riesgo**) in adventure travel at high altitudes, and the importance of emphasizing this in the brochures.

Prepara un folleto You may wish to have students include information in their brochures on vaccinations and what to do for acclimating to high altitudes. Students may find vaccination information (**información sobre vacunas**) on the Internet on the Centers for Disease Control and Prevention's website: www.cdc.gov.

Presenta la información Set aside sufficient class time to do a few presentations at a time until all students have had a chance to present.

The Affective Dimension Ask your students if they prefer giving their presentations live or on video, and why.

EVALUATION: Folleto

Criteria	Scale
Content	1 2 3 4
Organization	1 2 3 4
Accuracy	1 2 3 4
Creativity	1 2 3 4
Oral presentation	1 2 3 4

Scoring	
Excellent	18–20 points
Good	14–17 points
Satisfactory	10–13 points
Unsatisfactory	< 10 points

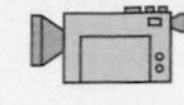

Section Goal

In **Panorama**, students will read about the geography and culture of Bolivia.

Instructional Resources
Transparencies, #5, #6, #55
WB/VM: Workbook, pp. 177–178; Video Activities, pp. 277–278
***Panorama cultural** DVD/Video*
Interactive CD-ROM
IRM: Videoscript, p. 134
Companion website: www.vistahigherlearning.com
Presentations CD-ROM

Suggestion Have students look at the map of Bolivia or project **Transparency #55**. Note that Bolivia is a completely land-locked country. Have students name the five countries that share its borders. Point out Bolivia's three main regions: the Andes region, the high plain (**altiplano**), and the Amazon basin. Ask students to read aloud the places labeled on the map, and to identify whether place names are in Spanish or in an indigenous language.

El país en cifras Have volunteers create a pie chart that represents Bolivia's ethnic makeup as described in the **Población** section. As students read about the **Ciudades principales**, have them locate each city on the map. As students read about **Idiomas**, point out that **quechua** was the language of the ancient Incan empire.

¡Increíble pero cierto! Visitors to La Paz and other Andean cities often experience **el soroche**, or altitude sickness. Andean natives typically develop increased lung capacity and a greater capacity for diffusing oxygen to the body, helping to compensate for decreased oxygen levels at these heights.

Bolivia

El país en cifras

- **Área:** 1.098.580 km² (424.162 millas²), *equivalente al área total de Francia y España*
- **Población:** 8.705.000

Los indígenas quechua y aimará constituyen más de la mitad° de la población de Bolivia. Estos grupos indígenas han mantenido sus culturas y lenguas tradicionales. Las personas de descendencia indígena y europea representan la tercera parte de la población. El 15% restante° es gente de descendencia europea nacida en Latinoamérica. Una gran mayoría de los bolivianos, más o menos el 70%, vive en el altiplano°.

- **Capital:** La Paz, sede° del gobierno, capital administrativa—1.662.000; Sucre, sede del Tribunal Supremo, capital constitucional y judicial—189.000
- **Ciudades principales:** Santa Cruz de la Sierra—1.286.000, Cochabamba—794.000, Oruro—202.000, Potosí—124.000

SOURCE: Population Division, UN Secretariat

- **Moneda:** peso boliviano
- **Idiomas:** español (oficial), aimará (oficial), quechua (oficial)

Bandera de Bolivia

Bolivianos célebres

- **Jesús Lara,** escritor (1898–1980)
- **Víctor Paz Estenssoro,** político y presidente (1907–2001)
- **María Luisa Pacheco,** pintora (1919–1982)
- **Matilde Casazola,** poeta (1942–)

la mitad *half* restante *remaining* altiplano *high plateau* sede *seat* paraguas *umbrella* cascada *waterfall*

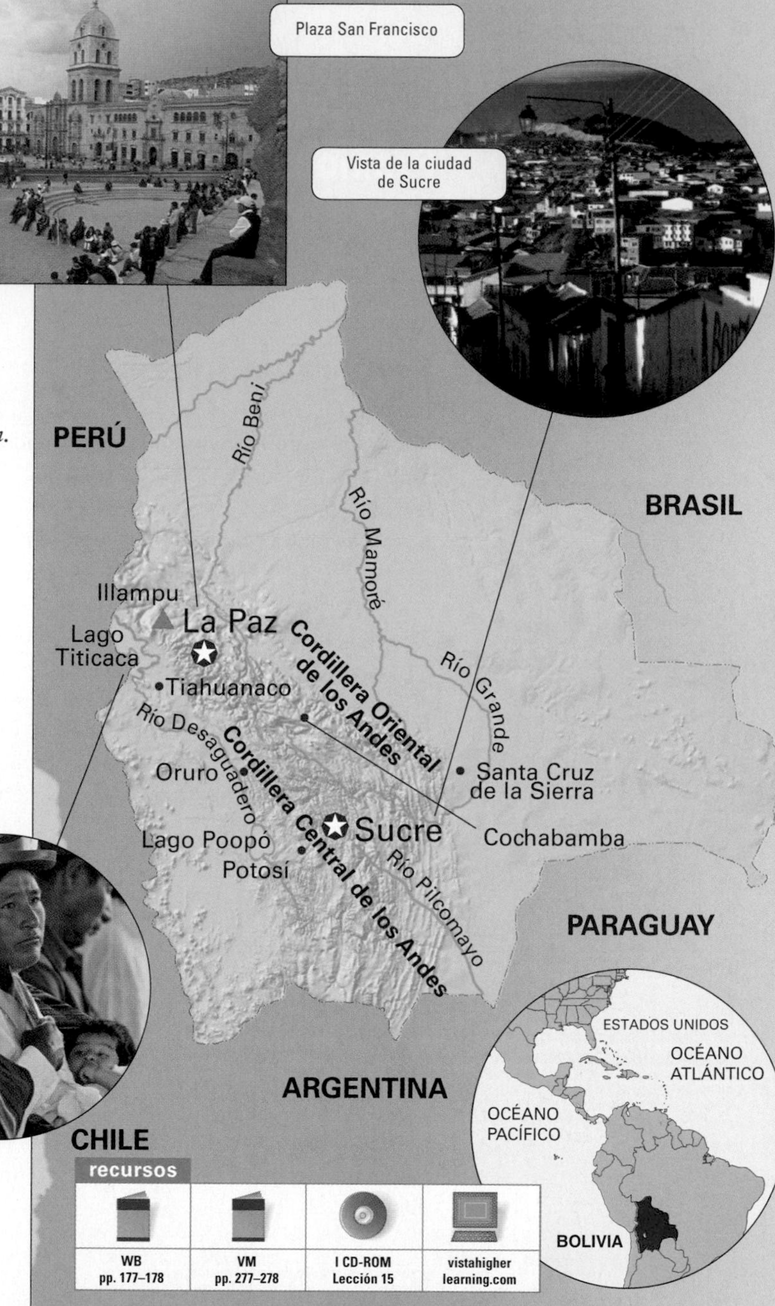

recursos

WB pp. 177–178	VM pp. 277–278	I CD-ROM Lección 15	vistahigherlearning.com

¡Increíble pero cierto!

La Paz es la capital más alta del mundo. Su aeropuerto está situado a una altitud de 3.600 m. (12.000 pies). Ah, y si viajas en carro hasta La Paz, ¡no te olvides del paraguas°! En la carretera, que cruza 9.000 metros de densa selva, te encontrarás con una cascada°.

TEACHING OPTIONS

Heritage Speakers Another way to become acquainted with the traditions of Bolivia's different regions is through regional dances. The **cueca collasuyo** is a traditional dance from the **altiplano** region, while the **cueca chapaca** is from the **Chaco** area. The **jiringueros del Beni** is traditionally performed by rubber tappers from the Amazon area. Invite students familiar with these traditional dances to share some of their basic steps with the class.

Worth Noting To give students the opportunity to listen to the sounds of **quechua** or **aimará**, as well as the music of the Andes, bring in recordings made by Andean musicians, such as **los Kjarkas** or **Inkuyo**. Some recordings may include lyrics in the original language and in translation.

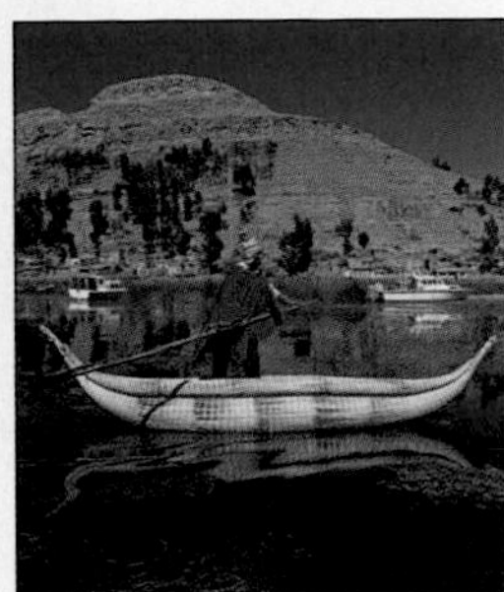

Lugares • El lago Titicaca

Titicaca, situado en los Andes de Bolivia y Perú, es el lago navegable más alto del mundo y está a una altitud de 3.815 metros (12.500 pies). También es el segundo lago más grande, después del lago Maracaibo, de Suramérica, con un área de más de 8.000 km^2 (3.000 millas^2). La mitología inca cuenta° que los hijos del dios° Sol emergieron de las profundas aguas del lago Titicaca para fundar° su imperio°. Los indígenas de la zona todavía hacen botes° de totora° a la manera° antigua y los usan para navegar las claras aguas del lago.

Artes • La música andina

La música andina, compartida por Bolivia, Perú, Ecuador, Chile y Argentina, es el aspecto más conocido de su folklore. Hay muchos conjuntos° profesionales que dan a conocer° esta música popular, de origen indígena, alrededor° del mundo. Uno de los grupos más importantes son los Kjarkas, que llevan más de veinticinco años actuando en los escenarios internacionales. Los instrumentos típicos que se usan son la zampoña y la quena (dos tipos de flauta°), el arpa°, el bombo°, la guitarra y el charango, que es una pequeña guitarra andina.

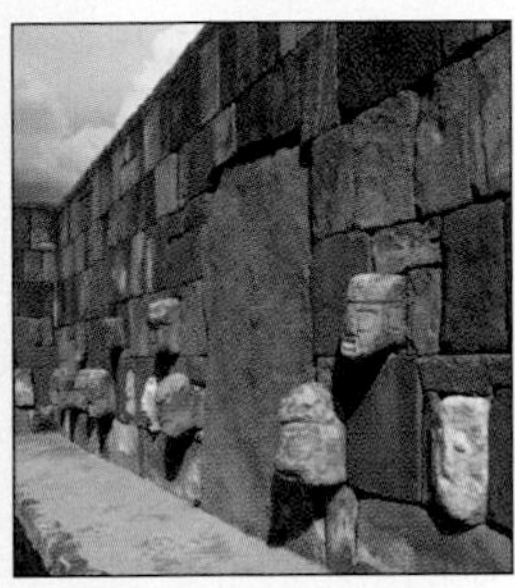

Historia • Tiahuanaco

Tiahuanaco, que significa "Ciudad de los dioses", es un sitio arqueológico de ruinas preincaicas situado cerca de La Paz y el lago Titicaca. Se piensa que los antepasados° de los indígenas aimará fundaron este centro ceremonial hace unos 15.000 años. En el año 1100, la ciudad tenía más o menos 60.000 habitantes. En este sitio se pueden ver el Templo de Kalasasaya, el Monolito Ponce, el Templete Subterráneo, la Puerta del Sol y la Puerta de la Luna. La Puerta del Sol es un impresionante monumento que tiene tres metros de alto y cuatro de ancho° y que pesa aproximadamente unas 10 toneladas.

¿Qué aprendiste? Responde a las preguntas con una frase completa.

1. ¿Qué idiomas se hablan en Bolivia? En Bolivia se hablan español, quechua y aimará.
2. ¿Dónde vive la mayoría de los bolivianos? La mayoría de los bolivianos vive en el altiplano.
3. ¿Cuál es la capital administrativa de Bolivia? La capital administrativa de Bolivia es La Paz.
4. ¿Cómo se llama la moneda de Bolivia? La moneda de Bolivia es el peso boliviano.
5. Según la mitología inca, ¿qué ocurrió en el lago Titicaca? Los hijos del dios Sol emergieron del lago para fundar el imperio inca.
6. ¿Qué hacen los indios con la totora? Los indios hacen botes de totora.
7. ¿Qué es la quena? La quena es un tipo de flauta.
8. ¿Qué es el charango? El charango es una pequeña guitarra andina.
9. ¿Qué es la Puerta del Sol? La Puerta del Sol es un monumento que está en Tiahuanaco.
10. ¿Cómo se llama el sitio arqueológico situado cerca de La Paz y el lago Titicaca? El sitio arqueológico situado cerca de La Paz y el lago Titicaca se llama Tiahuanaco.

Conexión Internet Investiga estos temas en el sitio **www.vistahigherlearning.com.**

1. Busca información sobre un(a) boliviano/a célebre. ¿Cuáles son algunos de los episodios más importantes de su vida? ¿Qué ha hecho esta persona? ¿Por qué es célebre?
2. Busca información sobre Tiahuanaco u otro sitio arqueológico en Bolivia. ¿Qué han descubierto los arqueólogos en ese sitio?

cuenta *tells the story* dios *god* fundar *to found* imperio *empire* botes *rowboats* totora *reed* manera *way* conjuntos *groups* dan a conocer *make known* alrededor *around* flauta *flute* arpa *harp* bombo *drum* antepasados *ancestors* ancho *wide*

El lago Titicaca Sitting more than two miles above sea level, Lake Titicaca is larger than the area of Delaware and Rhode Island combined.

La música andina Andean music is characterized by its plaintive, haunting melodies, often based in a minor or pentatonic scale.

Tiahuanaco The pre-Incan civilization that flourished at Tiahuanaco was probably a theocracy, governed by priest-kings. The primary deity was **Viracocha**, a sky and thunder god worshipped throughout much of the Andean world. The Tiahuanacan head of state was viewed as Viracocha's embodiment on earth.

Conexión Internet Students will find supporting Internet activities and links at **www.vistahigherlearning.com**.

TEACHING OPTIONS

Worth Noting Teams of scientists are currently extracting sediment samples from Titicaca's lakebed to study the history of climatological change in the region. Such research may help scientists build models to analyze contemporary trends in global climate change.

Worth Noting Students might like to learn this indigenous riddle about the **armadillo**, the animal whose outer shell is used to make the body of the **charango**, a small ten-stringed guitar used in Andean music:
Vive en el cerro, lejos del mar.
De concha el saco sin abrochar.
Cuando se muere... ¡pues a cantar!

Instructional Resources
Vocabulary CD
Lab Manual, p. 89
Lab CD/MP3 ***Lección 15***
IRM: Tapescript, pp. 67–70
Testing Program: ***Pruebas,*** *pp. 169–180*
Testing Program Audio CD
Test Files CD-ROM

El bienestar

el bienestar	*well-being*
la droga	*drug*
el/la drogadicto/a	*drug addict*
el masaje	*massage*
el/la teleadicto/a	*couch potato*
adelgazar	*to lose weight; to slim down*
aliviar el estrés	*to reduce stress*
aliviar la tensión	*to reduce tension*
apurarse, darse prisa	*to hurry; to rush*
aumentar de peso, engordar	*to gain weight*
disfrutar (de)	*to enjoy; to reap the benefits (of)*
estar a dieta	*to be on a diet*
(no) fumar	*(not) to smoke*
llevar una vida sana	*to lead a healthy lifestyle*
sufrir muchas presiones	*to be under a lot of pressure*
tratar de (+ *inf.*)	*to try (to do something)*
activo/a	*active*
débil	*weak*
en exceso	*in excess; too much*
flexible	*flexible*
fuerte	*strong*
sedentario/a	*sedentary; related to sitting*
tranquilo/a	*calm; quiet*

En el gimnasio

la cinta caminadora	*treadmill*
la clase de ejercicios aeróbicos	*aerobics class*
el/la entrenador(a)	*trainer*
el músculo	*muscle*
calentarse (e:ie)	*to warm up*
entrenarse	*to practice; to train*
estar en buena forma	*to be in good shape*
hacer ejercicio	*to exercise*
hacer ejercicios aeróbicos	*to do aerobics*
hacer ejercicios de estiramiento	*to do stretching exercises*
hacer gimnasia	*to work out*
levantar pesas	*to lift weights*
mantenerse en forma	*to stay in shape*
sudar	*to sweat*

La nutrición

la bebida alcohólica	*alcoholic beverage*
la cafeína	*caffeine*
la caloría	*calorie*
el colesterol	*cholesterol*
la grasa	*fat*
la merienda	*afternoon snack*
el mineral	*mineral*
la nutrición	*nutrition*
el/la nutricionista	*nutritionist*
la proteína	*protein*
la vitamina	*vitamin*
comer una dieta equilibrada	*to eat a balanced diet*
consumir alcohol	*to consume alcohol*
descafeinado/a	*decaffeinated*

Expresiones útiles	*See page 459.*

recursos

LM p. 89	Lab CD/MP3 Lección 15	Vocab CD Lección 15

El mundo del trabajo 16

Communicative Goals

You will learn how to:

- Talk about your future plans
- Talk about and discuss work
- Interview for a job
- Express agreement and disagreement

Lesson Goals

In **Lección 16** students will be introduced to the following:

- terms for professions and occupations
- work-related vocabulary
- future tense
- irregular future tense verbs
- future perfect tense
- past subjunctive tense
- recognizing similes and metaphors
- using note cards in preparation for writing
- writing a composition on personal and professional goals
- using background knowledge when listening
- listening for specific information
- developing a career plan or timeline
- cultural, geographic, and historical information about Nicaragua
- cultural, geographic, and historical information about the Dominican Republic

A primera vista Here are some additional questions you can ask based on the photo: **¿Has tenido un trabajo? ¿Dónde? ¿Qué hacías? ¿Te gusta trabajar? ¿Por qué? ¿Has sufrido presiones? Explica por qué. ¿Qué haces para aliviar el estrés?**

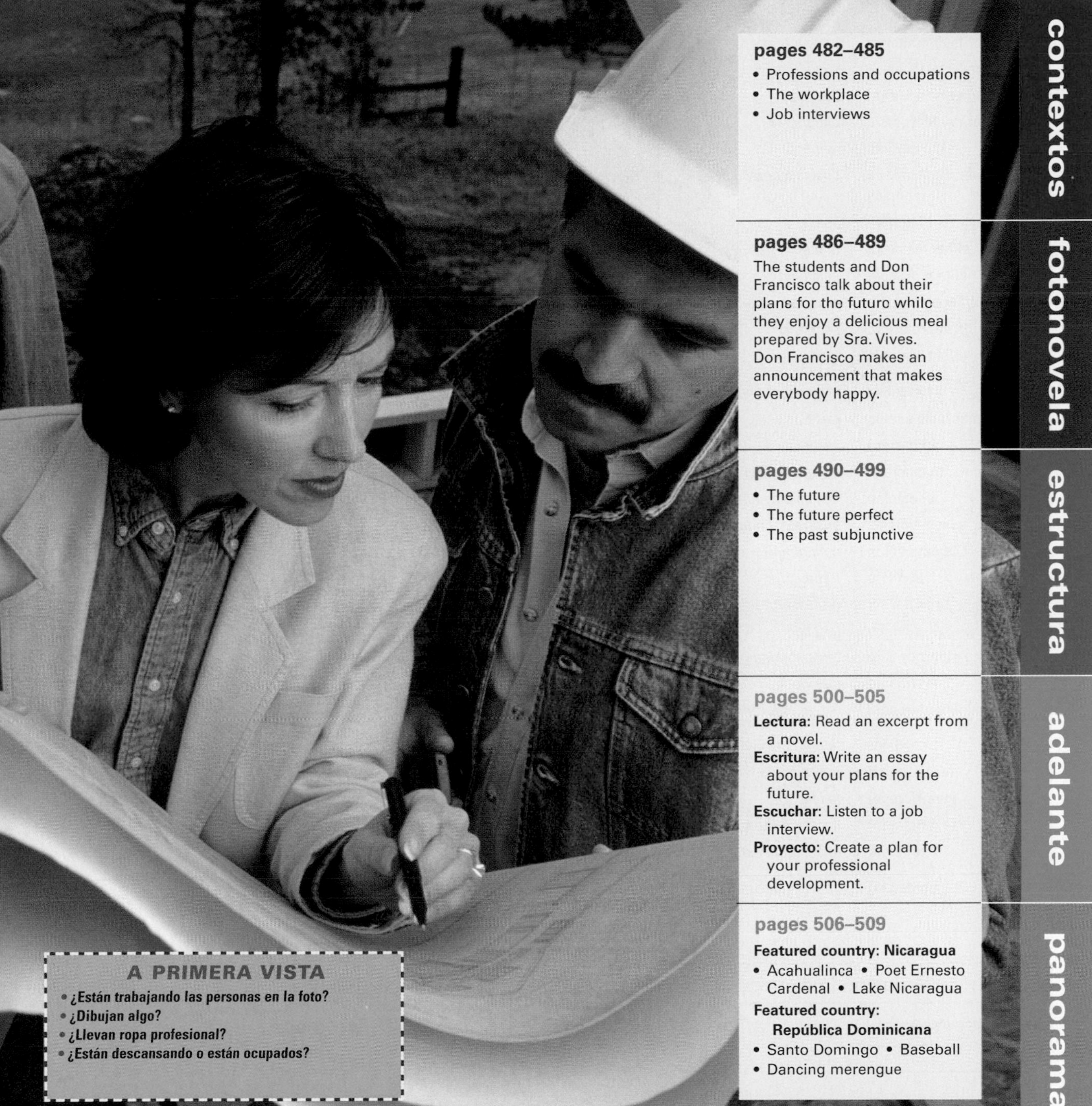

A PRIMERA VISTA

- ¿Están trabajando las personas en la foto?
- ¿Dibujan algo?
- ¿Llevan ropa profesional?
- ¿Están descansando o están ocupados?

INSTRUCTIONAL RESOURCES

Workbook/Video Manual: WB Activities, pp. 181–190
Laboratory Manual: Lab Activities, pp. 91–95
Workbook/Video Manual: Video Activities, pp. 243–244; pp. 279–282
Instructor's Resource Manual: **Hojas de actividades**, p. 173; **Vocabulario adicional**, p. 194; **¡Inténtalo! & Práctica** Answers, p. 222; **Fotonovela** Translations, pp. 147–148; Textbook CD Tapescript, p. 100; Lab CDs Tapescript, pp. 71–75; **Fotonovela** Videoscript, pp. 122–123; **Panorama cultural** Videoscript, p. 135
Info Gap Activities Booklet, pp. 61–64
Overhead Transparencies: #3, #4, #56, #57, #58
Lab Audio CD/MP3 **Lección 16**
Panorama cultural DVD/Video
Fotonovela DVD/Video
Testing Program, pp. 181–192z
Testing Program Audio CD
Test Files CD-ROM
Companion website
Presentations CD-ROM
Textbook CD
Vocabulary CD
Interactive CD-ROM
Video CD-ROM
Web-SAM

Section Goals

In **Contextos** students will learn and practice:

- words for professions and occupations
- labor-related terminology

Instructional Resources
Transparency #56
Textbook CD
Vocabulary CD
WB/VM: Workbook, pp. 181–182
Lab Manual, p. 91
Lab CD/MP3 ***Lección 16***
IRM: ***Vocab. adicional****, p. 194;*
Práctica *Answers, p. 222;*
Tapescript, pp. 71–75; p. 100
Interactive CD-ROM
Companion website:
www.vistahigherlearning.com
Presentations CD-ROM

Suggestions

- Using magazine pictures, ask volunteers to identify places of business and occupations. Ex: **¿Qué tipo de negocio es? (peluquería) La persona que trabaja en una peluquería se llama peluquero/a.** Write each job you mention on the board. Tell students they are now going to learn words associated with the world of work.
- Project **Transparency #56.** Ask questions that elicit the occupations. Ex: **¿Quién crea planos de edificios? (el/la arquitecto/a) Y, ¿quiénes usan los planos? (los carpinteros)** Then speak of yourself and ask students personalized questions about their career plans. Ex: **Cuando yo estudiaba, también trabajaba dos noches a la semana de cocinera en una pizzería. ¿Hay alguien en esta clase que estudie para arqueólogo/a? _____, ¿para qué profesión estudias? _____, ¿cuál es tu especialización?**

Note: At this point you may want to present **Vocabulario adicional: Más vocabulario para el mundo del trabajo**, from the IRM.

El mundo del trabajo

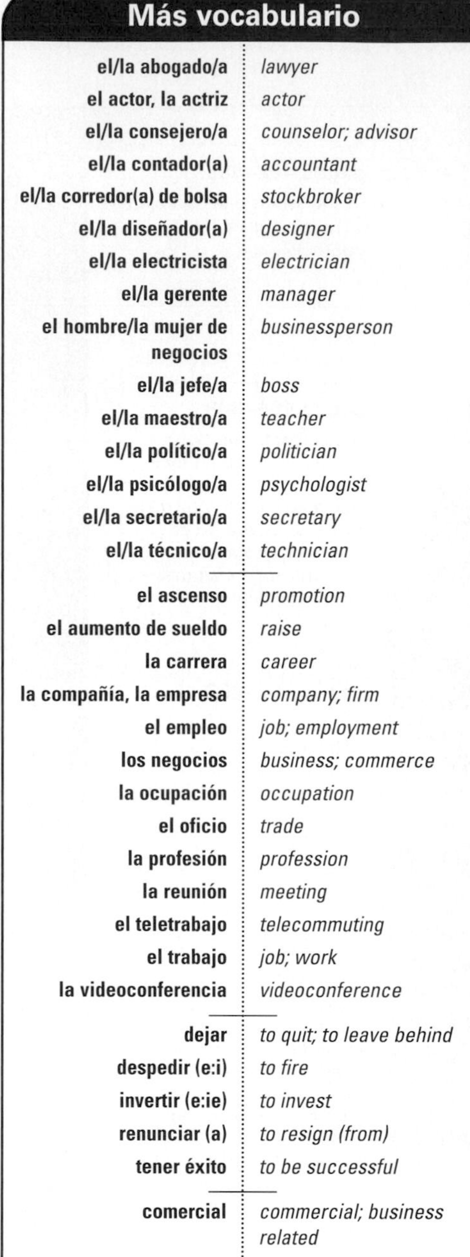

Más vocabulario

el/la abogado/a	*lawyer*
el actor, la actriz	*actor*
el/la consejero/a	*counselor; advisor*
el/la contador(a)	*accountant*
el/la corredor(a) de bolsa	*stockbroker*
el/la diseñador(a)	*designer*
el/la electricista	*electrician*
el/la gerente	*manager*
el hombre/la mujer de negocios	*businessperson*
el/la jefe/a	*boss*
el/la maestro/a	*teacher*
el/la político/a	*politician*
el/la psicólogo/a	*psychologist*
el/la secretario/a	*secretary*
el/la técnico/a	*technician*
el ascenso	*promotion*
el aumento de sueldo	*raise*
la carrera	*career*
la compañía, la empresa	*company; firm*
el empleo	*job; employment*
los negocios	*business; commerce*
la ocupación	*occupation*
el oficio	*trade*
la profesión	*profession*
la reunión	*meeting*
el teletrabajo	*telecommuting*
el trabajo	*job; work*
la videoconferencia	*videoconference*
dejar	*to quit; to leave behind*
despedir (e:i)	*to fire*
invertir (e:ie)	*to invest*
renunciar (a)	*to resign (from)*
tener éxito	*to be successful*
comercial	*commercial; business related*

Variación léxica

abogado/a ←→ licenciado/a (*Amér. C.*)
contador(a) ←→ contable (*Esp.*)

recursos

TEXT CD Lección 16	WB pp. 181–182	LM p. 91	Lab CD/MP3 Lección 16	I CD-ROM Lección 16	Vocab CD Lección 16

TEACHING OPTIONS

TPR Have students mime the work of different professionals. Write the name on a slip of paper (**actor, carpintero, arquitecto**) or whisper the name to the student. The rest of the class should guess what profession he or she is miming.

Pairs Say the Spanish term for a professional, such as **cocinero** or **bombero**. Students should write down as many words as possible that they associate with this job. Ex: **cocinero: cocina, cuchara, horno, restaurante**.

Práctica

1 Escuchar Escucha la descripción que hace Juan Figueres de su profesión y luego completa las frases con las palabras adecuadas.

1. Juan Figueres es __b__.
   a. actor b. hombre de negocios c. pintor
2. El Sr. Figueres es el __c__ de una compañía multinacional.
   a. secretario b. técnico c. gerente
3. El Sr. Figueres quería __a__ en la cual pudiera trabajar en otros países.
   a. una carrera b. un ascenso c. un aumento de sueldo
4. El Sr. Figueres viaja mucho porque __a__.
   a. tiene reuniones en otros países b. prefiere el teletrabajo
   c. utiliza las videoconferencias

2 Escoger Escoge la ocupación de la lista que corresponda a cada descripción.

la arquitecta	el corredor de bolsa
el bombero	el diseñador
la carpintera	la electricista
el científico	el maestro
la contadora	la técnica

1. Desarrolla teorías de biología, química, física, etc. el científico
2. Construye (*Builds*) armarios, sillas, mesas, casas y otras cosas de madera (*wood*). la carpintera
3. Nos ayuda a iluminar nuestras casas y arregla los electrodomésticos. la electricista
4. Combate los fuegos (*fires*) que destruyen edificios. el bombero
5. Ayuda a la gente a invertir su dinero. el corredor de bolsa
6. Trabaja con números y arregla las cuentas de diferentes negocios. la contadora
7. Enseña a los niños. el maestro
8. Diseña ropa. el diseñador
9. Arregla las computadoras. la técnica
10. Diseña edificios. la arquitecta

3 Asociaciones ¿Qué profesiones asocias con las siguientes palabras?

modelo
emociones *psicólogo/a*

1. pinturas pintor(a)
2. consejos consejero/a
3. elecciones político/a
4. comida cocinero/a
5. leyes abogado/a
6. teatro actor/actriz
7. pirámide arqueólogo/a
8. escuela maestro/a
9. periódico reportero/a
10. pelo peluquero/a

1 Suggestion Help students check their answers by reading the tapescript to the class and having volunteers give the correct choices to complete each statement.

1 Tapescript Yo soy de una familia de artistas. Mi madre es diseñadora gráfica, mi padre es pintor y mi hermano es actor. Pero yo me gradué con una especialización en negocios internacionales porque quería trabajar en otros países. Ahora soy el gerente de una compañía multinacional y viajo todos los meses. Sé que a muchos hombres de negocios no les gusta viajar y prefieren utilizar el correo electrónico, el teletrabajo y la videoconferencia para hacer negocios con empresas extranjeras. Yo, sin embargo, prefiero conocer a la gente personalmente; por eso yo viajo a sus países cuando tenemos reuniones importantes.
Textbook CD

2 Suggestion Model the activity by making a statement about a profession not listed. Ex: **Defiende a una persona acusada de un crimen.** Have volunteers identify the occupation that corresponds to your descriptions. (**la abogada**)

2 Expansion After students finish, ask them to write job descriptions for those professions not listed in the activity.

3 Suggestion Read the **modelo** and ask volunteers to suggest names of other associated professions. Ex: **consejero, psicólogo, artista.**

TEACHING OPTIONS

Pairs Ask students to categorize the professions according to two different paradigms. Ex: **trabajos al aire libre/trabajos en lugares cerrados; profesiones/ocupaciones; trabajos que requieren mucha fuerza/trabajos que no requieren mucha fuerza.** Have each pair read their categories aloud to the class.

Game Play a modified version of Twenty Questions. Ask a volunteer to think of a profession or occupation from the vocabulary drawing or list. Other students get one chance each to ask a yes/no question until someone guesses the profession or occupation correctly. Limit attempts to ten questions per item. Ex: **¿Es un oficio o una profesión? ¿Hay que tratar con mucha gente?**

Suggestion Introduce the vocabulary presented on this page by conversing with the class about their experience with interviews. Ex: **Algunas personas se ponen muy nerviosas antes de una entrevista. ¿Eso le pasa a alguno de ustedes? ¿Cómo te preparas para una entrevista?**

4 Suggestion Have pairs play the roles of **entrevistador** and **aspirante**. Each partner should look at the entire conversation but should only complete the lines that correspond to his or her role. Have pairs rehearse by reading their sentences to each other for peer correction. Once partners agree on all the answers, have pairs perform the conversation for the class.

5 Expansion Have pairs write logical sentences with the unused choices. Ex: **Me llamaron de una empresa porque me van a entrevistar.** Call on different pairs to read their sentences aloud.

6 Suggestion This activity may be done in pairs or in groups of three or four in round-robin fashion. Allow approximately ten minutes for completion of the activity. Afterward, call on different students to report on their group's responses.

4 **Conversación** Completa la entrevista con el nuevo vocabulario que se ofrece en la lista de la derecha.

ENTREVISTADOR Recibí la (1) solicitud (de trabajo) que usted llenó y vi que tiene mucha experiencia.

ASPIRANTE Por eso decidí mandar una copia de mi (2) currículum cuando vi su (3) anuncio en el periódico.

ENTREVISTADOR Me alegro de que lo haya hecho. Pero dígame, ¿por qué dejó usted su (4) puesto anterior?

ASPIRANTE Lo dejé porque quiero un mejor (5) salario/sueldo.

ENTREVISTADOR ¿Y cuánto quiere usted (6) ganar?

ASPIRANTE Pues, eso depende de los (7) beneficios que me puedan ofrecer.

ENTREVISTADOR Muy bien. Pues, creo que usted tiene la experiencia necesaria, pero tengo que (8) entrevistar a dos aspirantes más. Le vamos a llamar la semana que viene.

ASPIRANTE Hasta pronto, y gracias por la (9) entrevista.

Más vocabulario

el anuncio	*advertisement*
el/la aspirante	*candidate; applicant*
los beneficios	*benefits*
el currículum	*résumé*
la entrevista	*interview*
el/la entrevistador(a)	*interviewer*
el puesto	*position; job*
el salario, el sueldo	*salary*
la solicitud (de trabajo)	*(job) application*
contratar	*to hire*
entrevistar	*to interview*
ganar	*to earn*
obtener	*to obtain; to get*
solicitar	*to apply (for a job)*

5 **Completar** Escoge la respuesta que completa cada frase.

1. Voy a __b__ mi empleo.
   a. tener éxito b. renunciar a c. entrevistar
2. Quiero dejar mi __c__ porque no me gusta mi jefe.
   a. anuncio b. gerente c. puesto
3. Por eso, fui a una __b__ con una consejera de carreras.
   a. profesión b. reunión c. ocupación
4. Ella me dijo que necesito revisar mi __a__.
   a. currículum b. compañía c. aspirante
5. ¿Cuándo obtuviste __c__ más reciente?, me preguntó.
   a. la reunión b. la videoconferencia c. el aumento de sueldo
6. Le dije que deseo trabajar en una empresa con excelentes __a__.
   a. beneficios b. entrevistas c. solicitudes de trabajo
7. Y quiero tener la oportunidad de __a__ en la nueva empresa.
   a. invertir b. obtener c. perder

¡LENGUA VIVA!

Trabajo, **empleo**, and **puesto** all translate as *job*, but each has additional meanings: **trabajo** means *work*, **empleo** means *employment*, and **puesto** means *position*.

6 **Preguntas** Responde a cada pregunta con una respuesta breve. Answers will vary.

1. ¿Te gusta tu especialización?
2. ¿Lees los anuncios de empleo en el periódico con regularidad?
3. ¿Piensas que una carrera que beneficia a otros es más importante que un empleo con un salario muy bueno? Explica tu respuesta.
4. ¿Obtienes siempre los puestos que quieres?
5. ¿Te preparas bien para las entrevistas?
6. ¿Crees que una persona debe renunciar a un puesto si no se ofrecen ascensos?
7. ¿Te gustaría más un teletrabajo o un trabajo tradicional en una oficina?
8. ¿Piensas que los jefes siempre tienen razón?
9. ¿Quieres tener tu propia empresa?
10. ¿Cuál es tu carrera ideal?

TEACHING OPTIONS

Heritage Speakers Ask heritage speakers to describe a job that is unique to their cultural community. Ex: **gestor(a), aparejador(a), curandero/a, puestero/a.** Have them read their descriptions to the rest of the class. Write new vocabulary on the board.

Game Have students make a bingo card with the names of professions, and then ask them to exchange their boards with a classmate. Say a short description such as **Trabaja en una oficina.** If a student has a corresponding profession on his or her board, he or she makes a check mark in the corner of the box. To win, a student must have five professions in a row, read them back, and supply appropriate descriptions.

Comunicación

7 

Una entrevista Trabaja con un(a) compañero/a para representar los papeles de un(a) aspirante a un puesto y un(a) entrevistador(a). Answers will vary.

El/La entrevistador(a) debe describir...
- el empleo
- las responsabilidades
- el salario
- los beneficios

El/La aspirante debe...
- presentar su experiencia
- obtener más información sobre el puesto

Entonces...
- el/la entrevistador(a) debe decidir si va a contratar al/a la aspirante
- el/la aspirante debe decidir si va a aceptar el puesto

8 

Un(a) consejero/a de carreras En parejas, representen los papeles de un(a) consejero/a de carreras y una persona que quiere saber cuál es la mejor ocupación para él/ella. El/La consejero/a debe hacerle preguntas sobre su educación, su experiencia y sus intereses y debe sugerir dos o tres profesiones posibles. Después, intercambien (*swap*) los papeles. Answers will vary.

9 

Una feria de trabajo La clase va a celebrar una feria (*fair*) de trabajo. Unos estudiantes van a ser representantes de compañías que buscan empleados y otros van a estar buscando nuevos puestos. Los representantes deben preparar carteles con el nombre de su compañía y los puestos que ofrecen. Los que buscan empleo deben circular por la clase y hablar con tres representantes sobre sus experiencias de trabajo y el tipo de trabajo que están buscando. Los entrevistadores deben describir los puestos y conseguir los nombres y las referencias de los solicitantes. Answers will vary.

7 Suggestion Give students time to look at the photo and brainstorm. Then, ask volunteers to answer questions about the interviewing process. Ex: **En una entrevista, ¿quién explica las reponsabilidades del trabajo? ¿Quién pregunta sobre la experiencia de la otra persona?**

7 Expansion Ask volunteers to perform their **entrevista** for the class.

8 Suggestions
- Have the class brainstorm questions an employment counselor might ask. Write the questions on the board.
- Model the activity by providing information for an imaginary client. Ex: **Una joven busca trabajo. Le gustan mucho los niños, pero no tiene carrera universitaria. Tiene muchos hermanos y gana dinero cuidando a los niños de sus vecinos. ¿Qué trabajo le recomienda la consejera? (ayudante de maestra; trabajadora de guardería)**

9 Expansion After the **feria**, ask the **representantes de compañías** to say which one of the candidates they spoke with seems like the best match for their company. Then ask the **solicitantes** to say which one of the companies they looked into seems like the best match for them.

TEACHING OPTIONS

Small Groups Have groups of three write a résumé for a famous person. Write a suggested format on the board for the class. Ex: **Objetivos profesionales; Formación académica; Experiencia laboral**. Have groups exchange and critique the completed résumés. Later, have groups review their classmates' comments.

Game Divide the class into teams of four. Give groups five minutes to write a job announcement. Then have them take turns reading their announcements. The other teams must guess what job is being announced. Award one point for every correct guess and two points to the team who is able to stump the rest of the class.

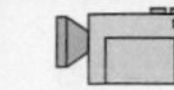

Section Goals

In **Fotonovela** students will:

- receive comprehensible input from free-flowing discourse
- learn functional phrases that preview lesson grammatical structures

Instructional Resources
WB/VM: Video Activities, pp. 243–244
***Fotonovela** DVD/Video (Start 01:29:11)*
Video CD-ROM
*IRM: **Fotonovela** Translations, pp. 147–148, Videoscript, pp. 122–123*
Interactive CD-ROM

Video Recap: Lección 15
Before doing this **Fotonovela** section, review the previous one with this activity.

1. ¿Qué hicieron Martín y los estudiantes en la montaña? (hicieron una excursión, sacaron fotos y disfrutaron del paisaje)
2. ¿Por qué sacó Javier mil fotos? (porque quería escenas para dibujar)
3. ¿Quién nunca había hecho una excursión antes? (Maite nunca había hecho una excursión)
4. ¿Les gustó la excursión a todos? (sí, les encantó)

Video Synopsis Over dinner, Don Francisco and the students discuss their career plans. Don Francisco is going to start a tourism company. Álex will start an Internet company. Maite is going to have her own interview show on TV. Javier will be a famous artist, and Inés will be an archaeologist. The group toasts to the future.

Suggestions

- Have your class glance at the video stills and scan the **Fotonovela** for words related to career plans. Then have students predict the content of this **Fotonovela** episode. Write down their predictions.
- Quickly review the predictions your students made about the **Fotonovela**. Ask a few questions to help your students summarize the plot.

¡Es un plan sensacional!

Don Francisco y los estudiantes hablan de sus ocupaciones futuras.

PERSONAJES

MAITE

INÉS

DON FRANCISCO

ÁLEX

JAVIER

1

MAITE La señora Vives es una cocinera magnífica.

DON FRANCISCO Me alegro de que les guste.

2

DON FRANCISCO Oigan, ¿qué me dicen del lugar donde fueron de excursión? ¿Qué les pareció?

MAITE ¡El paisaje es bellísimo!

INÉS Martín fue un guía excelente. Mostró mucho interés en que aprendiéramos sobre el medio ambiente.

3

DON FRANCISCO Sí, Martín es el mejor guía que conozco. Pero hablando de profesiones, ¿quieren saber cuáles son mis planes para el futuro?

MAITE ¡Me muero por saberlo!

DON FRANCISCO He decidido que el próximo verano voy a establecer mi propia compañía de turismo.

6

MAITE ¡Es un plan sensacional! Pero ahora escuchen el mío. Yo voy a ser periodista y tendré mi propio programa de entrevistas. Me verán en la tele entrevistando a políticos, científicos, hombres y mujeres de negocios y actores y actrices.

7

JAVIER No me cabe duda de que seré un pintor famoso. Todo el mundo querrá comprar mis cuadros y llegaré a ser más famoso que Picasso, que Dalí, que Velázquez...

8

INÉS Seré arqueóloga. Investigaré sitios arqueológicos en el Ecuador y en otros países. Escribiré libros sobre mis descubrimientos.

recursos

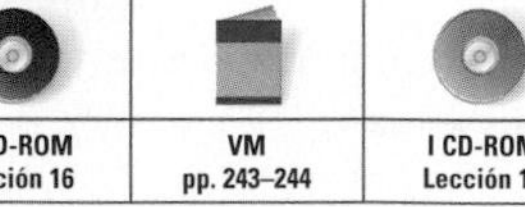

V CD-ROM Lección 16	VM pp. 243–244	I CD-ROM Lección 16

TEACHING OPTIONS

Video Tips General suggestions for using video clips in the classroom can be found on page IAE-12 of this Instructor's Annotated Edition.
¡Es un plan sensacional! Play the main video episode (but not including the **Resumen** segment) and have your students jot down key words. Then have them work in groups to prepare a brief plot summary using their lists of key words. Play the main video episode again, including the **Resumen** segment, and have students return to their groups to refine their summaries. Finally, discuss the plot with the entire class and correct any errors of fact or sequencing.

4

JAVIER ¡Buena idea, don Efe! Con su experiencia y talento, será un gran éxito.

ÁLEX Sí, estoy completamente de acuerdo.

DON FRANCISCO ¡Qué amables son! Pero, díganme, ¿cuáles son sus planes? Supongo que también ustedes han pensado en el futuro.

5

ÁLEX Pues claro, don Francisco. En cinco años habré establecido una compañía especializada en Internet.

INÉS Serás millonario, ¿eh?

ÁLEX Exactamente, porque muchísima gente habrá invertido montones de dinero en mi empresa.

9

MAITE ¡Fenomenal! Cuando sean famosos yo los invitaré a todos a mi programa. Y usted también vendrá, don Efe.

DON FRANCISCO ¡Enseguida! ¡Vendré conduciendo un autobús!

10

DON FRANCISCO ¡Por el porvenir!

ESTUDIANTES ¡Por el porvenir!

Enfoque cultural Las mujeres en el mundo del trabajo

Las mujeres en los países de habla hispana están trabajando en todas las ocupaciones posibles. Aunque todavía existe en muchas ocasiones una diferencia de sueldo entre hombres y mujeres, como ocurre prácticamente en todos los países del mundo, este problema va siendo cada vez más pequeño. En el mundo hispano muchas mujeres han ocupado altos puestos en la política, como Violeta Chamorro (Nicaragua) y Mireya Moscoso (Panamá), ambas presidentas de sus respectivos países.

Expresiones útiles

Talking about future plans

- ▶ **¿Quieren saber cuáles son mis planes para el futuro?** *Do you want to know what my plans for the future are?*
- ▷ **Me muero por saberlo.** *I'm dying to know.*
- ▶ **¿Cuáles son tus/sus planes?** *What are your plans?*
- ▷ **Seré un(a) pintor(a) famoso/a.** *I will be a famous painter.*
- ▷ **Tendré mi propio programa.** *I will have my own program.*
- ▶ **¿Dónde trabajarás?** *Where will you work?*
- ▷ **Trabajaré en México.** *I will work in Mexico.*
- ▶ **¿Qué piensas hacer después de graduarte?** *What do you intend to do after graduating?*
- ▷ **Pienso establecer mi propia compañía.** *I intend to start my own company.*

Agreement and disagreement

- **Estoy (completamente) de acuerdo.** *I agree (completely).*
- **Claro (que sí).** *Of course.*
- **Por supuesto.** *Of course.*
- **No estoy de acuerdo.** *I don't agree.*
- **No es así.** *That's not the way it is.*
- **De ninguna manera.** *No way.*

Giving a toast

- **¡Por el porvenir!** *Here's to the future!*

Suggestion To practice pronunciation, go through the **Fotonovela**, asking for volunteers to read the various parts. You may want to repeat this process with new volunteers so that more students participate.

Expresiones útiles Explain that **trabajaré, trabajarás, seré,** and **tendré** are future forms. Have the class scan the **Fotonovela** for more examples of the future **(será, serás, tendré, verán, querrá, llegaré, investigaré, escribiré, invitaré, vendrá, vendré).** Then have your students look at frame 2 of the **Fotonovela**. Tell them that **aprendiéramos** is an example of the past subjunctive. Now point out frame 5. Explain that **habré establecido** and **habrá invertido** are examples of the future perfect, which is formed with a future form of **haber** and a past participle. Tell your students that they will learn more about these concepts in **Estructura**.

TEACHING OPTIONS

Enfoque cultural Have your students work in groups to brainstorm lists of Hispanic women throughout the world who have made notable contributions in their professions. A few examples include Conchita Martínez (Spain, 1994 Wimbledon winner), Antonia Novello (former Surgeon General of the United States), Ellen Ochoa (first Hispanic female astronaut), and Rigoberta Menchú (Guatemala, winner of the Nobel Peace Prize). Have each group share its list with the class, explaining the accomplishments of each person. You may want to have your students create posters or give presentations about some of the women on their lists.

1 Expansion Give the class these additional items: **5. Maite dice que quiere ser actriz. (Falso. Maite quiere ser periodista.) 6. Javier dice que será un artista muy famoso. (Cierto.) 7. Inés dice que va a escribir sobre sus descubrimientos. (Cierto.) 8. Álex dice que va a establecer su propia compañía de turismo. (Falso. Don Francisco dice que va a establecer su propia compañía de turismo.)**

2 Expansion Give the class these additional items: **6. Tendré mis propios autobuses. (Don Francisco) 7. Voy a hablar con todos ustedes en mi programa de entrevistas. (Maite)**

3 Expansion Have pairs read their definitions aloud. Ask the rest of the class to guess the corresponding profession from the list in the activity.

4 Possible Response
E1: ¿Qué piensas hacer después de graduarte?
E2: Bueno, trabajaré en un colegio porque seré maestro. Voy a dar clases de inglés. Trabajaré en un colegio en el Ecuador.
E1: ¡Qué bien! ¿Quieres saber cuáles son mis planes para el futuro?
E2: Claro que sí. ¿Cuáles son tus planes?
E1: Pues, voy a ser una mujer de negocios. El próximo verano voy a trabajar en la oficina de mi tío pero pienso establecer mi propia compañía en cinco años.

Reacciona a la fotonovela

1 **¿Cierto o falso?** Indica si lo que dicen las siguientes frases es **cierto** o **falso**. Corrige las frases falsas.

	Cierto	Falso
1. Álex será millonario porque mucha gente invertirá en su compañía.	✓	○
2. Don Francisco preparó una comida deliciosa. La señora Vives preparó la comida.	○	✓
3. Martín insistió en que los estudiantes aprendieran sobre la historia del Ecuador. Martín insistió en que aprendieran sobre el medio ambiente.	○	✓
4. Inés será arqueóloga.	✓	○

2 **Identificar** Identifica quién puede decir las siguientes frases.

1. Con mi talento y experiencia en turismo, creo que mi compañía tendrá mucho éxito. don Francisco
2. Siempre me ha interesado mucho la historia de mi país. Inés
3. La comunicación y la tecnología me han gustado por mucho tiempo. Estableceré una empresa que se especialice en esas cosas. Álex
4. Voy a ser más famoso que Dalí. Javier
5. ¿Mi plan para el futuro? Trabajar en televisión y hablar con gente interesante. Maite

NOTA CULTURAL

El pintor español **Salvador Dalí** es uno de los máximos representantes del **surrealismo**, tendencia estética que refleja el subconsciente (*subconscious*) del artista. Las obras de Dalí están llenas de símbolos e imágenes fantásticas que muestran sus sueños y su propia realidad.

3 **Profesiones** Los protagonistas de la **fotonovela** mencionan las siguientes profesiones. En parejas, túrnense para definir cada profesión. Answers will vary.

1. arqueólogo/a
2. actor/actriz
3. científico/a
4. cocinero/a
5. hombre/mujer de negocios
6. periodista
7. pintor(a)
8. político/a

AYUDA

Remember that the indefinite article is not used with professions, unless they are modified by an adjective.

José es **pintor**.

José es **un buen pintor**.

4 **Mis planes** En grupos, hablen de sus planes para el futuro. Utilicen estas frases: Answers will vary.

- ▸ ¿Qué piensas hacer después de graduarte?
- ▸ ¿Quieres saber cuáles son mis planes para el futuro?
- ▸ ¿Cuáles son tus planes?
- ▸ ¿Dónde trabajarás?
- ▹ El próximo año/verano, voy a...
- ▹ Seré un(a)...
- ▹ Trabajaré en...

TEACHING OPTIONS

Extra Practice Ask your students a few questions about the **Fotonovela**. Ex: **¿Quién es el mejor guía que conoce don Francisco? (Martín) ¿Quién quiere ser más famoso que Picasso? (Javier) ¿Quién quiere hacer investigaciones arqueológicas en el Ecuador y en otros países? (Inés)**

Pairs Have your students interview each other in pairs about where they want to be and what they want to be doing in five years, in ten years, in 30 years, and so forth. Have each student take notes on his or her partner's plans. Then ask for a few volunteers to report on their partner's plans for the future.

Ortografía

Las letras y, ll y h

The letters **ll** and **y** were not pronounced alike in Old Spanish. Nowadays, however, **ll** and **y** have the same or similar pronunciations in many parts of the Spanish-speaking world. This results in frequent misspellings. The letter **h**, as you already know, is silent in Spanish, and it is often difficult to know whether words should be written with or without it. Here are some of the word groups that are spelled with each letter.

talla **sello** **botella** **amarillo**

The letter **ll** is used in these endings: **–allo/a, –ello/a, –illo/a.**

llave **llega** **llorar** **lluvia**

The letter **ll** is used at the beginning of words in these combinations: **lla-, lle-, llo-, llu-.**

cayendo **leyeron** **oye** **incluye**

The letter **y** is used in some forms of the verbs **caer, leer,** and **oír** and in verbs ending in **–uir.**

hiperactivo **hospital** **hipopótamo** **humor**

The letter **h** is used at the beginning of words in these combinations: **hiper-, hosp-, hidr-, hipo-, hum-.**

hiato **hierba** **hueso** **huir**

The letter **h** is also used in words that begin with these combinations: **hia-, hie-, hue-, hui-.**

Práctica Llena los espacios con **h, ll** o **y.** Después escribe una frase con cada una de las palabras.

1. cuchi_ll_o	3. cue_ll_o	5. estre_ll_a	7. destru_y_ó
2. _h_ielo	4. estampi_ll_a	6. _h_uésped	8. pla_y_a

Adivinanza Aquí tienes una adivinanza (*riddle*). Intenta descubrir de qué se trata.

Una cajita chiquita, blanca como la nieve: todos la saben abrir, nadie la sabe cerrar.[1]
Pista: Es una comida.

[1] El huevo

recursos

LM p. 92	Lab CD/MP3 Lección 16	I CD-ROM Lección 16

Section Goal

In **Ortografía** students will learn about the spelling of words that contain **y, ll,** and **h.**

Instructional Resource
Interactive CD-ROM

Suggestions

- Write the words **talla, sello, botella,** and **amarillo** on the board. Ask the class why these words are spelled with **ll.**
- Say the words **llave, llega, llorar,** and **lluvia** and ask for volunteers to spell them aloud in Spanish.
- Say the words **cayendo, leyeron, oye,** and **incluye** and ask for volunteers to write them on the board.
- Write the words **hiperactivo, hospital, hipopótamo,** and **humor** on the board and ask the class why these words are spelled with **h.**
- Say the words **hiato, hierba, hueso,** and **huir** and ask for volunteers to spell them aloud.
- Point out that **Ortografía** replaces **Pronunciación** in the Student Edition for **Lecciones 10–18**, but not in the Lab Manual. The **Recursos** box references the **Pronunciación** sections found in all lessons of the Lab Manual.

TEACHING OPTIONS

Group Work Have the class work in groups to make a list of six words that are spelled with **y, ll,** or **h** (two words for each letter). They shouldn't use the words that appear on this page. Have them write a creative, humorous sentence that includes all six of these words. Have a few groups share their sentences with the class.

Extra Practice Read aloud to your students a list of words that contain **y, ll,** or **h.** For each word, the class will say **i griega, elle,** or **hache** to indicate which letter is used in that word. Sample words: **ayer, llegaban, oyó, llamamos, humano, huésped, millonario, cayeron, leyó.**

Section Goals

In **Estructura 16.1** students will learn:

- the future
- irregular verbs in the future
- the future as a means of expressing conjecture or probability

Instructional Resources
WB/VM: Workbook, pp. 183–184
Lab Manual, p. 93
Lab CD/MP3 ***Lección 16***
IRM: ***¡Inténtalo!*** *&* ***Práctica*** *Answers, p. 222; Tapescript, pp. 71–75*
Info Gap Activities Booklet, pp. 61–62
Interactive CD-ROM
Companion website: www.vistahigherlearning.com
Presentations CD-ROM

Suggestions

- Ask students about their future activities using **ir a** + [*infinitive*]. After they answer, repeat the information using the future. Ex: **Mis amigos y yo almorzaremos a la una.**
- Review the **ir / ir a** + [*infinitive*] constructions to express the future in Spanish using the information in **Ante todo.** Then, work through the paradigm for the formation of the future. Go over regular and irregular verbs in the future point by point, calling students' attention to the information in **¡Atención!**
- Check for understanding by asking volunteers to give different forms of verbs not listed. Ex: **renunciar, ofrecer, invertir.**

16.1 The future

ANTE TODO You have already learned ways of expressing the near future in Spanish. You will now learn how to form and use the future tense. Compare the different ways of expressing the future in Spanish and English.

Present indicative

Voy al cine mañana.
I'm going to the movies tomorrow.

Present subjunctive

Ojalá **vaya al cine** mañana.
I hope I will go to the movies tomorrow.

ir a **+ [infinitive]**

Voy a ir al cine.
I'm going to go to the movies.

Future

Iré al cine.
I will go to the movies.

Future tense

		estudiar	aprender	recibir
SINGULAR FORMS	yo	estudiar**é**	aprender**é**	recibir**é**
	tú	estudiar**ás**	aprender**ás**	recibir**ás**
	Ud./él/ella	estudiar**á**	aprender**á**	recibir**á**
PLURAL FORMS	nosotros/as	estudiar**emos**	aprender**emos**	recibir**emos**
	vosotros/as	estudiar**éis**	aprender**éis**	recibir**éis**
	Uds./ellos/ellas	estudiar**án**	aprender**án**	recibir**án**

▶ In Spanish, the future is a simple tense that consists of one word, whereas in English it is made up of the auxiliary verb *will* or *shall*, and the main verb.

¿Cuándo **recibirás** el ascenso?
*When **will you** receive the promotion?*

Mañana **aprenderemos** más.
*Tomorrow **we will** learn more.*

▶ The future endings are the same for regular and irregular verbs. For regular verbs, simply add the endings to the infinitive. For irregular verbs, add the endings to the irregular stem.

Irregular verbs in the future

INFINITIVE	STEM	FUTURE FORMS
decir	dir-	dir**é**
hacer	har-	har**é**
poder	podr-	podr**é**
poner	pondr-	pondr**é**
querer	querr-	querr**é**
saber	sabr-	sabr**é**
salir	saldr-	saldr**é**
tener	tendr-	tendr**é**
venir	vendr-	vendr**é**

recursos

WB pp. 183–188
LM pp. 93–95
Lab CD/MP3 Lección 16
I CD-ROM Lección 16
vistahigherlearning.com

CONSÚLTALO

To review **ir a** + [*infinitive*], see **Estructura 4.1**, p. 112.

¡ATENCIÓN!

Note that all of the future endings have a written accent except the **nosotros/as** form.

TEACHING OPTIONS

Extra Practice To provide oral practice with the future, create sentences that follow the pattern of the sentences in the examples. Say the sentence, have students repeat it, then change the subject. Have students then say the sentence with the new subject, changing the verb as necessary.

Game Divide the class into groups of six. Each group should have a piece of paper. When you give an infinitive in Spanish, the first group member will write the **yo** form of the verb and pass the paper to the second member, who will write the **tú** form, and so forth. The first group to finish the entire paradigm correctly wins a point.

▶ The future of **hay** (*inf.* **haber**) is **habrá** *(there will be)*.

La próxima semana **habrá** dos reuniones.
Next week there will be two meetings.

Habrá muchos gerentes en la videoconferencia.
There will be many managers at the videoconference.

▶ Although the English word *will* can refer to future time, it also refers to someone's willingness to do something. In this case, Spanish uses **querer** + [*infinitive*], not the future tense.

¿Quieres llamarme, por favor?
Will you please call me?

¿Quieren ustedes escucharnos, por favor?
Will you please listen to us?

COMPARE & CONTRAST

In Spanish, the future tense has an additional use: expressing conjecture or probability. English sentences involving expressions such as *I wonder, I bet, must be, may, might,* and *probably* are often translated into Spanish using the *future of probability*.

—¿Dónde **estarán** mis llaves?
I wonder where my keys are.

—**Estarán** en la cocina.
They're probably in the kitchen.

—¿Qué hora **será**?
What time can it be? (I wonder what time it is.)

—**Serán** las once o las doce.
It must be (It's probably) eleven or twelve.

Note that although the future tense is used, these verbs express conjecture about *present* conditions, events, or actions.

CONSÚLTALO

To review these conjunctions of time, see **Estructura 13.3**, p. 412.

▶ The future may also be used in the main clause of sentences in which the present subjunctive follows a conjunction of time such as **cuando, después (de) que, en cuanto, hasta que,** and **tan pronto como.**

Cuando llegues a la oficina, **hablaremos**.
When you arrive at the office, we will talk.

Saldremos tan pronto como termine su trabajo.
We will leave as soon as you finish your work.

¡INTÉNTALO! Conjuga los verbos entre paréntesis en futuro.

1. (dejar, correr, invertir) yo *dejaré, correré, invertiré*
2. (renunciar, beber, vivir) tú renunciarás, beberás, vivirás
3. (hacer, poner, venir) Lola hará, pondrá, vendrá
4. (tener, decir, querer) nosotros tendremos, diremos, querremos
5. (ir, ser, estar) ustedes irán, serán, estarán
6. (solicitar, comer, repetir) usted solicitará, comerá, repetirá
7. (saber, salir, poder) yo sabré, saldré, podré
8. (encontrar, jugar, servir) tú encontrarás, jugarás, servirás

Suggestions

- Go over the future of **haber**. Remind students that **hay/habrá** has only one form and does not agree with any element in a sentence.
- Go over the explanation of **querer** + [*infinitive*].
- Explain the use of the future for expressing conjecture, which English generally expresses with the present tense. Use magazine pictures to get students to express speculation about what characters are thinking or going to do. Ex: **¿Qué estará pensando la mujer que está saliendo de la oficina? (Estará pensando en su entrevista.) ¿Quiénes serán esos chicos que corren por la calle? (Serán estudiantes de otra escuela.)**
- Go over the use of the future in the main clause of sentences in which the present subjunctive follows a conjunction of time. Check for understanding by asking individuals to supply the main clause to prompts of present subjunctive clauses. Ex: **En cuanto pueda... ; Tan pronto como me lo digas...**
- Have students open to **Fotonovela**, pages 486–487. Ask students to identify: 1) the use of the future to express upcoming actions; and 2) the use of the future as a means of expressing conjecture or possibility.
- Ask students answer questions about the future of the **Fotonovela** characters. Ex: **¿Quién tendrá la profesión más interesante? ¿Por qué? ¿Quién será más feliz?**

TEACHING OPTIONS

Pairs Ask pairs to write ten academic resolutions for the upcoming semester using the future. Ex: **Haré dos o tres borradores de cada composición. Practicaremos el español con los estudiantes hispanos.**

Extra Practice Ask students to finish the following sentences logically: **1. En cuanto encuentre trabajo,... 2. Tan pronto como termine mis estudios,... 3. El día que me toque la lotería,... 4. Cuando lleguen las vacaciones,... 5. Hasta que tenga un puesto profesional,...**

1 Suggestions
- Before beginning the activity, briefly explain the subtle difference between the future with **ir a** + [*infinitive*] and the simple future.
- Have two volunteers read the **modelo**. Change the subject of the sentence and ask a volunteer for the new sentence. Ex: **Celia va a consultar el índice de Empresas 500 en la biblioteca. (Consultará el índice de Empresas 500 en la biblioteca.)**

1 Expansion For further oral practice, read these additional items to the class: **7. Después de cinco años Álvaro y yo vamos a tener nuestro propio negocio. 8. El negocio va a estar en un lugar bonito. 9. Ustedes van a querer comprar los productos de nuestra compañía. 10. Vamos a jubilarnos cuando tengamos cuarenta años.**

2 Expansion Have partners tell each other about a real person they've seen somewhere but to whom they've never spoken. Have them speculate about that person. Ex: **Será el gerente del restaurante. Trabajará hasta muy tarde cada noche. Vivirá en las afueras de la ciudad.** Then, have pairs share their speculations with the class.

3 Suggestion Before beginning the activity, give students a few minutes to read the ads before assigning pairs.

3 Expansion Have students answer the same questions about the job of their dreams.

Successful Language Learning Ask your students how they could use Spanish in their present or future careers.

Práctica

1 **Planes** Celia está hablando de sus planes. Repite lo que dice, usando el tiempo futuro.

modelo

Voy a consultar el índice de Empresas 500 en la biblioteca.
Consultaré el índice de Empresas 500 en la biblioteca.

1. Álvaro y yo nos vamos a casar pronto. Nos casaremos...
2. Julián me va a decir dónde puedo buscar trabajo. Me dirá...
3. Voy a buscar un puesto con un buen sueldo. Buscaré...
4. Voy a leer los anuncios clasificados todos los días. Leeré...
5. Voy a obtener un puesto en mi especialización. Obtendré...
6. Mis amigos van a estar contentos por mí. Estarán...

2 **¿Quién será? ¿Qué hará?** En parejas, imaginen que están con un(a) amigo/a en un café y ven entrar a un hombre o una mujer. Imaginen cómo será su vida y utilicen el futuro de probabilidad en su conversación. Usen estas preguntas como guía y después lean su conversación delante de la clase. Answers will vary.

modelo

Estudiante 1: *¿Tendrá éxito en su profesión?*
Estudiante 2: *Creo que sí porque lleva ropa cara.*

- ¿Estará soltero/a?
- ¿Cuántos años tendrá?
- ¿En qué trabajará?
- ¿Será famoso/a?
- ¿Tendrá éxito en su profesión?
- ¿Con quién vivirá?
- ¿Estará esperando a alguien? ¿A quién?

3  **Preguntas** Imaginen que han aceptado uno de los puestos de los anuncios. En parejas, túrnense para hablar sobre los detalles (*details*) del puesto. Usen las preguntas de guía y hagan también sus propias preguntas. Answers will vary.

Laboratorios LUNA
Se busca científico con mucha imaginación para crear nuevos productos. Mínimo 3 años de experiencia. Puesto con buen sueldo y buenos beneficios. Tel: 492-38-67

SE BUSCA CONTADOR(A)
Mínimo 5 años de experiencia. Debe hablar inglés, francés y alemán. Salario: 120.000 dólares al año. Envíen currículum por fax al: 924-90-34.

SE BUSCAN
Actores y actrices con experiencia para telenovela. Trabajarán por las noches. Salario: 40 dólares la hora. Soliciten puesto en persona. Calle El Lago n. 24, Managua.

SE NECESITAN
Jóvenes periodistas para periódico nacional. Horario: 4:30 a 20:30. Comenzarán inmediatamente. Salario anual: 20.000 dólares al año. Tel. contacto: 245-94-30.

1. ¿Cuál será el trabajo?
2. ¿Qué harás?
3. ¿Cuánto te pagarán?
4. ¿Sabes si te ofrecerán beneficios?
5. ¿Sabes el horario que tendrás? ¿Es importante saberlo?
6. ¿Crees que te gustará? ¿Por qué?
7. ¿Cuándo comenzarás a trabajar?
8. ¿Qué crees que aprenderás?

TEACHING OPTIONS

Large Group Tell the class that everyone will soon have a new job. Using sticky notes, place the name of a profession on each student's back. Students will circulate around the class asking closed-ended questions to find out what their new jobs are going to be. They should use the future to form their questions, and they are only allowed to ask two questions per classmate. Ex: **¿Trabajaré al aire libre? ¿Me pagarán mucho? ¿Tendré que llevar uniforme?**

Video Show the video again to give students more input about the future. Stop the video where appropriate to discuss the use of the future to express coming events and as a means of expressing conjecture or probability.

Comunicación

4 

Conversar Tú y tu compañero/a viajarán a la República Dominicana por siete días. En parejas, indiquen lo que harán y no harán. Digan dónde, cómo, con quién o en qué fechas lo harán, usando el anuncio (*ad*) como guía. Pueden usar sus propias ideas también. Answers will vary.

NOTA CULTURAL

En la **República Dominicana** está el punto más alto y el más bajo de las Antillas. El Pico Duarte mide (*measures*) 3.175 metros y el lago Enriquillo está a 45 metros bajo el nivel del mar (*sea level*).

modelo

Estudiante 1: *¿Qué haremos el martes?*
Estudiante 2: *Visitaremos el Jardín Botánico.*
Estudiante 1: *Pues, tu visitarás el Jardín Botánico y yo caminaré por el Mercado Modelo.*

¡Bienvenido a la República Dominicana!

Se divertirá desde el momento en que llegue al **Aeropuerto Internacional de las Américas.**

- Visite la ciudad colonial de **Santo Domingo** con su interesante arquitectura.
- Vaya al **Jardín Botánico** y disfrute de nuestra abundante naturaleza.
- En el **Mercado Modelo** no va a poder resistir la tentación de comprar artesanías.
- No deje de escalar la montaña del **Pico Duarte** (se recomiendan 3 días).
- ¿Le gusta bucear? **Cabarete** tiene todo el equipo que usted necesita.
- ¿Desea nadar? **Punta Cana** le ofrece hermosas playas.

5 

Planear En grupos pequeños, hagan planes para formar una empresa privada. Usen las preguntas como guía. Después presenten su plan a la clase. Answers will vary.

1. ¿Cómo se llamará y qué tipo de empresa será?
2. ¿Cuántos empleados tendrá y cuáles serán sus oficios o profesiones?
3. ¿Qué tipo de beneficios se ofrecerán?
4. ¿Quién será el/la gerente y quién será el jefe/la jefa? ¿Por qué?
5. ¿Permitirá su empresa el teletrabajo? ¿Por qué?
6. ¿Dónde pondrá anuncios para conseguir empleados?

Síntesis

6  

El futuro de Cristina Tu profesor(a) va a darte una serie incompleta de dibujos sobre el futuro de Cristina. Tú y tu compañero/a tienen dos series diferentes. Háganse preguntas y respondan de acuerdo a los dibujos para completar la historia.

modelo

Estudiante 2: *¿Qué hará Cristina en el año 2010?*
Estudiante 1: *Ella se graduará en el año 2010.*

4 Suggestions

- Encourage pairs to review the ad before they complete the activity.
- If you have any students from the Dominican Republic in your class, or if any of your students have visited the Dominican Republic, ask them to talk about the places named in the ad.

4 Expansion Have several pairs present their conversation to the class.

5 Expansion Have groups develop a visual aid to accompany their presentation to the class.

6 Suggestion Divide the class into pairs and distribute the Info Gap Handouts from the Info Gap Activities Booklet that correspond to this activity. Give the students ten minutes to complete this activity.

6 Expansions

- Have students change partners, and have the new pairs use the future to retell the story without looking at the drawings. Later, ask students if any aspects of their second partner's version of the story differed from the version they created with their first partner.
- Have pairs pick a person who is currently in the news. Have them write predictions about his or her future and then share their predictions with the class.

TEACHING OPTIONS

Game Use a ball to play a game that practices the simple future forms. Say an infinitive of a known verb followed by a subject pronoun. Ex: **tener (Uds.)** Toss the ball to a student who must give the simple future of the verb in the indicated form. **(tendrán)** When the student has given the appropriate form, he or she tosses the ball back to you. Include verbs from all conjugations and those that have irregular futures. Keep the pace rapid.

Large Groups Assign a century to each corner of the room. Ex: 23rd century. Tell students they are going to go into the future in a time machine **(máquina de transporte a través del tiempo)**. They should pick which year they would like to visit and go to that corner. Once assembled, each group should develop a summary of life in their century. After groups have finished, call on a spokesperson in each group to report to the class.

Section Goal

In **Estructura 16.2** students will learn the future perfect.

Instructional Resources
WB/VM: Workbook, p. 185
Lab Manual, p. 94
Lab CD/MP3 ***Lección 16***
IRM: ***Hojas de actividades,***
p. 173; ***¡Inténtalo!*** *&* ***Práctica***
Answers, p. 222; Tapescript, pp. 71–75
Interactive CD-ROM
Companion website: www.vistahigherlearning.com
Presentations CD-ROM

Suggestions

- Write a series of dates on the board, making sure they correspond to key academic events, and use them in sample sentences with the future perfect. Ex: **Para el 15 de diciembre, el semestre habrá terminado. Para el 6 de junio, algunos de ustedes se habrán graduado.** Have volunteers give information about the other dates listed.
- Ask volunteers to read aloud the captions to the video stills and identify the future perfect verbs. Discuss **para** + [*time expression*]. Explain that the future perfect is also used to hypothesize about a past action. Ex: **Susana ya habrá salido de la oficina.**

16.2 The future perfect

ANTE TODO Like other compound tenses you have learned, the future perfect (**el futuro perfecto**) is formed with a form of **haber** and the past participle. It is used to talk about what will have happened by some future point in time.

Future perfect

		hablar	comer	vivir
SINGULAR FORMS	yo	**habré** hablado	**habré** comido	**habré** vivido
	tú	**habrás** hablado	**habrás** comido	**habrás** vivido
	Ud./él/ella	**habrá** hablado	**habrá** comido	**habrá** vivido
PLURAL FORMS	nosotros/as	**habremos** hablado	**habremos** comido	**habremos** vivido
	vosotros/as	**habréis** hablado	**habréis** comido	**habréis** vivido
	Uds./ellos/ellas	**habrán** hablado	**habrán** comido	**habrán** vivido

¡ATENCIÓN!
As with other compound tenses, the past participle never varies in the future perfect; it always ends in **–o.**

En cinco años habré establecido mi compañía de Internet.

Serás millonario, ¿eh?

Sí, porque mucha gente habrá invertido en mi empresa.

▶ The phrases **para** + [*time expression*] and **dentro de** + [*time expression*] are used with the future perfect to talk about what will have happened by some future point in time.

Para el lunes, habré hecho todas las preparaciones.
By Monday, I will have made all the preparations.

Dentro de un año, habré renunciado a mi trabajo.
Within a year, I will have resigned from my job.

¡ATENCIÓN!
The future perfect is also used like the future of probablility, except that it represents a past action.
¿Adónde habrá ido Raúl?
I wonder where Raúl has gone?

¡INTÉNTALO! Indica la forma apropiada del futuro perfecto.

1. Para el sábado, nosotros habremos obtenido (obtener) el dinero.
2. Yo habré terminado (terminar) el trabajo para cuando lleguen mis amigos.
3. Silvia habrá hecho (hacer) todos los planes para el próximo fin de semana.
4. Para el cinco de junio, ustedes habrán llegado (llegar) a Quito.
5. Para esa fecha, Ernesto y tú habrán recibido (recibir) muchas ofertas.
6. Para el ocho de octubre, nosotros ya habremos llegado (llegar) a Colombia.
7. Para entonces, yo habré vuelto (volver) de la República Dominicana.
8. Para cuando yo te llame, ¿habrás decidido (decidir) tú lo que vamos a hacer?
9. Para las nueve, mi hermana habrá salido (salir).
10. Para las ocho, tú y yo habremos limpiado (limpiar) el piso.

TEACHING OPTIONS

Small Groups Divide the class into groups of three. Ask each group to work together to write a description of a classmate's future success, using the future perfect. The group should not include the name of their subject. Then circulate the descriptions and ask the other groups to identify the name of the classmate whose future is being predicted.

Extra Practice To provide oral practice with the future perfect, give the students oral prompts with a future date. Ex: **Para el año 2010...** Say the prompt, have students repeat it, then call on individual students to add an appropriate ending using the future perfect. (**... habremos aprendido perfectamente el español.; ... usted se habrá jubilado.**)

Práctica

1 **Escoger** Juan Luis habla de lo que habrá ocurrido en ciertos momentos del futuro. Escoge los verbos que mejor completen cada oración y ponlos en el futuro perfecto.

casarse	leer	solicitar
comprar	romperse	tomar
graduarse	ser	viajar

1. Para mañana por la tarde, yo ya __habré tomado__ mi examen de biología.
2. Para la semana que viene, el profesor __habrá leído__ nuestros exámenes.
3. Dentro de tres meses, Juan y Marisa __se habrán casado__ en Las Vegas.
4. Dentro de cinco meses, tú y yo __nos habremos graduado__ de la universidad.
5. Para el fin de mayo, yo __habré solicitado__ un trabajo en un banco.
6. Dentro de un año, tú __habrás comprado__ una casa nueva.
7. Antes de cumplir los 50 años, usted __habrá viajado__ a Europa.
8. Dentro de 25 años, Emilia ya __habrá sido__ presidenta de los EE.UU.

Comunicación

2  **Encuesta** Tu profesor(a) te va a dar una hoja de actividades. Pregúntales a tres compañeros/as para cuándo habrán hecho las cosas relacionadas con sus futuras carreras que se mencionan en la lista. Toma nota de las respuestas y comparte más tarde con la clase la información que obtuviste sobre tus compañeros/as. Answers will vary.

modelo

Estudiante 1: *¿Para cuándo habrás terminado tus estudios, Carla?*
Estudiante 2: *Para el año que viene, habré terminado mis estudios.*
Estudiante 1: *Carla habrá terminado sus estudios el año que viene.*

Síntesis

3 **Competir** En parejas, preparen una conversación hipotética (8 líneas o más) que ocurra en una fiesta. Una persona dice lo que habrá hecho para algún momento del futuro; la otra responde, diciendo cada vez algo más exagerado. Prepárense para representar la conversación delante de la clase. Answers will vary.

modelo

Estudiante 1: *Cuando tenga 30 años, habré ganado un millón de dólares.*
Estudiante 2: *Y yo habré llegado a ser multimillonaria.*
Estudiante 1: *Para el 2020, me habrán escogido como la mejor diseñadora de París.*
Estudiante 2: *Pues, yo habré ganado el Premio Nobel de literatura.*

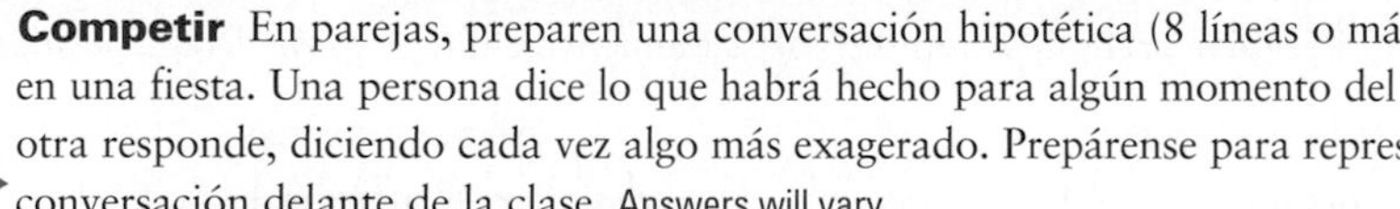

NOTA CULTURAL

El argentino Carlos Saavedra Lamas fue el primer latinoamericano en recibir un **Premio Nobel**. Lo recibió en 1936 por su trabajo como mediador en el conflicto entre Bolivia y Paraguay.

1 Expansion Use the same prepositional phrases to ask students personalized questions about their future plans. Ex: **Para mañana por la tarde, ¿qué habrás hecho? Para la semana que viene, ¿con quién habrás hablado?**

2 Suggestions
- Distribute the **Hojas de actividades** from the IRM that correspond to this activity.
- Have two volunteers model the activity by reading the **modelo,** noting as they do that the first example is the question asked, the second is the response, and the third is the rephrasing of the response by the first student.

3 Suggestion Read the **modelo** aloud with a volunteer who takes the role of **Estudiante 2**. Model adding another exaggerated claim to the exchange. Ex: **Pues, yo ya me habré jubilado del Comité del premio Nobel para esa fecha.**

3 Expansion After students have performed their conversations for the class, ask pairs to evaluate the claims. Ex: **La hipótesis de ____ es la más exagerada. La más ambiciosa es la de ____. La más original es la de ____.**

TEACHING OPTIONS

Pairs Have students work in pairs to prepare skits using the future perfect and a prediction theme. One student will play the part of a fortuneteller, a psychic, or another type of expert who claims to foresee the future. The other student will be the client. Encourage the students to bring props and/or costumes for the performance of their skit to the class.

Game Divide the class into groups of three. Write a future date on the board. Ex: **el 15 de noviembre de 2012**. Groups should confer and decide what will have happened by that date. When they have their answer, one student should stand up. The quickest group to respond with a correct answer wins a point. Ex: **Para el 15 de noviembre de 2012 habremos tenido otras elecciones presidenciales.**

Section Goal

In **Estructura 16.3** students will learn the past subjunctive.

Instructional Resources
WB/VM: Workbook, pp. 186–188
Lab Manual, p. 95
*Lab CD/MP3 **Lección 16***
*IRM: **¡Inténtalo! & Práctica** Answers, p. 222; Tapescript, pp. 71–75*
Info Gap Activities Booklet, pp. 63–64
Interactive CD-ROM
Companion website: www.vistahigherlearning.com
Presentations CD-ROM

Suggestions

- To demonstrate the use of the past subjunctive, ask volunteers to answer closed-ended questions about a recent event or popular movie. Ex: **¿Te sorprendió que la heroína se casara con el enemigo del protagonista? ¿Esperabas que el gobernador tomara esa decisión?** As students give you short answers, write the complete sentences on the board, underlining the past subjunctive form. Ex: **A todos nos sorprendió que la heroína se casara con el enemigo del protagonista. ____ no esperaba que el gobernador tomara esa decisión.**
- Explain that the past subjunctive is generally used in the same situations in which the present subjunctive is used, except to express past events.

16.3 The past subjunctive

ANTE TODO You will now learn how to form and use the past subjunctive (**el pretérito imperfecto de subjuntivo**), also called the imperfect subjunctive. Like the present subjunctive, the past subjunctive is used mainly in multiple-clause sentences which express states and conditions such as will, influence, emotion, commands, indefiniteness, and non-existence.

The past subjunctive

		estudiar	aprender	recibir
SINGULAR FORMS	yo	estudia**ra**	aprendie**ra**	recibie**ra**
	tú	estudia**ras**	aprendie**ras**	recibie**ras**
	Ud./él/ella	estudia**ra**	aprendie**ra**	recibie**ra**
PLURAL FORMS	nosotros/as	estudiá**ramos**	aprendié**ramos**	recibié**ramos**
	vosotros/as	estudia**rais**	aprendie**rais**	recibie**rais**
	Uds./ellos/ellas	estudia**ran**	aprendie**ran**	recibie**ran**

¡ATENCIÓN!
Note that the **nosotros/as** form of the past subjunctive always has a written accent.

▶ The past subjunctive endings are the same for all verbs.

-ra	**-ramos**
-ras	**-rais**
-ra	**-ran**

¡LENGUA VIVA!
The past subjunctive has another set of endings:

–se	**–semos**
–ses	**–seis**
–se	**–sen**

It's a good idea to learn to recognize these endings because they are sometimes used in literary and formal contexts.
Deseaba que mi esposo recibiese un ascenso.

▶ The past subjunctive is formed using the **Uds./ellos/ellas** form of the preterite. By dropping the **–ron** ending from this preterite form, you establish the stem of all the past subjunctive forms. To this stem you then add the past subjunctive endings.

INFINITIVE	PRETERITE FORM	STEM	PAST SUBJUNCTIVE
hablar	ellos habla~~ron~~	habla-	habla**ra**, habla**ras**, hablá**ramos**
beber	ellos bebie~~ron~~	bebie-	bebie**ra**, bebie**ras**, bebié**ramos**
escribir	ellos escribie~~ron~~	escribie-	escribie**ra**, escribie**ras**, escribié**ramos**

▶ For verbs with irregular preterites, add the past subjunctive endings to the irregular stem.

INFINITIVE	PRETERITE FORM	STEM	PAST SUBJUNCTIVE
dar	die~~ron~~	die-	die**ra**, die**ras**, dié**ramos**
decir	dije~~ron~~	dije-	dije**ra**, dije**ras**, dijé**ramos**
estar	estuvie~~ron~~	estuvie-	estuvie**ra**, estuvie**ras**, estuvié**ramos**
hacer	hicie~~ron~~	hicie-	hicie**ra**, hicie**ras**, hicié**ramos**
ir/ser	fue~~ron~~	fue-	fue**ra**, fue**ras**, fué**ramos**
poder	pudie~~ron~~	pudie-	pudie**ra**, pudie**ras**, pudié**ramos**
poner	pusie~~ron~~	pusie-	pusie**ra**, pusie**ras**, pusié**ramos**
querer	quisie~~ron~~	quisie-	quisie**ra**, quisie**ras**, quisié**ramos**
saber	supie~~ron~~	supie-	supie**ra**, supie**ras**, supié**ramos**
tener	tuvie~~ron~~	tuvie-	tuvie**ra**, tuvie**ras**, tuvié**ramos**
venir	vinie~~ron~~	vinie-	vinie**ra**, vinie**ras**, vinié**ramos**

¡LENGUA VIVA!
Quisiera, the past subjunctive form of **querer,** is often used to make polite requests.
Quisiera hablar con Marco, por favor.
I would like to speak to Marco, please.
¿Quisieran ustedes algo más?
Would you like anything else?

TEACHING OPTIONS

Extra Practice Write the following drill on the board. Students should change the verb according to each new subject. **1. estar: él/nosotros/tú 2. emplear: yo/ella/Ud. 3. insistir: ellos/Uds./él 4. poder: ellas/yo/nosotros 5. obtener: nosotros/tú/ella**

Heritage Speakers Ask heritage speakers to write ten sentences that use the past subjunctive to describe their experiences during their first days at your university or college. Ex: **Me sorprendió que la biblioteca fuera tan grande.** Ask them to write their sentences on the board and explain any unfamiliar vocabulary.

▶ **-Ir** stem-changing verbs and other verbs with spelling changes follow a similar process to form the past subjunctive.

INFINITIVE	PRETERITE FORM	STEM	PAST SUBJUNCTIVE
preferir	prefirie~~ron~~	prefirie-	prefiriе**ra**, prefirie**ras**, prefirié**ramos**
repetir	repitie~~ron~~	repitie-	repitie**ra**, repitie**ras**, repitié**ramos**
dormir	durmie~~ron~~	durmie-	durmie**ra**, durmie**ras**, durmié**ramos**
conducir	conduje~~ron~~	conduje-	conduje**ra**, conduje**ras**, condujé**ramos**
creer	creye~~ron~~	creye-	creye**ra**, creye**ras**, creyé**ramos**
destruir	destruye~~ron~~	destruye-	destruye**ra**, destruye**ras**, destruyé**ramos**
oír	oye~~ron~~	oye-	oye**ra**, oye**ras**, oyé**ramos**

▶ The past subjunctive is used in the same contexts and situations as the present subjunctive and the present perfect subjunctive, except that it generally describes actions, events, or conditions that have already happened.

Me pidieron que no **llegara** tarde.
They asked me not to arrive late.

Me sorprendió que ustedes no **vinieran** a la cena.
It surprised me that you didn't come to the dinner.

Salió antes de que yo **pudiera** hablar contigo.
He left before I could talk to you.

Ellos querían que yo **escribiera** una novela romántica.
They wanted me to write a romantic novel.

No pensé que pudiéramos terminar la excursión.

Martín mostró mucho interés en que aprendiéramos sobre el medio ambiente.

¡INTÉNTALO! Indica la forma apropiada del pretérito imperfecto de subjuntivo de los verbos entre paréntesis.

1. Quería que tú ___vinieras___ (venir) más temprano.
2. Esperábamos que ustedes ___hablaran___ (hablar) mucho más en la reunión.
3. No creían que yo ___pudiera___ (poder) hacerlo.
4. Se opuso a que nosotros ___invirtiéramos___ (invertir) el dinero ayer.
5. Sentí mucho que ustedes no ___estuvieran___ (estar) con nosotros anoche.
6. No era necesario que ellas ___hicieran___ (hacer) todo.
7. Me pareció increíble que tú ___supieras___ (saber) dónde encontrarlo.
8. No había nadie que ___creyera___ (creer) tu historia.
9. Mis padres insistieron en que yo ___fuera___ (ir) a la universidad.
10. Queríamos salir antes de que ustedes ___llegaran___ (llegar).

CONSEJOS

When a situation that triggers the subjunctive is involved, most cases follow this pattern:
main verb in present indicative → subordinate verb in present subjunctive
Espero que María **venga.**
main verb in past indicative → subordinate verb in past subjunctive
Esperaba que María **viniera.**

Suggestions

- Check comprehension by writing the infinitive of regular verbs from the three conjugations on the board. Ask a volunteer to give the **ellos** form of the preterite. Have the class then give the three distinct subjunctive forms.
- Follow the same procedure with verbs that have irregular preterite forms or are stem-changing in the preterite.
- Use pairs of examples such as the following to illustrate that the past subjunctive generally occurs in the same situations as the present subjunctive except that it deals with past events. Ex: **¿Es importante que estudies tanto? ¿Era importante que estudiaras tanto? Me sorprende que quieras ser político. Me sorprendió que quisieras ser político. No hay ningún teléfono que funcione. No había ningún teléfono que funcionara.**
- Ask volunteers to read the captions to the video stills and indicate the past subjunctive forms.
- Point out that the use of **quiero** instead of **quisiera** can seem rather blunt and could seem rude. Compare: **Quisiera hablar con Marco** and **Quiero hablar con Marco**, or **¿Quisiera usted algo más?** and **¿Quiere usted algo más?**

The Affective Dimension Tell the class that some students are intimidated by the past subjunctive. Point out that its forms are fairly easy to learn and that it is used in familiar contexts.

TEACHING OPTIONS

Video Show the video again to give students more input on the use of the past subjunctive. Stop the video where appropriate to discuss how and why the past subjunctive was used.

Extra Practice Write this cloze paragraph on the board, asking students to complete it using the correct forms of the following verbs: **querer, poder, estudiar, tener.**
Mis padres siempre querían que yo ____ (estudiara) una carrera universitaria. Nunca dudaron de que yo ____ (podía) llegar a ser lo que ____ (quisiera). Cuando ____ (tenga) hijos, espero tener la misma confianza en ellos.

1 Expansion Assign pairs one of the three conversations. Ask partners to work together to continue the conversation using the past subjunctive. Ex: **A mí me pasó algo igual. Me aconsejaron que dejara un trabajo que me gustaba mucho por otro que pagaba mejor.**

2 Suggestion Before assigning the activity, ask students what kinds of New Year's resolutions people usually make, encouraging them to use the future.

2 Expansion Assign pairs to groups of six. Ask the pairs to read their answers aloud to one another and pick the most original responses for each. Then ask them to write these responses on the board.

Práctica

1 **Diálogos** Completa los diálogos con el pretérito imperfecto de subjuntivo de los verbos entre paréntesis. Después representa los diálogos con un(a) compañero/a.

1. —¿Qué le dijo el consejero a Andrés? Quisiera saberlo.
   —Le aconsejó que __dejara__ (dejar) los estudios de arte y que __estudiara__ (estudiar) una carrera que __pagara__ (pagar) mejor.
   —Siempre el dinero. ¿No se enojó Andrés de que le __aconsejara__ (aconsejar) eso?
   —Sí, y le dijo que no creía que ninguna otra carrera le __fuera__ (ir) a gustar más.
2. —Qué lástima que ellos no te __ofrecieran__ (ofrecer) el puesto de gerente.
   —Querían a alguien que __tuviera__ (tener) experiencia en el sector público.
   —Pero, ¿cómo? ¿Y tu maestría? ¿No te molestó que te __dijeran__ (decir) eso?
   —No, no tengo experiencia en esa área, pero les gustó mucho mi currículum. Me pidieron que __volviera__ (volver) en un año y __solicitara__ (solicitar) el puesto otra vez. Para entonces habré obtenido la experiencia que necesito y podré conseguir el puesto que quiera.
3. —Cuánto me alegro de que tus hijas __vinieran__ (venir) ayer a visitarte. ¿Cuándo se van?
   —Bueno, yo esperaba que se __quedaran__ (quedar) dos semanas, pero no pueden. Ojalá __pudieran__ (poder). Hace mucho que no las veo.

2 **Año nuevo, vida nueva** El año pasado, Marta y Alberto querían cambiar de vida. Aquí tienen las listas con sus buenos propósitos para el Año Nuevo (*New Year's resolutions*). Ellos no consiguieron hacer realidad ninguno. En parejas, lean las listas y escriban por qué creen que no los consiguieron. Usen el pretérito imperfecto de subjuntivo.

modelo

obtener un mejor puesto de trabajo
Era difícil que Alberto consiguiera un mejor puesto porque su novia le pidió que no cambiara de puesto.

AYUDA

Puedes usar estas expresiones:
No era verdad que...
Era difícil que...
Era imposible que...
No era cierto que...
Su novio/a no quería que...

Alberto
- pedir un aumento de sueldo
- tener una vida más sana
- visitar más a su familia
- dejar de fumar

Marta
- querer mejorar su relación de pareja
- terminar los estudios con buenas notas
- cambiar de casa
- ahorrar más

TEACHING OPTIONS

Small Groups Ask students to write a plot summary of a movie they've seen, using the past subjunctive. Have them read their summaries in groups of five. Ex: **Su mamá no quería que se casara. Insistía en que la más joven de sus hijas se quedara soltera para cuidarla de vieja. No permitió que Tita aceptara la petición de matrimonio de Pedro. Tita tuvo que esperar hasta que se muriera su madre para ser feliz.**

Large Groups Ask students to think of a childhood fantasy they had about another person or a fictional character and create a sentence using the past subjunctive. Ex: **Yo quería que Santa Claus fuera mi abuelo. Yo insistía en que se pusiera la mesa para mis amigos imaginarios.** Then go around the room asking each person to say his or her sentence aloud, but repeating all the previous sentences first.

Comunicación

3 **Reaccionar** Manuel acaba de llegar de Nicaragua. Reacciona a lo que te dice, usando el pretérito imperfecto de subjuntivo. Escribe las oraciones y luego compáralas con las de un(a) compañero/a. Answers will vary.

modelo

El día que llegué, me esperaban mi abuela y tres primos.
¡Qué bien! Me alegré de que vieras a tu familia después de tantos años.

1. Fuimos al volcán Masaya. ¡Y vimos la lava del volcán!
2. Visitamos la Catedral de Managua, que fue dañada por el terremoto *(earthquake)* de 1972.
3. No tuvimos tiempo de ir a la playa, pero pasamos unos días en el Hotel Dariense en Granada.
4. Fui a conocer el nuevo museo de arte y también fui al Teatro Rubén Darío.
5. Nos divertimos haciendo compras en Metrocentro.
6. Eché monedas *(coins)* en la fuente *(fountain)* de la Plaza de la República y pedí un deseo.

NOTA CULTURAL

El nicaragüense **Rubén Darío** (1867-1916) es uno de los poetas más famosos de Latinoamérica. *Cantos de vida y esperanza* es una de sus obras.

4 **Oraciones** Haz cinco oraciones sobre lo que otros esperaban de ti en el pasado y cinco más sobre lo que tú esperabas de ellos. Luego, en grupos, túrnense para compartir sus propias oraciones y para transformar las oraciones de sus compañeros/as. Sigan el modelo. Answers will vary.

modelo

Estudiante 1: *Mi profesora quería que yo fuera a Granada para estudiar español.*
Estudiante 2: *Su profesora quería que él fuera a Granada para estudiar español.*
Estudiante 3: *Yo deseaba que mis padres me enviaran a España.*
Estudiante 4: *Cecilia deseaba que sus padres la enviaran a España.*

Síntesis

5 **¡Vaya fiesta!** Dos amigos/as fueron a una fiesta y se enojaron. Uno/a quería irse temprano, pero el/la otro/a quería irse más tarde porque estaba hablando con el/la chico/a que le gustaba a su amigo/a. En parejas, inventen una conversación en la que esos amigos intentan arreglar todos los malentendidos (*misunderstandings*) que tuvieron en la fiesta. Usen el pretérito imperfecto de subjuntivo y después representen la conversación delante de la clase.

modelo

Estudiante 1: *¡Yo no pensaba que fueras tan aburrido/a!*
Estudiante 2: *Yo no soy aburrido/a, sólo quería que nos fuéramos temprano.*

3 Suggestions
- Read the **modelo** aloud. Ask volunteers to give other possible responses to the prompt. Ex: **Fue estupendo que te recogieran en el aeropuerto.**
- Instead of having students compare their answers in pairs, have them do so in groups of four.

3 Expansion Ask students to find a poem by Rubén Darío and bring it to class. Or have them research the poet and **modernismo**.

4 Suggestions
- Ask four volunteers to read the **modelo.** Give your own responses to provide another example. Ex: **Mi hijo quería que le permitiera viajar solo a México.** Then have a volunteer rephrase the corresponding statement in the third person.
- Have individuals write their five sentences before dividing the class into groups of four.

5 Suggestion Ask the class to brainstorm suitable verbs for both the main and subjunctive clauses.

5 Expansion Have partners tell each other about a actual misunderstanding they had with someone. Ex: **Mi compañera de apartamento quería que yo limpiara el baño. Pero no era posible que yo lo hiciera en ese momento.** Then, have students relate their partner's story to the rest of the class.

Suggestion See the Info Gap Activities Booklet for an additional activity to practice the material presented in this section.

TEACHING OPTIONS

Extra Practice Write the following sentences on the board and ask students to complete them using the past subjunctive and the preterite. **1. Cuando era pequeño/a quería que ____, pero ____. 2. Me aconsejaron que ____, pero ____. 3. Durante mucho tiempo insistía en que ____, pero ____. 4. Siempre fue importante para mí que ____, pero ____.**

Game Divide the class into groups of four. Each group will write a description of a famous villain or group of villains using as many verbs in the past subjunctive as possible. Give the groups ten minutes to write their descriptions and ask the groups with the most verbs in the past subjunctive to read their descriptions aloud. The class will vote on the best description.

Section Goals

In **Lectura** students will:
- learn to recognize similes and metaphors
- read an excerpt from a Chilean novel

Instructional Resource
Companion website:
www.vistahigherlearning.com

Estrategia Review similes and metaphors. Then write the following sentences on the board: **Su cabello es como la seda. Sus palabras son poesía.** Ask volunteers which sentence is the simile and which is the metaphor. Ask students to make up a simile and a metaphor in Spanish and share them with the class.

Examinar el texto
- Before having students scan the text, remind them that Pablo Neruda was a Chilean poet who won the Nobel Prize for Literature in 1971. Neruda had retired to his home in Isla Negra when, in 1973, a violent coup d'état sponsored by right-wing elements of the Chilean armed forces overthrew the democratically elected government of president Salvador Allende. Neruda, a long-time member of the Communist Party, died not long after the coup.
- Students may note that the punctuation indicates that this excerpt is a dialogue.
- Point out this example of a simile in the text: **Pedalear con la bolsa sobre tu lomo es igual que cargar un elefante sobre los hombros.**

Lectura

Antes de leer

Estrategia
Recognizing similes and metaphors

Similes and metaphors are figures of speech that are often used in literature to make descriptions more colorful and vivid.

In English, a simile (**símil**) makes a comparison using the words *as* or *like*. In Spanish the words **como** and **parece** are most often used in similes. Example: **Mario estaba tan contento como un niño con zapatos nuevos.** (*Mario was as happy as a kid with new shoes.*)

A metaphor (**metáfora**) is a figure of speech that identifies one thing with the attributes and qualities of another thing. Whereas a simile says one thing is like another, a metaphor says that one thing *is* another. In Spanish, **ser** is most often used in metaphors. Example: **La vida es sueño.** (*Life is a dream.*)

Examinar el texto

Lee el texto una vez usando las estrategias de lectura de las lecciones anteriores. ¿Qué te indican sobre el contenido de la lectura? Toma nota de las metáforas y los símiles que aparecen. ¿Qué significan? ¿Qué te dicen sobre el tema de la lectura?

Contestar

1. ¿Quién es Pablo Neruda? (Ve a **Panorama** de la **Lección 9**, página 294.)
2. ¿Cuál es el significado de las siguientes oraciones?
   a. Su corazón y sus labios dijeron al unísono. —Sí.
   b. El cartero que lo atendía se jubiló jorobado como un camello.
   c. Soy de fierro.

recursos

vistahigherlearning.com

El cartero de Neruda
(un fragmento)

Antonio Skármeta

Antonio Skármeta nació en 1940 en Antofagasta (Chile). Estudió humanidades en la Universidad de Chile donde trabajó como actor y director de la compañía de teatro estudiantil CADIP. En 1975, se fue a vivir a Berlín y durante esos años fue profesor en la Academia de Artes, Cine y Televisión. Hoy día, Skármeta es conocido tanto por sus novelas y cuentos como por su labor cinematográfica. El gran éxito internacional que obtuvo la película Il Postino, *basada en su novela* El cartero de Neruda (Ardiente paciencia), *lo confirmó como uno de los escritores chilenos más célebres.*

Después de leer

Preguntas

Contesta las siguientes preguntas. Answers will vary.

1. ¿Quiénes son los personajes que hablan en este fragmento de la novela?
2. ¿Cómo son los personajes?
3. ¿Cuántos clientes va a tener el cartero? ¿Por qué?
4. ¿Es bueno el sueldo del cartero?
5. ¿Le importa a Mario el sueldo?
6. ¿Te gustaría ser el cartero de Neruda? ¿Por qué?
7. ¿Con qué persona famosa quisieras trabajar?
8. ¿Cuál es tu profesión ideal?

TEACHING OPTIONS

Pairs Ask pairs to work together to write the **anuncio** that Mario responded to. Then have them write ads for other professions, such as **chófer, actor(a), reportero/a, científico/a, arqueólogo/a, programador(a), maestro/a, abogado/a, peluquero/a, biólogo/a, escritor(a), traductor(a), cocinero/a.** Students should include details of job duties **(funciones o responsabilidades en el trabajo)**.

Extra Practice Have students research poetry by Pablo Neruda on the Internet. Encourage them to read his poetry, find their favorite poems, read them aloud, and discuss them in class.

Mario Jiménez jamás había usado corbata, pero antes de entrar se arregló el cuello de la camisa como si llevara una y trató, con algún éxito, de abreviar° con dos golpes° de peineta° su melena° heredada° de fotos de los Beatles.

—Vengo por el aviso° —declamó° al funcionario°, con una sonrisa que emulaba la de Burt Lancaster.

—¿Tiene bicicleta? —preguntó aburrido el funcionario.

Su corazón y sus labios° dijeron al unísono.

—Sí.

—Bueno —dijo el oficinista, limpiándose los lentes—, se trata de un puesto de cartero para isla Negra.

—Qué casualidad° —dijo Mario—. Yo vivo al lado, en la caleta°.

—Eso está muy bien. Pero lo que está mal es que hay un solo cliente.

—¿Uno nada más?

—Sí, pues. En la caleta todos son analfabetos°. No pueden leer ni las cuentas.

—¿Y quién es el cliente?

—Pablo Neruda.

Mario Jiménez tragó° lo que le pareció un litro de saliva.

—Pero eso es formidable.

—¿Formidable? Recibe kilos de correspondencia diariamente. Pedalear con la bolsa sobre tu lomo° es igual que cargar° un elefante sobre los hombros°. El cartero que lo atendía se jubiló jorobado° como un camello.

—Pero yo tengo sólo diecisiete años.

—¿Y estás sano?

—¿Yo? Soy de fierro°. ¡Ni un resfrío en mi vida!

El funcionario deslizó° los lentes sobre el tabique° de la nariz y lo miró por encima del marco°.

—El sueldo es una mierda°. Los otros carteros se las arreglan° con las propinas. Pero con un cliente, apenas te alcanzará° para el cine una vez por semana.

—Quiero el puesto.

—Está bien. Me llamo Cosme.

—Cosme.

—Me debes decir «don Cosme».

—Sí, don Cosme.

—Soy tu jefe.

—Sí, jefe.

El hombre levantó un bolígrafo azul, le sopló su aliento para entibiar la tinta°, y preguntó sin mirarlo.

—¿Nombre?

—Mario Jiménez —respondió Mario Jiménez solemnemente.

Y en cuanto terminó de emitir ese vital comunicado, fue hasta la ventana, desprendió° el aviso, y lo hizo recalar en lo más profundo del bolsillo trasero° de su pantalón.

abreviar *shorten* **golpes** *strokes* **peineta** *comb* **melena** *mop of hair* **heredada** *inherited* **aviso** *advertisement* **declamó** *he declaimed* **funcionario** *government employee* **labios** *lips* **casualidad** *coincidence* **caleta** *cove* **analfabetos** *illiterate* **tragó** *gulped* **lomo** *back* **cargar** *to carry* **hombros** *shoulders* **jorobado** *hunchbacked* **fierro** *iron* **deslizó** *slid* **tabique** *bridge* **marco** *frame* **una mierda** *crappy* **se las arreglan** *make it up* **alcanzará** *will be enough* **sopló su aliento para entibiar la tinta** *breathed on it to warm the ink* **desprendió** *took down* **lo hizo recalar en lo más profundo del bolsillo trasero** *stuck it in the deepest part of his back pocket*

Preguntas If students have trouble with the meaning of any word or phrase, help them identify corresponding context clues.

El diario de Mario Review the suggestions about information to include in the diary entry. You may wish to have students work in pairs to write an entry.

Terminar la historia Have heritage speakers work with those who are being exposed to Spanish for the first time. The heritage speaker can write the first paragraph.

Minidrama Give students time to write their scripts and practice their minidramas before performing them in front of the class. You may wish to create audio or video recordings of the performances.

El diario de Mario

Imagina que eres Mario Jiménez. Escribe en tu diario lo que pasó el día que conseguiste el trabajo de cartero de Pablo Neruda. Incluye la siguiente información:

- Una descripción del tipo de trabajo que buscabas
- Lo que pensabas del puesto después de leer el anuncio
- Lo que hiciste antes de la entrevista
- Una descripción de la persona que te entrevistó
- Lo que pasó durante la entrevista
- Lo que pensabas durante la entrevista
- Lo que sentías durante la entrevista
- Lo que hiciste después de la entrevista

Terminar la historia

Trabajen en grupos para escribir la continuación del fragmento de la historia "El cartero de Neruda". La primera persona escribe un párrafo y lo pasa a la próxima persona. Él/Ella añade un párrafo y así hasta terminar la historia. Incluyan todos los detalles posibles y asegúrense de que la historia sea coherente e interesante.

Minidrama

En parejas, preparen un minidrama basado en "El cartero de Neruda" y preséntenlo a la clase. Utilicen el diálogo que hay en el texto e inventen también una conversación más larga, basada en lo que saben de la personalidad de cada personaje.

TEACHING OPTIONS

Heritage Speakers Ask heritage speakers to share terms they use for *job* or *employment* and to talk briefly about how they are used and where they are used. Spanish speakers should mention that **trabajo** and **empleo** are probably the most common terms. **Oficio, ocupación,** and **profesión** are more formal. A very colloquial term used in parts of Latin America is **chamba**.

Game Have students describe the responsibilities of a particular profession. Their classmates will guess the profession they are describing.

Extra Practice Encourage students to view the video of *Il postino* (or show it in class). Encourage them to critique the film **(hacer una crítica de la película)** in Spanish.

Section Goals

In **Escritura** students will:

- learn to use note cards as a study aid
- use note cards to prepare to write a composition
- write a composition about professional and personal goals for the future

Estrategia Explain to students that using note cards in preparation for writing a composition will help greatly in organizing the information that they may want to include. Tell them they can use note cards to prepare to write the composition about their plans for the future. Suggest they use several note cards for each of the categories **(lugar, familia, empleo, finanzas, metas profesionales).** Remind them to number the cards by category.

Tema Go over the directions with the class, explaining that each student will write a composition on his or her plans for the future—professional and personal. In preparation for writing about professional goals they expect to have attained, have students review the conjugation of **haber** + [*past participle*] to form the future perfect tense.

Escritura

Estrategia

Using note cards

Note cards serve as valuable study aids in many different contexts. When you write, note cards can help you organize and sequence the information you wish to present.

Let's say you are going to write a personal narrative about a trip you took. You would jot down notes about each part of the trip on a different note card. Then you could easily arrange them in chronological order or use a different organization, such as the best parts and the worst parts, traveling and staying, before and after, etc.

Here are some helpful techniques for using note cards to prepare for your writing:

- Label the top of each card with a general subject, such as **el avión** or **el hotel.**
- Number the cards in each subject category in the upper right corner to help you organize them.
- Use only the front side of each note card so that you can easily flip through them to find information.

Study the following example of a note card used to prepare a composition:

3

En el aeropuerto de Santo Domingo

Cuando llegamos al aeropuerto de Santo Domingo, después de siete horas de viaje, estábamos cansados pero felices. Hacía sol y viento.

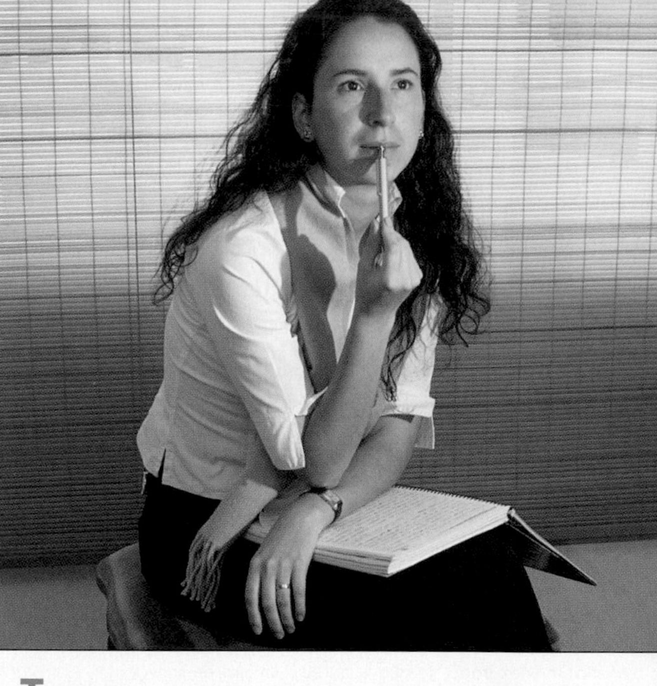

Tema

Escribir una composición

Escribe una composición sobre tus planes profesionales y personales para el futuro. Utiliza el tiempo futuro. No te olvides de hacer planes para estas áreas de tu vida:

Lugar

- ¿Dónde vivirás?
- ¿Vivirás en la misma ciudad siempre? ¿Te mudarás mucho?

Familia

- ¿Te casarás? ¿Con quién?
- ¿Tendrás hijos? ¿Cuántos?

Empleo

- ¿En qué profesión trabajarás?
- ¿Tendrás tu propia empresa?

Finanzas

- ¿Ganarás mucho dinero?
- ¿Ahorrarás mucho dinero? ¿Lo invertirás?

Termina tu composición con una lista de metas profesionales, utilizando el futuro perfecto.

Por ejemplo: **Para el año 2020, habré empezado mi propio negocio. Para el año 2030, habré ganado más dinero que Bill Gates.**

TEACHING OPTIONS

Proofreading Activity Copy on the board or onto a transparency the following items containing mistakes as a proofreading activity to do with the whole class.

1. **¡A las siete! A esa hora teneré sueño. ¿Habré café en la sala de conferencias?**
2. **Usted recibirá una yamada de parte nuestra, si decidimos ofrecerle el puesto.**
3. **Éste sará un trabajo ideal para mí. Yenaré la solicitud inmediatamente.**
4. **Me sorprendió que tú no llenaste la solicitud antes. Este proyecto le habrás interesado mucho.**
5. **El jefe izo la llamada en cuanto llegó en la oficina.**
6. **Por el año 2020 el banco haberá establecido una oficina el la luna.**

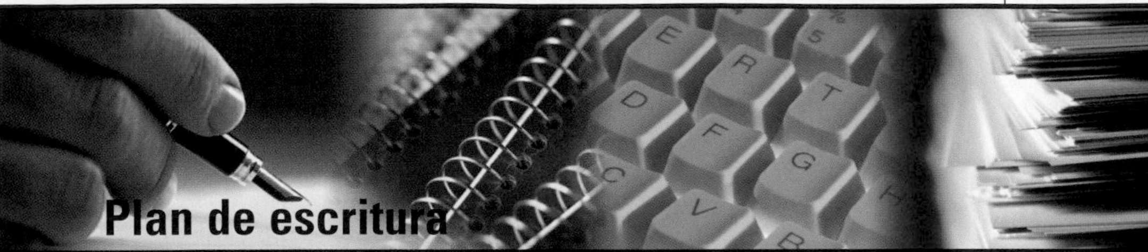

Plan de escritura

1 Ideas y organización
Utiliza unas fichas° para apuntar tus planes y metas° para el futuro. Dedica una ficha a cada plan o meta. No te olvides de asignar un año a cada meta.

2 Primer borrador
Utiliza tus apuntes de **Ideas y organización** para escribir el primer borrador de tu composición. Usa el diccionario sólo como último recurso.

3 Comentario
Intercambia tu composición con la de un(a) compañero/a. Lee su borrador y anota los aspectos mejor escritos de su composición. Compartan sus impresiones utilizando esta guía:

a. ¿Habla de metas específicas para su futuro?
b. ¿Ha organizado su información de una manera lógica?
c. ¿Qué sugerencias puedes darle al/a la escritor(a) para organizar mejor su descripción?
d. ¿Encuentras errores gramaticales u ortográficos?

4 Redacción
Revisa el primer borrador según las indicaciones de tu compañero/a. Antes de escribir tu versión final, revisa tu composición según la siguiente guía:

a. Subraya° cada verbo para comprobar el modo y el tiempo. Recuerda que el tema requiere el uso del futuro y del futuro perfecto.
b. Revisa la concordancia entre los sustantivos y los adjetivos en cada oración.
c. Revisa los pronombres para comprobar el uso correcto de cada uno.
d. Consulta tus **Anotaciones para mejorar la escritura** para evitar la repetición de errores previos.

5 Evaluación y progreso
Compartan su trabajo en grupos. Cada estudiante leerá su composición al grupo. Después, formulen una cronología° con las metas de cada estudiante. Cuando recibas los comentarios y las correcciones de tu profesor(a), anota tus errores en las **Anotaciones para mejorar la escritura** en tu **Carpeta de trabajos.**

fichas *note cards* metas *goals* Subraya *underline* cronología *timeline*

Comentario
- Go over guide questions a–d with the whole class so peer readers understand their task.
- Have students prepare **Redacción** as homework. Ask them to rewrite their drafts, incorporating the peer comments and following the directions in **Redacción**.

Evaluación y progreso Allow sufficient time for students to read their final drafts in groups.

Writing Sample Here is a sample composition that would constitute superior writing achievement.

Mi futuro

Después de graduarme, me mudaré a una ciudad grande que esté cerca del mar. Viviré al lado del mar por unos diez años y después me mudaré a un sitio en las montañas.

Estudio biología marina, así que el vivir al lado del mar tendrá sus ventajas. Trabajaré como ecóloga marina porque creo que es importante conservar los océanos, los lagos y los ríos. En cuanto pueda obtener el dinero necesario, estableceré mi propio laboratorio donde podré dedicarme a cualquier investigación que me interese. Habrá que hacer sacrificios, pero invertiré todo el dinero posible para poder jubilarme temprano.

Claro que tendré una familia también. Me casaré con mi mejor amigo. Después de cinco años, adoptaremos a dos niños.

Metas profesionales:
Para el año 2005, habré trabajado en tres proyectos. Para el año 2007, habré escrito un libro de texto sobre la ecología marina.

Para el año 2010, seré conocida como ecóloga famosa y habré conseguido mi propio laboratorio.

EVALUATION: Composición

Criteria	Scale
Content	1 2 3 4
Organization	1 2 3 4
Use of vocabulary	1 2 3 4
Accuracy and mechanics	1 2 3 4
Creativity	1 2 3 4

Scoring	
Excellent	18–20 points
Good	14–17 points
Satisfactory	10–13 points
Unsatisfactory	< 10 points

Section Goals

In **Escuchar** students will:

- use background knowledge and listen for specific information
- answer questions based on a recorded conversation

Instructional Resources
Textbook CD
IRM: Tapescript, p. 100

Estrategia
Script ¿Sufre usted de muchas tensiones? Con sólo una semana en el hotel El Retiro, usted podrá aliviar su estrés. Venga y disfrute de los espectaculares bosques que lo rodean, las habitaciones modernas y elegantes y las comidas sabrosas preparadas según su dieta. Además de los maravillosos baños térmicos volcánicos, se ofrecen masajes y sauna. El Retiro queda a 100 km de San José en un lugar que le traerá el descanso y la paz que usted necesita. Llame al 451-2356 para recibir más información.

Suggestion Have students say what they see in the photo.

Ahora escucha
Script SRA. SÁNCHEZ: Buenos días. Usted es Rafael Ventura Romero, ¿no? Soy la señora Sánchez, la jefa de esta compañía. Siéntese, por favor. • RAFAEL VENTURA: Buenos días, señora. Estoy muy agradecido de tener esta oportunidad de hablar con usted hoy. • S: Veo aquí que está solicitando el puesto de contador general. ¿Qué preparación tiene usted? • V: En diciembre me gradúo de contador en la Universidad Politécnica de Nicaragua. Durante los últimos tres años he trabajado en Dulces González aquí en Managua como contador durante las vacaciones. Es la carrera que siempre he querido y sé que voy a tener éxito si usted me da la oportunidad. • S: ¿Tiene usted algunas referencias? • V: Sí, señora. El gerente de la empresa donde he trabajado, el señor Héctor Cruz, y también el Profesor Armando Carreño de la Facultad de Contaduría Pública y Finanzas. Los teléfonos y direcciones están apuntados en el currículum. • S: Muy bien. Este puesto comienza con un salario mensual de 25.812 córdobas. Después de seis meses tiene la posibilidad de un aumento de sueldo. Ofrecemos beneficios excelentes. El horario es de 8:30 a 12:00 y de 2:00 a 6:00. ¿Está interesado? • V: Estoy sumamente interesado. • S: Pues, necesito unos días para comunicarme con las personas que usted ha dado de referencia. Si todo sale bien, lo llamaré antes del viernes. ¿Cuándo está dispuesto a comenzar a trabajar? Necesito a alguien lo más pronto posible. • V: No me gradúo hasta el 15 de diciembre. Pero puedo trabajar media jornada por las siguientes tres semanas hasta la graduación. • S: Creo que no va a haber ningún problema con eso. Entonces hablamos en unos días. • V: Muchas gracias por la entrevista, señora Sánchez. Estoy muy emocionado por la posibilidad de trabajar en esta gran empresa. Que tenga muy buen día.

Escuchar

Estrategia

Using background knowledge/ Listening for specific information

If you know the subject of something you are going to hear, your background knowledge will help you anticipate words and phrases you're going to hear, and will help you identify important information that you should listen for.

To practice these strategies, you will listen to a radio advertisement for the **Hotel El Retiro**. Before you listen, write down a list of the things you expect the advertisement to contain. Then make another list of important information you would listen for if you were a tourist considering staying at the hotel. After listening to the advertisement, look at your lists again. Did they help you anticipate the content of the advertisement and focus on key information? Explain your answer.

Preparación

Mira la foto. ¿De qué crees que van a hablar? Haz una lista de la información que esperas oír en este tipo de situación.

Ahora escucha 

Ahora vas a oír una entrevista entre la señora Sánchez y Rafael Ventura Romero. Antes de escuchar la entrevista, haz una lista de la información que esperas oír según tu conocimiento previo° del tema.

1. ____________
2. ____________
3. ____________
4. ____________

Mientras escuchas la entrevista, llena el formulario con la información necesaria. Si no oyes un dato° que necesitas, escribe *Buscar en el currículum*. ¿Oíste toda la información que habías anotado en tu lista?

Comprensión

Puesto solicitado contador
Nombre y apellidos del solicitante Rafael Ventura Romero
Dirección Buscar en el currículum **Tel.** Buscar en el currículum

Educación Universidad Politécnica de Nicaragua
Experiencia profesional: Puesto contador
Empresa Dulces González
¿Cuánto tiempo? 3 años durante las vacaciones de la universidad

Referencias:
Nombre Héctor Cruz
Dirección Buscar en el currículum Tel. Buscar en el currículum
Nombre Prof. Armando Carreño
Dirección Buscar en el currículum Tel. Buscar en el currículum

Preguntas

1. ¿Cuántos años hace que Rafael Ventura trabaja para Dulces González? tres años, durante las vacaciones
2. ¿Cuántas referencias tiene Rafael? dos
3. ¿Cuándo se gradúa Rafael? el 15 de diciembre
4. ¿Cuál es la profesión de Armando Carreño? es profesor
5. ¿Cómo sabes si los resultados de la entrevista han sido positivos para Rafael Ventura?
Los resultados fueron positivos porque la jefa quiere que él empiece a trabajar antes de que se gradúe.

conocimiento previo *prior knowledge* dato *fact, piece of information*

recursos
TEXT CD
Lección 16

Escribe una cronología° de tu carrera

Imagina que en el futuro trabajarás para una empresa multinacional que tiene sus oficinas más importantes en Nicaragua o en la República Dominicana. Vas a crear un plan o una cronología para tu futura carrera profesional.

1 Desarrolla una cronología

Prepara una cronología con texto y fotos de tu futura carrera. Usa los **Recursos para la investigación** para buscar información sobre industrias y compañías que operen en Nicaragua o en la República Dominicana. La cronología puede incluir las siguientes cosas:

- Una descripción de la empresa y sus productos
- Fotos relacionadas con la empresa y sus productos
- Una descripción de tu carrera, desde el comienzo hasta tu jubilación°, incluyendo los puestos que vas a tener en la empresa
- Fotos relacionadas con tu carrera

2 Presenta la información

Reúnete con un(a) compañero/a para explicarle tus planes para el porvenir. Usa la cronología que preparaste y muéstrale las fotos para informarle de tus planes para tu vida profesional.

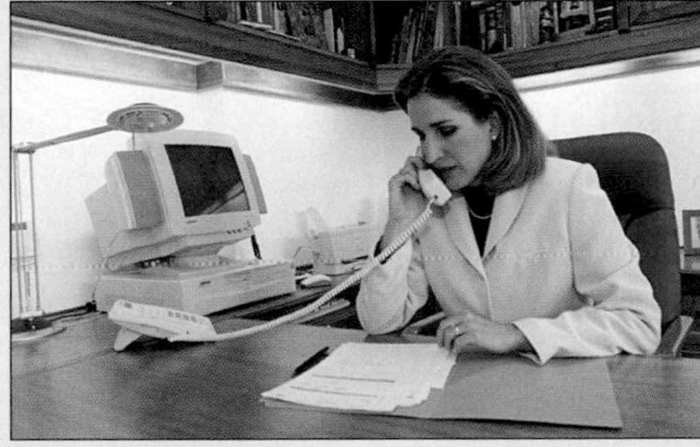

recursos para la investigación

Internet Palabras clave: Nicaragua, República Dominicana, empresa, industria, compañía multinacional

Comunidad Personas en la comunidad que han trabajado en Centroamérica o en el Caribe

Biblioteca Revistas, periódicos, libros de economía y de comercio

Otros recursos Investigar las industrias y empresas principales de Nicaragua y de la República Dominicana

cronología *timeline* **jubilación** *retirement*

Section Goals

In **Proyecto** students will:
- use Spanish as they research multinational companies
- develop a career plan or timeline for a position at a multinational company with headquarters in Nicaragua or the Dominican Republic

Suggestion Students might need a week to complete the project, so at the beginning of that time period, have them open their books to this page and glance over **Proyecto**. Tell them that they are going to use their Spanish skills as they conduct research on multinational companies with headquarters (**sede**) in Nicaragua or the Dominican Republic. Tell them that when they finish their research, they will develop a career plan from start date to retirement.

Desarrolla una cronología
- Students may wish to interview someone who works for a multinational company and may live in a Spanish-speaking country.
- If possible, provide students with articles or press releases written in Spanish about multinational companies and their products.
- Possible industries for Nicaragua include: **café, mariscos, plátanos, carne, petróleo**. Possible industries for the Dominican Republic include: **turismo, azúcar, minería de oro, cemento**.

Presenta la información
You may wish to have students present the timelines as though they were viewing a career history at a retirement party.

Successful Language Learning
Tell students they may want to consider study-abroad programs and internship opportunities in Spanish-speaking countries. Ask them if they would feel comfortable doing so, and why.

EVALUATION: Cronología

Criteria	Scale
Content	1 2 3 4 5
Organization	1 2 3 4 5
Accuracy	1 2 3 4 5
Creativity	1 2 3 4 5

Scoring	
Excellent	18–20 points
Good	14–17 points
Satisfactory	10–13 points
Unsatisfactory	< 10 points

Section Goal

In **Panorama**, students will read about the history and culture of Nicaragua.

Instructional Resources
Transparencies, #3, #4, #57
WB/VM: Workbook, p. 189;
Video Activities, pp. 279–280
***Panorama cultural** DVD/Video*
Interactive CD-ROM
IRM: Videoscript, p. 135
Companion website:
www.vistahigherlearning.com
Presentations CD-ROM

Suggestion Have students look at the map of Nicaragua or project **Transparency #57** and talk about the physical features of the country. Point out the concentration of cities along the country's Pacific Coast, and note the sparse settlement in the eastern part of the country and along the Caribbean coast. Remind students that before the construction of the Panama Canal, Nicaragua was the proposed site for an interoceanic canal.

El país en cifras After reading about the country's varied terrain and many volcanoes, tell students that Nicaragua's national slogan is **"El país de lagos y volcanes."** After students read about the capital, ask: **¿Qué porcentaje de nicaragüenses vive en Managua? (el 20%)** Tell students that one reason so many Nicaraguans live in the capital is due to the devastation experienced in much of the rest of the country over the past two decades due to war and natural disasters, such as Hurricane Mitch in 1998, and earthquakes and volcanic eruptions in 1999.

¡Increíble pero cierto! Lake Nicaragua is the largest lake in Central America. Over 40 rivers drain into the lake.

Nicaragua

National Standards: connections, cultures

El país en cifras

- **Área:** 129.494 km² (49.998 millas²), *aproximadamente el área de Nueva York*
  Nicaragua es el país más grande de Centroamérica. Su terreno es muy variado e incluye bosques tropicales, montañas, sabanas° y marismas°, además de unos 40 volcanes.
- **Población:** 5.359.000
- **Capital:** Managua—1.166.000
  Managua está en una región de una notable inestabilidad geográfica, con muchos volcanes y terremotos°. En décadas recientes, los nicaragüenses han decidido que no vale la pena° construir rascacielos° porque no resisten los terremotos.
- **Ciudades principales:** León—249.000, Masaya—149.000, Granada—113.000

SOURCE: Population Division, UN Secretariat

- **Moneda:** córdoba
- **Idiomas:** español (oficial), misquito, inglés

Bandera de Nicaragua

Nicaragüenses célebres

- **Rubén Darío,** poeta (1867–1916)
- **Violeta Barrios de Chamorro,** política y ex-presidenta (1930–)
- **Daniel Ortega,** político y ex-presidente (1945–)
- **Gioconda Belli,** poeta (1948–)

Pintada° en una pared de Managua

Típico hogar misquito en la costa atlántica

Río Coco
HONDURAS
Cordillera Isabelia
Saslaya
Chachagón
Piu
Río Tuma
Río Grande
Cordillera Darience
Sierra Madre
León
Océano Pacífico
Lago de Managua
Managua
Lago Nicaragua
Masaya
Granada
Isla Zapatera
Concepción
Maderas
Isla Ometepe
Archipiélago Solentiname
Río San Juan
COSTA RICA
ESTADOS UNIDOS
OCÉANO ATLÁNTICO
NICARAGUA
OCÉANO PACÍFICO
AMÉRICA DEL SUR

Violeta Barrios de Chamorro

recursos

WB pp. 189–190	VM pp. 279–280	I CD-ROM Lección 16	vistahigherlearning.com

sabanas *grasslands* marismas *marshes* pintada *political graffiti* terremoto *earthquake* no vale la pena *it's not worthwhile* rascacielos *skyscrapers* tiburón *shark* agua dulce *freshwater* bahía *bay* fue cercada *was closed off* atunes *tuna*

¡Increíble pero cierto!

En el lago Nicaragua está la única especie de tiburón° de agua dulce° del mundo. Los científicos creen que el lago fue antes una enorme bahía° que luego fue cercada° por erupciones volcánicas. Esta teoría explicaría la presencia de tiburones, atunes° y otras especies de peces que normalmente sólo viven en mares y océanos.

TEACHING OPTIONS

Worth Noting Managua is a city that has been destroyed and rebuilt multiple times due to wars and natural disasters. This has contributed to the unusual method used for listing street addresses in this capital city. Many places do not have an address that includes an actual building number and street name. Instead, the address includes a reference to a local landmark, and its relationship to other permanent features of the landscape, such as Lake Managua. Here's a typical Managua address: **De la Clínica Don Bosco, 2 cuadras al norte, 3 y media al sur.** Invite students who have lived in Managua to share other "typical" addresses.

Extra Practice Invite students to compare the romantic poetry of Rubén Darío to the contemporary work of Ernesto Cardenal and Gioconda Belli. Students can choose several poems to read aloud to the class, and then comment on differences in style and content.

Historia • Las huellas° de Acahualinca

La región de Managua se caracteriza por tener un gran número de sitios prehistóricos. Las huellas de Acahualinca son uno de los restos° más famosos y antiguos°. Se formaron hace más de 6.000 años, a orillas° del lago Managua. Las huellas, tanto de humanos como de animales, se dirigen° hacia una misma dirección, lo que ha hecho pensar a los expertos que éstos corrían hacia el lago para escapar de una erupción volcánica.

Artes • Ernesto Cardenal (1925-)

Ernesto Cardenal, poeta, escultor y sacerdote° católico, es uno de los escritores más famosos de Nicaragua, país conocido por sus grandes poetas. Ha escrito más de 35 libros y se le considera uno de los principales autores de Latinoamérica. Desde joven creyó en el poder de la poesía para mejorar la sociedad, y trabajó por establecer la igualdad y la justicia en su país. En los años 60, Cardenal estableció la comunidad artística del archipiélago Solentiname en el lago Nicaragua. Fue ministro de cultura del país desde 1979 hasta 1988, y también ha servido como vicepresidente de Casa de los Tres Mundos, una organización creada para el intercambio cultural internacional.

Naturaleza • El lago Nicaragua

El lago Nicaragua, con un área de más de 8.000 km^2 (3.100 $millas^2$), es el lago más grande de Centroamérica. Dentro del lago hay más de 370 islas, formadas por las erupciones del volcán Mombacho. La isla Zapatera, casi deshabitada ahora, fue un cementerio° indígena donde todavía se encuentran estatuas prehistóricas que parecen representar dioses. En el lago tambien se encuentran muchos peces exóticos.

¿Qué aprendiste? Responde a las preguntas con una frase completa.

1. ¿Por qué no hay muchos rascacielos en Managua?
   No hay muchos rascacielos en Managua porque no resisten los terremotos.
2. Nombra dos ex-presidentes de Nicaragua.
   Violeta Barrios de Chamorro y Daniel Ortega son dos ex-presidentes de Nicaragua.
3. ¿Qué especie única vive en el lago Nicaragua?
   La única especie de tiburón de agua dulce vive en el lago Nicaragua.
4. ¿Cuál es una de las teorías sobre la formación de las huellas de Acahualinca?
   Una teoría dice que las personas y los animales corrían para escapar de la erupción del volcán.
5. ¿Por qué es famoso el archipiélago Solentiname?
   El archipiélago Solentiname es famoso porque es el sitio de la comunidad artística establecida por Cardenal.
6. ¿Qué cree Ernesto Cardenal acerca de la poesía?
   Cardenal cree que la poesía puede mejorar la sociedad.
7. ¿Cómo se formaron las islas del lago Nicaragua?
   Las islas se formaron por erupciones volcánicas.
8. ¿Qué hay de interés arqueológico en la isla Zapatera?
   En la isla Zapatera existió un cementerio indígena en que todavía se encuentran estatuas prehistóricas.

Conexión Internet Investiga estos temas en el sitio **www.vistahigherlearning.com.**

1. ¿Dónde se habla inglés en Nicaragua y por qué?
2. ¿Qué información hay ahora sobre la economía y/o los derechos humanos en Nicaragua?

huellas *footprints* restos *remains* antiguos *ancient* orillas *shores* se dirigen *are headed* sacerdote *priest* cementerio *cemetery*

Las huellas de Acahualinca The **huellas de Acahualinca** were preserved in soft mud that was then covered with volcanic ash which became petrified, preserving the prints of bison, otter, deer, lizards, and birds—as well as humans.

Ernesto Cardenal After completing undergraduate studies in Nicaragua, **Ernesto Cardenal** studied in Mexico and in the United States, where he studied with religious poet Thomas Merton at the Trappist seminary in Kentucky. He later studied theology in Colombia, and was ordained in Nicaragua in 1965. It was shortly after that he founded the faith-based community of artists on **Solentiname** in **Lago Nicaragua.**

El lago Nicaragua Environmental groups in Nicaragua have been concerned about the recent introduction of a variety of **tilapia** into Lake Nicaragua. Although **tilapia** are native to the lake, this variety is a more prolific species. Environmentalists are concerned that the Nicaraguan-Norwegian joint venture responsible for this initiative has not done an adequate environmental impact study, and that the delicate and unique ecology of the lake may be negatively impacted.

Conexión Internet Students will find supporting Internet activities and links at **www.vistahigherlearning.com**.

TEACHING OPTIONS

Worth Noting On July 19, 1979, the FSLN (Frente Sandinista de Liberación Nacional), known as the Sandinistas, came to power in Nicaragua after winning a revolutionary struggle against the dictatorship of Anastasio Somoza. The Sandinistas began a program of economic and social reform that threatened the power of Nicaragua's traditional elite, leading to a civil war known as the **Contra** war. The United States became enmeshed in this conflict, illegally providing funding and arms to the **Contras**, who fought to oust the Sandinistas. The Sandinistas were ultimately voted out of power in 1990.

Section Goal

In **Panorama**, students will read about the geography and culture of the Dominican Republic.

Instructional Resources
Transparencies, #3, #4, #58
WB/VM: Workbook, p. 190; Video Activities, pp. 281–282
***Panorama cultural** DVD/Video*
Interactive CD-ROM
IRM: Videoscript, p. 135
Companion website: www.vistahigherlearning.com
Presentations CD-ROM

Suggestion Have students look at the map of the Dominican Republic or project **Transparency #58** and talk about the physical features of the country. Ask students to note that the majority of cities are located along the coast or close to it, and that there are few cities in the center of the island. Point out that there are rugged mountains through the center of the country, with fertile valleys interspersed.

El país en cifras After reading **Población**, point out to students that the neighboring country of Haiti is one of the poorest in Latin America and the Caribbean. Ask students to speculate about how that might impact the Dominican Republic. After reading **Idiomas**, the information that Kreyol is widely spoken should confirm that there is a major Haitian presence in the Dominican Republic.

¡Increíble pero cierto! The actual whereabouts of the remains of Christopher Columbus are a matter of dispute. While Santo Domingo claims to house them, the navigator died in Spain and there is an elaborate tomb said to be his in the Cathedral of Seville.

La República Dominicana

NATIONAL STANDARDS connections cultures

El país en cifras

- **Área:** 48.730 km² (18.815 millas²), *el área combinada de New Hampshire y Vermont*
- **Población:** 8.752.000

La isla La Española, llamada así tras° el primer viaje de Cristóbal Colón, estuvo bajo el completo dominio de la corona° española hasta 1697, cuando la parte oeste de la isla pasó a ser propiedad° francesa. Hoy día está dividida políticamente en dos países, La República Dominicana en la zona este y Haití en el oeste.

SOURCE: Population Division, UN Secretariat

- **Capital:** Santo Domingo—2.889.000

La mitad° de la población de la República Dominicana vive en la capital.

- **Ciudades principales:** Santiago de los Caballeros—1.632.000, La Vega—335.000, Puerto Plata—255.000, San Pedro de Macorís—213.000
- **Moneda:** peso dominicano
- **Idiomas:** español (oficial), criollo haitiano

Bandera de la República Dominicana

Dominicanos célebres

- **Juan Pablo Duarte,** político y padre de la patria° (1808–1876)
- **Celeste Woss y Gil,** pintora (1891–1985)
- **Juan Luis Guerra,** compositor y cantante de merengue (1956–)

tras *after* corona *crown* propiedad *property* mitad *half* padre de la patria *founding father* fortaleza *fortress* se construyó *was built* naufragó *shipwrecked* enterrado *buried*

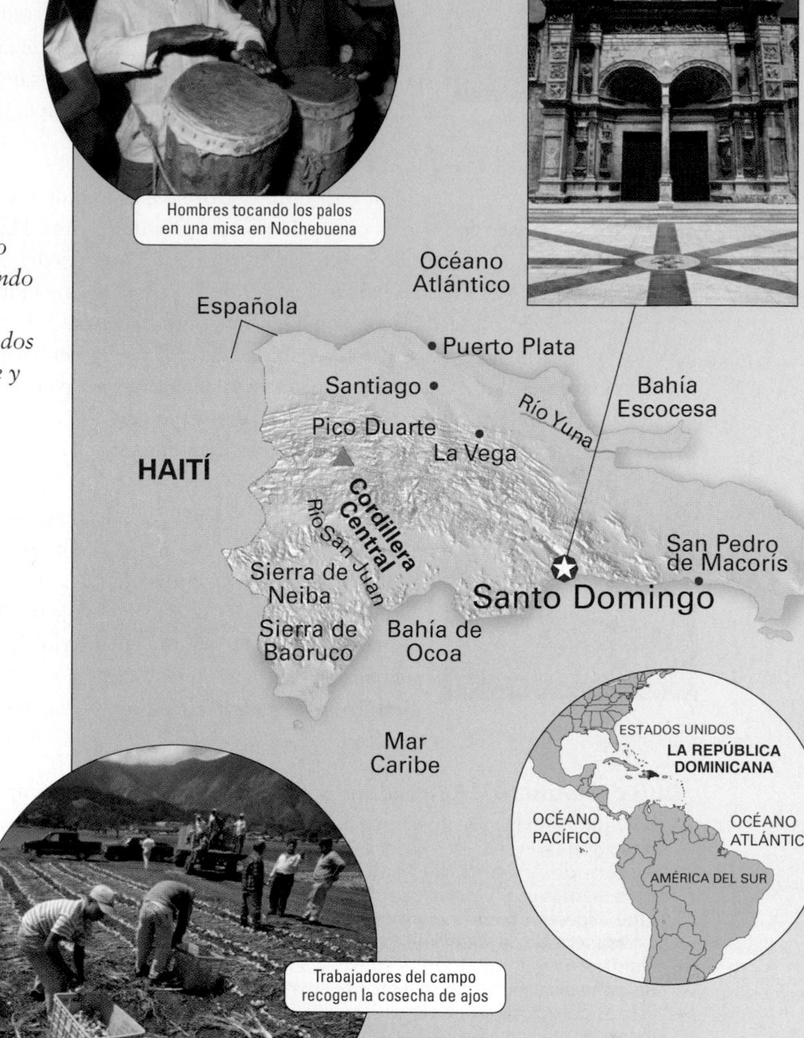

Hombres tocando los palos en una misa en Nochebuena

Catedral de Santa María la Menor

Trabajadores del campo recogen la cosecha de ajos

recursos

WB pp. 189–190	VM pp. 281–282	I CD-ROM Lección 16	vistahigher learning.com

¡Increíble pero cierto!

La primera fortaleza° del Nuevo Mundo se construyó° en la República Dominicana en 1492 cuando la Santa María, uno de los tres barcos de Cristóbal Colón, naufragó° allí. Aunque la fortaleza, hecha con los restos del barco, fue destruida por tribus indígenas, el amor de Colón por la isla nunca murió. Colón insistió en ser enterrado° allí.

TEACHING OPTIONS

Variación léxica Although the Arawak and Taíno people who were indigenous to Hispaniola were virtually eliminated following the European conquest, Caribbean Spanish continues to be marked by lexical items contributed by these cultures. Point out these words of Native American origin that have entered Spanish: **ají, cacique, canoa, hamaca, huracán** *(chili pepper, political leader, canoe, hammock, hurricane).*

Extra Practice Bring in recordings by Juan Luis Guerra, such as his 1998 release ***Ni es lo mismo ni es igual.*** Invite students to follow the printed lyrics as they listen to a track such as **"Mi PC."** Then, have students work together to create an English translation of the song.

Ciudades • Santo Domingo

La zona colonial de Santo Domingo, fundada en 1496, posee° algunas de las construcciones más antiguas del hemisferio. Gracias a las restauraciones°, la arquitectura de la ciudad es famosa no sólo por su belleza sino también por el buen estado de sus edificios. Entre sus sitios más visitados se cuentan° la Calle de las Damas, llamada así porque allí paseaban las señoras de la corte del Virrey; el Alcázar de Colón, un palacio construido por Diego Colón, hijo de Cristóbal, en 1509; y la Fortaleza Ozama, la más vieja de las Américas, construida en 1503.

Deportes • El béisbol

El béisbol es un deporte muy practicado en el Caribe. Los primeros países hispanos en tener una liga fueron Cuba y México, donde se empezó a jugar al béisbol en el siglo° XIX. Hoy día este deporte es una afición° nacional en la República Dominicana. Pedro Martínez y Manny Ramírez son sólo dos de los muchísimos beisbolistas dominicanos que han alcanzado° enorme éxito e inmensa popularidad entre los aficionados.

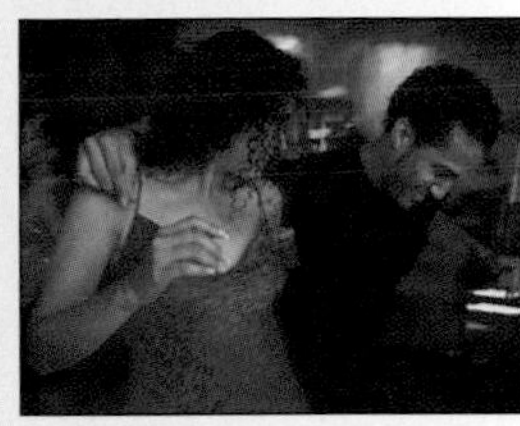

Artes • El merengue

El merengue, una música para bailar originaria de la República Dominicana, tiene sus raíces° en el campo. Tradicionalmente las canciones hablaban de los problemas sociales de los campesinos°. Sus instrumentos eran el acordeón, el saxofón, el bajo°, el guayano° y la tambora, un tambor° característico del lugar. Entre 1930 y 1960, el merengue se popularizó en las ciudades y adoptó un tono más urbano. En este período empezaron a formarse grandes orquestas. Uno de los cantantes más famosos y que más ha ayudado a internacionalizar esta música es Juan Luis Guerra.

¿Qué aprendiste? Responde a las preguntas con una frase completa.

1. Aproximadamente ¿qué porcentaje de la población vive en la capital?
   Aproximadamente el 50 por ciento de la población vive en la capital.
2. ¿Cuándo se fundó la ciudad de Santo Domingo?
   Santo Domingo se fundó en 1496.
3. ¿Qué es el Alcázar de Colón?
   El Alcázar de Colón es un palacio construido por Diego Colón, hijo de Cristóbal, en 1509.
4. Nombra dos beisbolistas famosos de la República Dominicana.
   Dos beisbolistas famosos de La República Dominicana son Pedro Martínez y Manny Ramírez.
5. ¿De qué hablaban las canciones de merengue tradicionales?
   Las canciones de merengue tradicionales hablaban de los problemas sociales de los campesinos.
6. ¿Qué instrumentos se utilizaban para tocar (*play*) el merengue?
   Se utilizaban el acordeón, el saxofón, el bajo, el guayano y/o la tambora.
7. ¿Cuándo se transformó el merengue en un estilo urbano?
   El merengue se transformó en un estilo urbano entre los años 30 y 60.
8. ¿Qué cantante ha ayudado a internacionalizar el merengue?
   Juan Luis Guerra ha ayudado a internacionalizar el merengue.

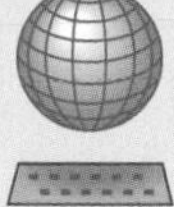

Conexión Internet Investiga estos temas en el sitio **www.vistahigherlearning.com.**

1. Busca más información sobre la isla La Española. ¿Cómo son las relaciones entre la República Dominicana y Haití?
2. Busca más información sobre la zona colonial de Santo Domingo: la Catedral de Santa María, la Casa de Bastidas o el Panteón Nacional. ¿Cómo son estos edificios? ¿Te gustan? Explica tus respuestas.

posee *possesses* restauraciones *restorations* se cuentan *are included* siglo *century* afición *love* han alcanzado *have reached*
raíces *roots* campesinos *rural people* bajo *bass* guayano *metal scraper* tambor *drum*

Santo Domingo UNESCO has declared Santo Domingo a World Heritage site because of the abundance of historical architecture. Efforts are being made to restore buildings to their original grandeur, and to "correct" restorations made in the past that were not true to original architectural styles.

El béisbol Like many other Dominicans, baseball player Sammy Sosa's first baseball glove was a milk carton, his bat was a stick, and the ball was a rolled-up sock wound with tape. Sosa has not forgotten the difficult conditions experienced by most Dominicans. After a devastating hurricane swept the island, Sosa's charitable foundation raised $700,000 for reconstruction.

El merengue The **merengue** synthesizes elements of the cultures that make up the Dominican Republic's heritage. The gourd scraper—or **güiro**—comes from the Arawak people, the **tambora**—a drum unique to the Dominican Republic—is part of the nation's African legacy, the stringed instruments were adapted from the Spanish guitar, and the accordion was introduced by German merchants. Once students hear this quick-paced music, they will understand how it came to be named after meringue—a dessert made by furiously beating egg whites!

Conexión Internet Students will find supporting Internet activities and links at **www.vistahigherlearning.com**.

TEACHING OPTIONS

Worth Noting Students may enjoy learning more about Latin American baseball. They can check out reports of Caribbean League baseball games on the Internet, with accounts of games by Dominican, Cuban, Venezuelan, and other teams. Encourage students to create a bilingual dictionary of baseball terms such as **jardinero, jardín, cuadrangular, jonrón, bateo, pitcheo, anotar carreras, ponchar, la goma, montículo,** and so forth. Encourage sports fans to help you identify Latin Americans currently playing in the Major Leagues.

Instructional Resources
Vocabulary CD
Lab Manual, p. 95
Lab CD/MP3 ***Lección 16***
IRM: Tapescript, pp. 71–75
Testing Program: ***Pruebas****, pp. 181–192*
Testing Program Audio CD
Test Files CD-ROM

Las ocupaciones

el/la abogado/a	*lawyer*
el actor, la actriz	*actor*
el/la arqueólogo/a	*archaeologist*
el/la arquitecto/a	*architect*
el/la bombero/a	*firefighter*
el/la carpintero/a	*carpenter*
el/la científico/a	*scientist*
el/la cocinero/a	*cook; chef*
el/la consejero/a	*counselor; advisor*
el/la contador(a)	*accountant*
el/la corredor(a) de bolsa	*stockbroker*
el/la diseñador(a)	*designer*
el/la electricista	*electrician*
el hombre/la mujer de negocios	*businessperson*
el/la maestro/a	*teacher*
el/la peluquero/a	*hairdresser*
el/la pintor(a)	*painter*
el/la político/a	*politician*
el/la psicólogo/a	*psychologist*
el/la reportero/a	*reporter; journalist*
el/la secretario/a	*secretary*
el/la técnico/a	*technician*

La entrevista

el anuncio	*advertisement*
el/la aspirante	*candidate; applicant*
los beneficios	*benefits*
el currículum	*résumé*
la entrevista	*interview*
el/la entrevistador(a)	*interviewer*
el puesto	*position; job*
el salario, el sueldo	*salary*
la solicitud (de trabajo)	*(job) application*
contratar	*to hire*
entrevistar	*to interview*
ganar	*to earn*
obtener	*to obtain; to get*
solicitar	*to apply (for a job)*

El mundo del trabajo

el ascenso	*promotion*
el aumento de sueldo	*raise*
la carrera	*career*
la compañía, la empresa	*company; firm*
el empleo	*job; employment*
el/la gerente	*manager*
el/la jefe/a	*boss*
los negocios	*business; commerce*
la ocupación	*occupation*
el oficio	*trade*
la profesión	*profession*
la reunión	*meeting*
el teletrabajo	*telecommuting*
el trabajo	*job; work*
la videoconferencia	*videoconference*
dejar	*to quit; to leave behind*
despedir (e:i)	*to fire*
invertir (e:ie)	*to invest*
renunciar (a)	*to resign (from)*
tener éxito	*to be successful*
comercial	*commercial; business-related*

Palabras adicionales

dentro de (diez años)	*within (ten years)*
en el futuro	*in the future*
el porvenir	*the future*
próximo/a	*next*

Expresiones útiles

Expresiones útiles	*See page 487.*

recursos

LM p. 95	Lab CD/MP3 Lección 16	Vocab CD Lección 16

Un festival de arte 17

Communicative Goals

You will learn how to:

- Talk about and discuss the arts
- Express what you would like to do
- Express hesitation

A PRIMERA VISTA
- *¿Estará trabajando el hombre de la foto?*
- *¿Es artista o arquitecto?*
- *¿Tendrá un oficio?*
- *¿Será una persona creativa o no?*

Lesson Goals

In **Lección 17** students will be introduced to the following:
- fine arts terms
- vocabulary for television and film
- conditional tense
- conditional perfect tense
- past perfect subjunctive tense
- summarizing a text in their own words
- finding biographical information
- writing a composition
- listening for key words and using context
- writing a report on Salvadoran and Honduran artists
- cultural and geographic information about El Salvador
- cultural, economic, and historical information about Honduras

A primera vista Here are some additional questions you can ask based on the photo: **¿En el futuro, tendrás un trabajo creativo? Explica tu respuesta. ¿Te interesa el arte? ¿Quién es tu artista favorito? Para el año que viene, ¿habrás visitado algunos museos de arte? ¿Cuáles? ¿Vas mucho al cine? ¿Cuál es tu película favorita?**

INSTRUCTIONAL RESOURCES

Workbook/Video Manual: WB Activities, pp. 191–200
Laboratory Manual: Lab Activities, pp. 97–101
Workbook/Video Manual: Video Activities, pp. 245–246; pp. 283–286
Instructor's Resource Manual: **Hojas de actividades**, pp. 174–176; **Vocabulario adicional**, p. 195; **¡Inténtalo!** & **Práctica** Answers, p. 223; **Fotonovela** Translations, p. 148; Textbook CD Tapescript, p. 101; Lab CDs Tapescript, pp. 76–79; **Fotonovela** Videoscript, p. 124; **Panorama cultural** Videoscript, p. 136
Info Gap Activities Booklet, pp. 65–68
Overhead Transparencies: #3, #4, #59, #60, #61
Lab Audio CD/MP3 **Lección 17**
Panorama cultural DVD/Video
Fotonovela DVD/Video
Testing Program, pp. 193–204
Testing Program Audio CD
Test Files CD-ROM
Companion website
Presentations CD-ROM
Textbook CD
Vocabulary CD
Interactive CD-ROM
Video CD-ROM
Web-SAM

Section Goals

In **Contextos**, students will learn vocabulary related to
- fine arts
- television and film

Instructional Resources
Transparency #59
Textbook CD
Vocabulary CD
WB/VM: Workbook, pp. 191–192
Lab Manual, p. 97
Lab CD/MP3 ***Lección 17***
IRM: ***Vocab. adicional****, p. 195;* ***Práctica*** *Answers, p. 223;*
Tapescript, pp. 76–79; p. 101
Info Gap Activities Booklet, pp. 65–66
Interactive CD-ROM
Companion website: www.vistahigherlearning.com
Presentations CD-ROM

Suggestions

- Begin a conversation by telling the class about some of your favorite artists and why you like them. Write unfamiliar vocabulary on the board as you use it. Ex: **¿Tienen ustedes un pintor favorito? A mí, Pablo Picasso me fascina. Pintaba de una manera muy original.** Be sure to mention singers, bands, and actors in the conversation. Tell students that they are going to learn vocabulary related to the arts.
- Project **Transparency #59**. Point to an object or person on the transparency and ask students to name it. When you point to a person, ask what he or she is doing. As you go through the items depicted, ask students about their opinions and feelings, eliciting the words in **Más vocabulario**. Ex: **¿Saben cuánto costó un boleto para el último concierto de U2? ¿Cuánto pagarías tú por una entrada, ____?** Also ask students who are studying the arts about their opinions. Ex: **____, estudias baile, ¿no? Para ti, ¿qué es lo más interesante del baile? Tienes que practicar muchísimo, ¿no?**

Note: At this point you may want to present **Vocabulario adicional: Más vocabulario para las artes**, from the IRM.

Un festival de arte

Más vocabulario

el/la compositor(a)	*composer*
el/la director(a)	*director; (musical) conductor*
el/la dramaturgo/a	*playwright*
el/la escritor(a)	*writer*
el personaje (principal)	*(main) character*
las bellas artes	*(fine) arts*
el boleto	*ticket*
la canción	*song*
la comedia	*comedy; play*
el cuento	*short story*
la cultura	*culture*
el drama	*drama; play*
el espectáculo	*show*
el festival	*festival*
la historia	*history; story*
la obra	*work (of art, music, etc.)*
la obra maestra	*masterpiece*
la ópera	*opera*
la orquesta	*orchestra*
aburrirse	*to get bored*
dirigir	*to direct*
presentar	*to present; to put on (a performance)*
publicar	*to publish*
artístico/a	*artistic*
clásico/a	*classical*
dramático/a	*dramatic*
extranjero/a	*foreign*
folklórico/a	*folk*
moderno/a	*modern*
musical	*musical*
romántico/a	*romantic*
talentoso/a	*talented*

Variación léxica

banda ⟷ grupo musical (*Esp.*)
boleto ⟷ entrada (*Esp.*)

recursos

TEXT CD Lección 17	WB pp. 191–192	LM p. 97	Lab CD/MP3 Lección 17	I CD-ROM Lección 17	Vocab CD Lección 17

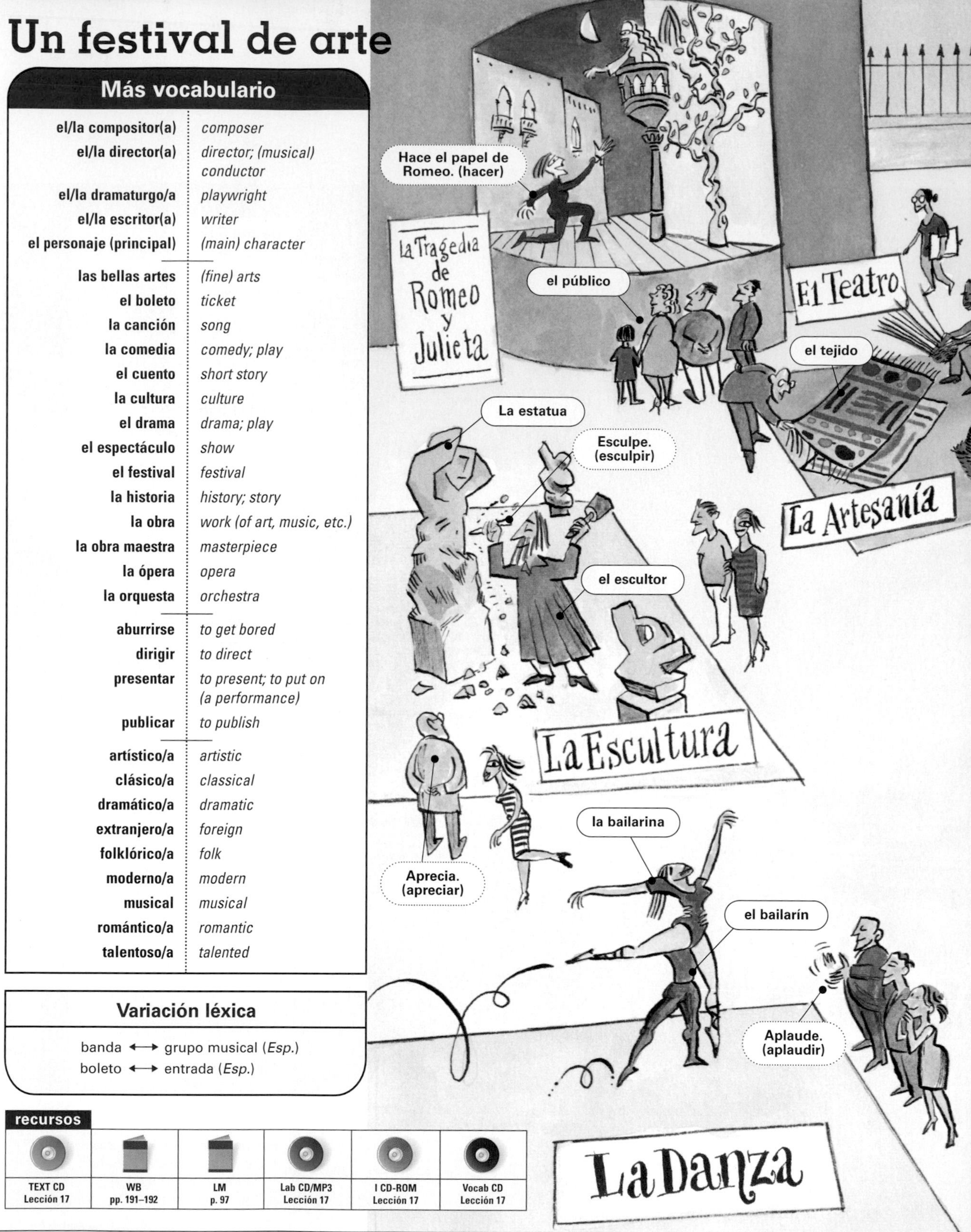

TEACHING OPTIONS

Variación léxica Tell students that, as well as **boleto** and **entrada**, they may also hear the word **billete** used to name a ticket for admission to a concert or museum. The ticket window where you buy your ticket is called **taquilla** in Spain, while in most of Latin America it is called the **boletería**.

Extra Practice Have students finish your statements with the vocabulary words from **Un festival de arte**. Ex: **Miguel Ángel esculpió muchas ____ importantes.** ***Carmen*** **es una ____ de Georges Bizet. Federico García Lorca es el ____ que escribió** ***Romancero gitano.***

Práctica

1 **Escuchar** Escucha la conversación y contesta las preguntas.

1. ¿Adónde fueron Ricardo y Juanita?
   Ellos fueron a un festival de arte.
2. ¿Cuál fue el espectáculo que más le gustó a Ricardo?
   Le gustó más la tragedia de *Romeo y Julieta.*
3. ¿Qué le gustó más a Juanita?
   A Juanita le gustó la banda.
4. ¿Qué dijo Ricardo del actor?
   Ricardo dijo que él era excelente.
5. ¿Qué dijo Juanita del actor?
   Ella dijo que él era guapo.
6. ¿Qué compró Juanita en el festival?
   Ella compró un disco compacto.
7. ¿Qué compró Ricardo?
   Ricardo compró dos libros de poesía.
8. ¿Qué poetas le interesaron a Ricardo?
   A Ricardo le interesaron Claribel Alegría y Roque Dalton.

2 **¿Cierto o falso?** Indica si lo que se afirma en las siguientes oraciones es **cierto** o **falso.**

	Cierto	Falso
1. Las bellas artes incluyen la pintura, la escultura, la música, el baile y el drama.	✓	○
2. Un boleto es un tipo de instrumento musical que se usa mucho en las óperas.	○	✓
3. El tejido es un tipo de música.	○	✓
4. La comedia es un tipo de orquesta.	○	✓
5. "Hacer un papel" quiere decir usar materiales como papel y pinturas de muchos colores.	○	✓
6. Un cuento es una narración corta que puede ser oral o escrita.	✓	○
7. Una obra maestra es un ejemplo del mejor trabajo de un(a) artista.	✓	○
8. Un compositor es el personaje principal de una obra de teatro.	○	✓
9. Publicar es la acción de hablar al público en grandes grupos.	○	✓
10. Los personajes principales de una ópera cantan.	✓	○

3 **Artistas** Indica la especialidad de cada uno de estos artistas.

1. Antonio Banderas actor
2. Frida Kahlo pintora
3. Gloria Estefan cantante
4. Octavio Paz poeta, escritor
5. William Shakespeare dramaturgo, poeta
6. Miguel de Cervantes escritor
7. Joan Miró pintor, escultor
8. Leonard Bernstein compositor
9. Toni Morrison escritora
10. Mikhail Baryshnikov bailarín

1 Suggestions
- Remind students to read the questions before listening to the audio. This will help them to know what information to listen for.
- Check answers orally with the class.

1 Tapescript JUANITA: Me encantó el festival de arte. Fue maravilloso, ¿verdad, Ricardo?
RICARDO: Sí. Me divertí mucho.
J: ¿Qué espectáculo te gustó más?
R: Pues, pienso que me gustó más la tragedia de *Romeo y Julieta.* El actor que hizo el papel principal fue excelente.
J: Y guapo.
R: Supongo que sí. Y tú, Juanita, ¿cuál fue tu favorito?
J: Sin duda alguna la banda. La cantante era magnífica.
R: Sí. Y los músicos tocaron con mucha pasión. Después, vendieron discos compactos. ¿Compraste uno?
J: Sí. Y tú, ¿compraste algo?
R: Sí, compré dos libros de poesía. Uno es de Claribel Alegría y el otro es de Roque Dalton.
J: Bueno, espero que el festival regrese el próximo año.
R: ¡Ojalá!
Textbook CD

2 Suggestion Ask volunteers to read each statement and say whether it is true or false. Have them correct any false statements.

2 Expansion Ask students to write six more statements, three true and three false. Have them read their statements to a partner who decides which are true or false.

3 Expansion After students have stated the profession of each person, ask them if they know the name of one of his or her works.

TEACHING OPTIONS

Heritage Speakers Have heritage speakers choose a Hispanic artist and research his or her life and works. Have students then present their findings in a short oral report. If the subject works in a visual medium, encourage the speaker to bring reproductions of his or her work, if possible.

TPR Play a game of charades. Ask volunteers to choose a vocabulary word. Students act out the word for the class to guess.

Large Groups Write the names of well-known artists on sticky notes and attach them to the backs of students, who then circulate around the room asking their classmates yes-no questions to determine their identity. Ex: **¿Soy escritor? ¿Escribo comedias? ¿Escribo novelas?**

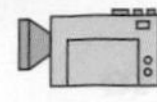

Section Goals

In **Fotonovela** students will:

- receive comprehensible input from free-flowing discourse
- learn functional phrases that preview lesson grammatical structures

Instructional Resources
WB/VM: Video Activities, pp. 245–246
***Fotonovela** DVD/Video (Start 01:35:56)*
Video CD-ROM
*IRM: **Fotonovela** Translations, p. 148, Videoscript, p. 124*
Interactive CD-ROM

Video Recap: Lección 16
Before doing this **Fotonovela** section, review the previous one with this activity.

1. ¿Qué hará don Francisco en el futuro? (establecerá su propia compañía de turismo)
2. ¿Quién será millonario? ¿Por qué? (Álex será millonario porque mucha gente habrá invertido dinero en su empresa)
3. ¿Quién tendrá un programa de tele? (Maite tendrá un programa de tele)
4. ¿Qué profesiones tendrán los estudiantes? (Álex será hombre de negocios, Maite será periodista, Javier será un pintor famoso e Inés será arqueóloga)

Video Synopsis Outside the theater, Álex and Maite chat about their artistic interests. After the performance, they return to the house. Javier and Inés catch them in the middle of a romantic moment.

Suggestions

- Have your students predict the plot of this **Fotonovela** episode, based on its title and the video stills. Write down their predictions.
- Quickly review the predictions your students made about the **Fotonovela**. Through discussion, help the class summarize the plot.
- Work through **Expresiones útiles**. Ask students what they would like to be in the future. Ex: **¿Te gustaría ser profesor(a) de español? ¿Qué te gustaría hacer?**

NATIONAL STANDARDS: communication, cultures

¡Ahí vienen Romeo y Julieta!

Álex y Maite van a ver una obra de teatro.

PERSONAJES

MAITE

ÁLEX

JAVIER

INÉS

1

ÁLEX Oye, ¿qué clase de películas te gustan? ¿las de acción? ¿las de horror? Para mí las mejores son las de ciencia ficción.

MAITE Eso no me sorprende. Mis películas favoritas son las películas románticas. ¿Pero sabes lo que me fascina?

2

ÁLEX No. Pero dime, querida, ¿qué es lo que más te fascina?

MAITE La poesía. Ahora estoy leyendo una colección de García Lorca... Es fenomenal...

3

ÁLEX ¡No me digas! A mí también me gusta la poesía. ¿Conoces a Octavio Paz, el poeta mexicano?

MAITE Pues, claro. Fue Premio Nobel de Literatura en 1990...

6

MAITE Oye, Álex, ¿te gustaría ser escritor?

ÁLEX Pues, creo que me gustaría ser poeta, pero publicaría todos mis poemas en Internet. ¿Te gustaría ser poeta?

7

MAITE Pues, no. Pero sí creo que me gustaría ser cantante. De no ser periodista, habría sido cantante de ópera.

ÁLEX ¿Cantante de ópera? Odio la ópera.

8

JAVIER Mira, ahí vienen Romeo y Julieta. ¡Míralos qué contentos! Ven conmigo... Vamos a sorprenderlos antes de que abran la puerta.

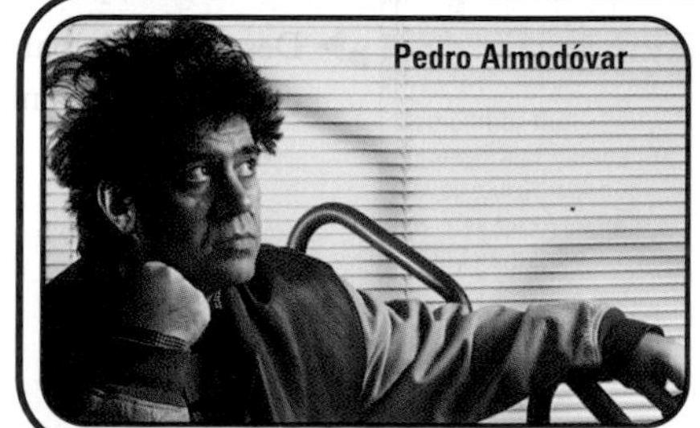
Pedro Almodóvar

recursos

V CD-ROM Lección 17	VM pp. 245–246	I CD-ROM Lección 17

TEACHING OPTIONS

Video Tips General suggestions for using video clips in the classroom can be found on page IAE-12 of this Instructor's Annotated Edition.

¡Ahí vienen Romeo y Julieta! Make copies of the script of the **¡Ahí vienen Romeo y Julieta!** segment of this lesson's video module and distribute them to your students. After your students have skimmed the script for the gist, ask them what this segment is about. Next, show the **¡Ahí vienen Romeo y Julieta!** segment and have your students circle all words related to music and the arts. Finally, ask your students to summarize this segment in their own words. You may want to ask a few questions to lead the class toward a correct plot summary.

ÁLEX ¡Uuuuyy! ¡Eres una experta en literatura!

MAITE Sí, leo de todo. Ahora en la mesita de noche tengo una colección de cuentos de Carme Riera, una española que también es periodista. En cuanto la termine te la dejo.

ÁLEX ¡Trato hecho!

Álex y Maite se besan.

JAVIER ¿Qué? ¿Les gustó la obra de teatro?

Expresiones útiles

Accepting an offer

- **¡Trato hecho!**
  You've got a deal!

Talking about things you would like to do

- **¿Te gustaría ser escritor(a)?**
  Would you (fam.) *like to be a writer?*
- ▷ **Creo que me gustaría ser poeta/cantante.**
  I think I would like to be a poet/singer.
- **De no ser periodista, habría sido cantante de ópera.**
  If I weren't a journalist, I would have been an opera singer.

Hesitating

- **Bueno...**
  Well...
- **Pues...**
  Well...
- **Este...**
  Umm...

Enfoque cultural El cine hispano

El cine hispano siempre se ha distinguido por su excelencia. El español Luis Buñuel fue uno de los primeros directores del cine de vanguardia (*avant-garde*). Su película *El perro andaluz* de 1929 es una obra maestra de este género. En el año 2000 Pedro Almodóvar, otro español de gran éxito, consiguió un Oscar con su película *Todo sobre mi madre.* En la generación más joven hay directores como el estadounidense de origen mexicano Robert Rodríguez, que ha hecho películas de éxito como *El mariachi, Desperado* y *Spy Kids*.

Suggestion Have the class work in groups of three to read the **Fotonovela** aloud. Each group member should play a different role. You may want volunteers to ad-lib this **Fotonovela** episode for the class.

Expresiones útiles Have the class look at frame 6 of the **Fotonovela**. Tell them that **gustaría** and **publicaría** are examples of the conditional, which is used to talk about what *would* happen. Point out frame 7, and explain that **habría sido** is an example of the conditional perfect, which is used to talk about what *would have happened.* Tell your students that they will learn more about these concepts in **Estructura**.

TEACHING OPTIONS

Enfoque cultural Point out that ***El perro andaluz*** was written in collaboration with Salvador Dalí. Point out that many Hispanics made significant contributions to the arts in the twentieth century, including Camilo José Cela (Spanish writer), Gabriel García Márquez (Colombian writer), Pablo Casals (Spanish cellist), Andrés Segovia (Spanish guitarist), Pablo Picasso (Spanish painter), Federico García Lorca (Spanish poet and playwright), Mario Vargas Llosa (Peruvian writer), Octavio Paz (Mexican writer), Jorge Luis Borges (Argentinian writer), Gabriela Mistral (Chilean poet), Diego Rivera (Mexican painter), and Frida Kahlo (Mexican painter), to name just a few. Ask your students if they know of other Hispanics who have distinguished themselves in the arts. You may want to have your students create posters or prepare presentations about some of these famous Hispanics.

1 Suggestion Have the class work through a few **cierto-falso** items before doing this activity. Ex: **1. A Maite no le gusta la ópera. (Falso.) 2. Maite quiere ser actriz. (Falso.) 3. A Álex le gustaría publicar poemas en Internet. (Cierto.)**

2 Expansion Give these additional items to the class: **7. ¿Has leído las obras de Octavio Paz? Es un escritor fascinante. (Álex) 8. Tengo un libro de cuentos en mi habitación. (Maite) 9. Sí, me gustaría mucho leer ese libro de cuentos. (Álex)**

3 Expansion Have your students write definitions in Spanish of the words **exposición, concierto, telenovela, ópera,** and **tragedia**. Have volunteers share their definitions with the class.

4 Possible Response
E1: ¿Qué te gustaría hacer este fin de semana?
E2: Pues, como a mí me gusta la música, creo que me gustaría ver una ópera.
E1: ¡Uy, odio la ópera! Además, los boletos son muy caros.
E2: Ay, sí, es cierto. Este... ¿te gustaría asistir a un concierto de la orquesta nacional?
E1: Buena idea. Me gusta la música clásica.
E2: Y a ti, ¿qué te gustaría hacer?
E1: Bueno, como me gusta tanto el arte, me gustaría ver una exposición de arte moderno.
E2: ¡Trato hecho!

Reacciona a la fotonovela

1 Seleccionar Selecciona la respuesta correcta.

1. Maite está leyendo ahora a los autores __a__.
   a. Riera y García Lorca b. Octavio Paz y García Lorca c. Octavio Paz y Riera
2. __c__ ganó el Premio Nobel de Literatura en 1990.
   a. García Lorca b. Carme Riera c. Octavio Paz
3. __b__ dice que le gustaría ser poeta porque le gusta mucho la poesía.
   a. Maite b. Álex c. Javier
4. Si no estudiara periodismo, Maite sería __a__.
   a. cantante de ópera b. escritora de novelas románticas c. poeta
5. "Romeo y Julieta" hace referencia a __c__.
   a. Javier e Inés b. el espectáculo que vieron Álex y Maite c. Álex y Maite

NOTA CULTURAL

El español **Federico García Lorca** (1898-1936) es uno de los escritores más reconocidos del mundo hispano. Entre sus obras se destaca (*stands out*) *Poeta en Nueva York*. Además de escribir poesía, Lorca escribió obras de teatro, como *La casa de Bernarda Alba*.

2 Identificar Identifica quién puede decir las siguientes frases.

1. Me encantan los cuentos de Riera. ¿Te interesa leer sus libros? Maite
2. Ya llegaron los románticos. ¿Por qué no los sorprendemos? Javier
3. ¡Parece que sabes muchísimo de poesía y de novelas! Álex
4. Oye, ¿qué tal la obra que vieron? ¿Me la recomiendan o no? Javier
5. Me gusta mucho la ópera. A veces creo que me gustaría cantar profesionalmente. Maite
6. Prefiero las películas de ciencia ficción a las de horror o de acción. Álex

ÁLEX

JAVIER

MAITE

3 Correspondencias ¿A qué eventos culturales asistirán Álex y Maite juntos?

una exposición de cerámica precolombina	un concierto	una ópera
una exposición de pintura española	una telenovela	una tragedia

1. Escucharán música clásica y conocerán a un director muy famoso.
   un concierto
2. El público aplaudirá mucho a la señora que es soprano.
   una ópera
3. Como a Inés le gusta la historia, la llevarán a ver esto.
   una exposición de cerámica precolombina
4. Como a Javier le gustaría ver arte, entonces irán con él.
   una exposición de pintura española

4 El fin de semana Vas a asistir a dos eventos culturales el próximo fin de semana con un(a) compañero/a de clase. Comenten entre ustedes por qué les gustan o les disgustan algunas de las actividades que van sugiriendo. Escojan al final dos actividades que puedan realizar juntos/as. Usen las siguientes frases y expresiones en su conversación.

Answers will vary.

- ¿Qué te gustaría ver/hacer este fin de semana?
- ¿Te gustaría asistir a...?
- ¡Trato hecho!
- Odio..., ¿qué tal si...?

TEACHING OPTIONS

Small Groups Have your students work in small groups to write a paragraph about the future of Maite and Álex's relationship. Give your students time to prepare, and ask a few groups to read their paragraphs to the class.

Pairs Have your students chat in pairs about what they would like to do or be in the future and why. Tell them to use **te gustaría** and **me gustaría** if possible. Then ask a few students to summarize what their partner told them.

Ortografía

Las trampas ortográficas

Some of the most common spelling mistakes in Spanish occur when two or more words have very similar spellings. This section reviews some of those words.

compro **compró** **hablo** **habló**

There is no accent mark in the **yo** form of **–ar** verbs in the present tense. There is, however, an accent mark in the **él/ella/Ud.** form of **–ar** verbs in the preterite.

este (adjective) **éste** (pronoun) **esté** (verb)

The demonstrative adjectives **esta** and **este** do not have an accent mark. The demonstrative pronouns **ésta** and **éste** have an accent mark on the first syllable. The verb forms **está** (*present indicative*) and **esté** (*present subjunctive*) have an accent mark on the last syllable.

jo-ven **jó-ve-nes** **bai-la-rín** **bai-la-ri-na**

The location of the stressed syllable in a word determines whether or not a written accent mark is needed. When a plural or feminine form has more syllables than the singular or masculine form, an accent mark must sometimes be added or deleted to maintain the correct stress.

No me gusta la ópera, sino el teatro.
No quiero ir al festival si no vienes conmigo.

The conjunction **sino** (*but rather*) should not be confused with **si no** (*if not*). Note also the difference between **mediodía** (*noon*) and **medio día** (*half a day*) and between **por qué** (*why*) and **porque** (*because*).

Práctica Completa las frases con las palabras adecuadas para cada ocasión.

1. Javier me explicó que ___si no___ lo invitabas, él no iba a venir. (sino/si no)
2. Me gustan mucho las ___canciones___ folklóricas. (canciones/canciónes)
3. Marina ___presentó___ su espectáculo en El Salvador. (presento/presentó)
4. Yo prefiero ___éste___. (éste/esté)

Palabras desordenadas Ordena las letras para descubrir las palabras correctas. Después, ordena las letras indicadas para descubrir la respuesta a la pregunta.

¿Adónde va Manuel?

y u n a s e d ó _ ◯ _ ◯ _ _ _ _

q u e r o p _ _ ◯ _ _ _

z o g a d e l a ◯ _ _ ◯ _ _ _ _

á s e t _ _ ◯ _

h a i t e s a b o n c i _ _ _ _ ◯ _ _ _ ◯ _ _ _

Manuel va _ _ _ _ _ _ _ _ _.[1]

Respuestas: desayuno, porque, adelgazo, esta, habitaciones

[1] Manuel va al teatro.

recursos

LM p. 98	Lab CD/MP3 Lección 17	I CD-ROM Lección 17

Section Goal

In **Ortografía** students will learn about Spanish words that have similar spellings.

Instructional Resource
Interactive CD-ROM

Suggestions

- Say the words **compro** and **hablo** and have volunteers write them on the board. Write the words **compró** and **habló** on the board and have volunteers pronounce them.
- Write the words **este, éste,** and **esté** on the board and have volunteers explain how the words are different. Have the class create a sentence that uses each word.
- Write the words **joven, jóvenes, bailarín,** and **bailarina** on the board and have the class explain why a written accent is needed in **jóvenes** but not in **bailarina**.
- Write the words **sino, si no, medio día, mediodía, por qué,** and **porque** on the board. Have volunteers explain what each word means. Have the class create a sentence that uses each word.
- Point out that **Ortografía** replaces **Pronunciación** in the Student Edition for **Lecciones 10–18**, but not in the Lab Manual. The **Recursos** box references the **Pronunciación** sections found in all lessons of the Lab Manual.

TEACHING OPTIONS

Small Groups Have your students work in groups to write an amusing example sentence or two for each of the spelling rules presented on this page. Circulate around the class to verify correct spelling. Then ask a few volunteers to write their sentences on the board.

Extra Practice Read aloud a few sentences that contain words presented on this page and have your students write them down. Then write the sentences on the board so that your students can check their work. Ex: **Si no compro la comida hoy, la compraré mañana. ¿Prefieres este vestido o éste? La señora Pardo no es vieja, sino joven.**

Section Goals

In **Estructura 17.1** students will learn:

- to use the conditional
- to make polite requests and hypothesize about past conditions

Instructional Resources
WB/VM: Workbook, pp. 193–194
Lab Manual, p. 99
Lab CD/MP3 ***Lección 17***
IRM: ***Hojas de actividades****, pp. 174–176;* ***¡Inténtalo!*** *&* ***Práctica*** *Answers, p. 223; Tapescript, pp. 76–79*
Interactive CD-ROM
Companion website: www.vistahigherlearning.com
Presentations CD-ROM

Suggestions

- Ask students to imagine they are attending an arts festival. Ask them what they would like to do there. Ex: **¿Qué te gustaría hacer o ver en el festival de arte? A mí me gustaría ver las comedias que dan. ¿Y a ti?** Tell students that **gustaría** is a polite form of **gustar** that they already know. The conditional is used to make polite requests.
- Ask volunteers to read the captions to the video stills and indicate which verbs are in the conditional.
- Point out that as in the future, there is only one set of endings in the conditional.
- Check for understanding by citing an infinitive and a subject pronoun while pointing to a specific student. The student should respond with the conditional form. Ex: **decir / nosotros (diríamos); venir / tú (vendrías)**
- Ask students what the future form of **hay** is. Then ask them what they would expect the conditional form to be.

17.1 The conditional

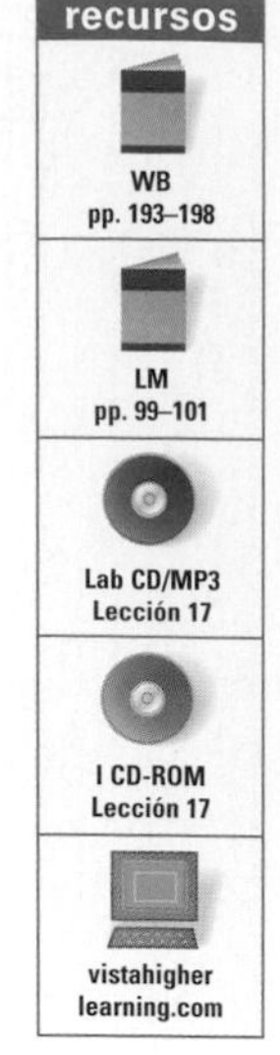

recursos
WB pp. 193–198
LM pp. 99–101
Lab CD/MP3 Lección 17
I CD-ROM Lección 17
vistahigherlearning.com

ANTE TODO The conditional tense in Spanish expresses what you *would do* or what *would happen* under certain circumstances.

The conditional tense

		visitar	comer	aplaudir
SINGULAR FORMS	yo	visitar**ía**	comer**ía**	aplaudir**ía**
	tú	visitar**ías**	comer**ías**	aplaudir**ías**
	Ud./él/ella	visitar**ía**	comer**ía**	aplaudir**ía**
PLURAL FORMS	nosotros/as	visitar**íamos**	comer**íamos**	aplaudir**íamos**
	vosotros/as	visitar**íais**	comer**íais**	aplaudir**íais**
	Uds./ellos/ellas	visitar**ían**	comer**ían**	aplaudir**ían**

Oye, Álex, ¿te gustaría ser escritor?

Pues creo que me gustaría ser poeta, pero publicaría todos mis poemas en Internet.

¡ATENCIÓN!
The polite expressions **Me gustaría...** (*I would like...*) and **Te gustaría** (*You would like...*) used by Álex and Maite in the **Fotonovela**, are another example of the conditional.

▶ The conditional tense is formed much like the future tense. The endings are the same for all verbs, both regular and irregular. For regular verbs, you simply add the appropriate endings to the infinitive.

▶ For irregular verbs add the conditional endings to the irregular stems.

INFINITIVE	STEM	CONDITIONAL	INFINITIVE	STEM	CONDITIONAL
decir	dir-	dir**ía**	querer	querr-	querr**ía**
hacer	har-	har**ía**	saber	sabr-	sabr**ía**
poder	podr-	podr**ía**	salir	saldr-	saldr**ía**
poner	pondr-	pondr**ía**	tener	tendr-	tendr**ía**
haber	habr-	habr**ía**	venir	vendr-	vendr**ía**

¡ATENCIÓN!
All forms of the conditional have an accent mark.
•••
The infinitive of **hay** is **haber**, so its conditional form is **habría**.

▶ While in English the conditional is a compound verb form made up of the auxiliary verb *would* and a main verb, in Spanish it is a simple verb form that consists of one word.

Yo no **me pondría** ese vestido.
I would not wear that dress.

¿**Vivirían** ustedes en otro país?
Would you live in another country?

TEACHING OPTIONS

Game Line students up in teams of six several feet from the board. Write an infinitive on the board and call out **¡Empieza!** The first team members race to the board and write the **yo** form of the verb in the conditional, then pass the chalk to the next team members, who write the **tú** form, and so on. The team that finishes first and has all the forms correct wins the round.

Extra Practice Ask students what they would or would not do over the next six months if they could do anything their hearts desired and money and time were no object. Ex: **Yo viajaría por todo el mundo.** Call on volunteers to read their sentences, then ask the class comprehension questions about what was said. Ex: **Clase, ¿qué harían Alicia y Tomás?**

- The conditional is commonly used to make polite requests.

¿**Podrías** abrir la ventana, por favor?
Would you open the window, please?

¿**Sería** tan amable de venir a mi oficina?
Would you be so kind as to come to my office?

- In Spanish, as in English, the conditional expresses the future in relation to a past action or state of being. In other words, the future indicates what *will happen* whereas the conditional indicates what *would happen.*

Creo que mañana **hará** sol.
I think it will be sunny tomorrow.

Creía que hoy **haría** sol.
I thought it would be sunny today.

- The English *would* is often used with a verb to express the conditional, but it can also mean *used to,* in the sense of past habitual action. To express past habitual actions, Spanish uses the imperfect, not the conditional.

Íbamos al parque los sábados.
We would go to the park on Saturdays.

De adolescentes, **comíamos** mucho.
As teenagers, we used to eat a lot.

CONSEJOS

Keep in mind the two parallel combinations shown in these sentences:
1) present tense in main clause → future tense in subordinate clause
2) past tense in main clause → conditional tense in subordinate clause

Sin ti, no sé qué haría.

Sólo tú sabes ordenar mi vida.

Computadoras de Bolsillo Vargas

MM-3000

COMPARE & CONTRAST

In **Lección 16**, you learned the *future of probability.* Spanish also has the *conditional of probability,* which expresses conjecture or probability about a past condition, event, or action. Compare these Spanish and English sentences.

Serían las once de la noche cuando Elvira me llamó.
It must have been (It was probably) 11 p.m. when Elvira called me.

Sonó el teléfono. ¿**Llamaría** Emilio para cancelar nuestra cita?
The phone rang. I wondered if it was Emilio calling to cancel our date.

Note that English conveys conjecture or probability with phrases such as *I wondered if, probably,* and *must have been.* In contrast, Spanish gets these same ideas across with conditional forms.

¡INTÉNTALO! Indica la forma apropiada del condicional de los verbos que están entre paréntesis.

1. Yo *escucharía, leería, esculpiría* (escuchar, leer, esculpir)
2. Tú apreciarías, comprenderías, compartirías (apreciar, comprender, compartir)
3. Marcos pondría, vendría, querría (poner, venir, querer)
4. Nosotras seríamos, sabríamos, iríamos (ser, saber, ir)
5. Ustedes presentarían, deberían, aplaudirían (presentar, deber, aplaudir)
6. Ella saldría, podría, haría (salir, poder, hacer)
7. Yo tendría, tocaría, me aburriría (tener, tocar, aburrirse)
8. Tú dirías, verías, publicarías (decir, ver, publicar)

Suggestions

- Discuss the use of the conditional in polite requests. Remind students of the forms **me gustaría** and **te gustaría**, which they have already learned. You might point out that usage tends to occur in set expressions, such as **¿Podrías... ? ¿Sería usted tan amable de... ? ¿Tendrían ustedes la bondad de... ? ¿Me harías el favor de... ?**
- Explain the concept of the conditional as *the future of the past.* Explain that the conditional is used to express some action that was yet to occur at some past time, and give examples. Ex: **Sé que el concierto será fabuloso. Sabía que el concierto sería fabuloso. Creo que el público llegará muy temprano. Creía que el público llegaría muy temprano.**
- Remind students of the future of probability. Point out that the conditional of probability functions just like it but in the context of the past. Compare the second example in the Compare & Contrast chart to the following: **Suena el teléfono. ¿Será Emilio para cancelar nuestra cita?**

TEACHING OPTIONS

Extra Practice Tell students to imagine that their family has come into a great deal of money. Ask them to write ten sentences describing what they and their family members would do with the money. Students should try to use as many different verbs and conjugations as possible. Ex: **Mi familia y yo ayudaríamos a los artistas de nuestra ciudad.**

Pairs Have students work together to role-play a reporter interviewing a candidate running for a seat on the arts council in their state. Reporters should ask the candidate about what he or she would do to help all artists statewide. Have students switch roles.

1 Suggestion Ask students to identify the verbs with irregular stems before they begin doing the activity.

1 Expansion Ask six volunteers to write the completed sentences on the board. Have six more volunteers correct any spelling or grammar errors.

2 Expansion Ask questions about the responses to practice all forms of the conditional. Ex: ____, **¿qué diría ____ en el concierto? (¿Podría sentarse, por favor?) ¿Cuántos diríamos lo mismo?**

3 Expansions

- Have partners choose their three best suggestions to present to the class. Write them on the board, then ask the class to vote on which are the most helpful.
- Have pairs create sentences to include in a letter of recommendation in support of Matilde. Have them use the conditional. Ex: **Matilde llegaría temprano todas las mañanas y terminaría todo su trabajo antes de irse a casa.** Ask pairs to share their sentences with the class, who will vote for the most persuasive ones.

Práctica

1 **De viaje** A un grupo de artistas le gustaría hacer un viaje a Honduras. En las siguientes oraciones nos cuentan sus planes de viaje. Complétalas con el condicional del verbo entre paréntesis.

1. Me ___gustaría___ (gustar) llevar algunos libros de poesía de Leticia de Oyuela.
2. Ana ___querría___ (querer) ir primero a Copán para conocer las ruinas mayas.
3. Yo ___diría___ (decir) que fuéramos a Tegucigalpa primero.
4. Nosotras ___preferiríamos___ (preferir) ver una obra del Grupo Dramático de Tegucigalpa. Luego ___podríamos___ (poder) tomarnos un café.
5. Y nosotros ___veríamos___ (ver) los cuadros del pintor José Antonio Velásquez. Y tú, Luisa, ¿qué ___harías___ (hacer)?
6. Yo ___tendría___ (tener) interés en ver o comprar cerámica de José Arturo Machado. Y a ti, Carlos, ¿te ___interesaría___ (interesar) ver la arquitectura colonial?

NOTA CULTURAL

Leticia de Oyuela (1935-) es una escritora hondureña. En sus obras, Oyuela combina la historia con la ficción, y sus personajes, por lo general, desafían (*challenge*) los problemas sociales de su país.

2 **¿Lo harías?** En parejas, pregúntense qué harían en las siguientes situaciones.

Estás en un concierto de tu banda favorita y la persona que está sentada delante no te deja ver.

Un amigo actor te invita a ver una película que acaba de hacer, y no te gusta nada cómo hace su papel.

Estás invitado/a a los Premios Ariel. Es posible que te vayan a dar un premio, pero ese día estás muy enfermo/a.

Te invitan, pagándote mucho dinero, para ir a un programa de televisión para hablar de tu vida privada y pelearte (*to fight*) con tu novio/a durante el programa.

NOTA CULTURAL

Los Premios Ariel de México son uno de los premios de cine con mayor proyección internacional. Cada año los entrega la Academia Mexicana de Ciencias y Artes Cinematográficas. Algunas películas que han ganado un Ariel son *Amores perros* y *El Crimen del Padre Amaro*.

3 **Sugerencias** Matilde busca trabajo. Dile ocho cosas que tú harías si fueras ella. Usa el condicional. Luego compara tus sugerencias con las de un(a) compañero/a.

Answers will vary.

modelo

Si yo fuera tú, buscaría trabajo en el periódico.

AYUDA

Here are two ways of saying *If I were you:*

Si yo fuera tú...

Yo en tu lugar...

TEACHING OPTIONS

Pairs Have students take turns asking each other for favors, using the conditional for courtesy. Partners respond by saying whether they will do the favor. If partners can't do it, they should make up an excuse. Ex: **¿Me podrías recoger del gimnasio a las cinco de la tarde? (Lo siento, pero no puedo. Tengo una clase de escultura hasta las cinco y media.)**

Heritage Speakers Ask heritage speakers to think of a Spanish-speaking writer or artist that they would like to meet. Have students give a short presentation describing what the meeting would be like, where they would meet, and what they would talk about with their celebrity.

Comunicación

4 **Conversaciones** Tu profesor(a) te dará una hoja de actividades. En ella se presentan dos listas con diferentes problemas que supuestamente tienen los estudiantes. En parejas, túrnense para explicar los problemas de su lista; uno/a cuenta lo que le pasa y el/la otro/a dice lo que haría en esa situación usando la frase "Yo en tu lugar..." (*If I were you...*)

Answers will vary.

modelo

Estudiante 1: ¡Qué problema! Mi novio/a no me habla desde el domingo.
Estudiante 2: Yo en tu lugar no le diría nada por unos días para ver qué pasa.

5 **Luces, cámara y acción** En grupos pequeños, elijan una película que les guste y después escriban una lista con las cosas que habrían hecho de manera diferente si hubieran sido los directores. Después, uno del grupo tiene que leer su lista, y el resto de la clase tiene que adivinar (*to guess*) de qué película se trata.

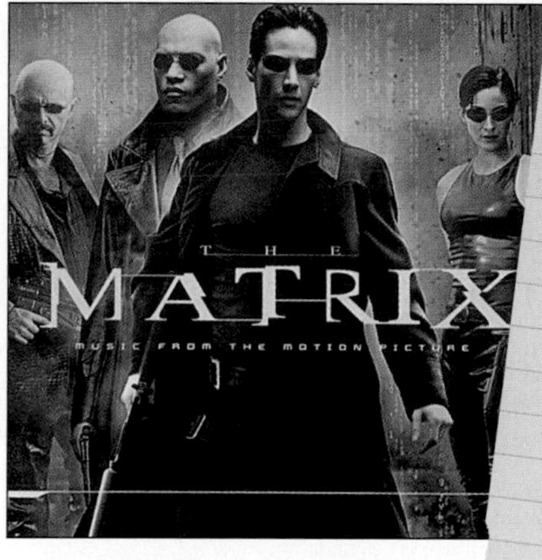

THE
MATRIX
MUSIC FROM THE MOTION PICTURE
Yo no contrataría a Keanu Reeves para ese papel.
Y tampoco haría muchas películas sobre el mismo tema.
Neo y Trinity, los protagonistas, se casarían y tendrían hijos.
Yo cambiaría el final de la historia.

Síntesis

6 **Encuesta** Tu profesor(a) te dará una hoja de actividades. Circula por la clase y pregúntales a tres compañeros/as qué actividad(es) de las que se describen les gustaría realizar. Usa el condicional de los verbos. Anota las respuestas e informa a la clase de los resultados de la encuesta. Answers will vary.

modelo

Estudiante 1: ¿Harías el papel de un loco en una obra de teatro?
Estudiante 2: Sí, lo haría. Sería un papel muy interesante.

4 Suggestion Distribute the **Hojas de actividades** from the IRM that correspond to this activity.

4 Expansion Working with the whole class, name a problem from one of the lists and ask several volunteers to share the suggestions they received. Encourage other students to comment on the suggestions, going through several problems this way.

5 Expansion Ask the class for titles of additional movies and write them on the board. Ask students to imagine they are going to produce a sequel (**una continuación**) for each one. Have them use sentences like those in the activity to name the attractive features that they would leave in the sequel. Ex: **Yo contrataría otra vez a Keanu Reeves para ese papel.**

6 Suggestion Distribute the **Hojas de actividades** from the IRM that correspond to this activity.

6 Expansion Encourage students to add two more activities to their list. Have them select from those listed on pages 512–513.

TEACHING OPTIONS

Small Groups Divide the class into groups of four. Have each one brainstorm a list of professions, both artistic and non-artistic. Each group member then chooses a different profession. Students take turns being interviewed by a three-person board about what they would do for their community in their chosen profession. Each board member should ask the interviewee at least two questions.

Extra Practice Ask students to write a short paragraph answering this question: **¿Qué harías para cambiar tu vida?** Call on volunteers to write their paragraphs on the board. Ask the class to check the paragraphs for correct usage and spelling.

Section Goal

In **Estructura 17.2** students will learn the use of the conditional perfect.

Instructional Resources
WB/VM: Workbook, p. 195
Lab Manual, p. 100
Lab CD/MP3 ***Lección 17***
IRM: ***¡Inténtalo! & Práctica*** *Answers, p. 223; Tapescript, pp. 76–79*
Info Gap Activities Booklet, pp. 67–68
Interactive CD-ROM
Companion website: www.vistahigherlearning.com
Presentations CD-ROM

Suggestions

- Briefly review the **yo** forms of the present, past, and future perfect tenses. Point out that they are all formed by a conjugated form of **haber** + [*past participle*]. Then make a true statement about yourself, using the conditional perfect. Ex: **De no ser profesor(a), yo habría sido periodista.** Ask a volunteer to identify the conditional perfect he or she heard in your statement.
- Ask a volunteer to read the captions to the video stills aloud, pointing out the conditional perfect. Then engage students in a conversation about what they might have done last night if they hadn't been studying. Ask: **De no haber estudiado para la clase de español anoche, ¿qué habrían hecho ustedes? ¿Habrían ido al cine? ¿Habrían salido con los amigos?**

17.2 The conditional perfect

ANTE TODO Like other compound tenses you have learned—the present perfect, the past perfect, and the future perfect—the conditional perfect (**el condicional perfecto**) is formed with **haber** + [*past participle*].

Y a ti, Maite, ¿te gustaría ser poeta?

Me gustaría ser cantante. De no ser periodista, habría sido cantante de ópera.

The conditional perfect

		pintar	comer	vivir
SINGULAR FORMS	yo	**habría** pintado	**habría** comido	**habría** vivido
	tú	**habrías** pintado	**habrías** comido	**habrías** vivido
	Ud./él/ella	**habría** pintado	**habría** comido	**habría** vivido
PLURAL FORMS	nosotros/as	**habríamos** pintado	**habríamos** comido	**habríamos** vivido
	vosotros/as	**habríais** pintado	**habríais** comido	**habríais** vivido
	Uds./ellos/ellas	**habrían** pintado	**habrían** comido	**habrían** vivido

▶ The conditional perfect is used to express an action that would have occurred, but didn't.

¿No fuiste al espectáculo? ¡Te **habrías divertido**!
You didn't go to the show? You would have had a good time!

Maite **habría preferido** ir a la ópera, pero Álex prefirió ir al cine.
Maite would have preferred to go to the opera, but Álex preferred to see a movie.

¡INTÉNTALO! Indica las formas apropiadas del condicional perfecto de los verbos entre paréntesis.

1. Nosotros habríamos hecho (hacer) todos los quehaceres.
2. Tú habrías apreciado (apreciar) mi poesía.
3. Ellos habrían pintado (pintar) un mural.
4. Usted habría tocado (tocar) el piano.
5. Ellas habrían puesto (poner) la mesa.
6. Tú y yo habríamos resuelto (resolver) los problemas.
7. Silvia y Alberto habrían esculpido (esculpir) una estatua.
8. Yo habría presentado (presentar) el informe.
9. Ustedes habrían vivido (vivir) en el campo.
10. Tú habrías abierto (abrir) la puerta.

TEACHING OPTIONS

Extra Practice Ask students to write five sentences describing how the life of their favorite writer or artist would have been different if he or she had lived in another century. Ex: **Stephen King habría escrito sus novelas con una pluma de cuervo.**

Small Groups Give students five minutes to work in groups of three to describe what would have happened to Cinderella had she not lost her glass slipper. Tell students that the translations for Cinderella, prince, and glass slipper in Spanish are **Cenicienta, príncipe,** and **zapatilla de cristal**.

Práctica

1 **Completar** Completa los diálogos con la forma apropiada del condicional perfecto de los verbos de la lista. Luego, en parejas, representen los diálogos.

divertirse	presentar	sentir	tocar
hacer	querer	tener	venir

1. —Tú ___habrías hecho___ el papel de Aída mejor que ella. ¡Qué lástima!
   —Sí, mis padres ___habrían venido___ desde California sólo para oírme cantar en Aída.
2. —Olga, yo esperaba algo más. Con un poco de dedicación y práctica la orquesta ___habría tocado___ mejor y los músicos ___habrían tenido___ más éxito.
   —Menos mal que la compositora no los escuchó. Se ___habría sentido___ avergonzada.
3. —Tania ___habría presentado___ la comedia pero no pudo porque cerraron el teatro.
   —¡Qué lástima! Mi esposa y yo ___habríamos querido___ ir a la presentación de la obra. Siempre veo tragedias y sé que ___me habría divertido___.

¡LENGUA VIVA!

The common expression **Menos mal que...** means *It's a good thing that...* or *It's just as well that...*. It is followed by a verb in the indicative.

2 **Combinar** En parejas, imaginen qué harían las siguientes personas en las situaciones presentadas. Combina elementos de cada una de las tres columnas para formar ocho oraciones usando el condicional perfecto. Answers will vary.

A	B	C
con talento artístico	yo	estudiar...
con más tiempo libre	tú	pintar...
en otra especialización	la gente	esculpir...
con más aprecio de las artes	mis compañeros y yo	viajar...
con más dinero	los artistas	escribir...
en otra película	Alejandro González Iñárritu	publicar...

NOTA CULTURAL

El director de cine **Alejandro González Iñárritu** ha conseguido destacar (*stand out*) dentro de la nueva generación de cineastas (*filmmakers*) mexicanos. Su película *Amores perros* fue nominada para el Oscar a la mejor película extranjera en el 2001.

3 **¿Qué habrías hecho?** Los siguientes dibujos muestran situaciones poco comunes. No sabemos qué hicieron estas personas, pero tú, ¿qué habrías hecho? Comparte tus respuestas con un(a) compañero/a. Answers will vary.

AYUDA

Some suggestions are:
Habría llevado el dinero a....
Yo habría atacado al oso (*bear*) **con....**
Yo habría...

1 Suggestion Before beginning the activity, model the use of **menos mal que...** Ex: **¿No estudiaron anoche? Menos mal que no tenemos examen hoy.**

1 Expansion Have pairs choose one of the three dialogues and write four additional lines. Call on volunteers to perform their expanded dialogues for the class.

2 Suggestion Have volunteers call out sentences using elements from each of the three columns. Have other volunteers act as secretaries, writing examples on the board. Ask the class to help you correct grammar and spelling as necessary.

3 Suggestion Before beginning the activity, ask students to describe each of the drawings. Write useful vocabulary on the board, including the expressions from **Ayuda**.

TEACHING OPTIONS

Pairs Ask students to tell their partner about the most embarrassing moment in their life. Partners respond to the stories by telling them what they would have done in their place. Ex: **En tu lugar, yo habría...**

Extra Practice Ask students to state what the following people would have done had they had more money: **mis padres, yo, mi mejor amigo, los estudiantes de la universidad, mi profesor(a) de español**. Ex: **Con más dinero, mis padres habrían comprado una casa más grande.**

4 Expansions
- Have students come up with four more questions to ask their partner.
- Have pairs give answers that are true for them today.
- Have pairs answer the same questions as an older member of their family would.

5 Expansion Ask students to respond to Mario's letter in writing. They should commiserate with him and state what they would have done differently.

6 Suggestion Encourage students to flesh out their conversations to justify their mistakes. Ex: **Aquel semestre, mi padre estaba en el hospital y yo no tenía mucho tiempo para estudiar.**

6 Expansions
- Have students share their mistakes and their partner's solutions with the class. If any mistakes are common to two or more students, compare the different solutions and ask the class to decide which one makes most sense.
- Use magazine pictures for additional practice with the conditional perfect, asking students what they would have done. Ex: **La ropa le queda pequeña. (Yo la habría lavado con agua fría.)**

Suggestion See the Info Gap Activities Booklet for an additional activity to practice the material presented in this section.

Comunicación

NATIONAL communication STANDARDS

4 **Preguntas** En parejas, imaginen que tienen cincuenta años y están hablando de sus años de juventud. ¿Qué habrían hecho de manera diferente? Answers will vary.

modelo

¿Te (interesar) aprender a tocar un instrumento?
Estudiante 1: ¿Te habría interesado aprender a tocar un instrumento?
Estudiante 2: Sí, habría aprendido a tocar el piano.

1. ¿Te (gustar) viajar por Latinoamérica?
2. ¿Qué escritores (leer)?
3. ¿Qué clases (tomar)?
4. ¿Qué tipo de música (escuchar)?
5. ¿Qué tipo de amigos/as (tener)?
6. ¿A qué fiestas o viajes no (ir)?
7. ¿Con qué tipo de persona (salir)?
8. ¿Qué tipo de ropa (llevar)?

5 **Pobre Mario** En parejas, lean la carta que Mario le escribió a Enrique. Digan qué cosas Mario habría hecho de una manera diferente de haber tenido la oportunidad.

modelo

Mario no habría hecho este musical.

Enrique:

Ya llegó el último día del musical. Yo creía que nunca iba a acabar. En general, los cantantes y actores eran bastante malos, pero no tuve tiempo de buscar otros, y además los buenos ya tenían trabajo en otras obras. Ayer todo salió muy mal. Como era la última noche, yo había invitado a unos críticos a ver la obra, pero no pudieron verla. El primer problema fue la cantante principal. Ella estaba enojada conmigo porque no quise pagarle todo el dinero que quería. Dijo que tenía problemas de garganta, y no salió a cantar. Conseguí a otra cantante, pero los músicos de la orquesta todavía no habían llegado. Tenían que venir todos en un autobús no muy caro que yo había alquilado, pero el autobús salió a una hora equivocada. Entonces, el bailarín se enojó conmigo porque todo iba a empezar tarde.

Quizás tuviera razón mi padre. Seguramente soy mejor contador que director teatral.

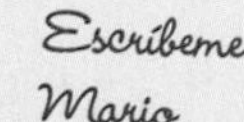

Escríbeme,
Mario

¡LENGUA VIVA!

The useful expression **de haber tenido la oportunidad** means *if I/he/you/etc. had had the opportunity.* You can use this expression in similar instances, such as **De haberlo sabido ayer, te habría llamado.**

Síntesis

NATIONAL communication STANDARDS

6 **Yo en tu lugar** Primero, cada estudiante hace una lista con tres errores que ha cometido, o tres problemas que ha tenido en su vida. Después, en parejas, túrnense para decirse qué habrían hecho en esas situaciones.

modelo

Estudiante 1: El año pasado saqué una mala nota en el examen de biología.
Estudiante 2: Yo no habría sacado una nota mala. Habría estudiado mucho más.

TEACHING OPTIONS

Pairs Have students make a list of everything they did last weekend. Then, ask students to tell their partners what they did, when they did it, and how they did it. Partners will counter with how they would have done each thing. Ex: **Bailé por cinco horas en una fiesta el sábado pasado. (Yo no habría bailado por tanto tiempo. Yo habría bailado sólo dos horas.)**

Large Groups Divide the class into three groups. Have each student answer the following question: **¿Qué habrías hecho de una manera diferente este semestre?** After everyone has spoken, have the group discuss which missed opportunities would have been the most important in making a difference in their lives.

17.3 The past perfect subjunctive

CONSÚLTALO

To review the past perfect indicative, see **Estructura 15.2**, p. 466.

To review the present perfect subjunctive, see **Estructura 15.3**, p. 469.

ANTE TODO The past perfect subjunctive (**el pluscuamperfecto de subjuntivo**), also called the pluperfect subjunctive, is formed with the past subjunctive of **haber** + [*past participle*]. Compare the following subjunctive forms.

Present subjunctive	Present perfect subjunctive
yo trabaje	yo haya trabajado
Past subjunctive	**Past perfect subjunctive**
yo trabajara	yo hubiera trabajado

Past perfect subjunctive

		pintar	comer	vivir
SINGULAR FORMS	yo	**hubiera** pintado	**hubiera** comido	**hubiera** vivido
	tú	**hubieras** pintado	**hubieras** comido	**hubieras** vivido
	Ud./él/ella	**hubiera** pintado	**hubiera** comido	**hubiera** vivido
PLURAL FORMS	nosotros/as	**hubiéramos** pintado	**hubiéramos** comido	**hubiéramos** vivido
	vosotros/as	**hubierais** pintado	**hubierais** comido	**hubierais** vivido
	Uds./ellos/ellas	**hubieran** pintado	**hubieran** comido	**hubieran** vivido

▶ The past perfect subjunctive is used in subordinate clauses under the same conditions that you have learned for other subjunctive forms, and in the same way the past perfect is used in English (*I had talked, you had spoken,* etc.). It refers to actions or conditions that had taken place before another action or condition in the past.

No había nadie que **hubiera dormido**.
There wasn't anyone who had slept.

Esperaba que Juan **hubiera ganado** el partido.
I hoped that Juan had won the game.

Dudaba que ellos **hubieran llegado**.
I doubted that they had arrived.

Llegué antes de que la clase **hubiera comenzado**.
I arrived before the class had begun.

¡INTÉNTALO! Indica la forma apropiada del pluscuamperfecto de subjuntivo de cada verbo entre paréntesis.

1. Esperaba que ustedes _hubieran hecho_ (hacer) las reservaciones.
2. Dudaba que tú _hubieras dicho_ (decir) eso.
3. No estaba seguro de que ellos _hubieran ido_ (ir).
4. No creían que nosotros _hubiéramos hablado_ (hablar) con Ricardo.
5. No había nadie que _hubiera podido_ (poder) comer tanto como él.
6. No había nadie que _hubiera visto_ (ver) el espectáculo.
7. Me molestó que tú no me _hubieras llamado_ (llamar) antes.
8. ¿Había alguien que no _hubiera apreciado_ (apreciar) esa película?
9. No creían que nosotras _hubiéramos bailado_ (bailar) en el festival.
10. No era cierto que yo _hubiera ido_ (ir) con él al concierto.

Section Goal

In **Estructura 17.3** students will learn the use of the past perfect subjunctive.

Instructional Resources
WB/VM: Workbook, pp. 196–198
Lab Manual, p. 101
Lab CD/MP3 ***Lección 17***
IRM: ***¡Inténtalo! & Práctica*** *Answers, p. 223; Tapescript, pp. 76–79*
Interactive CD-ROM
Companion website: www.vistahigherlearning.com
Presentations CD-ROM

Suggestions

- Briefly review the past perfect indicative and the present perfect subjunctive. Ask volunteers to identify cues that trigger the subjunctive mood in a subordinate clause (verbs of emotion; doubt, disbelief, denial; certain conjunctions; references to persons or things not known to exist; and so forth). Ask students to predict how the past perfect subjunctive is conjugated.
- Discuss the use of the past perfect subjunctive and examine the example sentences. Ask volunteers to identify the cue that triggered the subjunctive mood in each example. Then ask them to suggest other sentences that follow the pattern of the example sentences. Ex: **Se sorprendió de que nadie se hubiera dormido mientras tocaba aquella banda.**
- Point out that in many parts of the Spanish-speaking world, the past perfect subjunctive is used instead of the conditional perfect. Ex: **Maite hubiera preferido ir a la ópera, pero Álex prefirió ir al cine.**

TEACHING OPTIONS

Extra Practice Make a series of statements using the past perfect indicative, then begin reactions to the statements that call for the subjunctive. Have students complete the reactions. Ex: **Jorge había esculpido una estatua para el festival. Fue maravilloso que... (Jorge hubiera esculpido una estatua para el festival).**

TPR Make a series of statements using either the present perfect subjunctive or the past perfect subjunctive. If students hear a statement using the present perfect subjunctive, they raise one hand. If they hear one with the past perfect subjunctive, they raise two hands.

1 Expansion Write four cloze sentences on the board like those in the activity, leaving blanks only for verbs. Remember not to provide infinitives. Have pairs complete them and then read them aloud. The class should vote for the most creative sentences.

2 Expansion After practicing the present perfect and past perfect subjunctives in the activity, have students rewrite the items. This time they should use the present and past subjunctives. Then have them read all four versions of each item aloud. Ex: **Dudo que hayan cerrado el museo. Dudaba que hubieran cerrado el museo. Dudo que cierren el museo. Dudaba que cerraran el museo.**

3 Expansion Ask students to imagine they have been on the same spaceship as Emilio Hernández. Have them write six statements about what they hoped had changed over the past 30 years. Ex: **Esperaba que hubieran descubierto cómo reducir la contaminación.**

Nota cultural Ask students where else in Latin America volcanoes can be found. Have them research the role they have played in the myths and legends of Latin America.

Práctica

1

Completar Completa las oraciones con el pluscuamperfecto de subjuntivo de los verbos entre paréntesis.

1. Me alegré de que mi familia se hubiera ido (irse) de viaje.
2. Me molestaba que Carlos y Miguel no hubieran venido (venir) a visitarme.
3. Dudaba que la música que yo escuchaba hubiera sido (ser) la misma que escuchaban mis padres.
4. No creían que nosotros hubiéramos podido (poder) aprender tanto español en un año.
5. Los músicos se alegraban de que su programa le hubiera gustado (gustar) tanto al público.
6. La profesora se sorprendió de que nosotros hubiéramos hecho (hacer) la tarea antes de venir a clase.

2

Transformar María está hablando de las emociones que ha sentido ante ciertos acontecimientos (*events*). Transforma sus oraciones según el modelo.

modelo

Me alegro de que hayan venido los padres de Micaela.
Me alegré de que hubieran venido los padres de Micaela.

1. Es muy triste que haya muerto la tía de Miguel.
   Fue muy triste que hubiera muerto la tía de Miguel.
2. Dudo que Guillermo haya comprado una casa tan grande.
   Dudaba que Guillermo hubiera comprado una casa tan grande.
3. No puedo creer que nuestro equipo haya perdido el partido.
   No podía creer que nuestro equipo hubiera perdido el partido.
4. Me alegro de que mi novio me haya llamado.
   Me alegré de que mi novio me hubiera llamado.
5. Me molesta que el periódico no haya llegado.
   Me molestó que el periódico no hubiera llegado.
6. Dudo que hayan cerrado el Museo de Arte.
   Dudaba que hubieran cerrado el Museo de Arte.

¡LENGUA VIVA!

Both the preterite and the imperfect can be used to describe past thoughts or emotions. In general, the imperfect describes a particular action or mental state without reference to its beginning or end; the preterite refers to the occurrence of an action, thought, or emotion at a specific moment.

Pensaba que mi vida era aburrida.

Pensé que había dicho algo malo.

3

El regreso Usa el pluscuamperfecto de subjuntivo para indicar lo que el astronauta Emilio Hernández esperaba que hubiera pasado en su familia y en el mundo, durante los 30 años que había estado en el espacio sin tener noticias del exterior.

modelo

su esposa / no casarse con otro hombre
Esperaba que su esposa no se hubiera casado con otro hombre.

1. su hija Diana / conseguir ser una pintora famosa
   Esperaba que su hija Diana hubiera conseguido ser una pintora famosa.
2. los políticos / acabar con todas las guerras (*wars*)
   Esperaba que los políticos hubieran acabado con todas las guerras.
3. su suegra / irse a vivir a El Salvador
   Esperaba que su suegra se hubiera ido a vivir a El Salvador.
4. su hermano Ramón / tener un empleo más de dos meses
   Esperaba que su hermano Ramón hubiera tenido un empleo por más de dos meses.
5. todos los países / resolver sus problemas económicos
   Esperaba que todos los países hubieran resuelto sus problemas económicos.
6. su esposa / ya pagar el préstamo de la casa
   Esperaba que su esposa ya hubiera pagado el préstamo de la casa.

NOTA CULTURAL

En **El Salvador** hay varios volcanes activos. El volcán Izalco, el cual permaneció (*remained*) activo hasta 1957, era conocido por su producción constante de humo y de lava. Los marineros (*sailors*) le decían El faro (*lighthouse*) del Pacífico.

TEACHING OPTIONS

Pairs Have students make six statements about something that happened last year. Partners counter with statements declaring that the action had not really occurred. Ex: **El poeta Arturo Cruz se murió mientras leía su poesía. (No era cierto que Arturo Cruz se hubiera muerto mientras leía su poesía.)**

Small Groups Divide the class into groups of three. Have students take turns telling their group about things they wish had happened over the course of their lives. Ex: **¡Ojalá que hubiera aprendido a tocar el piano!**

Comunicación

4 **El robo** La semana pasada desaparecieron varias obras del museo. El detective sospechaba que los empleados del museo le estaban mintiendo. En parejas, siguiendo el modelo, digan qué era lo que pensaba el detective. Después, intenten descubrir qué realmente pasó. Presenten su teoría del robo a la clase. Answers will vary.

modelo

El vigilante (*security guard*) le dijo que alguien había abierto las ventanas de una sala.

El detective dudaba (no creía, pensaba que no era cierto, etc.) que alguien hubiera abierto las ventanas de la sala.

1. El carpintero le dijo que ese día no había encontrado nada extraño en el museo.
2. La abogada le dijo que ella no había estado en el museo esa tarde.
3. El técnico le dijo que había comprado una casa porque había ganado la lotería.
4. La directora del museo le dijo que había visto al vigilante hablando con la abogada.
5. El vigilante dijo que la directora había dicho que esa noche no tenían que trabajar.
6. El carpintero se acordó de que la directora y el vigilante habían sido novios.

5 **Reacciones** Imagina que los siguientes acontecimientos (*events*) ocurrieron la semana pasada. Indica cómo reaccionaste ante cada uno. Answers will vary.

modelo

Vino a visitarte tu tía de El Salvador.

Me alegré de que hubiera venido a visitarme.

1. Perdiste tu mochila con tus tarjetas de crédito y tus documentos.
2. Tu ex novio/a se casó con tu mejor amigo/a.
3. Encontraste cincuenta mil dólares cerca del banco.
4. Tus amigos/as te hicieron una fiesta sorpresa.

Síntesis

6 **Noticias** En grupos, lean los siguientes titulares (*headlines*) e indiquen cuáles hubieran sido sus reacciones si esto les hubiera ocurrido a ustedes. Luego escriban tres titulares más y compártanlos con los demás grupos. Utilicen el pluscuamperfecto de subjunctivo. Answers will vary.

Un grupo de turistas se encuentra con Elvis en una gasolinera.
El cantante les saludó, les cantó unas canciones y después se marchó hacia las montañas, caminando tranquilamente.

Tres jóvenes estudiantes se perdieron en un bosque de Maine.
Después de estar tres horas perdidos, aparecieron en una gasolinera de un desierto de Australia.

Ayer, una joven hondureña, después de pasar tres años en coma, se despertó y descubrió que podía entender el lenguaje de los animales.
La joven, de momento, no quiere hablar con la prensa, pero una amiga suya nos dice que está deseando ir al zoológico.

4 Suggestion Before beginning the activity, have the class brainstorm expressions of doubt that trigger the subjunctive in a subordinate clause.

4 Expansions
- Have pairs share with the class their theories of what really happened. After all theories have been presented, have the class decide which one is the most likely and which one is the least likely. Encourage students to defend their opinion.
- Have small groups write the police report the detective submitted to his superiors.

5 Suggestion Have students share a few reactions to what actually happened to them last week. Ex: **Me molestó que mis padres hubieran salido de vacaciones sin mí.**

6 Expansion Ask students to pick a fairy tale and write a five-sentence ending using the past perfect subjunctive. Ex: **No era verdad que el lobo hubiera comido a la abuela...** Write any unfamiliar vocabulary on the board for reference.

The Affective Dimension
Reassure students, who may be feeling overwhelmed, that many tenses are made up of forms they have already learned. Encourage them to review previously learned tenses regularly.

TEACHING OPTIONS

Extra Practice Tell students to write six sentences describing how they felt about what happened at an arts festival held last weekend. Ex: **Fue una lástima que mi cantante favorito no hubiera cantado en el festival.**

Small Groups Divide students into groups of three. Student A picks an event, such as final exams or a concert. Student B begins a statement in the past that triggers the subjunctive. Student C completes the sentence with a verb in the past perfect subjunctive. Ex: **el concierto de Ricky Martin / No había nadie que... / ... no se hubiera divertido.**

Section Goals

In **Lectura** students will:
- learn to summarize a text in their own words
- read a poem in Spanish

Instructional Resource
Companion website: www.vistahigherlearning.com

Estrategia Tell students that summarizing a text in their own words will greatly increase their comprehension of it. Explain that they may want to develop the habit of scanning a text, summarizing what they have read, taking notes, and then rereading the text. Tell them this strategy can help them understand any text they read.

Examinar el texto First, ask students to look at the format of the text and tell you what genre the text is. Then have students skim the poem. Read it aloud for the class, and ask students to say what the poem means to them. Encourage them to read it aloud in private to enjoy its lyrical nature.

Resumen Ask pairs to work together to complete the sentences. When they are finished, go over the answers orally with the whole class.

Preguntas Ask questions of the whole class. Ask volunteers to answer orally or to write their answers on the board.

Lectura

Antes de leer

Estrategia
Summarizing a text in your own words

Summarizing a text in your own words can help you comprehend it better. Before summarizing a text, you may find it helpful to skim it and jot down a few notes about its general meaning. You can then read the text again, writing down the important details. Your notes will help you summarize what you have read. If the text is particularly long, you may want to subdivide it into smaller segments so that you can summarize it more easily.

Examinar el texto

Lee la selección rápidamente. ¿Qué tipo de documento es? ¿De qué trata? Luego lee el texto una segunda vez para comprenderlo mejor.

Resumen

Después de leer la biografía, completa el siguiente resumen del texto usando las siguientes palabras:

literatura poema poesía poeta talentoso

1. El ___poema___ se llama "Entre lo que veo y digo...".
2. Esta obra es del ___poeta___ Octavio Paz y el tema es la ___poesía___.
3. El mexicano Octavio Paz es muy ___talentoso___.
4. Paz ganó el Premio Nobel de ___literatura___ en 1990.

Preguntas

1. ¿Te gusta la poesía? ¿Prefieres leerla o escribirla?
2. ¿Quién escribió este poema?
3. ¿Conoces a Octavio Paz?
4. ¿Se repiten palabras en el poema? ¿Cuáles?

recursos

vistahigherlearning.com

Entre lo que veo y digo

A Roman Jakobson

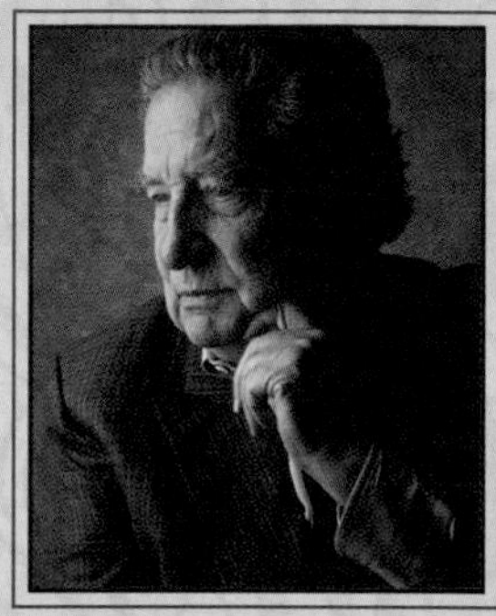

Octavio Paz

El ***escritor mexicano Octavio Paz*** *nació en 1914 y murió en 1998. Paz dejó su país por unos años para ir a estudiar literatura a España y a los Estados Unidos. Además, trabajó como diplomático en Francia, Japón y la India. Paz fundó la famosa revista de literatura* Letras Libres *y participó activamente en la vida literaria de Hispanoamérica. Uno de sus libros más conocidos es* El laberinto de la soledad, *en el que el autor escribe sobre los problemas sociales de su país. Publicó varios libros de poesía y de ensayos sobre crítica de arte y sobre la historia y la cultura de México. Las obras de Paz se premiaron en numerosas ocasiones. Recibió el Premio Cervantes en 1981 y el Premio Nobel de Literatura en 1990.*

TEACHING OPTIONS

Heritage Speakers Ask heritage speakers to prepare a brief presentation on their favorite Spanish-language poet. Students should include a short biography of the poet and be prepared to read for the class their favorite poem by him or her.

Extra Practice Ask students to write a biography of Octavio Paz. They should include a bibliography of his works and share other examples of his poetry with the class.

1

Entre lo que veo y digo,
entre lo que digo y callo°,
entre lo que callo y sueño,
entre lo que sueño y olvido,
la poesía.
Se desliza°
entre el sí y el no:
dice
lo que callo,
calla
lo que digo,
sueña
lo que olvido.
No es un decir:
es un hacer.
Es un hacer
que es un decir.
La poesía
se dice y se oye:
es real.
Y apenas digo
es real,
se disipa°.
¿Así es más real?

2

Idea palpable,
palabra
impalpable:
la poesía
va y viene
entre lo que es
y lo que no es.
Teje° reflejos
y los desteje°.
La poesía
siembra° ojos en la página,
siembra palabras en los ojos.
Los ojos hablan,
las palabras miran,
las miradas piensan.
Oír
los pensamientos,
ver
lo que decimos,
tocar
el cuerpo de la idea.
Los ojos
se cierran,
las palabras se abren.

callo *keep quiet* **desliza** *slides* **se disipa** *vanishes; dissipates* **Teje** *Weaves* **desteje** *unravels* **siembra** *plants*

Después de leer

Contestar

El poema contiene varias personificaciones como, por ejemplo, **"Los ojos hablan"**. Las personificaciones atribuyen a los objetos cualidades y acciones que sólo tienen los seres vivos.

Busca ejemplos de personificaciones en el poema y después inventa tú otros cuatro.

1. Los ojos hablan.
2. ______.
3. ______.
4. ______.
5. ______.
6. ______.
7. ______.
8. ______.

Octavio Paz nos dice que la poesía es una experiencia abstracta. ¿Crees que las personificaciones que has encontrado ayudan a ver esa abstracción? ¿Cómo?

Tú eres el/la poeta

Escribe un poema sobre un tema de tu elección. Para empezar, utiliza la primera parte de **"Entre lo que veo y digo"**. No olvides escribir un título. Cuando termines, comparte tu obra maestra con la clase.

(Título): ______
Entre lo que veo y digo,
Entre lo que digo y callo,
entre ______ y ______,
entre ______ y ______,
______.
______
______
______
______

Contestar

- Have students explain one or more of the personifications in the poem or rephrase them. Ex: **Los ojos hablan. En otras palabras, los ojos pueden expresar lo que alguien está pensando.**
- In small groups, have students write down two of the four examples of personification they invented, each one on a separate strip of paper. They should cut each strip into two pieces, one containing the subject and the other the predicate. Have the group mix up the pieces to create new examples of personification. Ask a group representative to read some of them aloud to the class, and ask volunteers to say how they might be interpreted.

Tú eres el/la poeta

- Before beginning the activity, ask students the following questions about their artistic interests: **¿Te gusta escribir poesía? ¿Por qué? ¿Te gustan otros tipos de arte? ¿Cuáles? ¿Te gusta pintar? ¿Esculpir? ¿O prefieres sólo admirar el arte? ¿Cómo expresas tus intereses artísticos?**
- Ask students these questions about this poem: **¿Te gusta "Entre lo que veo y digo"? ¿Por qué? ¿Qué nos dice el poema sobre el proceso creativo del poeta?**

The Affective Dimension Tell your students that reading poetry can be daunting, even in one's native language, because poetry is often written in very symbolic language. Point out that reading Spanish poetry will be less anxiety-provoking if students use the reading strategies they have learned so far.

TEACHING OPTIONS

Extra Practice Have students research the work of other types of artists in the Spanish-speaking world. Encourage them to present to the class what they learn and use as much lesson vocabulary as possible. They should also bring in samples of the artist's work.

Extra Practice Have students look at the poem again and decide how many of the five senses it alludes to: **vista** (*sight*), **tacto** (*touch*), **gusto** (*taste*), **olfato** (*smell*), **oído** (*hearing*). Then for each category, ask them to list as many vocabulary words from this lesson as they can that they associate with that sense.

Section Goals

In **Escritura** students will:

- learn to find biographical information
- integrate vocabulary and structures taught in **Lección 17**
- write a composition

Estrategia Explain to students that when they research biographical information, they may wish to start with general resources and work their way toward specific sources. Guide students on where to look for biographical information on the Mexican muralist Diego Rivera. Students should mention resources such as the Internet, books on Mexican muralists, or books specifically about Rivera, such as *Dreaming with His Eyes Open* by Patrick Marnham and *Diego Rivera: A Retrospective* by Cynthia Newman Helms, et al.

Tema Working with the whole class, brainstorm several artists, musicians, movie stars, scientists, historians, politicians, athletes, and others whom they would like to invite for dinner. Then have them brainstorm questions they may wish to ask their dinner guests. Model the pronunciation of the phrases on this page, asking students to suggest verbs in the conditional tense to complete them.

Escritura

Estrategia

Finding biographical information

Biographical information can be useful for a great variety of writing topics. Whether you are writing about a famous person, a period in history, or even a particular career or industry, you will be able to make your writing both more accurate and more interesting when you provide detailed information about the people who are related to your topic.

To research biographical information, you may wish to start with general reference sources, such as encyclopedias and periodicals. Additional background information on people can be found in biographies or in nonfiction books about the person's field or industry. For example, if you wanted to write about Jennifer López, you could find background information from periodicals, including magazine interviews and movie or concert reviews. You might also find information in books or articles related to contemporary film and music.

Biographical information may also be available on the Internet, and depending on your writing topic, you may even be able to conduct interviews to get the information you need. Make sure to confirm the reliability of your sources whenever your writing includes information about other people.

You might want to look for the following kinds of information:

- Date of birth
- Date of death
- Childhood experiences
- Education
- Family life
- Place of residence
- Life-changing events
- Personal and professional accomplishments

Tema

¿A quién te gustaría conocer?

Si pudieras invitar a cinco personas famosas a cenar en tu casa, ¿a quiénes invitarías? Pueden ser de cualquier° época de la historia y de cualquier profesión. Algunas posibilidades son:

- el arte
- la música
- el cine
- las ciencias
- la historia
- la política

Escribe una composición breve sobre la cena. Explica por qué invitarías a estas personas y describe lo que harías, lo que preguntarías y lo que dirías si tuvieras la oportunidad de conocerlas. Utiliza el condicional.

cualquier *any*

TEACHING OPTIONS

Proofreading Activity Copy the following sentences containing mistakes onto the board or a transparency as a proofreading activity to do with the whole class.

1. **Creíamos que un artista tan famoso haría pintado más cuadros esté año.**
2. **Luis compro un libro de poemas de Ernesto Cardenal por qué le gusta mucho a su obra.**
3. **La bailarína siguió bailando, pero dijo que se jubilara dentro de un mes.**
4. **De haberme preguntando a mí, había recomendado que la orquesta había tocado otro tipo de música.**
5. **Los dos jovenes habrían asistido al concierto en el parque sino hubiera llovido.**
6. **Miguel dijo que el querería ser autor de no ficción algun día.**

1 Ideas y organización

Busca información en Internet y en la biblioteca sobre las personas que escogiste°. Organiza la información de una manera lógica.

2 Primer borrador

Utiliza tus apuntes de **Ideas y organización** para escribir el primer borrador de tu composición.

3 Comentario

Comparte tu borrador y los datos° recogidos° en **Ideas y organización** con un(a) compañero/a de clase. Lee su información y su composición y ofrécele consejos basados en esta guía:

a. ¿Es interesante la composición?
b. ¿Contiene suficientes detalles?
c. ¿Está bien organizada?
d. ¿Hay errores ortográficos o gramaticales?

4 Redacción

Revisa el primer borrador según las indicaciones de tu compañero/a. Antes de escribir tu versión final, revisa tu trabajo según esta guía:

a. Busca los verbos en el condicional. ¿Están escritos correctamente?
b. Revisa la concordancia entre los sustantivos y los adjetivos en cada oración.
c. Subraya° los pronombres para comprobar el uso correcto de cada uno.
d. Consulta tus **Anotaciones para mejorar la escritura** para evitar la repetición de errores previos.

5 Evaluación y progreso

En grupos, compartan sus composiciones. Luego túrnense para crear diálogos basados en las cenas. Para cada diálogo, un(a) estudiante hará el papel del/de la entrevistador(a) y los/las otros/as estudiantes representarán a las personas famosas. Cuando el/la profesor(a) te devuelva° tu trabajo, lee sus observaciones para mejorar tu próxima composición. Como siempre, anota tus errores en las **Anotaciones para mejorar la escritura** en tu **Carpeta de trabajos**.

escogiste *you chose* datos *pieces of information* recogidos *collected* Subraya *Underline* devuelva *returns*

Comentario
- Go over guide questions a–d with the class and allow a few minutes for students to exchange their compositions.
- Have students prepare **Redacción** as homework.

Evaluación y progreso Give groups sufficient time to read the compositions and role-play dialogues based on them.

Writing Sample Below is a brief composition that would constitute superior writing achievement.

La cena de los famosos

Si yo tuviera la oportunidad de invitar a cinco personas famosas a cenar en mi casa, invitaría a las siguientes personas: Frida Kahlo, Pedro Almodóvar, Tim Berners-Lee, Pete Sampras y Albert Einstein.

Si una noche me encontrara con Frida Kahlo sentada en mi comedor, le preguntaría sobre los temas de su arte y le pediría que me contara algo interesante sobre cada cuadro.

Si pudiera cenar y charlar con Pedro Almodóvar, le diría que me encantan sus películas y le preguntaría sobre sus fuentes de inspiración.

Si conociera a Tim Berners-Lee, el inventor de Internet, le preguntaría sobre los planes futuros para Internet y si le gusta la rapidez con la cual está desarrollándose.

Si pudiera hablar con Pete Sampras, campeón de tenis, le preguntaría cuáles son sus estrategias para controlar los nervios bajo presión.

Si tuviera la oportunidad de cenar con Albert Einstein, el famoso científico, le pediría una explicación de la teoría de la relatividad.

En fin, ¡sería una cena inolvidable!

EVALUATION: Composición

Criteria	Scale
Content	1 2 3 4
Organization	1 2 3 4
Use of vocabulary	1 2 3 4
Grammatical accuracy	1 2 3 4
Creativity	1 2 3 4

Scoring	
Excellent	18–20 points
Good	14–17 points
Satisfactory	10–13 points
Unsatisfactory	< 10 points

Section Goals

In **Escuchar** students will:

- listen to a letter sent to a job applicant
- practice the strategies of listening for key words and using context
- listen to a film review

Instructional Resources
Textbook CD
IRM: Tapescript, p. 101

Estrategia
Script Estimada Srta. Negrón: Es un gran placer ofrecerle un puesto en el bufete de abogados Chirinos y Alemán. Como se mencionó durante su entrevista la semana pasada, el sueldo comenzará en $52.500 anuales. Los beneficios incluirán un seguro de salud, tres semanas de vacaciones pagadas y un seguro de vida. Quisiéramos que comenzara a trabajar el lunes, 17 de mayo. Favor de presentarse a las ocho en punto ese día. Si no le es posible comenzar ese día, favor de comunicarse conmigo lo más pronto posible.

Suggestion Guide students to see that the art is a poster for a horror movie.

Ahora escucha
Script Hoy viernes, como siempre, les vamos a ayudar a hacer sus planes para el fin de semana. Les traemos una reseña de la película que estrenó esta semana, *El fantasma del lago Enriquillo.* Esta película, en la cual regresa a la pantalla el famoso artista Jorge Verdoso, se anuncia como una película de ciencia ficción.
Es una lástima ver al talentoso Verdoso en esta película. Generalmente lo hemos visto en comedias románticas y su arte tanto como su apariencia se prestan más a ese tipo de obra que a *El fantasma del lago Enriquillo.* La trama es tan exagerada que acaba siendo una sátira.
La película tiene sus momentos especiales a pesar de sus limitaciones. Las escenas que Jorge Verdoso comparte con la estrella Lourdes del Río son destacadas y fascinantes. Hay una energía fabulosa entre estos artistas.
Los efectos especiales no son los que hoy día esperamos ver; parecen ser algo de una película de hace quince años. Pero la música del gran compositor Jaime Rebelde es espectacular.
Recomiendo la película pero con reservas. Los aficionados de las películas de Verdoso y del Río no se la van a querer perder. Pero vayan con el conocimiento de que algunos momentos supuestamente dramáticos son cómicos.

Escuchar

Estrategia

Listening for key words/ Using the context

The comprehension of key words is vital to understanding spoken Spanish. Use your background knowledge of the subject to help you anticipate what the key words might be. When you hear unfamiliar words, remember that you can use context to figure out their meaning.

To practice these strategies, you will now listen to a paragraph from a letter sent to a job applicant. Jot down key words, as well as any other words you figured out from the context.

JORGE VERDOSO
LOURDES DEL RÍO
EL FANTASMA DEL LAGO ENRIQUILLO

Preparación

Basándote en el dibujo, ¿qué palabras crees que usaría un crítico en una reseña° de esta película?

Ahora escucha 

Ahora vas a escuchar la reseña de la película. Mientras escuches al crítico, recuerda que las críticas de cine son principalmente descriptivas. La primera vez que la escuches, identifica las palabras clave° y escríbelas en la columna A. Luego, escucha otra vez la reseña e identifica el significado de las palabras en la columna B mediante el contexto. Answers will vary.

 A	 B
1. ________	1. estrenar
2. ________	2. a pesar de
3. ________	3. con reservas
4. ________	4. supuestamente
5. ________	5. la trama
6. ________	6. conocimiento

recursos
TEXT CD Lección 17

reseña *review* clave *key*

Comprensión

Cierto o falso

	Cierto	Falso
1. *El fantasma del lago Enriquillo* es una película de ciencia ficción.	✓	○
2. Los efectos especiales son espectaculares.	○	✓
3. Generalmente se ha visto a Jorge Verdoso en comedias románticas.	✓	○
4. Jaime Rebelde es un actor espectacular.	○	✓

Preguntas Answers will vary.

1. ¿Qué aspectos de la película le gustaron al crítico?
2. ¿Qué no le gustó al crítico de la película?
3. Si a ti te gustaran los actores, ¿irías a ver esta película? ¿Por qué?
4. Para ti, ¿cuáles son los aspectos más importantes de una película? Explica tu respuesta.

Ahora ustedes Answers will vary.

Trabaja con un grupo de compañeros/as. Escojan una película con actores muy famosos que no fue lo que esperaban. Escriban una reseña que describa el papel de los actores, la trama, los efectos especiales, la cinematografía u otros aspectos importantes de la película.

Escribe un informe

Imagina que estás escribiendo un informe sobre los mejores y más famosos artistas de Centroamérica. Tu informe debe incluir información sobre los artistas de El Salvador y de Honduras.

1 Escribe una sección del informe

Usa los **Recursos para la investigación** para buscar información de la historia del arte en Honduras y en El Salvador. Escoge tres o cuatro de los artistas más famosos de cada país. El informe debe incluir la siguiente información:

- Una descripción de las obras de cada artista
- Una explicación de por qué el artista fue escogido para aparecer en el informe
- Una foto de cada artista
- Fotos de las obras de cada artista (si no hay fotos disponibles° debes describir las obras más detalladamente°)

2 Presenta la información

Presenta el informe a la clase. Resume° lo que escribiste y muéstrales a tus compañeros/as las fotos que encontraste de los artistas y de su arte. Describe las obras y da tu opinión sobre ellas.

Iglesia con mural, El Salvador

Palabras útiles

el tema	*subject*
colorido/a	*colorful*
abstracto/a	*abstract*
informe	*report*

recursos para la investigación

Internet Palabras clave: Honduras, El Salvador, arte, museo, galería

Comunidad Profesores, estudiantes o personas en la comunidad que son de Honduras o El Salvador; profesores o estudiantes de arte

Biblioteca Libros, enciclopedias

Otros recursos El/La conservador(a)° del museo local o del museo de la universidad

disponibles *available* **más detalladamente** *in greater detail* **Resume** *Summarize* **conservador(a)** *curator*

Section Goals

In **Proyecto** students will:
- write a report on Salvadoran and Honduran artists
- use Spanish as they research and interact with the wider world

Suggestion Students might need a week to complete the project, so at the beginning of that time period, have them open their books to this page and glance over **Proyecto**. Explain that they are going to write a report about the most famous artists in El Salvador and Honduras.

Escribe una sección del informe

- You may wish to have students work in small groups. Have them determine what they will say about each artist and decide how to split up the work.
- Students can seek information on artists in El Salvador and Honduras by using the Spanish key words and phrases **arte El Salvador, arte Honduras, artistas salvadoreños, artistas hondureños,** and **artistas reconocidos de El Salvador y Honduras.**

Presenta la información

- Students will present their reports in small groups. You may wish to have groups display samples or pictures of the artists' work on tables or desks.
- You may wish to set aside sufficient class time to do a few presentations at a time until all students have had a chance to present.

EVALUATION: Informe

Criteria	Scale
Content	1 2 3 4
Organization	1 2 3 4
Grammatical accuracy	1 2 3 4
Creativity	1 2 3 4
Oral presentation	1 2 3 4

Scoring	
Excellent	18–20 points
Good	14–17 points
Satisfactory	10–13 points
Unsatisfactory	< 10 points

Section Goal
In **Panorama**, students will read about the geography and culture of El Salvador.

Instructional Resources
Transparencies, #3, #4, #60
WB/VM: Workbook, p. 199;
Video Activities, pp. 283–284
***Panorama cultural** DVD/Video*
Interactive CD-ROM
IRM: Videoscript, p. 136
Companion website:
www.vistahigherlearning.com
Presentations CD-ROM

Suggestion Have students look at the map of El Salvador or project **Transparency #60**. Draw students' attention to the number of active volcanoes in El Salvador. Tell students that because of the fertility of El Salvador's volcanic soil, the country has a strong agricultural sector which, in turn, has promoted a large population. Have students look at the inset map as you point out that El Salvador is the only Central American country without a Caribbean coast. Look at the photos and ask volunteers to read the captions.

El país en cifras El Salvador's overpopulation, chronic economic problems, and lack of social justice resulted, in the early 1970s, in social disturbances that the government put down with brutal force.

¡Increíble pero cierto! In the town of Concepción de Ataco, another legend claims that on the **Cerro la Empalizada** there is a cave containing plants that disorient anyone who steps on them.

El Salvador

El país en cifras

- **Área:** 21.040 km² (8.124 millas²), *el tamaño° de Massachusetts*
- **Población:** 6.519.000

El Salvador es el país centroamericano más pequeño y el más densamente° poblado. Su población, al igual que la de Honduras, es muy homogénea: casi el 95 por ciento de la población es mestiza.

- **Capital:** San Salvador—1.533.000
- **Ciudades principales:** Soyapango—252.000, Santa Ana—202.000, San Miguel—183.000, Mejicanos—145.000

SOURCE: Population Division, UN Secretariat

- **Moneda:** colón, dólar estadounidense
- **Idiomas:** español (oficial), náhuatl, lenca

Bandera de El Salvador

Salvadoreños célebres

- **Óscar Romero,** arzobispo° y activista por los derechos humanos° (1917–1980)
- **Claribel Alegría,** poeta, novelista y cuentista (1924–)
- **Roque Dalton,** poeta, ensayista y novelista (1935–1975)
- **María Eugenia Brizuela,** política (1956–)

Óscar Romero

tamaño *size* densamente *densely* arzobispo *archbishop* derechos humanos *human rights* laguna *lagoon* sirena *mermaid*

Ruinas de Tazumal

Salvadoreña secando hamacas (*hammocks*)

GUATEMALA · HONDURAS · Lago de Guija · Río de la Paz · Santa Ana · Río Lempa · Mejicanos · Ilobasco · Volcán de San Salvador · San Salvador · Soyapango · Río Torola · Río Goascorán · San Miguel · Volcán de San Vicente · Volcán de San Miguel · La Libertad · Océano Pacífico · Golfo de Fonseca

Aeropuerto Ilopango en San Salvador

ESTADOS UNIDOS · OCÉANO ATLÁNTICO · EL SALVADOR · OCÉANO PACÍFICO · AMÉRICA DEL SUR

recursos

WB pp. 199–200	VM pp. 283–284	I CD-ROM Lección 17	vistahigher learning.com

¡Increíble pero cierto!

El rico folklore salvadoreño se basa sobre todo en sus extraordinarios recursos naturales. Por ejemplo, según una leyenda, las muertes que se producen en la Laguna° de Alegría tienen su explicación en la existencia de una sirena° solitaria que vive en el lago y captura a los jóvenes atractivos.

TEACHING OPTIONS

Worth Noting Government repression in El Salvador intensified resistance, and by the mid-1970s a civil war was being fought between government forces and the FMLN, an armed guerrilla movement. Among the many martyrs of the war was the Archbishop of San Salvador, Óscar Romero. A descendent of the privileged class in El Salvador, Romero came to champion the cause of peace and social justice for the poor. This position made him the target of reactionary elements. On March 24, 1980, Archbishop Romero was assassinated while saying mass in the Cathedral of San Salvador. His life and death became an inspiration for those seeking social justice. Still, it was only in 1991 that a cease-fire brought an end to the civil war.

Deportes • El *surfing*

El Salvador, con unos 300 kilómetros de costa en el Océano Pacífico, se ha convertido en un gran centro de *surfing* por la calidad° y consistencia de sus olas°. *La Libertad* es la playa que está más cerca de la capital, y allí las condiciones son perfectas para el *surfing*. Por eso vienen surfistas de todo el mundo a este pequeño pueblo salvadoreño. Los fines de semana hay muchísima gente en *La Libertad* y por eso muchos surfistas van al oeste, por la *Costa del Bálsamo*, donde las olas son buenas y hay menos gente.

Naturaleza • El Parque Nacional Montecristo

El Parque Nacional Montecristo se encuentra en el norte del país. Es conocido también como El Trifinio porque es el punto donde se unen° Guatemala, Honduras y El Salvador. Este bosque está a una altitud de 2.400 metros (7.900 pies). Recibe 200 centímetros (80 pulgadas°) de lluvia al año y con frecuencia tiene una humedad° relativa del 100 por ciento. Sus altísimos árboles forman una bóveda° que la luz del sol no puede traspasar°. Allí hay muchas especies interesantes de plantas y animales, como orquídeas, hongos°, monos araña°, pumas, quetzales y tucanes.

Artes • La artesanía de Ilobasco

Ilobasco es un pueblo de grandes artesanos. Es famoso por sus objetos de arcilla° y por los artículos de cerámica pintados a mano. Los productos más tradicionales de Ilobasco son los juguetes°, los adornos° y los utensilios de cocina. Se ofrecen excursiones en las que se puede observar paso a paso° la fabricación de estos productos. Las "sorpresas" de Ilobasco, pequeñas piezas° de cerámica en cuyo interior están representadas escenas de la vida diaria, son especialmente populares.

¿Qué aprendiste? Responde a las preguntas con una frase completa.

1. ¿Qué es el náhuatl?
   El náhuatl es un idioma que se habla en El Salvador.
2. ¿Quien es María Eugenia Brizuela?
   María Eugenia Brizuela es una política salvadoreña.
3. Hay muchos lugares ideales para el *surfing* en El Salvador. ¿Por qué? Hay muchos lugares ideales para el *surfing* porque El Salvador recibe algunas de las mejores olas del océano Pacífico.
4. ¿A qué altitud se encuentra el parque Montecristo? El bosque nuboso se encuentra a una altitud de 2.400 metros.
5. ¿Cuáles son algunos de los animales y las plantas que se encuentran en el bosque nuboso?
   En el bosque nuboso hay orquídeas, hongos, monos araña, pumas, quetzales y tucanes.
6. ¿Por qué al Parque Nacional Montecristo se le llama también El Trifinio? Al Parque Nacional Montecristo también se le llama El Trifinio porque es el punto donde se unen Guatemala, Honduras y El Salvador.
7. ¿Por qué es famoso el pueblo de Ilobasco?
   El pueblo de Ilobasco es famoso por los objetos de arcilla y por los artículos de cerámica pintados a mano.
8. ¿Qué se puede ver en una excursión a Ilobasco?
   En una excursión a Ilobasco se puede ver la fabricación de los artículos de cerámica paso a paso.
9. ¿Qué son las "sorpresas" de Ilobasco? Las "sorpresas" son pequeñas piezas de cerámica en cuyo interior están representadas escenas de la vida diaria.

Conexión Internet Investiga estos temas en el sitio **www.vistahigherlearning.com.**

1. El Parque Nacional Montecristo es una reserva natural; busca información sobre otros parques o zonas protegidas en El Salvador. ¿Cómo son estos lugares? ¿Qué tipos de plantas y animales se encuentran allí?
2. Busca información sobre museos u otros lugares turísticos en San Salvador (u otra ciudad de El Salvador).

calidad *quality* olas *waves* se unen *come together* pulgadas *inches* humedad *humidity* bóveda *canopy* traspasar *pierce* hongos *fungi* monos araña *spider monkeys* arcilla *clay* juguetes *toys* adornos *ornaments* paso a paso *step by step* pieza *piece*

El *surfing* Tell students that La Libertad is a relatively small town that sees a large influx of beach-goers, not just surfers during the weekends and holidays. Black, volcanic sand covers the beach of La Libertad. About five miles east lies Zunzal beach, which, during Holy Week (**Semana Santa**) each year, is the site of international surfing competitions.

El Parque Nacional Montecristo The Montecristo cloud forest (**bosque nuboso**) is a protected area at the point where El Salvador, Honduras, and Guatemala meet. The point, at the summit of Montecristo, is called **El Trifinio**. The cloud forest receives close to 80 inches of rain per year and the average relative humidity is 100%. Visitors have access to Montecristo only between October and March. The rest of the year it is closed to visitors.

La artesanía de Ilobasco Ilobasco is a crafts village that specializes in ceramic ware. **Sorpresas** are one of the most famous items. They are miniscule, intricate scenes and figures inside egg-shaped shells about the size of a walnut. Every year on September 29th a crafts fair is held, drawing thousands of visitors from around the world.

Conexión Internet Students will find supporting Internet activities and links at **www.vistahigherlearning.com**.

TEACHING OPTIONS

Variación léxica Pupusa is the name given to the Salvadoran version of the **tortilla**. In fact, **pupusas** are made by putting a filling such as red beans, onions, garlic, and cheese on one uncooked tortilla, laying another tortilla over it, and pressing the two together so they adhere, and then frying both in hot oil until the pupusa is golden and crunchy. Served sizzling from the fryer, **pupusas** are delicious. They are so popular that in El Salvador there are many stores, called **pupuserías**, that specialize in them. And if you visit a neighborhood in the United States where Salvadorans have settled, you will inevitably find a **pupusería**.

Section Goal

In **Panorama**, students will read about the economy and culture of Honduras.

Instructional Resources
Transparencies, #3, #4, #61
WB/VM: Workbook, p. 200; Video Activities, pp. 285–286
***Panorama cultural** DVD/Video*
Interactive CD-ROM
IRM: Videoscript, p. 136
Companion website: www.vistahigherlearning.com
Presentations CD-ROM

Suggestion Have students look at the map of Honduras or project **Transparency #61** and talk about the physical features of the country. Hills and mountains cover three quarters of Honduras, with lowlands found only along coastal areas and in major river valleys. Deforestation is a major environmental challenge in Honduras. If deforestation continues at the current rate of 300 square kilometers per year, Honduras will have no trees left by 2020.

El país en cifras After reading about the indigenous populations of Honduras, tell students that the **miskito** people are also found along the Caribbean coast of Nicaragua. After students read about **Idiomas**, point out that **garífuna** speakers are descendants of indigenous Caribs who intermarried with African slaves following the shipwreck of a slaving ship some 300 years ago.

¡Increíble pero cierto! Honduras is not known for the fairness of its justice system. Many prisoners of the **Penitenciaría Central de Tegucigalpa** have never been officially sentenced for the crimes that landed them in prison! Severe overcrowding is another problem. Given these conditions, the works of the prison artisans of Tegucigalpa are all the more impressive.

Honduras

NATIONAL STANDARDS connections cultures

El país en cifras

- **Área:** 112.492 km^2 (43.870 $millas^2$), *un poco más grande que Tennessee*
- **Población:** 6.828.000

Cerca del 90 por ciento de la población de Honduras es mestiza. Todavía hay pequeños grupos indígenas como los jicaque, los miskito y los paya, que han mantenido su cultura sin influencias exteriores y que no hablan español.

- **Capital:** Tegucigalpa—1.120.000

Tegucigalpa

- **Ciudades principales:** San Pedro Sula—470.000, El Progreso—81.000, La Ceiba—72.000

SOURCE: Population Division, UN Secretariat

- **Moneda:** lempira
- **Idiomas:** español (oficial), miskito, garífuna

Bandera de Honduras

Hondureños célebres

- **José Antonio Velásquez,** pintor (1906–1983)
- **Argentina Díaz Lozano,** escritora (1917–1999)
- **Carlos Roberto Reina,** juez° y presidente del país (1926–2003)
- **Roberto Sosa,** escritor (1930–)

juez *judge* presos *prisoners* hamacas *hammocks*

Guacamayo

Hombres garífuna en Santa Fe

Islas de la Bahía
Mar Caribe
Golfo de Honduras
GUATEMALA
La Ceiba
Santa Fe
Laguna de Caratasca
San Pedro Sula
Río Ulúa
Sierra Rijol
Sierra de Payas
Río Patuca
Sierra Espíritu Santo
El Progreso
Montañas de Colón
Sierra Grita
Lago de Yojoa
Sierra Villasanta
Río Guayambre
Tegucigalpa
Río Coco
EL SALVADOR
Río Choluteca
Río Guayape
Océano Pacífico
NICARAGUA

Niños pescando en el lago de Yojoa.

recursos

WB pp. 199–200	VM pp. 285–286	I CD-ROM Lección 17	vistahigher learning.com

¡Increíble pero cierto!

Los presos° de la Penitenciaría Central de Tegucigalpa hacen objetos de madera, hamacas° y hasta instrumentos musicales. Sus artesanías son tan populares que los funcionarios de la prisión han abierto una pequeña tienda donde los turistas pueden regatear con este especial grupo de artesanos.

TEACHING OPTIONS

Worth Noting It was in Honduras, on his fourth voyage of discovery, that Christopher Columbus first set foot on the mainland of the continent that would become known as the Americas. On August 14, 1502, the navigator landed at a site near the town of Trujillo and named the country **Honduras** (*depths*) because of the deep waters along the northern Caribbean coast.

Extra Practice At this point in their studies, your students should be able to read and understand the poem **"La casa de la justicia,"** by Roberto Sosa, without difficulty. (You can find the text online.) Discuss it with your students, asking them what they think the poet's impression of the Honduran justice system is.

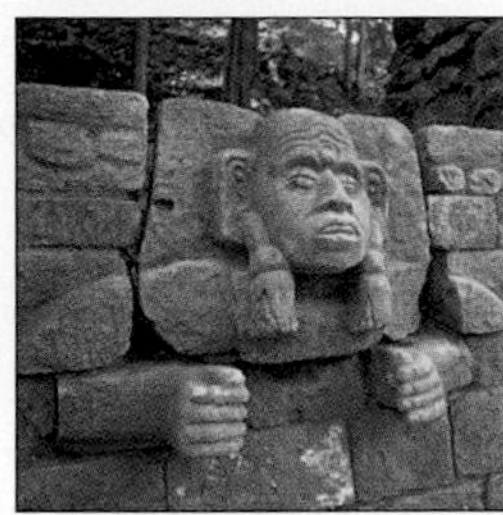

Lugares • Copán

Copán es el sitio arqueológico más importante de Honduras, y para los que estudian la cultura maya, es uno de los más fascinantes de la región. Aproximadamente en 400 d.C., la ciudad era muy grande, con más de 150 edificios y plazas, patios, templos y canchas° para el juego de pelota°. Copán es famoso por las esculturas pintadas que adornan sus edificios; por los cetros° ceremoniales de piedra finamente° esculpidos; y por el templo llamado Rosalila.

Economía • Las plantaciones de bananas

Hoy día las bananas son la exportación principal de Honduras. Hace más de cien años que tienen un papel fundamental en la historia económica y política del país. En 1889, la Standard Fruit Company empezó a exportar bananas a Nueva Orleans y la fruta resultó tan popular que rápidamente empezó a generar° grandes beneficios° para la Standard Fruit y para la United Fruit Company, otra compañía norteamericana. Debido al° enorme poder° económico que tenían en el país, estas compañías intervinieron° muchas veces en la política hondureña.

San Antonio de Oriente, 1957, José Antonio Velásquez

Artes • José Antonio Velásquez (1906–1983)

José Antonio Velásquez fue uno de los pintores primitivistas° más famosos de su tiempo. Se le compara con pintores europeos del mismo género°, como Paul Gauguin o Emil Nolde, porque en sus obras representaba lo más concreto de la vida diaria que lo rodeaba°. Se nota fácilmente el énfasis del pintor en los detalles° de la escena°. En su pintura desaparecen° casi totalmente los juegos de perspectiva, y los colores utilizados en los paisajes son puros.

¿Qué aprendiste? Responde a las preguntas con una frase completa.

1. ¿Qué es la lempira?
   La lempira es la moneda nacional de Honduras.
2. ¿Por qué es famoso Copán?
   Porque es el sitio arqueológico más importante de Honduras.
3. ¿Dónde está el templo Rosalila?
   El templo Rosalila está en Copán.
4. ¿Cuál es la exportación principal de Honduras?
   Las bananas son la exportación principal de Honduras.
5. ¿Qué es la Standard Fruit Company? La Standard Fruit Company es una compañía norteamericana que exportaba bananas de Honduras e intervino muchas veces en la política hondureña.
6. ¿Cómo es el estilo de José Antonio Velásquez?
   El estilo de Velásquez es primitivista.
7. ¿Qué temas trataba Velásquez en su pintura?
   Velásquez pintaba la vida diaria que lo rodeaba.

Conexión Internet Investiga estos temas en el sitio **www.vistahigherlearning.com.**

1. ¿Cuáles son algunas de las exportaciones principales de Honduras, además de las bananas? ¿A qué países exporta Honduras sus productos?
2. Busca información sobre Copán u otro sitio arqueológico en Honduras. En tu opinión, ¿cuáles son los aspectos más interesantes del sitio?

canchas *courts* juego de pelota *jai-alai* cetros *scepters* finamente *in a refined way* generar *to generate* beneficios *profits* Debido al *Due to* poder *power* intervinieron *intervened* primitivistas *primitivist* género *genre* rodeaba *surrounded* detalles *details* escena *scene* desaparecen *disappear*

Copán Recent archaeological studies have focused on the abrupt disappearance of the Mayans from Copán around the ninth century C.E. Findings indicate that the Mayan dynasty suffered a sudden collapse that left the Copán valley virtually depopulated within a century.

Las plantaciones de bananas When Hurricane Mitch struck Central America in November 1998, it not only wiped out much of the infrastructure of Honduras, but also destroyed 60% of the projected agricultural exports. Instead of the 33 million boxes of bananas projected for export in 1999, only 4 million boxes were exported. The banana industry is still trying to recover from this major setback.

José Antonio Velásquez The primitive style established by José Antonio Velásquez is now being carried on by his son, Tulio Velásquez. Tulio was taught by his father, and had his first exhibition in 1959. Since then, his primitive art has been exhibited throughout the Americas, in Europe, and in Asia. Have students view works by each artist and then write a brief comparison of their styles.

Conexión Internet Students will find supporting Internet activities and links at **www.vistahigherlearning.com**.

TEACHING OPTIONS

Worth Noting Honduras was among the hardest hit of the Central American nations when Hurricane Mitch struck in November 1998. Major roadways and bridges were destroyed, entire communities were covered in mud, and an air of hopelessness and desperation pervaded the country. With one of the lowest per capita income levels and one of the highest illiteracy rates in Central America, Hondurans were already struggling before the devastation of Mitch. Despite international aid, reconstruction is slow and the level of desperation in Honduras has been reflected in the increase in violent crime.

Heritage Speakers Ask heritage speakers to research one of the Honduran topics mentioned in **Panorama** and write a three-paragraph essay about it. They may then present their findings orally to the class.

Instructional Resources
Vocabulary CD
Lab Manual, p. 101
Lab CD/MP3 ***Lección 17***
IRM: Tapescript, pp. 76–79
Testing Program: ***Pruebas****, pp. 193–204*
Testing Program Audio CD
Test Files CD-ROM

Las bellas artes

el baile, la danza	*dance*
la banda	*band*
las bellas artes	*(fine) arts*
el boleto	*ticket*
la canción	*song*
la comedia	*comedy; play*
el concierto	*concert*
el cuento	*short story*
la cultura	*culture*
el drama	*drama; play*
la escultura	*sculpture*
el espectáculo	*show*
la estatua	*statue*
el festival	*festival*
la historia	*history; story*
la música	*music*
la obra	*work (of art, music, etc.)*
la obra maestra	*masterpiece*
la ópera	*opera*
la orquesta	*orchestra*
el personaje (principal)	*(main) character*
la pintura	*painting*
el poema	*poem*
la poesía	*poetry*
el público	*audience*
el teatro	*theater*
la tragedia	*tragedy*
aburrirse	*to get bored*
aplaudir	*to applaud*
apreciar	*to appreciate*
dirigir	*to direct*
esculpir	*to sculpt*
hacer el papel (de)	*to play the role (of)*
pintar	*to paint*
presentar	*to present; to put on (a performance)*
publicar	*to publish*
tocar (un instrumento musical)	*to touch; to play (a musical instrument)*
artístico/a	*artistic*
clásico/a	*classical*
dramático/a	*dramatic*
extranjero/a	*foreign*
folklórico/a	*folk*
moderno/a	*modern*
musical	*musical*
romántico/a	*romantic*
talentoso/a	*talented*

Los artistas

el bailarín, la bailarina	*dancer*
el/la cantante	*singer*
el/la compositor(a)	*composer*
el/la director(a)	*director; (musical) conductor*
el/la dramaturgo/a	*playwright*
el/la escritor(a)	*writer*
el/la escultor(a)	*sculptor*
la estrella (*m., f.*) de cine	*movie star*
el/la músico/a	*musician*
el/la poeta	*poet*

El cine y la televisión

el canal	*channel*
el concurso	*game show; contest*
los dibujos animados	*cartoons*
el documental	*documentary*
el premio	*prize; award*
el programa de entrevistas	*talk show*
la telenovela	*soap opera*
...de acción	*action*
...de aventuras	*adventure*
...de ciencia ficción	*science fiction*
...de horror	*horror*
...de vaqueros	*western*

La artesanía

la artesanía	*craftsmanship; crafts*
la cerámica	*pottery*
el tejido	*weaving*

Expresiones útiles	*See page 517.*

recursos

LM p. 101	Lab CD/MP3 Lección 17	Vocab CD Lección 17

Las actualidades 18

Communicative Goals

You will learn how to:

- **Talk about and describe your travel experiences**
- **Discuss current events and issues**
- **Talk about and discuss the media**

A PRIMERA VISTA

- **¿Qué profesión tendrán estas personas? ¿Son reporteros? ¿Periodistas?**
- **¿Es una videoconferencia?**
- **¿Hacen entrevistas?**
- **¿Es posible que hablen con estrellas de cine? ¿Con políticos?**

Lesson Goals

In **Lección 18** students will be introduced to the following:
- terms for current events
- political terms
- words for social issues
- **si** clauses in the subjunctive mood
- **si** clauses with verbs in the indicative mood
- review of subjunctive forms
- using the subjunctive, indicative, and infinitive in complex sentences
- recognizing chronological order
- writing strong introductions and conclusions
- writing a composition about improving the world
- recognizing genre and taking notes while listening
- writing a news article on current events in Paraguay and Uruguay
- cultural and geographic information about Paraguay
- cultural and geographic information about Uruguay

A primera vista Here are some additional questions you can ask based on the photo: **¿Ves mucho la tele? ¿Qué programas ves? ¿Para obtener información, prefieres leer el periódico y revistas o visitar sitios web? ¿Por qué? ¿Asistirías a un programa de entrevistas? ¿A cuál? ¿Harías un documental? ¿De qué?**

INSTRUCTIONAL RESOURCES

Workbook/Video Manual: WB Activities, pp. 201–212
Laboratory Manual: Lab Activities, pp. 103–106
Workbook/Video Manual: Video Activities, pp. 247–248; pp. 287–290
Instructor's Resource Manual: **Vocabulario adicional**, p. 196; **¡Inténtalo!** & **Práctica** Answers, p. 224; **Fotonovela** Translations, pp. 148–149; Textbook CD Tapescript, p. 102; Lab CDs Tapescript, pp. 80–83; **Fotonovela** Videoscript, p. 125; **Panorama cultural** Videoscript, p. 137
Info Gap Activities Booklet, pp. 69–72
Overhead Transparencies: #5, #6, #62, #63, #64
Lab Audio CD/MP3 **Lección 18**
Panorama cultural DVD/Video
Fotonovela DVD/Video
Testing Program, pp. 205–216; pp. 229–239; pp. 265–275
Testing Program Audio CD
Test Files CD-ROM
Companion website
Presentations CD-ROM
Textbook CD
Vocabulary CD
Interactive CD-ROM
Video CD-ROM
Web-SAM

Section Goals

In **Contextos**, students will learn and practice terminology related to:

- current events
- politics
- social issues

Instructional Resources
Transparency #62
Textbook CD
Vocabulary CD
WB/VM: Workbook, pp. 201–202
Lab Manual, p. 103
Lab CD/MP3 ***Lección 18***
IRM: ***Vocab. adicional****, p. 196;*
Práctica *Answers, p. 224;*
Tapescript, pp. 80–83; p. 102
Interactive CD-ROM
Companion website: www.vistahigherlearning.com
Presentations CD-ROM

Suggestions

- Bring in a current newspaper (Spanish-language if possible) and talk about the headlines and main stories. Ex: **¿Qué dice la prensa hoy? ¿Cuál es el reportaje principal? Anoche hubo un terremoto en… .** Show other headlines and ask volunteers to tell the class what they know about the story and what their opinions are.
- Project **Transparency #62**. Have students refer to the drawing to answer questions about news-making events. Ex: **¿Qué tiempo hace? ¿Quién se presenta como candidato en las elecciones? ¿Qué hace la señora sentada delante del banco? ¿Y el hombre que sale corriendo del banco?** As you continue, ask personalized questions. Ex: **¿Cuál es su opinión de los candidatos a ____? ¿Por qué creen eso? ¿Quién ha participado alguna vez en una huelga? ¿Cuál fue el resultado? ¿Cuántos leen el diario cada mañana? ¿Cuántos escuchan las noticias por la radio?**

Note: At this point you may want to present **Vocabulario adicional: Más vocabulario relacionado con las actualidades**, from the IRM.

Las actualidades

Más vocabulario

el acontecimiento	*event*
las actualidades	*news; current events*
el artículo	*article*
la encuesta	*poll; survey*
la experiencia	*experience*
el informe	*report; paper (written work)*
los medios de comunicación	*media; means of communication*
las noticias	*news*
la prensa	*press*
el reportaje	*report*
el desastre (natural)	*(natural) disaster*
el huracán	*hurricane*
la inundación	*flood*
el terremoto	*earthquake*
el desempleo	*unemployment*
la (des)igualdad	*(in)equality*
la discriminación	*discrimination*
la guerra	*war*
la libertad	*liberty; freedom*
la paz	*peace*
el racismo	*racism*
el sexismo	*sexism*
el SIDA	*AIDS*
anunciar	*to announce; to advertise*
comunicarse (con)	*to communicate (with)*
durar	*to last*
informar	*to inform*
luchar (por/contra)	*to fight; to struggle (for/against)*
ocurrir	*to occur; to happen*
transmitir, emitir	*to broadcast*
(inter)nacional	*(inter)national*
peligroso/a	*dangerous*

Variación léxica

informe ⟷ trabajo (*Esp.*)
noticiero ⟷ informativo (*Esp.*)

recursos

TEXT CD Lección 18	WB pp. 201–202	LM p. 103	Lab CD/MP3 Lección 18	I CD-ROM Lección 18	Vocab CD Lección 18
				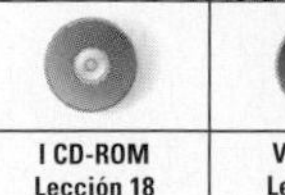	

TEACHING OPTIONS

Heritage Speakers Ask heritage speakers to watch a news broadcast on a Spanish station or surf the Internet for the latest news in their home communities. Have them summarize the report for the class.

Variación léxica Introduce common newspaper terms: **titular** (*headline*), **artículo regular** (*column*), **sección de deportes** (*sports page*), **carta al/a la director(a)** (*letter to the editor*).

Extra Practice Write the following groups of words on the board and have students indicate which word doesn't belong. **1. discurso elecciones política choque (choque) 2. televisión prensa locutora radio (locutora) 3. lluvia terremoto inundación tormenta (terremoto) 4. guerra desastre militar ejército (desastre) 5. peligroso huelga trabajador sueldo (peligroso)**

el tornado
el incendio
La política
el/la ciudadano/a citizen
el deber responsibility; obligation
los derechos rights
la dictadura dictatorship
las elecciones election
el impuesto tax
la política politics
el/la representante representative
declarar to declare; to say
elegir to elect
obedecer to obey
votar to vote
político/a political
BANCO
el diario
DIARIO
el noticiero
NOTICIAS CANAL 7
la locutora

Práctica

1 Escuchar Escucha las noticias y selecciona la frase que mejor completa las oraciones.

1. Los ciudadanos creen que __b__.
   a. hay un huracán en el Caribe
   b. hay discriminación en la imposición de los impuestos
   c. hay una encuesta en el Caribe
2. Los ciudadanos creen que los candidatos tienen __a__.
   a. el deber de asegurar la igualdad en los impuestos
   b. el deber de hacer las encuestas
   c. los impuestos
3. La encuesta muestra que los ciudadanos __c__.
   a. quieren desigualdad en las elecciones
   b. quieren hacer otra encuesta
   c. quieren igualdad en los impuestos
4. Hay __b__ en el Caribe.
   a. un incendio grande b. una tormenta peligrosa c. un tornado
5. Los servicios de Puerto Rico predijeron anoche que __c__ podrían destruir edificios y playas.
   a. los vientos b. los terremotos c. las inundaciones

2 Categorías Mira la lista e indica la categoría de cada uno de los siguientes términos. Las categorías son: **desastres naturales, política, medios de comunicación.**

1. reportaje — medios de comunicación
2. inundación — desastres naturales
3. incendio — desastres naturales
4. candidato/a — política
5. informe — medios de comunicación
6. ciudadano/a — política
7. encuesta — política
8. tornado — desastres naturales
9. noticiero — medios de comunicación
10. prensa — medios de comunicación
11. elecciones — política
12. terremoto — desastres naturales

3 Definir Trabaja con un(a) compañero/a para definir las siguientes palabras. Answers will vary.

1. guerra
2. crimen
3. ejército
4. desempleo
5. discurso
6. acontecimiento
7. sexismo
8. SIDA
9. huelga
10. racismo
11. locutor(a)
12. libertad

1 Suggestion Help students check their answers by reading the tapescript to the class and asking volunteers to read the completed sentences.

1 Tapescript Las noticias de hoy de Montevideo y de todo el mundo... En noticias políticas... Ahora que se acercan las elecciones, una encuesta nacional muestra que los ciudadanos creen que hay discriminación en la imposición de los impuestos. Se cree que los candidatos tienen el deber de asegurar la igualdad de los impuestos para todos o, por lo menos, explicar claramente por qué la desigualdad en ciertos impuestos ayuda a mejorar el bienestar nacional. En noticias internacionales... Esta noche una tormenta peligrosa que ha durado muchos días se acerca a las islas del Caribe, con vientos de más de 120 kilómetros por hora. Esta tormenta es casi un huracán. Los servicios de Puerto Rico y de la República Dominicana predijeron anoche que las inundaciones pueden destruir edificios, playas y productos agrícolas.
Textbook CD

2 Suggestion Model the activity by naming a term not listed. Ex: **huracán, impuesto, diario**. Have volunteers identify the category.

3 Expansions
- Have each pair join two other pairs and compare their definitions.
- Ask students to give antonyms for the first column of words. Possible answers: **paz, obediencia a las leyes, población civil, empleo, silencio, rutina**

TEACHING OPTIONS

Pairs Ask students to categorize all the nouns using different paradigms than those given. Ex: **fenómenos del tiempo relacionados con el agua: tormenta, huracán, inundación; conceptos democráticos: huelga, elecciones, derechos.** Have each pair read their categories aloud to the class.

Extra Practice Have students complete the following analogies. **1. locutora : ____ :: candidato : discurso (reportaje/noticias) 2. SIDA : salud :: ____ : libertad (dictadura) 3. pagar : impuesto :: ____ : candidato (votar) 4. lluvia : ____ :: viento : huracán (inundación/tormenta) 5. terminar : ____ :: desobedecer : obedecer (empezar/comenzar)**

4 Suggestion Have partners complete alternate sentences. Then ask them to check the other's responses.

4 Expansion Ask students to write a summary of a current news event using this activity as a model.

5 Expansion Have pairs convert the dialogue into a summary of events as reported by ***El País.*** Ex: **Hay cuatro artículos de interés en *El País* hoy. Agustín ha leído todos los artículos sobre los acontecimientos violentos, pero a Raúl le interesa el reportaje sobre los derechos humanos y la paz. Agustín no deja hablar a Raúl.**

6 Suggestions
- Go over the information in **Ayuda** before assigning this activity.
- This activity can also be done in small groups in round-robin fashion. Call on different students to report on their group's responses.

6 Expansion Assign students to groups of five, and ask them to develop a survey based on these questions. Have them survey students for the next class and present the results.

Successful Language Learning
Tell students that watching or listening to the news in Spanish is a good way to practice their comprehension skills. Point out that many of the words used in news broadcasts are cognates.

4 **Completar** Completa la siguiente noticia con los verbos adecuados para cada frase. Conjuga los verbos en el tiempo verbal correspondiente.

1. El grupo __anunció__ a todos los medios de comunicación que iba a organizar una huelga general de los trabajadores.
   a. durar b. votar c. anunciar
2. El presidente del país ha sugerido algunas soluciones para evitar que eso __ocurra__.
   a. ocurrir b. luchar c. elegir
3. Todos los representantes políticos les pidieron a los ciudadanos que __obedecieran__ al presidente.
   a. comer b. obedecer c. aburrir
4. La oposición, por otro lado, __eligió__ a un líder para promover la huelga.
   a. publicar b. emitir c. elegir
5. El líder de la oposición dijo que si el gobierno ignoraba sus opiniones, la huelga iba a __durar__ mucho tiempo.
   a. transmitir b. obedecer c. durar
6. Hoy día, el líder de la oposición declaró que los ciudadanos estaban listos para __luchar__ por sus derechos.
   a. informar b. comunicarse c. luchar

5 **Diálogo** Completa el siguiente diálogo con las palabras adecuadas.

artículo	derechos	peligrosa
choque	dictaduras	transmitir
declarar	paz	violencia

RAÚL Oye, Agustín, ¿leíste el (1)__artículo__ del diario *El País*?
AGUSTÍN ¿Cuál? ¿El del (2)__choque__ entre dos autobuses?
RAÚL No, el otro, sobre...
AGUSTÍN ¿Sobre la tormenta (3)__peligrosa__ que viene mañana?
RAÚL No, hombre, el artículo sobre política...
AGUSTÍN ¡Ay, claro! Un análisis de las peores (4)__dictaduras__ de la historia.
RAÚL ¡Agustín! Deja de interrumpir. Te quería hablar del artículo sobre la organización que lucha por los (5)__derechos__ humanos y la (6)__paz__.
AGUSTÍN Ah, no lo leí.
RAÚL Parece que te interesan más las noticias sobre la (7)__violencia__, ¿eh?

6 **La vida civil** ¿Estás de acuerdo con las siguientes afirmaciones? Comparte tus respuestas con la clase. Answers will vary.

1. Los medios de comunicación nos informan bien de las noticias.
2. Los medios de comunicación nos dan una visión global del mundo.
3. Los candidatos para las elecciones deben aparecer en todos los medios de comunicación.
4. Nosotros y nuestros representantes nos comunicamos bien.
5. Es importante que todos obedezcamos las leyes.
6. Es importante leer el diario todos los días.
7. Es importante mirar o escuchar un noticiero todos los días.
8. Es importante votar.

AYUDA
You may want to use these expressions:
En mi opinión...
Está claro que...
(No) Estoy de acuerdo.
Según mis padres...
Sería ideal que...

TEACHING OPTIONS

TPR Have students stand. Say an expression at random (**Eres locutor.**) and point at a student who should perform an appropriate gesture. Keep the pace rapid. Vary by pointing to more than one student (**Ustedes están en un huracán.**).

Game Have students write in Spanish five trivia questions and answers concerning news events. Ask them to number their questions from 1 (**la más fácil**) to 5 (**la más difícil**). Use these questions and the format of any popular television game show, but have the students compete in teams rather than as individual contestants.

Comunicación

7 **Las actualidades** En parejas, describan lo que ven en las fotos. Luego, escriban una historia para explicar qué pasó en cada foto. Answers will vary.

8 **Un noticiero** En grupos, trabajen para presentar un noticiero de la tarde. Presenten por lo menos tres reportajes sobre espectáculos, política, crimen y temas sociales. Answers will vary.

¡LENGUA VIVA!

Here are four ways to say *to happen:*
acontecer
ocurrir
pasar
suceder

9 **Las elecciones** Trabajen en parejas para representar una entrevista entre un(a) reportero/a de la televisión y un(a) político/a que va a ser candidato/a en las próximas elecciones. Antes de la entrevista, hagan una lista de los temas de los que el/la candidato/a va a hablar y de las preguntas que el/la reportero/a le va a hacer. Durante la entrevista, la clase va a hacer el papel del público. Después de la entrevista, el/la reportero/a va a hacerle preguntas y pedirle comentarios al público. Answers will vary.

7 Suggestions
- Allow the class two minutes to note details in the photos and think of scenarios for the events.
- Ask volunteers to answer closed-ended questions about each picture. Ex: **¿Ocurrió en la ciudad o en el campo? ¿Fue un acontecimiento político o un desastre natural? ¿Hubo muchas víctimas? ¿Es reciente el acontecimiento?**

7 Expansion Ask volunteers to summarize one of their descriptions.

8 Suggestion Point out **¡Lengua viva!** and give example sentences of the four ways to say *to happen* in Spanish. Then have groups of four use idea maps to brainstorm different ideas for their news reports.

8 Expansion Ask groups to choose one of their reports and present it to the class. Alternatively, have all groups present their news report during the next class meeting, encouraging them to bring props to enrich their presentations.

9 Suggestions
- Pick a prominent politician and ask students what questions they would ask him or her. Write their suggestions on the board.
- Videotape the **entrevistas** and show parts during the next class or check the tape out to students for private viewing.

TEACHING OPTIONS

Small Groups Assign groups of three for a debate on a current campus issue. Give the teams some time in class to prepare their strategy, but ask each team member to prepare his or her argument of two to three minutes as homework. Have the rest of the class judge the debate.

Game Divide the class into teams of four. Give groups five minutes to write a job announcement. Then have them take turns reading their announcements. The other teams must guess what job is being announced. Award one point for every correct guess and two points to the team who is able to stump the rest of the class.

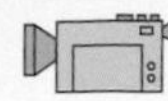

Section Goals

In **Fotonovela** students will:

- receive comprehensible input from free-flowing discourse
- learn functional phrases that preview lesson grammatical structures

Instructional Resources
WB/VM: Video Activities, pp. 247–248
***Fotonovela** DVD/Video (Start 01:42:43)*
Video CD-ROM
*IRM: **Fotonovela** Translations, pp. 148–149, Videoscript, p. 125*
Interactive CD-ROM

Video Recap: Lección 17
Before doing this **Fotonovela** section, review the previous one with this activity.

1. ¿A quién le gustan las películas románticas? (a Maite)
2. ¿Dónde publicaría Álex sus poemas? (los publicaría en Internet)
3. ¿De quiénes habla Javier cuando dice "ahí vienen Romeo y Julieta"? ¿Por qué? (habla de Maite y Álex porque salieron juntos)
4. ¿Quiénes se besan? (Álex y Maite)

Video Synopsis Upon the students' return to the university, Maite's friend Roberto interviews the group about their experiences on the excursion. Then Don Francisco and the students say good-bye to each other.

Suggestions

- Have the class read the title, scan the captions for cognates, and look at the stills. Ask students to predict what they think the episode will be about.
- Quickly review the predictions your students made about the **Fotonovela**. Ask a few questions to help them summarize the plot.
- Practice the active vocabulary in **Expresiones útiles** by asking your students a few questions about recent vacations they have taken. Ex: **¿Adónde fuiste de vacaciones el verano pasado? ¿Cuál fue tu experiencia favorita?**

¡Hasta la próxima!

NATIONAL STANDARDS connections cultures

Los estudiantes comparten con Roberto sus recuerdos (*memories*) favoritos de la aventura.

PERSONAJES

MAITE

INÉS

DON FRANCISCO

ÁLEX

JAVIER

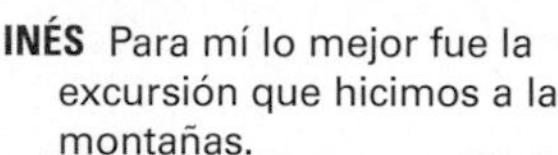
SRA. RAMOS

ROBERTO

1

SRA. RAMOS ¡Hola! Espero que todos hayan tenido un magnífico viaje.

JAVIER ¡Lo hemos pasado maravillosamente!

SRA. RAMOS ¿Qué tal, don Francisco? ¡Qué gusto volver a verlo!

2

MAITE ¡Roberto! ¿Cómo estás?

3

MAITE Álex, ven... es mi amigo Roberto. Nos conocimos en clase de periodismo. Es reportero del periódico de la universidad. Roberto, éste es mi novio, Álex.

ROBERTO Mucho gusto, Álex.

ÁLEX El gusto es mío.

6

ROBERTO A ver... Inés. ¿Cuál fue tu experiencia favorita?

INÉS Para mí lo mejor fue la excursión que hicimos a las montañas.

ROBERTO ¿Fue peligroso?

JAVIER No... Pero si nuestro guía no hubiera estado allí con nosotros, ¡seguro que nos habríamos perdido!

7

ROBERTO ¿Qué más ocurrió durante el viaje?

MAITE Pues figúrate que un día fuimos a comer al restaurante El Cráter. A la hora del postre la señora Perales, la dueña, me sorprendió con un pastel y un flan para mi cumpleaños.

8

JAVIER También tuvimos un problema con el autobús, pero Inés resolvió el problema con la ayuda de un mecánico. Ahora la llamamos La Mujer Mecánica.

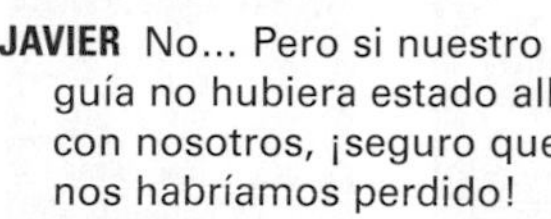

recursos

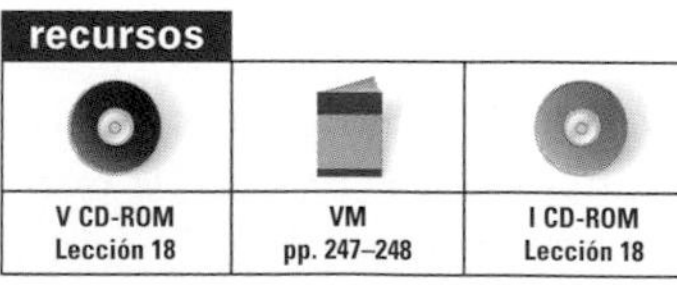

V CD-ROM Lección 18	VM pp. 247–248	I CD-ROM Lección 18

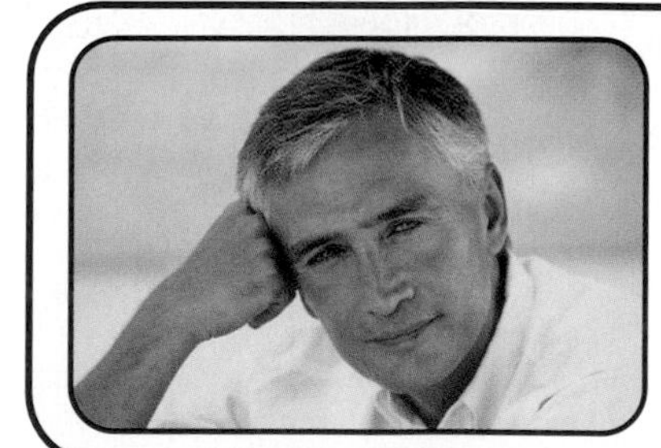

TEACHING OPTIONS

Video Tips General suggestions for using video clips in the classroom can be found on page IAE-12 of this Instructor's Annotated Edition.

¡Hasta la próxima! Before you play the **¡Hasta la próxima!** segment of this video module, give your students a list of questions about it. Tell them to read the questions and listen for the answers as they watch the video. After playing the segment, go over the questions with the class. If necessary, replay it. Sample questions: **¿Quiénes esperan a los estudiantes en la universidad? (señora Ramos, Roberto) ¿Quién es Roberto? (un amigo que Maite conoció en la clase de periodismo)**

MAITE Y éstos son mis amigos. Inés... Javier...

JAVIER & INÉS ¡Hola!

MAITE Pero, ¿qué estás haciendo tú aquí?

ROBERTO Ay, Maite, es que estoy cansado de escribir sobre crimen y política. Me gustaría hacerles una entrevista sobre las experiencias del viaje.

MAITE ¡Fenomenal!

ROBERTO Si pudieran hacer el viaje otra vez, ¿lo harían?

ÁLEX Sin pensarlo dos veces. Viajar es una buena manera de conocer mejor a las personas y de hacer amigos.

DON FRANCISCO ¡Adiós, chicos!

ESTUDIANTES ¡Adiós! ¡Adiós, don Efe! ¡Hasta luego!

DON FRANCISCO ¡Hasta la próxima, señora Ramos!

Enfoque cultural Los medios de comunicación

El periódico en español que más se vende en el mundo es *El País*, de Madrid. Se venden más de un millón de ejemplares (*copies*) cada día. En cuanto a la televisión, una de las cadenas (*networks*) más importantes es Univisión, de gran popularidad en los Estados Unidos.

Desde 1986, Jorge Ramos es el conductor titular del Noticiero Univisión. Ramos es considerado uno de "los hispanos más influyentes de Norteamérica" (*Hispanic Trends*) y uno de "los 10 Latinos más admirados en Estados Unidos" (*revista Latino Leaders*).

Expresiones útiles

Saying you're happy to see someone

- **¡Qué gusto volver a verte!**
  I'm happy to see you (fam.) *again!*
- **¡Qué gusto volver a verlo/la!**
  I'm happy to see you (form.) *again!*
- **Gusto de verte.**
  It's nice to see you (fam.).
- **Gusto de verlo/la.**
  It's nice to see you (form.).

Saying you had a good time

- **¡Lo hemos pasado maravillosamente!**
  We've had a great time!
- **¡Lo hemos pasado de película!**
  We've had a great time!
- **Lo pasamos muy bien.**
  We had a good time.
- **Nos divertimos mucho.**
  We had a lot of fun.

Talking about your trip

- **¿Cuál fue tu experiencia favorita?**
  What was your favorite experience?
- ▷ **Lo mejor fue la excursión que hicimos a las montañas.**
  The best thing was the hike we went on in the mountains.
- **¿Qué más ocurrió durante el viaje?**
  What else happened on the trip?
- ▷ **Lo peor fue cuando tuvimos un problema con el autobús.**
  The worst thing was when we had a problem with the bus.
- **Si pudieran hacer el viaje otra vez, ¿lo harían?**
  If you could take the trip again, would you do it?
- ▷ **Sin pensarlo dos veces.**
  I wouldn't give it a second thought.

Suggestion Work through the **Fotonovela** by having volunteers read the various parts aloud. Ask a few of them to ad-lib the interview portion of the **Fotonovela**.

Expresiones útiles Have the class locate the sentence **Si pudieran hacer el viaje otra vez, ¿lo harían?** Tell students that this sentence contains a **si** clause that uses the past subjunctive, followed by a clause containing a conditional form. Have the class identify the two verb forms. Then have students look at the caption for frame 6 of the **Fotonovela** and find the sentence **Pero si nuestro guía no hubiera estado allí con nosotros, ¡seguro que nos habríamos perdido!** Explain that this sentence contains a **si** clause that uses the past perfect subjunctive, followed by a clause containing a conditional perfect form. Have the class identify the two verb forms. Tell your students that they will learn more about these concepts in **Estructura**.

The Affective Dimension Ask students if they feel more comfortable watching the video now than when they started the course. Recommend that they view all the episodes again to help them realize how much their proficiency has increased.

TEACHING OPTIONS

Enfoque cultural Tell the class that there is a substantial Spanish-language media presence in the United States. Have the class work in small groups to brainstorm lists of the specific Spanish-language media that they are aware of, including local, regional, and national television networks, radio stations, magazines, and newspapers. Ask a few groups to tell the class about the media outlets on their lists. If possible, have your students bring examples of Spanish-language newspapers and magazines to class. They should be prepared to tell their classmates where each one is published and what audience it hopes to reach.

Reacciona a la fotonovela

1 **¿Cierto o falso?** Decide si lo que se afirma en las siguientes frases es **cierto** o **falso.** Corrige las frases que sean falsas.

	Cierto	Falso
1. Roberto es reportero; escribe artículos para el periódico de la universidad.	✓	○
2. Los artículos sobre el crimen y la política ya no le interesan tanto a Roberto.	✓	○
3. Para Inés, la mejor experiencia fue cuando cenaron en el restaurante El Cráter. Para Inés, la mejor experiencia fue la excursión que hicieron a las montañas.	○	✓
4. La señora Ramos sabe mucho de autobuses; por eso la llaman La Mujer Mecánica. Inés sabe mucho de autobuses; ella es "La Mujer Mecánica".	○	✓
5. A Álex le encantó el viaje pero es algo que sólo haría una vez en su vida. Álex haría el viaje otra vez, sin pensarlo dos veces.	○	✓

2 **Identificar** Identifica quién puede hacer las siguientes afirmaciones.

1. ¿Te acuerdas del problema mecánico con el autobús? Qué bueno que estaba Inés allí, ¿no? Javier
2. Si quieres hacer amigos y conocer mejor un país, tienes que viajar. Álex
3. ¡Hola! Qué bueno volver a verlos. Me imagino que tuvieron un viaje maravilloso. Sra. Ramos
4. Creo que el mejor día fue cuando fuimos a un restaurante y me prepararon un pastel. Maite
5. Ya no quiero escribir sobre cosas negativas. Prefiero hacer entrevistas sobre experiencias interesantes. Roberto

JAVIER

ROBERTO

ÁLEX

MAITE

SRA. RAMOS

3 **Preguntas** Responde a las siguientes preguntas.

1. ¿Dónde se conocieron Maite y Roberto?
Se conocieron en la universidad, en la clase de periodismo.
2. Normalmente, ¿sobre qué cosas escribe Roberto?
Escribe sobre el crimen y la política.
3. ¿Piensa Javier que el viaje fue peligroso? ¿Qué habría pasado si Martín no hubiera estado con ellos?
No. Si Martín no hubiera estado con ellos, se habrían perdido.
4. ¿Cuál fue la mejor experiencia de Maite? ¿Por qué? Fue cuando comieron en el restaurante El Cráter porque la sorprendieron con un pastel para su cumpleaños.
5. ¿Qué piensa Álex sobre viajar?
Viajar es una buena forma de conocer mejor a las personas y de hacer amigos.

4 **Mis experiencias** Tú y un(a) compañero/a de clase son unos amigos que no se han visto en algunos años. Hablen de las experiencias buenas y malas que tuvieron durante ese tiempo. Utilicen estas frases en la conversación: Answers will vary.

- ¡Qué gusto volver a verte!
- Gusto de verte.
- Lo pasé de película/maravillosamente/muy bien.
- Me divertí mucho.
- Lo mejor fue...
- Lo peor fue...

1 Expansion Give the class these additional items:
6. Roberto es el novio de Inés. (Falso. Roberto es un amigo de Maite.) 7. Javier se divirtió mucho durante el viaje. (Cierto.) 8. Roberto quiere hablar con los estudiantes sobre el viaje. (Cierto.)

2 Suggestion Have your students skim the **Fotonovela** before completing this activity.

2 Expansion Give this additional item to the class:
6. ¿Tuvieron experiencias interesantes durante el viaje? (Roberto)

3 Expansions
- In small groups, have students tell each other about their favorite episodes or scenes from the entire **Fotonovela**. Discuss the most popular ones with the whole class and ask students to share the reasons for their choices.
- Have pairs pick two of the **Fotonovela** characters and create a story about what will become of them in the future. Have volunteers share their stories with the class and compare them with those of other students.

4 Possible Response
**E1: ¡Hola! ¡Qué gusto volver a verte!
E2: Sí, gusto de verte. ¿Cómo has estado?
E1: Muy bien, gracias. Hice un viaje a Asia en junio.
E2: ¿Te divertiste?
E1: Sí, lo pasé de película.
E2: ¿Cuál fue tu experiencia favorita?
E1: Para mí lo mejor fue el viaje que hice a Tailandia. Vi muchas cosas fascinantes y comí muy bien.
E2: ¿Y cuál fue la peor experiencia?
E1: Lo peor fue cuando nos quedamos sin gasolina en una carretera en China. Oye, ¿qué has hecho tú este verano?
E2: Yo acabo de volver de Europa…**

TEACHING OPTIONS

Extra Practice Scramble the order of these events from the **Fotonovela** and have the class put them back in order: **1. El autobús llega a la universidad. 2. Roberto le pregunta a Inés sobre el viaje. 3. Maite habla de su fiesta de cumpleaños. 4. Javier recuerda el problema con el autobús. 5. Don Francisco se va.**

Pairs Have students write a short paragraph about a memorable trip, real or imaginary. Tell them to be sure to describe the best and worst parts of the trip. You may want to have your students share their paragraphs with the class, along with photographs, if possible.

Ortografía

Neologismos y anglicismos

As societies develop and interact, new words are needed to refer to inventions and discoveries, as well as to objects and ideas introduced by other cultures. In Spanish, many new terms have been invented to refer to such developments, and additional words have been "borrowed" from other languages.

bajar un programa *download*	**borrar** *to delete*	**correo basura** *junk mail*
en línea *online*	**enlace** *link*	**herramienta** *tool*
navegador *browser*	**pirata** *hacker*	**sistema operativo** *operating system*

Many Spanish neologisms, or "new words," refer to computers and technology. Due to the newness of these words, more than one term may be considered acceptable.

cederrón, CD-ROM **escáner** **fax** **zoom**

In Spanish, many anglicisms, or words borrowed from English, refer to computers and technology. Note that the spelling of these words is often adapted to the sounds of the Spanish language.

jazz, yaz **rap** **rock** **walkman**

Music and music technology are another common source of anglicisms.

gángster **hippy, jipi** **póquer** **whisky, güisqui**

Other borrowed words refer to people or things that are strongly associated with another culture.

chárter	**esnob**	**estrés**	**flirtear**
gol	**hall**	**hobby**	**iceberg**
jersey	**júnior**	**récord**	**yogur**

There are many other sources of borrowed words. Over time, some anglicisms are replaced by new terms in Spanish, while others are accepted as standard usage.

Práctica Completa el diálogo usando las siguientes palabras.

borrar	**correo basura**	**esnob**
chárter	**en línea**	**estrés**

GUSTAVO Voy a leer el correo electrónico.
REBECA Bah, yo sólo recibo correo basura. Lo único que hago con la computadora es borrar mensajes.
GUSTAVO Mira, cariño, hay un anuncio en Internet—un viaje barato a Punta del Este. Es un vuelo chárter.
REBECA Últimamente tengo tanto estrés. Sería buena idea que fuéramos de vacaciones. Pero busca un hotel muy bueno.
GUSTAVO Rebeca, no seas esnob, lo importante es ir y disfrutar. Voy a comprar los boletos ahora mismo en línea.

Dibujo Describe el dibujo utilizando por lo menos cinco anglicismos.

recursos

LM p. 104	Lab CD/MP3 Lección 18	I CD-ROM Lección 18

Section Goals

In **Ortografía** students will learn about
- recently invented Spanish words
- anglicisms

Instructional Resource
Interactive CD-ROM

Suggestions

- Ask the class to give you a few neologisms that refer to computers and technology. Then have students invent a few sentences that use these words. Write a few of their sentences on the board.
- Ask the class to give you a few anglicisms. Ask students to create a few sentences that use these words, and have volunteers write a few of their sentences on the board.
- Write the words **gángster, hipi, póquer, whisky, gol, yogur, récord,** and **esnob** on the board. Ask for volunteers to explain what each word means and use it in a sentence.
- Point out that **Ortografía** replaces **Pronunciación** in the Student Edition for **Lecciones 10–18**, but not in the Lab Manual. The **Recursos** box references the **Pronunciación** sections found in all lessons of the Lab Manual.

TEACHING OPTIONS

Small Groups Have the class work in groups of three or four to write a humorous paragraph using as many neologisms and anglicisms as possible. Then have a few volunteers read their paragraphs to the class.

Extra Practice Have students write questions using neologisms and/or anglicisms. Have volunteers write their questions on the board. Then work through the questions with the class.

Worth Noting New technology has long been the source of neologisms and cross-cultural borrowings. Most of the words of Arabic origin in Spanish, for instance, named "new technology" or products of their day. Ex: **azúcar** (*sugar*), **zafra** (*harvest of sugar cane*), **alberca** (*artificial pond, swimming pool*), **algodón** (*cotton*), **alquiler** (*rent*), **almohada** (*pillow*), **aduana** (*customs*)

Section Goals

In **Estructura 18.1** students will learn:

- **si** clauses in the subjunctive mood
- **si** clauses with verbs in the indicative mood

Instructional Resources
WB/VM: Workbook, pp. 203–204
Lab Manual, p. 105
Lab CD/MP3 ***Lección 18***
IRM: ***¡Inténtalo! & Práctica*** *Answers, p. 224; Tapescript, pp. 80–83*
Info Gap Activities Booklet, pp. 69–70
Interactive CD-ROM
Companion website: www.vistahigherlearning.com
Presentations CD-ROM

Suggestions

- Ask students to look at the caption to the first video still on this page. Ask a volunteer to identify the tense and mood of the verb in the first clause and the one in the second clause. Ask another volunteer to translate the sentence into English.
- Compare and contrast hypothetical and contrary-to-fact statements using the example sentences on this page. Check understanding by providing main clauses and having volunteers finish the sentence with a **si** clause. Ex: **No lo haría... (si fuera tú.) El huracán habría destruido tu casa... (si no hubieras tomado precauciones.) No lo habría hecho... (si hubiera sido tú.)**
- Do the same with clauses that express conditions or events that are possible or likely to occur. Ex: **Iré contigo... (si vas a participar en la huelga.)**
- Use magazine pictures to reinforce **si** clauses. Ex: **Si hubiera sido este señor, me habría puesto un abrigo.**

18.1 Si clauses

recursos
WB pp. 203–208
LM pp. 105–106
Lab CD/MP3 Lección 18
I CD-ROM Lección 18
vistahigherlearning.com

ANTE TODO **Si** *(if)* clauses describe a condition or event upon which another condition or event depends. Sentences with **si** clauses consist of a **si** clause and a main (or result) clause.

Si pudieran hacer el viaje otra vez, ¿lo harían?

▶ **Si** clauses can speculate or hypothesize about a current event or condition. They express what *would happen* if an event or condition *were to occur.* This is called a contrary-to-fact situation. In such instances, the verb in the **si** clause is in the past subjunctive while the verb in the main clause is in the conditional.

Si **cambiaras** de empleo, **serías** más feliz.
If you changed jobs, you would be happier.

Iría de viaje a Suramérica si **tuviera** dinero.
I would travel to South America if I had money.

¡ATENCIÓN!
Remember the difference between **si** (*if*) and **sí** (*yes*).

▶ **Si** clauses can also describe a contrary-to-fact situation in the past. They can express what *would have happened* if an event or condition *had occurred.* In these sentences, the verb in the **si** clause is in the past perfect subjunctive while the verb in the main clause is in the conditional perfect.

Si **hubiera sido** estrella de cine, **habría sido** rico.
If I had been a movie star, I would have been rich.

No **habrías tenido** hambre si **hubieras desayunado.**
You wouldn't have been hungry if you had eaten breakfast.

▶ **Si** clauses can also express conditions or events that are possible or likely to occur. In such instances, the **si** clause is in the present indicative while the main clause uses a present, near future, future, or command form.

Si **puedes** venir, **llámame.**
If you can come, call me.

Si **puedo** venir, **te llamo.**
If I can come, I'll call you.

Si **terminas** la tarea, **tendrás** tiempo para mirar la televisión.
If you finish your homework, you will have time to watch TV.

Si **terminas** la tarea, **vas a tener** tiempo para mirar la televisión.
If you finish your homework, you are going to have time to watch TV.

¡LENGUA VIVA!
Note that in Spanish the conditional is never used immediately following **si.**

TEACHING OPTIONS

Extra Practice Create additional sentences that follow the pattern of the example sentences. Say the main clause, then have students suggest different **si** clauses. Ex: **... tendría que caminar a las clases. (Si no tuviera bicicleta,...) ... hablaríamos español todo el día. (Si estuviéramos en México,...) ... pondría el noticiero de la tarde. (Si estuviera en casa,...)**

Heritage Speakers Ask heritage speakers to write a composition entitled **"Si yo no hablara español..."** The piece should describe how the student's life would have been different if he or she had not been born into a Spanish-speaking family. The compositions should have at least ten hypothetical and contrary-to-fact complex sentences with **si** clauses. Have students present their compositions to the rest of the class.

▶ When the **si** clause expresses habitual past conditions or events, *not* a contrary-to-fact situation, the imperfect is used in both the **si** clause and the main (or result) clause.

Si Alicia me **invitaba** a una fiesta, yo siempre **iba**.
If (Whenever) Alicia invited me to a party, I would (used to) go.

Mis padres siempre **iban** a la playa si **hacía** buen tiempo.
My parents always went to the beach if the weather was good.

▶ The **si** clause may be the first or second clause in a sentence. Note that a comma is used only when the **si** clause comes first.

Si tuviera tiempo, iría contigo.
If I had time, I would go with you.

Iría contigo **si tuviera tiempo.**
I would go with you if I had time.

Summary of *si* clause sequences

Condition	*Si* clause	Main clause
Possible or likely	**Si** + present	Present
Possible or likely	**Si** + present	Near future (**ir a** + infinitive)
Possible or likely	**Si** + present	Future
Possible or likely	**Si** + present	Command
Habitual in the past	**Si** + imperfect	Imperfect
Contrary-to-fact (present)	**Si** + past (imperfect) subjunctive	Conditional
Contrary-to-fact (past)	**Si** + past perfect (pluperfect) subjunctive	Conditional perfect

¡INTÉNTALO! Cambia los tiempos y modos de los verbos que aparecen entre paréntesis para practicar todos los tipos de oraciones con **si** que se muestran en la tabla anterior.

1. Si usted ___va___ (ir) a la playa, tenga cuidado con el sol.
2. Si tú ___quieres___ (querer), te preparo la merienda.
3. Si ___hace___ (hacer) buen tiempo, voy a ir al parque.
4. Si mis amigos ___iban___ (ir) de viaje, sacaban muchas fotos.
5. Si ella me ___llamara___ (llamar), yo la invitaría a la fiesta.
6. Si nosotros ___quisiéramos___ (querer) ir al teatro, compraríamos los boletos antes.
7. Si tú ___te levantaras___ (levantarse) temprano, desayunarías antes de ir a clase.
8. Si ellos ___tuvieran___ (tener) tiempo, te llamarían.
9. Si yo ___hubiera sido___ (ser) astronauta, habría ido a la Luna.
10. Si él ___hubiera ganado___ (ganar) un millón de dólares, habría comprado una casa en la playa.
11. Si ustedes me ___hubieran dicho___ (decir) la verdad, no habríamos tenido este problema.
12. Si ellos ___hubieran trabajado___ (trabajar) más, habrían tenido más éxito.

TEACHING OPTIONS

Pairs Ask students to reflect on the past semester(s) studying Spanish. Then assign them partners to write a list of eight complex sentences to express what they wish they had done and why. Ex: **Si hubiera hablado español con mi amiga puertorriqueña, ahora podría hablar mejor.**

Extra Practice Ask students to finish the following sentences logically: **1. Si tomas español otra vez el año próximo,... 2. Si hubieras estudiado periodismo,... 3. Si la tormenta no pasa pronto,... 4. Si no hubiera llegado el ejército,... 5. Si quieres ser locutor(a) de televisión,...**

Suggestions

- Have students open to **Fotonovela**, page 546 and read Javier's remark under frame 6. Make a question from his statement. Ex: **Si el guía no hubiera estado con ellos en las montañas, ¿qué habría pasado?** Have a volunteer state the mood and tense of the verbs and another one translate the sentence.
- Go over the use of the indicative in a **si** clause when it expresses something that is likely to happen or habitual past conditions or events. Give additional examples.
- After going over the summary of **si** clause sequences, give the students a complex sentence in the indicative, and have them work in pairs to form seven sentences using **si** clauses as per the chart. Ex: **Cuando viene un tornado, bajamos al sótano. (Si viene un tornado, bajaremos al sótano. Si viniera un tornado, bajaríamos al sótano. Si hubiera venido un tornado, habríamos bajado al sótano.** etc.**)**
- Point out that a contrary-to-fact situation in the present sometimes implies that the opportunity still exists, whereas this chance is no longer possible in a contrary-to-fact situation in the past. Ex: **Si tuviera tiempo, viajaría a Montevideo.** (Implies: *I don't have time, but there might still be a chance.*) **Si hubiera tenido tiempo, habría viajado a Montevideo.** (Implies: *I didn't have time, and the opportunity has passed.*)

The Affective Dimension

Ask your students if they feel intimidated by the variety of **si** clauses that can be created in Spanish. Tell them that the chart on this page will help them sort out the possibilities and that they will feel more comfortable with **si** clauses with time and practice.

1 Expansion Change the tense and/or mood in the **si** clauses, and have students change the main clause accordingly. Ex: **Si aquí hubiera habido terremotos,... (... no habríamos permitido edificios altos.) Si me informara bien,... (... podría explicar el desempleo.) Si me hubieras dado el informe,... (... se lo habría mostrado al director.)**

2 Suggestion In pairs, one partner fills in Teresa's answers and the other Anita's. Later, partners read and correct each other's answers.

2 Expansion Ask questions about the **minidiálogos** and have students answer in complete sentences. Ex: **¿Cuándo visitará Teresa a sus parientes? ¿Qué haría Teresa si tuviera tiempo?**

3 Suggestions
- Model the activity by having three or four volunteers complete the first sentence in different ways.
- Encourage students to ask their partner follow-up questions. Ex: **¿Por qué llamarías primero a tus padres si tuvieras un accidente de carro?**

3 Expansion Ask students to share their partner's responses with the class.

Práctica

1 **Emparejar** Empareja frases de la columna A con las de la columna B para crear oraciones lógicas.

A	B
1. Si aquí hubiera terremotos, _e_	a. se lo muestro al director.
2. Si me informo bien, _d_	b. habrían muerto muchos más.
3. Si me das el informe, _a_	c. muchos van a pasar hambre.
4. Si la guerra hubiera continuado, _b_	d. podré explicar el desempleo.
5. Si la huelga dura más de un mes, _c_	e. no permitiríamos edificios altos.

AYUDA

Remember these forms of **haber**:
(si) hubiera *(if) there were*
habría *there would be*

2 **Minidiálogos** Completa los minidiálogos entre Teresa y Anita. Some answers may vary.

TERESA ¿Qué (1) _habrías_ hecho tú si tu papá te (2) _hubiera_ regalado un carro?
ANITA Me (3) _habría_ muerto de la felicidad.

ANITA Si (4) _viajas_ a Paraguay, ¿qué vas a hacer?
TERESA (5) _Voy_ a visitar a mis parientes.

TERESA Si tú y tu familia (6) _tuvieran_ un millón de dólares, ¿qué comprarían?
ANITA Si nosotros tuviéramos un millón de dólares, (7) _compraríamos_ tres casas nuevas.

ANITA Si tú (8) _tuvieras_ tiempo, ¿irías al cine con más frecuencia?
TERESA Sí, yo (9) _iría_ con más frecuencia si tuviera tiempo.

NOTA CULTURAL

Paraguay es conocido como "El Corazón de América" porque está en el centro de Suramérica. Sus lugares más visitados son la capital Asunción, que está ubicada a orillas del río Paraguay y la ciudad de Itaguá, en donde se producen muchos textiles.

3 **Completar** En parejas, completen las frases de una manera lógica. Luego lean sus oraciones a sus compañeros. Answers will vary.

1. Si tuviera un accidente de carro...
2. Me volvería loco/a *(I would go crazy)* si mi familia...
3. Me habría ido al Cuerpo de Paz *(Peace Corps)* si...
4. No volveré a ver las noticias en ese canal si...
5. Habría menos problemas si los medios de comunicación...
6. Si mis padres hubieran insistido en que fuera al ejército...
7. Si me ofrecen un viaje a la Luna...
8. Me habría enojado mucho si...
9. Si hubiera un desastre natural en mi ciudad...
10. Yo habría votado en las elecciones pasadas si...

TEACHING OPTIONS

Pairs Have pairs write ten sentences about what they would do to improve their community or society. First, ask them to list the problems they would change and how they would do so. Then have them form their sentences as contrary-to-fact statements. Ex: **Si no se permitieran las contribuciones grandes a los candidatos, habría menos corrupción en el gobierno. Habría menos delincuencia si hubiera más lugares donde los jóvenes pudieran entretenerse. Si la universidad construyera más residencias, los alquileres no serían tan altos en nuestra comunidad.**

Video Show the video again to give students more input about **si** clauses. Ask students to write each one down as they hear it. Afterward, have them compare their notes in groups of four.

Comunicación

4 **Situaciones** Trabajen en grupos para contestar las siguientes preguntas. Después deben comunicar sus respuestas a la clase. Answers will vary.

1. ¿Qué harías si fueras de vacaciones a Uruguay y al llegar no hubiera habitaciones en ninguno de los hoteles?
2. ¿Qué haces si encuentras dinero en la calle?
3. Imagina que estuviste en Montevideo por tres semanas. ¿Qué habrías hecho si hubieras observado un crimen allí?
4. ¿Qué harías tú si fueras de viaje y las líneas aéreas estuvieran en huelga?
5. ¿Qué haces si estás en la calle y alguien te pide dinero?
6. ¿Qué harías si estuvieras en un país extranjero y un reportero te confundiera *(confused)* con un actor o una actriz de Hollywood?

NOTA CULTURAL

En **Uruguay**, se encuentra uno de los destinos más exclusivos de Latinoamérica, Punta del Este. En esta zona del país, hay muchos hoteles elegantes, preciosas playas, islas tranquilas y reservas forestales.

5 **Oraciones** En parejas, túrnense para hablar de lo que hacen, harían o habrían hecho en estas circunstancias. Answers will vary.

1. Si ves a tu novio/a con otro/a en el cine
2. Si hubieras ganado un viaje a Uruguay
3. Si mañana tuvieras el día libre
4. Si te casaras y tuvieras ocho hijos
5. Si tuvieras que cuidar a tus padres cuando sean mayores
6. Si no tuvieras que preocuparte por el dinero

6 **¿Qué pasaría?** En parejas, hagan seis oraciones con **si** basándose en las ilustraciones. Primero, deben buscar la ilustración de la causa y la del efecto correspondientes a cada oración. Su profesor(a) les va a dar a cada uno de ustedes una hoja distinta con la información necesaria para completar la actividad.

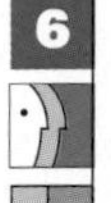

modelo

Estudiante 1: (*causa*) Si el presidente declarara una guerra,
Estudiante 2: (*efecto*) los ciudadanos lucharían por la paz.

Síntesis

7 **Entrevista** En grupos, preparen cinco preguntas para hacerle a un(a) candidato/a a la presidencia de los Estados Unidos. Luego, túrnense para hacer el papel de entrevistador(a) y de candidato/a. El/La entrevistador(a) reacciona a cada una de las respuestas del/de la candidato/a. Answers will vary.

modelo

Entrevistador(a): ¿Qué haría usted sobre el sexismo en el ejército?
Candidato/a: Pues, dudo que las mujeres puedan pelear en una guerra. Creo que deben hacer trabajos menos peligrosos.
Entrevistador(a): ¿Entonces usted no haría nada para eliminar el sexismo en el ejército?
Candidato/a: Si yo fuera presidente/a...

TEACHING OPTIONS

Large Group Ask each student to write a question that contains a **si** clause. Then have students walk around the room until you signal them to stop. At your cue each student should turn to the nearest classmate. Give students three minutes to ask and answer one another's question before having them begin walking around the room again. Each time you say "stop," they ask a new partner their question.

Small Groups Ask students to bring in the most outlandish news report they can find. Assign students to groups of four and have them write a list of statements that use **si** clauses about each report. Ex: **Si los extraterrestres vuelven para reunirse con el presidente, deben entrevistarlo personalmente.**

4 Expansion Ask groups to write a short description of what they would do if they took a group trip to Uruguay. Write a prompt on the board to get them started. Ex: **Si nosotros hiciéramos un viaje al Uruguay,...**

5 Suggestion Ask students to formulate a multiple-choice survey with the sentence fragments given. Then have them survey one another and record the answers. Ex: **Si ves a tu novio/a con otro/a en el cine,... 1. empiezas a llorar. 2. haces un escándalo. 3. los ignoras.**

6 Suggestion Divide the class into pairs and distribute the Info Gap Handouts from the Info Gap Activities Booklet that correspond to this activity. Give the students ten minutes to complete this activity.

6 Expansion Ask students to explore a Spanish-language news website and choose a story to bring to class. Assign students to groups of three, and have each one summarize his or her story for the group. Then each group should pick the strangest, saddest, or funniest story and write six **si** clauses based on it. Ex: **Si los impuestos suben más, tendré que ahorrar más dinero para pagarlos. Si pudiera hablar con el presidente, le diría exactamente lo que pienso.**

7 Suggestion Before beginning the activity, ask students to identify different political issues. Ex: **problemas sociales, el sexismo en el trabajo**, and so forth. Write these general categories on the board.

7 Expansion Ask groups to develop an assessment tool for the evaluation of the **entrevista**. Then have each group present the interviews to the class. The other groups will evaluate each presentation by using their assessment tool. Have all groups share their evaluation results with the class.

Section Goals

In **Estructura 18.2** students will review:

- the forms of the subjunctive
- the use of the subjunctive, indicative, and infinitive in complex sentences

Instructional Resources
WB/VM: Workbook, pp. 205–208
Lab Manual, p. 106
Lab CD/MP3 ***Lección 18***
IRM: ***¡Inténtalo! & Práctica*** *Answers, p. 224; Tapescript, pp. 80–83*
Info Gap Activities Booklet, pp. 71–72
Interactive CD-ROM
Companion website: www.vistahigherlearning.com
Presentations CD-ROM

Suggestions

- Review the subjunctive by summing up the year in statements that use the subjunctive. Ex: **En cuanto pasen unas semanas, habrá terminado el semestre. Espero que todos ustedes hayan aprendido mucho español. Antes de que nos despidamos, quisiera desearles a todos buena suerte.** Ask volunteers to identify the subjunctive form in each sentence.
- Before working through the summary of the subjunctive forms, review the tenses of the subjunctive, using the same sentence restated in each tense. Ex: **Cuando termine la discriminación, habrá justicia. Si terminara la discriminación, habría justicia. Si hubiera terminado la discriminación, ya habría habido justicia. Ojalá haya terminado la discriminación.**
- Have students look over the simple forms of the subjunctive of regular verbs. Ask them on which form the present subjunctive is based (present tense **yo** form) and on which one the past subjunctive is based (preterite **ellos/ellas/ Uds.** form). Then ask them to give the past or present subjunctive of common irregular verbs such as **decir, traer, introducir, conocer,** and **tener**. Finally, review the irregular verbs **dar, estar, haber, ir, saber,** and **ser**.

18.2 Summary of the uses of the subjunctive

ANTE TODO Since **Lección 12**, you have been learning about subjunctive verb forms and practicing their uses. The following chart summarizes the subjunctive forms you have studied. The chart on page 555 summarizes the uses of the subjunctive you have seen and contrasts them with uses of the indicative and the infinitive. These charts will help you review and synthesize what you have learned about the subjunctive in this book.

¡Hola! Espero que todos hayan tenido un magnífico viaje.

Si nuestro guía no hubiera estado allí con nosotros, ¡seguro que nos habríamos perdido!

Summary of subjunctive forms

–ar verbs		–er verbs		–ir verbs	
PRESENT SUBJUNCTIVE	PAST SUBJUNCTIVE	PRESENT SUBJUNCTIVE	PAST SUBJUNCTIVE	PRESENT SUBJUNCTIVE	PAST SUBJUNCTIVE
hable	hablara	beba	bebiera	viva	viviera
hables	hablaras	bebas	bebieras	vivas	vivieras
hable	hablara	beba	bebiera	viva	viviera
hablemos	habláramos	bebamos	bebiéramos	vivamos	viviéramos
habléis	hablarais	bebáis	bebierais	viváis	vivierais
hablen	hablaran	beban	bebieran	vivan	vivieran

–ar verbs	–er verbs	–ir verbs
PRESENT PERFECT SUBJUNCTIVE	PRESENT PERFECT SUBJUNCTIVE	PRESENT PERFECT SUBJUNCTIVE
haya hablado	haya bebido	haya vivido
hayas hablado	hayas bebido	hayas vivido
haya hablado	haya bebido	haya vivido
hayamos hablado	hayamos bebido	hayamos vivido
hayáis hablado	hayáis bebido	hayáis vivido
hayan hablado	hayan bebido	hayan vivido
PAST PERFECT SUBJUNCTIVE	PAST PERFECT SUBJUNCTIVE	PAST PERFECT SUBJUNCTIVE
hubiera hablado	hubiera bebido	hubiera vivido
hubieras hablado	hubieras bebido	hubieras vivido
hubiera hablado	hubiera bebido	hubiera vivido
hubiéramos hablado	hubiéramos bebido	hubiéramos vivido
hubierais hablado	hubierais bebido	hubierais vivido
hubieran hablado	hubieran bebido	hubieran vivido

CONSÚLTALO

To review the subjunctive, refer to these sections:
Present subjunctive, **Estructura 12.3**, pp. 378–380.
Present perfect subjunctive, **Estructura 15.3**, p. 469.
Past subjunctive, **Estructura 16.3**, pp. 496–497.
Past perfect subjunctive, **Estructura 17.3**, p. 527.

TEACHING OPTIONS

Small Groups Bring in or prepare a news report in Spanish about a recent natural disaster. Go over it with the class, clarifying any unfamiliar vocabulary. Then ask small groups to write a summary of the article in which they use at least three sentences in the subjunctive.

Game Divide the class into groups of three. Ask groups to think of an important historical event. Have them write two contrary-to-fact statements about the event without naming it. Each group will read its statements and the others will try to guess the event. Award one point for every correct guess. Ex: **Si el Norte no hubiera atacado al Sur, no habríamos entrado en la guerra. Si Nixon no hubiera sido presidente, la guerra habría terminado antes. (la guerra de Vietnam)**

The subjunctive is used...

1. After verbs and/or expressions of will and influence, when the subject of the subordinate clause is different from the subject of the main clause	Los ciudadanos **desean** que el candidato presidencial los **escuche.**
2. After verbs and/or expressions of emotion, when the subject of the subordinate clause is different from the subject of the main clause	Alejandra **se alegró** mucho de que le **dieran** el trabajo.
3. After verbs and/or expressions of doubt, disbelief, and denial	**Dudo** que **vaya** a tener problemas para encontrar su maleta.
4. After the conjunctions **a menos que, antes (de) que, con tal (de) que, en caso (de) que, para que,** and **sin que**	Cierra las ventanas **antes de que empiece** la tormenta.
5. After **cuando, después (de) que, en cuanto, hasta que,** and **tan pronto como** when they refer to future actions	**Tan pronto como haga** la tarea, podrá salir con sus amigos.
6. To refer to an indefinite or nonexistent antecedent mentioned in the main clause	Busco un empleado que **haya estudiado** computación.
7. After **si** to express something impossible, improbable, or contrary to fact	**Si hubieras escuchado** el noticiero, te habrías informado sobre el terremoto.

The indicative is used...

1. After verbs and/or expressions of certainty and belief	**Es cierto** que Uruguay **tiene** unas playas espectaculares.
2. After the conjunctions **cuando, después (de) que, en cuanto, hasta que,** and **tan pronto como** when they do not refer to future actions	Hay más violencia **cuando hay** desigualdad social.
3. To refer to a definite or specific antecedent mentioned in the main clause	Busco a la señora que me **informó** del crimen que ocurrió ayer.
4. After **si** to express something possible, probable, or not contrary to fact	Pronto habrá más igualdad **si luchamos** contra la discriminación.

The infinitive is used...

1. After expressions of will and influence when there is no change of subject from the main clause to the subordinate clause	Martín **desea ir** a Montevideo este año.
2. After expressions of emotion when there is no change of subject from the main clause to the subordinate clause	**Me alegro de conocer** a tu esposo.

Suggestions

- Before working through the summary of subjunctive usage, review the concepts of indicative and subjunctive. Explain that in most discourse the verbs are in the indicative, the mood used for making statements and asking questions. Then ask volunteers to tell you when the subjunctive is used. Write their statements on the board, revising them for clarity and correctness.
- Work through the summaries of the use of the subjunctive, indicative, and infinitive comparatively. After you have worked through the comparison of subjunctive vs. indicative with expressions of influence, emotion, and doubt and certainty, discuss cases where the infinitive is used instead of the subjunctive. Compare and contrast the use of subjunctive and indicative with conjunctions.

TEACHING OPTIONS

Large Group Prepare sentences based on the example sentences. Break each sentence into two clauses or fragments and write each one on an index card. Distribute the index cards and have students form sentences by finding a partner. Ex: **Me alegro mucho de que… /… hayan publicado tu artículo sobre el SIDA. Quisiera… /… visitar Montevideo algún día.**

Extra Practice To provide oral practice, create sentences that follow the pattern of the sentences in the examples. Say the sentence, have students repeat it, then change the tense of the main clause. Have students then say the sentence, changing the subordinate clause as necessary. Ex: **Dudo que terminemos el proyecto pronto. Dudaba que… (… termináramos el proyecto pronto.)**

1 Expansions
- Ask volunteers to read the completed sentences and state their reason for choosing either the subjunctive or the indicative form.
- Have students summarize the conversation in the third person.

2 Suggestion Give students two minutes to study the 12 phrases given. Then have them write down the main idea of their piece and three supporting ideas on the basis of the sentence fragments.

2 Expansion Have students read and comment on each other's paragraphs in groups of three.

3 Suggestions
- Go over the expressions listed in **Ayuda**, asking volunteers to give example sentences using each one.
- Have two volunteers read the **modelo** aloud. Provide a second response using an infinitive. Ex: **No pienso preocuparme por eso.**

3 Expansion Call on several pairs to read their conversations to the class.

Práctica

1 **Conversación** Completa la conversación con el tiempo verbal adecuado.

EMA Busco al reportero que (1) publicó (publicar) el libro sobre la dictadura de Stroessner.

ROSA Ah, usted busca a Miguel Pérez. Ha salido.

EMA Le había dicho que yo vendría a verlo el martes, pero él me dijo que (2) viniera (venir) hoy.

ROSA No creo que a Miguel se le (3) olvidara/haya olvidado (olvidar) la cita. Si usted le (4) hubiera pedido (pedir) una cita, él me lo habría mencionado.

EMA Pues no, no pedí cita, pero si él me hubiera dicho que era necesario yo lo (5) habría hecho (hacer).

ROSA Creo que Miguel (6) fue (ir) a cubrir un incendio hace media hora. No pensaba que nadie (7) fuera (ir) a venir esta tarde. Si quiere, le digo que la (8) llame (llamar) tan pronto como (9) llegue (llegar). A menos que usted (10) quiera (querer) dejar un recado...
(Entra Miguel)

EMA ¡Miguel! Amor, si hubieras llegado cinco minutos más tarde, no me (11) habrías encontrado (encontrar) aquí.

MIGUEL ¡Ema! ¿Qué haces aquí?

EMA Me dijiste que viniera hoy para que (12) pudiéramos (poder) pasar más tiempo juntos.

ROSA *(En voz baja)* ¿Cómo? ¿Serán novios?

NOTA CULTURAL

El general **Alfredo Stroessner** es el dictador que más tiempo ha durado en el poder en un país de Suramérica. Stroessner se hizo presidente de Paraguay en 1954 y en la madrugada del 3 de febrero de 1989 fue derrocado (*overthrown*) en un golpe militar (*coup*). Después de esto, Stroessner se exilió a Brasil.

2 **Escribir** Escribe uno o dos párrafos sobre tu participación en las próximas elecciones. Usa por lo menos cuatro de las frases que siguen. Answers will vary.

- Votaré por... con tal de que...
- Quisiera saber...
- Si gana mi candidato/a...
- Espero que la economía...
- Estoy seguro/a de que...
- A menos que...
- Mis padres siempre me dijeron que...
- Si a la gente realmente le importara la familia...
- No habría escogido a ese/a candidato/a si...
- Si le preocuparan más los impuestos...
- Dudo que el/la otro/a candidato/a...
- En las próximas elecciones espero que...

3 **Explicar** En parejas, escriban una conversación breve sobre cada tema de la lista. Usen por lo menos un verbo en el subjuntivo y otro en el indicativo o en el infinitivo. Sigan el modelo. Answers will vary.

modelo

un tornado
Estudiante 1: *Temo que este año haya tornados por nuestra zona.*
Estudiante 2: *No te preocupes. Creo que este año no va a haber muchos tornados.*

unas elecciones	una huelga	una inundación	la prensa
una guerra	un incendio	la libertad	un terremoto

AYUDA

Some useful expressions:
Espero que...
Ojalá que...
Es posible que...
Es terrible que...
Es importante que...

TEACHING OPTIONS

Heritage Speakers Have heritage speakers write a description of a particular news event that impacted their cultural community. Remind them to use complex sentences. Check for correct verb forms in the independent clauses before asking them to read their accounts to the class.

Pairs Have students create an informative bulletin in Spanish with a description and emergency instructions in case of a natural disaster. Focus on problems typical in your region. Remind students to use complex sentences with various subjunctive, indicative, and infinitive verb forms.

Comunicación

4 **Preguntas** Entrevista a un(a) compañero/a usando las siguientes preguntas. Answers will vary.

1. ¿Te irías a vivir a un lugar donde pudiera ocurrir un desastre natural? ¿Por qué?
2. ¿Te gustaría que tu vida fuera como la de tus padres? ¿Por qué? Y tus hijos, ¿preferirías que tuvieran experiencias diferentes a las tuyas? ¿Cuáles?
3. ¿Te parece importante que elijamos a una mujer como presidente? ¿Por qué?
4. Si hubiera una guerra y te llamaran para entrar en el ejército, ¿obedecerías? ¿Lo considerarías tu deber? ¿Qué sentirías? ¿Qué pensarías?
5. Si sólo pudieras recibir noticias de un medio de comunicación, ¿cuál escogerías y por qué? Y si pudieras trabajar en un medio de comunicación, ¿escogerías el mismo?

5 **Consejos** En parejas, lean la guía turística. Luego túrnense para representar los papeles de un(a) cliente/a y de un(a) agente de viajes. El/La agente le da consejos al/a la cliente/a sobre los lugares que debe visitar y el/la cliente/a da su opinión sobre los consejos. Answers will vary.

¡Conozca Uruguay!

La **Plaza Independencia** en **Montevideo**, con su **Puerta de la Ciudadela**, forma el límite entre la ciudad antigua y la nueva. Si le interesan las compras, desde este lugar puede comenzar su paseo por la **Avenida 18 de Julio**, la principal arteria comercial de la capital.

No deje de ir a **Punta del Este**. Conocerá uno de los lugares turísticos más fascinantes del mundo. No se pierda las maravillosas playas, el **Museo de Arte Americano** y la **Catedral Maldonado** (1895) con su famoso altar, obra del escultor **Antonio Veiga**.

Sin duda, querrá conocer la famosa ciudad vacacional de **Piriápolis**, con su puerto que atrae barcos cruceros, y disfrutar de sus playas y lindos paseos.

Tampoco se debe perder la **Costa de Oro**, junto al **Río de la Plata**. Para aquellos interesados en la historia, dos lugares favoritos son la conocida iglesia **Nuestra Señora de Lourdes** y el chalet de **Pablo Neruda**.

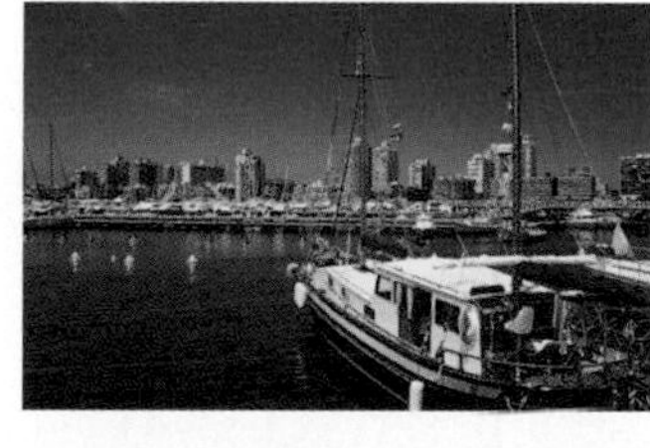

NOTA CULTURAL

Uruguay tiene uno de los climas más moderados del mundo: la temperatura media es de 22° C (72° F) en el verano y de 13° C (55° F) en el invierno. La mayoría de los días son soleados, llueve moderadamente y nunca nieva.

Síntesis

6 **Dos artículos** Tu profesor(a) les va a dar a ti y a tu compañero/a dos artículos: uno sobre una huelga de trabajadores, y otro sobre la violencia en las escuelas. Trabajando en parejas, cada uno escoge y lee un artículo. Luego, háganse preguntas sobre los artículos. Answers will vary.

4 Suggestion Tell students to take notes on what their partner says. Ask questions about the responses they received after the completion of the activity.

4 Expansions
- Ask students to create two more questions for the interview, keeping within the framework of natural disasters and sociopolitical issues.
- Survey responses to find those on which there is general agreement and those on which there is not.

5 Expansion Have the **clientes** sit on one side of the room and the **agentes de viajes** on the other. Then ask individual students about the advice they gave or were given. Ex: **¿Qué monumentos te aconsejó que visitaras? ¿Qué consejos le diste sobre los museos?**

6 Suggestions
- Divide the class into pairs and distribute the Info Gap Handouts from the Info Gap Activities Booklet that correspond to this activity. Give the students ten minutes to complete this activity.
- Go over the directions before dividing the class into pairs. Have partners skim the articles and choose the one with which they want to work.

6 Expansion Have partners develop three more questions they would ask about each article.

TEACHING OPTIONS

Pairs Have students write a news article about the end of the semester. The article should highlight the positive points of the class as well as the contributions of the students. Tell them to use the articles from **Actividad 6** as a guide.

Extra Practice Write this cloze paragraph on the board, asking students to complete it with the correct forms of **ver, llegar, creer, hacer,** and **aprender**.

Es difícil ____ (creer) que ____ (lleguemos/hayamos llegado) al final del semestre. Espero que todos ustedes ____ (hayan aprendido) mucho, no sólo español, sino sobre el lenguaje en general. Si deciden seguir estudiando el español, ____ (van a ver/verán) que se ____ (hace/hará) más fácil con el tiempo.

Section Goals

In **Lectura** students will:
- learn to recognize chronological order
- read an excerpt from a Spanish novel

Instructional Resource
Companion website:
www.vistahigherlearning.com

Estrategia Tell students that understanding the order of events allows a reader to follow what is happening in the narrative.

Successful Language Learning Tell your students to look for connecting words and transitions, because they are helpful in following a chain of events.

Examinar el texto Explain that Miguel de Cervantes Saavedra is thought to be Spain's greatest writer and that the novel ***El ingenioso hidalgo don Quijote de la Mancha*** is considered his masterpiece. Ask volunteers to tell what they know about the plot. Then have students scan the text. Explain any unfamiliar vocabulary. You may wish to have students read the excerpt aloud to aid comprehension.

Ordenar If students have trouble putting the events in order, have them refer to portions of the text and help them find the passages that contain the information.

Lectura

Antes de leer

Estrategia
Recognizing chronological order

Recognizing the chronological order of events in a narrative is key to understanding the cause and effect relationship between them. When you are able to establish the chronological chain of events, you will easily be able to follow the plot. In order to be more aware of the order of events in a narrative, you may find it helpful to prepare a numbered list of the events as you read.

Examinar el texto

Lee el texto usando las estrategias de lectura que has aprendido.

- ¿Ves palabras nuevas o cognados? ¿Cuáles son?
- ¿Qué te dice el dibujo sobre el contenido?
- ¿Tienes algún conocimiento previo° sobre don Quijote?
- ¿Cuál es el propósito° del texto?
- ¿De qué trata° la lectura?

Ordenar

Lee el texto otra vez para establecer el orden cronológico de los eventos. Luego ordena los siguientes eventos según la historia.

3 Don Quijote lucha contra los molinos de viento pensando que son gigantes.
5 Don Quijote y Sancho toman el camino hacia Puerto Lápice.
2 Don Quijote y Sancho descubren unos molinos de viento en un campo.
4 El primer molino da un mal golpe a don Quijote, a su lanza y a su caballo.
1 Don Quijote y Sancho Panza salen de su pueblo en busca de aventuras.

recursos

vistahigher learning.com

Don Quijote y los molinos de viento

Miguel de Cervantes

Fragmento adaptado de
El ingenioso hidalgo don Quijote de la Mancha

Miguel de Cervantes y Saavedra, el escritor más universal de la literatura española, nació en Alcalá de Henares en 1547 y murió en Madrid en 1616, tras° haber vivido una vida llena de momentos difíciles, llegando a estar en la cárcel° más de una vez. Su obra, sin embargo, ha disfrutado a través de los siglos de todo el éxito que se merece. Don Quijote representa no sólo la locura° sino también la búsqueda° del ideal. En esta ocasión presentamos el famoso episodio de los molinos de viento°.

Entonces descubrieron treinta o cuarenta molinos de viento que había en aquel campo°. Cuando don Quijote los vio, dijo a su escudero°:

—La fortuna va guiando nuestras cosas mejor de lo que deseamos; porque allí, amigo Sancho Panza, se ven treinta, o pocos más, enormes gigantes con los que pienso hacer batalla y quitarles a todos las vidas, y comenzaremos a ser ricos; que ésta es buena guerra, y es gran servicio de Dios quitar tan malos seres° de la tierra.

—¿Qué gigantes?

—Aquellos que ves allí —respondió su amo°— de los brazos largos, que algunos normalmente los tienen de casi dos leguas°.

Después de leer

¿Realidad o fantasía?

Indica si las siguientes afirmaciones sobre la lectura pertenecen a la realidad o la fantasía.

1. Don Quijote desea matar° a los enemigos. realidad
2. Su escudero no ve a ningún ser° sobrenatural. realidad
3. El caballero ataca a unas criaturas cobardes y viles. fantasía
4. Don Quijote no ganó la batalla porque los gigantes fueron transformados en molinos de viento. fantasía
5. El sabio Frestón transformó los gigantes en molinos de viento. fantasía

conocimiento previo *prior knowledge* propósito *purpose*
¿De qué trata...? *What is... about?* matar *to kill* ser *being*

TEACHING OPTIONS

Variación léxica Explain to students that **Quijote** has an alternative, older spelling, **Quixote**. In addition, point out that Quijote's eccentric behavior became emblematic, so that several terms derived from his name have entered the Spanish language. Among them are **quijote** (*a dreamer, hopelessly unrealistic person*), **quijotada** (*quixotic act*), **quijotesco** (*quixotic*), **quijotismo** (*quixotism*).

Extra Practice Ask students to research Miguel de Cervantes and to write a brief biography on the literary figure. Students should include a bibliography of his works.
Game Students give clues about characters in ***Don Quijote*** **(don Quijote, Rocinante, Dulcinea, Sancho Panza, los gigantes, Frestón)** for the class to guess. Ex: **el amigo que trata de convencer a don Quijote que los molinos no son gigantes (Sancho Panza).**

—Mire usted —respondió Sancho— que aquéllos que allí están no son gigantes, sino molinos de viento, y lo que parecen brazos son las aspas°, que movidas por el viento, hacen andar la piedra del molino.

—Bien veo —respondió don Quijote— que no estás acostumbrado a las aventuras: ellos son gigantes; y si tienes miedo, quítate de ahí y reza° mientras yo voy a combatir con ellos en fiera° batalla.

Y diciendo esto, dio de espuelas° a su caballo Rocinante, sin oír las voces que su escudero Sancho le daba, diciéndole que, sin duda alguna, eran molinos de viento, y no gigantes, aquellos que iba a atacar. Pero él iba tan convencido de que eran gigantes, que ni oía las voces de su escudero Sancho, ni se daba cuenta, aunque estaba ya muy cerca, de lo que eran; antes iba diciendo en voz alta:

—No huyáis°, cobardes° y viles criaturas, que sólo os ataca un caballero°.

Se levantó entonces un poco de viento, y las grandes aspas comenzaron a moverse, y cuando don Quijote vio esto, dijo:

—Pues aunque mováis más brazos que los del gigante Briareo, me lo vais a pagar.

Y diciendo esto, y encomendándose de todo corazón° a su señora Dulcinea, pidiéndole que le ayudase en esta difícil situación, bien cubierto de su rodela°, con la lanza en posición de ataque, fue a todo el galope de Rocinante y embistió° el primer molino que estaba delante: y dándole con la lanza en el aspa, el viento la giró con tanta furia, que la rompió en pequeños fragmentos, llevándose con ella al caballo y al caballero, que fue dando vueltas por el campo. Fue rápidamente Sancho Panza a ayudarle, todo lo rápido que podía correr su asno°, y cuando llegó encontró que no se podía mover: tan grande fue el golpe° que se dio con Rocinante.

—¡Por Dios! —dijo Sancho—. ¿No le dije yo que mirase bien lo que hacía, que sólo eran molinos de viento, y la única persona que podía equivocarse era alguien que tuviese otros molinos en la cabeza?

—Calla°, amigo Sancho —respondió don Quijote—, que las cosas de la guerra, más que otras, cambian continuamente; estoy pensando que aquel sabio° Frestón, que me robó el estudio y los libros, ha convertido estos gigantes en molinos por quitarme la gloria de su vencimiento°: tan grande es la enemistad que me tiene; pero al final, sus malas artes no van a poder nada contra la bondad de mi espada°.

—Dios lo haga como pueda —respondió Sancho Panza.

Y ayudándole a levantarse, volvió a subir sobre Rocinante, que medio despaldado estaba°. Y hablando de la pasada aventura, siguieron el camino del Puerto Lápice.

tras *after* cárcel *jail* locura *insanity* búsqueda *search* molinos de viento *windmills* campo *field* escudero *squire* seres *beings* amo *master* leguas *leagues (measure of distance)* aspas *sails* reza *pray* fiera *vicious* dio de espuelas *he spurred* No huyáis *Do not flee* cobardes *cowards* caballero *knight* encomendándose de todo corazón *entrusting himself with all his heart* rodela *round shield* embistió *charged* asno *donkey* golpe *knock* Calla *Be quiet* sabio *magician* vencimiento *defeat* espada *sword* que medio despaldado estaba *whose back was half-broken*

Personajes

1. En este fragmento, se mencionan los siguientes personajes. ¿Quiénes son?
   - don Quijote
   - Rocinante
   - Dulcinea
   - Sancho Panza
   - los gigantes
   - Frestón
2. ¿Qué puedes deducir de los personajes según la información que se da en este episodio?
3. ¿Quiénes son los personajes principales?
4. ¿Cuáles son las diferencias entre don Quijote y Sancho Panza? ¿Qué tienen en común?

¿Un loco o un héroe?

En un párrafo da tu opinión del personaje de don Quijote, basándote en la aventura de los molinos de viento. Ten en cuenta las acciones, los motivos y los sentimientos de don Quijote en su batalla contra los molinos de viento.

Una entrevista

Trabajen en grupos de tres para preparar una entrevista sobre los acontecimientos de este fragmento de la novela de Cervantes. Un(a) estudiante representará el papel del/de la entrevistador(a) y los otros dos asumirán los papeles de don Quijote y de Sancho Panza, quienes comentarán el episodio desde su punto de vista.

¿Realidad o fantasía? Have partners take turns reading the statements aloud and deciding whether the statement is **realidad** or **fantasía**.

Personajes Have partners pick a celebrity or someone they know personally who, like Don Quijote, is an idealist with his or her head in the clouds. Ask them to tell each other about this person, then have students share their partner's response with the class.

¿Un loco o un héroe? Have heritage speakers work with students who are being exposed to Spanish for the first time. When they are finished writing, ask them to read their paragraphs aloud.

Una entrevista Have groups brainstorm their questions and write them out on cards. Ask them to practice asking and answering questions and to perform their interviews for the class.

Successful Language Learning Ask your students if they approach reading in Spanish or English differently after learning the strategies presented in **VISTAS**.

TEACHING OPTIONS

Extra Practice Ask students to write a paragraph about someone they consider to be a hero or heroine (**héroe, heroína**). Students should explain why they think that person is a hero and describe at least one heroic act (**acto heroico**) carried out by him or her.

Heritage Speakers Ask heritage speakers to write five contrary-to-fact statements about the episode. Ex: **Si don Quijote no hubiera leído tantos libros, no se habría vuelto loco.** Have them share their statements with the class.

Section Goals

In **Escritura** students will:

- learn to write strong introductions and conclusions
- write a composition

Estrategia Explain that to write a strong introduction, one should briefly outline the topic and tell readers of the important points that will be addressed. Ask students to tell why an introduction to a biography of Miguel de Cervantes that does not mention ***Don Quijote*** is not a strong introduction. Explain that a strong conclusion summarizes the information in the body of the composition and inspires the reader to find out more about the topic. Ask students to tell how the following conclusion could be stronger: **Cervantes fue un gran escritor.**

Introducciones y conclusiones Write weak introductions and conclusions on the board for each of the three topics. Discuss these with the class, calling on volunteers to give suggestions and change or edit the introductions and conclusions to make them stronger.

Tema Read through the list of possible topics with the students and have them choose one. Have students who have chosen the same topic get together and brainstorm ideas about the changes they would make.

Escritura

Estrategia

Writing strong introductions and conclusions

Introductions and conclusions serve a similar purpose: both are intended to focus the reader's attention on the topic being covered. The introduction presents a brief preview of the topic. In addition, it informs your reader of the important points that will be covered in the body of your writing. The conclusion reaffirms those points and concisely sums up the information that has been provided. A compelling fact or statistic, a humorous anecdote, or a question directed to the reader are all interesting ways to begin or end your writing.

For example, if you were writing a biographical report on Miguel de Cervantes, you might begin your essay with the fact that his most famous work, *Don Quijote de la Mancha,* is the second most widely published book ever. The rest of your introductory paragraph would outline the areas you would cover in the body of your paper, such as Cervantes' life, his works, and the impact of *Don Quijote* on world literature. In your conclusion, you would sum up the most important information in the report and tie this information together in a way that would make your reader want to learn even more about the topic. You could write, for example: "Cervantes, with his wit and profound understanding of human nature, is without peer in the history of world literature."

Introducciones y conclusiones

Trabajen en parejas para escribir una frase de introducción y otra de conclusión sobre los siguientes temas.

1. El episodio de *Don Quijote de la Mancha*
2. La definición de la locura
3. La realidad y la fantasía en la literatura

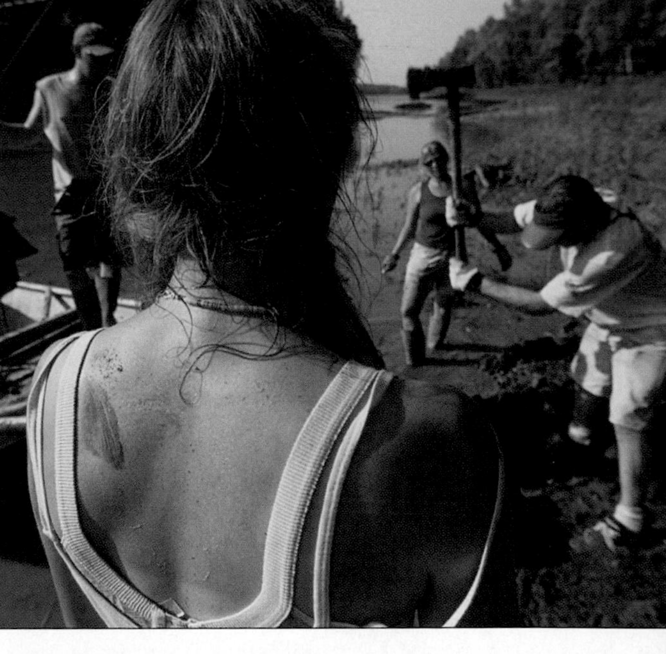

Tema

Escribir una composición

Si tuvieras la oportunidad, ¿qué harías para mejorar el mundo? Escribe una composición sobre los cambios que harías en el mundo si tuvieras el poder° y los recursos necesarios. Piensa en lo que puedes hacer ahora y en lo que podrás hacer en el futuro. Considera estas preguntas:

- ¿Pondrías fin a todas las guerras? ¿Cómo?
- ¿Protegerías el medio ambiente? ¿Cómo?
- ¿Promoverías° la igualdad y eliminarías el sexismo y el racismo? ¿Cómo?
- ¿Eliminarías la corrupción en la política? ¿Cómo?
- ¿Eliminarías la escasez de viviendas° y el hambre?
- ¿Educarías a los demás sobre el SIDA? ¿Cómo?
- ¿Promoverías el fin de la violencia entre seres humanos?
- ¿Promoverías tu causa en los medios de comunicación? ¿Cómo?
- ¿Te dedicarías a alguna causa específica dentro de tu comunidad? ¿Cuál?
- ¿Te dedicarías a solucionar problemas nacionales o internacionales? ¿Cuáles?

poder *power* Promoverías *Would you promote* escasez de vivienda *homelessness*

TEACHING OPTIONS

Proofreading Activity Copy on the board or onto a transparency the following items containing mistakes as a proofreading activity to do with the whole class.

1. **Si el periodista podría escribir sobre este tema otra vez, ¿lo hiciera?**
2. **Si sería usted periodista con una agencia internacional, viajara por todo el mundo.**
3. **El presidente aceptaría recibir la prensa si tuviera tiempo suficiente.**
4. **Si tenía que hacer reportajes sobre violencia, no me gustara hacerlo.**
5. **Espero que me das un libro que me explica la política.**
6. **A menos que acaban las inundaciones, los agricultores no podían plantar sus campos.**

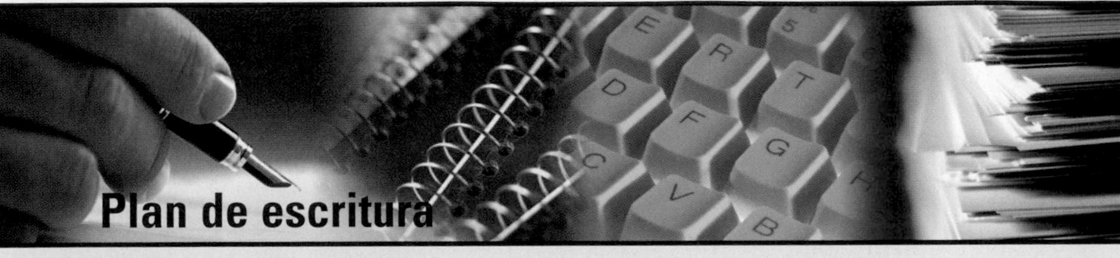

Plan de escritura

1 Ideas y organización

Antes de escribir, organiza de una manera lógica la lista de los cambios que efectuarías° para mejorar el mundo.

2 Primer borrador

Utiliza tus apuntes° de **Ideas y organización** para escribir el primer borrador de tu composición. Empieza y concluye con un hecho° o una pregunta que despierte el interés de tu lector(a). Utiliza el diccionario sólo como último recurso.

3 Comentario

Intercambia tu composición con la de un(a) compañero/a. Lee su borrador y coméntalo, usando estas preguntas como guía:

a. ¿Es interesante la introducción? ¿Cómo se puede mejorar?
b. ¿Es interesante la conclusión? ¿Cómo se puede mejorar?
c. ¿Hay errores gramaticales u ortográficos?
d. ¿Está organizado de una manera lógica?

4 Redacción

Revisa el primer borrador según las indicaciones de tu compañero/a. Antes de escribir tu versión final, revisa tu trabajo según la siguiente guía:

a. Subraya° los verbos para comprobar° que están en el modo y el tiempo adecuados. ¿Has utilizado el subjuntivo y el condicional correctamente?
b. Revisa la concordancia° entre el sujeto y el verbo en cada oración.
c. Revisa la concordancia entre los sustantivos y los adjetivos en cada oración.
d. Subraya los pronombres para comprobar el uso correcto de cada uno.
e. Consulta tus **Anotaciones para mejorar la escritura** para evitar la repetición de errores previos.

5 Evaluación y progreso

En grupos de tres o cuatro estudiantes, intercambien sus composiciones. Cada persona debe leer la composición de un(a) compañero/a y resumirla oralmente en tres o cuatro oraciones. Cuando tu profesor(a) te devuelva° sus comentarios, léelos con cuidado. Repasa tu **Carpeta de trabajos** para poder apreciar tu progreso en la escritura. No te olvides de mirar tus **Anotaciones para mejorar la escritura.** Seguramente te sorprenderás de ver que hoy parece fácil lo que hace unos meses parecía tan difícil.

efectuarías *you would put into effect* apuntes *notes* hecho *fact* Subraya *Underline* comprobar *to confirm* concordancia *agreement* devuelva *returns*

Comentario
- Go over guide questions a–d with the whole class. Then have pairs exchange compositions. Allow five minutes for comments.
- Have students prepare **Redacción** as homework.

Writing Sample This composition would constitute superior writing achievement.

¡Comida y casas para todos!

Cada 3,6 segundos una persona muere de hambre. El 75% de estas personas son niños. ¿Cómo es posible que se permita que una persona viva sin suficiente comida? El hambre crea graves problemas de salud. También puede causar problemas en la sociedad como el crimen, la violencia y la desigualdad. Si hay suficiente comida para alimentar a toda la gente, ¿por qué no se hace?

La falta de viviendas es otro problema grave. Sólo en los Estados Unidos hay más o menos 600.000 personas que no tienen dónde vivir. La cifra sube en el resto del mundo. ¿Por qué viven los ricos en mansiones y los pobres viven en sus carros o en la calle? Tenemos que construir más casas y apartamentos para nuestra gente.

Si pudiera dar a todos una vivienda y comida, yo lo haría sin pensarlo dos veces. ¡Qué injusticia! Tenemos que trabajar juntos para eliminar el hambre y la falta de viviendas. Hay que escribir cartas a los políticos y votar por aquéllos que tengan soluciones a estos problemas. ¡Si trabajamos juntos podemos lograr estas metas!

Successful Language Learning Ask your students if they approach writing in Spanish or English differently after using the strategies presented in **VISTAS**.

EVALUATION: Composición

Criteria	Scale
Content	1 2 3 4 5
Use of vocabulary	1 2 3 4 5
Grammatical accuracy	1 2 3 4 5
Use of introductions/conclusions	1 2 3 4 5

Scoring	
Excellent	18–20 points
Good	14–17 points
Satisfactory	10–13 points
Unsatisfactory	< 10 points

Section Goals
In **Escuchar** students will:
- practice recognizing genre and taking notes as they listen
- jot down the types of information they hear in a news broadcast

Instructional Resources
Textbook CD
IRM: Tapescript, p. 102

Estrategia
Script Con la nueva pasta de dientes BrillaBoca, usted gozará de dientes blancos y una boca fresca. Este producto le cambiará la vida. Nunca más estará solo en casa un sábado por la noche. ¡Disfrute de su vida! ¡Use pasta de dientes BrillaBoca!

Successful Language Learning Ask your students if they approach listening to Spanish or English differently after using the strategies presented in **VISTAS**.

Suggestion Have students look at the photo and guess who the woman depicted is. Guide them to recognize that she is a newscaster. Have them list the types of information they would expect to hear about in a news broadcast.

Ahora escucha
Script Buenas tardes. Les habla Sonia Hernández, dándoles la bienvenida al Noticiero del Mediodía. Y ahora las actualidades del miércoles, 21 de abril. El candidato presidencial Jaime Pantufla del Partido Colorado anunció en su discurso ante los ciudadanos de Salto su plan para mejorar la recaudación de impuestos en vista de la necesidad de mejorar la situación económica del país. Ahora la noticias internacionales. La tormenta que ha dejado más de 17 centímetros de lluvia sobre las Filipinas ha causado desastrosas inundaciones. Reportan que aproximadamente 12.000 personas han perdido sus casas y sus bienes. Las inundaciones también han traído gran peligro de enfermedades. Seguimos con los más importantes acontecimientos de arte y cultura. Pasado mañana, el conocido grupo de rock, Maná, presentará un concierto en el estacionamiento del Centro Comercial Portones en Montevideo. Hoy comienza la nueva exposición de las obras del pintor Ugo Nespolo en el Museo Nacional de Artes Visuales de Montevideo.
Regresamos después de unas breves noticias con el pronóstico del tiempo de Montevideo y sus alrededores.

Escuchar

Estrategia
Recognizing genre/
Taking notes as you listen

If you know the genre or type of discourse you are going to encounter, you can use your background knowledge to write down a few notes about what you expect to hear. You can then make additions and changes to your notes as you listen.

To practice these strategies, you will now listen to a short toothpaste commercial. Before listening to the commercial, write down the information you expect it to contain. Then update your notes as you listen.

Preparación

Basándote en la foto, anticipa lo que vas a escuchar en el siguiente fragmento. Haz una lista y anota los diferentes tipos de información que crees que vas a oír.

Ahora escucha 

Revisa la lista que hiciste para **Preparación.** Luego escucha el noticiero presentado por Sonia Hernández. Mientras escuchas, apunta los tipos de información que anticipaste y los que no anticipaste.

Tipos de información que anticipaste

1. Answers will vary.
2. Answers will vary.
3. Answers will vary.

Tipos de información que no anticipaste

1. Answers will vary.
2. Answers will vary.
3. Answers will vary.

Comprensión

Preguntas

1. ¿Dónde está Sonia Hernández?
   Está en una estación de televisión en Montevideo, Uruguay.
2. ¿Quién es Jaime Pantufla?
   Es un candidato presidencial.
3. ¿Dónde hubo una tormenta?
   Hubo una tormenta en las Filipinas.
4. ¿Qué tipo de música toca el grupo Maná?
   Toca música rock.
5. ¿Qué tipo de artista es Ugo Nespolo?
   Es un pintor.
6. Además de lo que Sonia menciona, ¿de qué piensas que va a hablar en la próxima sección del programa?
   Answers will vary.

Ahora ustedes

En parejas, usen la presentación de Sonia Hernández como modelo para escribir un breve noticiero para la ciudad donde viven. Incluyan noticias locales, nacionales e internacionales. Luego compartan el papel de locutor(a) y presenten el noticiero a la clase. Pueden grabar el noticiero si quieren.

recursos

TEXT CD
Lección 18

Proyecto

Prepara un reportaje

Imagina que eres un(a) reportero/a que está cubriendo el Cono Sur° para una emisora de radio° y un diario. Te han pedido un reportaje de noticias sobre Paraguay y/o Uruguay.

1 Escribe un artículo periodístico

Escribe un artículo sobre las últimas noticias de Uruguay y/o de Paraguay. Usa los **Recursos para la investigación** para informarte de lo que está pasando en esos países. El artículo puede incluir las siguientes cosas:

- Un titular°
- Una descripción del/de los acontecimiento(s), con una explicación de cuándo y dónde tuvieron lugar, quiénes participaron, etc.
- Un pequeño mapa que indique dónde tuvo lugar el acontecimiento
- Fotos de los acontecimientos

34F

Comienza el Carnaval

Hoy viernes, comienzan las grandes fiestas del Carnaval en Encarnación, capital del departamento de Itapúa, Paraguay. Esta ciudad es famosa por la música, los desfiles° y las bailarinas de su Carnaval. Es tan popular que vienen a esta celebración muchas personas de otras partes del país y del extranjero. Todos los hoteles y pensiones están llenos en esta época del año.

¡Se prohíbe tirar° agua a los participantes de los desfiles! La policía estará pendiente.

2 Presenta la información

El locutor de la emisora de radio está enfermo y te toca a ti° presentar el noticiero. Usa el artículo que escribiste para hacer un reportaje radial. Recuerda que el reportaje debe ser más corto que el artículo. Presenta el noticiero a la clase en vivo° o en una grabación°.

recursos para la investigación

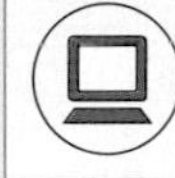	**Internet** Palabras clave: Uruguay, Paraguay, periódico, diario, noticias		**Comunidad** Profesores, estudiantes o personas en la comunidad que son de Uruguay o Paraguay
	**Biblioteca** Periódicos, revistas, mapas		**Otros recursos** Profesores de la Facultad de Asuntos Internacionales o de Estudios Latinoamericanos; embajadas° o consulados°

Cono Sur *Southern Cone* emisora de radio *radio station* titular *headline* te toca a ti *it is up to you* en vivo *live* grabación *tape recording* desfiles *parades* tirar *throw* embajadas *embassies* consulados *consulates*

Section Goals

In **Proyecto** students will:
- use Spanish as they research current events in Uruguay and/or Paraguay
- write a news article on current events in Uruguay and/or Paraguay

Suggestion Students might need a week to complete the project, so at the beginning of that time period, have them open their books to this page and glance over **Proyecto**. Tell them that they are going to use their Spanish skills as they carry out research on current events in Uruguay and Paraguay. Tell them that when they finish their research, they will write a newspaper article on current events.

Escribe un artículo periodístico
- Provide students with examples of articles written in Spanish about current events. Many Spanish-language newspapers can be found on the Internet. Tell students the abbreviations in URLs for Uruguay and Paraguay are **uy** and **py**, respectively.
- Students can seek information on Uruguay or Paraguay by using the Spanish key words and phrases **Cono Sur, actualidades Uruguay o Paraguay, noticias del Uruguay o Paraguay**.

Presenta la información
You may wish to set aside sufficient class time to do a few presentations at a time until all students have had a chance to present.

EVALUATION: Reportaje

Criteria	Scale
Content	1 2 3 4
Organization	1 2 3 4
Grammatical accuracy	1 2 3 4
Creativity	1 2 3 4
Oral presentation	1 2 3 4

Scoring	
Excellent	18–20 points
Good	14–17 points
Satisfactory	10–13 points
Unsatisfactory	< 10 points

Section Goal

In **Panorama**, students will read about the geography and culture of Paraguay.

Instructional Resources
Transparencies, #5, #6, #63
WB/VM: Workbook, p. 209;
Video Activities, pp. 287–288
***Panorama cultural** DVD/Video*
Interactive CD-ROM
IRM: Videoscript, p. 137
Companion website:
www.vistahigherlearning.com
Presentations CD-ROM

Suggestion Have students look at the map of Paraguay or project **Transparency #63**. Note that the major population centers lie east of the Paraguay River, which divides the country in two. West of the river is the **Gran Chaco,** a sparsely populated and largely infertile region.

El país en cifras As you read **Idiomas**, point out that **guaraní** is also spoken in neighboring Bolivia, Brazil, and Argentina. However, as an officially bilingual nation, Paraguay has the largest concentration of Guaraní speakers. As students read **Paraguayos célebres**, let them know that writer **Augusto Roa Bastos** is well known throughout Latin America as both a poet and novelist. His novels ***El Supremo*** and ***Hijo de hombre*** deal with the turbulent and difficult history of Paraguay.

¡Increíble pero cierto! Like Paraguay, several other Spanish-speaking countries impose fines on citizens for not voting. Ask students to research and name these countries. Ask the class if they think that such a measure should be implemented here to improve voter turnout at the polls.

Paraguay

NATIONAL STANDARDS connections cultures

El país en cifras

- **Área:** 406.750 km² (157.046 millas²), *el tamaño° de California*
- **Población:** 5.778.000
- **Capital:** Asunción—1.472.000
- **Ciudades principales:** Ciudad del Este—134.000, San Lorenzo—133.000, Lambaré—100.000, Fernando de la Mora—95.000

SOURCE: Population Division, UN Secretariat

- **Moneda:** guaraní
- **Idiomas:** español (oficial), guaraní (oficial)

Las tribus indígenas que habitaban la zona antes de la llegada de los españoles hablaban guaraní. Ahora el 90 por ciento de los paraguayos habla esta lengua, que se usa con frecuencia en canciones, poemas, periódicos y libros. Varios institutos y asociaciones, como el Teatro Guaraní, se dedican a preservar la cultura y la lengua guaraníes.

Bandera de Paraguay

Paraguayos célebres

- **Agustín Barrios,** guitarrista y compositor (1885–1944)
- **Josefina Plá,** escritora y ceramista (1909–1999)
- **Augusto Roa Bastos,** escritor (1917–)
- **Olga Blinder,** pintora (1921–)

recursos

WB pp. 209–210	VM pp. 287–288	I CD-ROM Lección 18	vistahigherlearning.com

tamaño *size* multara *fined*

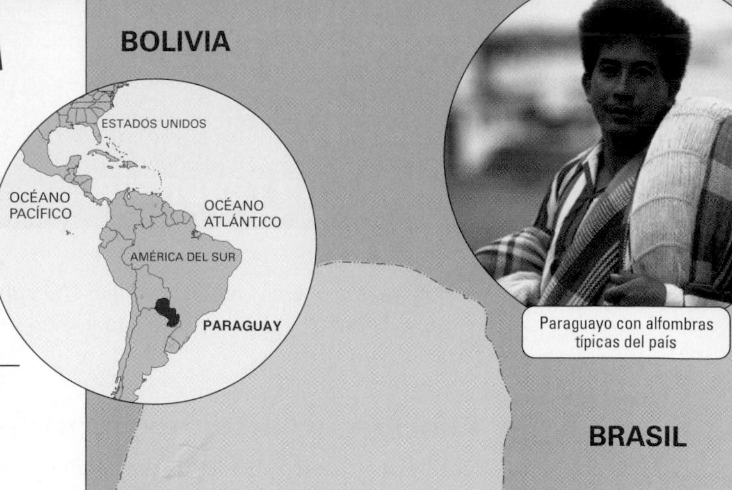

Paraguayo con alfombras típicas del país

Agricultor indio de la tribu maca

Itapúa

¡Increíble pero cierto!

¿Te imaginas qué pasaría si el gobierno multara° a los ciudadanos que no van a votar? En Paraguay, es una obligación. Ésta es una ley nacional, que otros países también tienen, para obligar a los ciudadanos a participar en las elecciones. En Paraguay los ciudadanos que no van a votar tienen que pagar una multa al gobierno.

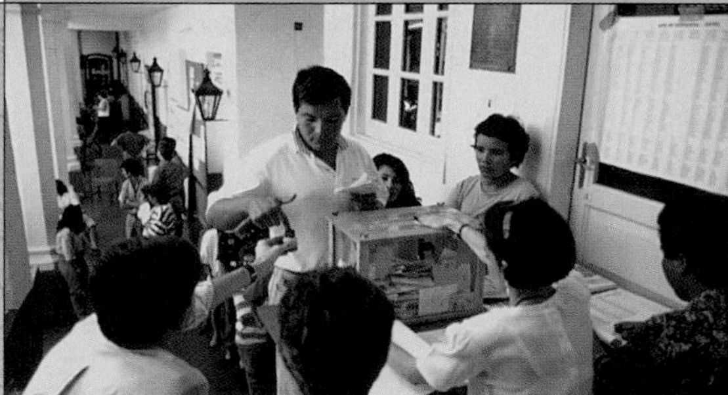

TEACHING OPTIONS

Worth Noting Students can get some flavor of the Guaraní language by reading aloud the names of these typical Paraguayan dishes: **chipa** (a baked good flavored with **anís**), **kiveve** (a stew made from **andaí**, a type of squash), and **pastel mandi'o** (turnovers made with the South American staple, manioc flour, and filled with **so'o ku'í,** chopped meat). Invite students who have visited or lived in Paraguay to share other information about traditional Paraguayan fare. Don't forget to have them mention the national drink of Paraguay (as well as of Uruguay, Argentina, and Rio Grande do Sul in Brazil), **yerba mate.** This is an infusion made from the leaves of a tree native to Paraguay and is sometimes called Paraguay tea in English.

Artesanía • El ñandutí

El ñandutí es la forma artesanal más conocida de Paraguay. Es un fino encaje° hecho a mano, que generalmente tiene forma circular. En guaraní, su nombre significa telaraña° y se llama así porque imita su trazado°. Estos encajes suelen ser blancos, pero también los hay de colores, y sus diseños pueden tener formas geométricas o florales. Aunque el ñandutí es originario de Itaguá, con el tiempo ha llegado a ser muy conocido en toda Suramérica.

Ciencias • La represa Itaipú

La represa° Itaipú, la obra hidroeléctrica más ambiciosa hasta nuestros días, se encuentra en la frontera entre Paraguay y Brasil. Su construcción se inició en 1974 y duró once años. Durante los primeros cinco años, se usó suficiente concreto como para construir un edificio de 350 pisos. El proyecto dio trabajo a 100.000 paraguayos. En 1984 se puso en funcionamiento la Central Hidroeléctrica de Itaipú, la mayor del mundo. Gracias a su cercanía a las famosas Cataratas de Iguazú, muchos turistas visitan la Central, atraídos por lo imponente de su construcción.

Naturaleza • Los ríos Paraguay y Paraná

Los ríos Paraguay y Paraná sirven de frontera natural entre Paraguay y Argentina, y son las principales rutas de transporte dentro de Paraguay. El río Paraná tiene unos 3.200 km navegables, y por esta ruta pasan barcos de más de 5.000 toneladas que pueden ir desde el estuario° del Río de la Plata hasta la ciudad de Asunción. El río Paraguay divide el Gran Chaco, una zona poco poblada, de la meseta° Paraná, donde vive la mayoría de los paraguayos.

¿Qué aprendiste? Responde a las preguntas con una frase completa.

1. ¿Quién es Augusto Roa Bastos?
   Augusto Roa Bastos es un escritor paraguayo.
2. ¿Cómo se llama la moneda de Paraguay?
   La moneda de Paraguay se llama guaraní.
3. ¿Qué es el ñandutí?
   El ñandutí es un tipo de encaje.
4. ¿De dónde es originario el ñandutí?
   El ñandutí es originario de Itaguá.
5. ¿Qué forma imita el ñandutí?
   Imita la forma de una telaraña.
6. En total, ¿cuántos años tomó la construcción de la represa Itaipú?
   La construcción de la represa Itaipú tomó 11 años.
7. ¿A cuántos paraguayos dio trabajo la construcción de la represa?
   La construcción de la represa dio trabajo a 100.000 paraguayos.
8. ¿Qué países separan los ríos Paraguay y Paraná? Los ríos Paraguay y Paraná separan a Argentina y Paraguay.
9. ¿Qué distancia se puede navegar por el Paraná?
   Se pueden navegar 3.200 km.

Conexión Internet Investiga estos temas en el sitio **www.vistahigherlearning.com.**

1. Busca información sobre Alfredo Stroessner, el ex-presidente de Paraguay. ¿Por qué se le considera un dictador?
2. Busca información sobre la historia de Paraguay. En tu opinión, ¿cuáles fueron los episodios decisivos en su historia?

encaje *lace* telaraña *spiderweb* trazado *outline; design* represa *dam* estuario *estuary* meseta *plateau*

El ñandutí In recent years, the number of traditional **ñandutí** makers has been in serious decline. The artisans of **Itaguá** grew tired of the low levels of compensation they received, and many have turned to other more profitable sources of income. Formal instruction in the skill of making **ñandutí** has even been incorporated in the curriculum of local handicraft schools in an effort to keep this traditional art alive.

La represa Itaipú The **Itaipú** dam project is a joint venture between Brazil and Paraguay, and has been remarkably successful. By 1995, four years after it went into production, the dam generated 25% of Brazil's energy supply, and 78% of Paraguay's. Annual electrical output continues to increase yearly.

Los ríos Paraguay y Paraná The Paraná River in particular was a highway for the settlement of Paraguay. Along its banks, between the 16th and late 18th centuries, the Jesuits organized their Guaraní-speaking parishioners into small, self-supporting city-states built around mission settlements, similar to the Franciscan mission system in California during the same period.

Conexión Internet Students will find supporting Internet activities and links at **www.vistahigherlearning.com**.

TEACHING OPTIONS

Worth Noting Paraguay has eight national parks, encompassing over 11,000 square miles. In addition, there are eight ecological reserves dedicated to the preservation of endangered flora and fauna. The rich diversity of plant and animal life, and the government's commitment to preserving these natural wonders, have made Paraguay a popular destination for ecotourists. The parks cover a wide spectrum of ecology. The **Parque Nacional Defensores del Chaco** and **Parque Nacional Teniente Enciso** are located in the semi-arid Chaco. Other parks, like **Parque Nacional Caaguazú** southeast of Asunción are covered with subtropical rainforest.

Section Goal

In **Panorama**, students will read about the geography and culture of Uruguay.

Instructional Resources
Transparencies, #5, #6, #64
WB/VM: Workbook, p. 210; Video Activities, pp. 289–290
***Panorama cultural** DVD/Video*
Interactive CD-ROM
IRM: Videoscript, p. 137
Companion website: www.vistahigherlearning.com
Presentations CD-ROM

Suggestion Have students look at the map of Uruguay or project **Transparency #64** and talk about the physical features of the country. Point out the long coastline that runs along the Río de la Plata, separating Uruguay from neighboring Argentina. Point out that Uruguay and Argentina have a great deal in common culturally.

El país en cifras After reading the text in italics, tell students that at the time of European contact, the area from Punta del Este northward up the coast of Brazil to Rio Grande do Sul was one enormous, uninterrupted beach. Early explorers were awestruck by the natural beauty of the Uruguayan landscape, which had rich and varied wildlife, including the ostrich-like **ñandú**, the jaguar, and many marine mammals. After reading **Uruguayos célebres**, point out that Horacio Quiroga's ***Cuentos de la selva*** are set amidst Uruguay's natural flora and fauna.

¡Increíble pero cierto! One **ñandú** egg can be over five inches long, weigh one pound, and equal 12 chicken eggs. Males typically incubate the eggs until they hatch and then watch fiercely over the chicks. Their paternal instinct is so intense that they might even raise other males' chicks and protect them as if they were their own.

Uruguay

El país en cifras

- **Área:** 176.220 km² (68.039 millas²) *el tamaño° del estado de Washington*
- **Población:** 3.385.000
- **Capital:** Montevideo—1.352.000

Casi la mitad° de la población de Uruguay vive en Montevideo. Situada en la desembocadura° del famoso Río de la Plata, esta ciudad cosmopolita e intelectual es también un destino popular para las vacaciones, debido a sus numerosas playas de arena° blanca que se extienden hasta la ciudad de Punta del Este.

- **Ciudades principales:** Salto—77.000, Paysandú—75.000, Las Piedras—61.000, Rivera—55.000

SOURCE: Population Division, UN Secretariat

- **Moneda:** peso uruguayo
- **Idiomas:** español (oficial)

Bandera de Uruguay

Uruguayos célebres

- **Horacio Quiroga,** escritor (1878–1937)
- **Juana de Ibarbourou,** escritora (1895–1979)
- **Mario Benedetti,** escritor (1920–)
- **Cristina Peri Rossi,** escritora y profesora (1941–)

tamaño *size* **mitad** *half* **desembocadura** *mouth* **arena** *sand* **avestruz** *ostrich* **no voladora** *flightless* **medir** *measure* **cotizado** *valued*

Gaucho uruguayo

Rivera, BRASIL, Río Arapey, Salto, Río Uruguay, Cuchilla de Haedo, Paysandú, Río Negro, Embalse del Río Negro, Laguna Merín, Cuchilla Grande, Río Yí, Cuchilla Grande Inferior, Colonia, Las Piedras, Río de la Plata, Montevideo, Punta del Este

ESTADOS UNIDOS, OCÉANO PACÍFICO, OCÉANO ATLÁNTICO, AMÉRICA DEL SUR, URUGUAY

Entrada a la Ciudad Vieja, Colonia del Sacramento

recursos

WB	VM	I CD-ROM	vistahigher learning.com
pp. 209–210	pp. 289–290	Lección 18	

¡Increíble pero cierto!

En Uruguay hay muchos animales curiosos, entre ellos el ñandú. De la misma especie del avestruz°, el ñandú es el ave no voladora° más grande del hemisferio occidental. Puede llegar a medir° dos metros. Normalmente, va en grupos de veinte o treinta y vive en el campo. Es muy cotizado° por su carne, sus plumas y sus huevos.

TEACHING OPTIONS

Variación léxica Montevideo looks out across the wide estuary of the Río de la Plata at Buenos Aires, Argentina, and the Spanish of Uruguay's major city has much in common with the **porteño** Spanish of its neighbor. When speaking, Uruguayans tend to use **vos** as frequently as **tú**, as well as all the corresponding verb forms. The plural of both forms is **ustedes**, as in the rest of Latin America. In the northern part of Uruguay, along the border with Brazil, the majority of residents are bilingual in Portuguese and Spanish.

Costumbres • La carne y el mate

La gran importancia de la producción ganadera° en las economías de Uruguay y Argentina se refleja en sus hábitos culinarios. Para los uruguayos, como para los argentinos, la carne de res es un elemento esencial de la dieta diaria. Algunos platos representativos son el asado°, la parrillada° y el chivito°. El mate, una infusión similar al té, es también muy típico de esta región. Es una bebida de origen indígena que está muy presente en la vida social y familiar de estos países aunque, curiosamente, no se puede consumir en bares o restaurantes.

Deportes • El fútbol

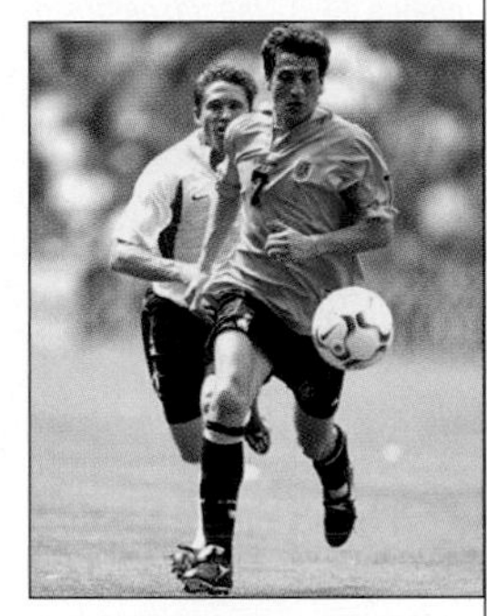

El fútbol es, sin lugar a dudas, el deporte nacional de Uruguay. La afición a este deporte se inició hace mucho en Uruguay. En 1891, se formó el primer equipo de fútbol uruguayo y, en 1930, el país fue la sede° de la primera copa mundial. A partir de los años treinta se inició el período profesional del fútbol uruguayo. El equipo nacional ha conseguido grandes éxitos a lo largo de los años: dos campeonatos olímpicos en 1923 y 1928, y dos campeonatos mundiales en 1930 y 1950. De hecho, los uruguayos ya están trabajando para que la Copa Mundial de 2030 se celebre en su país.

Costumbres • El Carnaval

El Carnaval de Montevideo es el más largo del mundo y uno de los mejores de Suramérica. Dura unos cuarenta días y cuenta con la participación de casi todos los habitantes de la ciudad. Durante el Carnaval, los uruguayos disfrutan de desfiles°, bailes y música en las calles de su capital. La celebración más conocida es el *Desfile de las Llamadas*, en el que participan bailarines que desfilan al ritmo del candombe, un colorido baile de tradición africana.

¿Qué aprendiste? Responde a las preguntas con una frase completa.

1. ¿Qué tienen en común los uruguayos célebres mencionados en la página 566?
   Son escritores.
2. ¿Cuál es el elemento esencial de la dieta uruguaya?
   La carne de res es esencial en la dieta uruguaya.
3. ¿En qué países es importante la producción ganadera?
   La producción ganadera es importante en Uruguay y Argentina.
4. ¿Qué es el mate?
   El mate es una bebida indígena que es similar al té.
5. ¿Cuándo se formó el primer equipo uruguayo de fútbol?
   En 1891 se formó el primer equipo de fútbol uruguayo.
6. ¿Cuándo se celebró la primera Copa Mundial de fútbol?
   La primera Copa Mundial se celebró en 1930.
7. ¿Cómo se llama la celebración más conocida del Carnaval de Montevideo?
   La celebración más conocida del Carnaval de Montevideo se llama El Desfile de las Llamadas.
8. ¿Cuántos días dura el Carnaval de Montevideo?
   El Carnaval de Montevideo dura unos cuarenta días.

Edificio del Parlamento en Montevideo

Conexión Internet

Investiga estos temas en el sitio **www.vistahigherlearning.com**.

1. Uruguay es conocido como un país de muchos escritores. Busca información sobre uno de ellos y escribe una biografía.
2. Investiga cuáles son las comidas y bebidas favoritas de los uruguayos. Descríbelas e indica cuáles te gustaría probar y por qué.

ganadera *cattle (adj.)* asado *barbecue* parrillada *beef platter* chivito *goat* sede *site* desfiles *parades*

La carne y el mate A legend from the **guaraní** people of Uruguay says that **yerba mate** was a gift from the god **Pa-i Shume.** Traditionally, the **yerba mate** leaves are packed into a **mate**—a cup made from a gourd—and hot water is poured over them. The infusion is sipped through a **bombilla**—a metal straw with a built-in tea strainer. The **mate** is refilled and drained several times, passing from hand to hand among a group of friends or family.

El fútbol Uruguayan women have begun to make their mark in soccer. Although the International Federation of Football Association (FIFA) established a women's league in 1982, it wasn't until 1985 that the first women's league—from Brazil—was formally established. The women's league of Uruguay now participates in international soccer play, showing that Uruguayan women can be just as fanatical as the men when it comes to **fútbol**.

El Carnaval Like the rest of Latin America, Uruguay also imported slaves from Africa during the colonial period. The music of the African-influenced **candombe** culture is popular with Uruguayans from all sectors of society.

Conexión Internet Students will find supporting Internet activities and links at **www.vistahigherlearning.com**.

TEACHING OPTIONS

Worth Noting Uruguay is similar to its larger, more powerful neighbor, Argentina, in many ways: the Uruguayans also love the **tango** and **yerba mate**, they play the Argentine card game **truco**, and they are devoted carnivores. Historically, cattle ranching, the culture of the **gaucho**, and the great cattle ranches called **estancias** have been important elements in the Uruguayan national fabric. Another, less pleasant, similarity was in the Dirty War (**Guerra sucia**) waged by an Uruguayan military dictatorship against domestic dissidents during the 1970s and 80s. In 1984 the military allowed the election of a civilian government. In 1989 that government was peacefully succeeded by another. Today, presidential and parliamentary elections are held every five years.

Instructional Resources
Vocabulary CD
Lab Manual, p. 106
Lab CD/MP3 ***Lección 18***
IRM: Tapescript, pp. 80–83
Testing Program: ***Pruebas,*** *pp. 205–216;* ***Exámenes,*** *pp. 229–239, pp. 265–275*
Testing Program Audio CD
Test Files CD-ROM

Successful Language Learning Tell your students that they may want to review all the end-of-lesson vocabulary lists at this time. Tell them to imagine how they would use each lesson's vocabulary in everyday life.

The Affective Dimension Tell your students to consider their feelings about speaking Spanish at the beginning of the course and think about how they feel about speaking Spanish now. Tell them that this is a good time to consider their motivations and set new goals as they continue learning the language.

Los medios de comunicación

el acontecimiento	*event*
las actualidades	*news; current events*
el artículo	*article*
el diario	*newspaper*
el informe	*report; paper (written work)*
el/la locutor(a)	*(TV or radio) announcer*
los medios de comunicación	*media; means of communication*
las noticias	*news*
el noticiero	*newscast*
la prensa	*press*
el reportaje	*report*
anunciar	*to announce; to advertise*
comunicarse (con)	*to communicate (with)*
durar	*to last*
informar	*to inform*
ocurrir	*to occur; to happen*
transmitir, emitir	*to broadcast*
(inter)nacional	*(inter)national*
peligroso/a	*dangerous*

Las noticias

el choque	*collision*
el crimen	*crime; murder*
el desastre (natural)	*(natural) disaster*
el desempleo	*unemployment*
la (des)igualdad	*(in)equality*
la discriminación	*discrimination*
el ejército	*army*
la experiencia	*experience*
la guerra	*war*
la huelga	*strike*
el huracán	*hurricane*
el incendio	*fire*
la inundación	*flood*
la libertad	*liberty; freedom*
la paz	*peace*
el racismo	*racism*
el sexismo	*sexism*
el SIDA	*AIDS*
el/la soldado	*soldier*
el terremoto	*earthquake*
la tormenta	*storm*
el tornado	*tornado*
la violencia	*violence*

La política

el/la candidato/a	*candidate*
el/la ciudadano/a	*citizen*
el deber	*responsibility; obligation*
los derechos	*rights*
la dictadura	*dictatorship*
el discurso	*speech*
las elecciones	*election*
la encuesta	*poll; survey*
el impuesto	*tax*
la política	*politics*
el/la representante	*representative*
declarar	*to declare; to say*
elegir	*to elect*
luchar (por/contra)	*to fight; to struggle (for/against)*
obedecer	*to obey*
votar	*to vote*
político/a	*political*

Expresiones útiles	*See page 547.*

recursos

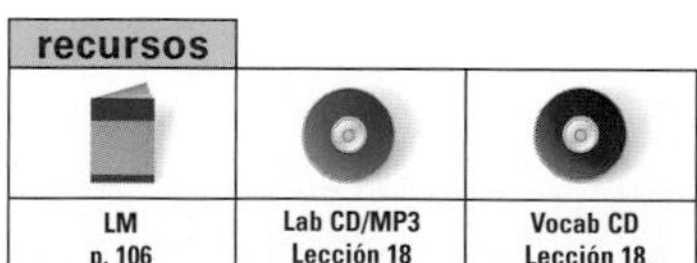

LM p. 106	Lab CD/MP3 Lección 18	Vocab CD Lección 18

Spanish Terms for Direction Lines and Classroom Use

Below is a list of useful terms that you might hear your instructor say in class. It also includes Spanish terms that appear in the direction lines of your textbook.

En las instrucciones	*In direction lines*
Camina/Caminen por la clase.	*Walk around the classroom.*
Ciertas o falsas	*True or false*
Cierto o falso	*True or false*
Circula/Circulen por la clase.	*Walk around the classroom.*
Completa las oraciones de una manera lógica.	*Complete the sentences logically.*
Con un(a) compañero/a...	*With a classmate...*
Contesta las preguntas.	*Answer the questions.*
Corrige las frases falsas.	*Correct the false statements.*
Di/ Digan...	*Say...*
En grupos...	*In groups...*
En parejas...	*In pairs...*
Entrevista ...	*Interview...*
Forma oraciones completas.	*Create/Make complete sentences.*
Háganse preguntas.	*Ask each other questions.*
Haz el papel de...	*Play the role of...*
Haz los cambios necesarios.	*Make the necessary changes.*
Indica/Indiquen si las oraciones...	*Indicate if the sentences...*
Lee/Lean en voz alta.	*Read aloud.*
...que mejor completa...	*...that best completes...*
Reúnete...	*Get together...*
Toma nota...	*Take note...*
Tomen apuntes.	*Take notes.*
Túrnense...	*Take turns...*

Palabras útiles	*Useful words*
el anuncio	*advertisement/ad*
los apuntes	*notes*
el borrador	*draft*
la concordancia	*agreement*
el contenido	*contents*
eficaz	*efficient*
la encuesta	*survey*
el equipo	*team*
el esquema	*outline*
el folleto	*brochure*
las frases	*statements*
la hoja de actividades	*activity sheet/ handout*
la hoja de papel	*piece of paper*
la información errónea	*incorrect information*
el/la lector(a)	*reader*
la lectura	*reading*
las oraciones	*sentences*
la ortografía	*spelling*
las palabras útiles	*useful words*
el papel	*role*
el párrafo	*paragraph*
el paso	*step*
la(s) persona(s) descrita(s)	*the person (people) described*
la pista	*clue*
por ejemplo	*for example*
el própósito	*purpose*
los recursos	*resources*
el reportaje	*report*
los resultados	*results*
según	*according to*
siguiente	*following*
la sugerencia	*suggestion*
el sustantivo	*noun*
el tema	*topic*
último	*last*
el último recurso	*last resort*

Verbos útiles *Useful verbs*

adivinar	*to guess*
anotar	*to jot down*
añadir	*to add*
apoyar	*to support*
averiguar	*to find out*
combinar	*to combine*
compartir	*to share*
comprobar (o:ue)	*to check*
corregir (e:i)	*to correct*
crear	*to create*
devolver	*to return*
doblar	*to fold*
dramatizar	*to act out*
elegir	*to choose/select*
emparejar	*to match*
entrevistar	*to interview*
escoger	*to choose*
identificar	*to identify*
incluir	*to include*
informar	*to report*
intentar	*to try*
intercambiar	*to exchange*
investigar	*to research*
marcar	*to mark*
preguntar	*to ask*
recordar (o:ue)	*to remember*
responder	*to answer*
revisar	*to revise*
seguir	*to follow*
seleccionar	*to select*
subrayar	*to underline*
traducir	*to translate*
tratar de	*to be about*

Expresiones útiles *Useful expressions*

Ahora mismo.	*Right away.*
¿Cómo no?	*But of course.*
¿Cómo se dice ________ en español?	*How do you say ________ in Spanish?*
¿Cómo se escribe ________?	*How do you spell ________?*
¿Comprende(n)?	*Do you understand?*
Con gusto.	*With pleasure.*
Con permiso.	*Excuse me.*
De acuerdo.	*Okay.*
De nada.	*You're welcome.*
¿De veras?	*Really?*
¿En qué página estamos?	*What page are we on?*
¿En serio?	*Seriously?*
Enseguida.	*Right away.*
Más despacio, por favor.	*Slower, please.*
Muchas gracias.	*Thanks a lot.*
No entiendo.	*I don't understand.*
No hay de qué.	*Don't mention it.*
No importa.	*No problem./It doesn't matter.*
¡No me digas!	*You don't say.*
No sé.	*I don't know.*
¡Ojalá!	*Hopefully!*
Perdone.	*Pardon me.*
Por favor.	*Please.*
Por supuesto.	*Of course.*
¡Qué bien!	*Great!*
¡Qué gracioso!	*How funny!*
¡Qué pena!	*What a pain!*
¿Qué significa ________?	*What does ________ mean?*
Repite, por favor.	*Please repeat.*
Tengo una pregunta.	*I have a question.*
¿Tiene(n) alguna pregunta?	*Do you have any questions?*
Vaya(n) a la página dos.	*Go to page 2.*

Glossary of Grammatical Terms

ADJECTIVE A word that modifies, or describes, a noun or pronoun.

muchos libros
many books

un hombre **rico**
a rich man

las mujeres **altas**
the tall women

Demonstrative adjective An adjective that specifies which noun a speaker is referring to.

esta fiesta
this party

ese chico
that boy

aquellas flores
those flowers

Possessive adjective An adjective that indicates ownership or possession.

mi mejor vestido
my best dress

Éste es **mi** hermano.
This is my brother

Stressed possessive adjective A possessive adjective that emphasizes the owner or possessor.

Es un libro **mío**.
It's my book./It's a book of mine.

Es amiga **tuya**; yo no la conozco.
She's a friend of yours; I don't know her.

ADVERB A word that modifies, or describes, a verb, adjective, or other adverb.

Pancho escribe **rápidamente**.
Pancho writes quickly.

Este cuadro es **muy** bonito.
This picture is very pretty.

ARTICLE A word that points out a noun in either a specific or a non-specific way.

Definite article An article that points out a noun in a specific way.

el libro
the book

la maleta
the suitcase

los diccionarios
the dictionaries

las palabras
the words

Indefinite article An article that points out a noun in a general, non-specific way.

un lápiz
a pencil

una computadora
a computer

unos pájaros
some birds

unas escuelas
some schools

CLAUSE A group of words that contains both a conjugated verb and a subject, either expressed or implied.

Main (or Independent) clause A clause that can stand alone as a complete sentence.

Pienso ir a cenar pronto.
I plan to go to dinner soon.

Subordinate (or Dependent) clause A clause that does not express a complete thought and therefore cannot stand alone as a sentence.

Trabajo en la cafetería **porque necesito dinero para la escuela.**
I work in the cafeteria because I need money for school.

COMPARATIVE A construction used with an adjective or adverb to express a comparison between two people, places, or things.

Este programa es **más interesante** que el otro.
This program is more interesting than the other one.

Tomás no es **tan alto como** Alberto.
Tomás is not as tall as Alberto.

CONJUGATION A set of the forms of a verb for a specific tense or mood or the process by which these verb forms are presented.

Preterite conjugation of **cantar:**

canté	cantamos
cantaste	cantasteis
cantó	cantaron

CONJUNCTION A word used to connect words, clauses, or phrases.

Susana es de Cuba **y** Pedro es de España.
Susana is from Cuba and Pedro is from Spain.

No quiero estudiar **pero** tengo que hacerlo.
I don't want to study, but I have to.

CONTRACTION The joining of two words into one. The only contractions in Spanish are **al** and **del**.

Mi hermano fue **al** concierto ayer.
*My brother went **to the** concert yesterday.*

Saqué dinero **del** banco.
*I took money **from the** bank.*

DIRECT OBJECT A noun or pronoun that directly receives the action of the verb.

Tomás lee **el libro**. | La pagó ayer.
*Tomás reads **the book**.* | *She paid **it** yesterday.*

GENDER The grammatical categorizing of certain kinds of words, such as nouns and pronouns, as masculine, feminine, or neuter.

Masculine
articles **el, un**
pronouns **él, lo, mío, éste, ése, aquél**
adjective **simpático**

Feminine
articles **la, una**
pronouns **ella, la, mía, ésta, ésa, aquélla**
adjective **simpática**

IMPERSONAL EXPRESSION A third-person expression with no expressed or specific subject.

Es muy **importante**. | **Llueve** mucho.
*It's very **important**.* | *It's **raining** hard.*

Aquí **se habla** español.
*Spanish **is spoken** here.*

INDIRECT OBJECT A noun or pronoun that receives the action of the verb indirectly; the object, often a living being, to or for whom an action is performed.

Eduardo **le** dio un libro **a Linda**.
*Eduardo gave a book **to Linda**.*

La profesora **me** dio una C en el examen.
*The professor gave **me** a C on the test.*

INFINITIVE The basic form of a verb. Infinitives in Spanish end in **-ar**, **-er**, or **-ir**.

hablar | **correr** | **abrir**
to speak | ***to run*** | ***to open***

INTERROGATIVE An adjective or pronoun used to ask a question.

¿**Quién** habla? | ¿**Cuántos** compraste?
***Who** is speaking?* | ***How many** did you buy?*

¿**Qué** piensas hacer hoy?
***What** do you plan to do today?*

INVERSION Changing the word order of a sentence, often to form a question.

Statement: Elena pagó la cuenta del restaurante.

Inversion: ¿Pagó Elena la cuenta del restaurante?

MOOD A grammatical distinction of verbs that indicates whether the verb is intended to make a statement or command or to express a doubt, emotion, or condition contrary to fact.

Imperative mood Verb forms used to make commands.

Di la verdad. | **Caminen** ustedes conmigo.
***Tell** the truth.* | ***Walk** with me.*

¡**Comamos** ahora!
***Let's eat** now!*

Indicative mood Verb forms used to state facts, actions, and states considered to be real.

Sé que **tienes** el dinero.
*I know that **you have** the money.*

Subjunctive mood Verb forms used principally in subordinate (dependent) clauses to express wishes, desires, emotions, doubts, and certain conditions, such as contrary-to-fact situations.

Prefieren que **hables** en español.
*They prefer that **you speak** in Spanish.*

Dudo que Luis **tenga** el dinero necesario.
*I doubt that Luis **has** the necessary money.*

NOUN A word that identifies people, animals, places, things, and ideas.

hombre | **gato**
man | ***cat***

México | **casa**
Mexico | ***house***

libertad | **libro**
freedom | ***book***

NUMBER A grammatical term that refers to singular or plural. Nouns in Spanish and English have number. Other parts of a sentence, such as adjectives, articles, and verbs, can also have number.

Singular	Plural
una cosa *a thing*	**unas** cosas *some things*
el profesor ***the** professor*	**los** profesores ***the** professors*

NUMBERS Words that represent amounts.

Cardinal numbers Words that show specific amounts.

cinco minutos
***five** minutes*

el año **dos mil cuatro**
*the year **2004***

Ordinal numbers Words that indicate the order of a noun in a series.

el **cuarto** jugador
*the **fourth** player*

la **décima** hora
*the **tenth** hour*

PAST PARTICIPLE A past form of the verb used in compound tenses. The past participle may also be used as an adjective, but it must then agree in number and gender with the word it modifies.

Han **buscado** por todas partes.
*They have **searched** everywhere.*

Yo no había **estudiado** para el examen.
*I hadn't **studied** for the exam.*

Hay una **ventana abierta** en la sala.
*There is an **open window** in the living room.*

PERSON The form of the verb or pronoun that indicates the speaker, the one spoken to, or the one spoken about. In Spanish, as in English, there are three persons: first, second, and third.

Person	Singular	Plural
1st	**yo** *I*	**nosotros/as** *we*
2nd	**tú, Ud.** *you*	**vosotros/as, Uds.** *you*
3rd	**él, ella** *he/she*	**ellos, ellas** *they*

PREPOSITION A word or words that describe(s) the relationship, most often in time or space, between two other words.

Anita es **de** California.
*Anita is **from** California.*

La chaqueta está **en** el carro.
*The jacket is **in** the car.*

Marta se peinó **antes de** salir.
*Marta combed her hair **before** going out.*

PRESENT PARTICIPLE In English, a verb form that ends in *-ing*. In Spanish, the present participle ends in **-ndo**, and is often used with **estar** to form a progressive tense.

Mi hermana está **hablando** por teléfono ahora mismo.
*My sister is **talking** on the phone right now.*

PRONOUN A word that takes the place of a noun or nouns.

Demonstrative pronoun A pronoun that takes the place of a specific noun.

Quiero **ésta**.
*I want **this one**.*

¿Vas a comprar **ése**?
*Are you going to buy **that one**?*

Juan prefirió **aquéllos**.
*Juan preferred **those** (over there).*

Object pronoun A pronoun that functions as a direct or indirect object of the verb.

Te digo la verdad.
*I'm telling **you** the truth.*

Me lo trajo Juan.
*Juan brought **it** to **me**.*

Reflexive pronoun A pronoun that indicates that the action of a verb is performed by the subject on itself. These pronouns are often expressed in English with *-self: myself, yourself*, etc.

Yo **me bañé** antes de salir.
***I bathed (myself)** before going out.*

Elena **se acostó** a las once y media.
*Elena **went to bed** at eleven-thirty.*

Relative pronoun A pronoun that connects a subordinate clause to a main clause.

El chico **que** nos escribió viene a visitar mañana.
*The boy **who** wrote us is coming to visit tomorrow.*

Ya sé **lo que** tenemos que hacer.
*I already know **what** we have to do.*

Subject pronoun A pronoun that replaces the name or title of a person or thing, and acts as the subject of a verb.

Tú debes estudiar más.
***You** should study more.*

Él llegó primero.
***He** arrived first.*

SUBJECT A noun or pronoun that performs the action of a verb and is often implied by the verb.

María va al supermercado.
***María** goes to the supermarket.*

(**Ellos**) Trabajan mucho.
***They** work hard.*

Esos **libros** son muy caros.
*Those **books** are very expensive.*

SUPERLATIVE A word or construction used with an adjective or adverb to express the highest or lowest degree of a specific quality among three or more people, places, or things.

De todas mis clases, ésta es la **más interesante**.
*Of all my classes, this is the **most interesting**.*

Raúl es el **menos simpático** de los chicos.
*Raúl is the **least pleasant** of the boys.*

TENSE A set of verb forms that indicates the time of an action or state: past, present, or future.

Compound tense A two-word tense made up of an auxiliary verb and a present or past participle. In Spanish, there are two auxiliary verbs: **estar** and **haber**.

En este momento, **estoy estudiando**.
*At this time, **I am studying**.*

El paquete no **ha llegado** todavía.
*The package **has** not **arrived** yet.*

Simple tense A tense expressed by a single verb form.

María **estaba** mal anoche.
*María **was** ill last night.*

Juana **hablará** con su mamá mañana.
*Juana **will** speak with her mom tomorrow.*

VERB A word that expresses actions or states-of-being.

Auxiliary verb A verb used with a present or past participle to form a compound tense. **Haber** is the most commonly used auxiliary verb in Spanish.

Los chicos **han** visto los elefantes.
*The children **have** seen the elephants.*

Espero que **hayas** comido.
*I hope you **have** eaten.*

Reflexive verb A verb that describes an action performed by the subject on itself and is always used with a reflexive pronoun.

Me compré un carro nuevo.
*I **bought myself** a new car.*

Pedro y Adela **se levantan** muy temprano.
*Pedro and Adela **get (themselves) up** very early.*

Spelling change verb A verb that undergoes a predictable change in spelling, in order to reflect its actual pronunciation in the various conjugations.

practicar	c→qu	practico	practi**qué**
dirigir	g→j	dirigí	diri**j**o
almorzar	z→c	almorzó	almor**c**é

Stem-changing verb A verb whose stem vowel undergoes one or more predictable changes in the various conjugations.

entender (i:ie)	ent**ie**ndo
pedir (e:i)	p**i**den
dormir (o:ue, u)	d**ue**rmo, d**u**rmieron

Verb Conjugation Tables

The verb lists

The list of verbs below, and the model-verb tables that start on page 578 show you how to conjugate every verb taught in **VISTAS**. Each verb in the list is followed by a model verb conjugated according to the same pattern. The number in parentheses indicates where in the verb tables you can find the conjugated forms of the model verb. If you want to find out how to conjugate **divertirse**, for example, look up number 33, **sentir**, the model for verbs that follow the **e:ie** stem-change pattern.

How to use the verb tables

In the tables you will find the infinitive, present and past participles, and all the simple forms of each model verb. The formation of the compound tenses of any verb can be inferred from the table of compound tenses, pages 578–585, either by combining the past participle of the verb with a conjugated form of **haber** or by combining the present participle with a conjugated form of **estar**.

abrazar (z:c) like cruzar (37)
abrir like vivir (3) *except* past participle is abierto
aburrir(se) like vivir (3)
acabar de like hablar (1)
acampar like hablar (1)
acompañar like hablar (1)
aconsejar like hablar (1)
acordarse (o:ue) like contar (24)
acostarse (o:ue) like contar (24)
adelgazar (z:c) like cruzar (37)
afeitarse like hablar (1)
ahorrar like hablar (1)
alegrarse like hablar (1)
aliviar like hablar (1)
almorzar (o:ue) like contar (24) *except* (z:c)
alquilar like hablar (1)
andar like hablar (1) *except* preterite stem is anduv–
anunciar like hablar (1)
apagar (g:gu) like llegar (41)
aplaudir like vivir (3)
apreciar like hablar (1)
aprender like comer (2)
apurarse like hablar (1)
arrancar (c:qu) like tocar (43)
arreglar like hablar (1)
asistir like vivir (3)
aumentar like hablar (1)
ayudar(se) like hablar (1)
bailar like hablar (1)
bajar(se) like hablar (1)
bañarse like hablar (1)
barrer like comer (2)
beber like comer (2)
besar(se) like hablar (1)
borrar like hablar (1)
brindar like hablar (1)
bucear like hablar (1)
buscar (c:qu) like tocar (43)
caber (4)
caer(se) (5)
calentarse (e:ie) like pensar (30)
calzar (z:c) like cruzar(37)
cambiar like hablar (1)
caminar like hablar (1)
cantar like hablar (1)
casarse like hablar (1)
cazar (z:c) like cruzar(37)
celebrar like hablar (1)
cenar like hablar (1)
cepillarse like hablar (1)
cerrar (e:ie) like pensar (30)
cobrar like hablar (1)
cocinar like hablar (1)
comenzar (e:ie) (z:c) like empezar (26)
comer (2)
compartir like vivir (3)
comprar like hablar (1)
comprender like comer (2)
comprometerse like comer (2)
comunicarse (c:qu) like tocar (43)
conducir (c:zc) (6)
confirmar like hablar (1)
conocer (c:zc) (35)
conseguir (e:i) like seguir (32)
conservar like hablar (1)
consumir like vivir (3)
contaminar like hablar (1)
contar (o:ue) (24)
controlar like hablar (1)
correr like comer (2)
costar (o:ue) like contar (24)
creer (y) (36)
cruzar (z:c) (37)
cubrir like vivir (3) *except* past participle is cubierto
cuidar like hablar (1)
cumplir like vivir (3)
dañar like hablar (1)
dar (7)
deber like comer (2)
decidir like vivir (3)
decir (e:i) (8)
declarar like hablar (1)
dejar like hablar (1)
depositar like hablar (1)
desarrollar like hablar (1)
desayunar like hablar (1)
descansar like hablar (1)
descargar like hablar (1)
describir like vivir (3) *except* past participle is descrito
descubrir like vivir (3) *except* past participle is descubierto
desear like hablar (1)
despedirse (e:i) like pedir (29)
despertarse (e:ie) like pensar (30)
destruir (y) (38)
dibujar like hablar (1)
dirigir (g:j) like vivir (3) *except* (g:j)
disfrutar like hablar (1)
divertirse (e:ie) like sentir (33)
divorciarse like hablar (1)
doblar like hablar (1)
doler (o:ue) like volver (34) *except* past participle is regular
dormir(se) (o:ue) (25)
ducharse like hablar (1)
dudar like hablar (1)
durar like hablar (1)
echar like hablar (1)
elegir (e:i) like pedir (29) *except* (g:j)

emitir like vivir (3)
empezar (e:ie) (z:c) (26)
enamorarse like hablar (1)
encantar like hablar (1)
encontrar(se) (o:ue) like contar (24)
enfermarse like hablar (1)
engordar like hablar (1)
enojarse like hablar (1)
enseñar like hablar (1)
ensuciar like hablar (1)
entender (e:ie) (27)
entrenarse like hablar (1)
entrevistar like hablar (1)
enviar (envío) (39)
escalar like hablar (1)
escoger (g:j) like proteger (42)
escribir like vivir (3) *except* past participle is escrito
escuchar like hablar (1)
esculpir like vivir (3)
esperar like hablar (1)
esquiar (esquío) like enviar (39)
establecer (c:zc) like conocer (35)
estacionar like hablar (1)
estar (9)
estornudar like hablar (1)
estudiar like hablar (1)
evitar like hablar (1)
explicar (c:qu) like tocar (43)
explorar like hablar (1)
faltar like hablar (1)
fascinar like hablar (1)
firmar like hablar (1)
fumar like hablar (1)
funcionar like hablar (1)
ganar like hablar (1)
gastar like hablar (1)
grabar like hablar (1)
graduarse (gradúo) (40)
guardar like hablar (1)
gustar like hablar (1)
haber (hay) (10)
hablar (1)
hacer (11)
importar like hablar (1)
imprimir like vivir (3)
informar like hablar (1)
insistir like vivir (3)
interesar like hablar (1)
invertir (e:ie) like sentir (33)
invitar like hablar (1)
ir(se) (12)
jubilarse like hablar (1)
jugar (u:ue) (g:gu) (28)
lastimarse like hablar (1)
lavar(se) like hablar (1)
leer (y) like creer (36)
levantar(se) like hablar (1)
limpiar like hablar (1)
llamar(se) like hablar (1)
llegar (g:gu) (41)
llenar like hablar (1)
llevar(se) like hablar (1)
llover (o:ue) like volver (34) *except* past participle is regular
luchar like hablar (1)
mandar like hablar (1)
manejar like hablar (1)
mantener(se) (e:ie) like **tener** (20)
maquillarse like hablar (1)
mejorar like hablar (1)
merendar (e:ie) like pensar (30)
mirar like hablar (1)
molestar like hablar (1)
montar like hablar (1)
morir (o:ue) like dormir (25) *except* past participle is muerto
mostrar (o:ue) like contar (24)
mudarse like hablar (1)
nacer (c:zc) like conocer (35)
nadar like hablar (1)
navegar (g:gu) like llegar (41)
necesitar like hablar (1)
negar (e:ie) like pensar (30) *except* (g:gu)
nevar (e:ie) like pensar (30)
obedecer (c:zc) like conocer (35)
obtener (e:ie) like tener (20)
ocurrir like vivir (3)
odiar like hablar (1)
ofrecer (c:zc) like conocer (35)
oír (13)
olvidar like hablar (1)
pagar (g:gu) like llegar (41)
parar like hablar (1)
parecer (c:zc) like conocer (35)
pasar like hablar (1)
pasear like hablar (1)
patinar like hablar (1)
pedir (e:i) (29)
peinarse like hablar (1)
pensar (e:ie) (30)
perder (e:ie) like entender (27)
pescar (c:qu) like tocar (43)
pintar like hablar (1)
planchar like hablar (1)
poder (o:ue) (14)
poner(se) (15)
practicar (c:qu) like tocar (43)
preferir (e:ie) like sentir (33)
preguntar like hablar (1)
preocuparse like hablar (1)
preparar like hablar (1)
presentar like hablar (1)
prestar like hablar (1)
probar(se) (o:ue) like contar (24)
prohibir like vivir (3)
proteger (g:j) (42)
publicar (c:qu) like tocar (43)
quedar(se) like hablar (1)
quemar like hablar (1)
querer (e:ie) (16)
quitar(se) like hablar (1)
recetar like hablar (1)
recibir like vivir (3)
reciclar like hablar (1)
recoger (g:j) like proteger (42)
recomendar (e:ie) like pensar (30)
recordar (o:ue) like contar (24)
reducir (c:zc) like conducir (6)
regalar like hablar (1)
regatear like hablar (1)
regresar like hablar (1)
reír(se) (e:i) (31)
relajarse like hablar (1)
renunciar like hablar (1)
repetir (e:i) like pedir (29)
resolver (o:ue) like volver (34)
respirar like hablar (1)
revisar like hablar (1)
rogar (o:ue) like contar (24) *except* (g:gu)
romper(se) like comer (2) *except* past participle is roto
saber (17)
sacar (c:qu) like tocar (43)
sacudir like vivir (3)
salir (18)
saludar(se) like hablar (1)
secar(se) (c:q) like tocar (43)
seguir (e:i) (32)
sentarse (e:ie) like pensar (30)
sentir(se) (e:ie) (33)
separarse like hablar (1)
ser (19)
servir (e:i) like pedir (29)
solicitar like hablar (1)
sonar (o:ue) like contar (24)
sonreír (e:i) like reír(se) (31)
sorprender like comer (2)
subir like vivir (3)
sudar like hablar (1)
sufrir like vivir (3)
sugerir (e:ie) like sentir (33)
suponer like poner (15)
temer like comer (2)
tener (e:ie) (20)
terminar like hablar (1)
tocar (c:qu) (43)
tomar like hablar (1)
torcerse (o:ue) like volver (34) *except* (c:z) and past participle is regular; e.g. yo tuerzo
toser like comer (2)
trabajar like hablar (1)
traducir (c:zc) like conducir (6)
traer (21)
transmitir like vivir (3)
tratar like hablar (1)
usar like hablar (1)
vender like comer (2)
venir (e:ie) (22)
ver (23)
vestirse (e:i) like pedir (29)
viajar like hablar (1)
visitar like hablar (1)
vivir (3)
volver (o:ue) (34)
votar like hablar (1)

Regular verbs: simple tenses

		INDICATIVE					SUBJUNCTIVE		IMPERATIVE
	Infinitive	Present	Imperfect	Preterite	Future	Conditional	Present	Past	
1	hablar	hablo	hablaba	hablé	hablaré	hablaría	hable	hablara	
		hablas	hablabas	hablaste	hablarás	hablarías	hables	hablaras	habla tú (no hables)
	Participles:	habla	hablaba	habló	hablará	hablaría	hable	hablara	hable Ud.
	hablando	hablamos	hablábamos	hablamos	hablaremos	hablaríamos	hablemos	habláramos	hablemos
	hablado	habláis	hablabais	hablasteis	hablaréis	hablaríais	habléis	hablarais	hablad (no habléis)
		hablan	hablaban	hablaron	hablarán	hablarían	hablen	hablaran	hablen Uds.
2	comer	como	comía	comí	comeré	comería	coma	comiera	
		comes	comías	comiste	comerás	comerías	comas	comieras	come tú (no comas)
	Participles:	come	comía	comió	comerá	comería	coma	comiera	coma Ud.
	comiendo	comemos	comíamos	comimos	comeremos	comeríamos	comamos	comiéramos	comamos
	comido	coméis	comíais	comisteis	comeréis	comeríais	comáis	comierais	comed (no comáis)
		comen	comían	comieron	comerán	comerían	coman	comieran	coman Uds.
3	vivir	vivo	vivía	viví	viviré	viviría	viva	viviera	
		vives	vivías	viviste	vivirás	vivirías	vivas	vivieras	vive tú (no vivas)
	Participles:	vive	vivía	vivió	vivirá	viviría	viva	viviera	viva Ud.
	viviendo	vivimos	vivíamos	vivimos	viviremos	viviríamos	vivamos	viviéramos	vivamos
	vivido	vivís	vivíais	vivisteis	viviréis	viviríais	viváis	vivierais	vivid (no viváis)
		viven	vivían	vivieron	vivirán	vivirían	vivan	vivieran	vivan Uds.

All verbs: compound tenses

PERFECT TENSES											
INDICATIVE								SUBJUNCTIVE			
Present Perfect		Past Perfect		Future Perfect		Conditional Perfect		Present Perfect		Past Perfect	
he		había		habré		habría		haya		hubiera	
has	hablado	habías	hablado	habrás	hablado	habrías	hablado	hayas	hablado	hubieras	hablado
ha	comido	había	comido	habrá	comido	habría	comido	haya	comido	hubiera	comido
hemos	vivido	habíamos	vivido	habremos	vivido	habríamos	vivido	hayamos	vivido	hubiéramos	vivido
habéis		habíais		habréis		habríais		hayáis		hubierais	
han		habían		habrán		habrían		hayan		hubieran	

PROGRESSIVE TENSES					
INDICATIVE				SUBJUNCTIVE	
Present Progressive	Past Progressive	Future Progressive	Conditional Progressive	Present Progressive	Past Progressive
estoy estás está estamos estáis estan } hablando / comiendo / viviendo	estaba estabas estaba estábamos estabais estaban } hablando / comiendo / viviendo	estaré estarás estará estaremos estaréis estarán } hablando / comiendo / viviendo	estaría estarías estaría estaríamos estaríais estarían } hablando / comiendo / viviendo	esté estés esté estemos estéis estén } hablando / comiendo / viviendo	estuviera estuvieras estuviera estuviéramos estuvierais estuvieran } hablando / comiendo / viviendo

Irregular verbs

		INDICATIVE					SUBJUNCTIVE		IMPERATIVE
	Infinitive	Present	Imperfect	Preterite	Future	Conditional	Present	Past	
4	caber **Participles:** cabiendo cabido	**quepo** cabes cabe cabemos cabéis caben	cabía cabías cabía cabíamos cabíais cabían	**cupe** **cupiste** **cupo** **cupimos** **cupisteis** **cupieron**	**cabré** **cabrás** **cabrá** **cabremos** **cabréis** **cabrán**	**cabría** **cabrías** **cabría** **cabríamos** **cabríais** **cabrían**	**quepa** **quepas** **quepa** **quepamos** **quepáis** **quepan**	**cupiera** **cupieras** **cupiera** **cupiéramos** **cupierais** **cupieran**	 cabe tú (no **quepas**) **quepa** Ud. **quepamos** cabed (no **quepáis**) **quepan** Uds.
5	caer(se) **Participles:** **cayendo** **caído**	**caigo** caes cae caemos caéis caen	caía caías caía caíamos caíais caían	**caí** **caíste** **cayó** **caímos** **caísteis** **cayeron**	caeré caerás caerá caeremos caeréis caerán	caería caerías caería caeríamos caeríais caerían	**caiga** **caigas** **caiga** **caigamos** **caigáis** **caigan**	**cayera** **cayeras** **cayera** **cayéramos** **cayerais** **cayeran**	 cae tú (no **caigas**) **caiga** Ud. **caigamos** caed (no **caigáis**) **caigan** Uds.
6	conducir (c:zc) **Participles:** conduciendo conducido	**conduzco** conduces conduce conducimos conducís conducen	conducía conducías conducía conducíamos conducíais conducían	**conduje** **condujiste** **condujo** **condujimos** **condujisteis** **condujeron**	conduciré conducirás conducirá conduciremos conduciréis conducirán	conduciría conducirías conduciría conduciríamos conduciríais conducirían	**conduzca** **conduzcas** **conduzca** **conduzcamos** **conduzcáis** **conduzcan**	**condujera** **condujeras** **condujera** **condujéramos** **condujerais** **condujeran**	 conduce tú (no **conduzcas**) **conduzca** Ud. **conduzcamos** conducid (no **conduzcáis**) **conduzcan** Uds.

	Infinitive	INDICATIVE					SUBJUNCTIVE		IMPERATIVE
		Present	Imperfect	Preterite	Future	Conditional	Present	Past	
7	dar **Participles:** dando dado	**doy** das da damos dais dan	daba dabas daba dábamos dabais daban	**di** **diste** **dio** **dimos** **disteis** **dieron**	daré darás dará daremos daréis darán	daría darías daría daríamos daríais darían	**dé** **des** **dé** **demos** **deis** **den**	**diera** **dieras** **diera** **diéramos** **dierais** **dieran**	 da tú (no des) **dé** Ud. **demos** dad (no **deis**) **den** Uds.
8	decir (e:i) **Participles:** **diciendo** **dicho**	**digo** **dices** **dice** decimos decís **dicen**	decía decías decía decíamos decíais decían	**dije** **dijiste** **dijo** **dijimos** **dijisteis** **dijeron**	**diré** **dirás** **dirá** **diremos** **diréis** **dirán**	**diría** **dirías** **diría** **diríamos** **diríais** **dirían**	**diga** **digas** **diga** **digamos** **digáis** **digan**	**dijera** **dijeras** **dijera** **dijéramos** **dijerais** **dijeran**	 **di** tú (no **digas**) **diga** Ud. **digamos** decid (no **digáis**) **digan** Uds.
9	estar **Participles:** estando estado	**estoy** estás está estamos estáis están	estaba estabas estaba estábamos estabais estaban	**estuve** **estuviste** **estuvo** **estuvimos** **estuvisteis** **estuvieron**	estaré estarás estará estaremos estaréis estarán	estaría estarías estaría estaríamos estaríais estarían	esté estés esté estemos estéis estén	**estuviera** **estuvieras** **estuviera** **estuviéramos** **estuvierais** **estuvieran**	 está tú (no estés) esté Ud. estemos estad (no estéis) estén Uds.
10	haber **Participles:** habiendo habido	**he** **has** **ha** **hemos** **habéis** **han**	había habías había habíamos habíais habían	**hube** **hubiste** **hubo** **hubimos** **hubisteis** **hubieron**	**habré** **habrás** **habrá** **habremos** **habréis** **habrán**	**habría** **habrías** **habría** **habríamos** **habríais** **habrían**	**haya** **hayas** **haya** **hayamos** **hayáis** **hayan**	**hubiera** **hubieras** **hubiera** **hubiéramos** **hubierais** **hubieran**	
11	hacer **Participles:** haciendo **hecho**	**hago** haces hace hacemos hacéis hacen	hacía hacías hacía hacíamos hacíais hacían	**hice** **hiciste** **hizo** **hicimos** **hicisteis** **hicieron**	**haré** **harás** **hará** **haremos** **haréis** **harán**	**haría** **harías** **haría** **haríamos** **haríais** **harían**	**haga** **hagas** **haga** **hagamos** **hagáis** **hagan**	**hiciera** **hicieras** **hiciera** **hiciéramos** **hicierais** **hicieran**	 **haz** tú (no **hagas**) **haga** Ud. **hagamos** haced (no **hagáis**) **hagan** Uds.
12	ir **Participles:** **yendo** **ido**	**voy** **vas** **va** **vamos** **vais** **van**	**iba** **ibas** **iba** **íbamos** **ibais** **iban**	**fui** **fuiste** **fue** **fuimos** **fuisteis** **fueron**	iré irás irá iremos iréis irán	iría irías iría iríamos iríais irían	**vaya** **vayas** **vaya** **vayamos** **vayáis** **vayan**	**fuera** **fueras** **fuera** **fuéramos** **fuerais** **fueran**	 **ve** tú (no **vayas**) **vaya** Ud. **vamos** id (no **vayáis**) **vayan** Uds.
13	oír (y) **Participles:** **oyendo** **oído**	**oigo** **oyes** **oye** **oímos** **oís** **oyen**	oía oías oía oíamos oíais oían	**oí** **oíste** **oyó** **oímos** **oísteis** **oyeron**	oiré oirás oirá oiremos oiréis oirán	oiría oirías oiría oiríamos oiríais oirían	**oiga** **oigas** **oiga** **oigamos** **oigáis** **oigan**	**oyera** **oyeras** **oyera** **oyéramos** **oyerais** **oyeran**	 **oye** tú (no **oigas**) **oiga** Ud. **oigamos** oíd (no **oigáis**) **oigan** Uds.

	Infinitive	INDICATIVE					SUBJUNCTIVE		IMPERATIVE
		Present	Imperfect	Preterite	Future	Conditional	Present	Past	
14	poder (o:ue) **Participles:** **pudiendo** podido	**puedo** **puedes** **puede** podemos podéis **pueden**	podía podías podía podíamos podíais podían	**pude** **pudiste** **pudo** **pudimos** **pudisteis** **pudieron**	**podré** **podrás** **podrá** **podremos** **podréis** **podrán**	**podría** **podrías** **podría** **podríamos** **podríais** **podrían**	**pueda** **puedas** **pueda** podamos podáis **puedan**	**pudiera** **pudieras** **pudiera** **pudiéramos** **pudierais** **pudieran**	**puede** tú (no **puedas**) **pueda** Ud. podamos poded (no podáis) **puedan** Uds.
15	poner **Participles:** poniendo **puesto**	**pongo** pones pone ponemos ponéis ponen	ponía ponías ponía poníamos poníais ponían	**puse** **pusiste** **puso** **pusimos** **pusisteis** **pusieron**	**pondré** **pondrás** **pondrá** **pondremos** **pondréis** **pondrán**	**pondría** **pondrías** **pondría** **pondríamos** **pondríais** **pondrían**	**ponga** **pongas** **ponga** **pongamos** **pongáis** **pongan**	**pusiera** **pusieras** **pusiera** **pusiéramos** **pusierais** **pusieran**	**pon** tú (no **pongas**) **ponga** Ud. **pongamos** poned (no **pongáis**) **pongan** Uds.
16	querer (e:ie) **Participles:** queriendo querido	**quiero** **quieres** **quiere** queremos queréis **quieren**	quería querías quería queríamos queríais querían	**quise** **quisiste** **quiso** **quisimos** **quisisteis** **quisieron**	**querré** **querrás** **querrá** **querremos** **querréis** **querrán**	**querría** **querrías** **querría** **querríamos** **querríais** **querrían**	**quiera** **quieras** **quiera** queramos queráis **quieran**	**quisiera** **quisieras** **quisiera** **quisiéramos** **quisierais** **quisieran**	**quiere** tú (no **quieras**) **quiera** Ud. **queramos** quered (no queráis) **quieran** Uds.
17	saber **Participles:** sabiendo sabido	**sé** sabes sabe sabemos sabéis saben	sabía sabías sabía sabíamos sabíais sabían	**supe** **supiste** **supo** **supimos** **supisteis** **supieron**	**sabré** **sabrás** **sabrá** **sabremos** **sabréis** **sabrán**	**sabría** **sabrías** **sabría** **sabríamos** **sabríais** **sabrían**	**sepa** **sepas** **sepa** **sepamos** **sepáis** **sepan**	**supiera** **supieras** **supiera** **supiéramos** **supierais** **supieran**	sabe tú (no **sepas**) **sepa** Ud. **sepamos** sabed (no **sepáis**) **sepan** Uds.
18	salir **Participles:** saliendo salido	**salgo** sales sale salimos salís salen	salía salías salía salíamos salíais salían	salí saliste salió salimos salisteis salieron	**saldré** **saldrás** **saldrá** **saldremos** **saldréis** **saldrán**	**saldría** **saldrías** **saldría** **saldríamos** **saldríais** **saldrían**	**salga** **salgas** **salga** **salgamos** **salgáis** **salgan**	saliera salieras saliera saliéramos salierais salieran	**sal** tú (no **salgas**) **salga** Ud. **salgamos** salid (no **salgáis**) **salgan** Uds.
19	ser **Participles:** siendo sido	**soy** **eres** **es** **somos** **sois** **son**	**era** **eras** **era** **éramos** **erais** **eran**	**fui** **fuiste** **fue** **fuimos** **fuisteis** **fueron**	seré serás será seremos seréis serán	sería serías sería seríamos seríais serían	**sea** **seas** **sea** **seamos** **seáis** **sean**	**fuera** **fueras** **fuera** **fuéramos** **fuerais** **fueran**	**sé** tú (no **seas**) **sea** Ud. **seamos** sed (no **seáis**) **sean** Uds.
20	tener (e:ie) **Participles:** teniendo tenido	**tengo** **tienes** **tiene** tenemos tenéis **tienen**	**tenía** **tenías** **tenía** **teníamos** **teníais** **tenían**	**tuve** **tuviste** **tuvo** **tuvimos** **tuvisteis** **tuvieron**	**tendré** **tendrás** **tendrá** **tendremos** **tendréis** **tendrán**	**tendría** **tendrías** **tendría** **tendríamos** **tendríais** **tendrían**	**tenga** **tengas** **tenga** **tengamos** **tengáis** **tengan**	**tuviera** **tuvieras** **tuviera** **tuviéramos** **tuvierais** **tuvieran**	**ten** tú (no **tengas**) **tenga** Ud. **tengamos** tened (no **tengáis**) **tengan** Uds.

#	Infinitive	INDICATIVE					SUBJUNCTIVE		IMPERATIVE
		Present	Imperfect	Preterite	Future	Conditional	Present	Past	
21	traer	**traigo**	traía	**traje**	traeré	traería	**traiga**	**trajera**	
		traes	traías	**trajiste**	traerás	traerías	**traigas**	**trajeras**	trae tú (no **traigas**)
	Participles:	trae	traía	**trajo**	traerá	traería	**traiga**	**trajera**	**traiga** Ud.
	trayendo	traemos	traíamos	**trajimos**	traeremos	traeríamos	**traigamos**	**trajéramos**	**traigamos**
	traído	traéis	traíais	**trajisteis**	traeréis	traeríais	**traigáis**	**trajerais**	traed (no **traigáis**)
		traen	traían	**trajeron**	traerán	traerían	**traigan**	**trajeran**	**traigan** Uds.
22	venir (e:ie)	**vengo**	venía	**vine**	**vendré**	**vendría**	**venga**	**viniera**	
		vienes	venías	**viniste**	**vendrás**	**vendrías**	**vengas**	**vinieras**	**ven** tú (no **vengas**)
	Participles:	**viene**	venía	**vino**	**vendrá**	**vendría**	**venga**	**viniera**	**venga** Ud.
	viniendo	venimos	veníamos	**vinimos**	**vendremos**	**vendríamos**	**vengamos**	**viniéramos**	**vengamos**
	venido	venís	veníais	**vinisteis**	**vendréis**	**vendríais**	**vengáis**	**vinierais**	venid (no **vengáis**)
		vienen	venían	**vinieron**	**vendrán**	**vendrían**	**vengan**	**vinieran**	**vengan** Uds.
23	ver	**veo**	**veía**	**vi**	veré	vería	**vea**	**viera**	
		ves	**veías**	**viste**	verás	verías	**veas**	**vieras**	**ve** tú (no **veas**)
	Participles:	ve	**veía**	**vio**	verá	vería	**vea**	**viera**	**vea** Ud.
	viendo	vemos	**veíamos**	**vimos**	veremos	veríamos	**veamos**	**viéramos**	**veamos**
	visto	veis	**veíais**	**visteis**	veréis	veríais	**veáis**	**vierais**	ved (no **veáis**)
		ven	**veían**	**vieron**	verán	verían	**vean**	**vieran**	**vean** Uds.

Stem-changing verbs

#	Infinitive	INDICATIVE					SUBJUNCTIVE		IMPERATIVE
		Present	Imperfect	Preterite	Future	Conditional	Present	Past	
24	contar (o:ue)	**cuento**	contaba	conté	contaré	contaría	**cuente**	contara	
		cuentas	contabas	contaste	contarás	contarías	**cuentes**	contaras	**cuenta** tú (no **cuentes**)
	Participles:	**cuenta**	contaba	contó	contará	contaría	**cuente**	contara	**cuente** Ud.
	contando	contamos	contábamos	contamos	contaremos	contaríamos	contemos	contáramos	contemos
	contado	contáis	contabais	contasteis	contaréis	contaríais	contéis	contarais	contad (no contéis)
		cuentan	contaban	contaron	contarán	contarían	**cuenten**	contaran	**cuenten** Uds.
25	dormir (o:ue)	**duermo**	dormía	dormí	dormiré	dormiría	**duerma**	**durmiera**	
		duermes	dormías	dormiste	dormirás	dormirías	**duermas**	**durmieras**	**duerme** tú (no **duermas**)
	Participles:	**duerme**	dormía	**durmió**	dormirá	dormiría	**duerma**	**durmiera**	**duerma** Ud.
	durmiendo	dormimos	dormíamos	dormimos	dormiremos	dormiríamos	**durmamos**	**durmiéramos**	**durmamos**
	dormido	dormís	dormíais	dormisteis	dormiréis	dormiríais	**durmáis**	**durmierais**	dormid (no **durmáis**)
		duermen	dormían	**durmieron**	dormirán	dormirían	**duerman**	**durmieran**	**duerman** Uds.
26	empezar	**empiezo**	empezaba	**empecé**	empezaré	empezaría	**empiece**	empezara	
	(e:ie) (c)	**empiezas**	empezabas	empezaste	empezarás	empezarías	**empieces**	empezaras	**empieza** tú (no **empieces**)
		empieza	empezaba	empezó	empezará	empezaría	**empiece**	empezara	**empiece** Ud.
	Participles:	empezamos	empezábamos	empezamos	empezaremos	empezaríamos	**empecemos**	empezáramos	**empecemos**
	empezando	empezáis	empezabais	empezasteis	empezaréis	empezaríais	**empecéis**	empezarais	empezad (no **empecéis**)
	empezado	**empiezan**	empezaban	empezaron	empezarán	empezarían	**empiecen**	empezaran	**empiecen** Uds.

	Infinitive	INDICATIVE					SUBJUNCTIVE		IMPERATIVE
		Present	Imperfect	Preterite	Future	Conditional	Present	Past	
27	entender	**entiendo**	entendía	entendí	entenderé	entendería	**entienda**	entendiera	
	(e:ie)	**entiendes**	entendías	entendiste	entenderás	entenderías	**entiendas**	entendieras	**entiende** tú (no **entiendas**)
		entiende	entendía	entendió	entenderá	entendería	**entienda**	entendiera	**entienda** Ud.
	Participles:	entendemos	entendíamos	entendimos	entenderemos	entenderíamos	entendamos	entendiéramos	entendamos
	entendiendo	entendéis	entendíais	entendisteis	entenderéis	entenderíais	entendáis	entendierais	entended (no entendáis)
	entendido	**entienden**	entendían	entendieron	entenderán	entenderían	**entiendan**	entendieran	**entiendan** Uds.
28	jugar (u:ue)	**juego**	jugaba	**jugué**	jugaré	jugaría	**juegue**	jugara	
	(gu)	**juegas**	jugabas	jugaste	jugarás	jugarías	**juegues**	jugaras	**juega** tú (no **juegues**)
		juega	jugaba	jugó	jugará	jugaría	**juegue**	jugara	**juegue** Ud.
	Participles:	jugamos	jugábamos	jugamos	jugaremos	jugaríamos	juguemos	jugáramos	juguemos
	jugando	jugáis	jugabais	jugasteis	jugaréis	jugaríais	juguéis	jugarais	jugad (no juguéis)
	jugado	**juegan**	jugaban	jugaron	jugarán	jugarían	**jueguen**	jugaran	**jueguen** Uds.
29	pedir (e:i)	**pido**	pedía	pedí	pediré	pediría	**pida**	**pidiera**	
		pides	pedías	pediste	pedirás	pedirías	**pidas**	**pidieras**	**pide** tú (no **pidas**)
	Participles:	**pide**	pedía	**pidió**	pedirá	pediría	**pida**	**pidiera**	**pida** Ud.
	pidiendo	pedimos	pedíamos	pedimos	pediremos	pediríamos	**pidamos**	**pidiéramos**	**pidamos**
	pedido	pedís	pedíais	pedisteis	pediréis	pediríais	**pidáis**	**pidierais**	pedid (no **pidáis**)
		piden	pedían	**pidieron**	pedirán	pedirían	**pidan**	**pidieran**	**pidan** Uds.
30	pensar (e:ie)	**pienso**	pensaba	pensé	pensaré	pensaría	**piense**	pensara	
		piensas	pensabas	pensaste	pensarás	pensarías	**pienses**	pensaras	**piensa** tú (no **pienses**)
	Participles:	**piensa**	pensaba	pensó	pensará	pensaría	**piense**	pensara	**piense** Ud.
	pensando	pensamos	pensábamos	pensamos	pensaremos	pensaríamos	pensemos	pensáramos	pensemos
	pensado	pensáis	pensabais	pensasteis	pensaréis	pensaríais	penséis	pensarais	pensad (no penséis)
		piensan	pensaban	pensaron	pensarán	pensarían	**piensen**	pensaran	**piensen** Uds.
31	reír(se) (e:i)	**río**	reía	**reí**	reiré	reiría	**ría**	**riera**	
		ríes	reías	**reíste**	reirás	reirías	**rías**	**rieras**	**ríe** tú (no **rías**)
	Participles:	**ríe**	reía	**rió**	reirá	reiría	**ría**	**riera**	**ría** Ud.
	riendo	**reímos**	reíamos	**reímos**	reiremos	reiríamos	**riamos**	**riéramos**	**riamos**
	reído	**reís**	reíais	**reísteis**	reiréis	reiríais	**riáis**	**rierais**	reíd (no **riáis**)
		ríen	reían	**rieron**	reirán	reirían	**rían**	**rieran**	**rían** Uds.
32	seguir (e:i)	**sigo**	seguía	seguí	seguiré	seguiría	**siga**	**siguiera**	
	(gu)	**sigues**	seguías	seguiste	seguirás	seguirías	**sigas**	**siguieras**	**sigue** tú (no **sigas**)
		sigue	seguía	**siguió**	seguirá	seguiría	**siga**	**siguiera**	**siga** Ud.
	Participles:	seguimos	seguíamos	seguimos	seguiremos	seguiríamos	**sigamos**	**siguiéramos**	**sigamos**
	siguiendo	seguís	seguíais	seguisteis	seguiréis	seguiríais	**sigáis**	**siguierais**	seguid (no **sigáis**)
	seguido	**siguen**	seguían	**siguieron**	seguirán	seguirían	**sigan**	**siguieran**	**sigan** Uds.
33	sentir (e:ie)	**siento**	sentía	sentí	sentiré	sentiría	**sienta**	**sintiera**	
		sientes	sentías	sentiste	sentirás	sentirías	**sientas**	**sintieras**	**siente** tú (no **sientas**)
	Participles:	**siente**	sentía	**sintió**	sentirá	sentiría	**sienta**	**sintiera**	**sienta** Ud.
	sintiendo	sentimos	sentíamos	sentimos	sentiremos	sentiríamos	**sintamos**	**sintiéramos**	**sintamos**
	sentido	sentís	sentíais	sentisteis	sentiréis	sentiríais	**sintáis**	**sintierais**	sentid (no **sintáis**)
		sienten	sentían	**sintieron**	sentirán	sentirían	**sientan**	**sintieran**	**sientan** Uds.

		INDICATIVE					SUBJUNCTIVE		IMPERATIVE
	Infinitive	**Present**	**Imperfect**	**Preterite**	**Future**	**Conditional**	**Present**	**Past**	
34	volver (o:ue)	**vuelvo**	volvía	volví	volveré	volvería	**vuelva**	volviera	
		vuelves	volvías	volviste	volverás	volverías	**vuelvas**	volvieras	**vuelve** tú (no **vuelvas**)
	Participles:	**vuelve**	volvía	volvió	volverá	volvería	**vuelva**	volviera	**vuelva** Ud.
	volviendo	volvemos	volvíamos	volvimos	volveremos	volveríamos	volvamos	volviéramos	volvamos
	vuelto	volvéis	volvíais	volvisteis	volveréis	volveríais	volváis	volvierais	volved (no volváis)
		vuelven	volvían	volvieron	volverán	volverían	**vuelvan**	volvieran	**vuelvan** Uds.

Verbs with spelling changes only

		INDICATIVE					SUBJUNCTIVE		IMPERATIVE
	Infinitive	**Present**	**Imperfect**	**Preterite**	**Future**	**Conditional**	**Present**	**Past**	
35	conocer	**conozco**	conocía	conocí	conoceré	conocería	**conozca**	conociera	
	(c:zc)	conoces	conocías	conociste	conocerás	conocerías	**conozcas**	conocieras	conoce tú (no **conozcas**)
		conoce	conocía	conoció	conocerá	conocería	**conozca**	conociera	**conozca** Ud.
	Participles:	conocemos	conocíamos	conocimos	conoceremos	conoceríamos	**conozcamos**	conociéramos	**conozcamos**
	conociendo	conocéis	conocíais	conocisteis	conoceréis	conoceríais	**conozcáis**	conocierais	conoced (no **conozcáis**)
	conocido	conocen	conocían	conocieron	conocerán	conocerían	**conozcan**	conocieran	**conozcan** Uds.
36	creer (y)	creo	creía	**creí**	creeré	creería	crea	**creyera**	
		crees	creías	**creíste**	creerás	creerías	creas	**creyeras**	cree tú (no creas)
	Participles:	cree	creía	**creyó**	creerá	creería	crea	**creyera**	crea Ud.
	creyendo	creemos	creíamos	**creímos**	creeremos	creeríamos	creamos	**creyéramos**	creamos
	creído	creéis	creíais	**creísteis**	creeréis	creeríais	creáis	**creyerais**	creed (no creáis)
		creen	creían	**creyeron**	creerán	creerían	crean	**creyeran**	crean Uds.
37	cruzar (c)	cruzo	cruzaba	**crucé**	cruzaré	cruzaría	**cruce**	cruzara	
		cruzas	cruzabas	cruzaste	cruzarás	cruzarías	**cruces**	cruzaras	cruza tú (no **cruces**)
	Participles:	cruza	cruzaba	cruzó	cruzará	cruzaría	**cruce**	cruzara	**cruce** Ud.
	cruzando	cruzamos	cruzábamos	cruzamos	cruzaremos	cruzaríamos	**crucemos**	cruzáramos	**crucemos**
	cruzado	cruzáis	cruzabais	cruzasteis	cruzaréis	cruzaríais	**crucéis**	cruzarais	cruzad (no **crucéis**)
		cruzan	cruzaban	cruzaron	cruzarán	cruzarían	**crucen**	cruzaran	**crucen** Uds.
38	destruir (y)	**destruyo**	destruía	destruí	destruiré	destruiría	**destruya**	**destruyera**	
		destruyes	destruías	destruiste	destruirás	destruirías	**destruyas**	**destruyeras**	**destruye** tú (no **destruyas**)
	Participles:	**destruye**	destruía	**destruyó**	destruirá	destruiría	**destruya**	**destruyera**	**destruya** Ud.
	destruyendo	destruimos	destruíamos	destruimos	destruiremos	destruiríamos	**destruyamos**	**destruyéramos**	**destruyamos**
	destruido	destruís	destruíais	destruisteis	destruiréis	destruiríais	**destruyáis**	**destruyerais**	destruid (no **destruyáis**)
		destruyen	destruían	**destruyeron**	destruirán	destruirían	**destruyan**	**destruyeran**	**destruyan** Uds.
39	enviar	**envío**	enviaba	envié	enviaré	enviaría	**envíe**	enviara	
	(envío)	**envías**	enviabas	enviaste	enviarás	enviarías	**envíes**	enviaras	**envía** tú (no **envíes**)
		envía	enviaba	envió	enviará	enviaría	**envíe**	enviara	**envíe** Ud.
	Participles:	enviamos	enviábamos	enviamos	enviaremos	enviaríamos	**enviemos**	enviáramos	enviemos
	enviando	enviáis	enviabais	enviasteis	enviaréis	enviaríais	**enviéis**	enviarais	enviad (no **enviéis**)
	enviado	**envían**	enviaban	enviaron	enviarán	enviarían	**envíen**	enviaran	**envíen** Uds.

	Infinitive	INDICATIVE					SUBJUNCTIVE		IMPERATIVE
		Present	Imperfect	Preterite	Future	Conditional	Present	Past	
40	graduarse	**gradúo**	graduaba	gradué	graduaré	graduaría	**gradúe**	graduara	
	(gradúo)	**gradúas**	graduabas	graduaste	graduarás	graduarías	**gradúes**	graduaras	**gradúa** tú (no **gradúes**)
	Participles:	**gradúa**	graduaba	graduó	graduará	graduaría	**gradúe**	graduara	**gradúe** Ud.
	graduando	graduamos	graduábamos	graduamos	graduaremos	graduaríamos	graduemos	graduáramos	graduemos
	graduado	graduáis	graduabais	graduasteis	graduaréis	graduaríais	graduéis	graduarais	graduad (no graduéis)
		gradúan	graduaban	graduaron	graduarán	graduarían	**gradúen**	graduaran	**gradúen** Uds.
41	llegar (gu)	llego	llegaba	**llegué**	llegaré	llegaría	**llegue**	llegara	
		llegas	llegabas	llegaste	llegarás	llegarías	**llegues**	llegaras	llega tú (no **llegues**)
	Participles:	llega	llegaba	llegó	llegará	llegaría	**llegue**	llegara	**llegue** Ud.
	llegando	llegamos	llegábamos	llegamos	llegaremos	llegaríamos	**lleguemos**	llegáramos	**lleguemos**
	llegado	llegáis	llegabais	llegasteis	llegaréis	llegaríais	**lleguéis**	llegarais	llegad (no **lleguéis**)
		llegan	llegaban	llegaron	llegarán	llegarían	**lleguen**	llegaran	**lleguen** Uds.
42	proteger (j)	**protejo**	protegía	protegí	protegeré	protegería	**proteja**	protegiera	
		proteges	protegías	protegiste	protegerás	protegerías	**protejas**	protegieras	protege tú (no **protejas**)
	Participles:	protege	protegía	protegió	protegerá	protegería	**proteja**	protegiera	**proteja** Ud.
	protegiendo	protegemos	protegíamos	protegimos	protegeremos	protegeríamos	**protejamos**	protegiéramos	**protejamos**
	protegido	protegéis	protegíais	protegisteis	protegeréis	protegeríais	**protejáis**	protegierais	proteged (no **protejáis**)
		protegen	protegían	protegieron	protegerán	protegerían	**protejan**	protegieran	**protejan** Uds.
43	tocar (qu)	toco	tocaba	**toqué**	tocaré	tocaría	**toque**	tocara	
		tocas	tocabas	tocaste	tocarás	tocarías	**toques**	tocaras	toca tú (no **toques**)
	Participles:	toca	tocaba	tocó	tocará	tocaría	**toque**	tocara	**toque** Ud.
	tocando	tocamos	tocábamos	tocamos	tocaremos	tocaríamos	**toquemos**	tocáramos	**toquemos**
	tocado	tocáis	tocabais	tocasteis	tocaréis	tocaríais	**toquéis**	tocarais	tocad (no **toquéis**)
		tocan	tocaban	tocaron	tocarán	tocarían	**toquen**	tocaran	**toquen** Uds.

Guide to Vocabulary

Note on alphabetization

Formerly, **ch**, **ll**, and **ñ** were considered separate letters in the Spanish alphabet, **ch** appearing after **c**, **ll** after **l**, and **ñ** after **n**. In current practice, for purposes of alphabetization, **ch** and **ll** are not treated as separate letters, but **ñ** still follows **n**. Therefore, in this glossary you will find that **año**, for example, appears after **anuncio**.

Abbreviations used in this glossary

adj.	adjective	*form.*	formal	*pl.*	plural
adv.	adverb	*indef.*	indefinite	*poss.*	possessive
art.	article	*interj.*	interjection	*prep.*	preposition
conj.	conjunction	*i.o.*	indirect object	*pron.*	pronoun
def.	definite	*m.*	masculine	*ref.*	reflexive
d.o.	direct object	*n.*	noun	*sing.*	singular
f.	feminine	*obj.*	object	*sub.*	subject
fam.	familiar	*p.p.*	past participle	*v.*	verb

Spanish-English

A

a *prep.* at; to 1
¿A qué hora...? At what time...? 1
a bordo aboard 1
a dieta on a diet 15
a la derecha to the right 2
a la izquierda to the left 2
a la plancha grilled 8
a la(s) + *time* at + *time* 1
a menos que unless 13
a menudo *adv.* often 10
a nombre de in the name of 5
a plazos in installments 14
A sus órdenes. At your service. 11
a tiempo *adv.* on time 10
a veces *adv.* sometimes 10
a ver let's see 2
¡Abajo! *adv.* Down! 15
abeja *f.* bee
abierto/a *adj.* open 5, 14
abogado/a *m., f.* lawyer 16
abrazar(se) *v.* to hug; to embrace (each other) 11
abrazo *m.* hug
abrigo *m.* coat 6
abril *m.* April 5
abrir *v.* to open 3
abuelo/a *m., f.* grandfather; grandmother 3
abuelos *pl.* grandparents 3
aburrido/a *adj.* bored; boring 5
aburrir *v.* to bore 7
aburrirse *v.* to get bored 17
acabar de (+ ***inf.*****)** *v.* to have just *done something* 6
acampar *v.* to camp 5
accidente *m.* accident 10
acción *f.* action 17
de acción action (genre) 17
aceite *m.* oil 8
ácido/a *adj.* acid 13
acompañar *v.* to go with; to accompany 14
aconsejar *v.* to advise 12
acontecimiento *m.* event 18
acordarse (de) (o:ue) *v.* to remember 7
acostarse (o:ue) *v.* to go to bed 7
activo/a *adj.* active 15
actor *m.* actor 16
actriz *f.* actor 16
actualidades *f., pl.* news; current events 18
acuático/a *adj.* aquatic 4
adelgazar *v.* to lose weight; to slim down 15
además (de) *adv.* furthermore; besides; 10
adicional *adj.* additional
adiós *m.* good-bye 1
adjetivo *m.* adjective
administración de empresas *f.* business administration 2
adolescencia *f.* adolescence 9
¿adónde? *adv.* (to) where? (destination) 2
aduana *f.* customs 5
aeróbico/a *adj.* aerobic 15
aeropuerto *m.* airport 5
afectado/a *adj.* affected 13
afeitarse *v.* to shave 7
aficionado/a *adj.* fan 4
afirmativo/a *adj.* affirmative
afueras *f., pl.* suburbs; outskirts 12
agencia de viajes *f.* travel agency 5
agente de viajes *m., f.* travel agent 5
agosto *m.* August 5
agradable *adj.* pleasant
agua *f.* water 8
agua mineral mineral water 8
ahora *adv.* now 2
ahora mismo right now 5
ahorrar *v.* to save (money) 14
ahorros *m.* savings 14
aire *m.* air 5
ajo *m.* garlic 8
al (*contraction of* **a + el)** 2
al aire libre open-air 6
al contado in cash 14
(al) este (to the) east 14
al fondo (de) at the end (of) 12
al lado de beside 2
(al) norte (to the) north 14
(al) oeste (to the) west 14
(al) sur (to the) south 14
alcoba *f.* bedroom 12
alcohol *m.* alcohol 15
alcohólico/a *adj.* alcoholic 15
alegrarse (de) *v.* to be happy 13
alegre *adj.* happy; joyful 5
alegría *f.* happiness 9
alemán, alemana *adj.* German 3
alérgico/a *adj.* allergic 10
alfombra *f.* carpet; rug 12
algo *pron.* something; anything 7
algodón *m.* cotton 6
alguien *pron.* someone; somebody; anyone 7
algún, alguno/a(s) *adj.* any; some 7
alimento *m.* food
alimentación *f.* diet
aliviar *v.* to reduce 15
aliviar el estrés/la tensión to reduce stress/tension 15
allí *adv.* there 5
allí mismo right there 14
almacén *m.* department store 6
almohada *f.* pillow 12
almorzar (o:ue) *v.* to have lunch 4
almuerzo *m.* lunch 8

aló *interj.* hello (*on the telephone*) 11
alquilar *v.* to rent 12
alquiler *m.* rent (payment) 12
alternador *m.* alternator 11
altillo *m.* attic 12
alto/a *adj.* tall 3
aluminio *m.* aluminum 13
ama de casa *m., f.* housekeeper; caretaker 12
amable *adj.* nice; friendly 5
amarillo/a *adj.* yellow 6
amigo/a *m., f.* friend 3
amistad *f.* friendship 9
amor *m.* love 9
anaranjado/a *adj.* orange 6
andar en patineta to skateboard 4
animal *m.* animal 13
aniversario (de bodas) *m.* (wedding) anniversary 9
anoche *adv.* last night 6
anteayer *adv.* the day before yesterday 6
antes *adv.* before 7
antes (de) que *conj.* before 13
antes de *prep.* before 7
antibiótico *m.* antibiotic 10
antipático/a *adj.* unpleasant 3
anunciar *v.* to announce; to advertise 18
anuncio *m.* advertisement 16
año *m.* year 5
el año pasado *last* year 6
apagar *v.* to turn off 11
aparato *m.* appliance
apartamento *m.* apartment 12
apellido *m.* last name 3
apenas *adv.* hardly; scarcely 10
aplaudir *v.* to applaud 17
apreciar *v.* to appreciate 17
aprender (a + *inf.*) *v.* to learn 3
apurarse *v.* to hurry; to rush 15
aquel, aquella *adj.* that; those (over there) 6
aquél, aquélla *pron.* that; those (over there) 6
aquello *neuter, pron.* that; that thing; that fact 6
aquellos/as *pl. adj.* that; those (over there) 6
aquéllos/as *pl. pron.* those (ones) (over there) 6
aquí *adv.* here 1
Aquí está... Here it is... 5
Aquí estamos en... Here we are at/in... 2
aquí mismo right here 11
árbol *m.* tree 13
archivo *m.* file 11
armario *m.* closet 12
arqueólogo/a *m., f.* archaeologist 16
arquitecto/a *m., f.* architect 16
arrancar *v.* to start (*a car*) 11
arreglar *v.* to fix; to arrange 11; to neaten; to straighten up 12
arriba *adv.* up
arroba *f.* @ symbol 11
arroz *m.* rice 8
arte *m.* art 2
artes *f., pl.* arts 17
artesanía *f.* craftsmanship; crafts 17
artículo *m.* article 18
artista *m., f.* artist 3
artístico/a *adj.* artistic 17
arveja *m.* pea 8
asado/a *adj.* roast 8
ascenso *m.* promotion 16
ascensor *m.* elevator 5
así *adv.* like this; so (*in such a way*) 10
así así so so
asistir (a) *v.* to attend 3
aspiradora *f.* vacuum cleaner 12
aspirante *m. f.* candidate; applicant 16
aspirina *f.* aspirin 10
atún *m.* tuna 8
aumentar *v.* **de peso** to gain weight 15
aumento *m.* increase 16
aumento de sueldo pay raise 16
aunque although
autobús *m.* bus 1
automático/a *adj.* automatic
auto(móvil) *m.* auto(mobile) 5
autopista *f.* highway 11
ave *f.* bird 13
avenida *f.* avenue
aventura *f.* adventure 17
de aventura adventure (genre) 17
avergonzado/a *adj.* embarrassed 5
avión *m.* airplane 5
¡Ay! *interj.* Oh!
¡Ay, qué dolor! Oh, what pain!
ayer *adv.* yesterday 6
ayudar(se) *v.* to help (each other) 11, 12
azúcar *m.* sugar 8
azul *adj. m., f.* blue 6

B

bailar *v.* to dance 2
bailarín/bailarina *m., f.* dancer 17
baile *m.* dance 17
bajar(se) de *v.* to get off of/out of (a vehicle) 11
bajo/a *adj.* short (*in height*) 3
bajo control under control 7
balcón *m.* balcony 12
baloncesto *m.* basketball 4
banana *f.* banana 8
banco *m.* bank 14
banda *f.* band 17
bandera *f.* flag
bañarse *v.* to bathe; to take a bath 7
baño *m.* bathroom 7
barato/a *adj.* cheap 6
barco *m.* boat 5
barrer *v.* to sweep 12
barrer el suelo *v.* to sweep the floor 12
barrio *m.* neighborhood 12
bastante *adv.* enough; rather 10; pretty 13
basura *f.* trash 12
baúl *m.* trunk 11
beber *v.* to drink 3
bebida *f.* drink 8
bebida alcohólica *f.* alcoholic beverage 15
béisbol *m.* baseball 4
bellas artes *f., pl.* fine arts 17
belleza *f.* beauty 14
beneficio *m.* benefit 16
besar(se) *v.* to kiss (each other) 11
beso *m.* kiss 9
biblioteca *f.* library 2
bicicleta *f.* bicycle 4
bien *adj.* well 1
bienestar *m.* well-being 15
bienvenido(s)/a(s) *adj.* welcome 12
billete *m.* paper money; ticket
billón *m.* trillion
biología *f.* biology 2
bisabuelo/a *m.* great-grandfather/great-grandmother 3
bistec *m.* steak 8
bizcocho *m.* biscuit
blanco/a *adj.* white 6
bluejeans *m., pl.* jeans 6
blusa *f.* blouse 6
boca *f.* mouth 10
boda *f.* wedding 9
boleto *m.* ticket 17
bolsa *f.* purse, bag 6
bombero/a *m., f.* firefighter 16
bonito/a *adj.* pretty 3
borrador *m.* eraser 2
borrar *v.* to erase 11
bosque *m.* forest 13
bosque tropical tropical forest; rainforest 13
bota *f.* boot 6
botella *f.* bottle 9
botella de vino bottle of wine 9
botones *m., f. sing.* bellhop 5
brazo *m.* arm 10
brindar *v.* to toast (*drink*) 9
bucear *v.* to scuba dive 4
bueno *adv.* well 2, 17
buen, bueno/a *adj.* good 3, 6
¡Buen viaje! Have a good trip! 1
buena forma good shape

(*physical*) 15
Buena idea. Good idea. 4
Buenas noches. Good evening; Good night. 1
Buenas tardes. Good afternoon. 1
buenísimo extremely good
¿Bueno? Hello. (*on telephone*) 11
Buenos días. Good morning. 1
bulevar *m.* boulevard
buscar *v.* to look for 2
buzón *m.* mailbox 14

C

caballo *m.* horse 5
cabaña *f.* cabin 5
cabe: no cabe duda de there's no doubt 13
cabeza *f.* head 10
cada *adj. m., f.* each 6
caerse *v.* to fall (down) 10
café *m.* café 4; *adj. m., f.* brown 6; *m.* coffee 8
cafeína *f.* caffeine 14
cafetera *f.* coffee maker 12
cafetería *f.* cafeteria 2
caído/a *p.p.* fallen 14
caja *f.* cash register 6
cajero/a *m., f.* cashier 14
cajero automático *m.* ATM 14
calcetín *m.* sock 6
calculadora *f.* calculator 11
caldo *m.* soup 8
caldo de patas *m.* beef soup 8
calentarse *v.* to warm up 15
calidad *f.* quality 6
calle *f.* street 11
calor *m.* heat 4
caloría *f.* calorie 15
calzar *v.* to take size... shoes 6
cama *f.* bed 5
cámara digital *f.* digital camera 11
cámara de video *f.* videocamera 11
camarero/a *m., f.* waiter 8
camarón *m.* shrimp 8
cambiar (de/en) *v.* to change 9
cambio *m.* **de moneda** currency exchange
caminar *v.* to walk 2
camino *m.* road
camión *m* truck; bus
camisa *f.* shirt 6
camiseta *f.* t-shirt 6
campo *m.* countryside 5
canadiense *adj.* Canadian 3
canal *m.* channel (TV) 17
canción *f.* song 17
candidato/a *m., f.* candidate 18
cansado/a *adj.* tired 5
cantante *m., f.* singer 17
cantar *v.* to sing 2
capital *f.* capital city 1
capó *m.* hood 11
cara *f.* face 7
caramelo *m.* caramel 9
carne *f.* meat 8
carne de res *f.* beef 8
carnicería *f.* butcher shop 14
caro/a *adj.* expensive 6
carpintero/a *m., f.* carpenter 16
carrera *f.* career 16
carretera *f.* highway 11
carro *m.* car; automobile 11
carta *f.* letter 4; (playing) card 5
cartel *m.* poster 12
cartera *f.* wallet 6
cartero *m.* mail carrier 14
casa *f.* house; home 2
casado/a *adj.* married 9
casarse (con) *v.* to get married (to) 9
casi *adv.* almost 10
catorce *adj.* fourteen 1
cazar *v.* to hunt 13
cebolla *f.* onion 8
cederrón *m.* CD-ROM 11
celebrar *v.* to celebrate 9
celular *adj.* cellular 11
cena *f.* dinner 8
cenar *v.* to have dinner 2
centro *m.* downtown 4
centro comercial shopping mall 6
cepillarse los dientes/el pelo *v.* to brush one's teeth/one's hair 7
cerámica *f.* pottery 17
cerca de *prep.* near 2
cerdo *m.* pork 8
cereales *m., pl.* cereal; grains 8
cero *m.* zero 1
cerrado/a *adj.* closed 5, 14
cerrar (e:ie) *v.* to close 4
cerveza *f.* beer 8
césped *m.* grass 13
ceviche *m.* marinated fish dish 8
ceviche de camarón *m.* lemon-marinated shrimp 8
chaleco *m.* vest
champán *m.* champagne 9
champiñón *m.* mushroom 8
champú *m.* shampoo 7
chaqueta *f.* jacket 6
chau *fam. interj.* bye 1
cheque *m.* (bank) check 14
cheque (de viajero) *m.* (traveler's) check 14
chévere *adj., fam.* terrific
chico/a *adj.* boy/girl 1
chino/a *adj.* Chinese 3
chocar (con) *v.* to run into
chocolate *m.* chocolate 9
choque *m.* collision 18
chuleta *f.* chop (*food*) 8
chuleta de cerdo *f.* pork chop 8
cibercafé *m.* cybercafé
ciclismo *m.* cycling 4
cielo *m.* sky 13
cien(to) one hundred 2, 6
ciencia *f.* science 2
de ciencia ficción *f.* science fiction (genre) 17
científico/a *m., f.* scientist 16
cierto *m.* certain 13
Es cierto. It's certain. 13
No es cierto. It's not certain. 13
cinco five 1
cincuenta fifty 2
cine *m.* movie theater 4
cinta *f.* (audio)tape
cinta caminadora *f.* treadmill 15
cinturón *m.* belt 6
circulación *f.* traffic 11
cita *f.* date; appointment 9
ciudad *f.* city 4
ciudadano/a *adj.* citizen 18
Claro (que sí). *fam.* Of course. 16
clase *f.* class 2
clase de ejercicios aeróbicos *f.* aerobics class 15
clásico/a *adj.* classical 17
cliente/a *m., f.* customer 6
clínica *f.* clinic 10
cobrar *v.* to cash (a check) 14
coche *m.* car; automobile 11
cocina *f.* kitchen; stove 12
cocinar *v.* to cook 12
cocinero/a *m., f.* cook, chef 16
cofre *m.* hood 14
cola *f.* line 14
colesterol *m.* cholesterol 15
color *m.* color 6
comedia *f.* comedy; play 17
comedor *m.* dining room 12
comenzar (e:ie) *v.* to begin 4
comer *v.* to eat 3
comercial *adj.* commercial; business-related 16
comida *f.* food; meal 8
como like; as 8
¿cómo? what?; how? 1
¿Cómo es...? What's... like? 3
¿Cómo está usted? *form.* How are you? 1
¿Cómo estás? *fam.* How are you? 1
¿Cómo les fue...? *pl.* How did ... go for you? 15
¿Cómo se llama (usted)? *(form.)* What's your name? 1
¿Cómo te llamas (tú)? *(fam.)* What's your name? 1
cómoda *f.* chest of drawers 12
cómodo/a *adj.* comfortable 5
compañero/a de clase *m., f.* classmate 2
compañero/a de cuarto *m., f.* roommate 2
compañía *f.* company; firm 16
compartir *v.* to share 3

completamente *adv.* completely 16
compositor(a) *m., f.* composer 17
comprar *v.* to buy 2
compras *f., pl.* purchases 5
 ir de compras go shopping 5
comprender *v.* to understand 3
comprobar *v.* to check
comprometerse (con) *v.* to get engaged (to) 9
computación *f.* computer science 2
computadora *f.* computer 1
computadora portátil *f.* portable computer; laptop 11
comunicación *f.* communication 18
comunicarse (con) *v.* to communicate (with) 18
comunidad *f.* community 1
con *prep.* with 2
 Con él/ella habla. This is he/she. (*on telephone*) 11
 con frecuencia *adv.* frequently 10
 Con permiso. Pardon me; Excuse me. 1
 con tal (de) que provided (that) 13
concierto *m.* concert 17
concordar *v.* to agree
concurso *m.* game show; contest 17
conducir *v.* to drive 8, 11
conductor(a) *m., f.* driver 1
confirmar *v.* to confirm 5
confirmar *v.* **una reservación** *f.* to confirm a reservation 5
confundido/a *adj.* confused 5
congelador *m.* freezer 12
congestionado/a *adj.* congested; stuffed-up 10
conmigo *pron.* with me 4, 9
conocer *v.* to know; to be acquainted with 8
conocido *adj.; p.p.* known
conseguir (e:i) *v.* to get; to obtain 4
consejero/a *m., f.* counselor; advisor 16
consejo *m.* advice
conservación *f.* conservation 13
conservar *v.* to conserve 13
construir *v.* to build
consultorio *m.* doctor's office 10
consumir *v.* to consume 15
contabilidad *f.* accounting 2
contador(a) *m., f.* accountant 16
contaminación *f.* pollution 13
 contaminación del aire/del agua air/water pollution 13
contaminado/a *adj.* polluted 13
contaminar *v.* to pollute 13
contar *v.* to count; to tell 4
contar (con) *v.* to count (on) 12
contento/a *adj.* happy; content 5
contestadora *f.* answering machine 11
contestar *v.* to answer 2
contigo *fam. pron.* with you 9
contratar *v.* to hire 16
control *m.* control 7
 control remoto remote control 11
controlar *v.* to control 13
conversación *f.* conversation 2
conversar *v.* to converse, to chat 2
copa *f.* wineglass; goblet 12
corazón *m.* heart 10
corbata *f.* tie 6
corredor(a) *m., f.* **de bolsa** stockbroker 16
correo *m.* mail; post office 14
 correo electrónico *m.* e-mail 4
correr *v.* to run 3
cortesía *f.* courtesy
cortinas *f., pl.* curtains 12
corto/a *adj.* short (*in length*) 6
cosa *f.* thing 1
costar (o:ue) *f.* to cost 6
cráter *m.* crater 13
creer *v.* to believe 13
 creer (en) *v.* to believe (in) 3
 no creer (en) *v.* not to believe (in) 13
creído/a *adj., p.p.* believed 14
crema de afeitar *f.* shaving cream 7
crimen *m.* crime; murder 18
cruzar *v.* to cross 14
cuaderno *m.* notebook 1
cuadra *f.* (city) block 14
¿cuál(es)? which?; which ones? 2
 ¿Cuál es la fecha (de hoy)? What is the date (today)? 5
cuadro *m.* picture 12
cuadros *m., pl.* plaid 6
cuando when 7; 13
¿cuándo? when? 2
¿cuánto(s)/a(s)? how much/how many? 1
 ¿Cuánto cuesta...? How much does... cost? 6
 ¿Cuántos años tienes? How old are you? 3
cuarenta forty 2
cuarto de baño *m.* bathroom 7
cuarto *m.* room 7; 12
cuarto/a *adj.* fourth 5
 menos cuarto quarter to (time)
 y cuarto quarter after (time) 1
cuatro four 1
cuatrocientos/as *m., f.* four hundred 6
cubiertos *m., pl.* silverware
cubierto/a *p.p.* covered
cubrir *v.* to cover
cuchara *f.* (table or large) spoon 12
cuchillo *m.* knife 12
cuello *m.* neck 10
cuenta *f.* bill 9; account 14
 cuenta corriente *f.* checking account 14
 cuenta de ahorros *f.* savings account 14
cuento *m.* story 17
cuerpo *m.* body 10
cuidado *m.* care 3
cuidar *v.* to take care of 13
 ¡Cuídense! Take care! 14
cultura *f.* culture 17
cumpleaños *m., sing.* birthday 9
cumplir años *v.* to have a birthday 9
cuñado/a *m., f.* brother-in-law; sister-in-law 3
currículum *m.* résumé 16
curso *m.* course 2

D

danza *f.* dance 17
dañar *v.* to damage; to breakdown 10
dar *v.* to give 6, 9
 dar direcciones *v.* to give directions 14
 dar un consejo *v.* to give advice
 darse con *v.* to bump into; to run into (something) 10
 darse prisa *v.* to hurry; to rush 15
de *prep.* of; from 1
 ¿De dónde eres? *fam.* Where are you from? 1
 ¿De dónde es usted? *form.* Where are you from? 1
 ¿De parte de quién? Who is calling? (*on telephone*) 11
 ¿de quién...? whose...? (*sing.*) 1
 ¿de quiénes...? whose...? (*pl.*) 1
 de algodón (made of) cotton 6
 de aluminio (made of) aluminum 13
 de buen humor in a good mood 5
 de compras shopping 5
 de cuadros plaid 6
 de excursión hiking 4
 de hecho in fact
 de ida y vuelta roundtrip 5
 de la mañana in the morning; A.M. 1
 de la noche in the evening; at night; P.M. 1
 de la tarde in the afternoon; in the early evening; P.M. 1
 de lana (made of) wool 6
 de lunares polka-dotted 6
 de mal humor in a bad mood 5
 de mi vida of my life 15
 de moda in fashion 6
 De nada. You're welcome. 1
 De ninguna manera. No way. 16
 de niño/a as a child 10
 de parte de on behalf of 11
 de plástico (made of) plastic 13
 de rayas striped 6
 de repente suddenly 6

de seda (made of) silk 6
de vaqueros western (genre) 17
de vez en cuando from time to time 10
de vidrio (made of) glass 13
debajo de *prep.* below; under 2
deber (+ *infin.***)** *v.* should; must 3; **Debe ser...** It must be... 6
deber *m.* responsibility; obligation 18
debido a due to (the fact that)
débil *adj.* weak 15
decidido/a *adj.* decided 14
decidir (+ *infin.***)** *v.* (to decide) 3
décimo/a *adj.* tenth 5
decir *v.* **(que)** to say (that); to tell (that) 4, 9
decir la respuesta to say the answer 4
decir la verdad to tell the truth 4
decir mentiras to tell lies 4
decir que to say that 4
declarar *v.* to declare; to say 18
dedo *m.* finger 10
deforestación *f.* deforestation 13
dejar *v.* to let 12; to quit; to leave behind 16
dejar de *(+ inf.) v.* to stop *(doing something)* 13
dejar una propina *v.* to leave a tip 9
del (*contraction of* **de + el)** of the; from the
delante de *prep.* in front of 2
delgado/a *adj.* thin; slender 3
delicioso/a *adj.* delicious 8
demás *adj.* the rest
demasiado *adj., adv.* too much 6
dentista *m., f.* dentist 10
dentro de (diez años) within (ten years) 16; inside
dependiente/a *m., f.* clerk 6
deporte *m.* sport 4
deportista *m.* sports person
deportivo/a *adj.* sports-related 4
depositar *v.* to deposit 14
derecha *f.* right 2
derecho *adj.* straight (ahead) 14
a la derecha de to the right of 2
derechos *m.* rights 18
desarrollar *v.* to develop 13
desastre (natural) *m.* (natural) disaster 18
desayunar *v.* to have breakfast 2
desayuno *m.* breakfast 8
descafeinado/a *adj.* decaffeinated 15
descansar *v.* to rest 2
descargar *v.* to download 11
descompuesto/a *adj.* not working; out-of-order 11
describir *v.* to describe 3
descrito/a *p.p.* described 14
descubierto/a *p.p.* discovered 14
descubrir *v.* to discover 13
desde from 6
desear *v.* to wish; to desire 2
desempleo *m.* unemployment 18
desierto *m.* desert 13
(des)igualdad *f.* (in)equality 18
desordenado/a *adj.* disorderly 5
despacio *adv.* slowly 10
despedida *f.* farewell; good-bye
despedir (e:i) *v.* to fire 16
despedirse (de) (e:i) *v.* to say good-bye (to) 7
despejado/a *adj.* clear (*weather*)
despertador *m.* alarm clock 7
despertarse (e:ie) *v.* to wake up 7
después *adv.* afterwards; then 7
después de after 7
después de que *conj.* after 13
destruir *v.* to destroy 13
detrás de *prep.* behind 2
día *m.* day 1
día de fiesta holiday 9
diario *m.* diary 1; newspaper 18
diario/a *adj.* daily 7
dibujar *v.* to draw 2
dibujo *m.* drawing 17
dibujos animados *m., pl.* cartoons 17
diccionario *m.* dictionary 1
dicho/a *p.p.* said 14
diciembre *m.* December 5
dictadura *f.* dictatorship 18
diecinueve nineteen 1
dieciocho eighteen 1
dieciséis sixteen 1
diecisiete seventeen 1
diente *m.* tooth 7
dieta *f.* diet 15
comer una dieta equilibrada to eat a balanced diet 15
diez ten 1
difícil *adj.* difficult; hard 3
Diga. Hello. (*on telephone*) 11
diligencia *f.* errand 14
dinero *m.* money 6
dirección *f.* address 14
dirección electrónica *f.* e-mail address 11
direcciones *f., pl.* directions 14
director(a) *m., f.* director; (*musical*) conductor 17
dirigir *v.* to direct 17
disco compacto compact disc (CD) 11
discriminación *f.* discrimination 18
discurso *m.* speech 18
diseñador(a) *m., f.* designer 16
diseño *m.* design
disfrutar (de) *v.* to enjoy; to reap the benefits (of) 15
diversión *f.* fun activity; entertainment; recreation 4
divertido/a *adj.* fun 7
divertirse (e:ie) *v.* to have fun 9
divorciado/a *adj.* divorced 9
divorciarse (de) *v.* to get divorced (from) 9
divorcio *m.* divorce 9
doblar *v.* to turn 14
doble *adj.* double
doce twelve 1
doctor(a) *m., f.* doctor 3
documental *m.* documentary 17
documentos de viaje *m., pl.* travel documents
doler (o:ue) *v.* to hurt 10
dolor *m.* ache; pain 10
dolor de cabeza *m.* headache 10
doméstico/a *adj.* domestic 12
domingo *m.* Sunday 2
don/doña *title of respect used with a person's first name* 1
donde *prep.* where
¿Dónde está...? Where is...? 2
¿dónde? where? 1
dormir (o:ue) *v.* to sleep 4
dormirse (o:ue) *v.* to go to sleep; to fall asleep 7
dormitorio *m.* bedroom 12
dos two 1
dos veces *f.* twice; two times 6
doscientos/as two hundred 6
drama *m.* drama; play 17
dramático/a *adj.* dramatic 17
dramaturgo/a *m., f.* playwright 17
droga *f.* drug 15
drogadicto/a *adj.* drug addict 15
ducha *f.* shower 7
ducharse *v.* to shower; to take a shower 7
duda *f.* doubt 13
dudar *v.* to doubt 13
no dudar *v.* not to doubt 13
dueño/a *m., f.* owner; landlord 8
dulces *m., pl.* sweets; candy 9
durante *prep.* during 7
durar *v.* to last 18

E

e *conj. (used instead of* **y** *before words beginning with* **i** *and* **hi***)* and 4
echar *v.* to throw 14
echar (una carta) al buzón *v.* to throw (a letter) in the mailbox 14
ecología *f.* ecology 13
economía *f.* economics 2
ecoturismo *m.* ecotourism 13
Ecuador *m.* Ecuador 1
ecuatoriano/a *adj.* Ecuadorian 3
edad *f.* age 9
edificio *m.* building 12
(en) efectivo *m.* cash 6
ejercicio *m.* exercise 15
ejercicios aeróbicos *m.*

aerobic exercises 15
ejercicios de estiramiento stretching exercises 15
ejército *m.* army 18
el *m., sing., def. art.* the 1
él *sub. pron.* he 1; *adj. pron.* him
elecciones *f. pl.* election 18
electricista *m., f.* electrician 16
electrodoméstico *m.* electric appliance 12
elegante *adj. m., f.* elegant 6
elegir *v.* to elect 18
ella *sub. pron.* she 1; *obj. pron.* her
ellos/as *sub. pron.* they 1; them 1
embarazada *adj.* pregnant 10
emergencia *f.* emergency 10
emitir *v.* to broadcast 18
emocionante *adj. m., f.* exciting
empezar (e:ie) *v.* to begin 4
empleado/a *m., f.* employee 5
empleo *m.* job; employment 16
empresa *f.* company; firm 16
en *prep.* in; on 2
en casa at home 7
en caso (de) que in case (that) 13
en cuanto as soon as 13
en efectivo in cash 14
en exceso in excess; too much 15
en línea in-line 4
¡En marcha! Let's get going! 15
en mi nombre in my name
en punto on the dot; exactly; sharp (*time*) 1
en qué in what; how 2
¿En qué puedo servirles? How can I help you? 5
enamorado/a (de) *adj.* in love (with) 5
enamorarse (de) *v.* to fall in love (with) 9
encantado/a *adj.* delighted; pleased to meet you 1
encantar *v.* to like very much; to love (*inanimate things*) 7
¡Me encantó! I loved it! 15
encima de *prep.* on top of 2
encontrar (o:ue) *v.* to find 4
encontrar(se) (o:ue) *v.* to meet (each other); to run into (each other) 11
encuesta *f.* poll; survey 18
energía *f.* energy 13
energía nuclear nuclear energy 13
energía solar solar energy 13
enero *m.* January 5
enfermarse *v.* to get sick 10
enfermedad *f.* illness 10
enfermero/a *m., f.* nurse 10
enfermo/a *adj.* sick 10
enfrente de *adv.* opposite; facing 14
engordar *v.* to gain weight 15
enojado/a *adj.* mad; angry 5
enojarse (con) *v.* to get angry (with) 7
ensalada *f.* salad 8
enseguida *adv.* right away 9
enseñar *v.* to teach 2
ensuciar *v.* to get (something) dirty 12
entender (e:ie) *v.* to understand 4
entonces *adv.* then 7
entrada *f.* entrance 12; ticket 17
entre *prep.* between; among 2
entremeses *m., pl.* hors d'oeuvres 8
entrenador(a) *m., f.* trainer 15
entrenarse *v.* to practice; to train 15
entrevista *f.* interview 16
entrevistador(a) *m., f.* interviewer 16
entrevistar *v.* to interview 16
envase *m.* container 13
enviar *v.* to send; to mail 14
equilibrado/a *adj.* balanced 15
equipado/a *adj.* equipped 15
equipaje *m.* luggage 5
equipo *m.* team 4
equivocado/a *adj.* wrong 5
eres *fam.* you are 1
es he/she/it is 1
Es bueno que... It's good that... 12
Es de... He/She is from... 1
Es extraño It's strange 13
Es importante que... It's important that... 12
Es imposible It's impossible 13
Es improbable It's improbable 13
Es malo que... It's bad that... 12
Es mejor que... It's better that... 12
Es necesario que... It's necessary that... 12
Es obvio. It's obvious. 13
Es ridículo. It's ridiculous. 13
Es seguro. It's sure. 13
Es terrible. It's terrible. 13
Es triste. It's sad. 13
Es urgente que... It's urgent that... 12
Es la una. It's one o'clock. 1
Es una lástima. It's a shame. 13
Es verdad. It's true. 13
esa(s) *f., adj.* that; those 6
ésa(s) *f., pron.* those (ones) 6
escalar *v.* to climb 4
escalar montañas *v.* to climb mountains 4
escalera *f.* stairs; stairway 12
escoger *v.* to choose 8
escribir *v.* to write 3
escribir un mensaje electrónico to write an e-mail message 4
escribir una (tarjeta) postal to write a postcard 4
escribir una carta to write a letter 4
escrito/a *p.p.* written 14
escritor(a) *m., f* writer 17
escritorio *m.* desk 2
escuchar *v.* to listen to
escuchar la radio to listen (to) the radio 2
escuchar música to listen (to) music 2
escuela *f.* school 1
esculpir *v.* to sculpt 17
escultor(a) *m., f.* sculptor 17
escultura *f.* sculpture 17
ese *m., sing., adj.* that 6
ése *m., sing., pron.* that (one) 6
eso *neuter, pron.* that; that thing 6
esos *m., pl., adj.* those 6
ésos *m., pl., pron.* those (ones) 6
España *f.* Spain 1
español *m.* Spanish (*language*) 2
español(a) *adj. m., f.* Spanish 3
espárragos *m., pl.* asparagus 8
especialización *f.* major 2
espectacular *adj.* spectacular 15
espectáculo *m.* show 17
espejo *m.* mirror 7
esperar *v.* to hope; to wish 13
esperar (+ *infin.*) *v.* to wait (for); to hope 2
esposo/a *m., f.* husband/wife; spouse 3
esquí (acuático) *m.* (water) skiing 4
esquiar *v.* to ski 4
esquina *m.* corner 14
está he/she/it is, you are
Está (muy) despejado. It's (very) clear. (*weather*)
Está (muy) nublado. It's (very) cloudy. (*weather*)
Está bien. That's fine. 11
esta(s) *f., adj.* this; these 6
esta noche tonight 4
ésta(s) *f., pron.* this (one); these (ones) 6
Ésta es... *f.* This is... (*introducing someone*) 1
establecer *v.* to start, to establish 16
estación *f.* station; season 5
estación de autobuses bus station 5
estación del metro subway station 5
estación de tren train station 5
estacionamiento *m.* parking lot 14
estacionar *v.* to park 11
estadio *m.* stadium 2

estado civil *m.* marital status 9
Estados Unidos *m.* (EE.UU.; E.U.) United States 1
estadounidense *adj. m., f.* from the United States 3
estampado/a *adj.* print
estampilla *f.* stamp 14
estante *m.* bookcase; bookshelves 12
estar *v.* to be 2
  estar a (veinte kilómetros) de aquí. to be (20 kilometers) from here 11
  estar a dieta to be on a diet 15
  estar aburrido/a to be bored 5
  estar afectado/a (por) to be affected (by) 13
  estar bajo control to be under control 7
  estar cansado/a to be tired 5
  estar contaminado/a to be polluted 13
  estar de acuerdo to agree 16
    Estoy (completamente) de acuerdo. I agree (completely) 16
    No estoy de acuerdo. I don't agree. 16
  estar de moda to be in fashion 6
  estar de vacaciones *f., pl.* to be on vacation 5
  estar en buena forma to be in good shape 15
  estar enfermo/a to be sick 10
  estar listo/a to be ready 15
  estar perdido/a to be lost 14
  estar roto/a to be broken 10
  estar seguro/a to be sure 5
  estar torcido/a to be twisted; to be sprained 10
  No está nada mal. It's not at all bad. 5
estatua *f.* statue 17
este *m.* east 14; umm 17
este *m., sing., adj.* this 6
éste *m., sing., pron.* this (one) 6
  Éste es... *m.* This is... (introducing someone) 1
estéreo *m.* stereo 11
estilo *m.* style
estiramiento *m.* stretching 15
esto *neuter pron.* this; this thing 6
estómago *m.* stomach 10
estornudar *v.* to sneeze 10
estos *m., pl., adj.* these 6
éstos *m., pl., pron.* these (ones) 6
estrella *f.* star 13
  estrella de cine *m., f.* movie star 17
estrés *m.* stress 15
estudiante *m., f.* student 1, 2
estudiantil *adj. m., f.* student 2
estudiar *v.* to study 2
estufa *f.* stove 12
estupendo/a *adj.* stupendous 5
etapa *f.* stage 9
evitar *v.* to avoid 13
examen *m.* test; exam 2
  examen médico physical exam 10
excelente *adj. m., f.* excellent 5
exceso *m.* excess; too much 15
excursión *f.* hike; tour; excursion
excursionista *m., f.* hiker 4
éxito *m.* success 16
experiencia *f.* experience 18
explicar *v.* to explain 2
explorar *v.* to explore
expresión *f.* expression
extinción *f.* extinction 13
extranjero/a *adj.* foreign 17
extraño/a *adj.* strange 13

F

fabuloso/a *adj* fabulous 5
fácil *adj.* easy 3
falda *f.* skirt 6
faltar *v.* to lack; to need 7
familia *f.* family 3
famoso/a *adj.* famous 16
farmacia *f.* pharmacy 10
fascinar *v.* to fascinate 7
favorito/a *adj.* favorite 4
fax *m.* fax (machine) 11
febrero *m.* February 5
fecha *f.* date 5
feliz *adj.* happy 5
  ¡Felicidades! Congratulations! (*for an event such as a birthday or anniversary*) 9
  ¡Felicitaciones! Congratulations! (*for an event such as an engagement or a good grade on a test*) 9
  ¡Feliz cumpleaños! Happy birthday! 9
fenomenal *adj.* great, phenomenal 5
feo/a *adj.* ugly 3
festival *m.* festival 17
fiebre *f.* fever 10
fiesta *f.* party 9
fijo/a *adj.* fixed, set 6
fin *m.* end 4
  fin de semana weekend 4
finalmente *adv.* finally 15
firmar *v.* to sign (*a document*) 14
física *f.* physics 2
flan (de caramelo) *m.* baked (caramel) custard 9
flexible *adj.* flexible 15
flor *f.* flower 13
folklórico/a *adj.* folk; folkloric 17
folleto *m.* brochure
fondo *m.* end 12
forma *f.* shape 15
formulario *m.* form 14
foto(grafía) *f.* photograph 1
francés, francesa *adj. m., f.* French 3
frecuentemente *adv.* frequently 10
frenos *m., pl.* brakes
fresco/a *adj.* cool 5
frijoles *m., pl.* beans 8
frío/a *adj.* cold 5
frito/a *adj.* fried 8
fruta *f.* fruit 8
frutería *f.* fruit store 14
frutilla *f.* strawberry 8
fuente de fritada *f.* platter of fried food
fuera *adv.* outside
fuerte *adj. m., f.* strong 15
fumar *v.* to smoke 15
  (no) fumar *v.* (not) to smoke 15
funcionar *v.* to work; to function 11
fútbol *m.* soccer 4
  fútbol americano *m.* football 4
futuro/a *adj.* future 16
  en el futuro in the future 16

G

gafas (de sol) *f., pl.* (sun)glasses 6
gafas (oscuras) *f., pl.* (sun)glasses 6
galleta *f.* cookie 9
ganar *v.* to win 4; to earn (money) 16
ganga *f.* bargain 6
garaje *m.* garage; (mechanic's) repair shop; 11 garage (*in a house*) 12
garganta *f.* throat 10
gasolina *f.* gasoline 11
gasolinera *f.* gas station 11
gastar *v.* to spend (*money*) 6
gato *m.* cat 13
gemelo/a *m., f.* twin 3
gente *f.* people 3
geografía *f.* geography 2
gerente *m., f.* manager 16
gimnasio *m.* gymnasium 4
gobierno *m.* government 13
golf *m.* golf 4
gordo/a *adj.* fat 3
grabadora *f.* tape recorder 1
grabar *v.* to record 11
gracias *f., pl.* thank you; thanks 1
  Gracias por todo. Thanks for everything. 9, 15
  Gracias una vez más. Thanks again. 9
graduarse (de/en) *v.* to graduate (from/in) 9
gran, grande *adj.* big 3
grasa *f.* fat 15
gratis *adj. m., f.* free of charge 14

grave *adj.* grave; serious 10
gravísimo/a *adj.* extremely serious 13
grillo *m.* cricket
gripe *f.* flu 10
gris *adj. m., f.* gray 6
gritar *v.* to scream 7
guantes *m., pl.* gloves 6
guapo/a *adj.* handsome; good-looking 3
guardar *v.* to save (on a computer) 11
guerra *f.* war 18
guía *m., f.* guide
gustar *v.* to be pleasing to; to like 7
  Me gustaría... I would like...
gusto *m.* pleasure 17
  El gusto es mío. The pleasure is mine. 1
  Gusto de verlo/la. *(form.)* It's nice to see you. 18
  Gusto de verte. *(fam.)* It's nice to see you. 18
  Mucho gusto. Pleased to meet you. 1
  ¡Qué gusto volver a verlo/la! *(form.)* I'm happy to see you again! 18
  ¡Qué gusto volver a verte! *(fam.)* I'm happy to see you again! 18

H

haber *(aux.) v.* to have (*done something*) 15
  Ha sido un placer. It's been a pleasure. 15
habitación *f.* room 5
  habitación doble double room 5
  habitación individual single room 5
hablar *v.* to talk; to speak 2
hacer *v.* to do; to make; 4
  Hace buen tiempo. The weather is good. 5
  Hace (mucho) calor. It's (very) hot. (*weather*) 5
  Hace fresco. It's cool. (*weather*) 5
  Hace (mucho) frío. It's very cold. (*weather*) 5
  Hace mal tiempo. The weather is bad. 5
  Hace (mucho) sol. It's (very) sunny. (*weather*) 5
  Hace (mucho) viento. It's (very) windy. (*weather*) 5
  hacer cola to stand in line 14
  hacer diligencias to run errands 14
  hacer ejercicio to exercise 15
  hacer ejercicios aeróbicos to do aerobics 15
  hacer ejercicios de estiramiento to do stretching exercises 15
  hacer el papel (de) to play the role (of) 17
  hacer gimnasia to work out 15
  hacer juego (con) to match (with) 6
  hacer la cama to make the bed 12
  hacer las maletas to pack (one's) suitcases 5
  hacer quehaceres domésticos to do household chores 12
  hacer turismo to go sightseeing 5
  hacer un viaje to take a trip 5
  hacer una excursión to go on a hike; to go on a tour 5
hacia *prep.* toward 14
hambre *f.* hunger 3
hamburguesa *f.* hamburger 8
hasta *prep.* until 6; toward
  Hasta la vista. See you later. 1
  Hasta luego. See you later. 1
  Hasta mañana. See you tomorrow. 1
  hasta que until 13
  Hasta pronto. See you soon. 1
hay there is; there are 1
  Hay (mucha) contaminación. It's (very) smoggy.
  Hay (mucha) niebla. It's (very) foggy. 5
  Hay que It is necessary that 14
  No hay duda de There's no doubt 13
  No hay de qué. You're welcome. 1
hecho/a *p.p.* done 14
heladería *f.* ice cream shop 14
helado/a *adj.* iced 8
helado *m.* ice cream 9
hermanastro/a *m., f.* stepbrother/stepsister 3
hermano/a *m., f.* brother/sister 3
hermano/a mayor/menor *m., f.* older/younger brother/sister 3
hermanos *m., pl.* siblings (brothers and sisters) 3
hermoso/a *adj.* beautiful 6
hierba *f.* grass 13
hijastro/a *m., f.* stepson/stepdaughter 3
hijo/a *m., f.* son/daughter 3
  hijo/a único/a *m., f.* only child 3
  hijos *m., pl.* children 3
historia *f.* history 2; story 17
hockey *m.* hockey 4
hola *interj.* hello; hi 1
hombre *m.* man 1
  hombre de negocios *m.* businessman 16
hora *f.* hour 1; the time
horario *m.* schedule 2
horno *m.* oven 12
  horno de microondas *m.* microwave oven 12
horror *m.* horror 17
  de horror horror (genre) 17
hospital *m.* hospital 10
hotel *m.* hotel 5
hoy *adv.* today 2
  hoy día *adv.* nowadays
  Hoy es... Today is... 2
huelga *f.* strike (labor) 18
hueso *m.* bone 10
huésped *m., f.* guest 5
huevo *m.* egg 8
humanidades *f., pl.* humanities 2
huracán *m.* hurricane 18

I

ida *f.* one way (*travel*)
idea *f.* idea 4
iglesia *f.* church 4
igualdad *f.* equality 18
igualmente *adv.* likewise 1
impermeable *m.* raincoat 6
importante *adj. m., f.* important 3
importar *v.* to be important to; to matter 7
imposible *adj. m., f.* impossible 13
impresora *f.* printer 11
imprimir *v.* to print 11
improbable *adj. m., f.* improbable 13
impuesto *m.* tax 18
incendio *m.* fire 18
increíble *adj. m., f.* incredible 5
individual *adj.* private (*room*) 5
infección *f.* infection 10
informar *v.* to inform 18
informe *m.* report; paper (*written work*) 18
ingeniero/a *m., f.* engineer 3
inglés *m.* English (*language*) 2
inglés, inglesa *adj.* English 3
inodoro *m.* toilet 6
insistir (en) *v.* to insist (on) 12
inspector(a) de aduanas *m., f.* customs inspector 5
inteligente *adj. m., f.* intelligent 3
intercambiar *v.* to exchange
interesante *adj. m., f.* interesting 3
interesar *v.* to be interesting to; to interest 7
(inter)nacional *adj. m., f.* (inter)national 18
Internet *m.* Internet 11
inundación *f.* flood 18
invertir (i:ie) *v.* to invest 16
invierno *m.* winter 5
invitado/a *m., f.* guest (*at a func-*

tion) 9
invitar *v.* to invite 9
inyección *f.* injection 10
ir *v.* to go 4
  ir a (+ *inf.*) to be going to do something 4
  ir de compras to go shopping 5
  ir de excursión (a las montañas) to go for a hike (in the mountains) 4
  ir de pesca to go fishing 5
  ir de vacaciones to go on vacation 5
  ir en autobús to go by bus 5
  ir en auto(móvil) to go by auto(mobile); to go by car 5
  ir en avión to go by plane 5
  ir en barco to go by boat 5
  ir en metro to go by subway 5
  ir en motocicleta to go by motorcycle 5
  ir en taxi to go by taxi 5
  ir en tren to go by train 5
irse *v.* to go away; to leave 7
italiano/a *adj.* Italian 3
izquierdo/a *adj.* left 2
  a la izquierda de to the left of 2

J

jabón *m.* soap 7
jamás *adv.* never; not ever 7
jamón *m.* ham 8
japonés, japonesa *adj.* Japanese 3
jardín *m.* garden; yard 12
jefe, jefa *m., f.* boss 16
joven *adj. m., f.* young 3
  joven *m., f.* youth; young person 1
joyería *f.* jewelry store 14
jubilarse *v.* to retire (*from work*) 9
juego *m.* game
jueves *m., sing.* Thursday 2
jugador(a) *m., f.* player 4
jugar (u:ue) *v.* to play 4
  jugar a las cartas *f. pl.* to play cards 5
jugo *m.* juice 8
  jugo de fruta *m.* fruit juice 8
julio *m.* July 5
jungla *f.* jungle 13
junio *m.* June 5
juntos/as *adj.* together 9
juventud *f.* youth 9

K

kilómetro *m.* kilometer 11

L

la *f., sing., def. art.* the 1
  la *f., sing., d.o. pron.* her, it, *form.* you 5
laboratorio *m.* laboratory 2
lago *m.* lake 13
lámpara *f.* lamp 12
lana *f.* wool 6
langosta *f.* lobster 8
lápiz *m.* pencil 1
largo/a *adj.* long (*in length*) 6
las *f., pl., def. art.* the 1
  las *f., pl., d.o.pron.* them; *form.* you 5
lástima *f.* shame 13
lastimarse *v.* to injure oneself 10
  lastimarse el pie to injure one's foot 10
lata *f.* (*tin*) can 13
lavabo *m.* sink 7
lavadora *f.* washing machine 12
lavandería *f.* laundromat 14
lavaplatos *m., sing.* dishwasher 12
lavar *v.* to wash 12
lavarse *v.* to wash oneself 7
  lavarse la cara to wash one's face 7
  lavarse las manos to wash one's hands 7
le *sing., i.o. pron.* to/for him, her, *form.* you 6
  Le presento a… *form.* I would like to introduce… to you. 1
lección *f.* lesson 1
leche *f.* milk 8
lechuga *f.* lettuce 8
leer *v.* to read 3
  leer correo electrónico to read e-mail 4
  leer un periódico to read a newspaper 4
  leer una revista to read a magazine 4
leído/a *p.p.* read 14
lejos de *prep.* far from 2
lengua *f.* language 2
  lenguas extranjeras *f., pl.* foreign languages 2
lentes de contacto *m., pl.* contact lenses 6
  lentes (de sol) (sun)glasses 6
lento/a *adj.* slow 11
les *pl., i.o. pron.* to/for them, *form.* you 6
letrero *m.* sign 14
levantar *v.* to lift 15
  levantar pesas to lift weights 15
levantarse *v.* to get up 7
ley *f.* law 13
libertad *f.* liberty; freedom 18
libre *adj. m., f.* free 4
librería *f.* bookstore 2
libro *m.* book 2
licencia de conducir *f.* driver's license 11
limón *m.* lemon 8
limpiar *v.* to clean 12
limpiar la casa *v.* to clean the house 12
limpio/a *adj.* clean 5
línea *f.* line 4
listo/a *adj.* ready; smart 5
literatura *f.* literature 2
llamar *v.* to call 11
  llamar por teléfono to call on the phone
  llamarse *v.* to be called; to be named 7
llanta *f.* tire 11
llave *f.* key 5
llegada *f.* arrival 5
llegar *v.* to arrive 2
llenar *v.* to fill 11, 14
  llenar el tanque to fill the tank 11
  llenar (un formulario) to fill out (a form) 14
lleno/a *adj.* full 11
llevar *v.* to carry 2; *v.* to wear; to take 6
  llevar una vida sana to lead a healthy lifestyle 15
  llevarse bien/mal (con) to get along well/badly (with) 9
llover (o:ue) *v.* to rain 5
  Llueve. It's raining. 5
lluvia *f.* rain 13
  lluvia ácida acid rain 13
lo *m., sing. d.o. pronoun.* him, it, *form.* you 5
  ¡Lo hemos pasado de película! We've had a great time! 18
  ¡Lo hemos pasado maravillosamente! We've had a great time! 18
  lo mejor the best (thing) 18
  Lo pasamos muy bien. We had a good time. 18
  lo peor the worst (thing) 18
  lo que that which; what 12
  Lo siento. I'm sorry. 1
  Lo siento muchísimo. I'm so sorry. 4
loco/a *adj.* crazy 6
locutor(a) *m., f.* (TV or radio) announcer 18
lomo a la plancha *m.* grilled flank steak 8
los *m., pl., def. art.* the 1
  los *m.pl., d.o. pron.* them, *form.* you 5
luchar (contra/por) *v.* to fight; to struggle (against/for) 18
luego *adv.* then 7; *adv.* later 1
lugar *m.* place 4
luna *f.* moon 13
lunares *m.* polka dots 6

lunes *m., sing.* Monday 2
luz *f.* light; electricity 12

M

madrastra *f.* stepmother 3
madre *f.* mother 3
madurez *f.* maturity; middle age 9
maestro/a *m., f.* teacher 16
magnífico/a *adj.* magnificent 5
maíz *m.* corn 8
mal, malo/a *adj.* bad 3
maleta *f.* suitcase 1
mamá *f.* mom 1
mandar *v.* to order 12; to send; to mail 14
manejar *v.* to drive 11
manera *f.* way 16
mano *f.* hand 1
  ¡Manos arriba! Hands up!
manta *f.* blanket 12
mantener *v.* to maintain 15
  mantenerse en forma to stay in shape 15
mantequilla *f.* butter 8
manzana *f.* apple 8
mañana *f.* morning, a.m. 1; tomorrow 1
mapa *m.* map 2
maquillaje *m.* make-up 7
maquillarse *v.* to put on makeup 7
mar *m.* sea 5
maravilloso/a *adj.* marvelous 5
mareado/a *adj.* dizzy; nauseated 10
margarina *f.* margarine 8
mariscos *m., pl.* shellfish 8
marrón *adj. m., f.* brown 6
martes *m., sing.* Tuesday 2
marzo *m.* March 5
más *pron.* more 2
  más de (+ *number*) more than 8
  más tarde later 7
  más... que more... than 8
masaje *m.* massage 15
matemáticas *f., pl.* mathematics 2
materia *f.* course 2
matrimonio *m.* marriage 9
máximo/a *adj.* maximum 11
mayo *m.* May 5
mayonesa *f.* mayonnaise 8
mayor *adj.* older 3
  el/la mayor *adj.* eldest 8; oldest
me *pron.* me 6
  Me duele mucho. It hurts me a lot. 10
  Me gusta... I like... 2
  No me gustan nada. I don't like them at all. 2
  Me gustaría(n)... I would like... 17
  Me llamo... My name is... 1
  Me muero por... I'm dying to (for)...
mecánico/a *m., f.* mechanic 11
mediano/a *adj.* medium
medianoche *f.* midnight 1
medias *f., pl.* pantyhose, stockings 6
medicamento *m.* medication 10
medicina *f.* medicine 10
médico/a *m., f.* doctor 3; *adj.* medical 10
medio/a *adj.* half 3
  medio ambiente *m.* environment 13
  medio/a hermano/a *m., f.* half-brother/half-sister 3
  mediodía *m.* noon 1
  medios de comunicación *m., pl.* means of communication; media 18
  y media thirty minutes past the hour (time) 1
mejor *adj.* better 8
  el/la mejor *m., f.* the best 8
mejorar *v.* to improve 13
melocotón *m.* peach 8
menor *adj.* younger 3
  el/la menor *m., f.* youngest 8
menos *adv.* less 10
  menos cuarto... menos quince... quarter to... (*time*) 1
  menos de (+ *number*) fewer than 8
  menos... que less... than 8
mensaje electrónico *m.* e-mail message 4
mentira *f.* to lie 4
menú *m.* menu 8
mercado *m.* market 6
  mercado al aire libre open-air market 6
merendar *v.* to snack 8; to have an afternoon snack
merienda *f.* afternoon snack 15
mes *m.* month 5
mesa *f.* table 2
mesita *f.* end table 12
  mesita de noche night stand 12
metro *m.* subway 5
mexicano/a *adj.* Mexican 3
México *m.* Mexico 1
mí *pron. obj. of prep.* me 8
mi(s) *poss. adj.* my 3
microonda *f.* microwave 12
  horno de microondas *m.* microwave oven 12
miedo *m.* fear 3
mientras *adv.* while 10
miércoles *m., sing.* Wednesday 2
mil *m.* one thousand 6
  mil millones billion
  Mil perdones. I'm so sorry. (*lit.* A thousand pardons.) 4
milla *f.* mile 11
millón *m.* million 6
millones (de) *m.* millions (of)
mineral *m.* mineral 15
minuto *m.* minute 1
mío(s)/a(s) *poss.* my; (of) mine 11
mirar *v.* to look (at); to watch 2
  mirar (la) televisión to watch television
mismo/a *adj.* same 3
mochila *f.* backpack 2
moda *f.* fashion 6
módem *m.* modem
moderno/a *adj.* modern 17
molestar *v.* to bother; to annoy 7
monitor *m.* (computer) monitor 11
  monitor(a) *m., f.* trainer
montaña *f.* mountain 4
montar a caballo *v.* to ride a horse 5
monumento *m.* monument 4
mora *f.* blackberry 8
morado/a *adj.* purple 6
moreno/a *adj.* brunet(te) 3
morir (o:ue) *v.* to die 8
mostrar (o:ue) *v.* to show 4
motocicleta *f.* motorcycle 5
motor *m.* motor
muchacho/a *m., f.* boy; girl 3
mucho/a *adj., adv.* a lot of; much 2; many 3
  muchas veces *adv.* a lot; many times 10
  Muchísimas gracias. Thank you very, very much. 9
  Mucho gusto. Pleased to meet you. 1
  (Muchas) gracias. Thank you (very much); Thanks (a lot). 1
muchísimo very much 2
mudarse *v.* to move (from one house to another) 12
muebles *m., pl.* furniture 12
muela *f.* tooth 10
muerte *f.* death 9
muerto/a *p.p.* died 14
mujer *f.* woman 1
  mujer de negocios *f.* business woman 16
  mujer policía *f.* female police officer
multa *f.* fine
mundial *adj. m., f.* worldwide
mundo *m.* world 13
municipal *adj. m., f.* municipal
músculo *m.* muscle 15
museo *m.* museum 4
música *f.* music 2, 17
musical *adj. m., f.* musical 17
músico/a *m., f.* musician 17
muy *adv.* very 1
  Muy amable. That's very kind of you. 5
  (Muy) bien, gracias. (Very) well, thanks. 1

N

nacer *v.* to be born 9
nacimiento *m.* birth 9
nacional *adj. m., f.* national 18
nacionalidad *f.* nationality 1
nada nothing 1; not anything 7
nada mal not bad at all 5
nadar *v.* to swim 4
nadie *pron.* no one, nobody, not anyone 7
naranja *f.* orange 8
nariz *f.* nose 10
natación *f.* swimming 4
natural *adj. m., f.* natural 13
naturaleza *f.* nature 13
navegar (en Internet) *v.* to surf (the Internet) 11
Navidad *f.* Christmas 9
necesario/a *adj.* necessary 12
necesitar (+ ***inf.*****)** *v.* to need 2
negar (e:ie) *v.* to deny 13
no negar (e:ie) *v.* not to deny 13
negativo/a *adj.* negative
negocios *m., pl.* business; commerce 16
negro/a *adj.* black 6
nervioso/a *adj.* nervous 5
nevar (e:ie) *v.* to snow 5
Nieva. It's snowing. 5
ni...ni neither... nor 7
niebla *f.* fog
nieto/a *m., f.* grandson/granddaughter 3
nieve *f.* snow
ningún, ninguno/a(s) *adj.* no; none; not; any 7
ningún problema no problem 7
niñez *f.* childhood 9
niño/a *m., f.* child 3
no no; not 1
No cabe duda de... There is no doubt... 13
No es así. That's not the way it is 16
No es para tanto. It's not a big deal. 12
No es seguro. It's not sure. 13
No es verdad. It's not true. 13
No está nada mal. It's not bad at all. 5
no estar de acuerdo to disagree
No estoy seguro. I'm not sure.
(no) hay there is (not); there are (not) 1
No hay de qué. You're welcome. 1
No hay duda de... There is no doubt... 13
¡No me diga(s)! You don't say! 11
No me gustan nada. I don't like them at all. 2
no muy bien not very well 1
¿no? right? 1
No quiero. I don't want to. 4
No sé. I don't know.
No se preocupe. (*form.*) Don't worry. 7
No te preocupes. (*fam.*) Don't worry. 7
no tener razón to be wrong 3
noche *f.* night 1
nombre *m.* name 1
norte *m.* north 14
norteamericano/a *adj.* (North) American 3
nos *pron.* us 6
Nos divertimos mucho. We had a lot of fun. 18
Nos vemos. See you. 1
nosotros/as *sub. pron.* we 1; *ob. pron.* us
noticias *f., pl.* news 18
noticiero *m.* newscast 18
novecientos/as *adj.* nine hundred 6
noveno/a *adj.* ninth 5
noventa ninety 2
noviembre *m.* November 5
novio/a *m., f.* boyfriend/girlfriend 3
nube *f.* cloud 13
nublado/a *adj.* cloudy 5
Está (muy) nublado. It's very cloudy. 5
nuclear *adj. m. f.* nuclear 13
nuera *f.* daughter-in-law 3
nuestro(s)/a(s) *poss. adj.* our 3; (of ours) 11
nueve nine 1
nuevo/a *adj.* new 6
número *m.* number 1
número (shoe) size 6
nunca *adj.* never; not ever 7
nutrición *f.* nutrition 15
nutricionista *m., f.* nutritionist 15

O

o or 7
o... o; either... or 7
obedecer (c:zc) *v.* to obey 18
obra *f.* work (*of art, literature, music, etc.*) 17
obra maestra *f.* masterpiece 17
obtener *v.* to obtain; to get 16
obvio/a *adj.* obvious 13
océano *m.* ocean 5
ochenta eighty 2
ocho *m.* eight 1
ochocientos/as *adj.* eight hundred 6
octavo/a *adj.* eighth 5
octubre *m.* October 5
ocupación *f.* occupation 16
ocupado/a *adj.* busy 5
ocurrir *v.* to occur; to happen 18
odiar *v.* to hate 9
oeste *m.* west 14
oferta *f.* offer 12
oficina *f.* office 12
oficio *m.* trade 16
ofrecer (c:zc) *v.* to offer 8
oído *m.* (sense of) hearing; inner ear 10
oído *p.p.* heard 14
oír *v.* to hear 4
Oigan. *form., pl.* Listen. (*in conversation*)
Oye. *fam., sing.* Listen. (*in conversation*) 1
ojalá (que) *interj.* I hope (that); I wish (that) 13
ojo *m.* eye 10
olvidar *v.* to forget 10
once eleven 1
ópera *f.* opera 17
operación *f.* operation 10
ordenado/a *adj.* orderly 5
ordinal *adj.* ordinal (*number*)
oreja *f.* (outer) ear 10
orquesta *f.* orchestra 17
ortografía *f.* spelling
ortográfico/a *adj.* spelling
os *fam., pl. pron.* you 6
otoño *m.* autumn 5
otro/a *adj.* other; another 6
otra vez again

P

paciente *m., f.* patient 10
padrastro *m.* stepfather 3
padre *m.* father 3
padres *m., pl.* parents 3
pagar *v.* to pay 6, 9
pagar a plazos to pay in installments 14
pagar al contado to pay in cash 14
pagar en efectivo to pay in cash 14
pagar la cuenta to pay the bill 9
página *f.* page 11
página principal *f.* home page 11
país *m.* country 1
paisaje *m.* landscape 5
pájaro *m.* bird 13
palabra *f.* word 1
pan *m.* bread 8
pan tostado *m.* toasted bread 8
panadería *f.* bakery 14
pantalla *f.* screen 11
pantalones *m., pl.* pants 6
pantalones cortos *m., pl.* shorts 6
pantuflas *f.* slippers 7
papa *f.* potato 8
papas fritas *f., pl.* fried

potatoes; French fries 8
papá *m.* dad 3
papás *m., pl.* parents 3
papel *m.* paper 2; *m.* role 17
papelera *f.* wastebasket
paquete *m.* package 14
par *m.* pair 6
para *prep.* for; in order to; by; used for; considering 11
para que so that 13
parabrisas *m., sing.* windshield 11
parar *v.* to stop 11
parecer *v.* to seem 8
pared *f.* wall 12
pareja *f.* (married) couple; partner 9
parientes *m., pl.* relatives 3
parque *m.* park 4
párrafo *m.* paragraph
parte: de parte de on behalf of 11
partido *m.* game; match (*sports*) 4
pasado/a *adj.* last; past 6
pasado *p.p.* passed
pasaje *m.* ticket 5
pasaje de ida y vuelta *m.* roundtrip ticket 5
pasajero/a *m., f.* passenger 1
pasaporte *m.* passport 5
pasar *v.* to go through 5
pasar la aspiradora to vacuum 12
pasar por el banco to go by the bank 14
pasar por la aduana to go through customs 5
pasar tiempo to spend time 4
pasarlo bien/mal to have a good/bad time 9
pasatiempo *m.* pastime; hobby 4
pasear *v.* to take a walk; to stroll 4
pasear en bicicleta to ride a bicycle 4
pasear por to walk around 4
pasillo *m.* hallway 12
pasta *f.* **de dientes** toothpaste 7
pastel *m.* cake; pie 9
pastel de chocolate *m.* chocolate cake 9
pastel de cumpleaños *m.* birthday cake 9
pastelería *f.* pastry shop 14
pastilla *f.* pill; tablet 10
patata *f.* potato; 8
patatas fritas *f., pl.* fried potatoes; French fries 8
patinar (en línea) *v.* to skate (in-line) 4
patineta *f.* skateboard 4
patio *m.* patio; yard 12
pavo *m.* turkey 8
paz *f.* peace 18
pedir (e:i) *v.* to ask for; to request 4; to order (*food*) 8
pedir prestado *v.* to borrow 14
pedir un préstamo *v.* to apply for a loan 14
peinarse *v.* to comb one's hair 7
película *f.* movie 4
peligro *m.* danger 13
peligroso/a *adj.* dangerous 18
pelirrojo/a *adj.* red-haired 3
pelo *m.* hair 7
pelota *f.* ball 4
peluquería *f.* beauty salon 14
peluquero/a *m., f.* hairdresser 16
penicilina *f.* penicillin 10
pensar (e:ie) *v.* to think 4
pensar (+ *inf.*) *v.* to intend to 4; to plan to (*do something*)
pensar en *v.* to think about
pensión *f.* boardinghouse
peor *adj.* worse 8
el/la peor *adj.* the worst 8
pequeño/a *adj.* small 3
pera *f.* pear 8
perder (e:ie) *v.* to lose; to miss 4
perdido/a *adj.* lost 14
Perdón. Pardon me.; Excuse me. 1
perezoso/a *adj.* lazy
perfecto/a *adj.* perfect 5
periódico *m.* newspaper 4
periodismo *m.* journalism 2
periodista *m., f.* journalist 3
permiso *m.* permission
pero *conj.* but 2
perro *m.* dog 13
persona *f.* person 3
personaje *m.* character 17
personaje (principal) *m.* (main) character 17
pesas *f. pl.* weights 15
pesca *f.* fishing 5
pescadería *f.* fish market 14
pescado *m.* fish (*cooked*) 8
pescador(a) *m., f.* fisherman/ fisherwoman
pescar *v.* to fish 5
peso *m.* weight 15
pez *m.* fish (*live*) 13
pie *m.* foot 10
piedra *f.* stone 13
pierna *f.* leg 10
pimienta *f.* black pepper 8
pintar *v.* to paint 17
pintor(a) *m., f.* painter 16
pintura *f.* painting; picture 12, 17
piña *f.* pineapple 8
piscina *f.* swimming pool 4
piso *m.* floor (*of a building*) 5
pizarra *f.* blackboard 2
placer *m.* pleasure 15
Ha sido un placer. It's been a pleasure. 15
planchar la ropa *v.* to iron the clothes 12
planes *m., pl.* plans 4
planta *f.* plant 13
planta baja *f.* ground floor 5
plástico *m.* plastic 13
plato *m.* dish (*in a meal*) 8; *m.* plate 12
plato principal *m.* main dish 8
playa *f.* beach 5
plaza *f.* city or town square
plazos *m., pl.* periods; time 14
pluma *f.* pen 2
población *f.* population 13
pobre *adj. m., f.* poor 6
pobreza *f.* poverty
poco/a *adj.* little; few 5
poder (o:ue) *v.* to be able to; can 4
poema *m.* poem 17
poesía *f.* poetry 17
poeta *m., f.* poet 17
policía *f.* police (force) 11
política *f.* politics 18
político/a *m., f.* politician 16; *adj.* political 18
pollo *m.* chicken 8
pollo asado *m.* roast chicken 8
ponchar *v.* to go flat
poner *v.* to put; to place 4; *v.* to turn on (*electrical appliances*) 11
poner la mesa *v.* to set the table 12
poner una inyección *v.* to give an injection 10
ponerse (+ *adj.*) *v.* to become (+ *adj.*) 7; to put on 7
por *prep.* in exchange for; for; by; in; through; around; along; during; because of; on account of; on behalf of; in search of; by way of; by means of 11
por aquí around here 11
por avión by plane
por ejemplo for example 11
por eso that's why; therefore 11
Por favor. Please. 1
por fin finally 11
por la mañana in the morning 7
por la noche at night 7
por la tarde in the afternoon 7
por lo menos *adv.* at least 10
¿por qué? why? 2
Por supuesto. Of course. 16
por teléfono by phone; on the phone
por último finally 7
porque *conj.* because 2
portátil *m.* portable 11
porvenir *m.* future 16
¡Por el porvenir! Here's to the future! 16
posesivo/a *adj.* possessive 3
posible *adj.* possible 13
Es posible. It's possible. 13
No es posible. It's not possible. 13
postal *f.* postcard 4

postre *m.* dessert 9
practicar *v.* to practice 2
practicar deportes *m., pl.* to play sports 4
precio (fijo) *m.* (fixed; set) price 6
preferir (e:ie) *v.* to prefer 4
pregunta *f.* question
preguntar *v.* to ask (*a question*) 2
premio *m.* prize; award 17
prender *v.* to turn on 11
prensa *f.* press 18
preocupado/a (por) *adj.* worried (about) 5
preocuparse (por) *v.* to worry (about) 7
preparar *v.* to prepare 2
preposición *f.* preposition
presentación *f.* introduction
presentar *v.* to introduce to put on (*a performance*) 17
Le presento a... I would like to introduce (name) to you... (*form.*) 1
Te presento a... I would like to introduce (name) to you... (*fam.*) 1
presiones *f., pl.* pressures 15
prestado/a *adj.* borrowed
préstamo *m.* loan 14
prestar *v.* to lend; to loan 6
primavera *f.* spring 5
primer, primero/a *adj.* first 5
primo/a *m., f.* cousin 3
principal *adj. m., f.* main 8
prisa *f.* haste 3
darse prisa *v.* to hurry; to rush 15
probable *adj. m., f.* probable 13
Es probable. It's probable. 13
No es probable. It's not probable. 13
probar (o:ue) *v.* to taste; to try 8
probarse (o:ue) *v.* to try on 7
problema *m.* problem 1
profesión *f.* profession 3; 16
profesor(a) *m., f.* teacher 1, 2
programa *m.* 1
programa de computación *m.* software 11
programa de entrevistas *m.* talk show 17
programador(a) *m., f.* programmer 3
prohibir *v.* to prohibit 10; to forbid
pronombre *m.* pronoun
pronto *adv.* soon 10
propina *f.* tip 9
propio/a *adj.* own 16
proteger *v.* to protect 13
proteína *f.* protein 15
próximo/a *adj.* next 16
prueba *f.* test; quiz 2
psicología *f.* psychology 2
psicólogo/a *m., f.* psychologist 16
publicar *v.* to publish 17
público *m.* audience 17
pueblo *m.* town 4
puerta *f.* door 2
Puerto Rico *m.* Puerto Rico 1
puertorriqueño/a *adj.* Puerto Rican 3
pues *conj.* well 2, 17
puesto *m.* position; job 16
puesto/a *p.p.* put 14
puro/a *adj.* pure 13

Q

que *pron.* that; which; who 12
¡Qué...! How...! 3
¡Qué dolor! What pain!
¡Qué ropa más bonita! What pretty clothes! 6
¡Qué sorpresa! What a surprise!
¿qué? what? 1
¿Qué día es hoy? What day is it? 2
¿Qué hay de nuevo? What's new? 1
¿Qué hora es? What time is it? 1
¿Qué les parece? What do you (*pl.*) think?
¿Qué pasa? What's happening? What's going on? 1
¿Qué pasó? What happened? 11
¿Qué precio tiene? What is the price?
¿Qué tal...? How are you?; How is it going? 1; How is/are . . . ? 2
¿Qué talla lleva/usa? What size do you wear? 6
¿Qué tiempo hace? How's the weather? 5
¿En qué...? In which...? 2
quedar *v.* to be left over; to fit (*clothing*) 7; to be left behind; to be located 14
quedarse *v.* to stay; to remain 7
quehaceres domésticos *m., pl.* household chores 12
quemado/a *adj.* burned (out) 11
quemar *v.* to burn (a CD) 11
querer (e:ie) *v.* to want; to love 4
queso *m.* cheese 8
quien(es) *pron.* who; whom; that 12
¿Quién es...? Who is...? 1
¿Quién habla? Who is speaking? (*telephone*) 11
¿quién(es)? who?; whom? 1
química *f.* chemistry 2
quince fifteen 1
menos quince quarter to (time) 1
y quince quarter after (time) 1
quinceañera *f.* young woman's fifteenth birthday celebration/ fifteen-year old girl 9
quinientos/as *adj.* five hundred 6
quinto/a *adj.* fifth 5
quisiera *v.* I would like 17
quitar la mesa *v.* to clear the table 12
quitarse *v.* to take off 7
quizás *adv.* maybe 5

R

racismo *m.* racism 18
radio *f.* radio (*medium*)
radio *m.* radio (set) 11
radiografía *f.* X-ray 10
rápido/a *adv.* quickly 10
ratón *m.* mouse 11
ratos libres *m., pl.* spare (free) time 4
raya *f.* stripe 6
razón *f.* reason 3
rebaja *f.* sale 6
recado *m.* (telephone) message 11
receta *f.* prescription 10
recetar *v.* to prescribe 10
recibir *v.* to receive 3
reciclaje *m.* recycling 13
reciclar *v.* to recycle 13
recién casado/a *m., f.* newlywed 9
recoger *v.* to pick up 13
recomendar (e:ie) *v.* to recommend 8, 12
recordar (o:ue) *v.* to remember 4
recorrer *v.* to tour an area
recurso *m.* resource 13
recurso natural *m.* natural resource 13
red *f.* network; Web 11
reducir *v.* to reduce 13
refresco *m.* soft drink 8
refrigerador *m.* refrigerator 12
regalar *v.* to give (a gift) 9
regalo *m.* gift 6
regatear *v.* to bargain 6
región *f.* region; area 13
regresar *v.* to return 2
regular *adj. m., f.* so so.; OK 1
reído *p.p.* laughed 14
reírse (e:i) *v.* to laugh 9
relaciones *f., pl.* relationships
relajarse *v.* to relax 9
reloj *m.* clock; watch 2
renunciar (a) *v.* to resign (from) 16
repetir (e:i) *v.* to repeat 4
reportaje *m.* report 18
reportero/a *m., f.* reporter; journalist 16
representante *m., f.* representa-

tive 18
reproductor de DVD *m.* DVD player 11
resfriado *m.* cold (*illness*) 10
residencia estudiantil *f.* dormitory 2
resolver (o:ue) *v.* to resolve; to solve 13
respirar *v.* to breathe 13
respuesta *f.* answer
restaurante *m.* restaurant 4
resuelto/a *p.p.* resolved 14
reunión *f.* meeting 16
revisar *v.* to check 11
  revisar el aceite *v.* to check the oil 11
revista *f.* magazine 4
rico/a *adj.* rich 6; *adj.* tasty; delicious 8
ridículo *adj.* ridiculous 13
río *m.* river 13
riquísimo/a *adj.* extremely delicious 8
rodilla *f.* knee 10
rogar (o:ue) *v.* to beg; to plead 12
rojo/a *adj.* red 6
romántico/a *adj.* romantic 17
romper (con) *v.* to break up (with) 9
romper(se) *v.* to break 10
  romperse la pierna *v.* to break one's leg 10
ropa *f.* clothing; clothes 6
  ropa interior *f.* underwear 6
rosado/a *adj.* pink 6
roto/a *adj.* broken 10, 14
rubio/a *adj.* blond(e) 3
ruso/a *adj.* Russian 3
rutina *f.* routine 7
  rutina diaria *f.* daily routine 7

S

sábado *m.* Saturday 2
saber *v.* to know; to know how 8
sabrosísimo/a *adj.* extremely delicious 8
sabroso/a *adj.* tasty; delicious 8
sacar *v.* to take out
  sacar fotos to take photos 5
  sacar la basura to take out the trash 12
  sacar(se) una muela to have a tooth removed 10
sacudir *v.* to dust 12
  sacudir los muebles to dust the furniture 12
sal *f.* salt 8
sala *f.* living room 12; room
  sala de emergencia(s) emergency room 10
salario *m.* salary 16
salchicha *f.* sausage 8
salida *f.* departure; exit 5
salir *v.* to leave 4; to go out
  salir (con) to go out (with); to date 9
  salir de to leave from
  salir para to leave for (*a place*)
salmón *m.* salmon 8
salón de belleza *m.* beauty salon 14
salud *f.* health 10
saludable *adj.* healthy 10
saludar(se) *v.* to greet (each other) 11
saludo *m.* greeting 1
  saludos a... greetings to... 1
sandalia *f.* sandal 6
sandía *f.* watermelon 8
sándwich *m.* sandwich 8
sano/a *adj.* healthy 10
se *ref.pron.* himself, herself, itself, *form.* yourself, themselves, yourselves 7
se *impersonal* one 10
  Se nos dañó... The... broke down. 11
  Se hizo... He/she/it became...
  Se nos pinchó una llanta. We had a flat tire. 11
secadora *f.* clothes dryer 12
secarse *v.* to dry (oneself) 7
sección de (no) fumar *f.* (non) smoking section 8
secretario/a *m., f.* secretary 16
secuencia *f.* sequence
sed *f.* thirst 3
seda *f.* silk 6
sedentario/a *adj.* sedentary; related to sitting 15
seguir (e:i) *v.* to follow; to continue 4
según according to
segundo/a *adj.* second 5
seguro/a *adj.* sure 5
seis six 1
seiscientos/as *adj.* six hundred 17
sello *m.* stamp 14
selva *f.* jungle 13
semana *f.* week 2
  fin *m.* **de semana** weekend 4
  semana *f.* **pasada** last week 6
semestre *m.* semester 2
sendero *m.* trail; trailhead 13
sentarse (e:ie) *v.* to sit down 7
sentir(se) (e:ie) *v.* to feel 7; to be sorry; to regret 13
señor (Sr.); don *m.* Mr.; sir 1
señora (Sra.) *f.* Mrs.; ma'am 1
señorita (Srta.) *f.* Miss 1
separado/a *adj.* separated 9
separarse (de) *v.* to separate (from) 9
septiembre *m.* September 5
séptimo/a *adj.* seventh 5
ser *v.* to be 1
  ser aficionado/a (a) to be a fan (of) 4
  ser alérgico/a (a) to be allergic (to) 10
  ser gratis to be free of charge 14
serio/a *adj.* serious
servilleta *f.* napkin 12
servir (e:i) *v.* to serve 8; to help 5
sesenta sixty 2
setecientos/as *adj.* seven hundred 6
setenta seventy 2
sexismo *m.* sexism 18
sexto/a *adj.* sixth 5
sí *adv.* yes 1
si *conj.* if 4
SIDA *m.* AIDS 18
sido *p.p.* been 15
siempre *adv.* always 7
siete seven 1
silla *f.* seat 2
sillón *m.* armchair 12
similar *adj. m., f.* similar
simpático/a *adj.* nice; likeable 3
sin *prep.* without 2, 13
  sin duda without a doubt
  sin embargo however
  sin que *conj.* without 13
sino but (rather) 7
síntoma *m.* symptom 10
sitio *m.* **web;** website 11
situado/a *p.p.* located
sobre *m.* envelope 14; *prep.* on; over 2
sobrino/a *m., f.* nephew; niece 3
sociología *f.* sociology 2
sofá *m.* couch; sofa 12
sol *m.* sun 4; 5; 13
solar *adj. m., f.* solar 13
soldado *m., f.* soldier 18
soleado/a *adj.* sunny
solicitar *v.* to apply (*for a job*) 16
solicitud (de trabajo) *f.* (job) application 16
sólo *adv.* only 3;
  solo *adj.* alone
soltero/a *adj.* single 9
solución *f.* solution 13
sombrero *m.* hat 6
Son las dos. It's two o'clock. 1
sonar (o:ue) *v.* to ring 11
sonreído *p.p.* smiled 14
sonreír (e:i) *v.* to smile 9
sopa *f.* soup 8
sorprender *v.* to surprise 9
sorpresa *f.* surprise 9
sótano *m.* basement; cellar 12
soy I am 1
  Soy yo. That's me. 1
  Soy de... I'm from... 1
su(s) *poss. adj.* his; her; its; *form.* your; their; 3
subir(se) a *v.* to get on/into

(*a vehicle*) 11
sucio/a *adj.* dirty 5
sucre *m.* Former Ecuadorian currency 6
sudar *v.* to sweat 15
suegro/a *m., f.* father-in-law; mother-in-law 3
sueldo *m.* salary 16
suelo *m.* floor 12
sueño *n.* sleep 3
suerte *f.* luck 3
suéter *m.* sweater 6
sufrir *v.* to suffer 10
sufrir muchas presiones to be under a lot of pressure 15
sufrir una enfermedad to suffer an illness 10
sugerir (e:ie) *v.* to suggest 12
supermercado *m.* supermarket 14
suponer *v.* to suppose 4
sur *m.* south 14
sustantivo *m.* noun
suyo(s)/a(s) *poss.* (of) his/her; (of) hers; (of) its; (of) *form.* your, (of) yours, (of) their 11

T

tal vez *adv.* maybe 5
talentoso/a *adj.* talented 17
talla *f.* size 6
talla grande *f.* large 6
taller *m.* **mecánico** garage; mechanic's repairshop 11
también *adv.* also; too 2; 7
tampoco *adv.* neither; not either 7
tan *adv.* so
tan pronto como as soon as 13
tan… como as… as 8
tanque *m.* tank 11
tanto *adv.* so much
tanto… como as much… as 8
tantos/as… como as many… as 8
tarde *adv.* late 7
tarde *f.* afternoon; evening; P.M. 1
tarea *f.* homework 2
tarjeta *f.* (post) card 4
tarjeta de crédito *f.* credit card 6
tarjeta postal *f.* postcard 4
taxi *m.* taxi 5
taza *f.* cup 12
te *fam. pron.* you 6
Te presento a... I would like to introduce you to... 1
¿Te gustaría? Would you like to? 17
¿Te gusta(n)... ? Do you like… ? 2
té *m.* tea 8
té helado *m.* iced tea 8
teatro *m.* theater 17
teclado *m.* keyboard 11
técnico/a *m., f.* technician 16
tejido *m.* weaving 17
teleadicto/a *m., f.* couch potato 15
teléfono (celular) *m.* (cell) telephone 11
telenovela *f.* soap opera 17
teletrabajo *m.* telecommuting 16
televisión *f.* television 11
televisión por cable *f.* cable television 11
televisor *m.* television set 11
temer *v.* to fear 13
temperatura *f.* temperature 10
temprano *adv.* early 7
tenedor *m.* fork 12
tener *v.* to have 3
tener... años to be... years old 3
Tengo... años. I'm... years old. 3
tener (mucho) calor to be (very) hot 3
tener (mucho) cuidado to be (very) careful 3
tener dolor to have a pain 10
tener éxito to be successful 16
tener fiebre to have a fever 10
tener (mucho) frío to be (very) cold 3
tener ganas de (+ *inf.*) to feel like (*doing something*) 3
tener (mucha) hambre *f.* to be (very) hungry 3
tener (mucho) miedo (de) to be (very) afraid (of); to be (very) scared (of) 3
tener miedo (de) que to be afraid that
tener planes *m., pl.* to have plans 4
tener (mucha) prisa to be in a (big) hurry 3
tener que (+ *inf.*) *v.* to have to (*do something*) 3
tener razón *f.* to be right 3
tener (mucha) sed *f.* to be (very) thirsty 3
tener (mucho) sueño to be (very) sleepy 3
tener (mucha) suerte to be (very) lucky 3
tener tiempo to have time 4
tener una cita to have a date; to have an appointment 9
tenis *m.* tennis 4
tensión *f.* tension 15
tercer, tercero/a *adj.* third 5
terminar *v.* to end; to finish 2
terminar de (+*inf.*) *v.* to finish (*doing something*) 4
terremoto *m.* earthquake 18
terrible *adj. m., f.* terrible 13
ti *prep., obj. of prep., fam.* you
tiempo *m.* time 4; weather 5
tiempo libre free time 4
tienda *f.* shop; store 6
tienda de campaña tent
tierra *f.* land; soil 13
tinto/a *adj.* red (wine) 8
tío/a *m., f.* uncle; aunt 3
tíos *m.* aunts and uncles 3
título *m.* title
tiza *f.* chalk 2
toalla *f.* towel 7
tobillo *m.* ankle 10
tocadiscos compacto *m.* compact-disc player 11
tocar *v.* to play (*a musical instrument*) 17; to touch 13
todavía *adv.* yet; still 5
todo *m.* everything 5
en todo el mundo throughout the world 13
Todo está bajo control. Everything is under control. 7
todo derecho straight (ahead) 14
¡Todos a bordo! All aboard! 1
todo/a *adj.* all 4; whole
todos *m., pl.* all of us; *m., pl.* everybody; everyone
todos los días *adv.* every day 10
tomar *v.* to take; to drink 2
tomar clases *f., pl.* to take classes 2
tomar el sol to sunbathe 4
tomar en cuenta take into account
tomar fotos *f., pl.* to take photos 5
tomar la temperatura to take someone's temperature 10
tomate *m.* tomato 8
tonto/a *adj.* silly; foolish 3
torcerse (o:ue) (el tobillo) *v.* to sprain (one's ankle) 10
torcido/a *adj.* twisted; sprained 10
tormenta *f.* storm 18
tornado *m.* tornado 18
tortilla *f.* kind of flat bread 8
tortillas de maíz flat bread made of corn flour 8
tos *f., sing.* cough 10
toser *v.* to cough 10
tostado/a *adj.* toasted 8
tostadora *f.* toaster 12
trabajador(a) *adj.* hard-working 3
trabajar *v.* to work 2
trabajo *m.* job; work 16
traducir *v.* to translate 8
traer *v.* to bring 4
tráfico *m.* traffic 11
tragedia *f.* tragedy 17
traído/a *p.p.* brought 14
traje *m.* suit 6
traje (de baño) *m.* (bathing) suit 6
tranquilo/a *adj.* calm; quiet 15
Tranquilo. Don't worry.; Be

cool. 7
transmitir to broadcast 18
tratar de (+ *inf.*) *v.* to try (*to do something*) 15
Trato hecho. You've got a deal. 17
trece thirteen 1
treinta thirty 1, 2
y treinta thirty minutes past the hour (time) 1
tren *m.* train 5
tres three 1
trescientos/as *adj.* three hundred 6
trimestre *m.* trimester; quarter 2
triste *adj.* sad 5
tú *fam. sub. pron.* you 1
Tú eres... You are... 1
tu(s) *fam. poss. adj.* your 3
turismo *m.* tourism 5
turista *m., f.* tourist 1
turístico/a *adj.* touristic
tuyo(s)/a(s) *fam. poss. pron.* your; (of) yours 11

U

Ud. *form. sing.* you 1
Uds. *form., pl.* you 1
último/a *adj.* last
un, uno/a *indef. art.* a; one 1
uno/a *m., f., sing. pron.* one
a la una at one o'clock 1
una vez más one more time 9
una vez once; one time 6
único/a *adj.* only 3
universidad *f.* university; college 2
unos/as *m., f., pl. indef. art.* some 1
unos/as *pron.* some 1
urgente *adj.* urgent 12
usar *v.* to wear; to use 6
usted (Ud.) *form. sing.* you 1
ustedes (Uds.) *form., pl.* you 1
útil *adj.* useful
uva *f.* grape 8

V

vaca *f.* cow 13
vacaciones *f. pl.* vacation 5
valle *m.* valley 13
vamos let's go 4
vaquero *m.* cowboy 17
de vaqueros *m., pl.* western (genre) 17
varios/as *adj. m. f., pl.* various 8
vaso *m.* glass 12
veces *f., pl.* times 6
vecino/a *m., f.* neighbor 12
veinte twenty 1
veinticinco twenty-five 1
veinticuatro twenty-four 1
veintidós twenty-two 1
veintinueve twenty-nine 1
veintiocho twenty-eight 1
veintiséis twenty-six 1
veintisiete twenty-seven 1
veintitrés twenty-three 1
veintiún, veintiuno/a *adj.* twenty-one 1
vejez *f.* old age 9
velocidad *f.* speed 11
velocidad máxima *f.* speed limit 11
vendedor(a) *m., f.* salesperson 6
vender *v.* to sell 6
venir *v.* to come 3
ventana *f.* window 2
ver *v.* to see 4
ver películas *f., pl.* to see movies 4
a ver *v.* let's see 2
verano *m.* summer 5
verbo *m.* verb
verdad *f.* truth
¿verdad? right? 1
verde *adj., m. f.* green 6
verduras *pl., f.* vegetables 8
vestido *m.* dress 6
vestirse (e:i) *v.* to get dressed 7
vez *f.* time 6
viajar *v.* to travel 2
viaje *m.* trip 5
viajero/a *m., f.* traveler 5
vida *f.* life 9
video(casete) *m.* video (cassette) 11
videocasetera *f.* VCR 11
videoconferencia *f.* videoconference 16
vidrio *m.* glass 13
viejo/a *adj.* old 3
viento *m.* wind 5
viernes *m., sing.* Friday 2
vinagre *m.* vinegar 8
vino *m.* wine 8
vino blanco *m.* white wine 8
vino tinto *m.* red wine 8
violencia *f.* violence 18
visitar *v.* to visit 4
visitar monumentos *m., pl.* to visit monuments 4
visto/a *p.p.* seen 14
vitamina *f.* vitamin 15
viudo/a *adj.* widower/widow 9
vivienda *f.* housing 12
vivir *v.* to live 3
vivo/a *adj.* bright; lively; living
volante *m.* steering wheel 11
volcán *m.* volcano 13
vóleibol *m.* volleyball 4
volver (o:ue) *v.* to return 4
volver a ver(te, lo, la) *v.* to see (you, him, her) again 18
vos *pron.* you
vosotros/as *form., pl.* you 1
votar *v.* to vote 18
vuelta *f.* return trip
vuelto/a *p.p.* returned 14
vuestro(s)/a(s) *poss. adj.* your 3; (of) yours *fam.* 11

W

walkman *m.* walkman 11

Y

y *conj.* and 1
y cuarto quarter after (time) 1
y media half-past (time) 1
y quince quarter after (time) 1
y treinta thirty (minutes past the hour) 1
¿Y tú? *fam.* And you? 1
¿Y usted? *form.* And you? 1
ya *adv.* already 6
yerno *m.* son-in-law 3
yo *sub. pron.* I 1
Yo soy... I'm... 1
yogur *m.* yogurt 8

Z

zanahoria *f.* carrot 8
zapatería *f.* shoe store 14
zapatos (de tenis) *m., pl.* (tennis) shoes, sneakers 6

English-Spanish

A

a **un/a** *m., f., sing.; indef. art.* 1
@ (*symbol*) **arroba** *f.* 11
A.M. **mañana** *f.* 1
able: be able to **poder (o:ue)** *v.* 4
aboard **a bordo** 1
accident **accidente** *m.* 10
accompany **acompañar** *v.* 14
account **cuenta** *f.*14
on account of **por** *prep.* 11
accountant **contador(a)** *m., f.* 16
accounting **contabilidad** *f.* 2
ache **dolor** *m.* 10
acid **ácido/a** *adj.* 13
acid rain **lluvia ácida** 13
acquainted: be acquainted with **conocer** *v.* 8
action (genre) **de acción** *f.* 17
active **activo/a** *adj.* 15
actor **actor** *m.*, **actriz** *f.* 16
addict (*drug*) **drogadicto/a** *adj.* 15
additional **adicional** *adj.*
address **dirección** *f.* 14
adjective **adjetivo** *m.*
adolescence **adolescencia** *f.* 9
adventure (genre) **de aventura** *f.* 17
advertise **anunciar** *v.* 18
advertisement **anuncio** *m.* 16
advice **consejo** *m.* 6
give advice **dar consejos** 6
advise **aconsejar** *v.* 12
advisor **consejero/a** *m., f.* 16
aerobic **aeróbico/a** *adj.* 15
to do aerobics **hacer ejercicios aeróbicos** 15
aerobics class **clase de ejercicios aeróbicos** 15
affected **afectado/a** *adj.* 13
be affected (by) **estar** *v.* **afectado/a (por)** 13
affirmative **afirmativo/a** *adj.*
afraid: be (very) afraid (of) **tener (mucho) miedo (de)** 3
be afraid that **tener miedo (de) que**
after **después de** *prep.* 7; **después de que** *conj.* 14
afternoon **tarde** *f.* 1
afterward **después** *adv.* 7
again **otra vez**
age **edad** *f.* 9
agree **concordar** *v.*
agree **estar** *v.* **de acuerdo** 16
I agree (completely). **Estoy (completamente) de acuerdo.** 16
I don't agree. **No estoy de acuerdo.** 16
agreement **acuerdo** *m.* 16
AIDS **SIDA** *m.* 18
air **aire** *m.* 13
air pollution **contaminación del aire** 13
airplane **avión** *m.* 5
airport **aeropuerto** *m.* 5
alarm clock **despertador** *m.* 7
alcohol **alcohol** *m.* 15
to consume alcohol **consumir alcohol** 15
alcoholic **alcohólico/a** *adj.* 15
all **todo/a** *adj.* 4
All aboard! **¡Todos a bordo!** 1
all of us **todos** 1
all over the world **en todo el mundo**
allergic **alérgico/a** *adj.* 10
be allergic (to) **ser alérgico/a (a)** 10
alleviate **aliviar** *v.*
almost **casi** *adv.* 10
alone **solo/a** *adj.*
along **por** *prep.* 11
already **ya** *adv.* 6
also **también** *adv.* 2; 7
alternator **alternador** *m.* 11
although *conj.* **aunque**
aluminum **aluminio** *m.* 13
(made of) aluminum **de aluminio** 13
always **siempre** *adv.* 7
American (*North*) **norteamericano/a** *adj.* 3
among **entre** *prep.* 2
amusement **diversión** *f.*
and **y** 1, **e** (*before words beginning with i or hi*) 4
And you?**¿Y tú?** *fam.* 1; **¿Y usted?** *form.* 1
angry **enojado/a** *adj.* 5
get angry (with) **enojarse** *v.* **(con)** 7
animal **animal** *m.* 13
ankle **tobillo** *m.* 10
anniversary **aniversario** *m.* 9
(wedding) anniversary **aniversario** *m.* **(de bodas)** 9
announce **anunciar** *v.* 18
announcer (*TV/radio*) **locutor(a)** *m., f.* 18
annoy **molestar** *v.* 7
another **otro/a** *adj.* 6
answer **contestar** *v.* 2; **respuesta** *f.*
answering machine **contestadora** *f.* 11
antibiotic **antibiótico** *m.* 10
any **algún, alguno/a(s)** *adj.* 7
anyone **alguien** *pron.* 7
anything **algo** *pron.* 7
apartment **apartamento** *m.* 12
apartment building **edificio de apartamentos** 12
appear **parecer** *v.*
appetizers **entremeses** *m., pl.*
applaud **aplaudir** *v.* 17
apple **manzana** *f.* 8
appliance (electric) **electrodoméstico** *m.* 12
applicant **aspirante** *m., f.* 16
application **solicitud** *f.* 16
job application **solicitud de trabajo** 16
apply (*for a job*) **solicitar** *v.* 16
apply for a loan **pedir** *v.* **préstamo** 14
appointment **cita** *f.* 9
have an appointment **tener** *v.* **una cita** 9
appreciate **apreciar** *v.* 17
April **abril** *m.* 5
aquatic **acuático/a** *adj.*
archaeologist **arqueólogo/a** *m., f.* 16
architect **arquitecto/a** *m., f.* 16
area **región** *f.* 13
arm **brazo** *m.* 10
armchair **sillón** *m.* 12
army **ejército** *m.* 18
around **por** *prep.* 11
around here **por aquí** 11
arrange **arreglar** *v.* 11
arrival **llegada** *f.* 5
arrive **llegar** *v.* 2
art **arte** *m.* 2
(fine) arts **bellas artes** *f., pl.* 17
article *m.* **artículo** 18
artist **artista** *m., f.* 3
artistic **artístico/a** *adj.* 17
arts **artes** *f., pl.* 17
as **como** 8
as… as **tan… como** 8
as a child **de niño/a** 10
as many… as **tantos/as… como** 8
as much… as **tanto… como** 8
as soon as **en cuanto** *conj.* 13; **tan pronto como** *conj.* 13
ask (*a question*) *v.* **preguntar** *v.* 2
ask for **pedir (e:i)** *v.* 4
asparagus **espárragos** *m., pl.* 8
aspirin **aspirina** *f.* 10
at **a** *prep.* 1
at + *time* **a la(s)** + *time* 1
at home **en casa** 7
at least **por lo menos** 10
at night **por la noche** 7
at the end (of) **al fondo (de)** 12
At what time…? **¿A qué hora…?** 1
At your service. **A sus órdenes.** 11
ATM **cajero automático** *m.* 14
attend **asistir (a)** *v.* 3
attic **altillo** *m.* 12
attract **atraer** *v.* 4
audience **público** *m.* 17
August **agosto** *m.* 5
aunt **tía** *f.* 3
aunts and uncles **tíos** *m., pl.* 3
automatic **automático/a** *adj.*

automobile **automóvil** *m.* 5; **carro** *m.;* **coche** *m.* 11
autumn **otoño** *m.* 5
avenue **avenida** *f.*
avoid **evitar** *v.* 13
award **premio** *m.* 17

B

backpack **mochila** *f.* 2
bad **mal, malo/a** *adj.* 3
It's bad that... **Es malo que...** 12
It's not at all bad. **No está nada mal.** 5
bag **bolsa** *f.* 6
bakery **panadería** *f.* 14
balanced **equilibrado/a** *adj.* 15
to eat a balanced diet **comer una dieta equilibrada** 15
balcony **balcón** *m.* 12
ball **pelota** *f.* 4
banana **banana** *f.* 8
band **banda** *f.* 17
bank **banco** *m.* 14
bargain **ganga** *f.* 6; **regatear** *v.* 6
baseball (*game*) **béisbol** *m.* 4
basement **sótano** *m.* 12
basketball (*game*) **baloncesto** *m.* 4
bathe **bañarse** *v.* 7
(bathing) suit **traje** *m.* **(de baño)** 6
bathroom **baño** *m.* 7; **cuarto de baño** *m.* 7
be **ser** *v.* 1; **estar** *v.* 2
be... years old **tener... años** 3
beach **playa** *f.* 5
beans **frijoles** *m., pl.* 8
beautiful **hermoso/a** *adj.* 6
beauty **belleza** *f.* 14
beauty salon **peluquería** *f.* 14; **salón** *m.* **de belleza** 14
because **porque** *conj.* 2
because of **por** *prep.* 11
become (+ *adj.*) **ponerse (+ *adj.*)** 7; **convertirse** *v.*
bed **cama** *f.* 5
go to bed **acostarse (o:ue)** *v.* 7
bedroom **alcoba** *f.*, **dormitorio** *m.* 12; **recámara** *f.*
beef **carne de res** *f.* 8
beef soup **caldo de patas** 8
been **sido** *p.p.* 15
beer **cerveza** *f.* 8
before **antes** *adv.* 7; **antes de** *prep.* 7; **antes (de) que** *conj.* 13
beg **rogar (o:ue)** *v.* 12
begin **comenzar (e:ie)** *v.* 4; **empezar (e:ie)** *v.* 4
behalf: on behalf of **de parte de** 11
behind **detrás de** *prep.* 2
believe (in) **creer** *v.* **(en)** 3; **creer** *v.* 13
not to believe **no creer** 13
believed **creído/a** *p.p.* 14
bellhop **botones** *m., f. sing.* 5
below **debajo de** *prep.* 2
belt **cinturón** *m.* 6
benefit **beneficio** *m.* 16
beside **al lado de** *prep.* 2
besides **además (de)** *adv.* 10
best **mejor** *adj.*
the best **el/la mejor** *m., f.* 8
lo mejor *neuter* 18
better **mejor** *adj.* 8
It's better that... **Es mejor que...** 12
between **entre** *prep.* 2
beverage **bebida** *f.*
alcoholic beverage **bebida alcohólica** *f.* 15
bicycle **bicicleta** *f.* 4
big **gran, grande** *adj.* 3
bill **cuenta** *f.* 9
billion: billion **mil millones**
biology **biología** *f.* 2
bird **ave** *f.* 13; **pájaro** *m.* 13
birth **nacimiento** *m.* 9
birthday **cumpleaños** *m., sing.* 9
birthday cake **pastel de cumpleaños** 9
have a birthday **cumplir** *v.* **años** 9
biscuit **bizcocho** *m.*
black **negro/a** *adj.* 6
blackberry **mora** *f.* 8
blackboard **pizarra** *f.* 2
blanket **manta** *f.* 12
block (city) **cuadra** *f.* 14
blond(e) **rubio/a** *adj.* 3
blouse **blusa** *f.* 6
blue **azul** *adj. m., f.* 6
boarding house **pensión** *f.*
boat **barco** *m.* 5
body **cuerpo** *m.* 10
bone **hueso** *m.* 10
book **libro** *m.* 2
bookcase **estante** *m.* 12
bookshelves **estante** *m.* 12
bookstore **librería** *f.* 2
boot **bota** *f.* 6
bore **aburrir** *v.* 7
bored **aburrido/a** *adj.* 5
be bored **estar** *v.* **aburrido/a** 5
get bored **aburrirse** *v.* 17
boring **aburrido/a** *adj.* 5
born: be born **nacer** *v.* 9
borrow **pedir prestado** 14
borrowed **prestado/a** *adj.*
boss **jefe** *m.*, **jefa** *f.* 16
bother **molestar** *v.* 7
bottle **botella** *f.* 9
bottle (of wine) **botella (de vino)** 9
bottom **fondo** *m.*
boulevard **bulevar** *m.*
boy **chico** *m.* 1; **muchacho** *m.* 3
boyfriend **novio** *m.* 3
brakes **frenos** *m., pl.*
bread **pan** *m.* 8
break **romper** *v.* 10
break (one's leg) **romperse (la pierna)** 10
break down **dañar** *v.* 10
The... broke down. **Se nos dañó el/la...** 11
break up (with) **romper** *v.* **(con)** 9
breakfast **desayuno** *m.* 2, 8
have breakfast **desayunar** *v.* 2
breathe **respirar** *v.* 13
bring **traer** *v.* 4
broadcast **transmitir** *v.* 18; **emitir** *v.* 18
brochure **folleto** *m.*
broken **roto/a** *adj.* 10, 14
be broken **estar roto/a** 10
brother **hermano** *m.* 3
brother-in-law **cuñado** *m., f.* 3
brothers and sisters **hermanos** *m., pl.* 3
brought **traído** *p.p.* 14
brown **café** *adj.* 6; **marrón** *adj.*6
brunet(te) **moreno/a** *adj.* 3
brush **cepillar** *v.* 7
brush one's hair **cepillarse el pelo** 7
brush one's teeth **cepillarse los dientes** 7
build **construir** *v.* 4
building **edificio** *m.* 12
bump into (*something accidentally*) **darse con** 10; (*someone*) **encontrarse** *v.* 11
burn (a CD) **quemar** *v.* 11
burned (out) **quemado/a** *adj.* 11
bus **autobús** *m.* 1
bus station **estación** *f.* **de autobuses** 5
business **negocios** *m. pl.* 16
business administration **administración** *f.* **de empresas** 2
business-related **comercial** *adj.* 16
businessperson **hombre** *m.* **/mujer** *f.* **de negocios** 16
busy **ocupado/a** *adj.* 5
but **pero** *conj.* 2; (rather) **sino** *conj.* (*in negative sentences*) 7
butcher shop **carnicería** *f.* 14
butter **mantequilla** *f.* 8
buy **comprar** *v.* 2
by **por** *conj.* 11; **para** *prep.* 11
by means of **por** *prep.* 11
by phone **por teléfono** 11
by plane **en avión** 5
by way of **por** *prep.* 11
bye **chau** *interj. fam.* 1

C

cabin **cabaña** *f.* 5
cable television **televisión** *f.* **por cable** *m.* 11
café **café** *m.* 4

cafeteria **cafetería** *f.* 2
caffeine **cafeína** *f.* 15
cake **pastel** *m.* 9
(chocolate) cake **pastel (de chocolate)** *m.* 9
calculator **calculadora** *f.* 11
call **llamar** *v.* 11
call on the phone **llamar por teléfono**
be called **llamarse** *v.* 7
calm **tranquilo/a** *adj.* 15
calorie **caloría** *f.* 15
camera **cámara** *f.* 11
camp **acampar** *v.* 5
can **lata** *f.* 13
can **poder (o:ue)** *v.* 4
Canadian **canadiense** *adj.* 3
candidate **aspirante** *m. f.* 16; candidate **candidato/a** *m., f.* 18
candy **dulces** *m., pl.* 9
capital city **capital** *f.* 1
car **coche** *m.* 11; **carro** *m.* 11; **auto(móvil)** *m.* 5
caramel **caramelo** *m.* 9
card **tarjeta** *f.* 4; (*playing*) **carta** *f.* 5
care **cuidado** *m.* 3
take care of **cuidar** *v.* 13
Take care! **¡Cuídense!** *v.* 15
career **carrera** *f.* 16
careful: be (very) careful **tener** *v.* **(mucho) cuidado** 3
caretaker **ama** *m., f.* **de casa** 12
carpenter **carpintero/a** *m., f.* 16
carpet **alfombra** *f.* 12
carrot **zanahoria** *f.* 8
carry **llevar** *v.* 2
cartoons **dibujos** *m, pl.* **animados** 17
case: in case (that) **en caso (de) que** 13
cash (a check) **cobrar** *v.* 14;
cash **(en) efectivo** 6
cash register **caja** *f.* 6
pay in cash **pagar** *v.* **al contado** 14; **pagar en efectivo** 14
cashier **cajero/a** *m., f.*
cat **gato** *m.* 13
CD-ROM **cederrón** *m.* 11
celebrate **celebrar** *v.* 9
celebration **celebración** *f.*
young woman's fifteenth birthday celebration **quinceañera** *f.* 9
cellar **sótano** *m.* 12
cellular **celular** *adj.* 11
cellular telephone **teléfono celular** *m.* 11
cereal **cereales** *m., pl.* 8
certain **cierto** *m.*; **seguro** *m.* 13
It's (not) certain. **(No) Es cierto/seguro.** 13
chalk **tiza** *f.* 2
champagne **champán** *m.* 9
change **cambiar** *v.* **(de)** 9
channel (*TV*) **canal** *m.* 17
character (*fictional*) **personaje** *m.* 17
(main) character *m.* **personaje (principal)** 17
chat **conversar** *v.* 2
chauffeur **conductor(a)** *m., f.* 1
cheap **barato/a** *adj.* 6
check **comprobar** *v.*; **revisar** *v.* 11; (*bank*) **cheque** *m.* 14
check the oil **revisar el aceite** 11
checking account **cuenta** *f.* **corriente** 14
cheese **queso** *m.* 8
chef **cocinero/a** *m., f.* 16
chemistry **química** *f.* 2
chest of drawers **cómoda** *f.* 12
chicken **pollo** *m.* 8
child **niño/a** *m., f.* 3
childhood **niñez** *f.* 9
children **hijos** *m., pl.* 3
Chinese **chino/a** *adj.* 3
chocolate **chocolate** *m.* 9
chocolate cake **pastel** *m.* **de chocolate** 9
cholesterol **colesterol** *m.* 15
choose **escoger** *v.* 8
chop (*food*) **chuleta** *f.* 8
Christmas **Navidad** *f.* 9
church **iglesia** *f.* 4
citizen **ciudadano/a** *adj.* 18
city **ciudad** *f.* 4
class **clase** *f.* 2
take classes **tomar clases** 2
classical **clásico/a** *adj.* 17
classmate **compañero/a** *m., f.* **de clase** 2
clean **limpio/a** *adj.* 5; **limpiar** *v.* 12
clean the house *v.* **limpiar la casa** 12
clear (*weather*) **despejado/a** *adj.*
clear the table **quitar la mesa** 12
It's (very) clear. (*weather*) **Está (muy) despejado.**
clerk **dependiente/a** *m., f.* 6
climb **escalar** *v.* 4
climb mountains **escalar montañas** 4
clinic **clínica** *f.* 10
clock **reloj** *m.* 2
close **cerrar (e:ie)** *v.* 4
closed **cerrado/a** *adj.* 5
closet **armario** *m.* 12
clothes **ropa** *f.* 6
clothes dryer **secadora** *f.* 12
clothing **ropa** *f.* 6
cloud **nube** *f.* 13
cloudy **nublado/a** *adj.* 5
It's (very) cloudy. **Está (muy) nublado.** 5
coat **abrigo** *m.* 6
coffee **café** *m.* 8
coffee maker **cafetera** *f.* 12
cold **frío** *m.* 5;
(*illness*) **resfriado** *m.* 10
be (*feel*) (very) cold **tener (mucho) frío** 3
It's (very) cold. (*weather*) **Hace (mucho) frío.** 5
college **universidad** *f.* 2
collision **choque** *m.* 18
color **color** *m.* 6
comb one's hair **peinarse** *v.* 7
come **venir** *v.* 3
comedy **comedia** *f.* 17.
comfortable **cómodo/a** *adj.* 5
commerce **negocios** *m., pl.* 16
commercial **comercial** *adj.* 16
communicate (with) **comunicarse** *v.* **(con)** 18
communication **comunicación** *f.* 18
means of communication **medios** *m. pl.* **de comunicación** 18
community **comunidad** *f* .1
compact disc (CD) **disco** *m.* **compacto** 11
compact disc player **tocadiscos** *m. sing.* **compacto** 11
company **compañía** *f.* 16; **empresa** *f.* 16
comparison **comparación** *f.*
completely **completamente** *adv.* 16
composer **compositor(a)** *m., f.* 17
computer **computadora** *f.* 1
computer disc **disco** *m.*
computer monitor **monitor** *m.* 11
computer programmer **programador(a)** *m., f.* 3
computer science **computación** *f.* 2
concert **concierto** *m.* 17
conductor (*musical*) **director(a)** *m., f.* 17
confirm **confirmar** *v.* 5
confirm a reservation **confirmar una reservación** 5
confused **confundido/a** *adj.* 5
congested **congestionado/a** *adj.* 10
Congratulations! (*for an event such as a birthday or anniversary*) **¡Felicidades!** 9; (*for an event such as an engagement or a good grade on a test*) *f., pl.* **¡Felicitaciones!** 9
conservation **conservación** *f.* 13
conserve **conservar** *v.* 13
considering **para** *prep.* 11
consume **consumir** *v.* 15
contact lenses **lentes** *m. pl.* **de contacto** 6
container **envase** *m.* 13
contamination **contaminación** *f.*
content **contento/a** *adj.* 5
contest **concurso** *m.* 17
continue **seguir (e:i)** *v.* 4

control **control** *m.*; **controlar** *v.* 13
be under control **estar bajo control** 7
conversation **conversación** *f.* 1
converse **conversar** *v.* 2
cook **cocinar** *v.* 12; **cocinero/a** *m., f.* 16
cookie **galleta** *f.* 9
cool **fresco/a** *adj.* 5
It's cool. (*weather*) **Hace fresco.** 5
corn **maíz** *m.* 8
corner **esquina** *m.* 14
cost **costar (o:ue)** *v.* 6
cotton **algodón** *f.* 6
(made of) cotton **de algodón** 6
couch **sofá** *m.* 12
couch potato **teleadicto/a** *m., f.* 15
cough **tos** *f.* 10; **toser** *v.* 10
counselor **consejero/a** *m., f.* 16
count (on) **contar** *v.* **(con)** 4, 12
country (*nation*) **país** *m.* 1
countryside **campo** *m.* 5; **paisaje** *m.* 5
(married) couple **pareja** *f.* 9
course **curso** *m.* 2; **materia** *f.* 2
courtesy **cortesía** *f.*
cousin **primo/a** *m., f.* 3
cover **cubrir** *v.*
covered **cubierto** *p.p.*
cow **vaca** *f.* 13
crafts **artesanía** *f.* 17
craftsmanship **artesanía** *f.* 17
crater **cráter** *m.* 13
crazy **loco/a** *adj.* 6
create **crear** *v.*
credit **crédito** *m.* 6
credit card **tarjeta** *f.* **de crédito** 6
crime **crimen** *m.* 18
cross **cruzar** *v.* 14
culture **cultura** *f.* 17
cup **taza** *f.* 12
currency exchange **cambio** *m.* **de moneda**
current events **actualidades** *f., pl.* 18
curtains **cortinas** *f., pl.* 12
custard (*baked*) **flan** *m.* 9
custom **costumbre** *f.* 1
customer **cliente/a** *m., f.* 6
customs **aduana** *f.* 5
customs inspector **inspector(a)** *m., f.* **de aduanas** 5
cybercafé **cibercafé** *m.* 11
cycling **ciclismo** *m.* 4

D

dad **papá** *m.* 3
daily **diario/a** *adj.* 7
daily routine **rutina** *f.* **diaria** 7
damage **dañar** *v.* 10
dance **bailar** *v.* 2; **danza** *f.* 17; **baile** *m.* 17
dancer **bailarín/bailarina** *m. f.* 17
danger **peligro** *m.* 13
dangerous **peligroso/a** *adj.* 18
date (*appointment*) **cita** *f.* 9; (*calendar*) **fecha** *f.* 5; (*someone*) **salir** *v.* **con (alguien)** 9
date: have a date **tener una cita** 9
daughter **hija** *f.* 3
daughter-in-law **nuera** *f.* 3
day **día** *m.* 1
day before yesterday **anteayer** *adv.* 6
deal **trato** *m.* 17
You've got a deal! **¡Trato hecho!** 17
It's not a big deal. **No es para tanto.** 12
death **muerte** *f.* 9
decaffeinated **descafeinado/a** *adj.* 15
December **diciembre** *m.* 5
decide **decidir** *v.* **(+ *inf.*)** 3
decided **decidido/a** *adj. p.p.* 14
declare **declarar** *v.* 18
deforestation **deforestación** *f.* 13
delicious **delicioso/a** *adj.* 8; **rico/a** *adj.* 8; **sabroso/a** *adj.* 8
delighted **encantado/a** *adj.* 1
dentist **dentista** *m., f.* 10
deny **negar (e: ie)** *v.* 13
not to deny **no dudar** 13
department store **almacén** *m.* 6
departure **salida** *f.* 5
deposit **depositar** *v.* 14
describe **describir** *v.* 3
described **descrito/a** *p.p.* 14
desert **desierto** *m.* 13
design **diseño** *m.*
designer **diseñador(a)** *m., f.* 16
desire **desear** *v.* 2
desk **escritorio** *m.* 2
dessert **postre** *m.* 9
destroy **destruir** *v.* 13
develop **desarrollar** *v.* 13
diary **diario** *m.* 1
dictatorship **dictadura** *f.* 18
dictionary **diccionario** *m.* 1
die **morir (o:ue)** *v.* 8
died **muerto/a** *p.p.* 14
diet **dieta** *f.* 15; **alimentación**
balanced diet **dieta equilibrada** 15
be on a diet **estar a dieta** 15
difficult **difícil** *adj. m., f.* 3
digital camera **cámara** *f.* **digital** 11
dining room **comedor** *m.* 12
dinner **cena** *f.* 2, 8
have dinner **cenar** *v.* 2
direct **dirigir** *v.* 17
directions **direcciones** *f., pl.* 14
give directions **dar direcciones** 14
director **director(a)** *m., f.* 17
dirty **ensuciar** *v.*; **sucio/a** *adj.* 5
get (something) dirty **ensuciar** *v.* 12
disagree **no estar de acuerdo**
disaster **desastre** *m.* 18
discover **descubrir** *v.* 13
discovered **descubierto** *p.p.* 14
discrimination **discriminación** *f.* 18
dish **plato** *m.* 8; 12
main dish *m.* **plato principal** 8
dishwasher **lavaplatos** *m., sing.* 12
disk **disco** *m.*
disorderly **desordenado/a** *adj.* 5
dive **bucear** *v.* 4
divorce **divorcio** *m.* 9
divorced **divorciado/a** *adj.* 9
get divorced (from) **divorciarse** *v.* **(de)** 9
dizzy **mareado/a** *adj.* 10
do **hacer** *v.* 4
do aerobics **hacer ejercicios aeróbicos** 15
do household chores **hacer quehaceres domésticos** 12
do stretching exercises **hacer ejercicios de estiramiento** 15
(I) don't want to. **No quiero.** 4
doctor **doctor(a)** *m., f.* 3; **médico/a** *m., f.* 3
documentary (*film*) **documental** *m.* 17
dog **perro** *m.* 13
domestic **doméstico/a** *adj.*
domestic appliance **electrodoméstico** *m.*
done **hecho/a** *p.p.* 14
door **puerta** *f.* 2
dormitory **residencia** *f.* **estudiantil** 2
double **doble** *adj.* 5
double room **habitación** *f.* **doble** 5
doubt **duda** *f.* 13; **dudar** *v.* 13
not to doubt 13
There is no doubt **No cabe duda de** 13; **No hay duda de** 13
Down with… ! **¡Abajo el/la…!**
download **descargar** *v.* 11
downtown **centro** *m.* 4
drama **drama** *m.* 17
dramatic **dramático/a** *adj.* 17
draw **dibujar** *v.* 2
drawing **dibujo** *m.* 17
dress **vestido** *m.* 6
get dressed **vestirse (e:i)** *v.* 7
drink **beber** *v.* 3; **bebida** *f.* 8; **tomar** *v.* 2
Do you want something to drink? **¿Quieres algo de tomar?**

drive **conducir** *v.* 8; **manejar** *v.* 11
driver **conductor(a)** *m., f.* 1
drug *f.* **droga** 15
drug addict **drogadicto/a** *adj.* 15
dry (oneself) **secarse** *v.* 7
due to **por** *prep.*
due to the fact that **debido a**
during **durante** *prep.* 7; **por** *prep.* 11
dust **sacudir** *v.* 12
dust the furniture **sacudir los muebles** 12
DVD player **reproductor** *m.* **de DVD** 11
dying: I'm dying to (for)... **me muero por...**

E

each **cada** *adj. m., f.* 6
eagle **águila** *f.*
ear (outer) **oreja** *f.* 10
early **temprano** *adv.* 7
earn **ganar** *v.*
earthquake **terremoto** *m.* 18
ease **aliviar** *v.*
east **este** *m.* 14
to the east **al este** 14
easy **fácil** *adj. m., f.* 3
eat **comer** *v.* 3
ecology **ecología** *f.* 13
economics **economía** *f.* 2
ecotourism **ecoturismo** *m.* 13
Ecuador **Ecuador** *m.* 1
Ecuadorian **ecuatoriano/a** *adj.* 3
effective **eficaz** *adj. m., f.*
egg **huevo** *m.* 8
eight **ocho** 1
eight hundred **ochocientos/as** 6
eighteen **dieciocho** 1
eighth **octavo/a** 5
eighty **ochenta** 2
either... or **o... o** *conj.* 7
eldest **el/la mayor** 8
elect **elegir** *v.* 18
election **elecciones** *f. pl.* 18
electric appliance **electrodoméstico** *m.* 12
electrician **electricista** *m., f.* 16
electricity **luz** *f.* 12
elegant **elegante** *adj. m., f.* 6
elevator **ascensor** *m.* 5
eleven **once** 1
e-mail **correo** *m.* **electrónico** 4
e-mail address **dirección** *f.* **electrónica** 11
e-mail message **mensaje** *m.* **electrónico**
read e-mail **leer** *v.* **el correo electrónico** 4
embarrassed **avergonzado/a** *adj.* 5
embrace (each other) **abrazar(se)** *v.* 11
emergency **emergencia** *f.* 10
emergency room **sala** *f.* **de emergencia** 10
employee **empleado/a** *m., f.* 5
employment **empleo** *m.* 16
end **fin** *m.* 4; **terminar** *v.* 2
end table **mesita** *f.* 12
energy **energía** *f.* 13
engaged: get engaged (to) **comprometerse** *v.* **(con)** 9
engineer **ingeniero/a** *m., f.* 3
English (*language*) **inglés** *m.* 2; **inglés, inglesa** *adj.* 3
enjoy **disfrutar** *v.* **(de)** 15
enough **bastante** *adv.* 10
entertainment **diversión** *f.* 4
entrance **entrada** *f.* 12
envelope **sobre** *m.* 14
environment **medio ambiente** *m.* 13
equality **igualdad** *f.* 18
equipped **equipado/a** *adj.* 15
erase **borrar** *v.* 11
eraser **borrador** *m.* 2
errand *f.* **diligencia** 14
establish **establecer** *v.*
evening **tarde** *f.* 1
event **acontecimiento** *m.* 18
every day **todos los días** 10
everybody **todos** *m., pl.*
everything **todo** *m.* 5
Everything is under control. **Todo está bajo control.** 7
exactly **en punto** 1
exam **examen** *m.* 2
excellent **excelente** *adj.* 5
excess **exceso** *m.* 15
in excess **en exceso** 15
exchange **intercambiar** *v.*
in exchange for **por** 11
exciting **emocionante** *adj. m., f.*
excursion **excursión** *f.*
excuse **disculpar** *v.*
Excuse me. (*May I?*) **Con permiso.** 1; (*I beg your pardon.*) **Perdón.** 1
exercise **ejercicio** *m.* 15
hacer ejercicio 15
exit **salida** *f.* 5
expensive **caro/a** *adj.* 6
experience **experiencia** *f.* 18
explain **explicar** *v.* 2
explore **explorar** *v.*
expression **expresión** *f.*
extinction **extinción** *f.* 13
extremely delicious **riquísimo/a** *adj.* 8
extremely serious **gravísimo** *adj.* 13
eye **ojo** *m.* 10

F

fabulous **fabuloso/a** *adj* 5
face **cara** *f.* 7
facing **enfrente de** *prep.* 14
fact: in fact **de hecho**
fall (down) **caerse** *v.* 10
fall asleep **dormirse (o:ue)** *v.* 7
fall in love (with) **enamorarse** *v.* **(de)** 9
fall (season) **otoño** *m.* 5
fallen **caído** *p.p.* 14
family **familia** *f.* 3
famous **famoso/a** *adj.* 16
fan **aficionado/a** *adj.* 4
be a fan (of) **ser aficionado/a (a)** 4
far from **lejos de** *prep.* 2
farewell **despedida** *f.*
fascinate **fascinar** *v.* 7
fashion **moda** *f.* 6
be in fashion **estar de moda** 6
fast **rápido/a** *adj.*
fat **gordo/a** *adj.* 3; **grasa** *f.* 15
father **padre** *m.* 3
father-in-law **suegro** *m.* 3
favorite **favorito/a** *adj.* 4
fax (machine) ***fax*** *m.* 11
fear **miedo** *m.* 3; fear **temer** *v.* 13
February **febrero** *m.* 5
feel **sentir(se) (e:ie)** *v.* 7
feel like (*doing something*) **tener ganas de (+ *inf.*)** 3
festival **festival** *m.* 17
fever **fiebre** *f.* 10
have a fever **tener** *v.* **fiebre** 10
few **pocos/as** *adj. pl.*
fewer than **menos de** (+ *number*) 8
field: major field of study **especialización** *f.*
fifteen **quince** 1
young woman's fifteenth birthday celebration **quinceañera** *f.* 9
fifteen-year-old girl **quinceañera** *f.*
fifth **quinto/a** 5
fifty **cincuenta** 2
fight (for/against) **luchar** *v.* **(por/contra)** 18
figure (*number*) **cifra** *f.*
file **archivo** *m.* 11
fill **llenar** *v.* 11
fill out (a form) **llenar (un formulario)** 14
fill the tank **llenar** *v.* **el tanque** 11
finally **finalmente** *adv.* 15; **por último** 7; **por fin** 11
find **encontrar (o:ue)** *v.* 4
find (each other) **encontrar(se)** *v.*
(fine) arts **bellas artes** *f., pl.* 17
fine **multa** *f.*
That's fine. **Está bien.** 11
finger **dedo** *m.* 10
finish **terminar** *v.* 2

finish (*doing something*) **terminar** *v.* **de (+*inf.*)** 4
fire **incendio** *m.*18; **despedir (e:i)** 16
firefighter **bombero/a** *m., f.* 16
firm **compañía** *f.* 16; **empresa** *f.* 16
first **primer, primero/a** *adj.* 5
fish (*food*) **pescado** *m.* 8; **pescar** *v.* 5; (*live*) **pez** *m.* 13
fish market **pescadería** *f.* 14
fisherman **pescador** *m.*
fisherwoman **pescadora** *f.*
fishing **pesca** *f.* 5
fit (*clothing*) **quedar** *v.* 7
five **cinco** 1
five hundred **quinientos/as** 6
fix (*put in working order*) **arreglar** *v.* 11
fixed **fijo/a** *adj.* 6
flag **bandera** *f.*
flank steak **lomo** *m.* 8
flat tire: We had a flat tire. **Se nos pinchó una llanta.** 11
flexible **flexible** *adj.* 15
flood **inundación** *f.* 18
floor (*of a building*) **piso** *m.* 5; **suelo** *m.* 12
ground floor **planta baja** *f.* 5
top floor **planta** *f.* **alta**
flower **flor** *f.* 13
flu **gripe** *f.* 10
fog **niebla** *f.* 5
foggy: It's (very) foggy. **Hay (mucha) niebla.** 5
folk **folklórico/a** *adj.* 17
follow **seguir (e:i)** *v.* 4
food **comida** *f.* 8; **alimento**
foolish **tonto/a** *adj.* 3
foot **pie** *m.* 10
football **fútbol** *m.* **americano** 4
for **para** *prep.* 11; **por** *prep.* 11
for example **por ejemplo** 11
for me **para mí** 8
forbid **prohibir** *v.*
foreign **extranjero/a** *adj.* 17
foreign languages **lenguas** *f. pl.* **extranjeras** 2
forest **bosque** *m.* 13
forget **olvidar** *v.* 10
fork **tenedor** *m.* 12
form **formulario** *m.* 14
forty **cuarenta** *m.* 2
four **cuatro** 1
four hundred **cuatrocientos/as** 6
fourteen **catorce** 1
fourth **cuarto/a** *m., f.* 5
free **libre** *adj. m., f.* 4
be free (of charge) **ser gratis** 14
free time **tiempo libre** 4; spare (free) time **ratos libres** 4
freedom **libertad** *f.* 18
freezer **congelador** *m.* 12
French **francés, francesa** *adj.* 3
French fries **papas** *f., pl* **fritas** 8 **patatas** *f., pl* **fritas** 8
frequently **frecuentemente** *adv.* 10; **con frecuencia** *adv.* 10
Friday **viernes** *m., sing.* 2
fried **frito/a** *adj.*8
fried potatoes **papas** *f., pl.* **fritas** 8; **patatas** *f., pl.* **fritas** 8
friend **amigo/a** *m., f.* 3
friendly **amable** *adj. m., f.* 5
friendship **amistad** *f.* 9
from **de** *prep.* 1; **desde** *prep.* 6
from the United States **estadounidense** *m., f. adj.* 3
from time to time **de vez en cuando** 10
He/She/It is from... **Es de...**; I'm from... **Es de...** 1
fruit **fruta** *f.* 8
fruit juice **jugo** *m.* **de fruta** 8
fruit store **frutería** *f.* 14
full **lleno/a** *adj.* 11
fun **divertido/a** *adj.* 7
fun activity **diversión** *f.* 4
have fun **divertirse (e:ie)** *v.* 9
function **funcionar** *v.*
furniture **muebles** *m., pl.* 12
furthermore **además (de)** *adv.* 10
future **futuro** *adj.* 16; **porvenir** *m.* 16
Here's to the future! **¡Por el porvenir!** 16
in the future **en el futuro** 16

G

gain weight **aumentar** *v.* **de peso** 15; **engordar** 15
game **juego** *m.*; (*match*) **partido** *m.* 4
game show **concurso** *m.* 17
garage (*in a house*) **garaje** *m.* 12; **garaje** *m.* 11; **taller (mecánico)** 12
garden **jardín** *m.* 12
garlic **ajo** *m.* 8
gas station **gasolinera** *f.* 11
gasoline **gasolina** *f.* 11
geography **geografía** *f.* 2
German **alemán, alemana** *adj.* 3
get **conseguir (e:i)** *v.* 4; **obtener** *v.* 16
get along well/badly with **llevarse bien/mal con** 9
get bored **aburrirse** *v.* 17
get off (a vehicle) **bajar(se)** *v.* **(de)** 11
get on/into (a vehicle) **subir(se)** *v.* **a** 11
get out of (a vehicle) **bajar(se)** *v.* **(de)** 11
get up **levantarse** *v.* 7
gift **regalo** *m.* 6
girl **chica** *f.* 1; **muchacha** *f.* 3
girlfriend **novia** *f.* 3
give **dar** *v.* 6, 9;
(*as a gift*) **regalar** 9
glass (*drinking*) **vaso** *m.* 12; **vidrio** *m.* 13
(made of) glass **de vidrio** 13
glasses **gafas** *f., pl.* 6
(sun)glasses **gafas** *f., pl.* **(oscuras/de sol)** 6
gloves **guantes** *m., pl.* 6
go **ir** *v.* 4
go away **irse** 7
go by boat **ir en barco** 5
go by bus **ir en autobús** 5
go by car **ir en auto(móvil)** 5
go by motorcycle **ir en motocicleta** 5
go by plane **ir en avión** 5
go by subway **ir en metro** 5
go by taxi **ir en taxi** 5
go by the bank **pasar por el banco** 14
go by train **ir en tren** 5
go down; **bajar(se)** *v.*
go fishing **ir** *v.* **de pesca** 5
go on a hike (in the mountains) **ir de excursión (a las montañas)** 4; **hacer una excursión** 5
go out **salir** *v.* 9
go out (with) **salir** *v.* **(con)** 9
go through customs **pasar** *v.* **por la aduana** 5
go up **subir** *v.*
go with **acompañar** *v.* 14
Let's go. **Vamos.** 4
goblet **copa** *f.* 12
going to: be going to (*do something*) **ir a (+ *inf.*)** 4
golf **golf** *m.* 4
good **buen, bueno/a** *adj.* 3, 6
Good afternoon. **Buenas tardes.** 1
Good evening. **Buenas noches.** 1
Good idea. **Buena idea.** 4
Good morning. **Buenos días.** 1
Good night. **Buenas noches.** 1
It's good that... **Es bueno que...** 12
good-bye **adiós** *m.* 1
say good-bye (to) **despedirse** *v.* **(de) (e:i)** 7
good-looking **guapo/a** *adj.* 3
government **gobierno** *m.* 13
graduate (from/in) **graduarse** *v.* **(de/en)** 9
grains **cereales** *m., pl.* 8
granddaughter **nieta** *f.* 3
grandfather **abuelo** *m.* 3
grandmother **abuela** *f.* 3
grandparents **abuelos** *m. pl.* 3
grandson **nieto** *m.* 3
grape **uva** *f.* 8
grass **césped** *m.* 13; **hierba** *f.* 13
grave **grave** *adj.* 10
gray **gris** *adj. m., f.* 6
great **fenomenal** *adj. m., f.* 5

great-grandfather **bisabuelo** *m.* 3
great-grandmother **bisabuela** *f.* 3
green **verde** *adj. m., f.* 6
greet (each other) **saludar(se)** *v.* 11
greeting **saludo** *m.* 1
Greetings to… **Saludos a…** 1
grilled (*food*) **a la plancha** 8
grilled flank steak **lomo a la plancha** 8
ground floor **planta baja** *f.* 5
guest (*at a house/hotel*) **huésped** *m., f.* 5 (*invited to a function*) **invitado/a** *m., f.* 9
guide **guía** *m., f.* 13
gymnasium **gimnasio** *m.* 4

H

hair **pelo** *m.* 7
hairdresser **peluquero/a** *m., f.* 16
half **medio/a** *adj.* 3
half-brother **medio hermano** 3;
half-sister **media hermana** 3
half-past… (*time*) **…y media** 1
hallway **pasillo** *m.* 12
ham **jamón** *m.* 8
hamburger **hamburguesa** *f.* 8
hand **mano** *f.* 1
Hands up! **¡Manos arriba!**
handsome **guapo/a** *adj.* 3
happen **ocurrir** *v.* 18
Happy birthday! **¡Feliz cumpleaños!** 9
happy **alegre** *adj.* 5; **contento/a** *adj.* 5; **feliz** *adj. m., f.* 5
be happy **alegrarse** *v.* **(de)** 13
hard **difícil** *adj. m., f.* 3
hard-working **trabajador(a)** *adj.* 3
hardly **apenas** *adv.* 10
haste **prisa** *f.* 3
hat **sombrero** *m.* 6
hate **odiar** *v.* 9
have **tener** *v.* 3
have time **tener tiempo** 4
have to (*do something*) **tener que (+ *inf.*)** 3; **deber (+ *inf.*)**
have a tooth removed **sacar(se) una muela** 10
he **él** 1
head **cabeza** *f.* 10
headache **dolor de cabeza** *m.* 10
health **salud** *f.* 10
healthy **saludable** *adj. m., f.* 10; **sano/a** *adj.* 10
lead a healthy lifestyle **llevar** *v.* **una vida sana** 15
hear **oír** *v.* 4
heard **oído** *p.p.* 14
hearing: sense of hearing **oído** *m.* 10
heart **corazón** *m.* 10
heat **calor** *m.* 5
Hello. **Hola.** 1; (*on the telephone*) **Aló.** 11; **¿Bueno?** 11; **Diga.** 11
help **ayudar** *v.* 12; **servir (e:i)** *v.* 5
help each other **ayudarse** *v.* 11
her **su(s)** *poss.* 3; (of) hers **suyo(s)/a(s)** *poss.* 11
here *adv.* **aquí** 1
Here it is. **Aquí está.** 5
Here we are at/in… **Aquí estamos en…** 2
Hi. **Hola.** 1
highway **autopista** *f.* 11; **carretera** *f.*11
hike **excursión** *f.* 4
go on a hike **hacer una excursión** 5; **ir de excursión** 4
hiker **excursionista** *m., f.* 4
hiking **de excursión** 4
hire **contratar** *v.* 16
his **su(s)** *poss. adj.* 3; (of) his **suyo(s)/a(s)** *poss. pron.* 11
history **historia** *f.* 2
hobby **pasatiempo** *m.* 4
hockey **hockey** *m.* 4
holiday **día** *m.* **de fiesta** 9
home **casa** *f.* 2
home page **página** *f.* **principal** 11
homework **tarea** *f.* 2
hood **capó** *m.* 11; **cofre** *m.* 11
hope **esperar** *v.* **(+ *inf.*)** 2; **esperar** *v.* 13
I hope (that) **Ojalá (que)** 13
horror (genre) **de horror** *m.* 17
hors d'oeuvres **entremeses** *m., pl.* 8
horse **caballo** *m.* 5
hospital **hospital** *m.* 10
hot: be (*feel*) (very) hot **tener (mucho) calor** 3
It's (very) hot **Hace (mucho) calor** 5
hotel **hotel** *m.* 5
hour **hora** *f.* 1
house **casa** *f.* 2
household chores **quehaceres** *m. pl.* **domésticos** 12
housekeeper **ama** *m., f.* **de casa** 12
housing **vivienda** *f.* 12
How… ! **¡Qué…!** 3
how **¿cómo?** *adv.* 1
How are you? **¿Qué tal?** 1
How are you?**¿Cómo estás?** *fam.* 1
How are you?**¿Cómo está usted?** *form.* 1
How can I help you? **¿En qué puedo servirles?** 5
How did it go for you…? **¿Cómo le/les fue…?** 15
How is it going? **¿Qué tal?** 1
How is/are…? **¿Qué tal…?** 2
How is the weather like? **¿Qué tiempo hace?** 15
How many? **¿Cuánto(s)/a(s)?** 1
How much does… cost? **¿Cuánto cuesta…?** 6
How old are you? **¿Cuántos años tienes?** *fam.* 3
however **sin embargo**
hug (each other) **abrazar(se)** *v.* 11
humanities **humanidades** *f., pl.* 2
hunger **hambre** *f.* 3
hundred **cien, ciento** *m.* 2, 6
hungry: be (very) hungry **tener** *v.* **(mucha) hambre** 3
hunt **cazar** *v.* 13
hurricane **huracán** *m.* 18
hurry **apurarse** *v.* 15; **darse prisa** *v.* 15
be in a (big) hurry **tener** *v.* **(mucha) prisa** 3
hurt **doler (o:ue)** *v.* 10
It hurts me a lot… **Me duele mucho…** 10
husband **esposo** *m.* 3

I

I **Yo** 1
I am… **Yo soy...** 1
I hope (that) **Ojalá (que)** *interj.* 13
I wish (that) **Ojalá (que)** *interj.* 13
ice cream **helado** *m.* 9
ice cream shop **heladería** *f.* 14
iced **helado/a** *adj.* 9
iced tea **té** *m.* **helado** 8
idea **idea** *f.* 4
if **si** *conj.* 4
illness **enfermedad** *f.* 10
important **importante** *adj.* 3
be important to **importar** *v.* 7
It's important that… **Es importante que…** 12
impossible **imposible** *adj.* 13
It's impossible. **Es imposible.** 13
improbable **improbable** *adj.* 13
It's improbable. **Es improbable.** 13
improve **mejorar** *v.* 13
in **en** *prep.* 2; **por** *prep.* 11
in the afternoon **de la tarde** 1; **por la tarde** 7
in a bad mood **de mal humor** 5
in the direction of **para** *prep.* 1;
in the early evening **de la tarde** 1
in the evening **de la noche** 1; **por la tarde** 7
in a good mood **de buen humor** 1
in the morning **de la mañana** 1; **por la mañana** 7
in love (with) **enamorado/a (de)** 5
in search of **por** *prep.* 11
in front of **delante de** *prep.* 2
increase **aumento** *m.* 16

incredible **increíble** *adj.* 5
inequality **desigualdad** *f.* 18
infection **infección** *f.* 10
inform **informar** *v.* 18
injection **inyección** *f.* 10
give an injection *v.* **poner una inyección** 10
injure (oneself) **lastimarse** 10
injure (one's foot) **lastimarse** *v.* **(el pie)** 10
inner ear **oído** *m.* 10
inside **dentro** *adv.*
insist (on) **insistir** *v.* **(en)** 12
installments: pay in installments **pagar** *v.* **a plazos** 14
intelligent **inteligente** *adj.* 3
intend to **pensar** *v.* **(+** ***inf.*****)** 4
interest **interesar** *v.* 7
interesting **interesante** *adj.* 3
be interesting to **interesar** *v.* 7
(inter)national **(inter)nacional** *adj. m., f.* 18
Internet **Internet** *m.* 11
interview **entrevista** *f.* 16; interview **entrevistar** *v.* 16
interviewer **entrevistador(a)** *m., f.* 16
introduction **presentación** *f.*
I would like to introduce (name) to you... **Le presento a...** *form.* **Te presento a...** *fam.*
invest **invertir (i:ie)** *v.* 16
invite **invitar** *v.* 9
iron (clothes) **planchar** *v.* **la ropa** 12
Italian **italiano/a** *adj.* 3
its **su(s)** *poss. adj.* 3, **suyo(s)/a(s)** *poss. pron.* 11
It's me. **Soy yo.** 1

J

jacket **chaqueta** *f.* 6
January **enero** *m.* 5
Japanese **japonés, japonesa** *adj.* 3
jeans **bluejeans** *m., pl.* 6
jewelry store **joyería** *f.* 14
job **empleo** *m.* 16; **puesto** *m.* 16; **trabajo** *m.* 16
job application **solicitud** *f.* **de trabajo** 16
jog **correr** *v.*
journalism **periodismo** *m.* 2
journalist **periodista** *m., f.* 3; **reportero/a** *m., f.* 16
joy **alegría** *f.* 9
give joy **dar** *v.* **alegría** 9
joyful **alegre** *adj.* 5
juice **jugo** *m.* 8
July **julio** *m.* 5
June **junio** *m.* 5
jungle **selva, jungla** *f.* 13
just **apenas** *adv.*
have just (*done something*) **acabar de (+** ***inf.*****)** 6

K

key **llave** *f.* 5
keyboard **teclado** *m.* 11
kilometer **kilómetro** *m.* 11
kind: That's very kind of you. **Muy amable.** 5
kiss **beso** *m.* 9; (each other) **besar(se)** *v.* 11
kitchen **cocina** *f.* 12
knee **rodilla** *f.* 10
knife **cuchillo** *m.* 12
know **saber** *v.* 8; **conocer** *v.* 8
know how **saber** *v.* 8

L

laboratory **laboratorio** *m.* 2
lack **faltar** *v.* 7
lake **lago** *m.* 13
lamp **lámpara** *f.* 12
land **tierra** *f.* 13
landlord **dueño/a** *m., f.* 8
landscape **paisaje** *m.* 5
language **lengua** *f.* 2
laptop (computer) **computadora** *f.* **portátil** 11
large (*clothing size*) **talla grande** 6
last **durar** *v.* 18; **pasado/a** *adj.* 6; **último/a** *adj.*
last name **apellido** *m.* 3
last night **anoche** *adv.* 6
last week **semana** *f.* **pasada** 6
last year **año** *m.* **pasado** 6
late **tarde** *adv.* 7
later **más tarde** 7
See you later. **Hasta la vista.** 1; **Hasta luego.** 1
laugh **reírse (e:i)** *v.* 9
laughed **reído** *p.p.* 14
laundromat **lavandería** *f.* 14
law **ley** *f.* 13
lawyer **abogado/a** *m., f.* 16
lazy **perezoso/a** *adj.*
learn **aprender** *v.* **(a+** ***inf.*****)** 3
least, at **por lo menos** *adv.* 10
leave **salir** *v.* 4; **irse** *v.* 7
leave a tip **dejar una propina** 9
leave for (*a place*) **salir para**
leave from **salir de**
leave behind **dejar** *v.* 16
left **izquierdo/a** *adj.* 2
be left over **quedar** *v.* 7
to the left of **a la izquierda de** 2
leg **pierna** *f.* 10
lemon **limón** *m.* 8
lend **prestar** *v.* 6
less **menos** *adv.* 10
less... than **menos... que** 8
less than **menos de (+** ***number*****)**
lesson **lección** *f.* 1
let **dejar** *v.* 12
let's see **a ver** 2
letter **carta** *f.* 4, 14
lettuce **lechuga** *f.* 8
liberty **libertad** *f.* 18
library **biblioteca** *f.* 2
license (*driver's*) **licencia** *f.* **de conducir** 11
lie **mentira** *f.* 4
life **vida** *f.* 9
of my life **de mi vida** 15
lifestyle: lead a healthy lifestyle **llevar una vida sana** 15
lift **levantar** *v.* 15
lift weights **levantar pesas** 15
light **luz** *f.* 12
like **como** *prep.* 8; **gustar** *v.* 7
I like... **Me gusta(n)...** 2
like this **así** *adv.* 10
like very much *v.* **encantar** 7
Do you like...? **¿Te gusta(n)...?** 2
likeable **simpático/a** *adj.* 3
likewise **igualmente** *adv.* 1
line **línea** *f.* 4; **cola** (*queue*) *f.* 14
listen (to) **escuchar** *v.* 2
Listen! (*command*) **¡Oye!** *fam., sing.*1; **¡Oigan!** *form., pl.*
listen to music **escuchar música** 2
listen (to) the radio **escuchar la radio** 2
literature **literatura** *f.* 2
little (*quantity*) **poco/a** *adj.* 5; **poco** *adv.* 10
live **vivir** *v.* 3
living room **sala** *f.* 12
loan **préstamo** *m.* 14; **prestar** *v.* 6, 14
lobster **langosta** *f.* 8
located **situado/a** *adj.*
be located **quedar** *v.* 14
long (in length) **largo/a** *adj.* 6
look (at) **mirar** *v.* 2
look for **buscar** *v.* 2
lose **perder (e:ie)** *v.* 4
lose weight **adelgazar** *v.* 15
lost **perdido/a** *adj.* 14
be lost **estar perdido/a** 14
lot, a **muchas veces** *adv.* 10
lot of, a **mucho/a** *adj.* 2, 3
love (*another person*) **querer (e:ie)** *v.* 4; (*inanimate objects*) **encantar** *v.* 7 ; **amor** *m.* 9
in love **enamorado/a** *adj.* 5
I loved it! **¡Me encantó!** 15
luck **suerte** *f.* 3
lucky: be (very) lucky **tener (mucha) suerte** 3
luggage **equipaje** *m.* 5
lunch **almuerzo** *m.* 8
have lunch **almorzar (o:ue)** *v.* 4

M

ma'am **señora (Sra.)** *f.* 1

mad **enojado/a** *adj.* 5
magazine **revista** *f.* 4
magnificent **magnífico/a** *adj.* 5
mail **correo** *m.* 14; **enviar** *v.*, **mandar** *v.* 14
mail carrier **cartero** *m.* 14
mailbox **buzón** *m.* 14
main **principal** *adj. m., f.* 8
maintain **mantener** *v.* 15
major **especialización** *f.* 2
make **hacer** *v.* 4
make the bed **hacer la cama** 12
make-up **maquillaje** *m.* 7
to put on make-up **maquillarse** *v.* 7
man **hombre** *m.* 1
manager **gerente** *m., f.* 16
many **mucho/a** *adj.* 3
many times **muchas veces** 10
map **mapa** *m.* 2
March **marzo** *m.* 5
margarine **margarina** *f.* 8
marinated fish **ceviche** *m.* 8
lemon-marinated shrimp **ceviche** *m.* **de camarón** 8
marital status **estado** *m.* **civil** 9
market **mercado** *m.* 6
(open air) market **mercado (al aire libre)** 6
marriage **matrimonio** *m.* 9
married **casado/a** *adj.* 9
get married (to) **casarse** *v.* **(con)** 9
marvelous **maravilloso/a** *adj.* 5
marvelously **maravillosamente** *adv.* 18
massage **masaje** *m.* 15
masterpiece **obra maestra** *f.* 17
match (*sports*) **partido** *m.* 4
match **hacer** *v.* **juego (con)** 6
mathematics **matemáticas** *f., pl.* 2
matter **importar** *v.* 7
maturity **madurez** *f.* 9
maximum **máximo/a** *m.* 11
May **mayo** *m.* 5
maybe **tal vez** 5; **quizás** 5
mayonnaise **mayonesa** *f.* 8
(to, for) me **me** *pron.* 6
meal **comida** *f.* 8
means of communication **medios** *m. pl.* **de comunicación** 18
meat **carne** *f.* 8
mechanic **mecánico/a** *m., f.* 11
mechanic's repair shop **taller mecánico** 11
media **medios** *m., pl.* **de comunicación** 18
medical **médico/a** *adj.* 10
medication **medicamento** *m.* 10
medicine **medicina** *f.* 10
medium **mediano/a** *adj.*
meet (each other) **encontrar(se)** *v.* 11; **conocerse(se)** *v.* 8
meeting **reunión** *f.* 16
menu **menú** *m.* 8
message (*telephone*) **recado** *m.* 11, **mensaje** *m.*
Mexican **mexicano/a** *adj.* 3
Mexico **México** *m.* 1
microwave **microonda** *f.*12
microwave oven **horno** *m.***de microondas** 12
middle age **madurez** *f.* 9
midnight **medianoche** *f.* 1
mile **milla** *f.* 11
milk **leche** *f.* 8
million **millón** *m.* 6
million of **millón de** *m.* 6
mine **mío(s)/a(s)** *poss.* 11
mineral **mineral** *m.* 15
mineral water **agua** *f.* **mineral** 8
minute **minuto** *m.* 1
mirror **espejo** *m.* 7
Miss **señorita (Srta.)** *f.* 1
miss **perder** *v.* 4
mistaken **equivocado/a** *adj.*
modem **módem** *m.*
modern **moderno/a** *adj.* 17
molar **muela** *f.* 10
mom **mamá** *f.*
Monday **lunes** *m., sing.* 2
money **dinero** *m.* 6
monitor **monitor** *m.* 11
month **mes** *m.* 5
monument **monumento** *m.* 4
moon **luna** *f.* 13
more **más**
more... than **más... que** 8
more than **más de (+** *number***)** 8
morning **mañana** *f.* 1
mother **madre** *f.* 3
mother-in-law **suegra** *f.* 3
motor **motor** *m.*
motorcycle **motocicleta** *f.* 5
mountain **montaña** *f.* 4
mouse **ratón** *m.* 11
mouth **boca** *f.* 10
move (*from one house to another*) **mudarse** *v.* 12
movie **película** *f.* 4
movie star **estrella** *f.* **de cine** 17
movie theater **cine** *m.* 4
Mr. **señor (Sr.)** *m.* 1
Mrs. **señora (Sra.)** *f.* 1
much **mucho/a** *adj.* 2, 3
very much **muchísimo/a** *adj.* 2
municipal **municipal** *adj. m., f.*
murder **crimen** *m.* 18
muscle **músculo** *m.* 15
museum **museo** *m.* 4
mushroom **champiñón** *m.* 8
music **música** *f.* 2, 17
musical **musical** *adj.* 17
musician **músico/a** *m., f.* 17
must **deber** *v.* (+ *inf.*) 3
It must be... **Debe ser...**6
my **mi(s)** *poss. adj.* 3; **mío(s)/a(s)** *poss. pron.* 11

N

name **nombre** *m.* 1
in the name of **a nombre de** 5
last name *m.* **apellido**
My name is... **Me llamo...** 1
be named **llamarse** *v.* 7
napkin **servilleta** *f.* 12
national **nacional** *adj. m., f.*
nationality **nacionalidad** *f.* 1
natural **natural** *adj. m., f.* 13
(natural) disaster **desastre** *m.* **(natural)** 18
natural resource **recurso** *m.* **natural** 13
nature **naturaleza** *f.* 13
nauseated **mareado/a** *adj.* 10
near **cerca de** *prep.* 2
neaten **arreglar** *v.* 12
necessary **necesario/a** *adj.* 12
It is necessary that... **Hay que...** 12, 14
neck **cuello** *m.* 10
need **faltar** *v.* 7; **necesitar** *v.* 2
negative **negativo/a** *adj.*
neighbor **vecino/a** *m., f.* 12
neighborhood **barrio** *m.* 12
neither... nor **ni... ni** *conj.* 7; neither **tampoco** *adv.* 7
nephew **sobrino** *m.* 3
nervous **nervioso/a** *adj.* 5
network **red** *f.* 11
never **nunca** *adj.* 7; **jamás** 7
new **nuevo/a** *adj.* 6
newlywed **recién casado/a** *m., f.* 9
news **noticias** *f., pl.* 18; **actualidades** *f., pl.* 18
newscast **noticiero** *m.* 18
newspaper **periódico** 4; **diario** *m.* 18
next **próximo/a** *adj.* 16
next to **al lado de** *prep.* 2
nice **simpático/a** *adj.* 3; **amable** *adj. m., f.* 5
niece **sobrina** *f.* 3
night **noche** *f.* 1
night stand **mesita** *f.* **de noche** 12
nine **nueve** 1
nine hundred **novecientos/as** 6
nineteen **diecinueve** 1
ninety **noventa** 2
ninth **noveno/a** 5
no **no** 1; **ningún, ninguno/a(s)** *adj.* 7
no one **nadie** *pron.* 7
No problem. **Ningún problema.** 7
no way **de ninguna manera** 16
nobody **nadie** 7

none **ningún, ninguno/a(s)** *adj.* 7
noon **mediodía** *m.* 1
nor **ni** *conj.* 7
north **norte** *m.* 14
to the north **al norte** 14
nose **nariz** *f.* 10
not **no** 1
not any **ningún, ninguno/a(s)** *adj.* 7
not anyone **nadie** *pron.* 7
not anything **nada** *pron.* 7
not bad at all **nada mal** 5
not either **tampoco** *adv.* 7
not ever **nunca** *adv.* 7; **jamás** *adv.* 7
not very well **no muy bien** 1
not working **descompuesto/a** *adj.* 11
notebook **cuaderno** *m.* 1
nothing **nada** 1; 7
noun **sustantivo** *m.*
November **noviembre** *m.* 5
now **ahora** *adv.* 2
nowadays **hoy día** *adv.*
nuclear **nuclear** *adj. m., f.* 13
nuclear energy **energía nuclear** 13
number **número** *m.* 1
nurse **enfermero/a** *m., f.* 10
nutrition **nutrición** *f.* 15
nutritionist **nutricionista** *m., f.* 15

O

o'clock: It's... o'clock **Son las...** 1
It's one o'clock. **Es la una.** 1
obey **obedecer (c:zc)** *v.* 18
obligation **deber** *m.* 18
obtain **conseguir (e:i)** *v.* 4; **obtener** *v.* 16
obvious **obvio/a** *adj.* 13
it's obvious **es obvio** 13
occupation **ocupación** *f.* 16
occur **ocurrir** *v.* 18
ocean **océano** *m.* 5
October **octubre** *m.* 5
of **de** *prep.* 1
Of course. **Claro que sí.** 16; **Por supuesto.** 16
offer **oferta** *f.* 12; **ofrecer (c:cz)** *v.* 8
office **oficina** *f.* 12
doctor's office **consultorio** *m.* 10
often **a menudo** *adv.* 10
Oh! **¡Ay!**
oil **aceite** *m.* 8
OK **regular** *adj.* 1
It's okay. **Está bien.**
old **viejo/a** *adj.* 3; old age **vejez** *f.* 9
older **mayor** *adj. m., f.* 3
older brother, sister **hermano/a mayor** *m., f.* 3
oldest **el/la mayor** 8
on **en** *prep.* 2: **sobre** *prep.* 2
on behalf of **por** *prep.* 11
on the dot **en punto** 1
on time **a tiempo** 10
on top of **encima de** 2
once **una vez** 6
one **un, uno/a** *m., f., sing. pron.* 1
one hundred **cien(to)** 6
one million **un millón** *m.* 6
one more time **una vez más** 9
one thousand **mil** 6
one time **una vez** 6
one way (*travel*) **ida** *f.*
onion **cebolla** *f.* 8
only **sólo** *adv.* 3; **único/a** *adj.* 3
only child **hijo/a único/a** *m., f.* 3
open **abierto/a** *adj.* 5, 14; **abrir** *v.* 3
open-air **al aire libre** 6
opera **ópera** *f.* 17
operation **operación** *f.* 10
opposite **en frente de** *prep.* 14
or **o** *conj.* 7
orange **anaranjado/a** *adj.* 6; **naranja** *f.* 8
orchestra **orquesta** *f.* 17
order **mandar** 12; (*food*) **pedir (e:i)** *v.* 8
in order to **para** *prep.* 11
orderly **ordenado/a** *adj.* 5
ordinal (*numbers*) **ordinal** *adj.*
other **otro/a** *adj.* 6
our **nuestro(s)/a(s)** *poss. adj.* 3; *poss. pron.* 11
out of order **descompuesto/a** *adj.* 11
outside **fuera** *adv.*
outskirts **afueras** *f., pl.* 12
oven **horno** *m.* 12
over **sobre** *prep.* 2
own **propio/a** *adj.* 16
owner **dueño/a** *m., f* 8

P

p.m. **tarde** *f.* 1
pack (one's suitcases) **hacer** *v.* **las maletas** 5
package **paquete** *m.* 14
page **página** *f.* 11
pain **dolor** *m.* 10
have a pain **tener** *v.* **dolor** 10
paint **pintar** *v.* 17
painter **pintor(a)** *m., f.* 16
painting **pintura** *f.* 12, 17
pair **par** *m.* 6
pants **pantalones** *m., pl.* 6
pantyhose **medias** *f., pl.* 6
paper **papel** *m.* 2; (*report*) **informe** *m.* 18
paper money **billete** *m.*
paragraph **párrafo** *m.*
Pardon me. (*May I?*) **con permiso** 1; (*Excuse me.*) Pardon me. **Perdón.** 1
parents **padres** *m., pl.* 3; **papás** *m., pl.* 3
park **estacionar** *v.* 11; **parque** *m.* 4
parking lot **estacionamiento** *m.* 14
partner (*one of a married couple*) **pareja** *f.* 9
party **fiesta** *f.* 9
passed **pasado/a** *p.p.*
passenger **pasajero/a** *m., f.* 1
passport **pasaporte** *m.* 5
past **pasado/a** *adj.* 6
pastime **pasatiempo** *m.* 4
pastry shop **pastelería** *f.* 14
patient **paciente** *m., f.* 10
patio **patio** *m.* 12
pay **pagar** *v.* 6
pay in cash **pagar** *v.* **al contado; pagar en efectivo** 14
pay in installments **pagar** *v.* **a plazos** 14
pay the bill **pagar la cuenta** 9
pea **arveja** *m.* 8
peace **paz** *f.* 18
peach **melocotón** *m.* 8
pear **pera** *f.* 8
pen **pluma** *f.* 2
pencil **lápiz** *m.* 1
penicillin **penicilina** *f.* 10
people **gente** *f.* 3
pepper (*black*) **pimienta** *f.* 8
per **por** *prep.* 11
perfect **perfecto/a** *adj.* 5
perhaps **quizás; tal vez**
permission **permiso** *m.*
person **persona** *f.* 3
pharmacy **farmacia** *f.* 10
phenomenal **fenomenal** *adj.* 5
photograph **foto(grafía)** *f.* 1
physical (*exam*) **examen** *m.* **médico** 10
physician **doctor(a), médico/a** *m., f.* 3
physics **física** *f. sing.* 2
pick up **recoger** *v.* 13
picture **cuadro** *m.* 12; **pintura** *f.* 12
pie **pastel** *m.* 9
pill (tablet) **pastilla** *f.* 10
pillow **almohada** *f.* 12
pineapple **piña** *f.* 8
pink **rosado/a** *adj.* 6
place **lugar** *m.* 4; **poner** *v.* 4
plaid **de cuadros** 6
plans **planes** *m., pl.* 4
have plans **tener planes** 4
plant **planta** *f.* 13
plastic **plástico** *m.* 13
(made of) plastic **de plástico** 13

plate **plato** *m.* 12
platter of fried food **fuente** *f.* **de fritada**
play **drama** *m.* 17; **comedia** *f.* 17; **jugar (u:ue)** *v.* 4; (*a musical instrument*) **tocar** *v.* 17; (*a role*) **hacer el papel de** 17; (*cards*) **jugar a (las cartas)** 5; (*sports*) **practicar deportes** 4
player **jugador(a)** *m., f.* 4
playwright **dramaturgo/a** *m., f.* 17
plead **rogar (o:ue)** *v.* 12
pleasant **agradable** *adj. m., f.*
Please. **Por favor.** 1
Pleased to meet you. **Mucho gusto.** 1; **Encantado/a.** *adj.* 1
pleasing: be pleasing to **gustar** *v.* 7
pleasure **gusto** *m.* 1; **placer** *m.* 15
It's a pleasure to... **Gusto de** (+ *inf.*) 18
It's been a pleasure. **Ha sido un placer.** 15
The pleasure is mine. **El gusto es mío.** 1
poem **poema** *m.* 17
poet **poeta** *m., f.* 17
poetry **poesía** *f.* 17
police (force) **policía** *f.* 11
police officer **policía** *m.*, **mujer policía,** *f.*
political **político/a** *adj.* 18
politician **político/a** *m., f.* 16
politics **política** *f.* 18
polka-dotted **de lunares** 6
poll **encuesta** *f.* 18
pollute **contaminar** *v.* 13
polluted **contaminado/a** *m., f.* 13
be polluted **estar contaminado/a** 13
pollution **contaminación** *f.* 13
pool **piscina** *f.* 4
poor **pobre** *adj.* 6
population **población** *f.* 13
pork **cerdo** *m.* 8
pork chop **chuleta** *f.* **de cerdo** 8
portable **portátil** *adj.* 11
portable computer **computadora** *f.* **portátil** 11
position **puesto** *m.* 16
possessive **posesivo/a** *adj.* 3
possible **posible** *adj.* 13
It's (not) possible. **(No) Es posible.** 13
post office **correo** *m.* 14
postcard **postal** *f.* 4; **tarjeta postal** *f.* 4
poster **cartel** *m.* 12
potato **papa** *f.* 8; **patata** *f.* 8
pottery **cerámica** *f.* 15
practice **entrenarse** *v.* 15; **practicar** *v.* 2
prefer **preferir (e:ie)** *v.* 4
pregnant **embarazada** *adj. f.* 10
prepare **preparar** *v.* 2
preposition **preposición** *f.*
prescribe (*medicine*) **recetar** *v.* 10
prescription **receta** *f.* 10
present **regalo** *m.*; **presentar** *v.* 17
pressure **presión** *f.*
be under a lot of pressure **sufrir muchas presiones** 15
pretty **bonito/a** *adj.* 3; **bastante** *adv.* 13
price **precio** *m.* 6
(fixed, set) price **precio** *m.* **fijo** 6
print **estampado/a** *adj.*; **imprimir** *v.* 11
printer **impresora** *f.* 11
private (*room*) **individual** *adj.*
prize **premio** *m.* 17
probable **probable** *adj.* 13
It's (not) probable. **(No) Es probable.** 13
problem **problema** *m.* 1
profession **profesión** *f.* 3; 16
professor **profesor(a)** *m., f.*
program **programa** *m.* 1
programmer **programador(a)** *m., f.* 3
prohibit **prohibir** *v.* 10
promotion (*career*) **ascenso** *m.* 16
pronoun **pronombre** *m.*
protect **proteger** *v.* 13
protein **proteína** *f.* 15
provided (that) **con tal (de) que** *conj.* 13
psychologist **psicólogo/a** *m., f.* 16
psychology **psicología** *f.* 2
publish **publicar** *v.* 17
Puerto Rican **puertorriqueño/a** *adj.* 3
Puerto Rico **Puerto Rico** *m.* 1
pull a tooth **sacar una muela**
purchases **compras** *f., pl.* 5
pure **puro/a** *adj.* 13
purple **morado/a** *adj.* 6
purse **bolsa** *f.* 6
put **poner** *v.* 4; **puesto/a** *p.p.* 14
put (a letter) in the mailbox **echar (una carta) al buzón** 14
put on (*a performance*) **presentar** *v.* 17
put on (*clothing*) **ponerse** *v.* 7
put on makeup **maquillarse** *v.* 7

Q

quality **calidad** *f.* 6
quarter **trimestre** *m.* 2
quarter after (*time*) **y cuarto** 1; **y quince** 1
quarter to (*time*) **menos cuarto** 1; **menos quince** 1
question **pregunta** *f.* 2
quickly **rápido** *adv.* 10
quiet **tranquilo/a** *adj.* 15
quit **dejar** *v.* 16
quiz **prueba** *f.* 2

R

racism **racismo** *m.* 18
radio (*medium*) **radio** *f.* 2
radio (set) **radio** *m.* 11
rain **llover (o:ue)** *v.* 5; **lluvia** *f.* 13
It's raining. **Llueve.** 5
raincoat **impermeable** *m.* 6
rainforest **bosque** *m.* **tropical** 13
raise (*salary*) **aumento de sueldo** 16
rather **bastante** *adv.* 10
read **leer** *v.* 3; **leído/a** *p.p.* 14
read e-mail **leer correo electrónico** 4
read a magazine **leer una revista** 4
read a newspaper **leer un periódico** 4
ready **listo/a** *adj.*
(Are you) ready? **¿(Están) listos?** 15
reap the benefits (of) *v.* **disfrutar** *v.* **(de)** 15
reason **razón** *f.*
receive **recibir** *v.* 3
recommend **recomendar (e:ie)** *v.* 8; 12
record **grabar** *v.* 11
recreation **diversión** *f.* 4
recycle **reciclar** *v.* 13
recycling **reciclaje** *m.* 13
red **rojo/a** *adj.* 6
red-haired **pelirrojo/a** *adj.* 3
reduce **reducir** *v.* 13
reduce stress/tension **aliviar el estrés/la tensión** 15
refrigerator **refrigerador** *m.* 12
region **región** *f.* 13
regret **sentir (e:ie)** *v.* 13
related to sitting **sedentario/a** *adj.* 15
relationships **relaciones** *f., pl.*
relatives **parientes** *m., pl.* 3
relax **relajarse** *v.* 9
remain **quedarse** *v.* 7
remember **acordarse (o:ue)** *v.* **(de)** 7; **recordar (o:ue)** *v.* 4
remote control **control remoto** *m.* 11
rent **alquilar** *v.* 12; (payment) **alquiler** *m.* 12
repeat **repetir (e:i)** *v.* 4
report **informe** *m.* 18; **reportaje** *m.* 18
reporter **reportero/a** *m., f.* 16
representative **representante** *m., f.* 18
request **pedir (e:i)** *v.* 4
reservation **reservación** *f.* 5
resign (from) **renunciar (a)** *v.* 16

resolve **resolver (o:ue)** *v.* 13
resolved **resuelto/a** *p.p.* 14
resource **recurso** *m.* 13
responsibility **deber** *m.* 18
responsabilidad *f.*
rest **descansar** *v.* 2
the rest **lo/los/las demás** *pron.*
restaurant **restaurante** *m.* 4
résumé **currículum** *m.* 16
retire (from work) **jubilarse** *v.* 9
return **regresar** *v.* 2; **volver (o:ue)** *v.* 4
return trip **vuelta** *f.*
returned **vuelto/a** *p.p.* 14
rice **arroz** *m.* 8
rich **rico/a** *adj.* 6
ride a bicycle **pasear** *v.* **en bicicleta** 4
ride a horse **montar** *v.* **a caballo** 5
ridiculous **ridículo/a** *adj.* 13
It's ridiculous. **Es ridículo.** 13
right **derecha** *f.* 2;
right away **enseguida** *adv.* 9
right here **aquí mismo** 11
right now **ahora mismo** 5
right there **allí mismo** 14
be right **tener razón** 3
to the right of **a la derecha de** 2
right? (*question tag*) **¿no?** 1; **¿verdad?** 1
rights **derechos** *m.* 18
ring (*a doorbell*) **sonar (o:ue)** *v.* 11
river **río** *m.* 13
road **camino** *m.*
roast **asado/a** *adj.* 8
roast chicken **pollo** *m.* **asado** 8
rollerblade **patinar en línea** *v.*
romantic **romántico/a** *adj.* 17
room **habitación** *f.* 5; **cuarto** *m.* 7; 13
living room **sala** *f.* 12
roommate **compañero/a** *m., f.* **de cuarto** 2
roundtrip **de ida y vuelta** 5
roundtrip ticket **pasaje** *m.* **de ida y vuelta** 5
routine **rutina** *f.* 7
rug **alfombra** *f.* 12
run **correr** *v.* 3
run errands **hacer diligencias** 14
run into (*have an accident*) **chocar (con)** *v.*; (*meet accidentally*) **encontrar(se) (o:ue)** *v.* 11; (*run into some thing*) **darse (con)** 10
run into (each other) **encontrar(se) (o:ue)** *v.* 11
rush **apurarse, darse prisa** *v.* 15
Russian **ruso/a** *adj.* 3

S

sad **triste** *adj.* 5; 13
It's sad. **Es triste.** 13
said **dicho/a** *p.p.* 14
sake: for the sake of **por**
salad **ensalada** *f.* 8
salary **salario** *m.* 16; **sueldo** *m.* 16
sale **rebaja** *f.* 6
salesperson **vendedor(a)** *m., f.* 6
salmon **salmón** *m.* 8
salt **sal** *f.* 8
same **mismo/a** *adj.* 3
sandal **sandalia** *f.* 6
sandwich **sándwich** *m.* 8
Saturday **sábado** *m.* 2
sausage **salchicha** *f.* 8
save (*on a computer*) **guardar** *v.* 11;
save (money) **ahorrar** *v.* 14
savings **ahorros** *m.* 14
savings account **cuenta** *f.* **de ahorros** 14
say **decir** *v.* 4
say (that) **decir (que)** *v.* 4, 9
say the answer **decir la respuesta** 4
scarcely **apenas** *adv.* 10
scared: be (very) scared (of) **tener (mucho) miedo (de)** 3
schedule **horario** *m.* 2
school **escuela** *f.* 1
science *f.* **ciencia** 2
science fiction **ciencia ficción** *f.* 17
scientist **científico/a** *m., f.* 16
scuba dive **bucear** *v.* 4
screen **pantalla** *f.* 11
sculpt **esculpir** *v.* 17
sculptor **escultor(a)** *m., f.* 17
sculpture **escultura** *f.* 17
sea **mar** *m.* 5
season **estación** *f.* 5
seat **silla** *f.* 2
second **segundo/a** *adj.* 5
secretary **secretario/a** *m., f.* 16
sedentary **sedentario/a** *adj.* 15
see **ver** *v.* 4
see (you, him, her) again **volver a ver(te, lo, la)** 18
see movies **ver películas** 4
See you. **Nos vemos.** 1
See you later. **Hasta la vista.** 1; **Hasta luego.** 1
See you soon. **Hasta pronto.** 1
See you tomorrow. **Hasta mañana.** 1
seem **parecer** *v.* 8
seen **visto/a** *p.p.* 14
sell **vender** *v.* 6
semester **semestre** *m.* 2
send **enviar; mandar** *v.* 14
separate (from) **separarse** *v.* **(de)** 9
separated **separado/a** *adj.* 9
September **septiembre** *m.* 5
sequence **secuencia** *f.*
serious **grave** *adj.* 10
serve **servir (e:i)** *v.* 8
set (*fixed*) **fijo** *adj.* 6
set the table **poner la mesa** 12
seven **siete** 1
seven hundred **setecientos/as** 6
seventeen **diecisiete** 1
seventh **séptimo/a** 5
seventy **setenta** 2
sexism **sexismo** *m.* 18
shame **lástima** *f.* 13
It's a shame. **Es una lástima.** 13
shampoo **champú** *m.* 7
shape **forma** *f.* 15
be in good shape **estar en buena forma** 15
stay in shape **mantenerse en forma** 15
share **compartir** *v.* 3
sharp (*time*) **en punto** 1
shave **afeitarse** *v.* 7
shaving cream **crema** *f.* **de afeitar** 7
she **ella** 1
shellfish **mariscos** *m., pl.* 8
ship **barco** *m.*
shirt **camisa** *f.* 6
shoe **zapato** *m.* 6
shoe size **número** *m.* 6
shoe store **zapatería** *f.* 14
tennis shoes **zapatos** *m., pl.* **de tenis** 6
shop **tienda** *f.* 6
shopping, to go **ir de compras** 5
shopping mall **centro comercial** *m.* 6
short (*in height*) **bajo/a** *adj.* 3; (*in length*) **corto/a** *adj.* 6
short story **cuento** *m.* 17
shorts **pantalones cortos** *m., pl.* 6
should (*do something*) **deber** *v.* **(+ *infin.*)** 3
show **espectáculo** *m.* 17; **mostrar (o:ue)** *v.* 4
game show **concurso** *m.* 17
shower **ducha** *f.* 7; **ducharse** *v.* 7; **bañarse** *v.* 7
shrimp **camarón** *m.* 8
siblings **hermanos/as** *pl.* 3
sick **enfermo/a** *adj.* 10
be sick **estar enfermo/a** 10
get sick **enfermarse** *v.* 10
sightseeing: go sightseeing **hacer turismo** 5
sign **firmar** *v.* 14; **letrero** *m.* 14
silk **seda** *f.* 6; (made of) **de seda** 6
silly **tonto/a** *adj.* 3
silverware **cubierto** *m.*
since **desde** *prep.*
sing **cantar** *v.* 2

singer **cantante** *m., f.* 17
single **soltero/a** *adj.* 9
single room **habitación** *f.* **individual** 5
sink **lavabo** *m.* 7
sir **señor (Sr.)** *m.* 1
sister **hermana** *f.* 3
sister-in-law **cuñada** *f.* 3
sit down **sentarse (e:ie)** *v.* 7
six **seis** 1
six hundred **seiscientos/as** 6
sixteen **dieciséis** 1
sixth **sexto/a** 5
sixty **sesenta** 2
size **talla** *f.* 6
shoe size *m.* **número** 6
skate (in-line) **patinar (en línea)** 4
skateboard **andar en patineta** *v.* 4
ski **esquiar** *v.* 4
skiing **esquí** *m.* 4
water-skiing **esquí** *m.* **acuático** 4
skirt **falda** *f.* 6
sky **cielo** *m.* 13
sleep **dormir (o:ue)** *v.* 4; **sueño** *m.* 3
go to sleep **dormirse (o:ue)** *v.* 7
sleepy: be (very) sleepy **tener (mucho) sueño** 3
slender **delgado** *adj.* 3
slim down **adelgazar** *v.* 15
slippers **pantuflas** *f.* 7
slow **lento/a** *adj.* 11
slowly **despacio** *adv.* 10
small **pequeño/a** *adj.* 3
smart **listo/a** *adj.* 5
smile **sonreír (e:i)** *v.* 9
smiled **sonreído** *p.p.* 14
smoggy: It's (very) smoggy. **Hay (mucha) contaminación.** 4
smoke **fumar** *v.* 8, 15
(not) to smoke **(no) fumar** 15
smoking section **sección** *f.* **de fumar** 8
(non) smoking section *f.* **sección de (no) fumar** 8
snack **merendar** *v.* 15; afternoon snack **merienda** *f.* 15
have a snack **merendar** *v.*
sneakers **los zapatos de tenis** 6
sneeze **estornudar** *v.* 10
snow **nevar (e:ie)** *v.* 5; **nieve** *f.*
snowing: It's snowing. **Nieva.** 5
so (*in such a way*) **así** *adv.* 10; **tan** *adv.*
so much **tanto** *adv.*
so so **regular** 1, **así así**
so that **para que** *conj.* 13
soap **jabón** *m.* 7
soap opera **telenovela** *f.* 17
soccer **fútbol** *m.* 4
sociology *f.* **sociología** 2
sock **calcetín** *m.* 6
sofa **sofá** *m.* 12
soft drink **refresco** *m.* 8
software **programa** *m.* **de computación** 11
soil **tierra** *f.* 13
solar **solar** *adj., m., f.* 13
solar energy **energía solar** 13
solution **solución** *f.* 13
solve **resolver (o:ue)** *v.* 13
some **algún, alguno/a(s)** *adj.* 7; **unos/as** *pron./ m., f., pl; indef. art.* 1
somebody **alguien** *pron.* 7
someone **alguien** *pron.* 7
something **algo** *pron.* 7
sometimes **a veces** *adv.* 10
son **hijo** *m.* 3
song **canción** *f.* 17
son-in-law **yerno** *m.* 3
soon **pronto** *adv.* 10
See you soon. **Hasta pronto.** 1
sorry: be sorry **sentir (e:ie)** *v.* 13
I'm sorry. **Lo siento.** 1
I'm so sorry. **Mil perdones.; Lo siento muchísimo.** 4
soup **caldo** *m.* 8; **sopa** *f.* 8
south **sur** *m.* 14
to the south **al sur** 14
Spain **España** *f.* 1
Spanish (*language*) **español** *m.* 2; **español(a)** *adj.* 3
spare (free) time **ratos libres** 4
speak **hablar** *v.* 2
specialization **especialización** *f.*
spectacular **espectacular** *adj. m., f.* 15
speech **discurso** *m.* 18
speed **velocidad** *f.* 11
speed limit **velocidad** *f.* **máxima** 11
spelling **ortografía** *f.*, **ortográfico/a** *adj.*
spend (*money*) **gastar** *v.* 6
spend time **pasar tiempo** 4
spoon (*table or large*) **cuchara** *f.* 12
sport **deporte** *m.* 4
sports-related **deportivo/a** *adj.* 4
spouse **esposo/a** *m., f.* 3
sprain (one's ankle) **torcerse (o:ue)** *v.* **(el tobillo)** 10
sprained **torcido/a** *adj.* 10
be sprained **estar torcido/a** 10
spring **primavera** *f.* 5
(city or town) square **plaza** *f.* 4
stadium **estadio** *m.* 2
stage **etapa** *f.* 9
stairs **escalera** *f.* 12
stairway **escalera** *f.* 12
stamp **estampilla** *f.* 14; **sello** *m.* 14
stand in line **hacer** *v.* **cola** 14
star **estrella** *f.* 13
start (*a vehicle*) **arrancar** *v.* 11; **establecer** *v.* 16
state **estado** *m.*
station **estación** *f.* 5
statue **estatua** *f.* 17
status: marital status **estado** *m.* **civil** 9
stay **quedarse** *v.* 7
stay in shape **mantenerse en forma** 15
steak **bistec** *m.* 8
steering wheel **volante** *m.* 11
step **etapa** *f.*
stepbrother **hermanastro** *m.* 3
stepdaughter **hijastra** *f.* 3
stepfather **padrastro** *m.* 3
stepmother **madrastra** *f.* 3
stepsister **hermanastra** *f.* 3
stepson **hijastro** *m.* 3
stereo **estéreo** *m.* 11
still **todavía** *adv.* 5
stockbroker **corredor(a)** *m., f.* **de bolsa** 16
stockings **medias** *f., pl.* 6
stomach **estómago** *m.* 10
stone **piedra** *f.* 13
stop **parar** *v.* 11
stop (*doing something*) **dejar de (+** *inf.***)** 13
store **tienda** *f.* 6
storm **tormenta** *f.* 18
story **cuento** *m.* 17; **historia** *f.* 17
stove **cocina, estufa** *f.* 12
straight **derecho** *adj.* 14
straight (ahead) **derecho** 14
straighten up **arreglar** *v.* 12
strange **extraño/a** *adj.* 13
It's strange. **Es extraño.** 13
strawberry **frutilla** *f.* 8, **fresa**
street **calle** *f.* 11
stress **estrés** *m.* 15
stretching **estiramiento** *m.* 15
to do stretching exercises **hacer ejercicios** *m. pl.* **de estiramiento** 15
strike (*labor*) **huelga** *f.* 18
stripe **raya** *f.* 6
striped **de rayas** 6
stroll **pasear** *v.* 4
strong **fuerte** *adj.* 15
struggle (for) **luchar** *v.* **(por)** 18
student **estudiante** *m., f.* 1, 2; **estudiantil** *adj.* 2
study **estudiar** *v.* 2
stuffed-up (*sinuses*) **congestionado/a** *adj.* 10
stupendous **estupendo/a** *adj.* 5
style **estilo** *m.*
suburbs **afueras** *f., pl.* 12
subway **metro** *m.* 5
subway station **estación** *f.* **del metro** 5
success **éxito** *m.* 16
successful: be successful **tener éxito** 16
such as **tales como**
suddenly **de repente** *adv.* 6
suffer **sufrir** *v.* 10
suffer an illness **sufrir una enfermedad** 10

sufficient **bastante** *adj.*
sugar **azúcar** *m.* 8
suggest **sugerir (e:ie)** *v.* 12
suit **traje** *m.* 6
suitcase **maleta** *f.* 1
summer **verano** *m.* 5
sun **sol** *m.* 5; 13
sunbathe **tomar** *v.* **el sol** 4
Sunday **domingo** *m.* 2
(sun)glasses **gafas** *f., pl.* **(oscuras/de sol)** 6; **lentes** *m. pl.* **(de sol)** 6
sunny: It's (very) sunny. **Hace (mucho) sol.** 5
supermarket **supermercado** *m.* 14
suppose **suponer** *v.* 4
sure **seguro/a** *adj.* 5
  be sure **estar seguro/a** 5
surf (*the Internet*) **navegar** *v.* **(en Internet)** 11
surprise **sorprender** *v.* 9; **sorpresa** *f.* 9
survey **encuesta** *f.* 18
sweat **sudar** *v.* 15
sweater **suéter** *m.* 6
sweep the floor **barrer el suelo** 12
sweets **dulces** *m., pl.* 9
swim **nadar** *v.* 4
swimming **natación** *f.* 4
  swimming pool **piscina** *f.* 4
symptom **síntoma** *m.* 10

T

table **mesa** *f.* 2
tablespoon **cuchara** *f.* 12
tablet (*pill*) **pastilla** *f.* 10
take **tomar** *v.* 2; **llevar** *v.* 6;
  take care of **cuidar** 13
  take someone's temperature **tomar la temperatura** 10
  take (*wear*) a shoe size *v.* **calzar** 6
  take a bath **bañarse** *v.* 7
  take a shower **ducharse** *v.* 7
  take into account **tomar** *v.* **en cuenta**
  take off **quitarse** *v.* 7
  take out (the trash) *v.* **sacar (la basura)** 12
  take photos **tomar fotos** 5; **sacar fotos** 5
talented **talentoso/a** *adj.* 17
talk *v.* **hablar** 2
  talk show **programa** *m.* **de entrevistas** 17
tall **alto/a** *adj.* 3
tank **tanque** *m.* 11
tape (audio) **cinta** *f.*
  tape recorder **grabadora** *f.* 1
taste **probar (o:ue)** *v.* 8
tasty **rico/a** *adj.* 8; **sabroso/a** *adj.* 8
tax **impuesto** *m.* 18
taxi **taxi** *m.* 5
tea **té** *m.* 8
teach **enseñar** *v.* 2
teacher **profesor(a)** *m., f.* 1; **maestro/a** *m., f.* 16
team **equipo** *m.* 4
technician **técnico/a** *m., f.* 16
telecommuting **teletrabajo** *n.* 16
telephone **teléfono** *m.* 11
  cellular telephone **teléfono** *m.* **celular** 11
television **televisión** *f.* 11
  television set **televisor** *m.* 11
tell **contar** *v.*; **decir** *v.* 4
tell (that) **decir** *v.* **(que)** 4, 9
  tell the truth **decir la verdad** 4
  tell lies **decir mentiras** 4
temperature **temperatura** *f.* 10
ten **diez** 1
tennis **tenis** *m.* 4
  tennis shoes **zapatos** *m., pl.* **de tenis** 6
tension **tensión** *f.* 15
tent **tienda** *f.* **de campaña**
tenth **décimo/a** 5
terrible **terrible** *adj. m., f.* 13
  It's terrible. **Es terrible.** 13
terrific **chévere** *adj.*
test **prueba** *f.* 2; **examen** *m.* 2
Thank you. *f., pl.* **Gracias.** 1
  Thank you (very much). **(Muchas) gracias.** 1
  Thank you very, very much. **Muchísimas gracias.** 9
  Thanks (a lot). **(Muchas) gracias.** 1
  Thanks again. (lit. Thanks one more time.) **Gracias una vez más.** 9
  Thanks for everything. **Gracias por todo.** 9, 15
that **que, quien, lo que** *pron.* 12
  that (one) **ése, ésa, eso** *pron.* 6; **ese, esa,** *adj.* 6
  that (*over there*) **aquél, aquélla, aquello** *pron.* 6; **aquel, aquella** *adj.* 6
  that which **lo que** *conj.* 12
  That's not the way it is. **No es así.** 16
  that's why **por eso** 11
the **el** *m.*, **la** *f. sing.*, **los** *m.*, **las** *f. pl.*
theater **teatro** *m.* 17
their **su(s)** *poss. adj.* 3; **suyo(s)/a(s)** *poss. pron.* 11
then **después** (*afterward*) *adv.* 7; **entonces** (*as a result*) *adv.* 7; **luego** (*next*) *adv.* 7; **pues** *adv.* 15
there **allí** *adv.* 5
  There is/are... **Hay...** 1;
  There is/are not... **No hay...** 1
therefore **por eso** 11
these **éstos, éstas** *pron.* 6; **estos, estas** *adj.* 6
they **ellos** *m.*, **ellas** *f. pron.*
thin **delgado/a** *adj.* 3
thing **cosa** *f.* 1
think **pensar (e:ie)** *v.* 4; (believe) **creer** *v.*
  think about **pensar en** *v.* 4
third **tercero/a** 5
thirst **sed** *f.* 3
thirsty: be (very) thirsty **tener (mucha) sed** 3
thirteen **trece** 1
thirty **treinta** 1, 2; thirty (*minutes past the hour*) **y treinta; y media** 1
this **este, esta** *adj.*; **éste, ésta, esto** *pron.* 6
  This is... (*introduction*) **Éste/a es...** 1
  This is he/she. (*on telephone*) **Con él/ella habla.** 11
those **ésos, ésas** *pron.* 6; **esos, esas** *adj.* 6
those (over there) **aquéllos, aquéllas** *pron.* 6; **aquellos, aquellas** *adj.* 6
thousand **mil** *m.* 6
three **tres** 1
three hundred **trescientos/as** 6
throat **garganta** *f.* 10
through **por** *prep.* 11
throughout: throughout the world **en todo el mundo** 13
throw **echar** *v.*
Thursday **jueves** *m., sing.* 2
thus (*in such a way*) **así** *adj.*
ticket **boleto** *m.* 17; **pasaje** *m.* 5
tie **corbata** *f.* 6
time **vez** *f.* 6; time **tiempo** *m.* 4
  buy on time **comprar a plazos** *m., pl.*
  have a good/bad time **pasarlo bien/mal** 9
  We had a great time. **Lo pasamos de película.** 18
  What time is it? **¿Qué hora es?** 1
  (At) What time...? **¿A qué hora...?** 1
times **veces** *f., pl.* 6
  many times **muchas veces** 10
  two times **dos veces** 6
tip **propina** *f.* 9
tire **llanta** *f.* 11
tired **cansado/a** *adj.* 5
  be tired **estar cansado/a** 5
title **título** *m.*
to **a** *prep.* 1
toast (*drink*) **brindar** *v.* 9
  toast **pan** *m.* **tostado**
toasted **tostado/a** *adj.* 8
  toasted bread **pan tostado** *m.* 8
toaster **tostadora** *f.* 12
today **hoy** *adv.* 2
  Today is... **Hoy es...** 2
together **juntos/as** *adj.* 9
toilet **inodoro** *m.* 7

tomato **tomate** *m.* 8
tomorrow **mañana** *f.* 1
See you tomorrow. **Hasta mañana.** 1
tonight **esta noche** *adv.* 4
too **también** *adv.* 2; 7
too much **demasiado** *adv.* 6; **en exceso** 15
tooth **diente** *m.* 7; tooth **muela** *f.*
toothpaste **pasta** *f.* **de dientes** 7
tornado **tornado** *m.* 18
tortilla **tortilla** *f.* 8
touch **tocar** *v.* 13, 17
tour an area **recorrer** *v;* **excursión** *f.* 4
go on a tour **hacer una excursión** 5
tourism **turismo** *m.* 5
tourist **turista** *m., f.* 1; **turístico/a** *adj.*
toward **hacia** *prep.* 14; **para** *prep.* 11
towel **toalla** *f.* 7
town **pueblo** *m.* 4
trade **oficio** *m.* 16
traffic **circulación** *f.* 11; **tráfico** *m.* 11
traffic signal **semáforo** *m.*
tragedy **tragedia** *f.* 17
trail **sendero** *m.* 13
trailhead **sendero** *m.* 13
train **entrenarse** *v.* 15; **tren** *m.* 5
train estation **estación** *f.* **(de) tren** *m.* 5
trainer **entrenador/a** *m., f.* 15
translate **traducir** *v.* 8
trash **basura** *f.* 12
travel **viajar** *v.* 2
travel agency **agencia** *f.* **de viajes** 5
travel agent **agente** *m., f.* **de viajes** 5
travel documents **documentos** *pl. m.* **de viaje**
traveler **viajero/a** *m., f.* 5
(traveler's) check **cheque (de viajero)** 14
treadmill **cinta caminadora** *f.* 15
tree **árbol** *m.* 13
trillion **billón** *m.*
trimester **trimestre** *m.* 2
trip **viaje** *m.* 5
take a trip **hacer un viaje** 5
tropical forest **bosque** *m.* **tropical** 13
truck **camión** *m.*
true **verdad** *adj.* 13
It's (not) true **(No) Es verdad** 13
trunk **baúl** *m.* 11
truth **verdad** *f.*
try **intentar** *v.;* **probar (o:ue)** *v.* 8
try (*to do something*) **tratar de (+** *inf.***)** 15
try on **probarse (o:ue)** *v.* 7
t-shirt **camiseta** *f.* 6
Tuesday **martes** *m., sing.* 2
tuna **atún** *m.* 8
turkey *m.* **pavo** 8
turn **doblar** *v.* 14
turn off (*electricity/appliance*) **apagar** *v.* 11
turn on (*electricity/appliance*) **poner** *v.* 11; **prender** *v.* 11
twelve **doce** 1
twenty **veinte** 1
twenty-eight **veintiocho** 1
twenty-five **veinticinco** 1
twenty-four **veinticuatro** 1
twenty-nine **veintinueve** 1
twenty-one **veintiún, veintiuno/a** 1
twenty-seven **veintisiete** 1
twenty-six **veintiséis** 1
twenty-three **veintitrés** 1
twenty-two **veintidós** 1
twice **dos veces** 6
twin **gemelo/a** *m., f.* 3
twisted **torcido/a** *adj.* 10; be twisted **estar torcido/a** 10
two **dos** 1
two hundred **doscientos/as** 6
two times **dose veces**

U

ugly **feo/a** *adj.* 3
uncle **tío** *m.* 3
under **bajo** *adv.* 7; **debajo de** *prep.* 2
understand **comprender** *v.* 3; **entender (e:ie)** *v.* 4
underwear **ropa interior** 6
unemployment **desempleo** *m.* 18
United States **Estados Unidos** *m. pl.* 1
university **universidad** *f.* 2
unless **a menos que** *adv.* 13
unmarried **soltero/a** *adj.*
unpleasant **antipático/a** *adj.* 3
until **hasta** *prep.* 6; **hasta que** *conj.* 13
up **arriba** *adv.* 15
urgent **urgente** *adj.* 12
It's urgent that... **Es urgente que...** 12
us **nosotros,** (to, for) us *pl. pron.* 6
use **usar** *v.* 6
used for **para** *prep.* 11
useful **útil** *adj. m., f.*

V

vacation **vacaciones** *f. pl.* 5
be on vacation **estar de vacaciones** 5
go on vacation **ir de vacaciones** 5
vacuum **pasar** *v.* **la aspiradora** 12
vacuum cleaner **aspiradora** *f.* 12
valley **valle** *m.* 13
various **varios/as** *adj. m., f. pl.* 8
VCR **videocasetera** *f.* 11
vegetables **verduras** *pl., f.* 8
verb **verbo** *m.*
very **muy** *adv.* 1
very much **muchísimo** *adv.* 2
(Very) well, thank you. **(Muy) bien gracias.** 1
vest **chaleco** *m.*
video **video** *m.*
video camera **cámara** *f.* **de video** 11
video(cassette) **video(casete)** *m.* 11
videoconference **videoconferencia** *f.* 16
vinegar **vinagre** *m.* 8
violence **violencia** *f.* 18
visit **visitar** *v.* 4
visit monuments **visitar monumentos** 4
vitamin **vitamina** *f.* 15
volcano **volcán** *m.* 13
volleyball **vóleibol** *m.* 4
vote **votar** *v.* 18

W

wait for **esperar** *v.* 2
waiter **camarero/a** *m., f.* 8
wake up **despertarse (e:ie)** *v.* 7
walk **caminar** *v.* 2
take a walk **pasear** *v.* 4; walk around **pasear por** 4
walkman ***walkman*** *m.* 11
wall **pared** *f.* 12
wallet **cartera** *f.* 6
want **querer (e:ie)** *v.* 4
war **guerra** *f.* 18
warm (oneself) up **calentarse** *v.* 15
wash **lavar** *v.* 12
wash one's face/hands **lavarse la cara/las manos** 7
wash oneself *v.* **lavarse** 7
washing machine **lavadora** *f.* 12
wastebasket **papelera** *f.* 2
watch **mirar** *v.* 2; **reloj** *m.* 2
watch television **mirar (la) televisión**
water **agua** *f.* 8
water pollution **contaminación del agua** 13
water-skiing *m.* **esquí acuático** 4
way **manera** *f.* 16
we **nosotros(as)** *m., f.* 1
weak **débil** *adj. m., f.* 15
wear **llevar** *v.* 6; **usar** 6
weather **tiempo** *m.*
The weather is bad. **Hace mal**

tiempo. 5
The weather is good. **Hace buen tiempo.** 5
weaving **tejido** *m.* 17
Web **red** *f.* 11
website **sitio** *m.* **web** 11
wedding **boda** *f.* 9
Wednesday **miércoles** *m., sing.* 2
week **semana** *f.* 2
weekend **fin** *m.* **de semana** 4
weight **peso** *m.* 15
lift weights **levantar** *v.* **pesas** *f., pl.* 15
welcome **bienvenido(s)/a(s)** *adj.* 12
well **pues** *adv.* 2, 17; **bueno** *adv.* 2, 17; (Very) well, thanks. **(Muy) bien, gracias.**
well-being **bienestar** *m.* 15
well organized **ordenado/a** *adj.*
west **oeste** *m.* 14
to the west **al oeste** 14
western (*genre*) **de vaqueros** 17
what **lo que** 12
what? **¿qué?** 1;
At what time...? **¿A qué hora...?** 1
What a... ! **¡Qué...!**
What a pleasure to... ! **¡Qué gusto (+** *inf.***)...** 18
What a surprise! **¡Qué sorpresa!**
What day is it? **¿Qué día es hoy?** 2
What did you say? **¿Cómo?**
What do you think? **¿Qué le/les** *form.* **parece?**
What happened? **¿Qué pasó?** 11
What is the date (today)? **¿Cuál es la fecha (de hoy)?** 5
What is the price? **¿Qué precio tiene?**
What pain! **¡Qué dolor!**
What pretty clothes! **¡Qué ropa más bonita!** 6
What size do you take? **¿Qué talla lleva (usa)?** 6
What time is it? **¿Qué hora es?** 1
What's going on? **¿Qué pasa?** 1
What's happening? **¿Qué pasa?** 1
What's. . . like? **¿Cómo es...?** 3
What's new? **¿Qué hay de nuevo?** 1
What's the weather like? **¿Qué tiempo hace?** 5
What's wrong? **¿Qué pasó?** 11
What's your name? **¿Cómo se llama usted?** *form.* 1
What's your name? **¿Cómo te llamas (tú)?** *fam.* 1
when **cuando** *conj.* 7; 13
When? **¿Cuándo?** 2
where **donde**
where? (*destination*) **¿adónde?** 2; (*location*) **¿dónde?** 1
Where are you from? **¿De dónde eres (tú)?** (*fam.*) 1; **¿De dónde es (usted)?** (*form.*) 1
Where is...? **¿Dónde está...?** 2
(to) where? **¿adónde?** 2
which **que** *pron.*
which? **¿cuál?** 2; **¿qué?** 2
which one(s)? **¿cuáles?** 2
while **mientras** *adv.* 10
white **blanco/a** *adj.* 6
white wine **vino blanco** 8
who **que** *pron.* 12; **quien(es)** *pron.* 12
who? **¿quién(es)?** 1
Who is...? **¿Quién es...?** 1
Who is calling? (*on telephone*) **¿De parte de quién?** 11
Who is speaking? (*on telephone*) **¿Quién habla?** 11
whom **quien(es)** *pron.*
whole **todo/a** *adj.*
whose **¿de quién(es)?** 1
why? **¿por qué?** 2
widower/widow **viudo/a** *adj.* 9
wife **esposa** *f.* 3
win **ganar** *v.* 4
wind **viento** *m.* 5
window **ventana** *f.* 2
windshield **parabrisas** *m., sing.* 11
windy: It's (very) windy. **Hace (mucho) viento.** 5
wine **vino** *m.* 8
red wine **vino tinto** 8
white wine **vino blanco** 8
wineglass **copa** *f.* 12
winter **invierno** *m.* 5
wish **desear** *v.* 2; **esperar** *v.* 13
I wish (that) **Ojalá (que)** 13
with **con** *prep.* 2
with me **conmigo** 4, 9
with you **contigo** *fam.* 9
within (ten years) **dentro de (diez años)** *prep.* 16
without **sin** *prep.* 2, 13, 15; **sin que** *conj.* 13
without a doubt **sin duda**
woman **mujer** *f.* 1
wool **lana** *f.*6
(made of) wool **de lana** 6
word **palabra** *f.* 1
work **trabajar** *v.* 2; **funcionar** *v.* 11; **trabajo** *m.* 16
work (*of art, literature, music, etc.*) **obra** *f.* 17
work out **hacer gimnasia** 15
world **mundo** *m.* 13
worldwide **mundial** *adj. m., f.*
worried (about) **preocupado/a (por)** *adj.* 5
worry (about) **preocuparse** *v.* **(por)** 7
Don't worry. **No se preocupe.** *form.* 7; **Tranquilo.** *adj.*; **No te preocupes.** *fam.* 7
worse **peor** *adj. m., f.* 8
worst **el/la peor, lo peor** 8, 18
Would you like to...? **¿Te gustaría...?** *fam.* 4
write **escribir** *v.* 3
write a letter/post card/e-mail message **escribir una carta/(tarjeta) postal/mensaje electrónico** 4
writer **escritor(a)** *m., f* 17
written **escrito/a** *p.p.* 14
wrong **equivocado/a** *adj.* 5
be wrong **no tener razón** 3

X

X-ray **radiografía** *f.* 10

Y

yard **jardín** *m.* 12; **patio** *m.* 12
year **año** *m.* 5
be... years old **tener... años** 3
yellow **amarillo/a** *adj.* 6
yes **sí** *interj.* 1
yesterday **ayer** *adv.* 6
yet **todavía** *adv.* 5
yogurt **yogur** *m.* 8
You **tú** *fam.* **usted (Ud.)** *form. sing.* **vosotros/as** *m., f. fam.* **ustedes (Uds.)** *form.* 1; (to, for) you *fam. sing.* **te** *pl.* **os** 6; *form. sing.* **le** *pl.* **les** 6
You don't say! **¡No me digas!** *fam.*; **¡No me diga!** *form.* 11
You are. . . **Tú eres...** 1
You're welcome. **De nada.** 1; **No hay de qué.** 1
young **joven** *adj.* 3
young person **joven** *m., f.* 1
young woman **señorita (Srta.)** *f.*
younger **menor** *adj. m., f.* 3
younger: younger brother, sister *m., f.* **hermano/a menor** 3
youngest **el/la menor** *m., f.* 8
your **su(s)** *poss. adj. form.* 3
your **tu(s)** *poss. adj. fam. sing.* 3
your **vuestro/a(s)** *poss. adj. form. pl.* 3
your(s) *form.* **suyo(s)/a(s)** *poss. pron. form.* 11
your(s) **tuyo(s)/a(s)** *poss. fam. sing.* 11
your(s) **vuestro(s)/a(s)** *poss. fam.* 11
youth *f.* **juventud** 9

Z

zero **cero** *m.* 1

F

G

H

I

J

L

M

N

Ñ

O

P

Q

R

Text Credits

416–417 © Gloria Fuertes. Reprinted by permission of Fundación Gloria Fuertes.
444–445 © Marco Denevi. Falsificaciones, Buenos Aires, Corregidor, 1999. Reprinted by permission of Editorial Corregidora.
472–473 © Giaconda Belli. Reprinted by permission of the author.
500–501 © Antonio Skármeta, 1985. Reprinted by permission of Agencia Literaria Carmen Balcells, S. A.
530–531 © By Octavio Paz. from COLLECTED POEMS 1957–1987, copyright © 1987 by Octavio Paz. Reprinted by permission of New Directions Publishing Corp.

Fine Art Credits

67 Diego Velázquez. *Las meninas*. 1656. Derechos reservados © Museo Nacional del Prado, Madrid.

101 Oswaldo Guayasamín. *Madre y niño en azul*. 1986. Cortesía Fundación Guayasamín. Quito, Ecuador.

132 Frida Kahlo. *Autorretrato con mono*. 1938. Oil on masonite, overall 16 X12" (40.64 x 30.48 cms). Albright-Knox Art Gallery, Buffalo, New York. Bequest of A. Conger Goodyear, 1966

539 José Antonio Velásquez. *San Antonio de Oriente*. 1957. Colección: Art Museum of the Americas, Organization of American States. Washington D.C.

Illustration Credits

Hermann Mejía: 5, 12, 13, 15, 16, 20, 21, 48, 55, 59, 73, 81 (b), 84, 92, 93, 113, 117, 124, 139, 150, 155, 159, 173, 191, 204, 205, 212, 222, 245, 259, 272, 280, 301, 311, 316, 317, 344, 347, 350, 351, 376, 385, 390, 410, 420, 443, 465, 467, 470, 525, 534, 558–559.

Pere Virgili: 2–3, 36–37, 56, 70–71, 81 (t), 104–105, 106, 136–137, 138, 151, 154, 164, 170–171, 202–203, 234–235, 236, 270–271, 298–299, 330–331, 332, 362–363, 364, 396–397, 398, 426–427, 428, 452–455, 456, 482–483, 512–513, 542–543.

Yayo: 9, 43, 77, 111, 145, 177, 209, 243, 277, 337, 369, 403, 433, 450–451, 461, 489, 519, 549.

Photography Credits

Martín Bernetti: 1, 2, 3, 4, 6 (b), 10, 14, 17, 28, 30, 31, 31 (b), 38, 40 (b), 46, 51, 52, 60, 61, 62, 64, 65, 71, 72, 74 (b), 80, 82, 85, 87 (r), 88, 94, 95, 98, 99, 100, 101 (t, ml, b), 105, 107, 108 (b), 120, 125, 126, 128, 130, 131, 132 (b), 149, 162, 183, 187, 188, 189, 194, 196, 197, 206 (b), 211, 213, 216, 217, 228, 229, 230 (tl, tr, tm), 231 (tl, br), 239, 262, 264, 273, 288 (t), 290, 302 (b), 309, 313, 322, 324, 334 (b), 341, 346, 365, 366 (b), 388, 432 (b), 439, 446, 448, 449, 457, 474, 476, 485, 486 (b), 502, 504, 505, 522, 532, 552.
Corbis: cover (tr) © Galen Rowell, (far lm) © Macduff Everton, (ml) © Danny Lehman, (rmc) © Douglas Peebles, (far rm) © Don Mason, (b) © Francesc Muntada. iii © Chuck Savage. **32** (tr) © Robert Holmes. **33** (tr) © Tony Arruza, (ml) © Owen Franken. **66** (tl, tr) © Patrick Ward, (m) © Elke Stolzenberg, (b) © Reuters/Heino Kalis. **67** (tl) © Paul Almasy, (tr) © Jean-Pierre Lescourret, (mr) © Tony Arruza, (br) © Dave G. Houser. **69** © Ariel Skelley. **87** (l) Warren Morgan. **96** © Tom & Dee Ann McCarthy. **101** (br) © Pablo Corral V. **103** © Jon Feingersh. **127** © AFP/Juan Barreto. **132** (tl) © George D. Lepp, (br) © Peter Guttman,

133 (tr) © Bettmann, (br) © Brian A. Vikander. 135 © Gary Kufner. 166 (b) Dave G. Houser. 167 (tr) © Steve Chenn. 199 (tr) © Richard Bickel, (bl) © Stephanie Maze, (br) © Ariel Ramerez. 201 © Michael Prince. 226 © Michael Pole. 230 (bm) © Charles & Josette Lenars, (lm) © Richard Smith, (b) © Yann Arthus-Bertrand. 231 (bl) ©Jeremy Horner. 233 © SIE Productions. 240 (b) © Owen Franken. 246 © José Luis Peleaz, Inc. 266 (t) © Bob Winsett, (ml, mr, b) © Dave G. Houser. 267 (tl) © Reuters NewMedia Inc./Jorge Silva, (tr) © Michael & Patricia Fogden, (bl) © Jan Butchofsky-Houser, (br) © Paul W. Liebhardt. 274 (b) ©Anders Ryman. 288 (b) © Pablo Corral V. 289 © Patrick Ward. 293 © AFP/Chris Bouroncle. 294 (tl) © Dave G. Houser, (tr, mtr) © Macduff Everton, (ml) © Pablo Corral V, (mbr) ©AFP/Macarena Minguell, (bl, br) © Bettmann. 295 (tl) © Wolfgang Kaehler, (bl) © Roger Ressmeyer, (br) © Charles O'Rear. 322 © Stuart Hughes. 325 © Stephanie Maze. 326 (tl) © Martin Rogers, (tr, m) Jan Butchofsky-Houser, (ml) © Bill Gentile, (mr) © Dave G. Houser, (b) © Bob Winsett. 327 (r, b) © Martin Rogers, (ml) © Jacques M. Chenet. 329 © PictureNet. 345 © Martin Bydalek Photography. 353 © Laurence Kesterson. 354 © Michael Prince. 357 © Kevin Fleming. 358 (t, b) © Pablo Corral V, (ml) © Arvind Garg, (m, mr) © Galen Rowell. 359 (t, b) © Pablo Corral V, (r) © Massimo Mastrorillo, (ml) © Tibor Bognár. 361 © José Luis Pelaez. 386 © Danny Lehman. 391 © Tim Page. 392 (tl) © Kevin Schafer, (tr, b) © Danny Lehman. 393 (tl) © Danny Lehman, (r) © Peter Guttman, (ml) © Ralph A. Clevenger, (b) © José Fuste Raga. 395 © Michael DeYoung. 397 (tl) © Richard Cummins, (tr) © Stephanie Maze, (bl) © Ray Juno, (br) © Paul A. Souders. 400 (b) © Staffan Widstrand. 406 © Carl & Ann Purcell. 416–417 © Japack Company. 420 © Ric Ergenbright. 421 © Kennan Ward. 422 (tr) © Carl & Ann Purcell, (ml, mr) © Jeremy Horner, (b) © Adam Woolfitt. 423 (tl) © Gianni Dagli Orti, (r) © Stringer/Mexico/Reuters, (bl) © Jeremy Horner. 425 © Macduff Everton. 450 (t) © John Madere, (mt) © Kevin Schafer, (mb) © Buddy Mays, (b) © Peter Guttman. 451 (tl) © Reuters NewMedia Inc./Kimberly White, (bl, br) © Pablo Corral V. 453 © Peter Barrett. 458 (b) © Pablo San Juan. 466 (b) © Pablo San Juan. 468 © Michael Keller. 472 © George H. H. Huey. 477 © Robert Weight. 478 (tl) © Anders Ryman, (m) Reuters NewMedia Inc./Sergio Moraes, (b) Pablo Corral V. 479 (tl) © Hubert Stadler, (r) AFP Photo/Gonzalo Espinoza, (bl) © Wolfgang Kaehler. 481 © Peter Beck. 498 © LWA-Stephen Welstead. 499 © Bill Gentile. 506 (tl) © Jeremy Horner, (tr, m) © Bill Gentile, (b) © Stephen Frink. 507 (tl) © Brian A. Vikander, (r) © Reuters NewMedia Inc./Claudia Daut, (bl) © Gary Braasch. 508 (tr) © Reinhard Eisele, (m) © Richard Bickel. 509 (tl) © Jeremy Horner, (r) © Reuters NewMedia Inc./Marc Serota, (bl) © Lawrence Manning. 516 (b) © Anna Clopet. 523 © Sygma. 530 © William Coupon. 536 (tl) © José F. Poblete, (tr) Peter Guttman, (ml) © Leif Skoogfors, (mr) © Lake County Museum. 537 (l) © Guy Motil. 538 (tl) © Stuart Westmorland, (tr, ml) © Macduff Everton, (mr) © Tony Arruza. 539 (tl) © Macduff Everton, (tr) © Owen Franken. 541 © Douglas Kirkland. 545 (t) © Owen Franken, (b) © Reuters NewMedia Inc./Andrew Winning. 557 (l) © Dave G. Houser. 560 © Layne Kennedy. 562 © John Lund. 564 (t) © Peter Guttman, (ml) © Paul Almasy, (b) © Carlos Carrion. 565 (r) © Joel Creed; Ecoscene. 566 (tl) © Bettmann, (tr) © Reuters/Andres Stapff, (m) © Diego Lezama Orezzoli, (b) © Tim Graham. 567 (tl) © Stephanie Maze, (r) © SI/Simon Bruty, (ml) © Reuters/Andres Stapff, (bl) © Wolfgang Kaehler.

DDB Stock: 565 (tl) Chris R. Sharp, (bl) Francis E. Caldwell.
Dominicanada: 33 (br).
Carlos Gaudier: 160, 161, 165, 166 (tl, tr, ml, mr), 167 (tl, bl).
Index Stock Imagery, Inc.: 269 © Network Productions. 511 © Leslie Harris.
Latin Focus: 35 © Jimmy Dorantes. 297 © Jimmy Dorantes.
PhotoDisc: 33 (tl), 167 (tr), 198 (t, b), 295 (tr),
Odyssey/Chicago: 198 (tl, mbr) © Robert Frerck. 199 (tl) © Robert Frerck.

106 Reprinted by permission of Juana Macías Alba.
515 Reprinted by permission of Julia Solomonoff.

About the Authors

José A. Blanco founded Vista Higher Learning in 1998. A native of Barranquilla, Colombia, Mr. Blanco holds degrees in Literature and Hispanic Studies from Brown University and the University of California, Santa Cruz. He has worked as a writer, editor, and translator for Houghton Mifflin and D.C. Heath and Company and has taught Spanish at the secondary and university levels. Mr. Blanco is also the co-author of several other Vista Higher Learning programs: **Panorama** at the introductory level, **Ventanas, Facetas**, and **Enfoques** at the intermediate level, and **Revista** at the advanced conversation level.

Philip Redwine Donley received his M.A. in Hispanic Literature from the University of Texas at Austin in 1986 and his Ph.D. in Foreign Language Education from the University of Texas at Austin in 1997. Dr. Donley taught Spanish at Austin Community College, Southwestern University, and the University of Texas at Austin. He published articles and conducted workshops about language anxiety management, and the development of critical thinking skills, and was involved in research about teaching languages to the visually impaired. Dr. Donley was also the co-author of **Aventuras** and **Panorama**, two other introductory college Spanish textbook programs published by Vista Higher Learning.

About the Illustrators

Yayo, an internationally acclaimed illustrator, was born in Colombia. He has illustrated children's books, newspapers, and magazines, and has been exhibited around the world. He currently lives in Montreal, Canada.

Pere Virgili lives and works in Barcelona, Spain. His illustrations have appeared in textbooks, newspapers, and magazines throughout Spain and Europe.

Born in Caracas, Venezuela, **Hermann Mejía** studied illustration at the *Instituto de Diseño de Caracas*. Hermann currently lives and works in the United States.

Mar Caribe
Barranquilla
Maracaibo
Caracas
Puerto España
Trinidad y Tobago
Venezuela
R. Orinoco
Georgetown
Guyana
Paramaribo
Surinam
Cayena
Guayana Francesa
Medellín
Colombia
Bogotá
Cali
R. Magdalena
Pasto
Quito
Ecuador
Guayaquil
R. Negro
R. Amazonas
Manaus
Belém
Iquitos
Perú
R. Madeira
Cordillera de los Andes
Recife
Lima
Cuzco
Lago Titicaca
Salvador
Brasil
Brasilia
Arequipa
La Paz
Bolivia
Arica
Sucre
R. Paraguay
Océano Pacífico
Iquique
Belo Horizonte
R. Paraná
Antofagasta
São Paulo
Río de Janeiro
Santos
Paraguay
Salta
Asunción
Chile
R. Uruguay
Córdoba
R. Paraná
Porto Alegre
Valparaíso
Mendoza
Rosario
Santiago
Uruguay
Buenos Aires
Montevideo
Concepción
Argentina
Océano Atlántico
Bahía Blanca
Puerto Montt
Cordillera de los Andes
N
O
E
S
Estrecho de Magallanes
Islas Malvinas
Punta Arenas
Tierra del Fuego
América del Sur
Islas Galápagos
Océano Pacífico
Isla Pinta
Isla Marchena
Isla Genovesa
Isla Isabela
Línea Ecuatorial
ECUADOR
Volcán Darwin
Isla Santiago
(San Salvador)
Isla Fernandina
Puerto Ayora
Isla San Cristóbal
Santo Tomás
Isla Santa Cruz
Puerto Barquerizo Moreno
Isla Santa María
Isla Española